W9-CTW-355

DATE DUE

			PRINTED IN U.S.A.

Poetry
Criticism

Guide to Gale Literary Criticism Series

For criticism on	Consult these Gale series
Authors now living or who died after December 31, 1959	*CONTEMPORARY LITERARY CRITICISM (CLC)*
Authors who died between 1900 and 1959	*TWENTIETH-CENTURY LITERARY CRITICISM (TCLC)*
Authors who died between 1800 and 1899	*NINETEENTH-CENTURY LITERATURE CRITICISM (NCLC)*
Authors who died between 1400 and 1799	*LITERATURE CRITICISM FROM 1400 TO 1800 (LC)* *SHAKESPEAREAN CRITICISM (SC)*
Authors who died before 1400	*CLASSICAL AND MEDIEVAL LITERATURE CRITICISM (CMLC)*
Black writers of the past two hundred years	*BLACK LITERATURE CRITICISM (BLC)*
Authors of books for children and young adults	*CHILDREN'S LITERATURE REVIEW (CLR)*
Dramatists	*DRAMA CRITICISM (DC)*
Hispanic writers of the late nineteenth and twentieth centuries	*HISPANIC LITERATURE CRITICISM (HLC)*
Native North American writers and orators of the eighteenth, nineteenth, and twentieth centuries	*NATIVE NORTH AMERICAN LITERATURE (NNAL)*
Poets	*POETRY CRITICISM (PC)*
Short story writers	*SHORT STORY CRITICISM (SSC)*
Major authors from the Renaissance to the present	*WORLD LITERATURE CRITICISM, 1500 TO THE PRESENT (WLC)*

ISSN 1052-4851

Poetry Criticism

Excerpts from Criticism of the Works of the Most Significant and Widely Studied Poets of World Literature

VOLUME 15

Christine Slovey
Editor

GALE

DETROIT · NEW YORK · TORONTO · LONDON

Riverside Community College
Library
4800 Magnolia Avenue
NOV '96   Riverside, California 92506

REF
PN1010 .P499
Poetry criticism : excerpts
from criticism of the works
of the most significant and
widely studied poets of
world literature.

STAFF

Christine Slovey, *Editor*

t Haerens, Jeff Hill, Drew Kalasky, Michael L. Lablanc,
Marie Rose Napierkowski, Mary K. Ruby, Larry Trudeau,
Associate Editors

Marlene S. Hurst, *Permissions Manager*
Margaret A. Chamberlain, Maria Franklin, *Permissions Specialists*

Diane Cooper, Michele Lonoconus, Maureen Puhl,
Susan Salas, Shalice Shah, Kimberly F. Smilay,
Permissions Associates

Sarah Chesney, Edna Hedblad,
Permissions Assistants

Victoria B. Cariappa, *Research Manager*

Julie C. Daniel, Tamara C. Nott, Michele P. Pica,
Tracie A. Richardson, Cheryl L. Warnock, *Research Associates*

Mary Beth Trimper, *Production Director*
Deborah Milliken, *Production Assistant*

Sherrell Hobbs, *Macintosh Artist*
Randy Bassett, *Image Database Supervisor*
Robert Duncan, *Scanner Operator*
Pamela Hayes, *Photography Coordinator*

Since this page cannot legibly accommodate all copyright notices, the acknowledgments constitute an extension of the copyright notice.

While every effort has been made to ensure the reliability of the information presented in this publication, Gale Research Inc. neither guarantees the accuracy of the data contained herein nor assumes any responsibility for errors, omissions or discrepancies. Gale accepts no payment for listing, and inclusion in the publication of any organization, agency, institution, publication, service, or individual does not imply endorsement of the editors or publisher. Errors brought to the attention of the publisher and verified to the satisfaction of the publisher will be corrected in future editions.

The paper used in this publication meets the minimum requirements of American National Standard for Information Sciences—Permanence Paper for Printed Library Materials, ANSI Z39.48-1984.

This publication is a creative work fully protected by all applicable copyright laws, as well as by misappropriation, trade secret, unfair competition, and other applicable laws. The authors and editors of this work have added value to the underlying factual material herein through one or more of the following: unique and original selection, coordination, expression, arrangement, and classification of the information.

All rights to this publication will be vigorously defended.

Copyright © 1997
Gale Research
835 Penobscot Building
Detroit, MI 48226-4094

All rights reserved including the right of reproduction in whole or in part in any form.

Library of Congress Catalog Card Number 91-118494
ISBN 0-7876-0474-7
ISSN 1052-4851

Printed in the United States of America
Published simultaneously in the United Kingdom
by Gale Research International Limited
(An affiliated company of Gale Research Inc.)
10 9 8 7 6 5 4 3 2 1

Contents

Preface vii

Acknowledgments xi

Preface

A Comprehensive Information Source on World Poetry

*P*oetry Criticism *(PC)* provides substantial critical excerpts and biographical information on poets throughout the world who are most frequently studied in high school and undergraduate college courses. Each *PC* entry is supplemented by biographical and bibliographical material to help guide the user to a fuller understanding of the genre and its creators. Although major poets and literary movements are covered in such Gale Literary Criticism Series as *Contemporary Literary Criticism (CLC), Twentieth-Century Literary Criticism (TCLC), Nineteenth-Century Literature Criticism (NCLC), Literature Criticism from 1400 to 1800 (LC),* and *Classical and Medieval Literature Criticism (CMLC), PC* offers more focused attention on poetry than is possible in the broader, survey-oriented entries on writers in these Gale series. Students, teachers, librarians, and researchers will find that the generous excerpts and supplementary material provided by *PC* supply them with vital information needed to write a term paper on poetic technique, examine a poet's most prominent themes, or lead a poetry discussion group.

Coverage

In order to reflect the influence of tradition as well as innovation, poets of various nationalities, eras, and movements are represented in every volume of *PC*. Each author entry presents a historical survey of the critical response to that author's work; the length of an entry reflects the amount of critical attention that the author has received from critics writing in English and from foreign critics in translation. Since many poets have inspired a prodigious amount of critical explication, *PC* is necessarily selective, and the editors have chosen the most significant published criticism to aid readers and students in their research. In order to provide these important critical pieces, the editors will sometimes reprint essays that have appeared in previous volumes of Gale's Literary Criticism Series. Such duplication, however, never exceeds fifteen percent of a *PC* volume.

Organization

Each *PC* author entry consists of the following components:

- **Author Heading:** the name under which the author wrote appears at the beginning of the entry, followed by birth and death dates. If the author wrote consistently under a pseudonym, the pseudonym will be listed in the author heading and his or her legal name given in parentheses in the lines immediately preceding the Introduction. Uncertainty as to birth or death dates is indicated by question marks.

- **Introduction:** a biographical and critical essay introduces readers to the author and the critical discussions surrounding his or her work.

- **Author Portrait:** a photograph or illustration of the author is included when available. Most entries also feature illustrations of people and places pertinent to an author's career, as well as holographs of manuscript pages and dust jackets.

- **Principal Works:** the author's most important works are identified in a list ordered chronologically by first publication dates. The first section comprises poetry collections and book-length poems. The second section gives information on other major works by the author. For foreign authors, original foreign-language publication information is provided, as well as the best and most complete English-language editions of their works.

- **Criticism:** critical excerpts chronologically arranged in each author entry provide perspective on changes in critical evaluation over the years. All individual titles of poems and poetry collections by the author featured in the entry are printed in boldface type to enable a reader to ascertain without difficulty the works under discussion. For purposes of easy identification, the critic's name and the publication date of the essay are given at the beginning of each piece of criticism. Unsigned criticism is preceded by the title of the journal in which it originally appeared. Publication information (such as publisher names and book prices) and parenthetical numerical references (such as footnotes or page and line references to specific editions of a work) have been deleted at the editor's discretion to enable smoother reading of the text.

- **Explanatory Notes:** introductory comments preface each critical excerpt, providing several types of useful information, including: the reputation of a critic, the importance of a work of criticism, and the specific type of criticism (biographical, psychoanalytic, historical, etc.).

- **Author Commentary:** insightful comments from the authors themselves and excerpts from author interviews are included when available.

- **Bibliographical Citations:** information preceding each piece of criticism guides the interested reader to the original essay or book.

- **Further Reading:** bibliographic references accompanied by descriptive notes at the end of each entry suggest additional materials for study of the author. Boxed material following the Further Reading provides references to other biographical and critical series published by Gale.

Other Features

Cumulative Author Index: comprises all authors who have appeared in Gale's Literary Criticism Series, along with cross-references to such Gale biographical series as *Contemporary Authors* and *Dictionary of Literary Biography*. This cumulated index enables the user to locate an author within the various series.

Cumulative Nationality Index: includes all authors featured in *PC,* arranged alphabetically under their respective nationalities.

Cumulative Title Index: lists in alphabetical order all individual poems, book-length poems, and collection titles contained in the *PC* series. Titles of poetry collections and separately published poems are printed in italics, while titles of individual poems are printed in roman type with quotation marks. Each title is followed by the author's name and the volume and page number corresponding to the location of commentary on specific works. English-language translations of original foreign-language titles are cross-referenced to the foreign titles so that all references to discussion of a work are combined in one listing.

Citing *Poetry Criticism*

When writing papers, students who quote directly from any volume in the Literary Criticism Series may use the following general formats to footnote reprinted criticism. The first example pertains to material drawn from periodicals, the second to material reprinted from books:

[1]David Daiches, "W. H. Auden: The Search for a Public," *Poetry* LIV (June 1939), 148-56; excerpted and reprinted in *Poetry Criticism*, Vol. 1, ed. Robyn V. Young (Detroit: Gale Research, 1990), pp. 7-9.

[2]Pamela J. Annas, *A Disturbance in Mirrors: The Poetry of Sylvia Plath* (Greenwood Press, 1988); excerpted and reprinted in *Poetry Criticism*, Vol. 1, ed. Robyn V. Young (Detroit: Gale Research, 1990), pp. 410-14.

Comments Are Welcome

Readers who wish to suggest authors to appear in future volumes, or who have other suggestions, are cordially invited to contact the editors.

Acknowledgments

The editors wish to thank the copyright holders of the excerpted criticism included in this volume and the permissions managers of many book and magazine publishing companies for assisting us in securing reprint rights. We are also grateful to the staffs of the Detroit Public Library, the Library of Congress, the University of Detroit Mercy Library, Wayne State University Purdy/Kresge Library Complex, and the University of Michigan Libraries for making their resources available to us. Following is a list of the copyright holders who have granted us permission to reprint material in this volume of *PC*. Every effort has been made to trace copyright, but if omissions have been made, please let us know.

COPYRIGHTED EXCERPTS IN *PC*, VOLUME 15, WERE REPRINTED FROM THE FOLLOWING PERIODICALS:

America, v. 134, February 28, 1976 for a review of "House, Bridge, Fountain, Gate" by Margaret Burns Ferrari. © 1976. All rights reserved. Reprinted with the permission of America Press Inc., 106 W. 56th Street, New York, NY 10019 and the author.—*The American Book Review,* v. 9, September-October, 1987; v. 12, September-October, 1990. © 1987, 1990 by The American Book Review. Both reprinted by permission of the publisher.—*American Poetry Review,* May-June, 1973 for "The Emerald Essay" by Diane Wakoski. Copyright © 1973 by World Poetry, Inc. Reprinted by permission of the author.—*The Antioch Review,* v. XXVI, Summer, 1966. Copyright © 1966 by the Antioch Review Inc. Reprinted by permission of the Editors.— *Ball State University Forum,* v. 16, Spring, 1975. © 1975 Ball State University. Reprinted by permission to the publisher.—*Books Abroad,* v. 46, Summer, 1972. Copyright 1972 by the University of Oklahoma Press. Reprinted by permission of the publisher.—*The Christian Science Monitor,* v. 65, February 28, 1973. © 1973 The Christian Science Publishing Society. All rights reserved. Reprinted by permission from *The Christian Science Monitor./* v. 72, January 2, 1980 for "Vicente Aleixandre Lights the Way" by Diana Der Hovanessian. © 1980 the author. All rights reserved. Reprinted by permission of the author.—*Comparative Literature,* v. 45, Winter, 1993 for "Violation of the Mother Tongue: Nishiwaki Junzaburo's Translatory Language in 'Ambarvalia'" by Hosea Hirata. © copyright 1993 by University of Oregon. Reprinted by permission of the author.—*Contemporary Literature*, v. 18, Winter, 1977. © 1977 by the Board of Regents of the University of Wisconsin System. Reprinted by permission of The University of Wisconsin Press.—*Dada/Surrealism,* n. 17, 1988. 1988 © Association for the Study of Dada and Surrealism. Both reproduced by permission of the publisher.—*Denver Quarterly,* v. 15, Fall, 1980 for "Rhetorical Strategy in the Surrealist Poetry of Vicente Aleixandre" by David Garrison. Copyright © 1980 by the University of Denver. Reprinted by permission of the author.—*Discurso Literario,* v. 6, Fall, 1988. Copyright © by Discurso Literario. Reprinted by permission of the publisher.— *ELH,* v. 47, Summer, 1980. Copyright © 1980 by The Johns Hopkins University Press. All rights reserved. Reprinted by permission of the publisher.—*Feminist Studies,* v. 10, Fall, 1984. Copyright © 1984 by Feminist Studies, Inc. Reprinted by permission of the publisher, c/o Women's Studies Program, University of Maryland, College Park, MD 20742.—*The Explicator,* v. 40, Summer, 1982. Copyright 1982 by Helen Dwight Reid Educational Foundation. Reprinted with permission of the Helen Dwight Reid Educational Foundation, published by Heldref Publications, 1319 18th Street, NW, Washington, DC 20036-1802.— *French Studies,* v. XIX, 1965. Reprinted by permission of the publisher.—*Hecate,* v. 1, July, 1975. Reprinted by permission of the publisher.—*Hispanic Review,* v. 56, Summer, 1988. Reprinted by permission of the publisher.—*The Hudson Review,* v. XXVI, Summer, 1973. Copyright © 1973 by The Hudson Review, Inc. Reprinted by permission of the publisher./v. 1, Winter, 1949. Copyright 1949, renewed 1977 by The Hudson Review, Inc. Reprinted by permission of the publisher.—*The Iowa Review,* v. 10, Fall, 1979 for "Past Halfway: 'The Retrieval System', by Maxine Kumin" by Sybil P. Estess. Copyright © 1979 by The University of Iowa. Reprinted by permission of the author.—*Latin American Literary Review,* v. X, Spring-Summer, 1982, v. XVIII, Fall-Winter, 1990. Both reprinted by permission of the publisher.—*Los Angeles Times,* July 18, 1982. Copyright, 1982, *Los Angeles Times.* Reprinted by permission of the publisher.—*Los Angeles Times Book Review,* October 16, 1986. Copyright, 1986, *Los Angeles Times.* Reprinted by permission of the publisher.—*The Los Angeles Times Book Review,* November 4, 1984; July 18, 1993. Copyright, 1984, 1993, *Los Angeles Times.* Both reprinted by permission of the publisher.—*The Massachusetts Review,* v. XVI, Spring, 1975. © 1975. Reprinted from *The Massachusetts Review,* The Massachusetts Review, Inc. by permission.—*MLN,* v. 105, March 1990. © copyright 1990 The Johns Hopkins University Press. All rights reserved. Reprinted by permission of the publisher.—*Modern Language Quarterly,* v. XXVIII, June, 1967. © 1969 University of Washington. Reprinted by permission of Duke University Press.—*Modern Poetry Studies,* v. XI, 1982. Copyright 1982, by Media Study, Inc. Reprinted by permission of the publisher.—*The Nation,* New York, v. 199, September 28, 1964. Copyright 1964, renewed 1992 *The Nation* magazine/The Nation Company, Inc. Reprinted by permission of the publisher.—New Letters, v. 49, Fall, 1982 for "Theodore Roethke Speaks" by Theodore Roethke. © copyright 1982 The Curators of the University of Missouri. Reprinted by permission of the publisher and the author.—*The New Republic,* v. 105, July 14, 1941. Copyright 1941, renewed 1968 The New Republic, Inc./v. 141, August 10, 1959. © 1959 , renewed 1987 The New Republic, Inc. Both reprinted by permission of *The New Republic.*—*The New York Quarterly,* 1970 for an interview with Mary Jane Fortunato by Diane Wakoski. Copyright © 1970 by *The New York Quarterly,* solely owned by The New York Quarterly Poetry Review Foundation, Inc. All rights reserved. Reprinted by permission of the publisher.—*The New York Times Book Review,* December 12, 1971; November 19, 1972; October 30, 1977; January 18, 1987. Copyright © 1971, 1972, 1977, 1987 by The New York Times Company. All reprinted by permission of the publisher./December 16, 1951; September 13, 1953. Copyright 1951, renewed 1979; copyright 1953, renewed 1981 by The New York Times Company. Both reprinted by permission of the publisher.—*The New Yorker,* v. XXIV, May 15, 1948 for "Verse" by Louise Bogan; v. XXVII, February 16, 1952 for "Praise to the End!" by Louise Bogan. Copyright 1948, renewed 1985; copyright 1952, renewed 1980 by The New Yorker Magazine, Inc. Both reprinted by permission of the Literary Estate of Louise Bogan./v. XXII, November 9, 1946. Copyright 1946, renewed 1973 by The New Yorker Magazine, Inc. Reprinted by permission of the publisher.—*Papers on Language and Literature,* v. 26, Fall, 1990. Copyright © 1990 by the Board of Trustees, Southern Illinois University at Edwardsville. Reprinted by permission of the publisher.—*The Paris Review,* v. 20, Fall-Winter, 1978 for "From the Prologue to the Second Edition of 'La Destruccion O Amor'"by Vicente Aleixandre, translated by David Prichard. © 1978 The Paris Review, Inc. Reprinted by permission of the author.—*Parnassus: Poetry in Review,* v. 1, Spring-Summer, 1973 for "Plentitude and Death" by Rosellen Brown; v. 1, Spring-Summer, 1973 for a review of "Up Country" by Ralph J. Mills, Jr. Copyright © 1973 Poetry in Review Foundation, NY. Both reprinted by permission of the respective authors.—*Perspectives on Contemporary Literature,* v. 9, 1983. Copyright © 1983 by The University Press of Kentucky. Reprinted by permission of the publisher.—*Poetry,* v. CLVI, April, 1990 for a review of "Nurture" by Henri Cole.; v. CLIX, November, 1992 for "Ecstasy and Irony" by David Baker. © 1990, 1992 by the Modern Poetry Association. Both reprinted by permission of the Editor of *Poetry* and the respective authors./January, v. 73, 1949 for "News of the Root" by Stanley Kunitz. Copyright 1949, renewed 1976 by the Modern Poetry Association Reprinted by permission of the Editor of *Poetry* and the author./June, 1959 for "The Cunning and the Craft of the Unconscious and the Preconscious" by Delmore Schwartz; v. XCIX, November, 1961 for "Revelations and Homilies" by William Dickey; v. XCIX, November, 1961 for "Down from the Forked Hill Unsullied" by Robert Wallace. © 1959, renewed 1987; © 1961, renewed 1989 by the Modern Poetry Association. All reprinted by permission of the Editor of *Poetry* and the respective authors.—Publishers Weekly, June 3, 1996. Copyright 1996 by Reed Publishing USA. Reprinted from Publishers Weekly, published by the Bowker Magazine Group of Cahners Publishing Co., a division of Reed Publishing USA.—*Romance Quarterly,* v. 36, August, 1989. Copyright © 1989 by The University Press of Kentucky. Reprinted with permission of The Helen Dwight Reid Educational Foundation. Published by Heldref Publications, 1319 18th St. N.W., Washington, D.C. 20036-1802.—*The Romanic Review,* v. 76, November, 1985; v. 81, March, 1990. Copyright © 1985, 1990 by the Trustees of Columbia University in the City of New York. Both reprinted by permission of the publisher.—*The Saturday Review of Literature,* v. 23, April 5, 1941. Copyright 1941, renewed 1968 Saturday Review Magazine. Reprinted by permission of Saturday Review Publications, Ltd.—*Shenandoah,* v. XVII, Winter, 1966 for "Weights and Measures" by Dabney Stuart. Copyright 1966 by Washington and Lee University. Reprinted from Shenandoah with the permission of the Editor and the author.—*Small Press,* v. 9, Fall, 1991. Copyright © 1991 by Meckler Corporation. All rights reserved. Reprinted by permission of the publisher.—*Sparrow,* v. 31, April, 1975 for "Creating a Personal Mythology" by Diane Wakoski. Copyright © 1975 by Diane Wakoski. Reproduced by permission of the publisher.—*The Texas Quarterly,* v. 21, Winter, 1988 for "Nature and Society in the Poetry of Vicente Aleixandre" by Miguel Gonzalez-Gerth. © 1988 by The University of Texas at Austin. Reprinted by permission of the author.—*Thought,* v. 65, December, 1990. Copyright © 1990 by Fordham University Press. Reprinted by permission of Fordham University Press, New York.—*The Times Literary Supplement,* n. 3459, June 13, 1968; n. 3820, May 23, 1975; n. 4230, April 27, 1984. © The Times Supplements Limited 1968, 1975, 1984. All reproduced from *The Times Literary Supplement* by permission.—*Victorian Poetry,* v. 14, Spring, 1976 for "Seeing Pied Beauty: A Key to Theme and Structure" by Amy Lowenstein. Reprinted by permission of the author.—*The Village Voice,* v. 17, December 21, 1972 for "The Poetess: Duel, Sigh, or Shrug?" by Shelia Weller. Copyright © The Village Voice, Inc. 1972. Reprinted by permission of The Village Voice and the author.—*The Virginia Quarterly Review,* v. 67, Summer, 1991. Copyright, 1991, by The Virginia Quarterly Review, The University of Virginia. Reprinted by permission of the publisher.—*The Western Review,* v. 18, Winter, 1954.—*The Women's Review of Books,* v. VII, October, 1989 for "Earth Mother, Earth Daughter" by Diane Wakoski; v. IX, May, 1992 for "Creature Comforts" by Diana Hume George. Copyright © 1989, 1992. All rights reserved. Both reprinted by permission of the respective authors.—*Women's Studies: An Interdisciplinary Journal,* v. 4, 1976. © Gordon and Breach Science Publishers. Reprinted by permission of the publisher.—*World Literature Today,* v. 52, Spring, 1978. Copyright 1978 by the University of Oklahoma Press. Reprinted by permission of the publisher.—*Yale French Studies,* n. 31, 1964. Copyright © Yale French Studies 1964, renewed 1992. Reprinted by permission of the publisher.

COPYRIGHTED EXCERPTS IN *PC,* VOLUME 15, WERE REPRINTED FROM THE FOLLOWING BOOKS:

Bowra, C. M. From *Inspiration and Poetry.* Macmillan & Co. Ltd., 1955. Reprinted by permission of Macmillan, London and Basingstoke.—Boyle, Robert R. From "The Thought Structure of the Wreck of Deutschland," in *Immortal Diamond: Studies in Gerard Manley Hopkins.* Edited by Norman Weyand. Sheed & Ward, 1949. Copyright, 1949, by Sheed & Ward, Inc.—Breton, Andre. From "Rano Raraku," translated by Wallace Fowlie, in *Xenophiles.* Gallimard, 1948. Reprinted by permission of the publisher.—Bump, Jerome. From *Gerard Manley Hopkins.* Twayne, 1982. Copyright © 1982 by G. K. Hall & Company. Reprinted with the permission of G. K. Hall, a division of Simon & Schuster, Inc.—Cabrera, Vicente. From "World Alone: A Cosmovision and Metaphor of Absent Love," in *Critical Views on Vicente Aleixandre's Poets.* Edited by Vicente Cabrera and Harriet. Society of Spanish and Spanish-American Studies, 1979. © copyright, Society of Spanish and Spanish-American Studies, 1979. Reprinted by permission of the publisher and the author.—Daydi-Tolson, Santiago. From *Vicente Aleixandre: A Critical Appraisal.* Edited by Santiago Daydi-Tolson. Bilingual Press/Editorial Bilingue, 1981. © 1981 by Bilingual Press/Editorial Bilingue. All rights reserved. Reprinted by permission of the publisher, Arizona State University, Tempe, AZ.—Donoghue, Denis. From *Connoisseurs of Chaos.* The Macmillan Company, 1965. Copyright © Denis Donoghue, 1965. All rights reserved. Reprinted by permission of Georges Borchardt, Inc., on behalf of the author.—Egan, Desmond. From *Saving Beauty: Further Studies in Hopkins.* Edited by Michael E. Allsopp and David Anthony Downes. Garland Publishing, 1994. Copyright © 1994 by Michael E. Allsopp and David Anthony Downes. All rights reserved. Reprinted by permission of the publisher.—Gardner, Thomas. From "Far from the Crash of the Long Swell: Theodore Roethke's North American Sequence," in *Discovering Ourselves in Whitman: The Contemporary Long Poem.* University of Illinois Press, 1989. © 1989 by the Board of Trustees of the University of Illinois. Reprinted by permission of the publisher.—George, Diana Hume. From "'Keeping Our Working Distance': Maxine Kumin's Poetry of Loss and Survival," in *Aging and Gender in Literature: Studies in Creativity.* Edited by Anne M. Wyatt-Brown and Janice Rossen. University Press of Virginia, 1993. Copyright © 1993 by the Rector and Visitors of the University of Virginia. Reprinted by permission of the publisher.—Heaney, Seamus. From *Preoccupations: Selected Prose, 1968-1978.* Farrar, Straus, Giroux, 1980, Faber & Faber, 1980. Copyright © 1980 by Seamus Heaney. All rights reserved. Reprinted by permission of Straus and Giroux, Inc. In Canada by Faber & Faber Ltd.—Hirata, Hosea. From "Return or No Return: Nishiwaki's Postmodernist Appropriation of Literary History, East and West," in *Literary History, Narrative, and Culture: Selected Conference Papers.* Edited by Wimal Dissanayake and Steven Bradbury. College of Languages, Linguistics and Literature, University of Hawaii, 1989. Copyright © 1989 by College of Languages, Linguistics and Literature, University of Hawaii. All rights reserved. Reprinted by permission of the publisher.—Jaffe, Dan. From Theodore Roethke: "In a Slow up-Sway," in *The Fifties: Fiction, Poetry, Drama.* Edited by Warren French. Everett/Edwards, Inc., 1970. Copyright © 1970 by Warren French. All rights reserved. Reprinted by permission of the author.—James, Clive. From *First Reactions: Critical Essays 1968-1979.* Knopf, 1980. Copyright © 1980 by Clive James. Reprinted by permission of Alfred A. Knopf, Inc. In Canada by the author.—John Hanak, Miroslav. From "Vicente Aleixandre's 'In a Vast Dominion': The Completion of a Submersion of Personality in the World Ground," in *La Chispa '85: Selected Proceedings.* Edited by Gilbert Paolini. Louisiana Conference on Hispanic Languages and Literatures, 1985. Copyright © 1985 by Gilbert Paolini. All rights reserved. Reprinted by permission of the publisher.—Keene, Donald. From *Dawn to the West: Japanese Literature of the Modern Era, Vol. 2.* Holt, Rinehart and Winston, 1984. Copyright © 1984 by Donald Keene. All rights reserved. Reprinted by permission of Henry Holt and Company, Inc. In the British Commonwealth by permission of Georges Borchardt, Inc. on behalf of the author.—Kumin, Maxine. From an interview in *To Make a Prairie: Essays on Poets, Poetry and Country Living.* University of Michigan Press, 1979. Copyright © by The University of Michigan Press 1979. All rights reserved. Reprinted by permission of the publisher.—Lauter, Estella. From "Diane Wakoski: Disentangling the Woman from the Moon," in *Women as Mythmakers: Poetry and Visual Art by Twentieth-Century Women.* Indiana University Press, 1984. Copyright © 1984 by Estella Lauter. Reprinted by permission of the publisher—Lewandowska, M. L. From "The Words of Their Roaring: Roethke's Use of the Psalms of David," in *The David Myth: in Western Literature.* Edited by Raymond-Jean Frontain and Jan Wojcik. Purdue University Press, 1980. Copyright © 1980 by Purdue Research Foundation, West Lafayette, Indiana 47907. All rights reserved. Reprinted by permission of the publisher.—Lorca, Frederico Garcia, and Pablo Neruda. From "Al Alimon," in *Selected Poems of Ruben Dario.* Translated by Lysander Kemp. University of Texas Press, 1965. Copyright © 1965 University of Texas Press. Reprinted by permission of the publisher, Frederico Garcia Lorca, and the Literary Estate of Pablo Neruda.—Mills, Ralph J., Jr. From "Theodore Roethke: The Lyric of the Self," in *Poets in Progress.* Edited by Edward Hungerford. Northwestern University Press, 1962. Copyright © 1962, 1967 Northwestern University Press. Reprinted by permission of the publisher.—Paz, Octavio. From "The Siren and the Seashell," in *The Siren & the Seashell and Other Essays on Poets and Poetry.* Translated by Lysander Kemp and Margaret Sayers Peden. University of Texas Press, 1976. Translation copyright © 1976 by Octavio Paz. All rights reserved. Reprinted by permission of the publisher and the translators.—Torres-Rioseco, Arturo. From *New World Literature: Tradition and Revolt in Latin America.* University of California Press, 1949. Copyright, 1949, by The Regents of the University of California. Reprinted by permission of the publisher.—Torres-Rioseco, Arturo. From "Ruben Dario: Classic Poet," translated by David Flory, in *Ruben Dario Centennial Studies.* Edited by Miguel Gonzalez-Gerth and George D. Schade. Institute of Latin American Studies, 1970. Copyright 1970 by the Department of Spanish and Portuguese, The University of Texas at Austin. Reprinted by permission of the publisher.—Vanderbilt, Kermit. From "Theodore Roethke," in *A Literary History of the American West.* Texas Christian University Press, 1987. Copyright © 1987 by The Western Literature Association. Reprinted by permission of the publisher.—Wakoski, Diane. From "Color Is a Poet's Tool," in *Poet's Perspectives: Reading, Writing, and Teaching Poetry.* Edited by Charles R. Duke and Sally A. Jacobson. Boynton/Cook Publishers, 1992. Copyright © 1992 by Boynton/Cook Publishers, Inc. All rights reserved. Reprinted by permission of the publisher.—Warren, Austin. From *Rage for Order: Essays in Criticism.* University of Chicago Press, 1959. Copyright 1948, 1959 by The University of Michigan. Renewed 1975 by Austin Warren. All rights reserved. Reprinted by permission of The University of Michigan Press.—Williamson, Alan. From *Introspection and Contemporary Poetry.* Harvard University Press, 1984. Copyright © 1984 by the President and Fellows of Harvard College. Excerpted by permission of the publishers and the author.

COPYRIGHTED IMAGES IN *PC*, VOLUME 15, WERE REPRINTED FROM THE FOLLOWING SOURCES:

Corrected typescript of "Feeding Time," by Maxine Kumin, photograph, **p. 205.** Reproduced by permission.—Cunningham, Imogen. Roethke, Theodore, portrait, **p. 243.** AP/Wide World Photos. Reproduced by permission.—Dario, Ruben. From a photograph in *Critical Approaches to Ruben Dario,* **p. 61.** By Keith Ellis. © University of Toronto Press.—Hopkins, Gerard Manley, **p. 169.** Harry Ransom Humanities Research Center, University of Texas at Austin, Photography Collection. Reproduced by permission.—Hopkins, Gerard Manley, photograph, **p. 122.**—Roethke, Theodore, **p. 285.** From a jacket of *The Far Field.* Doubleday, 1964. Used by permission of Doubleday, a division of Bantam Doubleday Dell Publishing Group, Inc.—Roethke, Theodore, photograph, **p. 243.** UPI/Corbis-Bettmann. Reproduced by permission.—Ruller, P. Dario, Ruben, drawing, **p. 76.**—Vicente, Aleixandre, photograph, **p. 1.** AP/Wide World Photos. © by AP/Wide World Photos. Reproduced by permission.—Wakoski, Diane, photograph by Fred W. McDarrah, **p. 337.** Reproduced by permission.—Kumin, Maxine, photograph by Layle Silbert, **p. 178.** Reproduced by permission.—Wakoski, Diane, photograph by Layle Silbert, **p. 359.** Reproduced by permission.—Wakoski, Diane, photograph by Robert Turney, **p. 322.** Reproduced by permission.

Vicente Aleixandre
1898–1984

Spanish poet, critic, journalist, and editor.

INTRODUCTION

Recipient of the Nobel Prize for literature in 1977, Aleixandre was a poet of the "Generation of 1927" whose prolific output has strongly influenced the work of subsequent Spanish poets. His selection for the Nobel Prize came as a surprise to much of the literary world although Aleixandre's first collection had appeared in Spain almost fifty years earlier and his reputation in his country was well established. Prior to 1977, Aleixandre's works available to English readers, including *Vicente Aleixandre and Luis Cernuda: Selected Poems* and *The Cave of Night: Poems*, had received little notice. Critical attention abroad increased following his reception of the award and several additional works of selected poems in translation have been published. Despite this interest and the vital role he has played in the evolution of Spanish-language poetry, the complexity of Aleixandre's work and the inherent difficulties in translating it have resulted in a limited general readership.

Biographical Information

Aleixandre was born in Seville and raised in Málaga, a nearby city that figures symbolically in much of his work. When he was eleven he moved with his family to Madrid, where he later received degrees in law and business administration and began a career in economic law. In 1925 Aleixandre contracted tuberculosis, thus beginning the series of illnesses that plagued him for the rest of his life. His health eventually forced him to abandon his career and he began to concentrate on writing poetry. His first book, *Ambito* (*Ambit*), published in 1928, was written in the tradition of *poésie pure* that was characteristic of Spanish poetry in the 1920s. Around the same time, Aleixandre began to associate with Pedro Salinas, Federico García Lorca, Jorge Guillén, and other poets based in Madrid, culminating in the innovative literary movement referred to as the "Generation of 1927." Writers in this group reacted against the provincialism of Spanish literature. They advocated poetry as a means to discover and explore the relationship between external reality and the poet's internal world, and, while they rejected sentimentality, love was a dominant theme in the work of Aleixandre and other members of the group. Unlike most other writers of his generation, Aleixandre remained in Spain during the Civil War and the subsequent reign of Francisco Franco. Although never a political poet, his works were banned in the postwar years due to his antifascist beliefs and his

independence from the official regime. Aleixandre's works were reinstated during the 1940s. As one of the few representatives of the earlier period still living in Spain, Aleixandre served as an inspiration to younger generations of Spanish poets, who viewed him as a great master. He continued to publish new works, including the critically heralded volumes *Poemas de la consumación* (*Poems of Consumation*) and *Diálogos del conocimiento* (*Dialogues of Knowledge*), the latter published when the poet was 76 years old. He died in 1984.

Major Works

Most of Aleixandre's poetry can be divided into three periods. The first includes *Pasión del la tierra* (*Passion of the Earth*, composed 1928-1929), *La destrucción o el amor* (*Destruction or Love*, composed 1933), and *Mundo* a solas (World Alone, composed 1934-1936). Most of the poems in these collections were written just prior to or during the Spanish Civil War, but they do not reflect current events. Rather they employ surrealistic imagery in presenting a cosmic, mystical vision of the world. Aleixandre's thematic focus during this period centers on the elemental forces of the human mind, a yearning for the solace of nature, and the inextricable connection between love and death and between the forces of creation and destruction. In contrast to *Ambit*, these volumes are more complexly constructed free verse, in which Aleixandre's sweeping, passionate meditations are given freer rein. Aleixandre's first post-Civil War collection, *Sombra del paraíso* (*Shadow of Paradise*), is a transitional volume leading to the second phase of his career. Poems in the middle period, which include those from *Historia del corazón* (*History of a Heart*) and *En un vasto dominio* (*In a Vast Dominion*), share with earlier ones a nostalgia for the lost union between humanity and nature, but a dramatic shift in focus is evident. Previously, Aleixandre had looked inside the individual, rejecting historical and social reality. During the middle period he reached outward, emphasizing temporal and physical connections between the self and the surrounding world and projecting a universal compassion for humanity. With a firmer grounding in earthly reality, surreal imagery and irrationalist techniques gave way to a more direct approach in which the affirmation of love predominates. Aleixandre's final period, consisting of *Poems of Consumation* and *Dialogues of Knowledge*, is characterized by a return to the structural and metaphysical complexity of his early work. In *Poems of Consumation*, the poet views the past from the perspective of old age and mourns the passing of love. In *Dialogues of Knowledge*, he attempts to comprehend the depths and limitations of human knowledge, a process marked by emotional intensity and somber brooding.

Critical Reception

Aleixandre has described his poetry as a "longing for the light." Many critics, and the poet himself, have noted the influence of Sigmund Freud on Aleixandre's exploration of the hidden passions and driving forces that operate beneath the surface of consciousness. Lewis Hyde, one of Aleixandre's noted translators, observed in his introduction to *Twenty Poems* that a desire to explore "the strong undertow beneath the accelerating tide of rationalism" connects Freud, surrealism, and the early poetry of Aleixandre. Of Aleixandre's poems, Hyde says: "[They] are not an affirmation. They are not working out a full and nourishing surreality, but away from the reality at hand. That . . . is part of their tension—they are the reflective mind trying to think its way out of coherence and precision."

PRINCIPAL WORKS

Poetry

Ambito [Ambit] 1928
Espadas como labios [Swords like Lips] 1932
Pasíon del la tierra [Passion of the Earth] 1935
La destrucción o el amor 1935; also published as Destruction or Love: A Selection from "La destrucción o el amor" of Vicente Aleixandre, 1976
Sombra del paraíso [Shadow of Paradise] 1944
Mundo a solas 1950; also published as World Alone, 1982
Poemas paradisiacos [Poems of Paradise] 1952
Nacimiento último [Final Birth] 1953
Historia del corazón [History of a Heart] 1954
Mis poemas mejores [My Best Poems] 1956
Poemas amorosos [Love Poems] 1960, revised 1970
Poesías competas [Complete Poems] 1960
Antigua casa madrileña [Ancient Madrid House] 1961
Picasso 1961
En un vasto dominio [In a Vast Dominion] 1962
Retratos con nombre [Portraits with Names] 1965
Obras completas [Complete Works] 1968, revised 1977
Poemas de la consumación [Poems of Consumation] 1968
Poems (bilingual edition) 1969
Antologia del mar y del la noche [Anthology of the Sea and the Night] 1971
Poesía superrealista [Surrealistic Poetry] 1971
Sonido del la guerra 1972
Diálogos del conocimiento [Dialogues of Knowledge] 1974
Vicente Aleixandre and Luis Cernuda: Selected Poems (bilingual edition) 1974
Antología total [Total Anthology] 1975
The Cave of Night: Poems (bilingual edition) 1976
Twenty Poems 1977
Poems-Poemas (bilingual edition) 1978
A Longing for the Light: Selected Poems of Vicente Aleixandre 1979
The Crackling Sun: Selected Poems of the Nobel Prize Recipient 1981
A Bird of Paper: Poems of Vicente Aleixandre 1982
Nuevos poemas varios [Selected New Poems] 1987

Other Major Works

Algunos caracteres de la poesía española contemporanea [Some Characteristics of Contemporary Spanish Poets] (criticism) 1945
Los encuentros [The Meetings] (critical and biographical sketches) 1958
Aleixandre para niños [Alexandre for Children] 1984

CRITICISM

Paul Ilie (essay date 1972)

SOURCE: A review of *Poesía superrealista*, in *Books Abroad*, Vol. 46, No. 3, Summer, 1972, pp. 455-56.

[*An American educator and critic specializing in Spanish literature, Ilie is the author of* The Surrealist Mode in Spanish Poetry *(1968) and* Documents of the Spanish Vanguard *(1969) and has published book-length studies of Camilo Jose Cela and Miguel de Unamuno. In the following excerpt, Ilie comments on the surrealist qualities of Aleixandre's poetry.*]

After more than a generation of denials that a surrealist mode of poetry and fiction existed in Spain, an important breakthrough seems to be taking place. Vicente Aleixandre himself, who once wrote that he was never a surrealist, has published an anthology [***Poesía superrealista***] designed to demonstrate the *secuenica irracionalista* of his poetic career. The reason for his change of heart is a radically revised definition of surrealism which Aleixandre formerly conceived of as automatic writing "and the consequent abolishment of artistic conscience." He now apparently regards superrealismo as characterized by "associations of verbal elements in which discursive logic breaks down, or approximations which, obeying another, more profound coherence, distort, on the altars of expression, their everyday sense." While this view is imprecise, it is a step forward in the direction of specifying the esthetic foundations and concrete practices of what I have called the "surrealist mode" in Spanish literature. Most critics have recognized ***Pasión de la tierra*** as belonging to this category, and now Aleixandre includes ***Mundo a solas*** and later poems as part of an irracionalismo linked to the surrealism of the early period.

The anthology itself is the best guide to the nature of Aleixandre's practices. One dominant characteristic is obsessive distortion. Themes of sterility and mutilation alternate with animal imagery: "Si yo acaricio un escarabajo / . . . el Sol se detiene, se alarga, se convierte en escala"; "besos amables a la cobra baja / cuya piel es sedosa o fría o estéril." Another characteristic is the resemblance many poems bear to surrealist painting: eery landscapes sometimes without men as in Tanguy ("No existe el hombre"); sometimes peopled with mannikins as in Chirico ("Un coro de muñecas, / cartón amable para unos labios fríos, / cartón de luna o tierra acariciada"); and sometimes luxuriant with disturbing vegetation as in Ernst ("Bajo tierra se vive . . . / Hay tubérculos que hacia dentro crecen como las flores"). A final characteristic is the theme of music, which is intertwined with eroticism and evocative of the search for a transcendent surreality found among the French surrealists ("Canción a una muchacha muerta"). To establish categories of esthetic practices is the more dispassionate means of arriving at a true understanding of a complex phenomenon. Fifty years from now critics will see the entire gamut of surrealist modes in different countries much the same way that we currently view the romantic movements of the 19th century: as a sensibility and not an orthodoxy defined by the manifestoes of one or two writers. Painting will also be recognized as perhaps the most useful key to this sensibility and its techniques as they appear in literature.

Guillermo Carnero (essay date 1973)

SOURCE: "'Knowing' and 'Known' in *Poems of Consummation* and *Dialogues of Knowledge*," in *Critical Views* on *Vicente Aleixandre's Poetry,* edited by Vicente Cabrera and Harriet Boyer, Society of Spanish and Spanish-American Studies, 1979, pp. 87-96.

[*A Spanish poet who began publishing in the late 1960s, Carnero is perhaps the most outspoken critic of the generation of native poets that preceded him for their single-minded focus on social issues and elevation of political content over such artistic concerns as form, style, and language. In the following essay, which was originally published in* Cuadernos Hispanoamericanos *in 1973, Carnero explains that Aleixandre's poetry contrasts vitality—exemplified by such traits as inquisitiveness, impulsiveness, and desire for new experiences—with dogmatism and detachment.*]

The major premise of Aleixandrine discourse is, as Carlos Bousoño has indicated in his excellent book [*La poesía de Vicente Aleixandre*], vitality, at least in what is considered the first stage of his poetic production which comes to a close with the publication of ***The History of the Heart.*** The vitality to which I refer is double: on the one hand it is the act of recognition of the world which surrounds the poet, or rather his intuition, since the word "recognition" is condemned in Aleixandre's universe as is manifest in the texts which serve as the subject of this study; on the other hand, it is evidence for the poet of his own vitality. In this way, existence in the world is, for Aleixandre, a harmony which is felt and enjoyed and does not need to be provoked because it is given between the being of the individual and the being of reality: between these there is more than communication (communication would presuppose the existence, at least at the beginning, of two expressivities which then turn out to be in agreement). There is a unique expression, which is the language of what is alive in the universe, of which the poet is a part differentiated only insofar as he is endowed with consciousness. I would dare say that there is no communication, because the relationship world-poet occurs at a level of greater identity in which the poet does not feel alien: "I am that happy earth that doesn't bargain for its reflection" (**"Ultimate Birth"**). The poet feels so full of life that, in a typical Aleixandrine vision, he grows until he touches the clouds and his extended arms take in the four cardinal directions.

As Bousoño has noted, this first long stage is a continuing canto to elemental beings, natural elements and animals, especially wild animals, including those which, like the beetle, wander serenely through a benevolent universe. In their massive, solid, motionless existence, the inorganic elements manifest evidence of life. The animals manifest the preeminence of impulse and instinct: Aleixandre calls "love" the energy of the tiger, endowed with "a heart that knows almost nothing, except love" (**"The Jungle and the Sea"**). As he states in **"The Poet,"** the vibrant poet sees himself reflected in nature:

> for you, poet, who felt in your breath
> the brutal charge of the celestial birds,
> and in whose words the powerful wings of eagles
>   fly as fast
> as the back of the warm fishes flash without sound:

After *History of the Heart,* the poet takes a step backwards; still immersed in the vital plan of the world, he no longer keeps step with it; he separates himself from things and, always ready to jump back into the world, he considers them from a certain distance in the two books which form the transitional stage in the development of his work: *In a Vast Dominion* and *Portraits with a Name*. In these two books, the attitude of Aleixandre could be summed up by what Bousoño has called "solidarity" to explain the way the poet approaches the characters of his *Encounters*. By "solidarity," I understand an attitude toward the world which is becoming tinged with nostalgia; it is not sad because the separation has been voluntary as well as recent: the poet does not yet feel it as an imposition (in all that follows I am referring to the two transitional works, not to the *Encounters*). The intensity of the relationship to the world diminishes and solidarity is another name for inertia. Separate from the poet, the characters in *Portraits with a Name* provoke in him an enormous sympathy. It is especially the first chapter in *In a Vast Dominion* where Aleixandre's fervor for young bodies, for the flesh in all of its manifestations, for youth, sustains an obvious trace of nostalgia: an inventory is made of a series of parts of the human body which Aleixandre contemplates now not with his normal exaltation but rather with amazement at its exact functioning and its perfect mechanisms. This is reminiscent of Leonardo's reflections on the appropriateness of anatomical organization; the enthusiasm has become intellectual, mixed in with the memory the senses bring to bear. This reflective attitude is not yet tinged with disillusion; but what the reading of *Poems of Consummation* will reveal to us about this attitude is that, in the first chapter of *In a Vast Dominion,* relationship between Aleixandre and the world is substantially modified.

In *In a Vast Dominion,* the poet's life pauses to be contemplated and acquires a clear meaning: it is the passage of time which contains moments of immersion into the universe. This immersion still seems possible, and the moment when the poet considers that his past is linked to the past itself there is no break in time because there is no separation from life; the poet thinks that he has simply made a stop on the way, and before resuming the journey, he looks back and takes comfort in it. As *Poems of Consummation* will show, this stop was not a pause, but rather a definitive stopping. **"The Old Man Is Like Moses"** well sums up the key idea of this work. Like Moses, the poet sees before him a future life which others will enjoy.

With *Poems of Consummation,* a new element in Aleixandre's world bursts forth: old age. It is not surprising that it is charged with dark tones if we recall the emphasis on life and on love, the gifts of youth, in the first eight books. Age sets margins: "But the one who passes alone, protected / by his age, crosses without being sensed" (**"The Years"**); and in **"Final Face"** it turns the being into a grotesque caricature:

> That is why, when the old man exhibits his hilarious
> vision he sees himself behind bars
> degraded, the recollection of some living, and there
> appears

the pointed nose, eaten on gnawed away, the thinning
hair,
a mat, the turbid drop that makes up the eye, and the
hollow or crack
where the mouth was . . .

Old age is the ongoingness of an incomplete existence, because living is loving and being loved: "The one who could have been was not. Nobody has loved him" (**"The One Who Was"**). The world is, by virtue of love, "Lyre opened of the world" (**"The Young Lovers"**). Life is linked to youth which is its indispensable requisite: "Life is being young and nothing more" (**"He Doesn't Know It"**). "I was young and I looked, I burned, / I touched, I sounded" (**"Sound of War"**). And the lesson of age is a paradox: one can only hope for immortality, unaltered permanence in time which is the negation of life: only dead things remain as they are and this state is the only one invulnerable to time: ". . . the leaves reflected fall. They fall and they last. They live" (**"If Anyone Had Told Me"**).

In *Poems of Consummation* it is stated clearly: "Knowing is not the same as to know" (first line of the poem **"A Term"**). As one continues reading the book it becomes evident that the two terms have a meaning which is not usual: Aleixandre goes polishing the meaning throughout the book which, from this perspective, turns out to be its progressive materialization. We witness this process of definition through which the attitude of Aleixandre toward the world becomes determined by the opposition between "knowing" and "known". Through the function of these two terms and their derivatives like "truth," the poet balances his life and exposes a new kind of relationship with the world. Furthermore, he assumes a concrete attitude toward the problem of writing. I shall try to expose the semantic content of these two key words: once the content is determined, *Poems of Consummation* will reveal a concrete meaning. The book is written in an alogical manner (which is very different from methodical illogicalness), nevertheless it is logically formulable and analyzable. I believe that these two characteristics, alogicalness in the writing and receptivity to logical analysis, permit the recognition of a great work rather than a mystification.

We know that in all of Aleixandre's work, life has been identified with the capacity for feeling love. This love can be understood in two ways: an animal loves when it sets itself in motion impelled by its instincts to communicate with its fellows and with nature: eating, killing, reproducing are episodes of this love. Man adds one ingredient to animal nature: his awareness of sharing animal instinct and especially his need to formulate in some way the attraction he feels toward what surrounds him and also the nature of this environment. Then, in the human being, there exists a supplementary manifestation of love: the desire for knowing and for knowing oneself in addition to knowing the other (*conocer*). For Aleixandre, love is, combined with sense perception and beginning with not-knowing, a need for knowing. In **"Lazarillo and the Beggar,"** Lazarillo says: "I love because I do not know" (*saber*). Knowing is not exclusive to man, since it occurs not only on a rational level, but also on an irrational level.

The feeling experience, although deprived of awareness, brings knowing; therefore, the bull comes to know his experience of the bullfight and of death: "That bull knows although he may be dying" (**"The Maja and the Old Woman"**). Although it may be impossible for him to elevate his experience to another level different from the level of feeling because of the limitations of his nature and because the feeling experience immediately precedes his death, he knows his experience. The verb "knowing" has, in the Aleixandrine context, an uncompleted value reinforced by the same value of the other verb which, in the same context, is closely connected to it: the verb "looking." "Knowing" and "looking" embody the unfinished process, the unsatisfied aspiration, the unfinished journey in the same way that "to know" and "to see" indicate termination and completion. "Looking" is the questioning and inquisitive attitude of the one who seeks to apprehend a meaning of which he is still ignorant, and "looking" is associated, in the Aleixandrine text, with youth: "the one who looked and who did not see . . . youth beating in his hands" (**"But Born"**); "Knowing, penetrating, inquiring: a passion that lasts as long as life" (**"Darkness"**); "the one who gropes, lives" (**"Sound of War"**). For this reason, "knowing," which is equivalent to being alive, is also equivalent to being uncertain about what one is trying to know: in the poem **"The Young Lovers"** (which I believe took its inspiration from the story of Calixto and Melibea [the young lovers in the Spanish masterpiece *La Celestina* (1499)]), he says: ". . . I glimpsed her: I am knowing her. And this garden hides from me behind its walls her form, / not her radiance." Love is born from a sudden vision, from a "radiance," and it impels one to apprehend the significance of the beloved and in this apprehension is its climax because, with the termination of the cognitive process, comes also the termination of the stimulus which attracts to the beloved: "Knowing is loving. To know, to die / I doubted. Never is love life" (**"The Old Lovers"**).

In April of 1925 a serious illness caused Aleixandre to retire to the countryside for two years. This illness left an indelible impression on his poetry, which concentrated on an evasion of reality and a preoccupation, at least in part, with his own physical necessities.

—*Kessel Schwartz, "The Sea, Love, and Death in the Poetry of Aleixandre," in* **Hispania,** *May, 1967*.

And life lasts as long as the desire to apprehend the world has not been satiated: "What insistence on living. I only understand it / as *formulation* of the impossible: the real / world" (**"The Old Lovers"**; italics mine). Let us stress the word *formulation*; a formula is a condensation of meaning which we consider definitive: a formula is the product of reason, and reason is proper to the old because it produces its edicts when the cognitive process has ended: "Only the

child is knowing" (**"The Comet"**); "I am young and I am knowing" (**"The Young Lovers"**).

When the cognitive process has ended, the one who undertook the process now has a wisdom: knowing is an activiy, and to know is a fixed result. Wisdom comes with age, and since old age is incompatible with vitality, and wisdom is acquired after the process of knowing has been completed, this wisdom is opposed to life: "The one who doubts exists. Only dying is science" (**"Without Faith"**); "Not knowing is living. To know, dying it" (**"Yesterday"**). I want to stress the transitive use of the verb "dying." This "it" does not mean the biological life of the poet but all that life means in Aleixandre's context; the transitive value of "dying" shows that death is not a state but rather the result of an activity. Aleixandre means that he is not dealing with the death of the body (that, in Spanish, would be the reflexive use of the verb to die) but with the annihilation of something larger than the body itself but so linked with its survival that the poet cannot say "kill it." With "killing it," he would also die; hence the great suggestive power of the transitive "dying it."

Wisdom is incompatible with youth and life as I have already said: "Because I know it I do not exist" (**"You Have a Name"**).

To know is to be born to science whose subject is the world and, at the same time, it is the death of life. What Aleixandre suggests is that he considers the evolution of the mind and of the body irreconcilable: the body advances through time driven by its senses and its desire for knowing and gradually it provides the mind with facts and experiences from which the mind induces wisdom. When the body stops functioning, the mind takes account and draws up conclusions: there are no conclusions until the acquisition of experience has ceased; these conclusions (to know–known) demonstrate that immersion into life (knowing) has stopped; the moment one "is born" (to the known), one "dies": "More young people see each other. They are the non-dead, since they are the non-born" (**"The Young"**). Swan, in **"That Swan's Way,"** says:

> . . . I climbed the ladder
> of that knowing. But I thought how useless
> it was to know it . . .

So once in possession of the known, the world loses its newness because each new experience becomes foreseeable and explainable by virtue of the known: "looking" becomes equivalent to "seeing" and the effort of "knowing" a new reality becomes frustrated in the "re-cognition" that that reality is similar to a previous reality already codified by the known. To know, which seemed to be the optimal relationship with the world because of the desire for knowing in the one who loves, turns out to be, once achieved, a wall between the lover and the beloved, between man and the world, and the poet tells us that the only desirable knowing would be that which results from an unpremeditated relationship with the world in which no knowing whatsoever was sought, in which only living was sought. Then one would have extracted from the world a known not subject to formulation and not accompanied by the signs of dying: ". . . the one who doesn't look is knowing" (**"You Are Waiting"**); "The light, once thought, deceives" (**"The Limit"**). The desire for the known grew out of a mistaken idea: to consider that the world had to be apprehended in scientific terms, that sensorial contact was not sufficient, that it was necessary to name it and to formulate it, as expressed in **"Present, Afterwards"**:

> To place my lips on your idea is to feel you
> a proclamation. Oh yes, terrible, you exist.
> I am the one who expired, the one who pronounced
>   your name
>   like form
> while I was dying.

Thus it turns out that to know is equivalent to being dead: "because I know I am falling asleep" (**"Lazarillo and the Beggar"**); "the one who remembers is the one who is dying" (**"The Young Lovers"**); here "to remember" is used with the meaning described above "to recognize": "the one who knows has already lived" (**"The Old Lovers"**). True wisdom would be, as I have previously stated, having "known" how to maintain an unpremeditated relationship with the world, relating to it in a perpetual knowing which can never be considered definitive, like the Rubén Darío Aleixandre sketched in **"Knowing Rubén Darío."** This wise man, always wandering and always alive, would be one of the "creatures of the dawn" of whom Aleixandre speaks in *Shadow of Paradise*: "You encountered the generous light of innocence" (first line of **"Creatures in the Dawn"**), "naked with majesty and purity facing the world's scream" (**"Message"**; this does not mean "deprived of majesty and purity," but invested with them by virtue of nakedness); ". . . being in the movement with which the great heart of men beats extended" (**"In the Plaza"**).

We can, then, establish two series of analogous terms through which the recent Aleixandre expresses himself and orders his vision of the world: on the one hand, knowing—youth—life—looking—experience of the senses; on the other hand, known—old—age—death—seeing—the conclusions of thought. If one undertakes to read *Poems of Consummation* and *Dialogues of Knowledge* taking these two master series into account, their deepest meaning emerges.

One could also establish that "light" and "air" used metaphorically, are associated with "knowing" while "sound" is associated with "known." The explanation could be that knowledge is formulated in words and words are articulated sounds. But I would rather pass over these associations which might not be valid, considering the very general value of natural elements in Aleixandre's poetry.

If wisdom is formulated in words, then Aleixandre has articulated the problems of expression and of writing and examined them with an essentially disenchanted view. Words are not always signs of death; they aren't when they rise spontaneously as a manifestation of vitality, as can be seen in **"The Words of the Poet"**:

> . . . words spoken
> in moments of delight or anger, of ecstasy or
>   abandon,
> when, the soul awakened looms in the eyes

In other situations, which are in fact the majority, words have a sterilizing quality, as in **"Sound of War"**:

> . . . (they) are merely words
> that drag you, a dust shadow,
> smoke exploded, human as you turn out
> like an idea dead beyond nothingness.

Already in *Swords like Lips,* Aleixandre had established the antithetical nature of words and elemental beings. In **"Words,"** he writes:

> Flower you, girl almost naked, alive, alive
> (the word, that mashed sand).
>   . . . . .
>
> (The word, the word, the word, what a clumsy
>   swollen womb).

In **"Message,"** from *Shadow of Paradise,* we read: ". . . without looking, cast far away the sad articles, sad clothes, words, blind stakes." The living word is characterized by being a nondefinitive formulation, an attempt to formulate; overly expert expression is symptomatic that one has reached the stadium of wisdom. As is seen in **"The Words of the Poet,"** living words are ordered according to their own logic:

> more like light than like expert sound.
>   . . . . .
>
>   . . . Not with supreme virtue,
> but yes with an order, infallible, if they want.

The wise man's desire is that his expert words recover the tremor and the fallibility they had when they were alive. Because wisdom as Aleixandre understands it, provides a kind of truth which the poet rejects after having sought it: only the incomplete and imperfect truth of knowing has value and radiates light and life: ". . . if it goes out, it is dead" (**"The Maja and the Old Woman"**).

Arthur Terry (essay date 1975)

SOURCE: "Kinds of Knowing," in *The Times Literary Supplement,* No. 3,820, May 23, 1975, p. 559.

[*An English educator and critic, Terry has published studies of the Spanish poets Joan Maragall and Antonio Machado and is the author of* Catalan Literature *(1972) and coauthor of* Introduccion a la lengua y la literatura catalanas *(1977). In the following review, he finds that in* Diálogos del conocimiento, *Aleixandre has continued to develop the style and insights of his poetry.*]

Vicente Aleixandre's most recent book of poems [*Diálogos del conocimiento*] is one of his best, and unmistakably different from any of the others. This is an unusual and gratifying thing to be able to say of a poet in his late seventies who for many years has been regarded as a master by younger generations of Spanish poets. His *Obras completas,* published seven years ago, seemed at the time to round off an achievement which could be seen to have grown naturally and organically from its earliest premises. This organic quality comes largely from Aleixandre's central preoccupation with the process of creation itself. In his earlier, Surrealist-influenced, poems, love becomes a metaphor for the self-destructive and self-renewing powers of the universe; later, from *Historia del corazón* (1945-53) onwards, the emphasis shifts to the contemplation of man in his human context, where the living and the dead are felt as parts of a single material, the "materia única" of one of his best-known poems.

These two phases, with their seemingly endless possibilities of inter-relationship, achieve their richest effect in *En un vasto dominio* (1958-62), the last collection to be included in the *Obras completas*. Yet, almost simultaneously, Aleixandre published a new book, *Poemas de la consumación* (1968), a series of bleak and moving lyrics on old age and the passing of love. In *Diálogos del conocimiento,* this most recent phase is taken a stage further: though the treatment of old age is no less intense than in the previous collection, the writing is deliberately less personal, as if Aleixandre were trying to accommodate his new vision to the more universal perspective of his earlier work.

Each of the fifteen poems is in dialogue form and runs to about a hundred lines. This relative spaciousness, together with the absence of complex imagery, may suggest that Aleixandre has returned to a more expansive mode after the austerities of his previous book. Yet the term "dialogue" is deceptive: the majority of the poems consist of two interwoven monologues, whose speakers make no direct contact with one another. In this way, the cumulative effect of genuine dialogue is avoided: instead of a steady linear development, there is a subtle interplay of contrasts and coincidences of which the speakers themselves are unaware. And the effect of this is to call into question the actual status of the words, as if the reader were gradually to become conscious of an unwritten poem behind the interrupted snatches of monologue.

The speakers themselves are differentiated through contrasts of age, sex and temperament, sometimes with the suggestion of a historical or literary context. Yet the most fundamental difference is between the experience of old age and that of youth. The key-word, as the title of the book implies, is "knowledge". In poem after poem, Aleixandre plays brilliantly on the nuances of the verbs *conocer* ("to know by experience or intuition", "to be acquainted with", "to discover") and *saber* ("to know for a fact,", "to be intellectually certain of"). Thus, for several of the speakers, the movement through life towards death is a question of passing from one kind of knowledge to the other, from the vital, though tentative, process of sense experience to

the certainties which come only when such experience is at an end. Or, as one of the speakers in **"Los amantes viejos"** puts it: "Conocer es amar. Saber, morir." ("To know by experience, is to love. To know intellectually is to die.")

In the poems themselves, however, nothing is as simple as that. Though Aleixandre renders the pathos of old age with great poignancy—the whole drift of his earlier poetry was towards the celebration of sense experiences he no longer finds available—there are moments when he seems to allow that abstract thought may be as "real", and therefore as vital, as intuition. And in **"Dos vidas"**, one of the few poems into which old age does not enter, he imagines two young poets, one a believer in the world of the senses, the other a more austere visionary for whom external reality must be filtered through the processes of the mind. Here it is as though, by admitting this second possibility, Aleixandre were recognizing a kind of poetry very different from his own which he had finally understood and might still come to practise.

The fact that he can convey such openness without sense of strain is perhaps the most obvious measure of his continuing vitality. More than ever, Aleixandre has, in Hugh Kenner's phrase, "the power to charge simple vocables with all that they can say". These latest poems, with their clarity of language and constantly shifting meanings, show that, after fifty years of writing, he is still capable of extending his range in unexpected and profoundly convincing ways.

From Aleixandre's "Nobel Lecture":

[The] poet is full of "wisdom"; but this he cannot pride himself on, for perhaps it is not his own. A power which cannot be explained, a spirit, speaks through his mouth: the spirit of his race, of his peculiar tradition. He stands with his feet firmly planted on the ground, but beneath the soles of his feet a mighty current gathers and is intensified, flowing through his body and finding its way through his tongue. Then it is the earth itself, the deep earth, that flames from his glowing body. But at other times the poet has grown, and now towards the heights, and with his brow reaching into the heavens, he speaks with a starry voice, with cosmic resonance, while he feels the very wind from the stars fanning his breast. All is then brotherhood and communion. The tiny ant, the soft blade of grass against which his cheek sometimes rests, these are not distinct from himself. And he can understand them and spy out their secret sound, whose delicate note can be heard amidst the rolling of the thunder.

Vicente Aleixandre, "Nobel Lecture," The Nobel Foundation, *1977.*

Robert Bly (essay date 1977)

SOURCE: "The Man Who Stayed Behind," in *The New York Times Book Review,* October, 30, 1977, pp. 3, 52.

[*One of the most prominent and influential figures in contemporary American poetry, Bly writes visionary and imagistic verse distinguished by its unadorned language and generally subdued tone. His poems are pervaded by the landscape and atmosphere of rural Minnesota, where he has lived most of his life, and are focused on the immediate, emotional concerns of daily life. In the following excerpt, Bly comments on the significance of Aleixandre's verse for the tradition of Western poetry.*]

How fitting it is that Vicente Aleixandre has won the Nobel Prize! He is one of the greatest poets alive and his work stands for endurance, the roots under the tree of consciousness, the slowly growing trunk. He receives the prize for all the others of his generation in Spain, especially Jorge Guillen and Rafael Alberti. His generation was the astounding one, a concentration of genius unheard of in Spain for centuries, amazing in any country. Federico García Lorca was the joyful bird of the group, composing poems on the piano; Rafael Alberti, the rationalist turned sailor, an ecstatic rationalist; Pedre Salinas, the gentle mason of love; Jorge Guillen, a worshipper of light; Luis Cernuda, who sang like a sad Job; and the enthusiastic Vicente Aleixandre, who was and is a kind of river, carrying trees torn up by the roots, everything turbid and wheeling, the things turned up frightening in the sunlight.

In his work you can see more clearly than in any poet in English the impact of Freud. The civilized Western man and woman has produced for several centuries a poetry that resembled a formal dance in a ballroom. Neruda, not being a European, had his dances outdoors, so it was left to Aleixandre to feel the full clash of Freud inside a drawing room. He evokes what it was like for a Westerner to read Freud's testimony of the immense and persistent sexual energy trying to rise into every vein and capillary of life and then go to a formal ball. He notices that

> The orchestra which stirs up
> my worries like a thoughtlessness,
> like an elegant witticism in a fashionable drawl,
> knows nothing of the down on the secret mound,
> knows nothing of the laugh which rises from
>   the breastbone like
>   an immense baton.

After Freud, moustaches become interesting in a public place:

> The ladies wait for their moment seated upon a tear,
> Keeping their dampness hidden with a stubborn fan,
> and the gentlemen, abandoned by their buttocks,
> try to draw all looks toward their moustaches.

That generation, some of whom published their first books in the late 1920's, came to be called "The Generation of '27." This generation welcomed Neruda when he came to Spain in the 30's, jumped feet first into surrealism, which they felt not as a clique but as an ocean, encouraged each other, tried to pull poetry simultaneously into surrealism and into song, and worked to help Spain feel in herself the new energy rising, both rebellious and sexual.

What happened? The rebellious energy they felt was felt also by the industrial workers and the farm workers. The defeat of the rebellious ended the energy flow. The Francoists shot Lorca, Alberti, Salinas. Cerauda, Guillen, Prades left Spain for the United States and Spanish America. Only Aleixandre, always in poor health, but stubborn, remained. The Franco people knew well where he stood, and he was kept silent by police and Control. In 1944 he was at last allowed to publish, and the book was the great *Shadow of Paradise*. By that time so much literature had been cut off near the ground, or torn up (Hernandez dead in prison, Spain isolated) that the younger writers felt abandoned, dead, in despair. It turned out that Aleixandre's decision to stay helped all that. He represented the wild energy still alive on Spanish soil. In fact, when I visited him in the late 60's, he was still living in the same house in the suburbs of Madrid where Lorca and Hernandez used to visit him.

All the young poets I met in Spain adored him; while I was visiting, there was a knock on the door, and a 20-year-old poet from Andalusia appeared, just arrived in Madrid. He had to see Aleixandre before he could settle down, what else could he do? Aleixandre gave him some practical advice, and showed him that he knew his poems. Aleixandre then read **"The Waltz"**—his ballroom poem— to both of us with terrific energy, and said happily, "Isn't it obscene!" He was hard to get hold of during those years, since he only answered the phone from 2 to 2:05 P.M. each day. One of the poets I was with the day before in a cafe suddenly cried out, "Oh God, it's 2:06! We missed it! Now we'll have to wait until tomorrow." So he preserved his privacy and yet remained open at the same time, a warm presence, a bridge between two Spains. Stephen Kessler, his translator from California, visited him last year and found the enthusiasm for him still increasing—the old grateful, the young dedicating their books to him.

After *Shadow of Paradise,* in 1944, Aleixandre gradually left the surrealist turmoil, and his poetry moved into what Lewis Hyde calls "Poems with White Light"—as contrasted with the "Red Light" Hyde senses in the earlier Freudian poems. A good example of the new style is his marvelous poem called **"The Man on His Death Bed."** This is Lewis Hyde's translation. A man is dying:

> He put his hand to his chest and said:
> Listen to me!
> No one could hear a thing. A strange smile lowered
>   its smooth mask like a veil
> over his face, rubbing it out.
> There was a little wind. Listen to me! Everyone,
>   everyone strained their delicate ears.
> Listen! And they heard it—pure and crystal tone—
>   the silence.

Here is how he describes an old man whom he used to see sitting in the sum each day:

> As the old man lived, as he waited, how the sun
>   thinned him out!
> How slowly it burned away the last wrinkles, his
>   sad lined skin, the record of his misery,
> how long it took, stripping and polishing
>   everything!
> In the silence the old man went slowly toward
>   nothing, slowly surrendering himself,
> the way a stone in a tumbling river gets sweetly
>   abraded
> and submits to the sound of pounding love.
> And I saw the powerful sun slowly bite at him with
>   great love, putting him to sleep
> so as to take him bit by bit, so as to dissolve him
>   with light bit by bit,
> the way a mother might bring her child very softly
>   back to her breast.

He continues to write these "poems of white light," poems with intellectual calm, with trust in the organic way of doing things, including the way people and creatures die, and a sweetness like that in Chaucer.

True to their famous myopia, none of the principal American publishing houses has printed a single book of Aleixandre's, and so he is virtually unknown here. As far as I know, only two books are in print, both provided by small presses. . . .

For the Nobel Prize to come to Aleixandre now is fitting, not only because of the energy and intensity of his own poetry, but because it comes at this moment in Spanish history. Spain is waking up after years of sleep, and Aleixandre's poetry and stubborn presence have a strong part in that awakening.

Miguel González-Gerth (essay date 1978)

SOURCE: "Nature and Society in the Poetry of Vicente Aleixandre," in *Texas Quarterly,* Vol. 21, No. 4, Winter, 1978, pp. 206-14.

[*A Mexican-born American educator, poet, and critic, González-Gerth has published several volumes of verse. Here, he examines Aleixandre's treatment of love, fellowship, and humankind's relationship to nature.*]

Vicente Aleixandre has been writing poetry for over half a century. To date he has written over thirty books and pamphlets of verse, and his collected poems and prose writings comprise two very substantial volumes. He belongs to an outstanding generation of Spanish poets, called the generation of 1927 because that year marked the tercentenary of Luis de Góngora's death and many young poets of the time visited Seville, where the Baroque master is buried, and gathered at the local Athenaeum to hold a ceremony. It was as if Spanish poetry, while reacting to the

latest European literary currents, were self-consciously reaching back in its own history and tradition to rediscover the metaphorical genius of Góngora. For metaphor was indeed the poetic currency of the day.

One of the immediate models, perhaps the main one, for the Spanish poets of 1927 was Juan Ramón Jiménez. In his *Segunda antolojía poética,* which had appeared in 1922, at the end of the book, there is a number of aphorisms and final notes written in prose. Those statements and much of the poetry in the volume together constitute a sort of new *ars poetica* which is a milestone in Spanish literary history. The nucleus of the new generation was composed of Pedro Salinas, Jorge Guillén, Federico García Lorca, Dámaso Alonso (also a well-known Góngora scholar), Gerardo Diego, Rafael Alberti, Luis Cernuda, Aleixandre, Emilio Prados, and Manuel Altolaguirre. Of these, Guillén, Alonso, Diego, Alberti, and Aleixandre are living. It was a brilliant and versatile group. Lorca and Alberti seem to have followed the trend, sensuous and fiery, set by Jiménez before the bridling effect of his second personal anthology. They were followed close behind by Cernuda and Aleixandre. In contrast, Salinas and Guillén adopted his subsequent mode, more thoughtful and precise, a mode which, for Jiménez, reached its apex in the dazzling unfinished poem entitled "Espacio." It is interesting to note, however, that Aleixandre, too, not only has practiced self-criticism in prefaces to his own books when reissued, but has written a very deliberate series of aphorisms entitled *Poesía, Moral, Público* (1950), not unlike that of Jiménez, yet expressing a totally divergent ethic. But after all, it is a question of evolution of sensibilities in the face of changing world situations.

Aleixandre's first period stretches from 1928, when he published *Ámbito,* to 1953, when *Nacimiento último* appeared. During that time the poet's view of reality was such that he would extol nature even in its most elemental plane. He gives us a vision that is vast and complex, both inviting and overwhelming, believable as well awesome. Earth and sky are teeming with meaningful life. The title of his first book, then, refers to the space encompassed by man's necessary awareness: "The boundaries are overrun," he says, "let the clear space shine." And later: "It is pleasant and beautiful to walk full of hope." The vastness is seen by the poet through the binoculars of imagined travel. Poor health and other circumstances have confined Aleixandre to Spain throughout his life, so maps became an essential means of poetic transportation in "the numberless countries I have touched with my hand, those dark-colored areas which I, dressed in black, have left far behind as I turned their back." Nature is evangelized and given the sensual but not the spiritual attributes of man: "A huge arm holds the jungle by the waist," we read, and yet "the whole rejected world withdraws as might a sea that bellowed without destiny." This seems to me an original variation of the neo-Platonism often identified by English scholars with the romantic poets, whose doctrine may have filtered to Aleixandre from its German source, since previous Spanish writers, such as Gustavo Adolfo B quer in the nineteenth century and Gabriel Miró and Jiménez, after the generation of 1898, manifested its attraction;

but our poet's ideology is determined by a personal conviction about the relations among things.

From the outset, Aleixandre's world appears balanced on an axis whose poles are nature and man. But, as Carlos Bousoño, the foremost Aleixandre authority today has amply pointed out, the poet's early work presents this polarization as a dichotomy to be overcome, as if social evolution had, in modern times, led to an abstraction from nature by human society, resulting in the empoverishment of the individual when it comes to ethics and esthetics. These qualities belong to the spirit, and man should strive to be in consonance with nature, deriving from it a well-ordered selflessness in exchange for his peculiarly human love. The opposite of communion is estrangement, and Aleixandre finds a ready image in the moon to convey that thought, as he also gives the human union of lovers a cosmic extension of highly charged nature imagery: "They suffered from the light . . . lips emerging from the hardened night . . . They loved each other on a seaborne bed . . . as flowers love the piercing thorns . . . A perfect noon, they loved each other and so deep. . . ." The desire to grasp, to encompass, to transcend limits reveals a sensuous character apparently not in harmony with the spiritual and contemplative, but only apparently, for as with many other poets past and present, the aim of Aleixandre is to make of his words an extension of himself, and for him the word *love* implies the destruction of all barriers and the experience of life to the full. From him, as for Novalis, the world is all one, and nature is the way of sensitizing man into communion: there is "a golden wind that would unite in purity all bodies on the sand," while unfortunately "a man does not know the godly green of the sea . . . his arms do not perceive the birds as they arrive." In order to be real and immediate, such communion must embrace matter itself. The human being must be alert to, that is, aware of everything around him. Thus he will not only live a richer life, in tune with the rest of creation, but also, upon dying he will experience what Aleixandre calls his "ultimate birth" in the bosom of ultimate reality. Man is a transitory creature only if his life and death are denied the proper relationship with the unity of the rest of creation, a vital link which the poet concretizes in what he calls a "goddess" whose "naked body risen in the woods and shining all alone" had a brief stay in his eyes because *they* were transient, but whose light and glow "never fade among men." This mythic vision or ideal reappears in another poem probably suggested by the recollection of a painting or tapestry.

Aleixandre's mission as a poet in this early period seems to be, then, to exhort his fellow human beings to discover the paradise they still have here on earth, if they will only regain it from neglect. Hence the title of his, until recently, most highly regarded book, *Sombra del paraíso* (1944).

It is a complex book, of extraodinary craftmanship, which casts the nature-man-love theme developed previously in imagery even more obscure though more technically brilliant than before and charged with a more evident Biblical symbolism. In the poem **"Tragic Destiny"** he says:

But you rose suddenly.
You had sensed the dark wings,
the magic message from the deep which calls to
  hearts.
You watched intently the incipient sound of the
  abyss.
What shapes did you behold? What virgin signs,
what precise words uttered by the foam,
sweet spittle from secret lips
that, half-open, invoke, submit, seduce?
The message said. . . .

And we are not told what the message was, unless it is the same as the one contained in the poem of that very title—**"Mensaje"**—appearing much later in the book and which states:

Friends, ask not of the joyful morning
why the intagible sun gives its strength to men.
Drink its bright gift, its brilliance in the shade,
in the amorous arms of that inspired blue,
and open your eyes upon the beauty of the sea, as
  that of love, . . .
you behold love, the cosmic urge in man,
and that fragrant abundance of the earth
where trees, brimming with urgent spring,
give their light or their apples to some thirsting
  lips . . .

Kiss ye the sand, echo of the sun perhaps,
  warm like a wine or a heavenly message . . .

Ah, my friends, cast away, without looking,
  all dismal artefacts,
dismal clothes, dismal words, all blind
  metals and sticks,
and naked with majesty, pure before the
  world's outcry,
plunge your body into the chasm of the sea,
  of light, of virgin joy,
while the universe, a sheer and final
  ember, burns away.

The relative obscurity found in this poetry, which can be defined as hermetic, though having some affinities with surrealism and its spin-offs then still prevalent in Europe, is more directly associated with and can be attributed to modern poetry in general, though in some cases, the prose collection **Pasión de la tierra** (1935), for example, a surrealistic intent is apparent. Bousoño, in his ample study of Aleixandre's poetry, has referred to the important part which the irrational element plays in it. Indeed, poetic vision and lyrical pull so predominate that the reader is hard put to detect a line of demarcation between experience and imagination in the imagery. As C. M. Bowra, in *The Creative Experiment*, says:

Most modern poets try to make poetry as full and as rich as possible in order to secure the maximum of truth and of poetical effect. An experience must be presented in its complexity, without the simplifications and the order which analytical thought gives . . .

The sense and the mind work so closely together and their interactions are so intricate that the poet cannot distinguish between them and must show how united they are in the moment of creative illumination.

Sombra del paraíso has been the object of much study and much praise. It is the acme of Aleixandre's first period and stands more or less midway within it. It therefore represents best the full range of the poet's vision at that time. His own sensitivity toward the cosmic fellowships he propounds is most directly expressed in poems about actual fields and actual country folk whom he calls "sons of the fields." He says to them: "I see you as the deepest of truths, humble and absolute inhabitants of earth . . . Oh sacred destiny! . . . In your continuance, you are the only certainty of fleeting eyes." Besides the peasant, other heroic figures in this lyrical scenario are: the lover, the loved one, and the poet; reminiscent of Rilke's hierarchy composed of the angel, the saint, the hero, the lover, and the poet. This first period closes with poems among which are some that offer discordant notes within an otherwise harmonious though by no means idyllic whole. Aleixandre's world of poetry had come in contact with a world at war. There is even a suggestion of unwanted death here, not the nirvana-like death through fusion with nature exalted in the previous books, but an ugly absence brought about by some wrongdoing: "Man does not exist."

A second period begins with the book entitled *Historia del corazón* (1954), "the heart's history." Here the poet turns from nature and natural man to society and the social individual. This does not mean that nature will disappear from his view; it will remain, and with the same value as before, but as a background for the drama of immediate human existence. There are many love poems in this volume, but they do not sing the joyous and mysterious links which love has with nature. Instead they express what love has in common with all human experience: transitoriness. The heart has always been the symbolic seat of the emotions. History is a vital structure peculiar to human beings. Thus this book is a reflection of those experiences which the poet considers most intense and which include the tribulations of love between persons, recollections of childhood and the emotions elicited by the death of children, the feeling of solidarity toward all individuals, and the conviction that the poet should speak for them all. Such love and fellowship, however, are no longer transcendent. Instead, the poet says, "everything conspires against the striving endurance of the hopeless flame" and "there are moments of loneliness when one's heart in amazement must admit it does not love." It might have been easy to engage in a loving fellowship with nature, but similar relations with fellow human beings become socially problematical. In the end, on what principle should we base such relations? According to Aleixandre, on the principle of commonality. We must "recognize" ourselves in one another. The use of that verb in that particular sense is essential to these poems. One which has been much discussed and frequently anthologized is **"On the Square."** It is not just characteristic of Aleixandre's new exhortation, it is a peculiarly urban poem, describing the social surroundings whence it comes, the

square being the heart of the city as humanity is the heart of history. When a man is seen walking into the crowd on the square, he quickly becomes one of the many people in the street; he remains in his heart an individual but becomes undifferentiated among the rest of humanity, lost from view of the deluded, discriminating eye, mindless of its own transitoriness. We are all Everyman in death, and so the poet seems to suggest that we should take comfort in exercising our will where we can, namely, in recognizing ourselves as Everyman in life. The poet himself is no exception. And in this feeling of solidarity with his fellow man can find the only comfort for his existential limitations, and so it is a question of turning the tables on the human condition. A beautiful thought, of course, and a commendable attitude, but as with all humanism, not likely to represent a challenge to traditional religion. As a purely social commitment, however, as a poetization of the social contract, **"On the Square"** contains a stirring message. Or is there more to its than that? Unfortunately, its particular rhetoric does not allow for good yet faithful English translation. But there is something here of the old message with just the scenery changed and the sound muffled:

> Go slowly, like a bather who afraid and
>   wary yet longing for the water,
> first lets his feet get wet . . .
> But then he holds out his arms and surrenders at
>   last.
> And there he finds himself, his strength grows as he
>   plunges forth. . . .

The "small, tiny heart" will be overtaken and absorbed by the "great, common heart" of the crowd in the waters of solidarity and commonality, instead of plunging into "the chasm of the sea, of light, of virgin joy" while fire burns away the world of the unloving. Communion among human beings alone has at this junction supplanted communion on a cosmic plane. Faith, hope, and love, to quote St. Paul, is summed up in the last, but it is human love turned to a sort of mystical egalitarianism. The statement "It is pleasant and beautiful to walk full of hope" found in the previous poem, has become the following:

> It is beautiful, beautifully comforting and humble,
>   revitalizing and true,
> to feel oneself in the sunshine, among others,
>   impelled,
> carried along, led, mingled, noisily pulled by the
>   crowd.

After *Historia del corazón* with its radical change of emphasis, Aleixandre published in 1962 a book entitled *En un vasto dominio*. For a poet so conscious of limits, the words "in a vast domain" can only mean expansion. During his first period his awareness of man's limitations was directed toward nature and man's apparent incapacity or unwillingness to break all barriers and commune freely, fuse with nature. In his second period, then, the focus on limits has to do with barriers between human beings and, by extension, between social classes. Aleixandre would have every human soul and body untrammeled and unfettered. But *En un vasto dominio,* the second book of this second period, does not move the poet's position in any direction, it merely expands it. In effect, it combines and synthesizes both positions previously assumed. And yet neither the dazzling beauty of nature nor the invigorating fraternity of human beings is particularly advanced. Both are present but diffused by new devices, such as historical, artistic and literary allusions, incidental parodies, social satire, and geographical settings. From the whole emerges the sensation that there is no going back to a youthful, optimistic, utopic vision of nature. Time, perhaps age, perhaps experience and memory have caught up with the singer-poet. We now have a narrator-poet who tells mostly sad stories, except for those provided with the barb of irony, the reflection of timeless lyricism or the symbolism of tradition and lore. Human primacy, for instance, blends with human transitoriness, and together they find embodiment in the sensual nature imagery with which we had already become familiar. In a human footprint the poet sees "still the naked foot, pressed like a kiss upon the ground" and in the human being that made it, "the perfect creature that was born, and grew, glimmered and vanished." Above all, however, this book offers poems which are remarkable in themselves and as examples of the subtle fusion of previous emphases. Human primacy and natural setting are suffused once again in the unity of creation which, nevertheless, becomes more than ever intelligible when it is restored through humble human experience. In **"Shepherd Bound for Mountain Pass"** we see this figure:

> His blended shape
> seemed dressed in corduroy, perhaps in tree bark . . .
>
> His foot was firm.
> His legs promised none else than hardness to the
>   toes.
> A flash of yellow lightning
> cracked and then rebuilt, ending in head,
> hair or smoke, everything real . . .
>
> A man under the sky,
> alone amid wool, among the middling oaks . . .
> feeling the blue of a new sky,
> the nightfall and its faithful stars,
> his foot asking for truth, his open arms
> a cross or just a call to beasts . . .
>
> He climbs the slope. The farm is
> near the mountain pass . . .
> the flock takes refuge, the fold is sleeping,
> and in turn, as on the only warmth,
> the tired shepherd too finds rest upon the ground.

Is the figure one of man or nature or of both? This is a poem without a message. **"On the Square,"** on the other hand, is a poem with a clear, obvious message; a moral lesson is to be learned from it, and the vocative modality should not put us off, since the poet addresses himself at least as much as anyone else. But the images that make up the poem are of an allegorical nature, while the ones that make up **"Shepherd Bound for Mountain Pass"** are, I think, of a symbolic nature.

In a piece entitled "Introduction" (*London Mercury,* July 1930) about Frederick Carter's *The Dragon of the Apocalypse,* D. H. Lawrence wrote the following:

> It is necessary for us to realize very definitely the difference between allegory and symbol. Allegory is narrative description using, as a rule, images to express certain definite qualities. Each image means something, and is a term in the argument and nearly always for a moral or didactic purpose, for under the narrative of an allegory lies a didactic argument, usually moral. Myth likewise is descriptive narrative using images. But myth is never an argument, it never has a didactic nor a moral purpose; you can draw no conclusion from it. Myth is an attempt to narrate a whole human experience, of which the purpose is too deep . . . in the blood and soul, for mental explanation or description . . . And images of myth are symbols. They don't "mean something"; they stand for units of human *feeling,* human experience. A complex of emotional experience is a symbol. And the power of the symbol is to arouse the deep emotional self, and the dynamic self, beyond comprehension, Many ages of accumulated experience still throb within a symbol. And we throb in response.

Human feeling, human experience, human throbbing, the **"Shepherd Bound for Mountain Pass,"** *The Man Who Died*: it would seem that Aleixandre and Lawrence have at one time been, surprisingly, on the same wave length. Every great poet invents for himself a kind of mythology. From figures and configurations of the past he may adopt and adapt a system that functions as the nucleus of his work's total structure. Aleixandre's, it seems to me, is neo-Biblical, starting with Genesis and ending with the Gospels and Revelation. Yet I am not suggesting that his poems are religious, only that the mythical charge of their imagery is undeniably Biblical and Evangelical though sometimes tinged with the pagan figures of art since the Renaissance. Such quality could also be the result of certain modes of neoromanticism. The wish for natural communion and human fellowship is evident in an artist like Franz Marc, whose animals might well be those frequently appearing in Aleixandre's poems, and who could easily personify, as described by his friend Wassily Kandinsky, the human-natural ideal propounded by our poet. "His free nature," wrote Kandinsky, in his *Reminiscences,* "was that of the countryside, and I always took a particular pleasure in watching him walk through the meadows, fields and woods with a rucksack on his back and a stick in his hand. His organic relationship with nature was reflected in his bond with his dog 'Russi,' a large white sheepdog, whose manner, strength of character and sweetness of temper made him a perfect four-legged copy of his master."

En un vasto dominio was followed by *Retratos con nombre* (1965), *Poemas de la consumación* (1969), and *Diálogos del conocimiento* (1974). This later poetry contains much reflection. There we find not merely experience but the philosophy of experience, old age in contrast with youth, the power and limitations of language. But there are also the constant themes of nature and love, as Wordsworthian "emotions recollected in tranquillity." Human death is a fact now to be grieved about. Heidegger's idea of poetry as commemorative language may be sufficient for life-experiences but not for death as the ultimate. And even the deepest fruition of living is beyond words. When it comes to the total of human experience only age yields the "truth" of life. It is highly significant that in these later poems, these poems of experience and old age, echoes of the earlier poems, the poems kindled by the fires of nature and love still ring. "Words die," the poet tells us. "Beautiful when said, they never last." Yet it is to be expected that his words, his words that make up his images, will last, especially those that can be categorized as mythical. Aleixandre's contribution to the poetic currents of his time includes the new ethic of social concern and commitment, which he expressed in his aphorisms and some of his later poetry. The trajectory of humanitarian and socio-political awareness in literature is a long one. There was the popular success of Edwin Markham, the Russian proletarian writers, the British war poets, the social poets of Spain and Spanish America, and now the American protest writers. All of them incorporate such themes into their poetry, reacting to the demands of a contemporary problematic by paying attention to what true poets have always known. But the lyric thrust must still transcend what other human enterprises can engage. When all is said and done, great poetry is not intended to elicit applause, not even social change; instead it is meant to produce astonishment.

On the style of Aleixandre's poetry:

Aleixandre's originality is radical and opposed to all symbolic tradition. And because the process is so virginal and different, the tone of the voice is also unheard-of. Aleixandre inaugurates in ***Diálogos del conocimiento*** a poetry of deaf and majestic slowness, spoken in the lowest chords, which I believe to be without precedent in our literature. This feeling of vast and obscure majesty at such a slow pace is quite simply a new feeling. All this achieved at the age of 76. Aleixandre's incessant creative capacity is truly amazing, even now in his glorious and fresh old age.

*Carlos Bousoño, "The Irrationalist Techniques of
Vicente Aleixandre," in* Vicente Aleixandre,
edited by Santiago Daydí-Tolson, 1981.

Manuel Durán (essay date 1978)

SOURCE: "Vicente Aleixandre, Last of the Romantics: The 1977 Nobel Prize for Literature," in *World Literature Today*, Vol. 52, No. 2, Spring, 1978, pp. 203-08.

[*Durán is a Spanish-born educator, critic, and poet who has published books on many Spanish and Latin American writers, including Pablo Neruda, Miguel de Cervantes, José Ortega y Gasset, Amado Nervo, Luis de León, and Francisco Quevedo. In the following overview of Aleixan-*

dre's career, Durán perceives a Romantic strain in the poet's verse.]

Why Aleixandre? More explicitly, why should the Nobel Prize for Literature be awarded to Vicente Aleixandre in 1977? Barbara Walters, speaking through a nationwide television program, declared that the poet was virtually unknown outside his native Spain (which only proves the lack of intellectual preparedness of our television announcers). And yet, if Lorca had been alive today, there is no question that the prize would have been his. The prize belongs not to a man, in this case, but to a whole generation, the generation of Lorca, Jorge Guillén, Rafael Alberti—perhaps the brightest and most original poetic generation in twentieth-century Western Europe. Not a restricted, disciplined group, as the French surrealists became, but rather a band of friends open to all influences.

I remember Aleixandre in the courtyard of his Madrid house, a great conversationalist who also knew when to listen. We talked about the romantics, dada, surrealism, the new trends: his blue eyes sparkled as he claimed that he had inherited from all movements, and by investing wisely he had increased the capital of poetry as a whole. Aleixandre is a tall man, with a noble face that seems to come out of a Michelangelo fresco, a modern prophet with a gravel voice and slow gestures. Wit and charm are part of his personality, and also personal warmth, yet the first impression is hard, almost overwhelming. The visitor is facing a giant, a giant who has attained the heights of poetic genius and is aware of it. Only slowly, step by step, the giant unwinds and becomes the most generous and cordial of hosts.

During our conversation I asked Aleixandre whether he could feel at home within any specific literary movement: he claimed the romantic movement came closest to his ideals. I both agreed and disagreed with his statement. Compared to an urbane and witty poet such as Pope, both Blake and Aleixandre, Keats and Baudelaire are brothers: a vast vision, a romantic sensitivity unites them. Yet compared to the other romantics, the style of Aleixandre's poems is clearly different. More difficult, more illogical, more mysterious, it is a style that has been profoundly influenced by surrealism.

There is an image which I feel can help us to understand the role of surrealism in contemporary poetry. If we think of a huge rocket as standing for the poetic vanguard movements in our century, then surrealism stands for the third stage of the rocket, the fastest and brightest stage. Every stage is marked by an increase in the anti-rational, illogical, subjective elements. Futurism, launched in 1909 by the Italian poet Marinetti in a manifesto written in French, wants to revolutionize subject matter, rhythm, rhyme, typography. Machines should be put on a pedestal; old legends and monuments should be put to the torch. Dadaism is invented by a Romanian, Tristan Tzara, in Zurich in 1916. Its aims are still more radical. As Stephen Spender puts it:

> Dada began in 1916, and consisted of the cultivated madness of gestures directed against the madness of

the war. Although Dada called itself revolutionary, its politics were not realistic or intended to be. Dada had no political program. The attitude of Dadaists was that mad and subversive and childish protests against the bourgeoisie were in themselves an already accomplished revolution in the lives of those who participated in them. ["Life Wasn't a Cabaret," *The New York Times Magazine,* Oct. 30, 1977.]

We are dealing, of course, with international movements. Writers such as Apollinaire, Alfred Jarry and Pierre Reverdy contributed to their launching, just at the time when the poems of the Chilean author Vicente Huidobro were helping to create a propitious climate for change both in Latin America and in Spain. And just as Picasso found inspiration in primitive American sculpture, Aleixandre brings to his observation of modern society the freedom, the power and the audacious sexual overtones that characterize his poems about the primitive world and the animals in the prehistoric jungle. In his poem **"The Waltz,"** for instance, the poet's X-ray eyes discover under the elegance and refinement of a modern ballroom, with ladies and gentlemen dancing faster and faster, carried away by the tidal wave of music, the passion of sexual desires, their pubic hair carefully hidden under the formal dress, the same heady mixture of sex and death:

> This is the instant the moment to say the word that
>   explodes
> the moment when long skirts become birds
> windows scream out
> light yells "help"
> and the kiss waiting in the corner between two
>   mouths turns into a thorn
> that will give out death by saying
> I love you.

In this poem, as in most other poems, Aleixandre destroys the distinction between subjectivity and objectivity, fuses the ideal and the real, the imaginary and everyday experience: these two realms are shown to be one and the same. This is why he can be at the same time a great poet of nature—nature as the outside world of spaces, rivers, forests, seas, dawns, animal life—and a great surrealist poet, delving into the unconscious, swimming in the stream of his own mind. He realizes, as most surrealist poets did, that the conventions of the rational world, as opposed to the desires and visions of the subconscious world of dreams and fantasies, tend to split into two mutilated halves what for primitive man was a whole and sound universe; hence the cult of voluntary hallucination and the sudden changes of subject and perspective, which can be baffling indeed to the average reader. There can be no doubt that Aleixandre is one of the most difficult poets ever to use the Spanish language. More than Lorca, Guillén and even Cernuda, in his generation, he employs every device that can free the mind of its rational categories. He wills a new reality whose truth is poetic rather than scientific, universal rather than particular. His main tool is his uncommon imagination, which faces the ordinary world and "derealizes" it. In other words, the conventional boundaries between ordinary perception and delirious hallucination are broken down, and every conceivable approach to experience becomes permissible.

Aleixandre knows instinctively that the modern poet must grow wings, must soar beyond everyday life, must see reality both from above and from below. He goes back in time and plunges into an abyss that opens both in the past and in his inner self. As a great critic of contemporary Spanish literature, Ricardo Gullón, puts it:

> Logically such an intense dreamer had to search for an answer where so many other poets before him looked for it, in the descent into Hell, in the underground where strange passions shed their dark light. Hell is now called the Subconscious, and the poet's guide is no longer Vergil or Orpheus but Rimbaud—yet a new name does not mean a new identity. And the traveler is called Surrealist, since under the outer layer of reality, beyond rational attitudes, in the abysses of dream, he is trying to discover the secret of Life and Death. From this dive into darkness Aleixandre came back a richer poet, both mysterious and lucid. His poems, like rivers, surround the reader slowly and inexorably, making him feel how much strength and vitality sparkle under the smooth surface of every word. [*Literature española contemporánea,* 1965]

It is difficult to know whether to characterize much of the nineteenth-century romantic verse as "religious." On the one hand, there is little overt reference to God or to religious subjects; on the other, many of the poems deal with experiences of a spiritual nature. Wordsworth, for instance, in "Lines Composed a Few Miles above Tintern Abbey," describes

> . . . that serene and blessed mood
> In which the affections gently lead us on,—
> Until, the breath of this corporeal frame
> And even the motion of our human blood
> Almost suspended, we are laid asleep
> In body, and become a living soul:
> While with an eye made quiet by the power
> Of harmony, and the deep power of joy,
> We see into the life of things.

These lines are inspired not by a supernatural power but by nature itself. What has caused in the poet an almost mystical trance are the trees, the fields, the sky.

The parallel between Aleixandre's poetry and William Blake's writings is even closer. They are both mystical and cosmic poets, visionary adventurers into the unknown. Blake's prophetic poems, like "The Four Zoas" and "The Book of Los" are extraordinarily complex, full of strange symbolism and self-created cosmologies. Aleixandre, in his **"The Jungle and the Sea"** (from *Destruction or Love*), likewise builds a vision of a primitive world through strange and powerful similes:

> Far away in a remote
> splendor of still virgin steel

there are tigers as large as hatred,
lions looking like a hirsute heart,
blood like placated sadness,
fighting against a yellow hyena shaped like the
    greedy sunset.

Aleixandre's cosmos, like Blake's, is animated by love. Yet the human elements in Blake are ever-present. His angels and titans are man himself writ large. Aleixandre goes back in his poetry to a primeval age in which man is a newcomer, almost an intruder. It is nature that rules man, not the other way around. And nature is restless— often, to the untrained human eye, pitiless. But there is love behind the destructive forces of nature. As I have noted elsewhere,

> [Aleixandre's] poems, if read from beginning to end, evaluate man's place in the cosmos, define all creation, and sing of the communion of men, as temporal beings, with the universe and with other men; only in such communion can man endure and become eternal. Through his difficult symbolic and visionary imagery, derived mainly from dreams and surrealism, Aleixandre has managed to unify realities that seemed irreconcilable. Not unlike William Blake, in Aleixandre the "marriage of Heaven and Hell" appears as a possibility; chaos is but one aspect of order; love and communion accept—and transcend—death.

Everything in nature is alive, as Keats knew, as Baudelaire and Rubén Darío had proclaimed (let us add here that Darío was for Aleixandre the poet who taught him the true meaning of poetry). Aleixandre writes:

> In the forest the trees sing just like birds do.
> An immense embrace caresses the jungle's waist.
> A bird that the unending light has turned to gold
> is still seeking the lips that will free him from his
>   jail.

("Come, Come Now," from *Destruction or Love*)

Perhaps the greatest book written by Aleixandre in the surrealist vein is *Sombre del paraíso* (*Shadow of Paradise*), begun in 1939, a year in which the whole of Spanish society lay in shambles. Jails and concentration camps were crowded. Most of the poet's close friends were dead or in exile. Life had to begin again from ground zero. Aleixandre took refuge in his memories of a happy childhood by the shores of the Mediterranean. As the critic Kessel Schwartz points out:

> Aleixandre deviates somewhat from the tumultuous and disparate ambivalence of *Destruction or Love,* but in the old familiar distinctions between man and nature, he continues to denigrate the former. The old fire remains in sublimated form, although from time to time the frenzy and naked passion of *Destruction or Love* shine through, and the poet employs new dimensions of supplementary imagery. He returns to his innocent world of infancy, to a Paradise beyond original sin and knowledge, to be one with the heavens and the creatures of the dawn. [Kessell Schwartz, *Vicente Aleixandre,* 1970]

Cosmic unity is the underlying theme of the book:

> Yes, poet: cast off this book which pretends to
> enclose in its pages a sparkle of sunlight,
> and look at the light face to face, while your head
> is supported on this rock,
> while your feet so far away feel the final kiss of the
>   setting sun
> and your uplifted hands sweetly touch the moon,
> and your hanging hair leaves a wake among the
>   stars.

("The Poet")

The poet is surrounded by innocent, virginal creatures. Hatred and sin have not yet been invented by Man:

> There each morning the birds were born,
> surprising, all new, full of life, celestial.
> Their tongues of innocence
> said no words . . .
> Birds of initial happiness, opening their selves,
> trying out their wings, without losing the virginal
>   drop of dew!

("Creatures in the Dawn")

Yet the poet's journey is not at an end. In *Historia del corazón* (*History of the Heart*), written between 1945 and 1953, Aleixandre comes back from Paradise in order to face all the ambiguity and anguish of our own times. As Kessel Schwartz describes it:

> The central theme concerns human solidarity and compassion for the victims of injustice. . . . Although he reserves his deepest and subtlest meanings for the description of historical and existential man, the poet also portrays his own life and personal past. No longer the creature of telluric forces . . . the poet, as a man, becomes all men, destined like him to live and die, without the assurance of Paradise or eternal life, in a world where death is always with us. [Schwartz, *Vicente Aleixandre*]

Nevertheless, it is not necessary to live desperate solitary lives, the poet exclaims with tenderness and optimism, as he signs for all mankind of fleeting time and human solidarity. Infants and oldsters mark the boundaries between being and not being, life and death. The poet recognizes that he is aging, but is without despair, empathizing with his neighbor who must also stoically face the end.

Rebellion, love and death are fused in one single existential vision:

> the lover knows that he passes and disappears,
> that love itself passes
> and that this generous fire that still endures in him
> witnesses pure the sweet passage of that which
>   eternally passes.

("Like the Thistledown")

The message is clear: man must learn to say "yes" both to life and love, on the one hand, and on the other, when it comes, to death and oblivion: "Oh dark night. I no longer expect anything. / Solitude does not lie to my senses. / The pure, calm shadow reigns" (**"Final Shadow"**).

Perhaps the main feature of Alexandre's poetry is the feeling of unity and organic growth that it creates in its readers. We are aware that each book has its own style, its peculiar characteristics, and at the same time that each book has a role to play in the corpus of Aleixandre's writings. The motto of this corpus could be "order and wisdom out of chaos"—yet an order and a wisdom that do not mask or conceal at any time the persistence of chaos, violence, anguish and ultimately death. Aleixandre's youthful poetry can be compared to a tornado, a nova exploding in the sky, a torrent of lava pouring into a primeval jungle. His later books are less violent and more nostalgic, as the poet opens his heart toward his own past and toward the suffering of his fellowmen.

The first period would stretch from 1928, the date of publication of his first book, *Ambito* (*Space*), to 1953, with *Nacimiento último* (*The Last Epiphany*). Its dominant trait is power: immense telluric and cosmic forces are deployed before us. They look for unity, love, ultimate fusion. The spectacle is at the same time fascinating and terrifying. The masterpieces of this period, *La destrucción o el amor* (*Destruction or Love*; 1935) and *Sombra del paraíso* (*Shadow of Paradise*; 1944), are organized around a main character which is basically not a human being but rather the whole cosmos, nature, the primeval creation of natural forces: man is only one of the many forces that nature deploys in its search for unity.

The second period, from *Historia del corazón* (1953) to *Poemas de la consumación* (*Poems of Consummation*; 1968), is less subjective, less irrational. The wild visions are replaced by an awareness of human time and human suffering. The first book belonging to this period, *Historia del corazón,* is basically the story of a love affair, in its daily moments of joy and anguish, and also the story of a growing awareness, a solidarity: the poet realizes that he is only one member of a vast society, the Spanish people, and that ultimately he is a part of mankind. Solidarity means a realization of finitude—the small, finite self is bound to disappear soon—and at the same time a source of strength: other human beings, very much like the poet, will go on living and loving. To this period belongs the book *Retratos con nombre* (*Portraits with Names*), thirty-seven poems each of which captures the physical and psychic essence of a friend of the poet: the poet's pen becomes a camera, one with great sensitivity and clear focus. One of the poems, **"Birthday,"** is a self-portrait: in it Aleixandre retraces step by step his own life as objectively and dispassionately as possible, and not without humor.

Self-knowledge is a door to wisdom: the last books by Aleixandre, *Poemas de la consumación* and *Diálogos del conocimiento* (*Dialogues of Knowledge*; 1974), are often desolate and tragic, yet serene. Human life has an end, old age is but the prelude to death, nothing—and nothingness—awaits us. The poet speaks with a soft voice, as in a confession or in evoking a memory too painful to explain in full detail. Often his sentences become brief, mysterious, contradictory. They remind us of the fragments of Heraclitus. Perhaps paradox and contradiction are the only weapons left to our mind: knowledge has to be paid for; logic can lead us only so far. For this last stretch of the journey the poet's mind must turn once again to irrational utterings. Yet the meaning of these books is not obscure: one must learn to say both "yes" and "no" to death and nothingness, the poet tells us. We must bow to what is and will be, and at the same time, as Dylan Thomas advised, we must not go too gently, too meekly, into the dark night of death: life is too precious for us not to regret its passing.

Organic growth is, as we have seen, the key feature in Aleixandre's poetry: *plus ça change, plus c'est la même chose,* since even in his philosophical poems dealing with death and old age we feel the fires of youth and desire burning under the smooth surface of each poem. Aleixandre's books encompass the "seven ages of man," and the remarkable feeling of unity, of growth within the frame of one individuality and one style, can be generated only because the poet is a master of Spanish poetic language and can thus clearly etch his own personality, his own vision of life, into each book, whether the book deals with the world as seen by an enthusiastic adolescent or whether we are listening to an old man waiting for death.

This is in itself a great merit—and yet it does not fully explain the range of Aleixandre's style. His poems are above all noble, "large," uplifting: we are always facing giants, a larger-than-life vision of the landscape and the figures in it. This feeling of *grandeur* can be attributed in part to some of the subjects; the sea, for instance, is a recurring theme. Yet there is more: Aleixandre has created, out of the influence of surrealism, a multi-layered style, one in which symbols are hidden behind words, and each line calls to mind a new group of symbols flying through the air toward the reader. For example, many of his nature poems can be read three ways, the first interpretation being that of a dream, a vision. And then the symbols begin to appear, both the Freudian and Jungian variety. The poem unfolds, new dimensions are added to it: it is a poem about a visionary poet, who at the same time is a child looking for his mother—and afraid of his parents—and a whole people remembering its past and the origins of the world. Thus in one of his earliest poems, in which he describes a stormy sea, menacing yet somehow attractive:

> The bituminous sea crushes shadows
> against itself. Hollows of deep blue
> remain frozen in every arch of the waves . . .
> Under lofty black skies the deep mouth bellows
> and demands night. The mouth, the sea, everything
> calls for darkness, deep, huge darkness,
> the horrible jaws want to eat, they show us
> all their white teeth of foam.
> A tongue huge as a pyramid, ominous, cold,
> rises up, demands. . . .
>
> (**"Sea and Night"**)

We see here how a positive symbol can acquire dramatically negative characteristics. The sea, symbol of fertility, of the feminine principle of fertility, is presented as something dark and menacing. In Cirlot's *Dictionary of Symbols* we read that the symbolic meaning of the sea "corresponds to the 'lower ocean,' to waters in motion. It is a transitive and mediating agent between the shapeless elements (air, gas) and the elements solidly shaped (earth, solidity) and by analogy between life and death. The sea, the oceans, are thus considered to be the fountain of life and also its end. 'To return to the sea' is like 'to return to the mother,' that is, to die." In Aleixandre the traditional symbols of the collective unconscious, the Jungian symbols, are reinforced very often, in a parallel system, by Freudian symbols: are not the "white teeth of foam" and the "tongue huge as a pyramid" the clearest poetic definitions of the "vagina dentata" which is a frequent motif of Freud's clinical writings?

Nostalgia is for the poet a normal and healthy reaching from our present consciousness toward the past, toward our roots. Human life is like a tree: its vast trunk, its leaves and flowers are easily seen, yet the roots are invisible, underground. We must always remember them, for without them, without the lost paradise of our unconscious world, our world of dreams, our childhood memories, we are no longer fully human. And yet another movement, a movement forward and upward, must also be emphasized: the open hand, the open arms, the solidarity with other human beings. After being long confined in his room, the poet goes out to the street, to the square, in order to mingle with other human beings and be a part of humanity:

It is a beautiful feeling, beautifully humble and
   buoyant, life-giving and deep,
to feel yourself beneath the sun among other people,
   propelled, carried forward, conducted,
blended, softly carried along.

   It is not good
to remain on the shore
like the jetty or like the mollusk stonily aping the
   rock.
Rather it is pure and serene to drown in happiness,
in the happiness of flowing and oblivion,
finding oneself in the movement with which the
   great heart of all men beats everywhere . . .

Don't look for yourself in the mirror,
in a dead dialogue where you cannot hear yourself.
Go down, go down slowly and search for yourself
   among the others.
There they all are, and you among them.
Get undressed, and fuse, and recognize yourself.
                                        (**"In the Square"**)

The poet can become a full-fledged member of mankind, can feel at home with the crowd, without losing his individuality. Paradise lost was not completely lost: a glimmer of the ancient light can be seen when we join arms with other human beings. The inescapable—and welcome—message is, we are not alone, if only we look

around. This message is made even more explicit in his next book, *En un vasto dominio* (*In a Vast Dominion*; 1962). Again we can find in Aleixandre's poetry an echo of the great romantic poets. Wordsworth had written,

Our birth is but a sleep and a forgetting;
The soul that rises with us, our life's Star,
   Hath had elsewhere its setting,
      And cometh from afar.
                  ("Intimations of Immortality")

Man is not alone, because—as Plato believed, as the theory of reincarnation holds—much wisdom, the untold knowledge of many previous lives, of previous beings, the experience even of animals, stones, water, infinite space, travels in our veins into our mind and heart. Man appears as an atom in a vast cosmos, but if the universe is curved about itself, man daring the vastness of time and space would then return on himself, perhaps from the route of the infinitesimally small.

Finally, if the world is created by the effort of arms and hands, and the earth itself, in a sense, is a product, a town also becomes a living unit, as do its citizens, a part of the landscape as they perform their daily tasks. Since things, life, man, love, history, spirit, and flesh are all material . . . Aleixandre stresses the need for collective participation in the process of salvation. Human life is still an arduous effort, but with the aid of men, both present and past, we may achieve continuity. [Schwartz]

In his recent work Aleixandre, once more, renews himself without changing his poetic personality. His two last books, *Poemas de la consumación* and *Diálogos del conocimiento,* with their short sentences, their paradoxes, their moments (flashes) of illumination, remind me of Heraclitus, of the Oriental mystics, of Schopenhauer. Wisdom, resignation, a sad acceptance, a stubborn resistance. From surrealism to wisdom: this is the trajectory—a long and fruitful journey—of our poet. As Robert Bly has written: "For the Nobel Prize to come to Aleixandre now is fitting, not only because of the energy and intensity of his own poetry, but because it comes at this moment in Spanish history. Spain is waking up after years of sleep, and Aleixandre's poetry and stubborn presence have a strong part in that awakening" [*The New York Times Book Review,* Oct. 30, 1977].

Vicente Cabrera (essay date 1978)

SOURCE: "World Alone: A Cosmovision and Metaphor of Absent Love," in *Critical Views on Vicente Aleixandre's Poetry,* edited by Vicente Cabrera and Harriet Boyer, Society of Spanish and Spanish-American Studies, 1979, pp. 53-70.

[*In the following essay, which was originally published in Spanish in* Journal of Spanish Studies: Twentieth Century *in 1978, Cabrera asserts that* Mundo a solas *(World Alone), is a pivotal work between the early and middle phases of Aleixandre's career.*]

The poetic work of Vicente Aleixandre from *Passion of the Earth* up to *Shadow of Paradise,* which makes up his first and perhaps richest period, is characterized as much by the unity of the elemental and cosmic conception of its theme as by the coherent and imaginative homogeneity of its diction. This substructure of vision and diction on which the poetry of this period rests is the result of an ongoing evolution in which each book becomes an outgrowth of the former one; that is, a lyrical step forward which, deriving from the earlier work, consolidates a new poetic vision. This evolution, however, is interrupted with the appearance of *Shadow of Paradise,* a work which, although it remains within the cosmic and elemental vision of the others, stylistically represents a change which had not previously occurred, for example, between *Passion of the Earth* and *Swords like Lips,* or between the latter and *Destruction or Love,* the work immediately preceding *Shadow of Paradise*.

There is no doubt that Aleixandre's silence between 1933 and 1944 led critics to suspect some sort of poetic crisis in the writer. But these speculations disappear with the publication of *World Alone* in 1950. Aleixandre says in the introductory note that this book was composed between 1934 and 1936, that is, between *Destruction or Love* and *Shadow of Paradise*. The author also explains that although "chronologically it antecedes it [*Shadow of Paradise*] in composition and therefore in style, in the development of a world to be expressed it is later." In his note to *My Best Poems,* he adds that *World Alone* is "perhaps the most pessimistic" of his books. This idea has been misinterpreted by critics as they attempt to deal with the whole as a simple negative canto and nothing more. The reason for this pessimism has not been explained nor have the other elements been explored. These new elements not only enrich the book's cosmovision but also make of this cosmovision a thematic outgrowth of the previously mentioned first period.

Seventeen poems were included in the first edition. Later one was added for the publication of the *Complete Works,* "Final Fire," and three more for the edition which in 1970 Aleixandre stated was the complete one: **"In a Cemetery," "Smoke and Earth,"** and **"Fallen Moon."** In the first poem, **"Final Fire,"** hope and even the certainty of surviving the final fire of death is found in love:

> You are as beautiful as the hope of living yet.
> As the certainty of loving you day after day.
>   . . . . .
>
>   Little girl small or sweet who are love or life,
>   a promise when the fire nears,
>   a promise of living, of living in May,
>   without having those flames which are burning the
>   world
>   reduce you to nothing. . . .

In the other three, especially in **"In a Cemetery,"** and **"Fallen Moon,"** the poetic vision is more ambiguous and severe because of the opposition of elements of life and death in the same equation and because of the juxtaposition of doubt and anguish with the drive to survive and integrate himself with the cosmos, expressed in **"In a Cemetery"** as follows:

> I still live, yes. I still live and seek earth,
> earth in my arms, while all the air
> is filled with its dark birds,

The poet feels that his cosmic reintegration achieved through death divests it of its negative nature. These four poems do not alter the general spirit of the book; they broaden it by adding new visions which emanate from its matrix: the being and the cosmos in their union and disunion.

The circumstances surrounding this work (the year of its publication, the apparent complications which its style represents in the poetic development of Aleixandre and the late-1970-inclusion of poems to complete it) have kept it from having the same popularity and impact as the earlier books. Also the enthusiasm and "stupefaction" [Carlos Bousoño, "Un nuevo libro de Aleixandre," *Insula,* No. 53, May, 1950] produced by *Shadow of Paradise* overshadowed its importance. But, as will be seen in this study, *World Alone* is intrinsically as artistic as the works published just before and after it.

There are three thematic currents in *World Alone*: love, the cosmos and man. Although it is impossible to separate one from the other, for the sake of clarity we shall try to study them separately here.

Love. The poet comes to feel or to comprehend that love is a means of knowing, a means of salvation and therefore a means of fulfillment. He comes to comprehend that love is knowing, not by reflecting on such a possibility, but by loving, by giving oneself over to one's marvelous fate or destiny which is to become elemental, as stated in **"Form without Love"**:

> I loved you . . . I don't know. I don't know what
>   love is.
> I suffered you gloriously like blood itself,
> like the painful hammer which gives life and kills.
>
>   I felt daily that life is death.
> I knew what it is to love because I died every day.
>
>   But I never died. One does not die. One dies . . .
> One dies on an emptiness, on an unloving shoulder.
> On an earth indifferent to the very kiss.

He does not know what love is; what he does know is that by suffering it, by dying, which is to say by living, he can know what it is to love. By living or dying or loving he comes to know himself. His existence would be a useless vacuum if he did not love. The blood which loves and the hammer which kills are on the same symbolic level. Death (unloving) is found only in an emptiness, on a sterile shoulder or on an indifferent world which ignores the dimension of a kiss. Time is introduced to intensify love: "I felt *daily* that life is death. / I knew what it is to love because I died *every day*" (italics mine). As a result, love comes to be a means of salvation when death or the indifferent world which is "burning up" becomes an immediate threat to the being. This is one of the underlying concepts of **"Final Fire."** In this poem, "the hope of living yet" is the "little girl small or sweet" with whom the self desires to unite in one single light or "swords in the shadow which motionless will burn up, / will melt united when the flames come." The world aflame which groans and perishes is paradoxically the salvation of the lovers because in their almost mystical union they create a new fusion or unity of loving transubstantiation: that of the sword which melts united.

Besides the concept of love as a means of knowledge and salvation, there are other conceptual components. On the one hand, there is the mysterious transformation of love into negative death with the concommitant metaphysical melancholy of the poet because of this change; on the other hand, there is the indifference of the world to the presence of and even to the call of love which requires the being to love. The disconsolate poet becomes irritated in the face of the indolent heart which does not respond. The complexity which these components add to the thematic vision of the book derives from the antithetical nature of love which comes, meets the lover, and abandons him, and from the love which, in coming, invites and is ignored by the lover. Furthermore, there is a painful double tension which is inferred from the conflict underlying each conceptual component within itself and from the antithetical relationship with each other: love comes, possesses the being and then abandons him; love comes and the being does not respond. This tension is one of the internal forces which forges the bitter and pessimistic character of *World Alone*.

The poems which develop the first thematic aspect or component are **"Form without Love," "Storm of Love, "Angry Love,"** and **"Human Burning,"** those which develop the second one are **"Edge of Love"** and **"To Love."** Among the poems of the first group **"Angry Love"** adds a new twist to the poet's insistence on love when it is discovered that "she" is the destructive "light and darkness":

> You were the light; the anger, the blood, the
>   cruelty, the lie you were.
>
> You, life which creaks in the bones,
> flowers, sending forth by fistfuls their aromas.
> Birds that enter through the eyes and blind
> the man, nude upon the earth, who looks.

But the lie he discovers in her will not overcome him; to the contrary, he will continue forward with greater impetus as if trying to redeem her and exalt his own self:

> I love you; I loved you, I loved you!
> I have loved you.
> I shall love you the way the body without skin
>   bleeds, ˙

like the last pure stripping of the flesh
that feeds the rivers reddened by anger.

It is important to point out that the negative character of this poem is suggested in its first lines: "I loved you the way one loves the furious light of a vibrant noon, / summer that hurts like a red whip." It is the same whip which at the end will leave him without skin but insisting in his loving desire. In comparison with this desperate situation, in **"To Love"** he goes on to lament the indifference and the indolence of the world's silence toward love which invites:

> But you came imitating the simple quiet of the
>   Mountain.
> You came the way the warm feather falls from a
>   shaken sky.
> The way a rose grows in blind hands.
> The way a bird spurts from an adored mouth.
> Just like a heart beats against another breast.

The sweet, tender, cosmic elementalness of love which has just arrived is supreme. The metaphors the poet uses to capture the nature of love and its manner of coming are effective: the mountain, the feather, the rose, the bird and the heart. All suggest elementalness and variety which are joined into one single loving unit. How does it come? Like the simple peace and quiet of the mountain, like the smooth and slow falling of the feather, like the sudden bursting forth of a bird and like the quick beating of a loving heart upon another. But this whole gift of loving grace will be ignored by man: "No one, no one knows you, oh Love, who arrive by a silence ladder, / by a road from another land invisible." But the poet transcends this ignorance and states clearly: "I felt you, I saw you, I divined you." He cannot be confused with the rest which is a formless mass, deaf to the outcry of the blood. From this point of view, love turns into the most effective means for the poet's individual affirmation and fulfillment as a man and as an artist:

The cosmos. In *World Alone* Aleixandre presents the cosmos as a refuge for the being who flees the indifferent world which, like Nineveh, burns sulphuriously, and also is the painful echo or reflection of the human void. The cosmic refuge can be up above as described in **"The Skies," "Smoke and Earth," "Birds without Descent," "The Victorious Sun"** and **"Celestial Freedom,"** whose last strophe reads:

> Round clear sky in which to live flying,
> in which to sing fluttering eyes that shine,
> in which to feel blood like blue firmament
> that circulates joyously copying free worlds!

Up above one lives, one sings, one feels; the being circulates freely like blood. In **"Smoke and Earth,"** he makes the same reference but with a painful reserve in his soul:

> I am the trace of an ended pain.
> I am the greeting to the purest atmosphere,
> to that transparent blue which like one single hand
> feels a silent smoke on its eternal skin.

Refuge is found in the depths of the earth, as is suggested in **"Under the Earth,"** in that:

> No. I am the dark shadow which, among the roots
>   of the trees
> coils like a serpent making music.
> A serpent thick like a tree trunk
> under earth breathes without imagining the grass.

At the end, the poet accuses those who live above of not feeling or knowing the destiny of man.

Refuge is found in the sea, as expressed in **"Birds without Descent"** and in **"The Skies,"** whose title contrasts paradoxically with the content of the poem in that the sea, not the sky, is exalted:

> Robust the sea rises without wings to love you,
> oh gradual sky where no one has lived.
>   . . . . .
> Robust, alien, like a Titan it holds up
> a whole sky or a breast of love in its arms.

The poet also laments because man without love, indifferent, does not feel the presence of this refuge. This he does in one of the most beautiful and expressive stanzas of **"Birds without Descent"**:

> That is why, stretched out here, on the beach.
> Stretched out there afterwards on the hard road.
> Stretched out beyond, on the enormous mountain,
> a man is unaware of the kind green of the seas,
> he is unaware of its melodious and empty surf
> and he does not know the eternal cannon of its
>   foam.

Besides his own lament, he has the sea punish the man by casting him far away: here on the beach, there on the road, and beyond on the mountain. By using the adverbs here, there, beyond, the sea's rejection becomes visualized.

The last cosmic refuge is the breast of the east, stated in **"Inhuman World"**:

> Everything flies ceaselessly on the way to the
>   east,
> on the way to the fast air towards the breast.
> There there are no birds but the clouds roll on
> as cautious as the foam of a total ocean.
>
> There, there, among the clear joys
> of that blue unknown by mortal men,

The poetic vision derives from the perspective of the western light through which everything flies toward the east, that is, toward the breast of the night unfelt by man.

If the poet takes pleasure in discovering these cosmic refuges (the breast of the heavens, of the earth, of the sea and of the night), at the same time he feels a great solitude because of the absence of the world which he imagines in

the distance from his refuge. In itself, the refuge is not a total communion. Thus, in that east which is the night, "there beats a sea which is not blood." In the breast of the earth it is not possible to imagine the life above; it is not perceived that "up above and free their petals / are pink, yellow, carmin or innocent." In the sea, life means only "an unstable flash, / deep darkness for a single breast." If the air is "greeting to the purest atmosphere," it is also "the trace of an ended pain" or a "silent smoke." This tension is another one of the internal forces which makes this book bitter, as clearly indicated in the title itself: *World Alone*.

Having examined the theme of the cosmos as a refuge for the being who flees the indifferent and unloving world, we must study the cosmos as an echo or a reflection of the emptiness of the world. Like this empty world, natural elements also manifest coldness and indifference toward love and life. **"Guitar or Moon," "It Is No Longer Possible"** and **"Fallen Moon"** are the poems which typify this attitude. In the latter:

> the moon, trackless, rolls like doubt,
> imitating a pain, a farewell to kisses,
> imitating a sadness revealed by dropping the head
>   on the breast,
> feigning that lilly torn off by the wind.

the moon feigns a pain it has never felt. It is a "terrible eye that does not shine, / because it looks within, abyss of the night, / the way dull steel that rolls looks." The moon is a lie, a void "like a severed hand / which held in its fingers a broken ring." All of the linguistic elements which make up this composition accumulate to express sharply the same negative idea; the same impact is felt in **"It Is No Longer Possible."** Here, the poet's pain and anger overflow to such a degree that he says "let the moon roll through the stones of the sky / like an already dead arm without an inflamed rose." Man and moon are placed on the same conceptual and symbolic level:

> But the moon is a bare bone with no accent.
> It is not a voice, it is not a celestial cry.
> It is its hard hollow, a wall where they resounded,
> thick walls where the sound of kisses used to break.

In the moon, the memories of a dead love only echo. Most likely these were the poems which led the critics to oversimplify the complexity and the importance of this book.

Man. Following our analysis of love and the cosmos, little remains to be said about man, given that the study of the former themes involved the study of man. Still, this is the thematic course most decried by the critics who, basing themselves on such obvious poems as **"Man Doesn't Exist"** (the first in the book), **"Inhuman World"** and **"Nobody,"** concluded that the work was pessimistic without examining the complexity of it. What is important is to discover why and how it is pessimistic. Aleixandre's visionary world in this book is not merely a pessimistic outcry. Each poem presents a variation of the same symphony of despair; each piece comprises an expansion which complements contradicts, questions, and endows the whole with a vital and artistic complexity.

. . . . .

Having studied the three thematic visions of *World Alone,* it is necessary now to analyze the technical elaboration of these themes, especially the various metaphoric forms and their effects.

Metaphoric contrasts. Frequently there appears at the beginning and end of the poem a chain of metaphors which through their poetic and real nature contrast with each other to such a degree that they seem to negate each other. The purpose is clear: to express the painful tension of the poet facing his intuition of the vision and to instill in the reader the unresolvable doubt inherent in the intuition. The first and next-to-last strophes of **"Human Burning"** exemplify this tension:

> Calm ship which floats along a river,
> at times I wonder if your body is a bird.
> At times if it is water, water or the river itself;
> but always I embrace you like a voice between lips.
>
> . . . . .
>
> But you who rest here the way light rests on a
>   summer afternoon,
> you are proud like nakedness without trees,
> violent like the reddened moon
> and burning like the river evaporated by a volcano.

In the first strophe, her loving serenity and calm are what fascinate and confuse the poet: She is "a calm ship," "bird," "water," "river," "voice between lips." These five metaphors are so interrelated that they lose their individuality and forge one single idea and emotion: peace and innocence. The elemental nature of the bird, the water, the river and the voice is transmitted to the ship turning it into a cosmic element. Although the ship is a product of man, the imagery makes it elemental through its contact with the calm the other images suggest.

To present a conceptual and an emotional antithesis, in the ending strophe, the beloved is the opposite: proud, violent and inflamed. These negative qualities stated in a first degree of a comparison will be raised to a second degree of intensity so that the contrast with the former calm becomes sharper. Her pride is compared with the treeless nakedness: sterile, monotonous, egocentric earth. Her violence is not loving but sterile like the anger of the "reddened moon." This is not the desired and loving violence which is perceived, for example, in **"To Love"**: "violent like doves who love, / cooing like those beasts unextinguished by a sunset." Here it is uselessly inflamed like a river full of lava and smoke which, in contrast with the first river, cannot be navigated. The clarity and innocence of the first river reflects the clarity and innocence of the water. The second, however, has lost even its river-qualities. The smooth serene rhythm of the first lines contrasts with the brusk irregularity of the end lines. In sum, these are the antitheses which create the painful tension of

this poem. It is important to point out that the "but" in the next-to-the-last strophe differs from the "but" which begins the last one: the first suggests the poet's confusion because of the change in his beloved, the second, resignation.

Metaphoric layering. Although this technical device is not, of course, exclusive to Aleixandre, it is important to explore how he uses it and what its effects are and herein lies his originality. This device is also typical of the Generation of '27 and of 17th century Spanish poetry. What happens with this linguistic device is that, using A. I. Richard's terminology, the vehicle of the first figurative level, becomes the tenor of the second; the vehicle of the second, in turn, becomes the tenor of the third which, in order to express it, has introduced a new vehicle [Vicente Cabrera, *Tres poetas a la luzde la Metáfora: Salinas, Aleixandre y Gullen,* 1975]. The poet says in **"Under the Earth"**:

> No. I am the dark shadow which, among the roots
>   of the trees
> coils like a serpent making music.
> A serpent thick like a tree trunk
> under earth breathes without imagining the grass.

There is a linking together of three metaphors whose tenors are transformed into vehicles in order to lead into the following figurative level. 1) The being is like the shadow which goes through the roots of trees. The idea of life begins to emerge because of the direct association of the shadow with the roots, the dark shadow ceases being that and becomes paradoxically luminous. 2) The shadow is like a musical serpent; that is, it has overcome the silence of the shadow. Furthermore, its vitality is communicated by means of music. 3) The musical serpent is thick like a trunk which breathes in order to nourish the tree. Again vitality is communicated. The two extremes, the *being* and the *tree,* expressed by a chain of transmitting metaphors, form a vital cycle. This chain is particularly reinforced by the long presence of the serpent which carries life from the *being* to the *tree.* Each metaphor linked to the previous one interconnects all the lines and, similarly, makes the entire strophe a continuous communication of life and love. The effect of this metaphoric layering produces an artistic and a conceptual pleasure. Hence, its unique use is original. It is not a mere technical virtuosity on the part of Aleixandre, but rather a necessary form of expression. This uninterrupted communication of life required such layering so that each level introduces into the next its tenor to be converted into a vehicle and thus continue the figurative layering.

Metaphoric proliferation. Aleixandre's poetry and especially his first period is primarily characterized by its imaginative force which pours forth with effusion—and with great artistic control—an abundance of metaphors. This is a typical of **Destruction or Love, Swords like Lips** (both before **World Alone**), and in **Shadow of Paradise** (after **World Alone**) it diminishes without disappearing altogether. This technique is still widely utilized in **World Alone**; as exemplified in **"Birds without Descent"**:

A blonde hair waves.
Remote beaches can be seen, happy clouds, a wind
   so golden
That it would connect bodies on the pure sand.
Birds without descent flee through the blue.
They are almost desires, they are almost foam.
They are the leaves of a sky radiant with beauty,
where a thousand throats sing light without death.

In this stanza which seems a whole poem in itself (notice the beginning, the development, and the conclusion) there are eleven independent and complementary metaphors: blonde hair (rays of the sun), light, desires, clouds, beaches, wind, sand, birds, foam, leaves, skies and a thousand throats (the musical birds). All are or allude to cosmic elements. Together with this elemental concert which the poet perceives in the radiant skies of any day are also suggested positive elemental states: freedom, love and life. The free verse and the quickness of its rhythm underline the content. One feels that the poet has let his flock of metaphors fly free through the sky of the poem. His enthusiasm in the presence of this elemental and loving world is evident in the overflowing spirit of his metaphoric creation; indeed the metaphoric profusion which is the expression or reflection of the profusion of cosmic elements creates the artistic unity which is similarly the reflection of the loving unity of the sky in the poem. It is important to add that when the poet says that from the sky "remote beaches can be seen," there is suggested a fusion of the sky with the sea creating another elemental union. On those beaches, the poet imagines that the "golden" wind would fuse, "would connect [loving] bodies on the pure sand." The fusion of sky and sea is expressed with the "music of a thousand throats which "sing light without death." The verbs linking these metaphors, to wave, to connect, to flee, to sing, are a projection of cosmic freedom and joy; the adjectives, blonde, golden, pure, radiant, pursue the same celestial clarity.

This has been a love poem, but the same metaphoric formula is used by the poet to express his anger and disconcertion facing the opposite situation, as is the case in **"Fallen Moon," "Nobody"** and **"Man Does Not Exist"**. What is ironic about the last poem is that it is precisely the moon, a vacuum in itself, that goes seeking man, another vacuum. From the metaphoric configuration of the poem, it is inferred that the more places the moon goes looking for the being, the more intensely the vacuum is felt. With the very same purpose the author, with thirty-five verbs of action (excluding the verb *to be*), gives the poem the proper sense of dynamism to capture the moon's mobility.

Metaphoric expansion. This device consists of the repeated and developed association of words which have to do, directly or indirectly, with the vehicle or tenor of the poem's central metaphor. We study it here because it is a device which requires great structural concentration and also because *World Alone* is a surrealist work. Indeed the author included thirteen poems from this book in his anthology of *Surrealist Poetry*. There are many poems which exemplify this phenomenon. In **"The Tree,"** the tenor is

man, and therefore the other metaphors with which the poem is constructed are; leg, thigh, knee, muscles, arm, veins, blood, heart and eyes. The purpose? Not only to humanize the tree, but to make it take the place of man. Thus the human being is supplanted by the tree. Only at the end does the poem take an unexpected turn when the tree "never cries out / nor does it ever cast its shadow on mortal men." This is its defect. Through expansion, the poem becomes a coherent, emotional, visual and conceptual experience in which the tree is transformed into a human reality. This technique will be further studied in **"Form without Love"** at the end of this [essay].

Metaphoric dynamism. (**World Alone** is a link between the first and the second poetic periods of Alexandre). This device, very typical of the second stage, consists of a gradual internal movement of the poem's structure. In the case of **"The Tree,"** the metaphoric dynamism reinforces the poetic construction of creation of the tree in human terms. One can actually see the poet, like a god, constructing the tree from the base of its trunk up to the top of its branches. Having finished, he proudly contemplates his creation.

In **"Under the Earth,"** the poet resorts to the same method to suggest a dynamism of inverse direction. That is, the poetic vision moves from the first subterranean level to the soil itself penetrating its deepest and most hidden strata. Notice the careful use of certain key words which the poet selects precisely for this effect. These words are underlined in the following lines: "*Under* earth one lives, the moisture is blood"; "*Beneath* the earth there exists *deeper,* the rock"; "There is water *under* the earth"; "*Deeper, deeper,* fire purifies." It is as if the poet were taking his reader on a flight through the deepest inwards of the earth, uncovering them to the world: the rock, the water, and the fire which "purifies," a verb which endows the journey with a religious or mystical tone. In these compositions, one feels how the dynamic structure of the poem reflects the dynamic desire of the poet which erects the three and which penetrates deeper and deeper into the earth.

In Aleixandre's poetic evolution, the use of this device becomes increasingly accentuated, starting with *Destruction or Love* until it becomes typical in *History of the Heart*. Hence, *World Alone* connects the two stages. It evolves together with the gradual poetic de-hermeticization of Aleixandre. Also visible in this evolution is the diminishing use of the conjunction "or." In *World Alone* there are approximately fifty identifiable uses of "or" in comparison with the two hundred in *Destruction or Love* and the ten or twelve in *Shadow of Paradise*. There are groups of negative formulas which, instead of negating, affirm. These do not exist in *Destruction or Love*; there are few of them in *World Alone*; and they abound in *Shadow of Paradise*. This indicates that *World Alone* is stylistically a link between the two books.

Metaphoric development in "Form without Love". Having examined the principal technical characteristics of *World Alone,* it is appropriate to analyze a typical poem in order to comprehend more throughly the effects which the various stylistic and metaphoric devices produce in the whole of Aleixandre's production. It is also important to analyze the various internal and external shades of structure and the gradual evolution of the intuition throughout the poem. The poem chosen for this purpose is **"Form without Love,"** which has forty-two lines. Its external and internal structure permits a division into nine poetic moments:

1. Line 1: With the emphatic "Enough, sadness, enough, enough, enough" there is as much evidence of sorrow because that body no longer loves as there is evidence of disgust because of the persistence of the sorrow. This moment presents the powerful psychological tension between wanting and not wanting to forget that loveless body.

2. Lines 2-4: The poet states that it is necessary to think no more of the eyes, or of the forehead, or of the beloved's blonde hair. The focus is on the luminousness of her face, the clarity with which he fell in love and which he now desires to cast aside. He is convinced about what he wants to do: abandon her.

3. Lines 5-8: But how to do it if he remembers the moment when he first possessed her, when he drank in light or sweet blood from her veins? Here, love is pain or sorrow; not an empty but a vital pain. This third moment negates the decision to abandon her stated in the second. Consequently the tension goes on tearing apart his being.

4. Lines 9-16: This moment is a reflection on the nature of the love he is suffering. He cannot define it rationally with logical formulas. But he does know what it is because of what he feels. Loving is dying every day. Dying is living. One only dies, one is only empty, when one does not love, when one does not live. He who lives and does not love is dead. This is the philosophical basis of *World Alone*.

5. Lines 17-190: He keeps reliving her: "You were so tender . . ." "sweet as the wind in the leaves / like a mound of roses for fixed lips." He makes her elemental by associating her with the wind and the roses. Connecting the "there" of line 17 with the "mound of roses" in line 19, the image of her body stretched out is suggested. This is the ideal posture described in many other poems in this book (for example in **"Edge of Love"**). It is, besides, a natural, unarranged heap. In **"Edge of Love"** she will be a "mound of nubile wheat." The wind and the roses are sweet because of the smoothness felt both on the leaves and on the lips. Notice the calmness and the delicacy of this crucial moment in the development of the inner world of the poet and his total surrender to his remote happiness.

6. Lines 20-28: The initial adverb "afterwards" introduces the unexpected and mysterious cause of her change into a form without love. "A vengeful flash, some enigmatic destiny" fell upon love, extinguishing it. There is not a clear reason. Through the metaphoric expansion the whole strophe acquires a dark tonality which corresponds with

the death of her as a lover: "vengeful flash," "cursed light," "stormy sky," "purple lightning." This fatal flash struck her face: eyes and forehead, the very same features he refused to think about in moment 2. The evocation continues. The poet goes on reliving those happy and painful moments. At the same time he seeks relief, he wounds himself.

7. Lines 25-28: The initial conjunction "and" likewise suggests what that explosion of evil did to her: the center of hatred and death. Her clear loving eyes now are "phosphorous" red eyes which glare hatred toward the heavens and the mountains which now are barren and sterile.

8. Lines 29-38: "Who are you? What face is that, what diamond hardness? / What marble reddened by the storm / unappeased by kisses or by sweet memory?" These are the questions with which this strophe erupts. No longer is it a matter of an evocation. The poet now confronts his present and hers. Because of the change, she is unknowable. He perceives that a transformation he cannot comprehend has occurred. That sweet "mound of roses" which represented her body surrendered to his lips in moment 5 has been turned into "reddened marble" and "a stone rose without blood" by the purple lightning. Now water and kisses slide off her marble body and the poet feels that kissing her is only kissing his own anguish and his own tears.

9. Lines 39-42: He does not cast her off. To the contrary, he embraces her knowing well that the body is a stone, a rock, a hard mountain, a dead body from which he seeks death. This moment expresses the metaphysical confusion of the poet who, having reviewed the history of his love, ends up asking for his own death. The various moments of this poem correspond to the different moods of the poet, who, reliving his past with the purpose of freeing himself from pain or sorrow, enters into his present reality even more confused than before. The dynamism is appropriate to the poet's gradual discovery of his inner world, memory by memory, until the arrives at the only possible conclusion from an aesthetic and emotional point of view.

World Alone, as was stated at the beginning of this essay, has suffered because of non-literary circumstances. They have directly affected its dissemination, popularity and the proper appreciation of its importance in the development of Aleixandre's first period. Regardless of what Aleixandre said, both thematically and stylistically, this book marks the transition between *Destruction or Love* and *Shadow of Paradise*. After completing *Destruction or Love,* what Aleixandre does in *World Alone* is focus his elemental cosmic vision from the perspective of the absent love. This aspect was defined already in several poems in the earlier book and what he does in the new one is carry this aspect to its final consequences. Furthermore, *World Alone* forces the poet to take, as a subsequent intuition, another step in his evolution toward what is expressed in *Shadow of Paradise* where, after having submerged himself in the depths of an indifferent and loveless world, he seeks the new paradisiacal light of childhood in a new world in which the being is affirmed and fulfilled as a loving and participating entity of the universe. The poet sings this world not with the surrealistic emphasis of his earlier works, but with a new, less hermetic diction no less effective than his earlier diction. This de-hermeticization becomes apparent in *World Alone*. In synthesis, the three moments of Aleixandre's evolutionary vision and creation are: loving destruction is life, in *Destruction or Love*; loveless destruction is death, in *World Alone*; from death the impetus to sing the new light of paradise will be reborn in *Shadow of Paradise*.

On the inadequacy of commentary on Aleixandre:

Due to the supposed obscurity of his text, critical approaches to Vicente Aleixandre have remained tentative, at times even fearful. Rarely do we encounter analyses that rise above generalized thematic explorations or sporadic stylistic commentaries. For over fifty years critics have suggested a hidden coherence to Aleixandre while evading in-depth, concrete explications of individual poems. . . . Such collective approaches, although not without merit, have tended to devalue specific interpretations that may open Aleixandre's text to new possibilities. To compound this problem, and perhaps as a result, critics have often portrayed Aleixandre as a relatively unsophisticated artist.

E. C. Graf, in Romanic Review, *March, 1994.*

Diana Der Hovanessian (essay date 1980)

SOURCE: "Vicente Aleixandre Lights the Way," in *The Christian Science Monitor,* January 2, 1980, p. 17.

[*Der Hovanessian is an American educator, poet, and translator. In a review of* A Longing for the Light: Selected Poems of Vicente Alxeixandre, *she asserts that Aleixandre moved definitively from the dark imagery of his early work toward more hopeful and humanist poems as his career progressed.*]

"The poet," according to Vicente Aleixandre, who won the Nobel Prize for literature in 1977, "is essentially a prophet. . . . His job is to illumine, to aim light."

Poetry, for Aleixandre, is "a longing for the light."

Lewis Hyde uses that existential phrase as the title for Aleixandre's first volume of selected poems in English [*A Longing for the Light*].

Why, we might ask, since Aleixandre is 81, did it take so long for his work to appear in English? The answer: This poet, prophet or not, was neither controversial enough nor political enough to interest a commercial publisher before he won the Nobel.

Some of his early poetry might tax a reader with its mysticism and disjointed style. But Aleixandre's poetry loses much of the disconnectedness in later years, and begins to address people directly—real people, and people of the past. Gone are the terrible black mountains at the bottom of the sea. Instead, we find the sunlit streets and classrooms of his childhood. Suddenly—light.

In **"The Old Man Is Like Moses"** Aleixandre assures us:

> . . . every man can be like that
> and deliver the word and lift his arms
> and feel how the light sweeps
> the old road dust from his face . . .
> his mouth full of light.

More and more he sees the world "exhaling a vegetable joy." **"On the Way To School,"** a poem about bicycling, ends with the boy-he-was folding his wings at the school door.

There also are Dickinson-like flashes: "Kill me sun, with your impartial blade." Wordsworthian messages: "inside the small boy is the man he will become." And fire everywhere: "I am the horse who sets fire to his mane."

Pedro Salinas said, "Vicente, delicate and apart, has discovered that love plus desperation equals poetry, deep, strangely moving poetry." To which we add, "poetry filled with light."

David Garrison (essay date 1980)

SOURCE: "Rhetorical Strategy in the Surrealist Poetry of Vicente Aleixandre," in *Denver Quarterly,* Vol. 15, No. 3, Fall, 1980, pp. 21-6.

[*In the following essay, Garrison provides a close reading of the poem "Vida" in order to demonstrate that Aleixandre employs a definite rhetorical strategy in his surrealist poetry, imbuing irrational images with an intrinsic, palpable coherence.*]

Surrealists in Spain, like their French counterparts, sought to liberate poetry and language itself from the confines of the rationalist tradition; they tried to express the subconscious, irrational side of life. Vicente Aleixandre, while disavowing the fundamental surrealist concept of automatic writing, has acknowledged surrealist images throughout his work. These images, he says, are governed not by logic but by "otra coherencia más profunda" ("another, more profound coherence") [*Poesía superrealista: antologia,* 1970]. Aleixandre's reference to this "otra coherencia" implies an ordering of irrational images; it implies that the poems are organized by some kind of rhetorical strategy. Although Aleixandre may not be fully aware of his use of such strategies, although he may bring images together by a process much like what psychologists call "free association," he nevertheless creates a coherence which we as readers can sense. We *feel* coherence, we *feel* communication when we read Aleixandre, but we often find it hard to explain our response in rational terms.

One of the ways in which he achieves this communication might be called a "strategy of imagistic tension." A set of images evokes a feeling or idea which by various means is brought into tension with the dominant feeling or idea of other sets of images in the poem. The tension between these sets is often expressed by a final set of images which synthesizes the conflicting patterns. This strategy quite clearly characterizes the poem **"Vida"** published in 1935 in one of his earliest and most famous surrealist works, *La destrucción o el amor*. This poem is central—both thematically and stylistically—to Aleixandre's work. Testimony to its important place within his poetry is provided in a much later volume, *Poemas de la consumación,* published in Barcelona in 1968, for there Aleixandre pays homage to **"Vida"** by explicitly alluding to it in three poems, thus making the poem, in effect, a kind of epigraph for *Poemas de la consumación*. In expressing the central theme of the book, the poem is thus a link between the early and late surrealist work of Aleixandre.

Vida

Un pájaro de papel en el pecho
dice que el tiempo de los besos no ha llegado;
vivir, vivir, el sol cruje invisible,
besos o pájaros, tarde o pronto o nunca.
Para morir basta un ruidillo,
el de otro corazón al callarse,
o ese regazo ajeno que en la tierra
es un navío dorado para los pelos rubios.
Cabeza dolorida, sienes de oro, sol que va a
       ponerse;
aquí en la sombra sueño con un rio,
juncos de verde sangre que ahora nace,
sueño apoyado en ti calor o vida.

Life

A bird of paper in my chest
says the time of kisses hasn't come.
To live, live, the sun crackles invisibly,
kisses or birds, late or soon or never.
To die a tiny noise will do:
as when another heart is silenced,
or that foreign lap on the earth
that is a gold ship for blond hairs.
Aching head, its gold temples, sun about to set,
here darkly I dream a river,
reeds of green blood being born,
I dream leaning on you, heat or life.
                    Translated by Willis Barnstone

The first line explodes with the alliteration of "p" sounds and the emphatic assonance of "a" and then "e." It is as if the sounds of the opening line are trumpeting for our

attention. Besides having a remarkable acoustic effect, the image in this first verse is conceptually complex in that it seems to express a unity consisting of two disparate ideas. On the one hand, the notion of "un pájaro en el pecho" ("a bird in my chest") suggests rapid heartbeat, strong emotion, desire, anticipation. If we simply visualize a bird inside a human chest, we sense a caged, desperate sort of power, a feeling of violence or rapid movement which could erupt at any moment. On the other hand, "pájaro de papel" ("bird of paper") suggests something delicate, fragile, vulnerable. Like the human heart, the "pájaro de papel en el pecho" is both powerful and fragile. It expresses the conflictive, ambivalent nature of many emotions such as anger, love, desire, fear. In this context the image quite literally says something—"el tempo de los besos no ha llegado" ("the time of kisses hasn't come")—thus reflecting primarily a sense of anticipation, of desire for fulfillment. Since the "time of kisses" is only desired, not reached, the striking sounds and ambivalent image of the first line seem to have heralded, anticlimactically, a negative announcement.

In the third and fourth lines, more alliteration and assonance are used to announce not the fulfillment of desire, not the time of kisses, but something else—"vivir, vivir, el sol cruje invisible" ("to live, live, the sun crackles invisibly"). The infinitive "vivir" stands out not only because it is repeated, but also because of its ambiguous syntactic relationship to the rest of the sentence. It is virtually unconnected grammatically to the other words, so it not only evokes the infinitive idea, "to live," but also the imperative meaning, "live!", and, at least implicitly, the nominative meaning, "life" or "living" ("el vivir" in Spanish). The sun is associated with the infinitives because of its presence next to them in the same verse and because of its archetypal value as a symbol of life. The repeated infinitive and the image of the sun are not formally compared, but rather juxtaposed so that they enrich each other and forge new meanings. The sound of the sun seems to suggest the sun's interaction with earth, the dynamic process which creates and sustains life. The image recalls another poem entitled **"El sol,"** from *Sombra del paraíso,* in which Aleixandre envisions the sun as a goddess whose invisible footsteps "crujen" ("crackle, rustle") on the earth. In both poems, the poet focuses on the invisible movement of the sun's rays over the earth, on the mysterious, powerful presence of the sun. In **"Vida,"** Aleixandre joins this symbol of life, drawn from nature, to an incantatory linguistic designation of the sun's symbolic meaning. He says, in effect, "Let there be life!" ("vivir, vivir"), and there it is in the dynamic sound and presence of the sun; language and symbol are joined together. Furthermore, within the context of this poem, the sun not only represents life, but also the passage of time, for in the next line the poet brings the image into tension with human concepts of temporality. The sun's steady circling gives life, but it continues without regard for man's desire or fulfillment, "besos o pájaros" ("kisses or birds"), in spite of human perceptions of time such as "trade o pronto o nunca" ("late or soon or never"). In effect the sun represents the unending cycle of cosmic time, of which man shares only a tiny portion within his brief life span.

If we now look at the first sentence as a whole (two sentences in the English version), we see that its images are linked together in that they all contribute to a dynamic, surging representation of life. The images of intense human desire and anticipation are associated with the dynamic process originated and sustained by the sun. Human living—*vivir*—has been framed within the life of the cosmos symbolized by the sun. The sun sets the stage for human activity, giving life and simultaneously marking the passage of time, warning of approaching death. It is this theme—*morir*—which the poet takes up in the next set of images.

The "p" sound which begins the fifth verse is but an echo of the opening alliteration. In dramatic contrast to the first sentence, the second begins with the shortest, most subdued line of the poem. The image is surprising not only for its originality, but also because it is stated so simply. Nothing is repeated, nothing is ambiguous about the syntax, there are no emphatic sound effects. The one noun of the line, a diminutive, refers to a "tiny noise," and there is indeed very little noise in the words. It is this contrast, this sudden quietness which heralds the theme of death. Here, as in many other Aleixandre poems, death is envisioned primarily as a peaceful experience, the final unification of man with the universe from which he came. This idea is even revealed in the title of the book from which **"Vida"** comes, where the author equates destruction and love—***La destrucción o el amor***. In this poem Aleixandre describes death simply as the last tiny noise and silence of a human heart. No trumpeting alliteration is necessary to announce it; "para morir basta un ruidillo" ("to die a tiny noise will do"). The second image of this part of the poem seems to suggest in the word "regazo" ("lap") the idea of comfort and peace. Although death seems foreign ("ajeno"), it is a lap which perhaps recalls the lap of a mother or father where a child dreamed; death is unknown, and yet it is like the comforting lap of a parent that was, for a child, "un navío dorado para los pelos rubios" ("a gold ship for blond hairs"). Or perhaps the image of the gold ship is a metaphor of the passage from life to death: the gold ship of life becomes the peace and comfort of the far-off lap of death. The image is a fertile one, suggesting many possible meanings.

The final sentence of the poem brings together images of both life and death. The sunset is the last in a series of images of gold color—"gold ship," "blond hairs," "gold temples," "sun"—which, like the third verse, links nature and man through juxtaposition. Here the attribution of a similar characteristic (the gold color) to nature, man, and death, adds even more unifying power. The sunset seems to remind the narrator of approaching death, as does his dream of the river, which in this context recalls the Medieval poet Jorge Manrique's metaphor, "Nuestras vidas son los ríos / que van a dar en la mar / que es el morir" ("Our lives are the rivers / that flow out into the sea, / which is death"). Again, Aleixandre uses archetypal symbols—the sun and the river—to express the passage of time and the approach of death; his narrator, framed within the darkening scene, watches the waning sunlight and dreams of the river. For a moment death seems to be

associated with the references to pain and darkness, but these images are followed by others which suggest growth and regeneration. The "juncos de verde sangre" ("reeds of green blood") simultaneously allude to the regenerative process of nature ("juncos") and of man ("sangre"). "Verde sangre" suggests at the same time the green color of plants and human blood; it implies the unity of natural and human life within the constant cycle of death and regeneration.

The poem ends with an enigmatic declaration, "sueño apoyado en ti calor o vida" ("I dream leaning on you, heat or life"), which seems to allude to the sun, for it is the sun which gives "calor" and "vida." It is the sun which counterbalances the awareness of pain and approaching death, thus "supporting" the narrator. It is the sun which creates and sustains the life of nature and man. Yet paradoxically the sun, as we have seen, is a dual symbol. Although it represents life, it also, like the river, stands for the flow of time which leads inexorably to death; the sun crackles with life-giving power, but it finally sets. The image of the sun obtains an ironic duality, referring to the constant regeneration of life—*vivir*—and also to approaching death—*morir*. The sun thus synthesizes the central tensions of the poem between life and death, between unending cosmic time and the brief span of a human life. It expresses the essence of the dialectial image pattern of the whole poem. At the same time the poem comes to an end, the final image points back to the very tension which was established throughout the first eight verses. Thus the poem, like the archetypal images contained within it, has an unending, cyclical pattern. The final synthesis does not actually resolve the tension, but rather sums it up in a unity which, ironically, points back to a duality. Like the sun, the dialectic of the poem suggests the cyclical process of life and death.

Although I have tried to clarify the coherence of the poem. I hope that in the process I have also indicated its multiplicity of meanings. These meanings stem primarily from the ambiguous nature of the images, such as the "pájaro de papel en el pecho," which points in many directions at once. Nevertheless that first image, and indeed all the images in the poem, are part of a pattern which emerges from what at first might seem to be a chaos. Although Leo Spitzer once referred to surrealism as a "callejón sin salida" ("blind alley") ["La enumeración caótica en la poesía moderna," *Lingüistica e historie literaria,* 1967], Aleixandre's surrealism is rather a profusion of streets with signs enough to allow the reader to proceed. Our way is lighted not by the clarity of reason, but by the flickering shadows of irrational insight. As Carlos Bousoño has pointed out, Aleixandre's images are "visionary" in that the elements of comparison are often not united by similarities that are easily recognizable at a rational level [*La poesía de Vicente Aleixandre,* 1968]. Rather than compare the brilliance of the sun to the beauty of a lady, as Renaissance poets often did, Aleixandre juxtaposes a reference to the sound of the sun with the sound of the infinitive "vivir." Rather than compare the passage of life to the flowing of the river, he has his narrator dream of a river while drawing support from "calor o vida." He juxtaposes and intermingles images which do not logically seem to belong together but which in fact play upon all kinds of symbolic, phonic, and syntactic relationships. He arranges these images in dialectical patterns—rhetorical strategies—which reveal the "otra coherencia más profunda" of his surrealist vision.

On the significance of Aleixandre's poetry:

Despite the variety of [Aleixandre's] writings, they have a unity stemming from the will to overcome all barriers between the I and the cosmos, between the I and humanity, and, finally, between the I and knowledge. Moreover, almost all of his books, from *Ambito* on, illuminate his total work, which, in turn, illuminates each individual book. Indeed, Aleixandre's poetry has a kind of Dantesque quality, not only in its massiveness or in the frequent asperity of its verse, but in the long search for light in the midst of darkness, or of knowledge in the midst of despair. It is in this sense that Aleixandre is an ethical poet. It seems fitting, then, that in his last published book, Aleixandre's belief in the dynamic nature of the act of knowledge is embodied in a literary form dialectic by definition, namely the dialog, and that, by choosing this form, he places himself in one of the most ethical of literary traditions.

Darío Fernández-Morera, "Vicente Aleixandre in the Context of Modern Poetry," in Symposium, *Summer, 1979.*

Santiago Daydí-Tolson (essay date 1981)

SOURCE: "Vicente Aleixandre: A New Voice of Tradition," in *Vicente Aleixandre: A Critical Appraisal,* edited by Santiago Daydí-Tolson, Bilingual Press/Editorial Bilingüe, 1981, pp. 1-34.

[*A Chilean-born American educator and critic, Daydí-Tolson is the author of* The Post-Civil War Spanish Poets *(1983) and* Five Poets of Aztlan *(1985). In the following excerpt, he traces Aleixandre's early career from* Ambito *to* Sombra del paraíso—*the collection that marks the arrival of artistic maturity for Aleixandre, according to Daydí-Tolson.*]

When in 1977 the Nobel Prize for literature was awarded to the Spanish poet Vicente Aleixandre, the name and works of the new laureate were little known outside of Spain and Latin America. He was mainly an author for hispanists, the poet for literary experts. Post-war Spanish poetry was represented in the mind of foreigners by Fe-

derico García Lorca and, in some cases, by the less popular poet Jorge Guillén, both of them contemporaries and good friends of Aleixandre. After the Civil War (1936-39) Spain had become for many a silent world, the domain of intellectual backwardness and governmental censorship; a Nobel Prize could not have been found in such a land, barren of literary greatness. But in later years Spain had begun to change, and no longer could it be considered a repressed society and a cultural wasteland—poetic voices were heard coming from the forgotten nation, and that of Vicente Aleixandre was the most resounding. Like a deep current flowing up from the years before the war, his voice filled the gap between those poets who had died or left the country and the younger generations of post-Civil-War Spain.

Since the nineteen twenties, Vicente Aleixandre has always been present in Spain's literary scene. He has lived through the years of the Republic, the Civil War, and the seemingly never-ending Franco era. He was one of the intellectuals of his generation who, although against the fascist regime, remained in his country after the war. Thus he became a model and master for the new poets who began to write in the cultural vacuum of the first years of dictatorship. His name alone could represent the tradition of poetry in a country that, having reached the excellence of an intellectual tradition in the twenties and thirties, preferred for a while the dictates of dogma and fanaticism over the freedom of art and spirit. Aleixandre stood, with his poetry and his personal attitude, in opposition to that state of affairs and kept alive the spirit of that earlier period of intellectual liberalism and aesthetic experimentation. Having now received the Nobel Prize, he understands the implicit indication that the recognition is not only for his personal work but also for the centuries-long tradition of Spanish literature, undeservedly forgotten in our days.

In his address to the Swedish Academy, Aleixandre states explicitly the idea that poetry is, above all, tradition ["Discurso de recepción del Premio Nóbel," *Insula,* No. 378, 1978]. The poet, then, is but a link between past and future, and his being great is conditioned by the literary and cultural circumstances in which he has to live. In Aleixandre's case, the past is represented by two different moments: the immediate one—the Generation of 1898 and its nineteenth-century predecessors; and the more remote one—the Spanish Golden Age. Through them, of course, the poet comes in contact with a wider range of influences, sometimes difficult to account for. The present circumstance—the horizontal tradition he talks about—encompasses a long period of more than fifty years of Spanish literary history. As a young man Aleixandre was part of a group of poets which included, besides Lorca and Guillén, the names of Luis Cernuda, Pedro Salinas, and Rafael Alberti. As a mature poet he took the responsibility to see that the younger generations could express themselves beyond the limitations of despair and conformism. In his old age he has become the sacred figure of the eternal poet, the voice that reincarnates itself in those few select men and women that have been given the gift of poetry. Today, Aleixandre himself is tradition.

His works, more that many other poets' productions, are a reflection of the circumstances in which the author lived. It could be said that Aleixandre's poetry evolves in harmonious correspondence with the main trends of Spanish lyric poetry from his first published poems, written in a period of highly technical and aesthetic literature, to the last collection of dramatic monologues, in some aspects related to late forms of lyric discourse in present-day Spain. In the last five decades Spanish poetry has passed through several alternate styles and modes of conceiving the poetic phenomenon and the poet's task. Aleixandre has been directly in contact with every new development, accepting with a clear conviction that man is determined by his being *here* and *now*. His work then is that of a writer who senses what the main current of poetic feeling is at a particular historical moment.

This somewhat vague characterization can be better illustrated by looking at what Aleixandre considers to be the essence of the poet. In his address to the Swedish Academy he defines the poet as a prophet, a seer. Reminiscent of the Platonic interpretation, Aleixandre's idea has its antecedent in Surrealism and can be traced back to Romanticism. This conception of the poet as a means for other voices to express themselves, as a superior being who can be in touch with the cosmos and with the essence of man, has a direct relation with the other concept also mentioned in the poet's address—the complete immersion of the writer in a particular tradition, because it is this tradition in which the seer finds the voices he has to assume as his: the voices of his people. Poetry, then, is a form of communication; it is the revelation of the common spirit of the people that takes the voice of the poet to make itself understood by all.

All of this is documented in Aleixandre's writings. In his address to the Swedish Academy he only restates what have always been the basic tenets of his poetic vocation. But it is not only in reference to concepts that the address corroborates a long-sustained idea of poetry; in it there is also a rhetorical device that has a meaningful value beyond its apparent common function as an expression of humility. Aleixandre refers to himself as "the poet" on several occasions when he should have used either the first person pronoun or his own name. A similar preference for impersonality is also manifest in Aleixandre's poetry, and particularly in the books written after the Civil War. Many of his poems convey a certain sense of anonymity, a feeling that the voice does not belong to a definite person. After reading the complete poems of Aleixandre, what seemed at first to be only a vague feeling ends up being a central characteristic of his poetic discourse. It will be of interest to follow, through fifty years of writing poetry, the development of that voice.

Born in 1898, Aleixandre began his literary career in the twenties, a great period in Spanish literature. His generation, besides being interested in Spanish tradition, was bewildered by the new aesthetic, philosophical and scientific ideas of post-war Europe. The climate of Spanish middle-class life was in those days defined by cultural interests, intellectual curiosity, and literary activity. In

Madrid, where Aleixandre had lived since boyhood, there were more than enough places to meet other intellectuals and be informed of new trends as well as the established and admired ideas of the older generations. Literary cafés, theaters, art galleries, the Ateneo, and the very important Residencia de Estudiantes were the meeting places for poets and writers, painters and artists, historians and philosophers, masters and disciples. Friendship was the common link among many of the young poets, artists, and intellectuals. In this spirit of comradeship Aleixandre found his poetic vocation and his first admiring readers and editors.

He had little interest in poetry before becoming a member of the literary group that today is known as the Generation of 1927. Although he was an avid reader, he did not like poetry and avoided reading it, convinced as he was from his high school years that such literature neither provided much enjoyment nor had any intellectual value. By eighteen his attitude had changed radically, thanks to the friendship of another young poet, Dámaso Alonso, who gave him an anthology of poems by Rubén Darío. The reading of that book was decisive for Aleixandre: ". . . that truly virginal reading—the poet writes later—produced a revolution in my spirit. I discovered poetry: my great passion in life was then revealed to me and took hold of me never to be uprooted again." He then began to write, but his first publications did not appear until almost ten years later. It is undoubtedly very important to record the fact that it was after reading Darío's poems that the young writer discovered his own poetic vein.

Critics see no noticeable traces of Darío's influence in Aleixandre's works. It has to be acknowledged, though, that Aleixandre has a spiritual correspondence with the Latin American poet and that he follows him in several ways that are not easy to trace and analyze because they are less a matter of stylistics than of general attitudes toward art and reality. For the young Spanish poet-to-be, Darío's works meant not only the fascinating discovery of the manifold possibilities of language but also the realization of the poetic view of man as a passionate lover who is consumed by love. Poetic language in Darío reaches a level of communicative effectiveness directly dependent on the poet's ability to create a purely fictional reality that represents, in metaphorical terms, an otherwise inexpressible understanding of man and existence. No less important to the effectiveness of this poetic language is the general tone of passionate materialism, an essential sensuality not at all alien to a desire for spiritual transcendence. These were aspects of Darío's literary accomplishment that Aleixandre could certainly have felt as profoundly inspiring because they found an echo in his own spirit.

The influence of Darío is not so evident in Aleixandre's first published compositions, for during the period in which he was working on them the author had an intense literary relationship with other young poets who declared their interest in favor of Juan Ramón Jiménez and the theories of "pure" poetry. Aleixandre's participation in the activities of the group that shared in the literary experimentations, discussions, and definitions typical of those times explains the influence of the ruling taste on *Ambito*, his first collection of poems. It also explains why that book came to be published. Aleixandre's interest in poetry not only began under the influence of a friend, but his actual career as a poet was launched by a few friends who took some of his poems to the then recently founded *Revista de Occidente,* where they appeared in 1926.

Aleixandre published *Ambito,* on which he had been working since 1922, in 1928. It was a typical product of that decade and for some critics seems to be totally unrelated to the rest of Aleixandre's work. But, in spite of its many debts to other poets highly considered at the time, *Ambito* is something more than an exercise in imitative writing. As the poet discovered years later, this first book represents a starting point of his whole production, a basis for later developments. A few analyses have demonstrated that in its pages are to be found several of the most characteristic aspects of Aleixandre's poetry.

If compared with the rest of the poet's books *Ambito* looks particularly different in its external characteristics, it is because following the examples of Juan Ramón Jiménez and other younger poets Aleixandre wrote a carefully structured book, not at all different, as Alonso points out, from many other books of poems published in those days [Dámaso Alonso, *Poetas españoles*]. Thirty-five poems closely related to each other form this highly structured work. Most of the compositions are written in traditional meters, some of them merely a variety of the "romance" or of other types of regular stanzas. His combined use of different meters in the same poem can be seen as a first step toward free verse, which will characterize Aleixandre's poetic language. Equally indicative of an evolution are several cases of enjambment and verse punctuation that break the fixed rhythm of the metric pattern. The basic model, however, was set by the careful treatment of rhythm and rhyme in Juan Ramón's post-modernist aestheticism.

Several other aspects of *Ambito* will be seen again in the rest of Aleixandre's work. In addition to technical details of a stylistic nature, perhaps the most important elements are the glimpses of irrational imagery, suggestive of Surrealism, and the cosmic vision of man and nature as identical in essence. Love is the central motive of these poems and represents a way for man to achieve fusion with all matter. Even though the book appears to narrate the personal experience of a deep understanding of the human condition on a cosmic level, the main subject of such experience is in some way veiled or diluted by a rather detached impersonality. The well-structured plan of the collection and the well-composed poems correspond to a stylistic restraint in no way different from that characteristic of some manifestations of "pure" poetry. In Aleixandre's literary career, *Ambito* represents a first attempt, the product of several years of apprenticeship in the active workshop of his generation: the cultural life of Madrid. His poetic ideas were not yet defined, and his style was not his own. To find in this book the first manifestations of traits characteristic of the future work of the author is not an unjustified critical procedure, as long as one does not overlook the fact that when published *Ambito* was more than anything else an imitative work. Its originality will emerge from a comparative reading of Aleixandre's later work.

Shortly after *Ambito* was published, Aleixandre began work on his second book, *Pasión de la tierra*. Although it was finished within a year, the new collection remained unknown in Spain until 1946. Only a few copies of a 1935 Mexican edition reached Spain, and hence the book could not have had any noticeable influence on the literary milieu. Even though *Pasión de la tierra* is totally different from *Ambito,* it is also a book representative of its time, a time of radical changes in aesthetic ideas and methods. If the book had been published in 1929, immediately after the author finished writing it, it would have become one of the most important surrealist books in Spanish literature. Most of its commentators consider *Pasión de la tierra* as the real starting point of Aleixandre's characteristic poetic language, viewing *Ambito* as a far less important antecedent. When Aleixandre wrote the latter he was able to resolve every stylistic problem by recurring to the well-known set of acceptable and already established solutions. The poet was acting within the predetermined patterns of a tradition. With *Pasión de la tierra,* those fixed channels of poetic expression are totally disrupted, and although language retains its functional coherence, the expression itself lacks the normal logical or sentimental aspects which might render it meaningful to a reader. By means of the new technique of free association of purely mental images, the poet tries to express within the limits of language a series of unedited visions belonging to a level of reality revealed by psychoanalysis and pointed out earlier by a few nineteenth-century poets who may be considered Aleixandre's literary antecedents. The contrast between *Ambito* and *Pasión de la tierra* is such that they seem to be the works of two completely different authors: a poet of the post-modernist aesthetic tradition and a surrealist.

Ample literary analysis has proved beyond any doubt the surrealistic character of *Pasión de la tierra*; but for a while the term "surrealism" was used in reference to this work only to deny any interpretation that would see the influence of the French school in Aleixandre's poetry. The poet was partial to that critical attitude and insisted that he was not a surrealist, although he made reference to his knowledge of Freud's writings. The truth of the matter is that for Spaniards it has seemed very important to make a clear distinction between French "surrealism" and Spanish "superrealismo," the difference being that in Spain there is no organized literary school, as in France. One of the characteristics of the poets of the Generation of 1927 is precisely their will to act as individuals; none of them belonged to or professed, knowingly, the principles of a particular literary school.

But it would be misleading to state that Aleixandre was creating completely on his own when he happened to write *Pasión de la tierra,* a book so clearly representative of Surrealism. The sudden change of style and of literary objectives apparent in this unprecedented book could not have originated as a sudden revelation but must have been the result of a well-informed confidence in the value of psychoanalytical theories and in the effectiveness of the technique of "automatic writing." By deciding on a surrealist form of expression rather than using the more conventional style of his first compositions, Aleixandre was, first of all, accepting the theoretical principles behind the surrealist method and stating, as well, his revolt against established tradition.

Aleixandre's poetic break with traditional ways of writing is not just another literarily playful experiment but a much more complex phenomenon, as would be the case with any sincerely serious writer. The attraction of aesthetic experimentation, so much a part of the literary scene of the thirties, did not touch the spirit of Aleixandre. On the contrary, he stated very distinctly his belief in the importance of message over form, thus presenting a good argument against his previous book, the product of a formalist and aestheticist composition. Between the carefully measured and well-combined verses of *Ambito,* the expression of a restrained voice, and the entirely loose prose of *Pasión de la tierra* there is a difference not only in external form and poetic techniques but more significantly in the attitude and tone of voice of the speaker, which, in turn, have their manifestation in the other, more visible distinctions. It is only natural that once tradition is attacked and abandoned by the artist, the attitude of the speaker changes from dutiful acceptance to rebellious opposition to the norm.

In Aleixandre's work this opposing force took the external form of prose, better suited than verse for the demanding verbal flux of his new voice. The model for it had already been set in the novel and the poet merely adapted it to a still deeper search in the human psyche and its world of fascinating dreams, fears, and desires. His reasons for using prose are to be sought in Aleixandre's own emotional experiences, his work being a journey into the inner self, a desperate and obsessive search for life and its meaning in an existence jeopardized by imminent dissolution: death. There is no need to speculate about particular motives behind each prose poem or even each dream-like image. Enough psychological analyses and commentaries are at hand to satisfy this type of curiosity. What really matters is to realize that by using the technique of automatic writing Aleixandre was rebelling against emotional restraint and aesthetic formality.

The prose in *Pasión de la tierra* is a sign of a truly new attitude; it is the obvious response to a need for expanding verse and its different possible combinations in order to express the new images and their concatenation in the freely associative flow of the discourse. And this, in turn, is the consequence of a renewed function of the voice. Surrealism had offered a philosophical basis and a technical device to the poet who was already in need of them. The almost mystical union of man with the cosmos as presented in *Ambito* does not have the same powerful conviction that is found in the prose poems of *Pasión de la tierra*. The attitude of the speaker is constrained by tradition in the first book and freed from any delimitations in the latter. This change has been possible thanks to the

discovery of the unconscious, an aspect of the self which has its own voice, an entity different from the author, although in this case it does not represent a completely conscious invention, as lyric voices normally do.

This voice of the unconscious follows its own rules, if it is possible to use such a term in reference to a discourse apparently devoid of any form of predetermined governing pattern. Bousoño has studied the basic formula of the irrational image as used by Aleixandre in his surrealist period ["Las técnicas irracionalistas de Aleixandre," *Insula,* No. 374-75, Jan.-Feb., 1978]. By following the critic's line of reasoning one can imagine the many other possible formulas that made the text a poetic text and not a mere piece of psychoanalytical monologue; the type of structure involved in the poetic text does show similarities to a psychiatric patient's discourse, but the two differ in that the poet's discourse follows a more intentionally artistic process of selection and organization. The poet is also consistent in maintaining the same level of illogicality throughout the concatenation of images, which appear in a seemingly breathless emission of unaccented speech. The utterance is that of an undetermined speaker who talks from the depths of the reader's inner being—the voice, as it were, of the speaker's own unconscious.

Prose reproduces, better than verse, the free flow of speech, the monotonous and uncontrolled wording of oneiric visions made up of a web of apparently unrelated images. A return, then, to versification in *Espadas como labios,* written after *Pasión de la tierra,* strikes one as a significant poetic decision. As Aleixandre declared years later, after writing the prose poems of his previous book he felt a strong desire to write again in verse—that is, to impose a certain control over the chaotic mass of images being formed in the unconscious. The verse transcription of the surrealistic associative images indicates a certain hesitancy in the author. Several compositions make use of traditional verses; others, in a procedure similar to the one used in some poems of *Ambito,* combine verses of different metric value. The result, as any reader of contemporary poetry can attest, is a rhythm and cadence not totally unheard before but more varied than the traditional metric patterns in order to appeal to a new sensitivity.

More than the choice between prose and verse, images and syntax are, to a great extent, responsible for the hypnotic or "possessed" tone of the voice both in *Pasión de la tierra* and *Espadas como labios*. Prose and verse in each case are only helpful transcriptions of the discourse. The use of hendecasyllabic and octosyllabic verses brings back to the voice the constraint found in *Ambito*. *Espadas como labios* exemplifies in its two types of metric preferences the poet's doubts and experimentations with his medium. The short poems, with a more or less regular metric form, embody a tone and attitude of control even when the images talk of strong emotions; from this duality emerges a feeling of tension quite in agreement with the general character of the book. The longer poems make use of free verse in accordance with a freer attitude of the speaker, who seems to allow his emotional state to appear in the poem. This second type of composition will be improved in the next book, *La destrucción o el amor,* and will continue to be a characteristic in Aleixandre's subsequent works.

It has been a common practice to describe free verse, or versicle, as a juxtaposition of basic rhythms already defined in traditional metrics. For Lázaro Carreter this kind of analysis does not help to define properly the rhythmic characteristics of the versicle because it implies that the free verse is nothing but a rather unsystematic variation of the same unchangeable patterns of old use ["El versículo de Vicente Aleixandre," *Insula,* Nos. 374-75, Jan.-Feb. 1978]. For him, the versicle is the expression of the emotive changing rhythm of the voice's discourse, and it is constituted by a series of varied kinds of repetitions, except rhyme and isosyllabism. Repetition is to be found in any of the different levels of the poetic discourse: the phonic, the syntactic, and the semantic levels. Any correspondence of the versicle with traditionally established meters is only circumstantial, and the many ruptures of the norm should be taken into account before trying to generalize about the metric nature of the versicle. The hendecasyllabic elements present in Aleixandre's poems are not only the consequence of a natural tendency of a poet well-versed in classical Spanish poetry to follow loosely the common rhythm of a poetic language but also the critic's habit of explaining the new by means of the old.

After *Espadas como labios,* published in 1932, Aleixandre does not make much use of regular versification, his preference being for the versicle. Although there are differences in the length and varieties of the versicles among some of the books, all of them have in common a series of reiterations and pauses which have no direct relation, in most cases, to traditional metrics. Essential to Aleixandre's versicle, then, are a series of stylistic devices which by repetition stress the value of resonance. Several of them are found in *Espadas como labios* and become truly characteristic of *La destrucción o el amor,* published in 1935. The obvious reiterative procedures are, of course, the anaphora, the repetition of words and clauses, alliterations, and assonances. Not so commonly seen as a case of repetition is apposition, used as a way of giving a new image to name that which the first image or word possibly did not express totally. In relation to this technique, very effective in the creation of a rhythmic pattern in the poem, there is the indecision of the speaker in choosing the appropriate way to express something. In some cases it is as if the speaker were almost stuttering or trying different ways to put his vision into words. But the most characteristically Aleixandrian of all the devices is the use of the conjunction or, not as a disjunctive property but as a means of identifying two words or two images. The constant use of this conjunction—present even in the title of one of the books—provides a great number of repetitions, or more exactly, of rhythmic pairings in the text.

Only a very detailed analysis of the poems would give an adequate idea of all the possibilities of the versicle in expressing the various attitudes and emotional states of the speaker. This type of versification has its first antecedent in the combination of traditional meters as seen in *Ambito.* The experience of the free prose of *Pasión de la tierra* taught the poet how to extend the common Spanish metric patterns to a much more flexible rhythmic use of the language. For Aleixandre, the versicle was the best available solution to communicate his particular conception of man and his destiny. The first book in which the versicle takes its most characteristic form is *La destrucción o el amor,* a book that puts into effect the poetic ideas of Aleixandre as stated in his note to the second edition of Gerardo Diego's anthology, published in 1934 [*Poesía españoles contemporánea*].

In the first edition of the anthology, published in 1932, the poet expresses his doubts about the function and value of poetry; two years later he has a more positive outlook. Without intending an explanation of a coherent poetic theory closely related to a general cosmic vision of man and nature, for Aleixandre all elements of creation, all matter, are only different manifestations of the one and only universal entity:

> Flor, risco o duda; o sed o sol o látigo:
> el mundo todo es uno, la ribera y el párpado
> **["Quiero Saber"]**

The chaotic enumeration of terms referring to human aspects—physical and emotional—and to animate and inanimate nature underlines the meaning of the statement. The same effect should be attributed to the repeated use of the conjunction "o" as identifier of unrelated terms, characteristic of Aleixandre's style in this period. The much commented conception of the unity of all existing matter has led critics to look for its antecedents in pre-Socratic philosophers and mystics. More contemporary equivalences besides surrealism could be found in philosophy, theology, psychology, and the natural sciences, insofar as all of these disciplines have advanced theories in this century of a similar unity of all existing matter, man included. For Aleixandre this universal identity explains the destructive power of love, the central force in the process of cosmic fusion. In the tradition of modern poetry, the Spanish author has looked to art for the true knowledge of the essence of reality and has tried to formulate in words his philosophical conviction.

Although man is part of that cosmic unity and as such will be fused with all creation, Aleixandre believes that man has little knowledge of his predicament and needs a way of becoming aware of it; thus poetry, which is the "clairvoyant fusion of man with creation, with that which perhaps has no name." The poet, then, is seen as a possible receptive "magnetic pole" of all the forces coming from the mysterious cosmos with which he becomes one. It is natural that Aleixandre should declare that "poetry is not a matter of words." What really matters for him is, paraphrasing his terms, not the false luminosity emanating from the crystal of poetic language, but the real light of knowledge. Language is unable to make this light visible if it has to conform to established patterns of expression; and since it has always been used under control, language has never had enough power to signify the profound and mysterious luminosity of true reality. The poet has to disregard the regular forms of poetic writing and create his own, in a daily effort to produce the "light of the poem." He runs away from the well-known toward the spheres of absolute truth.

As in *Pasión de la tierra,* Aleixandre is still driven by the desire for authenticity and looks for revelation on the level of the surreal, where words change their everyday meaning to make manifest in the poem the revealed truth. The poet is listening to the messages of the cosmos and makes of them a sensitive and communicating expression completely different from the normal aesthetic form of speaking. It is a form of surrealism, except that in this case the author no longer writes the utterances of an unconscious self, a first-person individuality, but becomes the voice of all life and matter expressing itself through the unconscious of someone who acts as a sibyl, a point of fusion between man and cosmos.

The reference to classical tradition does not come to mind as a mere rhetorical device. In *La destrucción o el amor* Aleixandre's poetry reaches a certain vaguely ancient tone of pagan pantheism. As if the relationship among books were the same one to be found among the poems of each book and the verses of each poem, every element of the total work is placed in reference to the rest. Thus, in *Ambito* the desire and search for a passionate embrace with nature is already expressed: the final poem of the collection narrates such an encounter. The next step takes the poet, freed from all previous prejudices of ideas and formulaic exteriorities, to the depths of existence as lived and experienced by man, every man. At this point the emotionally cautious voice of the first book has reached the level of a primal scream. Even though the writing is done in the first person singular, and in many cases the second person is dominant, there is a certain basic feeling of oneness that insinuates the possibility of the speaker being just that—humanness, or the reader's deeper self. This being the case, the next step in this voyage through man's essence is totally acceptable: the voice belongs now to an entranced speaker, to an individual who has been, or still is, in contact with those levels of reality that only a sibyl is allowed to reach and make known to the rest of men—a sibyl or a seer.

La destrucción o el amor has been one of the books preferred by critics because in it the poet's conception of reality is clearly stated and wonderfully expressed in poetic language. What has been termed the personal view of Aleixandre in this epoch of his life is nothing more than the coherent manifestation of a surrealistic conception made less illogical by the ordering capacity of the creative poetic mind. Aleixandre has conceived a metaphorical world, a pure literary construction, to make visible his own interpretative vision of man in nature. Obviously, due to the more controlled will to formulate an expressive metaphor, the book has a clearer and more logical structure than the two previous ones. The collection has been conceived as a totality, each poem being only part of the continuous flow of a slow-paced discourse, made rhythmically solemn by the use of long versicles. The tone is almost sa-

cred, but the images gain in clarity: Aleixandre is moving toward a more easily understandable lyric language. His world of primitive nature and dream-like situations is still reminiscent of *Pasión de la tierra,* but the new form of expression does not only refer to the level of subconscious knowledge but also to the deeply felt desire for intelligible communication.

It was to take the poet several more years to reach that desirable communicative language; years and experiences that cannot be ignored when discussing the evolution of his work. [In his prologue to Aleixandre's *Antología total*] Pere Gimferrer finds the age of the author to be an important factor—maturity brings a more coherent and better articulated interpretation of one's own condition as a human being, thus making less difficult its communication through language. But age alone will not explain everything; the critic's comment, though, is well-founded and directs attention to the life of the poet, somewhat forgotten in the discussion of his works. By 1936, the beginning of the Civil War, Aleixandre was 38 years old and had lived through a dangerous illness. For ten years he had been facing the limitations of a sick man; life and death, pleasure and pain, desire and fear must have been for him realities much more evident than for any other poet of his age. The sick man is doubly man because he is much more aware of his biological condition; in his body he sees, better than any healthy person, the slow process of decay and dissolution, and his mind wanders with enhanced anguish through the different available explanations of human life and death.

In his first books Aleixandre expresses precisely that anguished human search for a meaning to existence. In *Ambito,* limited by the demands of an aesthetic formalism, the inspiring force is not yet free to look for its own form of expression, which comes only with surrealism in *Pasión de la tierra.* Irrationalism is more a method than an objective, a poetic technique, not a rhetorical device. Confusion and chaos is the appropriate condition of a mind in a state of total uncertainty, but in the mass of images in the books considered to be properly surrealistic, one sees already the elements that in further developments will constitute a more logical, or logically understandable, message. At the beginning the poet himself does not know which elements those are, and only through the slow process of time does he come to have a more or less intelligible view of all creation. By then the poet is no longer young. Age means in his case having passed through the different stages of confusion to gain the conviction of a particular view, his own view.

With a more mature sense of his accomplishments, and conscious of the circumstances that surround him, in 1934 Aleixandre begins to write his fifth book, *Mundo a solas,* which he originally meant to entitle *Destino del hombre.* In a sense it is the first book that really develops what was set forth in the preceding one. Up to the time of the writing of *La destrucción o el amor* the poet was not completely in control of his subject, he did not have a clear concept of the world he was singing about; images and words were used more as searching tools than as means of purposeful communication. In *La destrucción o el amor* there is already a basic Weltanschauung from which the next book was to take its inspiration, focusing its interest on one aspect: man. This preference for the human aspect of creation was to become more important in the books written after the war. In pessimistic terms *Mundo a solas* talks about man's loss of his "primeval elemental state." Sad as it was, Aleixandre's vision of man as a fallen creature left his mind open to see the immediate circumstance of his world. It was in 1936, and the negative tones of his poetic vision were confirmed by the human violence of war.

During the violent years of the Civil War, Aleixandre did not write much. The book on which he had started to work in 1934 was finished in 1936, but adverse circumstances made its publication impossible. Instead, a few poems about war appeared in Republican literary magazines, never to be collected in any of his books. At the end of the war, the poet began to work on the first compositions of a new collection that would take him almost five years to complete. It was a time of sorrow and devastation. The war had taken most of what Aleixandre knew to be his world. His own house, half destroyed by the battle of Madrid, could very well symbolize the writer and his circumstances. The first moments of peace brought life back to the garden and rooms of the house which had been abandoned during the hostilities. But many friends of the pre-war years were gone: the most loved, Federico García Lorca, was dead; Cernuda, Guillén, Neruda, and others had left the country; Miguel Hernández, the youngest one, was dying in one of Franco's prisons. While their memories lingered in the renovated house, a new group started to replace them around the poet; it was not a generational group, not a school following the dictates of its leader, but the first members of an ever-growing group formed by most of the new Spanish poets who saw in Aleixandre the inspiring and most needed figure of the master. From that time, the poet accepted the responsibility of becoming a central figure in post-Civil-War Spanish literary life, and his house became the meeting place for everyone who was interested in poetry. The poet had reached maturity.

Coincidentally, in 1944 Aleixandre published his first book in almost ten years, *Sombra del paraíso,* a masterpiece which established without any doubt his reputation as the greatest poet of his generation living in Spain. In the midst of a literary scene filled with sonnets and other neo-classical "pastiches" inspired in a stale desire to believe in the reborn greatness of the Empire, the long versicles and sensuous images of Aleixandre's new book were the exception. Exceptional also was the world vision made concrete in the imagery of the poems. Conceived as a unity that took shape from the original inspiration of one poem, *Sombra del paraíso* continued, as is the case with almost every collection of Aleixandre's, the creative process developed in the previous books. *Mundo a solas* was still unpublished, and although it was not known by the public until 1950—when it appeared in a collector's edition—it has points of contact with *Sombra del paraíso* and should be taken into account as its immediate antecedent.

With *Mundo a solas* Aleixandre wanted to express his sad realization of man's fallen state; this idea, reminiscent of certain religious explanations of the apparent inadequacy of man in nature, is fully developed in *Sombra del paraíso,* as the title itself leads one to guess. But there are important differences between both books, differences which are made evident to the reader by the general tone of the voice in each collection. The first volume conveys a rather negative feeling of violent overtones, while the dominant tone in *Sombra del paraíso* leads to a more complex and richly sentimental feeling of human totality, or better stated, man's emotional being. For Pere Gimferrer this difference is indicative of two states in Aleixandre's understanding of reality. The first stage encompasses his first five books, which convey an idea of disorder and confusion; the poet's view is one of chaotic dispersion. The second stage, which begins with *Sombra del paraíso,* introduces a harmonious view of the universe. This change did not happen suddenly, nor did it come as a complete surprise—it is the sign of the writer's maturity. Essential to this new understanding of the relationship between man and the universe are Aleixandre's conceptions of poetry and the poet, although they are not much different from the ones he professed earlier in 1934.

In effect, the author's basic views in this matter had not changed. The only difference is to be found in the intensity of the conviction and its purposefulness. What a few years before had been a supposition and a desire was now an accepted fact, a definite ordering of the multiple components. Maturity is also responsible for this certainty about what to expect from poetry and its producer. The poet, for Aleixandre, continues to be viewed as a seer, as a man who can reveal to other men that ultimate knowledge of the otherwise inexpressible truth. In an image that says more than any abstruse explanation, the poet appears as a gigantic being whose feet are deep inside the earth and whose head is up above, touching the sky; his voice is that of mysterious forces. This figure cannot be more representative of a particular attitude toward poetry, and it explains in full the extent of Aleixandre's objectives in *Sombra del paraíso*.

It is only natural that the first reaction of the readers of this book was to compare it with a romantic work. Everything in it tends to underline emotion in its highest form; from the conception of poetry and the poet—developed in the first composition of the book—to the images and the versicles, *Sombra del paraíso* stands out as a document of man's eager acceptance of a degraded existence that is only a shadow of the original paradise. The speaker addresses nature, the cosmos, and other men as if he were indeed that gigantic poet of magnificent voice. Even those compositions in which the first-person speaker remembers—with the nostalgic tone of many of the poems—a past existence of paradisiacal beauty give an impression of a voice coming from a superior, or at least different, level of human consciousness; it is the voice of one possessed by a spirit of extreme sensitivity.

It is quite evident by this point in Aleixandre's literary career that his work has reached its originality by an unfailing and constant effort to relate poetry and the personal search for meaning; he has applied with all conviction the theory of poetic knowledge learned from surrealism and its predecessors. *La destrucción o el amor* and *Sombra del paraíso* are two perfect examples of poetry understood as a vocation, as a form of consciousness—spiritual, intellectual, emotional, social—in a word, a form of total life. For Aleixandre there are no other activities or devotions besides poetry; everything in the poet's life depends on it and finds in it its meaning, as in the case of a religious person whose particular belief provides an order and meaning to all creation. For Aleixandre the "religious" conviction in poetry does not respond to an already provided answer—he went step by step in search of it, in a journey he describes metaphorically as "an aspiration toward light."

On surrealist qualities in Aleixandre's poetry:

The work of Aleixandre that in aim, technique and achievement was closest to surrealism, as he himself has acknowledged, is *Pasión de la tierra,* which is composed of densely textured and highly imaginative prose poems whose capricious fluidity he did not control and whose excesses of language and fantasy he did not correct. To record his vision of primeval chaos, Aleixandre wrote his 'poetry "in a nascent state"' out of the 'subconscious elements' he harvested in the deep and inaccessible areas of his mind; this conscious pursuit of the mentally wayward and unformed made his original title *La evasión hacia el fondo* a more accurate label for an extravaganza that is one of the most unfathomable works of twentieth-century Spanish poetry.

C. B. Morris, in A Generation of Spanish Poets, 1920-1936, *1971.*

Miroslav John Hanak (essay date 1985)

SOURCE: "Vicente Aleixandre's *In a Vast Dominion*: The Completion of a Submersion of Personality in the World Ground," in *La Chispa '85: Selected Proceedings,* edited by Gilbert Paolini, Louisiana Conference on Hispanic Languages and Literatures, 1985, pp. 153-62.

[*In the following essay, Hanak discusses several poems from* In a Vast Dominion, *especially "Antigua casa madrileña," in order to support his contention that Aleixandre endorses a mystical view of fulfillment through the individual's submersion into a collective unconscious.*]

In a Vast Dominion is the ninth cyclus of poems in the

first volume of Aleixandre's *Obras completas* (1977). It first appeared under the title *En un vasto dominio* in 1962. The "vast dominion" in question is the spatiotemporal infinity of a strictly telluric dimension, the only true reality of existence. Space and time permeate each other without differentiation, for the here-and-now and the there-and-then are deceptive inventions of human self-consciousness that reveal the unreality of an egocentric world view. The following analysis gives a brief synopsis of six short poems as an introduction to a more detailed scrutiny of a seventh, a longer work entitled **"Antigua casa madrileña,"** which can be considered the culminating point of the cyclus.

"Materia humana" is the poet's exploration of humanity's spacial dimension. The poet's alter ego (referred to at first as *tú*) watches the city at night through a window. What the observer sees out there are sundry manifestations of "the one and only reality," the amorphous matter of which humanity is a part, an earthly phenomenon like any other. The difference in distances is existentially as irrelevant as any other spatial or temporal differentiation such as individuality, past, present and future. The people in the city are all "going far" and yet, all "go a short distance."

> All closely packed in the night. And all and each of them in
> his window, single and multiple.

Addressing "Mother Earth" as his inseparable alter ego, the poet pauses to muse at her "enormous body," referring to it with the metaphysical term "ground of being" which, until this poem, he chose not to define in exact philosophical or psychological terms:

> All this matter that from the *ground of existence*
> proceeds . . . (my italics)

Matter pauses for an instant in Earth's enormous body; this too is only an instantaneous act of individuation, for matter flows on as "Earth and her children" and "beyond," i.e., transcending each and every avatar so far achieved,

> propagating you and inheriting you, and through which you significantly are occurring.

It is thus in Earth's body as a matrix of becoming that each of its manifestations must participate, cutting across space and time, becoming thus a proof of the insignificance of the drive for individuation.

"El vientre" is the first poem in a series celebrating the human body as receptacle, sustainer and spiritual concentration of life forces. The belly has a particular affinity with the ground of being. Man's earthly condition is most convincingly represented by the belly, full of "hidden roots and running brooks" that wind through "dark rocks" and dissolve in "mire," in order to give man his most authentic grounding in living nature. Like a motionless but perfectly ground-attuned vegetable, man is thus "planted."

"El sexo," a poem dedicated to the two sexes, is self-explanatory. The "matter" making up the male sex divulges "one enduring truth": it has the longest maturation period among bodily organs. Coming to fruition in secret, it does not cease to manifest its urges until "the tree" of manhood "lies prostrate . . . on the ground." As the "fruit of flesh," it is a compact abstraction of the entire life phenomenon; it heats the blood that circulates through it, which in turn sets life on fire; it is like "the axle of the sun," the focal point of generation. If the male sex matures "concealed by a shadow," its female counterpart has an even more mysterious pall of secrecy about it. The poet uses the suggestive images of "flowing river," "insinuated berth," "fresh shadow or silent vapor" to conjur up the ineffable mystique of the seat of femininity

> Which in the smooth dusk stops immobile
> Between the thighs, time by itself, tranquil,

waiting, alluring, submitting, but never changing, like

> Time that doesn't pass, forever eternal,
> Immortal and unborn, between the shadows.

Here the female sex assumes the guise of quintessential femininity, usually represented in Aleixandre's imagery by the reclining female figure. The female sex becomes a "conjunction of life and beauty, of flower and blood," a "secret bud" that

> . . . in the light lends fragrance
> To the bright of light growing forth from
> Between the thighs of the stretched-out beauty.

Finally it becomes enbodied in the hub-like center of existence, an

> Unpolished coin or sun which the day is exhaling . . .

ready to receive its alter ego, "the adversary," pushed by the "sun in zenith," in its culminating peak.

"Estar del cuerpo" is the summary and concluding piece of the series of poems that extol the earthly condition of the human body. "Obscure is the heart" which is the center of the body's organic functions, because it is "buried," hidden and surrounded by matter, the same as its counterpart on a larger scale, the human body itself. Both are integral parts of the telluric material of life and, therefore, untouchable in their earth-like profundity. "Body" and "heart" are, in themselves, and isolated from conscious thoughts, immediate manifestations of the existential ground. The "heart" of "body"

> Like a dream . . . gives signals
> From great depths, the deepest.

"Pastor hacia el puerto" is a different approach to capturing the immediate and ineffable being of authentic, i.e., de-individuated existence. It revolves around the figure of an insignificant shepherd, an indifferent creature and, therefore, one closest to the roots of the pure phenomenon of existence. The ambience surrounding the shepherd's humble mode of self-expression is a simple tableau of rustic

Arcadia adorned with unpretentiously impressionist flashes. The author praises both the "silent lip" of nature that shows speech as an alienating articulation of the voice of the ground and the lip

> . . . That gives off a sound which is merely human . . .

The landscape comes alive through the enumeration of its self-evident features, quietly and simply complementing each other like the "indecisions" of the plain which alternates "the little grove" with "hillsides," a "green patch" with a "violet" patch and yet another one, a "large one, yellow." Against this setting of harmonious self-sufficiency and life-affirmation rises the figure of the shepherd, equally attuned to the becalmed, uninterrupted and smoothly flowing rhythm of being. Not surprisingly the shepherd's attributes are vegetal, rather than animal, maintaining a close linkage with the collective ground. The shepherd's figure blends in with the landscape to the point of being freed of all vestiges of personal consciousness. As he by-passes some pastures next to the pass, the ravine "rustles"; this acoustic phenomenon is often associated by Aleixandre with the presence of ineffable, unconscious being. Now totally transfigured into an elemental singular, "a single heat,"

> The exhausted shepherd to the ground
> surrenders, . . .

the last traces of conscious individuality thus being snuffed out—at least, for the duration of the night.

"Ciudad viva, ciudad muerta" summarizes in its opening statement one of the key principles of Aleixandre's metaphysics: "All lives as it is dying." Cast in a fairly regular blank verse, the poem calls forth visions that, except for their bare-bone economy, hark back to the poet's earliest *superrealismo*. The "burned-up living"—consumed already in its inception—proceeds slowly, under the "scorched clothing" of alienated self-consciousness, likely to be "divested" only in the moment of death,

> Between the crunch of bones that were
> extinguished.

In this dismal limbo of mutually deceiving appearances,

> Only shadows of derision hail us.

As a city of our time it is indeed a home fit only for the walking dead, a "city toward never . . . , city silent," which "wears a crown of birds that have no feathers." This necropolis perpetuates in its inhabitants the vital signs of genuine life and of dreams that transcend the human condition; and yet it lacks the requisite "feathers" to carry those dreams beyond the pull of earthly realities. The closing lines bring the poem close to the portentous visions of the early German expressionists Heym and Trakl. While the drift toward self-destruction continues, "deaf plumes. . . . in black" alone make good the escape from the city of shadows. Being what they are, dreamy frustrations materialized in sooty smoke, they are of little avail to the cause of life's rebirth and recon-firmation.

Like the idea of Castile, fundamentally conservative, Cath-olic, intransigent and defying time, so stands **"Antigua casa madrileña,"**

> Here, . . . fundamental. Stone pointing upward.

In one respect, this house, leading "from now to never," resembles the "city toward never" of the preceding poem, but while the latter was an indisputable token of society alienated from the ground of existence, this house in Madrid stands and endures precisely for the opposite rea-son: in it are embodied all the indestructible and static qualities of unconscious, immediate existence which made at one time Castilian Spain as unassailable as unconscious, unfeeling stone. The immovable sturdiness of simply *be-ing there* is explicitly formulated as the house's defiance against time: "But this house is still existing"; a fact which has nothing to do with

> . . . words, concepts which have nothing
> to do with presence . . .

as embodied in this house, or with "its matter."

That this sturdy relic of Castilian intransigence is a sym-bol of the equally irrepressible, sullen and impassive "ground" is borne out by the poet's emphasis on the house's undifferentiated compactness. It is "an enormousness" without *dis-traction,* which would imply centrifugal forc-es pulling its cohesion apart in all directions. Like the ground it represents, it steadfastly rejects the existence of anything real outside its reach. It simply declines to be-lieve that

> Anything on the outside exists: not dimension, not
> light. . . .

For the second time the poet insists on the first postulate of his ground-oriented metaphysics:

> Life is everything extending inward.

This then is the essence of Aleixandre's immanentist world view: the existence in soul only, sought and en-forced by this house, is that of a corporeal, embodied world soul. Such telluric soul is a "shadowy one," as befits the unconscious life exuberance that makes up the *world ground. The soul is* a base in whose "shadow light is lit and sighted," to continue to burn forever as self-perpetuating life,

> . . . continuous, enduring
> And vanquishes and is not extinguished
> Except in dying, which other flames sets flaring.

If the first part of the poem revolved around the fortress-like posture of the house *qua* barrier against the change of human things, the second part celebrates the "bars" of the "interlaced grating" that served at one time as a restraint

on lust and hence, on life. But now, they are a "support submissive / Of a flower, of a fragrance."

Like the house they guard even now against intrusion from the outside, the iron bars had been

> . . . put in place, turned together,
> To hold in check the impossible wishful thinking.

of some "dark eyes" burning inside with desire, and grate-ful for a mere

> . . . glimpse of a cape showing off gallantly
> . . . or a hat, in salutation sweeping
> The street in the shadows. . . .

The dark eyes alone, never hands and their tactile vulgar-ity, did "show the path" to the assiduous swain

> Flashing with light, breaking the darkness. . . .

If the bars had been a foolish check on "life, . . . perhaps without purpose," at least they are not entirely useless now; besides, "wills," at the instinct of procreation,

> . . . had never been completely
> Prisoners, and they break and they crush and they
> lay low, humbling.

The bars have found their life-sustaining role in giving support to flowers, to their "gleaming clear stalks" that "rise, climb, aspire," like all life springing directly from its ground, unchecked in its vegetal immediacy by any obstacles invented by conceptualizing consciousness. "Latched onto the bars," they aspire to what the house as "ground" cannot give them,

> . . . for light, light, for the sky, . . . searching.

The seasoned bars, "totally mute" as befits their nature of deep-rootedness, are transfigured by this vegetal enthusi-asm for upward growth; they grow "soft almost,"

> Almost like treelike branches of these full-grown
> roses. . . .

The third part is dedicated to the present, to the new re-ality which has penetrated even behind these compact walls and has transfigured the bars into pliant flower stalks. At last, some human element is added to the collective whole represented by the inanimate structure, now slightly vivi-fied by "vegetal" flowers and vine-like bars. But, like all of Aleixandre's ground-attuned counterparts of humanity, even the human element emerging here remains anony-mous and well-nigh unconscious. The touch of humanity in this house flows from two humble working hands, the poet's favorite symbol of tactile self-assertion. Unlike the hand image of his *superrealist* period which invariably conveyed the feeling of grasping egocentrism, here the hands remain unmediated by self-consciousness. They too have become tools of the ground, moving the flower stalks nearer to the life-giving light, "making possible" the growth of the roses. They give the unpretentious flowers the "little love" they require, for they are the hands of a seamstress. And so it is that once again human eyes are moved by admiration, although their object is no longer the gallant figure of a cavalier, only a dress mounted on a dummy.

> Empty, and there it shines. And eyes it admire.

The poet takes advantage of this admiration of a seemingly empty form to expound his theory of aesthetic creation.

> . . . The artist to admire is prone,
> To live the composite. To live it, means with life to
>   endow it.

Thus to produce a work of art is to put forms together into a composite that the artist's soul can live, admire, and hence, bring to life:

> To make is to be more alive.

Watching the artist infusing life into a composite of disparate parts, seeing "it made,"

> . . . is to watch it
> As it is near and different. . . .

The only true work of art is that which comes to life in this fashion. In this way, too, the artist-poet competes with a transcendent creator and, after the latter's withdrawal from this world in modern times, the artist replaces the old godhead with a new one, his own promise of perfection beyond the limitations imposed by human finiteness. A new participation ensues between the artist-creator and creation, a more intimate if painful one, for both of them belong to the one and only world of immanence. It is then that, once again,

> . . . its creator the creature
> Senses, as it is itself as well as the other. . . .

The former "Other," the alter ego of Aleixandre's earlier work which used to be a recumbent female nude, and became, on occasion, Mother Earth, has here grown to be the artist-creator vis-à-vis his work of art. Consequently it is the artistic creation as living creature that

> . . . doesn't admire but lives,
> Watching.

Straining out of "the patient clay" of the world ground toward the higher awareness promised by the artist-creator, the flowers are literally created by those hands. Their activity shines forth to the outside world through a "tall window" enabling it to show off life as its own and yet, not its own. Like all the earlier-enumerated elements of the ground, now amalgamated into a community of being without estranging categorization, the window too becomes "for an instant ephemeral" with the flux of becoming, and gives off "life's fragrance," thanks to these caring industrious hands. The transfiguration of the past and of the stony

mass into a present, palpitating life is complete, while the dream of a concrete individuation of the self is abandoned and absorbed in the phenomenon of unconscious being. The meaning of life has thus become reconfirmed through the intentional lapse into the unconscious. The artist participates in the world ground through his artwork which confirms its creator's life-enriching de-individuation.

Agnes Moncy Gullón (essay date 1988)

SOURCE: A review of *Shadow of Paradise,* in *Hispanic Review,* Vol. 56, No. 3, Summer, 1988, pp. 385-87.

[*In the following review of* Shadow of Paradise, *Gullón calls attention to light imagery in Aleixandre's poetic vision, and considers the difficulties faced by translators in rendering the vivid and precise imagery of Aleixandre's poems into English.*]

In the Foreward [to **Shadow of Paradise,** translated by Hugh A. Harter, 1987] Claudio Rodríguez indicates that opposing forces await the reader of this book:

> Clearly, **Shadow of Paradise** is a book about a paradise lost, about the loss of the innocence of love. Paradise and its absence, harmony and destruction, light and shadow, elegy and exaltation: the playing out of human destiny under the immortal canticle of trees, ocean foam, and moonlight: the glittering, unifying energy of erotic forces within a diversity of organic forms.

In the Introduction by Hugh A. Harter, a different view of Aleixandre's paradise is offered, one based on how a sense of loss in the postwar years—Madrid: dark, present—combines with bliss—Málaga: light, past—in a mind highly sensitive to beauty:

> For these poems present neither paradise nor a vision of it, but only the illusory, hallucinatory contours of its shadow—diaphanous, intangible, transitory—glimpses of primordial splendor tinged with the nostalgia for worlds that have vanished or perhaps never were, and vague remembrances and intuitions of a remote . . . utopia, the mythopoetic Málaga of childhood and contemplations of sea, foam, sand, bird, cloud, and stone. The insistent note of loneliness and deprivation acts as a poignant counterpoint to the gorgeous spectacle of nature.

Naturally, the poet evokes other hells, other Edens; as Harter says, Dante, Milton and English and German romantics enter into the elaboration of Aleixandre's poetic world, which also reveals an affinity with the Spanish mystics, Bécquer, Antonio Machado, Juan Ramón Jiménez, Rubén Darío. The themes shared are love, nature and solitude; the probing into the self, though, seems deeper in Aleixandre's case.

Fifty-two poems make up the bilingual edition, and each should ideally receive comment, for the translator "struggled sometimes night as well as day, with obtuse or resistant passages." The results were worth it: poems delicately crafted in English project not only their own atmosphere, but also peculiarly Aleixandrian qualities. I propose that we concentrate on several in which images of light and darkness appear, both because they are crucial to the theme and because, as Harter writes, the poems "are shot through with light, and the poet's rejoicing in it." Taking isolated images, we find "se ve brillar el lomo de los calientes peces sin sentido" rendered as "one sees the shining backs of silent fiery fish" (2-3); "un beso sin luz, un beso largo" as "a lightless kiss, a lengthy kiss" (2-3); and "carne mortal . . . que . . . arde en la noche" as "Yours is mortal flesh that . . . blazes in the night." Then comes a stanza (in the same poem, **"El poeta"**) locating light not in the world, but in the poet:

> No. Esa luz que en el mundo
> no es ceniza última,
> luz que nunca se abate como polvo en los labios,
> eres tú, poeta, cuya mano y no luna
> yo vi en los cielos una noche brillando.

> No. The light that in this world
> is not its final ash,
> a light that never melts like powder on one's lips,
> that light is you, poet, whose hand and not the
>   moon
> was what I saw one shining night up in the skies.

Even in these few snatches of magic we can appreciate the translator's struggle to achieve. Light in Aleixandre contains everything, is everything; it issues from natural or reflected sources and is seen by the poet who is light, the complex human kind that makes us see in a hand, a moon, essences reflecting each other. Located as a presence (fish) or an absence (kiss), this Aleixandrian light acts upon our mind, refracting and filling, eroticizing and inspiring awe as its many forms and varying intensities mesmerize, leaving us oblivious of the devices that create the effects, effects which must again, in English, function (albeit analogously at times) to enliven the page. In the stanza quoted, tone, rhythm, vowel, and consonant patterns: are these recreated? Yes, and beautifully so. The English version retains the confidence of the poetic voice; the sequenced pauses (before "The light" and "poet") are offset by a flowing image following each; the stressed *u*'s in Spanish are balanced by the stressed *s*'s in English: a sound pattern is preserved.

There is also the more problematic aspect of light, its literaturization, which is rejected:

> Sí, poeta; arroja este libro que pretende encerrar en
>   sus páginas un / destello del sol,
> y mira a la luz cara a cara, apoyada la cabeza en la
>   roca

which becomes:

> Yes, poet; throw aside this book which claims to
>   hold within
>   its pages a beam sent from the sun,

and face to face look at the light, your head against the rock.

Even naked light hitting a rock like a ball a wall, this, the poet wants to intercept, to capture for his book.

Essential differences between Spanish and English can change the feel of even a closely translated line such as the first verse of **"Creatures of the Dawn"**: "Vosotros conocisteis la generosa luz de la inocencia." The rhythm invalidates a polysyllabic synonym for "generosa" in the target language because the English line is built of monosyllables: "You knew the full rich light of innocence." The solution, the use of two short synonyms for one long adjective, is curious and effective, rhythmically.

Transparency is yearned for, and when captured in a paradisiacal kingdom it excites; touching produces light:

> Mouth against mouth I find release, transformed
>   into light,
> transformed into flame that flashes in the air.

For Aleixandre, pleasure from within happiness is suffused with light (**"Los Besos"** ends with "¡Oh mundo así dorado!"). And this line, rendered as "Oh glowing world thus touched with gold!" prompts the reflection that Harter's translation leans toward the archaic. A romantic style, as in "Oh world turned golden, golden!" (suggested to recall how relative an art literary translation is) would emphasize in a dramatic place—closure—the element usually disassociated with sensual pleasure in Aleixandre, but which in this particular poem envelopes the amorous experience.

In the final section, two poems register despair and ambivalence. In **"Destino de la carne,"** in a stanza full of shadowy dullness comes the sudden, irritated exclamation "¡Siempre carne del hombre, sin luz!"; and in **"Último amor"** the poet is no longer exalted by the moon: its radiance has left in him only an ember and he wonders "¿Es sólo muerte tu mirada?" Gone is the earlier vital cry, the one heard most often, most characteristically, in *Shadow of Paradise*:

> Light's destiny was love,
> to be a lover!

Jonathan Mayhew (essay date 1990)

SOURCE: "Vicente Aleixandre: 'Límites y espejo,'" in *The Poetics of Self-Consciousness: Twentieth-Century Spanish Poetry*, Bucknell University Press, 1994, pp. 52-65.

[*In the following essay, which was originally published in* Modern Language Notes *in 1990, Mayhew explores Aleixandre's concern with the limitations of language as a tool for describing reality.*]

The image of Vicente Aleixandre as a relatively unsophisticated creator has been remarkably tenacious, although no one has ever called into question his mastery of language. The stylistic analyses of Carlos Bousoño, the author of the first and most influential monograph on the poet, have provided ample demonstration of the subtlety and power of Aleixandre's poetic technique. Still, few studies of his poetry have emphasized his linguistic self-consciousness, his awareness of the verbal medium as a theoretical problem. In a recent study, Philip Silver has given voice to the widespread view that Aleixandre is essentially naive as a poetic thinker. For Silver, the author of *La destrucción o el amor* typifies the Hispanic poet who, like Antaeus in Greek mythology, derives all of his strength from his ties to the earth [Philip Silver, *Le casa de Anteo: Estudios de poética española,* 1985]. Aleixandre would thus lack the theoretical self-consciousness that is essential to the modern poet.

This assessment, I would argue, makes the poet a victim of his own rhetoric. Many of Aleixandre's statements about his own work give the initial impression of a resolutely antitheoretical poet, more concerned with the content of his poetic vision than with language per se. In a statement of his poetics written in the 1930s for Gerardo Diego's anthology, for example, he protests against what he perceives to be a widespread tendency in modern poetry to exalt language for its own sake: "Frente a la divinización de la palabra, frente a esa casi obscena delectación de la *Maestría* o dominio verbal del artífice que trabaja la talla, confundiendo el destello del vidrio entre sus manos con la profunda luz creadora, hay que afirmar, hay que exclamar con verdad. No, la poesía no es *cuestión de palabras*" ["In opposition to the deification of the word, to that almost obscene pleasure in the *mastery* or verbal skill of the artificer who fabricates his sculpture, confusing the gleam of glass in his hands with the profound creative light, it is necessary to affirm, to exclaim truthfully. No, poetry is not *a question of words*"].

Aleixandre appears to be exalting the content of the poet's vision at the expense of a concern for the verbal medium itself. He rejects the notion that the poet is primarily a wordsmith, refining language into a more perfect medium for the expression of thought. It could be argued, however, that Aleixandre's apparent denial of the linguistic nature of poetry reveals an obsession with language. His very distrust of words obliges him to consider the question of language in a way that a more obviously logophilic poet would not. I would argue that his attitude of suspicion is more characteristic of the modern poet than is the simple exaltation of poetic language. Aleixandre's poetry is indeed a "question of words," in the sense that it is both a quest for expression and a questioning of language. In his profession of the primacy of experience over words, Aleixandre aligns himself with one of the central currents of poetry since romanticism, the tradition that views language as an inherently defective system of signs that must continually be destroyed and recreated. Octavio Paz has succinctly summarized this attitude toward language in terms of a double imperative: "a un tiempo, destrucción y creación del lenguaje. Destruc-

ción de las palabras y de los significados, reino del silencio; pero, igualmente, palabra en busca de la Palabra." ["At once a destruction and a creation of language. A destruction of words and of signifieds, a realm of silence; but, equally, a word in search of the Word"] [*Corriente alterna,* 1967].

While adamantly denying that it is a question of words, Aleixandre concludes his statement by defining poetry in terms of language. He dismisses everyday words as "estrechos moldes previos" ["narrow, preestablished molds"] and "signos insuficientes" ["insufficient signs"] from which the poetic genius must escape:

> fuga o destino hacia un generoso reino, plenitud o realidad soberana, realidad suprasensible, mundo incierto donde el enigma de la poesía está atravesado por las supremas categorías, últimas potencias que iluminan y signan la oscura revelación para la que las palabras trastornan su consuetudinario sentido.

> a flight or a destiny toward a generous realm, a plenitude or sovereign reality, a reality superior to the senses, an uncertain world where the enigma of poetry is transfixed by supreme categories, ultimate powers that illuminate and seal that dark revelation for the sake of which words disturb their everyday sense.

Although the poet emphasizes the reality that lies beyond ordinary perception and ordinary language, this marvelous realm can be reached only through a specifically verbal act: the subversion of the accepted usage of words. This disturbance of sense implies the creation of a new and paradoxical poetic speech, one that will somehow correspond to the dark revelation, the paradoxically opaque unveiling, of poetic vision.

It has been customary to divide Aleixandre's poetic production into three major periods: the early surrealist-influenced poetry, the "realist" tendency of the postwar period, and the metaphysical investigations of *Poemas de la consumación* [*Poems of consummation*] (1968) and *Diálogos del conocimiento* [*Dialogues of knowledge*] (1974). Aleixandre's self-consciousness is most evident at the beginning and at the end of his long career. In many poems written during the 1930s, the poet expresses his view of language in terms very similar to those he employs in his *poética*. Words in their ordinary state impede the poet's expression of his vision, or even his access to it. In a poem from *Espadas como labios* [*Swords like lips*] (1932), **"Palabras,"** the speaker views language in essentially negative terms:

> Pero no importa que todo esté tranquilo
> (La palabra esa lana marchita)
> Flor tú muchacha casi desnuda viva viva
> (la palabra esa arena machacada)
>
> But it doesn't matter that everything is calm
> (The word that faded wool)
> Flower you girl almost naked alive alive
> (the word that pounded sand)

Once again, this denigration of words must be understood as part of a dialectical movement. Language is an obstacle to expression, but a necessary one, for without its interference or resistance there would be no tension between the words of the poem and the reality that they attempt to capture.

It could be argued that it is the tension between the poet's vision and its linguistic expression, rather than content of his vision per se, that most preoccupies the early Aleixandre. Paul Ilie, for example, has convincingly interpreted *Pasión de la tierra* [*Passion of the earth*] as an allegory of the poet's anxiety about his poetic gift [Ilie, "Descent and Castration," *Vicente Aleixandre: A Critical Appraisal,* edited by Santiago Daydí-Tolson, 1981]. The opening poem of *Espadas como labios,* entitled **"Mi voz,"** calls into question virtually every aspect of the communicative situation:

> He nacido una noche de verano
> entre dos pausas Háblame te escucho
> He nacido Si vieras qué agonía
> representa la luna sin esfuerzo
> He nacido Tu nombre era la dicha
> Bajo un fulgor una esperanza un ave
> Llegar llegar El mar era un latido
> el hueco de una mano una medalla tibia
> Entonces son posibles ya las luces las caricias la
>   piel el horizonte
> ese decir palabras sin sentido
> que ruedan como oídos caracoles
> como un lóbulo abierto que amanece
> (escucha escucha) entre la luz pisada

> I have been born one summer's night
> between two pauses Speak to me I listen to you
> I have been born If you could see what agony
> the moon effortlessly represents
> I have been born Your name was joy
> Beneath a brilliance a hope a bird
> To arrive to arrive The sea was a heartbeat
> the hollow of a hand a warm medal
> Then the lights the caresses the skin the horizon
>   become possible
> that speaking of senseless words
> that roll like ears snails
> like an open lobe that dawns
> (listen listen) amid the trampled light

In his landmark essay "Closing Statement: Linguistics and Poetics" [*Semiotics; An Introductory Anthology,* edited by Robert E. Innis, 1985], Roman Jakobson posited a model of communication consisting of six elements: addressor, addressee, contact, code, message, and context. According to Jakobson, different kinds of utterances privilege one or another of six functions. In Aleixandre's text, however, none of these elements is fully functional. The lyric speaker and his addressee—two isolated and vaguely defined personages—seem unable to establish contact with each other. Nor do they share any meaningful code, striving only to "decir palabras sin sentido." As in much modern poetry, the referential function (for Jakobson, a focus on the context of

utterance) is extremely weak. Of course, the text constitutes a "poetic" use of language, in that it focuses on the message for its own sake. Yet, because of the weakness of the other five elements, this poetic function has the effect of undermining rather than contributing to the act of communication.

It is interesting to note that Aleixandre's critics have tended to privilege *La destrucción o el amor* [*Destruction or love*], which contains fewer explicitly self-conscious poems, over *Pasión de la tierra* and *Espadas como labios,* his two earlier surrealist works. The poetic voice heard in this volume appears to be more confident of its communicative power, as Aleixandre develops a more powerful but also more predictable set of rhetorical devices. The resulting confidence in language ultimately leads, in Aleixandre's second period, to a very different kind of metapoetry. Words continue to be perceived as obstacles to the attainment of poetic vision. The most significant novelty in the books written during the forties and fifties, however, is that this linguistic interference is much more easily displaced. A relative clarity of expression replaces the tortured struggle with language characteristic of the earlier poetry. In a passage notable for its magnificent rhetoric, the speaker of **"El poeta,"** the initial poem in *Sombra del paraíso* [*Shadow of paradise*] (1944), instructs the poet who is about to read the book to throw it down, to reject it as an inadequate representation of the vitality of nature:

> Sí, poeta, arroja este libro que pretende encerrar en
>   sus páginas un destello del sol,
> y mira a la luz cara a cara, apoyada la cabeza en la
>   roca,
> mientras tus pies remotísimos sienten el beso
>   postrero del poniente
> y tus manos alzadas tocan dulce la luna,
> y tu cabellera colgante deja estela en los astros.

> Yes, poet, throw down this book which claims to
>   enclose in its pages a glimmer of sunlight,
> and look at the light face to face, with your head
>   resting on a rock,
> while your remote feet feel the last kiss of the west
>   wind
> and your raised hands touch the sweet moon,
> and your hair, hanging down, leaves its wake
>   among the stars.

The obvious paradox here is that these words do not have the effect of prompting the lyric addressee (or the real reader, for that matter) to stop reading the book. The result is likely to be exactly the opposite: the speaker's words create the illusion that the book in question is not really a text at all, but an unmediated encounter with the naked elements of Aleixandre's paradise. This passage contains an implicit message to its readers instructing them to ignore the linguistic medium of poetry, to look through the language as though it were a transparent glass that allowed them to come face to face with the light of the poet's transcendent vision.

The books that follow *Sombra del paraíso* continue to

elide the question of language. In *Historia del corazón* [*History of the heart*] (1954) and *En un vasto dominio* [*In a vast dominion*] (1962) Aleixandre no longer rejects everyday language as an impediment to a transcendent poetic vision. Rather, he accepts this language as an unproblematic channel of communication. Reading these books, one no longer senses any tension between language and its referents. The poet's lack of interest in poetic language as a problem corresponds to his desire to reach the largest possible audience. In the manifesto-like poem that opens *En un vasto dominio* [*In a vast domain*], "**¿Para quién escribo?**" ["**For whom do I write?**"], the speaker affirms that his goal is to give voice to the concerns of those who cannot speak. For such a poetics, diametrically opposed to that of *Espadas como labios,* language is no longer a problem or even a question. It becomes a mere tool for the expression of meaning. If the poet is not a goldsmith he is at least a blacksmith. What the Aleixandre of these years shares with the poet who conceives of his craft as fine metalwork is a certain complacency about the capacity of language to obey his will, to represent his vision of reality unproblematically.

In the final phase of his career Aleixandre returns to a more complex vision of language, one that is reminiscent to some degree of his earlier poetics. Aleixandre's renewed interest in metapoetry corresponds to a widespread awakening of self-consciousness in Spanish poetry of the sixties and seventies. Led by young poets such as Guillermo Carnero and Pere Gimferrer, poets of all generations and tendencies begin to call language into question with renewed fervor. It is no coincidence that Aleixandre is one of the major sponsors of these younger poets, or that Carnero and Gimferrer have both written intelligently and sympathetically about Aleixandre's later work.

Poemas de la consumación, like *Espadas como labios, Sombra del paraíso,* and *En un vasto dominio,* begins with a statement of poetics. "**Las palabras del poeta**" ["**The poet's words**"], however, is an elusive text, far from the programmatic statement of intentions of "**Para quién escribo.**" The poetic voice here is neither the vital, Whitmanesque singer of the former poem nor the Great Communicator of the latter. He is instead an old man whose words begin to fail him in the face of his impending end. At this point in the poet's career the mediation of words cannot be side-stepped: words are no longer direct representations of an available reality, as in Aleixandre's "realist" phase, but a medium for the preservation of memory:

> Después de la palabras muertas,
> de las aún pronunciadas o dichas,
> ¿qué esperas? Unas hojas volantes,
> más papeles dispersos. ¿Quién sabe? Unas palabras
> deshechas, como el eco o la luz que muere allá en
>   gran noche.

> After the dead words,
> those already pronounced or spoken,
> what do you expect? Some flying leaves,
> more dispersed papers. Who knows? Some words

undone, like the echo or the light that dies there in
    the great night.

This poem sets forward in discursive terms the implicit poetics of *Poemas de la consumación*. Language is no longer a transparent medium that can bring the poet and his readers into direct contact with a poetic vision of reality. Instead, it is an echo, a belated representation. As in both Aleixandre's early and middle periods, there is an implicit opposition between language and vitality. Here, however, the poet no longer has any access to this vitality outside of language. As a consequence, language is paradoxically identified with as well as opposed to life: "Morir es olvidar unas palabras" ["To die is to forget some words"].

While only a half-dozen poems after "**Las palabras del poeta**" explicitly address the linguistic theme, virtually all the poems in the volume touch upon it in some way. The structure of *Poemas de la consumación* allows a metapoetic reading of many poems that otherwise might not lend themselves to this approach. As with all of his books of poetry, with the exception of a few anthologies and miscellanies, Aleixandre has conceived the volume as an interdependent group of closely related poems, rather than a mere agglomeration of lyric poems. If anything, the book is even more tightly knit than the poet's previous efforts. For Gimferrer, Aleixandre's later poetry is "un arte combinatorio que procede por permutación, sustitución o superposición de un repertorio muy parco de elementos" ["An *ars combinatoria* that proceeds by permutation, substitution, or superposition of a very limited repertory of elements"; "La poesía última de Vicente Aleixandre," *Vicente Aleixandre,* edited by José Luis Cano, 1977]. Gimferrer goes on to make the surprising affirmation that the reiterative and paradigmatic structure of these books is imperceptible to the common reader, emerging only from the critic's analysis. I would argue, on the contrary, that this distinction is arbitrary, and that an awareness of the repetition of basic elements is an indispensable part of any reader's experience of the text. It is only by comparing and contrasting individual poems that one constructs a paradigm and thus makes sense of the larger whole. The "common reader" is a mere fiction in this case, given the already small audience for poetry and the difficulty of Aleixandre's final works.

Since terms that relate to language specifically and to representation in general have a crucial place within the densely woven semantic web of the book, it is not necessary or even desirable to concentrate exclusively on the poet's more explicit statements of poetics. I would begin charting the semantic system of *Poemas de la consumación* with the key word *palabra* [word], which relates directly to other types of signs—*signos, emblemas, nombres, textos* [signs, emblems, names, texts]—and to words that refer literally or metaphorically to poetry: *poeta, palabra, canción* [poet, word, song]. *Palabra* is also linked to words pertaining to orality: *voz, boca, beso, lengua, labios* [voice, mouth, kiss, tongue (or language), lips]. A line such as "roja pulpa besada que pronuncian" ["red kissed pulp that they pronounce"] conflates the speech-act and the kiss, so that the word becomes an explicitly erotic act. There is another set of terms having to do with sound: *son, sonido, eco, silencio, callar* [sound, echo, silence, to quiet]. Moving in another direction, language is linked metaphorically to other belated representations of reality: *espejo, imagen, reflejo, copia, sombra, huella, repetir* [mirror, image, reflection, copy, shadow, trace, to repeat]. The imperfection of linguistic representation finds expression in words such as *engaño, máscara, mentira, verdad, sueño* [deceit, mask, lie, truth, dream]. These terms lead us directly to the problem of knowledge that Guillermo Carnero has studied in Aleixandre's later work. This epistemological preoccupation is often expressed in imagery of light and darkness: *luz, oscuridad, mirar, ciego, ver, saber, conocer* [light, darkness, to look, blind, to see, to know, to be familiar with].

These chains of words could be extended into a complete glossary of the significant terms that appear in *Poemas*. The result of Aleixandre's technique is an implicit mode of poetic self-reflection that has not been widely appreciated. In order to demonstrate how this implicit self-consciousness functions in *Poemas de la consumación,* I have chosen to analyze a representative poem, **"Límites y espejo"** [**"Limits and mirror"**], which, aside from the presence of the word *palabras,* is not one of the half-dozen or so that explicitly address the question of the poet's language.

The same semantic structure that makes it difficult to interpret a single poem as an independent unit also allows such a poem to be representative of the larger whole. The opening lines of **"Límites y espejo,"** in the context of the volume as a whole, take on intertextual resonance. The abrupt way in which the poem begins, with a command to an unnamed interlocutor, implies the continuation of a previous dialogue. The enigmatic, aphoristic style and the brevity of the text, similarly, encourage the reader to look for help in the other poems in the book.

> No insistas. La juventud no engaña. Brilla a solas.
> En un pecho desnudo muere el día.
> No son palabras las que a mí me engañan.
> Sino el silencio puro que aquí nace.
> En tus bordes. La silenciosa línea te limita
> pero no te reduce. Oh, tu verdad latiendo aquí en
>   espacios.

> Don't insist. Youth does not deceive. It shines
>   alone.
> In a naked chest the day dies.
> What deceives me is not words.
> But the pure silence that is born here.
> On your edges. The silent line delimits you.
> But doesn't reduce you. Oh, your truth beating here
>   in spaces.

The first four lines recombine elements from the beginnings of the poems that immediately precede it in section 4 of the book: "La juventud engaña / con veraces palabras" ["Youth deceives / with true words"]. "Felicidad, no engañas. / Una palabra fue o sería, y dulce / quedó en el labio" ["Happiness, you don't deceive. / It was or would be a word, and sweetly / it stayed on my lip"]. "La juventud no lo conoce, por eso dura, y sigue" ["Youth does not know it, and because of this it lasts, and continues"]. These poems, variations on a theme, evoke two semantic networks: language and its deceptiveness, and the contrast between youth and old age that the majority of critics have seen as the major theme of Aleixandre's later poetry. **"Límites y espejo"** is a representative poem in *Poemas de la consumación* because of the way in which it fuses these two preoccupations. My thesis is that Aleixandre views the opposition between youth and old age in terms of a parallel opposition between reality and its imperfect linguistic representation. Old age is a pallid reflection of youth, just as language echoes but does not capture what it attempts to represent. The title of the poem, in this case, would suggest the *limits* of language's *mirroring*, which has the paradoxical effect of imitating reality while missing the essential truth.

Limits and borders in Aleixandre's poetry almost always have an ambiguous meaning. By definition they circumscribe and delimit. At the same time, to reach the limit is to come into contact with the absolute. The lover in *La destruccíon o el amor,* for example, feels "los hermosos límites de la vida" [the beautiful limits of life]. In the mirror's visual image, the poet attempts to have the benefits of mimesis without its drawbacks. He wishes to create a representation that limits without being reductive. The line, by defining the outlines of the image, also gives it its human, mortal dimension, and thus defines its essential truth. The "pure silence" of vision would appear to transcend the inherent deceptiveness of language. The mirror, of course, is a traditional symbol of pure, unmediated mimesis, though it can also represent the dangers of such mimesis, as in the myth of Narcissus. The second-person singular *tú* in these lines could be seen as a double of the poet. I would interpret this figure, however, as the poet's younger beloved, who appears in other poems of the volume. This female figure would thus stand in contrast to the older poet, who remains trapped within the less perfect medium of language.

The second stanza of **"Límites y espejo"** links the ambiguity of limits to another, similar paradox having to do with consummation, perfection, and death:

> Sólo un cuerpo desnudo enseña bordes.
> Quien se limita existe. Tú en la tierra.
> Cuán diferente tierra se descoge
> y se agrupa y reluce y, suma, enciéndese,
> carne o resina, o cuerpo, alto, latiendo,
> llameando. Oh, si vivir es consumirse, ¡muere!

> Only a naked body shows edges.
> He who limits himself exists. You on the earth.
> What a different earth unfolds
> and regroups and shines and, a summation, is lit,
> flesh or resin, or a high body, beating,
> flaming. Oh, if to live is to be consumed, die!

Consumación means "fulfillment, consummation, perfection." In Spanish, however, the word has the secondary meaning of "extinction, death, the end of time." Thus it combines the connotations of two distinct verbs, *consumar* and *consumir*. As the flame of life reaches its limits it consumes itself and at the same time reaches its point of consummation. This stanza describes the image of the beloved in the mirror in terms of Aleixandre's view of human life as a momentary state of exception in the universe. The limits are both spatial and temporal: they are the edges of her body, and the time frame that defines her existence as a "different kind of earth," one that only very briefly takes on human form. The brevity of life, its exceptionality in the context of the entire cosmos, is expressed in the virtual simultaneity of birth and death. By emphasizing the shortness of the human life span, the poet is able to minimize the possible difference in age between the poet and his beloved: if birth and death occur together, like the beginning and end of a lightning bolt, youth and old age become practically indistinguishable.

The third and final stanza of the poem returns to the idea of the imperfection of representation, striking a more subdued tone after the exaltation of the second section:

> Pero quien muere nace, y aquí aún existes.
> ¿La misma? No es un espejo un rostro aunque
>   repita
> su gesto. Quizá su voz. En el espejo hiélase una
>   imagen
> de un sonido. ¡Cómo en el vidrio el labio dejó
>   huellas!
> El vaho tan sólo de lo que tú amaras.

> But the one who dies is born, and here you still
>   exist.
> The same woman? A face is not a mirror although
>   it repeats
> its expression. Perhaps her voice. In the mirror the
>   sound of an image
> is frozen. How the lip left traces on the glass!
> Only the exhalation of what you had loved.

In contrast to the more optimistic tone of the beginning of the poem, the speaker now emphasizes the inadequacy of representation: a mirror is not the face it reflects. In the first stanza, the essential truth of the woman persists in the illusory three-dimensionality of the mirror's reflection ("Oh tu verdad latiendo aquí en espacios"). Now, however, the mirror freezes the reality that it reflects, converting even the poet's voice into an inert, spatial representation, twice removed from its source. The image of kissing the mirror calls to mind the lines from Pedro Salinas's *Presagios* . . . :

> 'Bésame', dices. Te beso,
> y mientras te beso pienso
> en lo fríos que serán
> tus labios en el espejo.

The situation in Aleixandre's poem, however, is almost the exact reverse. Instead of kissing the woman while

thinking of her reflection in the mirror, as does the speaker in the Salinas poem, Aleixandre's speaker conceives of his erotic encounter through the indirect medium of the mirror image. In the immediacy of the moment Salinas attempts to distance the kiss by converting it into a cold representation of itself. Aleixandre, in contrast, feels the last warmth of a past sexual union in the imprint of his lover's lips on the glass. We should remember that, in the semantic universe of *Poemas de la consumación,* kissing and speaking are often parallel acts. The poet, at the terminal point in his life, becomes the empty image of what his companion had loved.

The poem that immediately follows **"Límites y espejo"** in *Poemas de la consumación,* **"Rostro tras el cristal (Mirada del viejo)"** [**"Face behind the pane (An old man's gaze)"**] is another variation on the same theme:

> O tarde o pronto o nunca.
> Pero ahí tras el cristal el rostro insiste.
> Junto a unas flores naturales la misma flor se
>   muestra
> en forma de color, mejilla, rosa.
> Tras el cristal la rosa es siempre rosa.
> Pero no huele.
> La juventud distante es ella misma.
> Pero aquí no se oye.
>
> Sólo la luz traspasa el cristal virgen.

> Later or sooner or never.
> But there behind the glass the face insists.
> Next to the natural flowers the same flower is
>   revealed
> in form of color, cheek, rose.
> Behind the pane the rose is always a rose.
> But it has no odor.
> Distant, youth is itself,
> but here it can't be heard.
>
> Only light traverses the virgin crystal.

In this case a windowpane takes the place of the mirror. As in **"Límites,"** the poem is structured around the contrast between youth and old age, sight and sound (and in this case smell), reality and its sensory representation. The poet observes his beloved through a medium that preserves her image in its purified form, while separating him from its vitality. Unlike **"Límites y espejo,"** this poem does not explicitly mention language, "las palabras." Nevertheless, it forms part of Aleixandre's overall meditation on the limits of representation, and thus exhibits the self-reflexivity that characterizes all of the poet's later work.

The term *metapoetry* usually implies the existence of another kind of poetry, one that does not reflect upon itself. The implicit mode of self-reflection found in Aleixandre's later work, however, subverts any line the critic might wish to draw between metapoetry and other modes of poetic discourse. Theories of poetic self-consciousness are often based on the idea of the subversion of mimesis. It might be argued, though, that mimesis is not a generic norm for lyric poetry in the same way it is for other genres. Unlike prose narration or theater, where the reader might expect to find an illusion of reality, poetry is already an inherently self-reflexive genre, one that rarely claims to be referential. Thus any attempt to distinguish between ordinary poetic discourse and the self-conscious commentary on this discourse will beg the question of what constitutes poetic language in the first place.

In Aleixandre's later poetry, the question of poetic language becomes inseparable from the epistemological problem of the relation between reality and its representation, and the vital problem posed by the imminence of old age and death. In *Poemas de la consumación* the limits of language come to represent the limits of life itself. Poetic language reflects upon itself in the act of representation, or, more accurately, in the process of failing to represent a more essential reality. This "failure" is the consummate achievement of Aleixandre's later poetry.

FURTHER READING

Criticism

Bradford, Carole E. "From Vicente Aleixandre to Claudio Rodríguez: Love as a Return to the Cosmos." *Hispanic Journal* 4, No. 1 (Fall 1982): 97-104.
> Close reading of two poems, "Unidad en ella" by Aleixandre and "Ahí mismo" by Claudio Rodriquez, focusing on their treatment of love as a fundamental, unifying force of nature.

Cabrera, Vicente, and Boyer, Harriet, eds. *Critical Views on Vicente Aleixandre's Poetry*. Lincoln, Nebr.: Society of Spanish and Spanish-American Studies, 1979, 195 p.
> A collection of translated critical essays.

Cannon, Calvin. A review of *Presencias. Hispania* L, No. 2 (May 1967): 389-90.
> Considers an assertion in the preface of *Presencias* that Aleixandre's poetry is "objective," concluding that such a label must be understood "in a special sense, paradoxical, even ironical. Briefly, we may understand it as the surrender of self through love to the world (object) beyond self, as the submergence of the self in the object, in which the dualism of self-object is somehow transcended."

Daydí-Tolson, Santiago, ed. *Vicente Aleixandre: A Critical Appraisal.* Ypsilanti, Mich.: Bilingual Press, 1981, 353 p.
> Presents an overview of Aleixandre's career, the text of his Nobel Lecture, and several reprinted critical commentaries, including an essay by noted Aleixandre scholar Carlos Bousoño translated into English. This collection also contains an extensive primary and secondary bibliography.

DeAguilar, Helene J. F. "Clouds of Unknowing and Healthier Climates." *Parnassus* 8, No. 1 (Fall-Winter 1979): 64-83.
> Reviews two translated collections of Aleixandre's poems, *Twenty Poems* and *A Longing for the Light*. DeAguilar loosely categorizes Aleixandre as a "cosmic" poet.

Fernández-Morera, Darío. "Vicente Aleixandre in the Context of Modern Poetry." *Symposium* 33, No. 2 (Summer 1979): 118-41.
> Outlines several stages in Aleixandre's career as a poet, relating changes in his work to literary movements, cultural shifts, and the poet's internal life.

Graf, E. C. "May I Have This Dance? Unveiling Vicente Aleixandre's 'El Vals.'" *Romanic Review* 85, No. 2 (March 1994): 313-26.
> Provides a close reading of the poem "El vals," claiming: "Aleixandre's theoretical considerations of Freudianism and Surrealism force him to reexamine the question of sexuality, and often in conjunction with the very question of language."

Harris, Derek. "Spanish Surrealism: The Case of Vicente Aleixandre and Rafael Alberti." *Forum for Modern Language Studies* XVIII, No. 2 (April 1982): 159-71.
> Examines the use of automatism, a principal Surrealist technique, in the poems "Muñecas" by Aleixandre and "Adiós a las luces perdidas" by Alberti in an attempt to assess the relationship of Spanish poetry to French Surrealism.

Harvey, Sally. "Pastoral in *Sombra del paraíso." Bulletin of Hispanic Studies* LXIII, No. 2 (April 1986): 127-36.
> Reexamines the contention that *Sombra del paraíso* is concerned with paradise lost, asserting that the themes of this volume, emphasizing the simplicity of the natural world versus civilization's artificial complexity, fit squarely within the pastoral genre.

Morris, C. B. *A Generation of Spanish Poets 1920-1936.* Cambridge: Cambridge University Press, 1971, 302 p.
> Comparative study of the Spanish poets who comprised the "Generation of 1927." In one chapter, Aleixandre is contrasted with Jorge Guillén, while in another he is discussed with respect to Luis Cernuda, Rafael Alberti, and Federico García Lorca.

Poust, Alice. "Phenomenological Hermeneutics and Vicente Aleixandre's Self-Reading." *Revista de Estudios Hispanicos* 26, No. 3 (October 1992): 328-43.
> Asserts that readers can gain insight into Aleixandre's writing by understanding the literary theories that the poet applied to the creation and assessment of his own works.

Schwartz, Kessel. "The Sea, Love, Death in the Poetry of Aleixandre." *Hispania* L, No. 2 (May 1967): 219-28.
> Psychoanalytic interpretation of Aleixandre's works in which Schwartz asserts that "an examination of the sea symbolism in Aleixandre's poetry reveals the neurotic motivation behind and preoccupation with the equation that love equals death."

———. *Vicente Aleixandre*. New York: Twayne Publishers,
1970, 188 p.
    Overview of Aleixandre's life and works.

Additional coverage of Aleixandre's life and career is contained in the following sources
published by Gale Research: *Contemporary Authors,* Vols. 85-88, 114; *Contemporary Authors
New Revision Series,* Vol. 26; *Contemporary Literary Criticism,* Vols. 9, 36; *Dictionary of
Literary Biography,* Vol. 108; *Hispanic Writers*; and *Major 20th-Century Writers*.

André Breton
1896–1966

French poet, essayist, novelist, critic, and dramatist.

INTRODUCTION

Breton was the founder and primary theoretician of Surrealism, an influential literary and artistic movement dedicated to examining the irrational, paranormal, and subconscious aspects of the human mind. Originated in the 1920s, surrealism sought to replace established moral and ethical concepts with a philosophy of irrationality that Breton described as "exalting the values of *poetry*, *love*, and *liberty*." Accordingly, his poems are experiments in prose, free verse, and automatic writing; they draw upon socialist politics, the psychological theories of Sigmund Freud, and such mystical phenomena as alchemy and astrology.

Biographical Information

Breton was born in Tinchebray in the Normandy region of France. As a young boy he spent time in Lorient on the Brittany coast, the ocean, shore, and sky of which featured vividly in his poetic imagery. Prior to his literary career, he attended medical school at the University of Paris and became familiar with the ideas of such neurologists as Freud, Jean-Martin Charcot, and Pierre Janet. His psychiatric work in an army medical unit during World War I furthered his interest in the subconscious aspects of the human mind. Following the war, Breton became active in the Dadaist movement (a nihilistic philosophy of art and literature that proposed the cynical rejection of all established cultural values) and produced *Mont de piété* (*Pawnshop*), his first collection of poems. Breton soon became disenchanted with the limitations and destructiveness of Dadaism and sought to supplant it with Surrealism. His poetry collection *Les Champs magnétiques* (*Magnetic Fields*; coauthored with Philippe Soupault) has been called the first Surrealist text. Between the mid-1920s and World War II, Breton guided the rapid progress of the Surrealist movement, publishing manifestoes and editing Surrealist journals. Breton lived in self-imposed exile in North America during World War II and the German occupation of France. His memoirs (*Entretiens, 1913-1952*), published in 1952, give comprehensive coverage of his intellectual life, and explain his motives, his enthusiasms, and his often unstable relationships with friends and fellow artists. Breton returned to France at the end of World War II, where he lived until his death in Paris in 1966.

Major Works

In his early Surrealist poetry, collected in *Magnetic Fields*, *Clair de terre* (*Earthlight*), and *Poisson soluble* (*Soluble Fish*), Breton experimented with Pierre Janet's concept of psychic automatism, using a stream-of-consciousness approach known as automatic writing in which random, subconscious responses to self-induced dreams, hallucinations, and trances are transcribed into written form. Much of his poetry of the 1930s makes use of biological and botanical symbolism as well as contrasts between images of light, fire, and darkness. In the complex theatrical pieces collected in *Le Revolver à cheveux blancs* (*The White-Haired Revolver*) and in the ritualistic and erotic love poetry in *L'Air de l'eau* (*Airwater*), Breton evidenced a preference for bizarre metaphors and arcane language. The style of his poetic epics *Fata Morgana* and *Ode à Charles Fourier* (*Ode to Charles Fourier*) is considered more hermetic and less automatic than that of his early works and expresses in metaphoric and mythological terms Breton's self-exile during World War II. The prose poems in *Constellations*, written in 1940 and collected with drawings by Joan Miró, present images of the poet as craftsman, painter, and magician.

Critical Reception

Breton's interest in automatic writing, his adherence to surrealism, and his dense and arcane imagery have polarized critical assessment of his poems. Early judgment was particularly divided. Louise Bogan, for example, a poet and contemporary of Breton's, considered his work childish and formulaic; John Berryman dismissed it as ephemeral. Others, such as Anna Balakian and Wallace Fowlie, have seen Breton as an accomplished poet whose instincts were both original and timeless. One consistent focus has been on the complexity of his vocabulary, and the consensus among literary critics today is that Breton's poems deserve close study for the richness of the language they employ and for the way that language lends itself to a variety of critical interpretations.

PRINCIPAL WORKS

Poetry

Mont de piété [*Pawnshop*] 1919
Les Champs magnétiques (with Philippe Soupault) 1920; also published as *Magnetic Fields*, 1985
Clair de terre 1923; also published as *Earthlight*, 1990
Poisson soluble [*Soluble Fish*] 1924
Ralentir travaux [*Slow Down Construction*; with Rene Char and Paul Eluard] 1930
L'Union libre 1931
Le Revolver à cheveux blancs [*The White-haired Revolver*] 1932
L'Air de l'eau [*Airwater*] 1934
Fata Morgana 1940
Young Cherry Trees Secured Against Hares: Jeunes cerisiers garantis contre les lièvres (bilingual edition) 1946
Ode à Charles Fourier 1947; also published as *Ode to Charles Fourier*, 1969
Poémes 1948
Constellations 1959
Le La [*The Tone Setting*] 1961
Signe ascendent, suivi de Fara Morgana, les Etats Généreux, Dex Epingles tremblantes, Xénophiles, Ode á Charles Fourier, Le La 1968
Selected Poems 1969
Poems of André Breton: A Bilingual Anthology 1982
Oeuvres Complètes 1988

Other Major Works

Manifeste du surréalisme; Poisson soluble (manifesto) 1924
Les Pas perdus (essays) 1924
Nadja (novel) 1928
Le Surréalisme et la peinture (criticism) 1928
Second manifeste du surréalisme (manifesto) 1930
Les Vases communicants (novel) 1932
Qu'est-ce que le surréalisme? (lecture) 1934
Du temps que les surréalistes avaient raison (pamphlet) 1935
Position politique du surréalisme (lectures, speeches, and interviews) 1935

L'Amour fou (novel) 1937
Arcane 17 (novel) 1944
La Situation du surréalisme entre les deux guerres (lectures) 1945
Les Manifestes du surréalisme, [suivis de] Prolégomènes à un trosième manifeste du surréalisme ou non (manifestoes) 1946
Yves Tanguy (essays, poems, and photographs) 1946
Entretiens, 1913-1952 (interviews) 1952
La Clé des champs (essays) 1953
Manifestes du surrealisme (manifesto, complete edition) 1962
What Is Surrealism?: Selected Writings 1978

CRITICISM

Louise Bogan (essay date 1946)

SOURCE: A review of *Young Cherry Trees Secured Against Hares*, in *The New Yorker*, Vol. XXII, No. 39, November 9, 1946, pp. 121-23.

[*Bogan was an American lyric poet whose darkly romantic verse is characterized by her use of traditional structures, concise language, and vivid description. Bogan was also a distinguished critic known for her exacting standards and her penetrating analysis of many of the major poets of the twentieth century. In the following review, she accuses Breton's poetry of exhibiting the "student childishness" she finds typical of surrealism.*]

It is extraordinary how vital and adult the poetry of Arthur Rimbaud, who passed with the speed of a comet through the French literary world between his sixteenth and his nineteenth year (1870-73), now appears. Beside it, the poetry of the Surrealist André Breton, one of his successors, who was born in 1896 and has worked all his life as a literary experimenter, seems much more the work of an adolescent. This season [November 1946], we are able closely to compare the works of the young innovator and of this successor. View Editions has published a volume of André Breton's poetry, *Young Cherry Trees Secured Against Hares,* translated by Edouard Roditi (with drawings by Arshile Gorky and a cover designed by Marcel Duchamp), at the same time that New Directions has published a new translation, by Louise Varèse, of the prose poems from Rimbaud's *Illuminations*. The comparison brings out the truth that there are no short cuts to the world of the imagination. Rimbaud, in spite of occasional big talk about control over his subconscious processes, knew that he was only an instrument for them. ("It is wrong to say: I think. One should say: I am thought.") Breton has consciously applied every known method to get at *"le merveilleux,"* of which the subconscious seems to have the secret. But, at fifty, he seems undeveloped beside the wild youth who pushed into maturity in a flash, after attempting to live his life in accordance with his compelling and terrible vision. (The Surrealists, by the way, rejected Rimbaud long ago as being vulgar.)

Breton entered the Surrealist movement from French Dadaism. He has been its leader almost continuously, in spite of, or because of, his high-handed manner of leadership. The changes through which Surrealism has passed have Breton's intransigent nature behind them. Breton has, in fact, committed repeatedly what, according to early Surrealist doctrine, is one of the chief literary sins: he has taken himself too seriously. If the movement has now reached a blind alley, it is largely Breton's doing. He has multiplied his effects, rather than developed his gifts, and thus, after years of issuing manifestoes, diatribes, defenses, counterdefenses, of excommunicating disciples with the severity of a pontiff and inventing tactics with the ingenuity of a field marshal, he is beginning to assume the tone and features not of a master but of a rather bullying boy.

It is interesting to conjecture just why Surrealism, with its high aims—to change modern sensibility, to plumb the subconscious, to release the writer from isolation and a sense of futility and despair—has ended in smallness and dullness, without having "transformed the world" or "changed human life," as its adherents once planned. (Surrealist painting has been more successful in projecting various subliminal emotions.) It has thus always had the air of a turbulent schoolroom. The actual literary forms adopted by its members have often resembled caricatures of schoolroom tasks. There are poems made up of questions and answers, in the form of adages, proverbs, and definitions, of lists and catalogues—all close to the manner and matter of the examination paper. Or they have resembled the catechism and litanies familiar to those with a religious upbringing. Surrealists have played parlor paper games, like intelligent children; they have produced automatic writing and hypnotized each other; they have told each other their dreams, drawn up lists of literary ancestors and favorite writers. They have written insulting letters to the Pope, to eminent men of letters, and to their friends. The long squabbles, hairsplittings, and choosing of sides; the continual demotion of leaders and excommunication of followers; the practical jokes, the indiscriminate hatred of "culture," and the extreme sentimentality (on the whole) of their love poetry—all these preoccupations point to an emotional and intellectual fixation at a pre-adult level. Breton's . . . volume, which includes poems written from 1923 through 1944, preserves a good deal of this student childishness intact. He is a fine and eloquent rhetorician, but he is tiresome nonetheless. His subconscious, at least, seems never to have grown up.

Renee Riese Hubert (essay date 1964)

SOURCE: "Miró and Breton," in *Yale French Studies*, No. 31, 1964, pp. 52-9.

[*Hubert is a poet and scholar. In the following excerpt, she analyzes Breton's surrealist technique in* Constellations, *a volume consisting of twenty-two prose poems that parallel paintings by the artist Joan Miró.*]

Breton's Surrealist technique, unchanged since **Poisson soluble,** is very much in evidence in **Constellations**. An animated spectacle unfolds, several events happen simultaneously, and this multifarious animation provides the only unity. "**Le Lever du soleil**" suggests a solitary child's crossing of the threshold leading into a world of fantasy, legend, and heraldry. This movement coincides with the denouement of another more adult, fateful play. After this awakening, a further exploration of this newly discovered land is suggested by a series of unfolding movements, such as the sudden opening of poppies, the upward projection of an invisible ladder, the cries of chimneysweeps, mysterious skybound smoke rings. Then follow hoverings between light and dark, between labyrinths and evanescently defined roads. The world has the content and meaning of dreams and must be deciphered accordingly. To these evocations Breton attributes both intimacy and bewilderment, fatality and playfulness. He relates simultaneously old legends as well as everyday incidents.

The texts "**Femme à la blonde aisselle coiffant sa chevelure à la lueur des étoiles**" and "**Femmes sur la plage,**" far from attempting to rival the gouaches' multiplicity of erotic contours, suggest their gradual effacement. In a humorous dialogue between sand and a cork, the poet speaks of women's surrender, their liberation from conventions, their transgression of boundaries, their abandonment. Then, while the electrifying mystery persists, the gestures of the women embrace a lake, a castle and harvest fields. Undulating motions, creating a dreamlike fluidity, culminate in the final image of a nest woven of clematis leafage where secrecy renews its bond.

For the poet as well as for the painter, the world has become metamorphosed. In these texts objects and creatures maintain their identity in a veritable forest of symbols. The "Personnage blessé," undoubtedly an adult, gropes for rosy, sparkling, weightless elements and enigmatic fossils buried in caverns: the raw materials of future constellations. Surprise and illusion triumph over recognition. Humor adds a new dimension as night transforms a woman into a bird, but not with one stroke: "I'm halfwoman, but I've never been able to decide clearly whether the upper or the lower half suits me better" ("**Femme dans la nuit**"). Such metamorphoses both multiply and fuse images. A magnolia tree in "**Femme et oiseau**" embodies the sky and the earth, sound and sight, becomes a woman as well as a constellation while remaining a tree.

Magic festivities, games, disguises burst forth and overlap everywhere. Weightless creatures functioning as acrobats, dancers, stars, naiads graze the soil like shooting stars. Symphonic orchestrations, capable of endowing musical notations with the talent to perform by gestures the gay sounds they represent, enhance the show. Sparks and signs fly through the air, new life germinates on the milky way. The glitter moves ever more rapidly until the big dipper puts an end to the miracle. Forms and creatures subside, fuse and divide only to increase the animation. Reduced to their essential movements or outlines, all creatures are endowed with organic life. When joyful rites and other cults thus reach a climax, restlessness, pursuit, and destruction emerge to transform the nature of love. A relentless chase reduces woman, climbing the invisible ladder of the ideal, to a lacelike creature undistinguishable from the milky way. Fire and lightning dry the barren space until a black sun is spotted; bewitching erotic tunes persist. Later, in **"Vers l'Arc en ciel,"** love at last assumes its full range, extending from a child's exiguous heart to roses in full bloom, from the violent eroticism of a tauromachy to ultimate fulfillment. Moreover, destruction of, and detachment from, earthly elements are expressed through a series of verbs indicating separation, escape and fusion. Solid matter is strongly denied in **"Femmes au bord d'un lac à la surface irisée par le passage d'un cygne."** From the swan and the flower approaching fascinating stagnation (as opposed to movement characteristic of the majority of texts) radiates an unreal, nebulous, dreamlike atmosphere. The open eye, "l'oeil cyclopéen," is included as if the spectacle, which has been conjured, must now be immobilized. The mysterious bond between love and death emerges, carrying with it the seeds of rebirth. Women incarnating the domain of "inconnaissance" extend an invitation to dream, love and intuition with clear Baudelairian undertones.

Throughout the episodes of love, the festivities of the dream, the child's world has not been eclipsed. Bonnets, kites and cages fly through the air as dawn disbands or interrupts the spectacle. The fairyking Oberon appears, to offer his protection to Huon and Esclarmonde. Legends, mysterious creatures and games abound, signs and symbols will have to be deciphered. These games gradually become less casual and carefree. There is more and more determination, in counting, spelling, skipping the rope. There may even be danger in catching little birds. In **"Chiffres et constellations amoureux d'une femme"** and **"Le Bel oiseau déchiffrant l'inconnu au couple d'amoureux"** the wish to solve the riddle of musical, astrological and literary signs fuses with love and desire; the manifold harmony expresses itself in one language. Letters and numbers, birds and flowers undergo mutual transmutations. The effort towards unity is symbolized by the stringing of pearls on a thread. The poet strives to concatenate one endless garland which includes the smallest globule and extends to the sky. And each tiny globule in this endless succession takes the place of other elements, for identity becomes less significant than participation in the chorus of stars. Universal attraction dominates the scene, so much so that the embrace of love and desire can give a child's weightless balloon or an atom the same dimensions as the sun. It is just after the lyre and the rosebush musically and visually fused their masculine and feminine contours in the final prose-poem, **"Passage de l'oiseau divin,"** that Breton disbands "the world." Although gestures assume once more the complicity of marriage, although henchmen spread fear, although the insect devours the plant, and the bird the insect, we are as safe as in the world of fairytales, as safe as in a paradise of imagination and pure longing. The suite ends on a note of irony. It unravels like a drama. It disappears like a bird

whose very transparence reveals the presence of fish-shaped, flower-shaped and heart-shaped stars which never belonged to time-bound night.

Whether he takes the painter's representation as his immediate point of departure or derives his inspiration from other sources, Breton represents essentially the same poetic intent as Miró. Both bring day and night, desire and innocence, insect and comet into a single image. Breton, who wrote his prose-poems seventeen years after Miró had finished his twenty-two gouaches, has asserted the permanent traits of his own genius without betraying Miró's art. Strangely enough, the absence of spatial concepts characteristic of Breton's earlier poems, which are by no means lacking in painterly qualities, persists. Nonetheless, the barriers separating art from literature have perhaps never been as transparent as in *Constellations*.

Anna Balakian (essay date 1965)

SOURCE: "Metaphor and Metamorphosis in André Breton's Poetics," in *French Studies*, Vol. XIX, No. 1, 1965, pp. 34-41.

[*Balakian is an author and educator who has contributed many articles and reviews to language and literature journals. She has also published several book-length studies on Surrealism and Breton, including* Breton: Magus of Surrealism *(1971). In the excerpt below, Balakian explores Breton's poetical representation of the hermetic belief in metamorphosis and differentiates it from the theory of transcendentalism, two ideas that she feels are "too often and too carelessly . . . linked as part of a continuous chain in the history of poetics."*]

One of the major tenets of hermetism is metamorphosis. The occult art of the alchemist consists of transforming one type of material into another, and by extension one form of existence into the next. When Rimbaud talked of the alchemy of 'le Verbe' he saw in the power of words an effective agent of transmutation. Previously Baudelaire had been attracted to the theory of correspondences. Too often and too carelessly the two concepts are linked as part of a continuous chain in the history of poetics. They are, rather, opposite faces of the poetic coin. Correspondences imply a dualistic concept of the universe. During our sojourn here on earth certain emblems of nature give intimations of another plane of existence, and as we saunter along the pathways of our forest we recognize signs of a possible transcendence: 'the earth apparelled in celestial light', as Wordsworth so beautifully expressed it. In becoming more and more astute, the living creature comes closer and closer to this transcendence. Life, thus considered, consists of progressive steps rising higher and higher toward the kind of 'distant spheres' that Rossetti visualized. This transcendence is achieved through a moral purification in the case of many of the romanticists, or by virtue of a sharpening of the senses and an ultimate synaesthesia, as with the symbolists. Hence, among the symbols much in evidence to convey a poetic vision based on a dualistic philosophy, are the ladder, the wing or the chain in Hugo, the octave in the work of Claudel.

When we observe the alchemistic notion of life and its corresponding translation into poetry, we find something quite different. Although there is much unresolved discussion regarding the original character of the philosophy of Hermes, hermetism, as it is appropriated by modern poets and artists, is based on a monistic notion of the universe. It is not the same kind of alchemy as Shelley suggested in his *Defense of Poetry,* where it consisted of the purification of the objects around us and the cleansing of polluted waters. On the contrary, essence and substance become one, the material entity assumes a mystical function; Coleridge's 'milk of human paradise' has to be found here below. It is no longer a rising motion, but one of change and transformation. Transcendence is replaced by metamorphosis. The universe is not an octave, but, as André Breton puts it, a great circuit. The poet's mission is not to discover the signs that are reflections of another world, but to penetrate the disguises that obscure the way in the labyrinth or cryptograph of earthly existence. The act of interpreting reality actually consists of transforming it, as Breton suggests in *Les Vases Communicants.* One of the primary reasons for confusion of two so divergent poetic outlooks is that the power of metamorphosis is as dependent as that of transcendence upon the keenness of the senses and through the senses on the power of imagery. The means is similar, the goal quite different.

In the world of correspondences intuitive memory recalls previous existence to aid in the comprehension of the spiritual meaning of things. On the contrary, Breton considers memory an obstacle in the way of transformation. Memory can keep us in static form, while forgetting facilitates the passage to new experience and even to new existence. According to him it has been a fallacy to consider memory as a by-product of the imagination. Imagination reverts in his thinking to its original meaning, the act of creating images and making dreams become reality. It is the key with which man may attain whatever degree of liberty is possible here on earth.

> A rebours de l'opinion admise on n'était pas
> autorisé à tenir la mémoire
> Et tout ce qui se dépose de lourd avec elle
> Pour les sous-produits de l'imagination
> Comme si j'étais fondé le moins du monde
> A me croire moi d'une manière stable
> Alors qu'il suffit d'une goutte d'oubli ce n'est pas
> rare
> Pour qu'à l'instant où je me considère je vienne
> d'être tout autre et d'une autre goutte
> Pour que je me succède sous un aspect hors de
> conjecture
> Comme si même le risque avec son imposant
> appareil de tentations et de syncopes
> En dernière analyse était sujet à caution
> **Les États Généraux**

At the time when Breton unleashed his poetic fervour, all literature was suffering from an anaemia of the imagination. In the plastic arts alone there seemed to have been discovered a climate for creative ferment. Apollinaire sensed this, and Breton translated the disfigurations produced by the artists into a poetic credo of transfiguration; he attempted thereby to restore the faculty of imagination to its primary position in the literary act: a difficult position to hold against the popular, tried and tested means of literary communications, such as descriptive statement, symbolic interpretation, reminiscence, and confessional.

How did Breton's adherence to hermetism contribute to the art of writing poetry? Various technical procedures are used to suggest the metamorphosis latent in the imagery. There is a reversal of the correspondence technique: we find that instead of the concrete becoming abstract, the abstract is crystallized into the concrete. Disguise is another device much in use, the lifting of which produces poetic revelation. Here are a few examples from *Le Revolver à Cheveux Blancs*:

> Nous sommes les soupirs de la statue de verre qui
> se soulève sur le coude quand l'homme dort
> Et que des brèches brillantes s'ouvrent dans son lit. . .
> Nous te précédions alors nous les plantes sujettes à
> métamorphoses
> **'Facteur Cheval'**

> Les meubles font alors place à des animaux de
> même taille qui me regardent fraternellement
> Lions dans les crinières desquels achèvent de se
> consumer les chaises
> **'Vigilance'**

> Ces lumières qui bercent les choses irréelles
> Ces animaux dont les métamorphoses m'ont fait une
> raison
> **'Dernière Levée'**

The distinct divisions separating the animal, vegetable, and mineral worlds are broken down and a fluid passage occurs from one to the other as the barriers are dissolved. The physical elements, such as sun, wind, air, water, act as conjunctions between these various forms of existence. The most important among the key expressions on which the alchemy centres are all the words that suggest *fire,* for it is indeed the most basic agent of transformation, which does not destroy but turns one substance or form into another. Heat, high flame, lightning, burning coals are some of the variations. Light in its various forms, such as flares, lanterns, beacons, astral illuminations, are adjuncts to fire. The other important word is *water.* If fire transforms, water illuminates in turning the opaque translucent. Ice, crystal, glass are also transforming agents in the constant mutation which occurs.

In the world of correspondences the analogy is the axis of the poetic representation. The simile most faithfully translates the parallel between the material and its spiritual counterpart. Quite to the contrary, Breton tells us that *comme* is a word which does not mean 'such as'. Things and beings are not like other qualities or states; through the alchemy of the word they *become* something else, and the metaphor through which they are transformed draws them *not* from parallel spheres but from forms that are logically unrelated. For André Breton the same life-element penetrates all the ramifications of form, but without overflowing into the supernatural.

This state of mutation and fusion is produced by the sharpening and integration of the senses and the images which they conjure up. Breton wakens the drowsy senses with a beacon light, to borrow his metaphor, and plays on all of them. Synaesthesia occurs in the intermingling of sense perceptions, or, on the single plane of perception, one image flows into the other: a subterranean passage unites all perfumes, colours are diffused, sounds are prolonged, muted into rhythms perceptible only to the touch. A cluster of these can be gleaned in *Le Revolver*:

> Cette femme passe imperceptiblement dans un bruit
> de fleurs
> . . . des chanteuses dont la voix a la couleur du
> sable sur des rivages tendres et dangereux
> **'Les Écrits s'en vont'**

> Les réverbères mouillés bruissent encadrés d'une
> nuée d'yeux bleus
> **'Le Sphynx vertébral'**

> L'air de la chambre est beau comme des baguettes
> de tambour
> **'Le Verbe Être'**

And in the beautiful beginning of *Fata Morgana*:

> Ce matin la fille de la montagne tient sur ses
> genoux un accordéon de chauves-souris blanches

The resulting effect is a universal conciliation which even touches such concepts as presence and absence, manœuvering a complicity. The primary quality of life becomes the awareness of the inner rhythm produced by the unrelenting moulding of forms. The wider the radius of recognition of this interrelation, the more intense is the life-experience. And death is simply the prolongation of the radius beyond comprehensible limits. The process can also be reversed whereby resurrection may occur on a purely material basis. The poet's work thus envisaged is in a constant state of flux, producing unexpected transfigurations as they pertain to all the principal meditations of man: life, love, time, death, destiny, and social concern.

Life is ubiquitous and unconstrained. It is dynamic and ever in transition. Leaving its imprints in the same places as death, it is as a tangent to it rather than its antithesis. Form is a variable of life and not an identification. Life is an ever restless aspiration toward transformation, which can make the earth more translucid than water and let the metal ooze out of its shell. Such are the generalizations one can deduce from the galaxy of images expressed by brisk verbs suggesting change, such as cutting, escaping, throwing, flying, digging, overthrowing, or those which express penetration: diffusing, radiating, seeping, oozing, flowing, and all the fluids ranging from the blood of man

to the sap of the tree. And words like *cosse, coque, écorce* suggest the soluble confines that the life force is constantly breaking through.

> J'entends se déchirer le linge humain comme une
> grande feuille
> Sous l'ongle de l'absence et de la présence qui sont
> de connivence
> Tous les métiers se fanent il ne reste d'eux qu'une
> dentelle parfumée
> Une coquille de dentelle qui a la forme parfaite
> d'un sein
> Je ne touche plus que le cœur des choses je tiens le
> fil
> **'Vigilance', *Le Revolver à Cheveux Blancs***

To produce a powerful metaphor the long arms of the analogy do not merely touch but bear one on the other, and the interaction is expressed by the skilful manipulation of the verb at the centre of the image. This constant *becoming* rather than static *being* makes of *vitality* the primary theme.

Love is a magnetic process which draws the lovers into a conjugation with the varying forms of the earth. Instead of being raised above the material framework, here, on the contrary, they seem to become more entrenched in it, effecting an intimate communion with the earth. **'L'Union Libre'** is the most flamboyant example of this. But in the collection of *L'Air de l'eau,* there is a more subtle metamorphosis. When the poet says: 'monde dans un baiser', it is not a new world, but a fuller possession and a more concrete apprehension of the already familiar one. The loved one like a magnet draws to herself plants, insects, rocks, precious stones. On the surface it is the theme utilized by both Baudelaire and Verlaine wherein the beloved is compared to a beautiful landscape. But in the case of Breton love is a transformer almost in the technical, mechanical sense of the word. The loved one does not evoke but actually produces 'the far-off country', new suns, volcanoes steaming with snow. In one of these poems the erotic act is cadenced with ice, fire, and darkness, is freed of all evil with the appearance of a blossoming apple tree on the high seas. The meaning in terms of a conventional love poem would be, I suppose, that the love act transposes the poet to the threshold of a lost paradise and that original sin is erased in the vision of a new apple tree attired in pure blossoms. Vision would thus have proceeded from substance to essence and to quintessence. But no such gradation seems intended here. We first view the images resulting from the alchemy of love, and then we trace back to the generating force and the source of light, and thus we are encompassed in the entire magnetic field of operation. The most striking images of love are in *L'Air de l'eau* and in *Clair de Terre*:

> J'eus le temps de poser mes lèvres
> Sur tes cuisses de verre
> *L'Air de l'eau*

> Tes bras au centre desquels tourne le cristal de la
> rose des vents,

Ma fontaine vivante de Sivas

L'Air de l'eau

Ta chair arrosée de l'envol de mille oiseaux de
    paradis
Est une haute flamme couchée dans la neige

L'Air de l'eau

ses lèvres qui sont des pierres au fond de la rivière
    rapide

'Amour parcheminé', *Clair de Terre*

Several poems in the collection **Le Revolver à Cheveux Blancs** suggest the metamorphosis from life to death. In **'La Mort Rose'**, for example, we witness the passage of a living form from one state into another in a double metamorphosis: that of the being and that of the earth. One of the themes developed here was already suggested in Valéry's *Le Cimetière Marin*: 'the gift of living has passed into the flowers'. In Breton's poem the beloved's hair mingles with the sun and her hands are projected into a peach-tree in bloom. The echoes of voices linger in the landscapes and her footsteps are entrapped in the moss. But the earth changes in form and texture as well, as the comets burn down the forests, the horizon is enlarged and river beds overflow. The two transfigured beings move within a vegetation grown transparent and penetrate into each other's dreams and probe the depths of each other's tears.

In the **'Forêt dans la Hache'** we have an image of death in which it is the soul that disappears. The body becomes a transparent cavity in which doves and daggers fly. From this dwelling of his consciousness, the soul has been banished and with it the notion of duality; the physical world is freed of its arbitrary laws. He retains a sense of heat and cold, but the colours of the spectrum have been amalgamated and his body is inhabited by living forms, his brow is covered with crows, his eyes are made of mistletoe, his mouth is a dead leaf, and he takes on the characteristics of glass. In conformity with the notion that death is *change* rather than destruction, Breton has eloquently advised in the *Premier Manifeste* that at his own death he would wish to be carried away not by a hearse but by a moving-van.

Too little attention has been given to what is perhaps one of the truly philosophical poems of our age. *Fata Morgana,* written at Marseilles in December 1940, contains all the themes that have preoccupied Breton, as well as variations of his basic techniques. He celebrates the birth of a new day as he formulates the central concern: if I should escape my destiny. He ponders upon all the impossible metamorphoses and unreasonable states of being, which become plausible when, as he puts it: 'the lucid wind brings me the lost perfume of existence released at last of its limits', when yesterday is cast off with its contents like a miserable chest of drawers, and he sets out in his magnetized boat to decipher the great algebra of the universe where everything is pertinent to him and in which perfection is envisaged as 'the incessant fusion of imperfect creatures'. In an apostrophe to the hermetic bird of Egypt, the Ibis, he discovers his inner unity 'with all that no

longer is and waits to be'. And like a great spectacle, the convulsions of the natural world take place, impelled by the multiple appearances that water, fire, and light can assume.

Le vent lucide m'apporte le parfum perdu de
    l'existence
Quitte enfin de ses limites . . .
tout est là pour quelque chose qui me concerne . . .
la perfection qui appelle la fusion incessante des
    créatures imparfaites
Dans l'obliquité du dernier rayon le sens d'une
    révélation mystérieuse

Fata Morgana

Finally in **Les États Généraux** and **Ode à Fourier** the metamorphosis conveys social meaning. Allusions abound to nineteenth-century Utopians, such as Fabre d'Olivet and Fourier (whose concepts of universal harmony were inspired by theories of magnetic attraction). In these poems Breton defied the tone of despair of the time. The words *abattre* and *bâtir* are drawn to each other, surmounting as it were their contradiction in meaning. The conflagration takes on a mystical power of purification and the scattering of things and beings hastens the reorganization, the unveiling of the secrets of the universe. Above all, the peoples of the world rise to a universal and harmonious interdependence among nations and races:

Il suffisait que le peuple se conçût en tant que tout
    et le devînt
Pour qu'il s'élève au sens de la dépendance
    universelle dans l'harmonie
Et que la variation par toute la terre des couleurs de
    peau et des traits
L'avertisse que le secret de son pouvoir
Est dans le libre appel au génie autochtone de
    chacune des races

Les États Généraux

Again the verb is *devenir,* and the changes suggested in the images are the burning of the phœnix, the fire of the anvil, followed by the advent of the new magi and a sun man, as the poet contemplates the present and foresees the future:

En haut l'avenir il porte des cornes jaunes de
    taureau dardant des plumes de flamant
Il est surmonté d'un éclair de paille pour la
    transformation du monde

Les États Généraux

Amid a war-devastated humanity, Breton, the incorrigible dreamer, called upon poetry to rise from the ruins and bring about the most significant metamorphosis of all: the transformation of the world.

Edgar C. Knowlton, Jr. (essay date 1982)

SOURCE: "Breton's 'Rano Raraku,'" in *The Explicator,* Vol. 40, No. 4, Summer, 1982, pp. 50-2.

[*Knowlton is an American critic, translator, and educator. In this essay he stresses the importance of reading the poems in* Xénophiles *within their original context— as part of a catalog published for an exhibit of Oceanic art objects, and related directly to the objects and myths they describe. Within this context the critic interprets "Rano Raraku" as a statement against war.*]

RANO RARAKU

Que c'est beau le monde
La Grèce n'a jamais existé
Ils ne passeront pas
Mon cheval trouve son picotin dans le cratère
Des hommes-oiseaux des nageurs courbes
Volètent autour de ma tête car
C'est moi aussi
Qui suis là
Aux trois quarts enlisé
Plaisantant des ethnologues
Dans l'amicale nuit du Sud
Ils ne passeront pas
La plaine est immense
Ceux qui s'avancent sont ridicules
Les hautes images sont tombées

—ANDRE BRETON

How beautiful is the world
Greece never existed
They will not pass
My horse finds its feed in the crater
Bird-men curved swimmers
Fly around my head for
I too
Am there
Three quarters sunk
Joking with ethnologists
In the friendly night of the South
They will not pass
The plain is vast
Those who advance are ridiculous
The high images have fallen

—translated by WALLACE FOWLIE

Criticism has done little to clarify **"Rano Raraku"** or four other poems included in a section designated *Xénophiles* in a 1948 collection of André Breton compositions [*Poémes*]. This designation may be sufficient explanation for the presence of **"Rano Raraku"** here, but the poem is filled with allusions to Easter Island, where the volcano of that name is located, and comment on the poem may be helped by reference to relevant details.

The poem begins with an exclamation on the beauty of the world. This is followed by the cryptic remark to the effect that Greece, symbol of classical beauty to the Western and European part of the world, never existed. If one thinks of the title, **"Rano Raraku,"** one may interpret: the beauty of Easter Island owes nothing to the heritage of Greece.

The poet then injects himself into the poem with a reference to his horse feeding in the crater; we know that Rano Raraku is a volcano, and that there are more horses on Easter Island than human inhabitants. Tourist-like, the poet notes, in his imagination, figures of Easter Island's mythological and legendary tradition, bird-men and curved swimmers flying about his head. He has been transported to the Southern Pacific, to the friendly night of the South, in his jesting conversation with ethnologists, students of Easter Island's art, not completely, but as the poem states, three quarters of him sunk. The plain on which the huge and mysterious Easter Island statues or *moai* is immense; some of them have fallen. Against this appreciative background is set a typically French (or European) motto: "They will not pass," as the inspiring watchword of Verdun in 1916 may be translated. A courageous resistance against the enemy in war is suggested; if one remembers that the Spanish Civil War affected many French intellectuals like Breton, the Spanish echo of the watchword, *No pasaràn,* from the lips of La Pasionaria, may also come to mind. Easter Island also was torn asunder by the horrors of war— from outsiders, and civil war. Thus, the motto: "They will not pass" has relevance and unites France (or Spain) or the West with distant Easter Island. The line stating that those who advance are ridiculous may suggest the futility of war; in the case of Easter Island, at least, the statues have fallen, some physically, and others figuratively, since their function and meaning are lost, not only for the Westerner and the poet, but also for the Easter Islanders.

This poem, indeed, has intelligibility. It has been stated: "if Breton's later poetry is of interest by virtue of its intelligibility, it cannot be said to scale the heights of lyricism. On the contrary, its expository nature places it much nearer prose . . ." [Clifford Browder, *André Breton, Arbiter of Surrealism,* 1967]

The poem, and its four mates, had its motivation in 1948 because of an exposition of objects of art from Oceania in Paris; the catalogue for the exhibit had a preface from the pen of the surrealist writer, André Breton, as well as these five poems written for the occasion; most readers of the poems in this form, then, would have before them a listing of the art works in the collection and an opportunity to witness examples from Easter Island as well as the Marquesas, Hawaii, New Zealand, Dutch New Guinea, and New Ireland, for example. Such a reader might well expect that there would be a clear connection between the poems in the catalogue and the art objects on display; exposition, more than lyricism, is to be expected.

In the same year these poems appeared in the 1948 volume, torn from their context (the exposition and the catalogue of the Oceanic art works) and with no explanatory annotation. As a result of this, presumably, one critic has commented on the last two lines of the poem without reference to the appropriateness of an allusion to the Easter Island *moai* in the phrase: *les hautes images sont tombées,* as follows:

In *Xénophiles* (1948), Breton reaches the lowest possible depth of surrealist despair . . . Breton and the other surrealists put their entire confidence in the reconciling power of the image ("The image never deceives") and in the creative strength of the interior vision. When the images fall and the vision fails, they have no recourse. [Mary Ann Caws, *The Poetry of Dada and Sur-realism,* 1970]

After the first sentence quoted, the comment includes in French and English translation the last two lines of **"Rano Raraku":**

Those who go forward are ridiculous
The lofty images have fallen.

Fowlie's translation chooses "advance" for "go forward," and "high" for "lofty," and seems more suitable to the juxtaposition of the phrase recalling Verdun and the Spanish Civil War in the poem. It seems possible that neglect, whether intentional or otherwise, of the occasion for the poem and of the context of allusion in the poem, are responsible for interpreting these images as verbal and poetic, rather than as tangible and plastic. In any case, a rather different impression is made by the poem if one reads it, as originally intended, as part of the catalogue published in connection with the Paris exposition. Rather than the lowest possible depth of surrealist despair one has an appreciation of the oneness of man's experience, the evil of war.

Roger Cardinal (essay date 1984)

SOURCE: "Savage and Civilized," in *The Times Literary Supplement*, No. 4230, April 27, 1984, p. 450.

[*Cardinal is an English educator who specializes in French studies, surrealism, symbolism, and psychopathological creation. In the following excerpt, he assesses Breton's poetry as a brilliant exploration of the power of language.*]

Towards the end of his life, André Breton published a tiny book as his poetic testament. *Le La* consists simply of four enigmatic sentences which popped into Breton's mind while he was on the verge of sleep. Such samples of preconscious language are presented as touchstones of the poetic, inasmuch as they spring unmediated from the source and stimulate the incantatory process of surrealist automatism. These four brief phrases from the 1950s are the direct descendants of that celebrated dream-phrase of 1919 which first made Breton think about doing automatic writing: "Il y a un homme coupé en deux par la fenêtre".

What can now be seen as Breton's lifelong commitment to the principle of automatism or subliminal inspiration has been the locus of a series of misunderstandings and unjustified accusations. To refute some of the charges, it should simply be said: no, Breton didn't *only* write in an automatic manner; no, he didn't place unintelligibility above meaningfulness; no, he didn't sabotage beauty to protect a rigid ideological principle.

What Breton did do, as Jean-Pierre Cauvin and Mary Ann Caws's anthology amply demonstrates, was to explore language throughout his career in the light of a precept of unconstrained expression inseparable from the essentially ethical position on which the whole project of Surrealism is predicated. The automatic message floating into consciousness is nothing less than a signal from that reservoir of primal spontaneity which is the hidden or libidinal self in all its fertility. Breton's "man sliced in two" is the surrealist seeking to unite the two aspects of his being, the unconscious and the conscious, instinct and intelligence. Surrealist art in all its forms is an attempt to release the dormant savage within—but equally to reconcile him with the civilized man living with his eyes open to the real world.

Flamboyant and disquieting images are, of course, the best-known features of Breton's poetic style, and [*Poems of André Breton*] offers a ready selection of those "free unions" of discrepant realities which he so cherished as disruptive mental fixities.

—*Roger Cardinal*

Breton therefore prized the dream-utterance not because it was marvellously unintelligible, but because it was nonsense in transition towards sense—a form of language which epitomizes the expressive act as the passage from the shadows of inarticulacy to the light of communication and understanding. Again and again in his poems, Breton turns the tiller of his "phantom vessel" over to the obscure hand of automatism. Again and again, sense veers towards the rocks of meaninglessness; and yet it is out of this repeated veering that Breton is able to discover the shapes of a new meaning, mapping the precise outline of each island in the hitherto uncharted archipelago of emotion and intuition.

Flamboyant and disquieting images are, of course, the best-known features of Breton's poetic style, and [*Poems of André Breton*] offers a ready selection of those "free unions" of discrepant realities which he so cherished as disruptive of mental fixities. The "vertebral sphinx", the "glass-toothed wolf" and the "algebra-nostriled horses" are so many experimental species spawned in defiance of what seems reasonable.

More importantly, though, such images need to be read in context, as flashes or spasms in a dynamic of provocations. And, as Breton grew to understand the implications of his poetics, he tended more and more to relinquish arbitrary shock effects and to develop a grand style of long, oracular lines which set up a momentum below the flickering figures of the surface, stimulating an alertness to analogy and compatibility that goes beyond the bounds of prosaic literalness. This is utopian poetry on the Rimbaldian model, one that announces a new harmony lying on the far side of "present appearances".

Some readers of Breton's work will find his approach simply irritating. It is true that he has a penchant for flapdoodle. "It seems that the statue near which the wormwood of my nerve endings / Arrives at its destination is tuned every night like a piano" is a statement long on mischievous incongruity but rather short on lyrical resonance. On the other hand Breton's insistent word-spinning (often enhanced by the ritualistic insertion of rare words) can also summon the attentive—or acquiescent—reader to encounter something magnetizing and poignant, a convincing "presence" within the verbal concatenation. This occurs most often in his queerly de-centred effusions of sexual desire.

> Je caresse tout ce qui fut toi
> Dans tout ce qui doit l'être encore
> J'écoute siffler mélodieusement
> Tes bras innombrables
> Serpent unique dans tous les arbres

("I caress all that was you / In all that shall still be you / I can hear the melodious whistling / Of your numberless arms / Snake unique amid all the trees".)

There are, in fact, moments of true poetic revelation lying in wait in Breton's most unsettled texts. Perhaps his most assured longer poem is *Fata Morgana,* which he composed in Marseille in 1940, on the verge of exile; the poem employs an authoritative blend of automatism and willed structure that successfully mimes the attitudes of a mind hovering between anxiety and wisdom, puzzlement and discernment. Here lies Breton's achievement as a poet: he brings his reader into touch with the raw energy of words as they flow and cohere, to produce, image by image, a constellation of intuitively focused meanings and insights which allow him to glide over local incongruities.

Willard Bohn (essay date 1985)

SOURCE: "Semiosis and Intertextuality in Breton's 'Femme et Oiseau,'" in *The Romanic Review*, Vol. LXXVI, No. 4, November, 1985, pp. 415-28.

[*In the essay below, Bohn relates "Femme et Oiseau" to its corresponding Miró painting in order to demonstrate that the poems in* Constellations *are not descriptive but rather they represent Breton's subjective reaction to Miró's paintings.*]

In 1958 André Breton wrote twenty-two prose poems inspired by a series of gouaches that Joan Miró had created nearly twenty years earlier. Collected the following year in *Constellations,* each poem was juxtaposed with the appropriate painting in a mathematical progression based on skill and chance, intention and accident. If, as Anna Balakian states, "Breton's *Constellations* is a cosmic venture in which man joins nature through his manipulation of language" ["From *Poisson Soluble* to *Constellations:* Breton's Trajectory for Surrealism," *Twentieth Century Literature,* 21, February, 1975], the same may be said of Miró's paintings in which birds, women, and stars offer a privileged view of the universe. This is particularly true of **"Femme et oiseau"**—the eighth poem in the series—whose title unites two of the artist's favorite motifs. Throughout the volume verbal language complements visual language in an elaborate *pas de deux.* That Breton's intention is not simply to evoke Miró's art or to reproduce relevant themes may be seen from the term he chose to describe his creations: "proses parallèles." As such they represent independent meditations on subjects suggested by the paintings without any attempt to follow the path taken by the artist. Stressing the profound originality of Breton's undertaking, J. H. Matthews describes this reciprocal relationship as follows: "The image before his eyes liberates images within, and it is the latter that he seeks to capture, in acknowledgement of the former's evocative quality" ["André Breton and Joan Miró: *Constellations,*" *Symposium,* 34, 1980]. Located somewhere on the continuum between the *livre d'artiste,* which posits a close link between picture and text, and the institution of *poésie critique* based on poetic equivalents, Breton's poems are neither interpretive nor impressionistic.

According to Philippe Audoin each text takes its point of departure from one of three sources: the painting's title, its general tonality, or one or more graphic elements. This explains why the title **"Femme et oiseau"** makes no sense—it is entirely incidental. To be sure the poet refers to a woman toward the end, but she is only one of several characters who are equally important. Not only is the bird nowhere to be found, there is no indication that he will ever appear. Although Breton appropriates Miró's title for his poem, as he did throughout the book, it was clearly not the source of his inspiration. Continuing our inquiry in a similar vein, we can also rule out tonality as a potential source. Whereas the poem possesses a remarkable sensuality, which its leisurely rhythms and sonorous vowels accentuate, the painting is a sprightly composition whose bright patches of color and curved lines appear to be in constant motion. This leaves the plastic configurations which seem to lie at the root of the poem. Although Miró's characters are notoriously hard to identify, for our purposes this does not really matter. What we want are Breton's personal reactions to the picture, which seems to depict two women facing each other while two smaller creatures float between them. The woman on the right, whose breasts are evident, is carrying another animal on her shoulder. The woman on the left, recognizable from her triangular skirt, narrow waist, and long hair, is even more exceptional than her companion. Standing with her head thrown back, a mouth full of razor-sharp teeth, and a darting tongue, she seems about to swallow the fish-shaped creature before her. Below the latter the second creature— undoubtedly the bird of the title—is about to fly into her mouth.

Gradually we begin to understand how the painting is related to the poem. If the woman's torso is distinctly feminine, her ferocious expression and triangular teeth are markedly feline. In other words, as Breton clearly realized, the figure before us is that of a catwoman, whom we see devouring first a fish and then a bird. The entire poem derives from this seminal recognition scene. Once he chose his point of departure the poet turned his back on the rest of the painting, which is to say that its intertextual role is negligeable. What interested Breton was the unexpected presence of the catwoman whose dual nature was well known to him. To understand her appeal we have only to transpose elements to see that she is a variant of the *sphinx* whose eerie shadow, like the minotaur's, is one of the hallmarks of Surrealism. Like the latter, the sphinx represents the union of intellectual and physical power. The fact that both creatures mediate between the human and the animal makes them perfect vehicles for the *merveilleux* in which, as Breton tells us, "se peint toujours l'irrémédiable inquiétude humaine" [*Manifeste du surréalisme,* 1963].

In his *Semiotics of Poetry* Michael Riffaterre argues that every poem results from "the transformation of . . . a minimal and literal sentence into a longer, complex, and nonliteral periphrasis." If Riffaterre is right, that a poem is generated by a single phrase or "matrix," then the origins of Breton's **"Femme et oiseau"** are to be found in a statement such as "The sphinx is half cat and half woman." Structurally this sentence may be rendered as cat sphinx woman, where the sphinx's central position is dictated by its role as mediator in the human / animal dichotomy. Not only does the poem employ the same tripartite structure, it preserves the substantive nodes of the matrix and observes the same sequence. Seen in this perspective, Breton's strategy is relatively simple. Enumerating each element of the matrix, from cat to sphinx to woman, he pauses long enough for each image to generate a series of associations which he weaves together to form the poem. Utilizing conscious and unconscious impulses, this process is more complicated than it sounds. As the Structuralists have long noted, "a work can only be read in connection with or against other texts, which provide a grid through which it is read and [comprehended]" [Jonathan Culler, *Structuralist Poeties,* 1975]. The same strictures govern its creation as well. Among the numerous forces traversing a text Riffaterre focuses on a primary intertext that he calls a "hypogram." Consisting of a "pre-existing word group," the hypogram may be a quotation, a thematic configuration, a set of literary conventions, or a cliché. Situated midway between the matrix and the text, it distorts the former and produces the latter through conversion and expansion. With **"Femme et oiseau,"** as elsewhere in Breton's works, the hypogram seems to be a poem by Baudelaire, in this case "Les Chats." More precisely, as we will discover, it includes a whole complex in *Les Fleurs du mal* centered on this poem:

Les amoureux fervents et les savants austères
Aiment également, dans leur müre saison,
Les chats puissants et doux, orgueil de la maison,
Qui comme eux sont frileux et comme eux
    sédentaires.

Amis de la science et de la volupté
Ils cherchent le silence et l'horreur des ténèbres;

L'Erèbe les eût pris pour ses coursiers funèbres,
S'ils pouvaient au servage incliner leur fierté.

Ils prennent en songeant les nobles attitudes
Des grand sphinx allongés au fond des solitudes,
Qui semblent s'endormir dans un rêve sans fin;

Leurs reins féconds sont pleins d'étincelles
    magiques,
Et des parcelles d'or, ainsi qu'un sable fin,
Etoilent vaguement leurs prunelles mystiques.

As Riffaterre predicts, a number of Baudelaire's words and concepts are embedded in Breton's text, where they testify to its origins. One thing is immediately evident. What originally attracted him to "Les Chats" is the equation between cat and sphinx specified in the primitive sentence. Among other things this poem is the source of the sensuous language in **"Femme et oiseau"** and its langorous rhythms, which approximate the alexandrine. In tracing the evolution of Breton's imagery and ideas, we will see that many poetic features derive directly from the hypogram. Others are generated at the level of the text according to the principles of metaphor and metonymy identified by Roman Jakobson [in "Two Aspects of Language and Two Types of Aphasic Disturbances," in *Fundamentals of Language,* 1971].

The first sentence of **"Femme et oiseau,"** which is also the first line, illustrates Breton's method perfectly. Its alliterative play and twelve careful syllables underline the poet's debt to the author of "Les Chats." The initial portrait of the cat, who is dreaming and purring, is entirely conventional. Baudelaire not only evokes the animal's penchant for sleep, he stresses its endless capacity for reverie ("un rêve sans fin") which marks it as an avatar of the Poet. Although none of his cats actually purr, this is a metonymic characteristic which needs no justification. It is part of the baggage associated with the concept "cat." What is startling here is not the animal so much as its setting—a dusky music shop. If *lutherie* normally designates the stringed-instrument trade, here it is used metonymically to indicate the place where the instruments are made and sold. The next sentence corroborates this interpretation and develops it in more detail. Similarly, the fact that "brune" refers to twilight—on the model of "à la burne"—is confirmed by subsequent events in the poem. But why does Breton choose this location? Why this time of day? To find the answer we must return to Baudelaire who specifically associates cats with shadows and who makes Erebus, Lord of Darkness, their master. Clearly in touch with demonic forces, they function as intermediaries between mankind and the unknown. Breton replaces Baudelaire's demonic forces by those of the unconscious, but otherwise the animal's poetic vocation remains the same. The music shop itself has several possible sources. Looking back on Miró's painting, for instance, we find several shapes suggesting key signatures and musical notes. Moreover there may well be a metonymic link between the cat and the instruments, whose strings are probably made of catgut. The most likely explanation, however, is metaphoric, exploiting similarity rather than contiguity.

Thus Baudelaire devotes the first half of a two-part poem intitled "Le Chat" (No. LI) to celebrating the latter's delicate "voice" which he first compares to a verse of poetry. Continuing in the same vein, he exclaims:

> Non, il n'est pas d'archet qui morde
> Sur mon coeur, parfait instrument,
> Et fasse plus royalement
> Chanter sa plus vibrante corde,
> Que ta voix, chat mystérieux . . .
>
> (vv. 17-20)

Surely this explains why Breton's cat is in a music shop. The evolution of the image appears to be the following: from meow to voice the progression is metaphoric, based on functional similarity; from voice to violin bow it is also metaphoric, based on similar cause and effect. Thereafter the bow leads us metonymically to the violin which leads in turn to another metonym: the *lutherie*. In both cases the relationship is that of part to whole. If there is a common thread to the entire chain of events, it is musicality in its various forms. Once we begin to understand the poem's intricate background and its complexity of allusion, the seemingly banal first line comes alive. Radiating in every direction, from Baudelaire to Breton to us and back again, it is filled with virtual images operating at several levels. The image of the "lutherie brune" is especially resonant. Not only is the lute a traditional symbol of lyric poetry, as the *Petit Robert* insists, the adjective *brune* conjures up visions of Jeanne Duval who appears in yet another poem entitled "Le Chat" (No. XXXIV). Here the "corps électrique" of Baudelaire's cat suggests that of his mulatto mistress. "Je vois ma femme en esprit," he exclaims,

> Et, des pieds jusques á la téte,
> Un air subtil, un dangereux parfum
> Nagent autour de son corps brun.
>
> (vv. 9; 12-14)

Stated implicitly at the beginning, the themes of poetry and womanhood will gradually assume major proportions in the poem. It remains to discuss the unique atmosphere of the first line which is a function of its special setting. From the fact that the shop is dark we know it must be past closing time. The shopkeeper has turned off the lights and gone home, leaving his cat in the store until morning. This means that the initial scene takes place in total silence, broken only by the animal's purring, and that the shop is entirely empty. This too is characteristic of Baudelaire's cats who among other things "cherchent le silence et l'horreur des ténèbres" ("Les Chats"). For Breton then, as for Baudelaire, the cat serves as an emblem of the poet's solitude.

The second sentence evokes the animal's curiosity—a metonymic trait ignored by Baudelaire but exploited here to good effect. By providing, not one but two examples the poet increases the verisimilitude of his portrait and injects a certain humor into the poem. Without moving from its comfortable spot, the cat peers curiously at one of the nearby instruments, then begins to lick it. Both gestures are typical, both are convincing. The first clause, "Il scrute le fond de l'ébène," depicts the animal peering through the strings at the ebony fingerboard. Next the cat extends its tongue as far as it can to lick the instrument's body which is made of mahogany. The two prepositional phrases, "de biais" and "à distance," stress the exploratory nature of this gesture. Once we realize that it is the instrument's body that is "tout vif," we can visualize what has occurred. During its investigation the cat has brushed against the strings whose reverberations are amplified by the soundbox, causing it to "come alive." This sound, magnified by the stillness of the music shop, announces a change of scene and the introduction of a new character. The transaction from cat to catwoman is surprisingly smooth. "C'est l'heure où'" as Susan Harris Smith remarks, prepares the reader for the supernatural events to follow including the relaxation of the sphinx's suffocating coils around the fountain ["Breton's 'Femme of oiseau': An Interpretation," *Dada/Surrealism* No. 6, 1976]. As she also notes, this is the central action of the poem which corresponds to the sphinx's central position in the narrative sequence. The sphinx herself is subject to considerable mythological ambivalence. On the one hand no less an authority than Lévi-Strauss assures us that she is a female monster who attacks and rapes young men, "the personification of a female being with an inversion of the sign" [Vernon W. Gras, ed., *European Literary Theory and Practice, From Existential Phenomenology to Structuralism,* 1973]. We know from the Oedipus myth that she kills her victims when she is finished with them, which is confirmed by the etymology of her name: "the strangling one" [William Smith, *Smaller Classical Dictionary,* 1958]. On the other hand, "being the supreme embodiment of the enigma, the sphinx keeps watch over the ultimate meaning which must remain forever beyond the understanding of man" [J. E. Cirlot, *Dictionary of Symbols,* 1962]. As such she is the guardian of the cosmic mysteries and the key to the riddle of the universe.

Alan Brownjohn in a review of *Selected Poems*:

Breton was as vigorous and proselytic as ever in his post-war days (he died in 1966) but his great period of activity was the Thirties, and this book [*Selected Poems,* trans. by Kenneth White] wisely concentrates on it for a selection of his verse. Surrealist poetry—rapid, histrionic, volatile—really only varies according to the period, background and mental furniture of the poets—the tone and technique stay much the same. Only rarely, on the evidence of these translations, did Breton rise above the stock-in-trade of his own movement to produce genuinely powerful and compelling symbols. Mostly he deals in the images of contemporary surrealist art.

Alan Brownjohn, a review of Selected Poems *by André Breton, translated by Kenneth White, in* New Statesman, *August 15, 1969.*

This explains Breton's fascination with the sphinx whom he knew from previous encounters and who is best personified by the heroine of *Nadja*. If, as we have seen, the cat is the emblem of the Poet, the sphinx is the emblem of Woman whom Breton celebrates in all her diversity from *femme fatale* to femme-énigme. This is the subject of the third sentence in which the poet explores woman's dual nature. In her former aspect, presented at the beginning, the sphinx represents the emasculating, devouring female. The key to this interpretation lies in the word *garance* which designates 1) the madderwort plant and 2) a red dye made from its roots. Taken metaphorically, for example, the term suggests that the creature is stained red with the blood of her victims. Used metonymically, it indicates that she is stained red from eating the plant itself like the birds and animals that feed on it. Since, as Smith observes, the consumption of madder was an ancient remedy for the absence of menstruation, Breton implies that the sphinx is sterile, which makes her especially threatening. While either path is enough to account for the presence of red dye here, the image also seems to be associated with *Nadja*. Among several intertextual glimpses of this work in **"Femme et oiseau,"** we recall that Nadja's first address in Paris was the Hotel Sphinx, situated on the boulevard Magenta. At the very least the conjunction of the sphinx with ruddiness seems to be a constant in Breton's work.

The following section presents several difficulties. What is the sphinx doing in the department of Vaucluse, for instance, and how has she acquired a hunting horn wrapped around a fountain? That the author introduces a musical instrument at this point is understandable, for it may be traced back to the music shop described at the beginning. But why has he chosen a horn instead of a violin or guitar, which would be more in keeping with the *lutherie?* To answer this question we need to sift through the multifarious meanings of *trompe* which range from Eustachian tube to aspirator and squinch (an architectural term). The explanation seems to be that the word is taken from an alternate version of the sphinx—whose name also designates a large velvety moth. Bearing a prominent death's head on its back, which confirms the sphinx's reputation as a *femme fatale,* the creature extends its "proboscis" in anticipation of the magnolia blossoms in the last line. This word is also associated with a previous complex centered on *garance* in connection with the female reproductive system. For the fact that the sphinx is sterile suggests that she is suffering from blockage of her *trompes de Fallope.* Integrating the term into his musical context, Breton creates a fantastic brass horn with unusual flexibility. Like an elephant's trunk (*trompe d'éléphant*), it is capable of curling around objects and exerting pressure. This is consistent with the image of the hunting horn in particular which has a circular shape. The idea of constriction—and its subsequent relaxation—is provided by the sphinx's reputation as a strangler. Whether the author was familiar with the creature's etymology or whether he was thinking of its derivative "sphincter" does not really matter. From *corps* to *cor* the sphinx retains her ability to squeeze her prey to death.

Coupled with a singular subject: "sa trompe," the plural intensifier "par milliers" is troublesome until we attempt to visualize the scene. Despite our first impression the reference is not to thousands of horns (or tubes or trunks), but to a single horn twisted into thousands of coils. Curled around the fountain in a stupendous death grip, the sphinx represents a terrifying adversary. The fountain in **"Femme et oiseau"** presents relatively few problems. Smith argues convincingly that it is situated in the Vaucluse region because Petrarch tried to escape his obsession with Laura by taking refuge in the town of Fontaine-de-Vaucluse. Thus "Laura is the predator, the awful devouring beast, the compelling but destructive beauty that paralyzed the poet's mind." Freed from her constrictive presence but inspired by her memory, the poet composed some of his more enduring works. An interesting parallel exists here between the role of Petrarch's muse and that of Nadja who exerted a similar influence on Breton. Eventually committed to "l'asile de Vaucluse," she gave him a radically new perspective on the world.

The fountain of Vaucluse itself consists of an artesian spring situated near Avignon which serves as the origin of the Sorgue river. From *source* to source its symbolism in the poem is clear. Like Laura and Nadja, the fountain represents a source of poetic inspiration according to an age-old formula equating the two. What interests us here is its juxtaposition with the sphinx—a configuration that occurs elsewhere in Breton's work. As far back as *Les Champs magnétiques,* for example, we read that "L'antiquité est une fontaine nacrée par places, mais la gorge des sphinx a verdi." Whereas the latter example deplores the loss of classical wisdom, personified by the bronze sphinxes, in **"Femme et oiseau"** the situation is just the opposite. The sphinx becomes the source not only of inspiration but of a cosmic consciousness in which the difference between subject and object ceases to exist. The path to this final *point suprême* is indicated by the sphinx who as the source of ultimate wisdom plays an analogous role to that of the fountain. This explains why the two images are juxtaposed: each is a transform of the other. They are opposite sides of the same coin. In releasing her grasp on the poetic fountain, then, the sphinx releases the forces of the unconscious which are reflected in the cosmic enigma.

The poem itself is situated on the threshold between day and night, between the forces of repression and those of liberation. In passing from one realm to the other Breton introduces us to the third term of the matrix and his Surrealist vision of woman. The contrast between her and the sphinx is instructive. If one is cruel and destructive, the other is loving and creative. If one symbolizes suffocation and sterility, the other stands for freedom and fertility. Recalling the etymology of "sphincter," we may regard the sphinx as a classic anal retentive personality. Her successor, who gives birth to poetry at the end, is clearly vaginal expulsive. As such she represents the triumph of the life force over the destructive instinct, of Eros over Thanatos. To the extent that she combines the poetic with the enigmatic—poetry as enigma, enigma as poetry—she resolves two of the major themes in the poem and mediates between the cat and the sphinx. Among the homonyms and words used in more than one sense or context in *Constellations,* whose role has been noted by [Anna] Balakian, *calice* is a product of a twofold metaphorical process. A traditional symbol of purity, whose origins go back to the Holy Grail, the chalice is above all a receptacle for sacramental wine. As a receptacle, moreover, with a distinctly uterine form, it also functions as a sexual symbol. These facts lead us to discover a triple metaphorical bond between "femme" and "calice" based on the following semes (discrete semantic units): purity, holiness, and femaleness. From this we may deduce that the woman in question is a virgin priestess and that her mission is a sacred one.

An additional metaphorical link exists between the chalice and the fountain based on functional similarity. Both are containers which serve as sources of liquid. That this connection is deliberate is evident from the adjective "débordant" which stresses the fluidity of the vowels issuing from the priestess' mouth. These sounds function in turn on several levels. For one thing, there is an implicit metonymic link between the stream of vowels and the references to poetry earlier in the poem. Clearly this is the moment of poetic utterance we have been waiting for. For another thing, there is an implicit metaphorical link to the wine of the eucharist which is being poured from the chalice. Not only is the poetry divine, it partakes of immortality. Finally, the fact that the woman utters sounds rather than words suggests a third (metaphorical) interpretation. Caught in the throes of sexual passion, she is moaning incoherently. The intensity of her experience is indicated by the term "débordant" which suggests that it is uncontrollable and by the fact that she has lost the power of speech. That she utters *vowels* is particularly significant, for there is an extensive tradition linking the sequence AEIOU to the sounds of love-making. In **"Femme et oiseau,"** then, poetic delirium and sexual ecstasy merge into one.

So far so good, but how are we to reconcile the priestess' sexual activity with the fact that she is a virgin? Aren't these characteristics totally at variance with one another? To understand what is happening it is helpful to consider Valéry's poem "La Pythie" which features an identical conclusion. Like the Pythian oracle, of whom she seems to be a reincarnation, Breton's woman builds up to an orgasmic climax in which sexual release coincides with divine inspiration, birth, and poetic creation. Like Valéry's tragic heroine she is a virgin priestess of Apollo who is possessed by the god in the course of her divine office. The fact that she is a pythoness is especially intriguing and confirms the intertextual role of the earlier poem. What relates La Pythie to the sphinx—besides their enigmatic heritage—is their common association with serpents. For the former, seated on her tripod, the python is the emblem of the god's power. For the latter, coiled around the fountain, the python is a powerful form to be emulated.

Coupled with "la femme," the adverb "partout" is initially confusing. Is the subject of this section one woman or many women? In the context of the previous discussion we can affirm that both statements are true. The subject is simultaneously singular and plural. What this means is

that Breton's priestess is divided into countless images of herself according to a kaleidoscopic process. She is subjected to replication, expansion, and universalization until she becomes synonymous with Woman. Seen in this light the section suggests that all women become priestesses of Apollo as soon as night falls. Like the cat, whose sexuality is emphasized by Baudelaire, she is a creature of night attuned to the mysterious forces that surround us. Poised on the threshold of existence, she is ideally suited to serve as man's interpreter. Following the appearance of the priestess(es), Breton activates the second meaning of *calice* which is linked retroactively (and metaphorically) to "la femme." In passing from chalice to calyx (Latin for cup) he explores the word's etymology and continues the associations developed earlier. As the external envelope of a flower, the calyx encloses the latter's reproductive organs and thus stresses woman's sexual capacity.

By itself the calyx is enough to generate the final image of the flowering magnolia tree through metonymic association. However the latter is also connected to two other exotic trees, ebony and mahogany, which are evoked near the beginning. Together they contribute to the poem's sensuality and create a tropical ambience. From the fact that the magnolia is in bloom we know it is a warm spring evening. Like the woman-chalice overflowing with sounds, it exudes a heavy perfume that permeates the night air. As much as anything the fragrant tree illustrates the twin themes of connection ("en liaison") and expansion ("illimitable") with which the poem ends. Just as the magnolia's perfume expands to fill the garden, uniting everything in it, the priestess is multiplied infinitely and absorbed into the cosmic night. This is the event for which Breton has been preparing us: her ultimate apotheosis and fusion with the universe. Clearly woman's power is a function of her permeability, of her ability to open herself to external forces. On another level the magnolia serves as a metaphor for night itself whose descent brings the poem to a close.

The conclusion combines three separate images in a metaphoric *tour de force.* Interestingly, although these follow the progression "femme" "magnolia" "nuit," their structural order is the reverse. Thus in the phrase "le magnolia illimitable de la nuit" night functions as the tenor and the magnolia as the vehicle. Once we translate the image into visual terms we realize what is involved. Spanning the heavens from horizon to horizon, countless stars fill the sky with an unearthly radiance. Like a profusion of magnolia blossoms attached to a gigantic tree, they shimmer seductively in the night. The image is not only beautiful, it is majestic. Among other things it recalls the conclusion of the *Divine Comedy* where Dante beholds the Celestial Rose and perceives the unity of all creation. But if each of the blossoms represents a star, it just as surely represents a woman. This is the sense of "en liaison" at the metaphoric level. Each woman-calyx is *attached* to the magnolia tree, which means that each is actually a flower. Ultimately of course she is also a star, but this metaphoric transfer is too distant for the reader to perceive. Instead woman's position in the universe is rendered by her identification with the cosmic magnolia tree. Our last glimpse of the poem is peculiarly Surrealistic. Stretching toward infinity, a giant magnolia towers above us whose blossoms have been transformed into myriads of women.

The latter object illustrates two fundamental processes in **Constellations** which Balakian has drawn to our attention. Since these also serve as themes, the work finally becomes its own subject, an example of auto-illustrative poetry. The first process/theme revolves about the notion of containment—both containing and being contained—which Breton regarded as a universal structural characteristic. Here as elsewhere the play of "l'un dans l'autre" stems from a belief in the basic interdependence of all things. Aside from obvious containers such as the fountain, the chalice, and the calyx, images of syntactic containment abound in which "de" often substitutes for "dans." In some respects the poem resembles a series of Chinese boxes, each of which is nestled inside another. The first example, that of the cat in the room, is perfectly straightforward. The second involves the madder, one of numerous clinging plants in **Constellations** which Balakian has identified with the image of the embrace. Not only is the sphinx covered with red dye, she is enclosed by the plant itself. So far the images of containment exist side by side. Beginning with the fountain, they become more and more comprehensive, describing wider and wider circles as they spiral outward. We know that the latter is contained by the horn whose innumerable coils are wrapped around it like a python. The fountain, the horn, and the sphinx are embraced in turn by the Vaucluse region which possesses its own geographic identity. Finally the field of action is enlarged to include "partout"—presumably the entire world—which encompasses the Vaucluse itself. Following the central fountain episode "Femme et oiseau" includes two more examples of specific containment: the vowels contained by the *femme-calice* and the magnolia contained by the night. Despite its localized disguise, the last line opens at the very end to encompass the entire poem. Beyond the confines of the *lutherie,* beyond the Vaucluse itself, the magnolia night gathers the world and everything in it in a lasting embrace.

The second process theme is that of metamorphosis which informs the poem from beginning to end. Believing it to be the central mechanism of nature, Breton cultivates metamorphic imagery in an effort to duplicate this basic principle. In a sense metamorphosis is another form of containment. Exemplified by the *trompe* and the *calice,* which assume a multitude of forms, it inscribes one meaning inside another to create a transformational poetics. Above all metamorphosis is personified by the hybrid sphinx, who alternates between cat and woman and who acquires a prehensile appendage. So too the *femme-calice* becomes many women and fluctuates between chalice and calyx before losing herself in the magnolia. The latter image, as we have noted, involves a double transformation as the night sky becomes a magnolia tree bedecked with ecstatic women. . . .

It quickly becomes apparent that the first line serves as a paradigm for each of the succeeding sections according to the principle of structural equivalence. This means that each of the six segments is related to the others analogically, that each presents its own version of the initial event. With two exceptions the setting changes from scene to scene. The action that begins in the music shop is completed in the fragrant night after passing through the Vaucluse and the world beyond. Each episode features a being or an object that is the source of something else, leading one critic to conclude that the poem's subject is the creative act. The cat emits a purring sound, then causes the strings to vibrate. The sphinx relaxes its grip on the fountain, allowing water to well up. In half the cases it is a question of something intangible that is emitted by the subject itself. The magnolia's perfume and the woman's vowels are simply an extension of the cat's purring. In theory each of the six structures is autonomous, reflecting its companions while remaining separate from them. In practice no sharp line of demarcation exists. Like other features of the poem they possess a basic instability that subjects them to perpetual metamorphosis. The purring cat becomes the sphinx lounging in front of the fountain who is transformed into the babbling woman. The latter assumes the guise of a sacred chalice, reappears as herself, and vanishes into the magnolia night. And vice versa. The continual exchange of identities defeats all attempts to isolate the constituent parts. Metamorphosis goes hand in hand with indeterminacy.

These difficulties notwithstanding, we can identify certain evolutionary patterns in the poem which help to understand it better. From a metrical standpoint it is significant that the third sentence is three times as long as the second which is twice as long as the first. Rhythmically the poem constitutes an arithmetical progression ($1 \times 2 \times 3$), which accounts for the increasing momentum underlying the play of poetic forms. Against this rhythm **"Femme et oiseau"** follows two separate but complementary paths. Conceived in a moment of poetic solitude, which is documented in the first line, it brings us eventually to a point of total identification with the cosmos. As such it mediates between the two extremes and suggests that one is inevitably the product of the other. The second course extends from the initial meditative moment to the final burst of inspiration—indeed revelation—that concludes the poem. This path is entirely traditional and consists of the invocation of an internal Muse followed by the unveiling of unconscious processes.

It remains to consider the poem's narrative focus which varies from section to section and which is intimately linked to Breton's mission. From a relatively narrow focus in the first line, centered on the cat in the middle of the shop, the field of vision narrows even further to encompass the animal's head as it licks a single instrument. Thereafter it expands in concentric waves, as we have seen, to include the sphinx, the Vaucluse, and finally the universe. This series of events is far from accidental and reflects a fundamental concern with the creative process extending throughout **"Femme et oiseau."** In particular the movement from constriction to relaxation duplicates that of the sphinx who in slackening her hold on the fountain permits the poem to be born. The entire work is thus constructed around the image of birth which, like the poem itself,

Photo by Man Ray, c. 1930.

radiates out from its center. Viewed in this perspective the central action is identical to that of the poet who observes the same sequence of concentration and relaxation in the course of the creative act. But if the sphinx figures the poet, she also provides us with a glimpse of the reader. Confronted by the poetic text, the latter must focus intently on the signs before him as he puzzles out their meaning. Only then can he relax and allow the poem to engulf him like the boundless magnolia of the night.

Anna Balakian (essay date 1988)

SOURCE: An introduction to *Dada/Surrealism*, No. 17, 1988, pp. 1-11.

[*This excerpt was taken from Balakian's introduction to an issue of* Dada/Surrealism *that was devoted entirely to Breton. Balakian offers an overview of Breton's major poems and his best-known poetic techniques.*]

Viewed in its totality, the work of André Breton falls into three categories: the theoretical and philosophical essays, his narrative prose, and his poetry. The last two facets of

his writing substantiate his modernism, which the first category announces. In a somewhat gothically constructed eighteenth-century prose, the theoretical texts belie automatism; they are sometimes a rebuttal to hypothetical abuses, personal and impersonal, creating a one-sided debate, expressing personal passion, critical, existential, and political, in a tone eloquent and didactic. Unlike Mallarmé's theoretical prose, which consists primarily of an *a posteriori* ars poetica composed after his major poems were written, Breton's are *a priori* for the most part and as such very deceptive, because they do not totally predict the direction his own creative powers were to take in their subsequent development. . . .

[I] consider the poetry the most important part of the Breton corpus, although Breton was very modest about his poetic writings. He did not even mention them in a form he filled out for Biography News Services: Who's News, in 1962. He considered his poetry per se a lesser manifestation of his poetic act than his political pronouncements and his ideological writings, but authors are not necessarily the best judges of their works. Without hesitation I would posit that it is the poetry that makes Breton eligible for greatness, placing him in the lineage of the esoteric poets of Western civilization from Shakespeare to Blake, to Novalis, Hugo and Yeats. This poetic work beckons to literary critics for commentary on its structure and modus operandi. Stamos Metzidakis makes a move in that direction . . . in his essay on Breton's poetic originality as he probes Breton's propensities toward the primordial ["Breton and Poetic Originality," *Dada/Surrealism*, Vol. 17, 1988]. To date, commentaries on the poetry have been primarily thematic: love, death, liberty, types of imagery, and a few insights into his lexicon. . . .

The main target of close analysis has been the *Ode à Charles Fourier*, probably because its references are tangible and Breton's attraction to Fourier explicable; but one comes away from these exhaustive studies with more knowledge about Fourier than about Breton. Michel Beaujour's essay ["Breton's *Ode à Charles Fourier* and the Poetics of Genre," *Dada/Surrealism*, No. 17, 1988] points out a new direction. The fact that Breton tackled the epic genre and gave it a modern adaptation in this and in other post-World War II writings needs not only to be recognized but compared to the efforts of other modern poets engaged in this type of genre-mutation.

In responding to this dense, esoteric, erotic, semantically compact poetry one has to realize that its automatism is very partial, coming in spurts, that there is indeed dynamic variation in Breton's poetics, that his major poems belie many of his theoretical assumptions, and that there are affinities between Mallarmé and Breton in terms of structural premeditation and metaphoric progression in the construction of palimpsestic imagery in spite of the great differences in lifestyle and attitudes about life that have set them apart.

Following Breton's autoanalysis of his reconstruction of **"Tournesol"** we discover that his perception of reality has three concurrent registers. First, there is the objectification of desire, which makes him identify with objects in his aleatory path and brings him into confrontation with passing human figures. The second register consists of hermetic messages found hidden in Paris landmarks of statues and fountains serving as semiotic emblems. These and other hermetic images can generally be decoded by close reading of Fulcanelli's *Les Demeures philosophales* or other gnostic source books. His "one in the other" analogies, of which one part has its reference base in hermeticism, as in the case of the layered meanings of **"Tournesol,"** have not yet been explored in any extensive way. The third level lies in his analysis of his state of psychological motivation at each stage of his life. Most of the automatism of his early poetry involves references to this third and personal level, which in his analysis of **"Tournesol"** remains admittedly enigmatic even to himself.

When we come to his later poems, we find that they are much more structured, and the third and automatic level less innocent and more contrived. Michael Riffaterre has illustrated this structuring in relation to **"Guerre"** and *Fata Morgana* in an essay, "Intertextualité surréaliste" [in *Mélusine,* 1, 1979]. In fact, *Fata Morgana* is perhaps the best example of a technique which gives the illusion of automatism but turns out to be tightly structured. It is a tapestry of interwoven referential systems, representing war, exile, recuperation, without having direct reference to circumstantial data. In the absence of appreciable critical commentary on this major poem, it is appropriate to reveal here the response of Léon Pierre-Quint, his editor and prominent critic of his time, upon receipt of the poem on October 2, 1941: "*Fata Morgana* enchanted me; the poem has a rare gentleness and is perhaps the one where you express yourself the most completely. The rich and beautiful themes which succeed each other are impressive."

And what of *Les États généraux,* the poem of cataclysm and revolution, written in New York in 1943? Silence on both sides of the Atlantic Ocean in regard to a spiritual landmark so pertinent to both sides and a tribute to modern man's struggle for liberty. As for his final prose poem, *Constellations,* it was difficult of access for academic study before Breton's death except in Gérard Legrand's exquisite but rare anthology of Breton, *Poésie et autre.* This extraordinary serial response to Miró's gouaches by the same name is now readily available in *Signe ascendant,* a paperback collection of his later poetry. This prose poem should invite much critical attention since it is most indicative of the structuring methodology of Breton, illustrating his definition of poetry according to other than rhetorical gauges. It reflects his ultimate commitment to a monistic philosophy embracing the artist's ecological and cosmic habitat. It is in this vision that the linkage between Breton and Octavio Paz, as well as many remarkable and neglected poets of Latin America, becomes manifest. The sociologist-philosopher Michel Maffesoli, a half-century younger than Breton and one of the few writers outside of the literary and art disciplines aware of Breton's work as well as that of Paz, has written two books on the functioning of the human imagination in its responses to the activities of the cosmos. He concludes with his observation of

what he calls "transcendent immanence": "The precarious and the aleatory are in step with the irresistible continuation of things. The cosmic eroticism involved expresses in its own fashion the duality of death and life within a mixed infinite. . . . They [the generating divinities] remind us in a perfect manner, suggestive of the cosmic union which integrates the collective individual in a globality that surpasses him" [*L'ombre de Dionysos,* 1982]. He also gives an undiluted definition of the surreal: "a form of the real that is particularly concrete, which is involved to the highest point with everyday existence" [*La Conquête du present,* 1979].

In applying his philosophy of immanence to poetics, Breton's greatest contribution is probably his revolutionary modification cf the art of representation—a field of highest interest to the end-of-the-century critics. That much maligned poem, **"L'Union libre,"** myopically taken to refer "poetically to his wife's private parts" (note that it was written at a time when Breton had no wife!), implements the most important of Breton's aesthetic theories: that of poetic representation, whereby he transformed a stereotype blason into a courtship between human form and function and the ecology. Scholars currently searching for distinctions between mimetic versus transformational representation and so-called re-presentation are rethinking André Breton, yet most of them are admittedly unaware of Breton's work in this area. Any thinking on this subject could profitably use as preliminary texts **"L'Union libre"** and the essay "Signe ascendant."

He considered his poetry per se a lesser manifestation of his poetic act than his political pronouncements and his ideological writings, but authors are not necessarily the best judges of their works. Without hesitation I would posit that it is the poetry that makes Breton eligible for greatness, placing him in the lineage of the esoteric poets of Western civilization from Shakespeare to Blake, to Novalis, Hugo and Yeats.

—*Anna Balakian*

Among those who have written on Breton there have been two strong lines of approach: the ecstatic and the belligerent. On the one hand there occurs such an overwhelming empathy that the commentary assumes the very language of the commentated text and assimilates Breton's ideology. Such commentary often becomes heavy with Breton's intentionalities. The other tone is that of those who embrace Dada and Surrealism as part of the larger avant-grade movements of the time but are uncomfortable with Breton. They are apt to accuse him of hypocrisy, of superhuman posturing. They attack his *point sublime* but sound as if they discovered the expression in secondary sources.

Were they to go to *L'Amour fou* they would realize that in that supremely moving letter of Breton to his little daughter *point sublime* had to do with Breton's humble perception of the unattainable mountain peak: "There was never any question of my settling there. Besides, in that respect, it would have ceased to be sublime and I would have ceased to be a man."

What has not yet been clearly recognized is the role André Breton played in the global literary adjustment to the modern world. He started as an avant-grade writer but consolidated his position in a comprehensive accommodation to the concept of the relativity of reality over and above the ancient dichotomy between the real and the unreal. He was perhaps the only one in that first wave of the avant-garde of the twentieth century to proceed to the formation of a guard, knowing that this avant-garde is always preliminary.

Instead of rejecting beauty, as did many avant-garde writers and painters, Breton tried to redefine it in terms of "convulsive" beauty. Instead of rejecting mimesis, he established a non-anthropocentric relationship with the ecology, absorbing it into an elaborate, intricate system of analogies with the human sensorial system and in a deeper understanding of what nature has come to mean; and he also endeavored to explain the unpredictable manifestations of chance. In the questionnaire he was asked to fill out—that unique document I mentioned above—he stressed under the caption "Major areas of vocational interests, etc." his lifelong "struggle which aims to recast human understanding, starting with the proposition to modify sensibility." He ends the statement with an upbeat sense of success. Contrary to his initial instinct to abandon the notion of "literary" completely, he ultimately came to terms with a redefinition which he believed necessary to the term "literary" to make it acceptable in this age. It could survive as the expression of a close linkage with sociology to reveal a "passionate" knowledge of human behavior. This interest included a strong commitment to the salutary potential of women, which anti-Bretonian feminists might want to read before they accuse Breton of being anti-feminist. "This eternal power of woman, the only one before which I have ever bowed," he wrote in *L'Amour fou,* and he elaborated on this statement in *Arcane 17* after having written some of the most passionate love poems of this century. These two prose texts should be required reading in every bibliography of women's studies. José Pierre's essay in [*Dada/Surrealism,* Vol. 17, 1988], "Such Is Beauty," focuses on this motivating interface of Breton's life and work.

It is clear that scholarly activity on Breton is increasing although among academics in the U.S.A. he does not enjoy the popularity of Georges Bataille or Raymond Roussel. One might also note that a comprehensive avant-garde conference at Hofstra University in November 1986 demonstrated that among younger scholars interest in Duchamp and Dada far surpassed interest in Breton.

But among poets and artists, empathy with Breton runs much higher than among scholars. Linguists, psychocritics and reception theoreticians will no doubt enlarge our knowledge and enjoyment of Breton's work or assess Breton's contribution to the modern mentality and to the direction of intellectual change when they begin to treat his poetry—as they have Mallarmé's—with the methodology suitable for a polysemantic work, prohibitive of unilateral deciphering. Michael Riffaterre's explication of an excerpt from *Poisson soluble* illustrates here how far afield such decoding virtuosity can lead. Let us keep in mind in reading him that what he attributes to the reader's detective capacity is his own particular and personal interpretation, or as Dali would say, "delirium of interpretation," through "intertexts" which are of his choosing, spring out of his mind, and which do not have to limit the much broader range of the poetic field which Breton opens up to his readers. The power of the poetry of Breton to survive is precisely due to its dense character, which allows reception on multiple levels and is sustainable in different historical eras. Standard analytic methodologies are unlikely to reduce to rational, linear structures Breton's prisms and mosaics. The circularity of his work leaves him forever impermeable if he does not at the same time provoke passion in the respondent.

John Zuern (essay date 1988)

SOURCE: "The Communicating Labyrinth: Breton's 'La Maison d'Yves' as a Micro-*Manifeste*," in *Dada/Surrealism*, No. 17, 1988, pp. 111-20.

[*Below, Zuern reads Breton's poem "La Maison d'Yves" as a surrealist manifesto.*]

André Breton's **"La Maison d'Yves,"** in which Breton pays tribute to Yves Tanguy, presents itself as an inviting venue for the exploration of the surrealist aesthetic both in literature and the visual arts. The poem's interest lies not only in its testimony to Breton's enthusiastic support of the work of fellow avant-garde artists, but a careful reading reveals that in **"La Maison d'Yves"** Breton's tribute to Tanguy develops into an expression of the fundamental principles of surrealist aesthetics. The structure of the **"Maison"** shows itself to be essentially labyrinthine. The form of the labyrinth has close affinities to the images Breton himself uses to describe the surrealist orientation to the world, in particular the "tissu capillaire" which lies between the realms of the unconscious and external reality. The labyrinth has been observed as an organizational principle in a wide range of surrealist productions in the visual arts. An examination of the grammar in **"La Maison d'Yves"** reveals that the poem, in spite of its title, is as much concerned with a process as with a static structure; the process it describes is precisely the activity of the surrealist artist. The association of images in the poem is closely linked to its labyrinthine structure, and particular images, namely the references to mythological heroes, expand the parameters of the poem so that it will admit a reading which takes into account Breton's conviction that the surrealist world view is not limited to aesthetics, but has profound social ramifications. These considerations support a view of **"La Maison d'Yves"** as a comprehensive statement—and formal emblem—of the surrealist vision.

One variety of the labyrinth is a closed structure which contains within its parameters a number—ideally, an infinite number—of variables. In **"La Maison d'Yves,"** the closure is provided by the inaugurating rhymed couplet, "La maison d'Yves Tanguy / Où l'on n'entre que la nuit," and the final line, "C'est la maison d'Yves Tanguy," which, in fusing with the initial line to form the sentence "La maison d'Yves Tanguy, c'est la maison d'Yves Tanguy," effectively seals the poem: the poem's maze unfolds in the copula of this sentence. The five rhymed couplets which follow the first at intervals throughout the poem can be seen as additional structural support. It is in the intervals between the couplets that the volatile, variable, and *potentially infinite* dimension of the poem develops the pattern, reminiscent of certain children's songs, of cumulative, repeating lines that do not rhyme and, at first, seem to bear no semantic relation to one another. The couplets, formally closed and finite, contain the essentially open and perpetual form of the cumulative pattern. Thus, the most superficial observation of the physical "building" of **"La Maison d'Yves"** reveals the poem's labyrinthine nature.

If we focus our attention on the images contained both in the couplets and in the accumulating lines, we can observe a relationship between the two forms that is more than structural and spatial. The couplets do not simply contain the cumulative lines, but determine their content. The image set forward in each of the seven couplets in the series exerts an influence on the images contained in the next line in the accruing series; the image that bears no apparent relation to its immediate neighbors harks back to the foregoing couplet. From the standpoint of the distribution of images in the poem, the couplets might be likened to bar magnets placed under a page in a classroom demonstration of the gravitational force: metal filings spread over the page arrange themselves in looping patterns, clustering at the poles of the magnet; in a similar manner, each new image that appears, seemingly at random, in the cumulative sequence loops upward along a line of thematic force to the affiliated image in the couplet above it. The images that build **"La Maison d'Yves"** arrange themselves along three very general lines of force: the first encompassing the ideas of entry, piercing, and seeking; the second the ideas of enclosure, restriction, and the confounding of external and internal space; the third the idea of a guiding line.

The relationship between the first couplet and the first line in what will become the cumulative sequence is not difficult to determine. The lines "La maison d'Yves Tanguy / Où l'on n'entre que la nuit / Avec la lampe tempête" comprise the ideas of entry, darkness, and the light with which one pierces the darkness. These lines prescribe the conditions under which one may enter the "house": night, of course, is associated with dreams, the unconscious, and the unknown—the domain of the surrealist artist which he seeks to bring into contact with the external world. The

"lampe tempête" is a source of light in unusual, perhaps dangerous circumstances, and may indicate the Surrealist's supernormal vision, which is his guide as he enters the unknown and occasionally perilous realm of the unconscious and of dream.

The image of piercing vision is continued in the next couplet/line unit, "Dehors le pays transparent / Un devin dans son élément. . . . Avec la scierie si laborieuse qu'on ne la voit plus." The first line introduces the important opposition of inside and outside space. Here, the external appears to be clearly separate from the internal; the "pays" is "dehors." The image of the couplet is not difficult to understand; its first line calls to mind the limpid atmosphere of Tanguy's enigmatic landscapes, its second the frequent association of the surrealist artist with the seer, as well as the title of Breton's tribute to another of his contemporaries, *Picasso dans son élément*. The "scierie" is more startling, but it can be seen as a radical combination of the ideas of the couplet—transparency and piercing. The sawmill reminds us, too, that a house is being built—as a sawmill supplies the lumber for actual houses, "the scierie" here supplies another image in the structure that becomes the house of Yves Tanguy.

The third couplet is puzzling in that its lines seem unrelated: "Et la toile de Jouy du ciel / Vous, chassez le surnaturel." These lines, however, begin the enfolding of images of space that render the poem a labyrinth, as well as introduce the mythical figures who people it. The union of the decorative fabric "toile du Jouy" with the sky confounds inner, furnished space with the "pays" outside. The "toile de Jouy" may also refer to the "toiles" of Tanguy, which almost always depict objects distributed in an indeterminate space. The "vous" who is commanded to "hunt the supernatural" emerges, upon a rereading of the poem, as Theseus, who, aided by Ariadne, solves the labyrinth and defeats the Minotaur. The imperative here serves to reinforce the foregoing idea of entry: Theseus (and the surrealist artist, and the reader) is compelled to enter the labyrinth which is at this point in the poem beginning to take shape. The line associated with this couplet, "Avec toutes les étoiles de sacrebleu," takes up the sky image of the "toile de Jouy" and, with its confounded stars from which one cannot get one's bearings, continues to construct the maze. At this point in the poem the cumulative sequence has taken shape, and generates its own sense of imperative: the insistence of the repetition drives the reader onward to the anticipated new image and thus deeper into the poem and the poem's maze.

The relationship between the images in the couplets and those in the cumulative lines was described above as a loop; in the fourth—and therefore the central—couplet, the loop itself appears as an image: "Elle est de lassos et de jambages / Couleur d'écrivisse à la nage." In combination with its companion line in the sequence, "Avec les tramways en tous sens ramenés à leur seules antennes," this central couplet describes the actual structure of the poem's linked images—for "elle," that is, "la maison d'Yves," indeed reveals itself to be of "lassos and curlicues"—as well as introduces the motif of the guiding line.

The reference to the color of a swimming crayfish may relate to a particular painting's colors, but it would appear that the reference to a crayfish in motion contributes to the image of movement of—or is determined by—a line, whether a lasso, a written curl, the antennae of a crayfish or the guiding poles of the tramcar that attach it to its guiding wire. Connecting wires and antenna-like extensions can be found in many of Tanguy's paintings, particularly those which he produced around the time of this poem's composition, *Arrières pensées* (1939) and *Les Mouvements et les actes* (1937). The verb *ramener,* with its sense of bringing back, recalling, may play a part in the image of restriction to a particular space which is overtly stated in the following couplet.

As in the third couplet, both the labyrinth and the mythological adventurers associated with quests for the supernatural are presented in the fifth couplet/line conjunction. "L'espace lié, le temps réduit" describes the labyrinthine structure. A labyrinth "binds" space in that it concentrates it in a limited area; the radii of the plane are bent and folded in on themselves. In a like manner, the linear progress of time is enfolded in the structure of the labyrinth. Both "Ariane dans sa chambre étui" and "l'argonaute" of the line "Avec la crinière sans fin de l'argonaute" are figures involved in journeys ending in a confrontation with the surreal. The "crinière" picks up the image of the line, and here it is "endless," running through the infinite permutations of the labyrinth. The "chambre étui" in which we find Ariane is perplexing, for it seems to indicate that Ariane, rather than waiting outside the labyrinth as she does in the legend, is herself enclosed. The pattern of enclosing and enfolding may extend so far that that which proposes itself to be a guide through the maze is itself confounded in the maze. I will pick up this thread at a later point.

Interior and exterior space are confounded in the sixth couplet/line pair. The couplet, "Le service est fait par les sphinges / Qui se couvrent les yeux de linges," suggests, with its image of riddling attendants who cover their eyes with the linens, the interior space of the puzzling "house" the poem is constructing. This whimsical image gains a great deal of energy from the companion line in the accumulating sequence, "Avec le mobilier fulgurant du désert," which combines an image of great space, "désert," with a domestic image, "le mobilier." When brought together, the couplet and the line create an interconnected double image of the expanse of the Egyptian desert with the pyramids and the enigmatic sphinx and of a bizarrely furnished household maintained by servants whose only wish is to confound. Both of these physical spaces are contained in the maze that is the house of Yves Tanguy: "le mobilier fulgarant du désert," of course, refers to Tanguy's painted landscapes, in which strikingly clear—if puzzling—objects furnish an otherwise vacant and seemingly limitless plain.

In the final couplet the "on" of the first lines reappears: "On y meurtrit on y guérit / On y complote sans abri." This sudden description of activity effects an urgency, as does the "Vous, chassez le surnaturel" of the third cou-

plet, and unites this "vous" with the impersonal pronoun of the first couplet. The actor here is Theseus, and Theseus is the surrealist artist who must confront the Minotaur of the unconscious, the unknown, the dreamt. That the Minotaur is a compelling figure to the surrealist imagination is testified to by the title of one of the movement's longest-running reviews, *Minotaure,* which appeared with covers on which leading surrealist artists depicted the beast. The ambivalence with which Surrealism seems to regard its mascot is indicative of its recognition of the precariousness of the unconscious realm in which one can either achieve liberation or descend into madness. The Minotaur is attractive but dangerous, potentially both creative and destructive, a wounding and a healing force. This dialectical approach to the unconscious may well be figured in the line "On y meurtrit on y guérit." If the verbs are taken as transitive, however, the line can be read as a formula for the surrealist method: the Surrealist's "plot" against the mundane external world, involving a kind of violence, a radical dissociation and reassociation of elements which then "heal" into a fresh vision. This couplet is linked to the final line in the cumulative series, "Avec les signes qu'échangent de loin les amoureux," by means of the Theseus/Ariane theme. The words "de loin," the distance across which these lovers communicate, are particularly resonant, given the previous images of expanses in the poem—expanses which have been enfolded in the poem's labyrinth. As the last unit in a potentially infinite series, this line bears a great deal of weight. It consolidates the image of the labyrinth as an enfolded space—Theseus and Ariane are connected across its distance by the guiding line; it extends the human element of the poem to include "les amoureux," not only Theseus and Ariane but the poem's readers; and it returns us to Tanguy's paintings, in which indeterminate objects or beings stand at tremendous distances from one another but appear to "communicate," either along connecting lines or by means of unifying spatial relationships. Finally, the line closes the sequence with the idea of exchange, a dynamic activity that provides a clue to the function of this imaginary labyrinth.

"If Breton envisages himself as a Theseus forever closed within a labyrinth of crystal, at least he intends to confer upon the labyrinth a movement as perpetual as his within it," writes Mary Ann Caws in her biography of Breton. And indeed, Breton's labyrinth in **"La Maison d'Yves"** is in motion. In fact, a consideration of the grammar of the first lines and of the cumulative sequence will show that the poem is essentially about an activity. Each accumulating line is predicated grammatically on the first couplet, "La maison d'Yves / Où l'on n'entre que la nuit," in that each, beginning with "avec," indicates something brought *into* "la maison d'Yves." The additive sequences refer to the mode of entry into the "house," although at the end of the poem the "house" is built of their images, with the couplets—with their own images and oblique references to structure—serving as a formal skeleton. Thus, one constructs "la maison d'Yves" in the very act of entering it. This feature of the poem, highly satisfying from a surrealist point of view, depends upon the repetition/accumulation line pattern reminiscent of children's songs such as the English "House that Jack Built" and the French "Petit

Bricou," which relate a process made up of linked actions in sequence. Breton adopts this pattern, but fractures the sequence and creates a looping maze rather than a linear progression. Yet the urgent tempo of the pattern maintains the notion of activity and movement. **"La Maison d'Yves"** is ultimately a portrayal of surrealist liminality, of the process of creation and the artist's approach to the "pointe sublime" or the "point de l'esprit" at which oppositions "cessent d'être per us contradictoirement."

That the combinatory process of surrealist creation can be at least partially visualized with the image of a maze is evident in reading Breton's theoretical writings on Surrealism. In his discussions of the objectives of the movement, Breton himself often turns to images suggestive of labyrinthine structures. In *Les Vases communicants,* in which he attempts to lay the groundwork for a union of the external, physical realm with the realm of the unconscious and of dreams, he describes the unifying agent as a "tissu capillaire":

> Le rôle de ce tissu est, on l'a vu, d'assurer l'échange constant qui doit se produire dans la pensée entre le monde extérieur et le monde intérieur, échange qui nécessite l'interpénétration continue de l'activité de veille et de l'activité de sommeil. Toute mon ambition a été de donner ici un aperçu de sa structure.

Breton makes the statement, also in *Les Vases communicants*: "Je souhaite qu'il [le surréalisme] passe pour n'avoir tenté rien de mieux que de jeter un *fil conducteur* entre les mondes pas trop dissociés de la veille et du sommeil, de la réalité extérieure et intérieure, de la raison et de la folie, du calme de la connaissance et de l'amour, de la vie pour la vie et de la révolution, etc." The "fil conducteur" can be read as a "conducting wire," participating in the imagery of electricity of which Breton was fond, or as a "conducting thread," suggesting a "fil d'Ariane" that traverses the space between the two opposing realms, a dynamic in the surrealist dialectic. If the "tissu capillaire," suggestive of a conduit composed of convoluted passages, and the "fil conducteur" indicate the structure of the surrealist orientation to the two opposing "worlds," Breton's references to "le vertige" describe the experiential, active dimension of this orientation. The surrealist imagination must break down the accepted structures of the exterior world and reestablish them in new and unexpected combinations with elements from the interior world of the unconscious, and must always dismiss the actual in favor of the possible. The "ideal atmosphere," Breton writes in "L'Introduction sur le peu de réalité," ". . . would be one in which what could exist destroys at every step what does exist." In *Manifeste du surréalisme* Breton indicates that the imagination itself is labyrinthine in nature, and upholds the value of this quality:

> La seule imagination me rend compte de ce qui *peut être,* et c'est assez pour lever un peu le terrible interdit; assez aussi pour que je m'abandonne à elle sans crainte de me tromper (comme si l'on pouvait se tromper davantage). Où commence-t-elle à devenir mauvaise et où s'arrête la sécurité de l'esprit? Pour l'esprit, la

possibilité d'errer n'est-elle pas plutôt la contingence du bien?

The surrealist imagination's process of disorientation and reorientation simultaneously builds and unravels the labyrinth, but since the labyrinthine "tissu capillaire" is necessary to unite the two worlds in which the surrealist finds elements for his combinations, the imagination must immediately enter a new field of unlimited possibility. In his efforts to clarify a surrealist method in the visual arts, Hans Holländer provides two visualizations of the creative process, which, he argues, are detectable in surrealist productions, especially those of Tanguy and Max Ernst: "The methods of inventing and finding unknown, not visible constellations from elements of reality reflect themselves as models in surrealist iconography. One of their leitmotifs is the labyrinth, another is the game of chess, and the two are connected." The labyrinth, like the chessboard, presents a field of vast possibility, and it is this quality, as well as its ability to fuse contradictions, to muddle the ideas of interiority and exteriority, of progress and stasis, beginning and ending, that renders the labyrinth a useful metaphor for the dialectic at the heart of surrealist aesthetics.

Thus far, the form of the labyrinth as it develops in **"La Maison d'Yves"** has been regarded as a visualization of surrealist consciousness, of the Surrealist's way of seeing as it is acted upon in his creative production. To leave off here, and thus to limit the implications of the labyrinth to the realm of artistic creation, would be to insult Breton's vision of Surrealism. Breton viewed the movement not only as a revolution in artistic consciousness, but also as a participant in a revolution in political conscience. Although Surrealism had broken with the Communist party by the time Breton composed **"La Maison d'Yves,"** the movement maintained much of its revolutionary fervor, and a commitment to social change, perhaps even a utopian vision, is articulated in particular images in the poem.

The mythological figures named in the poem—Ariane, the Argonaut, and Theseus, who is implied in the "vous"—are all associated with an adventurous quest for the marvelous. In the case of Theseus, the marvelous is the Minotaur; for the Argonaut it is the Golden Fleece. The original myths in which these figures appear are folded into the labyrinth of the poem. Beyond the somewhat facile analogy of the quest lie the implications of the myths themselves: one must consider the social conditions within which these quests were undertaken. In the case of these two stories, the quest for the marvelous is an effort to effect liberating social change: the capture of the Golden Fleece permits Jason to unseat his pretender uncle; Theseus's victory over the Minotaur frees Athens from its terrible annual tribute of human lives to the government of Crete. Breton's particular adaptation of the Theseus myth in **"La Maison d'Yves"** retains the ultimate goal of the quest—liberation from tyranny—but changes the terms of the adventure.

It has already been noted that the Surrealists could not view the figure of the Minotaur as a wholly negative force.

(The Minotaur itself is an instance of radical recombination.) For the Surrealists the beast embodies the elements of the unconscious and the unknown, inhabiting the inviting and yet threatening world of dream. Associated thus with "le monde intérieur," the Minotaur in the surrealist myth is not so much imprisoned by the labyrinth as connected via the labyrinth to "le monde extérieur." In the poem, as was noted above, Ariane is enclosed, "dans sa chambre étui." Perhaps the "chambre étui," like the "lassos" and "jambages," offers a description of the poem itself—it is not outside the bounds of surrealist imagination to picture a labyrinth of vast possibilities reduced to a tiny box—so that Ariane, like Theseus, is within the labyrinth. This implies that the guiding line does not lead *out of* the maze, but itself originates *in* the maze—for it was Ariane who provided Theseus with the skein of thread—and can lead only back into the maze. So it is with the reader: upon reaching what he considers the end of the poem he finds himself at the beginning: the final line loops back to the first. As figured in **"La Maison d'Yves,"** the surrealist Theseus, the revolutionary, does not free the world from tyranny by entering the labyrinth and destroying the beast, but by taking the entire world into the labyrinth with him, where, confounded with the liberated unconscious, the world is transformed and "l'homme" is released from "le tour des objets dont il a été amené à faire usage, et que lui a livrés sa nonchalance, ou son effort, son effort presque toujours, car il a consenti à travailler. . . ." The labyrinth of **"La Maison d'Yves"** can be seen, then, not only as a "communicating vessel" joining the interior and exterior worlds for the purpose of the production of art, but as a region of consciousness in which the two worlds of human experience are combined so that the outside world, the political realm, is changed for the better as it is assumed into the structure of a revolutionary, freedom-affirming imagination.

"La Maison d'Yves" is much more than Breton's playful tribute to a fellow Surrealist: not only does it stand as an exemplar of Breton's verbal artistry, but it articulates, more through its intrinsic structure than by direct statement, the theoretical foundations and social conscience of the movement of which it is a product. **"La Maison"** is a communicating labyrinth within which the external world and the internal realm of dream are intertwined, and in which, in turn, the reader is confounded. As such it may serve as an emblem of "l'intuition *poètique* . . . débridée dans le surréalisme," which, Breton writes in a late essay, "se veut non seulement assimilatrice de toutes les formes connues mais hardiment créatrice de nouvelles formes—soit en posture d'embrasser toutes les structures du monde, manifesté ou non. Elle seule nous pourvoit du fil qui remet sur le chemin de la Gnose, en tant que connaissance de la Réalité suprasensible, 'invisiblement visible dans un éternel mystère.'"

Stamos Metzidakis (essay date 1990)

SOURCE: "Graphemic Gymnastics in Surrealist Literature," in *The Romanic Review*, Vol. 81, No. 2, March, 1990, pp. 211-23.

[*In the following excerpt, Metzidakis analyzes Breton's extraordinary use of language in* Poisson soluble.]

Although the term "surrealist" has come to be applied to many different kinds of writing—from the bizarre to the fantastic—the term itself was first defined and used extensively by the founder and eventual "pope" of the Surrealist movement, André Breton. For him the word referred specifically to the type of texts that he and his cohorts were producing *automatically,* beginning in the period that directly followed World War I. While similar to contemporary dadaist works in their apparent semantic incoherence, early surrealist texts constituted a literature that was nevertheless intended to serve a specific societal purpose, unlike the more anarchic, nihilistic dadaist works. Specifically, automatic texts were from the start of the Surrealist movement meant to help both readers and writers become more attuned to the common archetypal source of all thought, even though they had no preconceived plot or design to them. It was hoped that the artistic tapping of this source would eventually lead to a more harmonious, if not happier, society for all.

By engaging in automatic writing, the Surrealists wanted to exploit language in a positive way. They believed that through the use of automatic techniques, they could express themselves better, in the sense of expressing themselves more completely. This is not to say that surrealist literature was not "avant-garde" or otherwise revolutionary to a large extent. To suggest that the surrealist project was in certain respects utilitarian and societal is not to deny the need that Breton and his fellow poets felt to destroy quite a few literary idols and conventions of one kind or another all along the way. I would, however, contend that because of the ambitious nature and scope of their total project, the literature these writers produced cannot help but exhibit various innovative stylistic features related to this project. The features I refer to result from the fundamental desire shared by Breton and his friends to enlarge or expand the semiotic potential of the language in and with which they were working.

In light of this desire to open up the French language to greater signifying possibilities, it might, therefore, be supposed that surrealist texts both express *and* embody entirely new ways of viewing and describing the world. No longer satisfied "merely" to discover novel poetic techniques or elaborate philosophical solutions to old existential problems—the recently finished war had disabused them of any optimism they might have otherwise harbored in this regard—the Surrealists set out to write in such a fashion that, through the particular concatenation of words they put on the page, Reality itself would be transformed into a larger *Sur*reality. Because it combined both the conscious and unconscious realms of experience, Surreality was from this perspective a much wider and promising domain in which to work, and indeed, to live. In the eyes of these writers, literature no longer consisted just of a poetic, stylized representation of various concepts or feelings, but was instead to become an authentic presentation of a new, more complete, and, in some regards, better world. The literature they proposed to write was to be, quite simply, a way of putting into words the New (Psychic) World announced by the recent discoveries in psychoanalysis.

Consequently, when dealing with a collection of so-called "automatic" texts, like those of *Poisson soluble* published in 1924 by André Breton, we must take into account both the meaning of the words, and the specific shapes and forms these words take on the page. Lest there be any misunderstanding, let me hasten to say that collections like *Poisson soluble* or *Les champs magnétiques* (the very first collection of automatic texts published in 1919 by Breton and Philippe Soupault) are hardly good examples of what critics nowadays call "concrete poetry." They are not, that is, works that immediately strike their readers as having a significant visual or pictorialist dimension. By "pictorialist" dimension, I mean a typographical positioning or signifiers whose relevance to a text's general significance is wellnigh impossible to ignore or to deny. While it is true that French poets did become increasingly aware of the visual or iconic value of the words they used in their poems, starting with the Parnassians and continuing with the Symbolists, one should not confuse automatic texts with works like Mallarmé's *Coup de dés* (1897) or Apollinaire's *Calligrammes* (1918), i.e. deliberate writing experiments that made obvious use of the visual side of a poetic text.

Instead, the practice of automatic writing seems most often to have led to innovations of a different order, an essentially semantic, or even, thematic order. Some of the most rewarding and convincing contemporary readings of such writing have centered precisely around various subliminal narratives and intertextual networks that have been successfully recovered from a careful analysis of the words and images found in automatic texts. At first glance, therefore, surrealist literature as a whole has not induced most readers to consider at length the potential visual impact of the individual graphemes of which it is composed, as in the case of modern concrete poetry.

Yet, a close reading of specific automatic works reveals that one can, in fact, describe and delineate a significant graphemic dimension within their stylistic fabric. Although the "graphemic gymnastics" in question are not deliberate attempts to portray visually a preconceived, pre-existing idea or object—as with Apollinaire's *Calligrammes,* for instance—they do nonetheless point to an undoubtedly unconscious impulse on the part of a surrealist writer to expand *formally* various semantic and/or thematic aspects of his texts. Even when the latter have already been rendered much more complex than in non-automatic narratives, one can discover still more plays with and upon parts of words and individual letters, if one chooses to look carefully enough.

Looking "carefully," moreover, does not mean that one has to imagine these features into existence. It merely suggests that, like *all* stylistic features in a text, the perception of the graphemic aspects we will study here presupposes both a certain competence (in the Chomskyean sense) and predisposition or willingness on the reader's part to examine a bit more closely than usual the details of the words in front of him/her. Failing this competence and willingness, the stylistic traits proposed, not unlike more conventional or recognized features of literary style, may very well not come to light. We need not worry, therefore, about the ultimate validity of graphemic stylistic features (as if one could ever know unfailingly what should or should *not* be noticed within a text). So long as we demonstrate the function of graphemic features within a work, we can say that they are valid. For the more we succeed in demonstrating the stylistic role of these features in particular works, the more we acquire the necessary competence to discover such phenomena elsewhere in literature.

Provided we take these stylistic possibilities seriously then, any consideration of the conscious or unconscious play of graphemes (or what we shall call "graphemic gymnastics") should bring to our reading of surrealist literary texts further semiotic evidence and support for the particular interpretations we give of such works. In no case should one assume that the analyses presented here could or should be performed at random on any other literary text that one chooses to study. I am not proposing that one play graphemic games for the sake of playing Critical Pursuit or Trivial Criticism. I do insist, however, that in interpreting certain surrealist imagery, one often feels obliged, because of particular textual signs or forms present (here, graphemes), to respond to and follow up an extra-ordinary logic dictated by the letter of the texts under scrutiny. The logic in question or "narrative grammar," if one prefers, derives from the automatic writing process itself. It results from a kind of secondary elaboration of what a text already expresses somewhere else within its own margins, or in some other fashion. The letters, letter clusters, and accent marks of the works examined presently will thus be shown to add something more, a supplementary semiotic depth, so to speak, to what the texts already say elsewhere.

The scope of the present essay prevents us from providing any more theoretical background for our analyses, or from showing how poems by Baudelaire, Rimbaud, Mallarmé, Saint-Pol Roux, and other 19th-century poets exhibit analogous graphemic gymnastics *avant la lettre*. Fortunately, others have already begun to explore the use of such gymnastics in pre-automatic texts. Here, we shall instead limit ourselves to the one work, *Poisson soluble,* that Anna Balakian calls the finest and most authentic example of automatic writing [in her book, *André Breton,* 1971]. Our goal is to show that the term "surrealist" underscores an automatic work's *radical* tendency to play off certain graphemic and, a forteriori, lexical sequences fixed within a given stylistic context. In underlining the word "radical," I wish to suggest the degree to which such works disturb or otherwise upset the usual expectations of an uninitiated reader.

My hope in examining *Poisson soluble* is to suggest how this exemplary collection does what all automatic texts do: it forces readers to abandon certain unquestioned reading habits and to take on new ones. Specifically, it makes us ask ourselves whether we have truly understood the narrative implications of particular words, as well as the potential visual value of their formal make-up or constitution. Let us take for instance text no. 4, at the start of which we are told that: "Les oiseaux perdent leur forme après leurs couleurs." As if to explain this initial curious statement about birds, Breton then writes: "Ils sont réduits à une existence arachnéenne si trompeuse que je jette mes gants au loin." Being reduced to an arachnidan existence is, to be sure, already sufficiently unexpected an image to accept as one compatible with the reality of birds. But to read next that the narrator throws his gloves far away, presumably because this new existence for birds is "so deceitful," is to flirt with total absurdity.

Perhaps the constraints of some subtle internal logic justify this ostensibly inexplicable narration. Let us try to locate clues that might allow us to recover this logic. One must first consider the fact that the act of throwing gloves off traditionally signifies an act of defiance, an act meant to provoke a duel. In this sense, the narrator seems to be casting himself in the role of protector or avenger of wronged birds. Since the birds have somehow (or *by* someone) been transformed into spider-like beings, one might assume that it is because of this injustice that the narrator takes so heroic a stance vis-à-vis their metamorphosis.

On the other hand, it may be that the narrator does not seek so much to avenge the birds as to protect himself from the potential deceitfulness of such strange creatures. The rest of the prose poem does not, after all, develop the notion of any implied duel. No warrior or otherwise bold character arrives to take up the challenge represented by these cast gloves. Yet, the narrator does cross his arms and waits vigilantly ("Je guette"), presumably waiting for something bad to happen. Concerned more with what his gloves look like, and with the laughter that is said to be coming out of the earth, he spends his time watching the night fall, disappearing thereafter from the rest of this one-page text. The narrative appears thus to drift further and further away from the one idea—a duel—that appeared most likely to help us reconstitute the logic of the initial statement.

What then should we make of this now doubly bizarre twist to the story? At first, in keeping with "normal" reading habits, we thought that the best way to explain the fantastical opening statement was to be patient, to wait for the text to reveal the connections between the birds and the wary narrator. But, just as we begin to learn more about the clothing and actions of the narrator, he suddenly gets pulled into the fabric of the rest of the story, and drops out of sight. Given the arachnidan context, one could even say that he becomes entangled or gets caught in the narrative web or cloth (literally, the *text*) that he himself begins o weave from the beginning of the story.

Was he not, however, already implicated in this tale of metamorphosis from the moment he removed his gloves? Let us note that the text specifies the color and form of his gloves ("leur forme et couleur") as soon as he throws them, as if to signal to the reader and writer an *automatic* parallel between the birds and the narrator. Thus, no soon-

er do we read how birds lose their form after their color than we learn that the narrator, narrator, too, throws away his, I daresay, bird-like yellow gloves, gloves that have black stichings, "gants jaunes à baguettes noires". It would, therefore, appear that the entire text is stuck in its own textuality or autotransformation, a victim of its own (narrative) spider web. Unlike a "normal" narrative, the automatic text makes statement which are then consumed, as it were, by later statements, instead of being developed. One image drifts into another, just as in the Surrealists' favorite game of "L'un dans l'autre."

One might ask, though, why this text in particular functions in that way. Here, we finally discover how graphemic gymnastics help to explain the flow of words in an automatic text. For if there is a specific textual catalyst for this narrative metamorphosis it is surely located in the meaning *and* shape of the adjective "arachnéenne." Recalling the myth of Arachné, we can see how the bird metamorphosis in the opening sentence could have provoked an unconscious memory in the author (or vice versa) of that earlier tale, in which the young maiden Arachné is turned into a spider by her enemy Minerva. Given that the girl's crime was to have *weaved* better than the goddess, after she first accepted the goddess' challenge, we might hazard the opinion that Arachné functions metaphorically (if also subliminally) as a kind of poet who, like our poem's narrator, dares to accept a duel.

In any case, once we have accepted one possible link between Breton's text and the thematic or semantic dimension of the adjective "arachnéenne," we cannot discount that word's supplementary importance as what we could call a "pure" signifier as well. For its graphemic nature and usage-frequency in French (in English, too, we might add) are so rare that it is hardly surprising to find its very shape generating words that are formally related to it in this "automatic" context. What I mean is this. Though we seem, to a large extent, to have already justified thematically the narrator's actions, on the basis of the myth of Arachné, a question remains about the simultaneous occurrence in the same environment of so many words containing double-letter clusters. If we consider, however, that the previously noted unusual term "arachnéenne" contains two double-letter clusters side by side, then suddenly we discover an additional formal reason, an over-determining graphemic factor, for the lexical make-up of the passage that immediately follows this objective:

> . . . arach*née*nne si trompeuse que je je*tt*e mes gants au loin. Mes gants jaunes á bague*tt*es noires tombent sur une plaine dominée par on clocher fragile. Je croise alors les bras et je gue*tt*e. Je gue*tt*e les rires qui sortent de la te*rr*e et fleuri*ss*ent au*ss*itôt, ombelles. La nuit est venue, parei*ll*e à un saut de carpe á la surface d'une eau viole*tt*e . . .

The passage unfolds as if the graphemic form of the adjective, loomlike, generated figuratively *and* literally a narrative "thread" that runs throughout the beginning section of the poem. Other automatic texts have been shown to give rise to analogous phonemic parallelisms that have no narrative justification. We must then take seriously the possibility that a word's individual letters may often have as much to do with the imagery of an automatic narrative as does its mere meaning. Indeed, in some cases, I would contend that they could very well have more to do with it.

It is clear, therefore, that to read Surrealist prose one has to act differently than one does when reading most other prose. In a word, one must engage at some point or other in a type of reading activity normally associated with poetry, to wit, *scanning*. Scanning an automatic work for recurrent graphemic phenomena, either before, during, or after a more thematic consideration of it, turns up various stylistic features that might otherwise go unnoticed. Because these discoveries assist us in our retroactive recovery or understanding of other parts of the text, there is no reason not to avail ourselves of the hermeneutic tool, scanning, that makes them possible. To choose not to read such visual clues is tantamount to denying part of the apparent specificity of automatic writing.

With this in mind, let us now scan other prose poems from *Poisson soluble*. Our next examples of graphemic gymnastics are anagrammatic in nature. In these cases, a specific word that is either explicit in the text, or implicit in its words, has been spelled out more or less completely by different textual segments. In text no. 32, for instance, we find the following rather obvious play on the name of a northeastern suburb of Paris: "O propriétés *mal fermées* de *Montfermeil*" (my emphasis). What strikes us in this image is how the poet's pen has been pushed "automatically," so to speak, to describe the imagined properties of a real place on the sole basis of its name. That is, the sentence reads as though some type of material correspondence existed between the nature of this place and the shape of its name.

It may have been, however, the poet's initial evocation of a poorly enclosed estate that led him unconsciously, no doubt, to select that particular locale as the setting for his automatic story. In the opening section of the poem, the narrator claims that a fancy ball ended at five o'clock in the morning, and that at the ball, "les plus tendres robes se fussent égratignées á des *ronces* invisibles" (my emphasis). Is it because tender dresses of women were unduly scratched on brambles that should not have been present on an estate in Montfermeil (where, in this hypothesis, the ball took place) that Breton's pen singled out this name for its graphemic play? It is probably impossible to determine.

Whatever the case though, the fact remains that after a typical beginning to a story about an old love affair— "J'étais brun quand je connus Solange"—and a typical first encounter at a ball, the text suddenly escapes the trap of still greater narrative conventionality through its sudden and disruptive anagrammatic play with the name "Montfermeil." In this fashion, it underscores both the obvious formal automatism at its core and, at the same time, its presumption of surrealist creation. The reader can thereafter no longer justify his reading by reference to an already-known or even *knowable* place, a place like

Montfermeil. He must instead re-direct his attention to the signifiers he sees on the page and attempt to re-create within his own imagination a surreal world. This world lies somewhere between the reality these words conjure up in his mind (mimesis), and the linguistic system to which they as "pure" words refer back (semiosis).

Our second example of an anagram related to an explicit textual model functions similarly. Although again we cannot determine whether the island of Cyprus was already on Breton's mind before he began writing text no. 6 (and thus, in the course of this extended metaphor of the world qua newspaper, generated the following segment about a pleasant holiday spot), or whether the textual production worked in the reverse order, we can observe an insistent alliteration and internal repetition of the letters in that island's name throughout the paragraph preceding its otherwise arbitrary appearance. To the reader who asks then why the narrator plans to go to *Cyprus* rather than to another, perhaps more agreeable, vacation spot, we need only emphasize the graphemic make-up of the words forming this lexical choice's immediate linguistic environment:

> La *p*lus grande *p*artie de ce journal que je *p*arcours à *propre*ment *p*arler est consa*cr*ée aux déplacements et villégiatures, dont la ru*br*ique figure en bonne *p*lace au haut de la *p*remiére place. *Il y* est dit, notamment, que je me ren*dr*ai demain á Chypre.

In the light of all these repeated "p"'s and "pr"'s, as well as of the syllabic pattern $x + r$, the final sentence's opening syntactic pattern (the infrequent "Il y est dit") constitutes the final catalyst for the *automatic,* and otherwise, narratively unjustified, selection of "Chypre" in this spot of the story. One gets the distinct impression, therefore, that for whatever conscious or unconscious reasons Breton used the expression "Il y est" (as opposed to the much less unusual "Il y a," for example) at that juncture, the close occurrence of the graphemic pattern *capital letter + tall letter (e.g. "l" "h") + y* was all that was needed to provoke in him the memory of "Chypre."

As invalid as this reading may seem according to any conventional sense of literary style, the fact is that in this context, *no* other narrative allusion or cause that we can find removes the utter arbitrariness of that particular sign in this context. Of course, one might argue that the arbitrariness of the sign was precisely what the Surrealists were most interested in exploiting. I would not disagree with this potential objection. At the same time Breton composed the texts of *Poisson soluble* (1924), he himself brought up the same point in his *Manifeste*. There he says that the strongest surrealist image for him is "celle qui présente le degré d'arbitraire le plus élevé." Yet, immediately after making this statement, he explains that the surrealist image is as strong as it is because of how long it takes "á traduire en langage pratique." In other words, the arbitrariness of surrealist writing, to Breton's mind, *will* sooner or later disappear, even though the best of it will take a great deal of time. This is due to the fact that, in certain cases, Breton says, the only thing justifying these images is their ability to draw out of themselves "une justification *formelle* dérisoire." What more "derisory" formal justification, indeed, than one based on the shape and relative positions of certain graphemes!

In addition, Breton admits that in some instances, surrealist writing produces characters—or what A. J. Greimas would more precisely call "actants"—who are nothing more than the result of specific graphemic traits made on the page:

. . . vous n'aurez qu'à mettre l'aiguille de "Beau fixe" sur "Action" et le tour sera joué. Voici des personnages [or places like, say, Cyprus] d'allure assez disparates; leurs noms dans votre écriture sont une *question de majuscules* . . . (my emphasis)

What this means then is that when we find people, places, and things described in a surrealist text we must realize that they are often the graphemic result of the automatic writing itself, rather than that of any *genuine*, i.e. preconceived, narrative intent or strategy. Though they conjure up images from the phenomenological world we all live in, these images are only illusions created by textual beings, "êtres qui en vérité vous doivent si peu."

Let us consider now a case of just such a being whose presence in text no. 15 is occasioned by the similarity between his name *Hugues* and an absent word that summarizes the entire fantasy represented. This is an example of anagrammatic gymnastics around a word that does not actually figure in the text, as in our previous examples. The word is instead implied by other phrases and narrative situations surrounding it. The prose poem in question concerns small children in a Catholic school. Inexplicably, the children find their classroom suddenly and magically transformed. In the first sentence, for instance, the chalk is said to contain a sewing machine. A little later on, the blackboard becomes the sky. In a word, the children appear to be daydreaming about the outside world. Little wonder then that the narrator, in wonderfully pun-like manner, cannot resist saying: "C'est l'école buissonnière dans toute son acception." The kids, in other words, are, as the stereotype would have it, far more concerned with getting out of school than in staying in.

Significantly enough, the apparent leader of this group, whom Breton calls "le prince des mares," is named Hugues. Seeing how the entire narrative revolves around the kids' dreams of skipping school, or, more precisely, of *escaping* it once they arrive there, we might legitimately advance the following idea: as leader of these kids, the boy Breton realistically names "Hugues" presumably embodies both their wishes and their dreams. Since, however, he is supposedly a "real" child in an imaginary classroom that has somehow gone crazy, through the fantasy of the poet, it is narratively appropriate that his name indicate simultaneously the reality of these French children *and* their fantasy (escape). No other boy's name in French than Hugues so resembles the one word signifying perfectly these longed-for infantile evasions: *fugues*.

Another instance of this kind of implicit anagrammatic

derivation can be located in text no. 3, a tale of an enormous wasp found descending le boulevard Richard-Lenoir on its way to la place de la Bastille. The wasp is said to be singing loudly ("á tue-tête"). Not long after that, she asks the narrator how to get wherever it is she is going. After engaging the insect in conversation a bit more, the narrator then describes her buzzing as being "insupportable comme une congestion pulmonaire." At first glance, nothing is wrong or odd about this comparison. Congestion in one's lungs is, after all, difficult to endure. It could conceivably produce a respiness that might recall the buzzing of a wasp.

On the realistic application of Breton's Surrealist theory to poetry and painting:

It is doubtful . . . whether even the most subservient of the surrealist poets or painters paid much heed to Breton's decree, in the *Second Manifesto*, that "the activities of the surrealists" shall be motivated solely by "the hope of finding and fixing" a mythical "point of the mind at which life and death, the real and the imagined, past and future, the communicable and the incommunicable, high and low, cease to be perceived contradictorily." Yet this near-meaningless program is constantly being quoted seriously as a valuable pointer to the intentions of surrealist poetry or art. . . .

The exegetes would save themselves a great deal of tortured rationalization if they accepted the fact that the best of the surrealist poets and painters were entirely selective in their attitude to surrealist theory. In general, they retained from the theoretical apparatus, and adapted to their individual requirements, the basic mechanisms proposed by Breton as the means of liberating the psyche from its enslavement to "reason": hallucinatory and irrational thought associations and recollected dream images. But however effective the formulas for "jogging" inspiration, especially—in surrealist poetry and painting alike—the juxtaposition of disparate images, they can only feed an *immanent* inspiration. Only by exercising his intuitive intelligence and innate sensibility can the poet or painter select images whose confrontation will spark the magical transformation into surreality. Second-rate surrealist painting is easily recognizable by the banal or theatrical relationship between its constituent elements. The comparable vice among surrealist poets is a rudimentary automatism, involving the stringing together of endless non-rational associations.

Simon Watson Taylor, in a review of Selected Poems, *in* The New York Review of Books, *January 29, 1970, pp. 41-5.*

But if one looks carefully at the rest of the sentence in which the comparison is located, the reader would do well to reconsider his initial simple acceptance of it. According to the poet, the wasp's buzzing was so loud that it "couvrait à ce moment le bruit des tramways, dont le trolley était une libellule." Given that la place de la Bastille in 1924 was a major tramway intersection for trolley cars, one has no reason to doubt the aptness of Breton's comparison between the noise emitted by his huge fantastical creature and the *real* noise that trolleys must have actually produced at the time. To compare it in this case to a *pulmonary* congestion, however, appears retroactively to have been automatically generated, or textually inspired, if one prefers, by the word "Pullman." Pullman, of course, was *the* proper name par excellence in the code of trains, for Pullman cars were the most luxurious cars in passenger trains.

The pertinence of this detail must not go unnoticed. The wasp, after all, who is portrayed elsewhere in the text as a particularly attractive woman (amusingly, "á la taille de guêpe") is distinguished from another insect in the very sentence containing the now-problematic comparison. The "insect" we now have to consider is the trolley, who is called a dragonfly. The difference in insect code is thus reflected by an implied difference in train code (or possibly, the other way around). The latter is implied by the graphemic play between "pulmonaire" and the would-be adjective "Pullmanaire." The play is one between lung congestion and what would be an unsaid, though highly visible, train tie-up or train *congestion*. In this regard, it is important to remember that the American label "Pullman" was so well-known and widespread at the time that it passed into the French language without any graphemic transformation.

The last type of graphemic gymnastics we shall explore results from the narrative expansion of certain presuppositions of a word found in an automatic text. Since the word in question represents a part of a longer associative chain previously attached to that word—through native-speaker usage, dictionary entries, and other symbolic forms fixed in a particular culture—we shall call this kind of graphemic feature, *metonymic*. Our first example this time comes from . . . no. 7, the prose poem about the world as newspaper. In the course of the narrator's imagined peregrinations, he finds himself in command of what are essentially "aquatic ballons." Manipulating the different navigational devices, he states that the motive behind his various manoeuvrings is, paradoxically, to assure that all will be lost, "pour nous assurer que tout est perdu." Normally, one would expect such action by a commander to lead to a righting of a vessel's course, not a deliberate sabotaging of it.

Yet this phrase is emblematic of the nature of automatic writing. When given a (narrative) opportunity to produce something unexpected or ostensibly arbitrary, the surrealist writer usually will. In this example, the commander's intent to lose his way induces our poet to say the following about the ballon's compass:

cette boussole est enfin contrainte de prononcer le mot:

Sud, et nous rions sous cape de la grande destruction immatérielle en marche.

What interests us here is how the mere mention of the direction "Sud" arbitrarily pronounced by the compass gives rise to an extraordinary phrasal expansion. This expansion is located within the expression, "nous rions sous cape." It is notable for two reasons. First, the expression "rire sous cape" continues the apparent absurdity implied by the narrator's wish to lose himself. It accomplishes this by indicating that the crew is literally laughing in its sleeve about the great immaterial destruction this sudden turn of events provokes. However, as we have come to expect by now of automatic texts, the destruction at hand is described as being *im*material, not material. That is, in actuality, it is a nondestruction, or, in other words, an actual *improvement* of their surreal nautical voyage. In going South, the sailors will thus stay clear of the stormy weather that might otherwise ship-wreck them. (Earlier, they are said to be "créatures d'épaves.") This makes the otherwise paradoxical action of laughing consistent, albeit in reverse fashion, with the previous absurd narrative situation of wanting to lose, not find, one's way.

The second reason why the above expression is significant lies in the specific words "sous cape." Therein we find a significant graphemic manipulation of two variants of these words that are highly pertinent to this strange itinerary. In the first place, the word "cape" used in a nautical context refers to a specific manoeuvre whose goal is precisely to prepare a ship for stormy weather, as in the expressions "être à la cape" or "se mettre à la cape." The whole notion of good vs. bad weather is thereby evoked by a simple association of the word. At the same time, however, "cape" is very similar both phonemically and graphemically to the absent word "Cap," or Cape, in English. In the light of the *southern* direction already established (first and foremost by "Sud," but then secondarily and graphemically reinforced by "sous"), the many different southern Cape(s) recalled by that word thus only emphasize the idea that this crew is headed towards less dangerous seas. Southern capes are traditionally known by sailors and tourists alike for their calm, peacefulness, even promise of "Good Hope." (In passing, let us not forget also that in the past, the French term for "Le cap de Bonne-Espérance" was, in fact, "Le cap des Tempêtes.") Thus, the graphemic constitution of the phrase "nous rions sous cape" makes it the perfect lexical selection for this passage. By means of a kind of double negation, it describes a positive and promising nautical situation in seemingly negative terms ("tout est perdu," "nous rions sous cape," "destruction," etc.).

Another surrealist text, no. 17 in Breton's collection, expands its narrative in similar fashion. Thanks to a model provided by the initial image—which presents two men chatting about love while they walk in a park—the entire text is dialectically composed of two-part constructions. In some cases, these constructions are syntactical in nature, with different types of subordinate clauses occurring in pairs. In other instances, the doubling is more lexical. When the narrator begins to describe brushes or cigars, for example, the varieties of brush or cigar always come in groups of two.

The particular detail of interest to us involves the impossibly long ashes these cigars produce. The first man's cigar has an ash that measures one meter ten, while the second man's ash measures one meter thirty five. As if to challenge the reader's sense of reason, the narrator says boldly, "Expliquez cela comme vous pourrez quand je vous aurai dit qu'ils les [the cigars] avaient allumés en même temps." Retroactively, we understand that these unusual lengths are most likely related to the height of two women whose images appear immediately thereafter in the narrative. In any event, the narrator then creates a pair of metaphors according to which the younger man's ash is a blond woman, while the older one's is a brunette. Since the men were talking all along about love, the semantic associations of the word "allumé" (lust, passion, etc.) represent the probable lexical origin that sparked, as it were, the text's sudden production of female imagery.

But, in addition to this, there is a secondary or extended graphemic gymnastic of note in the choice of hair-color for these woman. Cigars, like cigarettes, we remember, can be made out of two kinds of tobacco, light or dark. In French, this distinction just happens to be rendered by the adjectives "blond(e)" and "brun(e)." It is no doubt a minor point, consequently, to insist that out of several possibilities (blond, red, etc.) the hair colors chosen from the metaphorical woman in this passage are blond and brown. Yet, in keeping within the scheme of a preliminary examination of such subtle stylistic features in surrealist literature, it is a point surely worth making.

In conclusion, I should like to repeat that the present essay has not been intended to be exhaustive in any sense. What remains for us to do first is to analyze how all these and other graphemic traits in automatic texts relate to and affect each other. In a second stage of research, one can envisage an eventual application of these findings to non-automatic works. The ultimate goal of such research would be to show how all literature exhibits similar graphemic gymnastics, though surely·not in all of the same ways and not to the same degree. Yet, if the latter were true, then clearly a re-assessment of literary style would be at least partially in order.

Christopher Merrill (essay date 1993)

SOURCE: "The Leading Surreal Light," in *The Los Angeles Times Book Review*, July 18, 1993, p. 5.

[*Merrill is an American poet and critic. In the following review, Merrill presents an overview of Breton's poetic achievement.*]

How many Surrealists does it take to screw in a light bulb? The answer—a fish—is at once inoffensive and to the point: Andre Breton and his friends wanted to reinvent man's relationship to life itself, and what better place to begin than with a simple mechanical operation? Illumination was their theme, humor their favorite means and the only problem with this joke, they might have said, is that it is not offensive. After all, these were the French poets and artists who greeted the advent of World War II with the publication of an anthology of black humor. "There's nothing more serious than a joke" goes the old saying, and the Surrealists turned that insight into the most revolutionary artistic program of the 20th Century. It is a commonplace to describe the events of our time as surreal; what is remarkable is that the considerable literary achievement of Andre Breton, the symbol of Surrealism, is so little known in this country. The recent publication of his *Conversations: The Autobiography of Surrealism* and a selection of his early poems, ***Earthlight,*** both in excellent translations, may win him the audience he deserves.

Breton was born in 1896 in Normandy, and he spent his early childhood in Brittany, whose moors had a profound influence on him: "They have often torn me apart," he admitted in one of the interviews collected in *Conversations,* "but I love that light of will-o'-the-wisp that they keep burning in my heart." Indeed, that light was what he tried to pass on in his writings, and in his sixth decade he declared, "all my pride comes from the fact that it hasn't yet gone out. At stake, as I saw it, were my chances of not failing the human adventure." That adventure took shape for him when World War I broke out. Drafted as a medical orderly, he worked with psychiatric patients, experimenting with the free associative methods he had read about in Sigmund Freud's works, exploring the unconscious in order to find what Octavio Paz calls "the primordial language."

His investigations, coupled with his readings of Guillaume Apollinaire and Pierre Reverdy, Arthur Rimbaud and Isidore Ducasse (or, as he was better known, Comte de Lautreamont), led him in 1919 to compose, with Philippe Soupault, ***Les Champs Magnetiques*** (***The Magnetic Fields***), the first automatic text. Written in the absence of conscious control to express what Breton believed would be "the real functioning of thought," ***The Magnetic Fields*** opened the verbal floodgates for the writers aligned first with Dada and then with Surrealism: Breton, Soupault, Paul Eluard, Louis Aragon, Robert Desnos, Benjamin Peret. It is true that automatic writing proved not to be their Holy Grail; nevertheless, it inspired them to produce much of their best work.

Certainly the practice was useful for Breton, who in these interviews as well as in his polemical writings revealed himself to be a highly rational thinker. His poetry, though, shines with a mysterious light: "I am born in the infinite disorder of prayers," he wrote in **"A Thousand Thousand Times."**

Destroying shackles of every kind was Breton's dream, and it was realized most often through love. "Each man according to his desires," he said, and his maxim—"Poetry is made in bed like love"—made him one of this century's great love poets. Here is how he begins **"The Writings Depart"**:

    The satin of pages we turn in
, books bodies forth a woman so
beautiful
    That when we aren't reading we
contemplate this woman sadly
    Without daring to speak to her
without daring to tell her that
    she's so beautiful
    That what we're going to find out
is priceless

Breton's commitment to liberation in the private realm had its counterpart in public life. Linking Rimbaud's desire to "change life" to Karl Marx's order to "transform the world," the Surrealists joined forces with the Communists, and this was what eventually tore the group apart. Breton was quick to denounce the strictures of Socialist Realism and the excesses of Stalinism, which cost him his friendships with Eluard and Aragon. Although he and his movement were eclipsed by the Existentialists, Breton continued to celebrate human freedom; and when he died in 1966, his obituary notice read, "I seek the gold of time." In his eulogy for his friend and mentor Octavio Paz wrote: "Every man is born several times and dies several times. This is not the first time that Breton has died. He knew, better than anyone, that we die more than once: Each one of his central books is the story of a resurrection." This translation of **Earthlight** tells that story once again and, along with *Conversations,* makes Breton's first American resurrection imminent.

FURTHER READING

Bibliography

Sheringham, Michael. *Andre Breton: A Bibliography.* London: Grant & Cutler Ltd., 1972, 122 p.
    Primary and secondary bibliography.

Adamowicz, Elza and Sheringham, Michael. *Andre Breton: A Bibliography (1972-1989).* London: Grant & Cutler Ltd., 1992, 147 p.
    Supplement to bibliography listed above.

Biography

Balakian, Anna. *André Breton: Magus of Surrealism.* New York: Oxford University Press, 1971, 289 p.
    Literary biography of Breton's life as it influenced his writing and the Surrealist movement which he founded. Includes a selected bibliography.

Criticism

Aspley, Keith. "André Breton's Poems for Denise." *French Studies* XLI, No. 1 (January 1987): 52-61.
    Suggests that the "Denise" poems, written in the early 1920s, may have been censored by Breton.

Balakian, Anna. "André Breton's *Les Etats Généraux*: Revolution and Poetry." *The French Review* 62, No. 6 (6 May 1989): 1008-16.
    Interprets Breton's poem as an epic on the theme of revolution.

Balakian, Anna, and Kuenzli, Rudolf E., eds. *André Breton Today.* New York: Willis Locker & Owens, 1989, 147 p.
    Selected critical and intrepretive essays on Breton's poetry and prose. Includes a selective bibliography, 1971-1988, of works by Breton as well as secondary material.

Berryman, John. A review of *Young Cherry Trees Secured Against Hares. Partisan Review* XIV, No. 1 (January-February 1947): 73-85.
    Considers the longevity of Breton's work.

Cauvin, Jean-Pierre. Introduction to *Poems of André Breton: A Bilingual Anthology,* by André Breton, translated and edited by Jean-Pierre Cauvin and Mary Ann Caws, pp. xvii-xxxviii. Austin: University of Texas Press, 1982.
    Defines Breton's poetry and its connection to life, and explains surrealist poetry's attempt to disconnect words and things from conventionality and the banal.

Caws, Mary Ann. "The Poetics of a Surrealist Passage." *A Metapoetics of the Passage,* pp. 27-35. Hanover: University Press of New England, 1981.
    Discusses Breton's poetry as a "defense of the passionate and the unique."

Caws, Mary Ann. *André Breton.* New York: Twayne Publishers, Inc., 1971, 133 p.
    Critical-analytical study of Breton's works. Includes a chronology of Breton's life and a selected bibliography.

Matzidakis, Stamos. "Picking up Narrative Pieces in a Surrealist Prose Poem." *Orbis Litterarum* 40, No. 4 (1985): 317-26.
    Examines narrative discontinuity in Breton's *Poisson Soluble.*

Paz, Octavio. "André Breton or the Quest of the Beginning." In *Alternating Current,* translated by Helen R. Lane, pp. 47-59. New York: The Viking Press, 1973.
    Originally published in Spanish in 1967, this essay is a reaction to Breton's death. Reviews Breton's poetic vocabulary, describing it as the language of passion and magic.

Scharfman, Ronnie. "Reading Breton Today: 'La Mort rose.'" *Dada/Surrealism* 17 (1988): 67-73.
    Extended critical reading of Breton's "La Mort Rose." Essay contains significant amounts of untranslated French.

Schjeldahl, Peter. Review of *Young Cherry Trees Secured Against Hares. Poetry* CXVII, No. 4 (January 1971): 262-64.
    Reevaluates the 1946 bilingual translation of Breton's poems in response to its republication in 1969.

Sheringham, Michael. "The Liberator of Desire." *Times Literary Supplement*, No. 4,462 (7-13 October 1988): 1125.
    Reviews Volume 1 of *Oeuvres complètes* (*Complete Works*), a Pléiade edition compilation of Breton's works up to 1930.

Additional coverage of Breton's life and career is contained in the following sources published by Gale Research: *Contemporary Authors*, **Vol. 19-20, 25-28 (rev. ed.);** *Contemporary Authors Permanent Series*, **Vol. 2;** *Contemporary Authors New Revision Series*, **Vol. 40;** *Contemporary Literary Criticism*, **Vols. 2, 9, 15, 54;** *Dictionary of Literary Biography*, **Vol. 65;** *Major Twentieth Century Writers*.

Rubén Darío
1867–1916

(Pseudonym of Félix Rubén García Sarmiento) Nicaraguan poet, short story writer, journalist, critic, essayist, autobiographer, and novelist.

INTRODUCTION

Though not widely known in the English-speaking world, Darío was one of the great Spanish poets and the leading figure of the late nineteenth-century Spanish-American *modernista* literary movement. Influenced by French Parnassian and Symbolist poetry, he revitalized Spanish poetics, which had essentially remained unchanged since the seventeenth century. A cosmopolitan blend of modernist formal experimentation, classical motifs, and Hispanic traditions, Darío's poetry is valued as much for its linguistic brilliance and technical and formal innovations as for its advocacy of Hispanic solidarity and concern about the universal human condition.

Biographical Information

Born Félix Rubén García Sarmiento on January 18, 1867, in Metapa, Nicaragua, Darío was a precocious writer, who began using his pseudonym at the age of fourteen. Dedicated to travel and literary pursuits, he emigrated in 1886 to Chile, where two years later he inaugurated the *modernista* movement with the publication of *Azul* (1888). After diplomatic service on behalf of Chile in Paris and Madrid, Darío arrived in Buenos Aires in 1893 as Colombian consul to Argentina, where he published *Prosas profanas y otros poemas* (1896). Following the Spanish-American War, Darío travelled throughout Europe as a correspondent for the Buenos Aires newspaper *La nación*, focusing his writing on more social, political, and contemporary themes. Between 1903 and 1907 Darío served as Nicaraguan consul to France; while in Paris Darío wrote *Cantos de vida y esperanza* (1905)—widely admired as his finest work—*El canto errante* (1907), and *Poema del otoño y otros poemas* (1910). After more than a decade of crisscrossing the Atlantic Ocean for diplomatic or literary purposes, Darío permanently left Europe in 1914 with plans for a North American lecture tour the following year. However, when Darío developed pneumonia in New York City, he returned to Nicaragua, where he died February 6, 1916.

Major Works

Darío's greatest fame derives from three major poetry collections. *Azul*, recognized as the defining work of the *modernista* movement, is a collection of prose and verse that represents Darío's interpretation of the artistic principles of the French Parnassian school—restraint, objectivity, precise description—in his native language. With its

exotic themes and simple, direct syntax, Darío's writings in *Azul* reanimated Spanish literature. In *Prosas profanas*, a collection of poems influenced by contemporary French Symbolism and marked by exotic aestheticism, Darío aimed for the formal purity of music by experimenting with unconventional but revolutionary metrical forms. *Cantos de vida y esperanza* reveals a change in Darío's poetic vision, a move away from aesthetic concerns toward political and social themes. The poetry in this collection ranges from meditations on the future of South America to expressions of Hispanic solidarity under the threat of North American imperialism. Other notable collections of Darío's poetry include *El canto errante*, which expounds his humanist views by addressing fundamental dilemmas of human existence, and *Poema del otoño*, which attempts to resolve the poet's own religious and metaphysical conflicts in a passionate celebration of both life and death.

Critical Reception

During his lifetime Darío was the toast of Spanish-speaking literati worldwide, and on his death he was mourned with eloquent eulogies extolling the vibrant language and technical virtuosity of his poetic vision. Salomón de la Selva called Darío "the Spanish Keats," and Pedro Henríquez Ureña remarked that "both Spain and Spanish America saw in him their representative poet." By midcentury, however, Darío's reputation had diminished somewhat among many scholars who suggested that for all its stylistic flair, his poetry sometimes lacked substance. C. M. Bowra found Darío's poetry explicitly derivative in its emulation of contemporary French verse, though Arturo Torres-Rioseco attributed a perceived critical neglect of the poet to a shift in readers' tastes. Other critics have interpreted and evaluated Darío's work on the basis of his biography, his socio-political position, or his place in literary history. Recent scholarship has continued to elaborate these aspects through close textual analysis, which in turn has highlighted other elements in Darío's poetry as diverse as Pythagorean philosophy and duality in his female imagery. As poet Octavio Paz once observed about Darío's literary significance, "Darío is present in the spirit of contemporary [Spanish] poets. He is the founder."

PRINCIPAL WORKS

Poetry

Abrojos 1887
Azul . . . (poetry and short stories) 1888
Prosas profanas y otros poemas [*Prosas Profanas, and Other Poems*] 1896
Cantos de vida y esperanza, Los cisnes, y otros poemas 1905
El canto errante 1907
Poema del otoño y otros poemas 1910
Canto a la Argentina y otros poemas 1914
Muy antiguo y muy moderno 1915
Eleven Poems 1916
Selected Poems of Rubén Darío 1965

Other Major Works

Primeras notas (letters and poetry) 1885
Emelina [with Edouardo Porier] (novel) 1887
Los raros (essays) 1893
Peregrinaciones (travel essays) 1901
Opiniones (criticism) 1906
El viaje a Nicaragua; e, Intermezzo tropical (travel essays) 1909
Autobiografia (autobiography) 1912

CRITICISM

Isaac Goldberg (essay date 1919)

SOURCE: "Rubén Darío: The Man and the Poet," in *The Bookman,* Vol. XLIX, No. 5, July, 1919, pp. 563-68.

[*In the following excerpt, Goldberg offers his estimation of Darío's role in Spanish literature.*]

Although it is but two years since his death, Rubén Darío is beginning to be looked upon not only as the greatest poet that Spanish America has produced, but as perhaps the greatest poet that has ever written in the Spanish tongue. Superlatives such as this always carry with them a trail of suspicion and mistrust; yet it is significant that they should be uttered at all, and doubly so when the utterance proceeds from a critic jealous of his standing, careful of his words and carrying conviction not only with the weight of his assertion but with the accumulation of his past services to letters. To Vargas Vila, the noted Colombian critic, Darío is even more: "One of the first in the world, if the world possesses another like him".

Assignment of rank, however, if it be one of the functions of criticism, is hardly the most important. What matters it if Darío be the greatest poet that ever wrote in Spanish, or merely the second or third, when we have the concrete and undebatable evidence of the immense influence he exerted upon the Spanish world of his time? To us of [the United States] Darío is important in more than one sense: not only is he the poet who summarizes an epoch and speaks for a continent; he is the man of the world who epitomizes a racial culture that we must surely understand better than we do now if we are to cement those ties with our Spanish-American neighbors which commercial relations only initiate but never fully tighten. Were it only from purely material motives we should know the cultural background of our prospective customers better, for it has become a platitude that in order to do business with our Southern neighbors we must be able to meet them socially and intellectually as well. But the [First World War] has emphasized another fact, one more fundamental to our present purpose: intellectual intercourse between different peoples leads to beneficial fertilization of one nation by another. In the past mere difference has too often been dismissed as inferiority; an increase in knowledge of one another must inevitably work toward a friendship that is founded on something more firm than a profitable interchange of commodities. Is there not something of silent reproach in the fact that North American poetry has nothing to match with Darío's **"Salutation to the Eagle"**, written in 1906 to welcome our delegates to the Pan-American Congress held that year in Brazil—a poem in which the proud fear of the United States as an invader of South America (expressed in his ode **"To Roosevelt"**) gave way to a more optimistic view? Such a note, which is more or less casual in Darío, is fundamental in the labors of José Santos Chocano, his successor. Yet did the completion of the Panama Canal elicit from our poets such a paean as Chocano's "Isthmus of Panama" or the same bard's "Song of the Future"? The war has done much to dissipate the atmosphere of distrust that is characteristic of certain of Darío's poems, but it is questionable whether Chocano's Pan-Americanism yet reflects the spirit of Spanish-America as a whole. Those of us who give thought to the matter at all cannot feel that we as a nation are totally blameless. Fortunately the situation, far from being hopeless, grows brighter every day. . . .

The Modernista movement in Spanish poetry, which Darío definitely established in 1888 with the appearance of his volume of mingled prose and poetry called *Azul* (*Blue*), had precursors in other Spanish-American countries. But Darío did more than merely crystallize the movement; he rapidly became the leader and pathblazer, finally carrying the revolution to Spain itself. The "modernistas" received their inspiration from France, the beloved renovator in all ages of Spanish letters. The revolution originated, under the influence of the Parnassians, decadents and symbolists, in a reaction against the cold formalism into which Spanish verse had fallen. That Poe and Walt Whitman should quickly have become favorites with the new Spanish school is hardly surprising; we learned really to appreciate these compatriots from the same source—France.

In a larger sense Darío is of no school but that of beauty. His technical innovations are numerous, and naturally receive much consideration from the Spanish critics; to foreigners, especially non-Latins, this phase of his work must remain subordinate. It is interesting to point out that the "modernistas" are not really so much innovators in this respect as they are revivers. They rescued Spanish verse from a slavery to a few meters by resuscitating others that had long lain dormant and by introducing French forms; one of the Iberian critics even avers that for free verse there was a prototype in old Spanish poetry. This same attitude of reviver rather than innovator is noticeable among the new poets of our own country. . . .

It is easy, too, to make of Darío a worshiper at the shrine of art for art's sake. Yet his poems are by no means sterile models of flawless technique. In his progress from the earliest exemplifications of his powers—in his autobiography he tells us that "I never learned how to write verses. It was organic, natural, inborn"—he makes a vast curve from the chiseled lines of classicism to the prophetic strophes of a Whitman. He was a classic by temperament, one writer tells us, and a modern by culture. His work exhibits the solidity of the classic style, with all the restlessness of the modern spirit. Yet his numerous critics agree in one thing, that his chief attribute is grace and delicacy rather than power. There is power in Darío, and plenty of it; he is by no means the poet of graceful swans and languid swains that a poem read here and there might make us imagine; but that power, for the most part, has been distilled into vibrant beauty. It is not the vigorous, self-confident, continental trumpeting of a Chocano; there is a classic repose about Darío's work that seems coldly perfect at first, like the cold perfection of a marble statue. Yet that statue has substance and solidity as well as grace; look at it long enough and it comes to life like a new Galatea under the loving caress of her Pygmalion.

> **Darío's work exhibits the solidity of the classic style, with all the restlessness of the modern spirit. Yet his numerous critics agree in one thing, that his chief attribute is grace and delicacy rather than power.**
>
> —*Isaac Goldberg*

At the very appearance of Darío's first significant volume, *Azul*, Juan Valera discerned in the youth a new spirit, and a "mental Gallicism" that was all the more surprising in that Darío had at that time been no nearer to France than Valparaiso, Chile. When his *Prosas Profanas* were issued eight years later, in 1896, it was seen that a great stride forward had been taken; in *Cantos de Vida y Esperanza* (*Songs of Life and Hope*, 1905) the singer stood forth in all the confidence of full maturity. The vitality of the poet's productions is indirectly attested by the criticism he has evoked. José Enrique Rodó's analysis of the *Prosas Profanas* ranks with the finest pages that South American criticism has produced. Gonzáles-Blanco's "Estudio Preliminar" of Darío's work is an exhaustive (and exhausting!) treatise by a Spaniard whose mania for citation cannot mar the thoroughness of his investigation and the general validity of his conclusions. I may be excused for pausing for a moment upon Gonzáles-Blanco, for no student of Spanish-American literature will go far in his investigations before coming upon that critic's valuable and voluminous studies. Page upon page of quotations from the most recondite and varied sources submerge the bark of his commentary in an ocean of allusion. What other critics are content to read, ponder and silently assimilate, he must needs place in formidable foot-notes that bristle with Latin, French, German, English and Greek, until the reader has stored up all the sensations necessary for a well-defined polyglot nightmare. And as if this were not sufficient, Gonzáles-Blanco annotates himself and deserts the subject of his study time and again in order to prove that he is justified in his multifarious quoting and to air his views upon the functions of criticism. Nevertheless, as I have said, he is a man that must be known, and has contributed valuable services to the cause of Spanish letters in the old world and the new. If only he had learned from Darío the art of writing Castilian prose! Rather the punctuation of a Vargas Vila than the plethoric citations of a Gonzáles-Blanco!

From these critics it is possible to make a composite photograph, so to speak, of what the great poet looks like to the cultured Spanish reader. In his varied manifestations he is called a Christian Olympian, a pantheist garbed in the Catholic liturgy, endowed with "Nipponism", "contemplative Asiaticism", and fundamentally pagan. Another terms him Greek in his cult of beauty and Hebrew in his strain of prophecy—a cosmopolitan lyrist, Catholic in sentiment only. The artist, however, is too expansive, too all-inclusive, to be included in any narrow hoop of classi-fication. The genius of Darío lies largely in the circum-stance that he so identified himself with an epoch that the epoch may now be identified with him. Many were the influences that he absorbed from his changing envi-ronments, yet he made them completely his own. He was a poet rich alike in harmonious responses to the past and the present, and in pregnant previsions of the world to come. . . .

The erotic element in Darío's poetry is treated by him with that same touch that transmuted everything else he laid hands upon. Barring the crude misogyny of some juvenile verses, the erotic in Darío is cleansed by the very flame of his art.

What of Darío's meaning to us? I do not refer to his political fears and hopes. I mean what has his poetry to bring to our spiritual life? Poetry has the great disadvan-tage of being much evaporated in the transit from one tongue to another; if it is at all possible, by all means read Darío, of all poets, in the original. Once granted, howev-er, that the happy poet may be found who can render this genius's music into our language, poetry has this advan-tage: that it deals with fundamental, universal emotions and reactions only less directly than music itself. To know Darío is to look differently upon men and women and the world about us after we have read him; to see a new beauty in an old theme; to discover new aspects of our inner life; to breathe a new atmosphere. It is not given to many men in any land to accomplish this so fully as did this noble spirit who was "not only the first among the great, but the first among the good", as Vargas Vila puts it; or, in the similar words of a lesser-known critic, Alber-to Tena, "a saint of goodness and a priest of beauty".

Arturo Torres-Rioseco (essay date 1949)

SOURCE: "A Reëvaluation of Rubén Darío," in *New World Literature: Tradition and Revolt in Latin America,* Uni-versity of California Press, 1949, pp. 120-37.

[*A Chilean-born scholar and poet specializing in Latin American fiction and verse, Torres-Rioseco was the au-thor of more than a dozen books about Spanish American literature, including three book-length studies of Darío. In the following excerpt, he traces the development of Darío's poetry, refuting claims that it is "superficial."*]

Today the thirty years that have passed since the death of Rubén Darío afford a perspective through which we may view his poetry afresh. I have always maintained that Darío is *the* great poet of our continent and one of the most eminent in the Spanish language. But since recent criti-cism of him has been increasingly adverse I should like to examine . . . the reasons for it.

I believe that, as a general rule, every writer who is not a man of genius diminishes in esteem with the course of time. It cannot even be said that each generation produces

a literary genius in any language. Hence the writers who compose the greater part of a nation's literary tradition are consigned to virtual oblivion; although their names recur in histories, anthologies, and even in conversation, their works do not command permanently the interest of readers. They are dying souls, who, though lingering on the brink, are nevertheless condemned without hope of reprieve.

Take, for example, the Spanish, Spanish American, and Brazilian romanticists. The names of Espronceda, the Duque de Rivas, Zorrilla, Echeverría, Mármol, Gonçalves de Magalhaes, Gonçalves Dias, and Castro Alves are known by all, but rare nowadays is the person of refined literary taste who will seek spiritual solace in the works of these poets. The bedside companion of yesterday graces the forsaken library shelf today. They are all drifting away on the stream of oblivion; some are still in sight, others already so far distant as almost to have disappeared. Time will carry them all from view; and when on occasion they are recalled in the future, it will be for reasons other than their purely poetic value.

Already this is beginning to happen to the Hispanic Amer-ican modernists. In Mexico, for example, present-day crit-ics are repudiating Gutiérrez Nájera and Amado Nervo, two poets who very recently were considered great; in Chile, the modernist Pedro Antonio González has been buried definitively; José Santos Chocano, who was once called the foremost poet of the continent, is now accused of superficiality and prosaism; Leopoldo Lugones faced disavowal even before his death; Herrera y Reissig is termed a verbalist; and so on down the list. Only Darío has remained erect on his pedestal; but already that emi-nence is challenged.

It would be pertinent to ask here: What type of poetry does the reader of today prefer, and which of the required poetic qualities are absent in Rubén Darío?

The reading public from 1890 to 1915 was accustomed to a type of poetry the prime elements of which were roman-tic sentiment and euphuistic style, mingled with an Orien-tal sensuousness of images and a warm French intonation. The romanticists had already popularized such melancholy, despairing poems as Lamartine's "Le Lac" (The Lake) and Musset's "Nuits" (Nights); José de Espronceda had written his "Canto a Teresa" (Song to Theresa); Bécquer, his intimately despondent verse; Manuel Acuna, his tor-mented "Nocturno a Rosario"; Gutiérrez Nájera, his fa-miliarly nostalgic "Serenata de Schubert," and José Asun-ción Silva, his voluptuous, mournful "Nocturnos." Thus, when there appeared such works as Darío's **"Sonatina," "Marcha triunfal" ("Triumphal March"), "Era un aire suave" ("It was a Gentle Breeze")**, and **"El Reino inte-rior" ("The Inner Kingdom")**, poems rich in color, re-splendent with dazzling images, exquisite elegance of dic-tion, and rhythm linked with purpose and idea, the Nica-raguan bard was acclaimed as the interpreter of the aes-thetic sensibility of the time. No poet of his period sur-passes him in brilliance or in refinement. For nearly thirty years he reigned, from Paris and Madrid, over the kingdom of decorative poetry, Parnassian-symbolistic in theme and expression. His celebrated **"Marcha triunfal"** is illustrative of the enthusiastic energy which captivated the American continent.

When González Martínez composed his famous sonnet, "Tuércele el cuello al cisne" ("Wring the Swan's Neck"), in which he condemns the baroque poetry of modernism and advocates instead the interpretation of the mysteries of life and nature, he revealed the birth of a new aesthetic sensibility; he proved that devotees of poetry were already tired of princesses, swans, winged steeds, nightingales, and roses. Rather, they were turning to a more intense poetry, to expression more akin to the suffering and struggle of life, to composition more daring in form. They were beginning to prefer free verse to the Alexandrine, brusque rhythm to monotonous cadence, social themes of vibrant import to Greek friezes and eighteenth-century drawings. In a word, they demanded that the poet be a man of his time and environment. If we had had a virile lover of democracy as was Walt Whitman, we would have turned toward him after the First World War.

To the generation of 1920, Rubén Darío was an artificial, courtly, Gallicized poet, totally alien to the life of his continent. His metrical reforms did not interest those new writers who proclaimed the destruction of poetic form; his verbal refinement sounded hollow in the ears of the revolutionary followers of Marinetti and Cocteau; the anachronism of his themes was interpreted as an evasion of reality.

I do not know what kind of poetry the cultured Spanish American reader of today prefers. It is highly probable that there exist as many tastes as there are cultural divisions. Besides, taste is often conditioned by elements foreign to creative production. For example, the poets of social themes—Vallejo, Neruda, Guillén León Felipe—are read frequently just because they are of the left, even though their comrades may not understand their works. Further, there is a group of people who sympathize with everything new, with all vanguard and leftist movements; and especially evident among them are students, those firm believers in social and racial revindications. If they could express themselves in verse, they would be social or political poets; this, in my opinion, constitutes, even as a doctrine, a serious menace to poetry.

Rubén Darío was not a social poet; he did not cultivate the Negro theme; he was not a Catholic poet, though he was a Catholic man; he was not even a democratic poet. Moreover, I am certain that these characteristics have nothing to do with poetry. But the public demands such elements nowadays; literature of the moment is in vogue, and therefore Darío is not the favorite poet of Spanish Americans today.

Curiously enough, we have let ourselves be lured by García Lorca's poetry, which is really as superficial as the most shallow moments of Darío; actually, García Lorca presents a mixture of Spanish classicism with a waggish touch of the Madrilenian dandy. His is poetry for recitation, a

characteristic from which the Spanish American seemed to flee in 1930, at least in the poetry of Rubén Darío. Within another twenty years all the poems of the *Romancero gitano* (*Gypsy Ballads*) of García Lorca will seem to us merely another literary fad. The admittance of the surrealist poetry of a Villaurrutia or of a Neruda would be more logical, since that mode is currently the most accepted in Europe and since its psychological significance invades the fields of sculpture and painting.

Rubén Darío does not meet fully the demands of today's reader, but part of the fault belongs to that reader and not to the poet. I have already stated that Darío is known essentially for his most superficial poems, for those in which there is more external luster than profound sensibility, more beauty of form than vital vibration. For example, we may recall **"La Bailerina de los pies desnudos"** (**"The Barefoot Dancer"**), **"El Clavicordio de la abuela"** (**"Grandmother's Clavichord"**), **"Cyrano en España"** (**"Cyrano in Spain"**), **"El Faisán"** (**"The Pheasant"**), **"La Marcha triunfal," "La Sonatina," "Margarita Debayle," "El Reino interior"** (**"The Inner Kingdom"**)—all very beautiful poems, but lacking in the anguish, the tremors of life.

But Darío was much more than this. Like Verlaine, he succeeded at times in penetrating the innermost recesses of the soul, in revealing the most intimate, most subtle emotions, and in expressing them without rhetoric, in the simple communication of sentiment. He created poetry of enduring beauty; even as early as in his *Prosas profanas*. . . .

Darío sought an interpretation of the designs of God in natural manifestations, approaching thus a kind of modern mysticism. He was always the exponent of the cultivation of internal rhythm as opposed to profane clamor. In fact, he was the profound, philosophical, carefully scrutinizing poet that González Martínez (who himself imitated Darío) demanded in his "Tuércele el cuello al cisne" ("Wring the Swan's Neck") . . .

> Darío succeeded at times in penetrating the innermost recesses of the soul, in revealing the most intimate, most subtle emotions, and in expressing them without rhetoric, in the simple communication of sentiment. He created poetry of enduring beauty. . . .
>
> —*Arturo Torres-Rioseco*

With the appearance of his *Cantos de vida y esperanza* (*Songs of Life and Hope*), in 1905, Darío became a social poet in the high sense of the word. He gives voice to the inner uneasiness of his continent in **"Salutación del optimista"** (**"The Optimist's Salutation"**) and **"A Roosevelt"** (**"To Roosevelt"**), and no longer can it be said that he is not the poet of America.

But it is in the constant probing into his soul that he displays best his greatness as a poet. Wounded to the core by the challenge hurled at him by José Enrique Rodó, he attempts not only to be the poet of his race, but also to reflect intensely all humanity.

> En mi jardín se vió una estatua bella;
> se juzgó mármol y era carne viva;
> un alma joven habitaba en ella;
> sentimental, sensible, sensitiva.

> [In my garden people saw a beautiful statue; they thought it marble and it was living flesh; a young soul lived within; sentimental, sympathetic, sensitive.]

The poet, keenly aware of the tragedy of his life, sums up his suffering in the words: "a vast pain, and minor cares." And he finds strength for resignation before his great doubts in the beauty of the world and in a vague mysticism [as in **"La dulzura del ángelus"**]. . . .

He had already spoken of his frustrated youth, of the bitter defloration of his existence, of the falsity of bohemian life: he had felt the terror of stumbling gropingly toward the unknown, the horror of the human slough, of feeling himself ephemeral in the world, of the terrible nightmare of the thought of death. But he does not want to know the answer to these enigmas. . . .

The innately Christian poet that Darío always was could well understand what he terms "the hopeless despair, the utter futility of a struggle with the infinite, in which the efforts of man are as fragile as butterfly wings, and the rhythm of his heart as potent as the descent of a snowflake." The simple soul redeems man, whereas the covetous, envious nature harbors a nest of burrowing moles. Imbued with a delightful pantheism, the lofty soul may discern the turbulent music of the world in the twilight, or even in the pupil of a cow's eye [as in **"Cleopompo y Heliodemo"**]. . . .

The simple soul of man should ever remain in an attitude of ineffable repose before the wondrous phenomena of nature; wrapped in a mystic quietism, sheltered in Franciscan retirement, it should blend inseparably with the beauties of the world. This mystic pantheism boasts a long history among Spanish peoples; it appeared among Spain's earliest poets as an instinctive exaltation of the motivating forces which failed of expression in words and ideas. . . .

Later, this pantheism became Spanish mysticism, which made itself felt widely in European thought. In Darío, this philosophy is tinged with Oriental fatalism. . . .

But actually, he was the first to forget his philosophy, for neither through this pantheism nor through his orthodox Catholicism did he ever achieve the tranquillity or the confidence of the mystics. His consciousness of original sin, his desire to encounter the living God, almost the human God, his absurd persistence in attempting to penetrate the ultimate mysteries of life, and his terror of death never gave him peace. His existence was one of inner torment, and upon giving expression to the fearful turmoil that reigned within him he rose to great poetic heights. . . .

Darío's excellent **"Poema del otoño"** (**"Poem of Autumn"**), published in 1907, revealed such dexterity of employment of the poetic idiom that he could well be considered our classic poet. This work may be compared favorably with the *Rubáiyát* of Omar Khayyám; it is a song of pagan optimism, an appeal to eternal youth and love. Lapidary strophes of exceptional lyricism succeed each other in amazing profusion. Forgetful of his old sorrows, the poet exclaims jovially:

> Y no obstante la vida es bella,
> por poseer
> la perla, la rosa, la estrella,
> y la mujer.

> [Nevertheless, life is beautiful, for it possesses pearl, rose, star, and woman.]

The overwhelming beauty of life makes him remark in an exaltation of crystalline purity:

> Y sentimos la vida pura,
> clara, real,
> cuando la envuelve la dulzura
> primaveral.

> [And we feel life to be pure, clear, genuine, when it is surrounded by spring-time sweetness.]

The Bacchic fervor of these words of Darío recalls to us Anacreon and Omar Khayyám:

> Gozad de la carne, ese bien
> que hoy nos hechiza
> y después se tornará en
> polvo y ceniza.
> Gozad del sol, de la pagana
> luz de sus fuegos;
> gozad del sol porque mañana
> estaréis ciegos.
> Gozad de la dulce armonía
> que Apolo invoca:
> gozad del canto, porque un día
> no tendréis boca.
> Gozad de la tierra, que un
> bien cierto encierra;
> gozad, porque no estáis aún
> bajo la tierra.

> [Enjoy the flesh, that treasure which bewitches us today and later will turn to dust and ashes. Enjoy the sun, the pagan light of its blaze; enjoy the sun, for tomorrow you will be blind. Enjoy the sweet harmony which Apollo invokes; enjoy singing, for one day you will

have no mouth. Enjoy the earth, which contains a positive good; enjoy the earth because you are not yet beneath it.]

We seem to catch glimpses of this modern poet of almost pagan sensuousness in a context of idyllic Grecian woodlands; we see him surrounded by nymphs and centaurs, oblivious of the Sphinx, yet heading fatally toward death, crowned with the laurel wreath and bearing the dove of Venus on his shoulder:

> En nosotros la vida vierte
> fuerza y calor.
> ¡Vamos al reino de la Muerte
> por el camino del Amor!

> [Life pours into us force and warmth. Let us go to the Kingdom of Death by the highway of Love.]

The day will yet come when we shall realize that this poem is worthy of comparison with the best in any literature, and that Darío was not only the superficial artisan of *Prosas profanas,* but the poet of depth, representative of the desires, the joys, and the anguish of his century. His **"Poema del otoño"** will remain the loftiest contribution of aesthetic sensibility from a continent which has inherited a great deal of the pagan temperament of Greece.

Only Góngora, that incomparable master of the lyric muse, equaled the great Nicaraguan poet in artistic agility in the Spanish language. It would seem impossible that the vigorous author of the **"Canto a la Argentina"** should be able to refine his poetic instrument, purify his prodigious wealth of expression, and sharpen his vision so ineffably; but in his **"Canción otoñal"** (**"Autumn Song"**) Darío's multiple gift, that capacity for emotional artistic adjustment which gives to his poetry its great variety, is clearly manifest; and we must confess that in purity of diction, in lightness of treatment, and in intimate harmony this poem is definitive. . . .

When Darío died in 1916, González Martínez had already proclaimed his defiance of the master; French iconoclastic poets were already known in America, and literary reform was clearly under way. In Spain, Juan Ramón Jiménez and Antonio Machado tried to forget the teachings of modernism and to create poetry reflecting their own lives. Miguel de Unamuno had given impetus to the reaction with his dry, tormented poetry, totally lacking in elegance and melody. José María Eguren had published some beautiful poems devoid of eloquence and of the superficial enhancement of music and color. Lugones was attempting by every means within his power to find a new literary orientation. José Juan Tablada almost accomplished this goal with his "hai kais" and his Japanese forms.

But after the death of Darío it was no longer a question of desire. Rather, the old masters were forced to yield their position to the renovators of the language and of poesy, to those who had never contracted the modernist vogue. And the field is dominated now by the Mexican López Velarde, by the Chilean Vicente Huidobro, the Peruvian

Valdelomar, the Argentinian Borges, and the Uruguayan Sabat Ercasty. In these writers, rebellion and originality are defining qualities—their reason for existence.

Synthesizing genius that he was, Darío could have been the leader of a new school if only he had not died exactly at the moment in which the great change was in process of formation. His last poems already give evidence of that zeal for novelty in which he had gloried during his youth. In his poem **"Caminos"** (**"Roads"**), for example, he approaches a patternless simplicity. . . .

In his last years Darío was intensely interested in Dante and especially devoted to the Bible. Attempting to express his apocalyptic visions, he veered toward the poetry of dreams. Rare combinations of images and reminiscences imbue it with the tone of mystery, the constant fluctuation between the visible world and the metaphysical, so essential to all great poetry. Here he ceases to be the diverse, sensational, voluptuous poet, fond of rapid shifts of sentimental states. Now he has found his source of moral and aesthetic unity, the former in an orthodox Catholicism, the latter in a bare form of rhetoric.

I recall here the words of the Spanish thinker Ramiro de Maeztu on Rubén Darío: "If, as he felt the dualism of pure form as opposed to impure, he had felt with the same perspicuity that of the pure life as opposed to the impure, Rubén would not be merely one of the greatest poets of our language, but another Milton (in my opinion, the greatest poet that the world has known), and his verses would reveal to men from now till the end of time the fount of life."

Actually, Rubén Darío was not far from that state of exaltation in which one goes through the world conscious of good and evil, of virtue and sin. He felt with absolute certainty the duality of life, and he expressed it in many poems. Nevertheless, only at the end of his life did he prefer the difficult road toward God, and then he followed it with fanatical ardor. In his poem **"Peregrinaciones"** (**"Peregrinations"**) he embarks on a long journey through the desolate shades of death. . . .

We have seen that the decorative, baroque style of Rubén Darío yielded before the sincerity of his poetic vision, becoming transformed into expression of perfect clarity. The monotonous rhythm based on regularity of accents effects the brusque movement inherent in the theme [of warfare in **"Pax"** (**"Peace"**)]. His very concept of poetry marks a definitive evolution, for Darío here abandons French or exotic themes in order to interpret his own suffering, his maladjustment, his ultimate faith in Christ, his constant awareness of the presence of death.

At the time of Darío's death that revolution in world literature . . . was already evident. Darío was neither the assailant of those new theories nor the defender of an obsolete aesthetic sensibility; on the contrary, more than one revolutionary poet was encouraged by the master.

Some critics assert that the true precursor of the lyrical vanguard was the Uruguayan poet Julio Herrera y Reissig.

This belief implies an error in vision. Herrera cultivated a form original to America but too close to the French model. Darío, on the other hand, possessed a formula of his own, developed in accord with his intimate artistic sense. He himself tells us: "My poetry is mine, within me." And that is why he once asked the young poets of America not to try to imitate him.

I have presented here a Darío whom few people know. The harmonious but cold poet of **Prosas profanas** has his well-defined place in our letters; the interpreter of the Spanish soul has been recognized by critics of the Iberian peninsula; Darío, composer of civic songs, has been called the "poet of America"; he has been studied as a classicist, as a romanticist, and as a modernist. The new Darío, whom I analyze here, though generally unknown in this aspect, may still be considered the greatest poet of the Spanish American continent.

C. M. Bowra (essay date 1951)

SOURCE: "Rubén Darío," in *Inspiration and Poetry,* Macmillan & Co. Ltd., 1955, pp. 242-64.

[*Bowra was an eminent English critic, literary scholar, and translator whose studies of classical and modern literature are known for their erudition, lucidity, and straightforward style. His books include* The Heritage of Symbolism *(1943) and* The Creative Experiment *(1949). In the following excerpt from the transcript of a lecture that was delivered in 1951, Bowra observes that Darío's fame may have exceeded his achievement, and suggests that the poet's aesthetic and literary goals likely hampered his natural talent.*]

Rubén Darío (1867–1916) presents a signal case of a man who had a remarkable influence on poetry but whose own achievement may seem in retrospect not fully to deserve its first renown. That he, more than anyone else, was responsible for the dazzling revival of Spanish poetry with the generation of 1898 is beyond question. At the time when Spain lost to the United States the last remnants of her once world-wide empire this stranger from Nicaragua brought a ringing message of confidence and a range of verbal melodies such as Spain had never heard before. His metrical innovations, his rippling, lucent language, his unquestioning devotion to his art, did something to comfort Spain for her territorial losses by providing her with a new poetry. Through him men of pre-eminent gifts like Antonio Machado and Juan Ramón Jiménez found their true selves and inaugurated an era of creative activity which lasted till the Civil War. Yet, great though Darío's influence undoubtedly was, its results were paradoxical. The poets whom he inspired reacted against his methods and were in no sense his disciples. There is no trace of his mellifluous ease in the Castilian austerity of Machado or the delicate impressionism of Jiménez. Nor has his reputation for originality weathered the years. It is true that he did something that had never been done before in Spanish and that he handled the language with a dexterity which

first shocked, and then enthralled, a generation which had come to believe that poetry was dying from inanition, but we can now see that much of his work was not ultimately original but a brilliant transposition into Spanish of French images and cadences. He absorbed with uncommon skill the most prominent qualities of French poetry from Hugo and Gautier to Mallarmé and Verlaine and presented them in an alluring Spanish dress, but the substance remained French. Even in this Gallicising task Darío was not influenced by those who were the greatest forces in the development of modern poetry. Rimbaud, Corbière, and Laforgue meant little or nothing to him, and though he was an ardent apostle of the Symbolists, we may doubt if he understood their essential aims. His achievement was largely derivative, and that no doubt is why he has lost some of his first glory.

It is not necessarily true that, because Darío's poetry is to some extent second-hand, it is therefore second-rate. European poetry presents many examples of men who have learned foreign manners and adapted them so skillfully and sincerely to their own languages that their work has a lasting appeal. The case against Darío is not so much that he derived his art from France as that he was too much concerned with the more superficial and more ephemeral qualities of his chosen masters. His metaphysical swans and butterflies, his Columbines and Pierrots, his figures from Greek myth, his *femmes fatales* like Herodias and Cleopatra, his scenes from Chinese vases and Japanese prints, his transposition of Catholic ritual to secular, erotic purposes, all betray their origins too candidly and suggest that Darío thought them to be essential elements of pure poetry, when in fact they were the fleeting fashions of an age whose other and richer resources escaped his attention. It is true that his debt to Verlaine was largely determined by a similarity of temperament, that Darío really had something of 'le pauvre Lelian' in his vagabond habits, his oscillations between gaiety and grief or between sin and repentance, and his childlike outlook on the world, but this similarity must not be pressed too far or made to justify too much. For Darío differed from Verlaine in several important respects. He was not a Parisian, not a European; he had nothing of Verlaine's cunning or love of mischief; his Catholicism was far less conscious and far less sophisticated; his literary training owed little to friends concerned with the same artistic problems as himself. If he was drawn to Verlaine by some similarity of personality and experience, he admired him chiefly because of his art. Much of Darío's poetry has lost its first appeal because, despite his unfailing technique, his excellent ear and abounding vitality, too much of it is concerned with matters which no longer touch us seriously but have passed into the limbo of lost curiosities.

Yet, when all this is said, something in Darío's work is still alive and compelling and undeniably serious; something still has more than a personal or historical interest and holds its own as original poetry. Amid all the flaunting stylishness, which has now rather faded, we come upon pieces which ring entirely true and have the authentic touch of a unique individual. But this individual has been misrepresented by false parallels and inapplicable standards.

It is easy to think of Darío as yet another gifted wastrel of the Nineties, a Bohemian genius, who wrecked his health with drink and trailed a sordid entourage of mistresses from one place to another, whose air of innocent candour was no more than the impertinence of an overgrown urchin, and whose lack of any central philosophy was the defiant gesture of a sceptical and defeated age. It is no less easy to treat him as the typical poet of Latin America, who turned to the mother country and to Paris, the capital of the world, because he believed that in them he could find roots and feel at home, and whose success in Europe was a tribute paid to a prodigal son who brought back to Spain some return for what she had spent in the extravagance of imperial expansion. Neither of these views is right. Darío was a Bohemian only because he came from a simpler, less organised, less departmental, and less self-conscious world. His self-indulgence was that of a child of nature confronted with unexpected opportunities for pleasure, and he found no difficulty in combining it with hard work and the friendship of the best Spaniards of his time. His lack of philosophy is the natural condition of a man who has given his first love to art in a country where art hardly exists, and who for that reason treasures it beyond everything else and feels no call to look outside it. Nor is he the national voice of Latin America. There were indeed times when he spoke nobly for it, but they were almost incidental. Spain and France meant quite as much to him as his own country, and the world of his dreaming fancies meant more than any of them. To see him in his right perspective we must remember that he was a stranger from an undeveloped land, that he had Indian blood in his veins and lacked the complexity and the sophistication which would belong to a European of his gifts and tastes. He differs from European poets of his time because he speaks for human nature at a very simple level and takes things as they come without shaping his life to a plan. Even his assumption of Parisian airs betrays his tropical love of bright colours and his desire to do the smart thing with rather too much emphasis and display.

Because Darío formed his art far away from Europe and saw in European models all that poetry ought to be, it was almost impossible for him to surrender gains which had been made at so much cost to himself and with so proud a sense of achievement. That no doubt is why he persisted almost to his death in writing verses which repeat the mannerisms of **Prosas profanas** (1896). This kind of poetry was not only an ingrained element in his life but a consolation for his personal troubles. If for long periods Darío retired into a secluded universe of dreams, he was well aware of it and not in the least ashamed. In his view this was all too natural and too necessary in a world which wounded and depressed him. . . .

That Darío should wish for an escape into imaginary worlds was natural enough. He was troubled not only by his own temperament but by the society into which he had been born. Those who saw in him a laureate of Latin America must have been painfully shocked when they read his poem **"A Colón,"** which he wrote in 1892 for the fifth centenary of the discovery of America by Columbus. For an occasion which might all too easily have been drenched in sentimental rhetoric Darío paints a melancholy, even tragic picture

of the New World which the great captain called into being. He dwells on its perpetual discords and wars, its perfidious ambitions and betrayed liberties, its destruction of ancient habits and its failure to put anything in their place. . . .

With this background behind him, and with all the music of French poetry in his head, Darío inevitably retired into fancies of his own making and was comforted by the thought that all over the world other poets were doing the same thing. He accepted from the start the view that poetry is an escape from the squalors of existence and must offer some harmonious alternative to them. When a poet does this, there is always a danger that his work will fail because it is insufficiently related to ordinary existence and lacks the substance which comes from a close contact with common life. When this poetry of escape succeeds, as it does in Coleridge's "Kubla Khan" or in Keats' "La Belle Dame sans merci," it is because the dream becomes a vehicle for something else which belongs to the waking consciousness, and expresses through forceful imagery what the considering mind expresses less happily through analytical abstractions. Poetry of this kind needs an intimate relation to events of every day and must appeal as a heightened, purified form of them. However ever mysterious and impalpable it may be, we must assume that it speaks of something intelligible and has a message of some importance. In the last resort the poetry of escape, of a search for an ideal order or a 'beyond', must reflect some deep need in ourselves and provide for it a satisfaction which is not mere dream or mere fancy but is more solid and more absorbing than what we find in the daily round. In this respect Darío often fails. Though his desire for escape was often prompted by powerful motives, he did not often write about it in its full strength, but disguised it in the imaginary scenes in which his fancy delighted but which were liable to omit much of the experience which preceded their creation. Indeed these scenes are some times insufficiently imagined. Neither by temperament nor by conviction was Darío really fitted to follow Mallarmé in his search for a mystical or ideal 'beyond'. He felt that he was committed to a search, but he did not always know what he sought, and was liable to be led astray by his august masters and to feel that quite ordinary objects of desire were more remarkable than they actually are. . . .

The dualism of Darío's character and life made it difficult for him to put the whole of himself into any single poem. Yet if he was to realise the full promise of his gifts, this was necessary, as he himself knew. Between dream and despair, between order and chaos, he had to find some compromise or adjustment. This was in the main a question for his art. In his own life he could turn to his Catholicism and find the consolation and the forgiveness which he required. Towards the end of his life, when the First World War brought home to him the hideous anarchy of human society, he resorted more consciously to his faith and shaped it into a more coherent structure. But this did not affect his poetry very profoundly. His last poems have indeed a touching simplicity, but they lack his earlier force and suggest that in his years his creative impulse had begun to lose some of its drive. But in the heyday of his powers, though sometimes he wrote poems of an exquisite and lucid

Christianity, as when he describes the angelus in the dawn or tells of the Three Wise Men, these are not very close to his which he faced his troubles with courage and candour and saw that what he found in himself something that permeated the whole world and deserved to be spoken of with all the sincerity that he could summon. By an apt choice of a subject which illustrated his own discords he was able to give his complete self to poetry and to show of what scope he was capable. . . .

It was Darío's fortune to be born at a time when the poetry of his own language had nothing to teach him, and he turned for help and inspiration to France. He found them indeed in abundance, and they made him a poet. Yet he was not altogether lucky in this, since his simple, natural character was better suited to a less elaborate, less sophisticated, and less ambitious art. His French schooling imposed on his extremely receptive spirit a manner which he wore with a remarkable brilliance and variety but which at times his inner life forced him to modify or to reject. This hampered the development of his talents and made him seem a minor disciple of the Symbolist school, when he might well have been something more original. More than this, his French attachments strengthened him in his desire for escape and his cult of dreams. Yet just because he cherished this, it provoked a conflict in him which was responsible for his best work, whether he spoke from the depths of melancholy about his falls from imaginative grace or wove together all the strands of his passionate personality into enchanting patterns of song.

On Darío's accomplishment as a poet:

As a prosodist, Rubén Darío is unique in Spanish. He is the poet who has mastered the greatest variety of verse forms. . . . Darío, and the *modernist* groups which sprang into action mainly through his stimulus, gave vogue, and finally permanence, to a large number of metrical forms: either verses rarely used, like the enneasyllabic and the dodecasyllabic (of which there are three types), or verses, like the alexandrine, to which Darío gave greater musical virtue by freeing the accent and the cæsura. Even the hendecasyllable acquired new flexibility when Darío brought back two new forms of accentuation that had been used by Spanish poets during three centuries but had been forgotten since about 1800. He also attacked the problem of the classic hexameter, which has tempted many great modern poets, from Goethe to Swinburne and Carducci, and, before these, a few of the Spanish in the XVIIth century, chiefly Villegas. He introduced, finally, the modern *vers libre,* the type in which the number of feet, but not the foot, changes (as in the **"Marcha triunfal"**), as well as the type in which both the number of syllables and the foot vary frequently.

Pedro Henríquez Ureña, in his introduction to Eleven Poems of Rubén Darío, *translated by Thomas Walsh and Salomón de la Selva, 1916.*

Octavio Paz (essay date 1965)

SOURCE: "The Siren and the Seashell," in *The Siren & the Seashell, and Other Essays on Poets and Poetry,* translated by Lysander Kemp and Margaret Sayers Peden, University of Texas Press, 1976, pp. 17-56.

[*A preeminent Mexican literary figure, Paz has earned international acclaim for works in which he seeks to reconcile divisive forces in human life. His works also reflect his knowledge of the history, myths, and landscape of Mexico as well as his interest in Surrealism, existentialism, Romanticism, Oriental thought—particularly Buddhism—and diverse political ideologies. In the following excerpt from an essay that was originally published in 1965, Paz discusses the Modernist context of Darío's poetry, commenting on its fundamental themes, sources, and archetypes.*]

Every language, not excluding that of liberty, eventually becomes a prison, and there is a point in the process at which speed becomes confused with immobility. The great Modernist poets were the first to rebel, and in their mature work they go beyond the language that they themselves had created. Therefore, each in his own way prepared for the subversion of the vanguard: Leopoldo Lugones was the immediate antecedent of the new poetry in Mexico (Ramón López Velarde) and Argentina (Jorge Luis Borges); Juan Ramón Jiménez was the guiding spirit of the generation of Jorge Guillén and Federico García Lorca; Ramón del Valle-Inclán is a presence in the modern theater and will daily become more influential. Darío's place is central, even if one believes, as I do, that of the great Modernists he is least a presence. He is not a living force but a point of reference, a point of departure or arrival, a boundary that has to be reached or crossed. To be like him or not: either way, Darío is present in the spirit of contemporary poets. He is the founder. . . .

Beginning in 1888, Darío used the word "Modernism" to designate the tendencies of the Spanish American poets. In 1898 he wrote: "The new spirit that today animates a small but proud and triumphant group of Spanish American writers and poets: Modernism." Later he would say "the moderns," "modernity." During his long and extensive activities as a critic he never stopped repeating that the distinctive characteristic of the new poets, their reason for being, was the will to be modern. Somewhat as the term "vanguard" is a metaphor revealing a conception of literary activities as warfare, the term "Modernist" reveals a kind of ingenuous faith in the superiority of the future or, to be more exact, of the present. The first implies a spatial vision of literature; the second, a temporal conception. The vanguard wants to conquer a location; Modernism seeks to locate itself in the present. Only those who feel that they are not wholly in the present, who sense that they are outside of living history, postulate contemporaneity as a goal. To be a contemporary of Goethe or Tamerlane is a coincidence, happy or otherwise, in which one's will plays no part; to desire to be their contemporary implies a will to participate, intellectually, in the actions of history, to share a history that belongs to others but that one somehow makes one's own. It is an affinity and a distance—and an awareness of that situation. The Modernists did not want to be French: they wanted to be modern. Technological progress had partially eliminated the distance between America and Europe. That nearness made our remoteness more vivid and perceptible. A trip to Paris or London was not a visit to another continent but a leap to another century. It has been said that Modernism was an evasion of American realities. It would be more accurate to say that it was a flight from the local present—which was, in their eyes, an anachronism—and a search for the universal present, which is the only true one. Modernity and cosmopolitanism were synonymous to Rubén Darío and his friends. They were not anti-Latin American; they wanted a Latin America that would be contemporaneous with Paris and London. . . .

Although the Modernists sang of the perpetual advent of the now, of its embodiment in this or that glorious or terrible form, their time marked time; it ran, but without moving. It lacked a future because it had been deprived of a past. Modernism was an aesthetic of luxury and death, a nihilistic aesthetic. However, that nihilism was more lived than assumed, more an affliction of the sensibilities than a confrontation by the spirit. A few of the Modernists, Darío first, recognized that the movement was simply a spin in the void, a mask with which the despairing consciousness both calmed and exacerbated itself. Their search, when it really was a search and not mere dissipation, was nostalgia for an origin. Man pursues his own self when he runs after this or that phantom: he seeks his beginning. Almost as soon as Modernism began to contemplate itself, it ceased to exist as a tendency. The collective adventure reached its end and individual exploration began. It was the supreme moment of the Modernist passion, the instant of lucidity that was also the instant of death.

Search for an origin, recovery of an inheritance: it might seem that nothing could be more unlike the earliest tendencies of the movement. In 1896, filled with reformist zeal, Darío cried: "The new American poets who write in Spanish have had to move swiftly from the mental independence of Spain . . . to the current that today, throughout the world, unites those distinguished groups that make up the cultivation and the life of a cosmopolitan and universal art." Unlike the Spaniards, Darío did not place the universal in opposition to the cosmopolitan; on the contrary, he held that the new art was universal because it was cosmopolitan. It was the art of the great city. Modern society, he said, "builds a Tower of Babel in which everyone understands everyone else." (I am not sure that the same is true in the new Babels, but contemporary reality, as one can see from the history of twentieth-century artistic movements, confirms Darío's view of the cosmopolitan character of modern art.) His opposition to Hispanism was a part of his love for modernity, and thus his criticism of the tradition was a criticism of Spain. His anti-Spanish attitude had a dual origin. On the one hand, it expressed a determination to break away from the ancient metropolis: "Our movement has given us a place apart, independent of Castilian literature." On the other, it identified Hispanism with traditionalism: "The evolution that brought Castilian to this renascence had to take place in America, since Spain is walled about by tradition, fenced and bristling with Hispanism."

Darío's place is central, even if one believes, as I do, that of the great Modernists he is least a presence. He is not a living force but a point of reference, a point of departure or arrival, a boundary that has to be reached or crossed. To be like him or not: either way, Darío is present in the spirit of contemporary poets.

—Octavio Paz

Modernism, a verbal reform, was a syntax, a prosody, a vocabulary. Its poets enriched the language with imports from French and English; they made excessive use of archaisms and neologisms; and they were the first to employ the language of conversation. Furthermore, it is often forgotten that the Modernists' poems contain a great many Americanisms and indigenisms. Their cosmopolitanism could include both the achievements of the French naturalistic novel and American linguistic forms. A part of their lexicon has become as dated as the furniture and other objects of Art Nouveau; the rest has entered the mainstream of the language. Instead of attacking the syntax of Castilian, the Modernists restored its naturalness and avoided Latinate inversions and overemphasis. They exaggerated rather than inflated; they were often slightly ridiculous but never rigid. In spite of their swans and gondolas, they gave Spanish poetry a flexibility and familiarity that were never vulgar and that would lend themselves admirably to the two main tendencies of contemporary poetry: a love for the unexpected image and for poetic prosaicness. . . .

Because of his age, Rubén Darío was the bridge from the initiators to the second Modernist generation; his travels and his generous activities made him the point of connection for the many scattered poets and groups on two continents; he not only inspired and captained the battle, he was also its spectator and its critic—its conscience; and the evolution of his poetry, from *Azul* [*Blue*] (1888) to *Poema del otoño y otros poemas* [*Poem of autumn and other poems*] (1910), corresponds to the evolution of the movement: it began with him and ended with him. But Darío's work did not end with Modernism: it surpassed it, went beyond the language of that school and, in fact, beyond that of any school. It is a creation, something that belongs more to the history of poetry than to the history of styles. Darío was not only the richest and most ample of the Modernist poets: he was also one of our great modern poets. He was the beginning. At times he makes one think of Poe; at other times, of Whitman. Of the first, in that portion of his work in which he scorns the world of the

Americas and is preoccupied solely by an otherworldly music; of the second, in that portion in which he expresses his vitalist affirmation, his pantheism, and his belief that he was, in his own right, the bard of Latin America as Whitman was of Anglo-America. In contrast to Poe, Darío did not enclose himself within his own spiritual adventure; neither did he have Whitman's ingenuous faith in progress and brotherhood. More than to the two great North Americans, he could be compared to Hugo: eloquence, abundance, and that continuous surprise, that unending flow, of rhyme. Like the French poet's, his inspiration was that of the cyclopean sculptor; his stanzas are blocks of animated matter, veined with sudden delicacies: the striation of lightning on the stone. And the rhythm, the continuous swing that makes the language one enormous aquatic mass. Darío was less excessive and prophetic; he was also less valiant: he was not a rebel and he did not propose to write the Bible of the modern era. His genius was lyric, and he professed a horror of both miniaturism and titanism. More nervous, more anguished, he oscillated between contradictory impulses: one could say that he was a Hugo attacked by "decadent" ills. Despite the fact that he loved and imitated Verlaine above all (and above all others), his best poems have little resemblance to those of his model. He had superabundant health and energy; his sun was stronger, his wine more generous. Verlaine was a provincial Parisian; Darío a Central American globetrotter. His poetry is virile: skeleton, heart, sex. Clear and rotund even when it is sad; no halftones. His work, born at the very end of the century, is that of a Romantic who was also a Parnassian and a Symbolist. Parnassian: nostalgia for sculpture; Symbolist: prescience of analogy. A hybrid, not only because of the variety of spiritual influences, but also because of the bloods that flowed through his veins: Indian, Spanish, and a few drops of African. A rare being, a pre-Columbian idol, a hippogriff. In America, both the Anglo and our own, these graftings and superimpositions are frequent. America is one great appetite for *being* and, for that reason, a historical monster. Modern beauty and the most ancient beauty, are they not monstrous? Darío knew that better than anyone: he felt that he was a contemporary of both Moctezuma and Roosevelt-Nimrod. . . .

In 1888 he published *Azul*. With that book, composed of stories and poems, Modernism was officially born. The prose, especially, was disconcerting, more daring than the poetry. In the second edition (1890), Darío reestablished the balance with the publication of several new poems: sonnets in alexandrines (an alexandrine never heard before in Spanish), others in different twelve-syllable lines, and another in a strange and rich meter of sixteen syllables. It was not only the unusual rhythms but also the brilliance of the words, the insolence of the tone, and the sensuality of the phrasing that irritated and bewitched. The title was almost a manifesto: was it an echo of Mallarmé ("Je suis hanté! L'azur, l'azur, l'azur, l'azur") or the crystallization of something that was in the air at the time? Max Henríquez Ureña points out that Manuel Gutiérrez Nájera had already demonstrated a similar fascination with colors. A spreading fan of preference and paths to follow. In *Azul* there are five "medallions" in the manner

of Heredia, dedicated to Leconte de Lisle, Mendès, Whitman, J. J. Palma, and Díaz Mirón; there is also a sonnet to Caupolicán, the first of a series of poems on "undiscovered America." All Darío: the French masters, Latin American contemporaries, pre-Hispanic civilizations, the shadow of the Yankee eagle ("The great old man lives in his iron country . . ."). In its time *Azul* was a prophetic book; today it is a historical relic. But there is one thing: a poem that is, for me, the first poem Darío wrote: I mean the first that is really a creation, a work. It is called **"Venus."** Every one of its lines is as sinuous and fluid as water seeking its path in the "profound extension" (because the night is not high, but deep). A black-and-white poem, a palpitating space in whose center opens the great sexual flower, "like a golden and divine jasmine inlaid in ebony." The final line is one of the most penetrating in our poetry: "Venus, from the abyss, looked at me with a sad gaze." Height becomes abyss and, from there, woman, fixed vertigo, watches us. . . .

In Buenos Aires he found what he had been searching for. Vivacity, cosmopolitanism, luxury. Between the pampas and the sea, between barbarism and the European mirage, Buenos Aires was a city more suspended in time than seated in space. Rootlessness but, at the same time, desire to invent itself, tension of creating its own present and its future tradition. The young writers had made the new aesthetic their own, and they crowded around Darío the moment he arrived. He was the indisputable leader. Years of agitation, polemics, and dissipation: the editorial room, the restaurant, the bar. Fervent friendships: Leopoldo Lugones, Ricardo Jaimes Freyre. Years of creation: *Los raros* and *Prosas profanas,* both in 1896. *Los raros* was the vade mecum of the new literature; *Prosas profanas* was and is the book that best defines the early Modernism: high noon, ne plus ultra of the movement. After *Prosas profanas* all openings closed: he must trim his sails or make the leap toward the unknown. Rubén Darío chose the former and reworked already known territory; Leopoldo Lugones risked the latter. Darío's *Cantos de vida y esperanza* [*Songs of life and hope*] (1905) and Lugones's *Lunario sentimental* [*Sentimental almanac*] (1909) are the two most important works of the second phase of Modernism, and from them derive, directly or indirectly, all the experiences and experiments of modern Spanish poetry.

Prosas profanas: the title, halfway between erudite and sacrilegious, caused even more irritation than that of the earlier book. To call a collection of predominantly erotic poems *prosas*—hymns that are sung at High Mass, following the gospel—was more than an archaism, it was a challenge. In addition, the title demonstrates a deliberate confusion between the vocabulary of the liturgy and that of pleasure. This persistent inclination, in Darío and other poets, is far from a caprice: it is one of the signs of the alternating fascination and repulsion that modern poetry experiences regarding traditional religion. The preface caused a scandal: it seemed to be written in another language, and everything it said sounded like paradox. Love of novelty, on condition that it not be of the present time; exaltation of the self and disdain for the majority; supremacy of the dream over the waking state and of art over reality; horror of progress, technology, and democracy ("If there is poetry in our America, it is in the ancient things, in Palenque and in Utatlán, in the legendary Indian, in the sensual and refined Inca, and in the great Moctezuma of the golden chair. The rest is yours, democratic Walt Whitman"); ambivalence, love, and mockery in regard to the Spanish past ("Grandfather, I must say it: my wife is from my country; my lover, from Paris"). Among all these declarations—clearsighted or impertinent, ingenuous or affected—those of an aesthetic nature stand out. First: the freedom of art and its gratuitousness; second, the negation of all schools, not excluding his own: "My literature is mine, in me; whoever slavishly follows my footsteps will lose his own personal treasure"; and rhythm: "As each word has a soul, there is in every verse, in addition to its verbal harmony, an ideal melody. Music, many times, comes only from the idea."

Formerly he had said that things have souls; now he says that words also have them. Language is an animate world and verbal music is the music of souls (Mallarmé had written: of the Idea). If things have souls, the universe is sacred; its order is that of music and dance, a concert formed of the harmonies, joinings, and separations of one thing with another, of one spirit with others. To this idea, as ancient as man man and always viewed with distrust by Christianity, modern poets add another: words have souls and the order of language is that of the universe: dance, harmony. Language is a magic double of the cosmos. Through poetry, language recovers its original being, becomes music again. Thus, ideal music does not mean the music of ideas but rather ideas that are in their essence music. Ideas in the Platonic sense, realities of realities. Ideal harmony: soul of the world; in its breast all things, all beings, are one same thing, one same soul. But language, although it is sacred by reason of participating in the musical animation of the universe, is also discord. Like man, it is contingency: the word is music and meaning at the same time. The distance between the name and the thing named, the meaning, is a consequence of the separation between man and the world. Language is the expression of consciousness of self, which is consciousness of the fall. Through the wound of meaning the whole being that is the poem bleeds and becomes prose: description and interpretation of the world. Despite the fact that Darío did not formulate his thought in exactly these terms, all his poetry and his attitude toward life reveal the tension of his spirit between the two extremes of the word: music and meaning. Through the first, the poet is "of the race that creates life with the Pythagorean numbers"; through the second, he has "the awareness of our human slime.". . .

In addition to several perfect poems and many unforgettable fragments, there is a grace and vitality in *Prosas profanas* that still charm us. It is still a young book. They criticize its artificialities and its affectations: have they noticed the exquisite and at the same time direct tone of the phrasing, a knowing mixture of erudition and conversation? Solemnity and pathos had numbed the muscles of Spanish poetry: with Rubén Darío, the language began to stride again. His poetry was the prelude to contemporary poetry, direct, spoken. It will soon be time to read that admirable and frivolous book with new eyes. Admirable because there is no poem that does not contain at least one impeccable or disturbing line, the fatal vibration of true poetry, music of this world, music of other worlds, always familiar and always strange. Frivolous because its manner is close to mannerism and its facility defeats its inspiration. Contortions, pirouettes: nothing to criticize in those exercises if the poet had danced them on the edge of the abyss. A book without abysses. And nevertheless . . .

Pleasure is the central theme of *Prosas profanas*. But pleasure, precisely because it is a game, is a rite from which sacrifice and pain are not excluded. "Dandyism," said Baudelaire, "borders on stoicism." The religion of pleasure is a rigorous religion. I would not reproach Darío for the hedonism of *Prosas profanas,* rather for its superficiality. Aesthetic exigency is not converted into spiritual rigor. On the other hand, passion glows in the best moments of the book, "black light that is more light than white light." Woman fascinates him. She takes all natural forms: hill, tiger, ivy, sea, dove; she dresses in water and fire, and, for her, nudity itself is vestment. She is a font of images: in bed she "becomes a curled-up cat," and as she loosens her hair "two swans with black necks" peer from beneath her blouse. She is the embodiment of the "other" religion: "Somnambulist with the soul of Eloise, in her there is the sacred frequency of the altar." She is the sensitive presence of that single and plural totality in which history and nature are fused:

. . . fatal, cosmopolitan,
universal, immense, unique, one
and all; mysterious and erudite;
she—sea and cloud, spume and wave—loves me.

Darío's eroticism is passionate. What he feels is perhaps not love for a single being but the attraction, in the astronomical sense of the word, of that incandescent star that is the apogee of all presences and their dissolution in black light. In his splendid "**Coloquio de los centauros**" ["**Colloquy of the centaurs**"], sensuality is transformed into passionate reflection: "All form is a gesture, a cipher, an enigma." The poet hears "the words of the mist," and the stones themselves speak to him. Venus, "queen of matrixes," rules in this universe of sexual hieroglyphics. She is All. Good and evil do not exist: "Neither is the wild pigeon benign, nor the crow perverse: they are forms of the enigma." Throughout his life Darío oscillated "between the cathedral and the pagan ruins," but his true religion was this blending of pantheism and doubt, exaltation and sadness, jubilation and fear. Poet of the astonishment of being.

The final poem of *Prosas profanas,* in my opinion the most beautiful in the book, is a résumé of his aesthetic and a prophecy of the future direction of his poetry. The themes of "**Coloquio de los centauros**" and other fine compositions here assume extraordinary density. The first line of the sonnet is a definition of his poetry: "I seek a form my style cannot discover." He seeks a beauty that is beyond beauty, that words can evoke but can never state.

All of Romanticism—the desire to grasp the infinite—is in that line; and all of Symbolism—an ideal, indefinable beauty that can only be suggested. That form, more rhythm than body, is feminine. It is nature and it is woman:

> The white peristyle is adorned with green palm
> trees;
> the stars have predicted that I shall see the goddess;
> and my soul reposes within the light, as the bird
> of the moon reposes upon the tranquil lake.

It is scarcely necessary to point out that these superb alexandrines recall those of "Delfica: Reconnais-tu le TEMPLE au péristyle immense . . ." The same faith in the stars and the same atmosphere of orphic mystery. Darío's lines evoke that "state of supernatural delirium" in which Gérard de Nerval was said to have composed his sonnets. In the sestet there is an abrupt change of tone. Doubt follows the certainty of the vision:

> and I find only the word that flies away,
> the melodious initiation that flows from the flute . . .

A feeling of sterility and impotence—I was going to write, of indignity—appears constantly in Darío, as in the other great poets of the epoch, from Baudelaire to Mallarmé. It is the critical consciousness, which at times resolves into irony and at others into silence. In the final line the poet sees the world as an immense question: it is not man who questions existence; it is existence that questions man. The line is worth the whole poem, as the poem is worth the whole book: "And the neck of the great white swan, that questions me.". . .

Although *Cantos de vida y esperanza* is his best book, the books that follow it continue in the same vein and contain poems that are equal to those of that collection. Thus, all these publications can be seen as a single book or, more exactly, as the uninterrupted flow of various simultaneous poetic currents. There is no break between *Prosas profanas* and *Cantos de vida y esperanza*. New themes appear, he expresses himself more soberly, more profoundly, but his love for the brilliant word does not diminish. Nor does his taste for rhythmic innovation disappear; on the contrary, these innovations are surer and more daring. Verbal plenitude, as much in the free verse as in those admirable re-creations of baroque rhetoric that comprise the sonnets of **"Trébol"** [**"Clover"**]: freedom, fluidity, continuous surprise of a language in perpetual movement, and, above all, communication between the written and the spoken language, as in the **"Epístola"** [**"Epistle"**] to the wife of Lugones, indisputable antecedent to what would be one of the conquests of contemporary poetry: the fusion of literary language and city speech. In sum, the originality of *Cantos de vida y esperanza* does not imply negation of the earlier period; it is a natural change, what Darío defines as "the profound work of an hour, the labor of a minute, and the prodigy of a year." Ambiguous portents, like those of the time.

The first poem in *Cantos de vida y esperanza* is a confession and a declaration. Defense of (and elegy for) his youth: "Was youth mine?"; exaltation and critique of his aesthetic: "The ivory tower tempted my desire"; revelation of the conflict that divides him and affirmation of his destiny as a poet: "Hunger for space and thirst for the heavens." The duality that manifests itself in *Prosas profanas* in aesthetic terms—the form that pursues and does not find its style—is now shown in its human truth: it is a schism of the soul. In order to express it, Darío uses images that burst almost spontaneously from what could be called his cosmology, if one understands by this not a system of thought but his instinctive vision of the universe. The sun and the sea rule the movement of his imagination; every time he looks for a symbol that defines the oscillations of his being, either aerial or aquatic space appears. To the first belong the heavens, light, stars, and, by analogy or sympathetic magic, the supersensitive half of the universe: the incorruptible and nameless region of ideas, music, numbers. The second is the domain of the blood, the heart, the sea, wine, woman, passions, and, also by magic contagion, the jungle, its animals and its monsters. Thus he compares his heart to a sponge saturated with the salt of the sea, and immediately after he compares it to a fountain in the center of a sacred jungle. That jungle is ideal or celestial: it is made not of trees but of harmony. It *is* harmony. Art extends a bridge between universes: the leaves and branches of the forest are transformed into musical instruments. Poetry is reconciliation, immersion in the "harmony of the great All." At the same time it is purification: "The soul that enters there should enter naked." For Darío poetry is practical or magical knowledge, a vision that is in itself a fusion of the cosmic duality. But there is no poetic creation without asceticism or spiritual combustion: "The star shines because of its nakedness." Darío's aesthetic is a kind of Orphism that does not exclude Christ (though it admits him as nostalgia rather than presence) or any of man's other vital and spiritual experiences. Poetry: totality and transfiguration.

A change of perspective corresponds to the change in the center of gravity. If the tone is deeper, the outlook is broader. History appears in its two forms: as living tradition and as struggle. *Prosas profanas* contains more than one allusion to Spain; the new books exalt it. Darío was never anti-Spanish, although the provincialism and conceit of Spain at the end of the century irritated him, as they did the majority of Latin Americans. But poetic renovation, at first received with distrust, had now conquered the young Spanish poets; at the same time, a new generation was initiating a rigorous and passionate examination of Spanish reality. Darío was not insensitive to this change, a change in which, incidentally, his influence had not been unimportant. And, lastly, his European experience had revealed to him the historical loneliness of the Spanish American. Divided by the harshness of geography and by the obtuse governments that prevailed in our countries, we were isolated from the world and also separated from our own history. This situation has scarcely changed today; and we know that the sensation of aloneness in space and time, the permanent basis of our being, becomes more painful outside our own countries. In the same way, contact with other Latin Americans, lost like us in the great modern cities, makes us immediately rediscover an identity that extends beyond the present artificial boundaries imposed by the combination of external power and internal oppression. Darío's generation was the first to be aware of this situation, and many of the Modernist writers and poets wrote passionate defenses of our civilization and attacks against imperialism. Darío abhorred politics, but the years of living in Europe, in a world indifferent to or disdainful of our own, caused him to turn his eyes toward Spain. He saw something more than the past in it, a still forceful element that gave unity to our disperseness. His vision of Spain was not exclusive: it embraced the pre-Columbian civilizations and the present of independence. Without either imperialist or colonialist nostalgia, the poet spoke with the same enthusiasm of the Incas, the conquistadors, and the heroes of our independence. He exalted the past but was distressed by Hispanic prostration, by the lethargy of our peoples, interrupted only by shudders of blind violence. He knew us to be weak and he looked with fear toward the north.

In those years, the United States, on the eve of becoming a world power, extended and consolidated its dominance in Latin America. In order to achieve this it used all measures—from Pan American diplomacy to the "big stick"—in a not infrequent mixture of cynicism and hypocrisy. Darío spoke out almost in spite of himself: "I am not a poet of the masses, but I know that unfailingly I must go to them." His anti-imperialism was not nurtured in the themes of political radicalism. He did not see the United States as the embodiment of capitalism nor did he conceive of the drama of Spanish America as a conflict of economic and social interests. The decisive element was the conflict between dissimilar civilizations in different historical periods: the United States was the youngest, most aggressive vanguard of a current—Nordic, Protestant, and pragmatic—in full ascent; our peoples, heirs of two ancient civilizations, were going through a period of decline. Darío did not close his eyes to Anglo-American greatness—he admired Poe, Whitman, and Emerson—but he refused to accept the possibility that that civilization was superior to our own. In the poem **"To Roosevelt"** he poses the progress-oriented optimism of the Yankees ("You think that . . . the future is wherever / your bullet strikes. No.") against a reality that is not of a material order: the Spanish American soul. It is not a dead soul: "It dreams, vibrates, loves." It is significant that none of these verbs designates political virtues: justice, liberty, energy. The Spanish American soul is a soul secluded in spheres that have little or nothing to do with human society: dreaming, loving, and vibrating are words that designate aesthetic, passional, and religious states. It was an attitude typical of the Modernist generation: José Enrique Rodó opposed Latin aesthetic idealism to Anglo-American pragmatism. These cursory definitions make us smile today. They seem superficial to us. And they are. But in them, in spite of their naïveté and the rhetorical presumption with which they were enunciated, there is something that modern ideologues do not suspect. . . .

Rubén Darío shared the feelings of the greater part of Latin America. In addition, he was not a political thinker and his character was flexible: neither in public nor in private life was he a model of strictness. Hence it is not strange that in 1906, on attending the Pan American Conference at Rio de Janeiro as a delegate of his country, he wrote **"Salutación al águila"** [**"Greetings to the eagle"**]. This poem, which celebrates something more than collaboration between the two Americas, might make us doubt his sincerity. We would be unjust: he was honorable in his understandable and spontaneous enthusiasm. It did not last long. He himself confesses this in his **"Epístola"** to Lugones's wife: "In Rio de Janeiro . . . I panamericanized / with a vague fear and very little faith." Proof of his supreme indifference toward political consistency: both poems appeared, a few pages apart, in the same book. . . .

All the work of Rubén Darío is bathed in a great sexual wave. He sees the world as duality, comprised of continuous opposition and copulation between masculine and feminine principles. The verb "love" is universal and to conjugate it is to practice the supreme science: it is not a knowledge of wisdom but of creation. But it would be futile to search for that passionate concentration that becomes an incandescent fixed point in his eroticism. His passion is disperse and tends to mingle with the fluctuation of the sea. In a very well known poem he confesses: "Plural has been the celestial / story of my heart." A strange adjective: if by "celestial" we mean that love that leads us to see in the loved one a reflection of the divine essence of the Idea, *his* passion does not easily respond to the qualifying word. Perhaps another acceptance of the word would be appropriate: his heart does not nourish itself from a vision of the motionless sky, but instead obeys the movement of the stars. The tradition of our love poetry, Provençal or Platonic, conceives of the loved one as reflected reality; the ultimate goal of love is not the carnal embrace, but contemplation, a prologue to the nuptials between the human soul and the spirit. That passion is a passion for unity. Darío aspires to the opposite: he wants to dissolve, body and soul, into the body and soul of the world. The story of his heart is plural in two senses: because of the number of women he loved and because of his fascination with the pluralism of the cosmos. For the Platonic poet the apprehension of reality is a gradual transition from the various to the one; love consists in the progressive disappearance of the apparent heterogeneity of the universe. Darío perceived this heterogeneity as the proof or manifestation of unity: every form is a complete world and, at the same time, is a part of totality. Unity is not one; it is a universe of universes, moved by erotic gravity: instinct, passion. Darío's eroticism is a magic vision of the world. . . .

The academic critic has generally preferred to close his eyes to the current of occultism that pervades Darío's work. This silence damages comprehension of his poetry. It is a question of a central current that constitutes a system of thought and also a system of poetic associations. It is his idea of the world or, rather, his image of the world. Like other modern creators who have used the same symbols, Darío transforms the "occult tradition" into vision and word. In a sonnet not collected in a volume during his lifetime, he confesses: "Pythagoras read the constellations.

/ I read the Pythagorean constellations." In the "confusion of his soul" his obsession with Pythagoras is mixed with his obsession with Orpheus, and both are mixed with the theme of the double. Duality now takes the form of personal conflict: who and what is he? He knows that he is "a felon, since the time of paradise"; he knows that he "stole fire and stole harmony," that he "is two inside himself," and that he "always wishes to be 'other.'" He knows that he is an enigma. And the answer to this enigma is another:

> The golden turtle on the sand shows me
> where he conducts the chorus of the Muses
> and where the will of God augustly triumphs. . . .

In **"Poema del otoño"** [**"Poem of autumn"**], one of his last and greatest creations, the two currents that nourish his poetry join together: meditations on death and pantheistic eroticism. The poem is presented as variations upon the old and exhausted theme of the brevity of life, the flower of the instant, and other such commonplaces; at the end, the tone becomes graver and more defiant: in the face of death the poet affirms, not his own life, but that of the universe. Earth and sun vibrate within his skull as if it were a seashell; the salt of the sea, the vitality of sirens and tritons, mixes with his blood; to die is to live a greater and more powerful life. Did he really believe that? It is true that he feared death; it is also true that he loved and desired it. Death was his Medusa and his siren. Dualistic death, like everything else he touched, saw, and sang. Unity is always duple. That is why, as Juan Ramón Jiménez saw, his emblem is the seashell, silent but swelling with sounds, infinity that fits into one hand. . . .

In 1914, with Europe at war, Darío returned to his native land. In addition to his physical and spiritual ailments, he was now suffering from financial difficulties. He conceived the idea of making a lecture tour throughout North America, assisted by a fellow countryman who was to serve as his business manager. He fell sick in New York and his companion deserted him. Mortally ill, he went to Guatemala. There the implacable Rosario Murillo [Darío's second wife] gathered him up and took him to Nicaragua. He died in her house on February 6, 1916. "The seashell is in the shape of a heart." It was both his living breast and his dead skull.

The Times Literary Supplement (essay date 1968)

SOURCE: "Master of Hispanic Modernism," in *The Times Literary Supplement,* No. 3459, June 13, 1968, p. 620.

[*In the following excerpt, the critic assesses Darío's career and literary influence, concluding that he "remains one of the most talked of and least understood of Latin American poets."*]

At the height of his career, the Nicaraguan poet, Rubén Darío, bestrode the Atlantic like a colossus. Although born in a remote corner of Central America, this most provincial of provincials was to become the focus of literary life in Central America, in Chile, in Buenos Aires and finally in Madrid; and the outstanding representative of the Modernist movement which ended the provincialism of nineteenth-century Hispanic literature and brought it into the mainstream of western culture.

Darío's success as a poet is inseparable from his personal history. From the moment when—still in his early teens—he was taken from León to the Nicaraguan capital of Managua, each new city broadened his opportunities and brought to bear increasingly sophisticated influences on his poetry. The poems of *Azul* (1888), published in Chile, were late romantic in style. The poems of *Prosas profanas* (1896) in which Parnassian and Symbolist contours can be traced, were mostly written in Buenos Aires; in *Cantos de vida y esperanza* (1905), published in Madrid, we have the self-assured prophet who had reached the goal dreamed of by many Latin Americans—the literary reconquest of Spain. If the note of inner anguish is evident in this collection and in the subsequent *El canto errante* (1907), perhaps this was only natural in a man who had achieved everything he set out to do except the discovery of his own soul. Not only his poetry but also all the articles, letters and essays which poured from his pen evidence his extraordinary powers of assimilation. They pulse with the beat of the moment, now with the names of Marx or Nietzsche, now with those of Léon Bloy or Zola, now Gambetta and Gladstone. Every durable and fleeting *fin-de-siècle* reputation is to be found in them. Those not familiar with the relationship between Latin American and European culture might be forgiven for seeing in Darío little more than a clever mime gesturing in the manner of Catulle Mendès, Hugo, Verlaine or Leconte de Lisle.

The suspicions are deepened when we observe the disparate roles he assumed and discarded in the course of his life. Friend of the poor and oppressed when in Chile, in Buenos Aires his sympathies with the workers wavered at the sight of their faces at an anarchist meeting. In Paris, he played the bohemian and decadent; in Mallorca, the Christian contemplative. Often his portraits give the impression of dressing up for a part. One shows him in diplomatic garb when he served briefly as Nicaraguan Minister in Madrid. Another, painted towards the end of his life, has him dressed as a monk. Were not the poetic styles he successively took on and discarded the literary equivalents of this role-playing?

Certainly he never held a consistent view even of his poetry. Sometimes he placed high value on sincerity, and on poetry as the direct expression of feeling. At other times, he regarded the poem as an artefact with tensions and inner relationships analogous to those found in experience. In his work, one style never grows organically into another. But this does not make him into the minah bird of Spanish literature. Nor is his work simply a receptacle of foreign influences. Rather, the vocabulary, verse forms and mythology he took from other cultures became the weapons of a prison break-out, a break away from a stale tradition that had lost touch with modern life.

Darío grew up in a society for which art and literature scarcely existed, a society in which the vast majority were illiterates, in which there were few publishing houses and virtually no literary public except among a small elite in the more important capitals. Among this elite, foreign books were not only preferred but often easier to obtain and more abundant than books by native writers. When Darío died in 1916, he and his fellow-Modernists had transformed the literary scene beyond recognition. There were literary magazines in abundance and new publishing houses had been founded. Poetry was no longer a marginal, dilettante activity but the passport to a fame, recognition and respect that few politicians could hope for.

But far more important than these social repercussions was the transformation Darío wrought on the literary language and forms he inherited. He came to a literature in which whole areas of modern experience were taboo and which had few forms for expressing the sensual. His foreign models helped to give him a language and mythology for what had hitherto been unexpressed in Spanish. His poetic development was not that of a man working within a tradition but consisted of a series of appropriations of elements which would help him to bridge the void in his own culture. In the early days of *Azul,* this appropriation was of vocabulary and myth that would clothe with a veil of allusiveness his message of the rightness of sexual fulfilment. In the stories and poems of this collection, the poet is the voice of nature and instinct.

Now that the novelty has been swept away, the deadness of much of his language is starkly apparent. In attempting to create a language as durable as marble, he often made it as dead as stone.

—The Times Literary Supplement

Azul introduces the reader to the guiltless naturalism of pre-Christian times. But there also lurks the shadow of cruelty and death which exist in the natural world and which could not be ignored by a man brought up in Latin America. To accept naturalism as Darío did in *Azul* was therefore to accept the chaos and barbarism which he, as a Latin American intellectual, was also trying to supersede. That is why, after *Azul,* he abandoned simple naturalism in favour of the "ideal wood" of art.

In *Prosas profanas,* his view of art is Pythagorean. Tension and conflict are chords which strike different notes but form part of the divine harmony. The poet perceives and recreates harmony out of conflicting elements. Behaving like a bohemian, dressing up as monk, may have dramatized Darío's personal conflicts but could not resolve them. But in poetry, conflict could be resolved for,

as he wrote, in this "ideal wood", "Psyche flies" and "the satyr fornicates". Language, form and symbol in *Prosas profanas* are thus intended to produce in the reader the sense of harmony and rest which are absent from living experience. In the poem, **"El reino interior"**, for instance, seven white princesses symbolize the virtues, seven scarlet princes the deadly sins. Images of white and purity balance images of scarlet and luxury, just as conflicting colours balance one another on a canvas. In other poems, Darío chooses myth figures which can symbolize this diversity within a whole. In the **"Coloquio de los centauros"**, for example, the centaurs symbolize the conflict of instinct, intellect and spirit and their dialogue presents the apparently contradictory aspects of experience. At the same time they also represent the harmony of disparate forces held within the circular framework of the poem.

Darío's universe is peopled with the myth figures of classical Greece; its flora and fauna are literary and mythological—Venus of Cyprus, Venus de Milo, Pierrot and Columbine, centaurs and satyrs, Leda and the swan, the rose and laurel and the myrtle. He chose these elements which were hallowed by tradition because he wanted "dreams and forms that come from afar and persist into the future". Their sensuality is formal, refined and elegant. The best poems, however, are often those which lean least heavily on the prop of mythology. In a poem addressed to Leda, for instance, in *Cantos de vida y esperanza,* the swan of the opening lines is a real swan observed preening itself at dawn. The brilliant plumage is contrasted with the receding shadows of night and as the sun rises is bathed in gold. It is at this moment of utmost beauty that the swan becomes Jupiter and rapes Leda while the eyes of the voyeur Pan sparkle in the green undergrowth. The poem shimmers with motion and light but the violence just below the surface is never allowed to break through the mythological associations serving to contain them. But this is Darío at his best. At other times, he cannot avoid the lifelessness of an Alma Tadema painting or the sort of pretentious vulgarity so well conveyed by the Spanish word *cursi*. And this leads us to wonder what kind of poetry he might have written if he had not resorted to Western myth. Darío himself provides the answer. In 1892 he published a poem based on a pre-Columban legend. But he did not include this poem either in *Prosas profanas* or *Cantos de vida y esperanza.* Indeed "Tutecotzimí" was not published in a complete form until 1907 when he included it in *El canto errante.* There are many lines in this poem which use natural rather than literary references to balance the conflicting elements of beauty and ugliness, transience and permanence, fertility and death. Here, for instance, three lines describe flies darting through the ground mist:

> Junto al verdoso charco, sobre las piedras toscas,
> rubi, cristal, zafiro, las susurrantes moscas
> del vaho de la tierra pasan cribando el tul.

The stagnant pool spreads a feeling of death and putrefaction, the steaming earth is warm and regenerative.

The flies, though vivid and alive, have sinister associations with death. Yet these contrasting forces are not allowed to jar and the total effect is one of brilliance. The modern reader often feels a preference for those poems in which mythological or literary associations are minimal, poems like **"Sinfonía en gris mayor"** or **"Allá lejos"**. But we cannot judge his work simply on the basis of contemporary preferences. Indeed, if we put ourselves in the position of the late nineteenth-century writer, we shall better appreciate how difficult it was for Darío—a provincial and a Latin American—to have taken any other course. For he was in search not only of an appropriate poetic language but also of a tradition. For a European writer to use classical myth may indicate nostalgia or a respect for hallowed values. For a Latin American the process was more positive and creative. By means of this system of references, Darío hoped to link Latin America to an existing tradition and bridge chaos and disorder with form, elegance and refinement.

Darío's position as a major influence on Hispanic literature is therefore unassailable. but his standing as a poet has suffered. Now that the novelty has been swept away, the deadness of much of his language is starkly apparent. In attempting to create a language as durable as marble, he often made it as dead as stone.

The impression that Darío has lost ground as a poet is confirmed by the manner in which the centenary of his birth was celebrated last year. Darío's poems do not seem to have been read either at the international congress in Los Angeles or at the Cuban "Encuentro con Rubén Darío". At the latter, the Chilean, Enrique Lihn, was not afraid to label Darío a second-rate poet. Not surprisingly critics and scholars who contributed to the many special Darío issues of periodicals were more circumspect in their judgments. Yet even here, the very conventionality of the majority of articles written in tribute to Darío seems to indicate a certain lack of enthusiasm. No major new interpretation has been offered. Nor does there exist a standard work which relates all the material available in articles and letters to Darío's poetry. Titles of articles published recently bear out the general reluctance to ask important questions. "García Lorca and Darío", "Rubén Darío in Mallorca", "Rubén Darío and the English language" are fair samples. The most welcome tribute to Darío is certainly the new edition of the *Poesías completas* which includes **"El salmo de la pluma"** and extra notes. The up-to-date bibliography published in the *Revista interamericana de bibliografía* was also an obvious necessity. Otherwise, it is Cuba which has paid homage most handsomely in a well produced issue of the *Casa de las Américas* with appropriate *art nouveau* illustrations. Here, the contributions have the merit of liveliness, many of them coming from practising poets. Only at the Cuban celebrations did critics try to separate what is dead from what is alive in Darío's work or attempt a phenomenology of his poetry. However, the questions raised in Cuba were too vast to be answered in the brief contributions allowed. The sad truth remains that, after a year of centenary tributes, Darío remains one of the most talked of and least understood of Latin American poets.

Arturo Torres-Rioseco (essay date 1970)

SOURCE: "Rubén Darío: Classic Poet," translated by David Flory, in *Rubén Darío Centennial Studies*, edited by Miguel González-Gerth and George D. Schade, Institute of Latin American Studies, 1970, pp. 85-96.

[*In the following excerpt, Torres-Rioseco explains elements of classical aesthetics in Darío's poetry and highlights the poet's emphasis of simplicity and clarity.*]

From his earliest youth, Rubén Darío acquired the aura of an exceptional poet, one already marked out for a singular and prodigious destiny. At first the indications were vague and superficial, as for example his precocious anti-clericalism, his infantile Voltairianism and his predilection for scientific problems. Later on we have evidence of his extraordinary facility for versification in his thirty-page poems, his improvisations on outlandish subjects and his versified journalism. His prolific output attracted attention even in his native tropics, where indeed it became confused with poetic genius. This mechanical facility for expression, on its own, would not have taken him anywhere, but the young man possessed a keen sensibility for the language, and little by little new and poetic words began to appear in these long and prosaic compositions: new poetic words which were to be the first manifestations of exoticism. When these efforts became more numerous, when the experimental linguistic process became more precise, the value of exoticism was defined in the mind of the writer. Each thread in this evolutionary process signifies a great victory for the poet, after an intense struggle, and the victory can sometimes be considered as a loss. In this case the exoticism of Darío leads him (at least in appearances) to hermeticism. Now hermeticism can take many forms: that of Góngora and of Mallarmé, that of Hopkins, or that of Eliot and Pound. The hermeticism of Darío, however, is more apparent than real, because his genius is actually that of simplicity and clarity. Such apparent hermeticism is due to a certain level of difficulty in understanding the mythological vocabulary of Rubén. This relative unintelligibility is the fault not of the poet, but of the reader, especially the ignorant and proud reader. The man who today has a great respect for science and praises Einstein without understanding his theory will not do the same for a great painter, a great composer, or a great poet. All art that he cannot understand is absurd and bad. The worst thing is that this man does not *want* to understand; he stubbornly persists in his ignorance and his pride.

In the case of Darío's work the resulting incomprehension was absolute and revealed a general lack of culture. Poems like **"A Verlaine"** were classified as incomprehensible. Stanzas such as the following were regarded as extravagantly silly:

> Padre y maestro mágico, liróforo celeste
> que al instrumento olímpico y a la siringa agreste
> diste tu acento encantador.
> Panida, Pan tú mismo, que coros condujiste
> hacia el propíleo sacro que amaba tu alma triste
> al son del sistro y del tambor.

How easy it would have been to find words like *liróforo, siringa, panida, propíleo, sistro* in a good dictionary! Can we wonder, however, that an uninitiated reader reacted against these words when Don Miguel de Unamuno himself made fun of the word *"siringa?"*

The entire concept of poetry evolved with Darío and not even his best friends in Chile could understand him. Perhaps the only exception is Pedro Balmaceda, although the character of his prose work lent itself less to stylistic evolution. One has only to cast a glance at the major themes of Darío's contemporaries to see a pseudo-philosophical, pseudo-religious, pseudo-political and pseudo-moral poetry, all without artistic plan, without aesthetic radiations. Rubén Darío was suffocating in this prosaic atmosphere of practical goings-on, politics, vulgar bohemia, tariffs, commercial enterprise and provincial journalism. He was predestined to be the exemplary author of his time, the synthesizer of a poetical language and an extremely refined artistic sensibility. For that reason he escapes from the real world to the world of imagination and daydreams, to the world of poetry. This was the magic universe of the French Parnassians, especially of Théophile Gautier. Darío began to create a new language, and this language, because of the lack of Spanish and Chilean literary models and because of the poverty of the language spoken in a society of incipient culture, was to be of a classical-mythological type. It is true that this style may be only somewhat genuine, and even a sort of classical *pastiche,* but over the years, as Darío matures, we see his style also acquiring the perfection of mature classicism.

After *Azul* Darío tends to *perfection of form,* to *spiritual maturity,* and to a *consciousness of the history of the Latin language.* It seems there may have been a certain contradiction at this period between the poet's eccentricity and his maturity, but later we see the fusion of all the creative elements. Being a poet of Greco-Latin tradition, Darío possessed a mental equilibrium which restrained the romantic impulses of his youth and thus enabled correct Spanish syntax to predominate in his writings; his images have a Renaissance precison and harmony, and his symbols are most properly those of a high Mediterranean culture. The proof of what I am saying is that the vulnerable point of his style, the only thing that betrays a weakness, is his well-known use of Gallicisms, a minor element in the Modernist form.

The first centennial of the birth of Rubén Darío makes us pause to think for a moment of the significance of his work and of his life, because Darío has become a miracle, poetry incarnate. At first he was considered a precocious child-poet, then a daring reformer of the poetry of his time, still later the master of his generation of writers, and finally the major figure of Spanish-American lyric poetry. I think all these opinions are just. His precocity is proverbial. His power of innovation took him quickly from **Abrojos** to **Azul** and from **Azul** to **Prosas Profanas**. No one has denied him the title of leader of Modernism, and today he is unanimously recognized as the great poet of Spanish America. It is true that precocity is not an absolute sign of future greatness, but in this case the augury

was fulfilled. His spirit of renovation could have run its course in mid-youth but it lasted until the end of his life. He synthesized the most profound qualities and characteristics of the movement which he initiated, and since 1916 his name has been held in the highest reverence.

Sometimes the glory of an artist derives from circumstances. Mysterious reasons accelerate or retard the growth of his fame. Rubén Darío is an example of true glory, based on the firm foundation of real values, which with the passage of time tend to become permanent, eternal.

Rubén Darío's life was simple. He did not create a courtly, luxurious, dramatic or heroic environment with which to surround himself. His loves were unfortunate; his love affairs, vulgar. Poverty was much more a reality to him than was opulence. The drama of his life developed in derisive forms. What could have been heroic became reduced to no more than empty gestures. His fame then grew on its own, as a result of those authentic values of artistic creation. He put it this way himself: "My poetry is mine within myself" (*mi poesía es mía en mí*). And thus it was, always: an extremely personal combination, organic product coupled with mental elaboration. Some artists create an artificial atmosphere in order to exist within it, and thus detract from their personalities either by inventing something false or expressing their thoughts and their dreams in a language foreign to their own experience. What long hours of labor Góngora must have spent in raising the scaffolding of his *Soledades* and what nightmares Sor Juana must have had when composing her *Primero Sueño*! On the other hand the pure aesthetic joy of San Juan is authentic in his *Cántico Espiritual* as is that of Garcilaso in his *Eglogas.*

After *Azul* Darío tends to perfection of form, to spiritual maturity, and to a consciousness of the history of the Latin language.

—*Arturo Torres-Rioseco*

The stylistic evolution of Rubén Darío goes hand in hand with his ever-increasing mental profundity and with the enriching of his thematic materials. Although he must have felt the fever of violent imaginative outbursts, he restrained his impulses and established the equilibrium of his classically conceived work. Many times I have been tempted to make the analysis of the creative mind of Rubén Darío: the struggle between the vital passion and the philosophical serenity of the mature man. In this essay, we will discuss some isolated characteristics of his creative processes, starting with his *simplicity,* an essential part of his classical attitude.

In the year of his poetic initiation (1880) Darío showed that simplicity is the dominant characteristic of his art. In one of the first poems of this period, he writes:

Las aves sus dulces trinos
iban alegres cantando.
Y blandamente saltando
de rama en rama, en los pinos. . . .

And in one of the last, in 1915, he says:

A Amy V. Miles
dedico este tomo
de versos galantes
muy siglo XVIII.

Darío follows his first lyric attempts with anti-clerical poems; later comes his poetry on political and didactic topics which requires nothing of exotic attitudes or complex rhetoric. Around the age of sixteen, the courtly theme begins to dominate his poetry, and it seems that a period of more difficult and *recherché* technique was initiated, but this in fact is nothing more than an enriching of oriental vocabulary. Any dictionary could have solved the most abstruse linguistic problem for the timorous reader. This is the period in which he employs words such as *ámbar, hastchis, sándalo, loto, cinamomo,* the period in which his poetic geography became enriched with *Golconda, Alejandría, Bassora,* the period of adjectives such as *marfileño* and *ebúrneo,* and yet a period in which his syntax retains its accustomed simplicity. Among the most frequent influences on the Darío of those days we note the names of Campoamor, Reina, Núñez de Arce, Bécquer and Martí, none of whom was given to stylistic extravagances of any kind.

Darío's desire for clarity is evident in the poem **"La Poesía Castellana"** of 1882 in which he praises "simple, harmonious, lusty" poets, condemns *culteranismo* and criticizes Góngora, who, he says,

con las ondas de su ingenio
antes tranquilo manantial de amores,
derramó de su mente los fulgores
de la española musa en proscenio.

Mas ¡ay! la ruda tempestad del genio
con sus horrendos rayos vibradores
de su alma en el vergel, tronchó las flores
que aromaron su dulce primigenio. . . .

which brings to mind the fact that years later he was to repeat the same thought in a masterful way, in the poem **"A los poetas risueños,"** from *Prosas Profanas*:

prefiero vuestra risa sonora, vuestra musa
risueña, vuestros versos perfumados de vino
a los versos de sombra y a la canción confusa
que opone el numen bárbaro al resplandor latino:
y ante la fiera máscara de la fatal Medusa
medrosa huye mi alondra de canto cristalino.

Around 1887 a desire for style (*voluntad de estilo*) manifests itself in Darío. In *Azul* (1888) it is evident in the prose of his stories, and it attracted the attention of the entire world. The fact that the simplicity of the poems of

"El año lírico" is maintained, indicates that essentially the poet's talent seeks the most direct forms of expression, while the prose writer is permitted the caprice of experimenting with new elaborations of syntax, youthful artifices which do not complicate the intention or disturb the measure of his composition. The novelty of the prose of *Azul* is never based on mysterious complexities or strange conceits. The verse (in the compositions added to the 1890 Guatemala edition) becomes increasingly rich because of the vocabulary that Darío was gathering along his poetic development and particularly because of the expert use of those words. Take, for example, his sonnet **"Caupolicán."** If we compare it with his "Central American" verses, we find an evident stylistic advancement. The harmonious quality of the composition is superior; the adjectives are chosen with exactness and propriety; the verses acquire a lightly symbolic sense; the historical references are more abundant. For the cultured reader there is no difficulty in understanding the meaning of the sonnet. In the remaining poems of this section the linguistic element livens the aesthetic, for example, in words such as *avatar, oarystis* and *cinegético.*

Darío arrived at the high point of his creative power in 1896, when his first great book, *Prosas Profanas,* appeared. His poetic language is now definitively formed. His inventions of syntax are unique in the history of Spanish literature; his vocabulary has a novelty and grace never before seen. It is not the formal syntactic richness of Góngora, mathematical and sometimes arbitrary, but rather a logical richness, with a sure movement toward excellence, with a high measure of reason, with the constant desire for perfection which always characterizes the work of the Nicaraguan poet. Darío had learned, assimilated, and improved. The superficially metaphoric became more profound and refined; it was transformed and became personal: "Most importantly, do not imitate anyone," declared the young master. With this, he created a cultured poetry of exemplary brilliance. And yet, he complained of the haste with which he wrote:

I have lacked the time and had too much weariness of heart and soul to make, like a good craftsman, my majuscules worthy of each page of the breviary. (*Prosas Profanas*)

Rubén penetrated this mythological artistic universe, assimilated it, and with his marvelous intuition turned it into something personal. In this way the ancient becomes modernized and that which was archeological is transformed into poetry.

In reviewing all the poems of *Prosas Profanas,* we find in **"Era un aire suave,"** that marvelous example of euphony, of rhythmic grace, of word-discovery, such structural purity that at times a verse is composed of a simple succession of nouns, while at other times by a repetition of one verb in different forms. Some of the most famous poems of Rubén are included in this book: **"Sonatina,"** a model of poetic elegance, so ingenuously conceived that today it appears in children's anthologies; **"Margarita,"** in which the florescence of form gives way to the intensity of passion; **"Heraldos,"** in which a chain of symbols is deciphered in natural form; **"Coloquio de los Centauros,"** a simple yet philosophical explanation of the myth of the divine beasts, **"Sinfonía en Gris Mayor,"** which presents a large quantity of new and strange images, difficult to interpret. In **"El Reino Interior"** Darío offers us one of his most beautiful allegories, in a perfect, transparent, classic structure.

It might be observed that Darío still favors the narrative form, the story-in-verse, which does not lend itself to the subtle distillation of style. In **"Recreaciones arqueológicas"** the greater or lesser capacity for comprehension corresponds once again to the proportional literary culture of the reader. This is due as much to the cultural geography of the poems as to their symbolism. It is apparent that Darío was familiar with René Ménard's *Mythologie dans l'art ancien et moderne* (1878) and that this book had a great influence on his style. To the knowledge of the Greek world through its poets, we must add what Darío obtains from the plastic arts, the painting of vases and bas-reliefs transmuted into lyric beauty by the words of the young poet.

In *Cantos de Vida y Esperanza* (1905) we find explicit statements concerning his manner of feeling and executing beauty. Everything within him is "anxiety, ardor, pure sensation and natural vigor"; there is in him no "falsehood, or make-believe, or literature." His soul is the essence of sincerity. There are in this work poems of such marvelous precision and simplicity, that Darío convinces us that this is indeed his most genuine creative vein. Consider, for example, **"La dulzura del ángelus," "Canción de otoño en primavera," "Letanía de nuestro señor Don Quijote," "Lo fatal,"** and many others. In the *Cantos* there are tortured verses, philosophical verses, sensual and mystic verses, but there are never abstruse or *conceptista* verses. He sometimes comes in contact with Góngora, but he never lets himself be seduced by him. It seems that his own poetical profundity kept him away from a poetic structure which was more brilliant, but which was also of limited duration and vitality.

In his "Dilucidaciones" (explanatory writings) in *El Canto Errante* (1907), Rubén affirms his belief in sincerity and simplicity, and continues to put it into practice. He buries himself in his interior world, he contemplates the mysteries of life, the accelerated anarchy of his day, and he develops a more philosophical attitude. His style, however, is always careful and exact.

And so Darío's poetic gift culminates in *Poema del Otoño* (1910), a poem of synthesis, the happiest artistic expression of the poet, his definitive philosophy of Man, in which we see life, in perfect harmony, in all its purity and clarity:

> Y sentimos la vida pura,
> clara, real,
> cuando la envuelve la dulzura
> primaveral.

A man who had suffered; who had written once of anguish in lines such as "Que no hay dolor más grande que el dolor de ser vivo" (there is no greater pain than the pain of being alive); "La camisa de mil púas sangrientas," (the shirt of a thousand bloodstained thorns); "La vida es triste, amarga, y pesa" (life is sad, bitter, hard to bear); says here—facing the moment of truth, and affirming the exaltation of the individual:

> Gozad del sol, de la pagana
> luz de sus fuegos;
> gozad del sol, porque mañana
> estaréis ciegos.
>
> En nosotros la vida vierte
> fuerza y calor.
> Vamos al reino de la muerte
> ¡por el camino del Amor!

Even though many of the poems written after 1910 are of great human significance and philosophical inspiration, in which the thought of death makes the poet's voice tremble, it would be futile to look through them for "reconditeness," for the obscurity, or for the metaphysical orientation of other poets. Quite the contrary, Darío's last poem, **"Divagaciones,"** shows us that his trajectory was unswerving:

> Mis ojos espantos han visto,
> tal ha sido mi triste suerte;
> cual la de mi Señor Jesucristo
> mi alma está triste hasta la muerte.
>
> Hombre malvado y hombre listo
> en mi enemigo se convierte;
> cual la de mi Señor Jesucristo
> mi alma está triste hasta la muerte.

The first poetic attempts of Rubén were imitative of the prosaic Campoamor (with a youthful and playful "bad taste") or of the exaggerated sentimentality of Bécquer's disciples or of the pseudo-philosophical tirades of Núñez de Arce, and they persist thus until his arrival in Chile. Shortly thereafter, the Parnassian note is sounded, first in prose and then in poetic anticipation of *Azul*. His pure literary taste still predominates; sophisticated French models replace old Spanish mentors.

But soon uncomprehending critics began to protest. Valera himself, basically fair in his study of Rubén dwelt at too great a length on his "mental gallicism"; Clarín (Leopoldo Alas) revealed his inability to understand contemporary poetic techniques; later Unamuno did not seem to realize the transcendental value of the renovation that was taking place in Spanish literary style.

Darío, then, turns out to be a strange poet to those used to traditional Spanish poetry, and a misfit of a poet, surrounded by the versifiers of America, who were busy singing the praises of political "caudillos," celebrating the beauty of the wives of presidents, deifying ministers and dissatisfied patrons. These versifiers, who were the first to applaud Darío's early compositions on themes such as those just mentioned, were also the ones who later began to give him a reputation as a difficult poet. His literary enemies were of three kinds: the masters of traditional taste, those who confused poetry with patriotism, who accepted a single artistic norm; the writers who envied him because they feared that Darío's triumph would end their local success, and finally, the ignorant poetasters for whom poetry was merely a social activity.

We can be thankful that Darío understood his mission, that he knew how to liberate himself from his initial literary environment, from the mediocrity of his friends and protectors, and from the vulgar bohemia that could have destroyed him. This is what he understood and said in his great poem **"Yo soy aquél"**:

> Mi intelecto libré de pensar bajo,
> bañó el agua castalia el alma mía,
> peregrinó mi corazón y trajo
> de la sagrada selva la armonía.

Today those to whom mythology and its vocabulary are unknown, whose knowledge of poetry is strictly limited, still speak of the complicated genius of the Nicaraguan poet. A basic lesson in good taste and a dictionary would be sufficient to show them their error.

I have tried to show that Rubén Darío is a classic poet, and I believe that he is just that. I see in him a case analogous to that of Lope de Vega, who, dazzled by the genius of Góngora, imitated him only to return to his own original simplicity. In the same way Darío imitated brilliant poets (although they were inferior to him) and later returned to his candor, to his sincerity, to his clear interpretation of the world and to his simple and perfect form.

Darío now ranks on the highest artistic level beside Garcilaso, because of his lyrical fluidity and his immense tenderness; beside San Juan de la Cruz, because of the psychological mastery with which he handles the poetic idiom; beside Quevedo, because of rigorous structure and formal perfection; beside Fray Luis de León, because of his serenity. In spite of the fact that the famous verses of Darío

> Amo más que la Grecia de los griegos
> La Grecia de la Francia, porque en Francia . . .

> Demuestran más encantos y perfidias
> las diosas de Clodión que las de Fidias . . .

> Verlaine es más que Sócrates y Arsenio
> Houssaye supera al viejo Anacreonte

seem to express a definitive predilection for modern French culture over the classical culture of the ancients, Vergil and Ovid dominate Rubén's aesthetic horizon during the epoch of **Prosas Profanas**, and Platonic sentiment is the essence of his feeling in the love poems. In all the work of the great Nicaraguan poet the intensity of his sense of classical beauty gives way only to the intensity of his fear of death.

Theodore W. Jensen (essay date 1982)

SOURCE: "Rubén Darío's Final Profession of Pythagorean Faith," in *Latin American Literary Review,* Vol. X, No. 20, Spring-Summer, 1982, pp. 7-18.

[*In the following essay, Jensen traces the influence of theosophic Pythagoreanism on Darío's poetry, noting his classical and Christian sources and the prevalent tensions in his works.*]

Because of their richness, and the multiple currents encountered in his works, and perhaps the paradoxes and eccentricities of his life, scholars have been reluctant to hypothesize that any one of countless *ideologías* [ideologies] or *manías* [whims] manifested in Rubén Darío's writings might be predominant. Consequently, while some analysts have begun to point to Pythagoreanism as a strong influence on the Nicaraguan bard, only Raymond Skyrme [in his *Rubén Darío and the Pythagorean Tradition,* 1975] and Erika Lorenz [in her *Rubén Darío bajo el divino imperio de la música,* 1960] have come close to a complete disclosure of its real importance. Yet it appears that even they have not presented a complete picture of the relationship between Darío and *lo pitagórico* [Pythagoreanism].

At the risk of seeming presumptuous, but in the interest of promoting deserved scrutiny of this aspect of the poet's art, this writer suggests that Rubén Darío was, in fact, a *modernista* Neopythagorean. Pythagoreanism was not just a poetic device, but a way of life for Darío, whose interest commenced at an early age and continued evolving until his death. Furthermore, Rubén's failure to attain Pythagorean harmony in his own life, due to conflict between his Christian up-bringing and his pagan yearnings, was one of his great disappointments, and is reflected in the melancholy lines and verses of his final works.

Since there is scarcely space here to consider the major elements of Old Pythagoreanism and their mutation over the centuries into Neo Pythagoreanism, let alone investigate their role in the twentieth century Pythagorean Society's esoterica, let us instead pause briefly to outline those characteristics associated with Rubén's *pitagorismo*, what we might loosely describe as "Theosophic Pythagoreanism":

> 1. A rhythmic conception of the universe. The universe consists of a series of dualisms, of opposing forces, unified and preserved from chaos by a divine cosmic harmony.

> 2. Number is the key and secret foundation of this harmony. Music represents the best example of the relation of number to harmony.

> 3. Immortality may be achieved through a series of reincarnations or transmigrations of the soul (metempsychosis), which need not reappear in human form.

> 4. A tendency to confuse Platonism, Orphism, and

Pythagoreanism.

5. Great interest in the occult sciences, and also in the esoteric doctrines of oriental religions, as manifestations of Pythagorean correspondences.

6. A preoccupation with the confrontation between Old Christian or Jewish cultures and the Hellenic or Roman ones.

7. A rejection of positivism through an attack on its excesses occasioned by an unlimited, and consequently (and pythagorically) evil science, and its rejection of faith in favor of reason.

These were not arbitrary ideas, nor did they just happen to occur to Rubén through divine illumination. The first three are traditionally Pythagorean; the unusual nature of the others is derived from a variety of sources which influenced Darío and other *modernistas* of the epoch, especially his friends Leopoldo Lugones and Amado Nervo. Before dealing with the Pythagorean elements of Darío's works, some of the background of his sources must first be reviewed.

Darío's Pythagorean core was based on readings of classical sources such as Ovid and Plotinus, Heraclitus, Plato, and others. But superimposed over those was a little-scrutinized, but vitally important, pseudo-Pythagorean influence: the Theosophical Society. Darío was touched deeply by Theosophy, in spite of a later disillusionment with its spokeswoman, Helena Petrovna Blavatsky. Darío became a theosophist, one especially interested in Blavatsky's *Isis Unveiled*. He drew from its doctrines many ideas and motifs, especially those of the Pythagorean kind, which soon found their way into his works. Theosophy had an immediate influence on his short stories, and Darío admitted that it contributed poetic inspiration. His theosophic poems, such as **"AÚN,"** are at least vestigially Pythagorean.

Theosophists believe that Theosophy was founded in the third century A.D. by the initiator of the Neoplatonist movement, Ammonias Saccas, and that the Neopythagoreans Porphyry, Plotinus, and Iamblichus were indeed theosophists. This would explain why there is a strong Pythagorean basis to theosophical doctrines, and yet also why—through the Neopythagorean influence—they stress the occult nature of those Pythagorean elements.

Darío encountered in Blavatsky's tomes many Pythagorean teachings, ones not set forth as theories, but rather as arcane truths, lost or concealed from general knowledge. For instance, Blavatsky discusses healing and medicinal powers of music, listing examples from ancient to modern times. She defends at length the Pythagorean theory of the music of the spheres, using scientific evidence of her era to substantiate it. She discusses the microcosmic nature of man, linking it to the Pythagorean Monad. She suggests that Pythagorean metempsychosis would supply "every missing link in the chain of evolution" if modern scientists could be induced to study it closely, and deliberates upon it herself in great detail. She reviews Pythagorean sacred

numbers and refers to Plato, who maintained that the Pythagorean 12 (Dodecahedron) was the geometrical figure employed in constructing the universe, as "the ardent disciple of Pythagoras." She states that all of Copernicus' theories were taken from Nicholas De Cusa's *De Docta Ignorantia,* and that De Cusa derived his data from "Hermes and the works of Pythagoras." Blavatsky also presents the Neopythagorean concept of the nature of the soul as a basis for spiritualist theories, and an explanation for vampirism, somnambulism, prophecy and clairvoyance, mesmerism, emphasizing that Pythagoras himself was a mesmerist. Pythagorean writings were done in code, said Blavatsky, so that to the initiate, mathematics—for example—really meant "Esoteric Science, Gnosis (magic)."

One of the most striking theosophic themes, which greatly influenced Darío, is the relationship established between Pythagorean and Christian metaphysics. St. Luke is presented as a Pythagorean Essene, and Christian ideas are seen as being derived from those Pythagorean Essenes. The Gospel of John is said to have been truly written by a Neopythagorean. Says Blavatsky, "All that is grand and noble in Christian theology comes from Neoplatonism." In fact Blavatsky comes very close to claiming that Jesus himself was a Pythagorean, noting that he spent his youth with the Pythagorean Essenes, and claiming that "All his sayings are in a Pythagorean spirit, when not verbatim repetitions." She compared sentences from "Sextus, the Pythagorean," with verses from the New Testament. And still there is more, including an association of Pythagoreanism with the Orient and Middle East. This assumes the form in Darío's works of a fascination for the meeting of pagan with Christian (**"Responso a Verlaine"**), and his often noted pagan-Christian bipolarity. And finally, Blavatsky's scathing attacks against positivism and Comte must have highly influenced Darío. In any case, by 1890 he was quite anti-positivist, and that became more evident as Darío's interest in Pythagoreanism, theosophy and other esoteric philosophies increased.

Another important source, although perhaps not as much so as Blavatsky, was Edouard Schuré, one of the leaders of spiritualism in later nineteenth century France. A significant fount of Pythagorean motifs, he is perhaps viewed too seriously by some scholars insofar as his Pythagorean expertise. While Schuré was a much more skillful writer than Blavatsky, their thoughts were very similar, they published in the same era, and—most intriguing—one chapter of Schuré's influential *Les Grandes Initiés* [*The Great Initiates*] was later published as *Pythagoras and the Delphic Mysteries,* with slight alterations so that Pythagoras is called a theosophist, and Pythagoreanism the "very heart of the theosophic doctrine, the arcanum of religious and philosophies . . . raising a corner of the veil of Iris to the light of Greek genius." All the previously noted theosophic-Pythagorean statements of Blavatsky, and more, are to be discovered in Schuré's *Les Grands Initiés*. Schuré stresses, moreover, an association of Christ with Pythagoras, and Pythagoras with Apollo. The Apollo connection is already superbly studied by Erika Lorenz, and is an esential hidden influence in Rubén's poetry, and behind his facination with Apollo and Orpheus. Indeed, a seeming confusion of Orpheus and Pythagoras in Darío's spirit may be noted in these verses from **"En las constelaciones"** (1980) [**"In the constellations"**]:

> En las constelaciones Pitágoras leía; Yo en las constelaciones pitagóricas leo, pero se han confundido dentro del alma mía el alma de Pitágoras en el alma de Orfeo.

> [In the constellations Pythagoras would read; in the Pythagorean constellations read I, but within my soul have become confused the soul of Pythagoras in the soul of Orpheus.]

This blend of Orphic and Pythagorean may be a direct influence of Schuré. Lorenz, in fact, sees a deeper meaning behind the main mythological images of Darío, which she believes mask a Pythagorean concept of universal harmony. Like Blavatsky, Schuré emphasizes the occult nature of Pythagorean teachings, noting that the term "esoteric" comes from the Pythagorean initiation ceremony. Schuré also links Pythagoras with the Egyptian "Mysteries," magic, theurgy, Chaldean magic, the Persian Magi, and the Jewish Kabal.

With sources like Blavatsky and Schuré, it becomes more comprehensible how Darío and other *modernistas* derived some of their more unconventional Pythagorean beliefs. Yet, there were still other sources, also, ones more of inspiration, perhaps, than information. Among these must be listed Victor Hugo, Gérard de Nerval, Honore de Balzac (*Seráphîta*), Louis Ménard, Leconte de Lisle ("Dies Irae"), Charles Baudelaire, Paul Verlaine, Eliphas Lévi, Franz Mesmer, Swedenborg, Antoine Fabre d'Olivet, Camille Flammarion, and Edgar Allan Poe. But let us now turn from Darío's Pythagorean sources, to his Pythagorean literature.

Darío's literary success is owed in part to the high artistic standards he set, ones rarely seen since the masters of the Spanish Golden Age. His works are beautiful in the Aristotelian manner: they elicit the highest pleasurable human experience, that of contemplation, the exercise of intellect upon concepts. The plots, when they exist, evince organization suggestive of design or appropriateness. Interior elements may appear to occur by chance, but there is ample evidence of a controlling desire. They evoke katharsis within the reader. At times this takes the form of pity or fear, but most often it is that less-talked of katharsis which gratifies one's sense of human dignity. For his works were not didactic vehicles, but rather, ones which explored the relation of man and universe. That exploration frequently is expressed in Pythagorean terms, and explores Pythagorean ideals.

Like the real Pythagoras, Darío usually made his an hermetic or symbolistic exploration, accessible only to the "initiate." These works are convertly Pythagorean, such as his poem **"La tortuga de oro"** [**"The Golden Tortoise"**]. But at times his emotions could not be contained within the hermetic shell, and burst forth in full view of the non-initiate, as overtly Pythagorean manifestations.

His very earliest Pythagorean elements tended to be chiefly ornamental in appearance, yet sometimes concealed covert Pythagorean explorations. Three early short stories, for instance—"La historia de un picaflor" (1886) ["The Blue Bird"], and "El palacio del sol" (1887) ["The Palace of the Sun"]—make use of Pythagorean-based Apollonian imagery and symbolism, and a beautiful manipulation of poetic space, which anticipates Gaston Bachelard, to disguise their Pythagorean core.

In a previous study we have noted a Pythagorean-based motive for Rubén's verbal mystification-illumination, his poetic musicalization, and his flirtation with the occult. But in this scrutiny, we will focus on some overt, and hence often strongly emotional, manifestations. This reduces the vast number of works to be considered, thereby perhaps overcoming one of the principal obstacles to understanding, since otherwise we might scarcely be able to view the forest because of the large number of trees. By so doing, we finally may uncover the bedrock of Darío's literary pythagoreanism.

As early as 1880, in poems such as **"A ti"** [**"To Thee"**], **"Una lágrima"** [**"A Tear"**], and **"El poeta"** [**"The Poet"**], Darío inserts Pythagorean elements. Yet it might be argued that these do not reflect a covert Pythagorean exploration, but perhaps only continue a long tradition of poetic ornamentation.

But in 1882, in his long poem **"El libro"** [**"The Book"**], appears his first Pythagorean manifestation which is decisively not ornamentation. Containing references to the harmony of the spheres, universal harmony, macrocosmic and microcosmic correspondences, it associates these with a god of harmony. Yet, not the Christian God, but the Old Testament god, a Pythagorean one, who is the First Principle, the Pythagorean Monad, the number One:

> "Hosanna" a Ti, Dios creador;
> Dios sin triángulo, Dios Uno,
> que no eres Siva ni Juno
> Dios que me gozo en amarte . . . ,
> que nunca llega a tocarte
> ni a comprenderte ninguno.

> [Hosanna to Thee, creator God;
> God without triangle, God one,
> Who are not Siva nor Juno; God
> whom I joy in loving . . . , whom
> no one will ever succeed in
> touching nor in comprehending]

Besides a brash rejection of Christian for pagan, in this poem the young poet also personifies and exalts "The Book" in such a way as to cause one to wonder if the Nicaraguan autodidact had in mind that *Apocalypsis Goliae* of the Middle Ages, wherein Pythagoras is characterized as a man transformed into a book.

In "El velo de la reina Mab" (1887) ["The Veil of Queen Mab"], Darío for the first time openly reveals his association of artistic perfection with Pythagorean ideals, when the musician in the story states:

yo escucho todas las armonías, desde la lire de Terpandro hasta las fantasías orquestales de Wagner. Mis ideales brillan en medio de mis audacias de inspirado. Yo tengo la percepción del filósofo que oye la música de los astros.

[I listen to all the harmonies, from the lyre of Terpander to the orchestral fantasies of Wagner. My ideals shine in the midst of my inspired audacities. I possess the perception of the philosopher who hears the music of the spheres.]

In the same year a most significant work appeared, his novelistic fragment *El hombre de oro* [*The Man of Gold*]. This work is a pivotal one, not only because for the first time in his narrative fiction he makes direct reference to Pythagoreanism, but because it reveals an intense psychological conflict within the great poet, which was deeply and indelibly to affect his work from this time onward.

In this narrative, Darío creates a purposeful dualistic point-counterpoint of opposing cultures: the pagan Greco-Roman (represented by a party in the home of a Roman aristocrat) and the Judeo-Christian (represented by a meeting of Christian who are hearing Malchus read a letter from Saint Paul). The meeting and the party occur simultaneously in Rome during the time of Tiberius. Lucius Varo is the novel's spokesman for what is good in the pagan culture, and Saint Paul—although not physically present—is the Christian prolocutor. This opposition of seeming opposites may be seen as Pythagorean in nature, denoting the initiation of another change of religions in the Pythagorean universe, in much the same manner that souls pass through different cycles. Schuré had noted that Pythagoras taught that entire races were reincarnated in cycles from planet to planet. Similarly, as Greek culture was succeeded by Roman, so now would Christian succeed Roman.

Yet the passing of the old is never total. A portion of the old culture is always assimilated into the new one. Darío causes us to ponder this, through Varo's ruminations about the replacement of Saturn by Jupiter, and his speculations as to whether Jupiter, now confronted with Christ, felt the same uneasy anticipation as had Saturn.

Not only elements of its religion and art, but also Hellenic (and Pythagorean) philosophy had been absorbed into the Roman. Darío, in his first direct reference to Pythagoreanism, emphasizes that through the following statement by one of his Roman characters:

Los astros del cielo están en relación con nuestros destinos. Nuestras almas están influídas por la música pitagórica: hay en nuestro ser una parte que nos viene de la altura luminosa. Pues bien, así como los celestes astros están en continuo movimiento—y si lo suspendiesen cesaría el orden en la máquina del universo—, nuestra naturaleza nos impulsa también a no permanecer fijos en un solo punto . . . necesario nos es la traslación.

[The stars of heaven are related to our destinies. Our souls are influenced by Pythagorean music: there is in our being a part that comes to us from the luminous heights. Well then, just as the celestial stars are in continual movement—and if they were stopped all order would cease in the machinery of the universe—our nature impels us also to not remain fixed in one place . . . movement is necessary for us.]

Some ideas of art, music and philosophy survive because they are good. Just as Darío encounters literary inspiration (and perhaps personal consolation) in Pythagorean themes, so too did Saint Augustine make use of some Pythagorean ideas to strengthen Christian theology. In this novel, Darío explores the use made of pagan ideas by the new Christians. For instance, Varo recalls how St. Paul—in an effort to convert him—claimed that he had seen Pan and his nymphs one day. Paul himself is a most intriguing figure for Darío to dramatize here, since he was at the same time a Jew, a Christian, and a Roman citizen. Darío seems to be using him here to symbolize the continuence and synthesis of all these within the Pythagorean cosmos. Paul is referred to as "the new philosopher," bringing to mind the man Aristotle termed the "first philosopher," Pythagoras. Furthermore, the poet, Varo (an obvious alter-ego for Rubén) perceives a hidden, covert, pagan core deep within Paul: "A través de su aspereza, de su terquedad, de sus relámpagos, creeríase oir un blando rumor de abejas" ["Through his gruffness, his stubbornness, and his brilliant flashes of wit, one could believe he heard a soft buzzing of bees"]. Bees, we recall, are symbols for souls in Neopythagorean writings, and have been used also as a Hellenic symbol in Darío's poem **"Interrogaciones"** (1907).

In this context, Varo / Darío suggests that not all that should have been absorbed into Christianity was, in fact, accepted by the Christians. *Eros* (carnal love) is to be succeeded in the new order by *ágape* (love of God): "El cristianismo llamaba a los desheredados a un ágape fraternal bajo el amparo del Señor" ["Christianity called the disinherited to a fraternal *ágape* under the protection of the Lord"]. When St. Paul attacks *eros* as Roman sexual license, Varo protests, and defends it. Varo / Darío is not against *ágape,* but he is for *eros,* which he perceives as a natural biological reality which should not be suppressed. Both are necessary in Darío's Pythagorean cosmos, and to exclude one is unnatural and disruptive. Pythagorean dualism advised that the universe is composed of opposite forces bound together by divine harmony. Excess if anything was evil; that was why Pythagoras taught continence and asceticism. Varo's defense of *eros* is clearly a reaction to what he perceives as an attempt by early Christians to totally eliminate it, while as the same time it may be rationalization for Rubén's libido.

Throughout this work Darío makes clear that he is not sympathetic with the Roman excesses in the name of *eros*: the homosexual advances upon helpless slaves, for instance, or the casual intent to rape the Christian girl, Lucila. This is evil, and he welcomes moral changes in this regard. But Paul's apparent design to completely eradicate *eros,* rather than simply restrain it, is in itself evil, from Varo's point of view. It is excessive, and goes beyond natural limits. Darío's defense here of carnal love becomes one of the most predominant and important themes of his works. Called "panerotismo" [paneroticism] or "misticismo erótico" [erotic mysticism] by Pedro Salinas, this phenomenon has its Pythagorean roots exposed by Salinas also, albeit from a different perspective, when he notes that: "el poeta siente en el placer carnal como un medio de llegar a la unión con el principio mismo del mundo" ["the poet senses, in carnal pleasure, a means of achieving union with the first principle of the world, itself"].

The dualistic structure and the *ágape-eros* conflict in *El hombre de oro* reflect an intense psychological conflict of Darío's. He is a modern hedonist. He loves pagan art, music, beauty, wine and carnal love. As a young man he rejects Christianity in **"El libro,"** brashly and stridently waving the banner of paganism. Yet five years later, in this novel, the latent alcoholic reveals that his Catholic up-bringing has begun to be felt through perceptions of guilt, and fear of heavenly retribution. Coupled with those is the drawing of compassion and admiration in him for the artistic, aesthetic and humanistic beauty of Christ the man, suffering and sacrificing himself for mankind. Rubén had been deeply drawn to Pythagoreanism because it was a beautiful pagan philosophy, one closely associated with both Apollo, patron of poets, and also with the Archetypal Musician, Orpheus. Pythagorean theories of dualism and harmony would seem to allow the coexistence of both *eros* and *ágape,* and metempsychosis would permit the "sinner" a second chance. Still . . . could Rubén somehow retain his Pythagorean beliefs, within the framework of a Christian context? *El hombre de oro* is the first and best of a series of narrative works wherein he attempts, throught his art (like Schuré and Blavatsky in their dogmas), to fuse Christian and Pythagorean. If an accommodation can be achieved in his art, then it might also succeed in life (reminiscent of Oscar Wilde's proposal that Life copies Art, in his essay "The Decay of Living"). A series of narrative explorations is launched concerning the occult in Christian miracles, the pagan metamorphosized into Christian, and other pagan-Christian confrontations: "La muerte de Salome" (1891) ["The Death of Salome"], "Palimpsesto I" (1893) ["Palimpsest I"], "En la batalla de las flores" (1893) ["In the Battle of Flowers"], "Voz de lejos" (1896) ["Voice from Afar"], "La leyenda de San Martín" (1897) ["The Legend of St. Martín"], "La fiesta de Roman" (1898) ["The Roman Party"], "Historia prodigiosa de la princesa Psiquia . . ." (1906) ["Prodigious History of the Princess Psiquia . . ."], "Palimpsesto II" (1908) ["Palimpsest II"], and "Huitzilopoxtli" (1915). Six others have Biblical settings: "Hebraico" (1888), "El árbol del rey David" (1891) ["The Tree of King David"], "Las pérdidas de Juan Bueno" (1892) ["The Losses of Good John"], "Cuento de Noche Buena" (1893) ["Christmas Eve Story"], "El Salomón Negro" (1889) ["The Black Solomon"], and "Las tres reinas magas" (1912) ["The Three Wise Women"]. Three have Greco-Roman settings: "El sátiro sordo" (1888) ["The Deaf Satyr"], "Respecto a Horacio" (1893) ["Re-

spect to Horace"], and "Las siete bastardas de Apolo" (1903) ["The Seven Bastards of Apollo"]. Yet three others, "La ninfa" (1887) ["The Nymph"], "Carta del país azul" (1888) ["Letter from the Blue Country"], and "Sor Filomela" (1894) reflect less obvious confrontations of pagan and Christian.

But in his later years we see Rubén in anguish at his failure to resolve the conflict between his pagan yearnings and his Christian fears. In his poem **"Divina Psiquis"** (1905) [**"Divine Psyche"**] for instance, his soul—characterized as Psyche and as a butterfly—is torn between pagan (and Pythagorean) and Christian: "Entre la catedral y las ruinas paganas/vuelas, ¡oh Psiquis, oh alma mía!" ["Between the cathedral and pagan ruins you fly, oh Psyche, oh my soul!"].

Still, spurred on by an eerie visitation by the ghost of his dead friend, Jorge Castro, and his anguish and guilt at his alcoholism, Rubén continued to manifest Pythagorean elements in his works. His **"Ama tu ritmo"** (1901) [**"Love Your Rhythm"**] was a totally Pythagorean statement by Rubén, almost as if from an initiation ceremony:

> Ama tu ritmo, y ritma tus acciones
> bajo su ley, así como tus versos;
> eres un universo de universos
> y tu alma una fuente de canciones.
> La celeste unidad que presupones
> hará brotar en ti mundos diversos,
> y al resonar tus números dispersos
> pitagoriza en tus constelaciones.
>
> Escucha la retórica divina
> del pájaro del aire y la nocturna
> irradiación geométrica adivina;
> mata la indiferencia taciturna
> y engarza perla y perla cristalina
> en donde la verdad vuelca su urna.

[Love your rhythm, and rhythm your actions under its law, as well as your verses; you are a universe of universes and your soul a fount of songs. The celestial unity you presuppose will cause to sprout in your diverse worlds, and upon echoing your dispersed numbers, pythagorize in your constellations. Listen to the divine rhetoric of the airborne bird and divine the nocturnal geometric emanation; kill taciturn indifference and link pearl after crystalline pearl where truth tips her urn].

Darío's poems **"Metempsicosis"** (1907) and **"En las constelaciones"** (1908) further substantiate the continuation of his Pythagorean ruminations. His short story "Mi Tía Rosa" (1913) ["My Aunt Rose"] is very important, since the narrator-poet is another obvious alter-ego for Rubén. In this tale he reveals again that his ideal music is Pythagorean; but even more significant, he links it for the first time with the erotic figure of Pan, proving that not only Apollo held that place of honor in Darío's kosmos: "Mi música, la pitagórica, que escuchaba en todas partes: Pan" ["My music, the Pythagorean music, that I would listen to everywhere: Pan"]. The context of the story implies that Rubén links Pythagorean music with *eros,* since Pan is usually so-associated, and appears here with Venus.

In his final works, Rubén communicates despair, fear of dying because of the excesses in his life, and sadness at having been unable to attain the solice of Christian belief. In his beautiful and brooding poem **"La Cartuja"** (1914) we experience one of Rubén's final Pythagorean professions, one which shows that he still is wistfully yearning for a synthesis of Christian and Pythagorean:

> Sentir la unción de la divina mano,
> ver florecer de eterna luz mi anhelo
> y oir como un Pitágoras cristiano
> la música teológica del cielo.

> [Oh to feel the unction of the divine hand, to see blossom from eternal light my longing and hear, like a Christian Pythagoras, the theological music of the heavens].

Rubén Darío's other final profession is found in *El oro de Mallorca* (1913-1914) [*The Gold of Mallorca*], a clearly autobiographical novelistic fragment. Appearing shortly before his death, it provides an invaluable insight into his thoughts. Chapter Two—published the same month as "Mi tía Rosa" (which, we recall, linked Rubén's concept of music and poetry with both eros and Pythagoras, and was also autobiographical)—discloses that Darío is still a *modernista* Neopythagorean. Through his alter-ego, the musician Benjamin Itaspes, Rubén reveals in this bitter-sweet novel that his religion is a passion for art, and that his art is Pythagorean:

> Pitágoras y Wagner tenían razón. La Música en su inmenso concepto lo abraza todo, lo material y lo espiritual, y por eso los griegos comprendían también en ese vocablo a la excelsa Poesía, a la Creadora. Y que el arte era de trascendencia consoladora y suprema sabía por experiencia propia, pues jamás había recurrido a él sin salir aliviado de su baño de luces y de correspondencias mágicas.

> [Pythagoras and Wagner were right. Music in its immense concept embraces everything, material and spiritual, and consequently the Greeks comprehended also in that word Sublime and Creative Poetry. And that art was of a consoling and supreme importance he [Benjamin Itaspes] knew through personal experience, since he had never turned to it without leaving soothed by its bath of lights and magical correspondences].

Two years before his death at age forty seven, in this final important work, Rubén has penned a poignant final profession of Pythagorean faith, undisguised, and even more forceful in maturity than that intimated by the brash young poet of fifteen years in **"El libro"**. We know from his last poems that he still wished to embrace Christian beliefs; yet he could not reject his Pythagorean ideals. A more clear statement of his views can scarcely be imagined, unless the timid Nicaraguan genius were to revert to a frightening and defiant gesture, such as that his friend and fellow Neopythagorean *modernista,* Leopoldo Lugones, would someday make on the Isle of the Tigers.

Priscilla Pearsall   (essay date 1983)

SOURCE: "Rubén Darío: Latin American Modernism and Literary Tradition," in *Perspectives on Contemporary Literature,* Vol. 9, 1983, pp. 36-42.

[*In the following essay, Pearsall contradicts the traditional view of Latin American modernism as an "isolated phenomenon" by revealing the movement's historical and contemporary literary significance as expressed in Darío's poetry.*]

The works of Latin American Modernism written at the beginning of the twentieth century are an ideal source for studying the problem of literary tradition in twentieth-century literature, for they represent a crisis in our cultural history, a transition between two periods: Romanticism and the twentieth century. The "traditionalist" view of Hispanic Modernism has been that it has very little to do with our own present-day literature. *Modernismo* has therefore tended to be seen as an isolated phenomenon, relatively separate from both earlier and later trends.

The work of the important revisionist critics of the contemporary period, including Juan Ramón Jiménez, Federico de Onís, Manuel Pedro González, Ricardo Gullón, and Iván Schulman, has helped to change the sense that Latin American Modernism has little to do with what has followed. They have insisted upon its periodicity and its nature not as a literary movement but as a period. Juan Ramón Jiménez insisted that Hispanic Modernism was a whole century. Iván Schulman makes clear that its importance in large part derives from the fact that it lies at the beginning of our own time, and that many of its characteristics link it strongly with our own modern sensibility. This vision links Latin American Modernism much more closely with the way in which the late nineteenth century has been perceived by major non-Hispanic critics like Monroe K. Spears and Irving Howe, who perceive Modernism internationally as a cultural crisis; i.e., as a reaction to the collapse of traditional social, religious, and esthetic values at the turn of the century.

One of the major reasons for the extremely narrow, traditionalist interpretation, which holds that Rubén Darío is the major influence upon the period and contends that Latin American Modernism is essentially an esthetic *estilo afrancesado,* limited to the years between the publication of *Azul* and Darío's death in 1916, is the writings of Darío himself. Darío was a great promoter of his own undeniable talent, and he wrote on various occasions in the early twentieth century that he was the founder of Hispanic Modernism. It is largely through the works of Darío, and the critics influenced by him, that the period has come to be

Darío in 1898.

viewed according to the terms of Renato Poggioli who, in his *Theory of the Avant-Garde,* characterized Modernism as the degeneration of modernity into its most superficial characteristics. Darío's self-serving and superficial characterizations of *modernismo,* however, present only a veneer with which he hid the profoundly modern sense of identity and art which emerges from his works, a sense which makes them an important part of a twentieth-century tradition.

Darío ended the 1901 edition of *Prosas profanas* with the poem **"Yo persigo una forma . . ."** which had not appeared in the earlier 1896 edition. He had concluded the "Palabras liminares" of the 1896 volume with the arrogant *desafío*: "Y la primera ley, creador: crear. Bufe el eunuco. Cuando una musa te dé un hijo, queden las otras ocho encintas." In the final poem of the 1901 collections, however, the bravado of the earlier introduction has disappeared. Darío confesses the extremely elusive quality of creation and, therefore, of his art when he writes: "Yo persigo una forma que no encuentra mi estilo / . . . Yo no hallo sino la palabra que huye . . .".

The traditional vision of *Prosas profanas* is that it represents the most superficial, French-inspired phase of

Latin American Modernism. This is in large part due to Darío's own rejection of *Azul . . .* and *Prosas profanas* in the opening lines of *Cantos de vida y esperanza,* which appeared in 1905: "Yo soy aquel que ayer no más decía / el verso azul y la canción profana . . .". The 1901 edition of *Prosas profanas,* with the new conclusion, can, however, in spite of Darío's own evaluation of the collection, be read as one of the first major works of Darío, and of the twentieth century, in which a radical esthetic of modernity is set forth and reflected in poetry. He repeatedly affirmed his commitment to the renewal of art through liberation. The Modernists, both in Latin America and beyond, often sought creative freedom in eroticism because of the sense of prohibited pleasure with which it was surrounded at the turn of the century. The erotic poem, **"Divagación,"** is essential to an understanding of the radical renewal of *Prosas profanas*. The eroticism of Darío's poem parallels that of Baudelaire's great erotic poems like "La Chevelure," "L'Invitation au voyage," and "Le beau Navire," works in which we find the French author's most complete and original expression of a psychology of mobile desiring fantasy. **"Divagación,"** like Baudelaire's "La Chevelure," is a luxuriant demonstration of sexuality as inseparable from fantasy. For Darío, as for Baudelaire, the woman exists not in order to satisfy his desires but in order to produce them.

In **"Divagación"** the woman becomes lost among the multiplicity of erotic fantasies; and yet it is not only the woman who becomes lost in the reverie, for if **"Divagación"** raises the question of where the woman is in the poet's desire for her, it also raises the question of where the poet is in his desire. In his study *Baudelaire and Freud,* Leo Bersani's assertion concerning Baudelaire's eroticism is also applicable to Darío's: "The mobility of the desiring imagination makes the identity of the desiring self problematic. Sexuality sets into motion a kind of fantasy-machine. But it is not only the woman as an identifiable, stable object of desire who gets lost in the turning of that machine; the poet himself is set afloat among his fantasies."

In Darío, as in Baudelaire, desire has an unanchoring effect upon the poet's and the woman's identities. This is especially apparent in the violent dispersal of the self in the penultimate verse of the poem:

> Ámame así, fatal, cosmopolita,
> universal, inmensa, única, sola
> y todas; misteriosa y erudita:
> ámame mar y nube, espuma y ola.

The plethora of adjectives in these lines explodes in a verbal orgasm. As a result, when the eroticism of **"Divagación"** reaches orgasmic intensity, it becomes overwhelmingly threatening to any coherent self-definition of the poet whose psyche floats among the fantasies. The vision of the self which emerges from **"Divagación"** is that modern identity is deeply problematic, and modern experience is fragmented.

The tenuous quality of modern art emerges from **"La página blanca,"** another poem from the earlier collection which Darío included in the 1901 edition of *Prosas profanas*. In **"La página blanca"** Darío reveals that the movements of his fantasies are only the contradictory and exacerbating flux of his being; they are no more than an accumulation of dreams and words which cross the desert of the blank page like slow dromedaries. For all the dynamism of his fantasies, all that remains is what there was in the beginning: nothing, the blank page, the desert:

> Y el hombre,
> a quien duras visiones asaltan,
> el que encuentra en los astros del cielo
> prodigios que abruman y signos que espantan,
>   mira al dromedario
>   de la caravana
> como el mensajero que la luz conduce,
> ¡en el vago desierto que forma la página blanca!

The words upon the page are not substantially different from the fantasies evoked by the poet. They both are evanescent, and tend to form a fragile mist which contrasts with the luminous and terrifying signs of the constellations.

Anthony Cussen, one of the most perceptive recent critics of *Prosas profanas,* notes the influence of Mallarmé upon Darío's use of blank spaces on the page, for Darío rearranges the typography to call attention to the poem itself as an esthetic object. Mallarmé elaborated a negative esthetic, for he approached, by means of hermetic paths, the nucleus of the poem filled with silence and nothingness. In *Un Coup de dés,* he concluded that the only possible language is the negation of language. Cussen compares **"La página blanca"** with the poetry of Mallarmé to reveal the way in which Dario, like the French poet, perceived the fragility and inefficacy of language, and questioned the essence of poetry itself.

These three poems from the 1901 *Prosas profanas*—**"Yo persigo una forma," "Divagación,"** and **"La página blanca"**—in their expression of the problematic nature of identity, the fragmentation of experience, and the tenuous quality of modern art, place Darío's Modernism squarely within a tradition which links him with contemporary Latin American writing. It is especially surprising that in Latin American criticism there has been so little sense of its *modernismo* as central to the tradition which culminates in the important work of today's Latin American authors. The period's deep sensitivity to the problems of defining modern identity, modern experience, and modern art has, in all probability, remained more vital in Latin American than in any other Western literature.

These three poems not only raise the question of Latin American Modernism's place within a twentieth-century literary tradition, but they also raise the question of its link with an Hispanic past. In the prologue to *Cantos de vida y esperanza,* Darío was viciously critical of the Spanish poetry of his time. The poet's words reveal the alienation of Hispanic writers from their own literary tradition at the turn of the century. Bernardo Gicovate has noted this disconcerting blindness to and rejection of one's own

cultural past: "No se descubre a sí mismo el hombre de habla española en la prosa de Sarmiento o en la de Pérez Galdós y cuando llega el momento no se oyen más que quejas acerca de la pobreza circundante." Darío also ignored the importance of Bécquer, or at least the deepest, most enduring themes of the Spanish poet's works: solitude, the complexity of his thought, the evocation of the musical qualities of his poetry, and the uncertain quality of being in a *ser* who exists in a nameless zone between the spiritual and the concrete. Darío's alienation from a specifically Hispanic literary tradition has led critics to look for the roots of the roots of the most experimental vein of his poetry in French literature, including Baudelaire and Mallarmé. And yet the French influences upon Darío necessarily lead one back to the Hispanic tradition from which he emerged.

The Frankfurt School critic and philosopher, Theodor Adorno, offers a specifically Hegelian insight into the problem of tradition and literary creativity:

> . . . artistic innovation . . . draws its legitimacy essentially from the tradition it negates. Hegel has taught that where something new becomes suddenly strikingly authentically visible, it has been long in developing and now shucks off its hull. Only that which has been nourished on the life blood of the tradition has any power to oppose it authentically; the rest become the helpless prey to forces it too little has overcome in itself.

The bond of tradition, however, is not equivalent to the simple sequence of events in history; rather, it is unconscious. Freud wrote in his late work, *Moses and Monotheism*:

> A tradition which was founded on communication could not produce the compulsive quality characteristic of religious phenomena. It would be heard, evaluated, eventually dismissed like every other piece of external information, and would never attain that privileged status necessary to liberate men from the sway of logical thought. It must have undergone the destiny of repression, the state of remaining in the unconscious, before it could develop a powerful enough influence, upon its return, to force the masses under its spell.

Adorno contends that the esthetic, no less than the religious tradition, "is the recollection of something unconscious, indeed repressed." Where an esthetic tradition has a strong influence, "it is the result not of a manifest, direct consciousness of continuity but rather of unconscious recollection which explodes the continuum. Tradition is far more present in works deplored as experimental than in those which deliberately strive to be traditional."

In spite of Darío's exaltation of a French tradition which undeniably had a positive influence on his development, the most original poems of the 1901 *Prosas profanas* link him deeply with an Hispanic past. His immediate Hispanic predecessor in the development of a concept of poetry as the attempt to express the ineffable is Bécquer, who placed at the beginning of *Rimas* his poem "Yo sé un himno gigante . . ." with its expression of the ineffableness of poetry. Before Bécquer, San Juan de la Cruz had written about the "no sé qué que quedo balbuciendo," which language is powerless to express.

Darío's poetry is filled with resistance to the mobile fantasies of *Prosas profanas*. He refused to accept his own vision of the fragmentation of modern experience, of identity, and of modern art, for at the same time that we see the development of a new sense of indeterminacy of being, we also find a deep nostalgia for traditional ways of perceiving literature and the self. At the beginning of the twentieth century, Darío repeatedly placed his Modernist esthetic within a larger, more "meaningful" view of art, which almost cancels it out. The poet reaffirms his commitment to the "lofty" aims of art in **"Al lector,"** his introduction to *Cantos de vida y esperanza* (1905): "Mi respeto por la aristocracia del pensamiento, por la nobleza del Arte siempre es el mismo." The schism between Darío's definition of literature, idealized and Romantic, and the radical esthetic of modernity of the most original poetry of *Prosas profanas* is evident also when we compare his poems with statements like the following from the "Dilucidaciones" to *El canto errante* (1907): "Yo he dicho: Es el Arte el que vence el espacio y el tiempo. He meditado ante el problema de la existencia y he procurado ir hacia la más alta idealidad."

Darío not only idealizes art in the poetry which follows *Prosas profanas*. In *Cantos de vida y esperanza,* we find a definition of the poet which contrasts sharply with the problematic nature of identity found in **"Divagación"**:

> ¡Torres de Dios! ¡Poetas!
> ¡Pararrayos celestes,
> que resistís las duras tempestades,
> como crestas escuetas,
> como picos agrestes,
> rompeolas de las eternidades!

Darío repeatedly undermined his own most original experiences in literature through his return to an essentially Romantic idealization of the self and art.

Paul de Man considers the ambivalence present in Darío central to all artistic creativity. Renewal is essential to the nature of literature; the appeal of modernity haunts all writing. Darío's tendency to undermine the renewal present in his own works, de Man finds to some extent in all writers: ". . . a curious logic that seems almost uncontrolled, a necessity inherent in the nature of the problem rather than in the will of the writer, directs their utterances away from their avowed purpose. Assertions of literary modernity often end up by putting the possibility of being modern seriously into question." Literature is necessarily both renewal and the erosion of that renewal in its own inescapably binding historicity, which is, after all, necessary in order for the possibility of renovation to exist. An image of creativity emerges from Darío's works in which literature is revealed to exist in both the fulfillment and denial of its own modernity. His writings, therefore, not only reflect a turn-of-the-century cultural crisis; they are exemplary of all literary creation, for art's immediacy and renewal are always both dependent upon, and undermined by, the very tradition from which they spring.

Stephen Kinzer (essay date 1987)

SOURCE: "Stranded by Politics and War: Nicaragua's Loved, Neglected Poet," in *The New York Times Book Review,* January 18, 1987, p. 3.

[*Kinzer is an American journalist who has served as a bureau chief in Nicaragua and Germany for the* New York Times. *While working in Managua, Nicaragua, for nearly thirteen years, he developed a native's perspective of Central America's complex politics that few American journalists have been able to duplicate. In the essay below, Kinzer laments the neglect suffered by Darío's poetry in contemporary Nicaragua.*]

One can hardly imagine how remote the newborn republic of Nicaragua must have been from the world's cosmopolitan centers during the last century. It was perceived, not quite correctly, as a tropical backwater, steamy, inert and destitute of learning and culture. Yet from a wretched Nicaraguan village, by some amazing mystery, emerged Rubén Darío, the vagabond poet who was to influence Latin American and Spanish literature forever and dazzle Europe as no provincial ever had. "That such a thing could happen makes you believe either in God or Darwin," said Carlos Martínez Rivas, a prominent Nicaraguan poet who, inescapably, has spent much of his life immersed in Darío's legacy.

Today is the anniversary of Darío's birth in 1867, and in his hometown, schoolchildren will declaim his poetry and official functionaries will read florid proclamations. Circles of his admirers will meet in Nicaragua and in the foreign capitals where he spent most of his life: Buenos Aires, Madrid and especially Paris. But at a book fair in Managua last month, not a single work of Darío, Nicaragua's major cultural figure and among the finest poets ever to write in Spanish, was to be found. Among those who guard the poet's memory, there is fear that he may become yet another victim of the war and political upheaval that has afflicted this country for the better part of a decade.

No single English-speaking writer has had an impact on poetry and sensibility comparable to Darío's in Spanish. Until he burst on an unsuspecting Europe in 1888 with the publication of his first great work, *Azul,* Latin America had produced only isolated examples of important or original literature. The Spanish language was emerging from a period of stiffness that Darío described as "mummification." Then suddenly, from a distant corner of the Spanish-speaking world, sprang a figure who was deeply versed in the classics, enamored of French and Italian culture and a master of a musical sense that allowed him to fashion some of the most melodic poetry written in any language.

"You have a very deep and unusual originality," the much-admired Spanish dramatist Juan Valera wrote Darío after *Azul* was published. "There is no author in Spanish who is more French than you." Praise was to follow the poet across two continents, and continue after his death in 1916. One of his greatest admirers, Pablo Neruda, sharing a Buenos Aires platform with Federico García Lorca in 1933, said both he and Lorca agreed that Darío "sang more highly than we do." Perhaps Darío's most direct literary influence was on the Spanish "generation of '98," which included such figures as Ramón del Valle-Inclán and Juan Ramón Jiménez, winner of the 1956 Nobel Prize in Literature.

Despite his position in the first rank of writers in Spanish, Darío is largely unknown in the English-speaking world. Part of the reason may be that his Latin heritage, which deeply affected him, distances him from Anglo-Saxon readers. Yet Darío touched many universal themes. In his early work, he was preoccupied with beauty, love and pleasures of the senses. "Every composition seems to be a sacred hymn to Eros," Juan Valera wrote of *Azul*. Later, Darío showed a more introspective side, alarmed at his destiny "to be, and to know nothing, and to have no certain path."

Another factor helps to explain Darío's relative anonymity among English speakers: the daunting challenge he poses to translators. His poetry owes its singular beauty to singsong rhythms and complex rhyme schemes, and therefore is exceedingly difficult to render into English or any other foreign language.

The first translators of Darío, reflecting the fashion of their age, tried to maintain some of his lyric cadences. In a small volume of translations published in 1916, Thomas Walsh has Darío describing himself as a product of varied influences,

> and very eighteenth-century; both old
> and very modern; bold, cosmopolite
> like Hugo daring, like Verlaine half-told
> and thirsting for illusions infinite.

Later, as Surrealism and other post-Darío movements led many poets away from classical structures and toward more conversational styles, Darío was translated into a form of free verse. The poet and essayist Lysander Kemp, in a translation published in 1965, rendered part of Darío's ode to spring-time this way, calling it

> month of roses. My poems
> wander through the vast forest
> to gather honey and fragrance
> from the half-opened flowers.

Although he spent most of his life in Europe and South America, Darío is an example of achievement cherished by all educated Nicaraguans. They do not read his work as much as scholars would like, but nonetheless hold him in an esteem that often reaches the point of veneration. The rightist regime in power in 1967, the centenary of his birth, mounted a major conference in Managua that at-

tracted Darío scholars from around the world, and minted a special gold coin to commemorate the occasion. Among the current Sandinista leadership, which has been in power since 1979, there are several literary figures who revere Darío, notably Vice President Sergio Ram ez Mercado and Minister of Culture Ernesto Cardenal.

Although political upheaval has taken its toll on the cult of Darío in Nicaragua, and although the "Rubén Darío honor guard" no longer meets for readings, there remain a number of Nicaraguans who are serious students of Darío and who continue to publish new studies of his work and his eventful, alcohol-shortened life. There are also dedicated amateurs like José Jirón Terán, a shopkeeper in León who has devoted 30 years to collecting editions of Darío's work and books about him. Mr. Jirón has more than 3,000 volumes crammed into musty bookcases that spill into his sister's adjoining house. He calls himself "a dilettante who loves Rubén Darío."

Mr. Jirón has a passionate mission these days. By 1992, the 500th anniversary of Columbus's first journey to the New World, he wants to see Darío's complete works assembled and published. A purportedly complete five-volume edition of Darío's prose and poetry was published in 1953 in Madrid, but Mr. Jirón and other "Darianos" can produce articles, critical essays, short stories and even poems that were overlooked.

"Rubén Darío is not being circulated here in Nicaragua, and this has to change," Mr. Jirón said as he showed a visitor a lavishly illustrated large-format book of selected Darío poems printed privately in Barcelona. "Many lesser poets have had their works systematically collected. Nicaragua owes it to Rubén to correct this injustice." Of course Nicaragua, its economy in shambles, is in no position to support such an undertaking. But some Government officials like the idea and hope they can persuade a foreign benefactor, perhaps the Government of Spain, to underwrite the project. Closer at hand, preparations will begin next month for a 1988 celebration to mark the centenary of *Azul*.

In contemporary Nicaragua, where Government-sponsored culture is expected to serve political ends, Darío's odes to forest nymphs and Greek goddesses, not to mention his brooding meditations on the ephemeral quality of life, are not immediately useful. But Darío, bohemian esthete though he was, never cut himself off from the world around him. He was a Nicaraguan diplomat and a passionate advocate of Central American and continental unity, and he proclaimed his beliefs in verse.

In 1905, he published **"To Roosevelt,"** a stirring condemnation of imperialism that is undoubtedly the Sandinistas' favorite Darío poem, the one they have reproduced on posters and reprinted time and again. A fragment of it, translated by Lysander Kemp, reads:

> You are primitive and modern, simple and complex;
> You are one part George Washington and one part
> Nimrod.

You are the United States,
Future invader of our naïve America
With its Indian blood, an America
That still prays to Christ and still speaks Spanish.

The following year, Darío wrote another poem on the same theme, **"Salutation to the Eagle,"** but it took a very different tone, and for that reason is officially ignored in Nicaragua today. In it, Darío sings to "Magic eagle, who loved Walt Whitman so much," and urges Latin America to "learn constancy, vigor and character from the Yankee." He spoke to the United States:

> May Latin America receive your magic influence
> And may a new Olympus be born, full of gods and
>   heroes!

Despite his virtual inaccessibility to English-speaking readers and the neglect his work has suffered in turbulent Nicaragua, Rubén Darío's place in Hispanic letters is secure. "There are those today who believe that poetry is a line of progress, like science or technology," said Enrique Anderson-Imbert of Harvard University, author of many books on Hispanic literature. "These people will tell you that Darío was great in his time, but that others have taken what they needed from him and moved onward. They consider some of Darío's poems frivolous, insincere, excessively formal. I am not of that school. I consider each poet as a star in the sky, and Darío is the greatest poet Spanish America has produced."

A tribute to Darío:

García Lorca: [Rubén Darío] gave us the murmur of the forest in an adjective, and being a master of language, like Fray Luis de Granada, he made zodiacal signs out of the lemon tree, the hoof of a stag, and mollusks full of terror and infinity. He launched us on the sea with frigates and shadows in our eyes, and built an enormous promenade of gin over the grayest afternoon the sky has ever known, and greeted the southwest wind as a friend, all heart like a Romantic poet, and put his hand on the Corinthian capital of all epochs with a sad, ironic doubt.

Neruda: His red name deserves to be remembered, along with his essential tendencies, his terrible heartaches, his incandescent uncertainties, his descent to the hospitals of hell, his ascent to the castles of fame, his attributes as a great poet, now and forever undeniable. . . .

García Lorca: Pablo Neruda, a Chilean, and I, a Spaniard, are one in our language and one in our reverence for that great Nicaraguan, Argentinian, Chilean, and Spanish poet Rubén Darío.

> *Federico García Lorca and Pablo Neruda, "Al Alimon" (originally a speech delivered to the Pen Club in 1933), in* Selected Poems of Rubén Darío, *translated by Lysander Kemp, 1965.*

John R. Burt (essay date 1988)

SOURCE: "Why the Dichotomy of Active and Passive Women in Darío's Poetry?" in *Discurso literario: revista de temas hispanicos,* Vol. 6, No. 1, Fall, 1988, pp. 137-49.

[*In the following essay, Burt compares images of active and passive women in several of Darío's poems, suggesting that the contrast arose from subconscious motivations in the poet.*]

Darío's poetry has received a great deal of critical attention over the years, and his relationship with women its full share as well. Almost all of the critics recognize the ubiquitous element of eroticism as the single most controversial theme of his poetry. Yet at the same time, none of them has noted an interesting and important dichotomy of feminine behavior.

In their relationships with the poet, either literally with Darío or with his poetic masculine alter ego, women exhibit two very different behavior patterns. One kind of woman behaves demurely, spending most of her time awaiting her lover only to awaken with a languorous submission to his wishes when he arrives (a passive, reactive role). The second kind of woman makes decisions for herself, changing her role in the situation at her own wish rather than at that of the poet, and becomes clearly the one who establishes control of the relationship (a decisive, active role).

Darío exemplifies both patterns quite clearly in eight representative poems selected from his *Poesías Completas*: **"De invierno"**, from *Azul*; **"Era un aire suave"**, and **"Sonatina"**, from *Prosas Profanas*; **"Canción de otoño en primavera"**, from *Cantos de vida y esperanza*; **"Mima"**, **"La monja y el ruiseñor"**, **"En Trinacria"**, and **"A Francisca"**. This broadly-based selection drawn from his major periods represents the pattern fairly while at the same time epitomizing the main thrust of his work.

In the poem, **"De invierno"**, Carolina, the feminine protagonist, rests curled up on the easy chair wrapped in her sable coat: ". . . mirad a Carolina. / Medio apelotonada, descansa en el sillón, / envuelta con su abrigo de marta cibelina". A short distance away, the fire blazes in the fireplace and her Angora cat nuzzles her skirt, while in the background repose a Japanese silk screen and Chinese porcelain jars—manifestations of the well-known Modernist penchant for Orientalia. All of this elegant and refined restfulness makes Carolina drowsy: "Con sus sutiles filtros la invade un dulce sueño". The poet himself, a short time later, enters and kisses her rosy face: "entro, sin hacer ruido; dejo mi abrigo gris; / voy a besar su rostro, rosado y halagüeño / como una rosa roja que fuera flor de lis". She reacts by opening her eyes with a smile, "Abre los ojos, mírame con su mirar risueño".

The poem depicts a Parnassian moment of sensual, luxurious repose with a heavy dream-like quality, and all of the several elements reproduce the quality of a painting of

Parisian elegance. The date of composition (1890) before Darío's first trip to Paris reveals with the certainty that the elements of the scene, including the lady, are imaginary. In her role as an idealized character, Carolina serves as an excellent example of what may be called the "passive" woman. She sensually waits amidst luxury for the return of the poet, and upon his return, awakens for him with a smile of welcome like Sleeping Beauty for Prince Charming. She does not perceptively make any decision about her life—she simply exists beautifully and responds sweetly to the poet.

An expanded version of the same type of "passive" woman is dramatized by the Princess in the famous **"Sonatina"**. Initially sad, she resembles Carolina in her silence, beauty and luxurious surroundings: "La princesa está pálida en su silla de oro, / está mudo el teclado de su clave sonoro, / y en un vaso, olvidada, se desmaya una flor". An imprisoned canary in a golden cage, the Princess does not view the banalities of her royal surroundings with amusement. She is much less fascinated by the sensual luxury than is the poet. Darío lingers in his descriptions of the exotic minutiae confining her which reflect her inner torment, and even takes delight in her petulant suffering, creating a pouting sound through the occlusives "p" and "t":

> ¡Ay!, la pobre princesa de la boca de rosa
> quiere ser golondrina, quiere ser mariposa,
> tener alas ligeras, bajo el cielo volar;
> ir al sol por la escala luminosa de un rayo.

Like a swallow or a butterfly, with fragile wings she would flee to taste the adventure of the heavens, a flight as evanescent as a luminous ladder made from a ray of light. With empathetic clarity of vision Darío emphasizes the frustration and unhappiness she feels at this moment in order to make it clear that at least one possible reason stems from her sexual frustration. This frustration makes her especially restless in the sexually charged environment where she finds herself, "el palacio soberbio que vigilan los guardas, / que custodian cien negros con sus cien alabardas, / un lebrel que no duerme y un dragón colosal". All these images are fraught with sexual energy—powerfully masculine guards, a lap dog (whippet) which like the Princess is tensely nervous and doesn't sleep, and a colossal dragon which not only reflects the exotic power and mystery of her kingdom but also conveys the hint of a powerful appetite for flesh. The moment of life that the Princess is experiencing, the moment of emergence into womanhood conveyed by "mariposa", "golondrina", "boca de fresa" and "boca de rosa", is expressed even more clearly in the line, "¡Oh, quién fuera hipsipila que dejó la crisálida!". She, like Hypsipyle, would break free of the cocoon of her adolescence.

Darío, however, does not allow her control over her own wishes; she cannot react actively to change her situation. Darío instead choreographs the entire situation so that she will be rewarded through her beauty, position and passive lifestyle. Her only consolation is the knowledge given her by her fairy godmother that she will soon be visited by a Prince Charming who will perform the noble coup de grâce and awaken her thus to life:

> el feliz caballero que te adora sin verte,
> y que llega de lejos, vencedor de la Muerte,
> a encenderte los labios con su beso de amor.

The active images, and real movement here, as in **"De invierno"**, are those of the male. The feminine role is to wait, eternally frozen at the moment of life when she is most physically beautiful, waiting for the male who will awaken her to the potential (sexual) pleasures of life with a single kiss. In this kind of role, the two women fit an image Darío finds quite attractive, the image common in folklore of Cinderella and Sleeping Beauty as outlined by Stith Thompson in *The Folktale*. The Princess is, in fact, the epitome of the "passive" woman in Darío: beautiful and silent, she is surrounded by elegance; her role in life is to wait, to wait for the ideal lover (the poet's surrogate), and then to blossom affectionately for him. Fictitious as Carolina of **"De invierno"** the Princess becomes an important, recurring symbol in Darío's poetry.

In **"La monja y el ruiseñor"**, (dated 1896), another beautiful female protagonist, this time a nun, waits silently and passively. In the form of a masculine alter ego, the Ruiseñor appears and informs her that he is her soul:

> Soy yo, el alma tuya,
> que esta forma tomé para, volando,
> recorrer distantes, luminosos países,
> cuyos prodigios mil, y mil encantos,
> vendré a contrate en las serenas noches . . .

On her behalf, like a chivalric knight, he wishes to traverse the earth to see all he can of life and then to return to recount for her a thousand enchantments. The nightingale then departs, and returns much later to tell of the wonders he has seen. The nun listens silently, until through him she is transported to mystic Heights. The Ruiseñor plays an active role, not unlike that of the "feliz caballero" in **"Sonatina"**, while the nun remains utterly passive.

The song of the nightingale is so beautiful and captivating that the nun enters into an unbreakable trance which removes her completely from the turmoil of life around her. When she does awaken at the end of the song, it is only to die, permitting thence the nightingale, her alter ego and her soul joined, to escape forever to the distant land of wonders.

"En Trinacria" (dated 1897), serves nicely to provide the transition between Darío's passive women and his active women. The opening stanza depicts a new kind of feminine behavior: "¡Oh mujer! / ¿Por qué te vas, sin volverte, / dejando flechas en las almas?". Having apparently abandoned numerous men already, this female demonstrates a more aggressively seductive attitude than has been seen heretofore. The poet implores:

> ¿Qué quieres? ¿Qué esperas de mí?
> Demasiado joven para darte la alegría,

demasiado joven también para darte oro,
yo no soy sino un niño aún.

and in his ravings, one apparent reason why this woman differs from the earlier ones rests clearly on the fact that for the first time the female seems to be older than the poet's persona. At the same time Darío's reference to his poetic self as a child underlines an attitude he will maintain throughout his poetry. In this poem, her confident behavior seems to result from chronological age. In later poetry, the same conceit recurs: the girl, the "experienced" teacher, and the poet, the "innocent" student. When not pertaining to a real age difference, it seems to convey a tangible difference in the level of experience in life.

In this poem the kind of relationship that exists between them becomes clear when the poet compares his father's simple background with that of the temptress he is addressing, "Pero él es pastor, lejos de los mares, / en la isla de Trinacria. / Tú que vendes todo, aun tu carne".

The woman, plying a living through selling her flesh as a courtesan, has much more experience in life than the poet whose innocence is especially underlined by his being the son of a shepherd.

> Pero tú, bella cortesana
> de rostro pálido,
> ¿Qué quíeres que te dé
> más que los más secretos arcanos de mi corazón?

Anxious to make a purchase of her favors, he offers her as payment the simple fruits of the land, but she responds negatively to his offer, preferring a different kind of payment:

> —No; yo quiero los besos de tu labio,
> joven y pueril niño;
> su frescura calmará mi fiebre.
> A ti yo te daré el amor, sabiamente.

She will offer him her love expertly, soothing her own (aging) fever with the balm of his youthful freshness.

It is, of course, one more version of the classic fantasy in which the sophisticated, yet still beautiful prostitute accepts the young innocent lover for one night without pay. For Darío it is a revealing fantasy nontheless. In the three poems examined earlier, the women performed the roles of young, passive innocents, and were the ones who needed to be guided.

The message of this poem, on the other hand, seems to be that the poet can accept a woman in an active role in his poetry provided it be noted that the male protagonist is young and less experienced in life than she ("joven y pueril niño"). If she be experienced especially in sexual matters, all the easier for him to allow her the decision-making, active role in the relationship.

In keeping with this understanding, another fantasy in which an active woman takes part may be found in **"Era un aire suave"** from *Prosas profanas* (1896). Eulalia, the central figure of the poem, remains probably the best example in Darío's poetry of the *belle dame sans merci*. At the same time, by drawing from what has been observed about the poem, **"En Trinacria"**, her role continues that of the sexually sophisticated, older woman.

She knowingly manipulates her lovers and then laughs at their plight, "Al oir las quejas de sus caballeros, / ríe, ríe, ríe la divina Eulalia". For her, the ability to play one lover against another is second nature, "La marquesa Eulalia risas y desvíos / daba a un tiempo mismo para dos rivales". All of this exaggerates her quality of desirability and demonstrates the expertise with which she deals with life.

When she actively destroys a flower at the ball, "Es noche de fiesta, . . . / La divina Eulalia, vestida de encajes, / una flor destroza con sus tersas manos", the symbolism is clear: the destruction of the flower represents the destruction of the lovers' hearts. As easily as she tears the petals from the flower, so it is that she shreds the hearts of those who chance to love her. One wonders only if she necessarily treats all men this away.

An answer comes at a moment near the end of the poem when Eulalia reaches the small woods at midnight for a secret rendezvous:

> la marquesa alegre llegará al boscaje,
> boscaje que cubre la amable glorieta
> donde han de estrecharla los brazos de un paje
> que, siendo su paje, será su poeta.

The pageboy receives her there with an embrace. As her "poet", he reveals Darío's emotional identity with the youthful protagonist. As with the courtesan of the previous poem, Eulalia here, by far the more sophisticated of the two, will endeavor to teach the young page (Darío's alter ego) all about love. Although Eulalia is chronologically young, she is still a bit "older" than the pageboy-poet.

Perhaps the best-known examples of active women in Darío's poetry are to be found in his well-known **"Canción de otoño en primavera"** from *Cantos de vida y esperanza* (1905). The three women portrayed in this poetic memoir are all active:

> Yo era tímido como un niño.
> Ella, naturalmente, fue,
> para mi amor hecho de armiño,
> Herodías y Salomé . . .

While sweet and young, "Era una dulce niña . . .", his first love was much more knowledgeable about love and sex than Darío, who portrays himself timid as a child, "Yo era tímido como un niño". As inferred from the line, "Herodías y Salomé", the girl, a captivating, dancing temptress who bewitched him, and by inference nearly cost him his head, is the one who directed the course of the relationship.

The second woman, even more agressively expressive, is outlined:

> Pues a su continua ternura
> una pasión violenta unía.
> En un peplo de gasa pura
> una bacante se envolvía . . .
> En sus brazos tomó mi ensueño
> y lo arrulló como a un bebé . . .
> Y le mató, triste y pequeño,
> falto de luz, falto de fe . . .

She too seemed to "dance" seductively, and treated his *ensueño* as if it were a baby, "y lo arrulló como a un bebé", suggesting again that the poet was still quite young physically and emotionally. She helped him to grow, if in no other way, at least in the way one grows by seeing the destruction of one's illusions, "Y le mató, triste y pequeño, / falto de luz, falto de fe". Like the first girl of this poem and the other active women observed previously, she too established the direction of their relationship while the young, timid poet responded submissively.

Because of her almost incessant frenzy, the third girl is described as if she were a virtual nymphomaniac:

> Otra juzgó que era mi boca
> el estuche de su pasión
> y que me roería, loca,
> con sus dientes el corazón
> poniendo en un amor de exceso
> la mira de su voluntad.

She is perhaps the most aggressive of all Darío's poetic females.

One wonders about the apparent anomolies presented in this poem, noting that these women are quite different from those of the first three poems (the passive nun, the Princess and Carolina). None of these active women is rich, noble, or surrounded by luxury, nor is any described as waiting for her lover. They choose to take part actively in the relationship. The reversal of roles noted here, when compared especially to **"De invierno"** and **"Sonatina"**, is important for what it seems to reveal of Darío's inner nature and of his own role in life. For one thing, these women in **"Canción de otoño en primavera"**, are by critical agreement based more on Darío's own life than are the Princess and the other passive women. Darío offers little information about his degree of participation, but one may easily surmise that he played a willing student to their role as able teachers. Darío is also a more mature poet at this juncture, and is able to tell a tale more truthfully, with less need for the self-flattering embellishments, such as the association with Prince Charming, he used as a younger poet.

An interesting, little known poem entitled, **"Mima: Elegía pagana"**, dedicated to Manuel Argerich in 1893, contains a brief portrait of another woman who actively took her love-life into her own hands. Like many of the women

Darío found most seductive, Mima was also a dancer:

> ¿Sabéis? La rusa, la soberbia y blanca rusa
> que danzó en Buenos Aires, feliz como una musa
> enamorada, y sonrió mucho, y partió luego
> a dar sol a sus rosas al Paraguay de fuego.

A beautiful Russian exile, she spent her life fleeing from one place to another and from one love to another, "la rusa más hermosa de las rusas viajeras". Continuing that patterns, she has just left Buenos Aires on her way to Paraguay.

In an apparent attempt to console her rejected lover, Manuel Argerich, for the loss of her affections Darío writes:

> ¿No recuerdas un día, amante que la lloras,
> en que gozosa y orgullosa fue mi rima,
> encuadernado el libro con un guante de Mima?
> Propiciatoriamente, yo invocaba a Himeneo . . .
> Aún veo el libro todo blanco y oro . . .

One speculates, based on Darío's poem, the book bound with Mima's glove, the invocation of Hymen (the god of weddings) that there is perhaps the hint of a momentary attraction between Mima and Darío. A dancer without a country, she was mistress of many nationalities, "la petersburguesa, parisiense y latina / tuvo todas las gracias, y además, la argentina". Then, as mysteriously as she came, she disappeared: "Como la Diana de Falguière, ella ha partido / virgen a lanzar flechas al bosque del Olvido . . . / a cazar imposibles entre la selva obscura". The Russian dancer, a real, evanescent woman, has departed, pursuing her dream. Unlike the first group of women in Darío's poetry but like those in **"Canción de otoño en primavera"**, she takes charge of her own destiny, deciding actively when and where to go, and with whom to become involved.

This poem provides a fundamental clue to the origin of the dichotomy of active and passive women in Darío's poetry. The primary reason why Mima differs from the passive women of the earlier poems is that her portrait is drawn from real life, and real women in Darío's poetry seem to behave differently from imaginary women.

In truth, at the simplest level, there seems to be a correlation in all of the poems between the apparent fact that the passive, princess-like females are women created from Darío's imagination. The active women tend to be real women who actually lived their relationship with the poet. The awareness that this pattern exists allows one to surmise as well that Darío's passive women may exist in poetry to allow him some manner of control which active women did not allow him in life. From what is known about his turbulent love-life, he often felt that his life was out of control.

One reason for this feeling, and one possible source for the dichotomy of feminine behavior may have its origin in the well-known circumstances of his early life. As a child he was abandoned by both parents, and felt especially devastated by a strange visit from his mother when still a young boy: "Un día, una vecina me llamó a su casa. Estaba allí una señora vestida de negro que me abrazó y me besó llorando . . . La vecina me dijo: 'Esta es tu verdadera madre. Se llama Rosa y ha venido a verte desde muy lejos'. No comprendí de pronto, como tampoco me di exacta cuenta de las mil palabras de ternura y consejos que me prodigara en la despedida aquella dama, para mí extraña. Me dio unos ducles, unos regalitos. Fue para mí rara visión. Desapareció de nuevo. No debía volver a verla hasta más de veinte años después". Darío's relationship with his mother is fraught with strangeness—on the day he received word of her death, "Curiosa reacción: el 19 escribe la '**Marcha triunfal**' en la isla de Martín García".

It is reasonable to surmise that, abandoned by his mother in childhood, he spent much of his life consciously or unconsciously looking for a surrogate. In his poetry, the women he chose to describe from his imagination conform to the mores of poetry and the tastes of his time, and as such are passive, beautiful, silent wisps. He has perfected the lyricism with which they are portrayed, and emotionally he has drawn them to satisfy his inner need for some control over his life. But the women he actually knew well enough to describe through their reactions to a real relationship are much more active. One critic resolves Darío's sexual dilemma by saying that is not describing individual women "con nombre propio, con alma propia y propiedad ante la vida. Su canción está enamorada donjuanescamente del sexo contrario, sin matices, sin exigente acoplamiento mental de la carne".

Quite to the contrary, however, is his psychological dilemma, for while he may love "womankind", the closer the specific woman is to real life and to Darío himself, as for example those women in "**Canción de otoño en primavera**" and "**Mima: Elegía pagana**", the more active and demanding she becomes. In these poetic memoirs, then, Darío becomes more the timid, shy figure he was in life, and the women in these poems the initiators of intimacy as they often were in his life.

The patterns of Darío's passive acceptance of active, aggressive females was established early in life in elementary school, and also in the well known seduction of him by the siren, Rosario Murillo, which led to their unhappy marriage.

Those poems addressed to Francisca Sánchez, his last mistress, reflect an almost conscious awareness that what he may have sought all his life in real women by his passivity was an active mother figure to take care of him. Torres Bodet agrees in essence, when he explains Francisca's role in Darío's life: "Sería su querida, su enfermera, su cocinera, su amiga, su ama de llaves y, en ocasiones, su Xantipa también, según algunos suponen y otros lo afirman . . . Aquí, procede una explicación. Rubén tuvo siempre las cualidades—y los defectos—del niño". Having the qualities and personality of a child, he desperately needed a mother.

In the poems "**A Francisca**" (dated 1914), Darío finds himself in great need of loving care, a care which Francisca apparently supplies. He urges her to be an unguent to cure

him, and later a Lazarillo to guide him, "Lazarillo de Dios en mi sendero, / Francisca Sánchez acompáñame. . . ." She replaces his thoughts of mourning and martyrdom with those of honey, "En mi pensar de duelo y de martirio, / casi inconsciente me pusiste miel". Francisca seems to provide the answer to his everlasting problem. As one of his early loves in "**Canción de otoño en primavera**" caused him to lose his faith and illusions, Francisca now returns them to him, "Seguramente, Dios te ha conducido / para regar el árbol de mi fe". Late in life, he found at last the mother-figure he sought. As with any real life situation, however, there were also many moments of disenchantment.

It may be argued that this could all simply be one more dramatic pose in Darío's pageant-like pilgrimage through life, but knowing about his personal life and especially about his abandonment as a child together with his frequent encounters with sexually-aggressive girls, it is reasonable to suspect that the diverse relationships depicted in his poems reveal a good deal of truth. He found women to take care of him, assuming for himself the child's role in the relationship, and the women assuming the mother's role.

The contrast too between real women and literary women might stem in part as well from the duality of character noted astately by Torres Bodet: "Y es que, en arte, Rubén fue siempre el maestro y el protector; en tanto que, en la vida, se resignó a ser el alumno y el protegido. Ello explica sus vehemencias juveniles de enamorado, sus infortunios de esposo y su paciente (o impaciente) apego a la compañía de Francisca Sánchez . . ." Ultimately his ideal woman would probably be one not unlike Francisca, who would willingly play Penelope to Darío's incessant Odysseus.

The poems all show a unity of thought, then, in that the active role always belongs to the mentor, and the passive role to the pupil, regardless of gender. One may fairly say that, while writing poetry showing very stereotypical feminine roles, Darío remains surprisingly tolerant of quite another kind of role in the women he actually knew, loved and lived with.

Darío's poetry ultimately reflects the duality of his life. In life, real women are independent and behave with minds of their own, accepting or rejecting love as they wish. It is only in literature that a passive, beautiful princess still waits for Prince Charming to come rescue her. By the time he wrote "**Canción de otoño en primavera**", Darío too seems to have realized this:

> En vano busqué a la princesa
> que estaba triste de esperar.
> La vida es dura. Amarga y pesa.
> ¡Ya no hay princesa que cantar!

Catherine Davies (essay date 1989)

SOURCE: "Woman as Image in Darío's *Prosas Profanas*," in *Romance Quarterly,* Vol. 36, No. 3, August, 1989, pp.

281-88.

[*In the following essay, Davies examines classical and Judeo-Christian images of woman in* Prosas profanas, *assessing the role of the archetypal female in Darío's verse.*]

Rubén Darío's **Prosas Profanas,** first published in Buenos Aires in 1896, was an audacious attempt to introduce the "aristocracia literaria" of European learned culture into what Darío considered a Philistine South America. It is significant that all but two of the thirty-three poems of the first edition involve gynaecomorphic images. Two-thirds of them take the female figure from Classical myth and the rest from Christian mythology and the Neo-classical reworkings of folk-tale—in short, from the quintessence of Western culture. It was into this highly contrived and erudite framework that Darío introduced the erotic and its apparent rejection of the narrow-minded, hypocritical mores of a sex-obsessed bourgeoisie. This was an idealistic eroticism, symptomatic of the end-of-century moral and spiritual malaise which the poet, in this case, attempted to overcome by means of "el culto por la belleza." Through a mystical appreciation of artistic creation Darío believed that the poet-idealist could transcend a banal, dualistic existence and aspire to universal harmony, preferably within himself. In *Prosas Profanas* the dominant sign of the poet's paradoxical endeavour to find the eternal and absolute in himself is the female figure, but because of the multiple and contradictory meanings attributed to it in Western culture, the female figure imposes itself on the text and finally subverts the poet's initial aesthetic undertaking.

Nowhere was the ancient practice of using female allegorical figures to represent abstract concepts more prolific than in the Paris of the Belle Epoque, the city of Darío's dreams, "la ciudad del Arte, de la Belleza y la Gloria; y sobre todo . . . la capital del Amor" which he finally visited in 1892. Only a handful of the poems of *Prosas Profanas* were written before this date. The voluptuous female classical iconography of the Parisian "statuomanie" and of the numerous other well-documented literary and artistic sources (Spanish Golden Age and French Neoclassical and nineteenth-century texts, translations of the Classics, books of Art such as Ménard's *Mythologie dans l'art ancien et modern,* etc.) which Darío scoured at the time, is reproduced in *Prosas Profanas*. Written "en pleno concepto clásico de lo erótico," according to Salinas, the collection recreates through myth a Parnassian illusion of eternal beauty in which sexual desire is enjoyed as both natural and good. From Góngora to Leconte de Lisle and Menéndez y Pelayo, Classical myth had perpetuated the deceptive vision of a world without contradictions, history or change, a superficial world which Barthes calls a "harmonious display of essences." The beauty and sensuality associated with a reputedly licentious Antiquity, where female sexuality bore no moral recrimination, is recreated through the "ninfas," "musas" and "bacantes" of *Prosas Profanas* as an acceptable and universal statement of Eros. The resulting female images, an amalgamation or distillation of Western cultural influences, can be compared to a series of holographs, three-dimensional pictures projected onto a flat surface giving simply an impression of depth. Mary Daly believes these are typical of patriarchal myth because they sustain the mystification of the female self. Certainly, in **Prosas Profanas** the most important female figure, Venus-Aphrodite, can be considered a fine, artistic distortion of femininity, the paragon of unchanging beauty, sexual charisma and carnal pleasure. Within the Classical vision of the collection she rules because of her beauty, "Ella es entre las reinas celestes la primera / pues es quien tiene el fuerte poder de la hermosura" (**"Coloquio de los Centauros"**). Beauty, like Art, has the ultimate power to deceive and transform and so "La Dea" comes to represent the poet's own "divina Idea", his own enigmatic concept of ideal beauty and his poetic creation through which he aspires to the absolute. But Venus is also the Goddess of Love and Fecundity who in **"Canto de la Sangre"** looks down with satisfaction on the spilt blood of virgins and the natural process of propagation. She represents Universal Harmony, and through her figure mere copulation acquires a transcendental and mystical significance. The female sign Venus indicates Art, Beauty and Poetry, man's most sublime ideals and creations, yet she is not autonomous, as she has emanated from the poet himself and the culture he attempts to absorb.

The illusory Classical world of charming delight, frozen for all time in polytheistic myth, allowed the erotic to enter "fin de siglo" refined tastes without vulgarity, censorship or remorse and is most apparent in the section "Recreaciones arqueol icas." In **"Friso,"** for example, the poet and his Eunice (sea-nymph), who is compared to the elegant "canéforas" or basket-bearers of Ancient Greece, contemplate a Neoclassical frieze which comes to life. The Dionysian procession draws the poet and his lover into the erotic vision where frenzied, intoxicated "ménades," half-naked, with nipples like "pomas ebúrneas," call for sex as a blossoming of Nature—like the daffodil (Narcissus) loved by Echo or the anemone (Adonis) loved by Aphrodite. The poet, hearing the cry of the self-castrated Atis, "triste pavor de la inviolada ninfa" and not wishing to disappoint his own nymph, proves his masculinity and celebrates his "regio triunfo" watched over by the voyeuristic "Dios viril," restrained in stone, and a host of strapping youths. The Classical mise-en-scène dispels any notion of moral reproach; sex in Antiquity was not taboo and chastity no great honour. In **"Friso"** the female figure embodies the natural principle of Eros, either as exalted womanhood (nymph) or uncontrollable sexual passion ("ménade") within a timeless patriarchy. However, the playful eroticism of this poem becomes more significant within the context of *Prosas Profanas* when it is associated with reproduction.

Reflecting the Ancient Greek assumption that the procreation of the father, Zeus, was a metaphor for the creation of the world, *Prosas Profanas* establishes an analogy between sexual and literary creation where man's sexual prowess is a metaphor for artistic endeavour and achievement. "Let the eunuch rant!" goads Darío in the Introduction to the collection, "Cuando una musa (woman) te de un hijo (poem), queden las otro ocho encinta." Female allegory represents not only the partner in this sexual/

textual union, i.e., poetic inspiration, but the Muse, like Venus, also represents the progeny of man, poetry itself. In **"Pórtico"** the "musa" is a simple personification of poetry, rhythm and, of course, music—the art of the Muses. Under the auspices of the goddess Harmonia she travels from Greece to Spain, symbolizing the creative energy which gave rise to Mediterranean lyricism, and she is finally approached by the young poet-warrior, Salvador Rueda, for whose book **"Pórtico"** was originally written. In **"El Cisne"** mortal woman is equated directly with poetry without the intermediate figure of the Muse. Making use of the myth in which Zeus, in the form of a swan, seduces Leda, who gives birth to Helen, in **"El Cisne"** the mortal Leda is replaced by "la nueva Poesía": "bajo tus alas blancas la nueva Poesía / concibe en una gloria de luz y harmonía / la Helena eterna y pura que encarna el ideal." In this address to the "Cisne wagneriano" the projected meaning on the female form is both poetry, or what Darío called in *Historia de mis libros* the new "manera de concebir y cultivar la belleza", as well as conceived, ideal beauty itself. But poetry, from the Greek word "to make" (and, implicitly "opera" from the Latin "work") is of man's making, in this case, Wagner's. "La nueva poesía" (Leda, Muse and Venus) is both actively created by the poet and then used as an instrument by means of which he can transcend banal existence. Any possible analogies with a female role in the creation of beauty are dispensed with. From this use of Classical myth in *Prosas Profanas* a Neoplatonic vision of the eternal feminine emerges in which the female form represents aspiration, the unrealizable, the non-existent, and erotic love is sublimated as creative process initiated by the poet. The analogy is most explicit in the poems **"Mía"** and **"Dice Mía,"** where the sole identity of the woman, whose name is "Mía," is to be possessed sexually by the poet. Moreover, Darío wrote in the Introduction to the collection, "Mi literatura es *mía* en mí"; he brings into existence poetry / woman and they stem from within himself. Like Zeus, who both engendered and brought forth his progeny, so the godlike "Pantocrator" of *Prosas Profanas* engages in a reversal of biological roles; he fathers woman-poetry-the text; he is the source of his own ideals.

However, this carefully constructed yet superficial mirage of self-sufficient perfection, of a man's world of sensuality where the poet is free from social and literary constraints and woman is the fabricated ideal to which he aspires, is insidiously undermined by just half a dozen poems introducing a conflicting strand of mythological references: the Judeo-Christian. Darío could not shake off the influence of an intense Jesuit education, nor the Christian values and images of woman this entailed. Neither could he step outside of nineteenth-century middle-class culture and its ambivalent attitude towards women, based on the precepts of the Church, despite his initial proposition. The Bible, Catholic liturgy and iconography taught that sex was sin and that the Fall, symbolized by the discovery of shame and the naked body, is personified by Eve. In Catholicism, virginity as a means of redemption acquires a moral value quite unknown in Antiquity and celibacy brings man closer to God. Chastity, a prime virtue, is incarnate in the Virgin Mary who, although never

explicitly named in *Prosas Profanas,* is ever-present. The holograph Venus is strongly contested by the equally insubstantial holograph Mary as patriarchy's representation of the ideal. Not surprisingly, such mutually incompatible female icons, belonging to quite different cultures and attitudes towards sex, give rise to tension and contradiction in *Prosas Profanas* present in the very title and Introduction. Here, religious and erotic terms are juxtaposed in an attempt to annual the opposition between the sacred and the profane posed by a dualistic interpretation of existence. The church bells call the poet-monk not to the mass of his youth with all its religious connotations ("fuegos divinos," "órgano," "antífonas," "breviario") but to the orgy of a mature man with sexual desires ("ojos de fuego," "fiesta," "clavicordio," "las rosas de las bocas"). Likewise, woman is "eterno incensario" (with the suggestion of Mary), yet "de carne." In the poem **"Ite, missa est"** Darío similarly inserts religious terminology into an erotic context to violate the Christian concept of sanctity. The poet worships not Mary but a snow-white virgin with Marian characteristics, and he sees the rituals of sex in terms of those of the Holy Mass where the consecrated host becomes the body of Christ and is offered to God as sacrifice. In the poet's "amorosa misa," it is his virgin's spirit which is made sacred and then offered as sacrifice to Love. The idealized, pure "sonámbula" is not only created by the poet; he is also the active agent of her deification. But this holy female figure of impenetrable mystery is not to his liking. Eroticism, "rojo beso ardiente," breaks the taboo and shatters the Neoplatonic icon; the virgin will become a growling "faunesa," beastlike with passion, yet, because the enigma of the Sphinx has been revealed, she will be "como convaleciente," dependent on the poet, "estupefacta." The virgin and the beast are contained within one female figure which is exalted or debased, idolized or sacrificed by the poet at will, although ultimately he can find no resolution between the two antithetical images of woman. In fact, by presenting the erotic as a detraction from the ideal an iconoclastic Darío again undermines his initial quest for Classical harmony. In **"Bouquet"** the "blanco serafín" to whom it is dedicated, Blanca Gomez Palacios, is also an idealized virgin who will celebrate her "bodas de nieve" with "el sueño," and virginity is once more synonymous with beatific purity (represented by the swans, white roses, lilies, candles and stars). But the poet, delighting in desecration, intends to rouse the virgin's passion: "¡Mira como mancha tu corpiño blanco / la más roja rosa que hay en mi jardín!" The subtle presence of Mary and the Church is most explicit in the poem **"El poeta pregunta por Stella"** written by Darío in memory of his first wife. The ambivalent "lirio divino," primarily a traditional symbol of purity and associated in this poem with Saint Gabriel, "lirio de las Anunciaciones," or with Christ himself, "lirio . . . que naces con la albura de las hostias sublimes," suggests Heaven and, in "la mano de las vírgenes," Mary, the Bride of Christ, the Church and her attributes: "lino sin mácula," "cándidas perlas." Heavenly beauty, the world to which the poet's ideal Stella belongs, can be seen in terms of the chaste, untainted with human passion, "la sangre de las rosas pecadoras." Yet even in this poem the phallic overtones of the "lirio, florido príncipe" indicate a more prurient interpretation which make a mockery of the Pre-Raphaelite image of impeccability.

The negation of the idolized Virgin is made even more explicit in *Prosas Profanas* through the figure of the sexually experienced Eve, the evil temptress wielding the dark power of the she-devil. Darío steps outside the bounds of Christian ethics and praises the dark beauty of Eve without compunction in **"Alaba los ojos negros de Julia."** Eve, associated in the original version of this poem with the Orient and the infidel, personifies the bewitching power of female sexual attraction which, the poet believes, can control and destroy man. Pentisilea, Queen of the Amazons, Judith the tyrannicide and Cleopatra, "encantadora de coronas," similarly abused their sexual charms, their "luz negra," subverting enlightenment for men and giving women "hoy más ciencia que los sabios." Yet, for the poet, this "luz negra" is "luz divina," "más luz que la luz blanca del sol," represented on this occasion by a blue-eyed Venus. Eve-like characteristics are also found in the "andaluza hechicera" of **"Elogio de la seguidilla"** and in the "maligna y bella" Eulalia herself. By exalting both Eve and Venus and by breaking the spell of virginal holiness with sexual desire, the poet attempts to annul the false dichotomy between evil sexuality and virtuous chastity in women, the basis of "fin de siglo" mores. Ironically, however, the mere allusion to Catholic and middle-class images of woman necessarily flaws the Classical facade of *Prosas Profanas* because it acknowledges and introduces into the mythical world of the text a contradictory, historical reality.

The common beliefs of the day regarding women are put in the mouth of the misogynist centaur Hipea in **"Coloquio de los centauros,"** whose soured comments are nevertheless outweighed later by Quirón's beautiful description of the birth of Venus:

HIPEA

Yo sé de la hembra humana la original infamia.
Venus anima artera sus máquinas fatales,
tras sus radiantes ojos ríen traidores males,
de su floral perfume se exhala sutil daño;
su cráneo obscuro alberga bestialidad y engaño.
Tiene las formas puras del ánfora, y la risa
del agua que la brisa riza y el sol irisa;
mas la ponzoña ingénita su máscara pregona:
majores son el águila, la yegua y la leona.

Even in the nineteenth century the Catholic Church could see woman as "the door of the devil, the way of iniquity . . . the ship-wreck of man, the clothed serpent, the ardent oven," although redeemable through motherhood. This too was the view of the sanctimonious, property-minded sectors who considered virginity an investment. The confluence of bourgeois and Christian morality meant that woman, cast as angel or whore, was dangerous, and her sexuality had to be controlled by chastity or the sacred institution of marriage. The middle-class myth of "passive womanhood," which had developed historically to justify

woman's place outside the secular world of productivity, meant that, although regarded intellectually inferior, she could embody the spiritual. But, as Ellen Pollack points out, "the spiritual and erotic attributes in a single woman" were therefore impossible, and the "decarnalization of female virtue" was as dear to the bourgeois as to the Medieval Church. It is this vulgar scenario of a society rife with sexual repression, hypocrisy, guilt and prostitution that *Prosas Profanas* attempts to transcend in order to sustain both the poet's female embodiment of the ideal and his mystical vision of sexual love. Thus the profound significance of the Venus image which encapsulates in one figure the sensuality of Eve and the goodness of Mary. As in **"El reino interior,"** the poet, faced with the deceptive polarization, the binary division of human experience into spiritual virtue and temporal vice, apparently no longer needs to opt for one or the other, but aspires to a harmony of the two.

However, the synthetic Venus, like Mary and Eve, is no more than a poetic construct, an incomplete image and one of various superimposed holographs of an imaginary eternal feminine. The Classical female allegory of perfection is a tool and is not only manipulated by the poet but is also flawed by the insidious presence of other contradictory meanings attributed to the female sign. Venus cannot stand alone as the personification of the final, ideal stage in *Prosas Profanas*'s mystical and erotic quest for oneness within the self. The ultimate answer to the enigma of life, the "arcano fatal," can only be androgyny. As the wise Quirón explains in **"Coloquio de los centauros,"** "Por suma ley un día llegará el himeneo / que el soñador aguarda. Cinis será Ceneo"; woman will be man, the mystery of the feminine Other will be revealed and the Sphinx—controlled by man and hence no longer feared—will release her secret to her "soberano." Androgyny heralds the absolute, the resolution of the enigma of life and the death of woman and passion. In this Classical concept of bisexuality the poet imagines a total, self-referential existence, in which sexual asceticism leads to the peace of death, "la victoria de la progenie humana."

In *Prosas Profanas,* then, the principal gynaecomorphic images of Western humanist culture are used to express a complex aesthetic undertaking fraught with underlying spiritual and moral conflict. The poet shapes his spiritual ideal in female form but cannot avoid or resolve the irreconcilable interpretations inherent in the sign. Despite his efforts to create a timeless, Classical vision of love, "fin de siglo" patriarchal assumptions inevitably infiltrate the text and the illusion is broken. Female allegory proves to be an inadequate poetic recourse for Darío, which helps explain his movement away from the Classical hedonism of *Prosas Profanas* after 1897 towards more reflective contemplation of life and death.

Cathy L. Jrade   (essay date 1990)

SOURCE: "Socio-Political Concerns in the Poetry of Rubén Darío," in *Latin American Literary Review,* Vol. XVIII,

No. 6, July-December, 1990, pp. 36-49.
[*In the following essay, Jrade identifies sociopolitical themes in Darío's poetry, focusing on the literary and political similarities between Spanish-American modernism and an emergent Spanish-American identity.*]

Critics who have set out to examine Rubén Darío's political poetry have tended to define politics in a narrow manner. They have confined themselves for the most part to those poems that deal explicitly with American themes. As a result of this focus, scholars as perceptive as Pedro Salinas, Arturo Torres-Ríoseco, and Enrique Anderson-Imbert, among others, have written about gaps in Darío's interest in politics—usually from the 1888 publication of *Azul . . .* [*Blue . . .*] to the 1905 publication of *Cantos de vida y esperanza* [*Songs of Life and Hope*]—and have tended to emphasize a few specific poems such as **"A Colón"** [**"To Columbus"**], **"Los cisnes"** [**"The Swans"**], **"Salutación al optimista"** [**"Greetings to the Optimist"**], **"A Roosevelt"** [**"To Roosevelt"**], **"Salutación al águila"** [**"Greetings to the Eagle"**], **"Raza"** [**"Race"**], **"Pax"** [**"Peace"**], and **"Canto a la Argentina"** [**"Song to Argentina"**]. But Darío's concern with social and political conditions in Latin America is present throughout his career. Much of his writing subtly deals with the search for a proper course and identity for the new Spanish American nations and their literature during the second half of the nineteenth century. His poetic vision offers a response to trends that simultaneously molded and alienated him. As an intellectual responding to his surroundings, Darío was not alone.

Aware of their extraordinary place in Spanish American history, Modernist poets broke with Spanish models which they understood to be both grandiose and inflexible. They turned their eyes instead toward Europe to bring themselves up to the present and into the future. This attitude is evident in Darío's selection in 1888 of the term "Modernism" to designate the tendencies of Spanish American poets. This choice underscores the Modernists' will to be modern, that is, to become contemporaneous with all of Europe but most especially with Paris. The poets sought to leave behind—either through their travels or their imagination—an anachronistic, local reality in order to establish for themselves a modern mode of discourse in which they could speak for the first time with their own voice and with a clear, critical vision of Spanish America.

Thus the most "escapist" of Modernist literature almost immediately became, as noted by Octavio Paz, a literature of exploration and return. Modernist writers turned their attention from the most up-to-date European trends towards home and resurrected, through flights of fancy as much as through historical fact, a Spanish American past that included ancient civilizations, indigenous peoples, and a Spanish American consciousness. This consciousness is clear in the Modernist attitude toward language and poetry. From the beginning, their concern for formal perfection reflected, along with Parnassian influences, a desire to formalize and to found a modern Spanish American discourse. Their pursuit of beauty throughout the centuries and across all borders was a manifestation of their desire to choose freely the elements of their ideal language. At the same time, Modernist authors struggled with the dominant poetic and prosaic modes of discourse in their attempt to find their own voice. This founding effort was simultaneously aesthetic and political, with the political becoming more pronounced when the pressures that gave rise to Modernism exploded in crisis in 1898 with the Spanish American War and later in 1903 with the creation of the state of Panama through United States intervention.

The social, economic, and political conditions that most directly affected the formation of Modernism of course vary from country to country. There were, however, certain key factors that consistently came into play. For the most part, the last decades of the nineteenth century saw a consolidation of power which brought about a new degree of political stability—despite the periodic resurgence of "caudillismo" and anarchistic tendencies. At the same time, economic reorganization and growth brought prosperity and affluence to the upper classes. In urban centers, wealth and international trade encouraged a perceptible Europeanization of life. As Roberto González Echevarría has expressed it, in exchange for its raw materials, Spanish America received culture, primarily in the form of manufactured products. The turn-of-the-century flood of luxury items filled the homes of the old landed aristocracy, the *nouveaux riches,* and the aspiring bourgeoisie. It also created an image of life that left a lasting impression upon the poetic imagination of the writers of the time, an image that evoked the sense of well-being, ease, and fashionable excess characteristic of the Parisian *Belle Epoque,* that is, of Paris during the three decades beginning with the 1880's.

Members of the ruling class allied themselves with foreign financiers and investors, and their primary ambition became the accumulation of capital at the expense of more traditional goals. The political philosophy of the day was the Positivism of Comte and later that of Spencer, both of which became linked with a type of social Darwinism. Comte had developed a philosophical system that rejected metaphysics and relied exclusively on the positive sciences. His final aim was to reform society so that all men could live in harmony and comfort. During the peace that followed the political consolidation of the 1860's, Positivism became the philosophy of order, promoting progress, science, and the "miracles" of free enterprise. Society in Spanish America was to be organized upon a more rational basis than ever before, and humanity was to find itself living in a world without problems. Scientists were believed to be the bearers of a demonstrable truth and trustees of the future. The evils of "modern life" and industrialization were accepted as necessary for national development. In reality, however, Positivism provided the ruling classes with a new vocabulary to legitimate injustice as liberal ideology was replaced by the struggle for existence and the survival of the fittest. Inequalities were now explained, not by race or inheritance or religion, but by science. The Mexican Porfirio Díaz and his "científicos," the oligarchy of the Argentine landowners, and the Chilean nitrate barons best represented the political scene during this era.

Positivism generated in most Modernists a strongly ambivalent attitude. They maintained a respect for science, its breakthroughs, and its contributions to progress; they rejected it, however, as the ultimate measure of all things. Despite the promises made, it became clear that, far from becoming more understandable, life appeared more enigmatic, and the great inventions and discoveries had not provided answers to the fundamental questions of existence. If anything, Spanish America's growing prosperity, and its increasing involvement with the industrial capitals of the world, brought about social dislocations that heightened the sense of crisis among its writers. Two essential elements in the social context of Modernist art were the disappearance of the old aristocracy along with its patronage of poetic production and the transformation of all products of human enterprise—including art—into merchandise. In this situation, poets had to earn their living producing a marketable commodity. Many supported themselves as journalists at the same time that they sought, through their well-crafted poetry, to assert themselves in a world where the items of highest esteem were luxurious, opulent, and usually imported. Some, like Julián del Casal, became marginalized, creating a bohemian response to the vulgarity and utilitarianism of bourgeois society. Others, like Darío in his famous "El rey burgués" ["The Bourgeois King"], scorned the materialism, mediocre conformity, and aesthetic insensitivity of the growing bourgeoisie. Still others, like José Martí, put their faith in the superior individual, "el hombre magno" [the great man], who could see beyond the pressures of rapid urbanization and commercialization.

With these conditions, modernity, as it is understood in Western culture, arrived in Spanish America—or, at the very least, to its great, cosmopolitan urban centers. Recent studies have emphasized that modernity, as a stage in the history of Western civilization, began as early as the second half of the eighteenth century. Its essential characteristics are linked to scientific and technological progress, the industrial revolution, and the sweeping economic and social changes brought about by capitalism. The ideological adjustments necessitated by these far-reaching alterations in the fabric of life have consistently generated a literary response or, as Octavio Paz notes in *Los hijos del limo,* modern poetry has always represented a reaction against the modern era and its various manifestations, whether they be the Enlightenment, critical reason, liberalism, positivism, or Marxism. Modernism is the literary response to Spanish America's entrance into modernity. It is a response to the spiritual and aesthetic vacuum created by the positivist abandonment of religion and metaphysics in favor of science as well as by the positivist support of materialistic, bourgeois values.

As the Modernists formulated their reaction to modernity and sought to deal with their feelings of alienation and anguish, they discovered appealing paradigms in the European literature that they had rushed to read in their attempt to create a modern poetic language consonant with the modern times. They found appropriate models in English and German Romanticism and French Symbolism,

for these literary movements too had been reactions to the spiritual upheavals generated by modern life. A primary design that the Romantics elaborated for possible recovery and that was later adapted by the Symbolists and the Modernists centers on analogy, that vision of the universe as a system of correspondences in which language is the universe's double.

The Modernist recourse to analogy sheds light on its cosmopolitanism, its obsession with verbal elegance and musicality, and its insistence on artistic freedom, formal experimentation, and heightened individuality. Many of these features, as well as others, were further fostered by the artistic rejection of what Calinescu calls "bourgeois modernity" [*Faces of Modernity: Avant-Garde, Decadence, Kitsch,* 1977]. As Spanish America entered the world economy, it came in touch with a tradition of modern values which encouraged faith in progress, pragmatism, and the beneficial effects of science and technology. Commercialization and commodification affected all aspects of life including art and time, and success was judged by the accumulation of wealth. Modernist authors responded to the resulting superficiality and vacuity of everyday existence with what had become another tradition, namely, the expression of defiantly hostile anti-bourgeois attitudes. This expression took many forms including art for art's sake, eccentricity, dandyism, and decadentism.

In their unrelenting search for the ideal poetic language, one with which they could address their concerns regarding the life and future of their countries, Modernist poets embraced and reconciled varying styles, images, religious beliefs, philosophic perspectives, and modes of discourse. Their ability and desire to incorporate a bewildering diversity of images and ideas is linked, in part, to the economic imperialism of the end of the nineteenth century. Surrounded by an overwhelming proliferation of imported manufactured items, the Modernists created a parallel poetic environment in which things proliferate not in a referential but in an artificial system. Nature is filtered through any number of aesthetic landscapes from any number of cultures, periods, or artistic media. Modernist art is filled with Versaillesque palaces, Oriental gardens and interiors, gods and nymphs, gold and pearls, folding screens (*biombos*), divans, lacquered pieces, urns, and tapestries. These places and things are described—especially in early Modernist verse—with sophisticated vocabulary and numerous adjectives that both reinforce a sense of wealth and accumulation and, more importantly, reflect the relationship that Modernist poets had with the materialism of bourgeois society. This relationship was strongly ambivalent. On the one hand, the values of the dominant classes are exalted in Modernism's rich language. On the other, however, the emphasis on wealth is criticized as superficial when it is seen as an end in itself and not recognized as subservient to the poets' profound search for transcendental beauty and universal harmony.

The impact of this socio-political context on Modernism has generally been overlooked in favor of literary factors. It is, however, precisely this context that forms the background to poems by Darío that have not been considered political but that now can be read as reflections of socio-political concerns. Darío's response to the spiritual and aesthetic vacuum in Spanish America resulting from the materialistic and positivistic orientation of bourgeois culture is present in his formulation of Modernist principles, goals, and ideals. The challenge presented to bourgeois society by these ideals is political in so far as through them Darío aspired to reorder dominant values, placing transcendental, poetic goals above materialistic ends. Yet the language of exaltation comes, at least at first, from the flood of luxury items and cultural models imported into Spanish America. Darío's struggle to find himself and a modern mode of discourse for Spanish America—one that is truly Spanish American—persists throughout both editions of *Azul . . .*, both editions of *Prosas profanas* [*Profane Proses*], and into *Cantos de vida y esperanza*. However, by the time he publishes *Cantos,* following the Spanish American War and U.S. intervention in Panama, certain elements have changed, and in his work the subtle discussion of socio-political tensions is replaced by boldly political statements.

While "politics" is easily found in Darío's earliest poetry, *Azul . . .* has generally been considered apolitically aesthetic and "esteticista" [preoccupied by aesthetic concerns]. The short stories and the vignettes of *En Chile* [*In Chile*] show Darío's eagerness to experiment with the styles of many periods, his enthusiasm for the creative possibilities of all the arts, and his audacity, like that of the Romantics before him, in breaking out of the traditional confines of specific genres. Equally important, however, was Darío's expression of disillusionment with the mundane and pedestrian, especially when everyday reality implied a withering of aesthetic and spiritual powers. "El rubí" ["The Ruby"], "El sátiro sordo" ["The Deaf Satyr"], "El palacio del sol" ["The Sun Palace"], "El rey burgués" ["The Bourgeois King"] and, perhaps most directly, the introductory section of *En Chile* all criticize the limited and limiting vision of bourgeois materialism, science, and technology. *En Chile* begins with a sentence-long paragraph that suggests the fundamental focus of Darío's writings at this point.

> Sin pinceles, sin paleta, sin papel, sin lápiz, Ricardo, poeta lírico incorregible, huyendo de las agitaciones y turbulencias, de las máquinas y de los fardos, del ruido monótono de los tranvías y el chocar de los caballos con su repiqueteo de caracoles sobre las piedras; del tropel de los comerciantes; del grito de los vendedores de diarios; del incesante bullicio e inacabable hervor de este puerto; en busca de impresiones y de cuadros, subió al Cerro Alegre, que, gallardo como una gran roca florecida, luce sus flancos verdes, sus montículos coronados de casas risueñas escalonadas en la altura, rodeadas de jardines, con ondeantes cortinas de enredaderas, jaulas de pájaros, jarras de flores, rejas vistosas y niños rubios de caras angélicas.

> [Without brushes, without palette, without paper, without pencil, fleeing the excitement and confusion, the machines and bundles, the monotonous noise of the trolleys and the jostling of horses with their ringing of hooves on the stones, the throng of merchants, the shouts of vendors, the incessant bustle and unending fervor of this port in search of impressions and scenes, Ricardo, an incorrigible lyric poet, climbed up to Happy Hill, which, elegant like a great flowering rock, displays its green sides, its mound crowned by smiling houses terraced at the summit, homes surrounded by gardens, with waving curtains of vines, cages of birds, vases of flowers, attractive railings, and blond children with angelic faces.]

The world of the modern, industrial city with its traffic, noise, and newspapers (the commercial side of writing) is left behind in search of "impressions and scenes," that is, in search of a nature filtered through, captured in (like the caged birds and cut flowers), and idealized by art (blond children with angelic faces). He leaves the Valparaíso "that performs transactions and that walks like a gust, that peoples the stores and invades the banks" in hopes of finding "el inmenso espacio azul" ["the immense blue space"]—not only the free, clear sky of beauty and tranquility, but also the source of artistic vision, which converts the author into a seer capable of recording the profound realities of existence, an existence that is in essence beauty and harmony, an existence that is offered as an alternative to the crass commercialization of the urban setting.

The poems of the first edition of *Azul . . .* reflect the same tensions and longings mixed with an additional element, that of erotic passion. **"El año lírico,"** [**"The Lyric Year"**] which begins the poetic selection, is an escape from the prosaic similar to that found in *En Chile* except the exotic, fanciful, and exquisite settings underscore a fundamental aspiration toward a harmony that is intimately linked to the fulfillment of sexual desire. Woman, more than the poet's Muse, is the Other that complements and completes and with whom the poet attains a vision of beauty, harmony, and artistic perfection that is simultaneously in tune with and supported by nature.

This exaltation of the seasons, of the natural order of things, and of sexuality is, as Paz recognized with regard to the Romantics, simultaneously a moral and political critique of civilization and an affirmation of a time before history. Erotic passion is a part of nature that has been inhibited and / or destroyed by the social order. Reclaiming its importance becomes linked with intuiting a primordial, more perfect world. As a result, these poems offer a vision that is atemporal and cosmopolitan (from classical antiquity in **"Primaveral"** [**"Spring"**], from British India in **"Estival"** [**"Summer"**], from the timeless world of art in **"Autumnal"** [**"Fall"**] and from South America in **"Invernal"** [**"Winter"**]) yet rooted in a reaction to a time and place. The political dimension is most evident in **"Estival."** Here the flow of sexual energy, which is portrayed as the animating force in nature and the inexorable bond between male and female, is disrupted by a cruel and senseless act on the part of the Prince of Wales. Power and modern technology burst upon a scene of lush sensuality and animalistic eroticism interrupting the natural order of things. The implications are both political and philosophic: human action must correspond to the natural harmony in life. Uninformed intervention destabilizes the balance of creation, unlocking violence, pain, and discord. Society must heed those who are in tune with the life force rather than those who blindly impose their will on it.

To the 1890 edition of *Azul* . . . Darío added poems that highlight his rapid maturation and his continued preoccupation with finding the "right" language for Spanish America. Most of the poems deal with literary figures and themes, with the exception of the first of the "Sonetos" ["Sonnets"] which describes the heroism of the Araucanian chief Caupolicán. The subject and placement of this initial poem colors the readings of those that follow, especially the sonnet on **"Salvador Díaz Mirón,"** which addresses the issue of the "newness" of the world for which the Modernists aspire to speak. Darío praises Díaz Mirón for the unfettered poetry with which the Mexican proclaims artistic strength and political freedom. The goal shared by both Modernists is to create a powerful new language that will speak for the nations of Spanish America, a language that breaks the chains of Spanish rule, that is up to date with Europe and North America, and that is, at the same time, faithful to Spanish America's originality and difference, that is, faithful to the ancient traditions and values represented by Caupolicán.

This new, Modernist language is in evidence with the subsequent publication of *Prosas profanas* in 1896. The struggles faced in the formulation of this new language appear in the form and substance of the prose introduction, "Palabras liminares," ["Liminal Words"] and in many of the poems of the collection. Despite the most widely held perceptions regarding *Prosas profanas,* these struggles continue to reflect a serious mix of social, economic, political as well as artistic considerations.

Prosas profanas is often described as a youthful, exuberant work full of exotic frivolity, playful imagination, and pleasure. When Darío himself refers to the content of the collection and its title he directs attention toward sexual passion—a sexual passion that is inextricably linked to art, poetic creation, music, and religion. He wrote: "Yo he dicho, en la misa rosa de mi juventud, mis antífonas, mis secuencias, mis profanas prosas." ["I have said, in the pink Mass of my youth, my antiphons, my sequences, my profane proses."] Darío plays with the medieval allusions, breaks expectations regarding the genre in question, and equates divine love and religious devotion with sexual exploits. While pleasure is certainly at issue here, so is a great deal more. As Javier Herrero has pointed out, this blasphemous religiosity consists of replacing the Christian gospel with a new one in which the altar is presided over by Venus. Darío aspires to a mystical experience—radically different from those of Catholic mystics—that reveals the meaning of the universe, life, and art. His poetic renovation proposes a revolutionary change in values.

It becomes clear that Darío's preoccupation with sexuality is linked to his fascination with the limits, restrictions, and constraints imposed on behavior, language, and vision by society. As a result, the socio-cultural context of Modernism is never far from his mind. He begins "Palabras liminares" with regret over the lack of understanding common to the general public and to professionals. It is art that sets him—and the others that he would rally to his cause—apart. Yet art is not imitation; it is the transgressing of limits; it is the reinterpretation and revitalization of habit and custom by each artist.

The art that Darío envisions is presented as an alternative to the dominant values of the day. Its aristocratic, exotic, and fanciful elements are offered in response to and escape from the vulgar materialism that flourished at the expense of aesthetic and spiritual concerns. This unstated dissatisfaction with the status quo forms the background to Darío's declaration that "yo detesto la vida y el tiempo en que me tocó nacer . . ." ["I detest the life and times to which I was born . . ."] This statement is not meant, however, as a rejection of Spanish America. Darío finds poetry in "our America," as he did in *Azul* . . ., in "the old things," in Palenke and Utatlán, in the sensual and refined Inca, and in the great Montezuma. The thrust is, nevertheless, toward the cosmopolis, exemplified by Buenos Aires, and toward the future, for in this envisioned milieu the Spanish, Spanish American, and European (Parisian) would find a balance that would facilitate the creation of a modern mode of discourse, that is, the creation of musical verses in which "each word has a soul."

The reference to the soul of language implies a body which, in Darío's poetry, is clearly female. She is—as seen before—the ideal other who promises love, happiness, erotic fulfillment, emotional and even spiritual salvation. She is also the lover of the poet, the "flesh" of poetry, poetic language. With her, the poet will achieve his ideal and visionary discourse—a discourse that fills the void left by positivism, materialism, and commercialization. He therefore concludes "Palabras liminares" with the mandate: "Y la primera ley, creador: crear. Bufe el eunuco. Cuando una musa te dé un hijo, queden las otras ocho encinta." ["And the first law, creator: create. Let the eunuch snort. When one muse gives you a child, let the other eight remain pregnant."] Despite the jocular tone of this command, Darío is never blind to the possibility that he may not find the language that would make possible his response to society and his vision for the future. This fear forms the background to the first three poems of *Prosas profanas*.

Darío begins with Eulalia of **"Era un aire suave. . ."** [**"It was a soft air . . ."**]. By characterizing her—or actually her golden laughter—as cruel, Darío softens the bold and ambitious declaration of artistic goals of the prose preface. He acknowledges the possible recalcitrance on the part of poetic language to be molded to the form he envisions. By calling her eternal, he affirms his aspiration to take Spanish American discourse out of its limited and anachronistic present and to have it become "modern" through a syncretic exaltation of the beauty and art of all ages—primarily as they come to him filtered through contemporary French sensibilities.

At the perfect point in the timeless evening of the poem, surrounded by auspicious music and an ivory-white swan, the poet will join with Eulalia, vanquishing his rivals, the "vizconde rubio" [the blond viscount] and the "abate joven" [the young abbot]. This reference to the defeat of his social and literary competitors is crucial. It underscores the poet's success in a society where artists are no longer rewarded, through patronage, for the nobility of their spirit but rather must compete in the marketplace producing a desirable commodity. It also emphasizes Darío's sense of having "caught up" with and even superseded those who courted Eulalia earlier, namely his literary role models—most specifically the Verlaine of *Fêtes galantes*. Unfortunately the poet's happiness is mitigated by the fact that there is no lasting amorous conquest. On the contrary, he remains her page, her servant. The first section of **"Era un aire suave . . ."** ends with Eulalia's mocking laughter.

With this emphasis on Eulalia's aloof nature and the possible intractability of poetic language, **"Era un aire suave . . ."** anticipates the lament as well as the images of **"Yo persigo una forma . . ."** [**"I pursue a form . . ."**], which was added as the last poem to the 1901 edition of *Prosas profanas*. But whereas **"Yo persigo una forma . . ."** pretends to decry the poet's limitations ("Yo persigo una forma que no encuentra mi estilo, / . . . / Y no hallo sino la palabra que huye, / la iniciación melódica que de la flauta fluye . . ." ["I pursue a form that my style does not find, / . . . / And I find only the word that flees, / the melodic initiation that flows from the flute . . ."]), **"Era un aire suave . . ."** suggests cautious optimism as Darío enters the *fêtes galantes* and competes with Verlaine and his other (imported) role models and rivals.

Darío's attempt to respond to and master the proliferation of cultural elements that dominated European and Spanish American values at the end of the nineteenth century is central as well to **"Divagación"** [**"Wandering"**], the second poem in *Prosas profanas*. **"Divagación"** is filled with cosmopolitan references, exquisite vocabulary, and esoteric proper names. And, like **"Era un aire suave . . . ,"** it deals with a beloved that is much more than a possible love interest. She is the other with whom Darío aspires to attain the perfect poetic vision. Yet, throughout his poetic journey across the globe, he finds that no one woman can satisfy, no one style can fulfill his longing for an original mode of discourse. The poet's aspiration to a comprehensive grasp of reality takes him through a literary "museum," which he ultimately leaves behind. He affirms instead the transcendental power of poetry, through which he claims divine knowledge and authority. He makes this claim in the final three stanzas of the poem in which he leads the reader off the map, out of the world of inhibiting cultural conventions, into the realm where all styles become one.

At the end, Darío's female Other evokes a male voice that speaks with mystical overtones. When Darío suggests that his love sleeps as he lights the censers, the quiet takes on a religious quality that is reinforced by the mention of a unicorn—associated with Christ—and dromedaries. He thus broadens his goals. He strives to create a poetry that is simultaneously Spanish American and universal, that is, a poetry that surpasses its artistic antecedents. He also aspires to achieve a divine mission. The poem concludes

with the savior of poetry—as does **"Sonatina"** [**"Sonatina"**], the next poem of the collection.

At the end of **"Sonatina"** the sad princess is given hope for happiness, love, life, and salvation in the form of "el feliz caballero que te adora sin verte, / y que llega de lejos, vencedor de la Muerte, / a encenderte los labios con su beso de amor!" ["the happy knight that adores you without seeing you, / and that arrives from far away, conqueror of Death, / to inflame your lips with his kiss of love!"] No matter how frivolous **"Sonatina"** appears at first with its nursery-rhyme rhythm and its fanciful gardens and palace, by the final stanza the profound nature of the fairy-tale couple becomes evident. The knight who arrives mounted on his winged steed, victor of Death, is more than the proverbial "prince charming" who appears in time to revive the love-sick princess. The linking of the hero / savior with Pegasus, the horse of the Muses, identifies the hero as an artist. The princess that awaits him is the female consort of the male creator, poetic language.

Darío holds that poetic language has lost its vitality and color; it is imprisoned in a golden vessel. The music that should be heard is silent; the atmosphere is stifling, unimaginative, and uninspired. Poetry's only escape is through dreams of freedom and flight. She longs to attain unmediated contact with the order of the cosmos. To this end, she rejects wealth and the reigning values of the day ("ya no quiere el palacio . . ." ["she no longer wants the palace . . ."]) because they interfere with her achieving the higher goal and greater pleasure of understanding the universe.

The objects that have come to be associated with the princess's imprisonment as well as with her physical and spiritual decline are boldly denounced. But Darío's detailed rejection is just the opposite of what it claims to be. It becomes a way of possessing, internalizing, and incorporating into his art those aspects that he pretends to disown—very much like the cultural patterns "superseded" in **"Divagación"** or the viscount and abbot "defeated" in **"Era un aire suave . . ."**. He disdains the palace and its wealth as incapable of providing spiritual gratification. In fact they appear as obstacles to knowledge and distractions that prevent the enlightened from seeing beyond the superficial trappings of life. At the same time, however, he takes possession of the opulence through description. This ambivalent position with regard to the riches of the palace reflects an even greater struggle—one common among Modernist authors. The poet challenges the superficial materialism of the bourgeois society in which he lives. He strives to assert the worth of his creation in an environment that tends to ignore the value of his art, knowledge, and spiritual insight. The poet fights for the respect and esteem that he feels he deserves by taking up the weapons of the enemy—wealth and opulence—and by poetically rendering them impotent.

The luxuries owned by the princess proliferate like the objects imported into Spanish America. Indeed, they are part of her attraction. She is a regal alternative to a bourgeois world, a means of reaching beyond the uninspired and prosaic. Darío's incorporation of these luxuries into his art indicate the degree to which he is part and parcel of his times and social context. He respects the art and objects brought from Europe and the Orient—like the many cultural possibilities considered in **"Divagación"**—while ultimately rejecting them as limited and disdaining those who fail to appreciate their transcendental worth. More importantly, the princess's wealth is made subservient to the spiritual wealth offered by the poet. The value of poetic vision and artistic achievement is thus doubly raised above everyday reality—"the life and times to which [he] was born." Only after the princess (poetic language) recognizes the appropriate (inferior) position of material wealth can the poet fulfill his superior destiny. In short, the poetic goals outlined in **"Sonatina"** and the other pieces examined point to a political and philosophic awareness behind the frivolity, musicality, and aesthetic play with which *Prosas profanas* has generally been characterized. In these works the passing pleasure of artistic experimentation and /or of the sexual *pas de deux* is an aspect of a profound, enduring response to a given social context, a response that reflects transcendental concerns.

This trajectory, which began with *Azul . . .* and continued in *Prosas profanas,* reaches its zenith in *Cantos de vida y esperanza,* in which Darío reveals himself to be a poet who is more sure of himself and more willing to express his sense of difference—his sense of being Spanish American. The imported models that dominated his poetic imagination in *Prosas profanas* have receded. His concerns reflect his sad awareness of the passage of time and of a youthful squandering of energies. At the same time, he directly addresses in a few powerful poems the socio-political context only alluded to previously. Darío discusses this change in the prose "Prefacio" ["Preface"] to *Cantos de vida y esperanza.* He wrote "Si en estos cantos hay política, es porque aparece universal. Y si encontráis versos a un presidente, es porque son un clamor continental. Mañana podremos ser yanquis (y es lo más probable); de todas maneras, mi protesta queda escrita sobre las alas de los inmaculados cisnes, tan ilustres como Júpiter." ["If there is politics in these songs, it is because it is universally present. And if you find verses to a president, it is because they are a continental clamor. Tomorrow we can all be *yanquis* (and that is what is most probable); at any rate, my protest remains written on the wings of immaculate swans, as illustrious as Jupiter."] Whether this willingness to express openly his political concerns is a result of external events—the Spanish American War or U.S. intervention in Central America—or his and Modernism's literary successes, Darío now speaks with his own voice.

The experimentation with rhythm and rhyme schemes, verse forms, styles, images, myths, religions, and philosophies that underpins the richness of Modernist art began as a search that inevitably turns back upon itself, that is, it is linked to the question of Spanish American modernity and, in broader terms, Spanish American identity. As the Modernist poets reflected upon the formation of nation states and the integration of Spanish America into the world economy, they confronted the issue of Spanish American

literature. From this perspective, the political impetus of Modernist literature becomes evident—even in the early Modernist verse that had been defined by Modernism's first commentators as escapist and superficial.

FURTHER READING

Criticism

Brotherston, Gordon. "Modernism and Rubén Darío." In *Latin American Poetry: Origins and Presence,* pp. 56-76. Cambridge: Cambridge University Press, 1975.
    Studies Darío's poetry within the context of the Modernist movement.

Cardwell, Richard A. "Darío and *El Arte Puro*: The Enigma of Life and the Beguilement of Art." *Bulletin of Hispanic Studies* XLVII, No. 1 (January 1970): 37-51.
    Examines philosophical attitudes in Darío's work.

Craig, G. Dundas. "Rubén Darío." In *The Modernist Trend in Spanish-American Poetry,* pp. 255-76. Berkeley: University of California Press, 1934.
    Comments on individual poems by Darío in a variety of contexts.

Ellis, Keith. *Critical Approaches to Rubén Darío.* Toronto: University of Toronto Press, 1974, 170 p.
    Treats various types of Darío criticism, including biographical, socio-political, literary tradition, philosophical, and structural analysis. This study also includes an appendix, "Rubén Darío as a Literary Critic."

Ellison, Fred P. "Rubén Darío and Brazil." *Hispania* XLVII, No. 1 (March 1964): 24-35.
    Examines the role that Brazil and Brazilian literature played in Darío's life and work.

Enguídanos, Miguel. "Inner Tensions in the Work of Rubén Darío," translated by Cecile Wiseman. In *Rubén Darío Centennial Studies,* edited by Miguel Gonzalez-Gerth and George D. Schade, pp. 13-30. Austin, Tex.: Institute of Latin American Studies, 1970.
    Discusses the tension between "the ugliness of life and the purity of Art" in Darío's poetry.

Fiore, Dolores Ackel. *Rubén Darío in Search of Inspiration: Greco-Roman Mythology in His Stories and Poetry.* New York: Las Americas Publishing Co., 1963, 178 p.
    Scholarly investigation of Darío's knowledge of the myths and languages of ancient Greece and Rome, concluding that his contact with these cultures was primarily through French and Spanish translations.

Fitzmaurice-Kelly, James. "Some Later Poets." In *Some Masters of Spanish Verse,* pp. 153-82. London: Oxford University Press, Humphrey Milford, 1924.
    Believes that Darío's chief accomplishment was extend-

ing the possibilities of meter in Spanish poetry.

Florit, Eugenio. "The Modernist Prefigurement in the Early Work of Rubén Darío," translated by John Wilcox. In *Rubén Darío Centennial Studies,* edited by Miguel Gonzalez-Gerth and George D. Schade, pp. 31-48. Austin, Tex.: Institute of Latin American Studies, 1970.

Examines Darío's pre-*Azul* poetics, focusing on the poet's struggle with form.

Franco, Jean. "The Many Faces of Modernism." In *A Literary History of Spain: Spanish American Literature since Independence,* pp. 111-20. New York: Barnes & Noble Books, 1973.

Discusses Darío's career in light of Latin-American Modernism, and analyzes spiritual, sensual, and political themes in his poetry.

Lee, Muna. "A Painful Example." *Poetry: A Magazine of Verse* XXII, No. III (June 1923): 165-68.

Negative review of *Prosas profanas*, primarily faulting the poor translation.

MacDonell, George N. "Rubén Darío, Poet of the Western World." *New Mexico Quarterly* XXXI, (Spring 1961): 105-12.

Summarizes Darío's life and career.

Mapes, E. K. "Innovation and French Influence in the Metrics of Rubén Darío." *Publications of the Modern Language Association* XLIX (March 1934): 310-26.

Asserts that Darío's metric technique derives from French sources.

————. "Rubén Darío's First Sonnets in Alexandrines." *Philological Quarterly* XIV, No. 4 (October 1935): 16-37.

Examines Darío's ideas on sonnet structure, discounting the notion that "Coupolican" is the first sonnet in alexandrines written by the poet.

McGuirk, Bernard. "On Misreading Mallarmé: Rubén Darío and *The Anxiety of Influence.*" *Nottingham French Studies* 26, No. 2 (October 1987): 52-67.

Applies principles of Harold Bloom's *The Anxiety of Influence* (1973) to Darío's "Yo persigo una forma," arguing that "Darío's poem constitutes a creative 'misreading' of Mallarmé's 'Mes bouquins refermes sur le nom de Paphos'."

Nims, John Frederick. "New World Man." *The New York Times Book Review* (26 December 1965): 16.

Mixed review of *Selected Poems of Rubén Darío.*

Rodriguez-Peralta, Phyllis. "Christian Elements and Aesthetic-Philosophic Expression in Darío's Poetry." *Kentucky Romance Quarterly* 32, No. 2 (1985): 185-99.

Analyzes the syncretic philosophic-religious background of Darío's poetry, positing that "Christian beliefs are interwoven on all levels of his poetry and prose."

Skyrme, Raymond. *Rubén Darío and the Pythagorean Tradition.* Gainesville: The University Presses of Florida, 1975, 107 p.

Relates themes and allusions in Darío's work to philosophical currents of the nineteenth century which had their source in the teachings of Pythagoras.

Torres-Rioseco, Arturo. "Modernism and Spanish American Poetry." In *The Epic of Latin American Literature,* pp. 103-10. New York: Oxford University Press, 1942.

Discusses Darío's poetry in terms of "the psychology of escape."

Trueblood, Alan S. "Rubén Darío: The Sea and the Jungle." *Comparative Literature Studies* 4, Nos. 1 & 2 (1967): 425-52.

Detailed analysis of sea and jungle motifs in Darío's works.

Umphrey, George W. "Spanish-American Poets of Today and Yesterday." *Hispania* II, No. 2 (March 1919): 64-81.

Appreciative survey of Darío's poetry.

Watland, Charles D. *Poet-Errant: A Biography of Rubén Darío.* New York: Philosophical Library, 1965, 266 p.

Well-documented and detailed survey of Darío's life and works.

Zavala, Iris M. "The Turn of the Century Lyric: Rubén Darío and the Sign of the Swan." In *The Crisis of Institutionalized Literature in Spain,* edited by Wlad Godzich and Nicholas Spadaccini, pp. 279-305. Minneapolis: The Prisma Institute, 1988.

Discusses the social function of lyric poetry in turn-of-the-century Latin America, focusing on transformations of the classic swan myth in Darío's poetry.

Additional coverage of Darío's life and career is contained in the following sources published by Gale Research: *Contemporary Authors,* **Vol. 131;** *Hispanic Literature Criticism,* **Vol. 1;** *Hispanic Writers;* *Major 20th-Century Writers;* **and** *Twentieth-Century Literary Criticism,* **Vol. 4.**

Gerard Manley Hopkins
1844–1889

English poet.

INTRODUCTION

Considered a major English poet, Hopkins's poems are distinguished by stylistic innovations, most notably his striking diction and his pioneering use of a meter he termed "sprung rhythm." Hopkins's radical departure from traditional poetics, coupled with his reluctance to publish his writings, caused his works to be almost completely unknown in the nineteenth-century. However, critics today agree that Hopkins is the author of some of the finest and most complex poems in the English language, and he is firmly established as a major figure in the development of modern poetry.

Biographical Information

Born in Stratford, Essex, to Manley and Kate Hopkins, Hopkins was the eldest of nine children. Beginning in 1854, he attended to Cholmeley Grammar School in Highgate, where he excelled in his courses and won a school poetry competition. In 1863, he obtained a scholarship to the prestigious Baillol College at Oxford University. His experiences at Oxford were to have a profound effect on his life: it was there he came under the influence of the teachings of John Henry Newman, a leading figure in the Oxford Movement and an important Catholic apologist and educator. In 1866, after months of soul-searching and against his family's wishes, he converted to Catholicism. The following year he graduated from Oxford. In the spring of 1868, he decided to enter the Jesuit order. He burned his poems, vowing to give up writing and dedicate himself fully to his religious calling. After his ordination in 1877, Hopkins served as a priest at parishes in London, Oxford, Liverpool, and Glasgow, and taught classics at the Jesuit Stonyhurst College. In 1884 he was appointed a fellow in classics at the Royal University of Ireland and professor of Greek at the University College in Dublin, positions he retained until his sudden death from typhoid fever in 1889. Hopkins was a dedicated priest and teacher, but was not, as most of his biographers agree, temperamentally suited to his work assignments, and, as time passed, he became progressively more isolated and depressed, plagued—particularly during his last years in Ireland—by spiritual doubts and ill-health.

Major Works

In 1876, when the German ship the *Deutschland* was lost at sea, carrying five Franciscan nuns exiled from Germany with it, one of Hopkins's superiors suggested that some-

one ought to write a poem about the incident. Hopkins took the hint and produced his first major work, *The Wreck of the Deutschland*. In the poem, Hopkins introduced the revolutionary sprung rhythm that he is credited with originating. Unlike conventional poetic meter in which the rhythm is based on the regular alternation of stressed and unstressed syllables, the meter of sprung rhythm is determined by the number of stressed syllables alone. In addition to experimenting with meter in *The Wreck of the Deutschland*, Hopkins also employed several other poetic techniques for which he has become known. His diction is characterized by unusual compound words, coined phrases, and terms borrowed from dialect, further complicated by intentional ambiguities and multiple meanings. Moreover, he frequently utilizes elliptical phrasing (often omitting, for example, relative pronouns), compression, internal rhyme, half-rhyme, assonance, alliteration, and metaphor. *The Wreck of the Deutschland* also introduced what were to become the central philosophical concerns of Hopkins's mature poetry. The poem reflects both his belief in the doctrine that human beings were created to praise God and his commitment to the Jesuit practices of meditation and spiritual self-examination. The teachings of the thirteenth-century Franciscan philosopher John Duns

Scotus also deeply influenced Hopkins's thinking. From Duns Scotus's teaching of "haecceitas" or the "thisness" of all things, Hopkins developed the concepts of "inscape," a term he coined to describe the inward, distinctive, essential quality of a thing, and "instress," which refers to the force that gives a natural object its inscape and allows that inscape to be seen and expressed by the observer.

After completing *The Wreck of the Deutschland*, Hopkins continued to experiment with style, language, and meter. He is perhaps most widely known for his shorter poems on nature, many of which were written during the early years of his priesthood. In such celebrations of natural beauty as "Spring," "Inversnaid," "Pied Beauty," "God's Grandeur," "The Starlight Night," and his most famous sonnet, "The Windhover," Hopkins strove to capture the inscape of creation as a means of knowing and praising God. His final poems, known as the "terrible sonnets," express his spiritual struggle. In "No Worst, There is None," "Carrion Comfort," "I Wake and Feel the Fell of Dark, Not Day," and "Thou Art Indeed Just, Lord," Hopkins chronicles the sense of sterility, isolation, and despair he appears to have frequently experienced toward the end of his life. In the sonnets "Spelt from Sibyl's Leaves" and "That Nature Is a Heraclitean Fire," he worked toward a resolution of his spiritual doubts. Although Hopkins feared that his poetic power was declining in his last years, the unguarded self-revelation and mastery of the sonnet form that critics perceive in these sonnets has led them to regard these poems highly.

Critical Reception

None of Hopkins' major works were published in his lifetime. In 1918 Robert Bridges compiled and published the first collection of Hopkins's poetry, *The Poems of Gerard Manley Hopkins*. His reservations about Hopkins's style, which he clearly voiced in his introduction to the volume, referring to "oddities," "obscurities," and "faults of taste" in the poems, set the tone for the early critical response to Hopkins. Critics tended to echo or to amplify Bridges's reservations. The idea that Hopkins's poetry was odd, obscure, and eccentric, in combination with both explicit and implicit rejoinders to that idea, was to constitute a running dialogue in Hopkins' criticism for at least two decades. A few reviewers of the collection praised his religious feeling, but the predominant response was one of bewildered incomprehension. The 1930s saw an enormous growth of interest in Hopkins's work, a growth that owed at least in part to a second, enlarged edition of the poems. Many critics of that period declared his modernity, and among young poets such as W. H. Auden, Robert Lowell, C. Day Lewis, and Dylan Thomas, he was revered as a model. By the early 1940s Hopkins's status as a major English poet was firmly established. With the centenary of his birth in 1944 numerous critical essays and appreciations appeared, and since that time his works have continued to attract extensive analysis from a myriad of literary critical schools of thought. Acclaimed for his powerful influence on modern poetry, Hopkins continues to be praised as an innovative and revolutionary stylist who wrote some of the most challenging poems in the English language on the subjects of the self, nature, and religion.

PRINCIPAL WORKS

Poetry

The Poems of Gerard Manley Hopkins 1918; also published as *Poems of Gerard Manley Hopkins* [enlarged editions] 1930, 1948, 1967
Gerard Manley Hopkins (poetry and prose) 1986
The Early Poetic Manuscripts and Note-Books of Gerard Manley Hopkins in Facsimile (poetry and prose) 1989
Poetical Works of Gerard Manley Hopkins 1990

Other Major Works

The Correspondence of Gerard Manley Hopkins and R. W. Dixon (letters) 1935
The Letters of Gerard Manley Hopkins to Robert Bridges (letters) 1935
The Note-Books and Papers of Gerard Manley Hopkins (prose) 1937
Further Letters of Gerard Manley Hopkins (letters) 1938
The Journals and Papers of Gerard Manley Hopkins (diary, journal, and notes) 1959
The Sermons and Devotional Writings of Gerard Manley Hopkins (sermons, journals, and notes) 1959
Gerard Manley Hopkins: Selected Prose (prose) 1989
Gerard Manley Hopkins: Selected Letters (letters) 1990

CRITICISM

John Middleton Murry (essay date 1919)

SOURCE: "Gerard Manley Hopkins," in *The Athenaeum*, No. 4649, June 6, 1919, pp. 425–26.

[*Murry is recognized as one of the most significant English critics of the twentieth century, noted for his studies of major authors and for his contributions to modern critical theory. Perceiving an integral relationship between literature and religion, Murry believed that the literary critic must be concerned with the moral as well as the aesthetic dimensions of a given work. In the following review of the first edition of Hopkin's poems, he suggests that the most distinguishing feature of Hopkins' poetry is its musical quality, but claims that it is devoid of substantial content and is, for that reason, an overall failure.*]

Modern poetry, like the modern consciousness of which it is the epitome, seems to stand irresolute at a crossways with no signpost. It is hardly conscious of its own indecision, which it manages to conceal from itself by insisting that it is lyrical, whereas it is merely impressionist. The value of impressions depends upon the quality of the mind which receives and renders them, and to be lyrical demands at least as firm a temper of the mind, as definite and unfaltering a general direction, as to be epic. Roughly speaking, the present poetical fashion may, with a few conspicuous exceptions, be described as poetry without tears. The poet may assume a hundred personalities in as many poems, or manifest a hundred influences, or he may work a single sham personality threadbare or render piecemeal an undigested influence. What he may not do, or do only at the risk of being unfashionable, is to attempt what we may call, for the lack of a better word, the logical progression of an *œuvre*. One has no sense of the rhythm of an achievement. There is an output of scraps, which are scraps, not because they are small, but because one scrap stands in no organic relation to another in the poet's work. Instead of lending each other strength, they betray each other's weakness.

Yet the organic progression for which we look, generally in vain, is not peculiar to poetic genius of the highest rank. If it were, we might be accused of mere querulousness. The rhythm of personality is hard, indeed, to achieve. The simple mind and the single outlook are now too rare to be considered as near possibilities, while the task of tempering a mind to a comprehensive adequacy to modern experience is not an easy one. The desire to escape and the desire to be lost in life were probably never so intimately associated as they are now; and it is a little preposterous to ask a moth fluttering round a candle-flame to see life steadily and see it whole. We happen to have been born into an age without perspective; hence our idolatry for the one living poet and prose writer who has it and comes, or appears to come, from another age. But another rhythm is possible. No doubt it would be mistaken to consider this rhythm as in fact wholly divorced from the rhythm of personality; it probably demands at least a minimum of personal coherence in its possessor. For critical purposes, however, they are distinct. This second and subsidiary rhythm is that of technical progression. The single pursuit of even the most subordinate artistic intention gives unity, significance, mass to a poet's work. When Verlaine declares "de la musique avant toute chose," we know where we are. And we know this not in the obvious sense of expecting his verse to be predominantly musical; but in the more important sense of desiring to take a man seriously who declares for anything "avant toute chose."

It is the "avant toute chose" that matters, not as a profession of faith—we do not greatly like professions of faith—but as the guarantee of the universal in the particular, of the *dianoia* in the episode. It is the "avant toute chose" that we chiefly miss in modern poetry and modern society and in their quaint concatenations. It is the "avant toute chose" that leads us to respect both Mr. Hardy and Mr. Bridges, though we give all our affection to one of them. It is the "avant toute chose" that compels us to admire the poems of Gerard Manley Hopkins; it is the "avant toute chose" in his work which, as we believe, would have condemned him to obscurity to-day, if he had not (after many years) had Mr. Bridges, who was his friend, to stand sponsor and the Oxford University Press to stand the racket.

Apparently Mr. Bridges himself is something of our opinion, for his introductory sonnet ends on a disdainful note:

> Go forth: amidst our chaffinch flock display
> Thy plumage of far wonder and heavenward flight!

It is from a sonnet written by Hopkins to Mr. Bridges that we take the most concise expression of his artistic intention, for the poet's explanatory preface is not merely technical, but is written in a technical language peculiar to himself. Moreover, its scope is small; the sonnet tells us more in two lines than the preface in four pages:

> O then if in my lagging lines you miss
> The roll, the rise, the carol, the creation. . . .

There is his "avant toute chose." Perhaps it seems very like "de la musique." But it tells us more about Hopkins' music than Verlaine's line told us about his. This music is of a particular kind, not the "sanglots du violon," but preeminently the music of song, the music most proper to lyrical verse. If one were to seek in English the lyrical poem to which Hopkins' definition could be most fittingly applied, one would find Shelley's "Skylark." A technical progression onwards from the "Skylark" is accordingly the main line of Hopkins' poetical evolution. There are other, stranger threads interwoven; but this is the chief. Swinburne, rightly enough if the intention of true song is considered, appears hardly to have existed for Hopkins, though he was his contemporary. There is an element of Keats in his epithets, a half-echo in "whorlèd ear" and "lark-charmèd"; there is an aspiration after Milton's architect tonic in the construction of the later sonnets and the most lucid of the fragments, **"Epithalamion."** But the central point of departure is the "Skylark." The **"May Magnificat"** is evidence of his achievement in the direct line:

> Ask of her, the mighty mother:
> Her reply puts this other
> Question: What is Spring?—
> Growth in everything—
>
> Flesh and fleece, fur and feather,
> Grass and greenworld all together;
> Star-eyed strawberry-breasted
> Throstle above her nested
> Cluster of bugle-blue eggs thin
> Forms and warms the life within. . . .
>
> . . . When drop-of-blood-and-foam-dapple
> Bloom lights the orchard-apple,
> And thicket and thorp are merry
> With silver-surfèd cherry,
>
> And azuring-over greybell makes
> Wood banks and brakes wash wet like lakes
> And magic cuckoocall
> Caps, clears, and clinches all. . . .

That is the primary element manifested in one of its simplest most recognizable, and some may feel most beautiful forms. But a melody so simple, though it is perhaps the swiftest of which the English language is capable without the obscurity which comes of the drowning of sense in sound, did not satisfy Hopkins. He aimed at complex internal harmonies, at a counterpoint of rhythm; for this more complex element he coined an expressive word of his own:

> But as air, melody, is what strikes me most of all in music and design in painting, so design, pattern, or what I am in the habit of calling *inscape* is what I above all aim at in poetry.

Here then, in so many words, is Hopkins' "avant toute chose" at a higher level of elaboration. "Inscape" is still, in spite of the apparent differentiation, musical; but a quality of formalism seems to have entered with the specific designation. With formalism comes rigidity; and in this case the rigidity is bound to overwhelm the sense. For the relative constant in the composition of poetry is the law of language which admits only a certain amount of adaptation. Musical design must be subordinate to it, and the poet should be aware that even in speaking of musical design he is indulging a metaphor. Hopkins admitted this, if we may judge by his practice, only towards the end of his life. There is no escape by sound from the meaning of the posthumous sonnets, though we may hesitate to pronounce whether this directness was due to a modification of his poetical principles or to the urgency of the content of the sonnets, which, concerned with a matter of life and death, would permit no obscuring of their sense for musical reasons.

> I wake and feel the fell of dark, not day.
> What hours, O what black hoürs we have spent
> This night! what sights you, heart, saw; ways you
>   went!
> And more must in yet longer light's delay.
>   With witness I speak this. But where I say
> Hours I mean years, mean life. And my lament
> Is cries countless, cries like dead letters sent
> To dearest him that lives, alas! away.

There is compression, but not beyond immediate comprehension; music, but a music of overtones; rhythm, but a rhythm which explicates meaning and makes it more intense.

Between the "**May Magnificat**" and these sonnets is the bulk of Hopkins poetical work and his peculiar achievement. Perhaps it could be regarded as a phase in his evolution towards the "more balanced and Miltonic style" which he hoped for, and of which the posthumous sonnets are precursors; but the attempt to see him from this angle would be perverse. Hopkins was not the man to feel, save on exceptional occasions, that urgency of content of which we have spoken. The communication of thought was seldom the dominant impulse of his creative moment, and it is curious how simple his thought often proves to be when the obscurity of his language has been penetrated. Musical elaboration is the chief characteristic of his work, and for this reason what seem to be the strangest of his experi-

ments are his most essential achievement. So, for instance, "**The Golden Echo**":

>   Spare!
> There is one, yes I have one (Hush there!);
> Only not within seeing of sun,
> Not within the singeing of the strong sun,
> Tall sun's tingeing, or treacherous the tainting of
>   the earth's air,
> Somewhere else where there is ah well where! one,
> One. Yes I can tell such a key, I do know such a
>   place,
> Where whatever's prized and passes of us,
>   everything that's fresh and fast flying of us,
>   seems to us sweet of us and swiftly away   with,
>   done away with, undone,
> Undone, done with, soon done with, and yet clearly
>   and dangerously sweet
> Of us, the wimpled-water-dimpled, not-by-morning-
>   matchèd face,
> The flower of beauty, fleece of beauty, too too apt
>   to, ah! to fleet
> Never fleets more, fastened with the tenderest truth
> To its own best being and its loveliness of youth. . . .

Than this, Hopkins truly wrote, "I never did anything more musical." By his own verdict and his own standards it is therefore the finest thing that Hopkins did. Yet even here, where the general beauty is undoubted, is not the music too obvious? Is it not always on the point of degenerating into a jingle—as much an exhibition of the limitations of a poetical theory as of its capabilities? The tyranny of the "avant toute chose" upon a mind in which the other things were not stubborn and self-assertive is apparent. Hopkins' mind was irresolute concerning the quality of his own poetical ideal. A coarse and clumsy assonance seldom spread its snare in vain. Exquisite openings are involved in disaster:

> When will you ever, Peace, wild wood dove, shy
>   wings shut
> Your round me roaming end, and under be my
>   boughs?
> When, when, Peace, will you, Peace? I'll not play
>   hypocrite
> To own my heart: I yield you do come sometimes;
>   but
> That piecemeal peace is poor peace. What pure
>   peace. . . .

And the more wonderful opening of "**Windhover**" likewise sinks, far less disastrously, but still perceptibly:

> I caught this morning morning's minion, king-
>   dom of daylight's dauphin, dapple-dawn-drawn
>   Falcon, in his riding
>   Of the rolling level underneath him steady air,
>   and striding
> High there, how he rung upon the rein of a
>   wimpling wing
> In his ecstasy! then off, off forth on swing,
>   As a skate's heel sweeps smooth on a bow-bend:

the hurl and
    the gliding
Rebuffed the big wind. My heart in hiding
Stirred for a bird,—the achieve of, the mastery of
    the thing!

We have no doubt that "stirred for a bird" was an added excellence to the poet's ear; to our sense it is a serious blemish on lines which have "the roll, the rise, the carol, the creation."

There is no good reason why we should give characteristic specimens of the poet's obscurity, since our aim is to induce people to read him. The obscurities will slowly vanish and something of the intention appear; and they will find in him many of the strange beauties won by men who push on to the borderlands of their science; they will speculate whether the failure of his whole achievement was due to the starvation of experience which his vocation imposed upon him, or to a fundamental vice in his poetical endeavour. For ourselves we believe that the former was the true cause. His "avant toute chose" whirling dizzily in a spiritual vacuum, met with no salutary resistance to modify, inform and strengthen it. Hopkins told the truth of himself—the reason why he must remain a poets' poet:

I want the one rapture of an inspiration.
O then if in my lagging lines you miss
The roll, the rise, the carol, the creation,
My winter world, that scarcely yields that bliss
Now, yields you, with some sighs, our explanation.

I. A. Richards (essay date 1926)

SOURCE: "Gerard Hopkins," in *The Dial,* Vol. LXXXI, No. 81, September, 1986, pp. 195-203.

[*Richards was an English poet and critic who has been called the founder of modern literary criticism. Primarily a theorist, he encouraged growth of textual analysis and during the 1920s formulated many of the principles that would later become the basis of New Criticism, one of the most important schools of modern critical thought. In the following essay first published in 1926, he analyzes the obscure and innovative nature of Hopkins's verse, maintaining that "it is an important fact that he is so often most himself when he is most experimental."*]

Modern verse is perhaps more often too lucid than too obscure. It passes through the mind (or the mind passes over it) with too little friction and too swiftly for the development of the response. Poets who can compel slow reading have thus an initial advantage. The effort, the heightened attention, may brace the reader, and that peculiar intellectual thrill which celebrates the step-by-step conquest of understanding may irradiate and awaken other mental activities more essential to poetry. It is a good thing to make the light-footed reader work for what he gets. It may make him both more wary and more appreciative of his reward if the "critical point" of value is passed.

These are arguments for some slight obscurity in its own right. No one would pretend that the obscurity may not be excessive. It may be distracting, for example. But what is a distraction in a first reading may be non-existent in a second. We should be clear (both as readers and writers) whether a given poem is to be judged at its first reading or at its *n*th. The state of intellectual enquiry, the construing, interpretative, frame of mind, so much condemned by some critics (through failure perhaps to construe the phrase "simple, sensuous, and passionate") passes away once its task is completed, and the reader is likely to be left with a far securer grasp of the whole poem, including its passional structure, than if no resistance had been encountered.

Few poets illustrate this thesis better than Gerard Hopkins, who may be described, without opposition, as the most obscure of English verse writers. Born in 1844, he became a Jesuit priest in 1868, a more probable fate for him then—he was at Oxford—than now. Before joining the Order he burnt what verses he had already written and "resolved to write no more, as not belonging to my profession, unless it were by the wish of my superiors." For seven years he wrote nothing. Then by good fortune this wish was expressed and Hopkins set to work. "I had long had haunting my ear the echo of a new rhythm which now I realized on paper. . . . However I had to mark the stresses . . . and a great many more oddnesses could not but dismay an editor's eye, so that when I offered it to our magazine . . . they dared not print it." Thenceforward he wrote a good deal, sending his poems in manuscript to Robert Bridges and to Canon Dixon. He died in 1889 leaving a bundle of papers among which were several of his best sonnets. In 1918 the Poet Laureate edited a volume of poems with an introduction and notes of great interest. From this volume comes all our knowledge of his work.

Possibly their obscurity may explain the fact that these poems are not yet widely known. But their originality and the audacity of their experimentation have much to do with the delay. Even their editor found himself compelled to apologize at length for what he termed "blemishes in the poet's style." "It is well to be clear that there is no pretence to reverse the condemnation of these faults, for which the poet has duly suffered. The extravagances are and will remain what they were. . . . it may be assumed that they were not a part of his intention." But too many other experiments have been made recently, especially in the last eight years, for this lofty tone and confident assumption to be maintained. The more the poems are studied, the clearer it becomes that their oddities are always deliberate. They may be aberrations, they are not blemishes. It is easier to see this to-day since some of his most daring innovations have been, in part, attempted independently by later poets.

I propose to examine a few of his best poems from this angle, choosing those which are both most suggestive technically and most indicative of his temper and mould as a poet. It is an important fact that he is so often most himself when he is most experimental. I will begin with a poem in which the shocks to convention are local and concern only word order.

Peace

When will you ever, Peace, wild wood dove, shy
    wings shut,
Your round me roaming end, and under be my
    boughs?
When, when, Peace, will you, Peace? I'll not play
    hypocrite
To own my heart: I yield you do come sometimes;
    but
That piecemeal peace is poor peace. What pure
    peace allows
Alarms of wars, the daunting wars, the death of it?

O surely, reaving Peace, my Lord should leave in
    lieu
Some good! And so he does leave Patience
    exquisite,
That plumes to Peace thereafter. And when Peace
    here does house
He comes with work to do, he does not come to
    coo,
        He comes to brood and sit.

Hopkins was always ready to disturb the usual word order of prose to gain an improvement in rhythm or an increased emotional poignancy. *To own my heart* = to my own heart; *reaving* = taking away. He uses words always as tools, an attitude towards them which the purist and grammarian can never understand. He was clear, too, that his poetry was for the ear, not for the eye, a point that should be noted before we proceed to **"The Windhover,"** which, unless we begin by listening to it, may *only* bewilder us. To quote from a letter: "Indeed, when, on somebody's returning me the Eurydice, I opened and read some lines, as one commonly reads, whether prose or verse, with the eyes, so to say, only, it struck me aghast with a kind of raw nakedness and unmitigated violence I was unprepared for: but take breath and read it with the ears, as I always wish to be read, and my verse becomes all right." I have to confess that **"The Windhover"** only became all right for me, in the sense of perfectly clear and explicit, intellectually satisfying as well as emotionally moving, after many readings and several days of reflection.

The Windhover

To Christ our Lord

I caught this morning's minion, king-
    dom of daylight's dauphin, dapple-dawn-drawn
    Falcon, in his riding
      Of the rolling level underneath him steady air, and
        striding
High there, how he rung upon the rein of a
    wimpling wing

In his ecstasy! then off, off forth on swing,
    As a skate's heel sweeps smooth on a bow-bend:
      the hurl and gliding
    Rebuffed the big wind. My heart in hiding
Stirred for a bird,—the achieve of, the mastery of
    the thing!

Brute beauty and valour and act, oh, air, pride,
    plume, here
    Buckle! AND the fire that breaks from thee then,
      a billion
Times told lovelier, more dangerous, O my
    chevalier!

    No wonder of it: shéer plód makes plough down
      sillion
Shine, and blue-bleak embers, ah my dear,
    Fall, gall themselves, and gash gold-vermillion.

The dedication at first sight is puzzling. Hopkins said of this poem that it was the best thing he ever wrote, which is to me in part the explanation. It sounds like an echo of the offering made eleven years ago when his early poems were burnt. For a while I thought that the apostrophe, "O my chevalier!" (it is perhaps superfluous to mention that this word rhymes strictly with "here" and has only three syllables) had reference to Christ. I take it now to refer only to the poet, though the moral ideal, embodied of course for Hopkins in Christ, is before the mind.

Some further suggestions towards elucidation may save the reader trouble. If he does not need them I crave his forgiveness. *Kingdom of daylight's dauphin*—I see (unnecessarily) the falcon as a miniature sun, flashing so high up. *Rung upon the rein*—a term from the *manège*, ringing a horse = causing it to circle round one on a long rein. *My heart in hiding*—as with other good poets I have come to expect that when Hopkins leaves something which looks at first glance as though it were a concession to rhyme or a mere pleasing jingle of words, some really important point is involved. Why in hiding? Hiding from what? Does this link up with "a billion times told lovelier, more dangerous, O my chevalier!"? What is the greater danger and what the less? I should say the poet's heart is in hiding from Life, has chosen a safer way, and that the greater danger is the greater exposure to temptation and error than a more adventurous, less sheltered course (sheltered by Faith?) brings with it. Another, equally plausible reading would be this: Renouncing the glamour of the outer life of adventure the poet transfers its qualities of audacity to the inner life. (*Here* is the bosom, the inner consciousness.) The greater danger is that to which the moral hero is exposed. Both readings may be combined, but pages of prose would be required for a paraphrase of the result. The last three lines carry the thought of the achievement possible through renunciation further, and explain, with the image of the ash-covered fire, why the dangers of the inner life are greater. So much for the sense; but the close has a strange, weary, almost exhausted, rhythm, and the word "gall" has an extraordinary force, bringing out painfully the shock with which the sight of the soaring bird has jarred the poet into an unappeased discontent.

> The more Hopkins's poems are studied,
> the clearer it becomes that their oddities
> are always deliberate. They may be
> aberrations, they are not blemishes.
>
> —*I. A. Richards*

If we compare those poems and passages of poems which were conceived definitely within the circle of Hopkins' theology with those which transcend it, we shall find difficulty in resisting the conclusion that the poet in him was often oppressed and stifled by the priest. In this case the conflict which seems to lie behind and prompt all Hopkins' better poems is temporarily resolved through a stoic acceptance of sacrifice. An asceticism which fails to reach ecstasy and accepts the failure. All Hopkins' poems are in this sense poems of defeat. This will perhaps become clearer if we turn to

Spelt From Sibyl Leaves

Earnest, earthless, equal, attunable, vaulty,
  voluminous, . . stupendous
Evening strains to be tíme's vást, womb-of-all,
  home-of-all, hearse-of-all night.
Her fond yellow hornlight wound to the west, her
  wild hollow hoarlight hung to the height
Waste; her earliest stars, earl-stars, stárs principal,
  overbend us,
Fíre-féaturing heaven. For earth her being has
unbound, her dapple is at an end, astray or aswarm,
  all throughther, in throngs; self ín self steepèd
  and páshed—quite
Disremembering, dísmémbering áll now. Heart, you
round me right
With: Óur évening is over us; óur night whélms,
whélms, ánd will end us.
Only the break-leaved boughs dragonish damask the
tool-smooth bleak light; black,
Ever so black on it. Óur tale, O óur oracle! Lét life,
wáned, ah lét life wind
Off hér once skéined stained véined varíety upon,
áll on twó spools; párt, pén, páck
Now her áll in twó flocks, twó folds—black, white;
right wrong; reckon but, reck but, mind
But thése two; wáre of a wórld where bút those twó
tell, each off the óther; of a rack
Where, selfwrung, selfstrung, sheathe- and
shelterless, thóughts agáinst thoughts ín groans
    grínd.

Elucidations are perhaps less needed. The heart speaks after "Heart you round me right" to the end, applying in the moral sphere the parable of the passing away of all the delights, accidents, nuances, the "dapple" of existence, to give place to the awful dichotomy of right and wrong. It is characteristic of this poet that there is no repose for him in the night of traditional morality. As the terrible last line shows, the renunciation of all the myriad temptations of life brought no gain. It was all loss. The present order of "black, white; right, wrong" was an afterthought and an intentional rearrangement; the original order was more orthodox. *Let life, waned*—the imperative mood carries through to the end; let life part, pen, pack, let life be aware of. *All throughter* = each through the other.

I cannot refrain from pointing to the marvellous third and fourth lines. They seem to me to anticipate the descriptions we hope our younger contemporary poets will soon write. Such synaesthesis has tempted several of them, but this is, I believe, the supreme example. Hopkins' technical innovations reach out, however, into many fields. As a means of rendering self-consciousness, for example, consider this:

            Only what word
Wisest my heart breeds dark heaven's baffling ban
Bars or hell's spell thwarts. This to hoard unheard,
Heard unheeded, leaves me a lonely began.

Or this:

Soul, self; come poor Jackself, I do advise
You, jaded, let be; call off thoughts awhile
Elsewhere; leave comfort root-room; let joy size
At God knows when to God knows what; whose
  smile
's not wrung, see you; unforeseen times rather—as
  skies
Betweenpie mountains—lights a lovely mile.

My last quotations must be the sonnets which most I think, represent the poet's inner conflict.

Not, I'll not, carrion comfort, Despair, not feast on
  thee;
Not untwist—slack they may be—these last strands
  of man
In me ór, most weary, cry *I can no more*. I can;
Can something, hope, wish day come, not choose
  not to be.
But ah, but O thou terrible, why wouldst thou rude
  on me
Thy wring-world right foot rock? lay a lionlimb
  against me? scan
With darksome devouring eyes my bruisèd bones?
  and fan,
O in turns of tempest, me heaped there; me frantic
  to avoid thee and flee?

Why? That my chaff might fly; my grain lie, sheer
  and clear.
  Nay in all that toil, that coil, since (seems) I
  kissed
  the rod,
Hand rather, my heart lo! lapped strength, stole joy,
  would laugh, chéer.
Cheer whom though? the hero whose heaven-
  handling flung me, fóot tród

Me? or me that fought him? O which one? is it
  each one? That night, that year
Of now done darkness I wretch lay wrestling with
  (my God!) my God.

No worst, there is none. Pitched past pitch of grief,
More pangs will, schooled at forepangs, wilder wring.
Comforter, where, where is your comforting?
Mary, mother of us, where is your relief?
My cries heave, herds-long; huddle in a main, a chief
Woe, world-sorrow; on an age-old anvil wince and
  sing—
Then lull, then leave off. Fury had shrieked "No
  lingering! Let me be fell: force I must be brief."

O the mind, mind has mountains; cliffs of fall
Frightful, sheer, no-man-fathomed. Hold them cheap
May who ne'er hung there. Nor does long our small
Durance deal with that steep or deep. Here! creep,
Wretch, under a comfort serves in a whirlwind: all
Life death does end and each day dies with sleep.

Few writers have dealt more directly with their experience or been more candid. Perhaps to do this must invite the charge of oddity, of playfulness, of whimsical eccentricity and wantonness. To some of his slighter pieces these charges do apply. Like other writers he had to practise and perfect his craft. The little that has been written about him has already said too much about this aspect. His work as a pioneer has not been equally insisted upon. It is true that Gerard Hopkins did not fully realize what he was doing to the technique of poetry. For example, while retaining rhyme, he gave himself complete rhythmical freedom, but disguised this freedom as a system of what he called Sprung Rhythm, employing four sorts of feet (-,- $\cup$,- $\cup\cup$,- $\cup\cup\cup$). Since what he called *hangers* or *outrides* (one, two, or three slack syllables added to a foot and not counting in the nominal scanning) were also permitted, it will be plain that he had nothing to fear from the absurdities of prosodists. A curious way, however, of eluding a mischievous tradition and a spurious question, to give them a mock observance and an equally unreal answer! When will prosodists seriously ask themselves what it is that they are investigating? But to raise this question is to lose all interest in prosody.

Meanwhile the lamentable fact must be admitted that many people just ripe to read Hopkins have been and will be too busy asking "does he scan?" to notice that he has anything to say to them. And of those that escape this trap that our teachers so assiduously set, many will be still too troubled by beliefs and disbeliefs to understand him. His is a poetry of divided and equal passions—which very nearly makes a new thing out of a new fusion of them both. But Hopkins' intelligence, though its subtlety with details was extraordinary, failed to remould its materials sufficiently in attacking his central problem. He solved it emotionally, at a cost which amounted to martyrdom; intellectually he was too stiff, too "cogged and cumbered" with beliefs, those bundles of invested emotional capital, to escape except through appalling tension. The analysis of his poetry is hardly possible, however, without the use of tech-

nical language; the terms "intellectual" and "emotional" are too loose. His stature as a poet will not be recognized until the importance of the Belief problem from which his poetry sprang has been noticed. He did not need other beliefs than those he held. Like the rest of us, whatever our beliefs, he needed a change in belief, the mental attitude, itself.

F. R. Leavis (essay date 1932)

SOURCE: "Gerard Manley Hopkins" in *New Bearings in English Poetry: A Study of the Contemporary Situation,* Chatto & Windus, 1938, pp. 159-93.

[*Leavis is an influential contemporary critic. In the following excerpt from an essay originally published in 1932, he claims that Hopkins' strength lies in his attempt to bring poetry closer to living speech.*]

Hopkins's originality was radical and uncompromising: there was, as he owns, some excuse for the dismay of his first readers. He could not himself, as the *Author's Preface* shows, be reconciled to his originality without subterfuge. His prosodic account in terms of Logaoedic Rhythm, Counterpoint Rhythm, Sprung Rhythm, Rocking Feet and Outriders will help no one to read his verse—unless by giving the sense of being helped: it merely shows how subtle and hard to escape is the power of habits and preconceptions. The prescription he gives when warm from reading his verse—'take breath and read it with the ears, as I always wish to be read, and my verse becomes all right'—is a great deal more to the point, and if we add 'and with the brains and the body' it suffices.

This is a measure of the genuineness of his originality. For the peculiarities of his technique appeal for sanction to the spirit of the language: his innovations accentuate and develop bents it exhibits in living use and, above all, in the writings of the greatest master who ever used it. Hopkins might have said about each one of his technical idiosyncrasies what he says about the rhythm of *The Wreck of the Deutschland*: the idea was not altogether new, but no one had professedly used it and made it a principle throughout as he had. Paradoxical as it may sound to say so, his strength was that he brought poetry much closer to living speech. How badly some such regeneration was needed may be judged from the inability of critics avowedly interested in him, as Bridges and Dixon were, to appreciate his significance: the habits and conventions he defeated were so strong. They are strong still: Mr. Charles Williams, the editor of the second edition of the *Poems,* concludes in his *Critical Introduction* that the poet to whom we should most relate Gerard Hopkins' is Milton. Now if one were seeking to define the significance of Hopkins by contraries, Milton is the poet to whom one would have recourse: the relation is an antithesis. But, alas! Mr. Williams leaves no room to suppose that he means that.

The way in which Hopkins uses the English language (that is the primary order of consideration; 'consciousness of the universe' is an unprofitable abstraction apart from it) contrasts him with Milton and associates him with Shakespeare. There is no essential characteristic of his technique of which it might not be said that it is a matter of 'using professedly' and 'making a principle' of something that may be found in Shakespeare:

> . . . the world-without-end hour
>
> [*Sonnet* 57]

> . . . bloody, bawdy villain!
> Remorseless, treacherous, lecherous kindless villain!
>
> [*Hamlet,* II. *ii*]

> . . . cabin'd, cribb'd, confined
>
> [*Macbeth,* III, *iv.*]

> what thou wouldst highly,
> That wouldst thou holily.
>
> [*Macbeth,* I. *v.*]

> If it were done when 'tis done, then 'twere well
> It were done quickly: if the assassination
> Could trammel up the consequence, and catch
> With his surcease success; that but this blow
> Might be the be-all and the end-all here,
> But here, upon this bank and shoal of time,
> We'd jump the life to come.
>
> [*Macbeth,* I. *vii.*]

—This last passage takes us beyond technical devices, found in embryo in Shakespeare. Indeed, it would be a mistake to insist too much on these (they could be exemplified indefinitely); it might distract attention from the more essential likeness illustrated by the passage as a whole. Hopkins's imagery, and his way of using the body and movement of the language, are like Shakespeare's.

> O the mind, mind has mountains; cliffs of fall
> Frightful, sheer, no-man-fathomed. Hold them
>   cheap
> May who ne'er hung there. Nor does long our small
> Durance deal with that steep or deep.

—That is Shakespearian, but quite un-Miltonic. And this ('what's not meet' being made to suggest at the same time 'not what's meet') handles grammar and syntax in the spirit of Hopkins:

> In a rebellion,
> When what's not meet, but what must be, was law,
> Then were they chosen: in a better hour,
> Let what is meet be said it must be meet,
> And throw their power in the dust.
>
> [*Coriolanus,* III. *i.*]

If we look for a parallel to a characteristic Shakespearian rendering of the very movement of consciousness—

> My thought, whose murder yet is but fantastical,
> Shakes so my single state of man, that function
> Is smother'd in surmise, and nothing is,

> But what is not
>
> [*Macbeth,* I. *iii.*]

—we shall find it easily in Hopkins:

> Only what word
> Wisest my heart breeds dark heaven's baffling ban
> Bars or hell's spell thwarts. This to hoard unheard,
> Heard unheeded, leaves me a lonely began.

It is not that he derives from Shakespeare (Shakespeare, we have often been told, is a dangerous model). We cannot doubt that he knew his Shakespeare well, but if he profited he was able to do so because of his own direct interest in the English language as a living thing. The bent of his genius was so strong that we are forced to believe that his experimenting would have taken much the same lines even if there had been no Shakespeare. The similarities arise out of a similar exploitation of the resources and potentialities of the language. Hopkins belongs with Shakespeare, Donne, Eliot and the later Yeats as opposed to Spenser, Milton and Tennyson. He departs very widely from current idiom (as Shakespeare did), but nevertheless current idiom is, as it were, the presiding spirit in his dialect, and he uses his medium not as a literary but as a spoken one. That is the significance of his repeated demand to be tested by reading aloud: 'read it with the ears, as I always wish to be read, and my verse becomes all right.' It is not merely the rhythm that he has in mind:

> I laughed outright and often, but very sardonically, to think you and the Canon could not construe my last sonnet; that he had to write to you for a crib. It is plain I must go no further on this road: if you and he cannot understand me who will? Yet, declaimed, the strange constructions would be dramatic and effective.

It is not only the constructions that gain, and the term 'dramatic' has a further sense here than perhaps Hopkins intended. His words and phrases are actions as well as sounds, ideas and images, and must, . . . be read with the body as well as with the eye: that is the force of his concern to be read aloud. He indicates now and then in notes the kind of thing he is doing. 'Here comes a violent but effective hyperbaton or suspension, in which the action of the mind mimics that of the labourer—surveys his lot, low but free from care; then by a sudden strong act throws it over the shoulder or tosses it away as a light matter.'—Effects of this order may be found on any page of his work. Even more significant is a note on a word in **"The Leaden Echo and the Golden Echo."** It is the more interesting in that Mr Sturge Moore paid this poem some attention in a recent number of *The Criterion* [July 1930]. The poem opens:

> How to kéep—is there ány any, is there none such,
>   nowhere known some, bow or brooch or braid
>   or brace, láce, latch or catch or key to keep
> Back beauty, keep it, beauty, beauty, beauty, . . .
>   from vanishing away?

Hopkins notes: '*Back* is not pretty, but it gives that feeling of physical constraint which I want.' This suggests fairly the spirit of his dealings with the English language. How alien to English poetry that spirit had become is illustrated by Mr Sturge Moore, a critic and verse-writer formed in the last century, who, writing on *Style and Beauty in Literature,* offers to improve Hopkins in this way:

> How to keep beauty? is there any way?
> Is there nowhere any means to have it stay?
> Will no bow or brooch or braid,
> Brace or lace
> Latch or catch
> Or key to lock the door lend aid
> Before beauty vanishes away?

There is no need to quote further. No reader of *The Criterion,* apparently, protested. Mr Sturge Moore remarks at the end that he has retained most of Hopkins's felicities, while discarding 'his most ludicrous redundancies.' He has discarded also 'back' and everything it represents; words as he uses them have no body. He has discarded, not merely a certain amount of music, but with the emotional crescendo and diminuendo, the plangent rise and fall, all the action and substance of the verse.

Not that **"The Leaden Echo and the Golden Echo"** is one of the poems in which the poet's greatness manifests itself. Remarkable as it is, if it were fully representative of Hopkins he would not demand much space in this study. In this kind of work he is elaborating and mastering his technical devices for more important purposes. It is not as mere musical effects (if such were possible in poetry)—melody, harmony, counterpoint—that these devices are important; they are capable of use for expressing complexities of feeling, the movement of consciousness, difficult and urgent states of mind. Take for instance the kind of word-play, the pattern and progression of verbal echo, alliteration, rime and assonance represented in the opening verse:

> How to kéep—is there ány any, is there none such,
>   nowhere known some, bow or brooch or braid,
>   or brace, láce, latch or catch or key to keep
> Back beauty . . .

—That need not be (indeed, is not) a mere musical trick, any more than conventional end-rime need be. Such devices may be used, as good poets use end-rime, to increase the expectancy involved in rhythm and change its direction, to control movement, to give words new associations and bring diverse ideas and emotions together, to intensify the sense of inevitability—in short, to get new, precise and complex responses out of words.

Of course, to be something convincingly more than word-play, to escape the limiting description, 'music,' these devices must have adequate work to do. The theme of **"The Leaden Echo and the Golden Echo"** does not offer very much resistance, and if this poem represented the height of Hopkins's achievement Mr Middleton Murry's judgment [in *The Athenaem,* June 6, 1919] would not be immediately absurd: 'If one were to seek in English the lyrical poem to which Hopkins's definition ['The roll, the rise, the carol, the creation'] could be most fittingly ap-

plied, one would find Shelley's "Skylark." A technical progression onwards from the "Skylark" is accordingly the main line of Hopkins's poetical evolution.' But if one looks at *The Wreck of the Deutschland,* which, says Bridges, 'stands logically as well as chronologically in the front of his book, like a great dragon to forbid all entrance,' it becomes plain that Hopkins has no relation to Shelley or to any nineteenth-century poet. This poem was his first ambitious experiment, and it is the more interesting in that his technical resources are deployed in it at great length: the association of inner, spiritual, emotional stress with physical reverberations, nervous and muscular tensions that characterizes his best verse is here explicitly elaborated in an account of the storm which is at the same time an account of an inner drama. The wreck he describes is both occasion and symbol. He realizes it so vividly that he is in it; and it is at the same time in him:

>   I did say yes
>   O at lightning and lashed rod;
>   Thou heardst me truer than tongue confess
>   Thy terror, O Christ, O God;
>   Thou knowest the walls, altar and hour and night:
>   The swoon of a heart that the sweep and the hurl
>   of thee trod
>   Hard down with a horror of height:
>   And the midriff astrain with leaning of, laced with
>   fire of stress.

He takes the actual wreck as the type of the worldly disaster that brings conviction, supernatural assurance, to the soul:

>   Stroke and a stress that stars and storms deliver,
>   That guilt is hushed by, hearts are flushed by, and
>   melt

—and identifies such experience mystically with Christ's Passion. In an audacious image he identifies the sudden overwhelming conviction, the insight, the illumination to the effect of a sloe bursting in the mouth:

>   The dense and driven Passion, and frightful
>   sweat;
>   Thence the discharge of it, there its swelling to
>   be,
>   Though felt before, though in high flood yet—
>   What none would have known of it, only the heart,
>   being hard at bay,
>   Is out with it! Oh,
>   We lash with the best or worst
>   Word last! How a lush-kept plush-capped
>   sloe
>   Will, mouthed to flesh-burst,
>   Gush!—flush the man, the being with it, sour or
>   sweet,
>   Brim, in a flash, full!—Hither then, last or first,
>   To hero of Calvary, Christ's feet—
>   Never ask if meaning it, wanting it, warned of it—
>   men go.

The conceit is Metaphysical, but the technique is pure Hopkins. It would be difficult to produce a more elaborate pattern of alliteration, echo, assonance and internal rime, but we do not feel of any element (except, perhaps, 'lush-kept plush-capped') that it is there for the sake of pattern. Even of 'lush-kept plush-capped' it might be said that by a kind of verbal suggestion (two different expressions sounding so like) it contributes to the sense of mystical identification that the passage is concerned to evoke—identification of 'the stress felt' with the Passion; helps also the metaphorical identification of the experience with the bursting of the sloe. Of the pattern generally it may be said that it issues out of and expresses emotional intensities in the same kind of way as 'cabin'd, cribb'd, confined' and

> bloody, bawdy villain!
> Remorseless, treacherous, lecherous, kindless villain!

and

>   . . . trammel up the consequence, and catch
> With his surcease success.

Particularly it may be pointed out how the words stressed by the pattern justify their salience.

>   Is out with it! Oh,
>   We lash with the best or worst
> Word last!

—'lash' (the highly-stressed 'out' carries on from the previous line) both suggests the inevitability (a lashing out on the stimulus of pain) of the response at this supreme testing moment ('last'), and gives the response a physical urgency. The moment is ripe ('lush'): and 'lush' applied to 'sloe' also suggests the paradoxical poignancy ('sour or sweet'?) of the revelation. In 'flesh-burst' we have both the physical disaster 'that storms deliver' and Calvary. The progression—'gush,' 'flush,' 'flash,' 'full'—is as much a matter of sense as sound: 'gush' describes the overwhelming onset of the experience, 'flush' the immediate bewildering immersion; 'flash'—it becomes illumination; 'full' suggests 'cup.'

Hopkins's words seem to have substance, and to be made of a great variety of stuffs. Their potencies are correspondingly greater for subtle and delicate communication.

—F. R. Leavis

Such an analysis is clumsy and inadequate: it is merely a means of indicating the kind of function that the more obvious technical devices serve. What Hopkins does here in this sustained and elaborated way he does in concentration in **"The Windhover"** and **"Spelt from Sibyl's Leaves"**.

Imagery that reminds us still more readily of the Metaphysical conceit (the characteristic Hopkins pattern is less insistent here) occurs in the fourth stanza:

>   I am soft sift
>   In an hourglass—at the wall
> Fast, but mined with a motion, a drift,
>   And it crowds and it combs to the fall;
> I steady as a water in a well, to a poise, to a
>   pane,
> But roped with, always, all the way down from
>   the tall
>   Fells or flanks of the voel, a vein
> Of the gospel proffer, a pressure, a principle,
>   Christ's gift.

—The superb metaphor in the first part of the stanza offers no difficulty. It conveys perfectly the inner sinking and dissolution, and then (with a subtle shift from sand to water) the steadying and recovery. The imagery in the last three lines is more complex, but, when (from the notes) we know that 'voel' is Welsh for 'bare hill,' not too difficult. The note adds: 'the meaning, obscured by *roped,* is that the well is fed by trickles of water within the flanks of the mountains.' This brief elucidation is a useful foil to the strength of Hopkins's imagery. The 'obscured' should imply no adverse criticism: the metaphorical 'roped' may make the original passage less immediately intelligible than Bridges' summary, but it also makes the mountain-rill something far more suggestive of power than a trickle, something capable of exerting pressure; it also suggests, illogically but not incompatibly (it is often the business of metaphor to reconcile opposed impulses, bents or emotions), that the 'pressure,' the 'principle,' can draw upwards. Nothing approaching this imagery in subtlety and strength can be found in any other poet of the nineteenth century.

Hopkins's technique justifies itself equally in the description of the storm in the second part of the poem—justifies itself obviously. Indeed, Bridges' 'dragon' exaggerates the general difficulty: a great deal of the poem is as inviting to the anthologist as the first stanza, which he printed in *The Spirit of Man*. The first stanza of the second part, for instance, is even less refractory to 'the grand style of our poetry':

>   'Some find me a sword; some
>   The flange and the rail; flame,
>   Fang, or flood' goes Death on drum,
>   And storms bugle his fame.
> But wé dream we are rooted in earth—Dust!
> Flesh falls within sight of us, we, though our
>   flower the same,
>   Wave with the meadow, forget that there must
> The sour scythe cringe, and the blear share come.

(The last line has six stresses.)

But remarkable as *The Wreck of the Deutschalnd* is it does not put his technical skill to the utmost stretch. This skill is most unmistakably that of a great poet when it is at the service of a more immediately personal urgency, when it expresses not religious exaltation, but inner debate. **"The Windhover"** is a poem of this kind. Since not only Mr Richards, in the essay already mentioned, but Mr Empson also, in *Seven Types of Ambiguity,* have dealt admirably with this poem, there is no need to analyse it here. Mr Empson's book is one that nobody interested in English poetry can afford not to have read. It is an implicit commentary on Bridges' complaint [in the ***Poems of Gerard Manley Hopkins***] that 'ambiguity or momentary uncertainty destroys the force of the sentence' and imposes on the reader a 'conscious effort of interpretation.' The kind of ambiguity that Mr Empson finds to be the essence of **"The Windhover"** is suggested here: `Thus in the first three lines of the sestet we seem to have a clear case of the Freudian use of opposites, where two things thought of as incompatible, but desired intensely by different systems of judgments, are spoken of simultaneously by words applying to both; both desires are thus given a transient and exhausting satisfaction, and the two systems of judgment are forced into open conflict before the reader.' It is in place at this point to observe that Hopkins's genius was as much a matter of rare character, intelligence and sincerity as of technical skill: indeed, in his great poetry the distinction disappears; the technical triumph is a triumph of spirit.

The inner friction expressed in the equivocal burden of **"The Windhover"** comes out more explicitly in **"Spelt from Sibyl's Leaves,"** which, if it represents a less difficult undertaking, is more indubitably a complete success. It is one of the finest things that he ever did, and since it exhibits and magnificently justifies most of the peculiarities of his technique, I will (though Mr Richards has analysed it) venture a brief commentary:

> Earnest, earthless, equal, attuneable, | vaulty, volu-
> 　　minous, . . stupendous
> Evening strains to be tíme's vást, | womb-of-all,
> 　　home-of-all, hearse-of-all night.
> Her fond yellow hornlight wound to the west, | her
> 　　wild hollow hoarlight hung to the height
> Waste; her earliest stars, earl-stars, | stárs principal,
> 　　overbend us,
> Fíre-féaturing heaven. For earth | her being has
> 　　unbound, her dapple is at an end, as-
> tray or aswarm, all throughter, in throngs; | self
> 　　ín self steepéd and páshed—qúite
> Disremembering, dismémbering | áll now. Heart,
> 　　you round me right
> With: Óur évening is over us; óur night | whélms,
> 　　whélms, ánd will end us.
> Only the beak-leaved boughs dragonish | damask
> 　　the tool-smooth bleak light; black,
> Ever so black on it. Our tale, O óur oracle! | Lét
> 　　life, wáned, ah lét life wind
> Off hér once skéined stained véined varíety | upon,
> 　　áll on twó spools; párt, pen, páck
> Now her áll in twó flocks, twó folds—black, white; |
> 　　right, wrong; reckon but, reck but, mind
> But thése two; wáre of a wórld where bút these |
> 　　twó tell, each off the óther; of a rack

Where, selfwrung, selfstrung, sheathe- and shelter-
less, | thóughts agaínst thoughts in groans
g.índ.

The poem opens with evening deepening into night. We are not merely told that evening 'strains,' we feel evening straining, to become night, enveloping everything, in the movement, the progression of alliteration, assonance and rime. This progression is associated with, and hardly distinguishable from, the development of meaning in the sequence of adjectives: evening is first sweetly solemn, serene, etherealizing and harmonizing, then becomes less tranquillizing and more awful, and finally ends in the blackness of night.

> Her fond yellow hornlight wound to the west, her
> 　　wild hollow hoarlight hung to the height
> Waste . . .

—The 'yellow hornlight' is, of course, the setting moon; 'fond'—tender, soft, sympathetic, clinging as if reluctant to go, the slow gentle sinking being felt in the movement and modulation of the verse. The 'hoarlight' is the cold, hard starlight, 'wild' and 'hollow'—remote, inhuman, a kind of emptiness in the hollow vault—in contrast to the 'fond yellow' moonlight. The verse-movement itself, with the inevitable rest upon 'height,' seems to hang. The 'dapple' of earth, the rich coloured variety that Hopkins loved so much (cf. **'Pied Beauty'**—'Glory be to God for dappled things') has gone, merged ('throughter'—each through other) into neutrality. That he is not concerned with 'pure description' the introduction of 'self' intimates, together with the unexpected strength of 'steepèd and páshed' and 'dismembering.'

He suddenly realizes the whole thing as a parable, not meditatively worked out, but immediate: he sees the outward symbol and the significance as one, in kind of metaphor. It is Blake's *Sun-flower* ["A Sun-Flower"] rather than Matthew Arnold's *Yes: in the sea of life enisled* ["To Marguerite—continued"].

> 　　Heart, you round me right
> With: Óur évening is over us; oúr night
> 　　whélms

—the heavy stress that his rhythm enables him to put upon 'our' brings home the poignant realization. His heart 'rounds' him, i.e. whispers (as in the ballads), and 'rounds upon him' with, the thought that he has sacrificed the 'dapple' of existence for the stark dichotomy of right and wrong.

> Only the beak-leaved boughs dragonish | damask
> 　　the tool-smooth bleak light; black,
> Ever so black on it.

—The trees are no longer the beautiful, refreshing things of daylight; they have turned fantastically strange, hard and cruel, 'beak-leaved' suggesting the cold, hard light, steely like the gleam of polished tools, against which they appear as a kind of damascene-work ('damask') on a blade. Then follows the anguished surrender to the realization:

. . . Oúr tale, O oúr oracle! | Lét life, wáned, ah
   lét life wind
Off hér one skéined stained véined varíety | upon,
   áll on twó spools; párt, pen, páck
Now her áll in twó flocks, twó folds—black, white; |
   right, wrong . . .

—The run of alliterations, rimes and assonances suggests the irresistible poignancy of the realization. The poem ends with a terrible effect as of unsheathed nerves grinding upon one another. The grinding might at first be taken to be merely that of 'right' against 'wrong,' the inner conflict of spirit and flesh, and the pain that which the believer knows he must face, the simple pain of renunciation. Yet we are aware of a more subtle anguish and a more desperate plight. And if we look closely we find that Hopkins is explicit about it:

   black, white; right, wrong . . .

—The first draft had 'wrong, right,' but he deliberately, and significantly, reversed the order. If he were merely 'ware of a world where but these two tell' his torment would be less cruel. But his consciousness is more complex; his absolutes waver and change places, and he is left in terrible doubt.

In comparison with such a poem of Hopkins's as this, any other poetry of the nineteenth century is seen to be using only a very small part of the resources of the English language. His words seem to have substance, and to be made of a great variety of stuffs. Their potencies are correspondingly greater for subtle and delicate communication. The intellectual and spiritual anaemia of Victorian poetry is indistinguishable from its lack of body. Hopkins is a very different poet from Dante, but a remark that Mr Eliot throws out in the discussion of Dante has a bearing here: 'that Hell, though a state, is a state which can only be thought of, and perhaps only experienced, by the projection of sensory images; and that the resurrection of the body has perhaps a deeper meaning than we understand.' The critical implications of this (they can be generalized and discussed apart from any theological context) deserve pondering. They relate to another remark of Mr Eliot's that has been quoted already and applies also to Hopkins: in his verse 'the intellect is at the tip of the senses.' And along with the qualities indicated by this phrase goes a remarkable control of tempo and modulation.

Austin Warren (essay date 1948)

SOURCE: "Instress of Inscape," in *Hopkins: A Collection of Critical Essays,* edited by Geoffrey H. Hartman, Prentice-Hall, Inc., 1966, pp. 168-77.

[*Warren was an American educator and literary critic with a special interest in theology and church history. In the following essay which was originally published in 1948, he explores the defining characteristics of Hopkins's mid-dle poems, emphasizing his penchant for "the sensuous, the concrete, and the particular."*]

The early Hopkins follows Keats and the "medieval school" (as he called the Pre-Raphaelites). The latest Hopkins, who wrote the sonnets of desolation, was a poet of tense, economic austerity. Their nearest parallel I can summon would be Donne's "holy sonnets": "Batter my heart" and "If poisonous minerals." For the mode of **"Andromeda"** and the later sonnets (1885-89), Hopkins himself projected "a more Miltonic plainness and severity": He was thinking of Milton's sonnets and the choruses of *Samson.* In 1887 he invoked another name: "My style tends always more towards Dryden."

The middle period, which opens with the *Wreck of the Deutschland* (1875) and closes with **"Tom's Garland"** and **"Harry Ploughman,"** both written in 1885, is the period of experiment. But it is also the most Hopkinsian—the most specially his own.

Middle Hopkins startles us by its dense rich world, its crowded Ark, its plenitude and its tangibility, its particularity of thing and word. There is detailed precision of image ("rose moles all in stipple upon trout that swim"). The poet is enamored of the unique, the "abrupt self."

The exploration of Middle Hopkins—its style, the view of life and art implicit in its style—may well start from the institutions and movements from which the poet learned, in which he participated. The motifs are the Ritualist Movement, Pre-Raphaelitism, Aestheticism, linguistic renovation, England, the Catholic church. In Hopkins' celebration of the sensuous, the concrete, the particular—his "instress of the inscapes"—all of these converge.

As a Catholic, Hopkins was an incarnationist and a sacramentalist: the sacraments are the extensions of the Incarnation. As a Catholic he believed that man is a compound of matter and form and that his body, resurrected, will express and implement his soul through all eternity. "Man's spirit will be flesh-bound when found at best. But unencumbered. . . ." Like all Catholic philosophers, he believed in an outer world independent of man's knowing mind—he was, in the present sense of the word, a "realist."

Hopkins was an Englishman, of a proud and patriotic sort. This is not always remembered, partly because he became the priest of a church viewed by other Englishmen as Continental, or Italian, or international. But there is an English way of being Catholic. Hopkins was not an "old Catholic" of the sturdy, unemotional variety nourished on Challoner's *Garden of the Soul;* no convert could be that. But, like his admired Newman, and unlike Manning and Faber (also converts), he was "Gallican," not ultramontane; British, not Italian, in his devotional life and rhetoric. He remembers when England was Catholic, when the pilgrims frequented the shrine of Our Lady of Walsingham.

   Deeply surely I need to deplore it,
   Wondering why my master bore it,

The riving off that race
So at home, time was, to his truth and grace
That a starlight-wender of ours would say
The marvellous Milk was Walsingham Way
    And one—but let be, let be:
More, more than was will yet be.

The four real shapers of Hopkins' mind were all Britons; we might go farther and say that all were British empiricists—all concerned with defending the ordinary man's belief in the reality and knowability of things and persons.

Two of them were encountered at Oxford. Pater, who remained his friend, was one of his tutors. Against the abstractions of the academic world, Pater boldly defended the concrete—in the visual arts and music, in perception. "Every moment some form grows perfect in hand or face, some tone on the hills or the sea is choicer than the rest . . ." Though Hopkins could not conceivably have written so representatively, abstractly ("hills . . . sea . . . choicer") the famous Conclusion to *The Renaissance* pleads for a stressing of the inscapes. Hopkins followed some lectures by Pater on Greek philosophy; perhaps he heard, in an earlier version, Pater's lectures on Plato and Platonism, in which, with monstrous effrontery, the Doctrine of Ideas was praised as giving contextual interest to the concrete.

With Ruskin, whose *Modern Painters* he read early and admiringly, Hopkins revolted against the neoclassical grandeur of generality praised by Johnson and expounded by Reynolds. The influence of Ruskin—art medievalist, devout student of clouds, mountains, trees—is pervasive in Hopkins' sketches (five of which are reproduced in the *Note-Books*) and in his journalizing, his meticulously technical descriptions of church architecture (often neo-Gothic) and scenery.

Hopkins follows the general line of Ruskin in more than art. He does not find the humanly satisfactory and well-furnished world such an effect of its Creator as the watch of the watchmaker. Nor does he, after the fashion of some mystics and Alexandrians, dissolve Nature into a system of symbols translating the real world of the Spirit. Like Ruskin, he was able to recover the medieval and Franciscan joy in God's creation. And, like Ruskin, he protested against an England which is "seared with trade . . . and wears man's smudge." His political economy, as well as it can be construed, was Ruskinian—what may be called tory socialist or distributist.

Hopkins' poems were written for an ideal audience, never existent in his day or ours, composed of literarily perceptive countrymen and of linguistically adept and folk-minded scholars.

—Austin Warren

It was to Newman, his great predecessor, that Hopkins wrote upon deciding to become a Roman Catholic. And Newman's closest approach to a philosophical work, his *Grammar of Assent* (1870), interested Hopkins enough so that in 1883 he planned to publish (had Newman agreed) a commentary on it. There were marked temperamental and intellectual differences between the men. Newman, much the more complex and psychologically subtle, could feel his way into other men's minds as Hopkins could not. Hopkins was the closer dialectician and scholar. He did not share Newman's distrust of metaphysics (including the scholastic), his tendency to fideism; but he was, like Newman—in words the latter used of Hurrell Froude—"an Englishman to the backbone in his severe adherence to the real and the concrete."

The great medieval thinker who most swayed Hopkins' spirit to peace, Duns Scotus, was also a Briton, had been an Oxford professor. He was "of reality the rarest-veinéd unraveler": he was able to analyze, disengage from the complex in which they appear, the thinnest, most delicate strands ("vein" may be either anatomical or geological). Perhaps "rarest-veinéd unraveler" is a kind of kenning for the philosopher's epithet, the Subtle Doctor. Scotus, the Franciscan critic of the Dominican Aquinas, was centrally dear to Hopkins as undertaking the philosophical validation of the individual. In the individual's relation to his species, Aquinas taught that the "matter" individuates, while the "form" is generic: that is, that the individuals of a species reproductively multiply their common originative pattern. Scotus insisted that each individual has a distinctive "form" as well: a *haecceitas,* or thisness, as well as a generic *quidditas,* or whatness.

After having discovered this medieval Franciscan, Hopkins, upon "any inscape of sky or sea," thought of Scotus. The word, of Hopkins' coinage, occurs already in his Oxford notebooks. Modeled presumably on "landscape," "inscape" stands for any kind of formed or focused view, any pattern discerned in the natural world. A central word in his vocabulary and central motif in his mental life, it traverses some range of meaning: from sense-perceived pattern to inner form. The prefix seems to imply a contrary, an outerscape: that is, an "inscape" is not mechanically or inertly present but requires personal action, attention, a seeing and a seeing into.

The earliest "Notes for Poetry" cite: "Feathery rows of young corn. Ruddy, furred and branchy tops of the elms backed by rolling clouds." "A beautiful instance of inscape *sided* on the *slide,* that is successive sidings on one inscape, is seen in the behavior of the flag flower." In 1873, two years before the "Deutschland," he "saw a shoal of salmon in the river and many hares on the open hills. Under a stone hedge was a dying ram: there ran slowly from his nostrils a thick flesh-coloured ooze, scarlet in places, coiling and roping its way down so thick that it looked like fat."

He made notes on ancient musical instruments and on gems and their colors: "beryl—watery green; carnelian—strong flesh red, Indian red. . . ." His love of precise

visual observation never lapsed, nor did his taste for re-
serach. Like Gray, he had a meticulous antiquarianism,
suited to botany or archeology, to notes and queries, details, studies in place names, amateur etymologies.

Perhaps his most brilliant prose celebrates the Self and
its wonders: "That taste of myself, of I and me above
and in all things, which is more distinctive than the taste
of ale or alum." Other selves were mysterious. As a shy
man, he found it easier to reach natural "inscapes." He
wrote no psychological portraits matching for sharpness
and delicacy his notations of ash trees. The men in his
poems are seen as from a distance—sympathetically but
generically.

But he gloried in the range and repertory of mankind.
Chesterton was concerned that, lying down with the lamb,
the lion should "still retain his royal ferocity"; and Hopkins, also, wanted monks to be mild and soldiers to be
pugnacious. He imagined Christ incarnate again as a soldier. He didn't want other men to be like himself; he was
drawn to his antitypes—to soldiers; miners; Felix Randall,
the blacksmith, and Harry, the ploughman; to manual laborers. Moreover, each of these men he wished to be
functioning not only characteristically but intensely, violently, dangerously—on their mettle, like the Windhover,
like Harry Ploughman, like the sailor of the "Eurydice"
who, "strung by duty, is strained to beauty."

In poetry he desired both to record inscapes and to use
words as objects. His was a double particularity.

Poetry, he wrote shortly before composing the *Deutschland,* is "speech framed to be heard for its own sake
and interest even over and above its interest of meaning.
Some [subject] matter and meaning is essential to it but
only as an element necessary to support and employ the
shape which is contemplated for its own sake. Poetry is in
fact speech for the inscape's sake—and therefore the inscape must be dwelt on."

In 1862 he was already collecting words. The earliest
entries in the *Note-Books* are gritty, harshly tangy words,
"running the letter,": "grind, gride, grid, grit, groat, grate"
and "crock, crank, kranke, crick, cranky." He collected
dialectical equivalents: "whisket" for "basket," "grindle-
stone" for "grindstone." He notes linguistic habits: that an
observed laborer, when he began to speak "quickly and
descriptively,—dropped or slurred the article." He attends
to, and tries to define, the sundry modes of Latin pronunciation. He inquires concerning the character of the Mal-
tese language; wants to learn Welsh—not primarily in order to convert the local Wesleyans back to their ancestral
faith.

In his early poetry Hopkins followed Keats and the "medieval school." Even in his middle style there remain
vestiges of the earlier decorative diction, frequent use of
"beauty," "lovely," "dear," "sweet" ("that sweet's sweeter
ending"). But as early as 1866, **"The Habit of Perfection,"** though dominantly "medieval," anticipates the later
mode:

> This ruck and reel which you remark
> Coils, keeps, and teases simple sight.

The Wreck of the Deutschland (1875) inaugurates Hopkins' middle period (his first proper mastery). The diction
is quite as extraordinary as the rhythm. Characteristic are
homely dialectal words, sounding like survivors from Old
English, and compound epithets suggestive of the same
archetype. From the concluding stanzas of the *Deutschland*
come these lines:

> Mid-numbered He in three of the thunder-throne!
> Not a dooms-day dazzle in his coming nor dark as
>   he came. . . .

and

> Dame, at our door
> Drowned, and among our shoals,
> Remember us in the roads, the heaven-haven of the
>   Reward. . . .

From **"The Bugler's First Communion":**

> Forth Christ from cupboard fetched, how fain I of
> feet
>   To his youngster take his treat!
> Low-latched in leaf-light housel his too huge
>   godhead.

That Hopkins was influenced by Old English poetry is an
easy assumption. In his excellent *New Poets from Old: A
Study in Literary Genetics,* Henry Wells observes that all
the technical features representative of that poetry appear
conspicuously in Hopkins; judges him far nearer to Cynewulf than to Chaucer; and finds a plausible parallel to a
passage in *Beowulf.* But, by his own statement, Hopkins
did not learn Anglo-Saxon until 1882 and seems never to
have read either *Beowulf* or Cynewulf. In any case, he was
already a student of Welsh poetry and an attentive reader
of linguistic monographs. Like Pound and Eliot, he belongs among the poets who can be incited to poetry by
scholars' prose.

In 1873-74, while teaching a course in rhetoric at Manre-
sa House, Hopkins wrote the observations collected in the
Note-Books. In his notes he used the 1859 *Lectures on the
English Language* by the American scholar, George P.
Marsh, a book calculated to incite a poet. Marsh has a real
interest in the future (as well as the past) of the language
and a real interest in the literary (as well as the pragmatic)
use of words. The whole direction of his book suggests
that literary experiment can find much to its purpose in
literary history and that new poetry can be engendered by
old. Ending his lecture on "Accentuation and Double
Rhymes," he urges: "We must enlarge our stock [of rhyming words] by the revival of obsolete words and inflec-
tions from native sources," or introduce substitutes for
rhyme; in the following chapter he excitingly discusses
alliteration (with illustrations from *Piers Plowman*), consonance, e.g., "bad, led"; "find, band" (with illustrations
from Icelandic poetry and invented English examples), and

assonance (with illustrations from the Spanish). Hopkins' quotations from *Piers* are Marsh's; only in 1882 did he study *Piers,* and then without admiration, regarding its verse as a "degraded and doggerel" form of Anglo-Saxon sprung rhythm.

To both Bridges and Dixon, curious concerning the new poetic method of the **Deutschland,** Hopkins says nothing of Old English or of *Piers Plowman* but speaks of nursery rhymes, the choruses of Milton's *Samson,* and his readings in Welsh poetry (which he began studying in 1875). "The chiming of the consonants I get in part from the Welsh, which is very rich in sound and imagery." Traits common to Old English and Middle Hopkins (scant use of articles, prepositions, and pronouns; constant use of compound words) are shared by both with Welsh poetry.

There is a third lineage for the diction of Hopkins. Through Barnes and Furnivall, at least, he derives from an imprecisely defined group of Victorian historians and philologists, who challenged the dominance of the Latin and Romance—the "civilized," learned, abstract—elements in our language. One of these linguistic protestants was the Oxford historian, E. A. Freeman, who chronicled the Norman Conquest and himself resisted it. As early as 1846 he was praising the Teutonic part of our language as affording "expressions mostly of greater strength than their Romance synonyms for all purposes of general literature"; and he used the phrase "pure English" for a diction purged of these synonyms. Another Anglicizer was F. J. Furnivall, a founder, in 1864, of the Early English Text Society, and a constant editor of texts, who began his intellectual career under the influence of Ruskin and Maurice and declared that his interest in early literature was not linguistic but social. Another founder of the E.E.T.S., R. C. Trench, gave a chapter of his *English, Past and Present* (1855) to a consideration of "English as it might have been" without a Norman Conquest. Though our present cerebral and technical words derive from the classical languages, he argues that the Anglo-Saxon might have developed—chiefly by compounding, as German has done—such a vocabulary. Even "impenetrability" could have been matched, accurately, by "unthoroughfaresomeness." And theological language would be understood by farm hand as well as by scholar if we said "again-buying" for "redemption."

In the tradition of Trench, but much more violent, William Barnes lamented the linguistic conquest of English and declared the old stock still capable of extension by compounding. Instead of "photograph," we should say "sunprint" or "flameprint." Indeed, all our current Latinisms we should replace out of the "wordstores of the landfolk." Barnes's nominations are all flavorsome; samples are "overyearn" (commiserate), "gleecraft" (music), "outclear" (elucidate), "faithheat" (enthusiasm). He regretted the loss of "inwit" in place of "conscience"; and to serve instead of "subjective" and "objective" (those psychological-philosophical terms which Coleridge introduced from Germany) he suggested "inwoning" and "outwoning."

Barnes had something of a following among literary people; was publicly praised by Patmore, Gosse, Bridges,

Hardy. His poetry, early read, Hopkins preferred to that of Burns, liking its "West Country instress." But he learned most from the prose. Barnes's *Speechcraft* [i.e., Grammar], says Hopkins, is "written in an unknown tongue, a soul of modern Anglo-Saxon, beyond all that Furnival in his wildest Forewords ever dreamed. . . . It makes one weep to think what English might have been, for in spite of all that Shakespeare and Milton have done with the compound ["impure" English] I cannot doubt that no beauty in a language can make up for want of purity. In fact, I am learning Anglo-Saxon and it is a vastly superior thing to what we have." He cites Barnes's wondrous "pitches of suchness" (for "degrees of comparison"): "We *ought* to call them so, but alas!"

Hopkins' characteristic critical and philosophical terminology follows closely the counsel of Trench and Barnes: that it, it is a compounding of Old English roots and suffixes to suit new needs and to replace Latinic terms. "Inwit" (for "conscience") and Barnes's "inwoning" (subjective) may have suggested "instress" and "inscape." Hopkins explains his special use of "sake" (the being a thing has outside itself) by analytic parallel of the compounds "forsake," "namesake," "keepsake." The terminology of the *Comments on the Spiritual Exercises* (1880) is particularly Hopkinsian (e.g., "pitch," "stress," "burl"). To Bridges, Hopkins wrote of his manuscript book on rhythm, "It is full of new words, without which there can be no new science."

His doctrine of the language for poetry, nowhere exposited, we can infer to have been quite different. Archaism—the use of obsolete words for literary effect—he repudiated. His oddities (like "pashed," "fashed," "tucked," "degged") are generally dialectal; and it is safe to assume that his words of Old English lineage were collected and used by him as dialectal, still-spoken English: not "inkhorn" terms but folk speech. Even when he thought he was improvising, he was—at least in one instance—remembering: his alleged coinage, "louched" (slouched, slouching) was, as Bridges observed, to be found in Wright's Dialect Dictionary.

Whenever Hopkins explained his words (as he always stood ready to do), their particularity, their compactness and detail, were manifest. "Stickles—Devonshire for the foamy tongues of water below falls." "Bole" is not only used by poets but seems technical and proper and in the mouth of timber merchants and so forth. Of "flit," questioned by a correspondent, he writes: "I myself always use it and commonly hear it used among our people. I think it is at least a North Country word, used in Lancashire, for instance."

Hopkins' experiments are yet more important than his achievement; his comparative failures more interesting than his good "whole poems."

—*Austin Warren*

His compoundings are another matter. Though analogues can be offered from Browning, Hopkins came to them, it is probable, by way of medieval poetry, English and Welsh, and by way of Marsh, Trench, and Barnes. His defense would doubtless be that to compound freely was to restore to the English language a power it once had possessed. But the words thus compounded, or the root and suffix or prefix, were separately familiar and oral. He writes "spend-savour salt" (the salt which is spending its savor and on its way to being the biblical salt which has lost its savor); "bloomfall"; "trambeam"; "backwheels"; "though worlds of *wanwood leafmeal lie*" ("leafmeal" is on the model of "piecemeal"; suffix means "by bits," "by portions").

Judged by its effect and its internal intent, Hopkins' poetry finds partial parallels in Holst, Delius, and Vaughan Williams. Avoiding the archaism of Warlock and Dolmetsch, they sought to resume the line of English music where its genuine succession was interrupted—at the Restoration, and to go creatively back to the English glory of folksong and madrigal and the modal scales, to Dowland, Bull, and Byrd. Similarly, Hopkins seems to be reaching back, while he is reaching forward, to an "English" poetry. Probably, we may add, to an "English Catholic" poetry; and suppose that his pushing back of the Elizabethans had some incentive in his desire to get back of the Reformation to an England at once Catholic and English.

Like the poetry of the bards and the scops, Hopkins' poetry is oral, yet not conversational but formal and rhetorical. It uses dialectal words without intending, like Barnes's *Poems of Rural Life,* to be local and homely; it uses folk words in "serious" poetry. Hopkins' poems were written for an ideal audience, never existent in his day or ours, composed of literarily perceptive countrymen and of linguistically adept and folk-minded scholars. What his poetry assumed as convention, he had, by artifice, to create. *The Wreck* and "Tom's Garland" suggest or predict a greater poetry than they achieve. Hopkins' experiments are yet more important than his achievement; his comparative failures more interesting than his good "whole poems."

The ideal of poetry must be to instress the inscapes without splintering the architecture of the universe and, expressionally, to make every word rich in a way compatible with a more than additively rich total poetic structure. But in Hopkins' poems, the word, the phrase, the "local excitement," often pulls us away from the poem. And in the more ambitious pieces, the odes as we may call them (*The Wreck,* "Spelt from Sibyl's Leaves," "Nature Is a Heraclitean Fire"), there is felt a discrepancy between texture and structure: the copious, violent detail is matched by no corresponding intellectual or mythic vigor. Indeed, *The Wreck of the Deutschland* is an "occasional," commissioned piece at which Hopkins works devotedly and craftfully, like Dryden at his *Annus mirabilis,* but which, like Dryden's poem, falls apart. Hopkins was not a story-teller, and he was not able to turn his wrecks into myths of wreck; they remain historical events accompanied by commentary. "**The Bugler-Boy**" and other poems suffer from the gap between the psychological naïveté and the purely literary richness.

To try prose paraphrases of the middle poems is invariably to show how thin the "thinking" is. Hopkins' mind was first aesthetic and then technical: he reasoned closely upon metaphysical and prosodic matters. But his reflections upon beauty, man, and nature—his humanistic thoughts—are not distinguished.

The meaning of Hopkins' poems hovers closely over the text, the linguistic surface. The rewarding experience of concern with them is to be let more and more into words and their ways, to contemplate the protopoetry of derivation and metaphorical expansion, to stress the inscapes of the English tongue.

Yvor Winters (essay date 1949)

SOURCE: "The Poetry of Gerard Manley Hopkins," in *The Hudson Review,* Vol. 1, No. 4, Winter, 1949, pp. 455-76.

[*Winters was an American poet and critic known for his negative opinion of Hopkins's work. In the following essay, he compares of Hopkins's sonnet "No Worst" to a poem by John Donne and Robert Bridges's "Low Barometer," concluding that Hopkins's poem suffers from its overemphasis of emotion and its failure to suggest a rational motivation for the feeling expressed in the piece. In the second part of the essay, he discusses the difficulties in determining the correct scansion of Hopkins's poetry in general.*]

It is my intention to begin by comparing three poems, a sonnet by John Donne, a short poem by Robert Bridges, and a sonnet by Gerard Hopkins, and to compare them with reference to a particular theory of poetry. The poems by Donne and Bridges conform to this theory and illustrate it perfectly; the poem by Hopkins deviates sharply and I believe suffers as a result. Hopkins provides an excellent example of deviation, however, for two reasons: in the first place, though his deviation is serious, it is not crude or ridiculous and thus differs from the deviations of many romantic poets before and after, even poets of genius; and in the second place, his gift for language, as far as his procedure will allow it to emerge, appears almost as great as that of Donne or Bridges, so that we may examine with a minimum of distraction the consequences of the deviation itself. The poems of Donne and Bridges deal with closely related themes, under different figures derived from different views of human history; the theme of Hopkins may be similar but is inadequately defined and one cannot be sure.

The theory of poetry may be summarized briefly as follows. A poem is a statement in words, and about a human experience, and it will be successful in so far as it realizes the possibilities of that kind of statement. This sentence may seem childishly obvious, but it states facts of which we must never lose sight if we are to understand poetry, and facts of which sight is very commonly lost. When we are discussing poetry, we should not beguile ourselves with analogies drawn from music, sculpture, architecture, or engineering; a poem is not a symphony, neither is it a structure made of bricks. Words are primarily conceptual; the words *grief, tree, poetry, God,* represent concepts; they may communicate some feeling and remembered sensory impression as well, and they may be made to communicate a great deal of these, but they will do it by virtue of their conceptual identity, and in so far as this identity is impaired they will communicate less of these and communicate them with less force and precision. It is the business of the poet, then, to make a statement in words about an experience; the statement must be in some sense and in a fair measure acceptable rationally; and the feeling communicated should be proper to the rational understanding of the experience.

Poetry has something, however, though relatively little, in common with music; namely, rhythm. Rhythm, with the other elements of sound which may be combined with it—in poetry these other elements are relatively few and simple—is to some extent expressive of emotion, and it may be used to modify the emotional content of language. The value of rhythm is not primarily in its power to intensify emotion, though it has this power; it is rather to modulate and define emotion, so that a finer adjustment of emotion to thought may be possible.

The poem thus differs from the statement of the philosopher or scientist in that it is a fairly complete judgment of an experience: it is not merely a rational statement, but it communicates as well the feeling which the particular rational understanding ought to motivate. It differs from the statement of the writer of imaginative prose, in that the poet's language is more precise and more flexible and hence can accomplish more in little space and accomplish it better. But with the development of romantic theory in the eighteenth, nineteenth, and twentieth centuries, there has been an increasing tendency to suppress the rational in poetry and as far as may be to isolate the emotional. This tendency makes at best for an incomplete poetry and makes at worst for a very confused poetry.
My first poem is by John Donne:

> Thou best made me, and shall thy work decay?
> Repair me now, for now mine end doth haste,
> I run to death, and death meets me as fast,
> And all my pleasures are like yesterday;
> I dare not move my dim eyes any way,
> Despair behind and death before doth cast
> Such terror, and my feeble flesh doth waste
> By sin in it, which it toward hell doth weigh;
> Only thou art above, and when toward thee
> By thy leave I can look, I rise again;
> But our old subtle foe so tempteth me,
> That not one hour myself I can sustain;
> Thy Grace may wing me to prevent his art,
> And thou like Adamant draw mine iron heart.

This poem is simple in conception: the poet looks forward a little way to death and backward on the sins of his life; he is oppressed with his helplessness and prays for God's grace that he may love God, repent, and be saved. The situation is a general one: we have an orthodox theological definition of a predicament in which every man is supposed to share; yet the poet knows it to be his own predicament, and the theological proposition becomes a personal experience. The language is plain, but is exact and powerful; it culminates in a pun which makes one of the greatest lines in English poetry.

My second poem, "Low Barometer," is by Robert Bridges:

> The southwind strengthens to a gale,
> Across the moon the clouds fly fast,
> The house is smitten as with a flail,
> The chimney shudders to the blast.
>
> On such a night, when Air has loosed
> Its guardian grasp on blood and brain,
> Old terrors then of god or ghost
> Creep from their caves to life again;
>
> And Reason kens he herits in
> A haunted house. Tenants unknown
> Assert their squalid lease of sin
> With earlier title than his own.
>
> Unbodied presences, the pack'd
> Pollution and Remorse of Time,
> Slipped from oblivion reënact
> The horrors of unhoused crime.
>
> Some men would quell the thing with prayer
> Whose sightless footsteps pad the floor,
> Whose fearful trespass mounts the stair
> Or bursts the lock'd forbidden door.
>
> Some have seen corpses long interr'd
> Escape from hallowing control,
> Pale charnel forms—nay ev'n have heard
> The shrilling of a troubled soul,
>
> That wanders till the dawn hath cross'd
> The dolorous dark, or Earth hath wound
> Closer her storm-spredd cloke, and thrust
> The baleful phantoms underground.

The theme of this poem, as I have said, is similar to the theme of the sonnet by Donne. Donne sees man as fallen from Grace and evicted from paradise, and as capable of salvation only through a return of Grace as an aid to his own imperfect ability; though he does not say so in this poem, his system depends in part on the right use of Reason, though Reason without Grace is insufficient, and the poem is a prayer for Grace. Bridges sees man as risen from brutality and as governed precariously by Reason. Both poets deal with man's unequal struggle with his lower nature, and with what we may call either literally or figuratively the effect of Original Sin. Bridges, like Donne, feels the need for supernatural aid in addition to Reason; unlike Donne, he cannot state this need directly and in theological language, for he is not a Christian, but he implies it in his figurative use of Air; ". . . when Air has loosed / Its guardian grasp on blood and brain." Through the figure of the storm, he indicates supernatural violence; as a result of the storm, the steady force of the air, like the pressure of water on submarine life, is relaxed, and man's nature is unbalanced, and man sees corpses "Escape from hallowing control"; Reason is overwhelmed by the ancient and powerful demonic forces in its fleshly habitation. This poem, like Donne's, deals with a common predicament; unlike Donne's, the poem does not profess to deal with a personal experience. Both poems deal with the experience in the most general of terms: Donne's despair, death, and sin could hardly be more general, but they are definite, for they have a body of theology behind them, and we know what they include and why Donne feels as he does; Bridges, without such a corpus of theology for direct reference, must limit his statement further:

> Unbodied presences, the pack'd
> Pollution and Remorse of Time,
> Slipped from oblivion reënact
> The horrors of unhoused crime.

These lines are the culmination of his account of sin as the subhuman, the archaic, and the chaotic; he is forced to greater particularity here than Donne, and he achieves greater power, but the statement is nevertheless general and very inclusive. What I wish to call to the attention at present is this: that though both poems are generalized, they are precise; that there is a great difference between generalization and uncertainty.

Let us now consider the sonnet by Hopkins:

> No worst, there is none. Pitched past pitch of grief,
> More pangs will, schooled at forepangs, wilder wring.
> Comforter, where, where is your comforting?
> Mary, mother of us, where is your relief?
> My cries heave, herds-long; huddle in a main, a chief
> Woe, world-sorrow; on an age-old anvil wince and sing—
> Then lull, then leave off. Fury had shrieked 'No ling-
> ering! Let me be fell: force I must be brief.'
>
> O the mind, mind has mountains: cliffs of fall
> Frightful, sheer, no-man-fathomed. Hold them cheap
> May who ne'er hung there. Nor does long our small
> Durance deal with that steep or deep. Here! creep,
> Wretch, under a comfort serves in a whirlwind: all
> Life death does end and each day dies with sleep.

This poem differs from the two preceding in that it deals primarily with a particular and personal experience; the difficulty consists in the fact that there is so little generalization that we can feel no certainty regarding the nature of the experience beyond the fact that it has generated a desperate emotion. This is not a poem about the effects of violent emotion in general; it is a poem about a particular violent emotion experienced by the poet. The nearest thing to a statement of motive occurs in the first line and a half

of the sestet; but what are these mountains of the mind? One does not enquire because one holds them cheap, but because one has hung on so many oneself, so various in their respective terrors, that one is perplexed to assign a particular motive. One is inclined to ask: "What do you know of these matters? Why are you so secretive? And above all, why are you so self-righteous in your secretiveness?" Hopkins' modern admirers have often assumed that the poem deals with a struggle to maintain what they consider an irrational and unwholesome faith, that it deals with the self-inflicted torture of the religious. There is nothing in the poem either to prove or to disprove the idea of such a struggle. The emotion might result from such a struggle, might result as in Donne's sonnet from a sense of sin either general or particular or both and for the need of Grace, from the contemplation of any of several metaphysical propositions, from the death of a friend, from betrayal by a friend, from the desperation of personal loneliness, from a mixture of some of these, or from something else. We have passed beyond the limits of generalization; we are in the realm of uncertainty; and the mind cannot organize itself to share Hopkins' experience with any real feeling of security.

It is interesting to observe the manner in which he achieves a part of the precision he needs, a small part which is managed with such skill that it gives a brief illusion of a great part, in the use of metaphor. Take, for example, his most brilliant phrase: "on an age-old anvil wince and sing—." The anvil is presumably God's discipline, and on it lies the poet as a piece of metal. The two verbs, the first with its sense of human suffering combined with metallic vibration, the second with its sense of metallic vibration combined perhaps with human triumph, make the metal suffer as metal under the hammer, and the suffering metal is terribly vivid. We suffer with the metal under the blow, and we forget that the literal metal does not suffer, that metal and blow are figurative, and that the human half of the figure is incomplete. Thus the poet conveys emotion for a moment, and conveys it with an illusion of motivation but with no real motivation. If the mountains of the mind were adequately identified, Hopkins' figure would have a power comparable to that of Donne's last line; but Donne's line has meaning, and Hopkins' figure the illusion of meaning.

The meter of the poem contributes to the difficulty, or at least emphasizes it. Hopkins' published explanation of his meter is incomplete and contradictory, and will help us only a little to understand his work. I will consider it in some detail presently, but for the moment I would like to give my own definition of sprung rhythm, which agrees only in part with that of Hopkins, and then proceed to an examination of the meter of the present sonnet. Sprung rhythm occurs when two stresses come together by means other than the normal inversion of a foot; it occurs freely in accentual meter and in syllabic meter; it may occur as a variant in standard English meter as a result of the dropping of an unaccented syllable with the resultant creation of a monosyllabic foot, or as a result of the equally heavy accentuation of both syllables of a foot. For example, when Barnaby Googe writes in an iambic pentameter poem: "Fair

A Vision of the Mermaids (1862), pen-and-ink drawing by Hopkins for his poem of the same title.

face show friends when riches do abound," the first two feet are sprung. It is most profitable, I think, to approach the sonnet under consideration as a variant on iambic pentameter, using Hopkins' remarks as occasional guides. I shall offer a scansion of the poem, with alternative readings of certain lines, and shall then comment on the scansion:

1. No worst/ *there* is/ *none*. Pitched/ *past* pitch/ *of* grief/, No *worst*/

2. More *pangs*/ will, *schooled*/ at fore/*pangs* wild/ *er* wring/.

3. Comfort/er where is/ *your* com/ *forting*/?

4. Mary/, mother/ of us/ where *is*/ *your* relief/?

5. My cries/ *heave*, herds/ *-long*; hud/*dle* in main/, *a* chief/
   (My) cries *heave*/ herds-*long*/; hud*dle*/ in a main/, *a* chief/

6. Woe, world sor/ (*row*); *on an* age/- *old* an/*vil* wince/ *and* sing/—
   Woe, world sor/*row*; *on an* age/

7. *Then* lull/, *then* leave/ off. Fu/ry *had* shrieked/ '*No* ling/-

8. *ering*/! Let *me*/ *be* fell/: force I/ *must be* brief/.'

9. O *the* mind/, mind/ *has* mount/*ains*: cliffs/ *of* fall/

10. Fright*full*/, sheer/, no-*man-fath*/omed. Hold/ *them* cheap/

11. May *who ne'er*hung/ *there*. Nor/ *does* long/ *our* small/
    May *who ne'er*/ hung *there*/. Nor *does*/ long/ *our* small/

12. Du*rance*/ deal *with*/ that steep/ *or* deep/. Here! Creep/,

13. Wretch, *un*/*der* a com/ *fort* serves/ *in a* whirl/ *wind*: all/

14. *Life* death/ *does* end/ *and* each/ *day* dies/ *with* sleep/.

The first line is normal, unless we read the first foot as reversed; in either version it defines the pattern. In the second line, the first two feet are reversed, and the last three are normal; the reversal of the second foot is unusual, as Hopkins says in his preface, and is the first indication of the violence to follow. In the third line the first and third feet are reversed and the rest normal, this being a more ordinary arrangement. The fourth line is composed of four reversed feet and a normal trisyllabic foot, the first four feet giving us what Hopkins calls counterpoint, or a heard rhythm running counter to the remembered norm. The fifth line may be scanned in either of two ways: as composed of four iambic feet (the first three and the fifth), with the fourth foot reduced to three syllables by the elision of *huddle* and *in;* or with *My* regarded as extra-metrical, a violent procedure from the standpoint of the ordinary metrist, but defensible in Hopkin's system of lines which are "rove over," and thereafter three reversed feet, a normal trisyllabic foot, and a normal dissyllabic. The two readings may be regarded as a case of counterpoint, perhaps, the first giving the theoretic norm and the second the heard rhythm. In regard to this and other elisions, real or possible, in Hopkins, one may suggest that Hopkins may have had a notion comparable to that of Bridges, whereby elision takes place for the eye and so pays its respects to regularity but does not take place for the ear: his elisions, or possible elisions, in any event, are usually preferable if seen but not heard. The sixth line contains seven inescapable accents, and so eliminates any possibility that the poem be scanned as regular accentual meter. I should be inclined to call the first three syllables, all of which are accented, a single sprung foot, of the same sort employed by Googe in dissyllabic units when he wrote, "Fair face show friends." I am acquainted with no poet save Hopkins who has used a sprung foot of three syllables, but the sprung foot of two syllables, employed as a variation on standard English meter, is fairly common in the sixteenth century. The second syllable of *sorrow* may then be regarded as extra-metrical, the position of the extra-metrical syllable before the caesura instead of at the line-end being natural enough in a system in which the line-end need not involve a pause and in which the caesural break may be heavy, that is in a system of lines which are "rove over," as I have said; or *sorrow* may be elided with *on;* thereafter we have a normal trisyllabic foot followed by two normal dissyllabics. The seventh line is simple except for the termination in mid-word, a procedure justified by Hopkins' theory and successful use of "rove-over" rhythm, and for which classical—and even, in a measure, Miltonic—precedent can be found if it is wanted; the fourth foot of this line is a normal trisyllabic, the others are normal dissyllabics. The eighth line contains an inverted foot in the difficult second position and another in the fourth, and for the rest contains two normal dissyllabics and a final normal trisyllabic, and thus brings the octet back more or less obviously to the iambic pentameter pattern.

In the ninth line, we have a trisyllabic, a monosyllabic, and three dissyllabics, the accents falling normally. The monosyllabic foot, as a method of achieving sprung rhythm, has, like the sprung dissyllabic, its precedents in the sixteenth century. It occurs in some of the poems of Wyatt which are based on a ten-syllable norm, and it occurs in some of the seven-syllable couplets of Greene: the reader may examine specimens of both, if he is curious, in *The Oxford Book of Sixteenth Century Verse*. In line ten we have an inverted dissyllabic, a monosyllabic, an inverted trisyllabic, and two normal dissyllabics. In the eleventh line we may read five dissyllabics, the first only being inverted; or we may read an inverted trisyllabic followed by two inverted dissyllabics, a monosyllabic, and a normal dissyllabic; the first reading giving the theoretic norm

and the second the heard rhythm, with another example of Hopkins' counterpoint as the result. The twelfth line consists of two inverted dissyllabics, a sprung dissyllabic, a normal dissyllabic, and a sprung dissyllabic, to give us another line of seven accents. The thirteenth line consists of an inverted dissyllabic, a normal trisyllabic, a normal dissyllabic, a normal trisyllabic, and a normal dissyllabic. The last line consists of five normal dissyllabics, although the long syllables in the first and fourth feet almost give the illusion of sprung feet: this line returns to the original pattern, yet echoes some of the more violent variations.

The poem, then, is not written in syllabic meter, for the number of syllables varies from line to line; if it is an attempt at accentual meter, it is irregular, for two lines contain extra accents. But it can be described, and without undue trouble, as a variant on standard English meter, a variant both learned and perverse but in which the rhythm is successfully maintained, in which the perversity is equalled by the skill.

Skill to what purpose, however? The rhythm is fascinating in itself, but it does not exist in itself, it exists in the poem. It is a rhythm based on the principle of violent struggle with its governing measure, and it contributes to the violence of feeling in the total poem. But it is this very violence which makes us question the motive, and I think one may add that the violence is in some degree the result of the inadequacy of the motive. When Bridges writes:

> Unbodied presences, the packed
> Pollution and Remorse of Time,
> Slipped from oblivion reënact
> The horrors of unhoused crime,

he is making a statement about human nature which is true and important; the concept and all its implications are clear; and he can make his statement quietly, for he knows that we should recognize its importance and be moved appropriately. I do not mean that the importance of the concept absolves him from the necessity of deliberately communicating the appropriate emotion, and in this passage the emotional weight of the language is great; I mean that his statement has the dignity of conviction. Hopkins has no such generating concept, or at least offers none; since he cannot move us by telling us why he himself is moved, he must try to move us by belaboring his emotion. He says, in effect: "Share my fearful emotion, for the human mind is subject to fearful emotions." But why should we wish to share an emotion so ill sponsored? Nothing could be more rash. We cannot avoid sharing a part of it, for Hopkins has both skill and genius; but we cannot avoid being confused by the experience and suspecting in it a fine shade of the ludicrous. Who is this man to lead us so far and blindfold into violence? This kind of thing is a violation of our integrity; it is somewhat beneath the dignity of man.

II

I have already indicated the most important general problem raised by Hopkins' meter, the problem of emotional overemphasis. My actual scansion of the poem in question, however, is one of which Hopkins might or might not have approved, although I suspect that he would have accepted it as reasonable. Before we can deal with Hopkins' meter in general, or at least with reference to his more curious and experimental structures, we must look at his own remarks, for the more difficult poems certainly cannot be scanned as variants on the iambic structure. There are two important documents: *Rhythm and Other Structural Parts of Rhetoric—Verse,* in *The Notebooks and Papers of Gerard Manley Hopkins,* a discussion which is merely a general survey of his speculations on the topic but which gives a fair idea of where his mind had roamed and paused, and the *Author's Preface* to the ***Poems,*** which was written as an explanation of his actual practice. The former document is only of incidental, though sometimes of real, interest: for example, in my own scansion of the sonnet which I have already discussed, I have indicated a foot of three accented syllables at the beginning of line six, and have noted that this resembles similar feet of two accented syllables which one can find in such Renaissance models as Googe and Nashe, but outdoes them; but Hopkins in the document mentioned lists the Greek *molossus,* or foot of three long syllables, among the various Greek constructions, and since he was aware that English feet resembled certain Greek feet if accent were substituted for length, and since he was all but obsessed with metrical theories of every kind, it is not unreasonable to suppose that he would attempt an English molossus if he were employing a metrical scheme which would at once sustain it and make it recognizable.

The *Author's Preface,* however, was written as an explanation of what Hopkins had actually done. It is unsatisfactory, but we must examine it briefly and point by point. Hopkins begins by naming two kinds of meter, Running and Sprung. The former he identifies with standard English meter; the latter he describes farther on. He states that Running rhythm may be more easily scanned if any unaccented syllable at the beginning of the line be regarded either as carried over from the preceding line or as extra-metrical, so that the accent will always fall in the first place in the foot. It seems obvious to me that such a system of scansion would introduce more difficulties than it would eliminate and further that it would disregard the natural genius of English rhythm. In the following paragraph, however, he proceeds to speak of standard English verse as if he had not made this suggestion: his discussion of reversed feet and of counterpoint rhythm rests on a recognition of the reality of iambic and anapestic feet, and he does not account in any way for this sudden change of theory. One does not know, therefore, how he prefers his own poems to be scanned, and one can only use what judgment one has with the individual poem.

He next takes up Sprung Rhythm, and he offers two distinct definitions for it. First, he says: "Sprung Rhythm, as used in this book, is measured by feet of from one to four syllables, regularly, and for particular effects any number of weak or slack syllables may be used. It [he refers here to the individual foot] has one stress, which falls on the only syllable, if there is only one, or, if there are more,

then scanning as above, on the first, and so gives rise to four sorts of feet, a monosyllable and the so-called accentual Trochee, Dactyl, and the First Paeon. And there will be four corresponding natural rhythms; but nominally the feet are mixed, and any one may follow any other." He adds that it will be natural in this rhythm for the lines to be *rove over,* "that is for the scanning of each line immediately to take up that of the one before, so that if the first has one or more syllables at its end the other must have so many the less at its beginning." This is partly a description of the way in which his own poems tend to move with little or no pause at the ends of lines, and it is partly a formal necessity, for if each foot is to start with an accented syllable, there must be some way to account for unaccented syllables when they occur at the beginning of a line, and the obvious method is to assign them to the last foot of the line preceding. What we have here, briefly, is a description of ordinary accentual verse, which commonly shall have a maximum of three unaccented syllables between accents, but which may sometimes have more. Near the end of the *Preface,* however, Hopkins remarks of certain old popular rimes and their modification by time, "however these may have been once made in running rhythm, the terminations having dropped off by the change of language, the stresses come together and so the rhythm is sprung." Here it appears that Sprung Rhythm is identified by the juxtaposition of stresses, and that we may have juxtaposition of stresses in meter other than accentual. For clarity of discussion, I shall use the term *Sprung Rhythm,* as I have used it in the past, to refer to rhythm in which two or more stresses come together, except where this occurs in standard English meter through the mere inversion of a foot.

Of Sprung Rhythm (apparently in either sense), Hopkins says: "Two licenses are natural to Sprung Rhythm. The one is rests, as in music; but of this an example is scarcely to be found in this book, unless in the **"Echoes,"** second line. The other is *hangers* or *outrides,* that is one, two, or three slack syllables added to foot and not counting in the nominal scanning. They are so called because they seem to hang below the line or ride forward or backward from it in another dimension than the line itself, according to a principle needless to explain here." This comment is characteristic. As to **"The Leaden Echo and the Golden Echo,"** it is metrically one of the most difficult of Hopkins poems, and I believe that there is no way of being certain what the pattern is, if there is indeed a fixed one; there is one insurmountable obstacle to certainty in this matter with regard to all the more difficult specimens, an obstacle which I shall presently discuss. And Hopkins himself appears uncertain as to whether there is a "rest" in the second line. As to *hangers* or *outrides,* he finds it needless to explain their principle; and it is hard to see how so many as six unaccented syllables could be attached to an accented syllable without confusion.

Hopkins cites Greene as having practiced Sprung Rhythm. The Sprung Rhythm which Greene practiced, however, can be classified properly as such according to my definition and to Hopkins' second, but not according to Hopkins' first. Greene's Sprung Rhythm occurs as a variant on standard English meter, when he drops an unaccented syllable, thus bringing two accented syllables together. The following passage, for example, comes from a poem written in ordinary couplets of seven-syllable lines:

> Up I start, forth went I,
> With her face to feed mine eye. . . .

Many similar lines can be found in Greene whenever he uses this form. I should judge that Hopkins must have had such lines by Greene in mind when he was writing his **"Lines for a Picture of St. Dorothea"** (Number 82, an early version of Number 1, **"For a Picture of St. Dorothea"**). I quote the first stanza, with the accents [in italics] as given in the published text:

> I bear a basket lined with grass.
> *I* am *so* ligh*t* and fai*r*
> Men are amazed to watch me pass
> Wi*th* the *b*asket I bea*r*,
> Which in newly drawn green litter
> Carries treats of sweet for bitter.

The meter of Hopkins' second line corresponds exactly to the meter of the first line quoted from Greene, and so does the meter of Hopkins' fourth if one reads the stress that is almost forced on the second syllable of *basket* in spite of its not having been indicated. But there is this difference: Greene's meter is based on the natural stress of the language and is plainly evident without artificial help, whereas no one would suspect the intentions of Hopkins if he had not marked the lines. A structure which is based on so willful a deformation of the language is indefensible, and it will often be grotesque, as it is here; yet Hopkins' more elaborate experiments often depend upon deformation equally fantastic, and the more elaborate structures make his intentions all but indecipherable.

The poem called **"Spring and Fall"** (Number 31) shows similar deformations in a comparably simple meter; and interestingly enough, most of the deformed lines are pleasanter, though less regular, if read in the normal rhythm of the language. The real difficulty inherent in such deformation, however, is apparent when we consider some of the more difficult poems. G. F. Lahey, for example, [in *Gerard Manley Hopkins,* 1930] gives a scansion of **"The Windhover,"** of which I shall offer only the first four lines. I do not know whether Lahey's scansion is merely a personal hypothesis or whether it is based on markings in a Hopkins ms. It does not correspond with the markings copied for me by a friend from one ms. version of the poem. I shall leave the unaccented syllables in italics and indicate the feet with cross-bars:

> *I* caught/ *this* morn/*ing* morn/*ing's* min/*ion*, king/-
>   dom *of* daylight's/ dau*phin*/, dap*ple-dawn-*
>   *drawn*/
>   Fal*con, in his*/ ri*ding*/
>   Of *the* rol*ling*/ lev*el* und*er*/ neath *him* steady/ air
>   *and*/ stri*ding*/

High *there, how he*/ rung *upon the*/ rein *of a*/ wimpl*ing*/wing/

Some of the difficulty in this reading can be eliminated if we pay more attention to Hopkins' theory of "rove-over" lines. That is, unless Hopkins is the ultimate authority for this reading, it would be better to put the first accents of lines three and four on *daylight's* and *rolling* respectively, and to consider the unaccented syllables preceding as parts of the last feet of lines one and two. However, the difficulties do not stop there. As nearly as I am able to pronounce the English language, the normal accentuation of these lines would proceed as follows:

> *I* caught *this* morning morn*ing's* min*ion*, king-
>   *dom of* day*light's* dau*phin* dap*ple-dawn-dawn*
>   Fal*con, in his* ri*ding*
>   Of *the* rol*ling* level un*der*neath *him* stea*dy* air,
>   *and* stri*ding*
> High *there, how he* rung *up*on *the* rein *of a*
>   wimpl*ing* wing.

Furthermore, I submit that this reading gives a better rhythm, in spite of the irregularity of meter (five accents in line one, six in two, seven in three, and six in four). On the other hand, if Lahey's version is defensible with regard to such feet as these—*dom* of daylight's, *Of* the rolling, *neath* him steady—then how are we to know that we should not read likewise: *caught* this morning, *morn*ing's minion? The presence of the unaccented syllable at the beginning of the line provides no obstacle, for Hopkins could easily have regarded it as extra-metrical; and these deformations are of exactly the same kind as those offered by Lahey and in fact are more conservative than some of Lahey's. If Lahey's reading is authoritative, then Hopkins expects us to change from normal accentuation to deformed accentuation merely at his own whim, and with no kind of warning, and his own markings of certain poems support this theory. Merely as a technical procedure, this is all but impossible; and if one manages to work it out one gets a mispronunciation of the language which renders the poem ludicrous. In the sonnet which I have already scanned according to my own lights, we found a meter which was very unusual, but which was at the same time comprehensible and pronounceable; its deviations from normal English meter, though made in the interests of an obscurely violent emotion, were structurally both learned and controlled. In **"The Windhover,"** however, the attempt to express violent emotion through violent meter has got out of hand and become merely preposterous. Lahey adds to this confusion when he tells us that *dapple-dawn-drawn Falcon in his* represent "outrides" or "hangers," though according to his own scansion they do not.

"The Windhover" is characteristic of Hopkins' more difficult metrical experiments, although it is not one of the most difficult. Other poems which exhibit a similarly confused meter are the following: *The Wreck of the Deutschland,* **"The Starlight Night," "Duns Scotus's Oxford," "Henry Purcell," "The Bugler's First Communion," "Spelt from the Sibyl's Leaves," "The Leaden Echo and the Golden Echo," "To What Serves Mortal Beauty," "The Soldier," "Carrion Comfort,"** and **"That**

Nature is a Heraclitean Fire." There is a good deal of difference in the degree of difficulty among these poems, and there are other poems which exhibit the difficulty. Some of the difficult poems, however, may be read with a fairly satisfactory rhythm, though with irregular meter, if Hopkins' theories are forgotten, although this is a melancholy compromise if one assumes that the poet really meant something by his rhythm.

Mr. Harold Whitehall, in one of the most interesting studies of Hopkins' meter which I have read ["Sprung Rhythm," in *Gerard Manley Hopkins,* by the Kenyon Critics, 1945], constructs a theory of his own on the fragmentary basis left by Hopkins. His theory, briefly and incompletely, is that Hopkins, without realizing it, was composing dipodic meter, or meter in double feet, of the sort described by Patmore, but was using this medium so freely and variously that Patmore did not recognize the results when he saw them. Put thus baldly, the theory may seem a trifle innocent, but actually Mr. Whitehall makes a fairly good case. I am not interested, however, either in attacking or in defending his theory, for in explaining his theory he makes the one admission which, in my opinion, renders his theory worthless as a defense of Hopkins' procedure, in spite of the fact that his theory may conceivably offer a true description of the procedure. He says:

> His sprung rhythm must be read as we read the words of a song when we happen to know the tune. If we do not know the tune—and Hopkins never furnishes it— the words may become, and in print frequently do become, a meaningless jumble of syllables.

But the "tune" of a poem is supposed to be constructed from the living material of the language, not imposed upon it arbitrarily, and Mr. Whitehall is here admitting the defect which I have already described, though he scarcely seems to recognize it as a defect. The double foot is composed of a major stress and a minor stress, and may have one or two unaccented syllables; it may be combined with the monosyllabic foot, especially when this falls in the last position. What one might call the classical form of the double foot is Hopkins' First Paeon, with the major stress on the first syllable and the minor on the third. A word employed by Mr. Whitehall will illustrate it: *Honeysuckle*. I will mark the scansion, on this basis, of two lines employed by Mr. Whitehall, the first from Alfred Noyes, the second from John Masefield, but will employ a simpler marking than his, one which merely indicates the major and minor accents and the feet. The [italics] will indicate the major stress, the single accent the minor:

> M*u*sic óf the/ st*a*rlíght/ sh*i*mmering ón the/ sea . . .
> S*a*ndalwóod,/ c*e*darwóod, and/ sw*ee*t white/ w*i*ne . . .

The double feet in these lines are real: that is, the poets have chosen their words in such a fashion that clearly recognizable light accents follow clearly recognizable heavy, in a rhythmic pattern which is unmistakable. That this is not, however, the basic pattern of English verse, as Patmore (and I should add Mr. Whitehall with him) would

seem to think, one may see readily enough from a brief examination of the following lines:

> Of M*a*n's/ first di /obe/dience ánd/ the fr*ui*t/
> Of thát/ forb*i*d/den tr*ee*/ whose m*o*r/tal t*a*ste/
> Brought d*ea*th/ ínto/ the w*o*rld/ and *a*ll/ our w*o*e/ . . .

If we regard the first syllable of the first line as extrametrical, we may arrange the feet of this line so that they resemble the feet of Masefield and of Noyes, but we shall be forcing the rhythm and ruining the line; the next two lines cannot be so arranged except by the most arbitrary of accentuation, which will render them ludicrous. The principle which is operating in these lines is different, therefore, from that which we found in the lines preceding. For purposes of the measure, only two kinds of syllable are recognized, the accented and the unaccented; the accented is recognized as such only with reference to the other syllable or syllables within its own foot; and different degrees of accent, since they do not affect the measure, can be infinitely variable and thus contribute to a flexible and perceptive rhythm; the poet is not bound to a simple drum-beat, he can write poetry instead of jingles. When Mr. Whitehall states that standard English meter is largely theoretical and does not lend itself to vocal reading, I can only think that he himself knows very little about the reading of verse.

Hopkins, however, is less simple than Noyes and Masefield. I will offer a few lines from Hopkins with Whitehall's accentuation:

> E*a*rnest, eárthless,/ *e*qual, attúneable,/ v*a*ulty, volúminous,/ stupéndous/

In this line nothing save forewarning of some kind can indicate that the heavy accents are heavier than the light; so long as one regards the language as it really exists, all of the stresses are equal, and their equality is emphasized by the grammatical parallels: the meter as indicated is a pure fiction. Whitehall runs into even greater difficulty with another line from the same poem:

> Her/ fond yellow hórnlight/ w*o*und to the wést, her/ w*i*ld hollow hóarlight/ h*u*ng to the héight./

The heavy and light accentuation is equally arbitrary here, and there is the additional confusion that the first syllables of *yellow* and *hollow,* which have a legitimate right to light accent marks, cannot be given them. The reader coming to this line with no previous theory except the realization that there were two kinds of accent involved, would inescapably mark these two syllables as light and every one of Mr. Whitehall's accented syllables as heavy.

We may observe the same kind of accentuation in the conclusion of **"The Lantern out of Doors,"** which I offer as accented by Hopkins himself according to the published text:

> Christ minds; Christ's interest, what to avow or amend
> There, éyes them, heart wánts, care háunts, foot

fóllows kínd,
Their ránsom, théir rescue / ánd first, fást, last
friend.

In the light of such scansion, it is curious to read this passage in one of Hopkins' letters to Bridges:

> Why do I employ sprung rhythm at all? Because it is the nearest to the rhythm of prose, that is the native and natural rhythm of speech, the least forced, the most rhetorical and emphatic of all possible rhythms.

It is even more curious to read the following comment upon this passage by so able a critic as Arthur Mizener:

> However much Hopkins crowded a sentence with repetitions, it never lost the cadence of actual speech; the sound of the voice speaking it is always there in the reader's ear to give the poems their incomparable immediacy.

It is this kind of thing which often makes poetry and the criticism of poetry in our day so baffling a study.

What we have in Hopkins' more difficult constructions, then, is a very complex accentual meter, in which the accents are for the most part the irresponsible inventions of the author rather than native elements of the language, and in which in addition we have "hangers" or "outrides," that is, groups of syllables which may or may not seem to the unassisted reader to have the characteristics of feet, and which are not to be counted in the scansion. Unless we have the author's marking to guide us or are willing to accept on faith the marking of some other authority, we commonly have no way of determining the scansion; and when we have such marking (and this is quite as true of Hopkins' own as of any other), we frequently find ourselves forced into deformations of language which are nearly unpronounceable and are often ridiculous. This metrical method, moreover, is devised in the interest of intensifying an emotion which is frequently unmotivated or inadequately motivated within the terms of the poem. It seems to me obvious that the poems so constructed should be regarded as ruins rather than masterpieces, whatever impressive fragments there may be lying loose among them; and furthermore that defensive explanation is quite foolish. Bridges has been repeatedly rebuked for failing to understand what Hopkins was doing. I am inclined to believe that Bridges understood as much as was necessary, and that the real failure was on the part of Hopkins.

Robert R. Boyle, S.J. (essay date 1949)

SOURCE: "The Thought Structure of the *The Wreck of the Deutschland*," in *Immortal Diamond: Studies in Gerard Manley Hopkins*, edited by Norman Weyand, S.J., Sheed & Ward, 1949, pp. 333-50.

[*In the following essay, Boyle examines the major themes of* The Wreck of the Deutschland, *asserting that it is not a poem about the problem of suffering but a poem about the answer to the problem of suffering.*]

In 1877 Sidney Lanier was distressed by a problem that has troubled the minds of most men at one time or another (*To Beethoven*):

> Th' indifferent smile that nature's grace
>   On Jesus, Judas, pours alike;
> Th' indifferent frown on nature's face
>   When luminous lightnings strangely strike
>
> The sailor praying on his knees
>   And spare his mate that's cursing God . . .

Hopkins had given his answer to that problem just a year or so before in *The Wreck of the Deutschland*. Perhaps Lanier would not have understood the answer even if he had had access to Hopkins' expression of it. But it is Christ's answer. It is St. Paul's answer. It is the answer of the Catholic Church. The mystery lies not in nature but in man. The mystery of God's grace in us, of Christ in us, of the mastery, the power of God in us—that is Hopkins' answer, and the subject of his masterpiece.

Hopkins is not dealing directly with the problem of suffering, but with the answer to that problem. His concern is with the power and the mastery of God. He takes the viewpoint of Christ:

> . . . but thou art above, thou Orion of light;
>   Thy unchancelling poising palms were weighing
> the worth,
>   Thou martyr-master; in thy sight
> Storm flakes were scroll-leaved flowers, lily
>   showers—sweet heaven
>   was astrew in them.

This is not a poem of the Passion, but of the Triumph which followed upon the Passion. It is not the lament of those who die, but the paean of those who seize the Life which follows death. It is not a wail expressive of suffering, but a song thrilling with triumphant joy.

The spirit of St. Paul shines through the poem from beginning to end. The power of God which St. Paul celebrated in everything he wrote is celebrated here:

> Thou mastering me
> God!

> Melt him but master him still.

> Make mercy in all of us, out of us all
> Mastery, but be adored, but be adored King.

> Thou Martyr-master . . .
> There then! the Master . . .

> I admire thee, master of the tides . . .

The mastery of God, in which all things work together for

good, is Hopkins' theme. According to Edith Sitwell [in *Aspects of Modern Poetry,* 1935], "The whole poem is inhabited by a gigantic and overwhelming power, like that of the element that inspired it." The power of the sea is a symbol, for Hopkins, of the power of God—"Stanching, quenching ocean of a motionable mind." The whole spirit of the poem is positive, not in any sense negative. It is the spirit of the Fourth Week of St. Ignatius' *Spiritual Exercises* where, in the concluding "Contemplation for Obtaining Divine Love," we behold God behind everything, God acting in and with everything, God working out His own transcendent glory in the universe.

The first part of the poem—which I will consider here rather briefly in relation to the poem as a whole, leaving consideration of its peculiar difficulties for the last part of my essay—gives the poet's qualifications for writing on this theme. He himself has experienced God's grace, the power of God working in him, and therefore he can know the experience of the nun. God's finger touched him, and almost unmade him. His heart was flushed by that stroke of God's finger, that "stress" of God felt in the innermost depths of his being, and his heart melted. The storm which brought this stress of God's power was not, in Hopkins' case, a physical storm, but a spiritual one, concerned not with "wild waters," but with "walls, altar and hour and night." He experienced it during a period of tremendous spiritual stress—"And the midriff astrain with leaning of, laced with fire of stress." I consider it probable that he refers here to his conversion to Catholicism, which must have cost him his greatest sacrifice up to the time when this poem was written. At any rate, he feared the power of God, he feared the "hurtle of hell," so he "whirled out wings that spell." I take this last phrase to mean that the image spells something, is significant, probably because the bird with extended wings forms a cross. The poet fled to Christ, to the "heart of the Host," and there found his strength and power. Christ gave him the grace to rise to ever new levels of the super-natural realms, sustained and lifted by that gift:

> My heart, but you were dovewinged, I can tell,
>   Carrier-witted, I am bold to boast,
> To flash from the flame to the flame then, tower
>   from
>   the grace to the grace.

His experience of grace is embodied in two striking figures: he seemed to be drained of himself like sand in an hourglass, and to be sustained from beneath like water in a well.

The following rather difficult stanzas are clarified somewhat by a quatrain written many years later (No. 73):

> What I know of thee I bless,
> As acknowledging thy stress
> On my being and as seeing
> Something of thy holiness.

What he can know of God begins with what he sees in nature, in stars and in storms, symbols of Christ's sweetness and power. He blesses and greets Christ, therefore, when he recognizes Him under nature's splendor and wonder. God's instressing of him, His finger's stroke upon his being, is delivered through nature; the stress, the activity of God which he feels within him is mediated by nature. God's grace, which is His power working in us, flows from the Cross of Christ, Who, by redeeming our fallen nature, made it possible for us to know more fully the Power Who lies under the power of nature. Nature speaks to us of God, and we are forced to hearken to her message when she drives us "hard at bay," holding us helpless in a superior power. Then we lash out with the best word, "yes," which is our acceptance of the mastery of that Power behind nature, or with our worst word, "no," which is our rejection of it. By that word the man makes known what side he takes, for or against God, and thus shows what he is (No. 67):

> What makes the man and what
> The man within that makes:
> Ask whom he serves or not
> Serves and what side he takes.

This revelation of his nature which each man experiences in his "yes" or "no" Hopkins compares to the experience of breaking the skin of a sloe which one has put whole into one's mouth. There is no escaping the rush of flavor, the "nature" of the fruit—sour or sweet. The metaphor represents a man's "conversion" or "non-conversion," his acceptance or rejection of God's mastery, in which act the true nature of the man, sour or sweet, appears. Response to Christ's power, His "stress," means life. Christ seeks to evoke that response even from the maliciously rebellious by the exercise of His power and mastery, thus forcing a decision:

> It is even seen, time's something server,
> In mankind's medley a duty-swerver,
>   At downright 'No or yes?'
> Doffs all, drives full for righteousness.
>   [**"The Loss of the Eurydice,"** 11.53-56]

Whether the man accepts or rejects that mastery, he must ultimately submit to it:

>   . . . Hither then, last or first,
>   To hero of Calvary, Christ's, feet—
>   Never ask if meaning it, wanting it, warned of it—
>   men go.

The first part of the poem concludes with a prayer to God that He should fulfill His glory in men. The apparent paradoxes ("lightning and love," "a winter and warm," "Father and fondler of heart thou hast wrung,") are identified in God, Who when He has His "dark descending" is then most merciful. The poet prays that He should make His mercy and mastery shine out through us by whatever means He will, whether by violence (storms) as in the conversion of Paul or by "a lingering-out sweet skill" (stars) as in that of Augustine. God appears to adapt His means to those with whom He deals. But the purpose of all things—of forces of nature, of the responses of men—is that God be glorified.

Hopkins is not dealing directly with the problem of suffering, but with the answer to that problem. His concern is with the power and the mastery of God.

—Robert R. Boyle, S.J.

The second part of the poem, which illustrates God's use of the violence of nature to achieve His ends, begins dramatically with the cry of Death, and a variant of the dread "Memento homo quia pulvis es . . ." The description of the boat's launching into the storm, of the wreck, and of the long terrible hours, is broken by the poet's cry to the "mother of being in me, heart." As in stanza seven, where the "heart" is said to utter truth not conceived before, the heart here finds the truth beneath the appearances. In the face of this seeming tragedy, the heart of the poet gives a gleeful, a "madrigal start." He inquires after the meaning of this glee. Does his heart have some interest there?

Yes, a sister calling their common Master. That is the interest. The flight of the nuns into exile and their seeming desperate loneliness recall Hopkins' sonnet on the Church (**"Andromeda"**):

> Her Perseus linger and leave her to her extremes?—
> Pillowy air he treads a time and hangs
> His thoughts on her, forsaken that she seems,
> All while her patience, morselled into pangs,
> Mounts . . .

But Christ was watching always; He was "weighing the worth"; the snowflakes in His sight were not cold signs of cruel fate but "scroll-leaved flowers, lily showers—sweet heaven was astrew in them."

"Martyr-master"—that name sounds the note of the next section. Christ is the Martyr Whose five wounds were scored on Him by men. He scores that cipher "himself on his own bespoken," that cipher of his wounds which is the "stigma, signal, cinquefoil token" for the lettering of the fleece of the Sacrificial Lamb, for the ruddying of the divine Rose. Hopkins celebrates the wounds of Christ in similar terms in **"Rosa Mystica."** The Blossom referred to here is Christ:

> What was the colour of that Blossom bright?
> White to begin with, immaculate white.
> But what a wild flush on the flakes of its stood,
> When the Rose ran in crimsonings down the Cross-
>   wood.
> In the Gardens of God, in the daylight divine
> I shall worship the Wounds with thee, Mother of
> mine.

> How many leaves had it? Five they were then,
> Five like the senses, and members of men;
> Five is the number by nature, but now

> They multiply, multiply, who can tell how.
> In the Gardens of God, in the daylight divine
> Make me a leaf in thee, Mother of mine.

The nuns were daughters of St. Francis, who himself bore the wounds of Christ, and here they share that privilege. The result of this triumph of Christ in them is their coming "to bathe in his fall-gold mercies, to breathe in his all-fire glances."

The poet notes the striking contrast between his own situation and theirs at the time of the wreck. He was at rest in the quiet countryside of Wales, where it was easy to know that Christ the shepherd was watching over him; the nun, helpless amid the wild waters, unfalteringly knew that the Good Shepherd was with her there.

Hopkins calls upon the Holy Spirit, "arch and original Breath," for light to understand the nun's cry. Did it signify that she desired to share the Passion of Christ, her lover? Or did she long for her suffering to cease that she might come to its reward, "the treasure never eyesight got, nor was ever guessed what for the hearing"? Not these. It is not sudden danger but a long period of suffering which "fathers" the plea for relief from the "sodden-with-its-sorrowing heart." Nor in such sudden danger does the Passion make its appeal. The nun has another motive. But it cannot be expressed. It is not a concept, but a vision, and that vision is Christ. She knew His power under the storm. She cries her "yes" and experiences His mastery within her. She is experiencing what Hopkins described of himself in the first part of the poem. She echoes the prayer which concluded the first part, calling upon Christ to ride in His triumph in her as in all the living and dead, to make His glory out of her.

This is the climax. The poet takes satisfaction in dwelling upon the perfect response of this creature to her God. She knew Him under the storm; the storm could not drive her from Him any more than a beacon of light can be blown from its course. She conceived Him, she bore Him within her ("I live now, not I, but Christ liveth in me"), she shared His sacrifice. She saw Christ in the storm and "worded it" by Him, as Simon Peter had seen the Godhead in the man Jesus before him, and had worded his vision for the ages. She was like Peter, too, in being a rock amid the storm, like the Tarpeian rock at Rome.

As a result of her sacrifice the nun shares Christ's glory, as does the "one woman without stain" who gave Christ birth. For the nun too has given Him new birth:

> But here was heart-throe, birth of a brain,
> Word, that heard and kept thee and uttered thee
>   outright.

Christ had said: "If anyone love me, he will keep my word, and my Father will love him, and we will come to him and make our abode with him" (John, 14:23).

The poet turns for a moment to consider the other passengers who perished, "the comfortless unconfessed of them."

His heart "bleeds at a bitterer vein" for them, who have also suffered the wreck and the storm and yet have not gained Christ. However, God was working also in these others; He was also their Father. And they heard the cry of the nun too. Perhaps that cry had moved them as it had moved the poet, and had "startled the poor sheep back."

Hopkins ends with passionate and almost incoherent praise of the majesty and mercy of God. He applies to Him various titles rising from the image of the storm: the master of the tides; the recurb and recovery of the gulf's sides, the girth of it and the wharf of it and the wall (an echo of St. Paul's "so that, being rooted and grounded in love, you may be able to comprehend with all the saints what is the breadth and length and height and depth . . ."); the "stanching, quenching ocean of a motionable mind," that is, God is the ocean which quenches the ever-changing desires of the human mind; the "ground of being, and granite of it," He of Whom alone it can be said, "I am Who am."

God is beyond all grasp, throned behind nature and behind death, which seems to us so conclusive. Yet in some measure the poet had grasped Him:

> I kiss my hand
> To the stars, lovely-asunder
> Starlight, wafting him out of it . . .

The nun had grasped Him:

> Ah! There was a heart right!
> There was single eye!
> Read the unshapeable shock night
> And knew the who and the why . . .

God is behind death with a "sovereignty which heeds but hides," that is, sees what is going on but does not clearly force His will upon men; Who "bodes but abides," that is, knows what will happen but does not therefore forestall the free acts of men. He is there with a mercy that will top the flood and be a saving ark to all who will listen to Him; with a love that goes even "lower than death and the dark"; with a vein (that is, a channel) for reaching the hopeless, the sinful, "the-last-breath penitent spirits," those rescued at the "uttermost mark" by Christ, striding across the stormy waters of the world.

The poet now quietly calls upon Christ to blaze in splendor before the world:

> Now burn, new born to the world,
> Double-naturèd name,
> The heaven-flung, heart-fleshed, maiden-furled
> Miracle-in-Mary-of-flame,
> Mid-numberèd He in three of the thunder-throne!

The storm is passed. Christ has reclaimed His own. This "storm of his strides" was not a punishment for the nuns, but a glorious fulfillment, "a released shower, let flash to the shire." He was not "a lightning of fire hard-hurled," as the disciples had wished to call down upon the unfriendly

Samaritans: "'Lord, wilt thou that we bid fire come down from heaven and consume them?' But he turned and rebuked them, saying, 'You do not know of what manner of spirit you are; for the Son of Man did not come to destroy men's lives, but to save them'" (Luke, 9:54–56).

Hopkins calls upon the nun to pray for the English, upon whose shoals she found her glory; to pray that Christ might again be the Sun of Britain, her high-priest, her warming fire.

The essential unity of the whole poem is achieved by a perfect structural parallelism in which part is proportioned to part. The two main divisions of the poem are labeled Part the First and Part the Second. In the former the power of God masters the poet, in the latter the same power masters the nun. Since the peculiar difficulties of Part the First will explain similar difficulties in Part the Second, I will consider here in detail only the problems which rise in relation to the first part.

Hopkins first discusses God's finger touching him, which is "the stress felt, the stroke dealt," of stanza six; in the second and third stanzas he describes his response and its results. In stanza four he expresses metaphorically the destruction of the old man and the support of the new, which is Christ's own life feeding and supporting him like the water from the mountain feeding and supporting the water in the well. The source of that life is the proffer of the gospel; the dynamic pressure of it lifts him; it is the principle of his new being; it is Christ's free gift to him—grace.

In the next stanza the poet points out that Christ speaks to him in all of nature—as in *Hurrahing in Harvest*:

> And, eyes, heart, what looks, what lips yet gave
>   you a
> Rapturous love's greeting of realer, of rounder
>   replies?

As a result of the touch of God's finger, he has been moved to acknowledge Christ behind nature, and this is the grace which Hopkins shares with the nun. This is Christ's gift (I Cor., 2:10–12):

> But to us God has revealed them through his Spirit. For the Spirit searches all things, even the deep things of God. For who among men knows the things of a man save the spirit of the man which is in him? Even so, the things of God no one knows but the Spirit of God. Now we have received not the spirit of the world, but the spirit that is from God, that we may know the things that have been given us by God.

The action of grace which Hopkins treats in the poem is that which causes the recipients to be "raised to the state when their deeds should be the doing of God in them" a statement which clarifies the difficult line of the twenty-eighth stanza, "Let him ride, her pride, in his triumph, despatch and have done with his doom there." So intimate is the union between Christ and the nun that her triumph is His doing, His triumph; her pride is Christ acting in her; the despatch of His doom, His plan, the sacrifice which He demands of her—"But he scores it in scarlet himself on his own bespoken"—this is the doing of God in her.

In his *Comments on the Spiritual Exercises* Hopkins calls this sort of action an activity of that form of grace which is "elevating, which lifts the receiver from one cleave of being to another and to a vital act in Christ: this is truly God's finger touching the very vein of personality, which nothing else can reach and man can respond to by no play whatever, by bare acknowledgment only, the counter-stress which God alone can feel ('subito probas eum'), the aspiration in answer to his inspiration. Of this I have written above and somewhere else long ago."

In this passage, I believe, lies the key to the whole poem, which thus becomes an illustration of that elevating grace. If this is true, the thought-structure of the poem centers about the line "His mystery must be instressed, stressed," which expresses the inspiration of God and the answering aspiration of man. To understand the full implications of the line, it is necessary to examine the terms "instress" and "stress" and so to derive Hopkins' conception.

The Wreck of the Deutschland is not a poem of Good Friday; it is an Easter poem. It is the record of the triumphant cry of a Christian who won the good fight, who received the crown of glory, who after glorious combat is dissolved and lives with Christ.

—Robert R. Boyle, S.J.

Dr. Pick—and in this he agrees with Mr. Gardner—takes the terms as synonyms: "Ordinarily Hopkins uses 'instress' verbally and 'stress' substantively; here, however, the first is an intensive form of the second, and the impact is heightened by the reversal of the expected word order." As Dr. Pick points out, such an interpretation is not in accord with Hopkins' ordinary use of the terms. There seems to be no good reason for supposing that Hopkins employs the terms in a sense different from his ordinary usage, which is here both appropriate and forceful. A consideration of Hopkins' usage of the terms in his other writings will make this clear.

Hopkins defines "stress" thus: "Stress appears so elementary an idea as does not need and scarcely allows of definition; still this may be said of it, that it is the making a thing more, or making it markedly, what it already is; it is the bringing out its nature" [*Further Letters*] (Nov. 7, 1883). He uses the term to denote emphasis of a word or syllable: "Its principle is that all rhythm and all verse consist of feet and each foot must contain one stress or verse-accent . . ." ([*The Correspondence of Gerard Manley Hopkins and Richard Watson Dixon*] Dec. 22, 1880).

He uses it further to denote the bringing out or the emphasis of a thing's or person's nature: "It is as if the blissful agony or stress of selving in God had forced out drops of sweat or blood . . ." ([*Note-Books and Papers*] 344). In this second usage the term "stress" is similar to the philosophical terms "act" and "perfection": "Nevertheless the being it has got has a great perfection, a great stress, and is more distinctive and higher selved, than anything else I see, except other such minds, in nature" ([*Note-Books and Papers*] 312). . . . "The word inspiration need cause no difficulty. I mean by it a mood of great, abnormal in fact, mental acuteness, either energetic or receptive, according as the thoughts which arise in it seem generated by a stress and action of the brain, or to strike into it unasked" ([*Further Letters*] Sept. 10, 1864). It is opposed to "slack," both in the sense of word emphasis—"So that wherever there is an accent or stress, there there is also so much unaccentuation, so to speak, or slack, and this will give a foot or rhythmic unit, viz. a stress with its belonging slack" ([*The Correspondence of Gerard Manley Hopkins and Richard Watson Dixon*] Feb. 27, 1879)—and in the sense of "nature" emphasis:

> Not, I'll not, carrion comfort, Despair, not feast
>   on thee;
> Not untwist—slack they may be—these last strands
>   of man
> In me or, most weary, cry *I can no more*
>
> (No. 40).

"Stress," then, is the general term which includes the terms "instress," "outstress," "distress," and "counter-stress."

"Instress" Hopkins defines as "throwing a stress on"— "The meaning of it is that you can without clumsiness instress, throw a stress on a syllable so supported which if it were unsupported would be drawling" ([*Note-Books and Papers*] 226)—or "coming to stress"—"And as more possibility, passive power, is not power proper and has no activity it cannot of itself come to stress, cannot instress itself" ([*Note-Books and Papers*] 310). When used verbally, "instress" means for him the process of bringing a thing to a state of stress, of actualising a thing: ". . . for the constant repetition, the continuity, of the bad thought is that actualising of it, that instressing of it, which he refused himself to be guilty of but which is carried out by a power not his doing him violence" ([*Note-Books and Papers*] 321). In this last passage, it is clear that the one concerned could instress himself with the bad thought, that is, could make it actual in himself, put himself in a state of stress towards it, or he can be instressed by a power other than his own. It is "active power" which instresses, not "passive power."

When used substantively, "instress" usually means that quality in a thing which brings about a state of stress or of act in the beholder: "Take a *few* primroses in a glass and the instress of—brilliancy, sort of starriness: I have not the right word—so simple a flower gives is remarkable" ([*Note-Books and Papers*] 142-143); ". . . light beating up from so many glassy heads, which like water is good to float their deeper instress in upon the mind" ([*Note-*

Books and Papers] 174); "(there is a simplicity of instress in the cinqfoil)" ([*Note-Books and Papers*] 209); "'The Woodpecker' reminds one of Cowper's poems in this metre and has the same sort of 'instress' of feeling but not quite the same satisfactory cadences" ([*The Letters of Gerard Manley Hopkins and Richard Watson Dixon*] Sept. 26, 1881). "Instress" in this substantive use might be called the "flavor" of a thing.

Hopkins further distinguishes the general term "stress" by means of the term "outstress," which refers to the act proceeding from the stress of the subject and terminating outside the subject: "The first intention then of God outside himself or, as they say, *ad extra,* outwards, the first outstress of God's power, was Christ . . ." ([*Note-books and Papers*] 344). "Outstress" is the act of the stress out from the self, as "instress" is the act of the stress, either one's own or the power of another's stress, towards the self.

Hopkins uses "distress" to signify a falling from stress, a de-emphasizing of the nature: "Michael and his angels instressed and distressed them with the thought of their unlikeness to the Most High . . ." ([*Note-books and Papers*] 351). The bad angels were instressed with the thought (that is, the thought was made actual to them) and were distressed, thrown off from stress, made even less what they should be. If their natures had not been in rebellion against truth, if they had said "yes" instead of "no," they would have been "stressed" as a result of that "instress," that is, their natures would have been emphasized, have been in more perfect act, have been more what they should be.

The line from the *Deutschland* states "His mystery must be instressed, stressed." God's mystery must be instressed, that is, made actual in us. After it has been made actual in us, it must be "stressed" by us, emphasized, made more what it already is. Note that as a result of the instress of God's mystery we are not, like the bad angels, "distressed," unless we say "no," refuse to accept and respond to that "instress." By saying "yes" we respond to the instressed mystery, we "stress" it, emphasize it, throw ourselves into act in regard to it. Hopkins refers to such action in the passage: ". . . this is truly God's finger touching the very vein of personality, which nothing else can reach and man can respond to by no play whatever, by bare acknowledgment only, the counter-stress which God alone can feel ('subito probas eum'), the aspiration in answer to his inspiration" ([*Note-books and Papers*] 337). Here "counter-stress" means our own stress or act as counter or opposed to God's stress or act. "Counter-stress" is distinguished not from "instress" or "outstress," but from the distinct stress of another. Taken in itself, without considering some outside stress, "counter-stress" means merely "stress." The "counter-stress" in this passage results from feeling the stress of God, from being "instressed" or touched by the finger of God. "Stress" refers to immanent activity, and our stress or counter-stress springs from our own being. Therefore, when God's power or stress acts upon us, that power must be responded to or "stressed" within us by our own "counter-stress", our own reaction, our aspiration answering His inspiration.

According to Hopkins' ordinary use of the terms "instress" and "stress," then, the line "His mystery must be instressed, stressed" means: "God's mystery must be made actual in us by his action, and must be responded to by our own." We can respond to His power "by bare acknowledgment only," by "blessing" and by "greeting" Him: "For I greet him the days I meet him, and bless when I understand." To say that God's "mystery must be instressed, stressed" is to say that although God is under the world's splendor and wonder, nevertheless the mystery of His being there must be made actual in me, and, having been made actual, must be responded to by my own response, my "greeting," my "kissing my hand" to Him, my saying "yes."

The sixth stanza states that the stress which we feel, the stroke dealt, does not spring from His bliss; it springs from nature, from time. This stress or stroke brings us to the recognition of Christ in nature. It is the absence of this recognition which terrifies the guilty when the stroke of God swings from the natural objects around us; it is the presence of this recognition of Christ which makes faithful hearts flush and melt. The stroke of lightning is the same for all, but the response to that stroke, the meaning of that stroke, differs with each man. The faithful may waver before the terror of God, as the poet described himself doing in the third stanza, ". . . where, where was a, where was a place." But those in whom Christ lives fully, those who have said "yes," are steady as a beacon of light: "But in all these things we overcome because of him who has loved us. For I am sure that neither death, nor life, nor angels, nor principalities, nor things present, nor things to come, nor powers, nor height, nor depth, nor any other creature will be able to separate us from the love of God, which is in Christ Jesus our Lord" (1 Cor., 1: 18).

The key to understanding that stress which we feel in stars and storms lies in the Incarnation of the Second Person of the Blessed Trinity, the God-Man Jesus Christ. From His life and passion swells that supernatural power of grace which carried the poet and the nun to selfsacrifice to God, and to salvation: "For grace is any action, activity, on God's part by which, in creating or after creating, he carries the creature to or towards the end of its being, which is its selfsacrifice to God and its salvation" ([*Note-books and Papers*] 332). We ordinarily are ignorant of this power acting within us, since it is the very life of our supernatural life (if we have it), the very current in which we move. We should always be ignorant of it unless we were driven hard at bay, knew our own strength as useless, and felt a greater power surging through us. That is the way the "heart, being hard at bay, is out with it." This is the point at which the man knows himself to be slipping away like sand in an hourglass, and feels the upsurge of divine power from underneath lifting him up "from the flame to the flame," towering "from the grace to the grace." In such an hour we lash out with our best or worst word; we "word" ourselves—we say what we are. We are mouthed to flesh-burst, and flooded with the taste of ourselves. In his *Commentary on the Spiritual Exercises,* Hopkins says, ". . . I consider myself-being, my consciousness and feeling of myself, that taste of myself, of *I* and *me* above and in all things, which is more distinctive than the taste of ale or alum, more distinctive than the smell of walnutleaf or camphor, and is incommunicable by any means to another man . . ." ([*Note-Books and Papers*] 309). In one of the later sonnets (No. 45) he develops the same thought:

> I am gall, I am heartburn. God's most deep decree
> Bitter would have me taste: my taste was me;
> Bones built in me, flesh filled, blood brimmed the
>   curse.
> Selfyeast of spirit a dull dough sours. I see
> The lost are like this, and their scourge to be
> As I am mine, their sweating selves; but worse.

Those in hell taste themselves forever, as they have chosen to do, and they are sour. They excluded the stress of God which would have instressed them, brought them to stress. They said "no" to Him, and their "no," when time is no more, is eternal.

The prayer which closes the first part of the poem is that God will master us all, exert His power in all, and in all of us be adored King. Our "yes" is all we can give, and it is the glory of man to give that "yes," the sublime opportunity of man to have a chance to say that "yes," to share the Sacrifice, the infinite "yes" of Christ. The poet was given that chance and "did say yes." The nun was given that chance, and "the call of the tall nun to the men in the tops and the tackle rode over the storm's brawling." It is clear, then, surely, how far this poem is from being one of sorrow, of penitence, of doubt, of suffering. I believe that Canon Dixon, admirable critic though he sometimes was, missed the essence of the poem, which lies far beyond the "elements of deep distress in it" which he mentions: "The Deutschland is enormously powerful: it has however such elements of deep distress in it that one reads it with less excited delight though not with less interest than the others" ([*The Letters of Gerard Manley Hopkins and Richard Watson Dixon*] 32-33, March 1, 1880). The **Deutschland,** as a matter of fact, concerns itself with elements of deep distress only as a prelude to the triumph which follows. It is not a poem of Good Friday; it is an Easter poem. It is the record of the triumphant cry of a Christian who won the good fight, who received the crown of glory, who after glorious combat is dissolved and lives with Christ.

David Sonstroem   (essay date 1967)

SOURCE: "Making Earnest of Game: G. M. Hopkins and Nonsense Poetry," in *Modern Language Quarterly,* Vol. XXVIII, No. 2, June, 1967, pp. 192-206.

[*In the following essay, Sonstroem draws an analogy between Hopkins and the nonsense poets of the late nineteenth-century.*]

In the poetry of Gerard Manley Hopkins, there is often a play with words and their sounds that comes very close to nonsense, a verbal play comparable to that of Lewis Carroll, Edward Lear, or Sir W. S. Gilbert. Hopkins loses nothing in the comparison with his fellow Victorians: play is seldom if ever trivial or meaningless, and it is entirely compatible with seriousness and reverence. Furthermore, the nonsense game that he plays is more ingenious, more difficult, and broader in scope than that of his contemporaries. The analogy between Hopkins and the nonsense poets is both interesting in itself and especially helpful in revealing Hopkins' method of composition and his motives for writing poetry. In pursuing the analogy, I shall let Edward Lear, the poet of the purest nonsense, serve as a foil to Hopkins, although any other nonsense poet would have served almost as well.

In professed intent, Hopkins and Lear are poles apart: one poet declares, "want of earnest I take to be the deepest fault a work of art can have" [*Further Letters*], and the other holds, "'Nonsense,' pure and absolute, [has] been my aim throughout" [*Introduction to More Nonsense Pictures, Rhymes, Botany Etc., 1872*]. But their poetic practices disclose their kinship. Hopkins' severity is tempered by occasional frolic—for example, in the octave of **"Spring"** (No. 33)—and a melancholy underlies Lear's superficial playfulness. Furthermore, there is something childlike in the verse of both. In Hopkins, the childlike resides in the poetic speaker, who responds with bright eyes and naïveté, suddenly and violently. Note the sixteen exclamation points in **"The Starlight Night"** (No. 32) and the frequent shouts that punctuate the poetry: "O," "Oh," "Gush!" "Ah!" "Five!" "there then!" "Ah!" "oh!" But the greatest similarity between the two is simply in the texture and flow of their lines:

> When the thing we freely fórfeit is kept with fonder
>   a care,
> Fonder a care kept than we could have kept it, kept
> Far with fonder a care (and we, we should have lost
>   it) finer, fonder
> A care kept.—Where kept? Do but tell us where
>   kept, where.—
>
> (No. 59)

> Lettuce! O Lettuce!
> Let us, O let us,
> O Lettuce leaves,
> O let us leave this tree and eat
> Lettuce, O let us, Lettuce leaves!
> [*The Complete Nonsense of Edward Lear*]

The basic likeness between **"The Golden Echo"** and "The History of the Seven Families of the Lake Pipple-Popple" is due to the fact that their authors are playing very similar games with their language.

Both fuse two words into one to form what Lewis Carroll called "portmanteau" words. Hopkins is more apt to juxtapose than fuse ("flockbells," "Amansstrength," "churlsgrace," "trambeams," "bloomfall"), but he does create "yestertempests" and "disseveral"; in Lear we find "grammarithmetic," "galloobious," and "howloudia." Also frequent in both are disparate words unexpectedly connected by means of alliteration or some other similarity in sound:

Hopkins writes "carrion comfort," "bow or brooch or braid or brace," "piecemeal peace is poor peace. What pure peace . . ."; Lear gives us "diaphanous doorscraper" and "comfortable, confidential cow." Both practice the forced rhyme:

> born, he tells me, of Irish
> Mother to an English sire (he
> Shares . . .)

> This very very day came down to us after a boon
> he on
> My late being there . . .
> Came, I say, this day to it—to a First Communion.
>   (No. 47)

> There was an old Lady of Winchelsea,
> Who said, "if you needle or pin shall see /. . . .

> There was an Old Man of Columbia,
> Who was thirsty, and called out for some beer.

Both are apt to split a word at the end of a line for an unusual rhyme. Hopkins writes:

> I caught this morning morning's minion, king-
> dom . . .
>   how he rung upon the rein of a wimpling
> wing. . . .
>   (No. 36)

> Some sleep unawakened, all un-
> warned, eleven fathoms fallen. . . .
>   (No. 41)

In Lear we find:

> Though you're such a Hoddy Doddy—
> Yet I wish that I could modi-
> fy the words I needs must say!

> How can I translate German Metaphys-
> Ics, if mosquitoes round my forehead whizz?

In both there is often a feeling for the rhyme at all costs, a release from convention, an allegiance to rhyme before sense.

Hopkins and Lear have a fondness for lists, lists of adjectives especially: "Cuckoo-echoing, bell-swarmèd, lark-charmèd, rook-racked, river-rounded" (No. 44); "Earnest, earthless, equal, attuneable, vaulty, voluminous, . . stupendous" (No. 62). Lear writes, "and then returned to their respective homes full of joy and respect, sympathy, satisfaction, and disgust" and "took an affecting and formal leave of the whole of their acquaintance, which was very numerous and distinguished, and select, and responsible, and ridiculous" The lists of both poets are especially remarkable for their unpredictability; each word of a series strikes us as a surprise.

Progressing from words in static arrangement to words in motion, we recognize additional similarities. One is a strong, regular, rhythmic beat. [*The Complete Nonsense of Edward Lear*]. Hopkins himself notes the relationship between his Sprung Rhythm and more childlike, less serious antecedents: "It is found in nursery rhymes, weather saws, and so on."

A final likeness is the quirky movement of their thought. Both poets forever leave us puzzling over how we got from there to here. Illustration is from Lear first for a change:

> G was Papa's new Gun,
> He put it in a box;
> And then he went and bought a bun
> And walked about the Docks.

This admirable stanza has been called "the perfect `non sequitur,'" [by Angus Davidson, in *Edward Lear: Landscape Painter and Nonsense Poet (1812-1888)*, 1938] and indeed one must maneuver sharply to keep on Lear's track. The properties of the words themselves (the principal ones, at least) are the key to the ordering relationship. What holds "Gun," "box," "bun," and "Docks" together is simply the pattern of sound that they form. There are two pairs of rhymes, the pairs themselves joined by the alliteration of "box" and "bun." When Lear writes unrhymed prose, alliteration and other chiming takes up the slack:

> all the Blue-Bottle-Flies began to buzz at once in a sumptuous and sonorous manner, the melodious and mucilaginous sounds echoing all over the waters, and resounding across the tumultuous tops of the transitory Titmice upon the intervening and verdant mountains, with a serene and sickly suavity only known to the truly virtuous.

Like Lear, Hopkins makes quirky progress through chiming chains. The complexity of his sound patterns and the extent to which he is preoccupied with them are extraordinary:

> We lash with the best or worst
> Word last! How a lush-kept plush-capped sloe
> Will, mouthed to flesh-burst,
> Gush!—flush the man, the being with it, sour or
> sweet. . . .
> (No. 28, st. 8)

With the aid of W. H. Gardner's complex (although incomplete) diagram [in *Gerard Manley Hopkins*, 1949], I estimate twenty-eight different "echoes" in these four lines. Unlike Lear, who gives the impression of falling into his resonances without effort and quite by accident, Hopkins is plainly struggling from word to word. Instead of setting forth directly in pursuit of his meaning, he makes his way incrementally, tortuously, along archipelagoes of sound. One critic has called his method "a sort of breathless hunt after assonant monosyllables [in *Studies* VIII (1919)]:

> How to kéep—is there ány any, is there none such, nowhere
>   known some, bow or brooch or braid or brace,

láce, latch or catch or key to keep
Back beauty, keep it, beauty, beauty, beauty,. . . .
from vanishing away?
(No. 59)

Surely the Jesuit Hopkins knew from the start the Christian answer to the question he was posing. That the question is not at all so significant as the questioning can be appreciated when Hopkins' lines are compared with an "improvement" upon them by T. Sturge Moore:

How to keep beauty? is there any way?
Is there nowhere any means to have it stay?
Will no bow or brooch or braid,
Brace or lace
Latch or catch
Or key to lock the door lend aid
Before beauty vanishes away?

Moore has attempted to discard Hopkins' "most ludicrous redundancies," but, as F. R. Leavis remarks [in *New Bearings in English Poetry,* 1950], "He has discarded, not merely a certain amount of music, but with the emotional crescendo and diminuendo, the plangent rise and fall, all the action and substance of the verse." By omitting the fumbling repetitions and the laborious stresses, he has lost the striving—the strenuous exertions of Hopkins' intense verbal play—which is the heart of the poem's dramatic effect.

Punning is another manifestation of quirky movement, and both poets practice it to a limited extent. Here is an example from Lear:

There was an Old Man in a tree
Who was horribly bored by a Bee.

Bees sting, although "bore" is a better nonsense word because it alliterates with "Bee." But "bored" can also mean "bored to tears," and this is its eventual primary meaning in the rhyme. Lear has, so to speak, boarded the word at one meaning, disembarked at another. To an even greater extent than Lear, Hopkins progresses by double meanings, entering a word through one, departing through another:

O look at all the fire-folk sitting in the air!
The bright boroughs, the circle-citadels there!
Down in dim woods the diamond delves!
(No. 32)

The constellations are seen as communities of fire-folk—"boroughs." If I am not mistaken, the movement from this image to that associated with the word "delves" is through "burrow," a homophone of the first word, a synonym of the second. A final example is the following:

Thy unchancelling poising palms were
weighing the worth,
Thou martyr-master: in thy sight
Storm flakes were scroll-leaved flowers, lily
showers—sweet heaven was astrew in them.

Five! the finding and sake
And cipher of suffering Christ.
(No. 28, sts. 21 and 22)

The apparently abrupt shift between stanzas and the interplay between Easter and Good Friday seem to hinge on the double meaning of "palms"—Christ's pierced hands and the fronds associated with Christ's triumph.

The list of likenesses completed, it must be remembered that, although Hopkins uses the devices of the nonsense poet, he is not a nonsense poet himself. No list of shared characteristics will persuade even the most casual reader of the two men that they are essentially kindred. Hopkins' agonizing moods, his lofty intentions, and his earnest personality are very different from Lear's. But the likenesses we have encountered are not specious ones. They have their explanation—one that accounts for the basic differences between the two men, as well as their extensive superficial similarities.

Let me begin the explanation with some observations on the nature of nonsense. Of course, nonsense is not what it says it is, senseless. Quite to the contrary. It might better be called double-sense or double-talk. One kind of sense is what we usually mean by the term: an arrangement of words that is governed by grammar, reason, and observation of the world at large. The second kind of sense is concerned exclusively with the properties of words themselves. It is simply an arrangement of words that is governed by the repetition (and, in the case of punning, coincidence) of their sounds.

> **Hopkins loses nothing in the comparison with his fellow Victorians: play is seldom if ever trivial or meaningless, and it is entirely compatible with seriousness and reverence. Furthermore, the nonsense game that he plays is more ingenious, more difficult, and broader in scope than that of his contemporaries.**
>
> **—David Sonstroem**

Nonsense, like all poetry, has something to do with both kinds of arranging, of making sense; but, unlike conventional verse, its first allegiance is to rhyme rather than reason. Or, rather, rhyme *is* its primary reason. The writer of nonsense—I describe an ideal procedure—first gives sound its head, arranging words into patterns according to the rules of prosody. Except for these strictures and the most rudimentary ones of grammar, the words, subject to chance, pour forth at random. (The "automatic writing" of Surrealism and the computer-poetry of the present moment come to mind as analogous.) Then the writer follows in his own tracks, tracing out whatever rational meaning is to be found there, observing what he has uttered with respect to the referents of the words that he has arranged.

The writer himself may well be as surprised and pleased as other readers at the "sense" thus derived, for its production has been largely accidental and spontaneous. In the introduction to *More Nonsense Pictures, Rhymes, Botany Etc.*, Lear speaks of his "uproarious delight and welcome at the appearance of every new absurdity"—as if his verses had appeared from without and he had had nothing to do with creating them.

The strength of nonsense poetry is its tidy self-consistency and its independence from referents. Its position relative to conventional poetry is much like that of mathematics to physics: although it can refer to the world at large, it can also mind its own business and do whatever it pleases, provided that it is true to itself. All poets customarily take advantage of the sounds of words to clinch an observation: "presume not God to scan; / The proper study of mankind is man" [A. Pope, *Essay on Man*]. The rhyme, the repetition of "man," and the forthright rhythm all give resonance to the sentiment. But the sound must always be only an echo to the sense, never its master; otherwise, the result is nonsense poetry:

> To act as if the yokes of rhyme were true
> Would mean that I fly by and you coo too—
> Contingencies our Sober Selves reject
> As poets' nonsense. What's Correct's Correct.
> But that is what verse tells us isn't so
> (And tells our Sober Selves where they can go). . . .
>   [Walker Gibson, in *The Reckless Spenders,* 1954]

I would modify Gibson's merry observation slightly: it is only nonsense verse that tells off our Sober Selves; the chimes of conventional verse must ever hide behind What's Correct and obediently wait upon it. Only nonsense lives upon the difference between the rule of rhyme and the rule of reason.

By letting the sound of words lord it over their meaning, the nonsense poet is playing a game with his referents. Twisting them and pushing them around is a way of mastering them, perhaps of getting even with them. The "opponents" that Lear has recruited are not hard to discern; the greatest number of his limericks treat of sickness, injury, death, ugliness of character, inadequacy, or distortion:

> There was an old man who screamed out
> Whenever they knocked him about. . . .

> There was an old person of Stroud,
> Who was horribly jammed in a crowd;
> Some she slew with a kick, some she scrunched
>   with a stick,
> That impulsive old person of Stroud.

> There was a Young Lady whose chin,
> Resembled the point of a pin. . . .

> There was a Young Person of Smyrna,
> Whose Grandmother threatened to burn her;
> But she seized on the Cat, and said, "Granny, burn

> that!
> You incongruous Old Woman of Smyrna!"

After his fashion, Lear is defeating these evils by demonstrating his power over them within the terms of his game. Deep feelings are muffled in foolery: the attitude of nonchalance with which the Young Person of Smyrna confronts her Granny is the typical one of these limericks. By busying himself with verbal tricks, rhyming "Smyrna" with "burn her," Lear is able to sail triumphantly through the rhyme and past the horrors—literally putting them in their place in the process.

Whereas the conventional poet's practice is first to make sense and yet have it come out rhyme, and the nonsense poet's practice is first to make rhyme and have it come out to the embarrassment of sense, Hopkins' practice is first to make rhyme and yet have it come out sense: "Poetry is . . . speech framed to be heard for its own sake and interest even over and above its interest of meaning" [in *Journals and Papers of Gerard Manley Hopkins,* edited by Humphry House and Graham Storey, 1959]. Like the conventional poet, Hopkins does not have to commit his allegiance either to rhyme or reason to the exclusion of the other, because he expects them to work in tandem. But, like the nonsense poet, he begins with the sounds of words and lets the sense come tumbling after. Using the practices of the nonsense poet, he yet expects his verse to fulfill the requirements of reason. Little wonder that his progress is more painful and tortuous than that of Lear, for he is playing a more demanding game.

His game has much in common with the old word-game whose object is to progress from one word to another of the same length through a series of words formed by changing only one letter of the previous word. For example, one might move from "black" to "white" by means of the series, -slack-shack-shark-share-shale-whale-while-. Hopkins "wins" his game by letting the accidents of his words carry him from black to white, from a pessimistic presentation of a problem to a reassuring answer:

> This Jack, joke, poor potsherd, patch matchwood,
>   immortal diamond,
>   Is immortal diamond.
>
>   (No. 72)

The rungs of sound are clear enough (an effect that might be overlooked is the running on of the chiming from the end of a line into the beginning of the next), except that there seems to be a break between "joke" and "poor potsherd." The break is only apparent, however: W. A. M. Peters, S.J. [in *Gerard Manley Hopkins: A Critical Essay towards the Understanding of his Poetry,* 1948] has remarked that Hopkins, here casting about for words to describe abject, miserable man, must have skipped from "joke" to "Job," and thence to the very potsherd with which the sufferer scraped his sores. If "potsherd" is permitted as a substitution for "Job," the ladder is an unbroken one.

Frequently the cheerful turn from black to white is abrupt, marked by a play on words:

> So be beginning, be beginning to despair.
> O there's none; no no no there's none:
> Be beginning to despair, to despair,
> Despair, despair, despair, despair.
>
>   Spare!
> There ís one, yes I have one. . . .
>
>   (No. 59)

The right word springs from the ashes of the old. A similar phonetic drama takes place in **"The Lantern out of Doors"** (No. 34):

> I cannot, and out of sight is out of mind.
>
> Christ minds. . . .

And again, in *The Wreck of the Deutschland* (No. 28), the insight that the poet has been searching for comes to him in the form of a pun. After trying to determine the significance of the drowning nun's cry, "O Christ, Christ, come quickly," he suddenly realizes that she was re-enacting verbally what Mary had performed physically—was uttering, giving birth to, Christ: she was

> Wording it how but by him that present and past,
> Heaven and earth are word of, worded by?
>
>   (st. 29)

The conventional Christian play on "Word" is what holds the analogy together. Addressing Christ, the poet remarks,

> For so conceivèd, so to conceive thee is done;
>   But here was heart-throe, birth of a brain,
> Word, that heard and kept thee and uttered thee
>   outright.
>
>   (st. 30)

We see that verbal play lies at the heart of Hopkins' method, serving as the means that permit him to move from quandary to Christian assurance.

His practice is not so silly, so unworthy of his argument, as it might seem, for the apparently accidental, fortuitous play that characterizes his poetic method is truly significant. To him nothing is haphazard, not even the most trivial of objects and events that we customarily relegate to chance: "All the world is full of inscape and *chance left free to act falls into an order as well as purpose:* looking out of my window I caught it in the random clods and broken heaps of snow made by the cast of a broom" (*Journals,* [Sonstroem's] italics). Every reader of Hopkins knows of the poet's continual quest for inscape—his term for the pattern of characteristics that reflects the inner nature of each object and event: "design, pattern or what I am in the habit of calling `inscape' is what I above all aim at in poetry" [*Letters of Gerard Manley Hopkins to Robert Bridges,* 1955]. And words proper, as well as events and other objects, have their inscapes: "Poetry is in fact speech only employed to carry the inscape of speech for the inscape's sake—and therefore the inscape must be dwelt on" (*Journals*). Besides their meanings, the inscape of words consists of their sounds, the likeness of their sounds to those of other words, coincidental relationships—in short, just those "casual" aspects with which we are concerned in this essay. Much of Hopkins' appreciation of inscapes is simple and spontaneous—his genuine joy at the fresh discovery of a pattern in a landscape, a cloud formation, or a group of words is direct and obvious—but the relationship between inscape and chance that he makes in the passage above shows his awareness that something more intricate is taking place.

Inscape is precious primarily for revealing the hand of God that fashions it: "All things therefore are charged with love, are charged with God and if we know how to touch them give off sparks and take fire, yield drops and flow, ring and tell of him" [*Sermons and Devotional Writings of Gerard Manley Hopkins,* edited by Christopher Devlin, 1959]:

> I walk, I lift up, I lift up heart, eyes,
>   Down all that glory in the heavens to glean our
>   Saviour;
>   And, éyes, heárt, what looks, what lips yet gave
>   you a
> Rapturous love's greeting of realer, of rounder
>   replies?
>
>   (No. 38)

Of course the sentiments are exactly those that we should expect of a good Jesuit, but our expectations may prevent us from appreciating an aspect of Hopkins that is very important. Let us not mistake his discoveries of God as rote expressions of automatic piety. He is out for signs and wonders. He is looking for "replies," and it is they that provoke his raptures. His search for inscape is a search for fresh tokens of God's continuing influence on the things of the world.

Desire for a reassuring sign from heaven is a strain that runs throughout his poems:

> My prayers must meet a brazen heaven
> And fail or scatter all away.
>
>   (No. 15)

> God, though to Thee our psalm we raise
> No answering voice comes from the skies;
> To Thee the trembling sinner prays
> But no forgiving voice replies;
> Our prayer seems lost in desert ways,
> Our hymn in the vast silence dies.
>
>   . . . . .
>
> Speak! whisper to my watching heart
> One word—as when a mother speaks
> Soft, when she sees her infant start,
> Till dimpled joy steals o'er its cheeks.
> Then, to behold Thee as Thou art,

I'll wait till morn eternal breaks.

(No. 22)

And my lament
Is cries countless, cries like dead letters sent
To dearest him that lives alas! away.

(No. 69)

On several occasions, too, he believed that he had received such a sign: "Also in some med. today I earnestly asked our Lord to watch over my compositions. . . . And this I believe is heard" (*Sermons*); "I received as I think a great mercy about Dolben" (*Journals*); "Do not make light of this, for it is perhaps the seventh time that I think I have had some token from heaven in connection with the death of people in whom I am interested" (Letter of 9 October 1877 to his mother, quoted in *Sermons*); "'I hear a voice you cannot hear' etc. We who are converts have all heard that voice which others cannot or say they cannot hear, have seen that beckoning finger which others etc" (*Sermons*); and finally:

When a man has given himself to God's service . . . he has fitted himself to receive and does receive from God a special guidance, a more particular providence. This guidance is conveyed partly . . . by direct lights and inspirations. If I wait for such guidance, through whatever channel conveyed, about anything, about my poetry for instance, I do more wisely in every way. . . . [*Correspondence of Gerard Manley Hopkins and Richard Watson Dixon*, edited by Claude Colleer Abbott, 1955]

I believe that it is not going too far to suggest that Hopkins is courting just such "mercies" as these in the very writing of his poems.

He deals out his words according to their sound, and then he expects them to turn up in a meaningful pattern that will serve as evidence of an unseen intelligence that is regulating them. He is, so to speak, giving God a free hand, so that He can declare Himself. Chance is not really chance, because it is superintended by God. Thus there is nothing fortuitous about the fact that "heaven" sounds much like "haven," "despair" embodies "spare," and "Jack" leads to "diamond"; God means them so.

The poet's and my card-talk is not out of place; the rationale surrounding his earnest word-play is the same as that behind the fortuneteller's Tarot Pack and, originally, behind many games:

behind many games lies magic of just this sort, divination—that expressive word. . . . So any game is at one and the same time an exercise of skill and manipulative ability, a way of finding out how God deals with the universe, and a dangerous make-believe with holy things [Elizabeth Sewell, *The Field of Nonsense*, 1952].

Like Lear, Hopkins is playing a game with words, but his is a somewhat different and more difficult one, with more profound implications. He has more at stake, for his prize, if he wins, is the recognition of the Power that makes the victory possible.

As a poetic method, Hopkins' game is unique but not so outrageous as it may seem. A poet's calling upon the gods for aid has its precedents, of course, and Hopkins' efforts may be seen as the wooing of a very special, Christian form of poetic inspiration. It is in these terms, rather than those of a game, that he sees his own practice:

He hath put a new song in my mouth.

(No. 7)

The fine delight that fathers thought; the strong
Spur, live and lancing like the blowpipe flame,
Breathes once and, quenchèd faster than it came,
Leaves yet the mind a mother of immortal song. . . .
  Sweet fire the sire of muse, my soul needs this;
I want the one rapture of an inspiration.

(No. 75)

For him there is no distinction to be made between poetic and religious inspiration. It is for his soul's sake that he pleads, and he calls to be his muse the Holy Ghost, who came upon the Disciples in the form of a tongue of flame and gave them the gift of tongues. Hopkins felt the "first and highest" kind of verse to be "the language of inspiration" (*Further Letters*), and he employed the term "Parnassian" (*Journals*) to indicate that verse written by a competent poet entirely on his own, of a high level but uninspired. Many of Hopkins' own poems would seem to be of this lower order of composition—**"To R. B.,"** for example, and the Terrible Sonnets (although his remark that some of the Terrible Sonnets came "unbidden and against my will" may indicate an entirely different and more sinister species of inspiration). They are marked by a *desire* for a visitation—"send my roots rain" (No. 74)—and a sharp reduction in sound effects, as we might expect. It is ironic that most of us prefer the later "Parnassian" poems to the "inspired" ones. Perhaps we find the "inspired" ones, with their movement from rhyme to reason, too perverse or obviously contrived to succeed in a grand way. But Hopkins was writing them for Christ, "the only just literary critic" (*Correspondence of Hopkins and Dixon*), rather than for us; and even we, appreciating the inner logic of the verse, can hardly refuse to admire.

Amy Lowenstein (essay date 1976)

SOURCE: "Seeing Pied Beauty: A Key to Theme and Structure," in *Victorian Poetry*, Vol. 14, No. 1, Spring, 1976, pp. 64-6.

[*In the following essay, Lowenstein asserts that the features that give "Pied Beauty" its distinctive quality are characteristic of Impressionist art.*]

As Francis Fike suggests [in *VP*, 1970], there is room for further exploration of Hopkins' relation to the art of painting. Hopkins' belief that poetry and painting are closely allied, that "inscape" or patterning is, to use Fike's word, "crucial" to both, sanctions such endeavors; but aside from Hopkins' complaint to Bridges about Millais' lack of "feeling for beauty in abstract design," there is little in the comments about painting that illuminates the distinctive quality of a poem like "**Pied Beauty.**"

Unlike the popular paintings of its day, the visual art in "**Pied Beauty**" is neither anecdotal nor literary. In itself, it is free of ideas or sentiment, and is constructed from optical data alone. The element of contrast, lights and darks particularly, is abstracted and presented instead of a whole object. A two-dimensional quality stresses surfaces rather than plastic form. The pictures are presented in rapid succession so that their transitory nature is intensified; the eye jumps from one to the next, taking in the alternating brushstrokes within each panel as well as the alternating images as they flash by.

These characteristics belong to Impressionist art which, at about mid-century, had begun to isolate the optical from the conceptual elements of experience. The first collective exhibition was one hundred years ago (1874), and, as I write, the centenary is being celebrated in Paris with an exhibition of the kind of academic painting shown that year in stern opposition to the new movement. Now that Impressionism is part of the Establishment, "we are unable even to imagine," says Arnold Hauser [in the *Social History of Art,* translated by Stanley Godman, 1951], "how helplessly the public confronted this medley of spots and blots"; he comments further, "the feeling of being jeered at may never have been so strong."

A similar feeling is unmistakable in Hopkins' well-known comment to Bridges that an artist who is true to his "inscape" or his own distinctive patterning risks becoming queer. In England Turner had been a target of public derision before Ruskin's spirited defense turned the tide. Twenty years later Monet, whose debt to Turner is established, exhibited his painting of a sunrise, "Impressions," a title which was applied derisively to a movement. And in 1877, the year Hopkins composed "**Pied Beauty,**" the jeering went on, this time against Whistler whose "Nocturne in Black and Gold: The Falling Rocket" owed much to the Impressionist imagination. Ruskin's accusation that Whistler was "flinging a pot of paint in the public's face" carried such weight that the famous *Whistler v. Ruskin* libel suit resulted.

Certainly the tenets of Impressionism and the resistance to them were "in the air" as Hopkins "painted" "**Pied Beauty,**" and there is no doubt that he was aware that he, too, was presenting images in a new way and that the new way was not a popular depiction of beauty. We are educated by the Impressionists and their heirs, the Neo- and Post-Impressionists, and can respond as Hopkins' contemporaries could not to "dappled things," purposely imprecise, immediately suggesting a fleeting world of sunlight and shadow. The "skies of couple-colour," huge alternating brushstrokes, themselves alternate strangely and unexpectedly with an image of a streaked, spotted cow. The point-

illist description of the trout, like the work of Seurat, emphasizes color contrast within form; yet it is not static—the trout "swim," the "finches' wings" flash by (their bandings of light and dark a possible association with the term for a streaked cow, "finch-backed"), the sparks shower down from the roasting chestnuts (Whistler's "Falling Rocket" in little?). The patched landscape with its diverse forms in field and fold, tool and plow, is not unfamiliar to sensibilities developed by Monet, Van Gogh, and Cezanne. And beyond the shifting, transitory quality of the designs themselves, their presentation in rapid succession, linked by the eye alone, breaks the world of experience into moments of delight in contrasts and forms abstracted from natural phenomena.

Nevertheless, these images, which are in themselves free from any emotion except the joy of translating sense experience into art, have a rhetorical as well as a deeply religious frame. The "argument" of the poem moves from the first line where the poet alone praises God for the beauty of "dappled things," to the last line in which the "viewer" is asked to join in such praise. Between these lines a series of images is presented which revolutionizes perception. In the penultimate line, "He fathers-forth whose beauty is past change," Hopkins sees God as the consummate harmonizer, the ideal artist in perfect control over his darting, speckled, freckled, spotted, striped, contrasting phenomena in all their transitory beauty. The greatest Impressionist, whose light dapples the world's landscape, is, paradoxically, beyond the impermanence, beyond time and change, perpetually avant-garde. Hopkins' visual images, abstracted from life, are returned to the source of life, but not before those who now have eyes to see, shocked out of their Victorian ideas of prettiness, have redefined beauty, and are therefore able, along with the artist, to "Praise him."

Jerome Bump   (essay date 1982)

SOURCE: "A New Style," in *Gerard Manley Hopkins,* Twayne, 1982, pp. 64-92.

[*Bump is an American critic with a special interest in Hopkins's work. In the following excerpt, he offers a stylistic analysis of his poetry, focusing on the recurrence or "parallelism" of certain sounds in Hopkins's work.*]

Hopkins's new style was developed in response to his question, "If the best prose and the best poetry use the same language . . . why not use unfettered prose?" [*Journals of Gerard Manley Hopkins*]. He answered, "It is plain that metre, rhythm, rhyme, and all the structure which is called verse both necessitate and engender a difference in diction and in thought." The first difference is "concentration and all which is implied by this. This does not mean terseness nor rejection of what is collateral nor emphasis nor even definiteness." Indeed, though Hopkins achieved a conciseness and concentration unusual among Victorian poets, he did so not by rejecting but by inviting collateral meanings of words, that is, not by an exclusiveness but by an inclusiveness of meaning. For him a word was not limited to one of its meanings: "every word may be considered as the contraction or coinciding-point of its definitions." Thus, if the first principle of his new poetics is concentration, the second is multiple levels of meaning or, to borrow a term from science, multivalence.

Poetry differs from prose by a greater concentration not only of meaning, moreover, but also of word-music and imagery, according to Hopkins. Inspired by the pervasiveness of parallelism throughout the Bible, Hopkins reduced these third and fourth features of his poetry to his principle of parallelism or recurrence in the sounds and thought in a poem:

> The artificial part of poetry, perhaps we shall be right to say all artifice, reduces itself to the principle of parallelism . . . in rhythm, the recurrence of a certain sequence of syllables, in meter, the recurrence of a certain sequence or rhythm, in alliteration, in assonance and in rhyme. Now the force of this recurrence is to beget a recurrence or parallelism answering to it in the words or thought and, speaking roughly and rather for the tendency than the invariable result, the more marked parallelism in structure whether of elaboration or of emphasis begets more marked parallelism in the words and sense. And moreover parallelism in expression tends to beget or passes into parallelism in thought . . . metaphor, simile, parable, and so on, where the effect is sought in likeness of things, and antithesis, contrast, and so on, where it is sought in unlikeness.

Such a definition of poetry supplies the broad parameters within which Hopkins developed the style that made him a great English poet, a style developed primarily between 1868 and 1875, seven years during which, paradoxically, he composed very few poems. The birth of the new style is apparent, however, in revisions of his earlier Pre-Raphaelite poems, especially **"For a Picture of St. Dorothea,"** and in the only new poems of this period, **"Ad Mariam"** and **"Rosa Mystica."** These initial attempts to discover his "authentic cadence" illustrate the practical effects of his definition of poetry and, relatively simple in their own right, they show us how to approach the more difficult poems which followed.

Hopkins's revisions of **"For a Picture of St. Dorothea,"** for example, demonstrate concisely how his definition of poetry as parallelism in sound led to his conception of poetry as speech, music, dramatic performance, and sacrament. **"Rosa Mystica,"** on the other hand, illustrates clearly the answering parallelism in the thought in a poem, especially that special kind of recurrence described by such terms as "type," "antitype," and "archetype" which imply a multiplicity of "vertical" parallels and movements between God and the world as well as a sense of mystery and, at times, even obscurity of meaning. **"Rosa Mystica"** also epitomizes Hopkins's conception of poetry as discourse on a higher level of generality than prose and illustrates how Hopkins's conventional imagery restricts his originality primarily to his parallelism in sound, that is, his word-music.

. . . . .

Confronted with the example of Christina Rossetti's songs of heaven, Hopkins began to consider which of the senses is most important in our response to words: seeing or hearing. Ever since the invention of the alphabet, the initial visualization of language in the Western world, there has been a propensity to regard literature as essentially a visual art. "Oral Literature" is in fact a contradiction in terms, for "literature" means "letters." Hopkins eventually became aware, however, of the danger of this overemphasis on the role of the eye in communication and began to modify the visual models of language he had inherited from Keats, Ruskin, and the Pre-Raphaelites in order to place more emphasis on the role of the ear.

Ironically it was his revision of **"For a Picture of St. Dorothea"** that generated much of his distinctive auditory poetics, including his first use of sprung rhythm, his first dramatic monologue, and his special use of word-music to "beget" metaphor. Though the title, **"For a Picture of St. Dorothea,"** proclaims the poem's genre as the verbal initation of the visual arts, Hopkins's revisions invoke the conventions of rival genres appealing to the ear more than the eye, that is, appealing more to the Victorians' fondness for reading aloud than to their love of word-painting, thus emphasizing the poem as speech, drama, and music.

Hopkins's aim was to revitalize the medieval legend of St. Dorothea. Just before her martyrdom, a lawyer named Theophilus jeeringly asked Dorothea to send him some fruits and flowers from the heavenly garden she believed awaited her. He converted when an angel delivered them. This legend became a favorite of the Pre-Raphaelites: Dante and Christina Rossetti, William Morris, Edward Burne-Jones, and A. C. Swinburne had all represented St. Dorothea in their art before Hopkins took her up in 1864. When a subject such as this was represented in a Pre-Raphaelite painting, moreover, they frequently accompanied it with a poem for the painting in Dante Rossetti's manner, often inscribed in the frame of the painting itself.

Hopkins's title reminds us that he originally wanted to be a painter and a poet after the fashion of Dante Rossetti and the Pre-Raphaelites. They obviously inspired both his subject and his choice of the genre of poems-for-pictures. Hopkins differed from them by substituting lilies, larkspurs, and a quince for the roses and apples in the legend, and by developing the exchange between Theophilus and Dorothea and/or her angel. His special emphasis on the role of speech and music, however, two auditory effects as likely to compete with visual sensations as to complement them, most clearly distinguished him from the Pre-Raphaelites.

Hopkins soon perceived that the ancient definition of poetry as a speaking picture is intrinsically dialectical, a contradition in terms. His decision to stress speech made his poem-for-a-picture not merely independent of an imaginable picture but distinctively different from any picture. As he put it, "the sensations of the eye are given in space, those of the ear in time." Speech, being invisible, with no existence in space, tended to force the imaginary picture of his title back into that world of time from which the spatial arts seem to escape.

Hopkins thus discovered how language has its own intrinsic generic propensities, especially a tendency to generate drama. In his first revision Hopkins's subtitle stressed the presence of two different speakers in the poem, and in his second he actually broke the poem up into five separate speeches. This incipient attraction to drama is more obvious in his plays—*Floris in Italy, Castara Victrix,* and *St. Winefred's Well*—but they, along with his more dramatic versions of **"For a Picture of St. Dorothea,"** remain unfinished. His theatrical tendencies, like those of many Victorian poets, blossomed instead in his lyrics, in the interpolated "oh's," "ah's," and exclamation marks which, like the outbursts of the narrator in Dickens's novels or the histrionic gestures of Victorian melodrama, emphasize climactic moments. In **"The Windhover"** and **"The Starlight Night"** (1877), for instance, his interjections dramatize his excited discoveries of unusually felicitous sacramental symbols.

This love of drama led to the invention of "sprung rhythm" and the sacrifice of many of the painterly effects in **"For a Picture of St. Dorothea"** (I). Seeking the more dramatic conciseness and directness of the sense-stress rhythms of Renaissance verse drama, Hopkins replaced regular rhythms in the poems such as "I am so light, I am so fair" and "And at the basket that I bear," with the more concise "sprung" rhythms, "I am so light and fair" and "With the basket I bear" (II). A comparison of the original lines with their revisions reveals the most striking feature of sprung rhythm: the freedom to vary the number of unaccented syllables, allowing more conciseness, and a more dramatic stress on the accented syllables. It is a rhythm, as Hopkins said of his use of it in **"Harry Ploughman,"** "which is altogether for recital, not for perusal (as by nature verse should be)" [*The Letters of Gerard Manley Hopkins to Robert Bridges*].

This realization of the dramatic potential of language encouraged the idea that poetry should not be merely word-painting, but also, as Wordsworth put it, "man speaking to men." This archaic sense of literature as "speaking," and thus reading as "reading aloud," the common usage in ancient and medieval cultures, was revived in the nineteenth century, apparently as a response to the accelerating mechanization of printing. Even novels were read aloud to families and large audiences. Philip Collins reminds us that a hundred years ago "much current literature was apprehended in this way—was indeed written with such a reception in mind," and thus "many people met contemporary literature as a group or communal, rather than an individual experience."

Hopkins in particular must have been conscious of the many parallels between the communal experiences of literature and religious ritual. At the time he was revising his Dorothea poem he was agonizing about his religious vocation and no doubt was aware that some of the most

popular Victorian public readers were clergymen—indeed, two of the most successful were Anglican priests who had gone over to Rome. Moving in the same direction himself, Hopkins was in fact experiencing two simultaneous and related conversions; he felt the necessity of restoring not only the medieval religion but also some of the oral traditions with which it was identified.

Hence in his version of the legend of St. Dorothea Hopkins concentrated on the speeches that led to the conversion of Theophilus and, in the process, developed his theory of sprung rhythm. As he explained to his brother Everard in 1885, sprung rhythm

> gives back to poetry its true soul and self. As poetry is emphatically speech, speech purged of dross like gold in the furnace, so it must have emphatically the essential elements of speech. Now emphasis itself, stress, is one of these: sprung rhythm makes verse stressy; it purges it to an emphasis as much brighter, livelier, more lustrous than the regular but commonplace emphasis of common rhythm as poetry in general is brighter than common speech.

In his revisions of the Dorothea poem, Hopkins uses sprung rhythm to stress the "parley," the debate between Dorothea and Theophilus, which ironically had the effect of the delivery of a "writ" to the pagan Theophilus, himself the Protonotary, writer of writs, now converted by the spoken rather than the written word.

Hopkins's representation of the "parley" making its "market here as well," moreover, increases our sense of a discussion with an audience, both inside and outside the poem, which is to be persuaded to strike a bargain, "to make market," to trade, to buy. This dramatization of the role of the audience led to the explicit exhortations and question and answer technique in the sequel to the Dorothea poem, **"The Starlight Night"**: "It is all a purchase, all is a prize. / Buy then! Bid then!—What?—Prayer, patience, alms, vows."

In many of Hopkins's subsequent poems the performance of the poem, the "parley" between the poem's speaker and the audience, is clearly intended to be the delivery of a "writ" for the audience's conversion. In other words, Hopkins replaced the modern axiom of the autonomy of the artistic imagination with the older idea of poetry as rhetoric. It can be argued that most of Hopkins's poetic techniques were developed to serve this clearly proselytical purpose. His most "modern" innovation, sprung rhythm, was obviously developed primarily for its rhetorical and oratorical potential: "Why do I employ sprung rhythm at all," Hopkins wrote to Bridges, "Because it is . . . the native and natural rhythm of speech, the least forced, the most rhetorical. . . . My verse is less to be read than heard, as I have told you before; it is oratorical, that is the rhythm is so." Along with the rhythm, the highly mnemonic sound structure of Hopkins's poems and their commonplace themes all suggest deep roots in the ancient tradition which defined poetry as a special kind of rhetoric, a tradition large enough to embrace even poems-for-pictures, for it prized *enargeia* (pictorial vividness) and *ecphrasis* (giving speech to an art object).

Hopkins's literary goal was a new genre of spoken lyric emphasizing poetry's affinities with speech and drama rather than the visual arts.

—Jerome Bump

As his commitment to medievalism in religion and art increased in the 1860s, Hopkins conceived of poetry not only as speech and drama but also as music. Music, the least representational, the most spiritual of the arts, generally replaced painting as the sister of poetry in the Middle Age. Thomas Aquinas's hymn, "Adoro Te Supplex," for instance, which Hopkins translated, asserts of God: "Seeing, touching, tasting are in thee deceived; / How says trusty hearing? that shall be believed" ("S. Thomae Aquinatis Rhythmus," undated). Aquinas's emphasis on the ear was reinforced in the eighteenth century by Edmund Burke and Gotthold Lessing, who reaffirmed Aristotle's assertion that poetry belongs with music as an art of temporal movement. This thesis was also supported by the German critics most important to Hopkins, those who promulgated romanticism as a medievalist movement animated by Christian spiritualism: Johann Herder, W. H. Wackenroder, Novalis, and the Schlegels. They praised music as the nonmimetic, expressive art to which lyric poetry should aspire.

The English romantics adapted their musical analogy, often in Aeolian harp imagery, and John Keble consecrated it for the Victorians. Thus, while Keats's "Ode on a Grecian Urn" epitomizes the romantic attraction to the visual arts, many other nineteenth-century poems emphasize affinities between poetry and music—so many, in fact, that romanticism has been defined as the shift from *ut pictura poesis* to *ut musica poesis*. In his revisions of his Dorothea poem, Hopkins was reconstructing this basic pardigm of romanticism.

He unified his own poem-for-a-painting through word-music rather than word-painting. Recognizing that we need to integrate a poem (which we usually apprehend first in discrete units) more than a painting (which we first perceive in one glance), Hopkins unified his poems with what he called "verbal parallelisms." Recurrent patterns of consonance and assonance, along with the audible rhythms of structural parallelism which he called "the figure of grammar," replace the Pre-Raphaelite painters' unifying techniques of ornamental designs and color harmonies. Perhaps the most obvious examples are the initial images of "a basket lined with grass" (I-III), in which "basket" and "grass" are audibly linked by *a* assonance and *s* consonance, and the later image of a "quince in hand" (I) which is integrated by *i* assonance and *n* consonance.

Similarly, it is the audible rhythm of structural parallelism ("the figure of grammar") that narrows the focus from St. Dorothea's basket of flowers to her lilies: "flowers I carry . . . Lilies I shew" (I). In addition to this kind of fugal iteration of structure, Hopkins also repeats sounds like "nor" to unify his picture, or in this case its disappearance: "We see nor fruit, nor flowers, nor Dorothy" (I).

The result is that although in fact we never see her, when the poem is read aloud we hear her music and that becomes the "message" of the poem. The impression of unity created by the word-music in **"For a Picture of St. Dorothea"** conveys the beauty of the final union with God in the realm in which Dorothea is "sphered": that heaven of "choice celestial music, equal to the motion of the spheres," invoked in Massinger's Renaissance drama of Dorothea, *The Virgin Martyr* (V, ii).

It was no doubt because music had such spiritual as well as formal powers that the musical analogy eventually became central to Hopkins's definition of poetry. He speculated that originally "music and verse were one" and such words as *"measure," "timbre," "melody," "air," "cadence," "rest," "modulation,"* and *"pitch"* pervade his discussions of poetry. Toward the end of his life he even preferred musical to rhetorical models for the performance of his poems: "above all remember what applies to all my verse, that it is, as a living art should be, made for performance and that its performance is not reading with the eye but loud, leisurely, poetical (not rhetorical) recitation, with long rests, long dwells on rhyme, and other marked syllables, and so on. This sonnet should be almost sung: it is most carefully timed in *tempo rubato*."

By aspiring to the condition of music, romantic poetry also sought to minimize the referential quality of language (which Victorian word-painting depended on), and thus lent itself to Hopkins's definition of poetry as "speech framed to be heard for its own sake and interest even over and above its interest of meaning. Some matter and meaning is essential to it but only as an element necessary to support and employ the shape which is contemplated for its own sake. (Poetry is in fact speech only employed to carry the inscape of speech for the inscape's sake—and therefore the inscape must be dwelt on)." In his own poetry Hopkins "dwells on" fugal repetition of the auditory inscape "to be heard for its own sake." Conventional syntax and clarity are consistently sacrificed for such musical effects, and the result in, say, **"The Leaden Echo and the Golden Echo,"** is an operatic performance which clearly subordinates the referential qualities of language to the musical.

This emphasis on language *qua* language and Hopkins's initial attraction to visual metaphors such as "the shape" of a poem, has naturally led us to associate his theories with modern criticism and its basic tenet of art for art's sake. The result, however, is often a misunderstanding of Hopkins's aims and methods. Many twentieth-century formalist critics, with basically spatial paradigms of language, naturally assume that language was primarily visual for

Hopkins too and therefore the essence of poetry for him was writing and reading silently, alone.

Yet Hopkins said that "such verse as I do compose is oral, made away from paper, and I put it down with repugnance." Hopkins's increasing emphasis on auditory rather than spatial effects often means that his poetry, for all its apparent modernity, cannot be read the way we normally read modern literature, as Hopkins himself discovered to his surprise: "When on somebody returning me the '**Eurydice,**' I opened and read some lines, reading, as one commonly reads whether prose or verse, with the eyes, so to say, only, it struck me aghast with a kind of raw nakedness and unmitigated violence I was unprepared for: but take breath and read it with the ears, as I always wish to be read, and my verse becomes all right." "**The Loss of the *Eurydice*,**" his other shipwreck poem, was also on his mind when he wrote to Everard: "I am sweetly soothed by your saying that you could make anyone understand my poem by reciting it well. That is what I always hoped, thought, and said; it is my precise aim. And thereby hangs so considerable a tale, in fact the very thing I was going to write about Sprung Rhythm in general."

Hopkins's considerable tale concerns the relationship between poetry and music. He took liberties with traditional grammar and diction in order to transform speech into something like music. "Some matter and meaning is essential" but we are to concentrate on the musical "shape" of the words, until the music itself becomes meaningful. Encouraged by onomatopoetic etymologies of contemporary linguists, Hopkins believed that similarity of sound in words "begets" similarity of meaning, that phonic harmony generates semantic harmony. Hopkins's choice of the word "begets," echoing the Nicene Creed's "Begotten not made, one in Being with," emphasizes not only the casual relationship, but the essential unity of sound and meaning.

This concept of the higher meaningfulness of the music of a poem had many nineteenth-century precedents. The romantics revived Pythagoras's theory of the music of the world, what Boethius called *musica mundana,* because they believed its sole aim is the Infinite. Pater defined this Pythagorean and Platonic "music of the spheres in its largest sense, its completest orchestration" as "the harmonious order of the whole universe." While contemporary musicologists related their studies to this music of the spheres and other mystical paradigms, Wordsworth asserted that "the roar of waters, torrents, streams / Innumerable" on top of Mt. Snowdon was "felt by the starry heavens."

The Platonic emphasis on the rhetorical and ethical effects of man-made music, what Boethius called *musica humana,* also remained popular. The romantics recalled Longinus's assertion that harmonious word-music makes us receptive to sublimity, and Newman claimed that the "perfection of the Intellect" has "almost the beauty and harmony of heavenly contemplation, so intimate is it with the eternal order of things and the music of the spheres." Similar ideas affected theorists both as modern as Valery,

who felt that the aim of music in poetry was to produce an extraordinary harmony in the listener, and as reactionary as the nineteenth-century medievalists, who resurrected many other traditional connotations of verbal harmony. Hopkins's word-music in his poem on Dorothea and her angel, for instance, may well be a response to Anna Jameson's insistence, in the book that inspired the cult of St. Dorothea, that "there is nothing more beautiful, more attractive in Art than the representation of angels" as the singers of the "music of the spheres."

Hopkins's word-music was designed to "beget a recurrence or parallelism answering to it in the words or thought," moreover, ultimately a recurrence of the music of heaven. These connotations of harmony in poetry suggest how Hopkins's word-music was designed to convey that sense of the possibility of a radically different order of time and experience that is one of the goals of most religions. Hopkins's Dorothea poem shows how, from the beginning of his career, even in his most conventional, mimetic phase, Hopkins was interested in representing not only nature but that which seemed to miraculosuly deviate from nature. Religion encouraged Hopkins to represent this independent reality, this world unto itself, this time out of time. "**For a Picture of St. Dorothea,**" like so many other Hopkins poems, is the music of this other word of centuries of religious traditions as well as the song of a particular self.

Ironically, while revising his poem-for-a-picture in search of new ways to tap the poetic power of these traditions, Hopkins's most important discovery was that the ear was more important than the eye. He sensed that the medieval age which his imaginary "picture" evoked was more alive than his own to the power of the spoken word, in the sacraments and in its oral traditions generally. Such traditions, as Walter Ong has shown [in *The Presence of the Word,* 1970], consisting of audible rather than visualized words, make the world more personal, for spoken words invoke the presence of speakers.

It is a sign of the ability Hopkins acquired to revive those traditions that his poems written for performance often evoke a world inhabited by personified presences, a vitalistic world in which all objects are animated by powers "deep down" inside them, a world very much like that resurrected by his ultimate revision of the Dorothea poem: "**The Starlight Night.**" In that poem as in so many others, Hopkins taps the extraordinary power of this vital oral tradition with a virtuoso auditory performance which rejuvenates and energizes the ancient metaphors. He extends their life in time in another sense as well: when the metaphors of "**The Starlight Night**" are spoken aloud, as they should be, they inevitably seem more successive and less simultaneous, for the tongue is much slower than the eye. But only by performing this and other poems by Hopkins aloud can a reader apprehend this aspect of his metaphors and feel the primary effect he aimed at in all his poetry: the parallelism of his sounds actually "begetting" the parallelism of his images, the integration of his word-music activating and reinforcing the unifying power of the metaphors.

Hopkins thus resurrected the original meaning of the term "sonnet"—like "sonata" it means "to be sounded or played." That his poems are based on a theory of poetry as performance was the rest of that "considerable tale" he adumbrated in his letter to Everard in 1885:

> Every art then and every work of art has its own play or performance . . . books play, perform, or are played and performed when they are read; and ordinarily by one reader, alone, to himself, with the eyes only. . . . Poetry was originally meant for either singing or reciting; a record was kept of it; the record could be, was, read, and that in time by one reader, alone, to himself, with his eyes only. This reacted on the art: what was to be performed under these conditions for these conditions ought to be and was composed and calculated. Sound-effects were intended, wonderful combinations even; but they bear the marks of having been meant for the whispered, not even whispered, merely mental performance of the closet, the study and so on. . . . This is not the true nature of poetry . . . *till it is spoken it is not performed,* it does not perform, it is not itself. . . .

Hopkins's use of the word "perform" here is full of echoes of the King James Bible familiar to most Victorians. These echoes include that sense of fulfilment of prophecy so basic to the typological imagination: "For I am the LORD I will speak, and the word that I shall speak shall come to pass . . . in your days . . . will I say the word, and will perform it" (Ezek. 12:25).

But the biblical "perform" is not limited to this typological meaning; it conveys all the connotations of speech as act: "I am the LORD that . . . confirmeth the word of his servant, and performeth the counsel of his messangers; that saith to Jerusalem, Thou shalt be inhabited; and to the cities of Judah, ye shall be built, . . . That saith to the deep, Be dry, and I will dry up thy rivers; That saith of Cyrus, He is my shepherd, and shall perform all my pleasure; even saying unto Jerusalem, Thou shalt be built, and to the temple, Thy foundation shall be laid" (Isa. 44:24-28). One of the reasons that the Bible is *the* book of Western civilization is that it is the one most in tune with those original oral traditions which endow our language with great power. The source of the ultimate performatives in our language, the Bible is the drama of word as event, speech as act, from the creation ("And God said, Let there be light: and there was light") to the New Testament: "In the beginning was the Word, and the Word was with God, and the Word was God." Biblical words are clearly kinetic, dynamic—they make things happen.

The emphasis is of course on speech, not writing, for the Hebrew tradition is oriented to the ears, not the eyes. The God of the ten commandments is heard, not seen: "And the LORD spake unto you out of the midst of the fire; ye hear the voice of the words, but saw no similitude; only ye heard a voice: And he declared unto his covenant, which he commanded you to perform" (Deut. 4:12-13). Other echoes of the word "perform" also stress the effect of the voice of the invisible God on the ear: "And the LORD said to Samuel; Behold, I will do a thing in Israel, at which both the ears of everyone that heareth it shall tingle. In that day I will perform" (Isa. 3:11-12).

To move closer to Hopkins's own situation, much of this sense of the power of the word is transferred to the poet when the word of the Lord comes to him and he accepts the role of the prophet with his "Amen" ("So be it"): "The word that came to Jeremiah from the LORD, saying, Hear ye the words of this covenant, and speak unto the men of Judah, and to the inhabitants of Jerusalem; And say unto them, Thus saith the LORD God of Israel; cursed be the man that obeyeth not the words of this covenant . . . Obey my voice, and do them, according to all which I command you; so shall ye be my people, and I will be your God: That I may perform the oath that I have sworn unto your fathers, to give them a land flowing with milk and honey, as it is this day. Then answered I, and said, So be it, O LORD" (Jer. 11:1-5).

So far we may seem to have stayed within the oral tradition, though the Bible is its visual transcription, but the biblical echoes of the word "perform" include explicit instructions on how to perform a written text: "And the king stood by a pillar, and made a covenant before the Lord, to walk after the Lord, and to keep his commandments and his testimonies and his statutes with all their heart and all their soul, to perform the words of this covenant that were written in this book" (2 Kings 23:3). In this model of reading, the performance of the words of a text demands the complete participation of the reader; his heart and soul are to embrace the heart and soul of the text: "I have inclined my heart to perform thy statutes alway, even unto the end" (Ps. 119:112). It is not enough to read the text, or even to speak it aloud; one must pour one's whole being into the performance of it: "That which has gone out of thy lips thou shalt keep and perform" (Deut. 23:23); "Now therefore perform the doing of it; that as there was a readiness to will, so there may be a performance also out of that which ye have" (2 Cor. 8:11).

This sense of the text as the script for a performance is clearly at the other end of the spectrum from the idea of the text as merely a visual object. Hopkins soon discovered that to read with the eyes only is to be deaf and dumb, to have one's organs closed to the magical or miraculous power of words in performance. In his sermon, "Cure of the Deaf and Dumb Man; Ephphetha," for instance, Hopkins recalls that "having made the organs ready to hear and speak he looked up to heaven and groaned. . . . *And said Ephphetha, Be opened*—The evangelist tells us the very word which had this magical or rather miraculous effect. . . . Much more should we admire what Christ has done for us—made us deaf hear, if we will hear . . . made us dumb speak."

Hopkins's literary goal was a new genre of spoken lyric emphasizing poetry's affinities with speech and drama rather than the visual arts. Anticipating H. Marshall McLuhan and Walter Ong, he suggested how the phonograph, which had been invented only seven years before, could help restore the human voice to literature:

I look on this as an infinite field and very little worked. It has this great difficulty, that the art depends entirely on living tradition. The phonograph may give us one, but hitherto there could be no record of fine spoken utterance. . . . the natural performance and delivery belonging properly to lyric poetry, which is speech, has not been enough cultivated, and should be. When performers were trained to do it (it needs the rarest gifts) and audiences to appreciate it it would be, I am persuaded, a lovely art. . . . With the aid of the phonograph each phrase could be fixed and learned by heart like a song.

As I have suggested elsewhere, the poetics expressed in this letter suggest our need to reevaluate how we teach literature and how we communicate generally.

Mary Anderson   (essay date 1990)

SOURCE: "Hopkins: Numinous Numbers in the Virgin Mary Poems," in *Papers on Language and Literature,* Vol. 26, No. 4, Fall, 1990, pp. 513–21.

[*In the following essay, Anderson points out that little attention has been paid to the numerical inscapes in Hopkin's poetry, and argues that the Virgin Mary poems demonstrate the development and complexity of the dialectic between verbal and numerical structures in his work.*]

While much has been written about Gerard Manley Hopkins's innovations in meter, such as sprung rhythm, inscape, and instress, little attention has been given the numerical structure that he builds into his work. Hopkins provides us with both verbal *and* numerical inscapes, and the "symmetry" between the two creates a "beauty" that "explodes" with revelations to reinforce the meaning. This dual structure acts as a kind of dialectic and conforms with Hopkins's theory of beauty in diversity, outlined in his essay "On the Origin of Beauty" (May 1865): "All poetry differs from prose by having a continuous and regular artificial structure . . . of continuous parallelisms. . . . A singularly beautiful expression of poetry has of its essence an antithetical shape:—for that the antithesis is essential to the beauty." The numerical structures unify a poetry that gives the appearance of randomness; the mathematical symmetry is directly related to Hopkins's world view as ordered and intelligible. Since Hopkins does not mention the numerical structure, we trust that it is a kind of code or riddle intended to be solved or experienced in some mystical way.

Hopkins makes one important reference to a book written by his father, Manley Hopkins, *The Cardinal Numbers* (1887), and states that he had some hand in it. Although the book has some limitations, it glosses some of the number symbolism discussed below, as does Bosman's *The Meaning and Symbolism of Numbers* and Hopper's *Medieval Number Symbolism.* Manley Hopkins discusses the psychological effect of the repetition of numbers:

Upon human beings, rhythm, or the regular repetition of numbers exerts an influence which is generally pleasing. . . . The mind keeps unconsciously a measure or account. . . . The Greek name for number is [arithmos], and rhythm, which originally means a certain number of pulses in a given time, is derived from the word [rhuthmizo], showing that rhythm is in direct relation to numbers. We can at least say . . . that an expectancy arises in the mind involuntarily and often unaccountably, for the return of sounds and ideas in the mind.

That Gerard Manley Hopkins shared this view is evident in the number symbolism that he weaves into his poetry to be experienced by the listener or reader. Numbers were very real for Hopkins; in his father's book he recounts his experience with "the very fantastic and interesting" circumstance of "apparition" or "spectral numbers."

The works that illustrate numerical structure and meaning are the Virgin Mary poems, which, taken in chronological order, show the development of Hopkins's verbal and numerical style and complexity. Certain key words or constructions are repeated according to the numbers from one to twelve. These repetitions conform to what Hopkins calls "aftering" and "oftening" and "over-and-overing," similar to the repeated tune or melody in music.

The first of the Virgin Mary poems, **"Ad Mariam"** (26), is one of the poems he dismissed as the "little presentation pieces" written during his seven-year poetic drought. The number symbolism in the poem begins with the duality in the word "Spring," which occurs twice, as a noun in the second line and as verb in the second-to-last line. The verb from of "spring" forces the reader back to the beginning in a circular motion, in order to glean this active meaning and to explore and "explode" both connections. The double meaning in "spring" is a typical Hopkins construction in which both noun and verb meanings reverberate in the same word; in fact, in the simplest terms, inscape can be seen as the noun and instress as the verb, and the beauty is in both the symmetry and dichotomy. Thus May-Mariam's inscape includes her relationship to the Old Testament maid and Queen of King David's house, who "sprang" from the tribe of Judah, and is the proverbial line from which the "son" (Christ) also "sprang." Hopkins may have in mind the scripture from Hebrews 7.14: "For it is evident that our Lord sprang out of Judah."

"Maiden," also repeated twice, symbolizes the dual nature of both virginity and potentiality. As such she is the duality in the physical world, objectified in matter, and is the "Mother-Substance of all things" [Leonard Bosman, *The Meaning and Philosophy of Numbers,* 1932]. Occurring twice, "Maiden" and "Spring" symbolize duality and symmetry, matter and spirit, which conforms with Hopkins's theory of beauty as interaction. Manley Hopkins also notes a similar "peculiar feature" of the poetic forms in Old Testament literature, in which a "parallelism," or "duplication" of an idea "forms an antithesis and a disjunctive conjunction." This difference of expression is necessary for "fulness and elegance."

The rhyme scheme of the first four stanzas, *ababccab,* changes in the fifth stanza to *ababaaab.* In all five octaves the *ab* rhyme occurs three times, suggesting the Trinity; it functions in its location at the beginning and end of each octave to represent an organic and circular order of continuity and completion. Manley Hopkins comments on just such a structure in music: "the third tone in union with the first produces the strongest harmony which two notes in the octave are capable of forming." In keeping with the lyrical quality of the poem, the rhyme scheme is slightly altered in the fifth and final stanza to emphasize the musical quality of the long "e" vowel sound ("we," "thee," and "tree"). "Thee" occurs nine times, a multiple of the trinitarian three, and forms an image of "perfect balance in all things" [Leonard Bosman, *The Meaning and Philosophy of Numbers,* 1932]. In the final stanza "thee" occurs seven times, the number of earthly completion and consummation. Hopkins thus emphasizes May-Mariam as the "May-hope of our darkened ways"—in the material world.

While Christ and Mary are not named in the poem, their presence "springs" out in the numerical structure. The structure of five stanzas suggests the number of Christ; there are five dots that form the cross; and "the stigmata, or five wounds of the crucifixion, have been held reverently dear to Christians." The number five is "the symbol of the creative Power of God, manifested in the `Word' or Logos in creation"; in Greek iconography the "Pythagoreans named it, *cardiatis . . .* the heart of things manifested, the centre of all things." Further, "May" and "month" are repeated five times, and May is the fifth month. Implicit in the poem is the image of Christ linked with the images of time, such as, "May," "month," "day," "hour," "year," "past," the seasons, and generation, all representing Christ's role in Creation and His birth into time as the ultimate beauty in duality—God made man.

Although Mary is unnamed, her presence is established in the numerical structure as well. The five stanzas contain eight lines each, forming five octaves, for a total of forty lines. At line twenty, at the very center, "Maid," "mother," and "May" come together in a triune, placing Mary at the very center of the birth process.

"Rosa Mystica" is also striking in its numerical form. Eight stanzas of six lines are divided into three rhyming couplets, with each final couplet a song-like refrain. [According to Bosman], Eight symbolizes a "Universal Harmony, Mother"; and "the simplest of all concords," to reflect the song-like character of the poem. The title of the poem, **"Mystica,"** and the use of "mystery" three times (including the title) express the mystery of the union of God and Christ in Mary. The three rhyming couplets symbolize Mary's role as the mother in whom Father and Son are combined: "Christ Jesus our Lord, her God and her son." The words "Mary," "Grace," "blossom," and "sweet(ness),", are each repeated three times, symbolic of Mary's role "for purposes of manifestation," for it is through her that God manifests the Son. "Mother" occurs nine times (a power of three), a number symbolic of "the final stage of preparation . . . in which all things are formed"; "God" occurs ten times, the number of spiritual

completion and perfection in which all are combined. The earthly completion of the creation process in Genesis is recalled in the seven repetitions of "Garden" and "Daylight."

Seventeen questions are raised in the poem, a number that at first glance appears relatively insignificant, except to restate seven and ten as the symbols of earthly and heavenly completion. However, Hopkins's placement is much more complex. There are fifteen questions up to stanza 7; then in stanza 7, other numbers and combinations call for interpretation. "Five" occurs three times—three and five respectively representing the Trinity and the number of Christ. Then Hopkins plants a curious clue to stimulate the questioning process: "Multiply, multiply, who can tell how?" But he has just told us how, for $3 \times 5 = 15$, which is precisely the number of questions to this point in the poem.

Further, the numerical structure of seventeen questions in eight stanzas leads to a scripture in Jeremiah 17.8 (note the numbers), which is appropriate to the meaning of the poem, and especially to stanza 7. In the scripture, as in the poem, we note the union of masculine and feminine in the image of the tree. Hopkins's "Make me a leaf in thee, mother of mine" recalls: "For he shall be as a tree planted by the waters, and that spreadeth out *her* roots by the river, and shall not see when heat cometh, but *her* leaf shall be green; and shall not be careful in the year of drought, neither shall cease from yielding fruit" (Anderson's emphasis). This tree is similar to the plant described by Manley Hopkins as a "wondrous five-leaved plant which exorcised demons, counteracted poisons, cured fevers, and contributed to the expiation of sin!"; and the number five and the mystical power of the plant are analogous to the miraculous and spiritual power of Christ.

The numerical structures unify a poetry that gives the appearance of randomness; the mathematical symmetry is directly related to Hopkins's world view as ordered and intelligible.

—Mary Anderson

The third poem, **"The May Magnificat,"** uses numerical structure in several significant passages. The poem has twelve stanzas, a number associated with time, season, and universality, and adumbrates Revelations 12.1 (again note the numbers): "And there appeared a great wonder in heaven; a woman clothed with the sun, and the moon under her feet, and upon her head a crown of twelve stars." "Wonder" appears at the beginning of the poem; "Twelve stars" are the twelve stanzas in "her" honour; and Mary's crown is associated with stars, since "Spring" has a "star-eyed strawberry-breasted / Throstle above her nested" (st. 5). Moreover, the "throstle" has triangular markings on its breast, and this symbol of unity is "nested" above her like a crown.

Four references to Mary—twice in the Mary-May sense (sts. 1, 9), and twice in the Mary-Christ sense (sts. 7-8, 12) suggest that her beauty lies in her dual nature, both temporal and divine, and analogize her with the forces of regeneration (st. 4). Four denotes "the form of the world" and the "signature of nature"; the "potentialities of objectivized Nature," and the "concretion of the Divine Idea working in Substance" (Bosman). "May" is represented four times in the poem, and shares in a parallel symbolism, while "Christ," "Lord," and "God" are each mentioned once only, in keeping with their spiritual perfection. In the last stanza, "Mary," "Christ," and "God" appear together, and Mary's reproductive role in Christ's birth is thus represented as the final or twelfth star in her crown. The poem opens with "May" and "Mary," and ends with "God" and "salvation," the path and provision for salvation. Just as Mary leads out from God, in Christ, she also leads back to God.

The fourth poem, **"The Blessed Virgin Compared to the Air we Breathe,"** appears to be a simple poem; its short lines, rhyming couplets and tercets give the poem a lilting character. However, the rhythm is sprung and the syntax requires much diligent reading. Its numerical structure is also more complex, reflecting a mature poet who has refined his style and technique. Consisting of 126 lines divided into six stanzas, the poem locates Christ's birth exactly in the middle, at line 63 in the third stanza, corresponding to His place in the Trinity. References to "Mary" and "mother" three times denote her spiritual unity and role as the mother of Christ, and conforms with the meaning of the poem. "Mother" also appears in several other forms, including compound words, such as "world-mothering" and "motherhood," for a total of six times (2X3), which may symbolize the function of "mother" in both the temporal and eternal spheres. Manley Hopkins notes that "in the Genesis of the world, the *sixth* day is prominent as being that on which man was created." Since man was created in the image of God, he also blends Spirit and Matter. For Bosman, "the `six-ing' process . . . relates the opposites, links triangle to triangle, trinity of Spirit to trinity of Matter. . . . Spirit and Matter are blended and synthesized."

The key word in the poem, "air," Hopkins uses twelve times. Its symmetry is further indicated in its occurrence three times in the first, and three in the last stanza, to represent the unity of the Trinity. Also, "air" and "Mary" are one, since "air" is contained within her name: "As if with air the same / Is Mary [Mairy], *more by name*" ([Anderson's] emphasis).

The emphasis on will, intellect, and revelation appears in a key numerical signal in the poem, which deals with the number 7 and leads to a scripture. This signal is similar to those found in the other three poems, but in this case the technique is perfected so that there can be no doubt about the poet's intention. We note that "air" is repeated seven times up to line 87, the point at which the poem states, "The seven or seven times seven / Hued sunbeam will transmit / Perfect, not alter it." The seven leads to a scriptural reading which unfolds the meaning both in word

and number: "The light of the sun shall be seven fold in the day of the Lord (it) bindeth up the breach of his people and healeth the stroke of the wound" (Isaiah 30.26). Seven symbolizes the open door between Heaven and Earth, and for this reason "the rainbow, and its seven colours . . . was considered a sign of the alliance between Earth and Heaven" (Bosman). Like the light of the sun in the rainbow, it heals the "breach" between heaven and earth, and signifies completion in the temporal world. Significantly, then, the poem follows the scripture at lines 89-102 with the analogy of the sunbeam that transmits "perfect" to dispel the "blackness bound" in the "grimy vasty vault." The reference to "vault" may signal Hopkins's reply to Plato's cave analogy, in which man sees only shadows in the cave; Hopkins demonstrates that man is not denied the perfection and light of God, but that he participates in the conception of "God's and Mary's Son" *in* Mary and thus becomes a "new self and nobler me."

It is important to the theme that it is the third stanza that deals with the Incarnation, since three is the number of unity. The stanza suggests that Mary conceives Christ continuously, and also conceives Christ "in us." We note the tentative approach at the beginning of the stanza, "If I have understood," before the poem continues:

> And makes, O marvellous!
> New Nazareths in us,
> Where she shall yet conceive
> Him, morning, noon, and eve;
> New Bethlems, and he born
> There, evening, noon, and morn—
>
> . . . . .
>
> Who, born so, comes to be
> New self and nobler me
> In each one and each one
> More makes, when all is done,
> Both God's and Mary's Son.
>
> (59–72)

This birth moves from flesh to spirit, "though much the mystery how," and emphasizes both the temporal and the spiritual in the circularity of the lines.

References to "God" seven times in the poem, and the numerical relationship with scripture, reveal Him as ultimately responsible for the provision of healing on earth and in time. The one instance of the "god" (lower case), which is a little puzzling in a Christian poem, may reveal that the historical function of the "god of old" in the Old Testament is also "God," even before redemption became possible when "A mother came to mould" in the New Testament.

The emphasis on knowledge in the poem and in the scripture is reinforced in Hopkins's punning of "wound" (34, 125). We are forced, in a "winding" motion, to go "round and round" and to perceive both the noun and verb meanings of "wound" (similar to "Spring" in **"Ad Mariam"**).

The reference to the homonymic "mind" shows that the noun "wound" and the "breach" represent man's limited knowledge, and suggests that duality and dichotomy precipitate the dialectic and the search for wisdom, and thus for "God." We are constantly reminded of Hopkins's equation: duality equals symmetry equals beauty. It is significant that "we are wound / With mercy round and round" and that "round" is repeated five times, the number of "the Lord" who appears in the scripture and in the poem. He is in Mary and "in us" and represents a synthesis. The beauty that explodes for us is that the wonder, winding, binding, and folding aspects of our limited knowledge can be seen as "wounds" that are healed in Mary and in Christ. The healing then is in the mind, in knowledge and in spirit. In the last stanza, therefore, the air is "live" and *speaks* into "my ears"—it is the Word made Flesh in an immaculate conception.

In all of his "Mary" poems, Hopkins uses names, images, and language in a nontraditional way, and thereby forces the reader to experience the meaning of Christian doctrine in a new form. The "mystery" of diction and syntax and the "riddle" of the numerical structure force the mind into a state of inquiry, meditation, and openness, which then "conceives" new associations and ideas "in us."

The numerical symbolism in Hopkins's "Mary" poems, derived from his father's book and traditional theories of religious number symbolism, not only supports the theme of each poem, but provides both a tool and a challenge to unravel its meaning. There can be little doubt that Hopkins's numerical structures are intentional. Their subtle, secret, and mystical purpose he never expressed, but left to be discovered by experience. The poet who abandoned conventional measuring techniques of rhythm also constructed an undergirding of numerical form to convey a hidden symmetry and proportion. Clues within the scheme suggest that Hopkins intended for us to discover the numerical structures as another "wonder"(ful) inscape to be explored and "exploded," and a game to be played in "ten thousand places."

Marylou Motto (essay date 1990)

SOURCE: "Uttering Truth: The Aphorism in the Poem," in *Thought*, Vol. 65, No. 259, December, 1990, pp. 544–49.

[*In the following essay, Motto describes how aphorism functions in Hopkins's poetry.*]

It is an often cited paradox that Gerard Manley Hopkins, a poet identified with a seemingly unstoppable lyrical onrush of imagery, is also the poet who fits that lyrical onrush into poems so short that they sit two on a page. Similarly, the concentrated stresses of Hopkins's sprung rhythm seem to cram the short space of his line with sound and meaning. And while Hopkins often had his eye on larger-than-life people in the midst of heroic effort—the nun, Harry Ploughman, Felix Randal at the forge and then

rising to God—he also trained his eye in admiration on the small and seemingly insignificant: the small child crying because leaves were falling, a skylark, a man who achieved sainthood by patiently waiting. That is, in any number of ways Hopkins seems to enjoy meeting the challenge of compression, of seeing and saying much in small. So the aphorism is a structure that suited him well.

The word "aphorism" comes from the Greek, and it means to set up boundaries. Hopkins liked, one suspects, the aphorism's definition, its marking of boundaries, and he perhaps especially liked that quality in a poetry that is elsewhere so propelled by dynamic motion. Hopkins' tendency toward aphorism—toward saying the large, general truth succinctly, memorably, neatly—is pronounced. In **"To his Watch,"** for example, the aphorisms and near-aphorisms are packed as closely as the gears on the watch he addresses:

> The telling time our task is; time's some part,
> Not all, but we were framed to fail and die—
> One spell and well that one. There, ah thereby
> Is comfort's carol of all or woe's worst smart.

The terse sayings of general principle are authoritative; the characteristic Hopkinsian play of sound gives the sayings their sharpness and wit. It's a decided pleasure in reading Hopkins, this coming upon aphorism.

The aphorism is a text of pleasure, not a text of bliss. As W. H. Auden and Louis Kronenberger wrote in the foreword to their anthology of aphorisms [in *The Faber Book of Aphorisms: A Personal Selection,* 1962], "Aphorisms are essentially an aristocratic genre of writing. The aphorist does not argue or explain, he asserts . . ." Aristocratic and elegant, the aphorism stands at arm's length, closing the reader out of the act of perception by asserting a polished conclusion. Its emphasis is not on the voice speaking but on the language said. In other words, the aphorism is "detachable" language, and it detaches itself from the poem, from the reader, and finally perhaps from the poet too. It is language within the poem that moves in the direction of autonomous sign.

THE APHORISM ITSELF

In an article on aphorism in Wallace Stevens [in *PMLA* 91, 1976], Beverly Coyle argues that Stevens liked and used aphorisms "despite his belief that such truth is tentative." Stevens aphorisms, as in "Thirteen Ways of Looking at a Blackbird," express a "momentary balance between reality and the imagination," a tentative truth-catching modified, deflected, or frankly contradicted by other equally valid aphorisms.

Of course, it is not so in Hopkins. Although Hopkins, like Stevens after him, is fond of beginning his poems with general principles and truths, his organization does not often depend on questioning the truth he has stated or considering a contradictory idea. Initiating statements in Hopkins are not likely to be phrased as aphorism and are almost never rejected in the poem's process. They are not used to create tensions or reversals. Instead, the poem is liable to deepen its opening statement through detailed exploration. "The world is charged with the grandeur of God"; "Glory be to God for dappled things"; "Nothing is so beautiful as Spring"—all these openings are poised as relatively uncomplicated statements waiting for the poet's lyrical substantiation.

These initiating statements of poems anchor the images to come. They mandate a momentary stability in their fresh discovery of old, known truth. They ordain the subsequent rhyming and assent to the world-design found. For all their decisiveness, abstraction, and stability, such statements are readiers (a fact often signalled by their punctuation), and they hold the reader and poem back in anticipation. To the practiced reader of Hopkins, they are felt as thematic setups, pressurized springboards before the plunge into the imagery that proves the principle. As initiatory statements, clearly, even loosely, phrased and occurring right before the densely figured language of lyricism, they suggest perhaps that the underlying truths of the world are easily discoverable, clearly offered by God to anyone paying attention.

Significantly then, the aphorisms in Hopkins occur not at the openings of poems but later in the poetic context; they occur in confirmation of ideas already introduced or developed. They exhibit concentration and polish. Bounded and defined in their meaning, the aphorisms assert truth irrefutable with self-confident authority. Much of the reader's pleasure derives from the integrity of the saying: "Self-yeast of spirit a dull dough sours." Or, "Nor mouth had, no nor mind, expressed / What heart heard of, ghost guessed."

Hopkins' aphorisms are efforts of language that reflect God-given truths, but they also exhibit a complicated, at times even dazzling, linguistic ability. Each is a linguistic performance, an exploit even, relating large ideas in few syllables. No less than the initiating statements, they speak of general principle, but they are now intensely charged by the poet's sensibility partly as a result of the foregoing experience of the world and of the poem:

> shéer plód makes plough down sillion
> Shine,
>
> ("**The Windhover**")

> Man Jack the man is, just;
> ("**The Shepherd's Brow**")

> meaning motion fans fresh our wits with wonder.
> ("**Henry Purcell**")

Each aphorism is self-sufficient, with a strong sense of closure. (We hear a period even when one does not exist.) Each takes a large, idea, a general principle, and locks it up—neatly, pleasingly—in a few words. And although Hopkins does not often employ traditional rhyme to achieve the encapsulation of aphorisms, he does use practically every other sound effect known to poet.

In, for example, "There lives the dearest freshness deep down things" in "**God's Grandeur**," the aphorism starts and ends with rather general abstract words, words relatively uncharacteristic of Hopkins: the enclitic "There" and the general "things." These two throwaway words that begin and end the line are alliterated and so come together in sense. The alliteration helps define the aphorism's boundaries, its endpoints. But it is at the line's center that we find its meaning: at the heart of all the old, known things is the revelation, the "dearest freshness." In other words, in addition to playing with sound, Hopkins is wittily playing with the pattern of his words, enacting the truth of the aphorism in the saying of his statement: "There lives the dearest freshness deep down things."

Again, in "shéer plód makes plough down sillion / Shine," we have the saying of a general truth (the truth seeming to have emerged from the image of the windhover's buckling) in the tersest form imaginable. And the terseness is revealing, even witty: Hopkins ploughs the sounds of "plód" into "plough down"; and "shéer" at the line's opening sheers off into "shine" at its end. Again, the first and last words, "shéer" and "shine," alliterate, marking the aphorism's outline, helping it to stand alone.

THE APHORISM IN THE POEM

So far, we have been discussing the aphorism as *in* the poem but not *of* it, and indeed, its capacity for standing single, as truth, gives it a curious isolationism today. In an age when closure is frowned upon, when even sentences in poems have a hard time getting themselves finished, the poetic experience is supposed to let us into the act of perception, to leave us "root room" to continue what the poet only begins.

On the face of it, the device of aphorism denies this whole romantic modern quest for inconclusiveness, incipience, and contingency. The aphorism instead objectifies an interior experience, holding forth a cool answer, a truth exterior to poet, poem, and reader. In this way, it is a denial of accessibility, a detachable saying that can be separated from its context and anthologized or inscribed on the wall.

Stevens found his way though this problem essentially by playing aphorism against aphorism and so focusing on the transience of any sense of finality. In effect, he made aphorism reflect a fragmentary existence, and filled his walls with illuminations that proclaimed themselves absolute *and* contradictory, because "The only emperor is the emperor of ice-cream." Hopkins' aphorisms are far more traditional, drawing firmly on the elegance of a poetry of statement. At the same time, Hopkins makes them work within poems, ever playing with Romantic ideas, patterns, and motions.

Hopkins knew well that his aphorisms were not starting places; they were not invitations into the poem either for the speaker or the reader. But he also knew that "Iron bars do not a prison make" and that "Nuns fret not in their

Hopkins in 1863.

then, before that quite comes clear, the aphorism yields to another saying that is likeness in unlikeness: "and blue bleak embers, ah my dear, / Fall, gall themselves, and gash gold-vermillion." The idea, the thought, of this clause is like that of the aphorism that precedes it, but the saying, the poetry, is something else again. The onwardness of "and" contradicts the finality of the aphorism while affirming its thought. And this, the second saying of the idea, is richer, fuller, and less aphoristic by virtue of the breathy, open-voweled exclamation at its center, and because now, this saying *seems* spontaneous, under the pressure of the moment as it opens up and out, spilling gold beyond neatness: "and blue bleak embers, ah my dear, / Fall, gall themselves, and gash gold-vermillion."

The poem moves from soil to fire. The conjunction, the "and," tells us that we are to hear the truth said again. It is the intervention of "ah my dear" that changes everything: "ah my dear" is a recovery of selfhood and voice, a recovery of poetic process, an intimate embrace that defies detachment from the poem, softens the harshness of the blow, and alleviates all the finality. Having seemingly surrendered his poetic authority to language in the aphorism, "shéer plód makes plough down sillion / Shine," the speaker then, in "ah my dear," recovers the poem for himself and for the reader. The aphorism, the stopping to gather and admire meaning, becomes but a temporary storage place, a gravity whose energy is drawn upon in the process onward.

> **In any number of ways Hopkins seems to enjoy meeting the challenge of compression, of seeing and saying much in small. So the aphorism is a structure that suited him well.**
>
> **—*Mary Lou Motto***

In Hopkins, the aphorism fixes what has come before into defined boundaries; it utters and confines explicatory truth. But it is not an ending; instead Hopkins takes the hardness and in many different ways liberates what he has enclosed. The result is that what follows the aphorism, the end of the poem in **"The Windhover,"** for example, seems to rise out of the ground, to fly all the more free for the stillness that preceded it.

In **"As kingfishers catch fire,"** Hopkins writes, "Each mortal thing does one thing and the same: / Deals out that being indoors each one dwells." Later in the same poem, he condenses the idea even further: "the just man justices." In this aphorism, the adjective, "just," unexpectedly becomes verb, "justices"; the statement thus turns characteristic into action, adjective into verb; the statement deals out *linguistically* what indoors dwells.

The concluding verb thus proves itself the principle of continuance, becoming a way out of self-enclosure, and

narrow convent walls." Hopkins explicitly chooses the density and closure offered by aphorism; he chooses the temporary linguistic imprisoning of poetic impulse. But if aphorisms are not starting places for his poems, neither do they serve as conclusions. If the poet seems to have surrendered voice to language momentarily, he calls it back again, always bringing the poem back to the reader, as in **"The Windhover."**

"Shéer plód makes plough down sillion / Shine": This aphorism captures the major idea of everything that precedes it in the poem. Its saying signals that the poet is turning to a more abstract voice, now formulating the meaning of all the previous imagery. In fact, the poem proclaims that the aphorism is explanation; the speaker signals that he is going to explain the windhover's buckling beauty: "No wonder of it: shéer plód makes plough down sillion / Shine." The aphorism is dense with sound and stress, and firmly closed, authoritative, so much so that on a first reading, the reader is probably aware of closure and sound before he makes sense of the thought.

Hopkins quickly moves to take advantage of the reader's imbalance. In the aphorism, in effect, Hopkins is saying, "Now I have hold of the idea—*this* is what it is," and into the further indwelling reason for all justicing: "the just man justices; / Keeps grace: that keeps all his goings graces; / Acts in God's eye what in God's eye he is—/ Christ."

In the octave of **"Felix Randal"** the speaker remembers and chronicles his association with Felix, and then blesses the farrier and seemingly dismisses him: "Ah well, God rest him all road ever he offended!" In the next line, the aphorism, the speaker seems to turn away in order to read his text by formulating the general truth, the lesson, out of their relationship: "This seeing the sick endears them to us." This is a distancing generality, subsuming the relationship of priest and farrier into one example of a general truth. But now, even before the speaker has finished the statement, poetic rather than aphoristic speaking has begun to take over: "us too it endears." Thus, "This seeing the sick endears them to us, us too it endears" turns back in on itself, moving forward and backward to illustrate the general truth of the relationship between the two men. The distancing generality cannot be maintained, and the speaker turns from general truth back to individual memory.

The aphorism then yields to memory, now renewed and in a different mode, of the intimacy between the two men. And the tercet ends in the speaker naming the farrier, individually, personally, affectingly: "child, Felix, poor Felix Randal." The point is that the aphorism cannot hold: it begins to turn as soon as it is said. And the turn is Hopkins' road onward from aphorism; the next line is firmly planted not in the universal Us and Them, but in the "I" and "Thou," the particular farrier and priest. Hopkins, of course, utters his truths in many ways, has disparate motions and modes of seeing and saying. Here he is speaking to himself at the very center of *The Wreck of the Deutschland*:

> Ah, touched in your bower of bone,
>   Are you! turned for an exquisite smart,
> Have you! Make words break from me here all
> alone,
>   Do You!—mother of being in me, heart.
> O unteachably after evil, but uttering truth,
> Why, tears! is it? tears;

Like the truth expressed by his unbidden tears, the words "mother of being in me, heart" are also unbidden. That phrase—"mother of being in me, heart"—reads as if it is "soft sift," words completely at one with the emerging self and spoken in a voice that seems wholly unself-conscious, stressless, and without any otherness.

In diametrical opposition to such truths are Hopkins' aphorisms: concentrated, articulated, forethought statements distancing themselves from the voice of the speaker. Centers of gravity, their truth-saying imposes discipline on the poem's motions and stays the poet's impulse for lyrical onrush. But for the most part the aphorism, however true in the poet's and reader's mind, functions in the poem as a place to stay only until the poet can again liberate the voice he has enclosed. The motion of liberation, the motion out of aphorism, is felt again and again, emerging as one of the characteristic and dynamic patterns of Hopkins' poetry.

Desmond Egan (essay date 1994)

SOURCE: "Hopkins' Influence on Poetry," in *Saving Beauty: Further Studies in Hopkins,* edited by Michael E. Allsopp and David Anthony Downes, Garland Publishing, 1994, pp. 59–93.

[*Egan is an Irish poet, critic, and the founder of the Hopkins Society in Ireland. In the following essay, he summarizes Hopkins's influence on several major poets.*]

When we compare the lines from Tennyson's "Requiescat" (pub. 1842):

> Fair is her cottage in its place
> Where yon broad water sweetly slowly glides
> It sees itself from thatch to base
> Dream in the sliding tides.

with these of Spender's poem "Rough" (c. 1930):

> My parents kept me from children who were rough
> Who threw words like stones and who wore torn
>   clothes.
> Their thighs showed through rags. They ran in the
>   street
> And climbed cliffs and stripped by the country
>   streams.

—we can notice a shift in consciousness and in technique. The latter quatrain owes something of its technical structure to Hopkins. To the new way of writing developed by Hopkins.

Owes quite a lot. Tennyson's lines are framed in the old metrics which had nourished poetry in English up to the end of the last century; Spender's on the other hand are in sprung rhythm.

Hopkins' style, in sprung rhythm, played a crucial part, expressed not only his own embodiment of anxiety and hope but also—a great artist does this as indeed Tennyson had done—that of his age. Sprung rhythm seemed a necessary device to Hopkins:

> Because it is the nearest to the rhythm of prose, that is the native and natural rhythm of speech, the least forced, the most rhetorical and emphatic of all possible rhythms, combining, as it seems to me, opposite and, one wd. have thought, incompatible excellences, markedness of rhythm—that is rhythm's self—and naturalness of expression (*Letters* I).

So, "scanning by accents or stresses alone, without any account of the number of syllables" (*Letters* II), will establish the kind of control and fluidity which he wished for. Other secondary tricks of style derive from this need:

inversion of word-order to put the most significant word in the most emphatic position; the coining of compound words; elision of less important relative pronouns, prepositions etc.; his ellipses, heavy alliterations, asyndeton, internal rhyming, far-stepping parentheses and preference for predicates . . . these with his other eccentricities of language derive from his concern for a less literary, more rhetorical or speech-oriented quality and serve as a reminder that, as he put it to Bridges, "My verse is less to be read than heard . . . it is oratorical, that is, the rhythm is so" (*Letters* I).

Hence the "expressive torque" (Hugh Kenner's telling phrase) of Hopkins' best work.

When Whitman introduced free verse into poetry he showed a revolutionary break with the syllable-stress tradition; Hopkins, however, showed how to combine freedom from the formality of the past with a sense of structure. The whole development of twentieth-century poetry traces back to these two progenitors. Whitman's contribution has, of course, been fully acknowledged; that of Hopkins, less so. (Neither of the recent biographies by Robert Bernard Martin and Norman White, for example, exhaustive as they are in other areas, have much to say on this subject though it is important for our understanding of Hopkins' achievement.) Interestingly, Hopkins had confessed in a letter to Bridges in October 1882 that Whitman had a mind, "more like my own than any other man's living" (*Letters* I).

In the same letter he allows that the nineteenth-century French school of landscape painting may trace back to Constable's *The Hay Wain,* which was exhibited in Paris in 1824; Hopkins' own impact on the development of modern verse has proved equally decisive. In two ways: the first (already averted to) that of technique; the other relating to the changing consciousness implicit in any technical revolution—that of philosophy. Hopkins' enormous influence has still not been fully recognized and codified. *Hopkins Among the Poets* (edited by Richard Giles) is a useful collection of short articles on this vast subject but it represents no more than a first step toward the sustained scholarly examination which is appropriate.

For a start, Hopkins' presence can be detected in a number of Robert Bridges' poems: [in *Hopkins among the Poets,* 1985] Donald Stanford counts at least seven borrowings of phrases in Bridges' verse, mostly in his early work. It was through Bridges that Hopkins' influence first showed itself. No doubt this contributed to the vogue in the Thirties for Hopkins' poetry, following the publication of the second edition. Yeats, though he confessed in a letter of 1935 to hating it, nevertheless experimented a little himself in sprung rhythm, notably in his plays, *The Herne's Egg* and *Purgatory.* Even for poets who felt little affinity, Hopkins was in the air, inescapable; and minor figures such as Monk Gibbon and Ivor Gurney (1890-1937) provide early evidence of the Victorian poet's growing modern legacy. William York Tyndall in his book on James Joyce suggests that the Dubliner was quite familiar with Hopkins' poetry. I find this easier to accept than

does Robert Boyle. There were too many points of interest for Joyce to overlook: the Newman connection; the Catholic University; Dublin; and, of course, the literary one. (Padraic Colum who knew Joyce better than most, told me in 1963 that the Jesuit link was one which Joyce valued: to the end of his life he looked on himself as a Jesuit boy.) Certainly in the last chapter of *Finnegans Wake* there is a direct echo of Hopkins' **"That Nature Is a Heraclitean Fire"**:

A flasch and, rasch, it shall come to pasch.

just before the resurrection of Finnegan. There are other echoes too: **"The Windhover," "Tom's Garland," "Heraclitean Fire"** (again), through Joyce's earlier two slim volumes, *Chamber Music* (1907), and *Poems Penyeach* (1927) came too early to have crossed Hopkins' path.

(I am not aware that another Dubliner, Samuel Beckett came under Hopkins' spell although the "terrible sonnets" with their bleakness, their sense of impotence and of failure, and their almost desperate commitment to persevering would surely have interested the Irishman—but Beckett was hardly an avid or systematic reader.)

Ezra Pound never quite got Hopkins in focus—although Hugh Kenner [in his *The Pound Era,* 1971] has spoken of an "eloquent eccentricity of diction akin to Hopkins in Pound's superb but underestimated version of *The Seafarer,* and again in one of the Cantos. [In *Hopkins among the Poets*] Hugh Witemeyer has shown that Pound was actually more interested in Bridges (for a short while) and grumbled, in his *Guide to Kulchur* (1938) that poets had become obsessed with imitating Hopkins.

In his inwardness, his self-consciousness, his modernity, Hopkins fits our age.

—*Desmond Egan*

It was the Modernists of the Auden generation who came strongly under the influence of Gerard Manley Hopkins, though the Hopkins craze had begun in Oxford and Cambridge just before 1930, when the second edition of his poems appeared. Auden himself parodied Hopkins, and when he published *A Certain World* in 1971, the anthology of his favorite writing—which he considered a kind of autobiography—he did not include Hopkins among the writers "from whom I have learned most" (although he did include Bridges). Nevertheless John Boly [in *Hopkins among the Poets*] argues that Auden owed a real debt to Hopkins, "from whom he learned the strategy of using biblically and religiously validated discourse to contend with the romantic repertoire." Comparing **"Thou art indeed just, Lord"** with Auden's "Sir, No Man's Enemy" (1929):

Sir, no man's enemy, forgiving all
But will his negative inversion, be prodigal:
Send to us power and light, a sovereign touch
Curing the intolerable neural itch . . .

Boly points out, "an indebtedness that reveals how he mastered and then extended Hopkins' strategy on very different levels of poetic achievement, I would add, but that's another story. . . ." At any rate, Hopkins had by now become a major force in the shaping of the poetic heritage nourishing the work of modern poets. Stephen Spender, as we have seen, was one such; Edwin Muir (1887-1959) another. Muir, a significant figure in British poetry, came under Hopkins' influence later in his career, but as a critic he also helped to promote the latter's reputation—a significant contribution in the 1930s.

A more important figure—though his somewhat overblown reputation has begun to reduce a little—was the Scottish poet, Hugh MacDiarmid (1892-1978). Hopkins' sense of the inscape, the *haecceitas* or individuality of things derived from, or rather was formulated after, his reading of Duns Scotus; we can catch an echo of this philosophy in MacDiarmid's emphasis on the particularity of an experience; in his statement that:

> Our opponents, Scotist opponents, are the Thomas Aquinas people who are trying to prematurely synthesize, whereas we are continuing to insist upon the individuality of the elements in a particular context.

MacDiarmid confuses Thomist with Scotist—whoever accused Aquinas of being a Scotist—(and is equally cavalier in his treatment of the infinitive), but his meaning comes across. The Scot even more tellingly reveals a debt to Hopkins, the unlikely darling of the Communist poets of the 1930s, in his own prosody, notably in the sprung rhythm he often employs and in other tricks of style which we recognize as Hopkinsian, *e.g.,* heavy alliteration, compound words etc. [In *Hopking among the Poets*] Harvey Oxenhorn argues that "Clearly, MacDiarmid's metrical techniques owe much to his great predecessor." But MacDiarmid's style is so variant and his interest in prosody so low-key that apart from the Scot's use of sprung rhythm it seems difficult to establish such a strong case. In poems such as "In Memoriam James Joyce" (1955) or "Second Hymn to Lenin" (1935), where various authors both loved and hated are mentioned, Hopkins' name does not crop up. Interestingly, MacDiarmid seems to come closer to the Hopkins mode when he writes in the Scots dialect, and here the example taken from Oxenhorn, "The Eemis Stane" (a lyric from *Sangschaw,* the first published collection of 1925) is convincing on many levels:

> I' the how-dumb deid o'the cauld hairst nicht
> The warl' like an eemis stane
> Wags i' the lift;
> An' my eerie memories fa'
> Like a yowdendrift.

David Jones, in Auden's opinion the author of "the greatest long poem written in English in this century," (*The*

Anathemata), was deeply influenced by Hopkins' poetry and wrote admiringly about it on many occasions. Jones, in *Epoch and Artist* (1959) described **The Wreck of the Deutschland** as ". . . a work full of significance for future English poets and one of the most exciting poems in the English language." Twenty years later, Jones saluted Hopkins for "his particular and uniquely important contribution to the common tradition of English poetry [*The Dying Gaul and other Writings,* edited by Herman Grisewood, 1978].

Samuel Rees highlights the affinities between Jones and the Victorian poet and the impact of Hopkins' aesthetic. Though Jones wrote in a different form, idiom, and mostly at greater length, nevertheless his use of language owed much to Hopkins. [In *Hopkins among the Poets*] Thomas Dilworth identifies Hopkins' impact under such headings as: use of ellipsis; compounding; disruption of syntax; alliteration; neologisms and the association of incongruous images. Of particular interest to an Irishman is Jones' belief that because he "felt" Welsh he was able to see through Hopkins' own Welsh influence to the Celtic tradition informing it, with its strange mixture of particularity and sense of the mutability of everything—the special quality of imagination we find, for example, in *The Book of Kells*. A sense of fantasy deriving I believe from the Celtic mystical vision of existence which can allow animals, words and human forms to transmute playfully into one another. Or, as Jones put it in a statement to H.S. Ede (1935), "There should always be a bit of lion in your lamb."

In his native country Hopkins also exerted a significant influence on the poetry of William Empson, and perhaps even more so on that of Elizabeth Jennings, whose poem "Sparrow" echoes Hopkins in more ways than one:

> Sparrow of "special providence" teach to us
> Your joy, your gladness, your success, for you
> Live in accord with that power which moves
> You fast and far. Your flights and pauses bring
> Delight to us. We are not surprised you were
>   chosen
> Specially, for even birds who sing
> With a rapture of angels lack your flare and fling.

Apart from the obvious influence of "Spring," the poems exhibits the even deeper debt of sprung rhythm.

Dylan Thomas certainly learned something from Hopkins, though he denied any conscious influence: David Jones would see the Welsh connection and the deeper Celtic metaphysics as significant links.

In Great Britain then, Hopkins' influence has been crucially important in shaping the technique, assumptions, and development of poetry in this century, so that even those who had little or no interest in his work were influenced indirectly in a fundamental way by him.

Hopkins had a comparable impact on American writing, but it began later, with Roethke, Lowell, Jarrell, Plath, Berryman, and the Modernists. When we compare this:

We chanced in passing by that afternoon
To catch it in a sort of special picture
Among tar-banded ancient cherry trees,
Set well back from the road in rank lodged grass. . . .
              (Robert Frost, "The Black Cottage")

with this:

Oil all my turbulence as at Thy dictation
I sweat out my wayward works.
Father Hopkins said the only true literary critic is
   Christ.
Let me lie down exhausted, content with that. . . .
          (Berryman, "Eleven Addresses to the Lord." 10)

we can sense that the lines by Frost, for all that they catch something of the speaking voice in tone and movement, are framed loosely within standard metrical forms; those by Berryman, on the contrary, are composed in sprung rhythm.

Indeed John Berryman (1914-1972), most of whose poetry tries to reconcile the need for a colloquial freedom with an equal desire for orderly structure (something that derives from Berryman's Catholic upbringing, in my opinion), was very obviously influenced by Hopkins: not surprisingly, in view of Berryman's obsession with style. Typical Berryman devices (especially in the *Dream Song* sonnets) include: ellipsis, omission of prepositions, conjunctions, relatives; straining syntax, including long separation of verb from object and interruptions with exclamations; and inversion of word order.

The shadow of Hopkins is here—so much so that when I was working, enthralled awhile by Berryman's example, on my own first collection of poetry *Midland* (1972), the Irish poet and critic Thomas Kinsella was able to see through the style of some of my poems to Hopkins—even though I was not then a Hopkins fan at all. In his Notes for Berryman's *Collected Poems: 1937-1971* (1991), Charles Thornbury comments on Berryman's use of the archaic "estop" in "The Dispossessed" that:

One of the functions of the poet, Berryman believed, is to disrupt our expectations of language so that we are given a new angle of perception.

Or, as Berryman himself puts it, in words which would have struck a chord with Hopkins:

Nouns, verbs do not exist for what I feel.
                                        (*Epilogue*)

Berryman was arguably the finest poet of his generation and exerted an enormous influence on the course of American poetry both then and since (Lowell's *Notebook* [1970] is little more than pastiche Berryman, for example), and "Father Hopkins" was arguably the poet who mattered most to Berryman.

Robert Lowell also came under the influence of Hopkins via the New Critics (Ransom, Eliot, Richards, Empson, Tate, and Winters) who trumpeted the Jesuit's poetry between the Wars. Steven Axelrod who has written about the subject in *Hopkins Among the Poets,* picks out a number of poems where Hopkins' influence is clear and relates *The Quaker Graveyard in Nantucket* to **The Wreck of the Deutschland** in terms of theme, treatment, and technique. Though Lowell later moves away from Hopkins, the latter does figure again in two of Lowell's confessional poems: "Skunk Hour" (1959), and "Night Sweat" (1964), in Lowell's parodying Hopkins in the latter (a double sonnet) in which the American finally tries to recover his independence, Axelrod argues, "by transforming the anxiety of influence into the aggression of parody."

Another American poet who fell under Hopkins' spell was Theodore Roethke. And even if, like Lowell, he moved away from that, he later returned to the "terrible sonnets" and some of his own dark poems show an indebtedness to Hopkins though a well-assimilated one.

Other Americans who crossed the Hopkins path in one way or another include Cummings, Randall Jarrell, Thomas Merton (a great influence here), and Sylvia Plath. Jon Rosenblatt in his study of Plath [*Sylvia Plath: The Poetry of Initiation,* 1979] highlights the quasi-religious element in the later poetry and also suggests that Plath's style, with its combination of emotional exuberance and formal control (which included such Hopkinsian devices as heavy alliteration, assonance, jerky rhythmic effects, and piling-up related ideas) owed no small debt to the English poet.

Gerard Manley Hopkins also exerted a powerful influence on Irish poetry. His presence may be detected in various ways in the work of Cecil Day-Lewis, Eugene Watters (who wrote in Irish as Eoghan O Tuairisc, and who was the most eclectic of his generation), Patrick Kavanagh (the only major Irish poet since Yeats), Michael Hartnett, Seamus Heaney, Desmond O'Grady . . . and indeed of myself. Heaney began as a slavish imitator, but even a 1979 collection reveals an influence not wholly assimilated and at odds with a plodding iambic pentameter more old-fashioned than Hopkins:

sirens of the tundra,
Of eel-road, seal-road, keel-road, whale-road raise
Their wind-compounded keen behind the baize.
                                  (*Glanmore Sonnets*)

Patrick Kavanagh—that towering figure whose reputation has continued to grow since his death in 1967—learned something from Hopkins both in terms of technique and approach. Kavanagh admired Hopkins' style and took from it a certain freshness of language and of syntax which shows itself in such devices as the formation of compound nouns and adjectives, occasional omission of unimportant words, the use of dramatic interjection, a readiness to cóin words or to push them to new use, and a willingness to find, "God's breath in common statement" ("Advent")—even to the point of using "religious" imagery in a secular sense. This last example highlights how, most importantly of all, Hopkins' example encouraged Kavanagh to give full expression to his own mystical sense of God's presence in the world—as in a poem like "Advent" or in the beautiful canal-sonnets:

> Leafy-with-love banks and the green waters of the
> canal
> Pouring redemption for me, that I do
> The will of God, wallow in the habitual, the banal,
> Grow with nature again as before I grew.
> The bright stick trapped, the breeze adding a third
> Party to the couple kissing on an old seat,
> And a bird gathering materials for the nest for the
> Word
> Eloquently new and abandoned to its delirious beat.
> O unworn world enrapture me, encapture me in a
> web
> Of fabulous grass and eternal voices by a beech,
> Feed the gaping need of my senses, give me ad lib
> To pray unselfconsciously with overflowing speech
> For this soul needs to be honoured with a new
> dress woven
> From green and blue things and arguments that
> cannot be Proven.
>
> ("Canal Bank Walk")

There is no anxiety in this influence. Though Hopkins' shadow lies there, Kavanagh's own voice is strong and unique enough to assimilate the audaciousness of his predecessor and turn it to his own purposes. Even the final couplet from "Lines Written on a Seat on the Grand Canal" which has been reproduced on the Kavanagh seat and which acts as kind of epitaph, owes something to Hopkins:

> O commemorate me with no hero-courageous
> Tomb—just a canal-bank seat for the passer-by.

Kavanagh in turn has had a major impact on modern Irish poetry.

Hopkins' influence as it spread around other countries has yet to be explored and certainly lies beyond my ken. In Nigeria, for example, Hopkins became such a dominant influence that an exasperated critic referred to it as "The Hopkins Disease" [Emeke Okeke-Ezigbo, in *Hopkins among the Poets*].

While it is easy to see Pound's influence on the work of priest/politician/poet Ernesto Cardenal of Nicaragua, I think that Hopkins has left his mark there too. And writing about Canadian poetry, John Ferns concludes, "Gerard Manley Hopkins had and has, I believe, a significant creative influence among Canadian poets," citing A. J. M. Smith and Ralph Gustafson (like Cardenal, another Poundian) as particular examples.

We can safely say that the influence of Hopkins on twentieth-century poetry in English has been enormous. I have concentrated on the stylistic, but Hopkins' has been more than just a matter of technical influence, crucial though that be. The more subtle matter of his revitalization of the language, just when English poetry needed it, must be

acknowledged; and the incalculable filtering of that newness into the consciousness of twentieth-century poetry. Hopkins' dislocations of syntax, nervous rhythms, and straining after expression do make heavy demands of us and, as W. H. Gardner puts it [in *The Poems of Gerard Manley Hopkins*, 1970] "do at times subject both the language and the reader to a strain all but disastrous." But Hopkins himself deals with that objection when he relays to Bridges:

> Obscurity I do and will try to avoid so far as it is consistent with excellences higher than clearness at a first reading (*Letters* I).

Returning to the subject nearly ten years later, he produces the clinching argument:

> Plainly if it be possible to express subtle and recondite thought on a subtle and recondite subject in a subtle and recondite way and with great felicity and perfection, the end, something must be sacrificed, with so trying a task, in the process, and this may be the being at once, nay perhaps even the being without explanation at all, intelligible (*Letters* I).

The assumptions behind this have had a vital bearing on the development of poetry. For one thing, Hopkins takes it for granted that musicality is not a defining principle of poetry; for another, he assumes that a poem represents an all-out attempt to capture in words the complexity of experience: an effort to *say something*. This philosophy—deriving partly from a Scotist reverence for the *quidditas* of things—distinguishes Hopkins' attitude to Nature from that of the Romantics. The result? David Downes puts it with real insight in his study *The Ignation Personality of Gerard Manley Hopkins*:

> That is why we think of Wordsworth as a poet of the poet's nature rather than a poet of Nature.

Hopkins accepted the intensity of existence and tried to express it as directly as he could, forcing language to go its way rather than vice versa. Such a rationale has special appeal for the modern writer, and poetry has tended towards severity and directness of utterance in which one prefers to avoid figurative speech and adjectival labelling: has tended towards the death of metaphor. For Hopkins (as for Patrick Kavanagh) such immediacy of acceptance was easier because of his mystical sense of God's presence in the world; for other writers of our century, caught by an awareness of chaos rather than of order, it had a different appeal. But the note of objectivity had been struck and heard:

> I caught this morning morning's minion, kingdom
> of daylight's dauphin,
> dapple-dawn-drawn Falcon, in his riding
> Of the rolling level underneath him steady air, and
> striding
> High there, how he rung upon the rein of a
> wimpling wing
> In his ecstasy! then off, off forth on wing.

There is a shift of consciousness here, as much as of technique; the emergence of a sensibility we have come to recognize as modern: in his inwardness, his self-consciousness, his modernity, Hopkins fits our age.

Not only that, but Hopkins' own experience seemed to reflect in advance something of the collapse of the old certainties of Victorian England and—with his gnawing sense of impotence, of being "time's eunuch" alienated in a life which did not seem to make sense and in which blind endurance appeared as the only grim option, he seems both to have anticipated the existential *angst* of the twentieth century and to have helped make its articulation possible. From,

> O the mind, mind has mountains; cliffs of fall
> Frightful, sheer, no-man-fathomed. Hold them cheap
> May who ne'er hung there. Nor does long our small
> Durance deal with that steep or deep. Here! creep,
> Wretch, under a comfort serves in a whirlwind: all
> Life death does end and each day dies with sleep.
>   **("No Worst, There Is None")**

—to Beckett's;

> Where I am I don't know, I'll never know, in the
>   silence
> you don't know,
> you must go on, I can't go on, I'll go on.
>   ("The Unnameable")

seems a lot closer than the three-quarters of a century which separates them.

FURTHER READING

Bibliography

Dunne, Tom. *Gerard Manley Hopkins: A Comprehensive Bibliography.* Oxford: Clarendon Press, 1976, 394 p.
Lists Hopkins scholarship through 1970.

Biography

Bump, Jerome. *Gerard Manley Hopkins.* Boston: Twayne Publishers, 1982, 225 p.
Biography with some critical commentary.

Lahey, G. F., S.J. *Gerard Manley Hopkins.* London: Oxford University Press, 1930, 172 p.
The first full-length biographical study of Hopkins.

Criticism

Allsopp, Michael E. and Downes, David Anthony, ed. *Saving Beauty: Further Studies in Hopkins.* New York: Garland

Publishing, 1994, 351 p.
Collection of critical essays on Hopkins's work.

Andreach, Robert J. "Gerard Manley Hopkins." In his *Studies in Structure: The Stages of the Spiritual Life in Four Modern Authors*, pp. 12-39. New York: Fordham University Press, 1964.
Traces Hopkins's spiritual development as evidenced in his poems.

Assad, Thomas J. "A Closer Look at Hopkins' `(Carrier Comfort).'" *Tulane Studies* 9 (1959): 91-102.
Explores the "overthought"—the literal meaning—of "Carrion Comforter," noting that while intensive critical attention has been given to the "underthought" of the poem, its "overthought" has not been adequately addressed.

Bender, Todd K. *Gerard Manley Hopkins: The Classical Background and Critical Reception of His Work.* Baltimore: Johns Hopkins Press, 1966, 172 p.
Posits that Hopkins's poetic innovations were at least partly derived from his classical and religious training.

Bottrall, Margaret, ed. *Gerard Manley Hopkins, Poems: A Casebook.* Casebook Series, edited by A. E. Dyson. London: Macmillan Press, 1975, 256 p.
Collection of critical essays on Hopkins's work.

Boyle, Robert, S.J. *Metaphor in Hopkins.* Chapel Hill University of North Carolina Press, 1960, 231 p.
Analyzes Hopkins's use of metaphor in his poetry.

Bump, Jerome. "Hopkins and Keats." *Victorian Poetry* 12, No. 1 (Spring 1974): 33-43.
Determines the influence of Keats on Hopkins's development as a poet.

Cotter, James Finn. "Inscaping *The Wreck of the Deutschland.*" *Renascence* 21, No. 3 (Spring 1969): 124-33, 166.
Offers a thematic and stylistic analysis of *The Wreck of the Deutschland.*

Deutsch, Babette. "The Forgèd Feature." In her *Poetry in Our Time*, pp. 286-311. New York: Columbia University Press, 1952.
Provides an overview of Hopkins' poetry.

Downes, David Anthony. *Gerard Manley Hopkins: A Study of His Ignatian Spirit.* New York: Bookman Associates, 1959, 195 p.
Studies Hopkins's poetry as an expression of Jesuit spirituality.

Ellsberg, Margaret. *Created to Praise: The Language of Gerard Manley Hopkins.* London: Oxford University Press, 1987, 160 p.
Explores Hopkins's use of language as a reflection of the tension between his vocations of poet and priest.

Fausset, Hugh I'Anson. "Gerard Hopkins: A Centenary Tribute." In his *Poets and Pundits: Essays and Addresses*,

pp. 96-113. London: Jonathan Cape, 1947.
Discusses the fundamental principles of Hopkins' poetry.

Foltz, William D. "Hopkins' Greek Fire." *Victorian Poetry* 18, No. 1 (Spring 1980): 23-34.
Provides a close reading of "That Nature is a Heraclitean Fire and of the Comfort of the Resurrection."

Gardner, W.H. "*The Wreck of the Deutschland.*" *Essays and Studies* XXI (1935): 125-52.
Offers a general reading of *The Wreck of the Deutschland*, arguing that the poem has "a completeness, an intellectual and emotional unity, a subtlety and variety of verbal orchestration which are unique not only in English but in the literature of the world."

Hallgarth, Susan A. "A Study of Hopkins' Use of Nature." *Victorian Poetry* 5, No. 1 (Spring 1967): 79-92.
Contends that Hopkins use of nature in his work differs from that of his contemporaries.

Hartmann, Geoffrey H. "Hopkins." In his *The Unmediated Vision: An Interpretation of Wordsworth, Hopkins, Rilke, and Valery*, pp. 49–67. New Haven: Yale University Press, 1954.
Offers a close reading of "The Windhover."

————, ed. *Hopkins: A Collection of Critical Essays.* Englewood Cliffs, N.J.: A Spectrum Book, 1966, 182 p.
Includes critical studies on Hopkins by several major scholars.

Heaney, Seamus. "The Fire i' the Flint: Reflections on the Poetry of Gerard Manley Hopkins." In his *Preoccupations: Selected Prose, 1968–1978*, pp. 79-97. New York: Fararr, Straus, Giroux, 1980.
Analyzes the composition of Hopkins's poetry, contending that "as opposed to the symbolist poetic, it is concerned with statement instead of states of feeling."

The Kenyon Critics. *Gerard Manley Hopkins.* The Makers of Modern Literature Series. Norfolk, Conn.: New Directions Books, 1945, 144 p.
Influential essays by Austin Warren, Herbert Marshall McLuhan, Harold Whitehall, Josephine Miles, Robert Lowell, Arthur Mizener, and F. R. Leavis. Most of these essays first appeared in the *Kenyon Review* in 1944.

Mackenzie, Norman. "Genius and Jobations." *Thought* 65, No. 259 (December 1990): 500-09.
Examines the factors that might have contributed to Hopkins' poetic eccentricities.

Milward, Peter, S.J., ed. *Readings of "The Wreck": Essays in the Commemoration of the Centenary of G. M. Hopkins' "The Wreck of the Deutschland."* Chicago: Loyola University Press, 1976, 172 p.
A selection of essays on "The Wreck of the Deutschland."

Motto, Marylou. *"Mined with a Motion": The Poetry of Gerard Manley Hopkins.* New Brunswick, N.J.: Rutgers University Press, 1984, 203 p.
Studies "the motions of voice" in the poetry of Hopkins.

Murphy, Michael W. "Violent Imagery in the Poetry of Gerard Manley Hopkins." *Victorian Poetry* 7, No. 1 (Spring 1969): 1-16.
Examines the violent imagery found in Hopkins verse, maintaining that these images "are the source of the tense, masculine, energetic quality which characterizes much of Hopkins's poetry."

O'Neill, George, S.J. "Gerard Hopkins." In his *Essays on Poetry*, pp. 117-38. Dublin: Talbot, 1919.
Discusses the odd and obscure aspects of Hopkins's poetry.

Phare, Elsie Elizabeth. *The Poetry of Gerard Manley Hopkins: A Survey and Commentary.* Cambridge: Cambridge University Press, 1933, 150 p.
Deals with the form and meaning of several of Hopkins's poems, with emphasis on his use of imagery.

Plotkin, Cary H. *The Tenth Muse: Victorian Philology and the Genesis of the Poetic Language of Gerard Manley Hopkins.* Carbondale: Southern Illinois University Press, 203 p.
Explores the relationship between Hopkins' poetic and philological activities, situating his work in the context of mid-nineteenth century debates about language.

Read, Herbert. "Inscape and Gestalt: Hopkins." In his *The True Voice of Feeling: Studies in English Romantic Poetry*, pp. 76-86. New York: Pantheon, 1953.
Argues that Hopkins' theories about poetry surpass most of the theories of poetry advanced in the nineteenth century.

Smith, Francis J., S.J. "Hopkins' Best Poem." *Victorian Newsletter* 83 (Spring 1993): 22-4.
Provides a stylistic analysis of "The Windhover."

Stonier, G. W. "Gerard Manley Hopkins." In his *Gog Magog and Other Critical Essays*, pp. 43-63. Reprint. Freeport, N.Y.: Books for Libraries Press, 1966.
Asserts that Hopkins's finest poetry was a result of his conflict between art and religion.

Sutherland, Donald. "Hopkins Again." *Prairie Schooner* 35, No. 3 (Fall 1961): 197-242.
Classifies Hopkins's poetry as baroque.

Wagner, Jennifer A. "The Allegory of Form in Hopkins' Religious Sonnets." *Nineteenth-Century Literature* 47, No. 1 (June 1992): 32-48.
Analyzes Hopkins's radical experimentation in meter and poetic form.

Walker, Ralph S. "An Introduction to the Poetry of Gerard Manley Hopkins." *The Aberdeen University Review* XXV, No. 15, (July 1938): 232-43.
Stresses the personal nature of Hopkins's poetry.

Weyand, Norman, S.J., ed. *Immortal Diamond: Studies in Gerard Manley Hopkins.* New York: Sheed & Ward, 1949, 451 p.

A collection of essays by Jesuit scholars on various aspects of Hopkins's work.

Wheeler, Michael. "Hopkins: *The Wreck of the Deutschland.*" In his *Death and the Future Life in Victorian Literature and Theology*, pp. 340–66. Cambridge: Cambridge University Press, 1990.

Explores the themes of death and future life in *The Wreck of the Deutschland* in terms of its specifically Roman Catholic content.

Additional coverage of Hopkins' life and career is contained in the following sources published by Gale Research: *Concise Dictionary of British Literary Biography*, 1890-1914; *DISCovering Authors*; *Dictionary of Literary Biography*, Vols. 35, 57; and *World Literature Criticism.*

Maxine Kumin
1925–

(Full name Maxine Winokur Kumin) American poet, novelist, short fiction writer, essayist, and author of children's books.

INTRODUCTION

Kumin is a Pulitzer Prize-winning poet whose verse often portrays the simple workings of day-to-day life at her Warner, New Hampshire, farm. Animals, children, the seasons, and neighbors are recurring subjects. Often classified as a transcendentalist, Kumin probes the human relationship to nature and celebrates the redemptive qualities of the natural world. Her writing has been compared to that of her late close friend, Anne Sexton, and in some aspects to the work of Sylvia Plath. Like Sexton, Kumin writes personal poems that focus on the inner lives of her characters. Unlike Sexton or Plath, however, she does not dwell on despair; thus, she is known for her survival poems.

Biographical Information

Kumin was born in Philadelphia, Pennsylvania. She earned a B.A. and an M.A. from Radcliffe College in 1946 and 1948 respectively, and married Victor Kumin in 1946. While awaiting the birth of her third child, she began to write children's stories. Her writing interests evolved to include poetry, novels, short fiction, and essays. She found encouragement for her writing at the Boston Center for Adult Education, where she met and befriended poet Anne Sexton. Kumin and Sexton's friendship was important to both women's poetry. The former possessed a technical ability honed from study; the latter wrote with a raw voice that was brilliantly fresh. They phoned each other daily, often writing a poem after ending the phone call. Each call was another session in their own continual workshopping. In fact, Sexton titled Kumin's *Up Country: Poems of New England*, and Kumin titled Sexton's *Transformations*. Kumin has received the most acclaim for her poetry, winning the Lowell Mason Palmer Award in 1960, a National Endowment for the Arts grant in 1966, and ultimately, the Pulitzer Prize for *Up Country* in 1973. Since 1958, she has served many distinguished posts as teacher, lecturer, and visiting fellow or artist; she was a consultant to the Library of Congress from 1981 to 1982. She continues to live on her farm in New Hampshire, tending to her horses and gardens.

Major Works

Halfway, her first collection of verse, was published in 1961 when Kumin was thirty-six and deals with topics she

has explored throughout her career: religious and cultural identity; the tenuousness of human life; loss or the threat of loss; and the human in relation to nature. Lessons learned in girlhood are always present in Kumin's work. The poet also searches for order in her poetry; she stated in an interview with Martha George Meek that ". . . there is an order to be discovered—that's very often true in the natural world—but there is also an order that a human can impose on the chaos of his emotions and the chaos of events. That's what writing poetry is all about." Highly personal material, another hallmark of Kumin's work, comes to life in *The Privilege*. The ties and separations inherent in families, especially "the privilege" of being a member of a family, are explored. In some of the poems of *Up Country* Kumin adopts the persona of a male hermit to particularize the universal solitude of man in nature. She continues in this vein with *House, Bridge, Fountain, Gate*. This volume's title, which originated from a quote from Rainer Maria Rilke, reflects Kumin's style of naming things in nature that are often overlooked. For her fastidious naming Kumin has been compared to Henry David Thoreau. Another volume that exhibits thoughtful naming is *The Retrieval System*, which was written as a memorial to Anne Sexton, who killed herself in 1974. Like *The Retrieval System*, *The Long Approach* and *Looking for Luck* reflect Kumin's experience of aging as well as her steadfast hope for chance encounters with the beneficence of all living things. Some of Kumin's pastoral themes in *Nurture* shift into the political realm: the earth and its inhabitants should be "nurtured," not endangered.

Critical Reception

Kumin's poetry has generally been favorably reviewed since her first book of verse appeared. Critics have noted that the poet's best poems in *The Privilege* are those that evoke her own childhood. In a review of *Up Country* in the 1973 Spring-Summer issue of *Parnassus*, Ralph J. Mills quoted John Ciardi: "[Kumin] teaches me, by example, to use my own eyes. When she looks at something I have seen, she makes me see it better. When she looks at something I do not know, I therefore trust her." Similarly, *The Long Approach* has been praised for Kumin's customary success in depicting the details of New England life. However, some of the poems in that volume and in *Nurture* have been criticized for venturing programmatically into social issues, an arena considered by some too large for Kumin's private voice. It is at such times that many critics feel she slips into blatant metaphor and prosaic lines of summation. But poet and reviewer Diane Wakoski defended Kumin as "best at . . . [m]aking images, wonderful images, that turn into big metaphors. Playing with dualities, and manipulating everyday language so that it works with complexity of idea and pattern."

PRINCIPAL WORKS

Poetry

Halfway 1961
The Privilege 1965
The Nightmare Factory 1970
Up Country: Poems of New England 1972
House, Bridge, Fountain, Gate 1975
The Retrieval System 1978
Our Ground Time Here Will Be Brief: New and Selected Poems 1982
Closing the Ring: Selected Poems 1984
The Long Approach 1985
Nurture 1989
Looking for Luck 1992
Connecting the Dots 1996

Other Major Works

Sebastian and the Dragon (juvenilia) 1960
Follow the Fall (juvenilia) 1961
Spring Things (juvenilia) 1961
A Summer Story (juvenilia) 1961
A Winter Friend (juvenilia) 1961
Mittens in May (juvenilia) 1962
No One Writes a Letter to the Snail (juvenilia) 1962

Archibald the Traveling Poodle (juvenilia) 1963
Eggs of Things [with Anne Sexton] (juvenilia) 1963
The Beach Before Breakfast (juvenilia) 1964
More Eggs of Things [with Anne Sexton] (juvenilia) 1964
Speedy Deigs Downside Up (juvenilia) 1964
Through Dooms of Love (novel) 1965; published in England as *A Daughter and Her Loves* 1965
Paul Bunyan (juvenilia) 1966
Faraway Farm (juvenilia) 1967
The Passions of Uxport (novel) 1968
The Wonderful Babies of 1809 and Other Years (juvenilia) 1968
When Grandmother Was Young (juvenilia) 1969
When Mother Was Young (juvenilia) 1970
The Abduction (novel) 1971
Joey and the Birthday Present [with Anne Sexton] (juvenilia) 1971
When Great-Grandmother Was Young (juvenilia) 1971
The Designated Heir (novel) 1974
The Wizard's Tears [with Anne Sexton] (juvenilia) 1975
What Color Is Caesar? (juvenilia) 1978
To Make a Prairie: Essays on Poets, Poetry, and Country Living (essays) 1980
Why Can't We Live Together Like Civilized Human Beings? (short fiction) 1982
The Microscope (juvenilia) 1984
In Deep: Country Essays (essays) 1987
Women, Animals, and Vegetables (essays and short stories) 1994

CRITICISM

William Dickey (essay date 1961)

SOURCE: "Revelations and Homilies," in *Poetry*, Vol. XCIX, No. 2, November, 1961, pp. 124-29.

[*Dickey was an American educator and poet who served as the Poetry Consultant to the Library of Congress, 1966-1968. In the following review of* Halfway, *he comments that "Kumin is more successful in personal poems than in those which attempt public stances."*]

[Maxine Kumin] defines her intention and accomplishment in a few lines from **"The Moment Clearly"**:

> Write, saying this much clearly:
> Nearly all, this is nearly all,
> The small sounds of growing, the impress
> Of unarrested time, raising
> The prized moment.

The realizations [of **Halfway**] are small, but they become important by reason of the care and precision with which they are expressed. Picking up her book and looking at the first poem, one might suppose that the images were going to be arbitrary. "Isosceles of knees" the poem starts, but it goes on "my boys and girls sit / cross-legged in blue

July / and finger the peel / of their sun-killed skin". The images return always to a strict visual accuracy; behind the startling word lies its solid justification. Consider Miss Kumin on bats: "until the terrible mouse with wings / notched like bread knives came skittering / down the chimney next to my bed". Or on travelling northward after a spring funeral in the south: "Homeward, the spendthrift streams pursed their mouths, / the trees unfleshed, the ground locked up its ruts, / and farther, death belonged / in this place. Weeks late, the rotten ice went out."

Miss Kumin is more successful in personal poems than in those which attempt public stances, as do **"Eleventh Century Doors,"** and **"For Anne at Passover."** She is wiser, too, when she avoids complex formal exercises; maybe all sestinas now have a slight lab-specimen smell. At her worst she can be trivially humorous, but she is seldom at her worst, and her humor can also show a grim sardonic force. I would be happy to have this book if only for **"Fräulein Reads Instructive Rhymes"**; I am happier yet to have it for **"The Lunar Probe."**

> Long before morning they waked me to say
> the moon was undone; had blown out, sky high,
> swelled fat as a fat pig's bladder, fit
> to burst, and then the underside had split.
>
> I had been dreaming this dream seven nights
> before it bore fruit (there is nothing so sweet
> to a prophet as forethought come true). They had
>   meant
> merely to prick when . . . good-bye, good intent!
>
> Dozing, I saw the sea stopper its flux,
> dogs freeze in mid-howl, women wind up their
>   clocks,
> lunatics everywhere sane as their keepers.
>
> I have not dreamed since in this nation of sleepers.

Dabney Stuart (essay date 1966)

SOURCE: "Weights and Measures," in *Shenandoah,* Vol. XVII, No. 2, Winter, 1966, pp. 91-102.

[*Stuart is an American educator and poet, and has served as poetry editor and eventually editor-in-chief of* Shenandoah *since 1976. Below, he admires Kumin's control of her subject matter, the domain of childhood, in* The Privilege.]

[T]he title of Mrs. Kumin's collection, ***The Privilege,*** [is taken] from one of Joseph Conrad's letters. The passage she cites closes, "One must drag the ball and chain of one's selfhood to the end. It is the price one pays for the devilish and divine privilege of thought."

For Mrs. Kumin, as the Conrad quote implies, the privilege is also a burden, and the poems in her book have an amazing internal balance of both these evaluations of

consciousness. Balance and control are central achievements of her poetry, won by an unflinching attempt to "bear out hope to the edge of pain."

It is impossible to communicate by commentary the world these poems make. It is a big world, a world of the self and the self's connections to things which help create it— parents, childhood, class, religion, war, space, love, domesticity. It is filled with dread and terror as well as expectancy, humor and praise. It is a world whose minutest details are observed with precision, whose smallest inhabitants are treated with purpose. Perhaps it is enough to say that *The Privilege* fulfills art's humblest and most difficult intention—to create a world within whose limitations a compelling and intelligent identity can realize itself. Specifically, the terms of Mrs. Kumin's world include, among others, the convent and the pawnshop, which become emblematic of Christianity and Judaism, two forces which were important in her childhood; and the cyclic experience of being a child and having children, from which comes a perspective on the loss of one's own parents and friends.

Though taking them out of context necessarily dissipates their effect, I want to quote a few passages to illustrate, finally, the kind of formal control Mrs. Kumin exercises upon these raw materials, emphasizing rather than destroying their force. One learns the power of a stallion more by trying to guide him than by letting him run free.

From **"Prothalamion,"** in which a tennis game is used figuratively in the direction the title suggests:

> We improve each other, quickening so by noon
> That the white game moves itself, the universe
> contracted to the edge of the dividing line
> you toe against, limbering for your service,
> arm up, swiping the sun time after time,
> and the square I live in, measured out with lime.

The first two stanzas of **"This Praying Fool"**:

> A prayer for a bad time
> ought, *pro forma,*
> to have God in it—
> a name, an apostrophe, Someone
> for *hasten the day*
> or *deliver me.*
>
> *Lord, Lord*
> for the children
> who turn in a little boat in bed,
> all-night sailors,
> while Mother and Father
> bob in the next room,
> already at anchor
> in the only harbor.

The penultimate stanza of **"The Pawnbroker"**;

> Firsthand I had from my father a love ingrown
> tight as an oyster, and returned it

as secretly. From him firsthand
the grace of work, the sweat of it, the bone-
tired unfolding down from stress.
I was the bearer he paid up on demand
with one small pearl of selfhood. Portionless,
I am oystering still to earn it.

Feet in the mud, Lady, fingers prying that tight, grinding
secret, keep on. Keep on.

Robert Wallace (essay date 1966)

SOURCE: "Down from the Forked Hill Unsullied," in
Poetry, Vol. CVIII, No. 2, May, 1966, pp. 121-24.

[*Wallace is an American educator and poet. In the following excerpt, he lauds* The Privilege *for its direct language.*]

Maxine Kumin's new poems [in **The Privilege**] are superb. She hardly makes a mistake. Her language always
catches the world into the poem, is deliciously prosy, direct, surprising—"fog thick as terry cloth"—as are her
strategies, which permit beginning a poem:

> The symbol inside this poem is my father's feet
> which, after fifty years of standing behind
> the counter waiting on trade,
> were tender and smooth and lay on the ironed sheet,
> a study of white on white, like a dandy's shirt.

Childhood and now, the halves of her world mirror equally
a vision of the isolation and enchantment of selfhood: in the
remembered games, streets, convent school, legless man
"who came / inside a little cart, inchmeal, / flatirons on his
hands, downhill"; in the adult lovers, "oyster killers who
live in a world / of sundown and gin and shellfish", and
cannot afford to count their "own small gift of bones"; in
fighting for sleep "by lying down" ("but the Walden of my
mind / fills up with berry pickers"); in the gin for a lady
dining on the past at the Ritz:

> It is much darker than that.
>
> She has come to the Ritz
> with dirty toes.
> Nothing she knows is dinner talk.
> Mother presses the buzzer.
> Father blesses the bread and pinches up salt.
> No one may cry at the table.

In **"Quarry, Pigeon Cove,"** "a makeshift amphibian",
"breathing out silver ball bearings", she dives into the city
that "waited, / hung upside down in the quarry" and

> might have swum down looking
> soundlessly into nothing,
> down stairways and alleys of nothing
> until the city took notice
> and made me its citizen,

except that life stirred overhead.
I looked up. A dog walked over me.

A dog was swimming and splashing.
Air eggs nested in his fur.

Joyce Carol Oates (essay date 1972)

SOURCE: "One for Life, One for Death," in *The New
York Times Book Review,* November 19, 1972, pp. 7, 14.

[*Oates is a prolific American educator, author, and critic. In the review below, she compares* Up Country *to Sylvia
Plath's* Winter Trees, *remarking on the similarities and
differences between the poets' writings and concluding
that "one book affirms life; the other affirms death."*]

Read together, these two excellent books cause us to ask
ourselves one of the riddles of life: Why is the experience
of one human being so vastly different from that of another? Why, in two sensitive, intelligent, gifted women poets
should the energies of art be so differently employed?
Where one discovers in nature a "presence" of "something
else that went before" (Kumin in **"The Presence"**), the
other discovers a helpless "blue dissolve" and shadows
"chanting, but easing nothing" (Plath in "Winter Trees").
Where one does not shy away from "populating symptoms" or from the stunning horrors of a physical world
gone into error, the other acquiesces to the symptoms, the
horrors, "the shriek in the bath, / The cloak of holes"
(Plath, "Purdah")—and seems perversely to honor them,
to insist upon them, to refuse to make any judgment that
might transpose the mysteries of nature into an adult, human
art.

Maxine Kumin's book acknowledges its debt to Thoreau,
though in my opinion Kumin's poetry gives us a sharp-
edged, unflinching and occasionally nightmarish subjectivity exasperatingly absent in Thoreau. The most valuable, because most powerful, statements of the transcendental experience are those rooted firmly in existence,
however private or eccentric. We are ready to believe
Miss Kumin's energetic praises of nature, her insistence
upon her own place in it—"we teem, we overgrow . . . we
are making a run for it"—because we have suffered along
with her the contraction of the universe to a child's nighttime horror of bats, her occasional despair, her speculations upon forms of mortality in an old burying ground.
When, in the book's final poem, she states firmly that
"We have our own constants" and "To be reasonable is to
let go," we are fully prepared to believe her. The experience of *Up Country*'s 42 poems is dramatic and visionary, but above all convincing.

The setting is rural New England, but the imagination is
boundless. Miss Kumin gets into the mind of a hermit
whose dog has been sprayed by a skunk ("Skunk is the
mother bed, the ripe taste / of carrion, the green kiss"),
she amuses us with an old handbook of "simples" (home
remedies for ailments), she dramatizes mud ("An army /

of lips works in its own ocean"), she effortlessly condemns the eating of meat, she takes us through a distinctively feminine / female experience of temporary loss, in which we hear not Anne Sexton's voice so much as the common, universal woman's voice that Sexton so powerfully dramatizes in her own way. Any group of poems that deal with nature is more or less committed to the honoring of cycles, the birth / death / birth wheel, the phenomenon of creatures giving way to creatures, "the pond's stillness . . . pocked with life" (**"Creatures"**); yet no poem really repeats another's theme, and it is a formidable feat for Miss Kumin to have attempted such a variety of points of view, none of them strained or artificial.

A typical success is **"Turning To,"** in which love forces the poet to think of Death "in these connections" and to imagine herself and her lover as frogs. They must die, presumably, but "Meanwhile / let us cast one shadow / in air or water" . . . "Let us turn to, until / the giant flashlight / comes down on us / and we are rammed home on the corkscrew gig / one at a time /and lugged off belly to belly." *Up Country* demonstrates beautifully how the transcendental vision is really the vision of imaginative existential life, available to anyone who seeks it. . . .

Both Sylvia Plath and Maxine Kumin would passionately affirm Thoreau's declaration "Be it life or death, we crave only reality." And both have investigated thoroughly the relationships between the self and the otherness of both an external environment and an interior, bewildering depthless world of the psyche. Yet one book affirms life; the other affirms death. We are ultimately mysterious to ourselves, as much as we are to one another. But perhaps we may say, hopefully, audaciously, that the "winter trees" of our experience make up one part—but only one part—of the "up country" of our time.

Victor Howes   (essay date 1973)

SOURCE: A review of *Up Country,* in *The Christian Science Monitor,* Vol. 65, No. 79, February 28, 1973, p. 9.

[*In the following review, Howes praises the "country ways" of* Up Country.]

Maxine Kumin is a poet attuned to country ways. She is heir to a tradition of pastoral poetry that reaches back through Robert Frost and Thomas Hardy all the way to its rural beginnings in Theocritus. Nature poetry, she comes to tell us, is alive and well and sinking its taproots in New Hampshire soil.

Whether she writes of a woodlot in winter, tadpoles hatching in the spring, of berrypicking or a night visit from a mosquito, she brings to her page what Wordsworth called "the harvest of a quiet eye." Her eye is on the object—the tininess of "the shrew's children, twenty to a teaspoonful;" the near invisibility of minnows—"a see-through army in the shallows / as still as grains in a rice bowl"; the ambiguity of strange markings left in new snow. What made the marks?

It could have been a raccoon
lugging a knapsack,
it could have been a porcupine
carrying a tennis racket,
it could have been something
as supple as a red fox
dragging the squawk and sputter
of a crippled woodcock.

Up Country is the fourth book of poems by this Boston-based poet and novelist. Neither surreal nor shrill, neither tragic nor transcending, Mrs. Kumin's poems sing with the music of the middle voice, sing of reality beheld with imagination, sing the world made meaningful by the perceptions of the beholder. *Up Country* is good news for all listeners to whippoorwills, inspectors of beaver dams, connoisseurs of the hazel nut and the honey mushroom.

Ralph J. Mills, Jr.   (essay date 1973)

SOURCE: A review of *Up Country,* in *Parnassus: Poetry in Review,* Vol. 1, No. 2, 1973, pp. 211-24.

[*Mills is an American poet who has written several critical studies on contemporary poets. In the following excerpt, he congratulates Kumin for her "marvelously etched, intricately textured pictures" of New England in* Up Country.]

Maxine Kumin is like [Denise Levertov,] a poet of the trained eye and the exact word, though without the visionary proclivities and the desire for new sonic and organic forms which Denise Levertov seeks. The poems of *Up Country* are selected from several sources, including previous books of Mrs. Kumin's, and compose a series of marvelously etched, intricately textured pictures of different aspects of New England life and countryside that fewer and fewer Americans know. The central location for these poems is a farm in southern New Hampshire where, one gathers, Mrs. Kumin and her family live part of each year; thus the poet's presence is that of a sympathetic inhabitant who also possesses a wider acquaintance with the world. Yet Mrs. Kumin, as is obvious from the first page on, has plunged like [Theodore] Roethke or [Robert] Frost, Edmund Blunden or Jon Silkin into the details of nature and rural living without stinting herself. We discover a capacity for *seeing* that places this poet in a direct line from the greenhouse poems of Roethke. I think the "Garden Master," as [John] Berryman called him, would surely approve the poem **"Mud"**:

You would think that the little birches
would die of that brown mouth sucking
and sucking their root ends.
The rain runs yellow.
The mother pumps in, pumps in
more than she can swallow.
All of her pockmarks spill over.
The least footfall

brings up rich swill.

The streams grow sick with their tidbits.
The trout turn up their long bellies.
The slugs come alive. An army
of lips works in its own ocean.
The boulders gape to deliver themselves.
Stones will be born of that effort.

Meanwhile the mother is sucking.
Pods will startle apart,
pellets be seized with a fever
and as the dark gruel thickens,
life will stick up a finger.

Whatever poetic company she keeps in such poems, Mrs. Kumin is no imitator but very clearly her own writer (and a distinctive novelist too). In these poems she steeps herself—sometimes adopting the figure of "the Hermit" to intensify the feeling of solitary humanity in the midst of nature—in the actualities of soil, pond, trees, beans, local topography, animal tracks in the snow, an ancient bathtub used for a watering trough, the gravestones of an old cemetery, the variety of insects frequenting a pond, the hundred-and-sixty-year-old markings in an attic, a handbook of simples, and so forth. As John Ciardi says of her accuracy with respect to the reality her poems render: "She teaches me, by example, to use my own eyes. When she looks at something I have seen, she makes me see it better. When she looks at something I do not know, I therefore trust her." That is high praise and also traditional praise. Many a younger poet at the present time should perhaps be compelled to earn it. The liberating changes which occurred in American poetry from the late 1950's into the 1970's have been of great value, but we are in danger of their being simply taken on by a newer generation which turns them into trite literary mechanisms, flicked on and off like light switches, and possibly losing touch altogether with the concreteness of the external world. How many of our legions of youthful poets can command both free *and* formal manners with the expertness of James Wright or Philip Levine?

Mrs. Kumin's writing stands as a masterful example of the middle style; her rhythmic sense, her ear and diction are above criticism. Of her kind, she is quite simply an excellent poet: one who looks, who names and who makes—all with astonishing and enviable craftsmanship. Like MacLeish, Eberhart and Denise Levertov, she labors her share of "the fields of imagination." I close with the moving declarations of her poem **"We Are,"** in the hope that it will provide a beginning for many new readers of her work:

Love, we are a small pond.
In us yellow frogs take the sun.
Their legs hang down. Their thighs open
like the legs of the littlest children.
On our skin waterbugs suggest incision
but leave no marks of their strokes.
Touching is like that. And what touches evokes.

Just here the blackest berries fatten

over the pond of our being.
It is a rich month for putting up weeds.
They jut like the jaws of Hapsburg kings.
Tomorrow they will drop their blood
as the milkweed bursts its cotton
leaving dry thorns and tight seeds.

Meanwhile even knowing
that time comes down to shut the door
—headstrong, righteous, time hard at the bone
with ice and one thing more—
we teem, we overgrow. The shelf
is tropic still. Even knowing
that none of us can catch up with himself

we are making a run
for it. Love, we are making a run.

Maxine Kumin with Anne Sexton and Elaine Showalter and Carol Smith (interview date 1974)

SOURCE: In a conversation on April 15, 1974, in *Women's Studies: An Interdisciplinary Journal,* Vol. 4, 1976, pp. 115-36.

[*In the following interview with Showalter and Smith, Kumin and poet Anne Sexton discuss their twenty-year-old friendship and its influence on their poetry.*]

Max and I
Two immoderate sisters,
Two immoderate writers,
Two burdeners,
Made a pact,
To beat death down with a stick.
To take over.
　　　　Anne Sexton, "The Death Baby"

This conversation between four women is about the friendship of Maxine Kumin and Anne Sexton, a friendship which began in the late 1950s, when they studied together in a poetry workshop in Boston led by John Holmes. Because they had young children, and were often unable to get out of the house, they developed a process of "workshopping" poems on the telephone, supplying for each other both detailed criticism and warm support. Both women won Pulitzer Prizes for books of poems. Anne Sexton in 1967 for *Live or Die,* and Maxine Kumin in 1973 for **Up Country: Poems of New England**. Their poetic styles are completely different; Kumin's poetry is exact, formal, intensely crafted, while Sexton wrote dramatically about breakdown and death. On October 5, 1974, Anne Sexton killed herself at her home in Weston, Massachusetts. . . .

[Showalter]: *Was John Holmes a difficult person for a woman to work with?*

[Sexton]: John Holmes didn't approve of a thing about me. He hated my poetry. I remember, even after Maxine had left, and I was still with Holmes, there was a new girl who came in. And he kept saying, oh, let us see *new* poems, *new* poems. We need them. And here I was giving him things that were later anthologized forever. I mean, really good poems.

[Smith]: *Didn't Holmes write comic verse as well, himself? And think you should move in the direction of comic verse, Maxine?*

A.S. No, no, she started with comic verse.

[Kumin]: I had already graduated from comic verse, Carol. I had started by writing light verse; that's how I became a poet. I started writing light verse for the slicks when I got pregnant with Danny, for a year.

A.S. Maxine, it was two or three years, it was no one year.

M.K. Wait a minute—he's now twenty-one. So it was twenty-one years ago. And I made a pact with myself that if I didn't sell anything by the time this child was born, I would chuck all my creative discontents. And in about my eighth month I started really landing with little four-liners, there, here and everywhere. *Saturday Evening Post* and *Cosmopolitan,* and so on. Then someone told me about John Holmes's class at the Center and in great fear and trembling I went and met Anne. We did that thing at the Center for a year and then we broke off and started a workshop of our own.

A.S. It was at least two years.

E.S. *And who was in the second workshop?*

M.K. It consisted of Sexton, Kumin, George Starbuck, Sam Albert, and John Holmes. And for a little while, Ted Weiss.

A.S. He was there for a while. And do you remember? the night we laughed so hard we were screaming, over women's girdles? I mean, we were hysterical. Ted Weiss was in Boston, and John wanted to bring him into the class, and he was nice. I'll never forget how we laughed. He just got us all onto women's girdles. I mean, in its own way it is a bit vulgar, and yet to me it isn't really vulgar at all. It's beauty, it's the girdle that's corrupting her. It was funny. But—I have to point this out, and you must too— John found me evil.

M.K. But I think it should also be said, that the reason for John's reaction, we *guess,* is that his first wife had *been* mentally ill, and had killed herself.

A.S. But I was writing about this subject. He kept saying, no no, too personal, or you musn't, or anything. Everything he said about my poems was bad, almost altogether. And yet, from the beginning, from the class, from him, I learned. And from Maxine. I must say Maxine, my best teacher—although for a while I was copying Maxine's flaws. I don't know how, I didn't know they were hers, although now I can see they were someone else's, an inversion here, or a noun. I got over that. I remember, I

didn't know her very well. I wrote "Music Swims Back to Me." I was playing a record, a 45, and I was leaning over my husband who was building a hi-fi set. I was climbing over him, in the kitchen, because I wrote in the dining room—I didn't really have a place to write, I wrote on a cardtable—to put on the 45 again. It's necessary to heat that song, because the song was taking me back to the mental institution where it constantly played. It was a very early poem, and I had broken all my ideas of what a poem should be, and I go to Maxine—very formal—we don't know each other very well. We hadn't started writing together yet. And I said, could you—? We sat together in the living room, stiffly on the couch. Sunday. It was a Sunday. And I said, is this a poem? And she said, yes.

M.K. Well, I get points for knowing it. I don't know how I knew it.

A.S. She knew. She knew. She responded. I had done this crazy thing, written this poem. Always Maxine responded to my poetry. Not John, but Maxine, although in spite of herself. Because it was hard for her.

M.K. Yes, it was hard. Here was my Christian academic daddy saying, stay away from her. She's bad for you.

E.S. *Did he actually say that?*

A.S. He would write letters saying, she's evil. He did, he said, be careful of her.

M.K. Oh, yes, he would write me letters. He was my patron; he got me a job at Tufts.

A.S. And for me, he was my daddy, but he was the daddy who was saying, you are no good.

M.K. And the fantastic thing is that it did not come between us. Of course, John then died terribly, terribly. He was told that his aches and pains were mental, that he needed a psychiatrist; meanwhile he had throat cancer and it had metastasized. Had totally invaded his chest and shoulders. I remember him talking about a shawl, a cape of pain. And he started drinking again. It was awful, awful.

A.S. It was awful. I remember calling his wife, Doris, and saying, what is it, what is it? He's not going to *die,* is he? And she said, well, it's funny, it's like psychiatry. What could she say?

C.S. *Who's that?*

M.K. She was a very good foil for John, because she's very warm, very outgoing, and she supplied a lot of things that John didn't. He was really quite reserved. I thought of him as very New England.

A.S. I remember one night Sam and me going to John's. It was sleeting out, but we make it. And he's on his way out—and he's so happy we were going out. I think maybe that moment he forgave me a little.

M.K. I was then teaching at Tufts, but we all read at Tufts, in the David Steinman series.

A.S. I never did. No, he wasn't going to ask *me*.

M.K. We used to go to parties at John's after all those readings—after John Crowe Ransom, and after Robert Frost. Frost said, don't sit there mumbling in the shadows, come up here closer. By then he was very deaf. And I was so awed.

C.S. *Was it out of that early relationship that you both began to work together?*

A.S. Yes, because we had to listen.

M.K. Because we had to listen to John Holmes read the poems—copies were not provided—and then we worked together on the telephone.

A.S. In our own workshop later we made copies. But then we worked on the phone. And sometimes my kids would be climbing all over me, and I'd say, shh! poem! Maxine! And I'd block my ear, and I could hear it. I could grasp the whole thing, and say change this, change that.

E.S. *Did you see it?*

M.K. Later. Maybe the following week, if we could get together, if one of us had a sitter.

A.S. She means did we see it in our minds. No, no, I just knew. I could tell the poem, and I could tell what she wanted to do. We still do it.

E.S. *You don't have to anymore. This was just because you couldn't get out of the house?*

A.S. Yes, because our kids were too small.

M.K. Yes. We did eventually do this wicked thing. We put in a second line, because our husbands complained that we were always on the phone.

A.S. We used to talk for two hours sometimes.

E.S. *When was it that you put in the phone? Was it before or after the Radcliffe Institute?*

M.K. Probably just then, because we both probably felt flush, and important.

C.S. *And you would talk about each other's poems, work-shop each other's poems?*

A.S. Yes, and also talk about our emotions and our feelings and what the day was like, what was going on.

C.S. *When you heard each other's poems, you said before you could enter the consciousness of the other person.*

A.S. Well, you see, we never tried to make the other sound like ourselves. We always saw in the other's voice, I'm sure of it.

M.K. We started with a recognition for and a respect for that separate identity. I would never meddle with what Anne is doing. I might be able to help her find a more effective way to do what she's doing.

E.S. *Did you ever find your own writing began to shade into the other person?*

M.K. No, no, we're different.

A.S. You can tell we're completely different.

E.S. *Yes, but was there ever a period when there was a struggle?*

A.S. No, there was never a struggle. It was natural, it wasn't hard.

M.K. It seems to be so normal. It wasn't ever an issue.

A.S. There was never any struggle. Don't you see—you enter into the voice of the poet, and you think, how to shape, how to make better, but not, how to make like me.

M.K. I think there is one conviction about the writing of a poem Anne and I share, although we may have come to it by separate routes. We both have very strong feeling about a poem ending definitively. We don't like poems that trail off. Real closure.

A.S. We both do. Oscar Williams said, anyone can write a poem, but who can end it? It's like slamming the door, And I said, you mean like having sex without orgasm? He didn't like that remark.

E.S. *Do you do this exchanging with your novels as well, Maxine?*

M.K. Anne reads sections. I ask a lot from her when I write prose, but not as much these days.

E.S. *Is the poetry workshopping diminishing too? Do you do this less, need this less, than you used to?*

A.S. No, not as long as we're writing.

M.K. I think the difference is that perhaps this year I haven't been writing as much.

A.S. I haven't been writing as much either; I've been having an upsetting time.

M.K. I think the intensity is the same, but the frequency has changed.

A.S. But just the other day Maxine said, well, that's a therapeutic poem, and I said, for god's sake, forget that. I want to make it a real poem. Then I forced her into helping me make it a real poem, instead of just a kind of therapy for myself. But I remember once a long time ago a poem called "Cripples and Other Stories." I showed it to my psychoanalyst—it was half done—and I threw it in the wastebasket. Very unusual because I usually put them away forever. But this was in the wastebasket. I said, would you by any chance be interested in what's in the wastebasket? And she said, wait a minute, Anne. You could make a real poem out of that. And you know how different that is from Maxine's voice.

M.K. I happen to really love that poem.

A.S. Really? I hate it. Although it's good. It reads well. But we're different temperatures, Maxine and I. I have to be warmer. We can't even be in the same room.

M.K. I'm always taking my clothes off and Anne is putting on coats and sweaters.

A.S. But you must remember it's not just a poetic relationship. It's been a great bond of friendship, growing, I suppose developing deeper and deeper. I mean, if one of us is sick, the other is right there. We tell each other everything that's going on. I tell her a dream to remember it, almost. Used to—I haven't been lately. We've both been so busy this year, we've kind of drifted apart, but it's because—

C.S. *When you talk about a poem, do you talk about ideas or techniques?*

M.K. Usually we don't start without a draft.

A.S. Well—I remember you talking to me about *Eighteen Days Without You,* helping me with the plot, the cabin. Although in the end I used none of it.

M.K. You had started though. You knew the shape.

A.S. No I didn't. I have the worksheets. First of all you had an apartment in Watertown and then I make it a cabin in Groton. Yet, she's fictionalized, helping me fictionalize the setting for the lovers. She did one thing, I did another. She started me.

M.K. It's always been this way.

A.S. Now can I tell this very personal thing, which we can cross out?

M.K. Probably not, but go ahead.

A.S. We might just be talking, and I'd say, we're just talking. Why the hell aren't we writing? And we'd get a line, a concept. I'd say, I'll call you back in twenty minutes. It is the most stimulating thing. It's a challenge. We've got this much time, and goddam it, I'm going to have something there. We hang up. In twenty-five minutes I call back. Have you got anything? She sure does. And so have I. It forces us. It's the challange of it. And with the workshop we had, we always had two poems, sometimes three.

M.K. There were certain people who need not be mentioned who always went over their allotted time span. My kids, when they would see some activity around the house would say, oh, the poets! now we'll *never* get any sleep! And they would fight for the privilege of sleeping over the garage, which was at the farthest remove, because the poets were so noisy. The poets came together and fought.

A.S. We'd scream and yell. Sam Albert said to Anne Hussey: There was no one who fought harder for her words in workshop than Anne Sexton and then went home and changed them. But I would fight—it was like they were taking my babies away from me. Actually I would write down who said what—like Max, no, George, this—and there were certain people I respected more. But Sam could be good at a sort of instinctive thing.

M.K. Well, we were a good group. George was icily cerebral. George would be sitting there counting the syllabics. But I could point to lines that I changed because of George. We've grown in different directions. We were very open and raw and new then. We were all beginners.

A.S. I think I had my first book published then. But the one time we didn't speak about writing poems was about John. We didn't workshop, we didn't talk, we were suddenly separate.

C.S. *Because your relationships with him were different?*

A.S. Yes, and I suppose our love for him was different.

M.K. Grief is private.

A.S. But our grief was never private in any other way. It was just with him, because he loved you, he didn't love me, and it probably made you feel guilty. Anyway, we discussed nothing. She wrote one poem, I wrote another. Mine was called "Somewhere in Africa."

E.S. *Has anything that's come out from the women's movement made you see the relationship you have in a different way?*

A.S. You see, when we began, there was no women's movement. We were it.

M.K. And we didn't know it.

E.S. *Because the relationship you have, and the relationship of Hallie and Sukey in* The Passions of Uxport *is totally new.*

A.S. I want to say—that is not me in *The Passions of Uxport.*

M.K. But certainly it takes something from our friendship.

E.S. *There are very few relationships in books that are like it. Women are generally supposed to destroy each other.*

A.S. I do support Maxine, although I've been a little weaker—

M.K. Of course you do. When I was writing my first novel, Anne was in Europe on a Prix de Rome. I sent Annie air mail, what? Forty pages? Three chapters. I said, please wherever you are, drop everything, read this, get back in touch with me. I don't know what I'm doing. Am I writing a novel? And Anne read it.

A.S. I started to cry. I was with Sandy. We had just driven out of Venice and I read the three chapters from *The Dooms of Love,* and I cried. She could do it.

M.K. I had to do all that without her. I think though that we're always proud of ourselves that we're not dependent on the relationship. We're very autonomous people, but it *is* a nurturing relationship.

E.S. *What difference would it have made if there had been a women's movement?*

M.K. We would have felt a lot less secretive.

A.S. Yes, we would have felt legitimate.

M.K. We both have repressed, kept out of the public eye that we did this.

A.S. I mean, our husbands, we could have thrown it at them.

E.S. *Why did you feel so ashamed of this mutual support?*

A.S. We did. We were ashamed. We had to keep ourselves separate.

M.K. We were both struggling for identity.

A.S. Also, it's a secret, we didn't want anyone to know. But I think it's time to acknowledge it.

C.S. *The separateness is evident and obvious.*

A.S. You should put that in, because the people who read this might never have read us, and think we're alike. I said to Maxine, write a book called *Up Country.*

M.K. Yes, you did. You tell yours and I'll tell mine.

A.S. I said write those country poems. It will be a book. Have it illustrated.

E.S. *By Barbara Swan. That's one of the external things that connects you, one of the few visible signs. Barbara Swan's illustrations for* **Up Country,** Transformations, The Death Notebooks, Live or Die.

A.S. She was at the Radcliffe Institute.

M.K. We were all there in the same year. Annie wrote the first transformation, and I said, god, that's fantastic. You could do a whole book of these. And Annie said I couldn't possibly. That's the only one, I know it. Of course, by the next day she had written another one. When she was done she said, what can I call it? And I said, call it *Transformations.*

A.S. Right in the middle I started a novel and you said, put that novel down and finish that book of poems! And thank you.

M.K. We titled each other's books. I titled *Transformations—*

A.S. It's a crappy title (laughing).

M.K. I love it.

A.S. And I named **Up Country**.

E.S. *You said you knew that could be a book. When you write do the poems come separately, or in a rush as a book?*

A.S. She had it in her to write masses of these country poems. I knew it.

I think there is one conviction about the writing of a poem Anne Sexton and I share, although we may have come to it by separate routes. We both have very strong feelings about a poem ending definitively. We don't like poems that trail off. Real closure.

—*Maxine Kumin*

E.S. *How do you organize the poems in the books?*

A.S. Well, we look at each other's things and say, do I have a book or do I not have a book? And we say, help me, help me, or this is crap.

C.S. *I assume* **Up Country** *came thematically. In the author's note you have to* Live or Die, *you say you're going to publish the poems chronologically. Were you interested in them as biography?*

A.S. No, I just thought it might be vaguely interesting to someone to see what dates they were written. They were all dated in the manuscripts, you see.

C.S. *How did they come together as a book?*

A.S. I remember George reading it, and there was no last poem. He said, all you need is a poem saying hello. And I wrote "Live."

M.K. Funny how we both went back to George. I sent George the manuscript of my third book, and he read through it with a great deal of care.

A.S. Some of his comments were damn wrong. He said, no one can write about operations but Anne Sexton. How ridiculous. A totally different kind of operation. I encouraged her to write it.

E.S. *There were a lot of nineteenth-century women writers who had partnerships like that, and critics tried to make them rivals. Charlotte Brontë once delayed the publication of a novel so it wouldn't come out at the same time as Elizabeth Gaskell's.*

A.S. Of course. We have books coming out at the same time next year.

M.K. We just found out.

A.S. It's all right. Maxine used to be horrified if we came out in the same year. But we're not compared.

E.S. *In a larger sense, now there's a female renaissance in poetry.*

M.K. Thank God. I think the fact that women are coming out of the closet is one of the most positive things that's happened in the century. Maybe the only good thing in a fucked-up world. I see such immense changes in women's perceptions. I grew up in an era when you went to a cocktail party and measured your success by how many men spoke to you. I really identified much more with the male side, but now I have such a feeling of sisterhood. I find that wherever I go, I meet splendid women, and I'd a hell of a lot rather be with them.

A.S. You know, this is also your analysis.

M.K. Yes, and the fact that I have two grown daughters with full-blown careers, and they have raised my consciousness. It was the work that I did with the analyst that helped me get past my awful difficulties with my own mother.

A.S. She had no close women friends, but I broke the barrier, because I'm a terrible breaker of barriers.

E.S. *Did you have a lot of close women friends?*

A.S. Yes.

E.S. *But in your books you have generations of women—the mother, the grandmother, the daughter. There aren't any women friends in it.*

A.S. You do see Max, and lists of names. There are the dedications.

E.S. *But then there are the blood relationships that are difficult, love you have to win back.*

A.S. My mother was very destructive. The only person who was very constructive in my life was my great-aunt, and of course she went mad when I was 13. It was probably the trauma of my life that I never got over.

E.S. *How did she go mad?*

M.K. Read "Some Foreign Letters."

A.S. That doesn't help. Do you know the *Nana Hex? Anna Who was Mad* in *Folly*? Notice the guilt in them. But the hex is a misnomer. I had tachycardia and I thought it was just psychological.

E.S. *Were you named for her?*

A.S. Yes, we were namesakes. We had love songs we would sing together. She cuddled me. I was tall, but I tried to cuddle up. My mother never touched me in my life, except to examine me. So I had bad experiences. But I wondered with this that every summer there was Nana, and she would rub my back for hours. My mother said, women don't touch women like that. And I wondered why I didn't become a lebian. I kissed a boy and Nana went mad. She called me whore and everything else.

I think I'm dominating this interview.

M.K. You are, Anne.

E.S. *Maxine, in* The Passions of Uxport *you describe the death of a child from leukemia—a death which has haunted me ever since. Do you think it's more difficult for a woman to write about the death of a child?*

M.K. In all my novels there's a death. In *The Abduction* there's a sixteen-year-old who dies in a terrible car crash. Perhaps as a mother I have a fear of a loss of a child.

A.S. We all know that a child going is the worst suffering.

M.K. Many years ago, my brother lost a child, and I remember this terrible Spartan funeral. That's the funeral in *The Passions of Uxport*, when he says the Hebrew prayer for the dead.

A.S. Do you remember we were young and going to a place called the New England Poetry Club, the first year we won the prizes, first or second. We were terrified. It was our first reading. Maxine's voice was trembling so, we couldn't hear her.

M.K. I couldn't breathe.

A.S. I couldn't stand up, I was shaking so. I sat on the table.

M.K. I wonder if there was a trembling in us—the wicked mother or the wicked witch, or whatever those ladies were to us.

E.S. *They were all women?*

M.K. There were a few squashy old men.

A.S. There were young men too. John was there. Sam was there.

E.S. *Did you have trouble with women writers of another generation? In Louise Bogan's* Letters—*she says about Anne? She doesn't seem to have been able to accept the subjects.*

M.K. This was the problem with a great many people. Women are not supposed to have uteruses, especially in poems.

A.S. To me, there's nothing that can't be talked about in art. But I hate the way I'm anthologized in women's lib anthologies. They cull out the "hate men" poems, and leave nothing else. They show only one little aspect of me. Naturally there are times I hate men, who wouldn't? But there are times I love them. The feminists are doing themselves a disservice to show just this.

M.K. They'll get over that.

A.S. Yes, but by then, they won't be published. Therefore they've lost their chance.

E.S. *When I anthologized you in my book,* Women's Liberation and Literature, *I chose "Abortion," "Housewife," and "For My Lover on Returning to His Wife." And I like all those poems very much; I'd choose them again.*

A.S. "For My Lover" is a help. It doesn't cost very much money to get "Housewife"—you can get it cheap. A strange thing—"a woman is her mother." That's how it ends. A housecleaner—washing herself down, washing the house. It was about my mother-in-law.

E.S. *A woman is her mother-in-law.*

Maxine Kumin with Martha George Meek (interview date 1975)

SOURCE: An interview in *The Massachusetts Review,* Vol. XVI, No. 2, Spring, 1975, pp. 317-27.

[*In the following interview, Kumin discusses her poetry. She declares that "in the process of writing, as you marshal your arguments, as you marshal your metaphors really, as you pound and hammer the poem into shape and into form, the order—the marvelous informing order emerges from it, and it's—I suppose, in a sense, it's in the nature of a religious experience."*]

Our formal subject is poetry as a principle of order in life, when oneself and the world are otherwise chaotic. As we discuss that difficult point where the art and the life of an artist coincide, Kumin reads aloud a quotation from Faulkner as a motto for confessional writers: "If a writer has to rob his mother, he will not hesitate. The 'Ode on a Grecian Urn' is worth any number of old ladies.". . .

[Meek]: *The hermit in the first eight poems of* **Up Country** *is so very alone. I wonder if for you, as well as for the hermit, if the tribe, the family, is the last unit in society that can be balanced between order and disorder?*

[Kumin]: Yes, I think very definitely.

It's no larger than that?

Well, it's the family and it's the larger family, by extension, of those whom you love. For me, it's certain writers I've been close to and who, in effect, speak the same language. Writers are all secret Jews; they all belong to the same tribe. We do talk a kind of language; well, we tend to talk a lot of shop talk. So there's the commonality of that. There's also the enormous commonality of the fact that to be a writer is to be a solitary. It's to be a hermit, by golly. It really is. It's to be shut off. Almost any other profession involves some sort of social intercourse with people, you know, with the world around you—medicine and law and so on. But to be a writer is to lock yourself up to do your job. So there's an awful lot of overage, and that's why I think writers like to get together and talk about how terrible it is, how lonely it is, how difficult it is.

This is a professional isolation for you, then, rather than a personal one?

I think by nature I am something of a solitary. I mean I'm capable of being perfectly sociable and amiable. But I need a lot of quiet; I need a lot of time when I'm not talking. Maybe more than other people do. I suppose what I'm saying is I don't put terribly much store by human nature. I don't think of us as infinitely perfectible as I might have twenty-five years ago. I think we're infinitely depraved, and brutish, and nasty. And this goes back to what you were saying about the family element, the saving nature of the close associations that you can feel within the family or, by extension, within the family of writers, plus a few close, tried-and-true friends.

Does your hermit repudiate modern life?

No, he doesn't repudiate it; he's just a cop-out. And it's a very selfish thing. I have this big thing about wanting to be totally self-sufficient. You know we've got this old farmhouse; I don't know what it is but I have this thing about always wanting to have the big vegetable garden we can live off of all year, and being really outside the mainstream. It's like being on an island as it is. Last summer I didn't have a car for a large part of the summer, and so, when we needed groceries, I'd go down to town on horseback. That worked out pretty well, except one day the carton of milk spilled onto the five-pound bag of flour in the knapsack, and by the time I got back on the hill, I had a knapsack full of paste. But it was sort of fun. I'd tie my horse to the V.F.W. flagpole and go to market.

Would you do it? Would you leave for good?

The affairs of the world? No, I couldn't. I wish I could. I don't know *how* I feel about it.

In the poem, "September 22nd," you speak of living as a "history of loss."

Yes. "I am tired of this history of loss! / . . . To be reasonable / is to put out the light. / To be reasonable is to let go." There's an old, old essay by Joseph Wood Krutch called "The Phantom of Certitude." It's about all the touchstones of Victorian times when there was the centrality of a belief in the one God and a kind of Calvinist faith in salvation through grace—all of those surenesses that imposed an order in which you could feel that you were growing in a tradition, in which you belonged to an ongoing tradition of the infinite perfectibility of man. I think all those certitudes have been taken from us. "To be reasonable is to let go"; it is really the only sane option that we have.

Do you find any hope for retrieving something from time? I think of "The Hermit Goes Up Attic," and "Cellar Hole in Joppa": There's "no word to keep you by."

Right, right. Except, of course, the word that the poet records. Always this sense the writer has, a kind of messianic thing: who will tell it if I do not? This is your assignment: to record it, to get it down, to save it for immortality.

Do you think that ultimately language fails us as a means of communication? I'm thinking about references in your poems to dreams, to signs, to messages, as a necessary language that is beyond words.

I have a lot of reverence for what goes on at the dream level in the unconscious—those symbolic events. I have tremendous reverence for raising it up into language, which I think is what it's all about, really. That's what poetry is all about, at any rate. Fiction is less so, because, for me at least, fiction is more a matter of invention and manipulation. Poetry is much closer to the wellspring. There's much less shaping, paradoxically, in being a poet than there is in being a writer of novels.

Frequently when you refer to dreams, it's an unbearable truth, though. It's one that's manageable possibly only through dream.

This may very well be so. Want to give me an example? Are you thinking of **The Nightmare Factory**?

Yes, certainly that. That this is a consideration, in fact, that the conscious mind would put aside.

The Nightmare Factory, as poems so often are, was a way of dealing with something very inchoate and very painful. I wrote it as a way of exorcizing a series of bad dreams about my recently dead father. I then had this fantasy that there is some distant Detroit-of-the-Soul where all bad dreams are created and that out of the warehouse of good, we are assigned certain recurrent nightmares that we have to—you know, it's like Conrad. He's talking about

the nightmare of one's choice and having to dream it through to the very end, if you remember that; I think it's *Heart of Darkness*. One must descend into the abyss and dream the nightmare of one's choice and dream it through to the very end. I think that's what I was trying to say about those dreams.

If I may quote you once again, from your column in The Writer *this time: "The man who writes out of an inner need is trying to order his corner of the universe; very often the meaning of an experience or an emotion becomes clear to him only in this way."*

Absolutely. That I still believe, very ardently. It happens to me over and over again.

The word "order" appears again in the poem, "Stones," in which you speak of the "dark obedient order" of the natural world. Is the crucial order in life an order invented by the writer, or is it a discovered order?

I think that there is an order to be discovered—that's very often true in the natural world—but there is also an order that a human can impose on the chaos of his emotions and the chaos of events. That's what writing poetry is all about. You begin with the chaos of impressions and feelings, this aura that overtakes you, that forces you to write. And, in the process of writing, as you marshal your arguments, as you marshal your metaphors really, as you pound and hammer the poem into shape and into form, the order—the marvelous informing order emerges from it, and it's—I suppose, in a sense, it's in the nature of a religious experience. It must be the same kind of feeling of being shriven that you would have if you were a true believer and you took communion. You feel, to that degree, reborn. Well, ideally, that's what writing a poem does.

The language becomes a part of, as well as a means to, the order which is achieved. Is that it?

It's hard to pin it down. It's what you find out while you're writing. I so often begin in total chaos, not knowing *what* it is I'm doing, just knowing that I have this recurrent phrase, or I have this insistent rhythm, or I have this concept, that I want to fiddle around with. And it isn't until I get the poem out, that I find out what it was saying, what I wanted to say. But I don't think that as a creative artist I'm all that conscious; and that gets back to that, you know, for God sakes, Oedipus, not-to-inquire-further thing. I think it's too much part of me. I don't want to know everything, because I'm afraid it will squat on my life and mess up everything that I do unconsciously.

I'm terrified by behavioral scientists. There's a group from Harvard who really wanted to come and sit around while I wrote a poem and see whether they couldn't change the way the poem was built by certain key things they would say or do. I was absolutely horrified. I thought that was the most voyeuristic, evil, X-rated-movie, porno idea I'd ever heard of. I hold this to be sacred; it's between me and my Book of Words, which is in my head. It's my own private method, and I don't even want to know too much about it. It's almost like inquiring into the mechanism of prayer. If you're really a mystic, or a saint, or somebody who makes things happen by ardently praying them into being, you don't want to investigate exactly what particular line of your incantation works or what particular aspect of your prayer to beseech the Almighty gets through to Him; because then you might come to rely on those and they might be constantly shifting. You might be all wrong.

You say that in a way it is a religious experience to work with language, as language creates form or order for you.

Well, words are the only "holy" for me. Any God that exists for me is in the typewriter keys. The only sanctity really, for me, is the sanctity of language.

You once wrote about the necessity of being as truthful and "clear" as a natural reticence will allow, even to the point of pain.

That's Marianne Moore, originally. She was a very reticent lady. I've largely outgrown my reticence, I think. That goes back to a period in my life when I felt very voyeuristic about what I was writing, daring to deal with interpersonal relationships, old family constellations and so on. There's a line from a Sexton poem: "The writer is essentially a crook. Out of used furniture he makes a tree." I really love that because it's the other side of the natural reticence. That, after all, is what art should do: create something that's natural out of all the used-up sticks and bureaus of our lives, the detritus of our lives.

At the same time, of course, I do very much respect that natural reticence. There has to be more than reticence; there has to be some psychic distance between the situation that you're dealing with and the time that you write about it. Now, how do you achieve that psychic distance? It may just be chronological; it may just be a number of years after a death that you finally write the elegy. Or it may be that you have grown beyond certain situations.

*You once said about an incident in the poem, "**Mother Rosarine**": "One association triggered another. Invented or real? Does it matter?" What is that particular authenticity that is crucial in any poem?*

I didn't think it mattered whether it was true that I had stolen the rosary or whether I simply imagined stealing the rosary. There's often very little distinction between thought and deed in a child's mind. My perceptions of my experiences at the convent seemed real to me. Whether some of them are invented or whether they were all true, authentic events, I didn't feel mattered for the purposes of making art out of it. They're all truly *felt*, whether they're true or not.

The authenticity resides in the feeling from which the poem springs?

Right.

I have to be pretty comfortable about what I'm writing, to write a free-verse poem; or else not terribly deeply involved. I almost always put some sort of formal stricture on a deeply-felt poem, maybe not rhyme, but at least a stanzaic pattern.

—*Maxine Kumin*

Do you tend to a particular use of form the more intimate the material, the more personal it is?

I generally choose something complex and difficult. The tougher the form the easier it is for me to handle the poem, because the form gives permission to be very gut-honest about feelings. The curious thing for me is that rhyme makes me a better poet. Invariably I feel it does. This is a mystic notion, and I'm not by any stretch a mystic, but it's almost as though I'm not capable of the level of language and metaphor that form enables me to achieve. It raises my language to heights that I wouldn't be up to on my own. When I'm writing free verse, I feel as though I am in Indiana, where it's absolutely flat and you can see the horizon 360 degrees around. You feel as though you have no eyelids, you can't blink. I lose, I have no sense of, the line. There are people who work so easily in this medium; they follow the breath rhythm and the normal pattern of speech. They feel totally at home and I feel totally bewildered. I have to be pretty comfortable about what I'm writing, to write a free-verse poem; or else not terribly deeply involved. I almost always put some sort of formal stricture on a deeply-felt poem, maybe not rhyme, but at least a stanzaic pattern.

Arbitrary?

In a formal sense it's arbitrary, but the poem finds its form early on, somewhere in the first or second stanza. And again, it's not a conscious thing. You just know the shape the poem's going to take and then you work the poem into that shape. There's that old thing the sculptor is supposed to say when he's carving a horse out of stone: he just chips away the parts that aren't horse.

Once again you're borrowing from a discovered form. You're leaning on it to help you discover it—that form—further.

Right. Right.

Would you say that, in addition to a stanzaic pattern or rhyme scheme, you tend to an understated diction, or a less "poetic" diction, when you're dealing with intimate material?—"The symbol inside this poem is my father's feet. . . ."

Very good example. It's the only time I ever did that, that

I'm aware of. That was the hardest poem I ever wrote, as you might well imagine. I wrote it quite a long time after my father was dead. And I *did* use that as a defense between me and the material. It's a way of standing back from the poem and saying: I as an artist am going to tell you a little secret about this poem; I have put a symbol in it. That was a way of getting going on the poem. I don't particularly approve of it; I don't particularly admire poems that are about poetry, for example. I think that some of the worst poems in the English language are written by poets about how they make a poem. I'm usually almost immediately offended by that; but I did do it. It does begin flatly. And it simply tells the details. It's a travelogue poem to a large extent. It relies on a thickness of listing things to carry the notion. I wrote that elegy, **"Pawnbroker,"** believe it or not, in syllabics as well as rhyme. That's how terrified I was of writing it.

This thickness of detail stands for feelings that you have. For example, in **"For My Son on the Highways of His Mind"**: that's the same kind of thing. The listing of the posters on the bedroom wall, the listing of the paraphernalia in the boy's room, are ways of speaking to the mother's feeling about the son. Without having to talk about emotion, you can use this.

You're talking about a defense between yourself and the emotion, rather than an attempt to make it seem genuine?

Well, I don't think that the attempt to make it seem genuine ever enters into it. It's not a conscious thing that happens. I don't ever say to myself, well now, in an attempt to make this seem genuine I will use the following details. I do think, on reflection, that they *are* a kind of defense against the expression of feeling.

Louis Simpson speaks about "the attitudes and tone of prose, in the form of verse," as a description of the volume, **Halfway***. Does that seem to you right, or somehow foreign, as a description?*

Well, of course, that was a first book. I have shifted a great deal, and I'm still evolving. That may be true of the poems in **Halfway,** but I'm not sure that it's generally true. It's funny that you bring up Simpson because the book that I'm putting together now will be called **House, Bridge, Fountain, Gate.** It's a direct quote from his partial autobiography, *North of Jamaica,* a lovely book. He says in it: "Poetry is a mixture of thoughts and objects; it is as though things are trying to express themselves through us. It may be, as a poet had said, we are here only to say house, bridge, fountain, gate." Well, that simply fascinated me, because I believe so strongly in the naming and the particularizing of things. I thought that would make a lovely title and was a little puzzled as to who the poet referred to was. Then, I was having drinks with Tony Hecht and his wife up at Bread Loaf, and I mentioned this quote; and Tony said, oh yes, of course that's from Rilke. Well, of course Tony would know because he's so marvelously erudite. So I went to the *Duino Elegies* and I searched and searched, and sure enough I found it. I'm going to put the German epigraph and then the quote from Simpson at the front of the book. Now, if the naming and the particularity of things is a function of prose more than it is of poetry, to that extent I suppose I do. I think that the one thing that's been consistently true about my poetry is this determination to get at that authenticity of detail.

That reminds me immediately of "The Spell," and Marianne Moore and the toads.

Do you know, when I wrote that poem I was not thinking of her "imaginary gardens with real toads in them." Not consciously. That's another one of those weird collisions that I tiptoe around the edges of. You know people find that very hard to believe—that a poet can be so naïve—but it's true. We are often very naïve.

What particular writers are you especially fond of?

The things that I like to read are very often the journals and letters, full of despair, of other writers. There's something very comforting in that—also something very voyeuristic. I'm enormously attracted to autobiographies or biographies such as the Bell book on Virginia Woolf, which I *just* got—a fascinating book.

What about ties with poets writing now?

Anne Sexton was a very close, personal friend. I know that sounds odd because we're so different; our voices are so different. But I think every poet needs a poet whose judgment he respects, to try things out on. Anne and I tried things out on each other quite constantly. I think the thing that saved our relationship, which had been going on for eighteen years, was that we didn't intrude on each other. We didn't try ever to moderate or tamper with the other's voice. We were there as a sounding board to say: that's very strained, that image is wrenched, this is dreadful, it's flat, that's an awful rhyme to end on, or whatever it was we said. That was my closest contact. There are some other poets I correspond with, and exchange poems with. One, who's really a dear friend of mine, an important pal-of-my-desk, is Bill Meredith, whose work I admire very much. I think he's one of the finest teachers of poetry; he's such a sensible human being. And a good poet. That's the family, the Mafia of the writing world.

There's nothing like a Boston school?

Well, if there is one, I'm not in it, let's put it that way. I don't belong to any group. I really never did—aside from those very first few years when we did have a writers' workshop of John Holmes and George Starbuck and Anne Sexton and me, from time to time. But not since those early days.

Would you say that John Holmes was one of the first to write in the mode of the intimate?

Well, he would turn over in his grave if he'd heard you say so, because he so detested it. He abhorred it, and he abhorred and was frightened of everything that Sexton wrote. He was very opposed to our developing friendship.

He thought it would be very destructive for me; and over the years we proved him wrong. I loved John. He was my Christian, academic Daddy. He really got me going, got me a job at Tufts where I was a part-time English instructor, equipped, in the eyes of the university, only to teach freshman composition to phys. ed. majors and dental technicians. That was how I began. And John did a superb job of running the workshop. He was a very good teacher. He had a way of eliciting the further detail without messing up somebody's voice. But he was very much opposed to what is now called "confessional" poetry. Anne frightened him a great deal because, I think, her hysteria and her suicidal nature reminded him of his first wife. Yet his best poems—the best poems he wrote—were the poems he wrote after we had an ongoing workshop; we were standing on our own legs, all of us, and we were pulling out of him poems more intimate than he had ever written before.

He was writing in response to you then.

We were all writing like mad in response to each other. It was divine and terrible all at once. It was a very yeasty and exciting time.

Where did confessional poetry begin?

In a very general way I think the quality of the *I* voice, the *moi* voice, that emerged out of the poetry of the Second World War, was the source that made Lowell, Snodgrass, Sexton, and so on, possible. There was a real loosening that took place in the war, maybe beginning with Shapiro, maybe beginning with Jarrell, maybe beginning God knows where, but somewhere in that group of poets whose poems came out of their experiences in the army or the navy.

What was it in the war?

That it was such a searing and such an intimate experience as well as a collective one. The best poems were the poems that particularized what was going on. I think of the Jarrell poem which has been so abused in anthologies, "The Death of the Ball Turret Gunner." It might very well be considered an ancestor to the poems in *Life Studies*. It's a funny link to be making, but it made the voice possible. It was the anguished voice of the soldier, that I think of as the forebear of the anguished voice in poetry.

Even for you as a woman?

Well, I don't know for me as a woman. I didn't really begin to be able to write womanly poems until, well, my consciousness was raised by my daughters. I started to grow up at about age thirty. I had a very long childhood, and a long and delayed adolescence. I was programmed into one kind of life, which was to say: get a college degree, get married, and have a family. It was just after the war, and this was what everyone was desperately doing; the tribe *was* kind of the saving centrality in a world that had gone totally awry. And I came to poetry as a way of saving myself because I was so wretchedly discontented, and I felt so guilty about being discontented. It just wasn't enough to be a housewife and a mother. It didn't

gratify great chunks of me. I came to poetry purely for self-gratification.

Do you feel that you and Anne Sexton have changed the face of poetry?

I think she has much more than I. She is a very original voice in American poetry. She certainly was responsible in large measure for the outpouring now of what I would call feminist verse. And I don't say "feminist" at all in a pejorative sense. She made it possible for women to write about the quality of womanhood in a way that just could not have been taken seriously twenty years ago. I don't put myself in that category; I don't know to what degree I may or may not have been an innovator. I think she has very clearly been an innovator, more so, I think, than Lowell. I think she went way beyond what he's doing.

Do you think that the confessional mode is dying out?

I don't think the confessional voice is dying out. That seems to me part of a long and honorable tradition in poetry: the voice of the *I*. I think we have that in every age in some degree or another.

One hears it asserted so often that with Sylvia Plath's suicide the impulse had been taken to its conclusion.

Certainly that was the logical conclusion to what Sylvia was doing, but it was, ironically, such a death by mistake.

She didn't intend to die?

I think that, as was true with Anne, there is half of the nature that wants to die, that needs to die, that needs to murder the self to get some release from the torment. But at the same time there remains the other part of that being, that wants very much to go on; and it's chancy, it's a steeplechase. Every time you try to die you're taking a risk; you might die, and then again you might be found. The impulse toward suicide is sometimes a sort of substitute punishment. Having made the attempt and then having been hauled back to life, the would-be suicide is in a way satisfied for a time. Death has been served. We've had so many poets die by their own hands. I don't know what the statistics are, poetic suicides as opposed, say, to suicides of bankers. But non-verbal people kill themselves, too. It's just that they haven't articulated their anguish ahead of time.

Do you suppose that's especially a twentieth-century impulse?

No, I don't think it's a twentieth-century impulse; it's just become more plausible with the relaxation of the hold of the church. As soon as you erode the sense of sin, the sin of dying by your own hand—you take away those certitudes we were talking about, and it gets more and more plausible to kill yourself. Like Kirillov in *The Possessed,* the only rational thing you can do is to kill yourself to prove there is no God.

N.B.: Maxine Kumin recently indicated to me that her final comments now seemed abrupt, particularly when read in the context of Anne Sexton's suicide. She wrote: they are too "coldly rational" and angry, although anger has its part in grief. I was reminded of a comment Kumin had made during our earlier discussion of the "history of loss" in a person's life. It is this, she had said, which continually exacts what she once called in **Halfway,** "the effort of consent."

Margaret Burns Ferrari (essay date 1976)

SOURCE: A review of *House, Bridge, Fountain, Gate,* in *America,* Vol. 134, No. 8, February 28, 1976, p. 165.

[*Below, Ferrari praises* House, Bridge, Fountain, Gate *for its "finely crafted structures" and "powerful, personal images."*]

Maxine Kumin won the Pulitzer Prize for her poems in **Up Country** in 1973. **House, Bridge, Fountain, Gate,** her newest collection, will not disappoint those who enjoy solid poetry that values life despite all its pain.

Two things seem immediately important: her dedication to her personal and poetic comrade, Anne Sexton, who took her own life in 1974, and her opening quotation from Rilke: "It may be as the poet has said, we are only here to say: House, Bridge, Fountain, Gate."

The dedication to Anne Sexton is particularly significant. I have read both women's works and have known each of them slightly, and I find in Kumin's latest poems a more Sexton-like directness. Though she still celebrates the positive, healing powers of nature, as she has always done in her poetry, she now confronts the macabre in her own life as well. Instead of shutting out the grotesque and unbearable pain life can bring, she faces it and incorporates it into a spirit of acceptance, however grim at times. But the horror is always understated, never dramatized or paraded for its shock value.

Her use of Rilke's quote, which seems to put a very minimal value on human life, is essential to the meaning of these poems. It is as if we were only here to cooperate with nature by naming things (that is, perhaps, by being conscious) and we might as well be content with our role.

Kumin orders the life around her by this naming, by a rhythmic participation in nature, by a reexamination of her life and family connections, of her childhood and motherhood, of time she spent alone in Kentucky and, finally, of her feeling for horses. She does this in finely crafted structures, put together as substantially as houses, bridges, fountains and gates must be. These structures are the order she has created to deal with the world.

I found the language in this collection particularly interesting because she weaves into it powerful, personal images: "In phrases lazy as marriage / running on, breaking off, beginning again / he tells me the geese are flying." There is a new colloquial earthiness in these poems: "Lately I am changing houses like sneakers and socks" and "Toads in their outsize skins / doze on stones. They line up / like old men in lumpy sweaters/ sunning themselves outside / the art museum."

The poems are often full of psychological truth, expressed in concrete imagery, as in the **"History Lesson"**: "That a man may be free of his ghosts / He must return to them like a garden. / He must put his hands in the sweet rot / uprooting the turnips, washing them / tying them into bundles / and shouldering the whole load to market." A person must work through and accept a painful past to live, and that unsentimental attitude is, in general, the life-affirming, positive voice of Kumin's poems.

Describing her stay as poet-in-residence at a small college in Kentucky, she underlines her isolation. She feels she must be the only Jew in town "looking for matzoh in the Safeway and the A&P" and is pressured by neon billboard messages and Sears Roebuck salesmen to accept Jesus or be damned.

Finally, in the Amanda poems, she gives a hint of an explanation for the strong emotional attachment she feels to horses. In **"The Horsewoman,"** she expresses a terrible disappointment with her father: "All this for the fantasy daddy / . . . when in fact the bona fide father / hunkered over his bourbon / and never went out of doors." Riding Amanda frees some thing in her: "What do I want for myself / dead center, bareback / on the intricate harp of your spine? / All that I name as mine."

The poems are not all equally strong, but there are many in this collection to delight the poetry reader. Maxine Kumin is a survival artist, and her poems are strong and honest.

Maxine Kumin with students (interview date 1977)

SOURCE: An interview in *To Make a Prairie: Essays on Poets, Poetry and Country Living,* The University of Michigan Press, 1979, pp. 35-46.

[*In the following interview conducted by high school students at Interlochen Arts Academy, Kumin answers questions about her work, in particular, her methods of writing. She also provides some advice for future writers.*]

[Students]: *Is everyday life experience the chief influence upon your poetry?*

[Kumin]: I would say that the distillation of everyday life experiences is exactly what I am trying to particularize and order in poetry.

When you write a poem, do you set down a chunk or block of words and then pare down from that, or do you build line on line?

I set down everything I can think of, everything that flies into my head, even though it may seem terribly digressive. I try to get it all because I'm afraid that if I don't get it all down on the page, it will evanesce and blow away. I tend to get a whole chunk that looks like prose, maybe three or four pages of it. While that's going on, I can already sense that certain of those things are lines, and then the next time through, I can begin to pick out the lines. By the end of the second session with the poem, I can see the order, the stanzaic pattern, if there's going to be one, and so on. It can happen the other way, too. Once in a while a poem will start with a compelling rhythm or line or just a phrase that you can't get rid of, and the poem will come from there.

When you talk about stanza patterns, do you mean the traditional one that someone like Auden would use?

Yes. I love Auden's work, and I think I learned a tremendous amount by imitating him, by deliberately cultivating that easy conversational tone of voice in which his poems are written, and by imitating to the best of my ability that deceptively easy-looking rhymed quatrain. The shorter the number of feet in a line the harder, of course, it is to work inside it. And he did so beautifully those short lines, some of them trimeter, some of them tetrameter.

Can you hinder your own work if you make too many drafts of it or rummage through it too many times?

Yes, I think you can. It's very hard to know when to stop because, you see, a poem is not like a watercolor. If you're painting a watercolor, you either have something in twenty minutes or you tear it up because you just "muddy" it if you go back over it. But you never lose anything by revising and recasting and trying different approaches, and so the problem is likely that with too much revision, the poem doesn't get finished. And yet, in truth, I would have to say immodestly that I think I always know when a poem is finished for me. It's taken me a long time to learn that, but I don't think I will worry a poem beyond its completion.

How do you begin your poems? Do you "think" them for a while before you write them down, do you sit down and try to write them, or do you get a line and start writing to see where it goes?

I don't think them before I write them, I know, because I'm always startled and often perplexed at what is building. I tend to just sit down and let it go. I think it starts in some very inchoate place, and the whole process of writing the poem is a process of elucidation. It's an attempt to find the truth for that particular corner of the universe.

You don't think you could force it, though.

Well, I did in the olden days when I was learning, when I was a beginner poet. I am a strong believer in the exercise poem and the workshop poem as a way of learning craft. I'm also old fashioned enough to believe that it's

very useful in workshop where the group dynamics are good and people are really constructive and loving with one another to write poems in common. I've worked with classes where we've written a sonnet in an hour, all of us together, to a predetermined end rhyme. Or I often use the device of group assignments where everybody has to write a dream poem or everybody has to write a descriptive poem of a person—you know, that kind of thing. And I think those things are useful. Sometimes exercise poems can turn into real true poems, and even if they don't, they've taught you something.

Have you ever given up on a poem?

Oh yes, lots of times. I have a great big box, a box that shirts used to come back from the laundry in before plastic bags were popular. That's my bone pile, and all the little snippets that failed and the aborted poems and stuff are in that. Don't ever throw those away because there'll be some wonderful phrase, maybe just two words in that box, but they're there. Going through your bone pile is often a very useful way to get started on a new poem. You can dip in there and find something that you couldn't deal with six months before. And suddenly it will right itself. That's a very mystic experience. I had once put away a poem in rhyming couplets. I think I had six or eight rhyming couplets. I had no way—no knowledge of how to complete this poem. I wrote probably forty-five wrong endings, and I put it away in the bone pile. Two years later I took it out, and I read through it. What came was like automatic writing. I just wrote the last three couplets, and there it was. It was an incredible experience. So this happens. It happens pretty frequently to a lot of poets.

How far do you think you should analyze a poem?

That's a very good question. Not quite to the point of pain. There is something known as "creeping exegesis" which is dissecting the poor poem until it wriggles around and is eventually killed. When I was young a lot of Robert Frost was killed for me in precisely that way. Almost all of Shakespeare was murdered in my high school days, and it was a long time before I could go back to him with anything other than a leaden sense of duty. Close examination of the text to understand what the poem is doing and how it works is fine because that heightens the poem, makes it much more meaningful. And then there has to be a point where the poem is something aesthetic, and you bring your own aesthetic judgment to bear on it.

In writing poems do you have a duty to yourself or to something else?

I'm really not sure. I'm not sure it's duty. I honestly think it's obsession. I mean, I don't think that I write poetry necessarily because I want to. I write it because I feel compelled. It's something I can't get away from—it's in me.

Have you ever felt that you've not been totally honest in a poem?

Well, it's hard to give an honest answer because there is a quality in poetry that I like to call poetic tact. There are some things that go unspoken. And a tremendous part of the punch of a good poem is in understatement, rather than hyperbole. Hyperbole has been so overused that it, like cliché, has lost its power to evoke feeling. If by understating, one is being not totally honest about the subject, then I guess I would have to say, yes, that I have not been totally honest in poems. But as far as telling the truth as I see it, I would have to say that I think I am always as honest as I can be.

Does your reference to I *in a poem relate the character's feelings or your own personal feelings?*

It can be either and it can be a little of both, because the *I* is the persona that the poet is hiding behind. There's an ancient and honorable tradition in poetry to use the *I,* or as the French call it, *le moi,* as a vehicle for conveying emotion or fact or whatever. Sometimes it can be very much a persona poem, and sometimes it can be quite an autobiographical poem.

Were you hiding behind the male persona in the hermit poems?

Yes. If I were writing them today, I would not employ the male persona. But when I was writing them I did not think that anyone could take a female hermit seriously, so I invented the hermit who, of course, is me. In the Amanda poems, however, that's no persona; there's nothing between me and the material.

Do you have to give yourself time between poems for something to build up?

Sometimes there's a great spate of them. Recently I was at the University of Arkansas doing a writers' workshop for a week, and I went from there to Washington for National Endowment meetings and then to read at the Folger Library. While I was in Arkansas I stayed in a dreary motel. It fronted right on a parking lot, and cars roared in and out at all hours. I was in that room quite a lot between student conferences and so on, and I started having nightmares. When I'm on the road I frequently have bad travel dreams in which everything is going wrong back at the farm. I wrote a whole poem in that motel, a poem I'm delighted with: in fact the *New Yorker* just bought it. I worked on it a little more after I got home because I cannot see in longhand what the poem will look like on the page. Then, while I was in Washington, I was taken to the King Tut Exhibit. It was hot and crowded, but the experience was overwhelming. I could have spent three days peering into those cases. And flying back to Boston I started another poem on the back of an airline ticket. It's called **"Remembering Pearl Harbor,"** and it's about seeing the King Tut Exhibit on Pearl Harbor Day. Now that may seem a very tenuous connection to you; it did to me. I could not find the connective link for the longest time. I sent the poem to a young poet friend of mine, someone who was not yet born when Pearl Harbor was bombed. I asked her whether it worked for her, because I was afraid that maybe it was just a generational poem. And she explained to me what the connections were. Now, of course, I see them, but I didn't see them while I was writing it. So I suddenly got those two poems, just all very unexpectedly. I hadn't gone seeking them, and there they were.

You have talked about being worried in Fayetteville—about the farm and having these nightmares. Have your husband and your children also affected your writing?

Oh, yes, very much so. I've written a great deal about family relationships. Although the children have grown and gone, they turn up in things.

Has your early family life greatly affected your later poetry, or do you feel it affected more your earlier poetry?

I think I'd have to say it's about fifty-fifty. You never get rid of family relationships, you know. I will always have a mother. My mother is eighty-two, but I still have her and, therefore, I'm still a child—I'm still a daughter. Such things carry through the generations, I think, forever. My father, for example, has been dead for fourteen years, but he still turns up in my dreams. It's astonishing how we are never really free of these relationships, of our position in the family. We carry these with us either as a burden or a joy.

I do not really have any faith, any coherent religious faith, and yet the one thing in my life that I feel passionate and evangelical about is poetry. I want to contribute to its well-being and to its future.

—Maxine Kumin

You've spoken before about a kind of falling out with the whole religious experience. Do you think that poetry is in some way a fulfillment of some sort of spiritual need?

You really are asking me very hard questions. I don't know how to answer that. I call myself an agnostic. I do not really have any faith, any coherent religious faith, and yet the one thing in my life that I feel passionate and evangelical about is poetry. I want to contribute to its well-being and to its future. And I suppose that speaking about the way poems occur is, if you read William James, something like the quality of a religious experience for me.

Do you worry about how your readers are going to read your poems?

I try not to worry about them. I try to put that out of my head, because if you once start worrying about how readers are going to react, it's a very short step from that to worrying about how listeners are going to perceive your poems, and from there it's only a half step to trying very hard to amuse and titillate them. Then pretty soon you are just pandering to an audience, and you're no longer a poet; you're just a performer. So you have to have some convictions about the worth of what you're doing, artistically. You cannot think of it as something that you're doing for the year 1977, but instead as something you hope will outlast you.

How much do you think a reader has to take to one of your poems to get something from it?

Well, I think he has to be reasonably intelligent and reasonably educated and reasonably sympathetic. At least that's what I would like.

Should you worry if he read it differently from what you intended?

I would probably be a little sorry, but if he got something out of it, that would be good. Poetry's a very fragile art form. I think it's the most fragile of all, and I think it requires the most preparation. There are so many dunces listening to music in this world and getting little from it that it rather appalls you when you stop to think. Everybody takes his little rug and cuddles up in pairs to hear Arthur Fiedler conduct the Boston Pops. But somehow more people listen to music with less comprehension than people read poetry. In other words, people don't bother to come to poetry unless they can work it through.

Do you like giving poetry readings?

I do not really like giving readings. I don't panic about them the way I once did. I used to endure agonizing anxieties before a reading, and I know a lot of poets who still do. For some mysterious reason, which I hope will never be clear to me, the terrible terror went away, just gradually eroded over a period of years of forcing myself to do it. What I'm left with is a generalized case of the jitters before I go on. And once I'm into a reading, if the audience is receptive, I could almost say I'm enjoying it—almost. But it's not something I would choose, occupationally. I have to be honest and say I do it for money. And there are some readings—at the Folger, the YMHA in New York, or the Library of Congress—readings like that to which one simply does not say no. You go and you do it.

Do you believe that a reading adds something to poetry?

Definitely, definitely. Poetry is an oral tradition. I think it immensely enhances the person's poetry for an audience to hear it in the poet's voice. I look back on occasions when I heard poets read (and I heard every one I could get to), and I can remember hearing Robert Frost in Sever Hall at Harvard when people were sitting six deep on the windowsills—there were thousands of people in that hall. I heard Auden innumerable times. I heard John Crowe Ransom read his own poetry in his last years, and that was

a fantastic experience. I can never again read a Ransom poem without hearing that marvelously rich southern voice, very controlled, used like an instrument. It gave me goose bumps. His poems gave me goose bumps to begin with, but now they're just immensely deepened. And I think I have felt that way about every poet I've heard read well. Marianne Moore read badly. She could not project her voice and she could not look at the audience, but even so it was exciting to see this great lady in her black cape and her big tricorne black hat. Some of these poets were great personages; some of them were real performers. I'm not sure I like the histrionic performances, but I like to hear the poet's breaks, where the emphasis is, where in the poet's head the interior of the line breaks, etc.

How does your poetry touch your fiction or your fiction touch your poetry?

All over the place and in many ways. I tend to steal from myself. The compass of the poem is so small and so demanding, you have to be so selective, and there are so many things that get left out that you feel cheated. So you take all those things that you couldn't really expatiate upon and they get into the fiction. If you read *The Designated Heir*, my new novel, you'll find probably lots and lots of points in which the text touches the poems and maybe even some recurring phrases, lifted, pirated out of poems that then I could go on with in fiction.

How much do you think a young writer should write? Should he write only as much as he feels like, or should he force himself to keep writing?

I think there's a real value to forcing. I do not think it hurts at all to write to assignment. Granted, the piece that you write for an assignment may not be as good as the piece that you wrote when you were moved to do so, but it will train something in you. Maybe it only trains your typing, but it does train something. I have heard fiction writers say that if you want to learn to write dialogue, get a volume of Hemingway's short stories, sit down at the typewriter, and copy, copy. Just type the text. Now that may sound ludicrous to you, but several things happen. In the first place, you learn how to punctuate conversation. In the second place, you begin to learn how terse and direct conversation can be on the page and how few attributives you really do need. You get out of all of those awful Tom Swifties: "he said, lovingly," "she said, languidly," "she said, contritely," etc. So you learn something about the concision and the terseness of style for which Hemingway is justifiably famous.

What advice would you give to young writers? What sort of reading should they do?

It's a good idea to get in the habit of keeping a notebook or journal, private or semiprivate. Get in the habit of jotting down states of mind or weather reports. It's habit forming and it's good. Also, I do not think anybody becomes a writer who is not a huge reader, omnivorous and wide-ranging. You have to be somebody who's turned on by reading. You have to love words, and you have to be willing to take lots of risks with words, and be willing to write really bad stuff in order to get to the good stuff. You only grow by doing, I think.

Maxine Kumin (essay date 1977)

SOURCE: "Kumin on Kumin: The Tribal Poems," in *To Make a Prairie: Essays on Poets, Poetry, and Country Living,* The University of Michigan Press, 1979, pp. 106-23.

[*In the essay below, written in 1977, Kumin surveys her "tribal poems" or "poems of kinship and parenting" and the examines the recurrent theme of parent-child separation.*]

A terrible ego, as rife among poets as roundworm in the barnyard, had caused all of us represented in this collection of essays by women writers to agree to examine critically some aspect of our own work. Some will argue that we leap to do so because we are women and only recently in the history of American letters has the woman writer been taken seriously. Since I began as a poet in the Dark Ages of the fifties with very little sense of who I was—a wife, a daughter, a mother, a college instructor, a swimmer, a horse lover, a hermit—a stewpot of conflicting emotions has given me some sympathy with that point of view.

But I suspect that the desire to be heard is purer, or more purely corrupt than that. Every poet everywhere longs to be understood, to plead his / her case before the tribunal. To explicate an image, to verify an attitude, to point out the intricacies of a rhyme scheme or stanzaic pattern is a far brighter fate than to take up a soap box in Hyde Park. And although I have not been unhappy with the epithet "pastoral" which is routinely applied to my work, although I do not deny that I write a poetry concerned with the smallest particulars in the natural world, I too have a thesis to advance.

I would like to discuss here in chronological order certain of my "tribal poems"—poems of kinship and parenting—that span two decades. Three of them are taken from **Halfway,** my first collection, long since out of print. They were written in the late fifties; it was not popular then to speak of the uterus or the birth canal. The Women's Movement was still unfounded. An editor of a national magazine wrote me with regret that he could not accept any more poems from me for six months or so because he had already published a woman poet the preceding month.

But what interests me about these poems now is not so much the sociology of the situation to which I was stupidly inured. I am more interested in reading the poet's opening statement of what is to be for her a recurring theme: the separation, for the sake of identity, of mother from child and child from the parental milieu, and her changing perceptions of that separation.

Indeed, I am going to speak of myself henceforth as "the poet" in hopes that the third person usage will cleanse memory and provide objectivity.

Nightmare

This dwelt in me who does not know me now,
Where in her labyrinth I cannot follow,
Advance to be recognized, displace her terror;
I hold my heartbeat on my lap and cannot comfort
    her.
Tonight she is condemned to cry out wolf
Or werewolf, and it echoes in the gulf
And no one comes to cradle cold Narcissus;
The first cell that divided separates us.

Eight lines, predominantly iambic pentameter, except for the longer fourth line which stands as the fulcrum of the poem, a poem rhyming in slant couplets. Two mythic allusions, one old English, the other classical Greek, neither of them difficult. These are the tools the poet uses to deal with strongly felt or painfully perceived material. She liked then, she likes to this day to cram hard thoughts into formal patterns, thereby rendering them malleable or at least bearable. It became her conviction over the years that form can provide a staunch skeleton on which to set the flesh and blood of feeling. Moreover, she came to believe that the exigencies of rhyme force her to a heightened level of language, especially of metaphor. A level she might not rise to on her own, so to speak. These, then, are her shibboleths.

"The first cell that divided separates us." The child must grow according to her own clock. The parent must make the effort of consent, must relinquish her offspring. If not gracefully, then a great ragged tearing will ensue.

The Journey
for Jane at thirteen

Papers in order; your face
accurate and on guard in the cardboard house
and the difficult patois you will speak
half mastered in your jaw;
the funny make-up in your funny pocketbook—
pale lipstick, half a dozen lotions
to save your cloudless skin
in that uncertain sea
where no one charts the laws—
of course you do not belong to me
nor I to you
and everything is only true in mirrors.

I help to lock your baggage:
history book, lace collar and pink pearls
from the five-and-ten,
an expurgated text
of how the gods behaved on Mount Olympus,
and pennies in your shoes.
You lean as bland as sunshine on the rails.
Whatever's next—
the old oncoming uses

of your new troughs and swells—
is coin for trading among girls
in gym suits and geometry classes.

How can you know I traveled here,
stunned, like you, by my reflection
in forest pools;
hunted among the laurel
and whispered to by swans
in accents of my own invention?

It is a dangerous time.
The water rocks away the timber
and here is your visa stamped in red.
You lean down your confident head.
We exchange kisses; I call your name
and wave you off as the bridge goes under.

Curiously, again allusions to Greek mythology, to Narcissus, Daphne, and Leda crop up, although here they are suggested by the actual I. A. Richards text referred to in the second stanza. Again, a prevailing formal pattern with more widely spaced rhymes. This time, the separation is viewed as a metaphorical journey. The daughter is not traveling off to boarding school, as one reviewer suggested. She is undertaking the rites of passage, making the necessary crossing from the innocence of childhood to the acute self-consciousness of adolescence. In her new life she will converse with her peers in their own patois. She goes forth armoured with the correct costume and the correct appurtenances. The sea, that sad, dying, all-mothering ocean that she must cross, is seen as "uncertain"; the time is "dangerous." But the daughter goes forth confidently, her visa (the menarche) already validated. No turning back. The bridge between mother and child serves no further function and it goes under.

There seems, perhaps a common enough phenomenon, to have been less fear on the poet's part that her daughters would be able to make the transition than fear for the fate of her son. In the following poem, rhythmically imitative of Auden, the poet remembers the boy's birth and the heroic measures required in the hospital to keep him breathing. No literary allusions here. The trimeter line and the *abab* rhyme scheme doubled or even trebled provide the reinforcing rods. The poet still likes this antique and sentimental poem. If only she could retract that dreadful "kiss" / "this" final couplet!

Poem for My Son

Where water laps my hips
it licks your chin. You stand
on tiptoe looking up
and swivel on my hands.
We play at this and laugh,
but understand you weigh
now almost less than life
and little more than sea.
So fine a line exists
between buoyance and stone
that, catching at my wrists,

I feel love notch the bone
to think you might have gone.

To think they smacked and pumped
to squall you into being
when you swam down, lungs limp
as a new balloon, and dying.
Six years today they bent
a black tube through your chest.
The tank hissed in the tent.
I leaned against the mast
outside that sterile nest.

And now inside the sea
you bump along my arm,
learning the narrow way
you've come from that red worm.
I tell you, save your air
and let the least swell ease you.
Put down, you flail for shore.
I cannot bribe nor teach you
to know the wet will keep you.

And cannot tell myself
unfasten from the boy.
On the Atlantic shelf
I see you wash away
to war or love or luck,
prodigious king, a stranger.
Times I stepped on a crack
my mother was in danger,
and time will find the chinks
to work the same in me.
You bobbled in my flanks.
They cut you from my sea.
Now you must mind your way.

Once, after a long swim
come overhand and wheezy
across the dappled seam
of lake, I foundered, dizzy,
uncertain which was better:
to fall there and unwind
in thirty feet of water
or fight back for the land.
Life would not let me lose it.
It yanked me by the nose.
Blackfaced and thick with vomit
it thrashed me to my knees.
We only think we choose.
But say we choose. Pretend it.
My pulse knit in your wrist
expands. Go now and spend it.
The sea will take our kiss.
Now, boy, swim off for this.

Here the poet seems to insist on, rather than protest over, her separation from the boy. She speculates today that the insistence was culturally imposed. Her expectations that the boy would "wash away / to war or love or luck, / prodigious king, a stranger" seem to her now to have been the standard maternal expectations of her era and should be viewed in that historical context. Nevertheless, it is painful to be old enough to speak of her past as an era.

In this poem the sea is a buoying but treacherous mother. Learning to float in it is a terrifying experience for the small boy who so nearly drowned at birth when fluid seeped into his lungs. Amnion and ocean both sustain and imperil. The poet remembers an incident when she too nearly drowned and discovered thereby how fierce the will to live, so fierce that she concludes we operate by instinct; "we only think we choose." She ends in a rhetorical burst, urging her small son forward metaphorically to make his own way on the strength of his genetic and God-knows-what-other inheritance. It is an overblown conclusion to an otherwise decent poem.

There is another motif. It emerges with the second book, *The Privilege,* published in 1965. For its epigraph the poet has taken some sentences from Joseph Conrad, who wrote to his aunt: "That's how it is! One must drag the ball and chain of one's selfhood to the end. It is the price one pays for the devilish and divine privilege of thought. . . ."

In two elegies for her father the poet comes again upon the desperate issue of autonomy, the ongoing and always paradoxical struggle for an identity separate from the parent. Now she looks back over her shoulder, as it were, at her own coming of age.

This is taken from **"The Pawnbroker."**

> Firsthand I had from my father a love ingrown
> tight as an oyster and returned it
> as secretly. From him firsthand
> the grace of work, the sweat of it, the bone-
> tired unfolding down from stress.
> I was the bearer he paid up on demand
> with one small pearl of selfhood. Portionless,
> I am oystering still to earn it.
>
> Not of the House of Rothschild, my father, my
>   creditor
> lay dead while they shaved his cheeks and blacked
>   his mustache.
> My lifetime appraiser, my first prince whom death
>   unhorsed
> lay soberly dressed and barefoot to be burned.
> That night, my brothers and I forced
> the cap on his bottle of twenty-year-old scotch
> and drank ourselves on fire beforehand
> for the sacrament of closing down the hatch,
> for the sacrament of easing down the ways
> my thumb-licking peeler of cash on receipt of the
>   merchandise,
>
> possessor of miracles left unredeemed on the shelf
> after thirty days,
> giver and lender, no longer in hock to himself,
> ruled off the balance sheet,
> a man of great personal order
> and small white feet.

Again, a strict rhyming pattern, a kind of enabling legislation to write the poem. It is interesting in retrospect to see the ocean once again, though obliquely, contained in the image of oyster and pearl and picked up on as a metaphor for the burial rites. In this instance, closing the lid on the father's body in the coffin is seen as the final act of battening down the hatches before setting sail. But the funeral is at the same time a beginning, a christening of a new ship for a new voyage as it is eased down the ways into the ocean.

Fortunately, the poet interjects, these illuminations of intent are not present at the time of composition.

A second elegy, **"Lately, at Night,"** written in alternating twelve and fourteen-line stanzas in a looser rhyme scheme, deals more directly with the funeral parlor experience, the business of burial: "I am pulled up short / between those two big boys your sons, my brothers / brave as pirates putting into / a foreign port." Even in death, it seems, the father's domain can only be entered by an act of plunder. Autonomy is arrived at by piracy. And the final stanza, expressing the anguish of the separated child who is condemned to relive the dying man's last hours in her dreams, returns to the pirate ship metaphor:

> Father,
> lately at night as I watch your chest
> to help it to breathe in
> and swear it moves, and swear I hear the air
> rising and falling,
> even in the dream it is my own fat lungs
> feeding themselves, greedy as ever.
> Smother, drown or burn, Father,
> Father, no more false moves, I beg you.
> Back out of my nights, my dear dead
>   undergroundling.
> It is time. Let the pirates berth their ships,
> broach casks, unload the hold, and let
> the dead skin of your forehead
> be a cold coin under my lips.

The poet would define these two themes—loss of the parent, relinquishment of the child—as central to her work. Once established they thrive like house plants but tend to branch off or hybridize as they grow.

By 1970, in *The Nightmare Factory,* the figure of the father is clearly an historical one, as in this excerpt from a poem called **"The New York Times."**

> Sundays my father
> hairs sprouting out of
> the V of his pajamas
> took in the sitdowns
> picket lines Pinkertons
> Bundists lend-lease
> under his mustache.
>
> In with the hash browns
> in with the double yolked
> once over lightly eggs

mouthfuls of bad news.
Nothing has changed, Poppa.
The same green suburban lawn.
The same fat life.

And the children are almost adults. The son, restless, dis-
affected, leaves home in a figurative sense. The mother is
no longer an authority figure; she is helpless against the
urgency of his craving to be gone:

Today the jailbird maple in the yard
sends down a thousand red hands in the rain.
Trussed at the upstairs window I
watch the great drenched leaves flap by
knowing that on the comely boulevard
incessant in your head you stand again
at the cloverleaf, thumb crooked outward.

Dreaming you travel light
guitar pick and guitar
bedroll sausage-tight
they take you as you are.

They take you as you are
there's nothing left behind
guitar pick and guitar
on the highways of your mind.

Even the tree has been taken prisoner. The mother too is
captive, "trussed" at the window. She can only speculate
about her son's future:

How it will be tomorrow is anyone's guess.
The Rand McNally opens at a nudge
to forty-eight contiguous states, easy
as a compliant girl. In Minneapolis
I see you drinking wine under a bridge.
I see you turning on in Washington, D.C.,
panhandling in New Orleans, friendless

in Kansas City in an all-night beanery
and mugged on the beach in Venice outside L.A.
They take your watch and wallet and crack your
    head
as carelessly as an egg. The yolk runs red.
All this I see, or say it's what I see
in leaf fall, in rain, from the top of the stairs today
while your maps, those sweet pastels, lie flat and
    ready.

[**"For My Son on the Highways of His Mind"**]

They are locked into this pattern, the mother and son, he
to take part in the "on the road" ethos of the sixties, she
to stand by grieving in the stereotype of mothers everywhere. The refrain lines, two trimeter quatrains, echo that
early poem, **"Poem for My Son."** Indeed, the poet had
wished to write the entire poem in trimeter, but found that
the expository material was so dense that she had to fall
back from the lyric line into iambic pentameter, which is
far better adapted to the kinds of cataloging she felt she
needed to do.

**Every poet everywhere longs to be
understood, to plead his / her case before
the tribunal. To explicate an image, to
verify an attitude, to point out the
intricacies of a rhyme scheme or stanzaic
pattern is a far brighter fate than to take
up a soap box in Hyde Park.**

—Maxine Kumin

In a sense, while the mother-son relationship has simpli-
fied itself, the mother-daughter one has grown more complicated. A darker outline emerges. It is no longer a matter of waving the child off into adolescence. Now the poet
must deal with a necessary rivalry developing between
mother and daughter, which ends, as it must, with the
metaphorical dismissal and death of the mother.

Metaphor is not smaller than life. It mediates between
awesome truths. It leaps up from instinctual feeling bearing forth the workable image. Thus in a sense the metaphor is truer than the actual fact.

In **"Father's Song"** the poet draws distinctions between
the father's attitude toward the son and toward the daughters. It is a feudal poem, not one the poet would wish to
save, but it points a direction:

I have not said there is the season
of tantrums when the throats of doors are cut
with cold slammings. Rooms fill with tears.
The bedclothes drown in blood
for these will be women. They will lie down
with lovers, they will cry out giving birth,
they will grow old with hard knuckles and dry
    necks.
Death will punish them with subtractions.
They will burn me and put me into the earth.

Although the persona is that of the male parent, the feeling tone clearly is shared with the mother.

Again, in **"The Fairest One of All,"** which alludes to,
indeed depends for its effect on the grisly outcome of this
fairy tale, the premonition of her own death calls forth
from the poet this concluding stanza to a love poem for
her older daughter:

So far so good, my darling, my fair
first born, your hair black as ebony
your lips red as blood. But let there be
no mistaking how the dark scheme runs.
Too soon all this will befall:
Too soon the huntsman will come.
He will bring me the heart of a wild boar
and I in error will have it salted and cooked
and I in malice will eat it bit by bit
thinking it yours.

And as we both know, at the appropriate moment
I will be consumed by an inexorable fire
as you look on.

The poet is given courage to press on by Yeats, who wrote:
"I must lie down where all the ladders start / In the foul
rag and bone shop of the heart." For these are harsh judgments, that the daughters, to come of age, must psychologically overwhelm their mothers, that they must canni-
balize across the generations one on another.

With the publication of **House, Bridge, Fountain, Gate** in
1975 the poet has, she now thinks, completed the tasks.
She has let go of the large children although she returns
thematically to them, evoking memory. In **"The Knot"**
she writes, addressing an absent daughter:

It's last summer in this picture, a day on the edge
of our time zone. We are standing in the park,
our genes declare themselves, death smiles in the
    sun
streaking the treetops, the sky all lightstruck . . .
In the dark you were packed about with toys,
you were sleeping on your knees, never alone
your breathing making little o's
of trust, night smooth as soapstone
and the hump of your bottom like risen bread . . .

and ends, coming to terms with the separation in time as
well as place:

          . . . I chew on the knot
we were once. Meanwhile, your eyes, serene
in the photo, look most thoughtfully out
and could be bullet holes, or beauty spots.

Similarly, in a poem addressed to the foster son who still
searches for his lost mother, she admonishes:

It is true that we lie down on cowflops
praying they'll turn into pillows.
It is true that our mothers explode
out of the snowballs of dreams
or speak to us down the chimney
saying our names above the wind

or scrape their legs like crickets
in the dead grass behind the toolshed
tapping a code we can't read.

That a man may be free of his ghosts
he must return to them like a garden.
He must put his hands in the sweet rot
uprooting the turnips, washing them
tying them into bundles
and shouldering the whole load to market.
                              [**"History Lesson"**]

Perhaps what she has said of the young man's ghosts can
also be said of her own? Hasn't this been the informing
thrust of her poetry? Particularly in this book she "returns
to them like a garden"; she has spread out the decade of

the thirties in which she was a small child, all of its "sweet
rot" exposed. Nor does it matter which details are invented, which are recorded. If everything coheres, the poem
has been served. Here is the central stanza from **"The
Thirties Revisited,"** full of those warring misconceptions:

Now I am ten. Enter Mamselle,
my mother's cut-rate milliner.
She is putting her eyes out in the hall
at thirty cents an hour
tacking veils onto felt forms.
Mamselle is an artist.
She can copy the Eiffel Tower
in feathers with a rolled-up brim.
She can make pyramids out of cherries.
Mamselle wears cheese boxes on her feet.
Madame can buy and sell her.

If daughters were traded among the accessories
in the perfumed hush of Bonwit Teller's
she'd have replaced me with a pocketbook,
snapped me shut and looped me over
her Hudson seal cuff: me of the chrome-wire mouth,
the inkpot braids, one eye that looks
wrongly across at the other.
O Lady of the Chaise Longue,
O Queen of the Kimono,
I disappoint my mother.

Yet it is in this collection that the poet begins—she is a
late beginner!—to come to terms with the ways in which
her own mother was shaped by the social constraints of
her young womanhood. **"Life's Work," "Sperm," "The
Deaths of the Uncles,"** narrative poems of some length,
take up the tantalizing mythology of her mother's family:

O Grandfather, look what your seed has done!
Look what has come of those winter night gallops.
You tucking the little wife up
under the comforter that always leaked feathers.
You coming perhaps just as the trolley
derailed taking the corner at 15th Street
in a shower of sparks, and Grandmother's
corset spread out like a filleted fish
to air meanwhile on the window sill.

She will make Galsworthian figures of them all, willy-
nilly. In **"Life's Work"** she contrasts her mother's rebellion against the aforementioned stern grandfather with her
own efforts to break away. Her mother, denied a musical
career, eloped with the man who became the poet's father.
Characteristically, when faced with his daughter's ambitions, he

swore on the carrots and the boiled beef
that I would come to nothing
that I would come to grief . . .

the midnights of my childhood still go on
the stairs speak again under your foot
the heavy parlor door folds shut
and "Au Clair de la Lune"

puckers from the obedient keys
plain as a schoolroom clock ticking
and what I hear more clearly than Debussy's
lovesong is the dry aftersound
of your long nails clicking.

So the mother is not the villain after all? So we are victims of our dailiness, in whatever archetypal roles we are
cast? As Jung tells us, there will always be the mother, the
father, the miraculous child. Everything we construct arises from these primordial images, very possibly inborn in
us. The poet is still doing her homework in the human
psyche. The children continue to appear in virtually every
new work she undertakes, sometimes viewed with acceptance, sometimes with distance. In **"Changing the Children"** she concludes:

> Eventually we get them back.
> Now they are grown up.
> They are much like ourselves.
> They wake mornings beyond cure,
> not a virgin among them.
> We are civil to one another.
> We stand in the kitchen
> slicing bread, drying spoons
> and tuning in to the weather.

"Sunbathing on a Rooftop in Berkeley" is addressed,
some fifteen years later, to the same daughter as was **"The
Journey."** But the lines are open and adopt a more relaxed, conversational tone. Stanzas match but there is no
rhyme scheme. The poet thinks her tone is no more or less
assured working in this freer way. She thinks only that it
befits the material, that the collision of particulars, observed and recalled, build up to and prepare for the unvar-
nished truth of the ending:

> O summers without end, the exact truth is
> we are expanding sideways as haplessly
> as in the mirrors of the Fun House.
> We bulge toward the separate fates that await us,
> sometimes touching, as sleeves will, whether
> or not a hug was intended.

> O summers without end, the truth is
> no matter how I love her, Death
> blew up my dress that day
> while she was in the egg unconsidered.

The poet wishes to make one final entry in this often
awkward disquisition on herself. A recent poem, **"The
Envelope,"** grew out of a chance encounter with a phrase
from Heidegger, "the fear of cessation." It was that curious Latinate usage, although very likely the Latinism was
acquired in translation, that triggered the opening line and
a half. The rest of the poem was carried forth by the
poet's ongoing preoccupation with the tribal notion of
succession. Her preoccupation, she concedes, is ever more
heavily tinged with intimations of her own mortality.
Nevertheless, the poet here records her perpetual astonishment at her good fortune in having had daughters. In

addition to the esthetic and emotional pleasure they provide, she feels agreeably improved on by them.

The Envelope

> It is true, Martin Heidegger, as you have written,
> *I fear to cease,* even knowing that at the hour
> of my death my daughters will absorb me, even
> knowing they will carry me about forever
> inside them, an arrested fetus, even as I carry
> the ghost of my mother under my navel, a nervy
> little androgynous person, a miracle
> folded in lotus position.

> Like those old pear-shaped Russian dolls that open
> at the middle to reveal another and another, down
> to the pea-sized, irreducible minim,
> may we carry our mothers forth in our bellies.
> May we, borne onward by our daughters, ride
> in the Envelope of Almost-Infinity,
> that chain letter good for the next twenty-five
> thousand days of their lives.

The womanly images persist. Just as there is an ovum in
"Sunbathing . . ." there is the fetus within the womb
here. But a peculiar transformation has taken place in the
childbearing process. Now it is our mothers, as well as
our children, whom we carry about with us, internalized
lares and *penates,* as it were. The poem concludes as a
prayer of sorts. Clearly, the poet's ego is speaking. She
wants to outlast her time frame. She prays to be carried
on.

Sybil P. Estess (essay date 1979)

SOURCE: "Past Halfway: *The Retrieval System,* by Maxine Kumin," in *The Iowa Review,* Vol. 10, No. 4, Fall,
1979, pp. 99-109.

[*Estess is an American poet and critic. In the following
essay, she analyzes the ways in which Kumin faces loss in*
The Retrieval System.]

The Retrieval System, Maxine Kumin's sixth book of poetry, is about surviving loss. It confirms things many of us
already knew about its author, a just-past-middle-age, increasingly refined, non-suicidal poet. The main value in
both her life and her poetry is preservation. That which is
retrieved in her system may be the simple life of fruits and
vegetables or it may be something in her unconscious. But
in ***The Retrieval System*** the things that most need to be
recovered, savored and saved are the memories of those no
longer within the poet's physical reach. This is the primary
kind of loss with which Kumin, in her mid-fifties, lives.

Kumin's courage in dealing with loss is evident in the
poems written about her friend Anne Sexton who died in
1974. After a lunch of tuna sandwiches and vodka at
Kumin's Boston house, Sexton drove to her own garage
and asphyxiated herself.

From all accounts, especially Kumin's—which she will be, as she says, "gathering up for years"—the friendship of these two women was extraordinary. Both came to writing late: Kumin at nearly thirty, pregnant with her third child, and Sexton around the same age, after her first mental breakdown. By the end of their time together they had shared much: the collaborative writing of several children's books; the pain of Sexton's ceaseless psychological strife; and their (remarkably different) poetry. In Boston, each had had a separate telephone installed for their daily, often day-long talks. Kumin remarked in a conversation with me, and later informed an interviewer, that these calls often lasted all day, beginning in the morning and continuing through temporary interruptions during which they kept each other "on the line" while each went about her routine. If either wished to resume the conversation she would whistle loudly into the receiver.

In **"Address to the Angels"** Kumin writes of her deep loss at Sexton's death: "Always / I think that no one / can be sadder than I am." Although such pain is absolute, Kumin's statement here is obviously exaggerated. Yet, as if to prepare for that blatant sentimentality, the poet precedes these lines with the admission that "Always it is passion that / confuses the issue." In any case, by staying with this poem, a reader locates its more crucial substance: the loneliness and anger which result from surviving middle-age and feeling left alone. The poet protests the absence of "angels, God's secret agents" who she is "assured by Billy Graham, / circulate among us to tell / the living they are not alone." Such beings might have protected her against, or at least helped her bear, so terrible a burden, but did not. Job-like, Kumin asks, "Angels, where were you when / my best friend did herself in?"

"Progress Report," another poem which deals with Kumin's grief over Sexton's death, begins with this long, sorrowful sentence:

> The middle age you wouldn't wait
> for now falls on me, white
> as a caterpillar tent, white
> as the sleetfall from apple trees
> gone wild, petals that stick
> in my hair like confetti
> as I cut my way through clouds
> of gnats and blackflies in the woods.

Kumin suggests to Sexton, now on "the other side," that "the idea of going on without you" seems so difficult that she might not be able to "carry on"

> Dear friend, last night I dreamed
> you held a sensitive position,
> you were Life's Counselor
> coming to the phone in Vaud or Bern,
> some terse one-syllable place,
> to tell me how to carry on.

But without Sexton's advice, Kumin does go on, seemingly because she determines, over and over, to survive:

> and I woke into the summer solstice
> swearing I will break
> your absence into crumbs
> like the stump of a punky tree
> working its way down
> in the world's evening
> down to the forest floor.

Kumin herself has stated that she wondered whether she would be able to write at all after Sexton died. But indeed she has, even after such loss, written some of her most plaintive poems.

Philip Booth has rightly noted [in "Maxine Kumin's Survival," *The American Poetry Review,* Vol. 7, No. 6, 1978] how "gently the ironies reverberate within" the "seeming facticity" of many lines from this book. We witness this phenomenon where subtle enjambment creates almost shocking irony, such as in "white / as a caterpillar tent, white / as the sleetfall from apple trees / gone wild. . . ." or in "swearing I will break / your absence into crumbs." In such ways this poet cuts her linguistic path through grief, "through clouds / of gnats and backflies in the woods."

In the fourth section, "Body and Soul," Kumin places two other poems about Sexton. In **"How It Is,"** a month after Sexton's death Kumin is wearing a blue jacket her dead friend left, becoming, in the first strophe, her suicide friend. Hauntingly, the poem begins, "Shall I say how it is in your clothes?" Then snapshot-like lines tell the reader part of how it is:

> The dog at the center of my life recognizes
> you've come to visit, he's ecstatic.
> In the left pocket, a hole.
> In the right, a parking ticket
> deliveered up last August on Bay State Road.
> In my heart, a scatter like milkweed,
> a flinging from the pods of the soul.
> My skin presses your old outline.
> It is hot and dry inside.

The poem concludes by suggesting just how intense the heat, how dry the terrain is in that lonely interior within which Kumin endures without and with Sexton:

> I will be years gathering up our words,
> fishing out letters, snapshots, stains,
> leaning my ribs against this durable cloth
> to put on the dumb blue blazer of your death.

"Gathering up," "fishing out," "leaning" are all downward motions which any solitary survivor recognizes as the person attempts to rebuild out of loss. More than this, what any poet works both with and against in order to attempt such a process is "dumbness." Kumin's metaphors transform pain into language, the essential groundwork for her ability to speak of and from Sexton's death.

Perhaps the saddest poem that Kumin writes about her recurring memories of Sexton is the complicated and chill-

Dark   *Winter Thoughts*

                    Feeding Time

Sunset. ————————→   *No sitting it out*
I pull on parka, boots,
mittens, hat,
Cross the road to the paddock ~~gate~~.
Cat comes.   *check latches, thermom—*
Horses are waiting.   *(7°) leave*
Each enters his ~~stall~~ *box*
in the order they've ~~all~~   *Re skinny, Feral Tom Cat*
agreed on, behind my back.   *who took us on last fall.*
Cat supervises from the molding cove.   *— stall*
Hay first. Water next.
Grain last. Hang up halters.   *13*
Check latches. Leave.
         turns   left a   *Purple sky left a royal bed*
Sky, purple, as ~~in~~ royal bed.   *Sky purple, blotched in*
Feed Dog next.   *felt*
I re-cross the road to woodshed. *Re*
Snappish moment with cat.   *Cat banished 10*
banished to top of stack.   *to top of*   *The world is grey down*
No real contest.   *on one knee*
Wag, wag, kerchunk! Polished
~~bowl~~. Dog asks for, receives rights
to go inside
lie by firelight.

Now ~~two~~ above. *Sky shows*
Meagre afterglow.
Feed Birds next. I wade
by way of footprint wells
in deep snow   *13*
to ~~fill~~ feeders in the glade
behind house. Cat follows
observing distribution   *high squeak*
of sunflower seeds, checks out each ~~hollow~~ heel-toe
I've stepped in, coming back
in case something *it needs,*
smelling small and foolish lurks.   *Turn piercing cold*
No luck.   *at 10 below, I hear*
                                                a horse cough
Cat gets
enormous supper:
chicken gizzards! Attacks
these like cougar *gulps;*   *8*
but does not ~~gobble~~, even at bay.
Retires to barn loft
to sleep in hay
maybe catch dessert.

Now us, Dear One.   of horse, pig, ~~goat~~ *sheep*
My soup, your bread *in bowls*   emerging from outcroppings
on old blue plates that will mourn/us   on these plates?   *13*
when we're dead, *I in bowls that probably*   Now, no one trespasses. ————
probably have written down   The house dozes.
much of what we've said   Later, I hear a horse cough
in thirty years of ~~slicings and~~ soppings;   and flash a message ~~texext~~: *worry*
Where are the children   *up slurps.*   Cat: are you warm enough?
who fought for the designs

Corrected typescript of Kumin's "Feeding Time."

ing **"Splitting Wood at Six Above."** As if she wishes unconsciously to postpone stating the grim finality of Sexton's death, it is not until the third line in the second strophe of the poem that the poet tells the reader what the real subject matter is: "You are four months dead." Until then, only the action of the title is described:

> I open a tree.
> In the stupefying cold
> —ice on bare flesh a scald—
> I seat the metal wedge
> with a few left-handed swipes,
> then with a change of grips
> lean into the eight-pound sledge.
>
> It's muslin overhead.
> Snow falls as heavy as salt.

Finally, in the thirty-third line of the poem, Sexton is addressed:

> See you tomorrow, you said.
> You lied.
> We're far from finished! I'm still
> talking to you (last night's dream);
> we'll split the phone bill.
> It's expensive calling
> From the other side.

"Splitting Wood at Six Above" alludes, of course, to former telephone conversations, to how dreams help or don't help Kumin work through memories, to her New England life which requires her to split wood to stay warm, and to a connection between the pain of "splitting wood" in six-degree weather and splitting a nightmare "phone bill," which costs her much. The underlying thematic question of the poem, however, is what happens to the "soul" of something after death. For Kumin, people, like wood, are another kind of matter. ("Time will do this as fair / to hickory, birch, black oak. . . .") Yet, "Even waking it seems / logical—" she writes, to assume that Sexton's "small round / stubbornly airborne soul" ascended, and "none the worse for its trip," arrived at "the other side."

> *The Retrieval System* will return to us and return us to Kumin's compassion; her dry-eyed sensitivity; her exemplary choices to live on, even with pain, rather than to give up; her transformation of matter into spirit, body into soul.
>
> —*Sybil P. Estess*

Having likened the sound of the departing souls of the dead wood she splits to a single "flap" which rises, the poet mysteriously and appropriately ends the poem with a subtle metaphor for what haunts her most about Sexton's death: "the sound of your going." **"Splitting Wood. . . ."** ends with five short, staccato lines:

> It is the sound
> of your going I drive
> into heartwood. I stack
> my quartered cuts bark down,
> open yellow-face up.

The chopping rhythm of this poem suggests the hard, flintlike reality of being split apart. The poem's very creation is analogous to chopping wood, for the will to go ahead into what is cold and inhospitable is characteristic of the will to endure a New England winter, the will to survive the death of a friend, the will to metamorphose suffering into art. The language of **"Splitting Wood"** is cold, brittle. Only ten lies out of fifty-three do not end with a monosyllabic, accented word. A few of those words ("eyelash," "ghost-puffs," "tightrope") comprise a spondaic foot. Others either end strongly ("puppet-squeak," "combine") or show the lightest sort of falling off ("nougat," "stammer," "hammer," "calling"). Both rhythm and language retrieve the experience of losing human contact, of being alone within the icy natural world.

"Remembering Pearl Harbor at the Tutankhamen Exhibit," also from the "Body and Soul" section, contrasts modern and ancient attitudes toward death. The poet wonders how many people in line with her to see the exhibit remember what became our planet's most horrible descent into irretrievability, Pearl Harbor and the start of World War II. The poem proceeds to a denial that anything survives the thoroughness of modern destruction:

> . . . the king is conveyed
> with a case for his heart
> and another magnificent
> hinged apparatus, far too small,
> for his intestines, all in place,
> all considered retrievable
>
> whereas if one is to be blown
> apart over land or water
> back into the Nothingness
> that precedes light, it is better
> to go with the simplest detail:
> a cross, a dogtag,
> a clamshell.

A major question that Kumin and *The Retrieval System* pose seems to be "Is lost life, for contemporary people, retrievable?" Her answer is a qualified "Yes": by imagination, and by metaphor, since metaphor allows imagination to emerge. The poet of the last lines of **"Remembering Pearl Harbor"** does not adhere to the belief in the resurrection of the body. But perhaps no American poet since Anne Bradstreet or Emily Dickinson—Kumin's New England ancestors—has been so concerned with showing that soul, or Spirit, both exists and survives the body's destruction. Stating in **"Body and Soul: A Mediation"** that she "ought to have paid closer / attention when Miss Bloomsberg / shepherded the entire fifth grade / into the Walk-Through Woman," the poet remembers something curious about the experience: "there was nothing about the soul." Kumin never locates the exact bodily home of psyche, yet she seems to think that souls are real:

> Still unlocated, drifting,
> my airmail half-ounce soul
> shows up from time to time
> like those old-fashioned
> doctors who used to cheer
> their patients in girls' boarding schools
> with midnight bedside visits.

What *The Retrieval System,* like Kumin's other books of poems, impresses us with is that only our unconscious and imaginative lives enable our bodies to house souls. On the other hand, Kumin, unlike Bradstreet or Dickinson, cannot imagine soul or Spirit apart from body or matter. In **"The Excrement Poem,"** Kumin writes, "I honor shit for saying: We go on." For her, the body gives evidence that Spirit is. It is the body, therefore, that she fears to lose.

In Kumin's best poems, descriptions—even descriptions of relationships—are best communicated by metaphor, the most likely system of retrieval. Not surprisingly, of the two poems to her daughters (to whom this volume is dedicated) the more poignant is the more metaphoric **"Seeing the Bones."** The mother receives "letters home that fall Fridays / in the box at the foot of the hill / saying the old news, keeping it neutral." She remembers:

> In junior high your biology class
> boiled a chicken down into its bones
> four days at the simmer in my pot.
> then wired joint by joint
> the re-created hen
> in an anatomy project
> you stayed home from, sick.

Then, the real pain, the pain of loss, appears. "Thus am I afflicted, seeing the bones." The final five lines of the poem read:

> Working backward I reconstruct
> you. Send me your baby teeth, some new
> nail parings and a hank of hair
> and let me do the rest. I'll
> set the pot to boil.

In **"The Envelope"** Kumin speaks of the pleasing affection which daughters often have for their mothers, of the lasting models which women become for their female offspring, and, most of all, of the tentative consolation which these truths afford one who ponders the irretrievability of one's mother's life, or one's own.

> Like those old pear-shaped Russian dolls that open
> at the middle to reveal another and another, down
> to the pea-sized, irreducible minim,
> may we carry our mothers forth in our bellies.

> May we, borne onward by our daughters, ride
> in the Envelope of Almost-Infinity,
> that chain letter good for the next twenty-five
> thousand days of our lives.

Even the nature poems in *The Retrieval System,* striking in their beauty or stirring in their forbodingness, reinforce the book's central theme: the pain of loss. In **"Territory"** Kumin recounts the death of the toad mangled by the power mower: ". . . he goes on / lopsidedly hopping until his mother runs out." **"How It Goes On"** concludes,

> The lamb, whose time has come, goes off
> in the cab of the dump truck, tied to the seat
> with baling twine, durable enough
> to bear her to the knife and rafter.

> O Lambs! The whole wolf-world sits down to eat
> and cleans its muzzle after.

Even poems which appear, at first, simply pastoral actually deal with either the acceptance of or strife against the life-death cycle that nature dramatizes. **"July, Against Hunger,"** an evocative description of haying time on a farm, proceeds in Proustian fashion as "The smell collects, elusive, sweet," into the poet's particular recollections

> of gray nights flicked with the snake tongue
> of heat lightning, when the grownups sat
> late on the side porch talking politics,
> foreclosures, war, and Roosevelt.

The poem's second strophe deals with the irretrievable losses of middle age as well as with the confusing yet inevitable merging of past and present as one grows older:

> Loneliness fills me like a pitcher.
> The old deaths dribble out. . . .
> . . . . .
> Meanwhile, a new life kicks in the mare.
> Meanwhile, the poised sky opens on rain.
> The time on either side of *now* stands fast
> glinting like jagged window glass.

The poem's final sentences are defiant—as if to strike back at the mental and spiritual hunger of this July:

> There are limits, my God, to what I can heft
> in this heat! Clearly, the Great Rat waits,
> who comes all winter to gnaw on iron
> or wood, and tears the last flesh from the bone.

But if **"July, Against Hunger"** protests loss, the final poems in the book are beautiful representations of what it means to accept how the natural world retrieves itself. After describing the many serendipitous mortal things which surprise with joy or horrify with their "naturalness"—a frog in the old outdoor bathtub; two white-throated sparrows, singing; a dog which "brings in one half a rank / woodchuck no angel spoke up for"—Kumin ends the final poem in the book, **"A Mortal Day of No Surprises,"** with thirteen lucky lines. They sum up some of her acceptance of the potentials for and limitations of mortal retrievability:

> When I'm scooped out of here
> all things animal
> and unsurprised will carry on.
> Frogs still will fall into those
> stained old tubs we fill
> with trickles from the garden hose.
> Another blue-green prince will sit
> like a friend of the family
> guarding the doomspout.
> Him asquat at the drainhole,
> me gone to crumbs in the ground
> and someone else's mare to call
> to the stallion.

In a poet's sixth book, we expect wise and purposeful construction. Within *The Retrieval System,* a sure and satisfying connection exists between the poems concerning Anne Sexton's death and those devoted to a portrait of Henry Manley, Kumin's rural neighbor. Henry Manley represents one who endures. He is a "rich example" of how to live a soul-building life. Manley does not suffer Kumin's kind of pain from loss, because he is even more connected to the natural world. In **"The Food Chain"** the poet describes Henry filling her pond with a "double tub of brookies" and warning her against kingfishers (of which he would rid himself with his air rifle) and martens:

> He stands there, busy with his wrists, and looking
>   savage.
>
> Knowing he knows we'll hook his brookies
> once they're a sporting size, I try for something
> but all the words stay netted in my mouth.
> Henry waves, guns the engine. His wheels spin
> then catch.

The last poem of the Manley sequence, **"Henry Manley, Living Alone, Keeps Time,"** describes how life, for the aging, narrows to the essentials. For Henry these are, ultimately, *"Coffee. Coffee Cup. Watch."* Henry sits

>   stiff
> at the bruised porcelain table
> saying them over, able
> to with only the slightest catch.

But even though "Terror sweeps him from room to room," Henry Manley seems to dwell with more submission to his fate than does metropolitan man:

> Knowing how much he weighed once
> he knows how much he has departed his life.
> Especially he knows how the soul
> can slip out of the body unannounced
> like that helium-filled balloon
> he opened his fingers on, years back.

There are dimensions of the poems in *The Retrieval System* which are more brilliantly "Kumin-esque" than ever

before: a language musical and lyrical, yet tough; reality re-imagined, as metaphor; a nearly fearless excavation into the unconscious; an attempt to make matter more palatable by locating spirit. Some of the poems here show flaws, of course. I notice most the occasional, forced tropes. It is arbitrary, for example, to compare time to a puppy (in **"Waiting Inland"**), and heavy-handed to say that one's time is like "unwashed dogfood cans" (**"Progress Report"**). Occasionally, there are lines which are much too flat, even when they are intended to represent a flaccidity or emptiness within the subject matter or theme of the poem. The lines ending **"Remembering Pearl Harbor at the Tutankhamen Exhibit,"** already quoted, fall into this category. Another example of this shortcoming occurs at the end of **"Making the Connection"**:

> Brother,
> Brother Dog, is that who you were?
> Is that who I was?

But the majority of Kumin's poems work well. Most of her music is fine, her ear for rhyme, and for the combination of melodious sounds, excellent. Listen, for instance, to the pleasing consonant consistencies, alliterations, and line breaks which create the right rhythms to describe a peaceful pastoral scene in its demise—the first strophe of **"The Henry Manley Blues"**:

> Henry Manley's house, unpainted for
> eighty years, shrinks as attached sheds crease
> and fold like paper wings. An elm tree sheers
> the sitting porch off in a winter storm.
> And Henry's fields are going under, where
> the beavers have shut down a local stream
> flooding his one cash crop, neat rows of pines
> he'd planned to harvest for Christmases to come.
> Their tips are beanpoles now, sticking up through
>   ice.
> We skate on the newborn pond, we thump on the
>   roof
> of the lodge and squat there, listening for life.

Maxine Kumin's life, as she knows, and her writing career, are indeed past their mid-point. Her poems in *The Retrieval System* are, in general, far better than those which she put in her first fine book, *Halfway*. Over twenty years later, Kumin's mature vision of what it means to sustain one's life is not only more compelling than it was in 1957, but her voice is less formal, more convincing, even more human, surely more "sincere." More than *Halfway,* more than *The Privilege* (1965), more than *The Nightmare Factory* (1970), more, even, than *Up Country* (1972), for which she won the Pulitzer Prize, more than *House, Bridge, Fountain, Gate* (1975), *The Retrieval System* will return to us and return us to Kumin's compassion; her dry-eyed sensitivity; her exemplary choices to live on, even with pain, rather than to give up; her transformation of matter into spirit, body into soul. Perhaps these poems will be discovered to be the best system by which to retrieve Maxine Kumin in decades to come.

Diane Wakoski (essay date 1989)

SOURCE: "Earth Mother, Earth Daughter," in *The Women's Review of Books,* Vol. VII, No. 1, October, 1989, pp. 20-1.

[*Wakoski is an American educator and poet. In the following review of* Nurture, *Wakoski—while stating that "Kumin's vision is sometimes limited"—admires the poet's Earth poetry, especially "the wonderful images, that turn into big metaphors."*]

If you had told me fifteen years ago that today I would assess Maxine Kumin as one of the ten best contemporary American poets, I probably would have smiled sceptically. However, my esteem for her work has continued to grow since publication of *The Retrieval System* (1978), work which seems to ground her right under a reader's bootsoles. In *Nurture,* she continues to explore American earth mythology as she offers her aging body as the aging earth itself.

Earth poets have fathers as well as mothers, and plainly Kumin's understanding of the world is from William Carlos Williams. Like Pound and Olson, she too has been telling the "tale of the tribe." Many of the best poems in this collection play in her smooth clear voice with the idea that holding on to things is human, but the real holding must be done for the community, the *polis*. And of course, there is father Whitman's ecstatic song of herself.

> Let us eat of the inland oyster.
> Let its fragrance intoxicate us
> into almost believing
> that staying on is possible
> again this year in
> benevolent blue October.
>   (**"Grappling in the Central Blue,"**)

Earth mythology is always about use and misuse. Thus the concerns of Maxine Kumin, as a person, become very central to the concerns of any twentieth-century citizen of the world—how can we survive the autumn, the fall of our misused earth? In this poem, she holds on to October, the month itself, the most beautiful (in her New England) season. Fall, of course, is the real season of death. When we "fall" out of the garden, the plants die or we harvest them, and recognize that winter is the time of sleep, of renewal, and preparation for the new generations to be born. "I declare you / Month I Will Not Let Go Of / October"; but what Kumin really affirms in this poem is that she accepts the season, the fall.

Over the years, some of Kumin's best poems have concerned her children and her Demeter-like role, grieving the loss of them as they grow up. However, what is most compelling in poems like **"Seeing the Bones"** is her willingness to accept evolution and change, replacing physical body with Williams' "body of light." Kumin, who at first may seem so simple in her sense of physical things, is a metaphysician too. Body is as transformable

as any other matter. "It's a simple world, full of crossovers," she says in **"In the Park."**

Kumin's vision is sometimes limited, and it makes her uncharacteristically bitter in a few of the poems which might better have been left out of this accomplished collection. *Nurture* is divided into three parts, and if I had been the editor I would have thrown out or seriously edited all the poems in Part One, except **"Sleeping with Animals," "Catchment"** and **"Encounter in August."** They are self-conscious (and self-righteous) you-are-raping-the-environment poems. While Kumin can fill even bad poems with her cool, dewy voice, poems like **"Repent,"** or **"Noted in *The New York Times,*"** and the title poem, **"Nurture"** depart from her rich, gentle, loving satire of the human condition. There is always irony in Kumin's work, the irony which comes out of Dionysian tragedy (and comedy). She writes about *hubris* as well as any classical poet, but when she goes Puritan and preachingly moralizes, the poetry becomes bitter, overstated, trivial.

Fortunately for us, when she grounds her poems in her personal life and myth, the goddess voice and stance returns. If there is a sense of loss or misuse, it is a sorrowing sense, as in **"Night Launch,"** which is studded with characteristic images:

> the rise-and-fall of ocean
> the lips of foam like seven-minute icing
> moon-pricked dots of plankton skittering

and an acceptance of the fall, as she thinks of the rocket launch at Cape Canaveral:

> On this warm seacoast tonight
> in the false dawn my neckhairs rose.
> Danger flew up to uncertain small applause.

In a typical and lovely ("Soft as beetpulp, the cover /of this ancient Baedeker") Kumin poem, **"On Reading an Old Baedeker in Schloss Leopoldskron,"** she speaks of the on-goingness of the world, both people and "swans / in their ninetieth generation." In **"'Primitivism' Exhibit"** and many of the best poems in this collection, she returns to her "retrieval system" theme.

> Longest I look at the dread
> dog fetish, whose spiky back
> is built of rusty razorblades
> that World War II GI's let drop
> on atolls in the South Pacific
> they were securing from the Japs
> who did not shave, but only plucked
> stray hairs from chin and jaw.
> I like the way he makes a funk-
> y art out of cosmetic junk
> standing the cutting edge of old steel
> up straight to say, *World, get off my back*

In another poem, my own particular favorite, earlier quoted, **"In the Park,"** it is clear that Kumin believes in the animal species and sees the human animal as having a chance.

> You have forty-nine days between
> death and rebirth if you're a Buddhist.
> Even the smallest soul could swim
> the English Channel in that time

But it is more than the optimism in this poem which is engaging. It is Kumin doing, as a poet, what she is best at doing. Making images, wonderful images, that turn into big metaphors. Playing with dualities, and manipulating everyday language so that it works with complexity of idea and pattern.

The third section of *Nurture* is called "More Tribal Poems," a phrase which takes on several meanings, as she writes often about her very large family and the community of poets and, finally, our earth-world human community. I sometimes wonder these days if Georgia O'Keeffe is the only painter poets even know the name of. There seem to be as many Georgia O'Keeffe poems now as there were "black hole" poems ten years ago. "**A Calling**" is not a bad poem, but it could be written to or about anyone, and its most vital image ("Oh Georgia! Sashaying between / first base and shortstop") actually would be better applied to Marianne Moore, whom we all know as having an abiding love for baseball. In fact, there is a fine poem in the collection, "**Marianne, My Mother, and Me,**" which defines poetry, for Kumin and for the tribe.

> "We
> must be as clear as our natural reticence
> will allow," she announces. Rapturously
>
> I try this statement on like a negligée
> that's neither diaphanous nor yet opaque.

With her poetic mother, Marianne Moore, to "shape her alphabet" Kumin has written a body of poetry which constantly reaffirms "no ideas but in things." She nurtures and offers to us her earthy world of trumpeter swans and the omnipresent horses, her private gardens which she turns and keeps separate from the wilderness she loves, as a good mother might, in this lyrical book. . . .

Henri Cole (essay date 1990)

SOURCE: A review of *Nurture,* in *Poetry,* Vol. 156, No. 1, April, 1990, pp. 48-50.

[*Here, Cole appraises* Nurture, *commending Kumin for her continued depiction of environmental issues and her modesty, which he describes as "divine translucence," in her verse.*]

Maxine Kumin is a senator for man and beast and earth. She speaks for the caribou, the manatee, the orca, the arctic fox, the Aleutian goose, the trumpeter swan, the dusky seaside sparrow, the broodmare, the grizzly bear, the Scotch Highland heifer, and all this only to begin a list, for there are also three generations of kin to consider and a plot of land to be worked. Please let me not be counted among those critics who devalue her "overabundance of maternal genes." In a world where dolphins are sacrificed daily for our light lunches of tuna fish salad, should there not be one among us to take up their cause? . . .

These sensible poems record the passage of seasons in the North Temperate Zone. In "**Surprises**" Kumin reports, "After fifteen summers // of failure . . ." a hundred California peppers cluster in her garden:

> Doubtless this means I am approaching
> the victory of poetry over death
> where art wins, chaos retreats, and beauty
>
> albeit trampled under barbarism
> rises again, shiny with roses, no thorns.

Such abundance, too, leads to Proustian recall of her mother's leftover stuffed peppers, served "every wash-day // Monday," reminding the reader that the poet's heart is not so tidily divided as the book's sections— "Catchment," "Place Names and Datelines," and "More Tribal Poems"—might suggest. For there is a complex "crossover" in the worlds that Kumin inhabits or that inhabit her. We see from the book's title piece that her urge to shelter both the "wild child" *and* the "bummer lamb" is equally strong. And later, in "**In the Park,**" she explains:

> I was raised on the Old Testament.
> In it God talks to Moses, Noah,
> Samuel, and they answer.
> People confer with angels. Certain
> animals converse with humans.
> It's a simple world, full of crossovers.

Further on one recognizes that as much for man, as for those with whom he shares the earth, it is a world of "good and harm." For all creatures, as newborns, must struggle to their feet, or into the air, or against a tide, and along the way nature can be a "catchment of sorrows." This perhaps explains the specter of war looming often in these pages. In the poem "**Grappling in the Central Blue,**" a "benevolent blue October" sky leads Kumin to call back an afternoon in 1940 with her "unemployed uncles / hangdog in the yard / playing touch football . . ." while they could not know the war that awaited them:

> One is to die by torpedo.
> One in a swamp on maneuvres.
> Only the oldest, at a great age
> a child again, outlasts my father
> to drift off alone in bed.

And elsewhere on these pages, as from an intaglio print of war's ravages or of German troops marching, the hellish past can dynamite quite suddenly into a poem's narrative.

The one longish poem in this collection **"Marianne, My Mother, and Me,"** is a litmus test of sorts for Kumin's easygoing prosaic style, which elsewhere can be clipped and sinewy in the best shorter lyrics (**"Nurture," "In Warm Rooms, Before a Blue Light," "Catchment," "Sleeping with Animals," "In the Park,"** and the wonderful **"A Game of Monopoly in Chavannes"**). It's fun to watch the rhymes unreel, yet they are not as exhilarating as the couplets which often conclude other poems, and the language finally remains peculiarly proselike. Unchallenged, Marianne Moore steals the limelight with her cameo appearances, and one longs for more morsels of her. Whatever the verdict on the poem (mine is a demurring *yea*), it does offer a useful glimpse at Kumin's poetic sympathies. We see her as a young woman, noting Marianne Moore's pronouncement, "'We / must be as clear as our natural reticence / will allow. . . .'" And later, after a Moore poetry reading, Kumin reports:

> We never meet. I am content to take
> to heart her praise of idiosyncrasy,
> exactitude, intensity, technique.
> Her "be accurate and modest" speaks to me.

Surely one cannot come away from *Nurture* without a sense of its accuracy and the author's affectionately modest demeanor. Detractors may translate modesty as thinness, yet in a world of shadow, thinness, too, can yield an agreeable, sometimes even divine translucence.

Kumin on ending poems:

All poems must close, even those that posit an infinity as the Frost poems do. Many poems succeed in shutting the door by turning back on themselves to unite beginning and ending. Pattern, rhyme, form of some sort probably serve their strongest purpose in this behest. It is possible for the poet to come down on an understatement that jars us to some apprehension of the truth; it is possible but perhaps more difficult to achieve the same goal with the anchor of prophecy, prayer, or shadow of the apocalypse. It is perhaps even harder to attain by turning or shifting the focus or tone or intent of the poem with a socket wrench just at the end.

Maxine Kumin, in To Make a Prairie, *The University of Michigan Press*, 1979.

Peter Harris (essay date 1991)

SOURCE: "Poetry Chronicle: Hunger, Hope, and Nurture: Poetry from Michael Ryan, the Chinese Democratic Movement, and Maxine Kumin," in *The Virginia Quarterly Review*, Vol. 67, No. 3, Summer, 1991, pp. 455-77.

[*In the following excerpt, Harris commends Kumin's intimate and tender poems in* Nurture. *He states that with this volume the poet is seeking "atonement."*]

Maxine Kumin labors under no immediate threat of being silenced for political reasons. But this has not tempted her to complacency. She has not had to look far in the modern world to discover ample cause for concern, ample provocation to resist evil and stupidity. In *Nurture*, Kumin focuses more strongly than ever on the animals passing from our lives. *Nurture* addresses the elemental subjects of birth, death, love, sex, the family, and violence but, as often as possible, it does so within the context of Kumin's long-standing concern for the welfare of animals. She mentions in the opening poem that a critic has accused her of suffering "from an overbundance of maternal genes." Her implicit response to this rather patronizing remark is that she agrees, and vows to suffer harder.

In a way that is not utterly unlike Shu Ting's "singing flower," Kumin claims for herself the role, or vocation, of nurturer. While its focus extends well beyond the animal world, *Nurture* gives animals pride of place. References to creatures from the natural world, usually mammals, appear in all 33 poems, although in one, a city poem, the flamingo is plastic. The first section, 13 poems, takes the fate of animals as their exclusive subject matter, though not always as their theme. Kumin touches on the subject of animals that are suffering, extinct or on the brink, animals that are struggling to reproduce, and animals that serve as playthings and foodstuff for humankind. Her list of concerns resembles the agenda of the Animal Welfare Institute, and Kumin at times bluntly criticizes instances of failed stewardship or human racism toward the natural world. In **"Repent"** she condemns the capture of killer whales for our amusement at marine parks, invoking as support a dictum of Immanuel Kant that "stupidity" is "caused by a / wicked heart." In **"Thoughts on Saving the Manatee,"** she describes the depredation of the Manatees' habitat—the choking effect of six-pack collars and the cutting effect of pop-tops—and then presents her "quick and humane" modest proposal: drop the pretense of our interdependence and simply proceed to "serve up the last few as steak marinara."

Driven by outrage and empathy, **"Repent"** and **"Thoughts on Saving the Manatee"** are fine polemical poems; they do not hide their designs on us. Witty and well made, they are not detached, highly qualified meditations on the intrinsically tragic nature of existence. It is not that Kumin rejects such a vision—in fact, some of her best poems, **"In Warm Rooms, Before a Blue Light,"** and **"Catchment,"** convey it—but she simply won't restrict herself to accepting in the short term what in the long term seems inevitable: a massive loss of diversity in the biosphere. In the face of such loss, Kumin celebrates the stunning, compelling fact of birth. **"Sleeping with Animals"** describes the poet's vigil outside the stall of her "vastly pregnant" brood mare. One part of her acknowledges that, for a woman in her sixties, sleeping in a mummy bag on the floor of a stable is evidence of imbalance, of "loving her animals too much." But it is just such an imbalance or, rather, overabundance that she embraces as her "covenant," her sacrifice. As both the content and the quality of the poem indicate, she is immensely rewarded for her sacrifice, by sensory and spiritual renewal. The vigil becomes an occasion for observation and reflection:

> I in my mummy bag just outside her stall
> observe the silence, louder than the catch
> in her breathing, observe gradations of
> the ancient noneditorial dark; against
> the open doorway looking south, observe
> the paddock posts become a chain gang, each
> one shackled leg and wrist; the pasture wall
> a graveyard of bones that ground fog lifts and
>   swirls.

Images of bondage and death impinge upon the manger and upon the poet's mind, prompting her recollection that, in seven previous vigils, two foals did not survive.

If death quickens her senses, and intensifies the signals from the muse, the imminent appearance of new life affords a holy communion, an interval of pure being:

> Restless, dozy, between occasional coughs
> the mare takes note of me and nickers. Heaves
> herself up, explores the corners of
> her feed tub. Sleeps a little, leg joints locked.
> I shine my light across the bar to watch
> the immense contours of her flanks rise and fall.
> Each double-inhale is threaded to the life
> that still holds back in its safe sac.
> What we say to each other in the cold black
> of April, conveyed in a wordless yet perfect
> language of touch and tremor, connects
> us most surely to the wet cave we all
> once burst from gasping, naked or furred,
> into our separate species.

Poets and mystics habitually invoke silence as the condition where, given psychic readiness, the gods descend, or ascend. The spiritually minded have long meditated on the paradox of trying to evoke the quality of such silence through language. While the phrase "wordless but perfect" might have been left unsaid, Kumin's dramatization of communion with the mare is nonetheless a vivid evocation of what may be borne and re-born in silence.

If Kumin had not called her book *Nurture,* it would have been as accurate, though less kinetic, to title it *Communion.* The former implies action, the latter a condition of being, though in Kumin's work they often come to the same thing. She wants, she craves, atonement, and if she cannot get it in fact, she'll have it in imagination, as in the poem **"With the Caribou,"** which begins with a series of exotic wishes. The speaker wants to ride a reindeer-driven troika at "the top of the world"; she also wants to speak passionately on behalf of the caribou at a meeting in the Yukon. When she goes on to say that she wants to talk to the Caribou themselves, so as to become a fellow-traveler, the gulf between her and the animal world clos-

es and she becomes a caribou, or at least a migratory animal. She handles this metamorphosis with such deft wit that it seems almost natural:

>   I want to advise the species
>   to set up new herds, to mingle and multiply,
>
>   else how can I hurtle with them across the Kobuk
>   River
>   at Onion Portage, be caught up in the streaming
>   southward,
>   the harsh crowding of antlers uplifted like thousands
>   of stump-fingered arms? I'm slithering backward in
>   time to
>   the Bering land bridge, awash at high tide, I cross
>   over
>   nibbling down to Nevada, down to New Jersey,
>   I rejoice to be circumpolar, all of us
>   on all fours obeying the laws of migration.

This poem shows a youthful, not to say primeval, spirit as it travels backward in time, reinvoking connections with our mammalian heritage as wanderers. In other poems in the volume, Kumin is equally "tribal," as she puts it, but the focus becomes her family.

"On Reading an Old Baedeker in Schloss Leopoldskron" springs from a trip to Austria partly designed to reconnect with the origins of her grandfather, a Jew who emigrated and avoided the holocaust. She reads the old guide book, visits old Jewish quarters hoping to see his double walking the streets. But when she visit an Austro-Hungarian venue that had been taken over by the Nazis, she reverses her purpose and, thus, paradoxically fulfills it. In Nazi headquarters, it is not his presence but his absence she craves, a banishing that brings his fate intensely to mind: "Never look back, Grandfather. / Don't catch my eye on this marble / staircase as wide as the 'gasse / you lived in." The ugliest fact in history obtrudes upon her desire for communion, but true to her vocation in this volume, Kumin will not let her connection resonate on a purely negative note. Searching for "a thin line of comfort . . . a weight-bearing bridge" to her grandfather, she settles for feeding stale bread in the rain "to the swans / in their ninetieth generation." Feeding the swans does not enact the vicarious cross-generational *deja vu* she'd hoped for, but it is a generous and touching gesture nonetheless, and one which allows us to see how nurturing others also serves her as solace for the depredations worked by the passage of time.

Kumin has always written well about her family, with a mixture of love, unsentimental piety, and almost parabolic detail. *Nurture* contains perhaps the longest, and most ambitiously inclusive, of these family poems, **"Marianne, My Mother, and Me."** It plays brief invocations of the major events of this century off against some turning points in the life of the three women mentioned in the title. Given its scope, the poem, even at six pages, is highly selective and impressionistic, a self-conscious sprint, which keeps us outside the sensibilities of the two elder women. But such distance has thematic relevance. Kumin's relationship to her mother is never directly dramatized, and her attitude is a bit chilly. Marianne Moore, whom Kumin never met, elicits a good deal more pathos from the speaker than does her mother. The most heartfelt, and precise, moments in the poem describe Moore's paradoxical presence and absence from Kumin's life as an undergraduate:

> "We
> must be as clear as our natural reticence
> will allow," [Moore] announces. Rapturously
>
> I try this statement on a like a negligee
> that's neither diaphanous nor yet opaque.
> Crisp lyrics from her quirky intellect
> flare across Modern Poetry Survey
> where she's sandwiched between Pound and
>   Ransom.
> But not once in my four years as a Cliffie,
> humble in Harvard Yard, do I find that phantom
> I long for, a woman professor, trailed by her covey.

Reticence as a virtue and as a form of self-repression are themes in the poem. Moore becomes a victim of her shyness. While her correspondence with the Ford Motor Company and her appearance in *Life* magazine make her, briefly, a cultural icon, it is mainly as a curiosity, a belated Victorian, outside history.

Despite these distances, Kumin, at the end of the poem, reverts to rhyme in order to assert kinship with both her mother and Moore:

> I claim them both as mine
> whose lives began in a gentler time and place
> of horse-drawn manner, parlor decorum
> —though no less stained with deception and
>   regret—
> before man split the atom, thrust the jet,
> procured the laser, shot himself through space,
> both shapers of my alphabet.

While in this conclusion Kumin owns her influences, it seems clear that the members of the previous generation serve her both as cautionary and as exemplary models. *Nurture* serves notice of Kumin's intention not to become irrelevant, not to stand outside history, not to abandon her interior life and her thirst for communion, not to stop nurturing.

The great strength of Kumin's poetry remains its capacity for intimacy. And yet what gives her intimacy its poise is exactly what she has inherited from her two mothers, a sense of grace and an element of reserve. Two closing examples I hope will make this clear. **"The Bangkok Gong"** describes the visit of someone Kumin loves deeply. The visitor, who goes unidentified, leaves her with a small gong. The speaker hangs the gong on her doorpost and, at the end of the poem, says just this:

> Some days I
> barely touch it.

Almost shyly, but to great effect, she implies a struggle for restrained equilibrium in a way that only intensifies the sense of loss and the desire for re-connection. The abundance of her longing comes through all the more clearly because of its litotes-like understatement.

A similarly restrained expression of strong emotion occurs in **"We Stood There Singing."** The poet is motoring in Switzerland with her daughter and grandson. They stop at a store, and when it becomes clear the boy needs his diaper changed, the proprietress invites them into her bedroom. After the boy is changed, the Swiss woman embraces and bounces him and soon the three women find themselves singing *le bon roi Dagobert*. About this moment of female intimacy and joyous solidarity with new life, Kumin comments:

> We stood there singing.
> I remember
> that moment of civility among women.

The very flatness of diction and spare straightforwardness of syntax absorb a great charge of emotion. Most interestingly, Kumin sees this scene as an instance of "civility," a word with much greater currency among members of her mother's generation than today, but a word which Kumin wants to renew and expand so as to include a generosity ready to break out into spontaneous high-spirited song. We may be thankful for Maxine Kumin's fiery civility.

Diana Hume George (essay date 1992)

SOURCE: "Creature Comforts," in *The Women's Review of Books,* Vol. IX, No. 8, May, 1992, p. 17.

[*George is a poet, educator, and critic. In the following review of* Looking for Luck, *she describes Kumin "as a survivor who knows her survival is only temporary, she uses poetry to come to terms with as many permanent losses as possible before the final one."*]

With *Looking For Luck,* her tenth volume of poetry, Maxine Kumin joins the Norton stable of writers. I'm usually uncomfortable with that term, but for Kumin, the horsewoman-poet of American letters, it's appropriate. For decades she has written about the connections between humanity and the rest of the folk who inhabit the world. In *Looking for Luck* she continues this and other themes— death and loss, family and legacy, how to survive devastation and celebrate life.

The poems here are often about the intervention of imagination in the natural world. The opening, **"Credo,"** announces Kumin's belief in magic—in the "rights of animals to leap out of our skins," as in an Indian legend in which suddenly *there was a bear where the boy had been.* The epilogue, **"Rendezvous,"** comes full circle to magic again, this time as a renewed, reclothed eros. Evoking a legend that says a male bear can feel shame, she writes that a woman encountering one is advised to remove her clothes, which will scare him away. But in Kumin's version the woman slips off her clothes while the bear removes his teeth. His pelt falls to the ground as a bed for them.

> He smells of honey
> and garlic.
> I am wet
> with human fear.
> How
> can he run away, unfurred?
> How can I, without my clothes?
>
> How we prepare a new legend.

Kumin's volume titles usually indicate a great deal about her intentions, with implications both ironic and serious. Here "luck" means coincidences she invests with meaning—but with a wry glance over her shoulder, a tongue sometimes so far in her cheek it's down her throat.

In **"Looking for Luck in Bangkok,"** Kumin describes a superstition in that country, where she apparently spent time: if you walk under an elephant, you'll have luck. People engage in the ritual at a market while she watches:

> They count out a few coins,
> then crouch to slip beneath
> the wrinkly umbrella that smells
> of dust and old age
> and a thousand miracles . . .

Kumin participates, with ironic reflections:

> I squat in his aromatic shade
> reminded of stale bedclothes,
> my mother's pantry shelves
> of cloves and vinegar,
> as if there were no world of drought,
> no parasites, no ivory poachers.
> My good luck running in
> as his runs out.

In **"Progress,"** luck continues to get bound up with nature. Kumin moves from Bunyan's Pilgrim who "attains his goal the way enough / ants can carry off an elephant/ and time will mend a migraine," to a horse, an injured "Indian paint," whose owners turn him out "to starve to death—the law of the West" and who "wander[s] into a distant slough instead," there to become "a champion cutting horse." Then she invokes the memory of Hiroshima:

> The boggy hollow is dark and perilous,
>
> sometimes language impedes, some times it helps.
> "Observe moon in first phase." The professor drops
> articles to be more easily
> comprehended by his Japanese
> students who say, "To you, Hiroshima
> is death. To us, is *beisbol* team,
> long life, Hiroshima Carp."

> They thrive in sloughs, these golden fish.
> Such luck they do not need it deep.

Pilgrim's luck is in his dogged persistence; the Indian paint would have died but he gets lucky—a champion cutting horse springs from his skin. It's the students' luck to be "golden fish" who thrive in the slough of catastrophe, thumbing their noses at death.

Kumin is at war with consciousness, the beloved enemy who must be embraced, who will help us make sense of things— but whose self-deceptions make us lie to ourselves about who we are. Her writing has a hard knot of realism, tending toward but never reaching cynicism.

—*Diana Hume George*

Progress in all its forms arouses a dry scepticism in Kumin. Not only do different generations and cultures understand it differently (for the teacher "progress" means enduring Western guilt over the bombing of Hiroshima, for the students, a jaunty amnesia), but progress itself is a human concept, and therefore limited. Only nature is limitless, dangerous ("The boggy hollow is dark and perilous") and flourishing. **"Praise Be,"** which immediately follows **"Progress,"** begins with the birth of a horse and ends with images of peace, natural abundance.

> I tear the caul, look into eyes
> as innocent, as skittery
> as minnows. Three heaves, the shoulders
>   pass.
> The hips emerge. Fluid as snakes
> the hind legs trail out glistering. . . .
>
> Let them prosper, the dams and their
>   sucklings.
> Let nothing inhibit their heedless
>   growing.
> Let them raise up on sturdy pastems
> and trot out in light summer rain
> onto the long lazy unfenced fields
>   of heaven.

1982 marked a watershed in Kumin's career: *Our Ground Time Here Will Be Brief* anthologized her six previous collections. In individual volumes since them (*The Long Approach* in 1986 and *Nurture* in 1989), she has developed the terms of survival first fully articulated during the late 1970s, when she wrote elegies to her closest friend, poet Anne Sexton. Life is full of losses, but we must get on with it, enduring—even thriving, as do the women in **"Voices from Kansas:"**

> You learn to pull out and pass, say the
>   Wichita women
>
> whom distance has not flattened,
>   who cruise at a cool
> 80 miles per hour toward the rolling-pin horizon. . . .
>
>   . . . Long hours at a stretch behind the wheel
> they zoom up to Michigan to speak at a conference,
>
> revisit a lover, drop in on old friends.
> They will not be sequestered by space. . . .
>
> As the grassland is rooted, so too are the
>   Wichita women.
> No absence among them may go unmarked into sleep.
> Like wind in the wheat, the boundary blurs but keeps.

Now in her sixties, Kumin often writes poems about the life cycle that brings together the family of other creatures with her own; these she calls her "tribal poems." In **"The Geographic Center,"** the poet watches a pair of pileated woodpeckers, "[l]ike us, a faithful couple." The speaker and her husband

> shoulder what this life has lots
> of, prisoners of hope as set
> in our own way as the woodpeckers
>
> whose bright red crests and red
>   mustaches
> glint against the flourishing bittersweet
> we say we should but never will rip
>   out.

The human family is both part of and separate from nature. What humans and horses "say to each other in the cold black / of April" is what "connects us most surely to the wet cave we all once burst from gasping, naked or furred" (**"Sleeping with Animals"**). We must comfort other creatures ("I believe in myself as their sanctuary," writes Kumin in **"Credo"**). They can offer us little comfort in return, of course, unless we relinquish our separation from them and lie down with horses, as would an old woman in one of the volume's most moving pieces, **"The Confidantes"**:

> Dorothy Harbison, *aetat* 91,
> stumps into the barn on her cane and my arm,
> invites the filly to nuzzle her face,
> her neck and shoulders, her snowdrift hair
> and would very likely be standing there
> still to be nibbled, never enough
> for either of them, so sternly lovestruck
> except an impatient middle-aged

> daughter
> waits to carry her mother off. . . .
>
> Leaving, Dorothy Harbison
> speaks to the foal in a lilting croon:
> *I'll never wash again, I swear.*
> *I'll keep the smell of you in my hair.*
> and stumps out fiercely young on her
>   cane.

Kumin is at war with consciousness, the beloved enemy who must be embraced, who will help us make sense of things—but whose self-deceptions make us lie to ourselves about who we are. Her writing has a hard knot of realism, tending toward but never reaching cynicism. It speaks to our fears in **"The Green Well,"** when she lets herself down.

> rung by rung into
> the green well of losses, a kitchen midden
> where the newly dead layer by layer
> overtake the long and longer vanished . . .

We're all destined for the midden heap ("It does / not end with us, not yet, though end it will"). Only "being with" and "being in" nature offer connectedness and continuity.

In Kumin's earlier work her gaze upon death was steady, yet often penetrated by anger and anxiety. Now there is an acceptance in which resignation is only part of the picture. A near-lightness suffuses some of her strongest poems. "Blindingly trite, this calling on the dead," she concludes with a half-smile in **"Visiting Flannery O'Connor's Grave."**

Kumin's poems to and about the dead continually play upon her own aging and her attempt to ready herself for death. She watches death and loss in the barn, the pasture, the woods, with clean-sighted toughness. In **"Porch Swing,"** the speaker sits with her one surviving brother: "Old orphans, our three middle siblings / dead, we look death straight / in its porcelain teeth, daring it / to squeeze onto the porch swing . . ."

While she is in no sense melancholic (she'd find that an intolerable indulgence in herself), the mourning of loss has become central to her poetic vision. We may know that we're mortal, but we don't have to like it. In **"Finding the One Brief Note,"** we sing, like the mockingbirds, "our single-minded still imperfect song. / We eulogize autumn." This mortal music, full of longing, betrays that "we mean, / roughshod and winged, to last forever."

Kumin's strength remains directly connected to celebration, for it is infinitely renewable life, as well as life's brutality, that she sings of and mourns. As a survivor who knows her survival is only temporary, she uses poetry to come to terms with as many permanent losses as possible before the final one.

David Baker (essay date 1992)

SOURCE: "Ecstasy and Irony," in *Poetry,* Vol. CLIX, No. 2, November, 1992, pp. 99-113.

[*In the following excerpt, Baker highly regards Kumin's work and points out that "it is nature that evokes her most passionate, exact writing, and provides a significant model for her to instruct or explain people to us."*]

Maxine Kumin is, and for a long time has been, one of our most widely praised poets. Her tenth collection of poems, *Looking for Luck,* is representative of her accomplishment, style, and vision. She writes like a lot of poets these days; or, more likely, many try to write like her. Her poems are never qualified by anything less than maturity, grace, and sureness of touch. It's as if her strong, good poems were found rather than composed. As if. Altogether appropriate for an *ars poetica* is Kumin's favorite figure of the horse, as companion and model:

> Whenever I caught him down in the stall, I'd
>   approach.
> At first he jumped up the instant he heard me slide
> the bolt. Then I could get the door open while
> he stayed lying down, and I'd go in on my hands
> and knees and crawl over to him so that
> I wouldn't appear so threatening. It took
> six or eight months before I could simply walk in
> and sit with him, but I needed that kind of trust.
>
> I kept him on a long rein to encourage him
> to stretch out his neck and back. I danced with him
> over ten or fifteen acres of fields with a lot
> of flowing from one transition to another.
> What I've learned is how to take the indirect route.
> That final day I felt I could have cut
> the bridle off, he went so well on his own.

"Could have." The conditional verb represents the gentle but knowing style of Kumin's work. To be sure, transparency and ease are rhetorical schemes, as purposeful as any baroque or neoclassical pattern. Her technique descends from the New England plain style, the quieter side of the romantic impulse, whose designs are humility and reverence rather than ecstasy and rapture. Here in *"Ars Poetica: A Found Poem,"* Kumin confirms an aesthetic preference to be (or to seem) closer to simplicity than clutter. The important, subtle paradox of such ease is that it is the product of hard work, training, a "kind of trust."

It is then more illustrative than contradictory that quite a number of these poems show Kumin to be fairly self-conscious about her unself-consciousness. **"Credo"** finds Kumin's speaker reciting a litany of aesthetic and personal values: "I believe in magic," she writes here: "I believe

in the rights / of animals to leap out of our skins." A few lines later, other favorite tropes are announced:

> I believe in living on grateful terms
> with the earth, with the black crumbles
> of ancient manure that sift through my fingers
>
> when I topdress the garden for winter.

A romantic faith in the magical capacities of nature, a reverence for animals and myth, a stewardship of the earth—these are Kumin's leitmotifs. A few pages later, in **"Taking the Lambs to Market,"** she reveals another aesthetic design. The character Amos, "who custom cuts and double wraps / in white butcher paper whatever we named, / fed, scratched behind the ear," earns her praise for his ability to take "something living" and provide sustenance for his patrons, though they "deplore his profession." He is, after all, "a decent man who blurs the line of sight / between our conscience and our appetite." The brusque honesty of his occupation elicits from Kumin more admiration than disgust, in part because she sees in his example her own imperative to render nourishment out of harsh necessity.

Kumin is, by temperament, a naturalist. Her speaker is as conversant with the garden or barn as with human company. It's not that Kumin avoids people in her poems; on the contrary, they clearly interest her—from the "chambermaids at the Marriott" to politicians and neighbors. But it is nature that evokes her most passionate, exact writing, and provides a significant model for her to instruct or explain people to us—not the other way around. She seems drawn to people out of responsibility and to nature out of desire. To me, her finest poems are those which ironize or fuse the relationship between the natural and the human, between the pastoral and the political. In **"The Geographic Center,"** for instance, a pair of pileated woodpeckers, "the Harpy-like great flappers," are among the bestiary of visitants to the speaker's winter yard where she and her husband have "put out 50 lbs. of birdseed . . . suet, sundry crusts and crumbs." This obligation to nature becomes transfigured, several stanzas later, into "a 50 lb. pack" the husband carried during basic training in World War II; and the birdseed they leave out is echoed in "the seedy back way / out of a hotel dining room" where Bobby Kennedy was shot. The yard's plentiful small dramas reiterate the political struggles of "[her] generation." This excellent poem is typical of Kumin's use of nature to provide the material impetus for a revelation about people, an equation she completes in the poem's closing:

> We shoulder what this life has lots
> of, prisoners of hope as set
> in our own way as the woodpeckers
>
> whose bright red crests and red mustaches
> glint against the flourishing bittersweet
> we say we should but never will rip out.

Throughout the thirty-six poems of *Looking for Luck* Kumin's method is anecdotal and representative. She moves expertly between free verse and formal prosody. Her speaker is stable, instructive, experienced, and much more like a real person than a construct of language. She works, in other words, fruitfully within the mainstream. Occasionally, despite her clear accomplishment, something in Kumin's work leaves me wanting more. I suppose that which we call mannerly or serene in a person can seem, in a poem, safe or usual. I wish Kumin's indignation, every now and then, were closer to anger or fury, her affections more fiery, more obsessed. I wish she approached extremity, oddity, or disorder a touch more willingly. But perhaps that is too uncharacteristic of this fine poet whose use of the plain style seems like a matter of faith. Modesty is a trait she holds high.

Diana Hume George (essay date 1993)

SOURCE: "'Keeping Our Working Distance': Maxine Kumin's Poetry of Loss and Survival," in *Aging and Gender in Literature: Studies in Creativity,* edited by Anne M. Wyatt-Brown and Janice Rossen, University Press of Virginia, 1993, pp. 314-38.

[*In the following essay, George examines how Kumin confronts the loss of friends and family and her own mortality in her later poetry.*]

> To be a poet in a destitute time means: to attend, singing, to the trace of the fugitive gods. This is why the poet in the time of the world's night utters the holy.
>
> —Martin Heidegger

A decade ago I began a sustained reading of modern and contemporary women poets on the subjects of memory, mortality, and aging in the literature of the life cycle. Exploring Denise Levertov, May Sarton, Marie Ponsat, May Swenson, and Muriel Rukeyser, I found that the writing of women poets on aging is confrontational, angry, tender, and unashamed. Their works indicate that they wish to do the work of aging, and of facing their own deaths, with fearlessness. But their poetry records the process of confronting their fear rather than the accomplishment of having defeated it. Theirs are poems of death and loss, and they would permit me no wishful projection that mature poets of demonstrated achievement, and presumably personal wisdom, had come entirely to terms with mortality or aging. What I did find was that such poets use their fears, deliberately and creatively. Their works embody the fact that we all, as we age, tally our losses, remember what has passed, think of our personal histories, our families, our unfinished business.

Memory and loss have always been among Maxine Kumin's primary subjects, and in that respect her poetry has consistently shared the preoccupation that becomes more concentrated in older poets. When Kumin was in her fifties, she wrote a series of elegies to deal with the loss of Anne Sexton, whose biography by Diane Wood Middlebrook was a controversial best-seller of 1991. Anne

Sexton and Maxine Kumin had been dear friends from the time they met in a Boston poetry workshop in the late fifties until Sexton's death by suicide in 1974. Their friendship surprised many people in the poetry community because they seemed to be opposites in almost every respect, both personally and poetically. Sexton, though she became a fine crafter of poetry, was unschooled and unintellectual, whereas Kumin was steeped in the great traditions of English formalism. Sexton's apprenticeship began in the mental asylum, Kumin's in universities and libraries. Sexton wrote uninhibitedly about her own madness and suicide attempts, but Kumin's early work was restrained, formal, decorous. In person Sexton was outgoing, often flamboyant, while Kumin's style was understated. Yet for seventeen years, they were inseparable, raising their children together, enduring deaths and losses, and always keeping the work at the heart of their lives. They workshopped their poems together over kitchen tables and telephones year after year, serving as each other's editors as well as soulmates and sisters.

The ultimate contrast between them became survival: Sexton chose to die, and Kumin chose to live. Cast by Sexton's death into the personal and poetic role of "survivor," Kumin spoke of endurance in direct connection to life-cycle issues. Now in her sixties, Kumin continues to represent and embody the survivor. In the late 1980s and early 1990s she makes it a matter of stubborn celebration as well as of constant, subtle, necessary mourning. The mourning of loss, particularly of loss generated by mortality, remains fundamental to her poetic vision. Her recent poetry, especially *Nurture* (1989) and *Looking for Luck* (1992), develops and sustains the terms of survival and endurance first fully articulated in the period following Sexton's death.

Here I discuss Kumin's elegies to Anne Sexton, especially as they apply to the issues of aging, loss, and survival for the living poet. I also look at the ways in which the representational aspects of poetic language make her poetry not only elegiac but in some respects epitaphic. The mourning of loss generated by mortality and the representation of absence remain fundamental to her recent poetry and to what I would call her poetics.

Kumin's poems to Sexton demonstrated the double haunting of lyric elegy—the poet haunted the dead as she herself was haunted. Through the dream site of elegy, Kumin attempted in the late 1970s and early 1980s to come to terms with her own middle age and her mortality. She "gathered up our words," both to fend off aging and to ready herself for it. While Sexton remained in the perpetual youth purchased by the flight from life, Kumin grew into the middle age that transformed her from the dead poet's "sister" into her "mother." Kumin's haunting by Sexton is overlaid by the living poet's words, carved as a monument to her (and our) mortality.

The five poems to Anne Sexton in *Our Ground Time Here Will Be Brief* (some reprinted from *The Retrieval System*) participate in an old poetic tradition: an address by a living poet to a dead poet much loved or admired.

Sexton's death left Kumin, as she says in **"Apostrophe to a Dead Friend,"** with a tremendous burden to carry, "like a large infant, on one hip": "I who am remaindered in the conspiracy, / doom, doom on my lips". The large infant is carried on the hip of a poet past her childbearing years, a woman experiencing the aging her friend escaped and preparing for the death Sexton embraced in an untimely hurry. Kumin knows she will never fully recover from this loss. How could it be otherwise, for the poet-sister left alive, who wears the dead poet's clothes, her shoes, who must "put my hands in your death / as into the carcass of a stripped turkey?" Yet this infant, this stripped carcass, instructs the survivor on how to endure into the night of life.

"Where Presence—is denied them, they fling their speech," wrote Emily Dickinson. Poetry has always taken as one of its domains the representation of loss, has always attempted to give body to memory, flesh to ghostly form. Karen Mills-Courts calls the spectral power of the written word essential rather than incidental to poetry; she suggests that poetic language is both epitaphic and elegiac, that every linguistic gesture can be seen as a kind of speaking monument. During the act of writing, every poet becomes, momentarily, a carver of gravestones. Even as one constitutes a self through writing, that self slips away at the moment of inscription, so that the haunting is always double, the gravestone carved always that of the poet as well as whom she intends to memorialize. Wordsworth called the human urge to memorialize in epitaphs our "tender fiction"—we bring the dead to life through the process of inscription.

Especially since Sexton's death, Kumin has engaged in the tradition of the "tender fiction," continuously developing and playing upon the extent to which her poems about the dead become a part of her attempt to ready herself for death. The voice in her poems is her own, however highly mediated it is by representational considerations. She observes death and loss in the barn, the pasture, the woods, as well as in the rooms of her life, with clear-eyed, clean-sighted toughness. Life is irrepressibly stubborn and delightful, and throughout her work she knows that it will renew itself, will go on without her. In **"A Mortal Day of No Surprises"**, the speaker watches the abundance of life—a frog in the pasture bathtub, weeds in the zucchini patch, sparrows making their "departmental claims," the dog bringing in "one half a rank / woodchuck no angel spoke up for"—and fits her own into the recurring cycle this way:

> When I'm scooped out of here
> all things animal
> and unsurprised will carry on . . .
> me gone to crumbs in the ground
> and someone else's mare to call
> to the stallion.

Kumin is thus elaborately aware of how she uses her observations in the natural world and their connection to the fact of her own death. Loss and death are Kumin's dominant themes in the poetry of the 1970s and 1980s, in

poems to and about her uncles, her brother, her animals, her Anne. And although many of these poems were written before Anne Sexton's death, that death seems to have allowed her to do sustained instead of intermittent mourning. When her poetry grows from solidity to stunning power, it does so in the elegiac tradition, as dirge; nor is this strength divorced from celebration, for it is the infinitely renewed mystery of life, as well as its brutality, that Kumin sings of and mourns. As the survivor who nevertheless knows that anyone's survival is only temporary, she uses her poetry to come to terms with as many permanent losses as she can before that final loss of self. Kumin's own statement on the purposes of poetry reflects her understanding: "I believe very strongly that poetry is essentially elegiac in its nature, and that all poems are in one sense or another elegies. Love poems, particularly, are elegies because if we were not informed with a sense of dying we wouldn't be moved to write love poems. The best love poems have that element of longing in them, that either they'll lose that love or that time will take it away. Behind the love poem there's always that sense of regret, that sense of doom." In this respect love poems are essentially elegiac, for they cast before them what Kumin calls "the premonitory shadow of your own mortality."

In Kumin's poems to Sexton in the early 1980s, the conversation between the live and the dead poet has gone on for nearly a decade; we overhear on occasion. Sexton joins Kumin in every activity of daily life: while she is walking in the woods, cutting and splitting logs, flying over Paris, listening to the pope in St. Peter's Square. Kumin picks up each conversation in medias res, lending a sense of immediacy and intimacy. In all of these poems Kumin entangles her complicated passions toward this dearest friend: she is loving, compassionate, bereaved, betrayed, sometimes ironic to the point of bitterness.

The first line of **"How It Is"** becomes an underlying theme for the series: "Shall I say how it is in your clothes?" The intimate paradoxes of their sisterhood are continually symbolized by this neat, biographical, entirely feminine detail: Kumin's and Sexton's shoe sizes were the same, their clothing sizes close enough that they could share everything from a blue jacket to "public-occasion costumes." Who shares clothes this way? Sisters and friends who call themselves sisters. When Kumin wears Sexton's clothing after her death—"A month after your death I wear your blue jacket"—she is in a sense trying on that other self who died by her own hand to escape old age and despair, to check the fit. "My skin presses your old outline." The question of identity between the living poet and the dead friend becomes and remains central. This otherwise self-possessed speaker, who knows perfectly well who she is, must keep calling into question that knowledge when she thinks of her friend. Repeatedly the poems declare: I know who I am; and then they ask: but since who I am has so much to do with you, then who am I without you?

Still in Sexton's jacket, Kumin runs the home movie backward, from "the death car idling in the garage," through the rituals Sexton used to prepare for her death that day, to "a space / we could be easy in, a kitchen place" where they sit and speak together, "our words like living meat." The unspoken allusion is perhaps to the dead meat of the body that no longer speaks, for both Sexton and Kumin had used the metaphor of the body as meat. "Our words" is the object of the poet's wish, and also the richly troubled legacy of Sexton's death, as Kumin says in the end of **"How It Is"**: "I will be years gathering up our words, / fishing out letters, snapshots, stains, / leaning my ribs against this durable cloth / to put on the dumb blue blazer of your death."

To "gather up our words" is to claim them, to put them back together, to hoard them as the only constants left, to use them both to mourn what has passed and to celebrate what still lives; it is also to claim them from and give them back to both poets' readers: writing this poem is part of the "gathering." In this first poem Kumin has conflated Sexton's dead absence and her living presence in the doubly haunted metaphors of clothing and words. Now that Sexton has gone, the living poet-friend must wear her clothing and speak their collective words from within the dumb blue blazer of Sexton's death. She must grow slowly, painfully, from within that death, to an acceptance of it; and she must also learn to lean into her aging body and its eventual death.

In **"Progress Report,"** Kumin keeps Anne Sexton informed about how life is without her, two years after her death, and it is here that she is first specific about the aging process. "The middle age you wouldn't wait / for now falls on me" as the speaker walks through the woods, fighting her way through gnats and blackflies. There is less time now, and perhaps less need, for comforting the absent friend or reassuring her that the one left behind understands. Kumin had expected, after all, to share this time of life with Anne Sexton, and since she is alone in the flesh, it is her own dilemma, and not Sexton's, that concerns her. Her eye watches what is permanent: time goes on, marked by regular rhythms and returns, and the only constant is this loss. Last year's scarlet tanager, "a red / rag flagging from tree to tree," lends a "rakish permanence to / the idea of going on without you." The smile in that line is grim; for her "empty times"

> still rust like unwashed dogfood cans
> and my nights fill up with porcupine
> dung he drops on purpose at
> the gangway to the aluminum-
> flashed willow, saying that
> he's been here, saying he'll come
> back with his tough waddle, his pig eyes,
> saying he'll get me yet.

The haplessly vicious porcupine is more than incidentally connected with Sexton's death: "He is / the stand-in killer I use / to notarize your suicide." No sun-yellow souls here—only the open-eyed, frankly acknowledged desperation of just how bad the bad times are, just how stupidly horrible the natural world becomes when seen through the refracting lens of this senseless death that would not await the natural process of aging.

From this grotesque image of the world gone unaccountably awry, Kumin turns to a vision of possible peace to be wrested from this moment of madness. She notes that Thomas Mann's permit to take refuge in Switzerland said, "For literary activities and the passage of life's evening." She wonders if his loved and dear dead came to him in reverie there, "he taking both parts, working it out." She sees that she has been doing much the same thing with Anne Sexton, "Me taking both parts in what / I suppose is my life's afternoon." She seems to find this both faintly ridiculous and comforting, this dialogue with the dead friend with whom she had always supposed she would have time to work it out. She is compelled to keep talking to this dead love, compelled to both ask the questions and answer them in words she imagines Sexton might say. As in **"Splitting Wood,"** the medium of their communication is dreaming:

> Dear friend, last night I dreamed
> you held a sensitive position,
> you were Life's Counselor,
> coming to the phone in Vaud or Bern,
> some terse one-syllable place,
> to tell me how to carry on.

For both Maxine Kumin and Anne Sexton, the dream is at the root of poetry. Kumin speaks of "the nightmare of one's choice," as described by Conrad in *Heart of Darkness*: "One must descend into the abyss and dream the nightmare of one's choice and dream it through to the very end." She will endure the decay of the organism, unpleasant though it be. For the period of her life beginning in 1974, Anne Sexton's death seems to be the nightmare of her choice. Waking from this dream, Kumin swears to Sexton that she

> will break
> your absence into crumbs
> like the stump of a punky tree
> working its way down
> in the world's evening
> down to the forest floor.

> ("**Progress Report**")

The movement of the metaphor is double and even contradictory, for Kumin will break Sexton's absence into crumbs that will finally, like the punky tree, disintegrate down into the forest floor. She seems to be saying both that she will finish with this loss once and for all by breaking down what's left of Sexton, forgetting her, learning to be done with the dead, and at the same time that it is only Sexton's absence that will break into crumbs, leaving the distillation of her presence, her very essence.

Another several years pass before **"Apostrophe to a Dead Friend."** As a continued progress report, **"Apostrophe"** has many confidences to impart. Everything is still the same; yet everything is different as Kumin ages, as Sexton's death and life recede:

> It fades, the glint of those afternoons
> we lay in the sun by the pond.
> Paler, the intimate confidences.

Even the distances we leapt in poems
have shrunk. No more parapets.

                    ("Apostrophe")

With flat frankness, Kumin details what happens when you stay alive and embrace the aging process. The men have "grown smaller, drier, / easier to refuse;" their mutual children, grown up into "exacting adults," are "no kinder or wiser than we." Kumin won't pretend otherwise. Yet the poem has begun with the same event that began **"How It Is"** years before; an interview with Sexton's biographer has stripped her back down to "the bones of this person / whose shoe size was your size / who traded dresses in our pool / of public-occasion costumes."

If the years have made her somewhat less sentimentally attached to "the glint of those afternoons," it still takes very little to bring her back to "How It Is." **"Apostrophe"** ends on the note of doubleness that began it, calling over the chasm of the distance that separates them, yet whispering into the ear right next to her mouth:

Soon I will be sixty.
How it was with you now
hardly more vivid than how
it is without you.

                    ("Apostrophe")

It has been nearly a decade, at the time of this poem, and Kumin has had to develop some distance from that death. As always, Kumin tells her dead friend the truth: that Sexton has faded, that life grows more constricted as we age. The time between Sexton's death and this poem is almost half the number of years of their friendship, and Kumin has been busy living in the intervening years—and changing. For these two women poets who came together over creative acts that included both poems and babies, the "large infant, on one hip" is an especially powerful image. Kumin, old enough to be a grandparent now, carries the weight of the "telling" of this old love like a baby who never grew up. Locked in the past, the "infant" of their relationship has not grown up, or older, with Kumin. Just as Sexton would not wait for her own middle age, Kumin will not be able to stop her own old age from arriving. Perhaps that is the "doom, doom on my lips": she, like Sexton, will someday die, and with her, their old conspiracy.

In **"Itinerary of an Obsession,"** Kumin speaks to Sexton in a voice as newly raw as it is familiar. The isolated notes of bitter irony in the other poems here gather into a chiding chorus of resentment, both good-humored and earnest. The **"Obsession"** of the title is the speaker's concern with Sexton's death—and with her own as she ages. She is telling Sexton the story of her trip to the Holy Land with a "planeload of pilgrims, / none under seventy."

All through the trip to the Holy Land that this poem describes, we might infer that Kumin, in however secular a fashion, is searching out some spiritual truth. Yet even here she is haunted by visions of Anne Sexton dead, Anne Sexton alive, Anne Sexton resurrected and restored to her.

Sexton's own search was for transcendent sacredness, for a patriarchal God of unquestionable authority and comfort. Kumin's search seems to be for connection of the human sort, transcendent over aging and time. While Sexton searched for God, Kumin searched for whatever it was she had, and lost, with Anne Sexton: a friendship stronger than death, a solidarity of souls that must continue. "Words are the only 'holy' for me. The only sanctity really, for me, is the sanctity of language." That language is the words between friends who are poets—"our words like living meat"—words turned by Sexton's death into a "carcass," which the living poet must try to reconstruct. She can do so, in these poems, only by bringing Sexton back from the grave. And she does so one final time in the last section of **"Itinerary,"** where she finds that even if she "dreams of you less," she is still obsessed:

Still, when the phone rings in my sleep
and I answer, a dream-cigarette in my hand,
it is always the same. We are back at our posts,
hanging around like boxers in
our old flannel bathrobes. You haven't changed.
I, on the other hand, am forced to grow older.
How I am almost your mother's age.
Imagine it! Did you think you could escape?
Eventually I'll arrive in her
abhorrent marabou negligee
trailing her scarves like broken promises
crying yoo-hoo! Anybody home?

                    ("Itinerary")

Recalling their old friendship, one of sisters and equals, the poet asks her dead friend to imagine the impossibility that she has been left to become the age of the monumental parental presence of Sexton's mother, Mary Gray. In these final lines of **"Itinerary,"** Kumin transforms herself into Mary Gray and follows Sexton to the grave, arriving as a gaudy, inappropriately dressed ghost who promises to continue disturbing Sexton's sleep. Because she is now Mary Gray's age, she can take on her identity by the same act through which she has taken on Sexton's identity throughout the series: she is wearing the dead woman's clothes.

> **Perhaps, a state of continuous and sustained mourning is the necessary province of the poet—in which case Kumin is among its most deliberate practitioners, believing, as we have seen, that poetry is essentially elegiac, that it casts before it that haunting "premonitory shadow of your own mortality."**
>
> **—*Diana George Hume***

As Kumin wanders up the mountain with her body, which she called **"Old Paint, Old Partner,"** in this "sedate roundup" in the "meander of our middle age," looking for the "same old cracked tablets," her "airmail half-ounce soul" touches tongues with "Old Paint"; but "somehow it seems less sure; / somehow it seems we've come / too far to get us there".

It was in part by working through Anne Sexton's death, and through the relationship between Sexton's body, so like Kumin's, and Sexton's soul, that small round entity like a "sun-yellow daisy heart," that Kumin tried in this middle period of her life and her poetry to unite her own body and soul, always uneasy partners. Sexton gave up the search. Kumin was left to puzzle her way through, aware that "our ground time here will be brief."

Since the mature period signaled by the publication of *The Retrieval System* and building through *Our Ground Time Here Will Be Brief, The Long Approach, Nurture,* and *Looking for Luck,* Maxine Kumin's poetry is fundamentally informed by the mourning of loss, such as we have seen in the Sexton elegies. While her earlier work included occasional poems of mourning for particular deaths or losses, *The Retrieval System* (1978) announced her clear intention to get down to the necessary business of confronting and then mourning loss, in the lived and in the written life. But this conscious embrace of mourning is not by any means a rejection of celebration. Quite the contrary: to live in the presence of a cultivated (self)-consciousness is to understand the necessity of loss, and to mourn it so that one may continue to live, so that one may experience delight.

The titles of three consecutive Kumin volumes clarify her position. "Fact: it is people who fade, / it is animals that retrieve them." The title poem of *The Retrieval System* indicates the nature of that system, i.e., the explicit, transmuted recovery of the dead. *Our Ground Time Here Will Be Brief* has its source in the pun on airport announcements between flights; the analogy, of course, is to the shortness of the human life span. And *The Long Approach* is the approach to death as well as from air to ground. The Sexton elegies appear in *Ground Time* and *Retrieval,* where fistfuls of other poems sustain the mood of mourning. **"In Memoriam P.W., Jr., 1921-1980,"** for instance, is a series of five poems for her dead brother.

The P.W. poems are different from the Sexton elegies in that the latter were composed over a period of years, thus most comprehensively signaling continuity in the mourning process; but in her two most recent collections, *Nurture* (1989) and *Looking for Luck* (1992), the beloved brother rises again, among the Kumin pantheon of dead aunts, cousins, parents, and living daughters, husband, son, and grandson, all the faces native to Kumin who form the core of the lifelong series she calls her "tribal poems." Even the mother-daughter poems, sustained over a period of decades, take mourning as their primary subject, beginning or ending in the leave-takings of physical or psychic separation.

Kathleen Woodward proposes the recognition of a state in between mourning and melancholia. As distinct from mourning, melancholia is a pathological state of mind, not a normal psychic process with a clear ending. Freud defined it as failed or unsuccessful mourning. Woodward finds that Freud "leaves us here with no room for another place, one between a crippling melancholia and the end of mourning." For some people, she argues, come to terms with their grief by learning to live with their pain. Moreover, she insists "that the distinction between mourning and melancholia has been cut too sharply, that we may point to something *in between* mourning and melancholia, that we may refer to a grief which is interminable but not melancholic in the psychoanalytic sense." Woodward contends that we all find mourning more difficult yet more familiar as we grow older and losses accumulate—and as we approach our own deaths. In the women poets whose work I explored ten years ago, Woodward's theory certainly holds true: the quality of a continuous, even a cultivated mourning suffuses many of their finest poems, but it is in no sense pathological, dysfunctional, or debilitating, not the symptom of a disorder or a diseased mind.

I propose an essential in-betweenness as central to Kumin's vision, even to what might properly be termed her poetics. Perhaps, indeed, a state of continuous and sustained mourning is the necessary province of the poet—in which case Kumin is among its most deliberate practitioners, believing, as we have seen, that poetry is essentially elegiac, that it casts before it that haunting "premonitory shadow of your own mortality." The best lyric poets have always known this. Wordsworth called his poetry a "speaking monument" in *The Prelude.* And Hopkins expressed it eloquently in "Spring and Fall: To a Young Child," where he asks, "Margaret, are you grieving / Over Goldengrove unleaving?" Kumin's speaker knows Hopkins's answer: "It is the blight man was born for, / It is Margaret you mourn for." I choose the examples of Wordsworth and Hopkins carefully in their connection to Kumin, for it is through the observation of nature, fundamental to the Romantic and post-Romantic vision, that she attempts to come to terms with the blight.

While Kumin herself eschews the practice of theory about poetry, she has commented in her poetry on one of the great theorists, Heidegger.

> It is true, Martin Heidegger, as you have written,
> *I fear to cease,* even knowing that at the hour
> of my death my daughters will absorb me, even
> knowing they will carry me about forever
> inside them, an arrested fetus, even as I carry
> the ghost of my mother under my navel, a nervy
> little androgynous person, a miracle
> folded in lotus position.
>
> ("The Envelope")

Heideggerean hermeneutics seeks meaning, while deconstruction insists that meaning is only an illusory effect of an illusory system. Karen Mills-Courts uses Heidegger and Jacques Derrida to discuss theories of language that are incarnative on the one hand and representational on the other. Heidegger's central figure is of "gathering" (which we have seen literalized in Kumin's "gathering up our words"), Derrida's of "dissemination." While Heidegger thinks of language as presentational and incarnative, Derrida and deconstruction treat it as ungrounded representation. And while Heidegger insists on the unconcealment of "meaning," Derrida dismantles the very concept. Caught between the fundamental conflicts about the nature of consciousness articulated in our time by these theories, many poets create poetry that is overtly intended to work as "unconcealment," as the incarnation of a presence, the embodiment of a voice in words. Yet, says Mills-Courts, he or she displays that voice as an inscription carved on a tombstone. Poetry must function between the presentational and representational workings of language. It attempts to incarnate meaning and intelligibility, even perhaps Truth; but "no choice between representational and incarnative language is genuinely possible." The speaking monument of poetry presents this contradiction: "The maintenance of presence and its undermining occur in the same gesture."

Poets, aware that their attempts to incarnate meaning are met with the limits of representation, grant poetry the same "privileges" one grants a gravestone. Having written extensively on burial stones, epitaphs, and iconography, I count the privileges of the monument, and our suspension of a certain kind of disbelief in its honor and presence, as considerable. If lyric poems share the province of the monument, their work is monumental in every respect. They assert, as does the memorial, that inscription makes a difference, points to or even creates significance, expresses or incarnates loss, gives body to the memory of spirit, stands meaningfully at the intersection between the living and dead, between consciousness and its end.

Poetry, for Heidegger, reveals to the self its relationship to its own death. "It is true," declares Kumin, *"I fear to cease."* Heidegger suggests that any evasion of this relationship creates a dearth of meaning. Poets must believe that their work offers, in one way or another, the lighting projection of truth: "This possibility motivates writing. Yet, most good poets have always understood that, as representation, poetry is always threatened by the possibility that words betray truth. As a result, poetry exists in an 'inbetween' state, located on a fine-honed edge between the desire to present the 'thing-itself' and the knowledge that language can only stand in place of that thing."

Maxine Kumin enacts the poetic form of this knowledge in any number of her mature works. She is explicit about the self-deceiving "tender fiction" Wordsworth associated with the epitaph form and with all poetic endeavor—and of its necessary attempt to embody presence in the process of composition:

> Poetry
> makes nothing happen.
> It survives
> in the valley of its saying.
> Auden taught us that.
> Next year another
> Consultant will sit
> under the hand with the arrow

that props the door ajar
for metaphor.
New poets will lie on their backs
listening in the valley
making nothing happen
overhearing history
history time
personal identity
inching toward Armageddon.
> **("Lines Written in the Library of Congress after the Cleanth Brooks Lecture")**

Brooks had spoken of history, time, and personal identity as three touchstones of poetry. Kumin was then the Library of Congress consultant in poetry, thus occupying a ritual place in the history of poetry she sometimes found faintly amusing, perhaps even self-parodic. In **"Revisiting the MacDowell Colony,"** she echoes Hopkins while acknowledging that poets behave as if poetry mattered and as if poetry were connected to Wordsworth's intimations of immortality instead of its opposite. Visiting poets have signed the plaque above the hearth, "as evidence of tenancy and worth," but there are "too many pale ones gone to smudges:" "Use a pen-knife, I advise my friend, / then ink each letter for relief /—as if a name might matter / against the falling leaf." (**"Revisiting"**).

It is such grim but light-hearted parody of poetic vocation that she deploys to make sure she does not take herself, or her vocation, too seriously. But of course she does take it seriously, because she believes in the sacredness of poetic language. What she cultivates is the in-betweenness expressed in poems such as **"The Envelope."** Here she confronts fear simply and cleanly, but then, once again with combined seriousness and self-parody (another kind of in-betweenness), she indulges in the fantasy of endurance through inheritance, embodying yet another "tender fiction" that is also, in Stevens's famous phrasing, supreme. The second section ends the poem with a half-tongue-in-cheek hope, intoned through a grammatical construction that both expresses a wish and confers a blessing: "May we, borne onward by our daughters, ride / in the Envelope of Almost-Infinity". This though she knows that it is through reproduction that death announces itself, as she wrote much earlier: "But let there be / no mistaking how the dark scheme runs." The huntsman brings the mother a heart, which she eats, thinking it is the daughter's. "And as we both know, at the appropriate moment / I will be consumed by an inexorable fire / as you look on" (**"The Fairest One of All"**). But she will have it both ways, alternating between a vision of death that seals a curse and another that confers a blessing. Her own mother's death was good. In her barn she hauls a hay bale, "and with my free hand pull / your easy death along" (**"February"**).

In the work she has completed in her sixties, Kumin contemplates mutability, aging, and mortality by intensifying her alternating gaze: inward toward family and heritage in variations of the tribal poems and outward toward the natural environment. This shifting gaze extends her essential in-betweenness; she looks outward, then inward, outward, then inward, as if to say that the two perspectives need each other in order to avoid sentimentality or self-absorption on the one hand or rigid detachment and objectification on the other. The result is what she herself calls her "working distance," one that allows for, even insists on, legitimate forms of intimacy within the constraints of individual consciousness and inevitable difference. The self mediates and interpenetrates the world of the other, the human the world of the nonhuman; body becomes, as nearly as she can envision, the domain of soul.

In the recent *Nurture,* a volume replete with the doubleness of her acknowledged fictions, Kumin conflates these issues with the other enduring subject of her poetry: the relationship of humanity to nature. The clear and present delights of the natural world and our connections with it as creatures who know we are part of it infuse her sense of responsibility toward more fragile forms of life on the planet we share. She continues to express the necessity of endurance in the face of odds we cannot finally beat.

Kumin's stature as a nature poet, far from distancing her work from the poet of "consciousness," unites the two endeavors in an emblematically modernist Romanticism. While she is largely without the sentimentality we associate with the Romantics in their efforts at union with, and idealization of, nature, they were perhaps less dedicated to that sentimental vision than we have thought. Wordsworth says that the end of the journey in *The Prelude* is not reunion with nature but a courageous self-consciousness. Much of his writing on nature is explicitly cast as the emblem of a mind, which he is careful not to create as a symbol of unification with nature. Returning to the notion of the "tender fiction," Wordsworth explicitly identifies the notion of simple presence within inscription as such a fiction and relates it to the "intervention of the imagination."

Kumin's consciousness of the interconnections among her visions of nature, mortality, and poetry is usually implicit, functioning as the subtle, never intrusive poetics underlying the poems. When she is explicit, as in **"Surprises"**, it is almost a surprise; but never to be caught treating such sacred terms with reverence—she must remain "in-between"—she couches her hope in the wry intonations of self-parody. For the first time in fifteen years, her red peppers grow and "hang / in clustered pairs like newly hatched sex organs /. . . . Doubtless this means I am approaching / the victory of poetry over death." A string of associations leads her through her mother's roses, her mother's memories of horses' names in old age, her own coming old age, her mother's baked peppers "full of the leftovers she called"—what else?—"surprises."

Kumin's recent poetry also delineates that we are part of nature as well as its observer, formulator, victim, and victimizer. We must nurture it as it has us, and as it also refuses to do; comfort its creatures even though they can offer us little comfort in return—unless we relinquish our separation from them and lie down with horses, acknowledging that the mortal body (theirs at the mercy of ours) is also the soul. I would say that Kumin—or her poetry,

at any rate—does not believe this for a minute, and also believes it utterly. The stakes are high, and consciousness (of mortality, in fact of anything) is the beloved enemy who must be embraced as well as extinguished.

She means us to ponder lovingly the webs of relationship that bind us to fates we both control and, ultimately, share. Stubborn celebration is the dominant tone: she bids us "rejoice to be circumpolar, all of us / on all fours obeying the laws of migration" (**"With the Caribou"**). She invites our gaze upon the parallels between us and her dog when he carries frogs from place to place in his mouth, "doing what he knows how to do / and we too, taking and letting go, that same story" (**"Custodian"**). We are better at taking than at letting go. But consciousness combines with nature to teach us that we must.

The animals she returns to most often are her own, who "run like a perfectly detached / statement by Mozart through all the other lines / of my life, a handsome family of serene / horses glistening in their thoughtlessness." She translates their conversation with her, "conveyed in a wordless yet perfect / language of touch and tremor" (**"Sleeping with Animals"**). Yet she eschews both moralism and sentimentality through an insistence on facing cruelty, predation, stupidity, whether committed by our fellow animal travelers or by us: "Nature a catchment of sorrows. / We hug each other. No lesson drawn" (**"Catchment"**).

The poet finds the tendency to anthropomorphize dangerous because sentimental and falsifying; but its opposite, complete detachment, is equally untenable because it begets the insensitivity that leads to imperialism and destruction. A "being with" and "being in" that approaches but does not reach identification with nature—crucially distinct from anthropomorphism—presents the opportunity to explore continuity in a world of mutability. It is significant that in the purest moments of this "being-with," the poet must relinquish words, which are always, after all, representations of separation brought into "being" by human consciousness. Relinquish words, yes, but not "language," which is more like Mozart's music. The "being-with" is expressed in that "wordless yet perfect / language." It is a language both beyond and before human speech, the only one that escapes consciousness, and therefore knowledge of death. Heidegger said: "Mortals are they who can experience death as death. Animals cannot do so, but animals cannot speak." Kumin would correct Heidegger: animals cannot speak, but they do have language. Ironically and appropriately, this indefinable concept, "language," that both includes and transcends poetry, that is shared by the beast and the bard, is one Kumin and Anne Sexton developed together decades ago.

Three poems, one near the end of *Nurture,* the other two the Prelude and Epilogue to Kumin's new collection, *Looking for Luck,* bring together Kumin's complex uses of nature in her confrontation with loss and mortality. **"Distance"** directly expresses the terms of her negotiation with aging. "What does it mean," she asks herself while mowing the lawn, "how / do I, who buried both my parents long ago, / attach my name and number to another birthday?" In part by detaching herself from exclusively gendered sexuality, the reproductive cycle that is also, ironically, the seal of death; she says the old are androgynous, which does not preclude a vision of eros but places it beyond the limitations of genital sex. And in part by acknowledging that life from now on will be that catchment of losses demonstrated to her by the natural cycles around her:

> Around me old friends (and enemies) are
>   beleaguered
> with cancer or clogged arteries. I ought to be
> melancholy inching upward through my sixties
> surrounded by the ragged edges of so many acres,
> parlaying the future with this aerobic mowing,
> but I take courage from a big wind staving off the
>   deerflies,
>
> ruffling and parting the grasses like a cougar if
>   there
> were still cougars. I am thankful for what's left
>   that's wild:
> the coydogs who howl in unison when a distant fire
>   siren
> or the hoot owl starts them up, the moose that
>   muddled
> through the winter in the swampland behind us, the
>   bears
> that drop their spoor studded with cherry pits in our
>   swales.
>
> If I could free a hand behind this Tuff-Cut
> I'd tug my forelock at the sow and her two cubs I
>   met
> at high noon last week on the trail to Bible Hill.
> Androgyny. Another birthday. And all the while
> the muted roar of satisfactory machinery.
> May we flourish and keep our working distance.
>
>   ("Distance")

Once again she shifts between intimacy and separation, claiming her essential in-betweenness. Yet in **Luck,** where almost half of the poems are concerned with death and loss and with the necessity of continuous mourning, her **"Credo"** announces that "I believe in magic." The nature of that magic? The "rights of animals to leap out of our skins." In an Indian legend "that instant a bear appeared where a boy had been." Rejoicing in the magic of the wild, she also draws near to the domesticated wildness inherent in "the gift of the horse," who reminds her of her custodianship.

> I believe in myself as their sanctuary
> and in the earth with its summer plumes of carrots,
>
> its clamber of peas, beans, masses of tendrils
> as mine. I believe in the acrobatics of boy
> into bear, the grace of animals
> in my keeping, the thrust to go on.
>
>   ("Credo")

In the Epilogue poem, **"The Rendezvous,"** that "thrust" will be expressed in a transmutation of the eros the poet,

now in her sixties, seemed to reject in **"Distance."** This renewed and reclothed, or newly naked, eros transcends the human by wishing for sexual / spiritual union with animals. Employing a legend that says a male bear is able to feel shame—a piece of anthropomorphism she would eschew outside of the poem—she says that a woman encountering a bear is advised to remove her clothes, causing him to run away. But in her rendezvous she slips off her skirt and blouse while he takes out his teeth. Then he works his way out of his pelt, casting it to the ground as a love-rug.

> He smells of honey
> and garlic. I am wet
> with human fear. How
> can he run away, unfurred?
> How can I, without my clothes?
>
> How we prepare a new legend.
>
>   ("Rendezvous")

The fiction is tender, incarnative as well as representational. If the epitaph genre records hope as well as fear, celebration as well as mourning, this one could be an epitaph of renewal for the ravaged world at the close of the century, attended to and recorded in the valley of vision where the poet lies down in a destitute time, at the edge of the world's night, uttering her only holy. She is singing the traces of the vanished gods in whom she does not believe, and in whom she believes.

Publishers Weekly **(essay date 1996)**

SOURCE: A review of *Connecting the Dots*, in *Publishers Weekly*, June 3, 1996, p. 73.

[Below, the reviewer notes themes similar to those in Kumin's previous work, in particular examining relationships among people, animals and nature; and "observing the moral responsibility of daily life."]

The process referred to in the title—and final—poem of Kumin's 11th collection [***Connecting the Dots***] is the ability to take care of one's businesses, personal and metaphysical. Here, the poet is aware that her grown children, on their visits home, gently assess her ability in this regard. Kumin is indeed still taking care of the same business that has absorbed her throught her career: noting the connections among family members; tracking the relations among people, animals and the natural world; and observing the moral responsibility of daily life. Her customary candor and irony are still present, as in her recollection of her youthful religious imagination and the demands her faith might make on her: "I didn't know how little risk I ran / of being asked to set my people free . . . I didn't know the patriarchy that spared me / fame had named me chattell, handmaiden." Although some poems are less substantive than others ("**Vignette**" is little more than its title suggests), others are memorably strong, particularly the poems about her mother and a number of vivid elegies. In "**New**

Year's Eve 1959," Jack Geiger is recalled dancing with Anne Sexton, ". . . pecking his head to the beat / swinging her out on the stalk of his arm / setting all eight gores of her skirt twirling." In **"After the Cleansing of Bosnia,"** Kumin constructs startling and sophisticated images that connect her expatriate daughter as a child and as an adult, the continuing cycle of world sorrow and the mysterious beauty of her rural life.

FURTHER READING

Biography

Gearhart, Jean B. "Courage to Survive—Maxine Kumin." *Pembroke Magazine*, No. 20 (1988): 272-75.

> A brief overview of Kumin's life and work.

Gould, Jean. "Anne Sexton-Maxine Kumin." In *Modern American Women Poets,* pp. 151-75. New York: Dodd, Mead & Company, 1984.

> Relates Kumin's career and life only by way of her friendship with Anne Sexton.

Criticism

George, Diana Hume. "Itinerary of an Obsession: Maxine Kumin's Poems to Anne Sexton." In *Original Essays on the Poetry of Anne Sexton*, pp. 243-266. Conway: University of Central Arkansas Press, 1988.

> Examines five of Kumin's poems to illustrate that after Anne Sexton's death, Kumin adopted some of the strengths of Sexton's poetic voice.

Kumin, Maxine. *To Make a Prairie: Essays on Poets, Poetry, and Country Living*, pp. 68-155. Ann Arbor: The University of Michigan Press, 1979.

> A compilation by Kumin containing personal interviews, essays, and lectures about poetry.

Interview

George, Diana Hume. "Kumin on Kumin and Sexton: An Interview." *Poesis* 6, No. 2 (1985): 1-18.

> Kumin comments on her lifestyle before discussing her former relationship with Anne Sexton and its influence on both poets' writing.

Additional coverage of Kumin's life and career is contained in the following sources published by Gale Research: *Authors in the News,* Vol. 2; *Contemporary Authors,* Vols. 1-4 (rev. ed.); *Contemporary Authors Autobiography Series,* Vol. 8; *Contemporary Authors New Revision Series,* Vols. 1, 21; *Contemporary Literary Criticism,* Vols. 5, 13, 28; *Dictionary of Literary Biography,* Vol. 5; *Major 20th-Century Writers*; and *Something about the Author,* Vol. 12.

Nishiwaki Junzaburō
1894–1982

Japanese poet, essayist, and critic.

INTRODUCTION

A scholar of medieval English literature, Japanese poet Nishiwaki is recognized for introducing literary modernism in Japan with the publication of his poetry collection *Ambarvalia.* Fluent in Latin, Greek, German, French, and English, Nishiwaki translated many works of Western literature into Japanese, including Geoffrey Chaucer's *The Canterbury Tales* and T. S. Eliot's *The Waste Land.* A devoted English professor for nearly sixty years, Nishiwaki was also a primary proponent of English literary scholarship at Japanese universities. In Donald Keene's estimation Nishiwaki "has probably exercised the greatest influence of any Japanese poet of the post-1945 generation."

Biographical Information

Born January 20, 1894 in Ojiya, Japan, Nishiwaki went to Tokyo in 1911 to pursue painting, but instead studied economics at Keiō University. Upon graduation in 1917 he had a brief stint writing for the English-language periodical *Japan Times.* In 1920 he began teaching in the English department at his alma mater. Two years later, Nishiwaki had the opportunity to travel to Oxford, England, where he studied Old and Middle English literature. Here, he became acquainted with the modernist writing and aesthetic theories of Eliot, Ezra Pound, James Joyce, and French surrealist poet André Breton; he also published his first poetry collection, *Spectrum* (1925). Nishiwaki returned to Japan in late 1925 and began his lifelong work as an English professor at Keiō University the next year. Between 1928 and 1931 he regularly contributed essays and poetry to the influential avant-garde literary journal *Shi to Shiron,* which he used to launch Surrealism in Japanese verse. In 1933 Nishiwaki was hailed as a new kind of Japanese poet with the publication of *Ambarvalia.* He continued his English literary studies through the 1930s, but during World War II he stopped writing to protest the fascist policies of Japan. Nishiwaki broke his silence in 1947 when he published *Tabibito kaerazu* (*No Traveller Returns*), which marked a departure from his earlier poetry. He published several more books of poetry and English literary scholarship during his lifetime, and he was named Person of Cultural Merit in Japan in 1971. He died June 5, 1982 in Ojiya.

Major Works

Nishiwaki's poetic debut, the disjointed and allusive *Spectrum,* was written in English and shows the influence of Eliot's early poetry. Nishiwaki published his first volume

of poems in Japanese under the Latin title *Ambarvalia,* which denotes the pagan springtime crop processions. The modernist language of *Ambarvalia* revolutionized Japanese poetics with its free associations and its surrealistic, convoluted verse. Nishiwaki's next book of Japanese poetry, *No Traveller Returns,* represents a transformation of his poetic language. Comprised of longer narrative poems, this collection turns to Eastern poetics with its primary concern of transience and the culture of his native Japan. Other notable verse collections include *Kundai no gūwa* (1953), *Raiki* (1967; *Record of Rites*), *Jūka* (1969), and *Jinrui* (1979). In addition, Nishiwaki published a study of William Langland, an introduction to Old English literature, and criticism on Charles Beaudelaire, among many other prose works.

Critical Reception

Despite publishing some poetry in English, Nishiwaki is relatively unknown among English-speaking readers. Revered in Japan, Nishiwaki "has been widely acclaimed as the founder and teacher of a modern Japanese poetry of the world," according to Keene. Critics have commented on the European influences in Nishiwaki's Japanese poetry, which has led others to question the "Japaneseness" of his canon, particularly of his later poetry. For instance, Hosea Hirata suggested that Nishiwaki appropriated both Japanese and Western literary history in his *No Traveller Returns* to construct the text's "Japaneseness." Hirata, perhaps the leading English-speaking critic of Nishiwaki's work, has also studied the "translatory" nature of Nishiwaki's poetic language in *Ambarvalia* and the similarities between Nishiwaki's theoretical writings and those of French deconstructionist Jacques Derrida.

PRINCIPAL WORKS

Poetry

*Spectrum 1925

*Poems Barbarous 1930

†Ambarvalia [Ambarvalia] 1933

Tabibito kaerazu [No Traveller Returns or The Traveler Does Not Return] 1947

Kindai no gūwa 1953

Dai san no shinwa 1956

Ushinawareta toki 1960

Eterunitasu 1962

Hōjō no megami 1962

Hōseki no nemuri 1963

Raiki [Record of Rites] 1967

Jūka 1969

Rokumon 1970

Shishū 1975

Jinrui 1979

Teihon, Nishiwaki Junzaburō zenshishu (collected poems) 1981

Other Major Works

‡Chōgenjitsushugi shiron [Surrealist Poetics] (criticism) 1929

Beiei shisoshi (philosophy) 1941

Koeinbungaku kenkyu josetsu (literary history) 1947

Shigaku (criticism) 1968

Nishiwaki Junzaburō zenshu 12 vols. (poetry, essays, criticism, history, and philosophy) 1982-83

*These works were written and published in English.

†This work was reissued in 1947 under the title *Anbaruwaria*.

‡Includes the essays "Profanus," "The Extinction of Poetry," and "Esthetique Foraine."

CRITICISM

Donald Keene (essay date 1984)

SOURCE: "Nishiwaki Junzaburō (1894-1982)," in his *Dawn to the West: Japanese Literature of The Modern Era,* Vol. 2, Holt, Rinehart and Winston, 1984, pp. 323-35.

[*In the following excerpt, Keene provides an overview of Nishiwaki's poetic career in terms of the European poetic tradition.*]

Nishiwaki has been acclaimed as the founder and teacher of a modern Japanese poetry that is part of the modern poetry of the world. A typical evaluation by an admirer states: "Nishiwaki Junzaburō played a decisive role in the fate of the Japanese modern poem. Together with Rilke, Valéry, and Eliot, he is one of four great poets who represent the twentieth century." He has probably exercised the greatest influence of any Japanese poet on the post-1945 generation. Some critics have claimed that Japanese poetry died at the end of the Taishō era in 1926, but many more believe that a great resurgence in Japanese poetry occurred at precisely that time, and that the central figure in the new poetry was Nishiwaki.

Nishiwaki was born in the town of Ojiya in Niigata Prefecture, where his father was a bank president. He displayed a precocious interest in English language and literature while still a middle-school student, even composing some poems in English at the time. He was also talented at drawing, and at one stage in his career went to Tokyo intending to become a professional artist; however, the decadent style of life expected of young artists in those day repelled him, and he gave up his plan. In 1912 he entered Keiō University in the Department of Economics, but spent most of his time reading literature and philology. He presented his graduation thesis in 1917; it was on economics considered as a form of sociology, and was written in Latin.

> **Nishiwaki has been acclaimed as the founder and teacher of a modern Japanese poetry that is part of the modern poetry of the world. A typical evaluation by an admirer states: "Nishiwaki Junzaburō played a decisive role in the fate of the Japanese modern poem. Together with Rilke, Valéry, and Eliot, he is one of four great poets who represent the twentieth century."**
>
> **—Donald Keene**

In 1922 Keiō University sent him as a research student to Oxford University, where he studied Old and Middle English. He associated with various young novelists and poets, and published his first poems in English periodicals. In 1925 a volume of his poetry in English, called **Spectrum,** appeared. It was well received, but it is an undistinguished collection of Georgian verse. He also wrote some poetry in French at this time. The chief significance of his stay in Europe was that his association on terms of equality with European literary figures of his own age made him "the only poet in Japan without a colonial complex toward European literature and artists."

Nishiwaki returned to Japan late in 1925. The next year he was appointed to a professorship at Keiō University, and soon afterward began contributing poetry and criticism to *Mita Bungaku,* the literary periodical of that university. He formed a literary salon where he exercised a strong influence as the most authoritative commentator on European Modernism. In particular, he used the journal *Shi to Shiron* as a platform for his views, especially his advocacy of Surrealism, the movement with which his name is associated.

Nishiwaki had written his early poetry in English or French because he felt it was impossible to express himself adequately in the Japanese language. In later years he recalled an experience of 1920:

> In that year I read *Howling at the Moon,* the collection of poetry by Hagiwara Sakutarō, and I felt for the first time an impulse to compose poetry in Japanese. Until then my resistance to Japanese style—to the elegant classical style—had kept me from composing poetry in Japanese. I had written poems almost exclusively in English or French, but as the result of the complete sympathy I felt with the colloquial, free verse in *Howling at the Moon,* I resolved henceforth to write in Japanese.

Nishiwaki's first collection of poems in Japanese (1933) appeared under the unfamiliar Latin name **Ambarvalia,** the designation of the pagan crop processions held in the spring. Classical European influences are certainly present, but they are less prominent than that of Hagiwara, with respect to Nishiwaki's poetic language, or of Keats in the imagery. Nishiwaki also acknowledged the influence of Nietzsche. **"Tenki"** (Fine Weather), the first poem in the section of **Ambarvalia** entitled "Greek Lyric Poems," suggests both his indebtedness and his personal vision:

> (Kutsugaesareta hōseki) no yō na asa
> Nampito ka toguchi ni te dare ka to sasayaku
> Sore wa kami no seitan no hi

The translation poses various problems, but this is a possible version:

> A morning like "an upturn'd gem"
> People are whispering with someone by a door
> It is the day of the god's nativity.

The quoted phrase in the first line is from *Endymion;* stained glass windows in a Gothic cathedral apparently called to the poet's mind the colors refracted in Keats's "upturn'd gem." The inclusion of this poem among the

"Greek Lyrics" suggests that the word *kami* in the third line refers to one or more Greek gods, but Nishiwaki, in response to an interviewer's question, stated that the scene was observed through a church window; in that case, the occasion would be Christmas. Nishiwaki's own note indicates that the second line refers not to people talking by the church door, but to a scene in front of an ordinary house on the street outside as observed through the stained-glass window. Nishiwaki remembered having seen such an illustration to a medieval story. But here, as in many poems, Nishiwaki was not trying to make up a puzzle that had to be solved by the ingenious reader; the images he presented were intended to stir the reader into creating a new and individual interpretation of the materials.

Nishiwaki's first important publication after his return to Japan was the article "Profanus" in the April 1926 issue of *Mita Bungaku.* In it he declared that Surrealist poetry, far from being a recent novelty, was typical of the great poets of the past. He cited especially Francis Bacon as a notable predecessor, and claimed that the views on poetry presented in *The Advancement of Learning* were completely realized only by the Surrealist and Dada poets. Although he insisted that the views set forth in his essay were not merely a restatement of the theories of Surrealism of Yvon Goll or André Breton, Nishiwaki followed quite closely Breton's famous manifestos; at one point he even stated as his own opinion Breton's "C'est du rapprochement en quelque sorte fortuit des deux termes qu'a jailli une lumière particulière, lumière de l'image. . . ." Nishiwaki went on:

> The Surrealism of Breton destroyed the cause and effect relationship between image and association. It did not merely evoke an obscure awareness, but attempted to raise the electric potential between the images included in the world of awareness and to produce a beautiful radiation of sparks. In short, the point of Surrealist poetry is to create a vast awareness of everything in our minds that cannot be reduced to definite cognition. Surrealist poetry constructs a world of chaotic consciousness, which consciousness itself could never construct. This last statement is not borrowed from the French Surrealists. It is entirely my own opinion.

Nishiwaki's poetry is often puzzling on first reading, and sometimes its meaning eludes to the end even the most determined annotators. This is not surprising in a poet who professed allegiance to such Surrealist principles as "automatic writing"; indeed, it is more surprising that so much of his poetry is not only easily intelligible but sensually pleasing. It is quite possible to read his poems, especially those of the later collections, without reference to any body of poetic doctrines. The surface beauty is so appealing that at times the reader may not trouble to unravel any ambiguities in the text. This is true of the early poem **"Ame"** (Rain):

> The south wind has brought soft goddesses.
> They have wet the bronze, wet the fountain,
> Wet the swallows' wings, wet the golden feathers,
> Wet the tidewater, wet the sand, wet the fishes,
> Gently wet the temples, baths and theaters;

This procession of gentle, soft goddesses
Has wet my tongue.

Obviously there is humor in the statements that rain has wet tide water, fishes, and other objects that are wet from the start, and the poetic conceit of imagining the raindrops are "goddesses" brought by the wind is also faintly comic. The scene of the poem is Mediterranean, possibly Rome, as suggested by the mention of bronze statues, fountains, temples, baths, and theaters. Perhaps there is an oblique reference to the Ambarvalia processions in honor of Ceres, the goddess of agriculture, in the words "this procession of gentle, soft goddesses." But even without such elucidations the poem is immediately attractive.

Another early poem, also from **Ambarvalia,** composed of seemingly disconnected fragments, evokes the emotions of a traveler, probably the poet himself. It is called **"Tabibito"** (Traveler):

> You, irascible traveler!
> Your excrement has flowed into the Hibernian sea,
> You have defiled the North Sea Atlantis the
>   Mediterranean.
> May you return to your village
> And bless the cliffs of your old home!
> That naked soil is your daybreak.
> Akebia fruits, like your soul,
> Have been dangling all summer.

Instead of explaining or describing the traveler's longing for home, Nishiwaki names the foreign seas he has defiled and suggests the restoration of his senses that his native soil will bring. The akebia fruits growing along the cliffs at home have dangled in the wind like his soul, all but forgotten and waiting for someone to discover them. In later years Nishiwaki wrote about this poem:

> The world of poetry is a world of faint awareness, I believe. If this were not the case, awareness would transcend the world of poetry. The world of poetry is a harmony of reality and dream. Humor and pathos must be faintly admixed to create a single, rare entity. . . . I should like to seek in poetry a faint humor and a faint pathos. That is the kind of poetry I like. Last November, in the mountains by the coast I tried sucking dockmackie (*gamazumi*) fruits with my children. They tasted like pomegranates, and stirred in me a faint pathos. I felt a faint pathos also in the red earth and the mossy boulders, the voice of a song thrush, the crooked saké bottle. Such things become poems for me in the same manner as poems made of words.

Nishiwaki continued his researches in English literature through the 1930s, publishing a study of Langland in 1935 and a massive volume on modern English literature in the following year. The next entry in the chronology of his work is for 1947. This long gap has not been satisfactorily explained; no doubt to many readers it must have seemed that Nishiwaki, like other Japanese poets of the twentieth century, had exhausted himself creatively while still in his thirties.

Anyone who had prophesied that Nishiwaki's career as a poet had ended would, however, have been gravely mistaken. Full recognition came only after the end of the war when he suddenly produced a rapid succession of collections of poetry, and when a new generation of poets discovered in his works the inspiration they needed as specifically modern poets. This was especially true of the *Arechi* (Wasteland) group of poets, who derived their name both from Eliot's poem and from the bleak postwar surroundings. The impressive revival of modern poetry after the war was linked by critics directly to the republication of **Ambarvalia** in 1947. This collection, which had seemed quite dead, proved to be a phoenix that guided the new men, a triumphant proof of the capability of modern Japanese to serve as a poetic language.

Nishiwaki's first new collection was **Tabibito Kaerazu** (**The Traveler Does Not Return,** 1947). He first began planning this collection toward the end of 1944, while evacuated to his native town in Niigata Prefecture. At this time, cut off from other poets, he read extensively in classical Japanese literature and resumed his old interest in ink drawings. Numerous commentators have noted the "oriental" cast of countenance to these poems, and some have deplored the "retrogression." However, Shinoda Hajime questioned the "Japaneseness" of Nishiwaki's later poetry; he believed that it was more accurate to say that this poetry was "a stage in the quest of the 'sensory thought' he had pursued ever since his debut as a poet." It is almost too easy when writing of a Japanese poet to note with satisfaction that, after his rebellious youth and infatuation with the West, he rediscovered in middle age the values of traditional Japan that he had hitherto overlooked. Undoubtedly Nishiwaki's long, unbroken residence in Japan after his return from Europe in 1925 made his choice of scenes for his poems more Japanese than they were in **Ambarvalia,** which consisted of poems written shortly after leaving Europe. But there is little to suggest the tanka or haiku in these poems; the "oriental" philosophical values noted by some commentators are personal, rather than traditional.

Miyoshi Tatsuji said of the collection, "In **The Traveler Does Not Return** the inscrutability of the poetic language, which had marked his previous poems, has all but disappeared, and the Surrealistic conceptions survive only vestigially." Certainly there is less need for exegesis, and some of the poems are transparently clear:

> The rains of an autumn night
> Collect in the mortars of stepping stones;
> They smell of chrysanthemums,
> A far-off smell of long ago.

Or, on a more complicated level of expression:

> From travel to return to travel,
> From earth to return to earth.
> If I break this jar
> It turns to eternal shards.
> Travel flows away:
> If I put out my hand and try to scoop it up,

It turns to foam and dreams.
Into this bamboo hat moistened by dreams
The autumn day leaks.

The prevalent themes in the collection deal with travel and eternity, as the opening poem announces:

Wait, traveler!
Before you moisten your tongue
In this insignificant stream,
Consider! traveler of life,
You too are only a water-spirit
Oozed from the rocks.
Even this thinking water will not flow forever;
At some moment in eternity it will dry up.
What a racket the jays make with their singing!
Sometimes from this water
A phantom man emerges, flowers held over his
    head.
"To seek eternal life is a dream.
To discard your thoughts in the murmuring brook
Of life flowing away, and finally to seek
To fall from the precipice of immutability
And vanish—that is reality."
So says the phantom water-sprite
Who comes to village and town from the water to
    play
When waterweeds are growing in the reflected
    clouds.

The meaning of this poem is unclear, but not because seemingly unrelated images have been brought together in Surrealist fashion; the ambiguity stems from Nishiwaki's use of a private image, the "phantom man." In the preface to the collection he explained, after describing the "modern man" and "primitive man" coexisting within him:

But there is yet another man lurking in me. Does he belong to the mystery of life or to the mystery of cosmic eternity? He is inexplicable, not to be resolved through normal intelligence or emotions.

I call him my "phantom man," and I think of him as the eternal traveler.

This "phantom man" comes to me at certain moments only to disappear. He is probably a recollection, miraculously preserved, of mankind before primitive man, a memory of human beings closer than ourselves to the world of eternity. . . .

I imagine this "phantom man" lurking in me is what makes me experience something like infinite recollections when I see fruit growing on a bush by the side of the road.

Even with this explanation the meaning of "phantom man" is not obvious. Murano Shirō explained the term as corresponding to the "gods of the road" that stir Bashō to leave on his *Narrow Road of Oku* journey. He added, "Nishiwaki in his poetry is constantly restless, moving from one place to another, from one time to another."

Murano said about another poem in *The Traveler Does Not Return,* which also mentions "eternity" (*eigō*) and the "phantom man" (*gen'ei no hito*):

For Nishiwaki God is the conception of eternity, but the existence of God is first revealed in the desolate world of cognition stirred by the pursuit of a "phantom man" through a forest of bushes drooping with fruit; to meditate on this phenomenon is to touch the secret of human existence, and is the sole way of approaching God. Nishiwaki's God, it goes without saying, is not the God of religion, but an ontological concept.

Such philosophical reasoning would certainly have been out of place in the discussion of earlier modern Japanese poets, but Nishiwaki is a scholar-poet whose critical writings are complex and sometimes obscure especially if the reader is not familiar with his vocabulary. His poetry is erudite, full of references that the average reader could not be expected to understand. His admiration for T. S. Eliot may have inspired some of this richness of allusion, but this is a characteristic not only of Eliot but of much poetry of a specifically modern nature. Unless readers are familiar with all of Nishiwaki's references they cannot be said to understand a poem fully, but most readers as might also be said of Eliot's readers are satisfied with less than complete comprehension. Perhaps even Nishiwaki himself could not define everything that is conveyed by a poem like the following one from *The Traveler Does Not Return*:

Akanomamma no saite iru
Doro michi ni fumimayou
Atarashii shinkyoku no hajime

I lost my way on a muddy road
Where red knotweed was blooming:
The start of a new Divine Comedy.

The brevity of the poem and the juxtaposition of two seemingly unrelated statements suggest a haiku, but the third line is an intellectual concept foreign to the world of haiku. The speaker, like Dante, is lost *nel mezzo del cammin di nostra vita*. He wanders onto a road, real or imagined, where he feels a helpless frustration at being bogged down in mud, even as weeds bloom insolently around him. At that moment perhaps he envisages a descent into the inferno, a private inferno with its particular torments; or it may be that he sees beyond the inferno immediately before his eyes to the creation of the poem that was the fruit of Dante's journey. No single meaning is intended. It is enough if the reader senses the anguish in the poet's heart.

Nishiwaki's mention of the red flowers may suggest the sensitivity of the Japanese poet to nature, despite the intellectual character of his thought, but his attitude toward nature was quite unlike that of the *Shiki* poets, whose sensitivity toward the traditionally admired flowers, birds, and the like fell into familiar patterns. The poet Ayukawa Nobuo stated: "Nishiwaki's nature is a nature discovered by destroying the order of the traditional sensitivity. He may be said in this respect to have discovered a new nature for modern poets. We find in Nishiwaki's world an instant of joy at the discovery of something fresh and quite different, even in the same sights of nature, because it has been freed from the spell of the old sensitivity."

In Nishiwaki's poetry the familiar elements of traditional Japanese poetry—not only the sights of nature but the awareness of the transience of the world and similar Buddhist concepts—acquired new meaning because of his fundamentally un-Japanese approach to the Japanese language itself. One critic put it: "Nishiwaki looked at the faculties of the Japanese language from the viewpoint of the European languages, rather than from within the tradition of the Japanese language itself; this enabled him to discover and open up an entirely new dimension in Japanese."

Nishiwaki has sometimes been called the "Eliot of Japan." Certainly there are elements in common between the two poets, such as the use of allusion and parody; but their differences are apparent from their attitudes toward tradition. Eliot stood on a foundation of Western European culture, and drew his references from what he considered to be the body of culture common to cultivated men in a half-dozen countries; but Nishiwaki's references are mainly to sources outside his own tradition. The distant past to which he refers is not that of his ancestors, the dancers gone under the hill of Eliot's poem, but "phantom men" of no country and no ascertainable time. He refers on occasion to Japanese poets and poetry, not to establish his spiritual descent so much as to demonstrate that Japanese poets, as sensitive human beings, shared certain basic, underlying beliefs with the great poets of other countries. In an article written in 1961 called "Surrealism and Myself," he described his early readings in Baudelaire, Poe, Rimbaud, and Eliot. He wrote:

> I came ultimately to the conviction that the lifeblood of poetry was what from long ago has been called "unanticipated juxtaposition," or what Baudelaire referred to as *surnaturalisme* or *ironie*. In short, the important elements in a poem are supernatural and surrealistic; the Surrealism of Goll and Breton was only one manifestation of this spirit. My views of Surrealism were not specifically derived from either Goll or Breton. I merely attempted to explain the general principles of modern poetry. The great Japanese poet Bashō was also a pioneer of Surrealism.

Nishiwaki describes Bashō as a pioneer, and no doubt he knew Bashō's works well, but he does not suggest any particular connection between himself and Bashō that is more intimate than his relationship with Baudelaire. He sees the same "phantom man" operating within Bashō, Baudelaire, and himself.

This approach to the past resulted in a different poetic stance from Eliot's. Eliot is intellectual, responding to and continuing tradition; but Nishiwaki is prevailingly lyrical, responding to the subconscious memory of "phantom men" close to the world of eternity.

Nishiwaki's poetry has sometimes been attacked for its aloofness from the problems afflicting the world. His tacit refusal to write poetry during the period of Japanese militarism of the 1930s and 1940s is grudgingly admired by his critics, but they find his withdrawal into silence no substitute for genuine resistance:

> The hellish advance of nationalism did not in the least intrude into the kingdom of uncertain nationality that was Nishiwaki's world of poetry. When the insane reality had mounted to such a degree that he could no longer protect his kingdom, he gave up overt acts in the form of poetry, and chose instead the blank of silence. But we cannot call this "poetic resistance." It was no more than an expression of the concentrated crisis in Japanese poetry, as symbolized in Nishiwaki's poems.

Nishiwaki's insistence on the "purity" of poetry, on the undesirability of making poetry serve any purpose other than its own, drew the fire of committed critics as early as 1930. He was denounced for harboring the escapist feelings of a man who has lost the courage to face reality, feelings he masked by his assertion that the poet must destroy humdrum reality before he can create new and fresh poetic insights. But Nishiwaki's long silence, broken only after the war ended, was more than escapism, and his decision to write poetry again involved more than a mere profiting by the favorable atmosphere for new poetry. The activities of the militarists dismayed him, but he was also dismayed when, in the bleak days after the end of the war, the Japanese attempted to forget Japan. Nishiwaki is said to have described his efforts in *The Traveler Does Not Return* as "gathering the fallen ears" left after the holocaust, and as "writing with a brush on the sooty shade of a lantern in a country inn" poems suited to a typically Japanese atmosphere. The poet Kitagawa Fuyuhiko said these poems were the product of "the mental state of Nishiwaki Junzaburō, a Japanese who, as the result of defeat in the war, no longer was in a mood (and no longer had the leeway) to be an avant-garde artist."

The best of Nishiwaki's postwar collections is probably *Kindai no Gūwa* (1953), to which he himself gave the English title *Modern Fable Poems*. The title poem was originally called **"April Fables,"** and the first line was "April fables are truly sad," an obvious reference to the opening line of *The Waste Land*. The collection as a whole, as Nishiwaki's preface stated, consisted of poems "written from time to time, from a single poetic viewpoint, with the object of comforting people."

The poems in the collection are marked by a stronger note of loneliness than before, but also by an irony and even a humor that gives them a uniquely bittersweet atmosphere. **"Ichigatsu" ("January")** is especially moving:

> The season of priests is upon us.
> Who was that priest
> Who first discovered the scent of the narcissus?
> When it comes to beauty, a naked tree
> Has it over a naked goddess.
> This is the season of crystals forming in the black
>   earth, of roots.
> A man sticks out his hand from a yellow clump of
>   bamboos

And snaps the jewels of fruit from the vines.
An oak, like a broken harp,
Lets droop a single strand of green hair.
No bees or women to sing the tune of lonely
　　spring.
That man is still among the thorn bushes,
Squatting and thinking.

Murano Shirō gave this interpretation of the poem: the mention of Buddhist priests (*bōzu*) in the first line can be taken as a symbol of dignity and control of the passions, but probably it is an abstract and somewhat comic way of expressing the "nothingness" of midwinter. The priest in the second line, on the other hand, is a member of humanity, rather than an abstraction; he has sniffed out the first faint fragrance of the narcissus to comfort himself in the bleakness of winter. The winter is depicted in terms of bare branches, of frost and ice, of roots in the earth. It is not the season of woman, preserver of the seed; and even the man stretching out his hand to pick a last fruit is a lonely, small figure.

"January" shows the traditional Japanese sensitivity to the seasons, but it is expressed in language that owes little to Japanese tradition, and the whole scene has been filtered through a Western sensibility. Other poems in the collection, though varied in subject and mood, confirm the general impression given by "January." The expression is indirect and sometimes even obscure, but the beauty of the imagery can be intuitively felt, and the mood of each poem is securely established. The effects achieved may suggest those of traditional Japanese poetry in the economy of means and the skillful juxtaposition of imagery, but Nishiwaki's poetic past is European rather than Japanese. Nevertheless, the language he uses is Japanese, the landscapes before his eyes or in his mind are Japanese, and he has found in such poetic features as an intense feeling for the seasons a congruence between his European tastes and Japanese tradition. He is an international poet who has exercised a profound influence on the poetry of one nation.

Hosea Hirata (essay date 1988)

SOURCE: "Return or No Return: Nishiwaki's Postmodernist Appropriation of Literary History, East and West," in *Literary History, Narrative, and Culture: Selected Conference Papers,* edited by Wimal Dissanayake and Steven Bradbury, University of Hawaii Press, 1989, pp. 122-31.

[*In the following essay, originally delivered at a conference in Honolulu in April, 1988, Hirata discusses the intertextuality of the poems in* No Traveller Returns *by suggesting that Nishiwaki appropriated both Western and Japanese literary traditions to construct the text's "Japaneseness."*]

After the dazzling display of modernist poetic language in *Ambarvalia* (1933), Nishiwaki Junzaburō's second book of Japanese poetry *Tabibito kaerazu* (*No Traveller Returns*), published in 1947, seemed to indicate his complete return to Eastern poetics with its central sentiment of *mujō* (transience). Indeed the surprising transformation of Nishiwaki's poetic language caused much indignation among the die-hard modernist poets of Japan at that time.

Yet, as recent source studies have revealed, the intertextuality of *Tabibito kaerazu* is far from a simple nostalgic return to the mode of classical Eastern literature. It is now evident that the text of *Tabibito kaerazu* traverses not one but many different traditions within Japanese literature and, more important, many Western "pre-texts" as well.

This paper attempts to show that in *Tabibito kaerazu,* Nishiwaki, despite the ostensible nostalgia for established "Japaneseness," has produced a uniquely "postmodernist" text that reveals not the modernist's outright attack on past literary traditions but a willful appropriation of literary history, Eastern as well as Western. Upon scrutiny, the text thus manifests a curious instability vis-à-vis its own specific historical time as well as its topos. The text becomes, as it were, a tenuous epidermis beneath which a network of intertextuality envelops an empty sign of *samishisa* (loneliness / desolation) at its very core.

Tabibito kaerazu is neither an Eastern nor a Western text. It is, rather, an allegory of fictionality itself—a deepening of the abyss of fictionality by means of the paradoxical figure of the *tabibito* (traveller) who must always return to the ever-receding ruins of home / memory / past. In the end, the traveller never returns, except to a deeper fictionality of interwoven pre-texts, pre-voices.

Nishiwaki Junzaburō was born in 1894 and died in 1982. He is commonly regarded as the father of literary modernism in Japan. By profession he was a professor of English and linguistics at Keio University. His main scholarly interest was Medieval English literature; but his artistic interest was clearly drawn towards modernism, which he absorbed during his stay in England from 1922 to 1925. His linguistic abilities were quite exceptional. He knew Latin, Greek, German, French, and English very well. In fact, he began writing poetry in foreign languages and did not even attempt to write poetry in his native tongue till he was in his late thirties. In 1933, Nishiwaki published his first volume of poems in Japanese, entitled *Ambarvalia,* whose luminous modernist language was to have a lasting and revolutionary impact on new generations of Japanese poets.

After the publication of *Ambarvalia,* there follows a fourteen-year period of silence until 1947, when Nishiwaki published *Tabibito kaerazu* along with *Amubaruwaria* (title in *hiragana*), a revised version of the original *Ambarvalia*. There is now a consensus among critics that *Amubaruwaria* is an inferior revision which took away the raw edges and surprising "unnaturalness" from the original version. In the epilogue of *Amubaruwaria* Nishiwaki wrote: "As I reread the poems [of *Ambarvalia*], now I understand how my mental state has changed." *Tabibito kaerazu* also appeared as a product of this change in Nishiwaki.

> **After the dazzling display of modernist poetic language in *Ambarvalia*, Nishiwaki Junzaburō's second book of Japanese poetry *Tabibito kaerazu* (No Traveller Returns), published in 1947, seemed to indicate his complete return to Eastern poetics with its central sentiment of *mujō* (transience). Indeed the surprising transformation of Nishiwaki's poetic language caused much indignation among the die-hard modernist poets of Japan at that time.**
>
> **—Hosea Hirata**

Reviewing the book, the prominent avant-garde poet Kitasono Katsue sharply criticized Nishiwaki's loss of modernist energy and his decline into a weakened, decadent poetic sensibility. Indeed, ***Tabibito kaerazu*** was a shock to those who had been familiar with Nishiwaki's prewar penchant for radical modernism. Another prominent poet, Miyoshi Tatsuji, observed: "In ***Tabibito kaerazu*** the previous incomprehensibility of Nishiwaki's poetic language has almost vanished. And his surrealist ideas have become nothing but ruins." What in fact bewildered readers at that time was Nishiwaki's seemingly complete return to the East, to its "philosophy" of *mujō* or *hakanasa* (transience), and to the traditions of Japanese classical literature.

Nishiwaki's insistence on *mujō*, however, can be traced back to one of his prewar writings on surrealist poetics. In his *Chōgenjitsushugi shiron (Surrealist Poetics)*, Nishiwaki argued that poetry is essentially an anti-expressive act. That is, poetry is the manifestation of an effort not to express (manifest). Poetry is, in fact, taken as an effort to abolish itself. Nishiwaki writes that the most advanced mode of poetry is that which is closest to its own extinction. At the same time, despite his ostensible endorsement of surrealism, Nishiwaki claims that poetry must be founded upon reality. But reality, he says, is "boring" *(tsumaranai)*. *Tsumaranai* is a very difficult word to translate. It can mean trivial, insignificant, trifling, unexciting, or boring. Nishiwaki writes, "To sense this fundamental yet supreme banality *(tsumaranasa)* constitutes the motivation for poetry." Poetry with its function of defamiliarization may render the "familiar / *tsumaranai*" reality interesting. But at the same time, and paradoxically, poetry must return to this *tsumaranasa*, to the fundamental non-meaning of reality.

In ***Tabibito kaerazu,*** however, the refreshingly colloquial expression of *"tsumaranasa"* is replaced by more classically coded literary expressions, such as *"samishiki"* (lonely, desolate), *"nagekawashiki"* (pitiful, lamentable), *"koishiki"* (longing for something, someone), and so on. The word *"samishiki"* (including its variations *"samishi"*

and *"samishisa,"* etc.) appears especially often over forty times throughout the one hundred and sixty-eight sections that comprise the work. The resulting textual matrix clearly manifests a strong link to the traditional Japanese literature of *hakanasa, mujō,* and *sabi*.

Not only the tone set by the repetition of *"samishiki"* but also the form of the poem suggests a return to tradition. ***Tabibito kaerazu*** is, as already mentioned, divided into one hundred and sixty-eight sections, whose lengths vary from a single word to over forty lines. There is no apparent lineal development or narrative progression from one section to the next. Thus each section can be considered an independent poem, though it is far more intriguing to regard each section as part of a more or less loosely orchestrated whole, which somehow reminds us of a *renga* sequence (Japanese linked verse). In some shorter sections, the trace of *haiku* is undeniable, though Nishiwaki does not conform to the metrical restriction of a 5-7-5 syllabic format. For example:

14

Kureru tomo naku kureru
Kokoro no haru

Dusk falling
    as if not falling
Heart's spring

15

Yukumichi no kasuka naru
Uguisu no oto

Faint,
    this road,
    a sound of
    a bush warbler.

16

Hisui no jōnen
Onna no yo no kasumu

The passion of jade
Women's realm fading.

By way of contrast, let us look at a typical poem from ***Ambarvalia***. We should be able to sense the surprising transformation in Nishiwaki's poetic language:

    Hand
    The spirit's artery snapped, God's film snapped—
    When I grope for the darkness of lips,
        taking the hand of ghostly ether dreaming
                    through withered timber,
    A honeysuckle reaches out
        spreading fragrance on rock,
            killing a forest.
    A hand reaching for a bird's neck and for the
        twilight of gems—

In this dreaming hand
                lies Smyrna's dream.
A rose bush flaring . . .

Can the text of **Tabibito kaerazu,** then, be summed up as
the result of Nishiwaki's nostalgia for the past and his
exhausted modernist voice? A closer reading of the text
reveals a far more complex and unstable textual structure
that defies such a simplistic conclusion. The key to this
complex textual structure is the intertextuality of **Tabibito
kaerazu.** A recent study by Niikura Toshikazu uncovers
an astonishing array of allusions that Nishiwaki employed
in constructing the text.

If this ostensibly "Japanese" text's citational practice were
limited to Eastern literary sources, Nishiwaki's "Return to
the East" would have been indisputable. After all, within
the tradition of classical Japanese literature, various methods of artful citation (such as *honmondori, honkadori,
honzetsu,* or *hikiuta*) were firmly established conventions.
What is intriguing about **Tabibito kaerazu,** however, is
the sheer number of hidden allusions to Western literary
sources. In fact, the range of Western as well as Eastern
allusions are so extensive that the uncovering of sources
begins to resemble a game of literary trivia.

Allusions to Japanese sources may be easier to detect. For
example, the last line of section 13 reads: *"Samishiki mono
wa wagami narikeri"* (What is lonely is my life). Anybody who is familiar with classical Japanese literature
would notice that the line is a slight modification of the
last line of a famous *waka* by Fujiwara no Kintsune collected in *Hyakunin isshu:*

Hana sasou
Arashi no niwa no
Yuki narade
Furiyuku mono wa
Waga mi narikeri

It is not snow
In the garden where the storm
Entices the blossoms
What drifts by
Is my life.

By contrast, Western sources are far more difficult to
uncover, for they are buried under Nishiwaki's unique
pseudo-classical Japanese diction and imagery. For example, what is the buried pre-text of the following?

131

Ishō   tetsugaku koso
Onna no tetsugaku nare
Onna no maruobi no
Uraganashiki

The philosophy of clothes
is the philosophy of women.
How sorrowful,
a woman's one-piece sash . . .

Reading this section, who would have thought of *Sartor
Resartus* by Thomas Carlyle, in which Carlyle's so-called
"clothes philosophy" is expounded? Another humorous
example can be seen in the following passage, the beginning of section 156:

Futokoro ni panko o ire
Hyōtan ni cha o ire
Kaki no ki no tsue o tsuki
Saka o nobotte iku . . .

. . . . .

Putting bread crumbs in my sleeves
tea in a gourd
walking up a hill
with a persimmon-wood cane . . .

. . . . .

This is a parody of a passage in *La Culture des idées* by
Remy de Gourmont:

L'homme malgré sa tendance au mensonge, a un grand
respect pour ce qu'il appelle la vérité; c'est que la
vérité est son bâton de voyage á travers la vie, c'est
que les lieux communs sont le pain de sa besace et le
vin de sa gourde.

What we witness here is a decisive shift from the destructive, anti-traditional language of **Ambarvalia** to a more
frivolous parodic mode of writing, in which the past traditions become not the object of destruction but of appropriation, of recycling by way of parody. Here, in this
parodic mode, the modernist impulse towards "purity,"
towards its autonomous status (that is, to be the object of
its own referent) is replaced by a postmodernist strategy
which problematizes the very activity of reference by revealing a referential *mise-en-abyme,* as it were, or to quote
Douglas Crimp, "strata of representation."

In **Tabibito kaerazu** the parodic mode does not limit itself
to passages where traditional pre-texts are hidden. The
ostensible seriousness of the elegiac tone that seems to
pervade the entire text is jolted by the sudden appearances
of the frivolous. In the same vein, the repetition of *samishiki* begins to appear self-parodying. Does the text not
achieve, through its over-repetition of *samishiki,* a parody
of its own voice, its own dominant message? Does the text
not deconstruct its most apparent feature, that is, its "return to the East / return to the classical past," by a subtle
strategy of fictionalizing its own ontological status, its
own historicity and topos? Let us analyze a section which
seems to reveal this postmodernist impulse towards self-
deconstruction, towards self-fictionalization:

38

Kugatsu no hajime
Kaidō no iwakake kara
Aoi donguri no sagaru

Mado no samishiki
Naka kara hito no koe ga suru

Ningen no hanasu oto no samishiki

"Danna konotabiwa Konpira mairi

Ni dekakerutte kotodaga

Kore wa tsumarane monodaga senbetsuda
Totte kunne"

"Mohaya shi ga kakenai
Shi no nai tokoro ni shi ga aru

Utsutsu no danpen nomi shi to naru

Utsutsu wa samishii
Samishiku kanzuru ga yue ni ware ari
Samishimi wa sonzai no konpon
Samishimi wa bi no hongan nari

Bi wa eigō no shōchō"

Early September
from a rock by the avenue
a green acorn hanging . . .

Desolate is the window.
Inside, there is someone's voice.
How desolate, the sound of human speech,
"Hey, mistah, dis time I hear you goin'a
prilgrimage to Konpira, eh? Please take dis wid ya.
No, no, it's nothin' mistah, just a partin' token.
Take it, take it."

"I can no longer write poetry.
Poetry exists where there is no poetry.
Only a shred of reality becomes poetry.
Reality is desolate.
I feel desolate, therefore I am.
Desolation is the root of existence.
Desolation is the ultimate desire for Beauty.
Beauty is the symbol of eternity."

The abrupt leaps of imagery seen in **Ambarvalia** have not entirely disappeared in **Tabibito kaerazu,** though what "leaps" here is not imagery but voice. The sudden intrusion of direct speech, made more vibrant, more "real" by the use of a rural dialect, disrupts the *"samishisa"* (desolateness / loneliness) which has been established in the previous lines. The speaker seems to be what Nishiwaki often calls a *"dojin"* ("native," or literally "man of soil"), whose voice contrasts sharply with the abstractions of the intellectual voice in the following lines—the voice of aporia, an internal soliloquy on loneliness and beauty. The stark contrast between the two voices is, to say the least, stunning. Their relation seems to be exactly that of "non-relation" (*kankei ga nai*), which Nishiwaki promoted in his theoretical writings as the essence of the surrealist text. Yet, at the same time, there is a certain incessant movement that traverses the whole section.

The first stanza is not a complete sentence. The last line *"Aoi donguri no sagaru"* (A green acorn hanging) may be considered to be modifying the first line *"Kugatsu no hajime"* (The beginning of September) though belatedly. Or it may be even modifying the first word of the second stanza *"mado"* (window). (This fluidity is also aided by the elimination of punctuation from the entire text of **Tabibito kaerazu**.) Or again, it may be modifying a certain vacuum created by the elimination of the possible final modified word (for example, it can be *hi* 'day,' thus, *"Aoi donguri no sagaru hi"* 'A day when a green acorn hangs'). The overall effect of the syntax of the first stanza is a sense of slight instability. On one hand, the *haiku*-like completed image of early autumn is clearly stressed by the cyclic movement of the syntax (the last line of the stanza returning to the first line). On the other hand, the elimination of the expected modified word brings out a certain empty space in the text. We do *read* this otherwise non-marked sign of vacuum. (Is the blank space of the stanza-break the sign of this vacuum?) And finally, there is a sense of continuation, the imagery of the first stanza spreading out to the next. As a result of all these different syntactical movements within the stanza, the text begins to "quaver," as it were, in its incompleteness. Perhaps this is where we may begin to hear the incessant murmuring of language Michel Foucault names "literature," which attempts to break the constraining shell of human speech, to supersede man, to transcend his aporia of poetry. Now a certain autonomous movement of language begins to flow, almost imperceptibly.

In the next stanza, *"samishiki"* is repeated twice, modifying first, *"mado"* and then *"ningen no hanasu oto"* (the sound of humans speaking). As mentioned before, *"samishiki"* is the central sign of the whole **Tabibito kaerazu,** establishing itself thus by its excessive repetition. What is the function of such excessive repetition? No doubt it creates a dominant mood. But we begin to suspect here that this excessive repetition may be a device to "exhaust" the repeated sign so that the signified (the sentiment of desolation) becomes "insignificant" like a cliché, too "familiar" like the sight of a window. The signifier, however, remains an empty shell on the surface of language. It becomes, in turn, the sign of this loss of meaning from the signified. Various subjects of the repeated modifier *"samishi"* also begin to lose their sentimental attachment to the signified of *"samishi."*

So the window is modified by an empty modifier, the non-significant signifier *"samishi."* But we are going around in a circle. Does not *"samishi"* signify from the beginning this state and feeling of loss, of "insignificance"? According to the *Kōjien* dictionary, *"sabishi"* (same as *samishi* means: 1) a sense of lacking the object of desire, not being content; 2) sad, not merry; 3) quiet and forlorn, not lively. In his theoretical writings Nishiwaki endorsed the notion of defamiliarization as the aim of poetry. The line, *"Mado no samishiki"* in a sense achieves this defamiliarization because not too many people would customarily associate *"samishiki"* (note also that it is in *bungotai*, classical literary style) with such a "familiar" object as a window. But now, because of the excessive repetition, *"samishiki"* has become as "familiar" and as *"tsumaranai"* as the window. At this point, therefore, the subject (window), the signifier (*samishiki*) and the signified (feeling of lack, desolation, loneliness) become curiously identical. They all become one in "familiarity," in "*tsumaranasa.*"

The subject of the next "*samishiki*" is "*ningen no hanasu oto*" (the sound of humans speaking). We must note here that what is *samishiki* is not "*hito no koe*" (human voice) of the preceding line, but "*oto*" (sound). The transition that occurs between these two lines is that from the man-centered "logocentric" voice to the neutral "sound," which is in fact, as Saussure indicated, a signifier *par excellence.* Thus what is to come as a quoted speech is defined not as a "voice" but as a signifier a "sound" (*oto*) yet to be attached to any signified.

The sound comes abruptly, carrying an irrelevant content. It has to be irrelevant because, dictated by the preceding transition from voice to sound, the arbitrary relation between the signifier and the signified is clearly underlined. Here the signified is cut off, floating. The content could have been anything, a slice of any human speech. Appropriate to the word "*oto,*" the speech's sound is emphasized and isolated by the use of a dialect. Thus both the signifier and the signified are isolated from each other as well as from the main text (context). This is where, so cunningly again, *samishiki* sneaks in. What is indeed *samishi* (lonely) is both this separation from context and the isolation of signifier and signified. Moreover, this is where the poet reaches his poetic aporia, trapped in this *samishisa,* in the "meaninglessness" of the sound and speech: "I can no longer write poetry / Poetry exists where there is no poetry."

How can we name this empty space gaping within the semiosis of language, this ultimate aporia of poetry? What kind of poetry can exist where there is no poetry? It is the impossible space of poetry, a gap between the signifier and signified, the limit of fictionality, non-meaning, *tsumaranasa.* Yet, from this aporia, the text of **Tabibito kaerazu** is woven. Aided by the incessant murmuring of language, a collage of scattered pre-texts, the text achieves an allegory of itself, that is, an allegory of fictionality / poetry. The fictive by definition differs from and defers the ultimate transparent revelation of the actual. By appropriating literary history, East and West, into its translatory citational strategy, the text of **Tabibito kaerazu** deconstructs its own originality. It is a fictive text citing and translating other fictive discourses of the past. It is, essentially, a story of its own fictiveness as well as of the limits of that abysmal fictionality.

Throughout the text of **Tabibito kaerazu,** through the reflecting (citational) strata of its intertextuality, the figure of a phantasmal traveller is evoked. He wanders around a fictive landscape of hidden citations and translations. He collects the ruins of language, the ruins of literary history. Where is he returning, if he ever is returning? Let us read the last section of **Tabibito kaerazu:**

168

Touching the roots of eternity,
passing the field's end

where the heart's quail cries,
where wild roses burst into bloom,
passing a village where a fulling block echoes,
passing through a countryside where a woodsman's
  path crosses,
passing a town where whitewashed walls crumble,
visiting a temple by the road,
viewing a mandala tapestry with reverence,
walking over crumbled mountains of dead twigs,
crossing a ferry where reed stalks are reflected in
  long shadows,
passing a thicket where grass-seeds hang,
the phantasmal man departs.
The eternal traveller never returns.

(255)

The traveller is the figure of what Roland Barthes calls "*écriture.*" He moves intransitively, towards the non-destination, taking detours (*michi kusa*), picking forgotten names of roadside weeds, reflecting and refracting voices from the past, writing again, writing again in translation of history. This may well be the destiny of postmodernist writing.

Hosea Hirata (essay date 1993)

SOURCE: "Violation of the Mother Tongue: Nishiwaki Junzaburō's Translatory Language in *Ambarvalia,*" in *Comparative Literature,* Vol. 45, No. 1, Winter, 1993, pp. 47-59.

[*In the following essay, Hirata suggests that Nishiwaki's "translatory writing"—his use of translation—in* Ambarvalia *effected "a radical deformation and foreignization of the Japanese language."*]

Baudelaire's "Invitation au voyage" evokes our nostalgia for a poetic (thus, oriental?) paradise where only the sweetest language of all, our mother tongue ("langue natale") is spoken. We could well assume that Nishiwaki Junzaburō (1894–1982), who was considered to be one of the best readers of Baudelaire in Japan, was well aware of the homesickness for a purer, more authentic language that would afflict any poet. Yet Nishiwaki's effort to create his own poetic voice took a completely opposite direction from the search for a more authentic, "oriental" mother tongue. Indeed, his first book of poetry written in Japanese, **Ambarvalia** (1933), presents itself as a surrendering of the mother tongue to the invasions of foreign tongues.

For anyone who would attempt to translate a text such as **Ambarvalia,** a series of questions will arise. What if the text to be translated is already a translation? What if the "sweet mother tongue" of the original text is already violated by foreign tongues? How can a translation of such an "original" text begin? Must we "un-translate" such a text, uncovering the invasions and the tattered ruins of the mother tongue? As foreign readers of Japanese literature, our translatory reading of the Nishiwaki text must begin with such anxieties.

Modern Japanese poetry in general started out by translating Western poetry. In order for Japanese poetry to become "modern," it had to free itself from the restrictions of traditional forms (*waka* and *haiku*) and adopt freer expressive imagery and styles from Western poetry. Soon after the Meiji restoration in 1868, pioneering collections of translations began to appear in succession: *Shintaishishō* (*A Selection of New Style Verse*) in 1882, *Omokage* (*Vestiges*) in 1889, *Kaichōon* (*Sound of Ocean Tides*) in 1905. The language of these translations remained, however, "authentically" Japanese, for the translators were mainly concerned with rendering Western poetry into the elegant literary style of the Japanese language.

These pioneering translations nurtured the growth of original modern Japanese poetry during *kindai* (the period from about the mid-nineteenth century to the end of World War II). Especially prominent among *kindai* poets was Hagiwara Sakutarō (1886-1942), whose *Tsuki ni hoeru* (1917) presented unprecedented skill and originality in using modern vernacular language as well as the style of the so-called *jiyōshi* (free verse). In fact, it was Hagiwara's new poetic language that made Nishiwaki envision the possibility of writing poetry in Japanese for the first time. However strange it may sound, Nishiwaki began his literary career by writing poetry in various foreign languages (Latin, French, and English) and did not even attempt to write poetry in Japanese until he was in his late thirties. Before encountering Hagiwara's experimental poetic language, Nishiwaki simply refused to associate the notion of modern poetry with the classically defined, elegant literary language that other *kindai* poets employed.

> **With *Ambarvalia*, an utterly new poetic language was introduced in Japan. Its newness, however, did not reside simply in the innovative employment of the existing Japanese language, whether colloquial or literary, but more importantly in Nishiwaki's idiosyncratic use of translation, effecting a radical deformation and foreignization of the Japanese language**.
>
> *—Hosea Hirata*

The transition from literary language to the vernacular as the vehicle of poetry was by no means easy. Even Hagiwara, abandoning the flexible vernacular language of *Tsuki ni hoeru,* had to resort to classical literary language in his last poetical work, *Hyōtō (Ice Land),* published in 1934. He acknowledges his failure: "After desperate attempts to discover a new language for Japanese poetry, I ended up returning to the age-old literary language. In doing so, I abandoned my cultural mission as a poet. I have aged. May new poets emerge and open a new road, a road I failed to build in my time."

Nishiwaki's *Ambarvalia* was published in 1933, a year before the publication of Hagiwara's *Hyōtō*. With *Ambarvalia,* an utterly new poetic language was introduced in Japan. Its newness, however, did not reside simply in the innovative employment of the existing Japanese language, whether colloquial or literary, but more importantly in Nishiwaki's idiosyncratic use of translation, effecting a radical deformation and foreignization of the Japanese language.

Ambarvalia was Nishiwaki's first collection of poems written in Japanese. He had earlier published two collections of English poems, *Spectrum* (London, in 1925) and *Poems Barbarous* (Tokyo, 1930), attempted to publish a volume of French poems, *Une montre sentimentale,* in Paris, and also had written an unpublished collection of English poems, entitled *Exclamations: Music of the Soul*.

It is now evident that some of the poems included in *Ambarvalia* are more or less direct translations of poems originally written in foreign languages by Nishiwaki himself. Consequently the text reveals a peculiar Japanese language, one willfully affected by Nishiwaki's sometimes extremely "literal" translations. In fact, the language of *Ambarvalia* shows some typically awkward expressions and mistakes commonly found in literal translations attempted by foreign students who have just begun studying the language with a dictionary. Such problems include the over-use of Chinese expressions where simpler Japanese expressions would suffice, the incorrect usage of counters, or the usage of grammatical constructions not "natural" in Japanese but possible in foreign languages.

For example, there is a line in a poem entitled **"Shitsurakuen"** ("Paradise Lost"): "Ikko no taripotto no ki ga onky o hassuru koto naku seichō shite iru." Its "original" version is found in Nishiwaki's French poem, **"Paradis Perdu."** The French reads simply, "Un palmier se grandit sans bruit." The first word in the Japanese line "Ikko no" must be the translation of the French article "Un." But "ikko no" is not the correct counter to use for a tree. It should be rather "ippon no." "Onkyō o hassuru" is an awkward expression displaying a somewhat forced use of Chinese instead of the simpler Japanese "oto o dasu."

As an example of foreign grammar invading the Japanese language, the following is illuminating: "Ore no yū jin no hitori ga kekkon shitsutsu aru." Literally translated into English, it becomes "One of my friends is getting married." This sounds natural enough. In fact, the original French simply reads: "Un de mes amis va se marier." But Nishiwaki willfully takes advantage of the ambiguous English construction—the copula followed by a present participle, indicating an action either in the present progressive or in the near future—and translates the English sentence in the sense of the present progressive into, again, a very "unnatural" Japanese sentence.

Nishiwaki's experiment with this peculiar style of literal translation can be seen in his earlier translations of European poems; he quotes them in his theoretical writings collected under the title of *Chōgenjitsushugi shiron (Sur-*

realist Poetics). His eccentric style can be best illustrated when we compare his translations with the elegantly "Japanized" renditions collected in *Kaichōon* by Ueda Bin, or in *Gekka no ichigun (A Moonlit Gathering)* (1925) by Horiguchi Daigaku. Horiguchi translates Jean Cocteau's lines, "Mon oreille est un coquillage / Qui aime le bruit de la mer" as "Watashi no mimi wa kai no kara / Umi no hibiki o natsukashimu." Nishiwaki's version is more literal, more "kanbun chō" ("Chinese style"): "Ore no mimi wa hitotsu no kaigara de aru/Umi no onkyō o aisu."

Paul Verlaine's "Chanson d'automne" may be considered the best known foreign poem in Japan, thanks to the beautiful translation by Ueda Bin:

> Les sanglots longs
> Des violons
> De l'automne
> Blessent mon coeur
> D'une langueur
> Monotone

Ueda's translation:

> Aki no hi no
> Vioron no
> Tameiki no
> Mi ni shimite
> Hitaburuni
> Uraganashi

(The sighs of a violin of an autumn day seeping into my body; and I am infinitely sad.)

Nishiwaki's translation:

> Aki no vioron no nagai shakurinaki wa
> Ore no tamashii o hitotsu no tanch na darusa o
>   motte kizutsukeru

(The long convulsive sobs of an autumnal violin injure my soul with a certain monotonous languor.)

Compared with the sentimental, lyrical tonality of Ueda's rendition, the violence of Nishiwaki's literal translation may appear simply grotesque at first. For a moment we seem to lose our cherished faculty of judgment we do not know whether to grimace or burst out laughing. Yet the vitality of this new "poetic" language, freed from the established Japanese literary styles and sensitivities, was to greatly influence new generations of *gendai* (contemporary) poets.

Ambarvalia is invaded not only by literal translations of his own works but also by other kinds of unannounced translations by Nishiwaki. We now know that some poems in *Ambarvalia* are Nishiwaki's translations of poems written by other poets. But the book itself does not reveal any indication that these poems are in fact not Nishiwaki's originals. Such translations include all the poems in the "Raten aika" ("Latin Elegies") section as well as **"Renka"** ("Love Song") in the "Le Monde Moderne" section. "Latin Elegies" consists of four poems: **"Catullus," "Ambarvalia," "Vinus sai no zenban"** ("Eve of the Venus Festival"), and **"Aika"** ("Elegy"). **"Catullus"** is a translation of a poem by Catullus. **"Ambarvalia"** is the translation of an elegy written by a Roman poet of the Augustan age, most likely Tibullus. **"Vinus sai no zenban"** is a translation of a Latin poem probably written by several anonymous poets around the second or third century A.D. **"Aika"** is composed of a "literary" translation of Nishiwaki's own poem originally written in Latin; it is followed by the original Latin text, which is in turn followed by a "literal" translation of the Latin text. **"Renka"** is Nishiwaki's translation of "Poèmes d'amour" by the French-German poet Yvan Goll.

The fact that these were translations was not revealed in *Ambarvalia*. Perhaps Nishiwaki did not feel that it was important to note the authorial sources, for, after all, *Ambarvalia* was meant to be a small publication. Only 300 copies were printed. Many readers discovered the existence of *Ambarvalia* after the war, by reading the revised version, *Amubaruwaria* (the Latin word transliterated into *hiragana*). Nonetheless, just as Ezra Pound's translations are highly regarded on their own, Nishiwaki's translations are very highly esteemed by critics. When the editors of *Gendaishi tokuhon (Contemporary Poetry Reader)* were put to the task of selecting thirty poems out of Nishiwaki's enormous corpus, they selected three translations from *Ambarvalia*: **"Vinus sai no zenban," "Aika,"** and **"Renka."**

Was Nishiwaki concerned with authorship as much as our "conscientious" modern scholarship concerns itself with the issues of copyright and plagiarism? Perhaps not. Could we then suspect that something else was at work behind these "author-less" translations? Here we must shift our critical attention from Nishiwaki's personal reason for not revealing the authors to a more strictly textual question: what made the authors disappear from the text? Let us here follow the path Michel Foucault, Roland Barthes, and others so boldly opened up with regard to the modern text. The modern text itself demands that the author disappear. *Ambarvalia,* then, could be regarded as an exemplary text in which the disappearance of the author is clearly enacted. In his essay "What is an Author?" Foucault aptly describes the situation:

> The writing of our day has freed itself from the necessity of "expression"; it only refers to itself. . . . [T]he essential basis of this writing is not the exalted emotions related to the act of composition or the insertion of the subject into language. Rather, it is primarily concerned with creating an opening where the writing subject endlessly disappears.

Accordingly, Nishiwaki's writing of *Ambarvalia* can be seen as an effort to lose his own as well as others' authorship by staging a radical violation of the mother tongue through his translatory textual strategies.

In his rare autobiographical note "Nōzui no nikki" ("Journal of a Brain"), Nishiwaki comments on his attitude towards the Japanese language:

> The reason I did not write poems in Japanese was that I was convinced that, in order to write poems in Japanese, one had to employ such an out-dated "literary" language (*bungakugo*) or "elegant" style (*gabuntai*). By writing poems in English, I could evade this problem. It was Hagiwara Sakutarō who taught me that we did not necessarily have to use elegant style to write poetry. I totally supported not only his use of language but also his naturalism. Before Hagiwara, Japanese poetry had been steeped in sentimental romanticism. Maybe my enthusiasm for Hagiwara came from my reaction against such poetry. Since I was in junior high school, I had felt embarrassed about such poetry. . . . I was already over thirty when I finally began writing poems in Japanese for the periodical *Mitabungaku*. But that was also accompanied by a feeling of embarrassment.

Nishiwaki's shyness with regard to his mother tongue reveals an essentially elusive subject. The subject refuses to use the mother tongue. By doing so, the subject eludes the risk of being constituted solely by the mother tongue. The subject must resist the sweet mother tongue that has always already nestled at its core. Nishiwaki, the author-subject, recoiled from the mother tongue, from his center. The text he was to produce was not to be the vehicle of the expression of the subject, as both Nishiwaki (in *Chōgenjitsushugi shiron*) and Foucault strongly demand. Rather, as Foucault's statement suggests, **Ambarvalia** becomes the text into which "the writing subject endlessly disappears." In **Ambarvalia,** the textual openings Foucault talks about are seen in the gaps between the invisible originals and Nishiwaki's translations, between the foreign tongues and the mother tongue. By employing translation as the primary means of deconstructing the established language of poetry, Nishiwaki thus succeeds not only in creating a new "poetic" language but also in making the author-subject disappear into the "porous" text. Catullus disappears, Tibullus disappears, Goll disappears. . . .

Let me quote a section of the poem entitled **"Shitsura-kuen"**:

Hinjaku na mado o hirakeba
Ore no rōka no gotoku hosoi ikko no niwa ga
  mieru
Yōkeijō kara tareru shabon no mizu ga
Ore no sōzō shita saboten no hana o ansatsu suru
Soko ni funsui mo nashi
Misosazai mo bengoshi mo shigā mo nashi
Rukaderarobia no wakaki shākatai no ukibori mo
  naku
Tenkū wa nanpito mo inai

(When I open a shabby window
I see a single garden as narrow as my hallway.
The soapy water dripping from the chicken-coop
Assassinates my imagined cactus flowers.
No fountains exist there.
No wrens, no lawyers, no cigars.

Neither are there the reliefs of choir boys by Luca
  della Robbia.
There is nobody in the heavens.)

What remains, therefore, is this subject-less textual surface "hardened" by the invasions of foreign languages. The expressions of the self, "the cactus flowers of my imagination," are "assassinated." The garden is unnaturally objectified and solidified by its strange modifiers: "ore no rōka no gotoku hosoi ikko no" ("as narrow as my hallway, a singular object . . ."). "Ikko" ("a singular object") is a grammatically incorrect counter for "garden." It should be rather "hitotsu." "Ikko" is an originally Chinese word given a Sino-Japanese pronunciation, which sounds "harder" than the Japanese word "hitotsu." Thus by putting "ikko" in place of "hitotsu," the garden acquires an "unnatural" sense of solidification. The word "niwa" ("garden") no longer refers to a garden in reality. It becomes a linguistically constructed new image, a piece of a solidified and objectified "garden." In this linguistically "unnatural" garden no presence is allowed. "No fountains exist there. / No wrens, no lawyers, no cigars. / Neither are there the reliefs of choir boys by Luca della Robbia. / There is nobody in the heavens."

Instances of the violation of the mother tongue can be seen on the orthographical level as well. The Japanese writing system involves three kinds of writing symbols: two *kana* phonetic syllabaries (*hiragana* and *katakana*) and a semantically functioning *kanji* (Chinese character). In modern Japanese, *katakana* is mainly used for writing transliterations of foreign words, as well as instances of onomatopoeia. Therefore, whenever one sees a word in *katakana,* the instant impression one receives is that of foreignness. Nishiwaki exploits this peculiar function of *katakana* to an extreme degree. Not only does he use transliterated foreign words often, but he even uses *katakana* for Japanese words commonly written in *hiragana* or *kanji.* For example (*katakana* italicized in the transliteration):

Waga tamashii no kegawa wa *kusugut*tai *manto* o
  kita
(My spirit's fur wore a cloak that was really
  ticklish.)

. . . . .

Yawaraka ni nemuru made jibun no *uchi* ni iru y ni
  sukoyaka ni nemuru
(sleeps soundly as if being at home / until he falls
  into a soft sleep)

The effect of such a contrived use of *katakana* is twofold: the foreignization of the word and the rendering of the word into a kind of onomatopoeia. In the first example, one adjective "kusuguttai" ("ticklish") is separated into two orthographical components "kusugut" written in *katakana* and "tai" in *hiragana;* thus the "skipping" sound (double consonant) "gutt" becomes emphasized and then is released into the softer sound and letters of "tai" in *hiragana.* An ordinary word is thus made into an onomatopoeia *of its own sound*. In the second example, the word "sukoyaka" is written in *katakana,* when it should be written in *hiragana* or *kanji.* The resulting effect is that suddenly the *sound* of the word rather than its "meaning" comes to the foreground. The text thus announces itself as a field of signifiers (sounds) rather than that of signifieds (meanings).

Other instances of Nishiwaki's peculiar use of *katakana* can be seen in the following poem from the "Girisha teki jojō shi" ("Greek Lyrics") section in *Ambarvalia:*

Taiyō

Karumojiin no inaka wa dairiseki no sanchi de
Soko de watashi wa natsu o sugoshita koto ga atta.
Hibari mo inaishi, hebi mo denai.
Tada aoi *sumomo* no yabu kara taiyō ga dete
mata *sumomo* no yabu e shizumu.
Sh nen wa ogawa de *dorufin* o toraete waratta.

The Sun

The countryside of Karumojin produces marble.
Once I spent a summer there.
There are no skylarks, and no snakes come out.
Only the sun comes up from bushes of blue damson
And goes down into bushes of damson.
The boy laughed as he seized a dolphin in a brook.)

"Karumojiin" written in *katakana* receives our first attention. By its context as well as by the fact that it is written in *katakana,* we infer that it is the name of a foreign place. Since the poem is in the section called "Greek Lyrics," this place is probably in Greece or its environs. The mentioning of "marble" confirms this inference. But "Karumojiin" was actually Nishiwaki's pure fabrication. There is no existing location named "Karumojiin." Reportedly, Nishiwaki coined the name by association from the brand-name of a popular sleeping medicine from Germany called "Calmotin." Of course, this fact is not provided with the text. What we see, therefore, is the *katakana* and the "sound" of "Karumojiin." There we fall into a beautiful vessel of fictionality induced by a proper noun without "property," without a real referent.

The *katakana* for "hibari" ("skylarks") may not seem so unnatural, for often names of animals and birds are written in *katakana.* But at the same time, "hibari" is not a foreign word like, say, "flamingo." Nishiwaki could have used either *hiragana* or *kanji* for it. In fact, in the revised version of the same poem published in 1947, "hibari" is written in *hiragana.* What the *katakana* does here, however, is to foreignize the bird.

The images of "skylarks" and "snakes" are presented negatively, as absences: "There are no skylarks, and no snakes come out." This way of representing absence must be very difficult in the visual arts. Only language seems to be capable of this paradoxical image-production. "Hibari" in *katakana* is many times removed from the real referent,

the real bird. First of all, as we have seen, it is "foreignized" by the *katakana.* Secondly, it does not exist in Karumojiin. Thirdly, Karumojiin does not actually exist. What exactly do we have left here? A ghostly trace of a trace of a trace?

Of course "hibari" is a very common bird in Japan, while both "skylarks" and "snakes" are heavily allegorized, familiar figures in Western literature. This is again a strangely paradoxical case in which such a "familiar" object is presented as an absence, but which in turn is already defamiliarized *before* it is even announced as an absence. The absence of skylarks is not simply the absence of a familiar presence. The presence of "hibari" has been already turned into an orthographically induced "trace." Here we may witness a case of Derridian *différance* at work in the process of writing.

We also see a similarly unusual employment of *katakana* for the word "sumomo" (a type of damson). Sumomo is a specifically Oriental plant, imported from China in ancient times. Therefore, it is usually written in *hiragana* or *kanji.* In the revised version in **Amubaruwaria,** Nishiwaki uses the *kanji* for it. In any case, it is most unusual to see this Oriental plant in this putatively Mediterranean scene. But it is so "foreignized" by the use of *katakana* that it fits in the scene. A gap opens up between the "Japaneseness" of the plant (the signified of the word) and the foreignness of the *katakana* (the signified of the script). Thus appears a certain negative space of fictionality on the very surface of the text.

"Only the sun comes up from bushes of blue damson / And goes down into bushes of damson." A slow cyclic movement of the cosmos is suggested. There are no animals. A hard landscape of marble is established. Then suddenly, "Shōnen wa ogawa de dorufin o toraete waratta" ("The boy laughed as he seized a dolphin in a brook"). "*A* boy" instead of "*The* boy" seems more natural in English because he has not been introduced. But in the original, his sudden appearance and the apparent shift in the narrative perspective make us feel that we have known him all along, that he has been the main character of this little story. For example, if the author had continued the first person narrative as he began ("Once I spent a summer there"), the last sentence would be, say, "Hitori no shōnen ga ogawa de dorufin of toraete waratte ita" ("A boy was laughing as he seized a dolphin in a brook"). This gives a sense of observation by the speaker. But, in the original line, the center of perspective suddenly shifts from the first-person narrator to the boy. The narration is now performed by the omnipresent third person for whom the boy is (has been) the main character. This effect must be due to the use of the particle *wa* instead of *ga. Wa* is generally considered to be the topic-marker as opposed to *ga,* which is the subject-marker. As the topic-marker, *wa* can be rendered something like "as for." Literally, then, the line can be translated as "As for the boy, he laughed as he seized a dolphin in a brook."

There are of course more factors in this line that make us feel strangely disoriented. For one thing, dolphins cannot inhabit a small brook! And again "dolphin" is presented by the transliteration of the English word "dolphin" in *katakana*. The usual Japanese word for "dolphin" is "iruka." Elsewhere (in **"Sara"**) Nishiwaki uses the *kanji* [characters for . . . "sea-pig"].

As a whole, **"The Sun"** presents itself as an exemplary space of literature constituted by the strata of various fictionalizing strategies. After the "real" referential sphere is disrupted by various purely linguistic displacements, what remains is a beautifully concerted movement of evocative images, traces, signifiers that refuse to be mere transparent media of meanings but rather fasten themselves to the very surface and movement of language itself.

What is this space of literature, the fictionality proper, towards which the modernist language seems inevitably drawn? Away from the real, away from the proper, away from the signified, Nishiwaki's language seems to direct itself to a tenuous epidermis we can only call "poetic text," where depth is no longer possible, yet paradoxically, the surface is already a trace of a trace of a trace . . . This space of literature is the field of signifiers where language begins to speak of itself, to play its own games. In this self-referentiality of language, a strange survival movement of language can be detected. In his essay "Language to Infinity," Foucault brings out the image of language's survival force discovering its own self-referentiality, its own *mise-en-abyme:*

> Before the imminence of death, language rushes forth, but it also starts again, tells of itself, discovers the story of the story and the possibility that this interpenetration might never end. Headed toward death, language turns back upon itself; it encounters something like a mirror; and to stop this death which would stop it, it possesses but a single power: that of giving birth to its own image in a play of mirrors that has no limits.

As we have seen, the fictionality (as opposed to mimetic referentiality) of Nishiwaki's text is enhanced by various workings of translation. How does this translation function in relation to the self-referential movement of language that Foucault talks about? Walter Benjamin's somehow Gnostic theory of translation developed in his essay "The Task of the Translator" may be helpful in this regard.

Benjamin posits the notion of "pure language," which denotes an absolute state of language, where "meaning" becomes unmediatedly and instantly truth. According to Benjamin, this absolute state of language can be intimated only by means of a violently literal translation, which allows a radical violation of the mother tongue by foreign tongues. Benjamin quotes Rudolf Pannwitz advocating this violation:

> Our translations, even the best ones, proceed from a wrong premise. They want to turn Hindi, Greek, English into German instead of turning German into Hindi, Greek, English . . . The basic error of the translator is that he preserves the state in which his own language happens to be instead of allowing his language to be powerfully affected by the foreign tongue. He must expand and deepen his language by means of the foreign language.

Benjamin goes further. All languages strive to become one in pure language, in the paradisal state of non-meaning. For Benjamin, a translation is not merely a means of transmitting the meaning of the original text. On the contrary, it purifies the original of its "meaning." The paradisal state of non-meaning, pure language, is already in the original text, in a poem. Benjamin writes: "No poem is intended for the reader, no picture for the beholder, no symphony for the listener." Thus poetry and pure language become synonymous in their refusal of the reader, that is, of meaning.

The "new" poetic language that Nishiwaki devised in *Ambarvalia* may be seen as a gateway to this pure language. It is a porous text. Many gaps are opened by the force of translation. Into these openings the author-subject falls, along with "sa douce langue natale" (Baudelaire, "L'Invitation au voyage"). This writing-subject's surrender to the flow of the translatory writing marked the birth of a Japanese modernist text. Yet since it is always already a translation, it transcends the boundaries of merely "Japanese" poetry. Along with Foucault and Benjamin, we may say that it is rather a manifestation of language's own movement to infinity, to poetry.

FURTHER READING

Criticism

Hirata, Hosea. "Pure Poetry and *Differance*: Negativity in Nishiwaki and Derrida." *Journal of The Association of Teachers of Japanese* 26, No. 1 (April 1992): 5-24.

> Discusses the similarities between Nishiwaki's theoretical writings about poetry and Derrida's theory of *differance*.

——— . *The Poetry and Poetics of Nishiwaki Junzaburo, Modernism in Translation.* Princeton, N.J.: Princeton University Press, 1993, 261 p.

> Translations of selections from Nishiwaki's work by Hirata, with revised essays which have been excerpted above.

Additional coverage of Nishiwaki's life and career is contained in the following source published by Gale Research: *Contemporary Authors*, Vol. 107. [obituary]

Theodore Roethke
1908-1963

(Full name Theodore Huebner Roethke) American poet, critic, essayist, and author of children's books.

INTRODUCTION

Roethke is among the most celebrated American poets of the twentieth century. His poetry employs dynamic, descriptive imagery to convey the process of self-realization and discovery. The concrete language of Roethke's poetry serves to present his personal themes as archetypal experiences, resulting in a highly original, symbolic body of work charged with semantic associations that must be intuitively comprehended by the reader. According to Rosemary Sullivan, Roethke's poetry conveys "his sensitivity to the subliminal, irrational world of nature; his relationship to his dead father, who occupies the center of his work . . . ; his attempts to explore other modes of consciousness which carried him to the edge of psychic disaster . . . ; his interest in mysticism . . . ; his debts, so well repaid, to the poetic ancestors from whom he learned his craft; and the calm joyousness which rests at the core of his work."

Biographical Information

Roethke was born in Saginaw, Michigan, to first generation German-American parents who operated a large floral greenhouse and produce business. He worked in his parents' greenhouse and attended Arthur Hill High School. Roethke began writing verse during his undergraduate years at the University of Michigan, Ann Arbor, though he did not submit poems for publication until he began pursuing a master's degree in literature, first at Michigan and then at Harvard. The Great Depression cut short Roethke's studies, as he was forced to withdraw from school to find a job. For four years—until 1935—he taught at Lafayette, a small college in Pennsylvania, where he was a popular teacher and hard drinker. During his time at Lafayette, Roethke began friendships with the poets Rolfe Humphries, Louise Bogan, and Stanley Kunitz and published nineteen poems in such magazines as *Poetry*, the *New Republic*, and the *Saturday Review*. He subsequently began teaching at Michigan State College in Lansing but suffered a mental breakdown in the fall of 1935 and went home to Saginaw to recuperate. Upon recovering, Roethke took a position as an instructor at Pennsylvania State, where he devoted much of his time and energy to his poetry. By 1939 he had enough poems to assemble *Open House*, which was eventually published in the spring of 1941. Roethke left Pennsylvania State in 1943 to join the faculty of Bennington College in Vermont. There he met the poets Leonie Adams and Kenneth Burke; the latter was an important influence on Roethke's next collection, *The Lost Son, and Other Poems*. Roethke experienced severe depression

toward the end of 1945 and once again returned to Saginaw to convalesce. Fortunately, he received a Guggenheim Fellowship, for which he had applied earlier that year, and was able to remain in Saginaw without having to worry about returning to work. He continued writing poetry while recovering and finished the poems to be included in *The Lost Son* by February 1947. In September of that year he went to Seattle to assume a teaching position at the University of Washington. Encouraged by enthusiastic reviews of *The Lost Son*, Roethke worked hard at teaching and began composing the poems that would constitute *Praise to the End!* In the fall of 1949 he again suffered intense mental agitation and was taken to a sanitarium. He sought and received a second Guggenheim Fellowship and was able to finish the poems for *Praise to the End!* in 1950. Roethke received many more awards in his career, including *Poetry* magazine's Levinson Prize, a Fulbright grant, two Ford Foundation grants, the Pulitzer Prize for *The Waking: Poems, 1933-1953*, the Bollingen Prize and the National Book Award for *Words for the Wind*, and the National Book Award for *The Far Field*. Despite his success, he also experienced at least two more mental breakdowns that required hospitalization. Roethke retained his post at the University of Washington until his death from a heart attack in 1963.

Major Works

Roethke's first volume, *Open House,* was warmly received by W. H. Auden and Louise Bogan, among others, who commended the poet's masterful command of conventional verse forms, meters, and rhymes. However, Auden, for one, noted that Roethke needed to develop his own style and distance himself from tradition. In his second collection, *The Lost Son, and Other Poems,* Roethke employed the evolutionary past—worms, slugs, snails, slime, and spiders—to represent unarticulated childhood fears and impulses submerged in his subconscious. By relaxing his dependence upon conventional structure and experimenting with free verse, Roethke evolved a form capable of examining his own psychological and emotional growth. Vegetative and nature imagery drawn from Roethke's experiences in his parents' greenhouse are central to the poem sequence "The Greenhouse Poems" as well as "The Lost Son," in which Roethke tries to come to terms with his ambivalent feelings for his father, who died when Roethke was only fourteen. *Praise to the End!* combines several long poems from *The Lost Son* with new poems that continue the themes and approach that the poet had explored in his second volume. Bogan described Roethke's subject here as "the journey from the child's primordial subconscious world, through the regions of adult terror, guilt, and despair, toward final release into the freedom of conscious being." Reprinting earlier poems with a selection of new verse, *The Waking* incorporates as yet unexplored metaphysical and spiritual themes, including the superiority of intuition and faith over rational thought. Similarly, in the new poetry of *Words for the Wind,* Roethke contrasts ideal and real love and considers the nature of humankind's spiritual and physical make-up. *The Far Field*—especially the poems in "North American Sequence"—presents the natural world as a mystical sanctuary in which the individual can join together with God and all of humanity.

Critical Reception

In *Open House* Roethke proved himself an accomplished technician and as a knowledgable student of earlier poets, but many critics have noted that the poetry in this volume is largely derivative. With the publication of *The Lost Son* he established himself as a highly creative and promising poet with a highly original yet controlled style well suited to his personal themes. In subsequent collections, Roethke returned to the traditional verse forms of *Open House* but adapted them to his artistic aims. Nevertheless, commentators have found evidence of heavy borrowing from William Butler Yeats and T. S. Eliot even in Roethke's later verse. Although his output is relatively small in comparison to other major poets of the twentieth century, Roethke is appreciated for creating such popular poems as "My Papa's Waltz," "The Waking," "Four for Sir John Davies," "Elegy for Jane," and other frequently anthologized works. Critics have often disagreed, however, in their attempts to classify Roethke's poetic style. His deeply personal images and the manner in which he utilizes nature to explore psychological territories have prompted scholars to associate Roethke's verse with either the Con-

fessional or the Romantic school of poetry. Ralph J. Mills, Jr., has argued that Roethke's verse does not fit neatly into any single category; comparing Roethke to other poets of his generation, Mills stated: "Of all these later poets Theodore Roethke appears the most considerable, in terms of imaginative daring, stylistic achievement, richness of diction, variety and fullness of music, and unity of vision. . . . We should not be surprised then in reading through Roethke's books to discover a wide range of moods and styles: tightly controlled formal lyrics, dramatic monologues and something like an interior monologue, nonsense verse, love lyrics, and meditative poems composed in a very free fashion. His experience reaches from the most extraordinary intuition of the life of nature to lightning flashes of mystical illumination."

PRINCIPAL WORKS

Poetry

Open House 1941
The Lost Son, and Other Poems 1948
Praise to the End! 1951
The Waking: Poems, 1933-1953 1953
The Exorcism 1957
Words for the Wind 1957
I Am! Says the Lamb (children's poems) 1961
Party at the Zoo (children's poems) 1963
Sequence, Sometimes Metaphysical 1963
The Far Field 1964
The Achievement of Theodore Roethke: A Comprehensive Selection of His Poems with a Critical Introduction 1966
The Collected Poems of Theodore Roethke 1966
Theodore Roethke: Selected Poems 1969
Dirty Dinky and Other Creatures: Poems for Children (children's poems) 1973

Other Major Works

On the Poet and His Craft: Selected Prose of Theodore Roethke (essays) 1965
Selected Letters of Theodore Roethke (correspondence) 1968
Straw for the Fire: From the Notebooks of Theodore Roethke, 1943-63 (notebooks) 1972

* This work is an illustrated edition of a poem sequence that was first published in 1957 as part of *Words for the Wind.*

CRITICISM

W. H. Auden (essay date 1941)

SOURCE: "Verse and the Times," in *The Saturday Review of Literature,* Vol. 23, No. 24, April 5, 1941, pp. 30-1.

[*Auden is recognized as one of the preeminent poets of the twentieth century. His poetry centers on moral issues and evidences strong political, social, and psychological orientations. In the following review, Auden hails* Open House *but expresses the opinion that Roethke needs to continue growing as a poet.*]

Both in life and art the human task is to create a necessary order out of an arbitrary chaos. A *necessary* order implies that the process of its creation is not itself arbitrary; one is not free to create *any* order one chooses. The order realized must, in fact, have been already latent in the chaos, so that successful creation is a process of discovery. As long as this remains latent and unconscious, conscious life must appear arbitrary; one grows up in the degree to which this unconscious order becomes conscious and its potentialities developed, to the degree that one's life ceases to be arbitrary, to the degree that one becomes both conscious of and true to one's fate. An artist is someone who is able to express his human development in a public medium.

A work of art, like a life, can fail in two different ways: either, in terror of admitting that there is any chaos, it takes refuge in some arbitrary conscious order it has acquired ready-made from others or thought up itself on the spur of the moment, some order which, because it ignores the chaos that exists can do nothing with it but suppress it; or, lacking the courage and the faith to believe that it is possible and a duty to bring the chaos to order, it contents itself with a purely passive idolization of the flux. In poetry, the first attitude leads to a lifeless academic rhetoric; the second to the formless, the vague, the nonsensical and boring stream-of-consciousness.

A good poet can be recognized by his tense awareness of both chaos and order, the arbitrary and the necessary, the fact and the pattern: as Angelus Silesius says:—

> Fuerwahr, wer diese Welt
> Recht nimmt in Augenschein,
> Muss bald Democritus,
> Bald Heraclitus sein.

By such a test, Mr. Roethke is instantly recognizable as a good poet. He is well aware of "Confusion's core set deep within," "The ugly of the universe," "the menace of ancestral eyes," and their terrifying laughter rumbling in one's belly. He is willing to acknowledge the facts of suffering, "the rubbish of confusion," whether it is his own or that of others, the poor and those unfortunate ones for whom

> Acceleration is their need:
> A mania keeps them on the move
> Until the toughest nerves are frayed.
> They are the prisoners of speed
> Who flee in what their hands have made

because he knows that "A scratch forgotten is a scratch infected," but he is not content to lie down and blubber, but accepts them as a challenge:

> With these I match my little wit
> And earn the right to stand or sit,
> Hope, love, create, or drink and die:
> These shape the creature that is I.

> The anger will endure.
> The deed will speak the truth
> In language strict and pure.
> I stop the lying mouth:
> Rage warps my clearest cry
> To witless agony.

Many people have the experience of feeling physically soiled and humiliated by life; some quickly put it out of their mind, others gloat narcissistically on its unimportant details; but both to remember and to transform the humiliation into something beautiful, as Mr. Roethke does, is rare. Every one of the lyrics in this book, whether serious or light, shares the same kind of ordered sensibility: *Open House* is completely successful.

The only question which remains, and it concerns the poet rather than the reader, is: "Where is Mr. Roethke to go from here? Having mastered, with the help of Herrick, Marvell, and Blake, a certain style of expression, how is he to develop it, to escape being confined to short, and usually iambic, lyrics?"

It is possible, I think, that Mr. Roethke is trusting too much to diction, to the poetic instrument itself, to create order out of chaos. For poetry is only an instrument; it can be sharpened, but it cannot by itself widen the area of experience with which it deals. Poe was quite right in saying that an interest in poetry alone, can only produce short lyrics, but wrong, I think, in concluding from this that only short lyrics are poetry. It is possible that Mr. Roethke has read quite enough English poetry for a bit, and should now read not only the poetry of other cultures, but books that are neither poetry nor about poetry. For every artist must be like one of his own characters who

> . . . cried at enemies undone
> And longed to feel the impact of defeat.

Otherwise he may be in danger of certain experiences becoming compulsive, and of either, like Emily Dickinson and A. E. Housman, playing more and more variations on an old theme, or, like Rimbaud, of coming to the end of his experiences and ceasing to write.

But this, as I have said, is Mr. Roethke's problem, not ours. In *Open House* he has already done more than enough to make us lastingly happy and grateful.

Rolfe Humphries (essay date 1941)

SOURCE: "Inside Story," in *The New Republic,* Vol. 105, No. 1, July 14, 1941, p. 62.

[*An American poet and translator, Humphries published*

several volumes of verse and translated works by the Spanish poet and dramatist Federico García Lorca and the classical writers Ovid, Virgil, Juvenal, and Lucretius. In the following review, Humphries declares Open House *an honest and impressive debut collection that demonstrates Roethke has much promise as a poet.*]

The title of [**Open House**], and the opening lines of the title poem, at once give the reader to understand that much of the material to follow will be largely self-centered:

> My secrets cry aloud.
> I have no need for tongue.
> My heart keeps open house,
> My doors are widely swung.
> An epic of the eyes
> My love, with no disguise.

Throughout the several sections of the book, varied as they are in manner and theme, the tendency is to revert to this type of preoccupation, in spite of the prayer of the poet, "Deliver me, O Lord, from all / Activity centripetal." Does it sound patronizing to say this is natural in a first book? What saves Roethke from producing sentimental, ordinary or painful results in the process is the blunt and obdurate honesty of statement, even at the cost of flexibility of technique, without embellishment or fancy business. He faces and acknowledges much that he knows or suspects to be wrong inside. His open house is indeed wide open, from attic to basement; you can have a good look not only at the Chippendale chairs, the rings and the relics, but the skeleton in the closet and the family bogeymen.

Some of this work Roethke will not wish to repeat or find profit in repeating. But the book is not padded with practice pieces, poems whose chief value was in the exercise; Roethke has been quite severe in his selection, and every specimen is *per se* valid. He knows, I should hope, that his personal-metaphysical rock will not yield ore indefinitely, but there are indications of other veins he has scarcely begun to exploit. In the poems of nature and the visible world, with the weight of the theme less heavy, the music is richer, more sensuous and deeper; the observation, turned outward, is sensitive, delicate and perceptive, if not yet passionate and intense. Roethke can grow in this direction; and I am sure that readers who enjoy poems like **"Academic"**:

> The stethoscope tells what everyone fears:
> You're likely to go on living for years,
> With a nursemaid waddle and a shopgirl simper
> And the style of your prose growing limper and
>   limper

or **"Vernal Sentiment,"** would like to see a further exercise of his really incisive satirical wit, or a fuller indulgence of his humor. It takes a pretty good poet to be funny without being frivolous.

Toward the end of the book, in **"Lull,"** for instance, or **"Highway: Michigan,"** the consciousness is social as well

as personal, and **"Idyll"** and **"Night Journey,"** the last two poems, speak the word of affirmation, reconciliation and praise. Roethke has not by any means exhausted the possibilities of entertaining with the exposition of his hates; when he learns to overcome a certain diffidence, to speak as bravely and finely of his joys and loves as he has of his terrors and doubts, the house will not be big enough to hold him; he can, as a poet, really go to town.

Louise Bogan (essay date 1948)

SOURCE: A review of "The Lost Son," in *The New Yorker*, Vol. XXV, No. 12, May 15, 1948, pp. 102, 105-06.

[*A major American lyric poet whose darkly romantic verse is characterized by her use of traditional structures, concise language, and vivid description, Bogan is recognized particularly for her honest and austere rendering of emotion. She was also a distinguished critic who served as poetry editor for the* New Yorker *from 1931 to 1970 and was known for her exacting standards and her penetrating analyses of many of the major poets of the twentieth century. In the following excerpt, Bogan praises* The Lost Son *as an exploration of emotion and "primordial experience."*]

Theodore Roethke's **The Lost Son** gains a good deal of coherence by sticking to a few absolutely personal themes. In the long poem that gives the book its title, he plunges into his subconscious as into a pond, and brings up all sorts of clammy and amorphous material. He often frames it in the language of the adage, the proverb, the incantation, and the nonsense rhyme. He is made, that is to say, almost inarticulate by the fears and pressures in which he has submerged himself. Where [Randall] Jarrell frequently only describes, Roethke relives. **The Lost Son** is written with complete conscious control. The effects have been manipulated, as all art is manipulated, but the method aids in the understanding of the material instead of befogging it. Throughout, true emotion gives the chosen style coloration and shape. The pattern of **The Lost Son** is ancient and satisfying as well—the pattern of light-found-after-darkness. The poet rises, at the end, to the surface of his obsessive dream to see the world in the light of day. This exploration of primordial experience is surely more effective than the putting down of detached items on the "state of the world." Roethke's complete documentation of his childhood and of his father's florist trade also proves fruitful in emotional reference. And he never pads poems out to conventional size or shape.

Jarrell and Roethke should be read together. Few seasons bring us works in which the virtues and faults of our enlightened younger poetic generation appear in such sharp relief. Roethke is full of virtues that are instinctive, or that can be acquired only with great difficulty. Jarrell also displays innate talent, but he is occasionally full of brilliant tricks that can be learned all too easily. Even in the new style, it is the temperament of the individual that counts. Young talents should not be pushed by the snobberies of the academic and the "intellectual" worlds into dealing with subjects that involve them only partially, or into too much adherence to too many poetic texts, no matter how admirable those texts, by themselves or in combination, may be.

Stanley Kunitz (essay date 1949)

SOURCE: "News of the Root," in *A Kind of Order, a Kind of Folly: Essays and Conversations,* Little, Brown and Company, 1975, pp. 83-6.

[*An American poet and critic, Kunitz won the Pulitzer Prize in 1959 for his* Selected Poems, 1928-1958. *His work is skillfully crafted, incorporating rhythms of natural speech, and evidencing a fine ear for the musical cadence of phrases. Often considered metaphysical, his poetry is intensely personal, exploring the mystery of self and the intricacies of time. In the following review, which originally appeared in* Poetry *in 1949, Kunitz enthusiastically endorses Roethke's poetic style in* The Lost Son, and Other Poems, *finding that "The ferocity of Roethke's imagination makes most contemporary poetry seem pale and tepid in contrast."*]

With *The Lost Son,* Theodore Roethke confirms what some of us have long suspected: that he stands among the original and powerful contemporary poets. In this remarkable collection he undertakes a passionate and relentless exploration of the sources of a life. The two major sections consist of a sequence of thirteen short poems that might be described, roughly, as botanical studies, and a quartet of long poems that are the record of a psychic adventure, the poet's quest of himself. For critical purposes the book needs to be examined as a whole: almost everything in it proliferates from a single root-cluster of images.

A greenhouse is the country of Roethke's childhood, the inevitable place of his return. This world under glass where, as a boy, small among "the lovely diminutives," he grubbed, weeded, pruned, transplanted, is bound in with his family, for whom it was, presumably, an economic as well as a physical center of gravity. In one of his most successful poems, which illustrates the naked precision and force of his vocabulary, he celebrates the ordeal of the greenhouse in the big wind, when he stayed with it all night, stuffing the holes with burlap. To him the structure, as will be seen, is not a *thing*; it has gender and personality; on this specific occasion it excites his admiration—he speaks of it *con amore*:

> But she rode it out,
> That old rose-house,
> She have into the teeth of it,
> The core and pith of that ugly storm
>
> . . . . .
>
> She sailed into the calm morning,
> Carrying her full cargo of roses.

The horticultural aspects of Roethke's work should be clearly defined. What absorbs his attention is not the in-

tricate tracery of a leaf or the blazonry of the completed flower, but the stretching and reaching of a plant, its green force, its invincible Becoming.

> This urge, wrestle, resurrection of dry sticks,
> Cut stems struggling to put down feet,
> What saint strained so much,
> Rose on such lopped limbs to a new life?

I do not wish to give the impression that Roethke's greenhouse world is rosy, innocent, optimistic. On the contrary, it swarms with malevolent forces. It is a place of scums, mildews, and smuts; of slug-soft stems; of obscenely lolling forms; a place moist and rank ("what a congress of stinks!"), engulfing, horribly fecund. The delicate slips keep coaxing up water; the sprouts break out, slippery as fish. Suddenly we are under ground, under water, in a grave, in a womb, in the deep ponds of the subconscious; plunged like Caliban into our creature-self; enduring the foetal throes. Underness is everywhere:

> Came to lakes; came to dead water,
> Ponds with moss and leaves floating,
> Planks sunk in the sand.
>
> . . . . .
>
> Nothing would sleep in that cellar, dank as a ditch.
>
> . . . . .
>
> What fish-ways you have, littlest flowers.
>
> . . . . .
>
> Where do the roots go?
>   Look down under the leaves.
>
> . . . . .
>
> The dark flows on itself. A dead mouth sings under
>   an old tree.
>
> . . . . .
>
> Last night I slept in the pits of a tongue.

As Roethke, with an almost nightmarish compulsiveness, makes his descent into the mythic regions of Father Fear and Mother Mildew, a furious energy activates his language; his metaphors whirl alive, sucking epithets into their centers of disturbance from the periphery of the phrase; his rhythms wrench themselves out of the fixed patterns of his earlier style and become protean, incantatory, organic; what will not submit itself to him he takes by storm, if he cannot take it by magic. The child encountered "under the concrete benches, Hacking at black hairy roots,—Those lewd monkey-tails hanging from drainholes," might serve as an image of the poet himself at his creative labor.

The ferocity of Roethke's imagination makes most contemporary poetry seem pale and tepid in contrast. Even his wit is murderous. He does not strain for cleverness, but he can achieve a concentration of phrase that is as brilliant as it is violent: "Dogs of the groin barked and howled" . . . "You will find no comfort here, In the Kingdom of bang and blab" . . . "I have married my hands to perpetual agitation, I run, I run to the whistle of money." His imagination is predominantly tactile and auditory (subject at times to the vice of echolalia). He is so aware of the transformations of the self that much of his imagery is palpably metamorphic: "This wind gives me scales, Have mercy, gristle" . . . "Call off the dogs, my paws are gone." At this depth of sensibility, far below the level of the rational, language itself breaks down, reverting to a kind of inspired nonsense, expressive of the childhood of the race as well as of the individual:

> Rich me cherries a fondling's kiss,
> The summer bumps of ha:
> Hand me a feather, I'll fan you warm,
> I'm happy with my paws.

Roethke's first volume, **Open House** (1941), was praised, deservedly, for its lyric resourcefulness, its technical proficiency, its ordered sensibility. The present collection, by virtue of its indomitable creativeness and audacity, includes much more chaos in its cosmos; it is difficult, heroic, moving, and profoundly disquieting. What Roethke brings us in these pages is news of the root, of the minimal, of the primordial. The sub-human is given tongue; and the tongue proclaims the agony of coming alive, the painful miracle of growth. Here is a poetry born of the maelstrom. It would seem that Roethke has reached the limits of exploration in this direction, that the next step beyond must be either silence or gibberish. Yet the daemon is with him, and there is no telling what surprises await us. I find it significant and highly encouraging that the volume ends triumphantly, luminously, with a thrust upward into "the whole air," into the "pierce of angels":

> To follow the drops sliding from a lifted oar,
> Held up, while the rower breathes, and the small
>   boat drifts quietly shoreward;
> To know that light falls and fills, often without our
>   knowing.
> As an opaque vase fills to the brim from a quick
>   pouring,
> Fills and trembles at the edge yet does not flow
>   over.
> Still holding and feeding the stem of the contained
>   flower.

Richard Eberhart (essay date 1951)

SOURCE: "Deep, Lyrical Feelings," in *The New York Times Book Review*, December 16, 1951, p. 4.

[*Eberhart is a highly regarded lyric poet whose verse examines fundamental questions about the nature of existence. His poems typically evoke quotidian images that illuminate conflicts between emotion and intellect, innocence and experience, chaos and order, and the spiritual and physical realms. Below, Eberhart uses the occasion of a review of* Praise to the End! *to extol Roethke's skill as a poet.*]

Theodore Roethke joins the ranks of the pure poets. His power is that his offering is clean-cut. His verse is pure. It is totally sensuous, totally personal, and his vision is totally contained. His poetry is not based on schematized

intellectualism but on blood-felt reports of sense experience known in memory, transmuted by imagination.

The limitation of his work makes for its purity and acts as a conscious good. The out-thrust and the in-check are held in a strong, positive balance. It is a highly lyrical style.

Roethke gives us the new, age-old excitement of a true poet uttering the feelings, the meanings deepest in him, in his own peculiar way, driven by compulsive force.

The verse is an incantation, a celebration—and it is often playful. Roethke is an interior monologist forever inviting his soul to the Self. He has delved into obscurest childhood and in mature complexity has drawn up marvels of tonal simplicity and penetration, gnomic flashes, witty self-criticisms, curious neologisms, all bestowed with fountainlike exuberance. His verbalism suggests Swinburne but a more resilient Swinburne of the times.

One of the rewarding feelings he gives is in his sense of strict economy and control. He has defined a world and mastered that world, a maker of magic combinations. It is an inner accurate world of feeling, not an outer world of things.

[**Praise to the End!**] reprints four fairly long poems, now well known, from **The Lost Son**: **"The Lost Son," "The Long Alley," "A Field of Light"** and **"The Shape of the Fire."** The early greenhouse pieces are not reprinted and all of the new poems are shaped like the above-mentioned ones, have their type of tone and intention and deal with similar subject-matter. The title poem, **"Unfold! Unfold!"** and **"I Cry, Love! Love!"** all have characteristic riches of device and make for uniform excellence throughout the book.

Some lines at random may serve to show the glint and thrust of the verse: "Fishing, I caught myself behind the ears!" "I was far back, farther than anybody else," "Speak to the stones, and the stars answer," "To have the whole air!" "Hello, thingy spirits," "I proclaim once more a condition of joy." The very next line to this brings in the critical, mocking, humorous spirit: "Walk into the wind, willie!"

Louise Bogan (essay date 1952)

SOURCE: A review of *Praise to the End!*, in *The New Yorker*, Vol. XXVII, No. 53, February 16, 1952, pp. 107-08.

[*In the following excerpt, Bogan compares Roethke's poetry to that of Richard Eberhart and applauds the symbolism that Roethke employs in* Praise to the End! *to suggest the journey from childhood into mature consciousness.*]

When Goethe stated that the shudder expressed mankind's best side, he was thinking not of the Gothic atmosphere fashionable in his day so much as of the general feeling of awe at the mysteries of the universe, to which the most hardened materialist is not entirely immune. In modern poetry, this larger emotion is rare indeed; the whole emotional set of the period is against it. The Gothic shudder, on the other hand, appears with fair regularity. The Surrealists revived it while exploiting the dark marvels of the subconscious, and traces of Surrealist influence continue to crop up in modern verse, although the movement, on the whole, is exhausted. . . . [Poets] who have published recent volumes illustrate the methods—precarious at best and open to failure more than to sucess—by which the modern imagination tries to project feelings of mystery and awe.

One method involves a putting on of masks, or personae, through which the poet speaks. . . .

Richard Eberhart, on the other hand, is a poet who can turn the cube of reality (in William James' phrase) so that another facet comes into view. At his best, he does this with the mystic's ease. His *Selected Poems* finally brings his gifts into focus. Eberhart, possessing the innocent unself-consciousness of one to whom the spirit is a reality, in earlier volumes displayed the faults of his virtues: tendencies toward diffuseness of language and dilution of idea. The poems in this collection are concentrated, both in mood and form, and the total effect is remarkable. . . . Eberhart continues to be original because his vision is constantly self-refreshing, and he needs no masks to enhance either his meaning or his impact.

If Theodore Roethke's poetry in *Praise to the End!* seems at first glance more consciously produced than Eberhart's, it is soon evident that the two poets share an unforced power of imaginative penetration into the obscure, the hidden, and the inarticulate, and that they are both capable of that larger awe of which Goethe spoke. Roethke has added several long poems to passages from *The Lost Son,* published a few years ago, and these additions accent his original theme—the journey from the child's primordial subconscious world, through the regions of adult terror, guilt, and despair, toward a final release into the freedom of conscious being. Roethke's description of this progress attaches itself to recognizable myth and legend hardly at all; his rendition of sub-or pre-conscious world is filled with coiling and uncoiling, nudging and creeping images that often can be expressed only with the aid of nonsense and gibberish. But it is witty nonsense and effective gibberish, since the poet's control over this difficult material is always formal; he knows exactly when to increase and when to decrease pressure, and he comes to a stop just before the point of monotony is reached. Behind Roethke's method exists the example of Joyce, but Roethke has invented a symbolism, in his searching out of these terrors, marginal to our consciousness, that is quite his own.

[*Carruth is a well-respected and prolific American poet whose verse is frequently autobiographical, varied in mood and form, and noted for its unadorned and precise language. His literary criticism, which is collected in such volumes as* Working Papers *(1982) and* Effluences from the Sacred Cave *(1983), is recognized for its directness and tolerance. In the following review, Carruth declares Roethke's poetic voice in* The Waking *original.*]

Above all others, Theodore Roethke is a poet to encourage and comfort us in our valley of literary conformism. He leads us back to the surprising upland. He makes us realize how rapidly our literature is flowing toward a dead center of accredited modernity. Worse, he makes us acknowledge, with a disconcerting twinge, that the grand oldsters, the experimentalists of the Twenties and the decade before, have been living on their original investments for thirty years or more, and that today experimental writing has been forfeited to juniority and dunderdom—the forlorn margin.

Roethke himself is, of course, the exception. He has turned, after a long apprenticeship in the techniques of standard English verse, to a personal idiom and a compressed, exclamatory line. He does not always avoid the pitfall of obscurity, but his writing is certainly more interesting and more provocative than any other current poetry. *The Waking,* which is a collection from his previous books plus a section of new poems, shows his development with remarkable clarity.

The author was forced into his later period by the demands of his subject. Among his earlier poems, the most interesting are those which evoke his childhood, his life as the son of a florist—i.e., a grower, not a seller, of flowers. These are poems of groping roots, straining tendrils, the turmoil of growth in a steamy greenhouse. From this Roethke passed to a consideration of all primitive life, the dark life of weed and minnow at the bottom of a woodland pond, the equally dark life of children.

The most interesting of Roethke's recent poems are those written from the point of view of a child. Usually children's sayings are a source of fun: when a child says something that sounds adult—or when a monkey smokes a cigar—we laugh. But Roethke's child says: "A kitten can / Bite with his feet: / Papa and Mamma / Have more teeth." This is the child's own intelligence which lives on in all of us; he is our spokesman for a fearful and murderous heritage.

Psychoanalysts have been telling us this for years, of course, but the poet has an advantage. Roethke gives us the actual experience of the child's insight. His poetry, far from being clinical, conveys the power and often the beauty that are only possible in the world of the imagination.

Hayden Carruth (essay date 1953)

SOURCE: "The Idiom Is Personal," in *The New York Times Book Review,* September 13, 1953, p. 14.

Hilton Kramer (essay date 1954)

SOURCE: "The Poetry of Theodore Roethke," in *Western Review,* Vol. 18, No. 2, Winter, 1954, pp. 131-46.

[*Kramer is a prominent art critic who has served on the staff of such journals as* Arts Digest, Arts Magazine, Nation, New Leader, New Criterion, *and the* New York Times. *In the following essay, which focuses primarily on the collection* Praise to the End!, *Kramer maintains that Roethke's treatment of prerational existence represents "the expression of a new primitivism."*]

Theodore Roethke is probably the most original poet to appear in America since the twenties. This is not always the highest praise for a poet, especially for an American poet of the last two decades. We know how often this "originality" means only Kenneth Patchen's rearrangement of the typography, or some new promiscuity with commas after the manner of José Garcia Villa. And further, it is not the kind of praise we are likely to reserve, say, for the poetry of Robert Lowell, one of the few poets of Roethke's generation who makes such large demands on our attention. But in Roethke's situation, it is large praise to make a claim for his originality. It is a situation which, until only a few decades ago, was quite unknown to American poets. We must refresh our memories to the fact (we are still so unused to it) that with the generation of poets which includes Eliot, Pound, Stevens, Crane, Moore, Cummings, Frost, Ransom, Tate, and Williams, we had for the first time in American poetry a spectacle of talents which allows us to speak without embarrassment of a renaissance. But the poet coming after such a generation must have the most ambivalent feelings about it: surely a kind of joy, even pride, that at last an American poet does not have to begin at the beginning all over again, that at last he can continue in a tradition which, though it does not provide him with what the French tradition supplied Baudelaire and Valéry, at least gives him some foundations (even Dickinson, Whitman, and Melville are recovered for the purpose); and surely, as well, a kind of despair at having so much to cope with in that perennial part of the poet's labor which always consists of, somehow, despite the usability of the past, beginning over again anew.

It seems to me that the two poets who emerge from this situation with the greatest success are Roethke and Lowell. And they are vastly different from each other. Lowell's poetry has been more readily accepted and understood because it seems to be in the genre of so much of the poetry (of the past and of the present) which forms the basis of our literary values. This does not mean that his poetry is derivative in the bad sense or that his style is not his own, but it does mean that his literary education (which is always a fund of values from the preceding generation) exercises a very special discipline on his writing and that his successes are the outcome of his struggle with this education, successes usually achieved by transforming something from the past into something new. And it is this past, this sense of history—New England history, Christian history, the history of his literary taste—which seems to give his poems their authority and power.

Roethke's poetry seems, if anything, to concern itself with pre-history. About his language, we can only guess, we are so uneducated to it: my guess is that it is the loose diction of a view which has not yet learned to recognize human moral history as anything separate from life as a primordial whole. Roethke had somehow to come up with a language which would not only render, but also itself be the medium of, the pre-rational. Lowell's poetry is bound to have a greater range, for that is what history is: the whole range of life as we recognize it objectively. And the sensibility which limits itself to a pre-historical sense of life, to all the urgent struggle which attends those stages by which the psyche seeks to free itself from the bondage (and the security) of its first dwelling place (the slime, the womb) and to commit itself sorrowfully to its destiny in the world of history—this view is bound to seem limited in comparison. Pre-history is a single episode in the human drama; whereas history, however motley or schematic its content, is a spectacle of great variety.

Roethke's first volume of poems, *Open House*, appeared in 1941. It was a brilliant book, notable for its clarity and humor; and although there were some influences rather heavily in evidence, such as Auden's in the poem called **"Lull (November, 1939)"** Roethke's style already announces itself. It is a style which is unencumbered by any distracting decorative elements; a style whose spare language delivers its poems to the reader with an admirable directness.

These qualities, of course, are characteristic of Roethke's style in his later volumes, **The Lost Son and Other Poems** (1948) and **Praise to the End!** (1951), but in a different way. What separates the poems in **Open House** and some of the shorter poems in the second volume from the later works is the changed relationship between language and subject. The sensibility of the earlier poems is the poet's; there is very little recourse to a persona, such as the child-figure in **"The Lost Son"** (and the cycle of poems in which it takes its place). Thus, language in these earlier poems has, as it were, a more conventional relationship to subject: it deals with this or that subject, calling attention to itself as little as possible. The storms, the landscapes, the emotions even, which occur in these poems are "objective," that is, they exist in the observable world, the world which our reason unfolds to us in waking experience. But in the later cycle of poems, first appearing in **The Lost Son and Other Poems** and brought together as a group in **Praise to the End!**, all this has changed. Here language and subject collide; they merge; and what we have as a result is the language which Roethke has created for a subject which does not ordinarily have a language.

The title of **Praise to the End!** is taken from Wordsworth. It appears in Book I of *The Prelude* in a passage which, if it does not anticipate Roethke's destination exactly, does presage the subject which is explored in these extraordinary poems. It is a passage in which Wordsworth interrupts his account of the education which the spirit receives in the hands of nature to acknowledge the antithesis between harmony (that "dark / Inscrutable workmanship that reconciles / Discordant elements") and the will to dissolution ("The terrors, pains, and early miseries, / Regrets, vexations, lasstudes") which characterizes the journey of the psyche in this world. And it is well to invoke the name of Wordsworth here, if only to recall the dilemma which he confronts so heroically and philosophically—not a dilemma only but an impasse, which recognizes that the world in which we find ourselves, its physical monstrousness and its moral chaos, and our own essential sense of life, above all the sense of life presided over by our feelings, are completely at odds.

Moreover, we should also recall the essential place which Wordsworth gives the *child* in his effort to recover a meaningful life of the emotions, and not the child only but, childhood itself in all its intimate identification with the life of nature. This identification has, for Wordsworth, both its maternal and its natural side, one not separated from the other. It is an image of childhood which in Roethke's poems is always in the memory, so to speak, as the hint of a lost Eden, and for which there is a great deal of filial longing. These are the lines, from another book of *The Prelude,* which gave the image in all its ideality:

> No outcast he, bewildered and depressed:
> Along his infant veins are interfused
> The gravitation and the filial bond
> Of nature that connect him with the world.

But the child who appears in Roethke's poems, sometimes as an immediate sensibility and sometimes as a recollection, is a lost child, a child without connections any longer, a child-hero wandering in the darkness of the soul to redeem what it has lost. There is an observation in Jung's essay on "The Psychology of the Child-Archetype" which has great relevance here. Jung is discussing the plight of the child-hero, and says,

> The hero's main feat is to overcome the monster of darkness: the long-hoped-for and expected triumph of consciousness over the unconscious. Day and light are synonyms for consciousness, night and dark for the unconscious. The coming of consciousness was probably the most tremendous experience of primeval times, for with it a world came into being whose existence no one had suspected before . . . Hence the 'child' distinguishes itself by deeds which point to the conquest of the dark.

This, stated in psychological terms, is also a moral effort, and the world "whose existence no one had suspected" is, of course, the moral world.

The Wordsworthian effort is not without its falsifications, however. And we are, I believe, naturally inclined to view skeptically a performance on a tight-rope which is fastened at one end to the reconstructed intuitions of a child and at the other to the perceptions of a philosophical poet writing in his middle age about the recovery of child-like intuitions. Wordsworth manages to survive the falsifications, but his success does not diminish our skepticism.

Roethke also addresses himself to the Wordsworthian subject: the spirit's education in the world of nature, and the recovery of human feelings. I remarked earlier that Roethke's poetry dwells on the pre-rational and the pre-historical sense of life, which is to say that he pursues the Wordsworthian subject into sources more primeval than

Wordsworth intended. And in carrying out this pursuit, of course, he parts company with Wordsworth, he leaves behind the serenity and philosophic discretion of Wordsworth's language; he chooses to take a lonely way and he can take very little with him.

Although several of the poems in *Praise to the End!* appeared in an earlier volume, the series here does seem to form a coherent development, which, stated most generally, is something like this: the first-person protagonist, frequently speaking out in anguished exclamations, nonsense songs, frenzied invocations, and even moments of contemplation, begins in a situation of death and desolation, undergoes the agony of coming alive again and of perceiving the world anew, and then ends with what is, however minimal and primitive, a vision of the triumph of life. Or to state it at an even more generalized level: these poems constitute the action of a soul undergoing its night-journey.

This general schema, while necessary, hardly gives any impression of the special kind of drama which takes place in each poem, of course. Probably no one since Saint Francis has lived so intimately with the sub-human forms of life, has had such an intense spiritual identification with them—and this, without personification and easy fable-izing. From the first, this intimacy and identification are achieved through the vehicle of the child-figure; and recurrently this figure, its innocent sensibility and its direct responses, is developed into, replaced by, and played off against, the memory of childhood and the agonized moment when the protagonist undergoes a kind of exalted "second childhood" of the emotions.

In the first poem of the group, **"Where Knock Is Open Wide,"** the protagonist is the child-figure. Roethke has elsewhere provided this note on the poem: "The earliest piece of all (in terms of the age of the protagonist) is written entirely from the viewpoint of a very small child: all interior drama; no comment; no interpretation." Here, even more strictly than in other poems, though it is one of the chief characteristics of his whole work, all intellectual matter is suppressed. The drama is the death of the father, and the "events" of the poems are perceptions and memories in which parental love and the security of home are jeopardized or in some moment of crisis. An uncle dies:

> I know who's got him
> They'll jump on his belly,
> He won't be an angel,
> I don't care either.

There is the memory of the child fishing with his father:

> We went by the river.
> Water birds went ching. Went ching.
> Stepped in wet. Over stones.
> One, his nose had a frog,
> But he slipped out.
> I was sad for a fish.
> Don't hit him on the boat, I said.
> Look at him puff. He's trying to talk.

Papa threw him back.

Bullheads have whiskers.
And they bite.

And there is the image of the father tending his greenhouse ("my symbol for the whole of life," Roethke has said):

He watered the roses.
His thumb had a rainbow.
The stems said, Thank you.
Dark came early.

This last line is a typical example of how Roethke can use the short line, the brief statement, to mean a great deal. *Dark came early*: the dark is death, and to this child, darkness has occurred early in life. Moreover, there is a momentary glimpse of the future and the wandering which the knowledge of death prefigures:

Nowhere is out. I saw the cold.
Went to visit the wind. Where the birds die.
How high is have?

And here we have another Roethkean habit: verb forms, prepositions, the most unlikely parts of speech, suddenly transformed in a Cummings-esque manner into conditions and situations. *How high is have?*: how high (in the sky? out of reach?) is have (to have a father? God?). Here the drama has really *become* words: it is as if Mallarmé's admonition to Degas—*"Mais, Degas, ce n'est pas avec des idées qu'on fait des vers, c'est avec des mots"*—had finally been heeded by the proper poet. It is indeed a poetry of words, words passionately wedded to their objects but totally divorced from telling any "anecdote" in the conventional way.

The poem concludes with a section in which is announced a whole cluster of motifs which recur throughout the entire series. And central to these is the figure of the father (now dead), presiding over his greenhouse (his home, too), as the earthly analogue of God the Father (now lost) presiding over all of life:

Kisses came back,
I said to Papa;
He was all whitey bones
And skin like paper.

God's somewhere else,
I said to Mamma.
The evening came
A long long time.

I'm somebody else now.
Don't tell my hands.
Have I come to always? Not yet.
One father is enough.

Maybe God has a house.
But not here.

The second poem, **"I Need, I Need,"** opens with the child's problematic relation to his mother (as always, the relations are rendered physically):

A deep dish. Lumps in it.
I can't taste my mother.

And there are images of a child's odd mourning, with the beginnings of those invocations which eventually (in later poems, when the protagonist is no longer a child) become the most intense moments of anguish:

Went down cellar,
Talked to a faucet;
The drippy water
Had nothing to say.

Whisper me over,
Why don't you, begonia,
There's no alas
Where I live.

And to the child there are also intimations of his dead father (and of God?): "Today I saw a beard in a cloud."

With the third poem, **"Bring the Day,"** begins the dark journey of growth, and this I think we must understand to be a double image: both the child's growth imaginatively recollected by the protagonist and the spiritual growth, symbolically rendered, of the protagonist himself. The final movement of the poem exclaims this beginning (are there so many exclamations in all modern poetry?), and what follows this beginning will all be episodes in the journey:

O small bird wakening,
Light as a hand among blossoms,
Hardly any old angels are around any more.
The air's quiet under the small leaves.
The dust, the long dust, stays.
The spiders sail into summer.
It's time to begin!
To begin!

In **"Give Way, Ye Gates"**—the title itself initiates a group of images, gates, caves, doors, etc., suggesting departures and returns, exits and entrances, not without erotic meanings—the protagonist enters into the underworld of sub-human and pre-rational forms of life, and carries on his dark romance with what we might call (after a recent poem by Anthony Hecht): *la condition botanique*. There is a constant shuttling back and forth between the vegetative life, the hero's identification with it ("I bleed like a tree"), and the sexual awakening which marks the passage out of childhood, an awakening intimated or observable everywhere in nature, everywhere celebrated with spontaneity, except in the human animal:

You tree beginning to know,
You whisper of kidneys,
We'll swinge the instant!—
With jots and jogs and cinders on the floor:
The sea will be there, the great squashy shadows,

Biting themselves perhaps;
The shrillest frogs;
And the ghost of some great howl
Dead in a wall.
In the high-noon of thighs,
In the spring-time of stones,
We'll stretch with the great stems.
We'll be at the business of what might be
Looking toward what we are.

But at the moment of awakening, of perceiving "what we are," there is the sudden regression back into the dark world, into the slime, the sub-human. *La condition botanique* and *la condition humaine*—these are the terms in the dialectic (if I may be permitted so intellectual a description of what is at every point a physical, albeit symbolical, drama) which contains the action. And from this point onwards there is no real "progress" in the action, only the variations and elaborations which assert themselves in terms of this antithesis, until the end.

The longest, most elaborate poem in the group, **"The Lost Son,"** occurs midway in the series, and seems to contain within its condensed form the whole spectrum of the series' action and of the larger action of the human psyche which it dramatises. The poem's narrative line (if it can be called such) is indicated by the four subtitles: The Flight, The Pit, The Gibber, The Return. The final movement of the poem is untitled, and contains the quiet meditation of a soul waiting to re-enter the world. The flight into the dark regions of sub-human life, into the sources of life, recalls Roethke's reading in fairy tale and folklore (I do not mean literary allusions *à la Eliot* but dramatic and symbolic equivalents):

At Woodlawn I heard the dead cry:
I was lulled by the slamming of iron,
A slow drip over stones,
Toads brooding in wells.
All the leaves stuck out their tongues;
I shook the softening chalk of my bones,
Saying,
Snail, snail, glister me forward,
Bird, soft-sigh me home.
Worm, be with me.
This is my hard time.

And there are compulsive invocations for some kind of other, further life:

Voice, come out of the silence.
Say something.
Appear in the form of a spider
Or a moth beating the curtain.

Tell me:
Which is the way I take;
Out of what door do I go,
Where and to whom?

There is then a moment in the Pit, a moment of immobility; and then the long Gibber, a frenzied movement of erotic agonies, filial uncertainties, economic doubts, and a whole drama of disconcerted anguish. There begins a hint of the life into which the Lost Son might be reborn:

At the wood's mouth,
By the cave's door,
I listened to something
I had heard before.

This expectancy is then restated in terms of sexual arousal, then disappointed:

Dogs of the groin
Barked and howled,
The sun was against me,
The moon would not have me.

The disappointment and loss are then transferred into filial anxiety and homelessness:

Hath the rain a father? All the caves are ice. Only
    the snow's here.
I'm cold. I'm cold all over. Rub me in father and
    mother.

There follows a frenetic questioning, implorations for some explanation of the growth which the hero feels taking place everywhere around him:

Is this the storm's heart? The ground is unstilling
    itself.
My veins are running nowhere. Do the bones cast
    out their fire?
Is the seed leaving the old bed? These buds are live
    as birds.

And even the economic motif is sounded, perhaps in a sudden intuition of the material world toward which this journey is moving:

Good-bye, good-bye, old stones, the time-order is
    going,
I have married my hands to perpetual agitation,
I run, I run to the whistle of money.

The Gibber finally ends in "a dark swirl."

The Return is pictured in closely autobiographical images generalized into a scene of homecoming. The return of the Lost Son to his father's greenhouse is both the return to his home and to *life*. Moreover, there is a dramatic heightening in this image of homecoming: the tension, never stated explicitly, between this image as a final stage in the action (and therefore as objective dramatization of a certain situation of the soul) and the image as a memory of the hero's (and the poet's) childhood. It is an image of Return which is depicted, with the kind of spiritual solidarity for *la condition botanique* exhibited throughout the poems, in terms of the greenhouse flowers giving themselves up to the light (which is their source of life) after their nocturnal drowse:

A fine haze moved off the leaves;
Frost melted on far panes;

The rose, the chrysanthemum turned toward the
light.
Even the hushed forms, the bent yellowy weeds
Moved in a slow up-sway.

The expectancy evidenced everywhere in the poem, and
especially given an alarming urgency in the Gibber, reaches its final transformation, in the last section, into a philosophic detachment. For once, there is not only the physical drama of the senses, the touching, knocking, stretching, and pushing of the physical life, but also the larger
view, the view of the whole spiritual landscape:

It was beginning winter,
An in-between time,
The landscape still partly brown:
The bones of weeds kept swinging in the wind,
Above the blue snow.

And there is in this vision of the landscape an intuition of
light, of the light which divides the day from the night,
which heralds birth, which symbolizes the dawning of
knowledge:

Light traveled over the field;
Stayed.
The weeds stopped swinging.
The wind moved, not alone,
Through the clear air, in the silence.

And then these final lines which signal the moment of
recovered life:

A lively understandable spirit
Once entertained you.
It will come again.
Be still.
Wait.

In trying to relate the symbolic action which underlies the
literal action of this poem (and others), I have quoted
extensively to guard against the impression that this poetry does not have a firm basis in literal images and actions.
I can think of no poet, in fact, who is more literal than
Roethke; it is his literality which strikes the reader from
the first; and after the symbolic levels rise to the surface,
and expand and transform our understanding of the literal,
it is still the literal which impresses us above all, and
which survives to haunt our minds, in which are now
embedded forms of odd living things we hardly expected
to contemplate.

The remaining poems in the series seem less self-con-
tained, and although I would not want to suggest that they
lack uniqueness, I think they might legitimately be taken
as larger foci of actions already observed. (Some of the
titles indicate this: **"The Long Alley," A Field of Light,"
"Praise to the End!," "Unfold! Unfold!,"** etc.)

However, there is an image in one of these later poems (it
occurs in **"The Shape of the Fire"** and is echoed many
times elsewhere) over which we might pause, for it con-

tains something essential to Roethke's whole order of
symbolic perception:

To be by the rose
Rising slowly out of its bed,
Still as a child in its first loneliness.

The image is of the growth of the flower in all its stages:
the flower's emergence out of the earth—"Rising slowly
out of its bed"—(the underworld, the sources of life, the
dark) and its development into the blossom, its becoming
a flower, always in this growth nourishing itself on and
straining itself toward the light, at last finding its place in
the whole scheme of life. This is Roethke's metaphorical
paradigm for the struggle to be reborn into the world. The
pattern is the flower's cyclical rebirth into the light. It is
a paradigm of resurrection.

But it is a paradigm which we shall do well to observe
with some misgivings once we have regarded its implications. The destination of the natural cycle which it recalls
is not the complex moment of adult sensibility; it must be
observed that despite the omnipresence of light imagery
in Roethke's poems there is no suggestion whatever that
this *light* embodies or encourages the light of the rational
faculties, and there are some forceful lines in the final
poem in the series which strengthen quite the opposite
view:

Reason? That dreary shed, that hutch for grubby
schoolboys!
The hedgewren's song says something else.

We have in this trope of the child and the rose, rather, a
saddened and reduced version of the Wordsworthian image: the stillness of "a child in its first loneliness." That
is, the destination is the moment of immobility which looks
back at the life of childhood and ahead to further growth.
But this immobility, indeed displaced in other poems by
sheer exhaustion, is the very margin of the paradigm which
Roethke evokes; it is as far as he goes in the recovery of
human feelings, and the burden of his intuitions is wholly
within the limits of this view.

Rilke in one of his letters remarks: ". . . inside my life
something is stirring, my soul is about to learn something,
it is beginning with new rudiments. . . . Perhaps I shall
now learn to become a little human . . . ," and in these
words he locates, with that extraordinary facility he had
for apprehending the dark moments of the soul, a stage in
a journey to which the whole of *Praise to the End!* is
devoted. It is a stage which has a formidable attractive-
ness about it, indeed—the theological term at least underscores what is at stake—a temptation. It is a stage at which
Rilke himself did not stop, and at which Wordsworth had
no interest in stopping. But it is a stage which a significant number of novelists of Roethke's generation have
occupied themselves with, and it is the stage at which
Roethke does stop in these poems. Moreover, it is a stage
which celebrates *la condition botanique* as an ideal, if
only by default, salvaging from Romanticism a certain
kind of melancholy and nostalgia for the pre-rational.

But before examining the implications of this view, I should like to advance a further observation to guard against some likely misunderstandings of Roethke's achievement.

Nearly all of the intellection in Roethke's poetry has been suppressed, but we must resist the error of believing that there is no intellection here or that the poems are pure intuitions. To suppress intellection in a poem is in no way the same as omitting it altogether. Not so long ago readers made the error of supposing that because Baroque poetry suppressed the passions, the Baroque sensibility failed in its perception of human nature. This was a prejudice which for the Romantics was programmatic and tactical, but it is a prejudice we no longer countenance. What is more likely to impress us now is the extent to which the Baroque mind held the passionate life of man in awe—an awe which found its inverse expression in forms which were constructed with architectural fastidiousness to hold the passions in check. In Roethke's style, something like the opposite motive needs to be recognized. It is the rational which is regarded with a kind of awe (not dissociated from distrust and cynicism) and which is suppressed by means of a style in which the rational impulse is necessarily diminished and easily denigrated.

Nor should we make the error of believing that the suppression of intellection in Roethke's poetry, and its radical commitment to unadorned images of the physical world,—"That anguish of concreteness!"—is another tricky incarnation of Imagism. So far as I know, Imagism never had any profound intellection to suppress. It performed a service for poetry: it reminded poets that the image is not simply the decorative aspect of poetry but the very *five senses* by which poetry perceives the world. It was a profound service; it has had great results with poets who were themselves not Imagists, and Roethke is among them. But as a literary movement, Imagism was curiously mindless. And because it discarded all but the most elementary materials of the intellect, Imagist verse was incapable of all the virtues which are most significant in Roethke, all that we shall henceforth regard as most Roethkean. Above all, it was incapable of that fragment of the tragic view of life which Roethke has recreated.

Yet, in the face of this we must concede that the Imagist movement had somehow prepared us for Roethke, and that with whatever (albeit feeble) authority it has, it provides his poetry with another kind of validity and interest. Moreover, one of the principles which Imagism forced us to recover (it was more a gratuitous result than a real intention) was the notion that a *trope* is actually a *judgment*, that perception in a poem embodies an evaluation of the object or the experience perceived. This is a principle which must weigh heavily in a poetry like Roethke's in which there is so little recourse to non-tropological language, and it is a principle which must ultimately determine our judgment of it.

All of the characteristics of Roethke's style—its suppression of the intellect, its attention to what we can only call the *life-force* seeking to emerge into the objective world, its curious dialectical struggle between *la condition botan-*

ique and *la condition humaine*, above all its effort to carry the Wordsworthian subject to a new extremity—all of this places upon us the burden of recognizing this poetry as the expression of a new primitivism. One does not enter willingly into a discussion of primitivism, for it is an area in which it is not difficult to speak nonsense. Writers as different as D. H. Lawrence and Gertrude Stein have been arraigned on this charge; and art criticism still fumbles (André Malraux is a notable exception) in making necessary distinctions between a great painter like Henri Rousseau and the folksy pictures of Grandma Moses, and between them and authentic primitive art, the art of primitive peoples. And futher, our notions of primitivism are peculiarly vulnerable to the modifications of history. Irving Babbitt charged Wordsworth with primitivism and wrote a long essay on the subject; but today we are more likely to find Wordsworth, as Lionel Trilling has suggested, hardly primitive enough.

I think this vulnerability is not simply a reflection of a change in the history of taste, though this it certainly is. More importantly, it is a reflection of the cultural crisis which calls primitivism into service in the first place: as we daily succumb to pressures which transform the primitivism of the past into the respectable culture of the present, we are pressed further to the margins of existence for any new notion of primitivism to play off, so to speak, against what we now accept as a matter of course.

It is in this light, I believe, that we shall have to understand Roethke's involvement with *la condition botanique*, for this would seem to be primitivism's final frontier. And it is not exactly foreign to the subject to inject the issue here, for Roethke himself in his notes on the opening movement of **"The Lost Son"** sounds the theme: ". . . the protagonist so geared-up, so over-alive that he is hunting, like a primitive, for some animistic suggestion, some clue to existence from the sub-human. . . . In a sense he goes in and out of rationality; he hangs in the balance between the human and animal." Of course, Roethke is discussing here only one passage in his most complex poem, but I think it hardly violates the context of the remark, or of the poem, to give these words a special importance, particularly as it is an observation which forces itself, sooner of later, on every attentive reader of Roethke's poetry; and also, since the primitive impulse is never actually transformed or resolved in the poem, but only modified, as I noted earlier, into an expectancy.

In assessing primitivism, we must make the distinction between those writers for whom the physical world does not cease to exist (though their values are not contained wholly within it) and who manage great success in depicting it in all its variousness and factuality, and writers for whom it is the only world which exists. Robinson Jeffers gives us the impression of being one of the latter, and I think it accounts for the lack of interest we show in him. Roethke is not one of the latter, but in committing his verse so drastically to the physical world he does somehow give the impression that it is the only world which survives, and in any case, it is chiefly that world which survives in our reading of him.

But we can extricate ourselves from some of the difficulties which Roethke's primitivism presents, I believe, if we arrive at this topic from, so to speak, the opposite direction. It is a direction which takes us full circle, which takes the view that despite the devotion with which Roethke concentrates on particulars and the sensuous intuition of objects, despite the suppression of intellection and the celebration of the visual and the tactile, (despite these, and because of them) Roethke's poetry is oddly *abstract*. Primitivism and abstraction—once they seemed to us polar opposites; and we have indeed come full circle when they meet in a single sensibility. (Still, we might remind ourselves that we can see, literally *see,* a similar convergence in the history of modern painting.) But what do we mean when we speak of abstraction in Roethke's poetry? I think Kenneth Burke has given the best answer to that question when he said, noting the antithesis we have observed, that, "Though Roethke has dealt always with very concrete things, there is a sense in which these very concretions are abstractions. Notably, the theme of sex in his poems has been highly generalized, however intensely felt . . ." ["The Vegetal Radicalism of Theodore Roethke," *Sewanee Review,* January-March, 1950]. It is this habit of dealing with an object in its generalized form which constitutes abstraction in Roethke's poetry; even the narrator, the "I" of the poems, seems at moments so universalized that it is difficult to imagine him (I almost said, imagine *it*) as a particular and human *I*. And this disposition toward abstraction is part of Roethke's indifference to history as a medium of human actions. We noted earlier that in contrast to the poetry of Robert Lowell, Roethke's does not take history as its medium, and what it means is that the personality and objects in his poetry, regardless of their imagistic precision, have none of the roughness, limitations, and irregularities, none of the material identity, which we associate with personalities and objects whose universality is compromised by their location in the historical world. Both abstraction and primitivism suppress history, and thereby suppress the human image in which our values subsist.

I do not believe it necessarily violates our sense of the physical sources of life, or even our belief (if we share it with Santayana) in the physical sources of values, to want to dissent from this suppression of the human image. But we are saved from the need to dissent by Roethke's latest poems, which, though they are clearly the creations of the same sensibility, transform the primitive impulse into a vitalism more human and intense than anything Roethke had written before. I doubt if there are any poems more beautiful than Roethke's **"The Partner"** (*Partisan Review,* Sept.-Oct. 1952) and **"The Wraith"** (*Hudson Review,* Winter, 1953) being written by an American just now. Moreover, Roethke abandons some of his tendency toward abstraction in a poem like **"Song for the Squeeze Box"** (*Hudson Review,* Winter, 1953)—incidentally, a very funny poem. Thus, in his latest poems Roethke affirms the human image by means which are largely denied in *Praise to the End!*—a lyricism of adult emotions, and a humor which is nothing if not social. Formally, it has meant Roethke's return to more orthodox stanzaic forms, which he used so expertly in *Open House* and which now re-

ceive the additional verve of his experiments in *Praise to the End!*

It is not too much to say that Roethke stands at the forefront of his generation, and among the most interesting poets of modern times.

To paraphrase Roethke is difficult because, in his search for transcendence, he seeks to find unity for the paradoxes of spirit and flesh, irrational and rational, female and male, darkness and light, unconscious and conscious, death and life.

—*Darlene Beaman, in "Roethke's Travels: An Overview of His Poetry,"* in Green River Review, *Vol. XIV, No. 2, 1983*.

Stephen Spender (essay date 1959)

SOURCE: A review of *Words for the Wind,* in *The New Republic,* Vol. 141, Nos. 6-7, August 10, 1959, pp. 21-2.

[*Spender was an English man of letters who rose to prominence during the 1930s as a Marxist lyric poet and as an associate of W. H. Auden, Christopher Isherwood, C. Day Lewis, and Louis MacNeice. His poetic reputation has declined in the postwar years, while his stature as a prolific and perceptive literary critic has grown. In the following review, Spender lauds the best verse in* Words for the Wind *but notes the need for Roethke to expand his range as a poet.*]

Poetry is an instrument which can be put to a great many uses, but as a medium it is sense-bound; however far the poetry goes beyond the senses, it is expressed in terms of them. This tells us something about the poet: that quite apart from his having a sensuous feeling for words, he has to live through his senses.

Sense-bound can easily mean self-bound. Not that the self which a poet expresses in his poetry need be exclusive. It can be a very representative self, as was the case with Wordsworth. It can dissolve into the social community, the national geography, and even the universe, as it did with Whitman. But all the same, the self-bound, sense-bound poets do have a particular kind of moral limitation. They inhabit purgatory. Wordsworth, Whitman, Hart Crane—to take the most obvious examples—have very much the kind of voice which Dante might have met down there: a voice for ever longing to become something else. Voices characterized by passionate yearning to reach out to some beyond—not the poet himself: the characteristic of this Otherness being its very strong resemblance to the poet himself, who finds the universe as a mirror in which he meets his own features:

> I have felt
> A presence that disturbs me with the joy
> Of elevated thoughts; a sense sublime
> Of something far more deeply interfused,
> Whose dwelling is the light of setting suns,
> And the round ocean and the living air,
> And the blue sky, and in the mind of man . . .

As Keats acutely observed the presence is the "egotistical sublime" of Wordsworth.

It is possible then for the purgatorial poet to create a world; but the world remains his world, himself, the drama his attempt to escape from it. This is very clear in the case of Theodore Roethke, who seems [in *Words for the Wind*] to be describing features which might be his own body, nostalgically viewed in retrospect, a garden seen through the eye of a child, a woman, perhaps a mother, or perhaps a bride.

> Mother of blue and the many changes of hay,
> This tail hates a flat path.
> I've let my nose out;
> I could melt down a stone,—
> How is it with the long birds?
> May I look too, loved eye?
> It's a wink beyond the world.
> In the slow rain, who's afraid?
> We're king and queen of the right ground.
> I'll risk the winter for you.
>
> You tree beginning to know,
> You whisper of kidneys,
> We'll swing the instant!—
> With jots and jogs and cinders on the floor:
> The sea will be there, the great squashy shadows,
> Biting themselves perhaps;
> The shrillest frogs;
> And the ghost of some great howl
> Dead in a wall.

Often as with "the great squashy shadows" and the "shrillest frogs," the observation is painterly and external enough. And yet it is the nightmarish or reptilian thing chosen which gives the poetry such an ambiguous aspect, the fusion of not-self with self. In a poem called **"Sensibility! O La!,"** Mr. Roethke begins "I'm the serpent of somebody else," which illustrates well the strong tendency of his world, in which emotions operate like forces leading to fusions and splittings—all too complete—of cellular life in the bottom of ponds.

At his best, Roethke's poetry is tragic in feeling and beautiful in operation. Tragic because the suffering and the way in which it is situated is so convincing. Mr. Roethke has really made a Noh drama of himself: a monologue in which, wearing a mask painted with a fixed smile of pain, he visits a pond in a wood which is haunted by a nymph-like ghost, and performs a very slow and solemn pirouet-

ting dance, whilst pronouncing some very strange serious-mock words:

> You all-of-sudden gods,
> There's a ghost loose in the long grass!
> My sweetheart's still in her cave.
> I've waked the wrong wind:
> I'm alone with my ribs;
> The lake washes its stones.
> You've seen me, prince of stinks,
> Naked and entire.
> Exalted? Yes,—
> By the lifting of the tail of a neighbour's cat,
> Or that old harpy secreting toads in her
>   portmanteau.

The nostalgia is not just simple nostalgia for childhood of the Dylan Thomas kind. It is rather a passionate regret that the desires of maturity cannot be fused with the beauty and innocence of youth, so as to avoid that accompaniment of mature desire—physical self-disgust.

Roethke's poetry moves in two directions—the centrifugal and the centripetal, and perhaps it is only completely successful when it is both of these at once. One can understand his desperate need to fly away from his own self-center, but when he effectively does so, as in some of the later poems, the images remain the same but the thought becomes salvationist and abstract:

> Who took the darkness from the air?
> I'm wet with another life.
> Yea, I have gone and stayed.
>
> What came to me vaguely is now clear,
> As if released by a spirit,
> Or agency outside me.
> Unprayed-for,
> And final.

It would be criticism to say that the later poems show a falling off from the middle ones. They are too explicit, too conscious, there is too much grammar of sense loosening up the thick and dense grammar of image working upon image. Such things have to be admitted between readers, but I doubt whether this is criticism of a kind that would help Mr. Roethke. His poetry has to develop, not repeat itself, and one can only develop in the direction of greater consciousness, absorbing and using more influences. One does not know how he will solve the very exceptional problems of a very exceptional talent. But one looks forward to his poems of the stage-after-next, and can be grateful for an achievement which is one of the most remarkable of the present century.

Delmore Schwartz (essay date 1959)

SOURCE: "The Cunning and the Craft of the Unconscious and the Preconscious," in *Selected Essays of Delmore*

Schwartz, edited by Donald A. Dike and David H. Zucker, The University of Chicago Press, 1970, pp. 197-99.

[*A prominent figure in American literature, Schwartz created poems and stories that are deeply informed by his experiences as the son of Jewish immigrants. His verse often focuses on middle-class New York immigrant families whose children are alienated both from their parents and from American culture and society. Schwartz explored such themes as the importance of self-discovery, the necessity of maintaining hope in the presence of despair, free will versus determinism, and the machinations of the subconscious. In the following review, which was originally published in 1959, he compares the verse in* Words for the Wind *to the poetry of William Butler Yeats.*]

It is sufficiently clear by now that Theodore Roethke is a very important poet. It is also more than likely that his reputation among readers of poetry is based, for the most part, upon the extraordinary lyrics in his second and third volumes. These poems appear, at first glance, to be uncontrollable and subliminal outcries, the voices of roots, stones, leaves, logs, small birds; and they also resemble the songs in Shakespearean plays, Ophelia's songs perhaps most of all. This surface impression is genuine and ought not to be disregarded. But it is only the surface, however moving, and as such, it can be misleading or superficial. The reader who supposes that Roethke is really a primitive lyric poet loses or misses a great deal. Perhaps the best way to define the substance of Roethke's poetry is to quote Valéry's remarkable statement that the nervous system is the greatest of all poems.

The enchanted depths beneath the chanting surface become more recognizable when the reader goes through this new collection with care from beginning to end. Throughout his work, Roethke uses a variety of devices with the utmost cunning and craft to bring the unconscious to the surface of articulate expression. But he avoids the danger and the temptation—which is greater for him than for most poets—of letting this attentiveness to the depths of experience become glib and mechanical, a mere formula for lyricism, which, being willed as a formula, would lose its genuineness and spontaneity. Roethke's incantatory lyrics are not, as they may first seem, all alike; on the contrary, each of them has a uniqueness and individuality.

In a like way, when, in his latest poems, Roethke seems to be imitating not only the manner but the subject-matter of Yeats—and even the phrasing—this too may very well be misleading if it is taken as *merely* imitation: for, first of all, it is paradoxical and true that the most natural and frequent path to true originality, for most good poets, is through imitating the style of a very great poet; secondly, Roethke has begun to imitate Yeats in mid-career, when he is at the height of his powers; and finally, since Yeats is a very different kind of poet than Roethke, the imitation is itself a feat of the imagination: Yeats discovered the concreteness and colloquialism which made him a very great poet only after many phases of vagueness, meandering through the long Celtic twilight; while Roethke's mastery of concreteness of image and thing has served

him in good stead from the very start. It is likely enough that the chief reason Roethke has followed Yeats's later style has been to guard against the deadly habit of self-imitation which has paralyzed some of the best poets in English—from Wordsworth to Edwin Arlington Robinson—soon after they enjoyed—at long last—the natural and longed-for recognition of the readers of poetry, after decades of misunderstanding, abuse, and very often the scorn of established critics.

If we compare one of Roethke's new, Yeatsian poems with the kind of poem which it appears to echo and imitate, we can hardly fail to discover not only the differences between the two writers, but something about all of Roethke's poems and about Yeats also.

Here is Roethke in his most Yeatsian phase: this is a stanza from a poem called **"The Pure Fury"**:

> The pure admire the pure and live alone;
> I love a woman with an empty face.
> Parmenides put nothingness in place;
> She tries to think and it flies loose again.
> How slow the changes of a golden mean:
> Great Boehme rooted all in yes and no;
> At times my darling squeaks in pure Plato.

And here is a stanza from *Among School Children,* one of the best of all poems of the language, which I quote for close reading, though it is or should be familiar to all readers of poetry:

> Plato thought nature but a spume that plays
> Upon a ghostly paradigm of things;
> Solider Aristotle played the taws
> Upon the bottom of a king of kings;
> World-famous golden-thighed Pythagoras
> Fingered upon a fiddle-stick or strings
> What a star sang and careless Muses heard:
> Old clothes upon old sticks to scare a bird.

The attitude and emotion in the latter poem is precisely the opposite of Roethke's; for Yeats, in this poem, as in so many of his later poems is full of a *contemptus mundi,* a scorn of nature, a detestation of history, which has left him an old man, however gifted: he took like the scarecrow face of the Leda-like beauty with whom he had been in love, has been by "the honey of generation betrayed." And this is why he ends his poem by saying: "How shall we know the dancer from the dance?", a Heraclitean statement that all is process and nothing is reality, except, as in other poems, the frozen artificial reality of Byzantium. And his poem is affirmative only in the sense of confronting despair and death: it is very close to Valéry's *La Cimitiére Marin,* where existence itself and the mind of the poet seem the sole flaw in the pure diamond of being, so that Valéry's affirmation too is hardly more than "Il faut tenter de vivre" and he too is appalled by the reality of process and unable to believe in another reality.

Roethke is capable of far greater affirmation—which is not to say that he is, as yet, as good as Yeats and Valéry, but that he is original and important enough to be compared to both poets, and to be regarded as having his own uniqueness. Thus he concludes this, one of his most Yeatsian poems, with the stanza:

> Dream of a woman, and a dream of death;
> The light air takes my being's breath away;
> I look on white and it turns into gray—
> When will that creature give me back my breath?
> I live near the abyss, I hope to stay
> Until my eyes look at a brighter sun
> As the thick shade of the long night comes on.

And it is worth adding that the difficulty of affirmation and hope, and the reality of the abyss have become more and more clear, more and more appalling, for poets alive today, as for all of us, than they were for Yeats when he wrote *Among School Children,* and for Valéry when he wrote *La Cimitière Marin.*

While he publicly downplayed the sweat and toil involved in writing poetry, Roethke worked privately in the notebooks which became his rich mines for poems. Anyone who has ever seen the Roethke notebooks, 277 of them altogether, must be struck with the man's obsessive dedication to poetry, his unwillingness to let any single word, idea, or statement that might contribute to a poem escape him.

—Neal Bowers, in Green River Review, Vol. XIV, No. 2, 1983.

Ralph J. Mills, Jr. (essay date 1962)

SOURCE: "Theodore Roethke: The Lyric of the Self," in *Poets in Progress,* Northwestern University Press, 1967, pp. 3-23.

[*An American poet and critic, Mills has published several volumes of verse and studies of such poets as Richard Eberhart, Edith Sitwell, and Kathleen Raine, in addition to Roethke. As well, he is the author of the studies* Contemporary American Poetry *(1965),* Creation's Very Self: On the Personal Element in Recent American Poetry *(1969), and* Cry of the Human: Essays on Contemporary American Poetry *(1975). The following essay, published in 1962, is a revised version of an article that first appeared in* Tri-Quarterly *in 1958. Here Mills outlines the exploration of selfhood and existence in Roethke's verse.*]

One of the dangers of any age that has produced important writers and literary revolutions such as our own is that the artists of generations immediately subsequent to the seminal one may not receive the attention they de-

serve. The focus of readers turns upon the task of assimilating the pioneers, the originators of new styles; and there follows a neglect of younger poets working in the light of the radical changes initiated by their predecessors. Several rough but distinguishable phases can be remarked in twentieth century poetry: one includes the post-symbolist revolutionaries who firmly established a modern tone and style—Eliot, Yeats, Pound, Rilke, Valéry, Stevens; another divides three ways, the first two developing the inheritance of their forerunners (Auden, Spender, Day Lewis in England, Tate, John Peale Bishop, Stanley Kunitz in America), the other in romantic reaction to this legacy (Dylan Thomas, George Barker, Kathleen Raine, David Gascoyne); a third consists of American poets who first became known during the second World War, among whom are Randall Jarrell, Karl Shapiro, Robert Lowell, and Theodore Roethke. Of these poets, Roethke has, it seems to me, demonstrated the most restless and exploratory impulse, a desire continually to plumb new areas of experience and to alter his style in accord with his discoveries. As a result of this impulse and his fine lyric gifts, the body of his writing has a strong cumulative effect upon the reader, for each successive stage of his work—and I mean thematically speaking, too—grows naturally out of the former. Reading his latest poems, one feels the weight of earlier ones as an actual presence. By means of this closely woven pattern, there is built up a scheme of meanings and values, what we might call a universe of discourse, in which the poems themselves fit and are comprehended.

Roethke's first book, *Open House* (1941), impresses the reader at the very start with this poet's natural ability to sing, his sharp, compact lines, his fundamental rhythmic sense. One is sure, having seen some of these short lyrics and descriptive pieces, that Roethke could never have stopped *here*; flexibility and incipient progress lurk everywhere under the surface of the words. In the title poem, one of the best in the volume, he announces the theme that will continue to occupy him and the artistic personality that is inseparable from it:

> My secrets cry aloud.
> I have no need for tongue.
> My heart keeps open house,
> My doors are widely swung.
> An epic of the eyes
> My love, with no disguise.
>
> My truths are all foreknown,
> This anguish self-revealed.
> I'm naked to the bone,
> With nakedness my shield.
> Myself is what I wear:
> I keep the spirit spare.
>
> The anger will endure,
> The deed will speak the truth
> In language strict and pure.
> I stop my lying mouth:
> Rage warps my clearest cry
> To witless agony.

The art proposed in these stanzas is peculiarly autobiographical, "naked to the bone," and, we might say, assumes the appearance of a journal—kept with great pain—which traces the path of a sensitive mind from bondage into the freedom of the open air. It seems as if much of the poetry evolves from a kind of curative effort on the poet's part—the exorcism of a demon, T. S. Eliot would call it—determining the direction his work will take. The pattern which emerges visibly from the writing as a whole is seen to fall into stages ranging from the psychological to the visionary and near-mystical. Such a classification must necessarily slight some excellent light verse and children's poems that appear peripheral to the author's main concerns. Roethke sets out upon a journey in his poems, a research into the origins of the psyche sometimes resembling the classical ordeals of legendary heroes since it involves a descent into the underworld of the mind, a confrontation of all the perils this voyage creates to the integrity of self. Having passed through these subterranean distances where the past history of the individual stands still and weighs secretly upon him, Roethke leads the way back into the world; the regenerated spirit discovers the physical universe anew. The development of Roethke's poetry is a record of the spirit's mutations, its division from nature and expansion into love and illumination, its final, anagogical disposition.

The series of brief poems opening *The Lost Son* (1948) serves as an introduction to later and longer pieces in the same book. Roethke has always stressed the eye as the most important organ (see his **"Prayer"**); and it is the eye of microscopic power trained on the minute, thriving vegetable life and mineral realm of the earth that determines the range and character of sensibility here. These poems remind us in part of Rimbaud's *Les Illuminations* or Whitman's *Leaves of Grass* not so much in subject matter and not at all in technique but because they are an affront to our habitual forms of perception. We are forced to look at things differently or reject the poetry altogether. The labor urged on us demands that we strip away those winding cloths of category and convention with which we deaden our sense of life, and that we regain our simplicity of vision: the belief in human possibility. Lying flat on the soil, our eyes level with the ground, we begin again in the poems with the elements of the natural world. Our origins are linked by correspondences with those elements. If this procedure of close attention to budding plants and tiny creatures clashes with our pretensions to adult dignity, Roethke shows us in **"Cuttings (later)"** that such observation has a striking relevance to our own estate:

> This urge, wrestle, resurrection of dry sticks,
> Cut stems struggling to put down feet,
> What saint strained so much,
> Rose on such lopped limbs to new life?

If we disclaim recognition of this struggle, we either fail to tell ourselves the truth or have not risen to life. Roethke constantly forces on us the images of grace and defection.

As he has often pointed out in commenting on his own writings, Roethke's youth was spent around his father's greenhouses in Michigan; and he absorbed their atmosphere and the minutiae of plant and vegetable life with an intensity, an affinity that has transformed them into both literal facts and dominant metaphors of his poetry. Early influenced by his reading of Wordsworth, John Clare, and Whitman, and later by Leonie Adams, quickly enough he found poetic counterparts to spur his personal fascination with the details and processes of nature. There is a human lesson to be learned that starts with a humility towards the lower orders of life and the knowledge of connections we have with them. True growth requires us to return along the way we came and touch once more the roots from which we sprang:

> When sprouts break out,
> Slippery as fish,
> I quail, lean to beginnings, sheath-wet.

Such imagery identifies man with a process in the natural world and relates him to the stubborn fecundity of the entire creation. This assertion of existence is evident in a poem like **"Root Cellar"** where

> Nothing would give up life:
> Even the dirt kept breathing a small breath.

The shorter poems of this period are all devoted to what Roethke calls "the minimal." Their recurrent themes and metaphors furnish a basis for more ambitious efforts and point to new departures. In a fine poem called "transplanting," we watch young plants set down in fresh soil and, as if through the eye of a camera equipped with a timing device, see them unfurl and bloom:

> Watching hands transplanting,
> Turning and tamping,
> Lifting the young plants with two fingers,
> Sifting in a palm-full of fresh loam,—
> One swift movement,—
> Then plumping in the bunched roots,
> A single twist of the thumbs, a tamping and
>   turning,
> All in one,
> Quick on the wooden bench,
> A shaking down while the stem stays straight,
> Once, twice, and a faint third thump,—
> Into the flat-box it goes,
> Ready for the long days under the sloped glass:
>
> The sun warming the fine loam,
> The young horns winding and unwinding,
> Creaking their thin spines,
> The underleaves, the smallest buds
> Breaking into nakedness,
> The blossoms extending
> Out into the sweet air,
> The whole flower extending outward,
> Stretching and reaching.

Roethke has realized how the same striving upwards is an essential movement of the spirit in man. This perception led him, in a series of longer poems, to explore the relationships between the unfolding inner life of the person and the objects and forces of physical nature. What is merely a proposed analogy between human and natural processes in earlier poems approaches identity in the ones that follow.

These longer poems, which extend and deepen Roethke's previous interests, appear as a full sequence in *The Waking* (1953), a volume which won for its author the Pulitzer Prize. In a feat of imaginative re-creation and poetic skill, he dramatizes by means of a technique close to the novelist's interior monologue the consciousness of a child as it slowly ascends from the mysterious regions of its origin toward a complete apprehension of the world and communion with it. As the body grows, the spirit grows with it; and the inter-action of the two, with the added consideration of the lives and things outside which impose upon the self, create the drama of the poems. An intimate connection with the animal, vegetable, and mineral levels of the universe is disclosed; and along with it, a tension in the human person between a persistent desire for his whole existence and a contrary pull downwards to death or the inanimate. In order to realize within the poems the immediacy of this evolution of self and spirit, Roethke turned away from the stricter forms of his preceding work to the looser form of what I have already indicated as a dramatic internal monologue—dramatic because it registers the impression of sensations from without on a shifting physiological and spiritual life within until there is a kind of dialectical arrangement between them. Thus these poems contain abrupt changes:

> Tell me, great lords of sting,
> Is it time to think?
> When I say things fond,
> I hear singing.
>   (**"O Lull me, Lull me"**)

the conflict of opposites:

> A worm has a mouth.
> Who keeps me last?
> Fish me out.
> Please.
>
> God give me an ear. I hear flowers.
> A ghost can't whistle.
> I know! I know!
> Hello happy hands.
>   (**"Where Knock Is Open Wide"**)

and unexpected juxtapositions everywhere:

> Such music in a skin!
> A bird sings in the bush of your bones.
> Tufty, the water's loose.
> Bring me a finger. This dirt's lonesome for grass.
>   (**"Give Way, Ye Gates"**)

In spite of superficial difficulties, which disappear once the reader surrenders himself to the purpose and rhythm of the poet's undertaking, we notice the same simple and

precise diction, the familiar musical gifts that mark Roethke's art. If the poems seem to lack the order we found in *Open House,* this lack must be attributed to the fluid reality they render. And so the adjustments demanded of us are more extreme than before. Entering the child's mind, we have to adopt a literalness in our apprehension and discard the adult's acquired skepticism. The world, from the new point of view Roethke provides, is transformed into a densely populated, because animistic, place where normal distinctions of object and subject, consciousness and unconsciousness, will and instinct are abolished, and synesthesia is an accepted mode of perception. Perhaps the license for such a radical departure in poetry can best be explained by a recent remark of the poet. "We must permit poetry to extend consciousness," Roethke says, "as far, as deeply, as particularly as it can, to recapture, in Stanley Kunitz's phrase, what it has lost to some extent to prose. We must realize, I think, that the writer in freer forms must have an even greater fidelity to his subject matter than the poet who has the support of form." Roethke, as a reading of his collected verse will prove, has labored in both these provinces; most of his newer poems display his fascination with experiment in "freer forms," as do the poems of the childhood sequence.

The poems, then, are composed on a rationale wholly their own, a logic nearer that of the dream or the ellipsis of thought and sensation than the calculating intelligence. Individually, they constitute stages of a journey into the hidden corners of the mind, the memories beneath everyday conscious thought; and so, too, they participate in a different temporal dimension by disturbing the apparently dormant experiences of the past. Roethke's poetic enterprise here involves him in something like the interpretation of the many layers of writing on a palimpsest; each one draws him farther back in time and into more obscure circumstances. But the journey is made with direction and, we feel, even with necessity. It is an attempt to gain a perspective on the general movement of personal existence from its remote beginnings by finding the "lost son" and recovering the moments of that long-abandoned life.

It would be simple on the basis of this description to discount these poems as clinical matters or the raw stuff of psychoanalysis, whereas they are nothing of the sort. However private the resources on which Roethke has called, the problems of understanding details of separate poems seldom appear to come from faults of privacy. Maybe the problems which arise are due to our own carelessness or impatience in reading. At any rate, a statement Roethke wrote for inclusion in *Twentieth Century Authors* should help to clarify the poet's intention:

> I have tried to transmute and purify my 'life,' the sense of being defiled by it, in both small and formal and somewhat blunt short poems, and, latterly, in longer poems which try in their rhythms to catch the very movement of the mind itself, to trace the spiritual history of a protagonist (not 'I,' personally), of all haunted and harried men; to make in this series . . . a true and not arbitrary order which will permit many ranges to feeling, including humor.

The universal character of Roethke's protagonist compels our participation in these inner travels. We are turned into partial actors of the drama his poems relate.

The uncovering of childhood exposes old sores; and anxiety over the questions of death, God, isolation, sexuality, and parental relations bulk large in these poems. An inclination to get up and out of the morass of such disturbances is the most pronounced characteristic of the protagonist, but he can attain this release only by facing directly all the hazards and powers—usually psychic ones—that endanger the gradually developing spirit. **"The Lost Son"** is possibly the most representative poem of the sequence for our purposes, because it contains within its carefully made order the major themes of the entire group, and so forms a paradigm of the inward journey. The plan of the poem falls into several sections which trace the narrator's progress: departure; the quest—with its accompanying ordeals; the return to a new harmony; the protagonist's expectation of another phase.

Any suspicion that **"The Lost Son"** follows the same cyclical motion as certain other works of modern literature and ends no farther on than it began ought to be dismissed, for the poem records the trial and the decided advance of the spirit. Beginning, ominously enough, with suggestions of death, gloom and ugliness, the poem drops us into the midst of the child's pursuit of freedom and singular identity, a pursuit frustrated by the continued shocks which experience administers the frail equilibrium of his psychic life:

> At Woodlawn I heard the dead cry:
> I was lulled by the slamming of iron,
> A slow drip over stones,
> Toads brooding in wells.

The proximity of destruction and the riddle of his own nature lure the protagonist into action, and he engages himself fully in the search for liberation:

> Which is the way I take;
> Out of what door do I go,
> Where and to whom?

But confusion dogs his tracks, for the animistic universe where each thing has an independent and ambiguous nature is nothing if not deceptive; like the magical forests of fairy tales, it presents more false leads than true paths. The creatures and plants and other elements populating this world, even the friendliest ones, haunt him, and yet he must inquire of them the way out. He seeks among the smallest creatures some reliable guides, though not always with the happiest results:

> All the leaves stuck out their tongues;
> I shook the softening chalk of my bones,
> Saying, Snail, snail, glister me forward,
> Bird, soft-sigh me home.

Under the prevailing conditions, movement offers the only relief available to the agonized spirit, which is also heir to the complaints of the flesh. The protagonist's search brings him at last to "the pit," in the section of the poem named after it, and there he reaches the lowest and most dangerous point in the journey. In fact, the pit, which needs partially to be viewed as a female symbol, signifies the place of origins but has now become a sign of defeat, even of death. As the protagonist approaches there to ask the fundamental question about life—"Who stunned the dirt into noise?"—he is answered with images of the womb and of birth, "the slime of a wet nest." A harsh music of warning jangles his nerves, accompanied in section three, **"The Gibber,"** by further alienation from his surroundings, sexual dilemmas, and shrill discord:

> Dogs of the groin
> Barked and howled,
> The sun was against me,
> The moon would not have me.
>
> The weeds whined,
> The snakes cried,
> The cows and briars
> Said to me: Die.

At the edge of annihilation, the protagonist passes through the "storm's heart" and glides beyond it into a state of calm, another level of existence. The spirit, having survived the threats to its growth, leaps forth in a gesture of exultation at the sheer pleasure of being:

> These sweeps of light undo me.
> Look, look, the ditch is running white!
> I've more veins than a tree!
> Kiss me, ashes, I'm falling through a dark swirl.

Body and spirit revel in their newly won harmony. The freed spirit, no longer fighting for its independence, dissolves all conflicts with the material world about it and, instead, elevates the things of the world by bringing them into communion with itself. The greenhouse, with its rich store of life, serves as the scene of this revelation and symbolizes both the unity and the potentiality of existence. The regenerative process is caught in the images of flowers:

> The rose, the chrysanthemum turned toward the
>   light.
> Even the hushed forms, the bent yellow weeds
> Moved in a slow up-sway.

In the final section of the poem, the protagonist meditates on his experience. This is "an in-between time" when he can do nothing but await further activity of the spirit. The imagery of the passage recalls *Ash Wednesday* and *Four Quartets,* and this is unquestionably purposeful, as it is in **"The Meditations of an Old Woman,"** which closes *Words for the Wind.* But Eliot's poems treat spiritual development as the result of prayer, contemplation, and self-denial. In Roethke's scheme, such development is the fruition of a *natural* struggle and is religious only in a much broader sense. The narrator hesitates to classify his experience; he will admit of no more than an indefinable visitation. I think it is clear that in stating his own attitude Roethke is replying to Eliot's:

> Was it light?
> Was it light within?
> Was it light within light?
> Stillness becoming alive,
> Yet still?

The allusion to Eliot's "still point of the turning world" seems obvious, but a certain amount of parody in these lines prevents them from being taken as a literal echo of the elder poet. Whatever generates the spiritual odyssey in Roethke's poem comes apparently from within, not from an external divine source:

> A lively understandable spirit
> Once entertained you.
> It will come again.
> Be still.
> Wait.

That spirit does return, again and again, in this poet's writings. Though Roethke continues to be preoccupied with the progress of the spirit, the conclusion of his sequence of monologues, with their radical technique, enables him to move off in a different direction. He does, of course, deal with the isolated self again in later poems, but in general the themes of childhood are replaced by mature considerations of love, death, and the larger meanings of human existence in the world.

With *The Waking* (1953), Roethke brought together a selection of his earlier verse and a number of new poems, some of them indicating a sharp departure from self-contemplation. These were, of course, the love poems; and more of them have appeared since, so that a section of *Words for the Wind* is devoted to an entire group. If we think of these poems solely in terms of the spirit, however, we shall misread them, for many are erotic and sensual. All the same, they do signify another stage of that theme: the change from consideration of self to fascination with the other. The woman of these poems is various. Sometimes she assumes the form of a wraith or entrancing spectre; sometimes she is purely physical. Her place in the poems can only be called that of the female or the opposite or the other, since her role involves metamorphosis. Observation of her beauties frequently means for the poet a rapport with creation:

> The breath of a long root,
> The shy perimeter
> Of the unfolding rose,
> The green, the altered leaf,
> The oyster's weeping foot,
> And the incipient star—
> Are part of what she is.
> She wakes the ends of life.
>
>   **("Words for the Wind")**

In some way, this beloved possesses the elusive secrets of existence and partakes of all that is. The style of these poems differs greatly from the psychological ones, but Roethke has certainly incorporated the informality and the discipline required by his previous experiments in these new pieces.

Fulfillment in love is the subject of a quartet of lyrics, **"Four for Sir John Davies,"** which extends the search for integration and harmony we saw in **"The Lost Son"** from an internal, psychological process to union with the beloved. Drawing its basic metaphor of dancing from Davies' sixteenth century poem, *Orchestra,* which explains the hierarchical order of the universe through that figure, and from Yeats, who saw in the dance an image of sexual and spiritual reconciliation, the poem leaves the poet's isolated dancing at the start to discover something of a transcendent completion in which both lover and beloved share. In the opening portion, the poet celebrates the vital energies of creation and of his own dance, but his movements are occasionally humorous and lack agility and purpose:

> I tried to fling my shadow at the moon,
> The while my blood leaped with a wordless song.
> Though dancing needs a master, I had none
> To teach my toes to listen to my tongue.

In spite of the joy of his single dance, which offers him the feeling of kinship with *things,* the poet seeks a deeper human relationship. The attraction for his newly found partner begins between "animal and human heat," but we soon realize that the meeting of the lovers physically has created a spiritual state corresponding to it.

> Incomprehensible gaiety and dread
> Attended all we did. Behind, before,
> Lay all the lonely pastures of the dead;
> The spirit and the flesh cried out for more.
> We two, together, on a darkening day
> Took arms against our own obscurity.

As traditionally befits such lovers, they receive, in the poem's third part, one identity. They remind us of that pair in Donne's "The Canonization" whose pure devotion to one another divorces them from the public world and invests them with a sacred or mystical aura, for here also, Roethke tells us, "the flesh can make the spirit visible." So this dance, though it originates in human love, is anything but ordinary and mundane. The vertical movement of the dancers and the successive alterations they undergo in their ascent lend the poems a religious quality, but only in a personal or loose way. It cannot be denied that the experience of love at its most intense which the poems portray is explicitly defined by the author as an event of the spirit, and, furthermore, an event of such magnitude that the lovers' connection with the cosmos is completely revised. And in **"The Vigil,"** the concluding poem, Dante's paradisiacal vision is introduced to set off Roethke's own version of an encounter with the eternal; but this seems, as it did in **"The Lost Son,"** a condition of inward blessedness, the gift of Eros rather than of God. What the poet calls elsewhere "a condition of joy," this moment renders the universe transparent to perception and mysteriously transfigures the couple:

The world is for the living. Who are they?
We dared the dark to reach the white and warm.
She was the wind when wind was in my way;
Alive at noon, I perished in her form.
Who rise from flesh to spirit know the fall:
The word outleaps the world, and light is all.

Roethke's poetry is dedicated much of the time to a search for moments like this. But such ecstatic assertions of being do not hide an inability to face the realities of human life. The later verse collected in *Words for the Wind* (1958) and the poems which have appeared in magazines after that book demonstrate the poet's effort to enlarge the range of his work, as well as to consolidate his gains in theme and style.

It is obviously impossible within this introductory essay to give a suitable or clear impression of the richness and variety of all of the more recent poetry of Roethke. He has been accused in the past few years of falling into, first, imitations of Yeats, then of Eliot; yet both these charges appear simple-minded and are founded on poor reading or a failure to understand the poet's aims. For a period Roethke uses Yeats as a point of departure for his own attitudes, and **"The Dying Man"** sequence is sub-titled as a memorial to Yeats. Even in that poem, though, we can hardly think the following passage—except for the third and possibly the second lines—sounds very reminiscent of the Irish master:

The edges of the summit still appal
When we brood on the dead or the beloved;
Nor can imagination do it all
In this last place of light: he dares to live
Who stops being a bird, yet beats his wings
   Against the immense immeasurable emptiness of
   things.

There are, of course, some poems which bear the marks of Yeats' influence; **"Four for Sir John Davies"** is one of them. For a further discussion of this matter, the reader should consult Roethke's own remarks in his essay "How to Write Like Somebody Else," in the *Yale Review*.

The question of Eliot is a rather different one and centers around the group of five poems called **"Meditations of an Old Woman,"** with which Roethke concludes *Words for the Wind*. Composed very freely with a prose-style line, the poems are sometimes said to be derivative from *Four Quartets*. Maybe so, though the influence of Whitman has seemed to me greater here, both in style and attitude, and this opinion the poet has recently confirmed in a letter to me. Yet the confusion is understandable when we recognize that the poems are in part—and in part only—an answer to *Four Quartets*. The old woman, though she is not a fictitious speaker and was a relative of the poet in life (as Roethke told me in a recent conversation), serves as an opposite to the mature Eliot in his poems. And the reflective conclusions at which she arrives have little in common with those of Eliot; in fact, some passages, like the following from **"What Can I Tell My Bones?"** can only be read as a direct answer to him—with slight overtones of parody:

It is difficult to say all things are well,
When the worst is about to arrive
It is fatal to woo yourself,
However graceful the posture.

   Loved heart, what can I say?
   When I was a lark, I sang;
   When I was a worm, I devoured.

   The self says, I am;
   The heart says, I am less;
   The spirit says, you are nothing.

Old age and the approach of death are themes of both Roethke's and Eliot's poems, but their final attitudes diverge widely. In contrast to the asceticism of *Four Quartets,* Roethke's old lady finally embraces in her memory and imagination the entire spectrum of life, its pleasures and delights, its sufferings and disappointments included. It is, at last, a series of poems which do more than merely affirm the unevenness of human existence; indeed, they celebrate the beauty of its variety and the horizons its possibilities open to view.

Though the narrator of the poem cannot be exactly identified with the poet, she is, in large measure, a voice for Roethke's beliefs. As I understand his use of her for dramatic purposes, she owes her *poetical* existence to what he makes her say; and, in her own life, she apparently coincided in outlook with the author. The poems shift with her mind's changing currents, touching on incidents and thoughts of a long life, and introducing many of Roethke's constant images and metaphors: the sun, the wind, the tiny creatures of earth, flowers and seeds and grass, water, and so on. But the range of the poem is not narrow; here is a brilliant and savage passage on the modern forms of destruction:

I think of the self-involved:
The ritualists of the mirror, the lonely drinkers,
The minions of benzedrine and paraldehyde,
And those who submerge themselves deliberately in
   trivia,
Women who become their possessions,
Shapes stiffening into metal,
Match-makers, arrangers of picnics—
What do their lives mean,
And the lives of their children?—
The young, brow-beaten early into a baleful silence,
Frozen by a father's lip, a mother's failure to
   answer.
Have they seen, ever, the sharp bones of the poor?
Or known, once, the soul's authentic hunger,
Those cat-like immaculate creatures
For whom the world works?

Perhaps the closing lines, full of the affirmative beauty of the world and the magical transformation or re-birth which the spirit works in man, indicate the lyrical power Roethke can command even in an informal order:

The sun! The sun! And all we can become!
And the time ripe for running to the moon!

In the long fields, I leave my father's eye;
And shake the secrets from my deepest bones;
My spirit rises with the rising wind;
I'm thick with leaves and tender as a dove,
I take the liberties a short life permits—
I seek my own meekness;
I recover my tenderness by long looking.
By midnight I lover everything alive.
Who took the darkness from the air?
I'm wet with another life.
Yea, I have gone and stayed.

The great beauty of this passage is quite characteristic of Roethke's recent verse; however, his newer poems are of many sorts. Some describe what Roethke calls the motions of the soul; others, such as the splendid **"Meditation at Oyster River"** (which appeared in *The New Yorker*) carry on the line of development opened up by **"Meditations of an Old Woman."** Without any doubt, Roethke is one of the most considerable American poets of the past half-century: his increase in range, power, and variety promise the kind of writing we must call major.

I should think that Roethke's life should scotch the notion of Eliot that in poetry there is no competition. Roethke realized that he was competing with everybody, and he was out to win. Not only was he competing with his contemporaries but he perceived that he was competing with the poets of the past, those who embodied the deepest truths in poetry.

—Richard Eberhart, "On Theodore Roethke's Poetry," in **Of Poetry and Poets,** *1979.*

Theodore Roethke (essay date 1963)

SOURCE: "Theodore Roethke Speaks: The Teaching Poet," in *New Letters,* Vol. 49, No. 1, Fall, 1982, pp. 7-25.

[*The following is a transcript of a spoken address. Roethke discusses such topics as teaching, his literary influences, the role of readers, and the poetic process. In the absence of further information regarding the date of composition, the year of Roethke's death has been substituted for the essay date.*]

THE TEACHING POET

I think teaching is one of the last resorts of the noble mind and is a whole, a profession, and in our times one of the ones that's least corrupted. It is a second order of creation, particularly visceral, romantic teaching of the sort that I go in for. Since I don't know anything, I have to use, make up for, energy, noise, and general pandemonium. It can get cumulative, and one can get this collective excitement going, and that's very dangerous, I found in bitter experience, well, in the first place for the teacher and secondly for the kids themselves. For instance at Bennington, I used to really teach like mad. I mean, it was the first time I'd ever been in a big-time operation. But these kids . . . I mean, I'd just walk around—"Ask me anything," you know, "about Hopkins." And I mugged up so much, and I worked so hard, and I puked before every class on Thursday. They'd come to me and say, "Look, don't knock yourself out; we're not worth it and besides, as soon as you get us to do something that's way beyond ourselves, you go away and then we can't do anything, or what we do is much less." Well, I'm not sure if I effect that kind of dent, make that kind of dent on kids anymore. At least I try to do it more quietly. But nonetheless, I feel it remains a second order of creation opposed to poetry. I think the very good teaching is like the dance. It's so related to a particular time and a place, and in a sense it can't be recaptured. I think, I mean, you know, Gestalt. On the other hand, I found that sometimes setting students' exercises has a chastening effect, in the sense that sometimes I just turn around and say, "If they say it's too hard, I say, 'Okay, I'll do it myself.'"

For instance a poem called **"The Cycle,"** which goes "Dark water underground, / Beneath the rock and clay, / Beneath the roots of trees, / Rose in a common day, / Rose from a mossy mound / In mist that sun could seize. / That fine rain coiled like a cloud / Turned by revolving air, / Far from that colder source / Where elements cohere, / Dense in the central stone. / The air grew loose and loud. / Then with diminished force, / The full rain fell straight down, / Tunneled with lapsing sound / Under the rock-shut ground, / Under primeval stone." I left out one line there. But we were working on the three-beat, and I wrote the piece, which I think is a good one of its kind. (The line Roethke omits is the penultimate one: "Under a river's source.")

It is true, of course, that you do find yourself clarifying your concepts and your attitudes. I find that good students are very good and very honest critics. There are certain areas of experience, or certain kinds of poems, of course, that they're not quite up to when they are, say 18, 19, 20, can't really get inside a complex metaphysical piece, or anything that approaches, what do you call it, preternatural experience, or shall we say, mystical experience. Why be frightened of that word?

There are a great deal of emotional pressures, particularly in modern teaching at its best, and I think the whole character of teaching in college has been changed in the last twenty years, primarily by writers. Now this point has never been made. They may not all be good teachers, but some of them are, and some of them are great ones, and I include old Winters, as nutty as he is, as a great teacher of this kind. That is, whatever he does, he makes a hell of a dent in them. Well, certainly Ransom was, is still, and Kunitz, I know, is, and I suppose that carries over into the arts. Now here the art department, frankly, I don't think is much, but it sort of seems chaotic and there are no, you know, no really big figures there.

LITERARY INFLUENCES

If you want to talk ancestors, it's mistake to set Yeats up as a central guy; for one reason, I resisted Yeats for a long time. I remember even saying to Bogan, "I don't get him." See, I came to Ann Arbor at 17, wanting to do what? To learn to write a chiseled prose. I had been trained by myself largely, and in part in a good high school, on the familiar essay. I read Stevenson *et cetera* . . . you know . . . Tomlinson, that sort of writing. I wanted these graceful essays. At home we didn't have a tremendous library. There was a leather-bound Emerson; there were a couple of good Thoreaus; there was a book called *Prose Every Child Should Know,* a book called *Heart Throbs,* but it was prose, you know. Between the greenhouses they had toilets put in and all that, but in piles, in these piles of pipe, there was this old backhouse and I'd go in there for meditation. On the wall was this epigram; it just said, "Enter softly and softly close the door, for beneath this floor lies many a noble dinner." Well now, it's a great sentence; it has the upward flow and the downward.

Thoreau, too, Emerson, Thoreau . . . but I was on to Emerson already, but I liked that aphoristic junk. And then some of the major essayists, I mean, of course, Thoreau. But the thing is when I got to Ann Arbor, I got a B plus in freshman rhetoric. As a freshman I read *all* of Stevenson, and wrote a paper without looking at any critical book, spent my whole vacation doing it and got A plus, marked my singular exactitude . . . would have A's. I'm a kid; I'm just 17; I didn't want to go to Michigan. I did because I'd be near Mom. But I thought, "Well, if I can't get A in a freshman rhetoric course, I can't be a writer; the hell with it, so I'll go through law school like Mama wants." So from then on I just took what I wanted. But I did have a guy, who went nuts, solemnly gave me a course in Wordsworth and also in American literature. But the Wordsworth—since I never like to repeat their damn fool ideas, and I used to learn great passages by heart, and I used to know hundreds of lines of Wordsworth, and I tried . . . I mean, he is there, yet I feel that actually Wordsworth didn't make much of a dent in. . . . It was supposed to be an opening up of unconsciousness, but I feel it's a very timid one. "I have felt a presence that disturbs me with a joy of elevated thought" and so on is always just the sense, or he's rowing and he has vague feelings. Oh, whatever . . . in my case, it seems to me, there should also be a focus on the minutiae of life, the little things of life.

Blake is a real guy for the beat. I've had I don't [know] how many editions of Blake. I can't explain those damn poems, exactly what they mean. But it's that beat, eh. And I was much more grounded in Blake, say, than I ever was with Yeats and also with some of the people that affected Yeats. You know, Yeats himself . . . I'm not trying to say that I wasn't influenced by Yeats; everyone was. But the particular poem where I give him this tribute, I'd been

reading Sir John Davies deeply and also Raleigh. (The poem referred to here is **"The Dance."**) Particularly, I wanted the 16th century guys. I wanted to get back to the plain, hard style. I said all this, by the way, in a piece, "How to Write Like Somebody Else," in which I pay tribute to certain early ancestors, people who have affected me technically. Mademoiselle Eleanor Wylie, who I think is in many ways a bad poet. And I wrote a pastiche of her. Then I did one of Léonie Adams; she was an influence. But oddly enough the contemporaries that affected me most when I started were Kunitz, whom I thought of as a superbrain—you know, *summa cum laude*—and Bogan, whom I caught just at the end of college. But what I mean, I went roaring around for four years with the richies, with the richies, with the dolls, and school for me was a kind of joke. I figured, well, you have to demonstrate you can do it, so I made Phi Beta Kappa by a cunt hair, to everybody's surprise. But it was only after getting out of college, I mean getting into the graduate school, that I began writing poems, and they were very bad at first. But then all of a sudden there was a real jump, say within six months, I mean. I published in the *New Republic, The Commonweal, Sewanee Review.* When I did that, and when Hillyer told me, "Why any editor who wouldn't print these is a fool," geez, well, at last I'm something. (Roethke introduced himself to Robert Hillyer at Harvard.)

I liked my prose all right, but I don't know—there's a combination of a deep unhappiness, a bust up of this real love affair. I mean, it went on four years and had, shall we say, all the ramifications . . . we might as well have been married, I mean, what the hell. But we each had more money than we . . . just pooled our money. Christ, some guys would go to Europe, and some of the chicks would go to the Evanston Cradle of Heaven, have an illegitimate kid, come back. Ann Arbor was unlike anything on land or sea, I mean. It's never been put down. We thought Scott Fitzgerald was a little shitass. I mean, that he was a little puke, and he was overwhelmed by money. Well, for Chrissake, some of the silly shits jumped around with him. Go across the street and this one guy in the Phi Delt house, he had seven million in his own name, which, of course, by Harvard standards isn't much, but he just had money in the closet like laundry.

In terms of immediate influence, I read a lot of Lawrence's prose, almost all of it, and I wrote a paper on him once. But, I mean, *The White Peacock* and *Sons and Lovers* dented me the most. When he got into those nutty phases—*The Plumed Serpent,* I thought, was far too strange—I didn't try to understand it. I think Lawrence's poetry is more important than the prose. And I think Eliot's all wrong about, you know, his sneering at him. Well, Lawrence talks about the immediate moment. That's what the poem, in a sense, should capture. I think Lawrence is, of course, often self-indulgent, but in the great runs we can feel into primordial kinds of life. I mean, that sense of identity.

I sometimes use that technique of dream, for instance "gliding shape / Beckoning through halls, / Fell dreamily down . . ." and so on. It's a combination of dream and even, you know, sexual—"my own tongue kissed / My lips awake" (**"The Lost Son"**). I mean, it's obviously onanistic, sweet myself.

THE ROLE OF THE READER

What happens in each reader, it is frequently said, is never the same, but nonetheless, it seems to me the reading of a good poem is in itself a re-creation of the poem, just like in looking at a picture, and that the experience itself is vicarious, and that's one of the reasons we have art, isn't it; that is that man can experience other men's experiences, to realize that this is there, this can happen.

I'm always writing, as it were, for as wide an audience as possible. That may sound fatuous, but perhaps I began wrong in deliberately courting the so-called popular audience in very plain, little poems about rather simple experiences. As I say, I began with verse, hoping that poetry would happen, and then went into things much more complex, but in a sense, I'm coming back to verse now, or I'm using the techniques and the longer line that I used originally. I think the capacity for poetry is much greater and much wider than most people realize, and I think that if the poetry can be made accessible to the so-called general reader, if it can be heard—and I've written almost everything I've done to be heard—once that occurs, there's usually understanding. I mean, I think a barrier has been erected against poetry. It isn't that poetry isn't being produced. I feel this is the greatest age, particularly for the shorter forms, in the language. We have no great drama but a body of lyrics of immense variety and a body of longer poems, but perhaps not so much full length drama; I mean, longer, meaning a hundred or two hundred lines. But everything sort of militates against . . . I mean, the radio, the television, the visual education. [To] bring up a whole generation trained, as it were, on TV is to abandon, as it were, part of the body, the ear. I mean, poetry is— or the use of language is—one of the differences between us and the apes, and if we're not careful of keeping that difference wide, we are going to have a retrogression, and certainly it is occurring in slovenly speech. Poetry is speech at its most memorable, at its best. And certainly it's human to desire the best, and that best is so accessible.

The best in the great complex poetry makes, in a sense, a profound and terrible demand; it says, "Change your life." That phrase is Rilke's, but other people have said it. And I think that's why the general public backs away from poets like Bogan or Kunitz and will read instead Millay or Brooke. They don't want their lives changed; they don't want to enter some other consciousness. They are, in a sense, consciously or unconsciously afraid of something. The best modern poetry is characterized by a terrible honesty of imagination. It is one of the things that we inherit from Blake. If one thinks of this in practical terms, we're supposed to be culture-mad America. Here is an area where we can really say we are the best in the world; that is lyrical poetry. It's available for 95 cents to usually four or five or six dollars. For 50 dollars a home can have a library of really choice, great poets that the young should have access to. Whereas people are willing to spend 1500, 2500 or 3500 for a lousy action painting, the idea of buying

a book seems to be abhorrent to them. Again, thinking in utilitarian terms, it's one of the ways in which we can defeat our great provinciality. We can't all get to the great opera; we can't all hear the great symphonies, but we can buy a book, or we can buy a good recording of poetry, and there are some.

The poet presumably is in the foreground of consciousness. He is aware of things, in a sense, before they happen, or before they generally happen. Now that isn't just falderal; it's simply so. I mean, a public poet like Auden, when he says, "We must love one another or die." He said it in a very few words . . . the central thing in our civilization. We are surrounded by all kinds of shoddy speech, by the clichés of advertising, by the kind of stylized prose of *Time, Life,* with the bromides of editorials. I mean, if someone can begin to hear good poetry, I don't mean serious or profound, but even "Mother Goose" or the poems in anthologies like *Come Hither.* They're part of the heritage of our race. If we cut ourselves off from them, we drift inevitably into a kind of obscene gobbledygook, of officialese, of jargon, and many of our courses in the university tend the same way, even some of the subjects themselves seem simply a waltzing with a special terminology. Whereas poetry is using the holy words, the words around which there's a great accretion of human association: "hill," "plow," "field," "mother." Furthermore, it's one of the ways we can, as it were, keep in touch with the subhuman, the other forms of life. I think the best modern poetry and some of the best modern painting still has a profound moral drive, not in the sense of a message, but it is written for the glory of man and the glory of God. It's the best we can do in our time, and we should be aware of it; even an indifferent or mediocre poem is more a human achievement than most prose.

THE POETIC PROCESS

I think the general genesis is one begins with a mood of some sort. And frequently I find that when I get grumpier and grumpier, and more and more irritable, that I . . . well, Beatrice, for instance, can say, "You had better write something pretty quick." The mood may not always be related to the piece, or it may be. But then the actual writing, the genesis of it, I think, for me, usually takes the shape of a line, or one or two or three lines, and these lines may accrete, I mean, sort of gather similar lines and images, you know. Then the actual composition of the poem for me . . . well, it isn't a fairly short . . . it is very rarely a thing that's just dashed off. But the only poem I ever wrote that I felt—well, there's been more than one— but as it were, a kind of seizure, is that one I wrote after Thomas' death (**"Elegy,"** included in *Words for the Wind*). That was for me almost a straight dictated poem, except that it had an extra stanza in it that I knocked out, and also that first poem **"The Dance."** But even there, I think, I usually have in the back of my mind the genesis of lines that, you know, that are skating around in your forebrain or in your fore-part of your consciousness or conscious mind. But it's the bringing together the whole thing into a coherent whole that's hard for me. I mean, that's the ultimate and the final work. Usually I can, in fact almost invariably I can tell when the thing is at least, shall we say, done, or in its final form; there may still be some fiddling or polishing with lines. But sometimes in an effort to describe an abstract thing, for instance these poems, "The spirit moves, / Yet stays: / Stirs as the blossom stirs" and so on . . . (**"A Light Breather"**). Well, that poem first was much longer, and then about twice, or more than twice its present length in the book. Then I cut it way down 'til it was almost nothing; then I sort of brought it back to its final shape.

Oddly enough, in **"The Adamant"** I had a kind of piece of luck. I fell into its form, which is three three-beat lines, and then a two-beat line each time. Originally they were all three-beat lines, and by cutting adjectives in the first and second stanza and changing the wording in the last stanza I came up with this curious cutoff effect which in a way sort of suggests the action of a rock crusher, and it gave it . . . well, it moved it from a poem that was just a poem into something where the rhythm was really integral with the feeling.

But writing for me is not an easy thing to do. I mean, it's always difficult. And I always am terrified, sort of, with the feeling that, well, the feeling after something that you know is really good, say, that well . . . "Is this the last time?" Well, I noticed that Auden said the same thing in his *The Making of Poetry*. As someone *that* gifted technically, whom I always think of as being able to write a poem at any time, on any subject, and within a very short time—that poem will always at the very least be readable—he would be the last person to worry or have that sense. To the public, anybody who has ever written a poem, a good poem, is regarded as a poet. But to the poet himself, it's that last, those last things that [matter].

I rarely can sit down and work from a very cold start. A poem that was written quite swiftly was **"In a Dark Time."** That's a villanelle, of course, slightly modified, and a damn tough form. And I remember writing that. I was reading a student notebook—well, by the way, there, in that sense, when I make them keep journals and whatnot, you sometimes . . . you know, they become your eyes and your ears and you do learn something from them. I believe very definitely the Kierkegaardian notion that education begins when the teacher starts learning from the student. That may sound like a paradox, but I'm sure you have had that same feeling, when it becomes, you know, a real reciprocity.

"In a Dark Time" was written while I was up really high (I mean high in the semantic or psychothalmic, constitutional-type sense). It took me about three days. It was in summer and I was sitting out there in the grass on a chaise lounge. Well, some of the lines were in notebooks before; the line, for me, sometimes will hang around for years. But I finally wrote it, as I say, in about three days, and I had the sense that this is one of the great poems of our time. I mean, I just knew it, and I shot it to Marianne Moore, who's tough if anyone is tough. Gee, she wrote back this card, saying, "an apocalypse and in mere language," *et cetera, et cetera,* see, and then Cal Lowell,

'cuz I thought, "Cal, ha, ha, think you know something about religious experience; get a load of this." Course this is Theodore's weakness still. I can't purge myself of playing, acting like I'm George Radermann or a quarterback, you know; I have to be cocky. But hell, that's 'cuz I had to grow up that way. After the old man died, there was me and Mama against the field. Everyone was trying to do us in, and I lived, well, I spent a lot of money. I lived in complete economic fear for years, hence that business "Money money money / Water water water" (**"The Lost Son"**). I mean, it's a cry from the very soul's depths. I mean, I have to live and I have to keep the creative, too. (Kenneth) Burke has some very good remarks there. Furthermore, we lived in the same house and his office was next to my class, and he used to sit there, when I was trampin' around teaching, [and say,] "Gee, you're going good today. I put a whole lot of things down." I said, "You son-of-a-bitch." But he wrote a thing called "The Vegetal Radicalism of Theodore Roethke," and he marches right through the first six poems, six of the long poems. There were some things in there; he says in our time that it's natural that the poet should make that equation, equation meaning water, all of fertility, all of life. Sounds nutty, but likewise, he draws a parallel, or contrast, with Eliot—Eliot using all the abstractions, whereas I use almost none. Now I'm moving more toward abstract language, but then again, that's another problem. This area which I'm puffing and blowing about . . . I say that because in most of those last short poems I feel I was the instrument, you see, as bleak as hell. Oh yea, that's rather good, "as bleak as hell." In a sense it is hell, and a dark night can be repeated, and there's no A-train to paradise. We don't grow up, older and and older, more and more benign, more and more full of wisdom and so on. I'm still death haunted, I'm afraid, in spite of saying death is an absurdity, it's an irrelevance.

The difference [between Yeats and me] is that I can dance, and Yeats can't. I mean, as somebody put it, 'cause—and I can say this without batting an eye—I know, in the final term, something and perhaps a good deal more than I realize about mystic experience. Yeats didn't. Sometimes people say that when I get rolling in the rhythm, in reading certain kinds, I start a thing that seems to approximate the dance. Of course there was a low point in the history of the modern dance when I was at Bennington where I was actually approached to be in under Martha Graham's . . . Well, of course, those pieces for Sir John Davies began out of a . . . probably the literary impulse came out of reading John Davies' "Orchestra," which is a long poem in praise of dancing and celebrating, and based on the whole Elizabethan notion of the cosmic dance. The whole thing is, you know, an improvisation. It was written in 15 days. But it has a wonderful rhythm. Kunitz introduced it to me originally. Arthur Smith quotes in one of his books about there are times that come in every living creature when the impulse to dance and to sing, or to sing and to dance—Oh gosh, I'm getting incoherent. This comes to all living things, I think, and I think it goes back, way back into the Dionysian experience.

There was the one time I played the Rimbaud business of really driving myself, seeing . . . you could really derange the senses, and it can be done, and let me tell you, I did it. I mean, I got in such good condition. I wasn't drinking at all. I was 27. This was in East Lansing, Michigan. I was running on those cinder pads four, five miles a day. Jesus, and teaching too. But you know I got in this real strange state. I got in the woods and started a circular kind of dance, and I've never put this down very . . . I refer to it in "I tried to fling my shadow at the moon" (**"The Dance"**). I kept going around and just shedding clothes. Sounds Freudian as hell, but in the end I had just sort of a circle— as if, I think, I understood intuitively what the frenzy is. That is, you go way beyond yourself, and this is not sheer exhaustion, but this strange sort of a . . . not illumination . . . but a sense of being again a part of the whole universe. I mean anything but quiet. I mean, in a sense everything is symbolical. In one of the Old Woman poems (**"Her Becoming"**) I just sort of put it in there, because I know if you put this down in prose, for God's sake, "Oh, this is merely clinical," I mean, "Obviously, he is crazy" and so forth. But it was one of the deepest and most profound experiences I ever had. And accompanying it was a real sexual excitement also . . . and this tremendous feeling of actual power. But finally, when coming back, I was just so exhausted that I could hardly walk, in as good condition as I was.

What happened to me eventually, well, one thing . . . you have this curious sense that you're actually being transformed literally into an animal. You start getting fantasies, I mean, of power, lion-like power. But the next night was much tougher, in a sense—I really thought my features were changing. Of course this was madness, you see, but the relationship between the ecstasy and madness is so . . . well, one of the things that the head-shrinkers know, or the good ones, that if these descents are too rapid, that can be chaotic, and I mean you knock. In other words, something could happen to you that you could get lost back there, because what you're doing is going right back into the history of the god-damn race. I mean, you're down to the animal, dog, and so forth, down to snake. It sounds nuts, but, well . . . fight your way out of that. What happened to me there, I simply blacked out, eventually. I knew I was teaching in real manic frenzy. Well, I woke up in the morning, somewhat like this, with very little sleep and decided I wanted to get to his office. (Probably a reference to Lloyd C. Emmons, Dean of Liberal Arts at Michigan State University.) I took a little walk on the edge of the city. There I got so cold I lay down and took off a shoe, and there I had . . . this is again real loony, and goes beyond . . . there was a curious crabhole, and I lay there and started whistling to this thing, as if you were really trying to call it out of the earth. Well, I knew what I was doing, that this was not a snakehole and so on and so on, but . . . and I put this down in one of those pieces, in one of those running ones (**"The Song"**). Then I got scared; it started getting cold; it was November and I started to run with only one shoe on. Jesus Christ, here you are, and I was barefoot . . . well, symbolically yet. I got into a gas station. There was a guy I again, I just associated with my father. I was out on my feet, see, just punchy from. . . . You know, I hadn't slept for five nights and I said, "Can . . . get me, drive me," and he said,

"Sure." He drove me to the campus and I came in, you know, just like someone who had been beaten for five rounds. I sat down in that god-damn office and I thought, "Jesus Christ, you're going to have to ad-lib now." But the trouble in these high states of consciousness is that *everything* gets heightened, so that sound particularly . . . somebody walking overhead, it just sounds like a concatenation. Well, I finally said, "Just bring me a coach and I'll try to explain on what happened to me physically." I was just going to say, "I'm not nuts. I'm just out on my feet because I've been working." I finally thought I'd died. There was a profound and beautiful experience, as if you . . . and you can hear the thing going, but you just die right then.

The *real* point is that this business of the dance accompanies exaltation of the highest, the human thing, and it also goes into the Dionysian frenzy, which in modern life hardly anyone even *speaks* of anymore. But the real profundity of that experience, I mean, in the sense of the mood itself, seemed to be, you know, the whole Islamic world. All the cultures were with you. This is exactly what they felt when they were rolling in the circular, you know, frenzy thing. And your perceptions, as I say, both in sight and particularly in sound *and* smell, and frequently also another is that you get the transfer of senses. Sometimes that comes even with memory. You know, Hopkins says in one of his . . . when he said that "I tasted brass in my mouth," well, that's the very essence, it seems to me, of metaphysical thinking. That is when the body itself . . . when Vaughan says, "When felt through all my fleshy dress, ripe shoots of everlastingness," well, *that's* the feeling. You feel one way that you are eternal, or immortal, and it doesn't seem to be a cheap thing either. And furthermore, death becomes, as it were, an absurdity, of no consequence. And also, the notion, conceptions, of time are completely subjective, and I've often thought sometimes that when the suicidal leaps from the window, when he hits that pavement and is just a blob, who knows, maybe he explodes into a million universes and he is happy. Who knows? That's behind, you know, the nuttier aspects of certain Hindu religions, when they'd start dancing and singing and finally in this ecstasy run right into the god-damn sea when they know all those sharks are there. Nothing could stop 'em. I mean, we can say that this is collective madness. It is, but it's part of the human psyche; it's there.

Well, maybe part of our problems, people nowadays, is that we have lost contact with both the ecstasy and the frenzy. "But the unconscious is a very funny thing," said he pontifically. I know, I know I'm supposed to have . . . as Kunitz says, "He sinks into the very bed of the self, and disorder itself has, takes on, its images or given images." Well, I think almost anyone could do that once they were willing to, shall we say, to pay the price. I mean, I think maybe this business about being able to tap the unconscious is a polite kind of way of saying you speak completely nutty, I mean, or potty, as it were.

Let me get back to this point—the unconscious, you can take a dive in and you come up with all kinds of garbage around your neck, or you can bring up something beautiful. I mean, in a sense it's like nature. I suppose it is nature, an interior nature. I mean, part of it's dead, irrational . . . dead. And when it's unlike nature, well, it can't be bullied. Maybe you can bully nature under some conditions. Does it sound like too cryptic a remark?

Eischler in New York has written on death, and Hoffer is one of the very great ones, and these things which sound sort of eerie and scary, to them are absolutely comprehensible. Well, what I mean is, we have modern man living as if he had no unconscious, as if he had none, and being ashamed of the impulse. That is, building up guilts about say, even masturbation and whatnot. Well, for God's sake, the most advanced thinking, as far as I can determine, is that any sexual expression, if done with love or even understanding is legitimate. I mean, therefore, of course, I suppose I'm no expert on the homosexual kick, but I mean, what the hell. Well, I don't mean to get mumbling about that, but the point is that once you neglect the unconscious and act as if isn't going to backfire personally it can backfire collectively, and that's certainly what happened with the Nazis, with the Germans, with a whole great, gifted people, in many ways more gifted, say, than the English.

Oh well, when I finally got into these poems, the first one, which was **"The Lost Son,"** came after a period of very intensive teaching, and also teaching particularly lyrics and long poems like "Anthony and Cleopatra." Then I began to realize what could be done by playing against the line, as it were, and also I saw certain forms of the diminishing kind in the Elizabethan songs. I wasn't conscious of that at the time. I wanted to write the kind of poem which would follow the action of the mind itself. And furthermore, a kind of poem which could represent the struggle—that is, between the two parts of one's personality, the self and the other self, daemon, call it what you will. So I began writing a style that had a considerable speed but still used monosyllables. But the shape of the stanzas was essentially as if I was composing for music. In other words, the poem would have a theme started and then that theme replied to, or answered to. There might be question, then answer, *et cetera*. The general design of these poems was cyclic. That is, frequently they began in the mire, in the depths, in a depressed state, if you will, and then they moved out. And often the eventual end came to a kind of resolution, or sometimes as euphoria, in other words, a poem of joy. The important thing to remember is that the euphoria, or euphorias, are not all the same, but they are conditioned by the very sights that are in the eye, and the mind's eye at the time. And I think it's rather odd that conditions of joy have much more variety than conditions of depression or despair, the blank grayness and sameness of the lower depths, as it were, although again, there are certainly degrees and depths of terror.

Well, as I say, (I) follow the movement of the mind itself, mind that is cyclic or, if you will, manic, to use an overworked or misunderstood term. But to take that movement and then to turn it into art, one takes only the general design of that movement, and there are times of interlude, times of rest, times of waiting. Then, of course, these

poems that followed were kind of soul's history, beginning with a small child. As Burke has pointed out, adolescence is peculiarly an interlude time, a time of being blurred or fuzzy or uncertain about what is happening, what's going on. I said someplace that "so much of adolescence is an ill-defined dying" (**"I'm Here"**). Of course, we are always dying into ourselves, and then renewing ourselves. That's perhaps as good a definition as any of what I do, or what I try to do. But this is simply one kind of poem. That is, I believe that a poet should show as many parts of his nature as he can in all decency reveal, and that includes the epigram, the aphorism, the joke, the song, the song-like poem, up to the very highly formalized lyric. It's there, perhaps, I come closest to old W.B. Yeats, but I think I do a different thing technically. I end-stop the lines much more than he ever did. In other words, I'm using a style that was more current—and the language was perhaps a little less sophisticated—in the 16th century, we'll say, in an effort to write a plain, bare, an even terrible statement. Whether one does it, of course, it always depends on the reader.

I think the deepest and most evocative images that come out of poetry are those, the things you saw and smelled and felt with the senses the earliest. But curiously enough I have rather a bad memory in the literal sense.

I sometimes try to render the object faithfully, to see it as intensely as I can, and turn that back into language, language that doesn't compete necessarily with the painter. In final terms, the purely imagistic poetry is decidedly limited if it remains nothing more than image, however good. But it is my belief that a thing perceived finally— and when one looks so long at the object or has looked at it habitually, or looked at it out of love as Rilke would look at an animal in the zoo for hours on end, until you become that object and it becomes you—is an extension of consciousness.

I can't profess to know. Well, maybe the kind of knowing that occurs in poetry is related at least to satori, as it were. I believe that one can suddenly become aware of another consciousness, a consciousness other than immediate; and sometimes that may happen to be a very trivial thing. And Proust has recorded this better than anyone when he stumbles going up to church, and he's suddenly aware that there's another world other than his, a consciousness that is higher. From what I gather from Japanese, our version of what is usually thought of as Zen is pretty superficial, to say the least. Suzuki himself is rather careless, and most of the Beats take Suzuki as their bible. It does represent a really rugged discipline, of course, so ritualized, so formalized. But let me see. It is possible that I might come close to it, if I can find . . . well, yea, in **"The Right Thing Happens to the Happy Man."** This is "His being single, that being all," or "he sits still, the solid figure when / "The self-destructive shake the common wall; / Takes to himself what mystery he can." This's possibly close to Zen notion . . . that's that sitting still which goes beyond mere quietism. I mean, quietism as such is noble enough, but it's a relatively low plane. Also, at the end of **"The Abyss,"** this, I don't know, this isn't Zen essentially, but is Buddhistic. I mean, there's deliberate allusion to the Buddha here: "I am most immoderately married: / "Lord God has taken my heaviness away; / I have merged, like the bird, with the bright air, / And my thought flies to the place by the bo-tree. / Being, not doing, is my first joy."

Hayden Carruth (essay date 1964)

SOURCE: "Requiem for God's Gardner," in *The Nation,* Vol. 199, No. 8, September 28, 1964, pp. 168-69.

[*In the following review, Carruth judges that in* The Far Field *Roethke achieved qualified success.*]

During the past year the fashion has been to praise Theodore Roethke to the skies. But what possible good can it do the poor guy now that he's dead and in the ground? He was a marvelous poet and apparently, in some of his moods, a charming, likable person. But he was not a Yeats or a Keats—he was too unsure of himself, technically and emotionally, to write the handful of absolute poems that one needs to enter the first rank—and we do an injustice to his memory and to our own worthiness as memorialists if we say otherwise. It will be better all around if we try instead to see exactly what he was.

This book [*The Far Field*] of his last work helps a good deal. Some of the poems, perhaps fifteen of the whole forty-eight, seem to be unfinished work. At least they contain errors of composition that Roethke almost certainly would have corrected, though since we aren't told how or by whom the book was assembled, conjecture is useless. It is best to disregard these poems. Ten or twelve of the rest are very good Roethke indeed, the equal, or nearly, of anything in his previous work. On every page one finds, as expected, something quite brilliant, even if only a line or a word. The poems are divided about equally among Roethke's three chief modes: the song; the longer poem in loose meters devoted to themes from nature, including human nature; and the denser poem in end-stopped pentameters, usually rhymed and usually philosophical in substance.

All the poems are about death. This was true of his earlier poems too, of course, the whole body of his work being a repeated failing defense against the fear of dying. But in these last poems the failures come more quickly, more insistently, and the fear deepens into a terrible malady.

Perhaps this is why the failures are so beautiful. In his last years he concentrated every ounce of his lyrical strength on the task of escaping, submerging the self in the universe, silencing the individual voice in the voice of nature. "I long for the imperishable quiet at the heart of form," he wrote, and again: Being, not doing, is my first joy." "I would be a stream . . . a leaf." "On one side [our side] of silence there is no smile; / But when I breathe with the birds, / The spirit of wrath becomes the spirit of blessing. / And the dead begin from their dark to sing in my sleep." The intention is unmistakable and quite con-

ventional, call it what you will: a Platonism of suburbia, the birdwatcher's transcendentalism; it is easy, too easy, to mock. The fact is that in his best poems about nature Roethke almost brought it off, partly through his verbal and imaginative power, partly through his individual synthesis of disparate pantheistic strains. He took his sources where he found them, Taoism, Amerindian poetry, Mother Goose; mostly he invented them.

A third factor was Roethke's skill as an amateur naturalist. He really was a birdwatcher, an excellent one, and his professional knowledge of flowers began in his father's greenhouses. (Who else would know that tulips "creak"?— yet they do.) In such a poem as **"All Morning"** he brings together in one catalogue the minute felicities of songbirds, even their cutenesses, the things we deprecate on greeting cards, and does it so unaffectedly that suddenly we realize he has touched the elemental force of the universe. When he writes of nature's larger aspects, such as the movements of waters and mountains, he evokes a sense of the cosmic resistlessness more compelling than that in any other recent poetry I can think of.

Yet these poems fail. They fail in their very brilliance and beauty. They do not do what Roethke wistfully hopes they do. When he says, "I lose and find myself in the long water," or "What does what it should do needs nothing more," these are statements only; highly poetic statements, often successful as such, but they were intended to transcend poetry. They do not. And since their intention is not only their meaning but their function—their place in the poem's completion—they destroy themselves. The individual voice is not silenced, the single consciousness still asserts its claims and fears, its tremulous and eternal devastation. Roethke's voice and consciousness; and ours. In weariness, vexation, and a kind of merriment, he sighs: "Running from God's the longest race of all." Then did he, at the end, return to God, as some reviewers have suggested? Of course he could not. Instead we see him, a huge melancholy man, laughing in shyness, stopping, peering around, continuing again, stumbling, quivering, dancing, crying, singing, up to the cemetery gate. This is his poem. It is the poem par excellence of his generation. And if he did not quite succeed in containing it within any of the individual forms that he titled his poems, it reveals itself clearly enough in the whole. It moves us deeply because Roethke was one of us, and it will continue to do so for a long time because Roethke had the ability to write lines that can be remembered; for example, several that I have quoted in this review, though I did not choose them with this in mind. Memorability isn't the only proof of fine poetry, nor the most important, but it is still rare enough to be distinguished, I think, and pleasing enough to be cherished.

Denis Donoghue (essay date 1965)

SOURCE: "Theodore Roethke," in *Connoisseurs of Chaos: Ideas of Order in Modern American Poetry,* The Macmillan Company, 1965, pp. 219-45.

[Donoghue is an Irish-born educator and literary critic. In his study The Arts without Mystery *(1984), he attacks the tendency of contemporary societies to reduce art to a commodity. In the following essay, Donoghue perceives Roethke's poetry as an attempt to discern order and purpose in a world that may seem meaningless.]*

There is a poem called **"Snake"** in which Theodore Roethke describes a young snake turning and drawing away and then says:

> I felt my slow blood warm.
> I longed to be that thing,
> The pure, sensuous form.
>
> And I may be, some time.

To aspire to a condition of purity higher than any available in the human world is a common urge. Poets often give this condition as a pure, sensuous form, nothing if not itself and nothing beyond itself. But it is strange, at first sight, that Roethke gives his parable in the image of a snake, because snakes tend to figure in his poems as emblems of the sinister. In **"Where Knock is Open Wide"** one of the prayerful moments reads: "I'll be a bite. You be a wink. / Sing the snake to sleep." In **"I Need, I Need"** the term "snake-eyes" is enough to send its owner packing. And there is this, in **"The Shape of the Fire"**:

> Up over a viaduct I came, to the snakes and sticks
>   of another winter,
> A two-legged dog hunting a new horizon of howls.

But this is at first sight, or at first thought, because Roethke, more than most poets, sought a sustaining order in the images of his chaos, and only those images would serve. If you offer a dove as answer to a snake, your answer is incomplete, an order not violent enough. Hence when the right time came, in **"I'm Here,"** Roethke would find that a snake lifting its head is a fine sight, and a snail's music is a fine sound, and both are joys, credences of summer. As Roethke says in **"The Longing,"** "The rose exceeds, the rose exceeds us all."

But he did not sentimentalize his chaos. He lived with it, and would gladly have rid himself of it if he could have done so without an even greater loss, the loss of verifiable life. When he thought of his own rage, for instance, he often saw it as mere destructiveness. In one of his early poems he said: "Rage warps my clearest cry / To witless agony." And he often resorted to invective, satire, pseudonymous tirades, to cleanse himself of rage and hatred. In one of those tirades he said, "Behold, I'm a heart set free, for I have taken my hatred and eaten it." But **"Death Piece"** shows that to be released from rage is to be—quite simply—dead. And the price is too high. This is one of the reasons why Roethke found the last years of W. B. Yeats so rewarding, because Yeats made so much of his rage, in the *Last Poems*, *The Death of Cuchulain*, and *Purgatory*. In one of his own apocalyptic poems, **"The Lost Son,"** Roethke says, "I want the old rage, the lash of primordial milk," as if to recall Yeats' cry, "Grant me an

old man's frenzy." And in **"Old Lady's Winter Words"** he says: "If I were a young man, / I could roll in the dust of a fine rage . . ."; and in **"The Sententious Man"**: "Some rages save us. Did I rage too long? / The spirit knows the flesh it must consume." Hence Roethke's quest for the saving rage. Call it—for it is this—a rage for order. He was sometimes tempted to seal himself against the rush of experience, and he reminds himself in **"The Adamant"** that the big things, such as truth, are sealed against thought; the true substance, the core, holds itself inviolate. And yet man is exposed, exposes himself. And, in a sense, rightly so. As Yeats says in the great "Dialogue of Self and Soul":

> I am content to live it all again
> And yet again, if it be life to pitch
> Into the frog-spawn of a blind man's ditch.

In **"The Pure Fury"** Roethke says, "I live near the abyss." What he means is the substance of his poetry. The abyss is partly the frog-spawn of a blind man's ditch, partly a ditch of his own contriving, partly the fate of being human in a hard time, partly the poet's weather. As discreetly as possible we can take it for granted, rehearsing it only to the extent of linking it with the abyss in other people. Better to think of it as the heart of each man's darkness. In **"Her Becoming"** Roethke speaks of it in one aspect:

> I know the cold fleshless kiss of contraries,
> The neverless constriction of surfaces—
> Machines, machines, loveless, temporal;
> Mutilated souls in cold morgues of obligation

And this becomes, in the **"Fourth Meditation,"** "the dreary dance of opposites." (But so far it is common enough.)

It is still common enough when Roethke presents it through the ambiguities of body and soul. In **"Epidermal Macabre"** Roethke, like Yeats in *The Tower*, wishes the body away in favor of a spirit remorselessly sensual:

> And willingly would I dispense
> With false accounterments of sense,
> To sleep immodestly, a most
> Incarnadine and carnal ghost.

Or again, when the dance of opposites is less dreary, Roethke accepts with good grace the unwinding of body from soul:

> When opposites come suddenly in place,
> I teach my eyes to hear, my ears to see
> How body from spirit slowly does unwind
> Until we are pure spirit at the end.

Sometimes the body is "gristle." In **"Praise to the End"** Roethke says, "Skin's the least of me," and in the **"First Meditation"** it is the rind that "hates the life within." (Yeats' "dying animal" is clearly visible.) But there were other moments, as there were in Yeats. In **"The Wraith"** the body casts a spell, the flesh makes the spirit "visible," and in the **"Fourth Meditation"** "the husk lives on, ardent as a seed."

Mostly in Roethke the body seems good in itself, a primal energy. And when it is this if features the most distinctive connotations of the modern element: it is a good, but ill at ease with other goods. Above all, it does not guarantee an equable life in the natural world. More often than not in these poems man lives with a hostile nature, and lives as well as he can. In **"I Need, I Need"** intimations of waste, privation, and insecurity lead to this:

> The ground cried my name:
> Good-bye for being wrong.
> Love helps the sun.
> But not enough.

"I can't marry the dirt" is an even stronger version, in **"Bring the Day,"** echoing Wallace Stevens' benign "marriage of flesh and air" while attaching to it now, as courageously as possible, the bare note, "A swan needs a pond"; or, more elaborately in another poem, "A wretch needs his wretchedness." The aboriginal middle poems have similar cries on every page: "These wings are from the wrong nest"; "My sleep deceives me"; "Soothe me, great groans of underneath"; "Rock me to sleep, the weather's wrong"; "Few objects praise the Lord."

These are some of Roethke's intimations of chaos. They reach us as cries, laments, protests, intimations of loss. Most of Roethke's later poems are attempts to cope with these intimations by becoming—in Stevens' sense—their connoisseur. In **"The Dance"** Roethke speaks of a promise he has made to "sing and whistle romping with the bears"; and whether we take these as animals or constellations, the promise is the same and hard to keep. To bring it off at all, Roethke often plays in a child's garden, especially in poems like **"O Lull Me, Lull Me,"** where he can have everything he wants by having it only in fancy. "Light fattens the rock," he sings, to prove that good children get treats. "When I say things fond, I hear singing," he reports, and we take his word for it; as we do again when we acknowledge, in a later poem, that "the right thing happens to the happy man." Perhaps it does. But when Roethke says, "I breathe into a dream, / And the ground cries . . . ," and again, "I could say hello to things; / I could talk to a snail," we think that he protests too much, and we know that his need is great. Roethke is never quite convincing in this note, or in the hey-nonny note of his neo-Elizabethan pastiche. Even when he dramatizes the situation in the **"Meditations of an Old Woman"** the answers come too easily. In two stanzas he has "the earth itself a tune," and this sounds like a poet's wishful dreaming. Roethke may have wanted the kind of tone that Stevens reached in his last poems, an autumnal calm that retains the rigor and the feeling but banishes the fretful note, the whine, the cry of pain. But Stevens earned this. And Yeats earned it too, in poems like "Beautiful Lofty Things." Roethke claimed it without really earning it. Here is a stanza from **"Her Becoming"**:

> Ask all the mice who caper in the straw—
> I am benign in my own company.
> A shape without a shade, or almost none,
> I hum in pure vibration, like a saw.

> The grandeur of a crazy one alone—
> By swoops of bird, by leaps of fish, I live.
> My shadow steadies in a shifting stream;
> I live in air; the long lights is my home;
> I dare caress the stones, the field my friend;
> A light wind rises: I become the wind.

And here is Stevens, in a passage from "The Course of a Particular":

> The leaves cry. It is not a cry of divine attention,
> Nor the smoke-drift of puffed-out heroes, nor
>   human cry.
> It is the cry of leaves that do not transcend
>   themselves,
> In the absence of fantasia, without meaning more
> Than they are in the final finding of the air, in the
>   thing
> Itself, until, at last, the cry concerns no one at all.

How can we compare these two passages except to say that Stevens speaks with the knowledge that there have been other days, other feelings, and the hope that there will be more of each, as various as before? Roethke speaks as if the old woman were now released from time and history and the obligations of each, released even from the memories that she has already invoked. There is too much fantasia in Roethke's lines, and this accounts for a certain slackness that fell upon him whenever he tried too hard to be serene. Stevens' poem is, in the full meaning of the word, mature; Roethke's is a little childish, second-childish. Stevens would affirm, when affirmation seemed just, but not before. Roethke longed to affirm, and when the affirmation would not come he sometimes—now and again—dressed himself in affirmative robes.

But only now and again. At his best he is one of the most scrupulous of poets. In **"Four for Sir John Davies,"** for instance, the harmony between nature and man that Davies figured—the orchestra, the dance, the music of the spheres—is brought to bear upon the poem, critically and never naïvely or sentimentally. The divinely orchestrated universe of Davies' poem is more than a point of reference but far less than an escape route. For one thing, as Roethke says, "I need a place to sing, and dancing-room," and for another, there is no dancing master, and for a third, there isn't even at this stage a dancing partner. So he must do the best he can in his poverty. And if his blood leaps "with a wordless song," at least it leaps:

> But what I learned there, dancing all alone,
> Was not the joyless motion of a stone.

But even when the partner comes and they dance their joy, Roethke does not claim that this makes everything sweet or that nature and man will thereafter smile at each other. In the farthest reach of joy he says:

> We danced to shining; mocked before the black
> And shapeless night that made no answer back.

The sensual cry is what it is, and there are moments when it is or seems to be final, but man still lives in the element of antagonisms. In "Four Quartets" the "daunsynge" scene from Sir Thomas Elyot testifies to modes of being, handsome but archaic; it answers no present problem. Nor does Sir John Davies, who plays a similar role in Roethke's sequence. And even before that, in **"The Return,"** man in the element of antagonisms feels and behaves like an animal in his self-infected lair, "With a stump of scraggy fang / Bared for a hunter's boot." And sometimes he turns upon himself in rage.

When Roethke thinks of man in this way, he often presents him in images of useless flurry. Like Saul Bellow's Dangling Man, he is clumsy, ungainly, an elephant in a pond. Roethke often thinks of him as a bat—by day, quiet, cousin to the mouse; at night, crazy, absurd, looping "in crazy figures." And when the human situation is extreme, Roethke thinks of man as a bat flying deep into a narrowing tunnel. Far from being a big, wide space, the world seems a darkening corridor. In **"Bring the Day!"** Roethke says, "Everything's closer. Is this a cage?" And if a shape cries from a cloud as it does in **"The Exorcism,"** and calls to man's flesh, man is always somewhere else, "down long corridors." (Corridors, cages, tunnels, lairs—if these poems needed illustration, the painter is easily named: Francis Bacon, keeper of caged souls.)

In **"Four for Sir John Davies"** the lovers, Roethke says, "undid chaos to a curious sound," "curious" meaning careful as well as strange and exploratory. In this world to undo chaos is always a curious struggle, sometimes thought of as a release from constriction, a stretching in all directions, an escape from the cage. In **"What Can I Tell My Bones?"** Roethke says, "I recover my tenderness by long looking," and if tenderness is the proof of escape, long looking is one of the means. In *King Lear* it is to see feelingly. In some of Roethke's poems it is given as, quite simply, attention. In **"Her Becoming"** Roethke speaks of a "jauntier principle of order," but this is to dream. What he wants, in a world of cages and corridors, is to escape to an order, an order of which change and growth and decay are natural mutations and therefore acceptable. In many of the later poems it will be an order of religious feeling, for which the punning motto is, "God, give me a near."

The first step, the first note toward a possible order, is to relish what can be relished. Listening to "the sigh of what is," one attends, knowing, or at least believing, that "all finite things reveal infinitude." If things "flame into being," so much the better. "Dare I blaze like a tree?" Roethke asks at one point, like the flaming tree of Yeats' "Vacillation." And again Roethke says, "What I love is near at hand, / Always, in earth and air." This is fine, as far as it goes, but it is strange that Roethke is more responsive to intimations of being when they offer themselves in plants than in people; and here, of course, he differs radically from Yeats. In the first version of **"Cuttings"** he is exhilarated when "the small cells bulge," when cuttings sprout into a new life, when bulbs hunt for light, when the vines in the forcing house pulse with the knocking pipes, when orchids draw in the warm air, when beetles, newts, and lice creep and wriggle. In **"Slug"** he rejoices in his kinship with bats, weasels, and worms. In **"A Walk in Late Summer"** being "delights in being, and in time." In the same poem Roethke delights in the "midnight eyes" of small things, and in several poems he relishes what Christopher Smart in *Jubilate Agno* calls "the language of flowers." Everywhere in Roethke there is consolation in the rudimentary when it is what it is, without fantasia. It is a good day when the spiders sail into summer. But Roethke is slow to give the same credences to man. Plants may be transplanted, and this is good, but what is exhilarating reproduction in insects and flowers is mere duplication in people. Girls in college are "duplicate gray standard faces"; in the same poem there is talk of "endless duplication of lives and objects." Man as a social being is assimilated to the machine; the good life is lived by plants. In the bacterial poems, weeds are featured as circumstance, the rush of things, often alien but often sustaining. "Weeds, weeds, how I love you," Roethke says in **"The Shape of the Fire."** In the **"First Meditation,"** "On love's worst ugly day, / The weeds hiss at the edge of the field . . . ." In **"What Can I Tell My Bones?"** "Weeds turn toward the wind weed-skeletons," presumably because "the dead love the unborn." But in **"Praise to the End!"** when the water's low and romping days are over, "the weeds exceed me."

There are two ways of taking this, and Roethke gives us both. Normally we invoke the rudimentary to criticize the complex: the lower organism rebukes the higher for falling short of itself, as body rebukes the arrogance of vaunting mind or spirit. This works on the assumption that what is simple is more "natural" than what is complex, and that lower organisms have the merit of such simplicity. Or, alternatively, one can imply that the most exalted objects of our human desire are already possessed, in silence and grace, by the lower organisms. Roethke often does this. In **"The Advice,"** for instance, he says:

> A learned heathen told me this:
> Dwell in pure mind and Mind alone;
> What you brought back from the Abyss,
> The Slug was taught beneath his Stone.

This is so presumably because the slug had a teacher, perhaps the dancing master who has retired from the human romp. Roethke doesn't commit the sentimentality of implying, however, that all is sweetness and light in the bacterial world, and generally he avoids pushing his vegetal analogies too far. In his strongest poems the bacterial is featured as a return to fundamentals, a syntax of short phrases to represent the radical breaking-up that may lead to a new synthesis. In grammatical terms, we have broken the spine of our syntax by loading it with our own fetishes. So we must begin again as if we were learning a new language, speaking in short rudimentary phrases. Or, alternatively, we learn in simple words and phrases, hoping that eventually we may reach the light of valid sentences. In this spirit Roethke says, in a late poem, "God bless the roots!—Body and soul are one!" The roots, the sensory facts, are beneath or beyond doubt; in **"The Longing"**

Roethke says, "I would believe my pain: and the eye quiet on the growing rose." Learning a new language in this way, we must divest ourselves at this first stage of all claims to coherence, synthesis, or unity. This is the secular equivalent of the "way of purgation" in "Four Quartets," and it serves a corresponding purpose, because here too humility is endless. If our humility is sufficient, if we attend to the roots, to beginnings, we may even be rewarded with a vision in which beginning and end are one, as in the poem **"In Evening Air"**:

> Ye littles, lie more close!
> Make me, O Lord, a last, a simple thing
> Time cannot overwhelm.
> Once I transcended time:
> A bud broke to a rose,
>   And I rose from a last diminishing.

We can see how this goes in the first stanzas of **"Where Knock is Open Wide"**:

> A kitten can
> Bite with his feet;
> Papa and Mama
> Have more teeth.

We can take this as pure notation, the primitive vision linking things that to the complex adult eye seem incommensurate. But the adult eye is "wrong," and it must go to school again if it is ever to say, "I recover my tenderness by long looking." Roethke's lines are "intuitions of sensibility," the ground of our beseeching, acts of the mind at the very first stage, long before idea, generalization, or concept. And this is the only way to innocence—or so the poem suggests. Then he says in the second stanza:

> Sit and play
> Under the rocker
> Until the cows
> All have puppies.

Here the aimlessness of the kitten stands for the innocence of game and apprehension. The play is nonchalant, and it conquers time by the ease of its reception. Time is measured by the laws of growth and fruition, not by the clock. In this sense it is proper to say, as Roethke does in the next stanza:

> His ears haven't time.
> Sing me a sleep-song, please.
> A real hurt is soft.

In Christopher Smart's "A Song to David" (the source of the title of the present poem) stanza 77 includes the lines:

> And in the seat to faith assigned
> Where ask is have, where seek is find,
> Where knock is open wide.

The cat's ears haven't time because they don't ask for it. If time is for men the destructive element, that is their funeral, and mostly their suicide. "Sing me a sleep-song,

please" is a prayer to be released from time. "A real hurt is soft" is an attempt to render human pain as pure description, to eliminate self-pity. And the appropriate gloss is the second stanza of **"The Lost Son"**—"Fished in an old wound, / The soft pond of repose"—to remind us that the primitive vision is at once harsh and antiseptic. (Roethke himself sometimes forgot this.) Hence these intuitions of rudimentary sensibility are exercises, akin to spiritual exercises, all the better if they are caustic, purgative, penitential. The exercises are never finished, because this is the way things are, but once they are well begun the soul can proceed; the energy released is the rage for a sustaining order.

The search for order begins easily enough in Roethke. Sometimes, as we have seen, it begins in celebration, relishing what there is to relish. Or again it may begin by sounding a warning note. The early poem **"To My Sister"** is a rush of admonition designed for survival and prudence. "Defer the vice of flesh," he tells her, but on the other hand, "Keep faith with present joys." Later, Roethke would seek and find value in intimations of change and growth, and then in love, normally sexual love. Many of the love poems are beautiful in an Elizabethan way, which is one of the best ways, and whether their delicacy is entirely Roethke's own or partly his way of acknowledging the delicacy of Sir Thomas Wyatt is neither here nor there. Some of the love poems are among Roethke's finest achievements. I would choose **"The Renewal," "I Knew a Woman," "The Sensualists," "The Swan," "She,"** and **"The Voice"**—or this one, **"Memory"**:

> In the slow world of dream,
> We breathe in unison.
> The outside dies within,
> And she knows all I am.
>
> She turns, as if to go,
> Half-bird, half-animal.
> The wind dies on the hill.
> Love's all. Love's all I know.
>
> A doe drinks by a stream,
> A doe and its fawn.
> When I follow after them,
> The grass changes to stone.

Love was clearly a principle of order in Roethke's poems, but it never established itself as a relation beyond the bedroom. It never became dialogue or *caritas*. Outside the bedroom Roethke became his own theme, the center of a universe deemed to exist largely because it had such a center. This does not mean that the entire universe was mere grist to his mill; he is not one of the predatory poets. But on the other hand, he does not revel in the sheer humanity of the world. Indeed, his universe is distinctly under-populated. Even Aunt Tilly entered it only when she died, thereby inciting an elegy. This is not to question Roethke's "sincerity"; poems are written for many reasons, one of which is the presence of poetic forms inviting attention. But to indicate the nature of Roethke's achievement it is necessary to mark the areas of his deepest response and to point to those areas that he acknowledged more sluggishly, if at all. I have already implied that he responded to the human modes of being only when a specific human relation touched him and he grasped it. He did not have that utter assent to other people, other lives, that marks the best poetry of William Carlos Williams or Richard Eberhart, the feeling that human life is just as miraculous as the growth of an orchid or the "excess" of a rose. Indeed, one might speculate along these lines: that Roethke's response to his father and mother and, in the love poems, to his wife was so vivid that it engrossed all other responses in the human world. It set up a monopoly. And therefore flowers and plants were closer to him than people.

Even when he acknowledged a natural order of things, Roethke invariably spoke of it as if it did not necessarily include the human order or as if its inclusion of that order were beside the point. The natural order of things included moss growing on rock, the transplanting of flowers, the cycle of mist, cloud, and rain, the tension of nest and grave, and it might even include what he calls, rather generally, "the wild disordered language of the natural heart." But the question of the distinctively human modes of life was always problematic. In Roethke's poems human life is endorsed when it manages to survive a storm, as in **"Big Wind,"** where the greenhouse—Roethke's symbol for "the whole of life"—rides the storm and sails into the calm morning. There is also the old florist, standing all night watering the roses, and the single surviving tulip with its head swaggering over the dead blooms—and then Otto.

To survive, to live through the weeds—in Roethke's world you do this by taking appropriate security measures. Property is a good bet. In **"Where Knock is Open Wide"** there is a passage that reads:

> That was before. I fell! I fell!
> The worm has moved away.
> My tears are tired.
>
> Nowhere is out. I saw the cold.
> Went to visit the wind. Where the birds die.
> How high is have?

The part we need is the last line, "How high is have?" This virtually identifies security with property. In several poems Roethke will pray for a close relation to God, and this will rate as security, but in the meantime even property in a material sense will help. And because he lived in our own society and sought order from the images of his chaos, security and property normally meant money. In **"The Lost Son,"** for instance, there is this:

> Good-bye, good-bye, old stones, the time-order is
>   going,
> I have married my hands to perpetual agitation,
> I run, I run to the whistle of money.
>
>   Money money money
>   Water water water

And even if he wrote two or three poems to make fun of this, the fact remains: property and the fear of dispossession, money and the lack of it, were vivid terms in his human image. Property was money in one's purse, more reliable than most things—more reliable than reason, for instance.

In his search for a viable and live order Roethke used his mind for all it was worth, but he would not vote for reason. He did not believe that you could pit the rational powers against the weeds of circumstance and hope to win. When he spoke of reason it was invariably Stevens' "Reason's click-clack," a mechanical affair. In one poem Roethke says, "Reason? That dreary shed, that hutch for grubby schoolboys!" Indeed, reason normally appears in his poems, at least officially, as a constriction. Commenting on his poem **"In a Dark Time,"** Roethke said that it was an attempt "to break through the barriers of rational experience." The self, the daily world, reason, meant bondage; to come close to God you had to break through. These things were never the medium of one's encounter with God, always obstacles in its way. For such encounters you had to transcend reason; if you managed it, you touched that greater thing that is the "reason in madness" of *King Lear*. The good man takes the risk of darkness. If reason's click-clack is useless, there remains in man a primitive striving toward the light. Nature, seldom a friend to man, at least offers him a few saving analogies, one being that of darkness and light. Much of this is given in the last stanzas of **"Unfold! Unfold!"**:

> Sing, sing, you symbols! All simple creatures,
> All small shapes, willow-shy,
> In the obscure haze, sing!
>
> A light song comes from the leaves.
> A slow sigh says yes. And light sighs;
> A low voice, summer-sad.
> Is it you, cold father? Father,
> For whom the minnows sang?
>
>   A house for wisdom; a field for revelation.
>   Speak to the stones, and the stars answer.
>   At first the visible obscures:
>   Go where light is.

To go where light is: the object is self-possession, sometimes featured as a relation to the world:

> I lose and find myself in the long water;
> I am gathered together once more;
> I embrace the world.

To be one's own man, to come upon "the true ease of myself," to possess oneself so fluently as to say, "Being, not doing, is my first joy"—these are definitive joys when "the light cries out, and I am there to hear." If it requires "the blast of dynamite" to effect such movements, well and good. At any cost Roethke must reach the finality in which, as he says in **"Meditation at Oyster River,"** "the flesh takes on the pure poise of the spirit." (This is his version of Yeats' "Unity of Being.") Hence he admires the tendrils that do not need eyes to seek, the furred caterpillar that crawls down a string, anything that causes movement, gives release, breaks up constriction. In the natural world there is growth, the flow of water, the straining of buds toward the light. And in the poet's craft these move in harmony with the vivid cadence, fluency, Yeats' "tact of words," the leaping rhythm.

For the rest, Roethke's symbolism is common enough. The life-enhancing images are rain, rivers, flowers, seed, grain, birds, fish, veins. The danger signals are wind, storm, darkness, drought, shadow. And the great event is growth, in full light. **"The Shape of the Fire"** ends:

> To have the whole air!
> The light, the full sun
> Coming down on the flowerheads,
> The tendrils turning slowly,
> A slow snail-lifting, liquescent;
> To be by the rose
> Rising slowly out of its bed,
> Still as a child in its first loneliness;
> To see cyclamen veins become clearer in early
>   sunlight,
> And mist lifting out of the brown cattails;
> To stare into the after-light, the glitter left on the
>   lake's surface,
> When the sun has fallen behind a wooded island;
> To follow the drops sliding from a lifted oar,
> Held up, while the rower breathes, and the small
>   boat drifts quietly shoreward;
> To know that light falls and fills, often without our
>   knowing,
> As an opaque vase fills to the brim from a quick
>   pouring,
> Fills and trembles at the edge yet does not flow
>   over,
> Still holding and feeding the stem of the contained
>   flower.

The flower, contained, securely held in a vase filled with water and light—with this image we are close to the core of Roethke's poetry, where all the analogies run together. The only missing element is what he often called "song," the ultimate in communication, and for that we need another poem, another occasion. One of his last poems, a love poem, ends:

> We met to leave again
> The time we broke from time;
> A cold air brought its rain,
> The singing of a stem.
> She sang a final song;
> Light listened when she sang.

If light listens, if light attends upon a human event, then the event is final. Kenneth Burke has pointed out that Roethke tends to link things, whenever there is a choice, by means of a word in the general vocabulary of communication. We need only add this, that when the relation is as close as a relation can be, the participants "sing,"

and there is singing everywhere, singing and listening. "The light cries out, and I am there to hear."

Pushed to their conclusion, or followed to their source, these analogies would run straight to the idea of God, or rather to the image of God. And taking such stock in the symbolism of creation and light, Roethke could hardly have avoided this dimension. Nor did he. One of his last and greatest poems is called **"The Marrow"**:

> The wind from off the sea says nothing new.
> The mist above me sings with its small flies.
> From a burnt pine the sharp speech of a crow
> Tells me my drinking breeds a will to die.
> What's the worst portion in this mortal life?
> A pensive mistress, and a yelping wife.
>
> One white face shimmers brighter than the sun
> When contemplation dazzles all I see;
> One look too close can make my soul away.
> Brooding on God, I may become a man.
> Pain wanders through my bones like a lost fire;
> What burns me now? Desire, desire, desire.
> Godhead above my God, are you there still?
> To sleep is all my life. In sleep's half-death,
> My body alters, altering the soul
> That once could melt the dark with its small breath.
> Lord, hear me out, and hear me out this day:
> From me to Thee's a long and terrible way.
>
> I was flung back from suffering and love
> When light divided on a storm-tossed tree;
> Yea, I have slain my will, and still I live;
> I would be near; I shut my eyes to see;
> I bleed my bones, their marrow to bestow
> Upon that God who knows what I would know.

The first stanza is all alienation—from nature and man and the self. The second is preparation for prayer, a relation with God as the light of light, source of the sun. The third is the prayer itself to the ground of all beseeching. In the fourth and last stanza the loss of selfhood is associated with the breakup of light on a storm-tossed tree, the emaciation of the human will; and then the last gesture—the voiding of the self, restitution, atonement (a characteristic sequence in late Roethke).

From the poems I have quoted, it might seem that Roethke was concerned with only one thing—himself. And this is true. But in his case it does not mean what it usually does. It does not mean that he is thrilled by his own emotions or that he spends much time in front of his mirror. The saving grace in Roethke, as in Whitman, is the assumption that he is a representative instance, no more if no less. When Roethke searches for value and meaning he assumes that this is interesting insofar as it is representative and not at all interesting when it ceases to be so. This is the source of Roethke's delicacy, as of Whitman's. When he says, in **"I Need, I Need," "The Trouble is with No and Yes,"** or when he says, in **"The Pure Fury," "Great Boehme rooted all in Yes and No,"** he advances this choice as a universal predicament rather than a proof of his own tender conscience. Again, in **"The Waking"** and other poems of similar intent, when he says, "I learn by going where I have to go," he is not claiming this as a uniquely sensitive perception; the line points to areas of feeling important because universal. And when he says, "Light takes the Tree; but who can tell us how?" the question is given with notable modesty, although indeed Roethke could have staked a higher claim for it, since it is the basis of several of his own religious poems. The motto for this delicacy in Roethke is a line from **"The Sententious Man"**: "Each one's himself, yet each one's everyone." And there is the **"Fourth Meditation"** to prove that Roethke was never really in danger of solipsism.

With these qualifications, then, it is permissible to say that he was his own theme and to consider what this means in the poems—with this point in mind, however, that Whitman's equations were not available to Roethke. Roethke was not content to think of the self as the sum of its contents, even if he had Yeats to tell him that a mind is as rich as the images it contains. He would try to accumulate property, but only because he thought of property as a protective dike; behind the dike, one could live. But he never thought of this as having anything to do with the "nature" of the self. The self was problematic, but not a problem in addition. In one of his last and most beautiful poems, **"In a Dark Time,"** he said:

> A man goes far to find out what he is—
> Death of the self in a long, tearless night,
> All natural shapes blazing unnatural light.
>
> Dark, dark my light, and darker my desire.
> My soul, like some heat-maddened summer fly,
> Keeps buzzing at the sill. Which I is *I*?

That is still the question. In the early poems Roethke held to the common romantic idea of "the opposing self," the self defined by its grappling with the weeds of circumstance; hence, as Hopkins said, "Long Live the Weeds." Much later, Roethke was to consider this more strictly, notably in a poem like **"The Exorcism,"** where he asks in a beguiling parenthesis, "(Father of flowers, who / Dares face the thing he is?)" And this question is joined to several bacterial images of man partaking uneasily of several worlds, beasts, serpents, the heron and the wren. In **"Weed Puller"** man is down in a fetor of weeds, "Crawling on all fours, / Alive, in a slippery grave."

Many of the middle poems feature a declared loss of self, often given as division, absence. In **"Where Knock is Open Wide"** Roethke says:

> I'm somebody else now.
> Don't tell my hands.
> Have I come to always? Not yet.
> One father is enough.
>
> Maybe God has a house.
> But not here.

There is a similar feeling in **"Sensibility! O La!"** and in **"The Shimmer of Evil"** perhaps the most explicit of all versions is, quite simply, "And I was only I"—which leads almost predictably but nonetheless beautifully to "There was no light; there was no light at all." The later poems tend to reflect upon the nature of the self by listing its demands; behind the love poems there is the assertion that "we live beyond / Our outer skin" even when the body sways to music. And much of this feeling culminates in the lovely **"Fourth Meditation,"** which begins with many intuitions of sensibility and goes on to this:

> But a time comes when the vague life of the mouth
>   no longer suffices;
> The dead make more impossible demands from their
>   silence;
> The soul stands, lonely in its choice,
> Waiting, itself a slow thing,
> In the changing body.
>
> The river moves, wrinkled by midges,
> A light wind stirs in the pine needles.
> The shape of a lark rises from a stone;
> But there is no song.

This is a later version of the predicament, loss of self, which cries through the middle poems. In **"The Lost Son"** he says:

> Snail, snail, glister me forward,
> Bird, soft-sigh me home.
> Worm, be with me.
> This is my hard time.

And a few lines later we read: "Voice, come out of the silence. / Say something." But there is no song in that "kingdom of bang and blab." In Roethke's poems song is proof that infinity clings to the finite. In **"Old Lady's Winter Words"** he says, "My dust longs for the invisible." What he wants is given in phrase, image, and rhythm: "the gradual embrace / of lichen around stones"; "Deep roots"; and, quite directly:

> Where is the knowledge that
> Could bring me to my God?

The only knowledge is reason in madness.

Theodore Roethke was a slow starter in poetry. He survived and grew and developed without attaching himself to schools or groups. He was never a boy wonder; he was never fashionable as the Beat poets were fashionable; most of the currents of easy feeling left him untouched, unmoved. He never set up shop as a left-wing poet or a right-wing poet or a Catholic poet or a New England poet or a Southern poet or a California poet. He never claimed privilege in any region of feeling. This was probably as good for his poetry as it was bad for his fame. He made his way by slow movements, nudgings of growth, like his own plants and flowers. But he grew, and his poems got better all the time—so much so, that his last poems were his greatest achievements, marvelously rich and humane.

Along the way he was helped by friends, often poets like Louise Bogan and Marianne Moore, but this is another story, not mine to tell. He was, however, helped also by other writers, earlier poets, and some of this story may be told, and the telling should disclose something of the poetry. Clearly, he was a careful, scrupulous poet. There are lines and phrases here and there that show that he was prone to infection, picking up things from lesser poets, like Dylan Thomas, and keeping them beyond the call of prudence. But the poets who really engaged him were those who offered him a challenge, a mode of feeling, perhaps, that he himself might not possess, or possessed without knowing that he did. The Elizabethan song-poets, and especially John Donne, challenged him in this way, and his own love poems reflect not only their own feeling but the strenuous competition of the Elizabethan masters. And then there were poets like Davies and Smart who disclosed certain modes of feeling and belief that were not so deeply a personal challenge but a measure of the time in which we live. And there were the great modern masters whom he could hardly have avoided hearing. He learned a lot from T. S. Eliot—mainly, I think, how to be expressive while holding most of his ammunition in reserve. And this often comes through the verse as a cadence, as in this passage from **"I'm Here"**:

> At the stream's edge, trailing a vague finger;
> Flesh-awkward, half-alive,
> Fearful of high places, in love with horses;
> In love with stuffs, silks,
> Rubbing my nose in the wool of blankets;
> Bemused; pleased to be;
> Mindful of cries,
> The meaningful whisper,
> The wren, the catbird.

Consider the rhetoric of the short phrase, at once giving and taking; Eliot is a great master in these discriminations. Think of this passage in "East Coker":

> In the middle, not only in the middle of the way
> But all the way, in a dark wood, in a bramble,
> On the edge of a grimpen, where is no secure
>   foothold,
> And menaced by monsters, fancy lights,
> Risking enchantment.

Other cadences Roethke got from other poets—from Hopkins, notably, especially from "The Wreck of the Deutschland," which Roethke uses in the poem about the greenhouse in a storm, **"Big Wind"**:

> But she rode it out,
> That old rose-house,
> She hove into the teeth of it,
> The core and pith of that ugly storm . . .

From Joyce Roethke learned one kind of language for the primitive, the rudimentary, the aboriginal, especially the Joyce of the *Portrait of the Artist as a Young Man,* bearing hard on the first chapter; and *Finnegans Wake* showed him one way of dealing with the unconscious. And there

is Wallace Stevens. Roethke disapproved of Stevens' procedures in argumentative theory, but in fact he learned some fundamental lessons from Stevens. When he says, "I prefer the still joy," he is Stevens' pupil, conning a lesson he could well have done without. And I think he found in Stevens a justification of, if not an incitement to, his own propensity for the "pure moment." In one of his later poems he says, "O to be delivered from the rational into the realm of pure song." And if pure song is pure expression or pure communication, it is also close to Stevens' "hum of thoughts evaded in the mind." Stevens seems to me to be behind those poems in which Roethke longs for essence, for an essential "purity," or finds it in a still moment. He records it in a passage like this, for instance, from the **"First Meditation"**:

> There are still times, morning and evening:
> The cerulean, high in the elm,
> Thin and insistent as a cicada,
> And the far phoebe, singing,
> The long plaintive notes floating down,
> Drifting through leaves, oak and maple,
> Or the whippoorwill, along the smoky ridges,
> A single bird calling and calling;
> A fume reminds me, drifting across wet gravel;
> A cold wind comes over stones;
> A flame, intense, visible,
> Plays over the dry pods,
> Runs fitfully along the stubble,
> Moves over the field,
> Without burning.
>   In such times, lacking a god,
>   I am still happy.

And Stevens is behind those poems in which Roethke presents the "single man" who contains everything:

> His spirit moves like monumental wind
> That gentles on a sunny blue plateau.
> He is the end of things, the final man.

When Whitman comes into the later poems, such as **"Journey to the Interior,"** he shows Roethke how to deal with natural forms without hurting them, so that "the spirit of wrath becomes the spirit of blessing"; or how to give one thing after another without lining them up in symbolist rivalry, so that he can say "Beautiful my desire, and the place of my desire"; or how to preserve one's own integrity even when beset by "the terrible hunger for objects." But Whitman was a late consultant to Roethke. Much earlier, and toward the end of his poetic life, he attended upon Yeats' poems and contracted debts handsomely acknowledged in the **"In Memoriam"** and again in **"The Dance."** To Roethke—or so it seems from the poems—Yeats stood for the imperious note, concentration, magnificent rhetoric clashing against the bare notation, the dramatic play of self and soul.

> What's madness but nobility of soul
> At odds with circumstance? The day's on fire!
> I know the purity of pure despair,
> My shadow pinned against a sweating wall.

That place among the rocks—is it a cave,
Or winding path? The edge is what I have.

It peters out somewhat. Yeats would not have praised the last line. But the rest is very much in Yeats's shadow, particularly the Yeats of "Coole Park and Ballylee, 1931." The dramatic occasion; the landscape, moralized with a large showing; the poet, finding correspondences and emblems in herons, wrens, swans; nature with her tragic buskin on—these are the Yeatsian gestures. And, to take them a little further, Roethke knows that if he proposes to learn a high rhetoric he must do it in earnest. So he begins with the magisterially rhetorical question, then the short declaration, not yet intimate, "The day's on fire!" and only then the despair. And even now it is given as knowledge rather than romantic exposure, so that even the shadow, the other self, is presented as an object of contemplation before the poet acknowledges the feeling as his own in "a sweating wall."

One of the odd things in this list of relationships, however, is that it is quite possible to think of Roethke as one of the best modern poets without troubling about the fact that he was, after all, an American poet. When reading Stevens or Frost or Williams or Robert Lowell we are constantly aware that we are reading American poets; but this is not an insistent element in Roethke. Indeed, it is quite clear that he bears no special relation to either of the dominant traditions in American poetry—New England and the South. Temperamentally he is not too far away from such writers as Hawthorne, Melville, or James. Like them, in his quite different way, he was concerned with the wounded conscience, the private hazard. But while it is obviously proper in some sense to relate the poems of Robert Lowell to this tradition, it has little bearing on Roethke's work. And the tradition of the South can be ruled out. This suggests that the discussion of American literature in terms of these two traditions may by now have lost much of its force. To think of the New England tradition as scholastic, autocratic, and logical, and the Southern tradition as humanistic, Ciceronian, grammatical, and rhetorical is fine as far as it goes, but its relevance clearly fades in regard to poets like Roethke. This may well be the point to emphasize, that Roethke and many of the poets of his generation took their food wherever they could find it. Yeats could well be more useful to them than, say, Hawthorne, because they saw their problems as being human, universal, in the first instance, and American problems only by application and inference. Roethke committed himself to his own life. He thought of it as a human event of some representative interest. And he set himself to work toward lucidity and order without turning himself into a case study entitled "The Still Complex Fate of Being an American." This is one aspect of Roethke's delicacy. Contemporary American poets, for the most part, are not going his way; they insist upon their complex fate and would not live without it. But Roethke's way of being an American is an eminently respectable way, and part of his achievement is that he makes it available to others.

"The Far Field" is a distinguished example of this delicacy. It has four unequal sections. The first is a dream of journeys, journeys without maps, featuring imprisonment, attenuation of being, the self "flying like a bat deep into a narrowing tunnel" until there is nothing but darkness. It is life in a minor key, diminished thirds of being. The second stanza translates these into major terms, images of force, aggression, suffering, death, dead rats eaten by rain and ground beetles. But the poet, meditating upon these images, thinks of other images, of life, movement, freedom, everything he means by "song." And these natural configurations lead to thoughts of life as cycle, evolution and return, proliferations of being, the whole process of life, which the poet calls "inifinity"; what Wallace Stevens in "The Bouquet" calls "the infinite of the actual perceived, / A freedom revealed, a realization touched, / The real made more acute by an unreal." In the third section the poet feels a corresponding change in himself, a moving forward, a quickening, and as he commits himself to earth and air he says, "I have come to a still, but not a deep center." Naturally it feels like a loss, another diminution of being, even if the sense of life-ordained process is strong. And this feeling leads straight into the fourth and last section:

> The lost self changes,
> Turning toward the sea,
> A sea-shape turning around,—
> An old man with his feet before the fire,
> In robes of green, in garments of adieu.
>
> A man faced with his own immensity
> Wakes all the waves, all their loose wandering fire.
> The murmur of the absolute, the why
> Of being born fails on his naked ears.
> His spirit moves like monumental wind
> That gentles on a sunny blue plateau.
> He is the end of things, the final man.
>
> All finite things reveal infinitude:
> The mountain with its singular bright shade
> Like the blue shine on freshly frozen snow,
> The after-light upon ice-burdened pines;
> Odor of basswood on a mountain-slope,
> A scent beloved of bees;
> Silence of water above a sunken tree:
> The pure serene of memory in one man,—
> A ripple widening from a single stone
> Winding around the waters of the world.

Roethke says: "The end of things, the final man"; Stevens asserts in **"The Auroras of Autumn"**:

> There is nothing until in a single man contained,
> Nothing until this named thing nameless is
> And is destroyed. He opens the door of his house
> On flames. The scholar of one candle sees
> An Arctic effulgence flaring on the frame
> Of everything he is. And he feels afraid.

The difference is that Stevens identifies the man with his imagination, and his imagination with his vision—and insists upon doing so. And the imagination feeds upon as much reality as it can "see" and values only that; what it can't see won't hurt or help it. The scholar has only this one candle. Roethke's man is not a scholar at all, or if he is, he is an amateur, perhaps a mere teacher. His imagination is partly his memory, which offers hospitality to sights, sounds, and smells, and partly his conscience, and partly his feeling for modes of being that he cannot command, directions that he cannot chart. Hence his poems are the cries of their occasions, but rarely cries of triumph. This is what makes his later poems the noble things they are, stretchings of the spirit without fantasia or panache. "Which is the way?" they ask, and if they include God in their reply they do so with due deference, knowing that one can be "too glib about eternal things," too much "an intimate of air and all its songs."

Another way of putting it is that the poems, especially the middle poems, are cries of their occasions, sudden, isolated cries. The later poems turn cries into prayers, praying for a world order, a possible world harmony of which the cries are part, like voices in polyphony. The self in exposure is monotone; a sustaining society is polyphony; God is the Great Composer. The poet's ideal is the part song, music for several instruments, what the Elizabethans called "broken music." In **"In Evening Air"** Roethke says, "I'll make a broken music, or I'll die." In such poems as **"The Marrow"** and **"In a Dark Time"** he made a broken music at once personal and—in Stevens' sense—noble. And then, alas, he died.

Theodore Roethke, like Yeats, was a romantic poet, but he was also a confessional poet in the very strictest sense of that term. His life, his fears, his dreams—these are the stuff of his poetry; consequently, much critical attention has been devoted to the biographical sources for his imagery. . . .

—*Julie M. Johnson, in* Massachusetts Studies in English, *Vol. IX, No. 1, 1983*.

Clive James (essay date 1968)

SOURCE: "On Theodore Roethke's *Collected Poems,*" in *First Reactions: Critical Essays 1968-79,* Alfred A. Knopf, 1980, pp. 59-62.

[*James is an Australian-born English critic, poet, and novelist who has written extensively about British culture and national politics but is perhaps best known for his commentaries on television and broadcast programming. Joseph Epstein, of* The New York Times Book Review, *has judged James "one of the brightest figures in contemporary English intellectual journalism" and the humourous and satirical qualities of his writing — including his poetry—have attracted many readers. In the following*

review, which was originally published in 1968, he states that a minority of Roethke's poems are highly original and accomplished, though most are derivative.]

When Theodore Roethke died five years ago, his obituaries, very sympathetically written, tended to reveal by implication that the men who wrote them had doubts about the purity and weight of his achievement in poetry. Now that his collected poems have come out, the reviews, on this side of the water at least, strike the attentive reader as the same obituaries rewritten. Roethke was one of those men for whom poetic significance is claimed not only on the level of creativity but also on the level of being: if it is objected that the poems do not seem very individual, the objection can be headed off by saying that the man was a poet apart from his poems, embodying all the problems of writing poetry "in our time." It is a shaky way to argue, and praise degenerates quickly to a kind of complicity when what is being praised is really only a man's ability to hold up against the pressures of his career. Criticism is not about careers.

From the small amount of information which has been let out publicly, and the large amount which circulates privately, it seems probable that Roethke had a difficult life, the difficulties being mainly of a psychic kind that intellectuals find it easy to identify with and perhaps understand too quickly. Roethke earned his bread by teaching in colleges and was rarely without a job in one. It is true that combining the creative and the academic lives sets up pressures, but really these pressures have been exaggerated, to the point where one would think that teaching a course in freshman English were as perilous to the creative faculties as sucking up to titled nobodies, running errands for Roman governors, cutting purses, grinding lenses or getting shot at. If Roethke was in mental trouble, this should be either brought out into the open and diagnosed as well as it can be or else abandoned as a point: it is impermissible to murmur vaguely about the problems of being a poet in our time. Being a poet has always been a problem. If the point is kept up, the uninformed, unprejudiced reader will begin to wonder if perhaps Roethke lacked steel. The widening scope and increasing hospitality of academic life in this century, particularly in the United States, has lured many people into creativity who really have small business with it, since they need too much recognition and too many meals. Plainly Roethke was several cuts above this, but the words now being written in his praise are doing much to reduce him to it.

[*Collected Poems*] is an important document in showing that originality is not a requirement in good poetry—merely a description of it. All the longer poems in the volume and most of the short ones are ruined by Roethke's inability to disguise his influences. In the few short poems where he succeeded in shutting them out, he achieved a firm, though blurred, originality of utterance: the real Roethke collection, when it appears, will be a ruthlessly chosen and quite slim volume some two hundred pages shorter than the one we now have, but it will stand a good chance of lasting, since its voice will be unique. In this respect, history is very kind: the poet may write only a few good poems in a thousand negligible ones, but those few poems, if they are picked out and properly stored, will be remembered as characteristic. The essential scholarly task with Roethke is to make this selection and defend it. It will need to be done by a first-rate man capable of seeing that the real Roethke wrote very seldom.

Of his first book, *Open House* (1941), a few poems which are not too much reminiscent of Frost will perhaps last. Poems like **"Lull"** (marked "November, 1939") have little chance.

> Intricate phobias grow
> From each malignant wish
> To spoil collective life.

It is not assimilating tradition to so take over the rhythms of poetry recently written by another man—in this case Auden. It is not even constructive plagiarism, just helpless mimicry. To a greater or lesser degree, from one model to the next, Auden, Dylan Thomas, Yeats and Eliot, Roethke displayed throughout his creative life a desparate unsureness of his own gift. In his second book, *The Lost Son,* published in 1948, the influence of Eliot, an influence which dogged him to the end, shows its first signs with savage clarity.

> Where's the eye?
> The eye's in the sty.
> The ear's not here
> Beneath the hair.

There are no eyes here, in this valley of dying stars. In his five-part poem **"The Shape of the Fire"** he shows that he has been reading *Four Quartets*, giving the game away by his trick—again characteristic—of reproducing his subject poet's most marked syntactical effects.

> To see cyclamen veins become clearer in early
>   sunlight,
> And mist lifting out of the brown cat-tails;
> To stare into the after-light, the glitter left on the
>   lake's surface,
> When the sun has fallen behind a wooded island;
> To follow the drops sliding from a lifted our,
> Held up, while the rower breathes, and the small
>   boat drifts quietly shoreward;

The content of this passage shows the pin-point specificity of the references to nature which are everywhere in Roethke's poetry. But in nearly all cases it amounts to nature for the sake of nature: the general context meant to give all this detail spiritual force usually has an air of being thought up, and is too often just borrowed. In the volume *Praise to the End!,* which came out in 1951, a certain curly-haired Welsh voice rings loud and clear. It is easy to smile at this, but it should be remembered that a poet who can lapse into such mimicry is in the very worst kind of trouble.

> Once I fished from the banks, leaf-light and happy:
> On the rocks south of quiet, in the close regions of
>   kissing,

> I romped, lithe as a child, down the summery
>   streets of my veins.

In the next volume, *The Waking* (1953), his drive towards introspective significance—and a drive towards is not necessarily the same thing as possessing—tempts him into borrowing those effects of Eliot's which would be close to self-parody if it were not for the solidly intricate structuring of their context.

> I have listened close
> For the thin sound in the windy chimney,
> The fall of the last ash
> From the dying ember.

There it stands, like a stolen car hastily resprayed and dangerously retaining its original number-plates. His fascination with Yeats begins in this volume—

> Though everything's astonishment at last,

—and it, too, continues to the end. But whereas with Yeats his borrowings were mainly confined to syntactical sequences, with Eliot he took the disastrous step of appropriating major symbolism, symbolism which Eliot had himself appropriated from other centuries, other languages and other cultures. The results are distressingly weak, assertively unconvincing, and would serve by themselves to demonstrate that a talent which has not learnt how to forget is bound to fragment.

> I remember a stone breaking the edifying current,
> Neither white nor red, in the dead middle way,
> Where impulse no longer dictates, nor the darkening
>   shadow,
> A vulnerable place,
> Surrounded by sand, broken shells, the wreckage of
>   water.

Roethke's good poems are mostly love poems, and of those, most are to be found in the two volumes of 1958 and 1964, *Words for the Wind* and *The Far Field*. Some of his children's poems from *I Am! Says the Lamb* are also included, and there is a section of previously uncollected poems at the very end of the book including a healthy thunderbolt of loathing aimed at critics. Roethke achieved recognition late but when it came the critics treated him pretty well. Now that his troubled life is over, it is essential that critics who care for what is good in his work should condemn the rest before the whole lot disappears under an avalanche of kindly meant, but effectively cruel, interpretative scholarship.

Seamus Heaney (essay date 1968)

SOURCE: "Canticle to the Earth: Theodore Roethke," in *Preoccupations: Selected Prose 1968-1978,* Farrar, Straus, Giroux, 1980, pp. 190-94.

[Heaney is widely considered Ireland's most accomplished contemporary poet and has often been called the greatest

Irish poet since William Butler Yeats. In the following essay, which was first published in 1968, Heaney praises Roethke for adhering to his own instincts as a poet and characterizes his poetry at various stages in his career.]

A couple of years ago, an American poet told me that he and his generation had rejected irony and artfulness, and were trying to write poems that would not yield much to the investigations of the practical criticism seminar. And another poet present agreed, yes, he was now looking at English poetry to decide which areas seemed most in need of renovation, and then he was going to provide experiments that would enliven these sluggish, provincial backwaters. As poets, both seemed to be infected with wrong habits of mind. They had imbibed attitudes into their writing life which properly belong to the lecturer and the anthologist: a concern with generations, with shifting fashions of style, a belief that their role was complementary and responsible to a demonstrable literary situation. For although at least one spirit of the age will probably be discernible in a poet's work, he should not turn his brain into a butterfly net in pursuit of it.

An awareness of his own poetic process, and a trust in the possibility of his poetry, that is what a poet should attempt to preserve; and whatever else Theodore Roethke may have lacked, he did possess and nourish this faith in his own creative instincts. His current flies continuously:

> Water's my will and my way,
> And the spirit runs, intermittently,
> In and out of the small waves,
> Runs with the intrepid shorebirds—
> How graceful the small before danger!

But the most remarkable thing about this watery spirit of his is that for all its motion, it never altogether finds its final bed and course. Through one half of the work, it is contained in the strict locks of rhyme and stanzaic form; through the other, it rises and recedes in open forms like floods in broad meadows.

His first book has the quiet life of an old canal. 'Vernal Sentiment' would not be an unjust title for the volume. All the conflicting elements in Roethke's make-up are toned down and contained in well-behaved couplets and quatrains. The sense of fun is coy, the sense of natural forces explicit and the sense of form a bit monotonous. It is partly a case of the young man putting a hand across his daimon's mouth, for although the first poem calls:

> My secrets cry aloud.
> I have no need for tongue.
> My heart keeps open house,
> My doors are widely swung

we have to read the whole book to believe it. Indeed the life's work is neatly bracketed by the first and last lines of [**Collected Poems**] We move from 'My secrets cry aloud' to 'With that he hitched his pants and humped away,' and between the rhetoric and the rumbustiousness the true achievement is located.

That achievement arrives from the boundaries of Roethke's experience: childhood and death are elements in which his best work lives. And love. He grew up in Michigan among his father's extensive greenhouses: 'They were to me, I realize now, both heaven and hell, a kind of tropics created in the savage climate of Michigan, where austere German-Americans turned their love of order and their terrifying efficiency into something truly beautiful. It was a universe, several worlds, which, even as a child, one worried about and struggled to keep alive.'

Growth, minute and multifarious life, became Roethke's theme. His second collection, *The Lost Son,* contained the famous greenhouse poems, a repossession of the childhood Eden. Now the free, nervous notation of natural process issues in a sense of unity with cosmic energies and in quiet intimations of order and delight. They are acts of faith made in some state of grace:

> I can hear, underground, that sucking and sobbing,
> In my veins, in my bones I feel it,—
> The small waters seeping upward,
> The tight grains parting at last.
> When sprouts break out,
> Slippery as fish,
> I quail, lean to beginnings, sheath-wet.

Such celebration, however, was prelude to disturbance and desperation. Out of Eden man takes his way, and beyond the garden life is riotous; chaos replaces correspondence, consciousness thwarts communion, the light of the world fades in the shadow of death. Until the final serenity and acceptance of all things in a dance of flux, which comes in the posthumous *The Far Field,* Roethke's work is driven in two opposite directions by his fall into manhood.

In the final poems of *The Lost Son* volume and in all the work of *Praise to the End* there is an apocalyptic straining towards unity. These are large, sectioned poems, ghosted by the rhythms of nursery rhyme. You feel that the archetypal properties are being manipulated a bit arbitrarily, that the staccato syntax is for effect rather than effective and that in general the sense of fractured relations between the man and his physical and metaphysical elements is deliberately shrouded. These poems are more like constructs for the inarticulate than raids upon it. Yet despite the occasional echo of Dylan Thomas, they retain the authentic Roethke note, the note of energy and quest:

> Everything's closer. Is this a cage?
> The chill's gone from the moon.
> Only the woods are alive.
> I can't marry the dirt.

In direct contrast to these wandering tides of the spirit, there follows a series of tightly controlled and elaborately argued meditations and love poems. After the fidgety metres and the surrealism, he begins to contain his impulses to affirmation in a rapid, iambic line which owes much to Raleigh and Sir John Davies, even though in a moment of exuberance he declares:

I take this cadence from a man named Yeats,
I take it, and I give it back again.

The poems tend to have a strict shape and lively rhythm
('the shapes a bright container can contain!') and deal
with the possibility of momentary order, harmony and illumination. Love and lyric are modes of staying the confusion and fencing off emptiness. Within the glass walls
of the poem, something of the old paradisal harmony can
be feigned:

> Dream of a woman, and a dream of death:
> The light air takes my being's breath away;
> I look on white, and it turns into gray—
> When will that creature give me back my breath?
> I live near the abyss. I hope to stay
> Until my eyes look at a brighter sun
> As the thick shade of the long night comes on.

There is a curious split in Roethke's work between the
long Whitmanesque cataloguing poem, which works towards resolution by accumulating significant and related
phenomena, and this other brisk, traditional artefact that
dances to its own familiar music. Perhaps the explanation
lies in Roethke's constant natural urge to praise, to maintain or recapture ecstasy.

The more relaxed and loaded form includes his best poems, all of which exhale something of a Franciscan love
of every living thing, and invoke the notion of a divine
unity working through them. They are canticles to the earth,
if you like, written in a line that has exchanged its 'bar-
baric yawp' for a more civil note of benediction. On the
other hand, when he is not in full possession of his emotion, when tranquillity is missing, then he employs the
artificer's resources of metre, stanza and rhyme to conduct himself and the poem towards a provisional statement. The stanzaic poems always sound as if they are
attempting something. The best Roethke, the praise poetry, always gives the impression that the lines came ripe
and easy as windfalls.

Ripeness is all in the latest work, which appeared in this
country two years after his death. In one of the poems he
mentions 'that sweet man, John Clare', and one is reminded how both poets lived near the abyss but resolved extreme experience into something infinitely gentle. In the
light of their last days, 'all's a scattering, a shining'. Their
suffering breeds something larger than masochism. Roethke reflects when his field-mouse departs for the hazard of
the fields:

> I think of the nestling fallen into the deep grass,
> The turtle gasping in the dusty rubble of the
>   highway,
> The paralytic stunned in the tub, and the water
>   rising,—
> All things innocent, hapless, forsaken.

He is outside movements and generations, and his work is
a true growth. He seems destined to grudging notice because he echoed the voices of other poets, or because

people have grown afraid of the gentle note that was his
own, but the ***Collected Poems*** are there, a true poet's testament:

> Pain wanders through my bones like a lost fire;
> What burns me now? Desire, desire, desire.

Dan Jaffe (essay date 1970)

SOURCE: "Theodore Roethke: 'In a Slow Up-Sway'," in
The Fifties: Fiction, Poetry, Drama, edited by Warren
French, Everett/Edwards, Inc., 1970, pp. 199-207.

[*In the following excerpt, Jaffe highlights Roethke's
strengths as a poet.*]

It has become a cliché of the modern poetry class to point
out how divided critical and anthological opinion had
become by the end of the 50s. The so-called academic
anthologies excluded the Beat poets; the Beat collections
excluded the academics. Roethke might well have been
included in either kind of collection, it seems to me. Perhaps that's one reason why he was not sufficiently appreciated. Both camps probably found him suspect. During
the 50s Roethke had three books: ***Praise to the End*** (1951),
The Waking, Poems 1933-1953 (1953), and ***Words for
the Wind*** (1958), the last, a collection of new and earlier
work. Poems like **"The Shape of the Fire," "Praise to
the End," "I Cry, Love! Love!" "O, Thou Opening, O"**
follow from **"The Lost Son,"** Roethke's 1948 breakthrough. This group of poems is probably the most startling. Each of these poems contains many of the same
ingredients in different proportions. The poet's tactics are
similar in each. They are highly imagistic, contain only
minimum explanation of feeling or idea. Thematically, they
generally move from terror toward hope, from fearful
questioning toward tentative affirmation. Although single
lines may fall into easily scanned metrical patterns, the
line lengths are highly irregular and no metrical norms are
established. These are poems of creatures, plants, stones,
bits of flesh, childhood touches and gestures; only rarely
do the objects or the apparatus of our technological civilization get into the poems. Time and again the poems
turn back to close approximations of nursery rhythms and
rhymes. Repeatedly there are references to the elemental,
to Mother and Father, to earth and water, to growth. They
shift from the literal to the figurative unexpectedly, often
without warning.

But such generalizations, even if they are accurately descriptive fail to provide a sense of the poems. One feels
like saying, "The hell with prosody!" The experience is
the consequence of the poet's virtuosity; the poems are
linguistic performances. Who can deny it? But these are
poems beyond admiration, beyond even the "new" criticism, fine tool that it may be. They reach directly for
experience. Somehow the smaller the area between art
and the world, the less room there is for the critic to move

around in and justify himself. Roethke doesn't leave much room. Are his images symbols or psychic actualities? Do they represent ideas or are they the direct embodiment of feelings? The professor of poetry ordinarily selects the first of these alternatives. Even the poet talking about his own work discusses what he means to symbolize. But the discussion of symbols immediately introduces an intellectualization alien to the spirit of these poems. They take one down below the mind or out beyond it.

More important than any technical or thematic observations are the drench of feelings, the corporeal itch, the agony, in the colloquial and classic sense of that word. This is a poetry of stretch rather than repression. It accomplishes what the Beats maintain they mean to accomplish. It is flying or diving rather than an instruction pamphlet or a superbly fashioned machine. Here one is more aware of the pitch of feelings than the skill of achievement. What one wonders about is how he managed himself while making it, rather than how he made it, how he faced such dares of feeling and still functioned artistically. Each of these poems seems to be a return to a tightrope stretched in a heavy wind across an enormous abyss. The old notion of aesthetic distance breaks down. We become the poet, the dramatic voice, the renewed self, amazed by suffering and survival.

These poems do not provide us touchstones of correctness; they do not call attention to the erudition or prowess of the poet. By being most himself he becomes one with basic forces the American at mid-century may easily forget. His poems somehow seem a corrective for the time in which they were written. They reply to the strangulation of the spirit threatened by Senator Joseph McCarthy and the computer collective. These are not poems of quiet, good taste. They refuse to be prim. They don't even hide in the acceptable realms of intellectual achievement, though they are without a doubt justification for philosophizing and theological discussion. Roethke has craft; he has intellectual scope. But that comes later; the first thrust is the thrust of unleashed feeling, of the insides opened out, the wiggle, push, threat of living forms rather than the safety of a shaped fortress. The poems cry, "Risk," in a time devoted to security. And so in an indirect way they have social significance, although they point outward toward what Roethke calls "the kingdom of bang and blam" at only rare moments. I don't even want to quote, not even to prove my points. A few lines out of context will probably seem more epigrammatic than intended, more brilliant tidbits than part of a rush of psychic development, more proof than bite.

> Mother me out of here. What more will the bones
>   allow:
> Will the sea give the wind suck? A toad falls into a
>   stone.
> These flowers are all fangs. Comfort me, fury.
> Wake me, witch, we'll do the dance of rotten sticks.
>   (from **"The Shape of the Fire"**)

Dust jacket for the posthumously published collection of the poems Roethke wrote in his last years. This volume won a National Book Award.

A cursory look at **"The Shape of the Fire,"** however, may provide a sense of some of the tensions Roethke brings us to. In the opening section, from which the above lines are taken, the dramatic voice cries out. His is a cry of confusion, compensation, terror; he seeks nourishment amid the elemental forces that tremble around him and make him tremble. In section two, the dramatic voice reassesses the sources of fear: the self is a "varicose horror," "A two-legged dog hunting a new horizon of howls." The images are primitive, animalistic; underneath the human clothes are swamp instincts. He is trapped by his own flesh, but is that all? Section three answers symbolically with affirmations of glisten and rose-sway. It is a kind of epiphany: a promise of progress in "the journey from flesh." Section four is faintly reminiscent of shining passages of Dylan Thomas, whom Roethke admired. Light, birds, flowers—they sing life. Section five is a joyful recapitulation of the rising of the rose, the snail, the man, toward the sources of sustenance. Even such a simplistic summary ought to make clear that these poems are essentially psychic narratives drawing a great deal of force from the archetypal metaphor of the journey. But beware of phrases like "archetypal metaphor." They have the text book ring.

What matters most here is the movement from dream to dream. And these are real dreams, couched in fact. They leave sweat and sperm on the sheets. In our culture what could be more forbidding and embarrassing? Imagine our politicos owning up to their dreams, Mr. Nixon or Mr. Agnew disclosing to the nation something of their inner lives. This is akin to Allen Ginsberg stripping at Columbia. What could be more scandalous than such revelations? Ted Roethke threatens the self-assurance of the culture; he makes the men of cool, practiced efficiency look at themselves and their circumstances: Wrenched and fleshy feelings in an unpinned universe.

But Roethke was not a single minded poet who wrote a single kind of poem. ***Words for the Wind*** illustrates the fallacy of thinking of Roethke as simply a greenhouse poet of slugs and soil. There are those who would dump all modern poetry into one basket. It's not possible to do that with even a single poet of caliber. And certainly not with one of exceptional stature.

Set against the narrative-dramatic poems of the inner life that identify Roethke as a poet of energy and exuberance are poems of clasical grace, poems like **"I Knew a Woman,"** whose form is summed up in the line, "The shapes a bright container can contain!" Roethke can soothe with a gentle villanelle like **"The Waking."** Here the substance of the wilder poems is gentled within the confines of the strict iambic line, "The lowly worm climbs up a winding stair." In poems like the **"Four for Sir John Davies"** Roethke illustrates how well he can step to familiar cadences:

> Things loll and loiter. Who condones the lost?
> This joy outleaps the dog. Who cares? Who cares?
> I gave her kisses back, and woke a ghost.
> O what lewd music crept into our ears!
> The body of the soul know how to play
> In that dark world where gods have lost their way.

It's enough to melt the heart of any old academic to note the heavy rhyme, assonance, and alliteration. One can almost bring this safely into the classroom in order to discuss traditional poetic techniques.

Here the great energy has harnessed itself to shape, transformed itself into the most expressive kind of poise, the poise of performance and the poise of potential. These poems give us control, the matter caught; they also give us, to use Roethke's metaphor, a bird singing at the center of a tree, stir and ripple choreographed by a master.

So, **"All the Earth, All the Air"** might be a text book for those concerned with the glide of vowels and the shift of consonants. Poem after poem is a virtuoso performance without being a cheap tour-de-force. The skill is the kind that doesn't obtrude. Roethke juggles only to mean, but that does not diminish our admiration for his dexterity.

The poet tries to make form a liberator; uniqueness a habit. The Beats tried to break out of the straight jacket they felt the dictates of T.S. Eliot and Ezra Pound had imposed; the academic poets sought to preserve the virtues of craft. Ted Roethke managed the balance between energy and control; that is the measure of greatness.

He is a poet of wider resources and tactics than has been appreciated. He reaches from torment to joy, from absolute fear to mystical affirmation. He can provide the touch of the brute world and a sense of the indefinable. He can be witty and passionate at once. One moment he is on his nubs in the loam, the next soaring in meditation. He can be elliptical and conversational, and he seems to have constantly polished and reassessed his equipment so that while he developed new ways of going he never lost the techniques of the earlier poems. There is a lyrical, a dramatic, a discursive, and an epigrammatic Roethke. Many of his poems come clear on at least one level immediately. Others may baffle readers for long periods. His work can be viewed as a modern Divine Comedy: he moves from the Inferno to Paradise. One can read the poems as theological and philosophical examinations, forays into the nature of the human condition, the function of suffering, the sources of evil, even the generation gap. One can consider them psychological dramatizations.

Most importantly Roethke transforms language into actualization; the poems bombard us, stroke us, shake us. No American poet has approached the subject of physical love with such love, the body with such foreboding. Children, lady editors, lovers—he has poems for them all.

Critics, anthologists, and professors who ignore Roethke do so at the risk of offending posterity. The 50s gave us a major poet whose reputation is already moving "in a slow up-sway," the appropriate motion of Roethke's poems. The new generation of readers has already found Roethke provides what it needs: a sense of self; a willingness to report on the personal, emotional life, in order to share rather than to confess; a willingness to be different, even strange. And, at the same time, a kind of connective tissue that links us all.

Richard Wilbur (essay date 1973)

SOURCE: "Poetry's Debt to Poetry," in *The Hudson Review,* Vol. XXVI, No. 2, Summer, 1973, pp. 273-94.

[*Wilbur is an American poet and critic. Respected for the craftsmanship and elegance of his verse, he employs formal poetic structures and smoothly flowing language as a response to disorder and chaos in modern life. In the following excerpt, Wilbur comments on Roethke's emulation of other poets.*]

It is fatal for a writer to have one hero only; submitting to a single model, admiring but one syntax and lexicon, means that you will say what you don't mean, and that you will never find the right words for what you do mean. A commanding imagination, as many have said before me, steals not from one writer but selectively from all writers, taking whatever will help in the articulation of its own sense of things.

In this connection, the most precarious of the fine poets of our century was Theodore Roethke. The poems of his first book, **Open House**, are noticeably affected by certain woman poets whose work he loved—Louise Bogan, Elinor Wylie, Léonie Adams. Roethke was well aware of the fact, and in his essay "How to Write Like Somebody Else," he accounted for the fact in a remarkable way, saying that his early work had been touched by a compulsion to praise; out of his admiration for Léonie Adams, he said, he had felt driven "to create something that would honor her in her own terms." In the shorter poems of Roethke's next period, especially the wonderful greenhouse pieces, I find no moments of celebratory imitation, and the voice seems entirely the poet's own; the long poems of that time, such as **"The Shape of the Fire,"** have, as Roethke put it, certain "ancestors"—among them Mother Goose, the songs and rants in Elizabethan and Jacobean plays, Thomas Traherne, and (I should think) James Joyce and the psychology of Jung. But whatever means he may have borrowed for these poems of psychic struggle, of regression and rebirth, everything had been mastered and turned to his own fresh purposes. If the poems sometimes fail through a too unmediated subjectivity, they are nevertheless powerfully original. And therefore it is a shock to find Roethke, in the next phase of his work, succumbing frequently and totally to the style of William Butler Yeats, so much so that in one poem he must declare with a certain bravado,

> I take this cadence from a man named Yeats;
> I take it, and I give it back again. . . .

The candor is disarming, but still one feels like answering, *Why?* When Roethke writes in the voice of Yeats, the results are often felicitous, as in the stunning poem from which I have just quoted, and yet one is disquieted, as by those free translations in which Robert Lowell makes Rilke sound like Lowell, and provides him with additional stanzas. One thinks, "This is good, but what is it?" In cases of this kind it is impossible not to be nagged by the question of authenticity, the question of who, after all, is talking.

Delmore Schwartz, writing in 1959, asked himself why an exceptional poet, at the height of his powers, should take to imitating Yeats, and concluded that Roethke's chief reason was probably "to guard against the deadly habit of self-imitation." I think that may have been part of the story. I also think—indeed, I know—that his marriage in the early 1950's gave Roethke a new entrée to life calling for a new poetic vein, a vein which he could not at once invent. There are poets for whom the discovery of style is easy, because their purchase on the world is rational and social, and therefore readily expressed in some version of urbane discourse. But Roethke was not a rational, social poet; the great spur of his poetry was a romantic longing to escape the bounds of self, to escape the rational mind and its estranging formulations, and to become at one with the whole of life through communion and vision. A poetry of the subverbal and the supra-verbal, which pursues the wordless through the wordless, doesn't find its true voice, or modify that voice, without some floundering and casting-about.

One thing which moves a poet to translate from other tongues, as I know from my own experience, is the urge to broaden his utterance through imposture, to say things which he is not yet able to say in his own person. That sounds disgraceful, but it needn't be. You can't translate, after all, without having an affinity for the original. If you bring over the ghazals of Saadi into English, as one of my students is doing, then you have done three things: you have improved the English reader's access to the genius of Persia, you have provided English poetry with some new Persian tricks, and you have rendered more articulate that part of you which resembles Saadi. It was something like this last result, I think, which came of Roethke's impersonation of Yeats. What was it that Yeats could offer Roethke? Technically, he offered a muscular and often end-stopped pentameter line which Roethke was equipped to exploit—for Roethke was, above all, a poet of the striking line. Yeats offered also a ruggedly vatic style in which such words as "soul" could sound convincing and modern, in which one could get away with talking of visions, of "Heaven blazing into the head," and of that beatitude called "unity of being," wherein self and world miraculously agree. Furthermore, and much to Roethke's purpose, Yeats offered a physical mysticism of the dancing body and of the marriage-bed. Many of Roethke's Yeatsian poems succeed; some fail, as Yeats himself could fail, through the blustering rhetorical question, the wilful transport, the mantic resolution which does not ring true. In any case, Roethke's impersonation of Yeats seems to me to have kept him talking; to have limbered, emboldened and extended him, so that he became capable of those last poems which are better than ever and so much more his own.

Am I right about all that? Heaven knows. Let us agree that such a case is infinitely interesting and problematical. . . .

Jenijoy La Belle (essay date 1975)

SOURCE: "Martyr to a Motion Not His Own: Theodore Roethke's *Love Poems*," in *Ball State University Forum*, Vol. 16, No. 2, Spring, 1975, pp. 71-5.

[*In the following essay, La Belle asserts that Roethke's love poems place him in the tradition of John Donne, Andrew Marvell, and Dante Alighieri, among others.*]

For Theodore Roethke writing poetry was like making love: it was an activity requiring a partner. All of his poems are literary love children, the issue of a union between Roethke's own vision and the work of other poets whom he admired. This way of creating was not mere imitation. It was an attempt to connect with another sensibility, to merge, finally to "see and suffer [himself] in another being, at last."

Roethke's early spiritual romances did not produce "real" poems, only premature little verses scarcely able to stand on their own iambic feet. He began by falling in love with some of the better poetesses—Emily Dickinson, Elinor Wylie, Léonie Adams, and Louise Bogan. But the resulting poems seldom moved beyond mimicry to assimilation. During this period, for instance, he wrote a poem entitled **"The Buds Now Stretch"** and then proceeded to tell Léonie Adams it was one of the finest poems she had ever written. Miss Adams was not amused. Nor have most readers found the poem to be one of Roethke's better efforts. But Roethke later wrote that he hated "to abandon" that poem:

> I feel it's something Miss Adams and I have created. . . . I loved her so much, her poetry, that I just *had* to become, for a brief moment, a part of her world. For it *is* her world, and I had filled myself with it, And I *had* to create something that would honor her in her own terms.

Roethke continued throughout his career to pay homage to poets in their own terms, and eventually he created poems which were successful combinations of his individual talent and his sense of a tradition. Love became for Roethke one of his structural metaphors for this relationship between himself and his poetic partners, and in turn the writing of poetry became a metaphor for the act of love.

In his major sequence of love poems, which appeared in *Words for the Wind* (1958), Roethke's response to the woman he loves is simultaneously a response to the poets he loves. The presence to his naked lover transforms Roethke into that very poet whose sensibility suggests the proper response to the woman: "I am my father's son, I am John Donne / Whenever I see her with nothing on" (**"The Swan,"** *Collected Poems*). Donne exhorts in one of his poems, "Study me then, you who shall lovers bee at the next world." Few of his followers have studied him as intently as Roethke who learned from Donne a pattern for his love. Roethke's lines, however, leave the causal relationships between lover and poet ambiguous. Does the naked lover call forth emotions in Roethke's mind which he then associates with Donne, or does Donne's poetry conjure up the image of the woman? These images in **"The Swan"** embody that always complex relationship between the poet's personal experiences and his literary influences.

In the first poem of his sequence Roethke adopts both the title and the theory of one of Donne's love elegies. Louis L. Martz in *The Meditative Poem* suggests that Donne's "Elegy X," usually called "The Dreame," may "owe something to St. Augustine's theory that the soul always knows the 'image' of its beloved before meeting the beloved object." Roethke's **"The Dream"** begins, "I met her as a blossom on a stem / Before she ever breathed." With the movement from the mind, to sight, to an image of fire, the next few lines of Roethke's poem recall William Drummond of Hawthornden's sequence of similar images—also to describe the speaker's foreknowledge of the beloved:

> My Minde mee told that in some other Place
> It elsewhere saw the Idea of that Face,
> And lov'd a Love of heavenly pure Delight.
> No Wonder now I feele so faire a Flame,
> Sith I Her lov'd ere on this Earth she
>   came.
>
> (Drummond)

> The mind remembers from a deeper sleep:
> Eye learned from eye, cold lip from sensual lip.
> My dream divided on a point of fire.
>
> (Roethke)

Roethke, like Drummond, moves from self (mind) to other (fire), from inner to outer, through the organ of perception. The eye is also the portal through which love first enters man's soul in the traditions of neoplatonic and courtly love. The borrowings in any one of Roethke's love poems are seldom limited to a single poet: the doctrine of **"The Dream"** is from Donne and Drummond, the diction and the rhythm of some of the lines come from another Renaissance writer of love poetry—Sir Walter Ralegh. Compare, for example, Roethke's "She loved the wind because the wind loved me" with Ralegh's "I loved myself because myself loved you."

The celebration of the love relationship is in many of the poems in Roethke's sequence a kind of religious experience. In several poems such as **"The Dream,"** Roethke's method of describing a sexual relationship as a spiritual experience expressed through traditional literary images is very close to D. H. Lawrence, another twentieth-century writer who treats love as a central religious experience. Compare the following passage from Lawrence's novel *The Rainbow* with the end of Roethke's **"The Dream"**:

> Inside the room was a great steadiness, a core of living *eternity*. Only far outside, at the rim went on the noise and the destruction. Here at the *centre* the great wheel was *motionless, centered* upon itself. Here was a poised, unflawed stillness that was beyond time, because it remained the same, inexhaustible, unchanging unexhausted. . . . The *flames* swept him, he held her in sinews of fire. . . . He stood away near the door in blackness of *shadow* watching, transfixed. And with *slow* heavy movements she *swayed* backwards and forwards. . . .

> She held her body *steady* in the wind;
> Our *shadows* met, and *slowly swung* around;
> She turned the field into a glittering sea;
> I played in *flame* and water like a boy
> And I *swayed* out beyond the white seafoam;
> Like a wet log, I sang within a flame.
> In that last while, *eternity's* confine,
> I came to love, I came into my own.

Through words and expressions such as *point, encircled, the center, circles,* and *least motion,* Roethke images the love experience in terms similar to Lawrence's. The two poets, by describing love through the spatial metaphors of the circle and the point in the center of the circle, image secular love through Dante's metaphors for holy love in the *Paradiso*. Similarly, the states of "eternity" and "steadiness," in which the lover and his beloved reside, and the references to "fire" take on religious connotations. Roethke, following Lawrence and the seventeenth century metaphysical poets, carries the love relationship between man and woman to a higher level of spiritual insight by means of images and metaphors traditionally reserved for religious subjects. In **"The Dream"** Roethke writes of love primarily by joining in a poetically intimate relationship with other talents.

Lawrence's love poems, as well as his novels, furnish Roethke with points of departure for his own love lyrics. "I Wish I Knew a Woman" expresses Lawrence's desire for an ideal sexual relationship: Roethke's **"I Knew a Woman"** presents such a relationship in its consummation. Roethke not only draws upon the poets in his tradition for images and themes but also continually struggles to outdo these other poets. His well-known love poem begins,

> I knew a woman, lovely in her bones,
> . . . . .
> Of her choice virtues only gods should speak,
> Or English poets who grew up on Greek
> . . . . .
> How well her wishes went! She stroked my chin,
> She taught me Turn, and Counter-turn, and Stand;
> . . . . .
> She was the sickle; I, poor I, the rake. . . .

Since "English poets who grew up on Greek" are best able to sing this woman's praises, it is to these poets that Roethke turns for metaphors and images. One poet who fits the description and whom we are inevitably reminded of when we read Roethke's extended metaphor on "mowing" is Andrew Marvell. Though the "mowing" image is predominant in several of Marvell's poems ("The Mower against Gardens," "Damon the Mower," and "The Mower to the Glo-Worms") it is in the refrain to "The Mower's Song" that the description of scything is most clearly a metaphor for the sexual relationship with a woman: "When Julianna came, and She / What I do to the Grass, does to my Thoughts and Me." Roethke, like Marvell, brings new life to the convention-ridden pastoral love lyric through the injection into his poem of the intellectualized sensuality of metaphysical wit.

Roethke refers to another English poet who grew up on Greek when he writes, "She taught me Turn, and Counter-turn, and Stand." The source for this unusual way of naming the three divisions of an ode (commonly called strophe, antistrophe, and epode) is probably Ben Jonson's "To the Immortal Memorie, and Friendship of that Noble Paire, Sir Lucius Cary, and Sir H. Morison," in which the terms "the Turne," and "the Counter-Turne," and "the Stand" are used as titles for the various sections of the poem. The verbal echo in and of itself is slight, but it is only through a knowledge of this echo that we realize an important theme in Roethke's poem. By employing these literary terms in his line, Roethke describes the rhythm of love as a movement in poetry. He not only transforms life into art, but also perceives and thus images it as art. This metaphor, imaging sex as poetry, has its converse in a mocking title scribbled in one of Roethke's notebooks: "Thirteen Ways of Fornicating the Amphibrach." And in an even more general formulation of the union of poetry and sex, sex and poetry, Roethke wrote down a few pages later in this same notebook a line from Becquer: "Poetry is feeling and feeling is woman."

One of the most remarkable examples of Roethke's imagination coming to bear upon a text and transforming it into poetry is his use of St. Augustine's analysis of time in terms of bodily motion in the chapter on time and eternity in his *Confession*: "When a body is moved, I measure in time how long it is moved." Roethke's **"I Knew a Woman"** ends "But who would count eternity in days? / These old bones live to learn her wanton ways: / (I measure time by how a body sways)." Roethke takes "body" not just to mean a physical object, but to refer to the woman's body. In I. A. Richards' terms, he transforms the referential language of the philosopher and theologian into the emotive language of his poem. This converting of a sentence from Augustine at his most scientific into an image for a love poem shows the energy of Roethke's mind: he absorbed everything he read and with a few turns and counter-turns transmuted it into poetry. One can not help being reminded of Pablo Picasso's "Bull's Head" which is made out of nothing more than the seat and handlebars of an old bicycle. The great attraction of the piece is the viewer's realization of the shaping vision of the artist, rather than the actual materials before him. "What is far from simple," writes H. W. Janson in *Key Monuments of the History of Art,* "is the leap from the imagination by which Picasso recognized a bull's head in these unlikely objects. . . . clearly, then we must be careful not to confuse the making of a work of art with manual skill or craftsmanship." Similarly, what we marvel at in Roethke's lines (so close to Augustine's) is not so much his technical skills as the genius and wit of his creative powers.

Although the immediate source for Roethke's image may be Augustine, the master of the method which Roethke uses to handle this image is Donne. Roethke, like Donne, takes sensual experiences and deals with them through scientific and theological imagery. Roethke is thoroughly eclectic in searching out and in inventing specific images to describe the love experience, but his methodology is consistently in the tradition of Donne—that line of wit in love poetry that extends from the master of seventeenth-century metaphysical poetry through Lawrence and up to Roethke. This is indeed **"Love's Progress"**—as Roethke was well aware when he borrowed this title from Donne for one of his own poems—and simultaneously it is the progress of poetry.

The underlying pattern in metaphysical love poetry is the continual interplay between the mind and the body, between the thoughts of an inherently philosophical speaker and his emotions which form the heart of the love experience. The metaphysical poem moves out of this dramatic conflict and into its own drama of images, most characteristically in the extended conceit where the elements of mind and body are fused. Roethke saw this same basic drama enacted in Yeats' poetry. Although usually we do not think of Yeats as essentially in the Donne tradition of love poetry, Roethke responds to him in a way which does point out the sympathies between the love poems of Yeats and the tradition of Donne. Compare the first stanza of Roethke's **"The Pure Fury"** with two passages from Yeats:

> Stupor of *knowledge lacking* inwardness—
> *What book, O learned man,* will *set* me *right?*
> Once I read nothing through a fearful night,
> For *every* meaning had grown meaningless.
> *Morning,* I saw the world with second *sight,*
> As if *all* things had died, and *rose again.*
> I *touched* the stones, and they had my own skin.
>
> [Roethke]

> it sails into the *sight*
> And in the *morning's* gone, no *man* knows why,
> And is so lovely that it *sets* to *right*
> *What knowledge* or its *lack* had *set* awry,
> So arrogantly *pure.* . . .
>
> [Yeats]

> That *every morning rose* again
>   . . . . .
> For *what* mere *book* can grant a *knowledge*
>   . . . . .
> And must no beautiful woman be
> *Learned* like a *man?*
>   . . . . .
> That *all* must come to *sight* and *touch.* . . .
>
> [Yeats]

Both of Yeats' poems are about the powers of the body (and thus the powers of women) being radically different from and perhaps even superior to the powers of masculine intellect. Loving a woman can be therefore quite a dangerous venture as these two beings—the woman-body and the man-mind—come together. This same drama is basic to Roethke's poem both in the speaker's attitude towards the woman and in the very images used to describe this attitude. Even though Roethke's poem is titled **"The Pure Fury,"** it is still about Yeats' "complexities of fury" or "furies of complexity"—those intricate interrelationships between the physical and the spiritual. Though in calling it a "pure" fury, Roethke perhaps is trying to bring the metaphysical image to that ultimate plenum where mind and body become one. What Yeats does in his poems and what Roethke does also is not only to use the method of metaphysical love poetry but also to make this method a metaphor for love and finally the very subject of the poem.

By bringing Yeats into association with Donne, Drummond, Jonson, Marvell, and Lawrence, Roethke functions as both critic and poet: he offers us a new perspective on a major tradition in English love poetry. Many voices echo and breathe in unison through Roethke's love poems, and the harmonies that result reveal the underlying similarities between these diverse poets brought together by Roethke in a continuation of metaphysical wit to "sing [like lovers] in chorus, cheek to cheek."

On Roethke's accomplishment as a poet:

During the last years of his life, Roethke was still writing ardently, leaning on his belief in the authority of the poetic act to carry him through several illnesses. His famous class in "Verse Form" at the University of Washington continued to produce such poets as Carolyn Kizer and James Wright to extend Roethke's achievement. When Roethke died suddenly in 1963, the world was deprived of one of its toughest and most intense poets, a major figure who will be remembered and emulated for his strong rhythms, his sensual metaphor and earthy image, and his constant energetic vacillation from primordial slime to light and full fruit. "'Major American poet' describes Theodore Roethke well enough," William Martz observes, "because he succeeds in doing what a major poet has to do—he teaches us how to feel."

> R. T. Smith, "Critical Introduction to the Poetry
> of Theodore Roethke (1908-1963)," in Green
> River Review, Vol. XIV, No. 2, 1983.

Don Bogen (essay date 1980)

SOURCE: "From *Open House* to the Greenhouse: Theodore Roethke's Poetic Breakthrough," in *ELH*, Vol. 47, No. 2, Summer, 1980, pp. 399-418.

[*In the following essay, Bogen studies the evolution of Roethke's poetry as illustrated in the representative poems "Genesis," "On the Road to Woodlawn," and "Cuttings."*]

> My first book was much too wary, much too gingerly in its approach to experience; rather dry in tone and constricted in rhythm. I am trying to loosen up, to rite poems of greater intensity and symbolical depth. [Theodore Roethke, *Selected Letters of Theodore Roethke,* edited by Ralph J. Mills, Jr., 1968. Subsequent correspondences cited in this essay are reprinted in this volume.]

By the mid-1940s, Theodore Roethke had become aware of the limitations of his first volume and had immersed himself in new work of a significantly different order. The seven-year period between the publication of **Open House** in 1941 and **The Lost Son and Other Poems** in 1948 is considered pivotal by many critics. [In *Theodore Roethke,* 1963] Ralph J. Mills, Jr. refers to the "imaginative leap" Roethke made during this time, and [in "The Objective Ego," in *Theodore Roethke: Essays on the Poetry,* edited by Arnold Stein, 1965] Stephen Spender describes the poet's work after this "leap" as that which is "most uniquely Roethke." [In "Cult of the Breakthrough," *New Republic*, September 21, 1968] Kenneth Burke sees the period in which Roethke was working on his second volume as one centered on the poet's "most important breakthrough," citing Roethke's greenhouse poems in Part I of *The Lost Son* as the embodiment of the change. As Burke and others note, this break-through was not only stylistic but also psychological. Characterized by the development of what Mills calls an "intensely subjective vision," Roethke's less "wary" "approach to experience" after the breakthrough reflected a new relation between his writing and his sense of self. In this essay I want to discuss the nature of this change in Roethke's work by examining developments in the way he went about writing. The Theodore Roethke Papers at the University of Washington, an extensive collection of unpublished drafts, notebooks, letters, and other material, are the basis of the essay. My focus is primarily on the composition of three poems: **"Genesis,"** a representative example of Roethke's work from the mid-1930s; **"On the Road to Woodlawn,"** an intriguing transitional poem from the late '30s; and **"Cuttings,"** the opening piece in the greenhouse sequence, dating from the mid-'40s. Examining Roethke's work on these poems in his unpublished notebooks and drafts, we can see significant developments, in both the way he wrote and the way he felt about what he wrote, which are the underpinnings of the poet's extraordinary breakthrough.

Here is the final text of **"Genesis"** as it appeared in *Open House*:

> This elemental force
> Was wrested from the sun;
> A river's leaping source
> Is locked in narrow bone.
>
> This wisdom floods the mind,
> Invades quiescent blood;
> A seed that swells the rind
> To burst the fruit of good.
>
> A pearl within the brain,
> Secretion of the sense;
> Around a central grain
> New meaning grows immense.

This poem was first published in *The Nation* in 1936 and is typical of much of Roethke's early work. The end-stopped, metrical lines—there are no rhythmic substitutions—and the tight rhyme scheme give the feeling of fierce energy controlled by form. The central image of the poem, the "pearl within the brain," parallels that of two other *Open House* poems in iambic trimeter quatrains, **"The Adamant"** and **"Reply to Censure."** Based on a dichotomy between self and world which is announced in the title poem of *Open House,* **"Genesis,"** like the other two poems, develops the concept of an inviolable core of personal identity. **"Open House"** calls for "language strict and pure" which will "keep the spirit spare." Relying heavily on direct statements, unelaborated images, and abstractions, the language of **"Genesis"** meets this definition. As **"Open House"** indicates, the tightly controlled style derived from such "pure" language and strict adherence to the demands of rhyme and meter is a way of keeping the spirit "spare," constraining the self within the bounds of the conscious will. The style of **"Genesis"** and other early poems thus reflects not only Roethke's aesthetic preferences but also his sense of the self as an entity to be controlled and ordered through the process of writing.

The composition of poetry, however, is not entirely a function of the conscious will. The origins of **"Genesis"** in the poet's notebooks reveal at least a partial suspension of will as Roethke works toward his first sense of the poem. Roethke's use of rhyme and meter in this preliminary work is an example. In the completed text of **"Genesis,"** these formal aspects stress the poet's conscious, rational control over his material. However, in the primary stage of composition, Roethke's use of rhyme and a repeating rhythm shows his reliance on the sounds of words, not their meanings, as a way of generating poetic material. The notebook in which the first work on **"Genesis"** was done contains a number of disconnected lines and couplets—such as "A haze before the sun," "Arise from red-eyed ache," and "Its attributes are worn"—before Roethke puts together a recognizable stanza. These fragments are not unified by a particular concept, an idea the poet has consciously chosen to develop, but rather by their common iambic trimeter rhythm. At this early stage of composition, then, Roethke is using meter as a device to generate lines without a clear sense of what he wants to say; conscious acts of arrangement, clarification, and judgment are held in abeyance.

Rhyme is employed in a similar manner:

> What splits its way through rock
> Like subterranean fire
>
> The creeping flame, desire,
> Will seek its way through rock
>
> A ravenous tongue of flame
> Remote in deepest shock.

"Fire" leads the poet to "desire," and "rock" leads to "shock." But what differentiates Roethke's work with these three couplets from his work with the other fragments is that links of sound are used along with conscious considerations of image and meaning as Roethke develops the hackneyed metaphor of love as flame. It is significant that, despite the clichés inherent in them, Roethke selects these three couplets from a mass of less conscious but more imaginative material. Rejecting intriguing phrases like "The muscles of the wind" and "Colours scrape the eye," the poet settles on the lines most clearly molded by the conscious mind as the primary material for the conclusion of this early version of **"Genesis"**:

> This elemental force
> Was wrested from the sun;

A river's leaping source
Is locked in narrow bone.

This love is lusty mirth
That shakes eternal sky,
The agony of birth,
The fiercest will to die.
The fever-heat of mind
Within prehensile brute;
A seed that swells the rind
Of strange, impalpable fruit.

This faith surviving shock,
This smoldering desire,
Will split its way through rock
Like subterranean fire.

[This text is reproduced in Roethke's essay "Verse
in Rehearsal" in *On the Poet and His Craft:
Selected Prose of Theodore Roethke,* edited by
Ralph J. Mills, Jr., 1965.]

The stanzaic form of **"Genesis"** arises early in the process of composition. The fragmentary lines and couplets in Roethke's notebook are followed immediately by attempts to construct an *abab* quatrain. This early movement from fragments to the development of a stanza reflects Roethke's interest in working with consciously crafted material as soon in the writing process as possible. The stanza we see emerging, however, is not the one we might expect from the poet's attention to the "rock"–"shock" couplets but rather one for which there is no preliminary material in the notebook passage, the second quatrain in the draft cited above. In his three attempts to complete this stanza Roethke struggles to develop a single formal unit before he considers the implications in what he has previously written. His interest is clearly not so much in content, in developing a complete thought from the preliminary material, as it is in form. Looking back at this early notebook passage as a whole, we see that the fragmentary material before the quatrain—though it has no relation to the stanza's ideas or images—is nonetheless essential to the creation of the stanza because it provides a framework of rhythm and rhyme in which the poet can undertake more extensive work. Before this formal structure is established, the most developed units in the notebook passage are only a few lines long; after it, we find a group of some twenty lines on the same topic. The earliest work in the notebook, then, can be considered a kind of poetic "gearing up," in which the repetition of the basic trimeter rhythm and the alternate rhyming in the couplets are more important than the meanings of individual lines and images.

Once form has been established, however, the writing process changes. For one thing, deletions become much more frequent. Among the forty lines and fragments of preliminary material in the notebook passage, the poet has crossed out only two completely—both of these in his work on the quatrain—and made small deletions of single words or phrases in about a dozen more. At a later stage of composition, when Roethke has the first three stanzas of the draft version done and is working on the fourth only two complete lines out of ten are left untouched, and one-third of the lines are deleted completely. The poet's more critical attitude toward what he has written reflects his movement from the generation of poetic material—which involves, as we have seen, the partial suspension of the conscious will—to the transformation of the generated material into the artifice of the poem, a process which, at this stage of Roethke's career, is based on conscious, logical choice. In keeping with this change, Roethke no longer uses meter and rhyme as a way of developing new images and connections but rather employs them to gain control over his material by eliminating the parts that do not fit. For example, from the preliminary couplet "A ravenous tongue of flame / Remote in deepest shock" Roethke keeps the last line for consideration but not the first; other fragments ending in "flame" or "flames" are also deleted because they do not fit the "fire"–"desire," "rock"–"shock" rhyme scheme. Rhythmic irregularities too are removed, as in the deletion of "hot" from "This ant-like flame, hot desire." Roethke even includes a list of rhymes for "shock" on the right hand side of the page, setting up a tight structure which new alternate lines must fit.

In forming and polishing individual quatrains at this stage of composition, Roethke does not concern himself much with the order of stanzas in the work. As we have seen, he begins with the second stanza; some pages later in the same notebook is a draft of the first. The first complete draft of the poem, of course, contains two stanzas which do not appear in the published text and lacks the vital concluding stanza which makes **"Genesis"** what it is:

A pearl within the brain,
Secretion of the sense;
Around a central grain
New meaning grows immense.

In the first two stages of composition we have seen how Roethke generates poetic material and then forms and polishes stanzaic "pearls" from it. The poet's large-scale revisions of the first complete draft mark a third stage, in which the "New meaning" of the work is developed.

In his essay "Verse in Rehearsal" Roethke quotes the comments of his friend Rolfe Humphries on the early, four-stanza version of **"Genesis."** Humphries' remarks, though extensive, say little about the overall meaning of the work, concentrating instead on problems like the draft's "conventional rhymes," its "monogamous adjective–noun combinations," and the redundance of the phrase "strange, impalpable fruit" in the third stanza. Roethke must have considered these comments important, since he reprinted them in the essay; but the relation between Humphries' remarks and Roethke's revisions is not as direct as the essay might imply. The poet deals with most of the problems his friend notes, but instead of doing the technical "tinkering" that Humphries advises—finding a title to account for the standard rhymes; changing "strange, impalpable" to a four-syllable word—Roethke replaces everything in the poem except the opening stanza and one line in the third quatrain. One reason for this radical revision is that the poet had already done the kind of poetic polishing his friend suggests when he was working on the individual stanzas. Roethke's early sense that the draft was at least technically proficient is reflected in the fact that he submitted it to three periodicals before sending it to Humphries.

Roethke may have felt growing reservations about the craftsmanship of the piece as the rejection slips came in, but I think the main problems that bothered him at this final stage of the compositional process had to do with the overall meaning, tone, and stance of the poem. He expresses this dissatisfaction in his comments on the draft sent to Humphries: "Sophomoric straining? Just old tricks? Or fair traditional piece?" The last of these three remarks is, of course, wishful thinking. The second comment views the "traditional" aspects of the piece from a darker perspective. In this sense the remark could be taken primarily as a sign of doubts about the conventionality of the poem's technique, as Humphries appears to read it; but it also connects with Roethke's first comment. "Sophomoric straining?" shows the poet's worries about how he appears in the poem, about whether he seems immature or phony in it. I think Roethke is referring to a kind of pose of disembodied wisdom here, one which he has assumed before in uncollected poems like **"Prepare Thyself"**—"Prepare thyself for change, / The ever-strange, / Thy soul's immortal range."—and **"The Knowing Heart"**—"O this mortality will break / The false dissembling brain apart." This kind of poetic stance—in which the poet assumes a pompous, all-knowing attitude in order to claim broad metaphysical knowledge he has not earned in the poem or in his experience—must have seemed like an "old trick" to Roethke; it is an easy way for a young poet to take on large topics. It pervades the three stanzas the poet omitted from the final draft, with their references to "prehensile brute" and "eternal sky" and their confident statements about the results of "love" and "faith surviving shock."

It might be argued that the final version of **"Genesis"** is also pompous in tone, with its description of "wisdom flooding the mind" and the concluding image of the "pearl within the brain." But the published text is not "sophomoric straining"; we accept its claims partially because they are toned down and made more specific than those in the earlier draft but also, and more importantly, because we can see their relation to the poet who makes them. The final text clearly traces the movement of the "elemental force" of external energy inward to the individual mind and body and its development there into the substance of the growing "pearl." The title **"Genesis,"** which appears only after Roethke has begun work on the three-stanza version, clarifies this movement by focussing our attention on the poem as a description of a creative process, with the implication that the poem itself is the result of such a process. The earlier four-stanza draft—though it has elements of the basic external-internal, energy-matter dichotomies—includes neither this progression toward the individual self nor the im-

plied reference to the poet in the process of writing. Its tone seems impersonal and pompous, its claims unjustified by experience. In revising the poem after this draft has been completed, Roethke finds a new meaning in the work, as well as a new poetic stance, one which presents the self with more accuracy and honesty. As the title poem of **Open House** indicates, Roethke sees the self at this stage of his career as an entity essentially created in the act of writing. Thus it is not surprising that the version of **"Genesis"** which presents the self most accurately and with the least pomposity is also the best aesthetically, with a clear structure, language which has been made "strict and pure" by the deletion of confusing or unnecessary adjectives, total metrical regularity, and a rhyme scheme that is both tight and original.

"The great danger is *softness,"* Roethke wrote in a letter in 1935. What we find in **"Genesis"** and other early poems is a pose which counteracts this danger by projecting a spare and inviolable core of identity: a pearl; an adamant; even, as in **"Open House,"** a shield. This is the poetry of what Dennis E. Brown terms "the entrenched self" ["Theodore Roethke's 'Self-World' and the Modernist Position," *Journal of Modern Literature,* July, 1974], and behind the trenches we see few specifics of Roethke's individual identity. By the late 1930s, however, Roethke was becoming aware of the limitations of this kind of writing. In a review of Ben Bellit's *The Five-Fold Mesh* in 1939, Roethke raised some critical points which could apply to his own early work:

> Often instead of being truly passionate, he is merely literary; he shapes ingenious verbal patterns, but they are not always poetry. Too much of his work seems to spring from an act of will rather than from an inner compulsion. Except for half a dozen poems—and that is enough—he creates no more than remarkable artifice. [Roethke, *On the Poet and His Craft*]

As Richard Blessing notes [in *Theodore Roethke's Dynamic Vision,* 1974], Roethke began to feel dissatisfied with the "well made poem" in the late '30s. In seeking to develop his own work beyond mere "remarkable artifice," Roethke produced two intriguing poems in this period which found their way into **Open House**. Both **"The Premonition,"** with its reliance on unstressed line endings and half-rhyme, and **"On the Road to Woodlawn,"** with its rough hexameter rhythm, are formally looser than the other work in the volume; both poems too arise from an "inner compulsion" which becomes central in Roethke's work: the poet's drive to understand and communicate with his dead father. There are also significant differences in compositional method from that of the early work, as an analysis of the writing of **"On the Road to Woodlawn"** reveals.

The composition of **"On the Road to Woodlawn"** represents a transitional phase between Roethke's work on poems like **"Genesis"** in the mid-'30s and his work on the greenhouse poems in the early '40s. Here is the final text as it appeared in **Open House**:

On the Road to Woodlawn

I miss the polished brass, the powerful black horses,
The drivers creaking the seats of the baroque
 hearses,
The high-piled floral offerings with sentimental
 verses,
The carriages reeking with varnish and stale
 perfume.

I miss the pallbearers momentously taking their
 places,
The undertaker's obsequious grimaces,
The craned necks, the mourners' anonymous faces,
—And the eyes, still vivid, looking up from a
 sunken room.

As we might gather from the length and rhythmic variation of the lines, Roethke does not use a repeating rhythm
as a way of generating material for this poem. Rather the
poem has its origins in questions which lead to a gathering
of imagery:

 Where is the polished brass
 ~~Where are the~~
 Or the streamlined fenders the black flags
 The line, snipped by the traffic light,

 [notebook]

These questions reflect the process of memory which is at
the heart of Roethke's work on this and many subsequent
poems. While this conscious attempt to tap his own past
experience through memory is a technique not seen in the
preliminary work on "Genesis," we do find the same use
of rhyme as a generating tool in both poems:

 I miss the powerful black horses:
 The drivers in the creaking seats of the baroque
 hearses;
 The high piled Floral Offerings with sentimental
 verses,

 [notebook]

After this rhymed section, the poet returns in his notebook
to unrhymed fragments as he works to clarify details in his
memory of the funeral procession. Here, in contrast to
"Genesis," the scene of the poem, existing as it does in
the past, is determined considerably before the meter. On
the next page of the notebook, in fact, Roethke's examination of the scene has led him from the funeral procession to his dead father, whom he now addresses in trimeter: "Far and away above you / The hissing Planets whirl."
After these lines is a question in prose which concludes
the work on this poem in the notebook. When Roethke
asks himself, "Do the clues to our generation lie in the
diseased?" [quoted by Allan Seager in *The Glass House:
The Life of Theodore Roethke,* 1968]—a question I take
to refer to his father's slow death from cancer—he is thinking about neither the poem's form nor its descriptive detail. The question, unlike anything in the notebook work
on "Genesis," reflects Roethke's concern with the meaning of the experience before the poem is written.

The issue of the personal significance of the experience
for Roethke is held largely in abeyance as the poet works
on completing and polishing a draft of the poem. It is in
this second stage of composition that the work on this
poem most closely resembles that on "Genesis." The *aaab
cccb* rhyme scheme is established, and the poet tries out
different versions of lines to fit it. There is also some
rhythmic tinkering, though considerably less than with
"Genesis" because of the later poem's looser metrical
form. The basic work on the first stanza of "On the Road
to Woodlawn" is completed at this stage, but the second
stanza at this point is considerably different from the
published text:

 Now, as if performing a task that disgraces,
 The black-flagged cars, filled with anonymous faces,
 Hurry to where, among urns, a vacant place is,
 —As if that cemetery had insufficient room.

If Roethke had decided to retain this draft stanza as the
conclusion of "On the Road to Woodlawn," he would
have produced a poem not unlike "Highway: Michigan," "Idyll," or the other poems on social topics in
Open House, a piece beginning with observation and
description from the poet's own viewpoint and including
at the end a vision of the social problem—highway mania,
suburban anxiety, our inability to deal with death—expressed in a largely impersonal way. But the question of
the personal meaning of the scene begins to concern
Roethke again after he has completed this draft; beneath
the two typed stanzas on the draft sheet is new work in
pencil on what will become the second stanza of the
published text.

The most noticeable changes between the draft and published texts of the second stanza are the clear presence of
the poet himself in the final version, signalled by the "I
miss" which now repeats the directly personal opening of
the piece; and the replacement of an objective, thematically centered last line with one based on a haunting personal
image. This concluding hallucinatory vision of the father
staring up from the casket does not resolve the movement
of the poem the way the pearl image does in "Genesis";
it does not unify the pattern of images in the work or
clarify the overall meaning of the poem. Neither does it
develop the personal stance seen in the earlier work. In
"On the Road to Woodlawn" the self is presented as
vulnerable, and the experience is seen as essentially irre-
solvable. In revising this poem in the last stage of the
writing process, Roethke does not work toward creating a
vision of self as he had earlier, but rather toward describing personal experience specifically and honestly.

Based as it is on memory, the composition of "On the
Road to Woodlawn" involves more conscious work with
the subject matter, particularly in the early stages, than
does the writing of "Genesis." Paradoxically, however,
"Genesis" in its final version appears a more consciously
crafted poem than "On the Road to Woodlawn." The
personal stance developed in the earlier poem emphasizes
the conscious awareness of "meaning" in experience, in
contrast to the depiction in the later work of an emotional

event the self does not completely comprehend. Roethke's sense of the difference between these two modes of dealing with experience in poetry, as well as his increasing frustration with the **"Genesis"** mode, is summarized in this notebook entry: "I can suck something dry from experience, but I can't see it imaginatively."

The poet's progress toward a kind of writing which would allow him to "see experience imaginatively" was not easy. Here, for example, is some early notebook work on the greenhouse poem **"Old Florist"**:

> I cannot claim those acres,
> The benches knocked to stone,
> The hot beds smashed to kindling
> The rose house tumbled down.
>
> Those tall hard-fingered florists
> Swearers and drinkers, they
>
> The garish shanties creep across
> The fields once full of flowers

These lines are essentially a false start; after them come the fragments like "spitting tobacco juice" which are the actual raw material for the poem. The problems in the lines are related, I think, to Roethke's use of meter and, in the first quatrain, rhyme. In meeting these formal demands, Roethke assumes an odd melodramatic tone, in which the self is cast in a traditional elegiac role and the subject is glamorized. Diction suffers too, as in the inverted "Swearers and drinkers, they"; in another attempt to work on this material in meter Roethke even uses the contraction "shan't." Formal techniques, then, instead of generating authentic poetic material from memory, essentially replace careful examination of past experience with language and images based on a conventional pose. In an early poem like **"Genesis"** this process works because the poet's goal is not to examine his own self and past but to create an identity, a personal stance, through the act of asserting artistic control over largely impersonal material. But in the early 1940s, in order to use memory effectively and develop an accurate sense of self, Roethke had to eliminate the formal techniques which led him to conventional stances.

In Roethke's notebooks we can see important changes in the poet's working methods. While Roethke's biographer Allan Seager exaggerates the differences between the notebooks of the '30s and those of the early '40s, his basic point, that the poet began to "loosen up" in the late '30s, is valid. Even the earliest notebooks appear fragmentary and confusing, with drafts of different poems and parts of poems interspersed among teaching notes, addresses, fragments of letters, and other material. Like the later notebooks, they show evidence of Roethke's re-reading. But as the poet completes *Open House* and begins work on his second volume, the notebooks become even more confusing. For one thing, Roethke's work in them is much more extensive than earlier, involving not only a large increase in draft material for poems but many more prose fragments, questions, partial narratives, and other

related material. The re-readings become more frequent, with corrections and additions of new material. In his new, more extensive use of the notebooks, Roethke spends a great deal of time describing aspects of the greenhouse, often without an idea of one particular poem in mind. One notebook from the early '40s contains several pages of such work, including details that find their way into **"Root Cellar"**—"All the breathing of growing"—**"Weed Puller"**—"Weeds beneath benches, / The drain-holes festooned with mossy roots dripping"—and **"Transplanting"**—"To be pinched and spun quick by the florists' green thumbs." The evocation of images from memory is more important than artifice here. I do not mean to imply that Roethke is unconcerned with the composition of specific poems at this point; we can see this passage eventually leading into work on **"Forcing House."** But the artifice here, the separation of greenhouse experience into distinct units that will become poems, arises gradually from the description instead of guiding and focussing the writing from the beginning. There is neither the rush to complete a formal unit, as in the early work, nor the clear sense of a particular subject, as in **"On the Road to Woodlawn."** "The poem invents the form; it insists on the form," Roethke writes in one notebook. The poet's sense of artifice has become more organic; writing now involves discovery, not just conscious choice. Roethke's belief in this period that "A poem becomes independent of you" shows a new attitude toward the self in the writing process, a movement away from will and stance toward a more subtle and fluid sense of himself and his material. The new type of preliminary work in the poet's notebooks reflects Roethke's growing awareness that it is vital to keep the gates of memory open, the self open to past experience.

Related to this new openness in the writing process is the value Roethke now places on what can perhaps best be defined as "looking." This concept first appears in the mid-'30s in a letter from Roethke's friend Louise Bogan. Charging Roethke with a kind of fear of feeling in his early verse, she sent him a copy of Rilke's *Letters to a Young Poet* and advised, ". . . you will have to *look* at things until you don't know whether you are they or they are you" (Bogan's emphasis). Roethke echoed this idea many years later in the film *In a Dark Time,* noting Rilke's careful observation of animals and referring to long, intense "looking" as "an extension of consciousness." This "extension of consciousness," it is important to remember, arises not only from introspection, "looking" at the self, but also from close observation of entities outside the self. In the lengthy descriptive passages from the greenhouse notebooks we can see the poet "looking" as he writes. An example is Roethke's work on the memory of pulling weeds, which extends for more than a dozen pages. The scene is examined again and again; details are repeated; and, though practically all of the images and phrases in **"Weed Puller"** appear in the passage, there is little attempt to order the material as it is being written. Roethke is not just gathering lines here as he might have done earlier—the work is too repetitious and extensive for that. Rather, he is intensely "looking" at a memory in an attempt to "extend his consciousness" to include elements of the greenhouse experience of his younger self, to go beyond simple description toward "seeing it imaginatively." What the poet eventually learns from this "looking" is revealed in the general comment about weed pulling he makes in a later notebook: "Ambivalent / Spirituality & sensuousness."

Though the greenhouse notebooks show that Roethke has moved away from conscious, limiting structures in his concepts of self and artifice, there is nonetheless a great deal of conscious work involved in the writing of the greenhouse poems. Roethke's comment on weed pulling is an example: After "looking" at the experience until his present sense of self begins to merge with aspects of the greenhouse and his past identity, the poet steps back from what he has written, examines it, and states what he has learned. The knowledge gained through this examination is then used in developing the artifice of the poem. This more conscious work comes after a given poem has begun to emerge from the mass of greenhouse notes; it can thus be seen as part of a second stage in the compositional process. While it is necessary to discuss the preliminary greenhouse work with reference to several poems, as their origins are intermingled, the nest stage in the writing process is best seen in the poet's work on a single poem. Here is the final text of **"Cuttings"** as it appeared in *The Lost Son and Other Poems*:

> Sticks-in-a-drowse droop over sugary loam,
> Their intricate stem-fur dries;
> But still the delicate slips keep coaxing up water;
> The small cells bulge;
>
> One nub of growth
> Nudges a sand-crumb loose,
> Pokes through a musty sheath
> Its pale tendrilous horn.

Like the second stage in the composition of an early poem, Roethke's work in completing a draft of **"Cuttings"** involves the development and selection of material to fit his idea of the artifice of the poem. In the early poems, of course, Roethke uses meter and rhyme as tools in the process, deleting material that does not fit the pattern and listing rhyme words as a kind of boundary within which new lines might be written. The absence of these tools in the composition of the greenhouse poems makes Roethke's task more difficult. The poet discusses this problem in "Some Remarks on Rhythm":

> We must realize, I think, that the writer in freer forms must have an even greater fidelity to his subject matter than the poet who has the support of form. He must keep his eye on the object, and his rhythm must move as a mind moves, must be imaginatively right, or he is lost. [*On the Poet and His Craft*]

Comparing the composition of **"Genesis"** with that of **"Cuttings,"** we see in the later poem fewer lines completed and then revised for rhythmic regularity, more fragmentary beginnings which are not revised but just dropped. In one notebook passage, for example, there are more than twenty consecutive attempts at the third line of the poem. It is clear from some of these fragments that Roethke knows the basic movement he wants to develop at this transitional point in the poem—the gradual transformation, within a continuous natural process, of dormant stems into slips actively drawing up water—but he cannot develop the details until he is satisfied with the beginning phrase of the transition. Unlike Roethke's work on the individual stanzas of **"Genesis,"** the completion of a part of **"Cuttings"** is bound up with the poet's idea of the whole, his awareness that the clause beginning with "But" is central to the poem's entire movement. Working toward a line which is not formally metered but "imaginatively right," he repeats the opening "But" again and again, trying out different alternatives for the subject of the clause—"the sliced wedge of a stem," "the planted end," "the face"—in an attempt to start a train of thought and a corresponding rhythm which will carry him through this part of the poem. Roethke's difficulty in getting past the beginning of the line at this point reflects the fact that the process involved here is not a simple one of summarizing or reproducing experience. It is an attempt, rather, to re-create in the act of writing the movement of the poet's mind. In **"Genesis"** and other early poems a tough personal stance arises directly from Roethke's strict formal style and adamantine imagery, but in the greenhouse poems this process is essentially reversed: The imaginative attempt to re-live the act of perception determines the lines and phrases which make up the artifice; only when the poem's rhythms "move as a mind moves," following the self in the process of perception and cognition, are they "imaginatively right."

The concrete details and perceptions we find in the finished poem represent only a fraction of the total amount generated by Roethke's intense observation of greenhouse experience. The final stage of composition, after the poet has completed a draft, involves careful selection of lines and images, along with revision and rearrangement of material. The composition of **"Cuttings"** provides a clear example of this kind of work, as the first draft of the poem is vastly different from the final text. Here is the draft, with its early title:

Propagation House

> Slivers of stem, minutely furred,
> Tucked into sand still marked with thumb-prints,
> Cuttings of coleas, geranium, blood-red fuchsia
> Stand stiff in their beds.
> The topsoil crusts over like bakery sugar.
>
> The delicate slips keep coaxing up water,
> Bulging their flexible cells almost to bursting.
> Even before fuzzy root-hairs reach for their gritty
>   sustenance,
> One pale horn of growth, a nubby root-cap,
> Nudges a sand-crumb loose,
> Humps like a sprout,
> Then stretches out straight.

"Propagation House" has the overall structure of **"Cuttings,"** most of its details, and several of the specific images. But, compared to the final text, it is wordy and slow-moving. Such an overabundance of detail is a natural result of Roethke's reliance on memory and extensive "looking" in the early stages of composition. It is also related to the poet's shift from formal to free verse, as a letter from William Carlos Williams suggests:

> The thing sought is the essence and for this we need to be saying (as poets!) what we are saying. But in releasing ourselves, in that feeling of confident release the difficulty is that we say too much, we say more than is distinctively ourselves, we slop over a little.

In paring down his draft to express no more than is "distinctively himself," Roethke uses what he has learned of himself and greenhouse experience in the earlier stages of writing to clarify and condense his material. In the case of **"Weed Puller,"** for example, Roethke uses his discovery that the experience involved "Ambivalent / Spirituality & sensuousness" to select the combination of sensuous images and spiritually oriented abstractions which will make up the finished poem.

Returning to **"Cuttings,"** we find that the poet is most conscious of the artifice at this final stage of composition. Aesthetic concerns—redundance, awkward rhythms, too many adjectives, irrelevant details—merge with Roethke's drive to present himself and his perceptions honestly and directly. Most of the first stanza, for example, is discarded because its specific flower names and references to transplanting detract from the focus of the poem and the experience. As we have seen from Roethke's early work on the transition in the third line of the published text, the gradual change from apparent lifelessness to the beginnings of growth is central to the poet's perception of the scene, and the irrelevant material in the first stanza of "Propagation House" blurs this perception. Other details which distort the experience include the exaggeration of the phrase "almost to bursting" in line 7, the redundance of "flexible" in the same line and the appositive at the end of line 9, and the rather fussy effect produced by the accumulation of adjectives ending in "y" in lines 8 and 9. The rhythms of "Propagation House," with its abundance of unstressed syllables, lengthy lines, and feminine line endings, feel cluttered and overly elaborate. Roethke's goal in revising the draft is to pare them down, making them "natural," as he puts it. In addition to removing these distorting, unnatural elements, Roethke tightens the structure of the poem to clarify the experience presented. The strong separation between the seemingly lifeless stems and the "slips coaxing up water" created by the stanza break in "Propagation House" is reduced in **"Cuttings,"** in keeping with Roethke's sense of the change as part of a continuous natural process. In the final text the stanza break serves to emphasize the time between the drawing up of water and the first growth, reflecting the process more accurately. These revisions all show the "greater fidelity to his subject matter" Roethke develops in the third stage of composition.

The term "subject matter" should not be defined narrowly. In his letters to editors and friends in the mid-'40s, Roeth-ke insisted that the greenhouse poems went "beyond mere description" of natural phenomena and suggested "at least two levels of experience." The level beneath that of greenhouse description includes Roethke's presentation of self in the sequence. **"Cuttings,"** the shortest and least anthropomorphic of the greenhouse poems, presents something of a special case here: The second level is not brought out directly in the poem itself but rather through the interaction between **"Cuttings"** and the poem which follows it in the sequence and shares its title, **"Cuttings (later)."** While **"Cuttings"** has its origins in the poet's observation of a natural process, **"Cuttings (later)"**—even in its early stages—involves the relation between nature and the self. Here is the text as it appeared in *The Lost Son and Other Poems*:

Cuttings (later)

This urge, wrestle, resurrection of dry sticks,
Cut stems struggling to put down feet,
What saint strained so much,
Rose on such lopped limbs to a new life?

I can hear, underground, that sucking and sobbing,
In my veins, in my bones I feel it,—
The small waters seeping upward,
The tight grains parting at last.
When sprouts break out,
Slippery as fish,
I quail, lean to beginnings, sheath-wet.

As we might expect from the subject and images—"sticks," water, and "sheath"—common to both poems, Roethke worked on **"Cuttings"** and **"Cuttings (later)"** simultaneously. Both poems were primarily composed in 1944, although, like most of the greenhouse poems, they include details which appeared earlier in the undifferentiated greenhouse material of the notebooks. As I mentioned, the connection between nature and the self is at the core of **"Cuttings (later)"** from the beginning, but in bringing the piece to its final state Roethke makes the poem more specifically personal, moving from this rather rhetorical version of the concluding stanza—

> Who could shun this hump and scratch,
> The close sweat of growth,
> Not quail to the same itch,
> Not stir, lean to beginnings, sheath-wet?

to a stanza which anchors the link with nature firmly in the experience of "I," the poet himself, and expresses it not as a question but as an affirmative statement. While the connection between self and nature is clarified in the revisions of **"Cuttings (later),"** it is consciously excluded from **"Cuttings."** In one instance, Roethke uses details from the draft material of **"Cuttings (later)"** to revise the other poem from its "Propagation House" stage. The opening line of **"Cuttings"** appears among this draft material as "The best of me droops, in a drowse." In reworking this line, Roethke removes the personal pronoun from the material, keeping **"Cuttings"** focussed on nature, not the self. The fact that **"Cuttings"** concentrates on description without a perceiving "I" is no accident. As Jarold Ramsey notes [in "Roethke in the Greenhouse," *Western Humanities Review,* Winter, 1972], Roethke "suppresses all possible human implications" in **"Cuttings"** in order to establish an objective perspective. In doing this, the poet asserts that the connection between self and nature comes from close observation of greenhouse life and is not applied to the material from the beginning in a kind of arbitrary analogy. The "two levels" Roethke develops in the greenhouse poems are connected organically, as "looking"—even if not specifically directed toward the self—is intrinsically linked to an "extension of consciousness." In their position as the opening poems of the greenhouse sequence, **"Cuttings"** and **"Cuttings (later)"** clearly announce the relation between natural processes and the development of self which is at the heart of the sequence and the volume as a whole.

In a statement made at Northwestern University in 1963 Roethke characterized the title poem of *Open House* as "a clumsy, innocent, desperate asseveration" and contrasted it to his subsequent work:

> The spirit or soul—should we say the self, once perceived, *becomes* the soul?—this I was keeping "spare" in my desire for the essential. But the spirit need not be spare: it can grow gracefully and beautifully like a tendril, like a flower [Roethke's italics]. ["On 'Identity'," in *On the Poet and His Craft*]

In working toward this organic sense of self, Roethke went through basic changes in the way he wrote. In the late '30s and early '40s he began to rely more on memory and extensive "looking" at objects and experiences as a way of generating poetic material. Rhyme, meter, and even the awareness of artifice itself were downplayed as Roethke examined his past, attempting to re-create the process of perception in the act of writing. Dropping the support of formal verse, he worked toward rhythms which would "move as a mind moves" and a corresponding new sense of self: The artificial stance assumed in the early poems is replaced by a consciousness, open to experience, which grows in the process of writing and leads to an accurate expression of personal identity in the finished text. In a notebook kept as he was completing the greenhouse poems, Roethke wrote, "You must learn to walk before you can dance; you can't be a master of suggestion unless you are a master of description." The greenhouse poems are descriptive in the richest sense of the term. "Learning to walk" in these poems was, for Roethke, an essential prelude to the "dance" of more complex self-discovery in the "Lost Son" sequence.

M. L. Lewandowska (essay date 1980)

SOURCE: "The Words of Their Roaring: Roethke's Use of the Psalms of David," in *The David Myth in Western Literature,* edited by Raymond-Jean Frontain and Jan Wojcik, Purdue University Press, 1980, pp. 156-67.

[*In the following essay, Lewandowska claims that the poems in* Praise to the End! *evince the influence of the Bible's Psalms.*]

Theodore Roethke's long *Praise to the End!* sequence is probably best approached through Roethke's own guide to perception: "We think by feeling. What is there to know?" Indeed, it is one of the few long sequences in modern poetry that can be read aloud, dramatically, and erupt into meaning solely by means of its sounds and images. Yet, for those of us who must know as well as feel, the sequence is extremely complex and thus difficult to explicate. Though Roethke insisted he did not "rely on allusion," he suggested many of the ancestors for these poems and among the sources he first mentions is the Bible. He notes one direct quotation from Job, but the more fertile source material is that of the Psalms, especially those traditionally attributed to David. Although their authorship is debated by modern biblical scholars, these songs have for centuries formed part of the mythical and literary reality of that heroic figure, a man who knew triumph and despair, power and persecution, and who ordered his most intense experiences by shaping them with music. It is toward that persona, that popular image of the lyric side of David, that Roethke reaches in his own unique way. The Psalms contain dramatic emotional correlatives for Roethke's protagonist and their rhetoric and images provide the means by which the two voices can blend in their singing.

An immediate link between the Psalms and the *Praise* sequence is suggested by parallels in rhetorical patterns. A great many Psalms begin with invocation: "Hear the right, O Lord," "Plead my cause, O Lord," "Our Lord, Our Lord, how . . . ," "Help, Lord," "My God, my God . . ." The protagonist in Roethke's poems uses similar invocations, "God, give me a near" (**"Where Knock is Open Wide"**), but the object addressed soon becomes quite different: "Hear me, soft ears and roundy stones" (**"I Need, I Need"**), "Voice, come out of the silence" (**"The Lost Son"**). As the sequence progresses, Roethke invokes metaphoric spirits which come from dreams or the unconscious: "You child with a beast's heart," and "Mother of blue and many changes of hay," and "You tree beginning to know" (**"Give Way, Ye Gates"**).

Another example, "Worm, be with me," is a perfect echo of David and the pattern found so often in the Psalms: the address follows, or is followed by, the imperative. "Bow down thine ear, O Lord" (86:1), "Judge me, O Lord" (26:1), "Preserve me, O God" (16:1), "O Lord, rebuke me not" (6:1). There is much of the same in Roethke, and the pattern creates an immediacy, a rare sense of drama. "Delight me otherly, white spirit," he says in **"I Cry Love! Love!"** and "Lave me, ultimate waters" (**"Praise to the End!"**), or, in another mood, "Renew the light, lewd whisper" (**"The Shape of the Fire"**).

The pattern is used for both exhortation and supplication. When David wishes revenge on his enemies, the tone is tense and demanding: "Destroy, O Lord, and divide their tongues; for I have seen violence and strife in the city" (55:9); "Arise, O God, plead thine own cause: remember how the foolish man reproacheth thee daily" (74:22). When he laments, the tone of the Psalmist is one of supplication: "Be merciful unto me, O God, be merciful unto me; for my soul trusteth in thee" (57:1), and, "O Lord, rebuke me not in thy wrath" (38:1). Roethke also uses exhortation and supplication, more and more often as the *Praise* sequence progresses and the poems gain intensity. For example, "Believe me, knot of a gristle, I bleed like a tree" (**"Give Way, Ye Gates"**), or "Mamma! Put on your dark hood: / It's a long way to somewhere else" (**"Sensibility! O La!"**). In the softer tones: "Sooth me, great groans of underneath, / I'm still waiting for a foot" (**"O Lull Me, Lull Me"**); "Voice, come out of the silence, / Say something, / Appear in the form of a spider" (**"The Lost Son"**). Or simply: "Father, forgive my hands" (**"Praise to the End!"**).

To read this sequence aloud is to become acutely aware of how often Roethke uses these patterns, how strong the biblical echoes are. And we might well ask why a modern poet would choose such "archaic" forms in which to deliver his very contemporary song. An answer is immediately clear: the effect is incredibly powerful. Speech is formalized and intensified and all verbal excesses, all temptations to philosophize, are eliminated. The short, tight forms present the emotion with an immediacy that touches us far more quickly than any metaphor could. Indeed, there is a literalness in this language which is rare in modern poetry, and yet the mystery remains. When Roethke or David uses invocation, the object addressed, be it the Lord or a "white way to another grace" metamorphoses, quickens, as we are forced to focus on it so sharply. In marvelous contrast to the dramatic lines such rhetoric produces, the lyric passages in Roethke become all the more musical. Listen, for example, to the contrast in two stanzas from **"I Cry Love! Love!"**:

Mouse, mouse, come out of the ferns,
And small mouths, stay your aimless cheeping:
A lapful of apples sleeps in this grass.
That anguish of concreteness!—
The sun playing on loam,
And the first dust of spring listing over backlots,—
I proclaim once more a condition of joy.
Walk into the wind, willie!

　　. . . . .

A fish jumps, shaking out flakes of moonlight.
A single wave starts lightly and easily shoreward,
Wrinkling between reeds in shallower water,
Lifting a few twigs and floating leaves,
Then washing up over small stones.

There is another rhetorical connection. Mitchell Dahood, in *The Anchor Bible,* mentions that "the dominating principle of . . . Biblical poetry is . . . that of balance or symmetry, the famous *parallelismus membrorum.*" This balance shows most clearly in pairs of synonyms: rejoice-exault, foe-adversary, devoted ones-faithful ones. But the translators of the Psalms usually provide a balance in rhythm or rhetorical structure also. Thus we hear David sing "I will praise thee, O Lord, among the people; and I

Louise Bogan on *The Waking*:

Theodore Roethke, whose book, **The Waking,** is a volume of selections running from 1933 to the present, shares with Robert Penn Warren a strong sense of origins. His descriptions of a childhood spent in and out of his father's greenhouses stand as models of time recaptured without the slightest touch of sentimentality. It was after the delicacy and pathos of these vignettes that Roethke turned to describing another kind of journey—his return to the subconscious of child and man. Here again he deals with difficult material in language that renders it exactly; his seemingly irrational lyrics are as neatly put together as sonnets, and we hear the wit and laughter of the subconscious as well as its nightmare mutterings about terror and guilt. The collection ends with several new poems. In them, Roethke goes back to a traditional formality which has reached the point of accomplishment and control that seems effortless but, of course, is not. Amid the dreary and abstract poetry of Roethke's generation, it is a pleasure to come upon such well-made, humane, and wise lyrics.

Louise Bogan, The New Yorker,
October 24, 1953.

will sing praises unto thee among nations" (108:3), and "All night I make my bed to swim; I water my couch with tears" (6:6).

Again, Roethke takes advantage of the Psalms pattern, especially as he moves from entreaty to celebration. The effect is incantatory. "You tree beginning to know, / You whisper of kidneys" (**"Give Way, Ye Gates"**) leads to "In the high noon of thighs / In the springtime of stones" in the same poem. In **"Praise to the End!"** the youth urges: "Speak to me, frosty beard. / Sing to me, sweet," and, having heard the singing, prays: "Wherefore O birds and small fish, surround me. / Lave me, ultimate waters." The repetition sometimes intensifies, sometimes clarifies, as it does when the poet balances an abstraction in one line with something quite concrete in the next: "I could say hello to things; / I could talk to a snail" (**"O Lull Me, Lull Me"**).

Such rhetorical similarities invite a more direct comparison of the two protagonists, but the relationship is subtle, oblique. The ancient heroic lad who faced Goliath with only a sling in his hand lends his voice to a modern child whose battles are all internal and whose giant is a ghost. This protagonist struggles slowly and painfully toward some understanding of his personal tragedy and his present condition. When Roethke reaches toward the David image, therefore, he seeks not a literal but an emotional reference for his sequence. The Psalms create for us David the singer, the poet-king who tells us of his great sorrows and his great joys, a lost son who seeks understanding and forgiveness from his Father. There is no lasting triumph for this singer; instead, the shifts of mood and tone and spiritual condition come through the powerful lyric poetry and we find ourselves alternately rejoicing or weeping as we read. And so we do for the lost son of this Roethke sequence, of which the poet says, ". . . at least you can see that the method is cyclic. I believe that to go forward as a spiritual man it is necessary first to go back. Any history of the psyche . . . is bound to be a succession of experiences, similar yet dissimilar. There is a perpetual slipping back, then a going forward; yet there is some 'progress.'"

There are certain "facts" which become clear as the sequence progresses, however, that relate to those in the Psalms: events, themes, plot, and images. A central event is the death of the father, seen through the eyes of a very young child at the end of the first poem, **"Where Knock is Open Wide."** "He was all whitey bones / And skin like paper," the child says, sharing with us the traumatic event which colors all his perceptions. His instinctive emotional response to this event, "Kisses come back, / I said to Papa," establishes the intense feelings of loss, separation, and lack of love and communion which determine the child's response to all external sights and sounds. His rational response to the event, "God's somewhere else" and "Maybe God has a house. / But not here," explains his sense of isolation and his continuing quest for a place or a time in which he can be enclosed by love.

The poems which follow in the sequence record that quest, described by John Wain as central to art, "an endeavor to break down the isolation of the human being . . . to bring us into a fruitful contact with *something*" ["The Monocle of My Sea-Faced Uncle," *Theodore Roethke: Essays on the Poetry,* edited by Arnold Stein, 1965]. Wain goes on to say that Roethke is an "evangelical writer," that "the intensity of his lyric gift sprang directly from the hunger that raged at its center—a hunger for salvation." Such hunger is also at the center of the Psalms, and the implied dramatic situation—of a passionate, lonely person with great emotional gifts and needs, awaiting and seeking reconciliation, union—could provide Roethke with just enough structure to shape his account of the restless psyche.

As Karl Malkoff notes [in *Theodore Roethke: An Introduction to the Poetry,* 1966], "the main themes of the entire sequence—birth and death, sexual guilt and confusion, separation from the father and God (the 'lost son' motif)—are explicitly considered in the first poem." The themes are reiterated constantly, but always from a different point of reference and usually with some novel linguistic rendering. As the child grows up, he seeks solace from the mother, from associations with his past, from all elements of nature. His understanding comes after numerous descents to the "pit," a place familiar to David. To Roethke, the pit symbolized the far reaches of a regressive journey, a place of mire, of primordial slime. These journeys are often accompanied by scenes of masturbation and consequent guilt, until the protagonist finally comes to realize a union with all things, which is sensual and ultimately sexual, for the regressive journeys have set off

a fish-sperm association and, by extension, a fish-father-death-womb-water-life-light sequence. The young man's awareness of the cycle brings him, finally, to a sense of his own identity and to the understanding that "What the grave says, / 'The nest denies" (**"Unfold! Unfold!"**), that

> We met in a nest. Before I lived.
> The dark hair sighed.
> We never enter
> Alone.
>
> **["I Cry Love! Love!"]**

The profound perception is reiterated in the final poem of the sequence, **"O, Thou Opening, O"**:

> The dark has its own light.
> A son has many fathers.
> Stand by a slow stream:
> Hear the sigh of what is.

There is much more. The physical growth of the persona is accompanied by a parallel spiritual development; the union is mystical also. So too with the protagonist's aesthetic progress, for the child moves from a "small sing" in the first poem to a point where the grown persona cries in **"Unfold! Unfold!"**:

> Sing, sing, you symbols! All simple creatures,
> All small shapes, willow-shy,
> In the obscure haze, sing!

As Roethke's sequence opens, the tie to David is immediate, albeit indirect. The title of the first poem, **"Where Knock is Open Wide,"** is from Christopher Smart's *A Song to David.* Smart asserts "Strong is the lion . . . ," and in verse 77:

> But stronger still, in earth and air,
> And in the sea, the man of pray'r;
>   And far beneath the tide;
> And in the seat to faith assign'd,
> Where ask is have, where seek is find,
>   Where knock is open wide.

The unique diction renders Smart's version of Matthew 7:7, "Ask, and it shall be given you; seek, and ye shall find; knock, and it shall be opened unto you." Roethke's debt to Smart went beyond the use of that line for the title poem, for he also practices some of Smart's grammatical conversions and thus enlivens the rhetoric of the child protagonist. The title has implications which go beyond the original context, of course; it can have sexual connotations or even refer to the literal as well as the spiritual birth of a child. But the important thing, Smart's devotion to David, cannot be denied. His *Song* has 86 verses and he also did poetic "translations" of a number of the Psalms, many of which were set to music. Surely Roethke knew of this homage.

Interestingly, another poet whom Roethke cites was also especially devoted to David. Traherne was mentioned the first time Roethke spoke of "ancestors" for this sequence, and in a letter to John Crowe Ransom, Roethke mentions that it was Traherne's prose that most influenced him. In the "Third Century" Traherne says,

> but as I read the Bible I was here and there Surprised with such Thoughts and found by Degrees that these Things had been written of before, not only in the Scriptures but in many of the fathers and that this was the Way of Communion with God in all Saints, as I saw Clearly in the Person of David. Me thoughts a New Light Darted in into all his Psalms, and finally spread abroad over the Whole Bible. [*Traherne: Centuries, Poems, and Thanksgivings,* edited by H. M. Margoliouth, 1958]

After speaking of his new vision, Traherne wrote his own poem about David and then explicated some of the Psalms, giving contemporary exegetical associations. In *Thanksgivings,* Traherne echoes David strongly, seeing with David's poetic vision.

When Roethke was working on this sequence, with just a few of the poems done, he wrote to Kenneth Burke, "But God, I need a larger structure; something dramatic: an old story,—something. Most of the myths are a bore, to me. Wish I could talk to you about it." His search quite obviously took him to the Bible, for his long poem, **"The Lost Son"** (first done for a collection with that title and later placed at the center of the *Praise to the End!* collection), contains a direct quote from Job 30:28, "Hath the rain a father?" And perhaps the words of Elihu to Job inspired the "plot" of the sequence: "His flesh shall be fresher than a child's: he shall return to the days of his youth" (Job 33:25), and "Lo, all these things worketh God oftentimes with man," "To bring back his soul from the pit, to be enlightened with the light of the living" (Job 33:29, 33:30).

The path from the pit to the places of light is long and difficult for adolescent or king, and Roethke fills his journey with an amazing number of images which are also found in the Psalms. Many of these images are traditional symbols, found often in our Western literature, but the Psalms provide an original emotional context for our poet. When Roethke echoes the pleading and anguish of David, he assimilates David's images and invests them with modern psychological symbolism. Thus the pit, for example, is not a place where evildoers are punished, as David saw it, but a dark, subconscious area in the psyche of the boy. It is a necessary stop on the journey of the spirit, and its exploration, however painful, can lead to union.

As we saw, it is easy to tie the theme of return to childhood to some later verses in Job, but the Psalms also open with images of generation and birth: "I will declare the decree: the Lord hath said unto me, Thou art my Son; this day have I begotten thee" (2:7). In the first poem of Roethke's sequence the child tells us: "Once upon a tree / I came across a time," and most critics agree that the time the child comes to is a prenatal time, a point at which he can ask "What's the time, papa-seed?" and when he can tell us "My father is a fish." The tree image is reiterated throughout the sequence, connected most often with

sexual awakening or awareness. In an early poem he tells us, "When I stand, I'm almost a tree. / Leaves, do you like me any?" (**"Bring the Day!"**), and later we hear "Believe me, knot of gristle, I bleed like a tree," and mention of "You tree beginning to know" (**"Give Way, Ye Gates"**). In **"Sensibility! O La!"**—in a time of joy—he notes, "I'm a twig to touch," and in **"Unfold! Unfold!"** he says "I stretched like a board, almost a tree." The idea of potency, caught by the image of a tree, is introduced early in the Psalms: "And he shall be like a tree planted by the rivers of water, that bringeth forth his fruit in his season; his leaf also shall not wither" (1:3). Later, with joy, David tells us "But I am like a green olive tree in the house of God" (52:8).

Roethke's choice of the voice of a child for these early poems is surely striking and appropriate, for David tells us, in Psalm 8:2, "Out of the mouth of babes and sucklings hast thou ordained strength because of thine enemies, that thou mightest still the enemy and the avenger." The enemy of Roethke's child is the ghost of the father, a ghost he must "still" and one that he finds in the wind or in the long grass. David's spiritual Father flies "on the wings of the wind" (18:10) and we know he spoke to Job from a whirlwind. Though Roethke's child comes to accept the wind later in the sequence, his first utterances are tense and compressed, showing the grammatical conversions Christopher Smart was so fond of. "How high is have?" he asks, "Have I come to always?" Or he sighs "Nowhere is out," or pleads "God, give me a near." This last clause has often been misprinted "God, give me an ear," an error which indicates just the kind of audible ambiguity Roethke intended. But it also echoes a number of David's cries: "Hear me when I call, O God" (4:1); "Give ear to my words, O Lord" (5:1); "Hear my prayer, O Lord, give ear to my supplication" (143:1); and finally, "Give ear to my voice, when I cry unto thee" (141:1).

At another moment the child begs, "Fish me out. / Please." A strange image for a child to use, and difficult to explain, until we see that the Psalmist also used it: "He sent from above, he took me, he drew me out of many waters" (18:16), and again: "Deliver me out of the mire, and let me not sinketh: let me be delivered from them that hate me, and out of the deep waters" (69:14). David, in that same Psalm, moans "I am weary of my crying," a condition we noted before, in Psalm 6:6, where he tells us "I am weary with my groaning; all the night I make my bed to swim; I water my couch with my tears." In a beautiful contraction, intensified by the unusual rhetoric, the child tells us simply "My tears are tired."

In a regressive stage, Roethke's protagonist often mentions "a worm." In the first poem he cries, "A worm has a mouth. / Who keeps me last?" and later: "It's still enough for the knock of a worm" (**"Praise to the End!"**). In **"The Lost Son"** is an early incantation, "Worm be with me. / This is my hard time." The image and the rhetoric belong to David also, in a song spoken from the same despairing mood: "But I am a worm, and no man; a reproach of men," and a few lines later: "Be not far from me; for trouble is near" (22:6 and 11). Similarly, and just as much a puzzle, is the boy's plea, "Bird, soft-sigh me home" (**"The Lost Son"**). The object of this address seems very general, until we note that David often cried to the Lord to hide him "in the shadow of thy wings," and connected the image with the soul in 11:1: "In the Lord put I my trust: how say ye to my soul, Flee as a bird to your mountain." For the modern poet, the image carries the weight of physical and spiritual connotations and is offered in terms as lovely. In **"Give Way, Ye Gates"**: "Such music in a skin! / A bird sings in the bush of your bones." And in the poem just previous:

> O small bird awakening,
> Light as a hand among blossoms,
> Hardly any old angels are around any more.
>
> [**"Bring the Day"**]

Often repeated in Roethke's sequence is the image of bones, a reminder to readers of his very first book of published poems. There, in the first poem, **"Open House,"** he presented himself as utterly open, "naked to the bone." This kind of nakedness meant total involvement for the persona, and the image grew in meaning in a later poem, **"Cuttings (later),"** when the speaker felt in his veins and in his bones the "sucking and sobbing" of the plant beginning to root. In the most intimate moments of the *Praise* sequence, Roethke uses the bone imagery to express the intense emotions felt by the persona. At first the association is frightening: papa, dead, is "all whitey bones," and later he tells us "I dreamt I was all bones; / The dead slept in my sleeve." As he regresses in this poem, **"Praise to the End!"** he asks "Can the bones breathe? This grave has an ear." At the end of **"The Lost Son,"** in a time of communion, he sees the light moving slowly "over the dry seed-crowns, / The beautiful surviving bones / Swinging in the wind," but just previous to this, in the heart of a "storm," he says "My veins are running nowhere. Do the bones cast out their fire?" At the very beginning of this poem, in fact, in a time of fear and longing for understanding, he tells us "I shook the softening chalk of my bones."

The Psalmist uses almost the same words in his expression of his fear and impotence: "I am poured out like water, and my bones are out of joint" (22:14). In fact, the bone imagery appears throughout the Psalms, just as it does in the Roethke sequence. In 31:10, David moans: "My strength faileth because of my iniquities, and my bones are consumed"; in 32:3, "When I kept silence, my bones waxed through my roaring all the day long"; and, in a joyful song, "He [the righteous] keepeth all his bones: not one of them is broken" (34:20). In the depths again: "Our bones are scattered at the grave's mouth" (141:7).

The most impressive connection of the sequence with the Psalms is probably the abundance of imagery associated with the pit or the mire. For Roethke, the journey backward was also a journey into the dark, the pit. He tells us: "Each poem . . . is complete in itself; yet each in a sense is a stage in a kind of struggle out of the slime, part of a slow spiritual process; an effort to be born, and later, to become something more." When he wrote the **"Lost Son"**

poem, before the others in this long sequence, he titled one of the sections **"The Pit,"** indicating that **"The Flight"** of the previous section would take one to this dark interior. Any reading of the Psalms is bound to impress one with the same imagery, for the fear of the pit was omnipresent and we see that the wicked are always condemned to it (30:3, 30:9, 28:1, etc.). For David, the pit is dug by the offender, as we see in 7:15: "He made a pit, and digged it and is fallen into the ditch which he made." We feel his joy in his deliverance in 49:2: "He brought me up also out of the horrible pit, out of the miry clay, and set my feet upon a rock." When Roethke's protagonist comes to understanding, it is in reconciliation with the images of the pit, the "miry clay," as well as all else. He tells us in **"Unfold! Unfold!"**: "I was far back, farther than anybody else," and describes how far that was:

> I was privy to oily fungus and the algae of standing
>   waters;
> Honored, on my return, by the ancient fellowship of
>   rotten stems.

Those images announce the move toward joy and light, a place both singers knew very well. In later poems Roethke often uses images of dancing to exclaim his joy; at one point he tells us "And everything comes to One, / As we dance on, dance on, dance on" (**"Once More, The Round"**). But the steps of that dance start here, in the final parts of this sequence, when his protagonist "danced in a simple wood." David also danced as he spoke to the Lord, "Thou has turned for me my mourning into dancing" (30:11). And the joy extends into new songs, too, as we see when David announces his faith in the Lord: "And now shall mine head be lifted up above mine enemies round about me: therefore will I offer in his tabernacle sacrifices of joy; I will sing, yea, I will sing praises unto the Lord" (22:7). In 40:3 we see that he has been brought up out of the pit, and immediately he says: "And he hath put a new song in my mouth." Again, in 144:9, the same impulse: "I will sing a new song unto thee, O God." For Roethke's protagonist the awakening brings a new awareness:

> I'm more than when I was born;
> I could say hello to things;
> I could talk to a snail;
> I see what sings!
> What sings!
>
> [**"O Lull Me, Lull Me"**]

In the final poem of the sequence he tells us "I've crept from a cry," "I sing the green, and things to come, / I'm king of another condition, / So alive I could die!" (**"O, Thou Opening, O"**).

Such joy, such exaltation, is possible for all men, as David sees them in 103:15: "As for man, his days are as grass: as a flower of the field, so he flourisheth"; and it extends to all creation, too, for we see in Psalm 65 that God touches all things on earth and in the heavens, so that "the pastures are clothed with flocks; the valleys also are covered over with corn; they shout for joy, they also sing" (65:13).

The realization comes also for the persona of Roethke's sequence, sometimes in the wild joy we have seen above, sometimes in the same image of the field which emanates life. The blessings were there, around him all the time, but the knowledge of such glory was hard to accept. In the first poem the child cried "Maybe God has a house. / But not here." At the end of the sequence he sees

> A house for wisdom: a field for revelation.
> Speak to the stones, and the stars answer.
> At first the visible obscures:
> Go where the light is.
>
> ["Unfold! Unfold!"]

Theodore Roethke's work remains largely untouched by this investigation. The *Praise* sequence has many fathers, and is enormously rich in other themes and images, yet Roethke knew the wealth the Psalms held and was not afraid to sing with David's voice when he needed it. He acknowledged his debt to all his "ancestors" when he said: "In their harsh thickets / The dead thrash. / They help." I believe he was thinking of David when he wrote

> See what the sweet harp says.
> Should a song break a sleep?
>
> ["O, Thou Opening, O"]

He answered affirmatively, awaking the harpist, so they could sing together.

A tortured man—with psychological characteristics both paranoid schizophrenic and manic-depressive—Roethke used his madness, his tenuous sense of self, to become a spokesman for us all. He articulated what is generally repressed: the struggle of the naked self to persist in its existence, of the isolated man to become part of something greater than himself.

—*Karl Malkoff, in "Theodore Roethke: The Darker Side of the Dream," in* American Writing Today, *edited by Richard Kostelanetz, 1991.*

Neal Bowers (essay date 1982)

SOURCE: "Theodore Roethke: The Manic Vision," in *Modern Poetry Studies*, Vol. XI, Nos. 1-2, 1982, pp. 152-64.

[In the following essay, examines the connection between Roethke's manic-depression and evidence of mystical themes in his works.]

Although Theodore Roethke's manic depressive syndrome, which troubled him most of his adult life, and his interest in mysticism, particularly during his last decade, have been fairly well documented, no one has ever commented on the significant connection between these two things. This is a curious oversight because the relationship, far from being remote, is a causal one, with Roethke's manic experiences leading him inevitably to mystical literature in search of a parallel for his own unusual perceptions. He found in the writing of mystics and scholars of mysticism validation of his manic-depressive experiences and a way to order the manic vision which, without a larger context, must initially have appeared aberrant and chaotic. Because the relationship between manic-depression and mysticism was apparent to Roethke from the earliest stages of his career, an evaluation of that relationship should lead to a greater understanding of his work and, beyond that, to a more complete view of the poet himself, as a man who turned a personal handicap into a rich source for poetry.

Although several critics (William Heyen and Jay Parini, in particular) have touched upon Roethke's mysticism, no one has seemed eager to deal with it in detail, perhaps because no one feels very comfortable with the term "mysticism" and because most critics would agree with Richard Allen Blessing that Roethke was "not much of a mystic if, indeed, he was one at all" [*Theodore Roethke's Dynamic Vision*, 1974]. Nevertheless, certain mystical qualities are so apparent in the poetry, particularly in the final book, *The Far Field*, as to be unavoidable. And Roethke's interest in mysticism is undeniable, for his working notebooks (in the University of Washington's collection) abound, from the first to the last, with references to mystical doctrine. Such references frequently take the form of apparent outlines or notes transcribed from other sources, as in the following:

> The inward flight
> and frozen night
>
> . . . . .
>
> St. John of the Cross
> Suffer
>
> . . . . .
>
> Orthodox mystic spiritual marriage
> to God
>
> . . . . .
>
> *Unitive mysticism* "complete fusion of
>   soul with the divine"
>
> . . . . .
>
> epithalamic mysticism
> Soul cannot partake of God, but only
> resemble God.
>
> —Ruysbroeck

These notations, recorded in 1939, are sketchy, but subsequent entries are more explicit. For example, in a 1942 notebook Roethke presents thorough summaries of the discussions of mysticism found in Denis De Rougemont's

Love in the Western World. His notes reveal a familiarity with such well-known mystics as Meister Eckhart, St. Francis, and St. Theresa and preserve comments from their writings that Roethke apparently found significant: *e.g.,* "True mystics are [the] essence of prudence, rigor & clear-sighted obedience" and "All mystics have complained of a want of new words."

In addition to the abundance of references scattered throughout the notebooks, lengthy notes on mysticism can be found elsewhere in the Roethke manuscripts, sometimes entered on loose leaf paper, sometimes in spiral notebooks, and, in at least one instance, in a tablet of typing paper. These writings appear to be notes for teaching, but on many occasions it becomes apparent that Roethke was writing as much for himself as for his students. For example, on one page beneath the heading "Mysticism" appear the following remarks:

> The business is Love. A total dedication of the Will.
> For silence is not God, nor speaking is not God, etc. . . . But he is hid between them.
> Such a blind shot with the sharp dart of longing may never fail of the prick, the which is God.
> —The Cloud of Unknowing
> Come out of the theological tree. Intelligence must rest without.

These entries seem designed primarily to jog the memory. If they were used in class, no doubt Roethke had pages of extemporaneous commentary to offer on each statement, and perhaps the last remarks functioned as an exhortation to his students: "Come out of the theological tree. Intelligence must rest without." But in many ways, these notes on mysticism resemble those found in the notebooks, and they were probably more valuable to Roethke than to his students. It seems likely that Roethke introduced his students to the arcane study of mysticism because of his own fascination with the material.

Roethke's reading in mysticism intensified during the last ten years of his life, as did his interest in philosophy in general, but he read steadily and broadly in mystical literature from the late 1930's and early 1940's onward. And his reading was more than merely casual, as the following note found inside the cover of his copy of *The Soul Afire: Revelations of the Mystics,* edited by H. A. Reinhold, indicates: "Nowadays those who are near God must keep quiet. An extraordinary book: praised by nobody." This inscription indicates that Roethke not only read the book and read it thoroughly but also took it to heart, found something of value within its covers. His interest in mysticism did not come late in life, as has often been supposed, but is traceable from the earliest phases of his career, long before the publication of *Open House* in 1941. Thus, the following entry, attributed to Saroyan, appears in a 1935 notebook: "For an eternal moment he was all things at once: the bird, the fish, the rodent, the reptile, and man." This comment is, in many ways, peculiarly Roethkean because it describes the mystical sense of unity often encountered in Roethke's poetry—in the later poetry,

however, from *The Lost Son* on, not in the poems of *Open House.* Similarly, the following entry, found in the same notebook, connects more directly with the poems of a later period:

> What a sweet ineffable aura lay upon all experience at the time, when the merest act, the lifted finger, the barest lift of the brow, was suffused with tenderness.

These entries are striking for several reasons. First, both describe in rather standard language what has been indentified throughout the centuries as the mystical experience. The language is standard because mystics usually emphasize the paradoxical ("an eternal moment") and ineffable nature ("a sweet ineffable aura") of their perception. Second, both comments seem to have more in common with Roethke's later poetry than with anything he was writing in 1935. In fact, while they tell little about the *Open House* poems, they may serve as a gloss for most of the poems in "The Lost Son" sequence (**"A Field of Light"** for example, or **"Praise to the End!"**). Roethke's experience (as recorded in the notebooks) was running considerably ahead of his poetry. Time would be needed to assimilate what he had felt, that he had "Stood on the threshold of a mystic experience."

It is not merely coincidental that the entries which reveal something of mystical awareness appear in the same notebook in which Roethke recorded certain observations about his first mental breakdown. In fact, it seems obvious that whatever unusual perception Roethke may have had was a direct product of his collapse. It is interesting to note that Roethke himself described his breakdown as a mystical experience. According to Roethke's biographer Allan Seager, Roethke told Peter De Vries that "he had a mystical experience with a tree and he learned there the 'secret of Nijinsky'" [*The Glass House: The Life of Theodore Roethke,* 1968]. It is, of course, impossible to say exactly what Roethke meant by this, but Seager's speculations are reasonable: that Nijinsky's encounter with the tree (described in his *Diary*) emphasized "the primacy of emotion over reason," an ordering Roethke himself believed in. Whatever Roethke meant, it is clear that he felt he had encountered some transcendent truth during his manic excursion into the Michigan woods that cold November night. Some nine years later, he would remember it this way:

> For no reason I started to feel very good. Suddenly I knew how to enter into the life of everything around me. I knew how it felt to be a tree, blade of grass, even a rabbit. I didn't sleep much. I just walked around with this wonderful feeling. [*The Glass House*]

This feeling of euphoria and unity is equivalent to the mystical experience, in which "the self perceives an added significance and reality in all natural things: is often convinced that it knows at last 'the secret of the world'" [Evelyn Underhill, *Mysticism,* 1955]. If the episode was in some ways terrifying for Roethke and bore terrible consequences for him at Michigan State (where his job hung in the balance), it was also a revelation for him. In a 1946 notebook, he wrote of the experience, "Breakdown, hell, that was a break-up."

To illustrate just how profound the experience was for Roethke, a fairly long account of the episode given by him during the last year of his life is presented below. This commentary, recorded in conjunction with the film *In a Dark Time,* was not included in the sound-track recording and has never before been published. It is presented here, with a minimum of editorial changes, as evidence of how vividly the experience remained with Roethke even after the passage of some 28 years. His remarks, which run in almost stream-of-consciousness fashion, reveal an intensity and excitement which underscore the significance of the event in his life:

> There was the one time I played the Rimbaud business of really driving myself, seeing . . . you could really derange the senses, and it can be done, and let me tell you, I did it. I mean, I got in such good condition, I wasn't drinking at all. I was twenty-seven. This was in East Lansing, Michigan. I was running on those cinder pads four, five miles a day. Jesus, and teaching, too. But you know I got in this real strange state. I got in the woods and started a circular kind of dance, and I've never put this down very . . . refer to it in "I tried to fling my shadow at the moon." I kept going around and just shedding clothes. Sounds Freudian as hell, but in the end, I had sort of a circle—as if, I think, I understood intuitively what the frenzy is. That is, you go way beyond yourself, and . . . this is not sheer exhaustion but this strange sort of a . . . not illumination . . . but a sense of being again a part of the whole universe. I mean, anything but quiet. I mean, in a sense everything is symbolical. In one of the Old Woman poems I just sort of put it in there, because I know if you put this down in prose, for God's sake [people will say], "Oh, this is merely clinical"—I mean, "Obviously, he is crazy" and so forth. But it was one of the deepest and most profound experiences I ever had. And accompanying it was a real sexual excitement also . . . and this tremendous feeling of actual power. But finally, when coming back, I was just so exhausted that I could hardly walk, in as good condition as I was.

> What happened to me eventually . . . well, one thing, you have this curious sense that you're actually being transformed literally into an animal. You start getting fantasies—I mean, of power, lion-like power. But the next night was much tougher, in a sense—I really thought my features were changing. Of course, this was madness, you see, but the relationship between the ecstasy and madness is so . . . well, one of the things that the head-shrinkers know, or the good ones, that if these descents are too rapid [they] can be chaotic, and I mean, you knock. In other words, something could happen to you: you could get lost back there, because what you're doing is going right back into the history of the goddamn race. I mean, you're down to the animal, dog, and so forth, down to snake. It sounds nuts, but, well . . . fight your way out of that What happened to me there, I simply blacked out eventually. I knew I was teaching in real manic frenzy. Well, I woke up on the morning, somewhat like this, with very little sleep, and decided I wanted to get to his

office. I took a little walk on the edge of the city. There I got so cold I lay down and took off a shoe, and there I had . . . this is again real loony, and goes beyond—there was a curious crabhole, and I lay there and started whistling to this thing, as if you were really trying to call it out of the earth. Well, I knew what I was doing, that this was not a snake-hole, and so on and so on, but . . . and I put this down in one of those pieces, in one of those running ones. Then I got scared; it started getting cold; it was November, and I started to run with only one shoe on. Jesus Christ, here you are, and I was barefoot . . . well, symbolically, etc. I got into a gas station. There was a guy—I again—I just associated with my father. I was out on my feet, see, just punchy from . . . you know, I hadn't slept for five nights, and I said, "Can . . . get me, drive me," and he said, "Sure." He drove me to the campus, and I came in, you know, just like someone who had been beaten for five rounds. I sat down in that goddamn office and I thought, "Jesus Christ, you're going to have to adlib now." But the trouble in these high states of consciousness is that *everything* gets heightened, so that sound particularly . . somebody walking overhead . . . it just sounds like a concatenation. Well, I finally said, "Just bring me a coach and I'll try to explain on what happened to me physically." I was just going to say, "I'm not nuts. I'm just out on my feet because I've been working." I finally thought I'd died. There was a profound and beautiful experience, as if you . . . and you can hear the thing going, but you just die right then.

> The *real* point is that this business of the dance accompanies exaltation of the highest, the human thing, and it also goes into the Dionysian frenzy, which in modern life hardly anyone *speaks* of anymore. But the real profundity of that experience, I mean, in the sense of the mood itself, seemed to be, you know, the whole Islamic world. All the cultures were with you. This is exactly what they felt when they were rolling in the circular, you know, frenzy thing. And your perceptions, as I say, both in sight and particularly sound *and* smell, and frequently also . . . another is that you get the transfer of senses. Sometimes that comes even with memory. You know, Hopkins says in one of his . . . when he said, "I tasted brass in my mouth" . . . well, that's the very essence, it seems to me, of metaphysical thinking. That is when the body itself . . . when Vaughan says, "When felt through all my fleshy dress, Ripe shoots of everlastingness," well, that's the feeling. You feel one way that you are eternal, or immortal, and it doesn't seem to be a cheap thing either. And furthermore, death becomes, as it were, an absurdity, of no consequence. And also the notion, conception, of time is completely subjective, and I've often thought sometimes that [when] the suicidal leaps from the window, when he hits that pavement and is just a blob, who knows, maybe he explodes into a million universes and he is happy. Who knows? That's behind, you know, the nuttier aspects of certain Hindu religions, when they'd start dancing and singing and finally in this ecstasy run right into the goddamn sea when they know that all those sharks are there. Nothing could stop 'em. I mean, we can say that this is collective madness. It is, but it's part of the human psyche; it's there.

This account goes far beyond Seager's, which describes only what could be seen by an observer or a biographer not caught up in the experience: Roethke's frenzied walk in the cold, in the middle of the night, with only one shoe on. Such behavior looks like purest madness, and that is the way it was viewed by the administrators at Michigan State who chose not to reinstate Roethke after his release from Mercywood Sanitarium. But from Roethke's perspective, the episode went beyond madness to ecstasy, to the point where he could feel "a sense of being again a part of the whole universe." This sensation is identical to the mystic's heightened sense of unity. No wonder then that the experience overwhelmed him and remained imprinted upon his memory, for one of the chief characteristics of the mystical insight is its indelibility. What Roethke saw and felt during his manic flight into the countryside was transcendent truth, a reality beyond what is normally regarded as real. His perception marked a kind of initiation, an awakening, which inevitably modified everything.

To what extent Roethke willed his mental collapse is difficult to determine. Seager, who is willing to accept Roethke's claim that he induced the episode at Michigan State, cites Roethke's drinking, pill taking, and going without sleep as possible causes. But he also observes that manic-depressives characteristically insist that they bring on their attacks themselves. Perhaps Roethke was trying to achieve a "break-up;" perhaps he was pushing toward something like Rimbaud's *"dereglement de tous les sens."* An entry in a 1934 notebook reveals quite clearly that Roethke felt the need to make some changes in his life for the good of his poetry:

> I think God has sterilized me so I can't have any more poems. Maybe I had some poetic Spanish fly—some nightingale guano? Perhaps I've written all I can write in my present state of physical & moral development. Perhaps I should become a homosexual?

This passage, written approximately sixteen months before the first breakdown, lends credence to Roethke's claim that he induced his first episode "to reach a new level of reality." It is not improbable that Roethke became so disenchanted with his work that he determined to alter his "state of physical and moral development." Certainly, no one could doubt that the abusive way he treated himself during the time immediately preceding his collapse was at the least a contributing factor to his first episode. Unquestionably, he invited the episode, felt that he had induced it himself, and seemed convinced that it was in some way related to the production of his art.

That Roethke saw a positive relationship between his mental disorder and his poetry is revealed in a number of places in the notebooks. For example, in a draft of his contribution to the Ostroff-edited symposium on **"In a Dark Time,"** Roethke makes the following observations:

> A "descent" can be willed—or at least the will—the human will—can be a factor. The real danger lies in the preceding euphoria, in the exhilaration getting out of hand. My first "breakdown" was in a very real sense deliberate. I not only asked for, I prayed that it would happen. True, I had used a tough resilient athlete's

body as if it were rubber: had gone without any sleep at all for months, etc., etc.

Perhaps he had "prayed" for the breakdown because he was determined to escape from what he perceived to be stagnation in any way he could, even at great risk to his own well-being. As he writes in another notebook during the same year:

> All I care about is achievement: but it must be real achievement in its absolutely final terms: how achieved—at least in terms of the cost to the self—I do not care.

And in an earlier notebook he enters a similar remark in dialogue:

> "I can't go flying apart just for those who want the benefit of a few verbal kicks. My god, do you know what poems like that *cost?* They're not written vicariously: they come out of actual suffering; *real* madness."
>
> "I've got to go beyond. That's all there is to it."
>
> 'Beyond what?'
>
> "The human, you fool. Don't you see what I've done: I've come this far and now I can't stop. It's too late, baby, it's too late."

Roethke knew what he was doing, realized that his personal risks could be translated into poetic accomplishments, and he was even prepared to induce the manic-depressive cycle himself. He took the risk because the manic stages were periods of heightened activity and awareness during which he participated in the mystical feeling of "oneness," a feeling he claimed to have experienced "so many times, in so many varying circumstances, that I cannot suspect its validity." The overall result of Roethke's self-exploitation, his daring risk taking, was a poetry that is richly mystical. His manic-depressiveness afforded him a perception which was parallel or identical to mystical apprehension, and he utilized that perception to its fullest in his search for identity. He was not about to let the opportunity pass. As he comments in the middle of one notebook entry about mysticism: "Blake, too, was not of the type to let slip what he had learned."

According to Seager, Roethke was diagnosed variously as a "manic-depressive psychotic, but not typical," a "manic-depressive psychotic, but not typical," and as a "paranoid schizophrenic." The consensus was that Roethke was a manic-depressive, though the type was in dispute, and Roethke himself accepted that diagnosis. Certainly, the following textbook description of manic-depression seems to apply directly to Roethke's behavior during his manic episodes:

> The characteristic manifestations are psychomotor overactivity, elation of mood, distractibility and delusions with an omnipotent and omniscient content. The psycho-

motor overactivity is to be observed in the rapid speech, the pressure of talk, the continuous movement and the distractibility. As far as the mood state is concerned, the patient is not continually elated for there are occasions when there is depression with the lowering of self-esteem and self-criticism. When frustrated in his intentions the patient may become aggressive in word and action. [Thomas Freeman, "Observations on Mania," in *Manic Depressive Illness*, edited by Edward A. Wolpert, 1977]

There are many echoes here of Roethke's behavior: his insistence that he "started to feel very good" for no reason at all at the outset of his first breakdown, his grandiose business schemes (primarily those involving J. Robert Crouse and the utopian Hartland Area Project), his delusions about the Mafia, and his aggressive attitude toward various authority figures (for example, Dean Lloyd Emmons at Michigan State, whom he called a "Harvard son-of-a-bitch"), among other behavior characteristics cited by Seager in the biography. And perhaps the most significant element of the description concerns the mood state: the psychosis is characterized by movements from states of mania to states of depression. For Roethke, the depressed states were apparently not so long or so terrible, but then he always remained in a hospital where his depression was somewhat controlled by treatment and medication. Still, he did vacillate between up and down phases, and the vacillation is significant because it is very similar to the swing from heightened states of awareness to deep troughs of despondency ordinarily associated with the mystic temperament. The "typical mystic seems to move toward his goal through a series of strongly marked oscillations between 'states of pleasure' and 'states of pain'" [Evelyn Underhill].

Another element common to both manic-depression and mysticism is the "merging phenomenon." The manic-depressive may sometimes identify so strongly with other people or objects around him that he loses his identity and sense of self. In this condition, "he no longer regards himself as an entity distinct from other entities" [Thomas Freeman]. This aspect of the disorder is seen in Roethke's claim that he "knew how it felt to be a tree, a blade of grass, even a rabbit" [quoted in *The Glass House*]. And perhaps this, too, is the secret of Nijinsky and the explanation for Roethke's mystical encounter with the tree. Certainly, this phenomenon appears throughout the poetry, as in **"A Field of Light"**—"I moved with the morning"—or in **"Praise to the End!"**—"Many astounds before, I lost my identity to a pebble." The mystic, too, senses this merging, for he is acutely aware of the unity of all things. His perception of the oneness of creation causes him to strive to give up his ego in favor of merging with that singleness he perceives. In fact, the determined movement of the mystic is toward a blending with what he views as the One, the Ultimate, or the Absolute.

The relationship between mysticism and various psychotic states has been observed before, and the question of whether the mystical experience is merely another kind of psychotic state or a truly higher level of consciousness re-

mains unresolved. There is much to be said for the theory that mystical states are essentially periods of regression, returning to the infantile condition where "the self and the world have not yet been separated from one another" [Raymond Prince and Charles Savage, "Mystical States and the Concept of Regression," in *The Highest State of Consciousness*, edited by John White, 1972]. This notion brings mysticism and manic-depression into even closer proximity since the latter is also characterized by a return to infancy:

> The manic patient returns to a stage in which his impulses had not succumbed to repression, in which he foresaw nothing of the approaching conflict. It is characteristic that such patients often say that they feel themselves "as though new-born." [Karl Abraham, "Notes on the Psycho-Analytical Investigation and Treatment of Manic-Depressive Insanity and Allied Conditions," in *Manic-Depressive Illness*, edited by Edward A. Wolpert, 1977]

Significantly, the mystical also speaks of rebirth, of starting over again in a completely new world. Obviously, the regression to infancy bears directly upon Roethke's work, especially "The Lost Son" poems, where the protagonist is followed not only from infancy but from the womb. That Roethke himself was aware of some of the psychological views of mysticism is revealed in the following comment found in a 1942 notebook: "Material psychologists from Voltaire to Freud have said mystics are victims of sexual aberrations."

Roethke's first breakdown, whether he willed it or not, was a welcome disruption, a stimulating disarrangement of his senses. It provided him with a new perspective on the world, which revealed itself to him during the episode as inherently harmonious and unified. The resulting insights were of the type that can change a life, and they changed Roethke's. The numerous notebook entries and Roethke's stimulated interest in mystical reading material immediately following the first breakdown indicate that he saw a clear relationship between his episode and the mystical experience. Further, it is obvious that he exploited that relationship for poetic insights and produced from his manic experiences a poetry that is richly mystical.

The primary thematic concern in Theodore Roethke's poetry is with the evolution and identity of the self, its beginnings with an individual's birth, its organic growth which resembles the growth of things in nature, and its attainment of a maturity and independence that bring it into a new, harmonious relationship with creation.

—Ralph J. Mills, Jr., "In the Way of Becoming: Theodore Roethke's Last Poems," in Cry of the Human, *1975.*

Kermit Vanderbilt (essay date 1987)

SOURCE: "Theodore Roethke," in *A Literary History of the American West,* Texas Christian University Press, 1987, pp. 447-55.

[*In the following essay, Vanderbilt considers evidence of regionalism in Roethke's poetry.*]

Since Theodore Roethke's sudden, untimely death in summer of 1963, his work has been the subject of a steadily rising flood of critical assessments. The consensus of most of them is that his career can best be explained as an intense search for identity, wholeness, and grace. He shaped his private meditations into increasingly powerful esthetic forms that are at once original and charged with echoes from his various American and English poet-masters. A further aspect of Roethke's imaginative vision, however, remains to be adequately explored, namely his significant response to a regional America—the Midwest of his youth and, climactically, the Pacific Northwest where he lived his final sixteen years.

Roethke arrived in the Northwest in autumn of 1947 to teach poetry at the University of Washington, which remained his academic address until his death. The move from Penn State westward marked the crucial turning point in his career and the beginning of a serious identification with place in America. There were, of course, hints of regional identity in Roethke from the earlier period as he alternately suppressed, deplored, and finally embraced his Midwest origins. Born in 1908 in Saginaw, Michigan, the son of a strong-willed, Germanic father who operated the local greenhouse, he lived an introverted, troubled childhood that bred lifelong demons of guilt and insecurity. His biographer Allan Seager portrays, and somewhat oversimplifies, Roethke as a self-absorbed youth who scarcely felt a spirit of place in his Upper Midwest:

> There is no memory of Roethke hanging around the old folks listening, like Faulkner, and his old folks were German, anyway. Their stories would have led him back to the Old Country which never interested him. He also ignores all the vivid racy tales of the lumber boom, tales that expressed courage, will, and cunning that might have engaged another man. Unlike Allen Tate or Robert Lowell, he ignores in his poetry the events of his region's history. He must have been aware of the Indians, for he collected a shoebox full of flint arrowheads in his rambles along the riverbanks. But, of course, many boys did that. [*The Glass House: The Life of Theodore Roethke,* 1968]

Still, the environs of Saginaw and the Upper Midwest were implanted in a young poetic consciousness as a seminal force in the work to come. After graduation from Michigan and a year at Harvard, Roethke taught at Lafayette, returning home in 1935 to teach at Michigan State. In fall semester, he suffered a first mental breakdown. During convalescence, he recorded the following insight about himself in a long medical questionnaire: "Afraid of being localized in space, i.e. a particular place like W. E. Leonard in Madison. Question: What is the *name* of this? Hate some rooms in that sense, a victim of claustrophobia (sp)? Wasn't Dillinger a victim of this? Aren't many of the criminal leader types of this sort [*sic*]." (The illuminating reference to Dillinger discloses Roethke's self-image of the poet as an outsider in the Midwest community, and recalls the alienation he felt even earlier: in one of his college essays at the University of Michigan, he had discussed "the poet as criminal," the instance being François Villon.)

His first two books of poetry firmly support a one-sided thesis that the maturing Roethke was never a midwestern regionalist, either by sympathetic identity or literary example. The year before *Open House* appeared in 1941, ten of the poems were anthologized in a volume titled *New Michigan Verse.* Hungry for a reputation, Roethke was delighted to be published, but he worried, too, that he might be regarded as a merely regional poet. Yet shortly after, he applied for a Guggenheim grant to write "a series of poems about the America I knew in my middle-western childhood. . . . poems about people in a particular suburbia." Though he failed to receive the grant, Roethke persisted, and in his successful Guggenheim application three years later, he described two of his three projects as the writing of a distinctively regional verse:

> (1) a dramatic-narrative piece in prose and verse about Michigan and Wisconsin, part and present, which would center around the return of Paul Bunyan as a kind of enlightened and worldly folk-hero.

> (2) a series of lyrics about the Michigan countryside which have symbolical values. I have already begun these. They are not mere description, but have at least two levels of reference.

To William Carlos Williams, who would understand this regional program, Roethke worried over "the Paul Bunyan idea. The more I think about it, the less I like it. But I've got to get some device to organize some of my ideas & feelings about Michigan, etc.—not too solemn or God bless America or Steve Benétish. Maybe it's worth trying, anyway." When *The Lost Son* appeared in 1948, readers would not discover Roethke's early "ideas & feelings about Michigan" to be organized around the Bunyan folk-hero; instead, he had created a primordial myth of the child's Edenic greenhouse world. But the urge to regional description and symbolization, as well as to natural immersion and union, had begun. After 1947 in his adopted Northwest, Roethke increasingly drew from Michigan scenes of his childhood. The Midwest lived in the residue of memory, at times bitter yet also positive and cherished, to sustain the older poet and enrich the strong poems that grace his final, prize-winning years.

As it would predictably have to be for the mercurial Roethke, the final period in the Pacific Northwest became an intense love-hate affair with the regional culture and geography. After only a few months there, his life amounted to a sort of physical and spiritual exile. "I tell you, Kenneth," he wrote to Burke, "this far in the provinces you get a little nutty and hysterical: there's the feeling that all life is going on but you're not there." Within the year, he had reverted to the earlier self-characterization of the poet as at best an outlaw celebrity in his tame middle-class community. "As the only serious poet within 1,000 miles of Seattle," he wrote another friend in the East, "I find I have something of the status of a bank robber in Oklahoma or a congressman in the deep south." Throughout his tenure at the University of Washington, he inquired into jobs elsewhere or applied for Fulbrights and other grants that might bring him relief or delivery from the scene at Seattle and the University. This alienation was caused, in part, by what to him was a psychologically depressing climate in the Northwest. The region also affected him physically, exacerbating the arthritis in his knees, the "spurs" in his shoulders, and the bursitis in his tennis elbow (the fiercely competitive poet had been tennis coach both at Lafayette and Penn State).

Yet the Northwest had an immediate, salutary effect on the poet as well. Some eleven years before, a bookless Roethke in Michigan had lamented to Louise Bogan on his twenty-eighth birthday, "No volume out and I can't seem to write anything. You can say what you want, but *place* does have a lot to do with productivity." By contrast, he exploded with ideas and poems after he arrived in Seattle, as one discovers from the Northwest images and tropes coming alive in the extant notebooks, in their disciplined growth amid the felicitous prunings of the manuscript poems, and in the final harvest of the published work. Through the 1950s, the huge, unlikely poet-teacher had caused an excited flowering of poetry on the Washington campus and in the Seattle community. By the end of the decade he brought home to the Northwest all the major literary prizes in America. He was earning a place among the distinguished regional poets of our literature.

The nature of Roethke's regional expression has only begun to be appreciated. His first book of poems in the Northwest appeared in 1951. *Praise to the End!* is a "tensed-up" version of Wordsworth's *Prelude,* according to Roethke, and carries nine new poems which can be read, in one sense, as his completing the "lean-to beginnings" in the previous *Lost Son* collection. Once more he tracks his voyage of the mind's return to the dream logic, Mother Goose rhythms, and purposeful gibberish of childhood, and then back again to the varieties of rebirth after these mythic descents. Oblique and occasionally even direct influences from his early Northwest years can be recognized here and there in the expression and form of these verses.

A stronger promise of the regional poems to come appears in the new verses of his next book, *The Waking: Poems 1933-1953* (1953). **"A Light Breather,"** to select one, reveals a joyous dynamism of the spirit, "small" and "tethered" as before but now "unafraid" and "singing." Symptomatic of a new phase, too, are poems like **"Elegy for Jane,"** totally inspired from Northwest experience, and the more ambitious efforts which show the poet escaping from his former prison of the self to engage the circumambient world and the being of other living creatures. Just before the book appeared, he had married Beatrice O'Connell, his student during the year at Bennington a decade before. Seager believes that Roethke's marriage presently led him to a decisive awareness of the Northwest surroundings. As his capacity for feeling reached out to his young Beatrice, "hesitantly, even reluctantly perhaps, he admitted her into those labyrinths within himself where his father still lived, and he began to love her, not in the same way that he loved his father but with a true love nevertheless. And from this time forward, she participated in his growth, encouraged and supported it. Then he could see the mountains, the siskins, the madronas, and begin to use them." Viewed in this regard, segments of the next book, *Words for the Wind* (1958), and especially the "Love Poems," when thoroughly studied for their passionate metaphors of wind and seafoam, light and stones and rippling water as "spirit and nature beat in one breastbone," reveal the true beginnings of that distinctive Northwest sensibility which fully emerges in Roethke's subsequent poems, gathered in the posthumous *The Far Field* (1964).

The title poem of Roethke's final volume comes from the **"North American Sequence,"** the great achievement of this last book and Roethke's finest effort in the vein of literary regionalism. In the years to come, the six interlaced long poems of the **"North American Sequence"** may rank among the great ambitious poetic works of the language. The genesis of the sequence may be traced, in one fashion, to the summer of 1950. Roethke had bought his first car and had driven it back to Seattle. The trip created the stirrings of a "symbolical journey," his own spiritual version of a Northwest passage. It suggested "for next or possibly later book . . . a happy journey westward"; but there would be a uniquely Roethkean variation of this traditional passage—"in a word, a symbolical journey in my cheap Buick Special toward Alaska and, at least in a spiritual sense toward the east of Russia and the Mongolian Plains whence came my own people, the Prussians. . . ."

By the end of the decade, Roethke had modified this journey to an exclusively North American and ultimately regional experience. What he developed, in fact, is an intricate triple motif of outer-inner journeys. First is the Northwest passage to the dark oceanic "stretch in the face of death," and the periodic resolution experienced at the Pacific Coast shoreline, a journey out to the physical "edge" and metaphysical "beyond" and then back to reconciliation "where sea and fresh water meet" in the Northwest corner. The second passage or journey is a return to his origins, a movement eastward to the Michigan of his father's greenhouse and childhood years. Third is a "journey to the interior," imaged in an inland American geography perhaps equivalent, temporally, to the middle period of Roethke's initial breakdown in what he once termed that "Siberian pitilessness, the essential ruthlessness of the Middle West."

Of the three journeys, the Northwest passage is by far the richest and most dominant in the six poems of the sequence. Roethke gathers within it the shifting motifs of selfhood within the Northwest's natural plenitude, identifications with birds, fish, trees, and flowers (and occasionally as relief, with the stillness of rocks, clam shells, driftwood, and nature's minimals); the imagery of edges, abysses, and thresholds; the desire for convergence, resolution and union with the natural scene of salt water, fresh water, air, and earth; and on occasions, when blessedly aided by the soft regional light and wind, a felt convergence, with shimmerings of transcendence and beatitude.

Roethke establishes these interwoven journeys and themes and alternating rhythms in the first poem, **"The Longing,"** and then carries the reader forward to a longed-for passage, finally with an American Indian vigor of exploration, toward the threshold of full spiritual awareness. The poem opens in bleak rain as the Northwest scene, natural and manmade, fumes in its putrefaction. We are then launched on one more characteristic Roethkean voyage of the mutilated modern soul in its tormented quest for light and wholeness, but this time through a heightened relationship with a western landscape at once visible, personal, and charged with historical memory. The speaker anticipates a version of the legendary Indian vision-quest, a rite of passage into the North American interior.

> . . . the mouth of the night is still wide;
> On the Bullhead, in the Dakotas, where the eagles
>   eat well,
> In the country of few lakes, in the tall buffalo grass
>   at the base of the clay buttes . . .

Does the aging spirit dare to go primitive? No, if subjected to the ruthless plains of the interior. Yes, if sustained amid the inland waters.

> Old men should be explorers?
> I'll be an Indian.
> Ogalala?
> Iroquois.

"Meditation at Oyster River," the second poem, begins at twilight on the east coast of Vancouver Island. Roethke's explorer looks eastward to the "first tide-ripples," briefly immerses his feet in the water, and then partakes of earth and air as well by ascending to a perch on the cliffside. In the Northwest "twilight wind, light as a child's breath," the spirit quivers with alertness. A soundless pause has readied the time for meditation after urgent longing in the previous poem. The speaker takes us now on a backward motion toward the source, to "the first trembling of a Michigan brook in April." He feels the quickenings of a younger spirit which, like the melting Tittebawasee in early spring, could awaken, expand, and burst forward into a new season of becoming. The meditation returns to Oyster River and closes with the harmonious resolution of youth and age as he is "lulled into half-sleep" in a Whitman-like sea-cradle. After his journey back to Michigan and forward once more to the waters of the Northwest, he merges now in quiet joy with the waves and the intrepid birds of the coastline.

Arrivals on the threshold of naturalistic grace are momentary and precarious. In the third poem, **"Journey to the Interior,"** the speaker returns to the yawning mough of the night which awaited him at the close of **"The Longing."** He now embarks on a second American journey into the past, between Michigan beginnings and Northwest consummations, which takes the form of an actual trip westward through the North American interior. The second section concludes as he advances through the western prairies and beyond the Tetons. The past merges with the present, the random fluidity of the land journey is abated, and "time folds / Into a long moment" for the youth become, in the remembrance, confident father of the troubled man. In the final section, he still feels his "soul at a still-stand," but this time with a difference. Reconciled to change and death, united with the soft elements of his region, he can "breathe with the birds" while he stands "unperplexed" looking out on the Pacific scene. All extremes dissolve on that "other side of light," and

> The spirit of wrath becomes the spirit of blessing,
> And the dead begin from their dark to sing in my
>   sleep.

"The Long Waters" was apparently written after but appears before **"The Far Field."** Presumably, Roethke felt the need for a tranquil, sustained meditation piece to separate **"Journey to the Interior"** from **"The Far Field"** (which was once titled "Journeys"). **"The Long Waters"** occurs in a setting closely resembling Oyster River. The poem moves quietly among three Roethkean stages—retrogression (closing at times to infantile regression), thresholds, and convergence. These movements are experienced largely in Northwest images without the backward journey motifs of the previous poems. Roethke creates, instead, an alternating rhythm of gentle ebbing and flowing, action and reaction, that climaxes when the undulant long waters attenuate in the long poetic line and shape for the speaker a transformed moment of union and renewal:

> My eyes extend beyond the farthest bloom of the
>   waves;
> I lose and find myself in the long water;
> I am gathered together once more.
> I embrace the world.

With **"The Far Field,"** the journey becomes an extended return to a timeless childhood, presumably in Michigan, and to moments of immanence in that "far field, the windy cliffs of forever, / The dying of time in the white light of tomorrow." When he returns to the adult's present, the speaker can sense "a weightless change, a moving forward." The poem rises into gentle transcendence. The "finite things" which in previous lines of the sequence recalled "a vulnerable place" or a disturbing juxtaposition of death and life, now compose a constellation of Northwest images that the tranquil mind discovers to be the shape of "infinitude."

The final poem, **"The Rose,"** sums up and completes the **"North American Sequence."** All three of the American journey-motifs are here, together with all of the inner stages of the soul and their supporting images. More fully than any of the preceding single poems, **"The Rose"** is Roethke's Northwest poetic creation par excellence. He begins at the Northwest seacoast:

> There are those to whom place is unimportant,
> But this place, where sea and fresh water meet,
> Is important—

He then draws the bountiful natural life into this ultimate song of himself. In the next fifteen lines, he describes some dozen Northwest birds and at the same time, predictably, he unites them to air, earth, and water. He no longer requires the agonizing interior journey through and out of the perplexed self. He can "sway outside myself / Into the darkening currents" with the quiet grace of the intrepid hawks he has just described.

Still, in its apparently buoyant ease of passage, his spirit feels obscurely troubled, somehow adrift and incomplete. The realization he is seeking now approaches on the Northwest shoreline before his feet. His guide to final union and grace is the single "rose in the sea-wind," the transcendent rose he had briefly invoked in **"The Longing."** Its own excuse for being, the wild rose silently instructs by a dynamic staying "in its true place," by "flowering out of the dark," widening in noonday light, and stubbornly resisting encroachment upon its solitary life. The meditation upon the individualized wild rose leads the speaker associatively to one final journey to the greenhouse world of his childhood. In the reminiscence, the aged man reposesses the glories he had known when "those flowerheads seemed to flow toward me, to beckon me, only a child, out of myself." The child had merged with the roses and both had flourished in the bountiful Eden created by his sufficient, protective father.

The childhood memory then triggers the other, or later, journey into the past. Section three first echoes the early morning "sound and silence" of the Northwest scene in the opening lines of the poem. We are then taken on a last journey into the "interior," to gather up and catalog the inland "American sounds in this silence"—a Whitmanian excursion among industrial noises, the bravuras of birds, "the ticking of snow around oil drums in the Dakotas, / The thin whine of telephone wires in the wind of a Michigan winter," and more. His second journey eastward into the past completed, the old explorer has reached the final definition of himself. His question in **"The Longing"** had been "How to transcend this sensual emptiness?" He has discovered the answer: the sensual emptiness has been transcended in the sensual fullness of the Whitman–Roethke gatherings of American plenitude, as in these fluid interior "American sounds in this silence." And this possession, be it noted, has occurred within a primary context of the regional. Thanks to the final journeys of private and native—and esthetic—self-realization that were stimulated by the rose's expansive self-containment, he has again embraced his present world, his Northwest, and can rejoice equally with the bird, the lilac, and the dolphin in the calm and change which they accept in air, land, and water. In the lovely closing lines, he absorbs in his controlling solitary symbol the diversity of experience and imagery in this climactic poem.

> [I rejoiced] in this rose, this rose in the sea-wind,
> Rooted in stone, keeping the whole of light,
> Gathering to itself sound and silence—
> Mine and the sea-wind's.

And so ends an intensive drive toward definition of the many Roethkean selves, of the perplexed American in his country and his region. Even Roethke's "drive toward God" was climaxed in the ultimate landscape of the **"Sequence."** The northern coast and oceanic far field of his adopted region served him perfectly to frame and extend his religious journeys in and out of time and space and even to resolve them in fleeting moments of joyous, tranquil union.

"The Rose" appeared in a magazine one month before Roethke died of a heart attack while swimming in a private pool on Bainbridge Island, Washington. Returned to the physical regimen of earlier years, the restless, hard-driving poet was seriously charting in his notebook a new approach to western experience, this time through an epic poem on the North American Indian. His structural device would be, once more, a passage across the nation's heartland. The speaker would stop to commemorate the scenes of tragic undoing which various tribes suffered at the hands of the white marauders and military. In this epic drama, which he hoped to create "through suggestive and highly charged symbolical language," the heroic figures, indicated in his notes, were to include the Nez Percé's Chief Joseph, the Oglala's Black Elk and Crazy Horse, as well as white adversaries like Generals Custer and Crook. Six large notebook pages are all that remain among his papers to suggest the mood, landscape, and action of his projected saga. Conceived at the full maturity of his powers, the poem may well have exceeded in imaginative range even the regional poems of *The Far Field*. At his death, Roethke had only begun to open the way to a new enrichment of western American literature. The extraordinary verses of his final book, however, remain an invaluable legacy for regional writers of the future to build upon as they embark on their own poetic journeys toward discovery and definition of a Northwest ethos.

Thomas Gardner (essay date 1989)

SOURCE: "Far from the Crash of the Long Swell: Theodore Roethke's 'North American Sequence'," in *Discovering Ourselves in Whitman: The Contemporary Long Poem,* University of Illinois Press, 1989, pp. 78-98.

[*In the following essay, Gardner classifies Roethke's "North American Sequence" in the long poem genre and compares the method and style of the sequence to Walt Whitman's "Song of Myself," which Gardner perceives as a model of the American long poem.*]

Theodore Roethke shares with [John] Berryman and [Galway] Kinnell a commitment to [Walt] Whitman's embrace as a means of singing forth what is "in me" but "without name." "It is paradoxical," he writes in an essay on "establishing a personal identity," "that a very sharp sense of the being, the identity of some other being—and in some instances, even an inanimate thing—brings a corresponding heightening and awareness of one's own self. . . ." For Roethke as well, that increased awareness is the result of gaining or developing a language. What Kinnell describes as filling out the "languished alphabet" of another, and Berryman pictures as dressing "up & up" in different costumes, Roethke understands as the act of expanding another's "terms"—as in this early response to the work of Leonie Adams: "I loved her so much, her poetry, that I just had to become, for a brief moment, a part of her world. For it is her world, and I had filled myself with it, and I had to create something that would honor her in her own terms. . . . That poem is a true release in its way. I was too clumsy and stupid to articulate my own emotions." Unlike Berryman and Kinnell, however, what complicates and limits the embrace for Roethke—what needs to be acknowledged and worked with before any "release" of the spirit into articulation occurs—is the "sharp sense" of difference between "one's own self" and "some other being." Where Kinnell and Berryman assumed that the embrace was disrupted by problems with the perceiver—and that its reformulation thus depended on the poet's clarity in examining his own personal struggles—Roethke sees a more fundamental disruption or gap, one more usefully addressed by asking about technique. As he puts it: "The human problem is to find out what one really is: whether one exists, whether existence is possible. But how?" If self and medium are separate, Roethke's struggle, like Whitman's in sections 30-38 of "Song of Myself," is to work out what sort of indirect approach might yet prompt the "flights of a fluid and swallowing soul."

The problematic nature of making contact with another and thereby singing the self has, of course, been central to Roethke's work throughout his career, although perhaps only his extended **"North American Sequence"** works out and puts into practice all of the implications of that process. The two **"Cuttings"** poems from his early greenhouse sequence, however, quite dramatically frame Roethke's approach to the problem. The first poem points to the occurrence of a progressively deeper embrace—and thus "a corresponding heightening and awareness of . . . [the] self"—by tracing the movements of the poet's eye. We see the just-reviving cuttings from a distance as "Sticks-in-a-drowse," then are brought close enough to notice their "intricate stem-fur," moved inside to notice how the "small cells bulge" as water is gradually absorbed, and finally are brought to rest under the soil—face up against "one nub of growth" that actively "nudges a sand-crumb loose." Two things happen: the poet struggles through to a fuller, more participatory way of seeing, and the cutting comes back to life.

What this parallel implies but never states is that the struggle with medium—the struggle to see it, use it, enter it—has led to growth in the perceiver as well as in the cutting.

If that was so, the next poem speculates, turning to the same cuttings "(later)," what sort of poetic implications would follow? Roethke is of two minds in answering. His first try is the traditional one: ignoring his own struggle to see, he turns the slips into tortured, reviving saints, declaring his own distance from them to be a non-issue: "This urge, wrestle, resurrection of dry sticks, / Cut stems struggling to put down feet, / What saint strained so much, / Rose on such lopped limbs to a new life?" Then he revises himself: if that distance *was* the issue, then what those changes in seeing accomplished was the spurt of his own new beginning:

> I can hear, underground, that sucking and sobbing,
> In my veins, in my bones I feel it,—
> The small waters seeping upward,
> The tight grains parting at last.
> When sprouts break out,
> Slippery as fish,
> I quail, lean to beginnings, sheath-wet.

Rather than stepping back from the problem of distance, this second attempt insists that in acknowledging the gap between himself and the cuttings, then working by observation and imagination to cut that separation down, his initial response had suggested a new way of speaking. That these two opposing responses to what is "sharp" and vibrant in something other are simply juxtaposed here suggests that Roethke hasn't yet explored the full implications of embracing and working with a medium. But, as the following reading of **"North American Sequence,"** his strongest work, argues, the techniques developed near the end of his career to weave himself into something external are quite similar to what is proposed in the last stanza of **"Cuttings (later)."**

"The Longing," first poem of the sequence, presents a blasted landscape that functions as an obvious correlative for the initial condition of Roethke's consciousness. Like the drowsing cuttings, all is asleep or decaying, slowed to a decidedly uneasy rest with no "balm" or promise anywhere apparent: "A kingdom of stinks and sighs, / Fetor of cockroaches, dead fish, petroleum, / . . . The slag-heaps fume at the edge of the raw cities: / The gulls wheel over their singular garbage." The longing of the poem's title is touched on by suggestions that an earlier state has exhausted itself, leaving only memories of a once-vibrant world: "The great trees no longer shimmer; / Not even the soot dances." In parallel fashion, Roethke notes that his own spirit—fatigued by sterile lust, drained by unfulfilled dreams of contact—is also unable now to engage the world actively: "Less and less the illuminated lips, / Hands active, eyes cherished; / Happiness left to dogs and children—." Without the possibility of embracing this landscape, his spirit cannot develop and takes on the shape of a slug—a creature Roethke has described in another poem as simply "the cold slime come into being": "And the spirit fails to move forward, / But shrinks into a half-life, less than itself, / Falls back, a slug, a loose worm / Ready for any crevice, / An eyeless starer." As Richard Blessing notes [in *Theodore Roethke's Dynamic Vision,* 1974], Roethke's pun on "eyeless" is quite important, for without the eyes actively responding to the world, the poet's internal "I" must always be less than itself. Unable to touch another and so approximate its inner world, the spirit is simply asleep, deep within a crevice.

The memory of shimmering landscape and responsive soul in the poem's first section and the prediction of that state regained in the second section ("How comprehensive that felicity! . . . / A body with the motion of a soul. / . . . The light cries out, and I am there to hear—" suggest that exhaustion and waking of the spirit are joined cyclically. In fact, the shock of finding oneself inarticulate and being forced to gain speech again seems, in Roethke, to be a necessary condition for an increase in consciousness: "Are not some experiences so powerful and profound (I am not speaking of the merely compulsive) that they repeat themselves, thrust themselves upon us, again and again, with variation and change, each time bringins us closer to our own most particular (and thus most universal) reality? We go, as Yeats said, from exhaustion to exhaustion. To begin from the depths and come out—that is difficult; for few known where the depths are or can recognize them; or, if they do, are afraid." Continually lifting himself from the depths and giving body to what was shapeless gives Roethke the opportunity, through the "variation and change" of each new act of formation, to unfold more and more of his own "most particular . . . reality." In this opening poem, Roethke finds himself stalled and the impulse to embrace exhausted. As the sequence continues, he will continually drop back to this state, often by raising new questions and fears about the embrace itself, in order to give himself an opportunity to work himself out of the mire once again. Repeatedly made shapeless, repeatedly forced to confront his "wretched" inability to take in the world, he will both define a self and think through the act of definition by flowering, petal after petal: "To this extent I'm a stalk. / —How free; how all alone. / Out of these nothings / —All beginnings come."

The first movement out of emptiness that comes is a detailed expression of longing for the embrace's return:

I would with the fish, the blackening salmon, and
  the mad lemmings,
The children dancing, the flowers widening.
Who sighs from far away?
I would unlearn the lingo of exasperation, all the
  distortions of malice and hatred;
I would believe my pain: and the eye quiet on the
  growing rose;
I would delight in my hands, the branch singing,
  altering the excessive bird;
I long for the imperishable quiet at the heart of
  form;
I would be a stream, winding between great striated
  rocks in late summer;
A leaf, I would love the leaves, delighting in the
  redolent disorder of this mortal life,

The "imperishable quiet" that Roethke longs for here seems to be a core of identity—an imperishable core known only as it manifests itself in perishable ("mortal") form. As in

On Roethke's view of himself as a poet:

Roethke's poetics hark back to German Romantic theory and Coleridge, though his personal sources were Wordsworth and Emerson. Fundamental to this system is the concept of poet as *vates,* the role of prophet. The poet becomes a priest of the imagination, a secular clergyman. But the burden of alienation from the mainstream of society attends this special role; the seer appears to outsiders as a madman, the *poet maudit* of nineteenth-century French letters. The example of Whitman shows how swiftly this Romantic idea took hold in American, for Whitman was indeed at times a caricature of the prophetic bard. There is no doubt Roethke thought of himself as one of the "mad poets" and even embraced the idea. In the late poem **"In a Dark Time"** he asks, rhetorically: "What's madness but nobility of soul / At odds with circumstance?"

Jay Parini, "Theodore Roethke: The Poetics of Expression," in Ball State University Forum, *Winter, 1980.*

section 5 of "Song of Myself," Roethke links an intuition of the soul's boundlessness with its possible approximation in the world external to it. By moving with the fish, dancing with the children, or widening with the flowers; by becoming a stream or a drifting leaf, part of the "disorder of this mortal life," the unformulated heart, Roethke proposes, will be made to take on shape. A "body" will be created which, indirectly, moves like the "soul." The image of the "eye quiet on the growing rose," with another pun on "eye," is a statement of the wish to move with the growing rose in order to become aware of the "I's" own quiet places. As we will see, that longing to again embrace the world is put into play in the next five poems, each of which is identically set "where the sea and fresh water meet." In the last poem of the sequence, Roethke describes this setting as "the place of my desire"—a landscape, almost a laboratory, where his desire, in all of its inescapable complication, might be acted upon, and his sleeping spirit be awakened.

"Meditation at Oyster River" begins with Roethke sitting on a rock at the edge of a bay, the mouth of a river at his back. Although the world around him steadily increases in activity, he seems as weary and tentative as at the beginning of **"The Longing."** The "first tide-ripples" slowly move toward where he waits, protected by "a barrier of small stones" and a "sunken log." When he is surrounded by water and "one long undulant ripple" has broken through, he responds: "I dabble my toes in the brackish foam sliding forward, / Then retire to a rock higher up on the cliff-side." In short, he refuses the embrace, and in a deliberate manner that calls attention to his refusal. Cary Nelson observes [in *Our Last First Poets,* 1981] that, "The decision is a partial rejection. He resists the natural world even while reaffirming his need for it." This twin rejection and reaffirmation insists that the problem—what he longs to do, he cannot—must be dealt with before there can be any movement of the spirit. The problem is made clear again a few lines later when the world outside comes back to life ("The dew revives on the beach-grass; / The salt-soaked wood of a fire crackles") while the poet remains unmoving. Eventually, in a pattern that will be repeated throughout the sequence, the problem of the failed embrace triggers an unstated question—why am I refusing contact?—that the second section of the poem begins to investigate:

> The self persists like a dying star,
> In sleep, afraid. Death's face rises afresh,
> Among the shy beasts, the deer at the salt-lick,
> The doe with its sloped shoulders loping across the
>   highway,
> The young snake, poised in green leaves, waiting
>   for its fly,
> The hummingbird, whirring from quince-blossom to
>   morning-glory—
> With these I would be.

The problem expressed, anticipated by the "disorder of this mortal life" in **"The Longing,"** is fundamental to the poem: although Roethke would be part of the "loping," "whirring" world surrounding him, he is unable to break away from a persistent awareness of himself. To relax his attention on his own boundaries and become totally absorbed in something other is, he fears, to risk the dissolution of what makes him a self. Thus, "death's face" insistently includes itself in the catalog of animals Roethke would be with. As James McMichael writes [in "Roethke's North America," *Northwest Review,* Summer, 1971] "What he desires is outside him, outside the self. But this desire is blunted by the unavoidable awareness and fear that to be lured out of the confines of the self is to court death, the absolute loss of self."

What the structure of the sequence suggests is that such a confrontation with "the absolute loss of self" must have occurred before **"The Longing"** began—the no longer "illuminated" lips and sterile "dreams" of that poem marking a near total retreat from an overreaching attempt at full absorption in an other. A way to think about this would be to recall the experimental overimmersion Whitman risked in section 26 and 28 of "Song of Myself." Where Whitman was whirled wide by the "orbic flex" of an orchestra which, when too fully embraced, wrenched such previously hidden "ardors" from him that he was left puzzled and silent, "throttled in fakes of death" by his own self-betrayal ("I talk wildly, I have lost my wits, I and nobody else am the greatest traitor, / I went myself first to the headland, my own hands carried me there," so Roethke, reacting to just such a confrontation with the "death's face" of his own boundlessness, insistently holds on to the "dying star" of his established self even when listing the shy beasts he longs to embrace. . . .

How to move beyond this fear? As Whitman did in section 29 and 38, Roethke silently reformulates the manner

in which one embraces in more indirect, and thus more limited, terms. Rather than turning on himself and addressing his fear of immersion, . . . Roethke uses his awareness that he cannot give himself fully to the sea as a prompt in developing a new means of contact. Playfully, and at a distance, he muses about water. "I shift on my rock, and I think," he writes: first, of a "trembling . . . Michigan brook in April, / Over a lip of stone, the tiny rivulet," then of a "wrist-thick cascade tumbling from a cleft rock," and finally of the Tittebawasee River, poised, "between winter and spring, / When the ice melts along the edges in early afternoon. / And the midchannel begins cracking and heaving from the pressure beneath, / The ice piling high against the iron-bound spiles, / Gleaming, freezing hard again, creaking at midnight—." As with the **"Cuttings"** poems, these increasingly powerful images testify to Roethke's growing ability to work with the moving tide; acknowledging by his fear that he can't be the same as the swirling currents, he yet develops a way of speaking and moving:

> And I long for the blast of dynamite,
> The sudden sucking roar as the culvert loosens its
>   debris of branches and sticks,
> Welter of tin cans, pails, old bird nests, a child's
>   shoe riding a log,
> As the piled ice breaks away from the battered
>   spiles,
> And the whole river begins to move forward, its
>   bridges shaking.

The longing is so precisely rendered that both reader and poet do experience, momentarily, a movement forward. By becoming aware through the failed embrace of the distinction between himself and the sea and creating a series of metaphors in response to that tension, Roethke has also enabled himself to become more a part of the seaside setting. That is, working with an aspect of this landscape "small enough to be taken in, embraced, by two arms," he has avoided a dissolving of boundaries while yet opening himself to that world. As will be seen throughout the sequence, each such increase in consciousness is signalled by an increasing ability to join with ocean. Here, he records a steady rocking of the spirit ("I rock with the motion of morning") as he leans to move forward then pulls himself back, finally "lull[ing]" himself into a "half-sleep." He is in between, no longer sealed off by his barrier of rocks, but quite careful to claim only a "small" embrace of his surroundings: "And the spirit runs, intermittently, / In and out of the small waves, / Runs with the intrepid shorebirds— / How graceful the small before danger!"

The next poem in the sequence, **"Journey to the Interior,"** takes place later in the evening, in "the moonlight," and uses the word "rehearse" ("I rehearse myself for this: / The stand at the stretch in the face of death" to describe the weave of memory and speculation that Roethke constructs in order to prepare to confront the sea without fully dissolving the boundaries of self. Again, the structure is a response to the problem raised by the failed embrace; as with the rivulet-cascade-river memories of the previous poem, this is a rehearsal, a construct—not a direct approach to the landscape (which would be "death"), but an indirect unfolding of one of its problematic implications. The poem begins by comparing the movement out of the self and toward the world to a journey, one constantly interrupted by dangerous, "raw places" that send the self off on long, circuitous detours:

> In the long journey out of the self,
> There are many detours, washed-out interrupted raw
>   places
> Where the shale slides dangerously
> And the back wheels hang almost over the edge
> At the sudden veering, the moment of turning.

What has caused *his* "sudden veering" away from what one might have thought would be a simple and direct "journey" from self to something other, Roethke goes on to suggest, are two problems of which he is now "wary." The first is the risk of violent, surging expansion: "The arroyo cracking the road, the wind-bitten buttes, the canyons, / Creeks swollen in midsummer from the flash-flood roaring into the narrow valley." The second is the risk of reduction and annihilation:

> —Or the path narrowing,
> Winding upward toward the stream with its sharp
>   stones,
> The upland of alder and birchtrees,
> Through the swamp alive with quicksand,
> The way blocked at last by a fallen fir-tree,
> The thickets darkening,
> The ravines ugly.

Both threats might usefully be compared to the risks of overpowering contact Whitman imagines in sections 26 and 28—the sudden expansion of being whirled "wider than Uranus flies" followed by his "windpipe [being] throttled."

Roethke counterbalances this fear of annihilation by recounting a long, circuitous journey that, he remembers, gently led him out of himself. The journey—successfully taking Roethke from self-absorption to union with the external—is a rehearsal for the present decision to make or refuse contact with the sea: a rehearsal, or (as we learn only after thirty-four absolutely convincing lines), a "detour"—an indirect, long way around which, avoiding the "raw places" of direct contact with the other, works out a way to eventually allow the "journey out of the self" to proceed. Emphasis is given first to the remembered dangers of the road ("dangerous down-hill places, where the wheels whined beyond eighty—"), then to the boy's sense of pride at his mastery of the terrain:

> The trick was to throw the car sideways and charge
>   over the hill, full of the throttle.
> Grinding up and over the narrow road, spitting and
>   roaring.
> A chance? Perhaps. But the road was part of me,
>   and its ditches,
> And the dust lay thick on my eyelids,—Who ever
>   wore goggles?—

Gradually, the speaker disappears, and the landscape, a blur of small towns and discarded objects, takes over: "An old bridge below with a buckled iron railing, broken by some idiot plunger; / Underneath, the sluggish water running between weeds, broken wheels, tires, stones." This is the sort of exhausted landscape that Roethke had turned away from in **"The Longing."** Now, however, transfixed by the rhythm of the speeding car, he begins to lose himself to the flashing scenery. He seems to be still, with the world flowing by ("The floating hawks, the jackrabbits, the grazing cattle—I am not moving but they are") until, finally forgetting himself, he becomes a part of his surroundings, both still and moving: "I rise and fall in the slow sea of a grassy plain, / The wind veering the car slightly to the right, / Whipping the line of white laundry, bending the cottonwoods apart." With the same wind moving the car and the cottonwoods, inside and outside are joined. Although the memory itself is quite powerful, the reference to the "slow sea" reminds the reader that this journey is being recounted and worked with as a way around Roethke's current failure to embrace the waves around him.

The memory concludes with what Roethke has called "the first stage in mystical illumination":

> I rise and fall, and time folds
> Into a long moment;
> And I hear the lichen speak,
> And the ivy advance with its white lizard feet—
> On the shimmering road,
> On the dusty detour.

Although several commentators have cited this passage as a mystical culmination to the sequence, the word "detour" is a reminder that this moment of union in which "all is one and one is all" is only one of several possible results of the journey out of the self. Roethke is investigating the problem of whether one can move out of the self and not be destroyed, not simply describing the possibility of illumination. This memory serves as a demonstration that the journey might be made safely if indirectly and round-aboutly. That is, as the tense change reminiscent of that in Whitman's gradual participation in his grandmother's father's sea fight—from past ("the road was part of me") to present ("And all flows past")—suggests, working with the memory has led the poet to experience a similar union with a greatly enlarged world here, beside the ocean: "I see the flower of all water, above and below me, the never receding, / Moving, unmoving in a parched land, white in the moonlight." By making his way down this detour, skirting the "raw places" it seeks to avoid, Roethke has increased his technical resources and brought himself to a point where he can make a decision about moving beyond the soul's "still-stand." What is the result? Here in the present, claiming only a blind man's intuition, Roethke changes position, moving away from his fear of death and, with his "body thinking," out toward the world:

> As a blind man, lifting a curtain, knows it is
>   morning,
> I know this change:

> On the one side of silence there is no smile;
> But when I breathe with the birds,
> The spirit of wrath becomes the spirit of blessing,
> And the dead begin from their dark to sing in my
>   sleep

From a position of silence and immobility, Roethke has gazed at the disastrous, unsmiling face of the journey out of the self ("the spirit of wrath"), then at the breathing, singing aspect of the journey, and has chosen to risk contact. And it is this rehearsal, which has indeed "made something" out of his first contact with the sea, that has made possible that greater, although indirect, embrace.

Roethke, by continually raising new questions about his ability to embrace this world directly, repeatedly gives himself opportunities to struggle out of the mire by refining his ability to work with it indirectly, as a medium different from him. Once again, **"The Long Waters,"** the next poem in the sequence, opens with an acknowledgment of fearfulness—Roethke again retreating from the "advancing and retreating waters" he is drawn to make contact with. He begins by suggesting that the sense, as demonstrated by innumerable small creatures, seem to provide both contact and a means of making and expressing newly-discovered distinctions: "Whether the bees have thoughts, we cannot say, / But the hind part of the worm wiggles the most, / Minnows can hear, and butterflies, yellow and blue, / Rejoice in the language of smells and dancing." It seems to Roethke that the languages (wiggling, dancing) employed by these creatures illustrate a kind of thinking that he might use himself. Roethke has pursued this idea further in an essay in which he speculates that for the poet who "thinks with his body: an idea for him can be as real as the smell of a flower or a blow on the head. And those so lucky as to bring their whole sensory equipment to bear on the process of thought grow faster, jump more frequently from one plateau to another . . ." The senses then, he proposes, might provide an entrance into the external world and a language to give his ideas shape—make them "real." To choose this manner of thinking is to choose not to rely on those extraordinary insights into our world or those intuitions of some other world beyond the range of the senses:

> Therefore I reject the world of the dog
> Though he hear a note higher than C
> And the thrush stopped in the middle of his song.
> And I acknowledge my foolishness with God,
> My desire for the peaks, the black ravines, the
>   rolling mists
> Changing with every twist of the wind,
> The unsinging fields where no lungs breathe,
> Where light is stone.

Instead, he situates himself at that place of his desire, a world full of potential where the senses might be fully engaged:

> I return where fire has been,
> To the charred edge of the sea
> Where the yellowish prongs of grass poke through

>   the blackened ash,
> And the bunched logs peel in the afternoon
>   sunlight,
> Where the fresh and salt waters meet,
> And the sea-winds move through the pine trees,
> A country of bays and inlets, and small streams
>   flowing seaward.

This is a complete world where the four elements—fire, water, earth, wind—all meet and interpenetrate. Grass pokes "through" the fire's ash, winds "move through" the pines, fire touches the sea, fresh waters meet salt. In short, this is a universe no longer immediately threatening, as in **"Oyster River,"** but open to the senses' penetration.

Characteristically, however, Roethke immediately retreats from this decision to immerse himself in the sea-edge world. Discovering a familiar problem implicit in his description of the charred, reviving landscape, he thrusts himself away, back into the depths, and gives himself another opportunity to climb out. Addressing Mnetha, Blake's guardian of two "perpetual infants" who are kept forever innocent, he acknowledges his fear of the flurry of change and new birth that the natural world offers him. He reaches back, in fact, to the language-bearing worm and butterfly of the opening lines of the poem and sees them again, now as examples of disorder and retreat: "Mnetha, Mother of Har, protect me / From the worm's advance and retreat, from the butterfly's havoc, / From the slow sinking of the island peninsula, the coral efflorescence, / The dubious sea-change, the heaving sands, and my tentacled sea-cousins." Once articulated, however, these fears of the flowering ("coral efflorescence"), changing, and self-dissolving world can be countered. Roethke does so by calling attention to another, unnamed deity who might intensify and shape that about-to-dissolve world rather than free him from it:

> But what of her?—
> Who magnifies the morning with her eyes,
> The star winking beyond itself,
> The cricket-voice deep in the midnight field,
> The blue jay rasping from the stunted pine.

Magnifying the morning—these examples indicate—involves adding the presence of the viewer to an otherwise unmarked world, that of night sky, "midnight field," and "stunted pine." Her presence, voicing the world while not being overwhelmed by it, seems to be a standin for the poet, for Roethke immediately turns to his own faculties of imagination and memory that might intersect the changing world and magnify its potential. A remembered "pleasure," he argues in the next stanza, dies slowly; it lasts like a "dry bloom" still holding its battered shape under the coming "first snow of the year," and in doing so gives depth and richness to his present contact with the world: "Feeling, I still delight in my last fall." This opening expression of doubt, then, forcing Roethke to acknowledge the havoc of the sensual world, has also led him to assert the role of human memory and imagination in deepening, and thus rendering nonthreatening, the order of that world. In a sense, he has spelled out, in the image of memory as a magnifier, what the indirect contact of the two previous poems simply demonstrated.

The final three sections of **"The Long Waters"** investigate this combined use of memory and the senses in contacting the world, and do so with a similar pattern of statement, challenge, and a deepened restatement. Roethke begins by repeating his commitment to enter the "rich desolation of wind and water" stretching before him. To move toward that world, he reminds himself, is to enter the advancing and retreating world of time:

> *In time* when the trout and young salmon leap for
>   the low-flying insects,
> And the ivy-branch, cast to the ground, puts down
>   roots into the sawdust,
> And the pine, whole with its roots, sinks into the
>   estuary,
> Where it leans, tilted east, a perch for the osprey,
> And a fisherman dawdles over a wooden bridge,
> These waves, in the sun, remind me of flowers:
> (emphasis mine)

In the world of time, advance is cyclically linked to decline; trout leap as insects fly low; a newly cast down branch roots itself while established roots are pried out whole; as a pine tree sinks, an osprey uses its perch to lift itself. Previously, this "dubious" movement would have inspired retreat; now the poet realizes that this cyclical pattern also lifts human memory out of worlds cast down. The presence of his memory, then, "magnifying" the sea's waves into the familiar shapes of lilies and morning-glories, helps him to engage his senses and, "Blessed by the lips of a low wind," come forward to enter this "rich desolation." Once again, however, this insight must be tested. The blessing is followed by a quivering moment of doubt where, as another "long swell, burnished, almost oily" washes toward him, he fearfully erects a barrier and uses memory not to deepen his response to water but to find an emblem for his feelings of vulnerability at loosening his boundaries. What would it be like to enter this world without the tools of memory and desire to reshape it?

> I remember a stone breaking the eddying current,
> Neither white nor red, in the dead middle way,
> Where impulse no longer dictates, nor the darkening
>   shadow,
> A vulnerable place,
> Surrounded by sand, broken shells, the wreckage of
>   water.

Immediately though, as if his momentary tendency to remain inert and stonelike "in the dead middle way" proved no match for the combination of slowly dying memory and the whispering sea, Roethke finds himself awakened again:

> As a fire, seemingly long dead, flares up from a
>   downdraft of air in a chimney,
> Or a breeze moves over the knees from a low hill,
> So the sea wind wakes desire.
> My body shimmers with a light flame.

And wonderfully, now that his senses are in contact with the world, his spirit is able to awake, move, and (reaching back to **"The Longing"** for the term) shimmer. The awakening of desire—the method Roethke has developed for entering and shaping the world through memory—has been a slow process bringing him to a union that has been doubted, lost, and won several times over.

Interestingly, Roethke chooses to end **"The Long Waters"** not with these striking lines, but with a passage that Cary Nelson rightly characterizes as "mere posturing." Roethke concludes by claiming that, set loose from his fear of dissolution, he is able to "Become another thing," disperse himself to the gathering waters, and "embrace the world." This progression neatly completes the sequence's major themes, but the strikingly pat presentation contrasts noticeably with the painstaking advance and retreat we have just followed. This manner of presentation seems to be a deliberate signal of another intensification of the problem, a signal supported by an additional claim that although he senses in the sea's waves a "shape" that corresponds to an aspect of his sleeping spirit, Roethke is unable to label it clearly. That is, he signals his inability, at this stage, to make more than a striking pose out of his union with the waves.

> I see in the advancing and retreating waters
> The shape that came from my sleep, weeping:
> The eternal one, the child, the swaying vine branch,
> The numinous ring around the opening flower,
> The friend that runs before me on the windy
>   headlands,
> Neither voice nor vision.

The last line is particularly telling. To see the shape as a montage of traditional images—alternately the "one," a child, a branch, a numinous ring, a friend running—is deliberately to "conceive too much of articulation," suggesting that although a union has been established, there has not yet been a proper assessment of its limits. To achieve "Neither voice nor vision" is to have put nothing into useful form and to indicate both a temporary end to one poem and the need for further meditation.

"The Far Field" attempts to think through the necessary limits to embracing "the advancing and retreating waters" by linking the sea of the previous poems with the far field of eternity in order more forcefully to bring to awareness the problem of "immensity.". . . Is it too much to claim that a single individual might comprehend and articulate such an expanse? The poem begins, as has become customary, by answering that unspoken question with an expression of fear that temporarily negates the previous union and provides the poet with another opportunity to remake his answer to that problem. Roethke imagines driving out a "long peninsula," alone, in a frightening thrust away from the mainland and out toward the sea: "Ending at last in a hopeless sand-rut, / Where the car stalls, / Churning in a snowdrift / Until the headlights darken." Roethke responds to the fear of what "Journey to the Interior" called those "interrupted raw places" where one could be overwhelmed and diminished by remembering a series of equivalent "ends" he experienced as a child: a culvert at the end of a field; a pile of discarded cans and tires; the decayed face of a dead rat; the entrails of a cat, blasted by a night watchman. The images parallel the stalled car, but, by placing them in a larger context of constantly changing shapes, Roethke understands why, as a child, his "grief was not excessive": the field's end was also the "nesting-place of the field-mouse"; and both the flower dump and the "twittering restless cloud" of an elm tree insisted that the world was "ever-changing." In a similar manner, he also "learned of [his own place in] the eternal" through viewing his own body in that larger context. Lying "naked in the sand," "fingering a shell," sinking "down to the hips in a mossy quagmire," or sitting with bare knees "astride a wet log" were all ways of indirectly "thinking" himself into contact with an older world by reliving his earlier shapes: "Once I was something like this, mindless, / Or perhaps with another mind, less peculiar." As a child, then, he reminds himself, he "learned not to fear infinity, / . . . The sprawl of the wave, / The oncoming water" by developing an artistic, sensual means of thinking about, and thereby indirectly participating in, the constant movement of time and shapes. He learned to give himself to "infinity" in a way that "was not excessive."

This reminder—this rehearsal—frees him from his opening fear of being overwhelmed; now able to entertain imaginatively and indirectly the "thought of my death" and his subsequent connection with "earth and air" as the simple loosing of the scents of a garden or fire to the air, he is "renewed by death" and experiences a forward movement of the spirit: "I feel a weightless change, a moving forward / As of water quickening before a narrowing channel / When banks converge, and the wide river whitens." This forward movement is made possible by the poet teaching himself again how to think about the broad, surrounding expanses. Roethke returns to the combination of stillness and movement first introduced in **"The Longing"** in order to explain this manner of participating without being dissolved:

> I have come to a still, but not a deep center,
> A point outside the glittering current;
> My eyes stare at the bottom of a river,
> At the irregular stones, iridescent sandgrains,
> My mind moves in more than one place,
> In a country half-land, half-water.

Holding himself out of the force of the main current, Roethke insists that he is able to join it by looking at it ("my eyes stare") and, most importantly, by flexibly thinking about it ("my mind moves in more than one place"). That outward movement, or embrace, has made possible, in turn, an insight into what **"The Longing"** called "the imperishable quiet at the heart of form"—an insight now carefully qualified, however, as an approach to "a still, but not a deep center." Full insight, for both Whitman and Roethke, is an overpowering deepness—an approach to an "infinity" beyond words and articulation.

The quiet tone of these lines is convincing and prepares the reader for a second, and more limited, attempt to define the shape discovered in the union between the individual and the long waters: "The lost self changes, / Turning toward the sea, / A sea-shape turning around,—." The lost self, the self that has loosened its hold on its original boundaries, turns toward the sea and, identifying with the waves it faces but also remaining a thinking creature, becomes both a man and a "sea-shape turning around." To realize that one has the potential to merge with such an expanse is to awaken to one's own immensity without being overwhelmed by it: "A man faced with his own immensity / Wakes all the waves, all their loose wandering fire." He wakes these waves within himself, but, because he has approached them indirectly, through "finite things [which] reveal infinitude" without themselves carrying the infinite's full weight, he finds himself no longer threatened by "The murmur of the absolute"; it simply "fails on his naked ears." So, Roethke can claim that, as a single man, he is, through such a merger, also an "old man" in the sea's "robes of green" or, more abstractly, "the end of things, the final man." Touching those long waters, working with them without fully embracing them, his work is a limited thrust into immensity: "A ripple widening from a single stone / Winding around the waters of the world."

The final poem of the sequence, **"The Rose,"** is both a summary of the sequence's overall movement and a demonstration of what Roethke has learned about how to embrace the other. Its central image is a wild rose blowing in the sea wind, a figure, as Nelson remarks, "for a self exceeding the limits of time and space, yet supremely flowering in its place." Indeed, the sea rose, which "Stays in its true place," "Rooted in stone," yet also unfolds its petals, extends its tendrils, and drops down to the waves—"struggling out of the white embrace of the morning-glory," "Moving with the waves, the undulating driftwood"—is a completed version of the spirit that has been given struggling form in the sequence. The rose functions as an ideal image (unlike the poet, it is bound by no limitations and thus embraces "the whole of light," all of "sound and silence") to which Roethke may compare himself, and thus assess where his poem has arrived. In a sense, the ideal rose and *his* apparent distance from its fully realized potential are the problems that spur both the meditation and demonstration of this poem and of the entire sequence.

The poem begins with a long description of "this place, where sea and fresh water meet." Everything is in movement: hawks sway in the wind, eagles sail, gulls cry, the tide rises, birds flash and sing. In time, as the poet watches and listens, this motion gradually diminishes until "The old log subsides with the lessening waves, / And there is silence." Summarizing his carefully developed abilities to join with this world, Roethke writes: "I sway outside myself / Into the darkening currents, / Into the small spillage of driftwood, / The waters swirling past the tiny headlands." Deliberately, this embrace, in effect the entire sequence, is described in quite modest terms. Both the limited context for the movement—"small spillage," "tiny headlands"—and the contrast, in the next lines, to a grander, remembered union complete with a "crown of birds," place this embrace in carefully limited perspective, exactly that developed by the many discussions of such a connection throughout the sequence. Through "change and variation," that is, the embrace has been refined.

The next two sections focus on this modest union with "the darkening currents"—demonstrating and assessing the technique that has made this connection possible. This is done quite precisely. Comparing the spirit's constantly adjusting sense of itself to the movement of a ship ("rolling slightly sideways, / The stern high, dipping like a child's boat in a pond— / Our motion continues"), Roethke immediately juxtaposes that rolling, piecemeal sense of development to that of the ideal rose that "Stays, / Stays in its true place" and knows itself whole. How is that human, non-ideal movement achieved? Like Whitman in section 33 calling deliberate attention to the act of flinging his fancies out toward an arctic world, Roethke returns to the gradually silenced world of section 1 and quite consciously shows us *how* that connection was accomplished. "What do they tell us, sound and silence?" he writes—that is, what does this observed distinction give him that might be worked with or "used?" How might memory or desire or other forms of indirect participation "magnify," and thus make accessible, that aspect of this potentially overpowering landscape? "I think of American sounds in this silence: / On the banks of the Tombstone, the wind-harps having their say, / The thrush singing alone, that easy bird, / The killdeer whistling away from me." A long, Whitmanesque catalog follows in which Roethke demonstrates how one fills silence with sound, seasons, and occupations. He moves outward, as he has learned to do in the course of this poem, through use of his full mental powers: enumeration ("I think of American sounds"), memory ("the catbird / Down in the corner of the garden"), and the careful discrimination and patterning of the various sounds. Magnifying and working a problem posed by the distinctness of the other is how a poet, in contrast to a rose, embraces, however indirectly, the world. Interestingly, as Roethke completes this demonstration and returns to the darkening "place of my desire," he once again distinguishes his achievement—approximating the "single sound" at the "heart of form" with a "twittering" of multiple movements—from an impossibly removed ideal:

> I return to the twittering of swallows above water,
> And that sound, that single sound,
> When the mind remembers all,
> And gently the light enters the sleeping soul,
> A sound so thin it could not woo a bird.

This distinction is referred to again in the sequence's conclusion, where Roethke celebrates "the place of my desire," the place where his desire has been focused and given form:

> I live with the rocks, their weeds,
> Their filmy fringes of green, their harsh
> Edges, their holes
> Cut by the sea-slime, far from the crash
> Of the long swell,

The oily, tar-laden walls
Of the toppling waves,

By living "with the rocks," Roethke points to the way he has, like the Indian of **"The Longing,"** become absorbed by this particular setting in the course of the sequence, but he also insists, in using that phrase, that his proper place is at the edge of the sea, rather than in the middle of crashing swells. He has been out in those waves, of course, but in a way that needs to be carefully set forth:

> Near this rose, in this grove of sun-parched, wind-
>   warped madronas,
> Among the half-dead trees, I came upon the true
>   ease of myself,
> As if another man appeared out of the depths of my
>   being,
> And I stood outside myself,
> Beyond becoming and perishing,
> A something wholly other,
> As if I swayed out on the wildest wave alive,
> And yet was still.

Once, Roethke writes, "near this rose," he had an insight into "the true ease" of himself. But like Whitman's full contact with his soul in section 5, that was in the past: "once we lay such a transparent summer morning." And if—again like Whitman in that section—that full insight into the "depths of my being" seemed *as if* he had realized his connections with the full range of created things (Roethke with "the wildest wave alive," far on the horizon; Whitman with "all the men ever born"), now Roethke lives at the edge of the sea, "far from the crash of the long swell," working out a series of more limited and more indirect contacts with those waves and his "being." If, then, what is in him remains "something wholly other," Roethke has, at the same time, worked out a way to bring us "nearer" to it.

FURTHER READING

Biography

Seager, Allan. *The Glass House: The Life of Theodore Roethke.* 1968. Reprint. Ann Arbor: The University of Michigan Press, 1991, 301 p.

> The only book-length biography on Roethke, written by a friend who was a distinguished novelist. Roethke's bibliographers James McLeod and Judith Sylte have stated: "Although critical consensus suggests that Seager's work is far from satisfactory, it remains an important point of reference in the developing critical understanding of Roethke's art" (*Contemporary Authors Bibliographical Series,* Vol. 2, Gale Research).

Criticism

Blessing, Richard Allen. *Theodore Roethke's Dynamic Vision.* Bloomington: Indiana University Press, 1974, 240 p.

Asserting that Roethke "experienced life in terms of speed, energy, whirl—as unceasing and often violent motion," Blessing attempts to ascertain *"by what techniques* Theodore Roethke was able to present dynamism successfully in a work of art."

Burke, Kenneth. "The Vegetal Radicalism of Theodore Roethke." *Sewanee Review* 58 (January-March 1950): 68-108.
Seminal essay on Roethke. Burke contends that Roethke uses simplicity, concrete language, and tangible nature imagery in such a way as to lend a symbolic and mystical depth to his subjects.

Heyen, William, ed. *Profile of Theodore Roethke.* Columbus, Ohio: Charles E. Merrill, 1971, 116 p.
Including pieces by Kenneth Burke, Delmore Schwarz, and Stanley Kunitz, this collection, observes Heyen, contains "some of the most perceptive estimates of Roethke's achievement." Furthermore, Heyen has selected material that is not readily or conveniently available.

Hoey, Allen. "Some Metrical and Rhythmical Strategies in the Early Poems of Roethke." *Concerning Poetry* 15, No. 1 (Spring 1982): 49-58.
Studies the use of traditional meter and rhyme in Roethke's early poems in order to better understand the techniques employed in his free verse.

Kunitz, Stanley. *A Kind of Order, a Kind of Folly: Essays and Conversations.* Boston: Little, Brown, 1975, 320 p.
Includes four essays on Roethke: a reminiscence, a review of *The Lost Son, and Other Poems,* an explication of the poem "In a Dark Time," and a discussion entitled "Poet of Transformations" about the motif of change in Roethke's poetry.

La Belle, Jenijoy. *The Echoing Wood of Theodore Roethke.* Princeton, N.J.: Princeton University Press, 1976, 174 p.
La Belle attempts to determine "why Roethke saw himself to be writing in the tradition of certain poems and poets, how he established his own cultural tradition, and what effect this tradition had upon his achievement as a poet."

Malkoff, Karl. *Theodore Roethke: An Introduction to the Poetry.* New York: Columbia University Press, 1966, 245 p.
Comprehensive survey of Roethke's work. According to Malkoff, it is best not to approach the poetry poem-by-poem, because Roethke "created a world in terms of a consistent and obsessive symbolism, which links poems and often makes them dependent on each other for full understanding."

Mazarro, Jerome. "The Failure of Language: Theodore Roethke." In his *Postmodern American Poetry,* pp. 59-84. Urbana: University of Illinois Press, 1980.
States the Roethke was confronted throughout his career with the failure of language to adequately bridge the gap between his internal life and the external world.

Mills, Ralph J., Jr. "Theodore Roethke." In his *Seven American Poets from MacLeish to Nemerov: An Introduction,* edited by Denis Donoghue, pp. 92-131. Minneapolis: University of Minnesota Press, 1963.
An overview of Roethke's works and literary themes. According to Mills, "His art shows this poet's will to extend himself, to try his skill and imagination at every turn, and his growth was organic and true."

Nelson, Cary. "The Field Where Water Flowers: Theodore Roethke's 'North American Sequence'." In his *Our Last First Poets: Vision and History in Contemporary American Poetry,* pp. 31-61. Urbana: University of Illinois Press, 1981.
In the preface to his book, Nelson states that "my analysis of 'North American Sequence' shows it to be a major accomplishment, however flawed. I also argue . . . that in 'North American Sequence' Roethke's self-prized naiveté becomes a highly self-conscious verbal artifice."

Parini, Jay. *Theodore Roethke: An American Romantic.* Amherst: University of Massachusetts Press, 1979, 203 p.
Claiming that Roethke was a Romantic, Parini demonstrates that "Roethke saw himself as working within a great tradition, modifying and extending it after his own fashion. . . . His work abounds in references to Blake, Wordsworth, and Yeats, especially, but my stress is upon the American quality of his Romanticism with Emerson and Whitman as primary ancestors, with Stevens as a strong contemporary influence."

Scott, Nathan A. Jr. "The Example of Roethke." In his *The Wild Prayer of Longing: Poetry and the Sacred,* pp. 76-118. New Haven, Conn.: Yale University Press, 1971.
Finds that Roethke is perhaps the most "sacramental" contemporary American poet because "almost everywhere, it seems, the poet's voice is lifted up in jubilant alleluias announcing 'the soul's immediate joy' and praising the glory and greatness of the world."

Snodgrass, W. D. "'That Anguish of Concreteness': Theodore Roethke's Career." In his *In Radical Pursuit: Critical Essays and Lectures,* pp. 101-16. New York: Harper & Row, 1975.
Maintains that Roethke's experimentation with verse forms and conventions paralleled his ongoing struggle to come to terms with his self-identity.

Stein, Arnold, ed. *Theodore Roethke: Essays on the Poetry.* Seattle: University of Washington Press, 1965, 199 p.
A collection of important early pieces on Roethke by notable figures such as the poets Stephen Spender, John Wain, William Meredith, and W. D. Snodgrass.

Sullivan, Rosemary. *Theodore Roethke: The Garden Master.* Seattle: University of Washington Press, 1975, 220 p.
Approaches Roethke's work chronologically but, through constant reference to "those images, ideas, memories, and obsessions that constitute the core of his creative personality," emphasizes the continuing development of his poetry.

Vernon, John. "Theodore Roethke." In his *The Garden and the Map: Schizophrenia in Twentieth-Century Literature and Culture,* pp. 159-90. Urbana: University of Illinois Press, 1973.

Declaring in the preface to this volume that Western culture is "schizophrenic" because "it chooses to fragment its experience and seal certain areas off from each other," Vernon claims that Roethke's poetry offers a remedy: a vision of "a totally unrepressed world in which all things open upon each other and exist in a kind of intimate erotic community."

Additional coverage of Roethke's life and career is contained in the following sources published by Gale Research: *Contemporary Authors*, Vols. 81-84; *Contemporary Authors Bibliographical Series*, Vol. 2; *Concise Dictionary of American Literary Biography, 1941-1968*; *Contemporary Literary Criticism*, Vols. 1, 3, 8, 11, 19, 46; *Dictionary of Literary Biography*, Vol. 5; and *Major 20th-Century Writers*.

Diane Wakoski

1937–

American poet, essayist, and critic.

INTRODUCTION

Wakoski's unified poetic vision has earned her a distinguished position in contemporary American literature. Her poems are personal narratives through which she weaves repeated images and themes, forming a rich texture of metaphor and critical reflection based in individual experience. Wakoski describes the poet's mission as "carving out a territory, creating the subject matter or content which helps to the reader to identify his voice or style as poet." For Wakoski, this poetic territory is based on the events of her own life, but the resulting work transcends the limitations of factual representation in order to emphasize the most interesting and universal qualities related to the experience. Her work is inhabited by such fantastic characters as George Washington, The King of Spain, and The Man Who Shook Hands, all of whom attain mythical stature and embody the concepts central to Wakoski's vision.

Biographical Information

Wakoski speaks frequently of her difficult childhood and adolescence in a poor working-class family in Southern California. She recalls being one of the poorest children in her schools, but also one of the most academically gifted. Her father had made a career of the Navy and was frequently away from home, leaving her mother to care for Wakoski and her sister. Eventually, her parents divorced, and the failure of Wakoski's father to provide the nurturing attention she needed figures significantly in many of her poetic works. In her high school and college years, she endured other significant experiences, including two unwanted pregnancies. In both cases, she gave the babies up for adoption and continued to pursue her education. After earning a B.A. from the University of California, Berkeley, in 1960 she relocated to New York City and immersed herself in the artistic circles of the city. While developing her poetic skills and attaining her first publications, she worked as a clerk in a bookstore and, later, as a teacher in the New York Public Schools. Beginning in the late 1960s, she supported herself by giving poetry readings and teaching workshops around the country. These activities developed into a series of temporary positions at various universities. In 1975 she accepted a permanent position at Michigan State University, where she continues to teach.

Major Works

Wakoski's first two volumes, *Coins and Coffins* and *Discrepancies and Apparitions,* established her, according to Sheila Weller, as a "poet of fierce imagination." In *The George Washington Poems,* published in 1967, Wakoski uses the figure of George Washington to develop a number

of themes, including that of an absent father who is romanticized by his daughter. In an interview, Wakoski called her next major collection, *Inside the Blood Factory,* "the turning point in my career from being a young poet, perhaps talented and perhaps accomplished, in certain ways, to someone who . . . had established a real and original voice, different from anyone else." In this book, Wakoski explores rejection and betrayal, themes further expanded upon in *The Motorcycle Betrayal Poems.* The latter volume also contains the poem "I Have Had to Learn to Live with This Face," in which Wakoski develops another of her primary concerns—what she perceives as her lack of physical beauty. With *Virtuoso Literature for Two and Four Hands* and *The Man Who Shook Hands,* music becomes a dominant theme in Wakoski's work. In many of the poems in these volumes, Wakoski employs a digressive technique similar to that in musical compositions, allowing her naturally associative verse to wander away from its central concerns then eventually return to its main themes. The publication of *The Collected Greed, Parts 1-13* in 1984 represented the culmination of an ongoing project. The "Greed" poems had previously been published in four separate volumes, at irregular intervals, beginning in 1968. The series documents Wakoski's struggles with self-definition and with her sometimes conflicting desires. In the 1990s, the poet undertook another multi-volume series of related poems. The series, including the collections *Medea the Sorceress, Jason the Sailor,* and *The Emerald City of Las Vegas,* intersperses poems with letters and prose fragments in order to consider the metaphoric implications of a wide range of topics, including popular films, literature, and quantum physics.

Critical Reception

Wakoski's poetry generates extreme reactions. Her detractors accuse her of adopting a sometimes irritating tone of self-pity and for obsessively reworking her favorite themes of betrayal, anger, and envy. She has also been criticized of overwriting, of producing poems that are too long and are too great in number, with the result that her best imagery and most important ideas are lost in the sheer mass of words. Several feminist critics have complained about the persona put forth in her work, a female "victim" who requires a man to make her life meaningful. On the other hand, a large number of critics have praised her work for its intelligence, wit, and imagination and for its fantastic, often surreal, imagery. Others emphasize the determined, resilient persona in her work who, while often emotionally wounded or angry, also possesses a wry sense of humor. Wakoski's ongoing experimentation with form and mythic archetypes are frequently viewed as complex and innovative, and the powerful intensity of her poetic voice has been appreciated by supporters and detractors alike.

PRINCIPAL WORKS

Poetry

Coins and Coffins 1962
Four Young Lady Poets [with Rochelle Owens, Barbara Moraff, and Carol Berge] 1962
Discrepancies and Apparitions 1966
The George Washington Poems 1967
The Diamond Merchant 1968
Greed, Parts 1 and 2 1968
Inside the Blood Factory 1968
Greed, Parts 3 and 4 1969
The Lament of the Lady Bank Dick 1969
The Moon Has a Complicated Geography 1969
Thanking My Mother for Piano Lessons 1969
Greed, Parts 5-7 1970
Love, You Big Fat Snail 1970
The Magellanic Clouds 1970
Exorcism 1971
The Motorcycle Betrayal Poems 1971
On Barbara's Shore 1971
This Water Baby: For Tony 1971
The Purple Finch Song 1972
Smudging 1972
Sometimes A Poet Will Hijack the Moon 1972
Dancing on the Grave of a Son of a Bitch 1973
Greed, Parts 8, 9, 11 1973
The Owl and the Snake: A Fable 1973
Stillife: Michael, Silver Flutes, and Violets 1973

Winter Sequences 1973
Abalone 1974
Looking for the King of Spain 1974
The Wandering Tattler 1974
The Fable of the Lion and the Scorpion 1975
Virtuoso Literature for Two and Four Hands 1974
George Washington's Camp Cups 1976
The Laguna Contract 1976
The Last Poem 1976
Waiting for the King of Spain 1976
Overnight Projects with Wood 1977
The Ring 1977
Spending Christmas with the Man from Receiving at Sears 1977
The Man Who Shook Hands 1978
Pachelbel's Canon 1978
Trophies 1979
Cap of Darkness 1980
Making A Sacher Torte: Nine Poems, Twelve Illustrations [with Ellen Lanyon] 1981
Divers 1982
The Lady Who Drove Me to the Airport 1982
The Magician's Feastletters 1982
Saturn's Rings 1982
The Collected Greed, Parts 1-13 1984
Why My Mother Likes Liberace 1985
Emerald Ice: Selected Poems 1962-1987 1988
Medea the Sorceress 1991
Jason the Sailor 1991
The Emerald City of Las Vegas 1995

Other Major Works

Toward a New Poetry (essays and interviews) 1979

CRITICISM

Dick Allen (essay date 1966)

SOURCE: "Of Exhibitionist Poetry, Redwoods, and the Fluid Narrative Dramatic," in *The Antioch Review,* Vol. XXVI, No. 2, Summer, 1966, pp. 265-80.

[*In this excerpt, Allen reviews* Discrepancies and Apparitions, *admiring the directness of Wakoski's work and calling her "our most exciting younger American poetess."*]

Surely when Diane Wakoski says, "I think it [poetry] is *only interesting* in proportion to how interesting the person who writes it is," she is attacking new criticism at one of its weakest stomachs. I don't fully agree with her, but the *nerve* of the girl! The happy thing is, most of her poems [in ***Discrepancies and Apparitions***] work wonderfully, work because they are direct perceptions of a sensitive contemporary female, because this particular woman is terribly interesting. For her, "the sense of disguise is a / rattle-snake and / it's easy to wake up and find it curled in your shoe"—as she says beginning a poem called **"Follow that Stagecoach."**

This poem, one of the best in *Discrepancies and Apparitions,* shows her "swimming in Dry Gulch Hollow thinking of Sheriff / Stanley / who did not love me but left to start the Pony Express." It is a weird and beautiful mixture of fantasy and open reaction to the basic unreality of the Other. The poem concludes:

> Mr. Sheriff Day she writes you this poem from her
>   dusty house
> Walking naked is her most frequent disguise it
>   disarms everyone
> The world by now is confused with all the costumes
> The world by now takes her up and tried to make
>   her wear the right
>   disguises she says no no no I will go where I
>   want when I want to
> So I'll write you a love poem if I want to. I'm a
>   Westerner and
> not afraid
> of my shadow.

We notice, of course, the freedom of the line, the tone of natural breathlessness, the Walt Whitman base. But mainly we sense a *directness,* coupled with impossibility of cutting this poem apart line by line.

In other poems, Miss Wakoski rides a donkey in the desert, watches bumblebees, imagines herself as a belly dancer, tries playing the guitar ("When I sat down / to play the guitar / I found both hands had been cut off / at the wrist"), goes inside a painter's "eyes that change like a snowflake every second" and asks, in **"The Oedipus Within"**:

> Is there some way to accept the truth,
> to face it directly
> as we would a nude statue in the museum,
> Without the fear we feel looking at our own
>   unrobed bodies,
> full and warm as summer lake water?

Her book ends with these lines, from Part VI of **"Procession Poem"**:

> If I ever had one complaint in this world
> it is that my mechanism
> was not quite perfect;
> that, as a machine,
> I was almost a failure.

Here, as throughout her entire book, Miss Wakoski laments the human inability to hold anything really steady. It is this realization of a world in continual flux, a world subject to "discrepancies and apparitions" (in which a person would have to be a machine to operate perfectly) that makes her poems so striking and fluid. In affirming her inability to be a machine, she mourns the failure which defines the particularly human aspects of existence.

Discrepancies and Apparitions announces Diane Wakoski, at twenty-nine, as our most exciting younger American poetess. A feeling of its overall genius cannot be given in an omnibus review—that is its strength. It must be read whole.

Paul Hannigan (essay date 1969)

SOURCE: "A Word about Diane Wakoski," in *Sumac,* Vol. 2, No. 1, Fall, 1969, pp. 141-42.

[*In the following review, Hannigan discusses several of Wakoski's collections and pronounces her "a first rate poet" who demonstrates a command of wit, "stagecraft," and technical poetic skills.*]

Four years ago Diane Wakoski let it be known publicly that she thought, ". . . poetry is the completely personal expression of someone about his feelings and reactions to the world. I think it is only *interesting* in proportion to how interesting the person who writes it is." There is no poetic power dead or alive to absolve that sort of fatuity; but Diane Wakoski has, amazingly enough, justified all the bravado. If **you** accept the idea of literature in time, then you will find every literary utterance 'interesting' in its context—much as Plekhanov could find bank statements and prison torture chambers "ochen' interesno." Yeats, Duncan, Aram Saroyan, and John Ciardi are all—to be sure *interesting.* Wakoski is a fine poet. She is, so far, a first rate poet. And this is not to be confused with first rate poetess (there are plenty of culls in the basket waiting for that grey laurel).

She is a moralist and her tools—excepting her shaky moral authority—are her beautiful wit and her amazing stagecraft. Her subjects are her life and her loves. The tenors of her imagery are arbitrarily selected facts of the world. Since she lives when she does and knows whom she knows they are often the hieratic, the hermitic, and the arcane—the Tarot pack, Egyptian stuff, the birthday of the Buddha. But, of course, there is *The George Washington Poems,* which is her best book and which, I understand, is all but out of print. She uses these tenors—arcane or commonplace—not to enrich some tradition of symbolism but to decorate her own fine speeches, her revilings of herself, her lovers, husbands, country, for their various failures to satisfy a minimal vision of normal human happiness and decency. Her best poems are usually rather long and in very very free verse. Technically she is amazing because she uses so little of the armory poets have available to them now; she is not interested in sounds or forms or epigrams. Her surface-texture is closer to Whitman than any poet I can think of—but this is a historical propinquity, true but adventitious.

Inside The Blood Factory is a fair selection of her poetry but no selection can give a sense of her cleverness and emotional range with a single image (as *The George Washington Poems* does). But there are five splendid poems in this book **"The Father of My Country," "Rescue Poem," "Filling the Boxes of Joseph Cornell," "Ringless,"** and **"The Ice Eagle."** Her effects are built so slowly that it is impossible to quote from these long poems and demonstrate her power. They simply must be read whole. Any one of them is worth the price of the book.

Greed Parts I & II is a high-priced signature. Part I is not bad but it is not the best Wakoski. "Part II, of Accord and Principle," is worse but more 'interesting.' She establishes an image of poets as kissing fish and toys with it at some length. She worries the integrity of poets whose integrity has never been a matter of public record and is never likely to be a matter of concern to history. And then she comes up with this preposterous statement: "But that is the greed of all of us, the poets, who want our play considered work; want to be respected and paid for saying what we think and feel. Such luxury." The moral blindness of that statement is very odd, coming, as it does, from a moralist. In a world where we pay and admire tennis players, baseball players, weapons inventors, surgeons, generously and loudly, why should we not pay and admire poets? And whoever thought that we paid and admired them for their tedious personal agonies? We pay and admire them for writing well.

The Diamond Merchant is, like *Greed,* one of those instant rarities which are justifiable only because they bring some money to the poet and—I suppose—some pleasure to the collector. The title poem is somewhat thin and forced, but the second poem, **"Glass"** is a fine and rich poem more surreal than most of Wakoski's published work.

Exhorting people to read Diane Wakoski is rather a thankless task; it is her practice to publish her poems very often in places so obscure that neither moth nor rust has heard of them. The Buddha's birthday poems are in *odda tala 2* and *odda tala 3* is all Wakoski. *odda tala* indeed. Even obscurity can be an impertinence.

Paul Zweig (essay date 1971)

SOURCE: "The Motorcycle Betrayal Poems," in *The New York Times Book Review,* December 12, 1971, pp. 17-18.

[*Here, Zweig compares earlier collections of Wakoski's poetry with* The Motorcycle Betrayal Poems.]

When *Inside the Blood Factory* was published in 1968, it was clear that in the poetry of Diane Wakoski a new sort of energy had been tapped. A fierce impulse toward confession and autobiography moved through her poems, but it took unexpected detours into an imagery of elusive beasts, colors and bizarre precious stones. The "me" she confessed to was not contained by situations; it was not an object of complaint. Although her poems were stirred by angers and fears, they did not include gestures toward suicide, the madhouse or the pill bottle. Instead, she confessed to the hippogriff in her soul, which carried her like an exulting spirit among the men who loved her, or betrayed her. The blend of exotic shapes and swift spoken language was often startling, as in **"Blue Monday"**:

> the crystal in your arm cuts away
> the night, folds back ebony whale
>   skin
> and my face, the blue of new rifles,
> and my neck, the blue of Egypt,
> and my breasts, the blue of sand,
> and my arms, bass blue,
> and my stomach, arsenic;
> there is electricity dripping from me
>   like cream;

> there is love dripping from me I
>   cannot use like acacia or
> jacaranda—fallen blue and gold
>   flowers, crushed into the street.

Diane Wakoski wrote poems of loss. The loss of childhood; the loss of lovers and family; the perpetual loss a woman lives with when she thinks she is not beautiful. These losses created a scorched earth of isolation around her, which she described harshly and precisely:

> When he diagnosed
> my case,
> it left me with little
> hope.
> "You have an invisible telephone
>   booth
> around you,"
> he said.

From this vulnerable retreat, a stream of liberating images emerged to grapple with the world and mythify it.

But *Inside the Blood Factory* was also an erratic book. Many of the longer poems rambled inconclusively. Miss Wakoski's very exuberance tended to play tricks on her by allowing the intensely personal core of the poems to become stifled in a mesh of images that moved far away from any recognizable center. In a sense, the failures of the book were very much in the image of its power; the best and the worst belonged to each other, for both resulted from the poet's defiant commitment to her freedom. It might have been better if we'd been spared the bad poems, but their rambling may have formed the only ground from which Diane Wakoski's imposing inwardness could spring. There is, after all, a bravery that artists may need more than most people: a willingness to risk being ridiculous, in order to expose the reluctant figures in their lives.

During the years since *Inside the Blood Factory,* Miss Wakoski has written voluminously. She has published an extremely interesting volume entitled **"The Magellenic Clouds"**; several pamphlets containing sections of a long poem, **"Greed"**; and now another long volume, *The Motorcycle Betrayal Poems.* The accomplished energy, as well as the limitations of her work, appears even more strongly in these new poems. The same obsessive themes are present: the woman betrayed, the anger she feels at her frail body and her face which seems hard to love; the rescue performed by the imagination, which reaches around the bareness of her life to create the comfort of cleanly expressed needs. The book is haunted by a curious mythology composed of mustached lovers, "mechanics" who do not understand the engine humming under her skin, the great-grandfatherly warmth of Beethoven and George Washington, to whom she turns with humor but also with a sort of desperation.

The Motorcycle Betrayal Poems are more open than much of Miss Wakoski's earlier work. An example is **"Thanking My Mother for Piano Lessons,"** perhaps the most beautiful poem in the book, with lines in it like these:

The relief of putting your
  fingers on the keyboard,
as if you were walking on the
  beach
and found a diamond
as big as a shoe;

as if
you had just built a wooden
  table
and the smell of sawdust was
  in the air,
your hands dry and woody;

as if
you had eluded
the man in the dark hat who
  had been following you
all week . . .

The directness of these lines describing the combat that
art enables the poet to wage against the bitterness of her
life is one of the very best qualities in the book. In much
of it, Miss Wakoski achieves an intensity of simple speech
that is rare in contemporary poetry; for example, in the
opening poem, **"I Have Had to Learn to Live With My
Face"**:

Tonight I move alone in my
  face;
want to forgive all the men
  whom I've loved
who've betrayed me.
After all, the great betrayer is
  that one I carry around each
  day,
which I sleep with at night. My
  own face;
angry building I've fought to
  restore
imbued with arrogance, pride,
  anger and scorn.
to love this face
would be to love a desert
  mountain,
a killer, rocky, water hard to
  find, no trees anywhere/
perhaps I do not expect anyone
to be strange enough to love it;
but you.

The word "betrayal" crops up again and again self-betrayal and more often betrayal by others, so many others.
Sometimes the poet answers these failures of trust with
acts of self-understanding; sometimes, more rarely, with
self-pity. But most of all, it is with anger, flights of strident anger, whose intensity can be overwhelming, as in
"Love Letter Postmarked Van Beethoven," where she
describes herself drilling bullet holes into the bodies of the
lovers who have betrayed her, with a 38-caliber Thomson
Contender, "the one they recommend for shooting rattle-
snakes."

These poems are not declarations of feminine independence. Their rage is not ideological, as in many Women's
Liberation tracts. Miss Wakoski's tactic is different. She
digs her teeth into the slaveries of woman, she cries them
aloud with such fulminating energy that the chains begin
to melt of themselves. The rage is that of a prisoner whose
bitterness is her bondage but also her freedom.

In many poems, however, the anger becomes thin, repetitious, and this is perhaps the book's most serious weakness. All too often, the stridency does not turn into poetry;
the words are flattened almost into helplessness by the
very anger they express. The tone is set in Miss Wakoski's dedicatory sentence: "This book is dedicated to all
those men who betrayed me at one time or another, in
hopes they will fall off their motorcycles and break their
necks." The humor intended here does not quite come off.
The anger in many of the poems is too steely, and after a
while one feels a failure of generosity, a sort of blindness
that harms them.

But this is far from general in the book. Many poems
survive, and they are like nothing I know in contemporary
poetry. Often enough, the vindictive rage is rounded into
whimsy and self-knowledge, or into asides of sheer fantasy that charm the reader while they are chilling him with
insight. There is a remarkable short poem, **"Black Leather Because Bumblebees Look Like It,"** that begins:

When bumblebees ride their
  black motorcycles down to
  the
country to watch death
  swimming in the river, nude,
enjoying the summer, and me,
  gathering mushrooms in the
  shade
nearby,
everything is quiet and
  peaceful.
Death and I get along because
  we are not too personal.
And my life is like Chinese to
  him; he doesn't read it or
  understand.
But his black clothes and
  leather cap
thrown on the bank carelessly
remind me of my children, like
  hundreds of bee carcasses,
  tossed together
and dead from a storm that
  wrecked the hive.

This is what Miss Wakoski can do so well—reaching into
the hive of her angers, she plucks out images of fear and
delight that are transparent, yet loaded with the darkness-
es of life.

Yes, there are failures in *The Motorcycle Betrayal Poems*: But they are the sort of failures that lesser poets
could have avoided without improving themselves. At her

best—and the best is frequent enough—Diane Wakoski is an important and moving poet.

Sheila Weller (essay date 1972)

SOURCE: "The Poetess: Duel, Sigh, or Shrug?," in *The Village Voice,* Vol. 17, No. 51, December 21, 1972, p. 26.

[*In the following excerpt, Weller discusses Wakoski's poetry in regard to gender roles. The critic applauds Wakoski's treatment of the subject and declares that* The Motorcycle Betrayal Poems *addresses "the anxieties, fantasies and paradoxes which many women would rather hide."*]

[Today] as in the days of George Eliot, one of the highest compliments a woman poet or novelist can receive is: "Reading her work, you wouldn't necessarily know she was a woman." It's curious and encouraging, then, that Diane Wakoski—a poet who, through her own hard sensuality, has always been rescued from a gender typecast she herself has had contempt for—has achieved, in these highly personal poems of love and betrayal a very sharp distillation of the contemporary female sensibility with all its cultural baggage and contradictions. With a fury and earnestness that has no use for self-mockery or apology, the poet addresses those anxieties, fantasies, and paradoxes which many of today's women would rather hide. She thus risks being accused of masochism, bitterness, even sentimentality. Through the courage of her honesty she survives these risks. And through a rhythm alternatingly, jagged and languorous, an imagery of metal, reptiles, planets, and flesh, the complaint never dominates the peculiar pulse and landscape of the poet's imagination.

The woman speaking here is victim of a mythology she didn't make. She is self-sufficient, and she takes herself seriously enough to fire a bullet "for the men who run my country without consulting me . . . the man who says I am a fool to expect anyone to listen to me," yet, at the same time, she will not relinquish the romantic ramifications of the sexual metaphor. Man is reckless and assertive, the hirsute motorcyclist with hit-and-run morality; she, woman, is "the spiny starfish softer inside than evolution should allow." Yielding to this model, she glorifies

>   . . . The muscles
> that make a man's body have so much substances,
> that makes a woman
> lean and yearn in that direction
> that makes her melt

She romanticizes her vulnerability ("When you leave me for a few days/ the salt disappears / from my body"), and woman's role as encloser, entrapper of man.

> once I almost inspired a man to love me so
>   much
> he

almost changed his life
for me. What higher praise could
a woman have?

Yet she knows too much. The passive model is as instinctually appealing as it is actually unworkable. She is the woman "who needs, wants / cannot be / possessed."

Must we then demystify the sexual polarity in order for woman to be loved fairly, to love without pain, these poems ask. Probably, yes. But the poet will not accept this. Nor will she stop demanding that men, trapped in this same mythology but to better advantage, play by women's rules.

Women have the option today of acquiescing to emotional victimhood or masculinizing their perspective. These poems speak for the woman who will do neither, and from this comes their rage and frustration. Thus when she inevitably suffers from her machismo archetypes, it is not from the desire for pain, but from the stubbornness of a female morality that insists on surviving in a world governed by the male emotional set. In her vulnerability, she realizes, is her strength. And so when she dares her men—

> Love me
> if you can.
> I will not make it easy for you
> any more

—she is not threatening retribution; rather, she is proposing a duel of sensibilities in which men and women are "different kinds of rock" and "My rock doesn't crumble./ My rock is the mountain."

These poems clarify the strain our sexual romanticism puts on women's psyches. At the same time, they refuse to yield to the ethos of defensive rationality. They angrily insist—as many women are insisting today—that if love is to survive liberation, women cannot begin to think and react like men but, rather, men must begin to think and react more like women.

Diane Wakoski (essay date 1973)

SOURCE: "The Emerald Essay," in *Toward a New Poetry,* The University of Michigan Press, 1980, pp. 37-44.

[*In this excerpt, originally published in 1973, Wakoski discusses her concept that "poetry is mythology. And mythology is image." In the process, she outlines the some of the ways that she comes upon images and how they are used in her work.*]

I have spent the three days I have been here [The Boatwright Literary Festival in Richmond, Virginia] looking with fascination at the gigantic emeralds ringed with tiny diamond studs that Katherine Anne Porter wears on her pale birdlike hands. One, the smaller one, is shaped like a large teardrop and I think of those Southern catalpa trees that now, in winter, are bare with sexual pods hanging from the limbs like walking canes, and how in a few months they will be covered again with heart-shaped green leaves, like the green teardrop emerald on Katherine Anne's little finger of her right hand, a leaf seen through the rain or floating on some swollen stream. And then *The Ring*. A square or perhaps I should say rectangular one, an emerald that extends to her knuckle, that reaches over the sides of her middle and little fingers on her left hand, like the green awning over a porch, a stone you could look into and see a past of exotic fish swimming in it or the future, the canals of Mars, and the tiny diamonds surrounding it like commoners flocking to see the Queen of England.

These emeralds fascinate me. I can feel their substance which is part of their beauty, can fantasize a handful of them as if I were holding a handful of dripping wet seaweed at the beach, or I had reached my hand into a sack or barrel of grain and were letting the cool smooth kernels touch my closed palm, or I were holding my own silky hair in my hand, feeling it as if it were part of a silk drape. But their beauty and substance which tantalize me are not what obsesses me. I have thought about Katherine Anne Porter's emeralds for the last three days because they are symbols of her success as a beautiful woman and an influential writer. Peter Taylor told me, when I asked about the emeralds, that she had bought them with some of the handsome profits from *Ship of Fools*. Whether this is true or not is irrelevant. For me they are symbolic of the fact that women as writers are up to the same things men as writers are up to—that is, converting the imagination into something tangible and beautiful, big for its size and yet so small we can wear it on our two hands; that artists are like women in that when they receive wealth they turn it into something beautiful to look at, small and yet magnificent in its surroundings. The emeralds themselves make the diamonds surrounding them into mere background. They are symbols, images, and metaphors of their own reality. They are what comes out of life, not life itself.

When I have been tired or bored or feeling the need for poetry for the last three days, I have looked for Katherine Anne's emeralds. When the conversation has flagged, I have mentioned Miss Porter's emeralds. When I have felt that we have talked too much about art and poetry and not been living it, I mention her emeralds. "Have you seen her emeralds?" I have said to everyone. Not, "Have you read her books?" (because we have all read her books) but, "Have you seen her emeralds?"

These emeralds surrounded by diamond chips remind me of a set of dreams I had when I was in college in the fifties. I had a series of dreams, night after night, which I called my green silk dreams and which I recorded each day. In them, green represented poetry, and the floors were always draped with huge fine bolts of green silk; they were unusual dreams because each night they continued, like a serial story, and of course the green silk was the dominant fact of them. At that time, a roommate in the apartment several of us students lived in had a green paste ring which looked like an emerald. She used to let me wear it when I read poetry or painted little watercolors,

because I said that when I looked into it I could see a secret room, also green, in which my fantasies were played out. I have not been able to look at Katherine Anne's emeralds without thinking that she must sit alone with her feelings often and look into the liquid of those pieces of rock and visualize her fantasies also. Without fantasy, real life is incomplete and dull. Without some substantial real life, there is no fantasy possible.

One of the most beautiful poems I have ever read is Lorca's "Ballade Somnambule"—"green, green, I want you green, green wind, green branches."

Images are a way of shaping poems. I do not mean using images to decorate poetry. I mean images as icons. Images as the structure, the bones, gleaming behind the flesh. Katherine Anne's emeralds this week have been the structure on which I have tried to hang my flesh.

I like gleaming images. Here is a list of gleaming black things which I have used in poems:

eels

leeches

grand pianos

watermelon seeds

patent leather

obsidian

my black velvet coat

a Doberman pinscher

oil bubbling out of the ground

Women have always been the interior decorators, rather than the architects. I would like to propose that the image which used to be decoration in poetry is now becoming the building, the room itself. I would like to propose that Katherine Anne's emeralds are a room she's built and not a decoration on her fingers.

Let me tell you a story which is an obsession with me. I lived with a man, a mechanic, who was always covered with grease. I loved him very much. He had a Doberman with a gleaming black coat and clipped ears who lived with us, who was vicious and bit people though she loved us. This Doberman loved to look at herself in the bedroom mirror and in fact pawed a hole in the rug in front of the mirror over the years, looking at herself, black as obsidian in the mirror. I loved this dog very much and when the motorcycle mechanic left me to live alone in the woods he took his Doberman with him. But she apparently bit everyone who came to his cabin, and he finally had to shoot her. He loved his dog but hated her dependence on him. I am sure he shot her himself and did not take her to the pound. I am sure that it broke his heart but that he also liked shooting her. The image of this rugged man with a mustache and powerful shoulders who had lived with me and rejected me, shooting the Doberman pinscher whose body shone black as Chinese lacquer, is one that haunts me and appears in my mind every time I see a jewel, like Katherine Anne's emeralds.

I spent many months thinking about the look on the dog's face when she was hit with the bullet and the look on the man's face as he shot her. I spent a day this November walking on a beach by a lake which was covered with a thin layer of snow, walking in shiny black boots and wearing a black velvet coat, soft and shiny as a seal, with a red bandanna sticking out of the pocket, and wondering about these images, knowing that I could not really connect them, but still knowing that somehow they were a structure, a connection,

> The doberman, black as caviar,
> my coat, soft and black, like a panther,
> my boots, crunching the sand,
> the black muzzle of the gun—they blue the
>   barrel, powder burns are black,
> the red that must have appeared in the
>   hole as the bullet penetrated the
>   dog,
> my final understanding that love is not
>   something that goes away,
> nor anything which prevents pain or even
>   that can be lived with,
> that this man in his black leathers, riding
>   his Vincent Black Shadow
> or his BSA Gold Star into the night was
>   the Prince of Darkness,
> the Ishmael I loved
>   Motorcycle Mechanic
>   Woodsman
>   Plumber

and that the pain of losing him is an image that itself must be a structure in my life; and that I love another man, the man with the silver belt buckle, the elusive King of Spain as well, is also a structure composed of images. That a myth is a set of beautiful memorable images we string together with different narratives each time. That the constellations in the sky exist as stars which we outline into shapes with our pencils, imaginary lines as exciting to us as the stars themselves, but that the stars are the structure, the images are the skeleton, that concept rests in the image, that "There are no ideas but in things."

Let me tell you how poetry is mythology. And mythology is image. When I was in California for the summer in 1969 and very much alone, pining for the motorcycle mechanic, I met a man who had nothing dark in him at all. He was golden as only Californians can be golden. The first time I saw him, I felt like he came out of a fairy tale. I found out who he was and haunted the place where he worked to talk to him. I did not like talking to him. I liked looking at him. But I was still in love with the man in leathers, the motorcycle mechanic. Ironically, the golden

man cared even less about me than my betrayer. But in my poems, I began to imagine a man like the golden one whom I called the King of Spain. He was a mystery. Never quite there. Yet mysteriously appearing and disappearing in such a way as to make me know he followed me wherever I went. The next year a man whom I only met for a few hours one evening fell in love with me and began to fantasize that he was the King of Spain. When I met him again this year I told everyone I had found the King of Spain. I even wrote a poem called "**Discovering Michael as the King of Spain**." After a day, I told him I was going to meet the Man with the Silver Belt Buckle, and for days I would allude to going off to meet the Man with the Silver Belt Buckle. He too became a mysterious missing desirable character in my poems who loved me but was never there. Last week I sent the King of Spain a silver belt buckle. After looking at Katherine Anne's emeralds all week, I have decided that perhaps I would like to find the man with the emerald ring. Here is a little story about the Man with the Emerald Ring:

> Once there was a man whom all women fell in love with. He was invisible, except for a huge emerald ring which he wore on his right hand, on the ring finger. The ring was so large that the husbands of beautiful women whom the man with the emerald ring visited always noticed when he was there. It was hard for them to accuse their wives of infidelity when their rival was an invisible man. However, that ring flashed in and out of their lives in such a way as to make many of them more furious than when a certain handsome mustached young poet used to visibly visit their beautiful wives, sitting on the verandas at five drinking martinis.

How's that for the beginning of a story? Before I go on, I think I'd like to try out another beginning.

> A poem is a story in which the images are more important than the narrative. Once there was a man who became invisible because no one loved him. However, he had a magnificent emerald ring which everyone could see. Whenever he went anywhere he caused consternation as everyone could see the giant emerald, like a frog, wet from the pond, sitting in the middle of the room.

Or, how about this?

> Once there was a woman who was in love with a man who wore an emerald ring on his finger. However, she could not speak because she had a begonia in her mouth instead of a tongue, and when she tried to tell the man with the emerald ring that she loved him, petals fell out, but no words were formed.

Perhaps if the story begins with the emerald ring it could be hidden in a sugar bowl in the house of midget or a scholar of Urdu.

> Once there was a girl who lived with a Doberman pinscher and who fell in love with a shooting star. She wore an invisible emerald ring.

How can I tell you a story when I cannot decide on a good beginning? I know what the ending is, though: a statement about poetry:

> The poem is the image.

> It gives us some beauty to live for both when life is good and when it is not.

This week I am obsessed with Katherine Anne's emeralds. Have you seen her emeralds? I keep saying. Have you seen those magnificent emeralds? That *is* what women are up to.

There is a coda to this piece. After I had delivered it, George Garrett, the novelist, stood up and said that he had just remembered a story which he'd like to tell. When he was embroiled in the problems of writing his historical novel, a project which required about fifteen years, he met Katherine Anne Porter at a conference. She understood the problems he was having and was both encouraging and sympathetic. She took off the large emerald ring—The Ring—and put it in his hand. "Hold that," she said. "It's heavy, isn't it?"

Pause. "That's *Ship of Fools*. That's all it is."

Then she said to him, "Put the ring on, now," and she made him put it on the only finger it would fit. "Now wear it," she said. And he wore it all day.

He never forgot her emeralds. She too lives with the images and knows how it becomes reality.

Rosellen Brown (essay date 1973)

SOURCE: "Plenitude and Dearth," in *Parnassus: Poetry in Review,* Vol. 1, No. 2, Spring-Summer 1973, pp. 51-9.

[*In this excerpt from a larger article comparing four women poets, Brown notes the strength of Wakoski's poetic persona and her skillful blending of the commonplace with more fantastic and imaginative elements. The critic finds that Wakoski's work in* Smudging *suffers from other qualities, however, including wordiness, awkward prose, and a frequently "nagging" tone.*]

Twice in the last year I've encountered poems by college girls that refer in obvious fascination to Diane Wakoski's face; one, naming its source, referred readers to her poem, **"I Have Had to Learn to Live With My Face."** Referred to the poet, that is, through her poem, curious about what she "really" looks like, uncertain whether this admission of homeliness ("no one could love it . . . a desert mountain, a killer . . .") is an artful exaggeration or a hard, mean fact with which they will be able to go on identifying even after they've checked her out. Wakoski is a superstar of poetry in this sense, transcending the poems in which she stars, compelling people to think of *her.* When they do, they see themselves, not idealized but—in this

day of real girl-next-door movie stars with Barbra Streisand noses, men on the Alka Seltzer ads who look like the awful Joneses, or, worse, like the face in the mirror—as themselves.

Her poems create a persona who is not heroic but who is demanding nonetheless; the apotheosis of all our own plainness to a level where its other, presumably more basic, virtues *must* begin, mercifully, to be searched for. Because she lacks beauty, the man who lives with her, she says, "must see something beautiful

> Like a dark snake coming out of my mouth,
> or love the tapestry of my actions, my life.

That is the best hope of all adolescents, certainly, except (or maybe especially?) the beautiful ones whom everyone is happy enough never to bother to get to know. Before one is confirmed in believing in his value (or has it confirmed by love and work) one does a lot of worrying about one's face: as metaphor and as actuality. And at the risk of having this sound like the Eureka! in that Alka Seltzer advertising campaign, still I can see it's true; Wakoski has had the good sense to make her whole style out of this ordinariness, which she expresses in plain talk, no shit, an unadorned, "straight," anti-poetic voice—in skillful alternation with its opposite. For all her unfeigned simplicity and the accommodation to reality her lack of conventional, hence easy, beauty demands (as metaphor for all the other good reasons for being open and honest), it is hard to think of a poet who writes more lyrically: invoking jewels and flowing hair, exotic animals, landscapes as stylized and exaggerated as fairy tales—in these she is Diana of the moon. So, she has hit her readers, especially the young ones on the college circuits, twice: first precisely where they live and then where they go to dream. In this her poetry is more like Brautigan's prose than even his own poetry: cool, syntactically innocent, damn hard sometimes, fresh with the insights given only to the undeceived—while underneath beats a heart as sentimental as old gold.

(I should add, parenthetically, that her ideal in men, vigorously and endlessly and attractively detailed, is similarly double: much conventional machismo—motorcycles and mustaches, a Clyde to her Bonnie—crossed with the truest sweetness and patience; the warrior-prince, virile, a little menacing, but gentle up close, a tender lover of poets and plain women. There must be three men like him in America, and two probably have the wrong kind of mustache.)

Here are parts of a poem called **"The Duchess Potatoes"** that illustrates every one of these polarities of diction (and desire):

> my people grew potatoes,
> my hair is lanky and split edged and dishwater
> blonde.
> My teeth are strong but yellowish
> I am fleshy without muscles
> my energy is thin and sharp like gravy
> but I crawl into bed as if I were pulling a counter

of rubies
over me,
dream past all my lower class barbed wire
walk down the street in a silk glove
try to scrub myself to an aristocratic bone,
and always come back to the faded colors,
lumpy shape

. . . . .

And I,

peasant,
have no compassion for the lumps,
the lumpy mashed potatoes
that weren't beaten with enough butter and milk.
and made so fine
so fine
they were called "Duchess"

The same dichotomy is beautifully realized in the title poem which begins, ambiguously, "I come out of a California orange grove / the way a meteor might be/ plucked out of an Arizona desert." Struggling beyond the disastrous memories of a childhood in which warmth was uncertain, she, like the delicate orange trees that need smudging, sees her life undefended, in constant danger of a killing frost—so she ends by asserting herself in the face of the men who have constantly deserted her:

There is part of me that trembles,
and part of me that reaches for warmth,
and part of me that breaks open
like mythic fruit,
the golden orange every prince will fight
to own.

In this book as in much of Wakoski's previous work, I find myself fascinated and puzzled by what I think are lapses of a sort, but which in the end may pull with the general strategy of her writing; may be, in fact, part of what prods readers like the college girls I mentioned to look outside the poems at the poet as if *she* were an artifact, or as if the poems were not. In the midst of this tautly-constructed poem (half her poems are seem to work by causal accretion, the other half are "composed" and often more abstract), there will come a conjunction of voices like this:

and I who grew up in a little house
frightened of soot and angry
at the voices of men in the night,
long for you
with all the mystery of my childhood.
You threw me out once
for a whole year,
and I felt that all the masculinity I knew about was
    gone:
        saw blades humming through stiff wood,
        the hand that threaded wire into place and made
    light
        the soaking parts of motorcycles and cars which
        were sloshed free of old dirt and put

meticulously back
    into now running
    machines,
    the hands and mind which could fix the shower
    or the furnace if either
    didn't work.

("Smudging")

You are
that new snow covering our late-night street.
You are so different from me,
        a strong man who builds, thinks designs,
        a mechanic and architect,
        an important freeway in my life.

("A Winter Poem For Tony Weinberger Written
on the Occasion of Feeling Very Happy")

In one of the *Motorcycle Betrayal Poems,* during a fanciful (which is not to say un-serious) shooting, she imagines herself toppling her lover, "you big loud symphony who fell asleep drunk," and says:

I shoot you each time in that wide dumb back,
insensitive to me,
glad for the mild recoil of the gun
that relieves a little of my repressed anger
each time I discharge a bullet into you; . . . .

You too, betrayer,
you who will not give me your name as even a
    token of affection;

("Love Letter Postmarked Van Beethoven")

Two long poems, **"Greed.** Parts 3 and 4, are in fact a solid mass of just such extraordinarily laborious and awkward prose. (I haven't seen Parts 1 and 2, published a few years ago by Black Sparrow.) The first is an ironically self-excused raking over the coals of various of her poet friends for the assorted violences they have done her, their wives, themselves—naming the names, just as in the past she has enjoyed the bold naming of the men she's liked or wanted, with all the reasons why. (And later, in a parody of Anne Waldman's style, she apologizes, or at least has a laugh at herself for it.) But she doesn't manage to bring it off in **"Greed,"** though not because she has indulged meanness in herself or the voyeur in us: rather because the friend, not the poet, nags in her most abstract voice, a bloody bore. Her perceptions here are occasionally interesting:

Rarely do I express my hostilities
                without also defending the
person
                I feel anger towards.
                Sometimes defending him more
than
        he would himself.
But:

                Desire

for the purpose of control or
excluding others
or of total ownership
is greed
whether motivated out of extreme need
or sheer petulance.
The effect can only debase the spirit.

The Communist Manifesto is a lot more riveting than that.
When her list of disappointing friends is finished, she goes
on to complicate the role of "landlord of the emotions"
mightily and often subtly, dragging along every metaphor
she mentions, for later elaboration. Perhaps her intention
is to seem not to be able to let go of anything: greed
exemplified. In any event, there is a great deal of slackness to be got through; but there are few poets whose
styles have so much amplitude—like pockets and folds in
a huge garment into which all manner of encumbrance can
be stuffed. Add to this regrettably spontaneous (i.e., un-
worked-sounding) style which occasionally takes over,
Wakoski's other primitive quality—in content, not diction
and once again it appears that all of it, flaws and all,
works toward a larger picture of incredibly naive openness. But past a certain point it begins to resemble simple-
mindedness, and I begin to lose patience with it:

> You are going to ask me about my life now.
> Why it is such a failure,
> why I have never found a husband,
> a man to love me,
> why I have no family,
> why no one wants me
> very much.
> And I am going to tell you
> the story of a woman who collects wishbones.
> She is hard to talk to.
> She feels like a failure.
> She sometimes is very beautiful
> with long hair and a soft voice
> but she is often alone and
> she writes poems to keep from breaking her heart
>   all the time
> because she falls in love with men
> who don't take her seriously.
>
>   ("Wishbones")

With Wakoski's long wordy books, one can reach in anywhere for an illustration of flaccid writing. In "The Mar-
iachis—A Glimpse"—is the qualification meant to excuse a fragment, an unfinished poem? there is a line that
galled me out of all proportion to its significance: "I see
another party of local people—about twenty." Again, it's
a failure of ear, or sloppiness where her natural ear wasn't
working, by a poet who, granted, does not work for delicacy and subtle refinements (except in certain short, gem-
like poems which seem to announce themselves on the
page before you've read them: swimming in white margin,
they have been whipped into frugal form). Granted she
achieves her effects by building somewhat crudely with
big blocky statements. If one were to see Wakoski's poems as whole languages, they would be synthetic, rather
than analytic—structures that heap up and join words rath-

er than build long and complex and precise single words
which enclose meaning. This may seem irrelevant carping
about that kind of poet, but I've just been re-reading one of
my touchstones in useful criticism, the chapter of Hugh
Kenner's *The Pound Era* in which he looks closely at a
very spare William Carlos Williams poem and traces the
syntactic dependencies in the poem: how each "as" or "then"
pulls with it certain weights of expectation, sets whole systems of necessity in taut motion. And though this poem
(about a cat walking, setting his feet in a flowerpot) seems
just about the single most unlikely poem to cite in a discussion of Wakoski, who chats and ambles and declaims in full
voice, unashamed, raunchy, idealizing, nonetheless I find
myself, ungratefully, looking at this her twelfth book (153
pages; less of a solid structure than her last, also long,
Motorcycle Betrayal Poems, which was like variations on
a theme) and wondering, if there were less, would more of
it be strong and shapely? She is a marvelously abundant
woman who sounds, in her non-goddess moments (which
predominate), like some friend of yours who's flung herself
down in your kitchen to tell you something urgent and makes
you laugh and respect her good old-fashioned guts at the
same time ("So then I told him . . ."). Would that flow itself
be curtailed if less of it were to see the light of print?

She can write poems with extreme and immaculate care.
See the disciplined tone, no less "realistic" and conversational than in the lesser poems, of **"Steely Silence,"** of
"Sour Milk." See the tour de force **"Screw, A Technical
Love Poem,"** which manages in spite of its ostensible
subject, to be a poem about love, with all the other implications of its title held quite miraculously at bay. See
**"The Joyful Black Demon of Sister Clara Flies Through
the Midnight Woods on Her Snowmobile,"** whose title
is a joyous catalog of the remarkable contents of Wakoski's mind when it is really engaged; whose lines are a
richly orchestrated music which feels like a vastly extended sestina because of the tolling recurrence of words and
images.

Smudging contains so much that is good that I resent
being worn into satiety and inattention by its length, and
by all that is easy and disheveled and nagging in it. What
she is trying to do is well-served by her two kinds of
voices, the broad and profane and the more precise and
intellectualizing, and she deserves a lot of latitude in return for that versatility. ("Building up / in any way / a
structure that will permit you to say / no, / a structure that
will permit you to say / yes.") There is little this poet says
that is uninteresting per se; but she can and should be
more than interesting. She closes her book with an answer
to the likes of me. Speaking to a friend she says accurately about herself:

> There is music,
> poetry,
> dance,
> in this house.
> It is clean
> organized
> and direct in its meanings.
> My life has none of this poetry to frame it. . . .

All life is motion.
Mine is *the* quicksilver flash.
Yours
some more steady beam.
The ocean
is my background. Its motion
designing the sand,
carving the rocks,
offering life to simple things.

                                           (**"On Barbara's Shore"**)

So be it. But if, by design or default, she can't become a more consistent poet, then let her have a harsher editor. A fine poet three-quarters disciplined does not have to apologize.

Diane Wakoski (essay date 1974)

SOURCE: "Creating a Personal Mythology," in *Toward a New Poetry,* The University of Michigan Press, 1980, pp. 106-19.

[*In this essay, originally written in 1974, Wakoski discusses her belief that "form is an extension of content" in poetry, and also explains her ideas about personal mythology and what subjects and processes inform her work.*]

Once again I am writing about the subject which seems so simple to me and yet which confuses so many readers of contemporary poetry. When I say "form is an extension of content," I truly mean to be so simple as to be almost tautological. I mean the poet first has something to say and then he finds a mode for saying it. That's so simple a proposition as to be of almost no meaning or help at all. But it can be enormously helpful in looking retrospectively at a poet's work. It means you have to look at a body of it. You have to discover the territory that author was trying to carve out for himself, and at that point many of his stylistic choices will also begin to make sense. For example, Olson's concerns were with archeology, history, and language as it changes through history, so when he uses his city of Gloucester, Massachusetts, as a focus for these interests, open-ended lines which seem digressive become essential; and discovering that each subject led rapidly to another and left a field of discourse, a field of information to roam around in, his lines found themselves unhappy with simple subjects and predicates. Olson found that history doesn't have beginnings, middles, and ends, as the neat composer's mind would like to think. So each poem becomes a field, a landscape of ideas, and completely baffles the critic or reader whose reading techniques were formed by the New Criticism.

On the other hand, there is no reason why the premise "form is an extension of content" cannot be used for more orderly or traditional poetry as well. I propose it as a means of looking at all poetry in some consistent way, and not having to leave out the work of difficult poets like Ashbery, Olson, Duncan, or in fact any contemporary poet, because at times all of us are writing our own rules for the poem as we form the poem. And the reader can look for those forms and find them, I think. His only limitation is that he must look at a body of poems rather than just one to find this working in most cases.

I want to talk about the process for the poet of carving out a territory, creating the subject matter or content which helps the reader identify his voice or style as a poet. And the simplest thing for me to do is to try to discuss my own interests in this matter.

From 1963 to 1966, I taught junior high school in the slums of Manhattan. Like all of my other money-earning activities, it was a job I did as best I could but which I basically hated. However, I did have many interesting experiences on this job, which is more than I can say for the dozens of other jobs I've had since high school, as I've always had to earn my living, and I've done everything from working in the cafeteria to washing test tubes in a laboratory. The one thing all my jobs have had in common is that they have been menial and they have paid poorly.

After I was no longer teaching junior high school and was trying to make my living doing things I enjoyed, like giving poetry readings and poetry workshops, David Ignatow, a poet who has many fine poems about how awful menial jobs are, asked me if I had ever written any poems about my teaching experiences. I told him that I hadn't and that I was sure I never would. He was shocked because he professes to believe that our working experiences are our most meaningful. I felt like that was false in my case and told him so. I told him that I daydream my way through jobs I hate and that my imagination just wasn't caught by the customers in the bookstore or the impossible kids in a slum school English classroom. I also pointed out that his best poems were complaints about how demeaning and terrible bad jobs were to the spirit, and how the spirit could survive *in spite of,* not because of, impossible jobs. That he wrote about survival, not the so-called meaningful experiences of the work itself. I also told him that in my opinion my work was poetry, for that was what was most meaningful to me; and that everyone makes rules about the fact that we shouldn't write poems about writing poetry.

Naturally, we came to an impasse in this discussion. What he was doing was trying to define his own territory in poetry, one that I love and admire when it is written by David Ignatow. And what I was doing was trying to define my own territory and telling another poet that we owned different pieces of land and shouldn't insist on community property. One of my best poems is **"The Fable of the Fragile Butterfly"** which is precisely about the fact that my real life is a fantasy, dream life, even though I accept the proletarian concept that we all have to work for our daily bread (actually, when David Ignatow was talking to me ten years ago, for some reason he must have thought that I came from a middleclass family and like many young poets, in his eyes, wrote out of some decadent, bourgeois need).

After this conversation, it became important to me to try to understand what subjects I found suitable for poetry, from my life, and which ones I had rejected out of hand. Actually, I began this examination for another reason than what I am speaking of now—which is to define the content, the territory of my poems, which then extends itself into the voice or style of my writing. I actually felt that if I could understand why I chose some things as material for poems and rejected others, I might be able to rescue some of what I rejected as poem material after all. You see, poets really are stuck with themselves. For the poem is always the personal narrative and most of us have very limited selves. Most of us could write our autobiographies in one small volume. In my second book of poems, I wrote the line in the title poem, "the answer is to leave autobiography." For a poet you may think of as autobiographical or "confessional" (a term I wish we could get rid of), this is a strange line. And yet I believe it and still mean it. What I mean is that everything in one's life can be emblematic of something else. We are stuck with the facts of our life as a main body of information. But we are *not* stuck with talking about them literally or autobiographically. And what I had discovered was that some things, even a trivial incident like serving food in a cafeteria, became emblematic of something I could talk about with more of the accoutrements of my fantasy life, which was what was important to me. Whereas, the events of a day in a New York City junior high school were so complete with their own intrinsic meaning that they did not seem emblematic to me at all. In fact, most of the time I just wanted to forget them. If I could have written a book about my teaching experiences in the New York public school system, the book would have been *Up the Down Staircase*. But Belle Kaufman wrote it for all of us who taught then. And there was no poetry in it at all. None.

I also came to some definite conclusions while I was thinking about why I didn't write any poems about being a junior high school teacher, and that is that it takes a long time to digest material for poetry. It is seldom that you can write well about experiences that you are having for the first time. Any of you who write poetry will notice that sometimes you can use immediate experience—your love for someone, your feeling of hurt or rejection when someone leaves you, for instance—and what you may find is that it is an experience you have had *before,* perhaps in another form. And now the experience is available with some perspective. You may even be able to use the details of the current experience because they have become emblematic of details in previous experiences. Therefore it is not autobiography you are writing, but your life you are *using* in order to write about life as other people experience it too.

Two of the poets who were very important to me (though I didn't realize it at the time) when I was trying to understand these things about my own work were Allen Ginsberg and Robert Lowell—at least the Ginsberg of *Kaddish* and the Lowell of *Life Studies* and now of *The Dolphin*—because I began to realize that there was something happening in those works which transcended the act of writing about oneself. First of all, it involves using either the most dramatic and important details of one's life or the opposite, using something trivial, like a description of the furniture in your father's room. What this did was make the reader accept the emblematic reality of details and events. And what that leads to is a concept of personal mythology. Your father is not *your* father but an archetypal one. His room is not just a room but a place where important events occur.

The poet, then, is a person willing to see his life as more than itself and his autobiographical technique, ironically, should leave autobiography behind.

About this same time in my history when David Ignatow asked me why I didn't write poems about teaching junior high school, I made a statement in print which I still believe, but which is one of those ambiguities that haunt their authors all their lives. I said, "The poem is as interesting as the person who writes it." Of course I meant that the poet either invents his autobiography by selecting what is most important or interesting about his life to write about, or he in fact is smart enough to know that his life is dull but his mind isn't and he then gives his reader a fantasy self which *is* interesting. At any rate, you will never read a good poem that doesn't also make you think the poet was a fascinating person. And in fact a reader will reject an otherwise well formed poem if the speaker does not win him over in this way.

When I arrived at Hollins College a few months ago, I sat in on many pleasant conversations. By the third day I decided that if I stayed any length of time I would have to write about pets, for I don't think I heard a conversation which didn't turn to pets at some point. Now, this doesn't have anything to do with the way my mind selects material for poetry. I look for things which appear and reappear. I try to find subjects that somehow touch on everyone's lives and when I particularize them, I try to make my details become emblematic, not simply remain idiosyncracies of my life. I have to admit that I didn't write anything about pets while I was there, though I did finish a poem about a carnivorous plant and I'm now working on a poem called **"Annie's Arctic Snake"** which uses an image of a silver snake on the Antarctic ice. And I am also tempted to write about the albino junco which comes regularly to feed on the campus—for rarities are my interest, not the mundane. People are always surprised when I claim Stevens as an important influence on my poetry—they often suggest Williams—but actually what I have found to love in Stevens is the exotic. You will notice that when I choose a subject for a poem, even sour milk, I always have something about magic, about transformations, about rare objects, rare beauty, or if nothing else simply use images like a naked girl riding on a zebra, or clocks in my elbows.

Ignatow writes poems about accepting the dull and boring world we sometimes have to live in—by surviving and enduring it. He is a stoic and his poetry contains the power of stoicism. But my poetry is about beauty and how it rescues us, if only through our fantasy lives, from what is mundane and dull. So my poems always have gold and silver and diamonds from fairy tales in them, even if they are in the form of an orange or a flower or an animal. I could not write about teaching junior high school or most other jobs I've had because they were a landscape where my fantasy was denied rather than turned on. I had already invented a mythical Diane for the poems. She was a Cinderella figure. Beautiful but covered with ashes, so to speak. Waiting for the prince to come along and pick her out for her small foot (a sign of natural superiority) as opposed to the big clumsy feet of the rich, successful, and vulgar but happy other people. She was strong even though sensitive. She was shy but eloquent. She could hardly be a junior high school teacher, for we all know what *they* look like. They can't be too sensitive or the kids would run them out of the classroom. They mainly wear heavy shoes, sensible clothes (because they get covered with chalk during the day), have loud voices in order to coach the volleyball teams during recess, live in tract houses or middle-class condominiums, and teach remedial reading in their spare time.

No Ferraris, no lonely beaches, no motorcycle racers or Hollywood nightclubs or hikes in the woods. No, for me to write about teaching junior high school would have been more unthinkable than actually punching that time clock every morning at 7:30 and rexographing those thousands of improve-your-vocabulary exercises I really did. Just as I could not write a poem about the cats and dogs of Hollins College, for it would have to be a poem with a cat suffering from ataxia, a dog which steals chickens but which the owner still expects to sell for $10, the hour-long Thurberian monologue by Thomas Berger about his dachshund Schotsie, the Burmese cat which sat on my lap when I was feeling unwell . . . well, surely you can see that to write a poem about pets at Hollins College would be the same as writing a poem about teaching junior high school. My animals must be exotic—an imaginary silver snake, an albino junco—or have dramatic events surrounding them—being shot in the head by a devoted owner.

I have been having dreams about the poetry world. One night I dreamed that I left my book bag at a poetry reading and when I went back to get it, it was filled with animals. The man who gave it to me said, "Oh yes, all the people at the poetry reading had animals they needed to get rid of and instead of giving them to the SPCA where they might be killed they put them in your book bag for you to take away."

"But I can't take them," I said. "I travel and can't have any pets." Then I looked into my large bag and started pulling animals out. First a large black cat which had a dragon's head. Then a small white cat which was covered with blood from a wound on its back. Then there was a tiny soggy white shape, as big as a cake of soap. It was the embryo, perfectly formed, of a swan. Finally out of the bag came two little pea-sized pellets. They were the perfectly shaped fetuses of a collie and a horse. I threw all the animals away, saying "I can't take them with me."

I often make poems out of dreams but somehow that one did not seem like material for a poem to me. Yet I have

remembered it, and that is an essential item in the process of writing poetry, for me. I have never kept a pad by my bedside to jot down ideas when I think of them at night. I have never been able to keep notebooks or journals like Anaïs Nin or Annie Dillard, not because I don't admire the process but because some part of me has made a bargain (with the devil) only to write poetry out of experiences that are so vivid and memorable that they keep coming back to me. For me the test of material for a poem is an image, an idea, an anecdote, a phrase, a metaphor, a dream that *does* keep coming back, until I am sure that it means something more than itself. This is my test of what I can make interesting enough to be that mythical Diane I want in the poems. One such dream that I had while at Hollins was like that, and I will recite it to you for what it's worth, as I haven't yet made a poem out of it.

I have had a number of dreams about poets and poetry. I am sure this is because I received a copy of a strange, fascinating collection of poems called *Preferences* by Richard Howard. What has interested me most in various bedtime readings has been the photographs by Tom Victor. The first night I was there I dreamed that Richard Howard and I were laughing and talking, as at a party, having a good time, and he kept saying what beautiful poetry I wrote. Now, Richard Howard and I are friends but he has never said to anyone, including me, that I write wonderful poetry. So that was obviously a dream in which someone else appeared disguised as Richard Howard. But a few nights later I had a dream that seemed like a more significant one to me since it involved a real event which has troubled me. Once I wrote to Elizabeth Bishop, a poet whose work I admired and, though I had never met her, I wrote to her saying that I needed some recommendations for a grant I was applying for and that if she had read my books and liked my work it would be a great favor to me if she would write a recommendation. I expected that if she hadn't read my books she would either ask for copies or ignore the letter. That if she had read my work and not thought much of it, she would also ignore the letter. Instead, she sent me a gracious letter saying, as a matter of fact, I wrote "the kind of poetry" that she had spent her whole life fighting against and therefore could not recommend me. Needless to say, I have never figured out what "kind of poetry" that is, nor do I really think she's ever read my work or she could simply say she didn't like my poems. That idea—that people dismiss a whole body of work without reading it—has haunted me for a long time. And this is the dream I had:

I dreamed I was outside of the house I was staying in at Hollins College—a white two-story frame house with a glass door. In the dream I was coming into the front glass door. It was a sunny day and you could see reflections on the glass. As I reached the door, I saw on the other side Elizabeth Bishop just as she appeared in Victor's photo in *Preferences*. She was signaling me to go away, even though I had a guest apartment in the building. I said I wanted to come in, and she told me I shouldn't come in because I stood for the kind of poetry she had spent her life fighting against. I said she was wrong. She didn't understand what she was saying. The light glared on the flat glass sheet of the door, and as the light got stronger, I could no longer see her reflection, only my own.

I woke up with the image of my face flattened in a glaring reflection on the glass, as if I were a photograph burned into the door.

That is the kind of dream I would make into a poem. I almost always start with an image, as when I wrote about Katherine Anne Porter's emeralds [after seeing them at a writer's conference].

Sometimes the image comes from someone else's poetry. I agree with Robert Duncan that in some way every good writer is derivative. Yet my ethics for writing poetry require disguising what you take. Along with Stevens and Lorca, Yeats has been a very important poet to me. And I think I wrote my first important or adult or non-student poem as a result of being deeply impressed with his poem "Leda and the Swan." About the same time I had read Mann's *Holy Sinners* and also been impressed with that book. I suppose the combination of reading the poem and the novel, and also taking a course in Greek tragedy about that time, made me very interested in incest, rape, sex which causes guilty feelings, taboos, etc. I will not include here a copy of the poem I wrote which is called **"Justice Is Reason Enough,"** but let me say it is a short poem, autobiographical, about my twin brother, David, who committed suicide when we were still children after we had sex together. For years, people thought this was a true story, because when anyone asked, I averted my eyes, and said I didn't want to talk about it. Then later I let it be known that during that period of my life, I had a mental aberration and had really thought that the whole story was true, and that I had a brother. I believe (for here history is no longer terribly clear to me) that in writing that poem, I invented the whole thing but decided that in some mythic or psychic way, it was truer than my true history, part of which was boring and part of which I was ashamed of and felt I could never tell anyone. So I invented the emblematic experience. It is, I think, as much a part of my history now as whatever is real about my history. I can read lots of Freudian or Jungian interpretations into the poem now the male twin represents that part of me which could have functioned authoritatively in the world as men are privileged to do but which I myself killed, i.e. suicided, because I loved too much in a taboo way, as incest is taboo—and was forced to preserve the order of things in my own mind. The poem ends with the lines, "Justice is reason enough for anything ugly / It balances the beauty in the world."

For me, that poem represents the kind of content I insist on in poetry which shapes the poems, gives the formal dictates to my work. I must have a personal narrative because my poems are about *my* perceptions of the world. I must have an image which sticks in my mind, and in this poem, if you trouble to look it up, you will find the image of Yeats's raping swan, transposed into the shadow of a gull. And all of this is feeding into some means of talking about our lives as human. I spent many months before writing the poem sitting in a coffeehouse that students frequented (this was when I was an undergraduate at Berkeley), watching boys and girls as couples. I was alone. I was plagued with the feeling that I was not beautiful and yet equally plagued with the idea that physical beauty is an accident and not a virtue. About this time I began to discover dualistic philosophies like Zen Buddhism which posit that there is just the right amount of good in the world, since it balances the amount of evil. Looking at things in terms of balances began to create a morality for me, and this poem was the most passionate way I could think of describing it.

If you are interested in the written form of this poem you can notice that the first letters of each line of the poem (which is short) form the words, "He who once was my brother," which is part of the first line of the poem—"He who once was my brother, has died by his own hand / even now I see his thin form lying in the sand near the sheltered cliff / which he chose to die from." This acrostic was necessary because I was taking a writing workshop from Thom Gunn who insisted that we have formal structures in our poem until Christmas, when we could write free verse. He taught me, inadvertently, that all poems need some arbitrary forms, even if you have to invent them. I remember that this poem won general approval in the workshop with one exception: I had left the "h" out of brother because I cut the line that began with "h" when I revised the poem. So much for formal objections. It also forced me to write very long lines to work my way around to descriptive and narrative statements which also had words beginning with the needed letters for an anagram.

The sestina is a form which has also appealed to me because when you make long and short lines it is also fun to juggle the ends, as well as the beginnings. As a young poet, I started by writing many sonnets. However, what led me to free verse and its more conceptual forms was the fact that I more and more rebelled against the even-length line. The even meter was not a narrative tool because the personal narrative has so much digression in it.

I would like to end with a short poem that continues my personal mythology and embodies part of what I have been trying to talk about. It is published in my collection, ***Dancing on the Grave of a Son of a Bitch,*** and it is called **"Some Brilliant Sky."**

David was my brother
and killed himself
by the sea,
a dark night
without city lights
to obscure the milky way.

My hair glistens around me like stars
on the night when a man
cracks in half and falls
into the ocean.
Sheets of water,
as I come out of sleep,
no lover,
only the sweaty body of dreams

Wakoski in Greenwich Village in 1960.

he stands over my bed
as I wake up
silent,
whispering to himself,
"no scars"
"no scars"

but he forgets
David who died in the ocean
when the stars were visible in some brilliant sky,
and does not want to see my belly
mangled with scars
from childhood or birth.

Poetry is our history.
We study the stars
to understand temperatures.
Life and death are the only issues;
we often forget that—
arranging our furniture,
washing our cars.

When I look at the sky
I think of David
throwing himself off that cliff
into an ocean which moves with the moon,
dying,
the red blood in his mouth
in a night as black
as eels.

Diane Wakoski with Mary Jane Fortunato (interview date 1974)

SOURCE: An interview in *The Craft of Poetry: Interviews from "The New York Quarterly"*, edited by William Packard, Doubleday & Company, Inc., 1974, pp. 321-40.

[*Here, Wakoski discusses her beginnings as writer, the technical aspects of her work, including imagery, poem structure, and working habits, and the methods she employs in teaching poetry.*]

[Fortunato]: *Could you tell us when you began writing?*

[Wakoski]: I really did start writing when I was a little kid. I wrote my first poem when I was seven years old, about a rose bush, and then I wrote a lot of poetry when I was in high school. I got seriously involved in college, which was when I decided I would spend my life as a poet. Right about the time I was taking Thom Gunn's workshop. That workshop was a wonderful workshop because Thom was very gracious when he said I didn't need a teacher, but what he meant was that there was an unusual situation in that particular workshop. There really were five extremely talented people who would have learned from each other whether he had been there or not. He did what a gentleman and scholar would do. He quarreled with us enough to present his objective, but he also respected the fact that we all were just passionately in-

volved in what we were doing. And would do it. In the true sense, we didn't need him. On the other hand, he really did help us because he understood that. He didn't try to mold us or do anything else. That was a formative period. I was just beginning to find my voice and write the poems that—my publishable poems date from that year.

That was **Coins and Coffins***?*

Yes. You know, there really are events that happen in your life that are significant at the time they are happening. No one else may notice that they are significant, but they are obviously partly significant because you think they are. But you also felt they were because there was something significant about them. And the event that I will always remember from that period—and I date my poetry from that period, though I wrote poetry much longer than that—was the result of Thom's workshop being very prestigious in a strange sort of way. The Poetry Center, which was just beginning, invited him to pick five students from Berkeley or people who wrote poetry seriously, and obviously Berkeley had a reputation, and put us on a program in January of 1959 called "Berkeley Poets." For me it was a really significant event. The other poets—they were all men if that means anything—it didn't mean anything to me . . .

So you would say that that was your most important apprenticeship—that experience?

It really was. The first thing Thom Gunn made me realize was that there are lots of rules about poetry that have nothing to do with poetry in the abstract. Poetry is a human art, and we're really talking about our lives, and poetry which is most readable is that which is most intimate and touching. At the same time, it requires a tremendous kind of craft to walk that tightrope of talking intimately about feelings or talking feelings and not producing a certain amount of gush. Thom made me immediately aware of the fact that he didn't say this in so many words I had a proclivity to like beautiful things, that I thought poetry was about beautiful things. I still think that, by the way, but I have a different idea of what beautiful things are now. He made me realize that if I was going to get any tension at all in there I would have to stop writing those pretty things. I would have to write something more powerful. And he did this partly, I think, by being British. You know, Americans are very susceptible to a British accent. It carries a certain authority, especially when you're young.

Do you have your student poets read their own poems?

I do. I really very much subscribe to the idea that what contemporary poetry is about is partially an oral phenomenon which can only be understood and really appreciated if you hear it. I know for a fact that the experience of hearing the poetry reading is dynamic to many people who would not have had that experience reading the poems on the page. I'm not talking about the poet himself or the good reader of poetry or the scholar who obviously can find many kinds of pleasure in a poem. I really do think that if there is any such thing as a possible wider audience—and even for any of us who think of ourselves as experts having specialized in one poet—the experience of having been to a poetry reading is much more vivid to us than reading the book. Consequently, I think the people should learn to do it. I used to be very, very interested in the prospect of poetry as theatre and having some actors get involved in it. I am against it at the moment. I still believe it's an interesting prospect, but I've come to realize, from talking about this to many people, that isn't really what poetry is about these days. Poetry is about poetry, which means the poet reading his poems. This gives the poems another dimension in the same way that when you try to talk about film as an art as opposed to theatre as an art, you can make all kinds of generalizations. The point is that right now in the times we live most people find the film experience a more vivid one. It's only those of us who have certain kinds of knowledge and certain perceptions that like the theatre just as much. I think that's pretty generally true about poetry. I see no reason why if a person is really serious about poetry, it shouldn't be one dimension of his education. If he reads it, and reading it means presenting his personality as another dimension, and then that's part of the poem. There are poets who have resisted this and their argument is a perfectly good one, a good poem comes alive on the page. But perhaps that isn't really that much to think about right now. We do and we don't. We have a much different idea about poems lasting. It makes me think that if a poem lasts eighty years, it has really lasted a long time. And I do expect poems to last eighty years. Although they don't always. I know I tried to reread Shelley this summer, and found it impossible.

Do you have an imaginary audience in the back of your mind during a reading, the way you really want an audience to be, the way you'd like them to respond?

Yeah, I think so. I think I have several imaginary audiences. First of all, I always write my poems with the feeling that I am speaking to someone. Or some group of people. So I obviously have people in mind. And I wrote poetry because I had a very narrow and circumscribed deprived life, and it was a fantasy world. And the Diane who's in my poems is not a real person. She's a person I would like to be, that I can imagine myself being, even though I put all my faults in my poems, it doesn't mean I'm not a fantasy or imagined person. I didn't create a fantasy that was unreal. I'm smart enough not to have done that. But the Diane in my poems really is fantasy. I don't care how happy my life ever gets, there's always a part of all of us that feels deprived in some way or another. We don't have everything and what the poem speaks to is that fantasy part of ourselves—and no matter what my life is and no matter how it's fulfilled, there are many things that I will not be, and those are the things that I will fantasize. Part of my imaginary audience are always those people who have not loved me or are not in my life because I am not the Diane I fantasize. In a way I'm always having a kind of duel with my audience. I don't ever believe they'll ever like me. And they are the very people who in real life probably wouldn't like me.

Your early poems have been called "confessional poetry." What is your definition of confessional poetry?

I'll give you my parting line first, and then—the term "confessional" has been a real misnomer. A critical school, I don't know if it was M. L. Rosenthal who coined it or not. In general, people think that it is, when he was writing about Plath and Sexton and Lowell. The one thing that Plath and Sexton and Lowell all had in common, and most twentieth-century poets have this, is they liked physical imagery. They all had been in mental institutions and all had either suicidal impulses or alcoholic behavior. They had in some way had antisocial patterns in their lives. And I use the term advisedly because the term "confessional" is related to poems and poets who are talking about experiences that were not acceptable to normal people—the fact that you've been in a mental institution, the fact that you're an alcoholic, the fact that you tried to commit suicide, the fact that you were a conscientious objector—whatever. They were things that you were supposed to be ashamed of and so to talk about your impulses was to confess them. I think that's a real misnomer because first of all even Plath's poetry, which comes closer to that term than any other, is not confessional in the sense that none of those poets are ashamed of what they did or felt that anything they felt should be condemnatory. They felt they had human experiences. In Sexton's case her poetry was only made possible by her experiences of madness because what her personal experience did was obviously shatter a kind of bourgeois insulation—I don't mean that all bourgeois people are insulated but that life is one that insulates you very easily. And to break through to a kind of feeling perception of the world is something I'm sure she would never have arrived at without her nervous breakdowns. Plath has often been said to glorify suicide in her poems. She's certainly not confessing it as a bad thing. I think in order to read her poems with real sympathy you have to have a tragic vision of the world and it has to be a kind of grand thing accomplished by itself. Sexton's poems really do point to the fact that when you go to bedlam and back and get something good out of it, it isn't a bad thing at all. Lowell's poems, which are the source of that term, are simply autobiographical poems. What he does is speak about being an aristocrat with a certain amount of humility, showing that it wasn't all that it was cracked up to be either. But none of them are confessing. Lowell doesn't feel it was an original sin. He wants you to understand that whatever condition people have, it's a human condition and he glorified it.

Could you tell us about your George Washington poems? Why did you choose him?

Because I'm basically interested in symbol and allegory. And Washington is the father of our country. And we live in this very paternalistic society, and he stands for the kind of masculine values that have strengths but for many of us have their frustrations. They do stand for the opposite of what poetry is about. For me he's really the symbol of the material world that doesn't appreciate enough how you feel and for me the revelation that that frustration comes out of not any of the things like materialism or the kind of Philistine attitude that penalizes, but really comes out of our inability to communicate, which I equate with our unwillingness to communicate. For instance, nobody ever understands anybody else. The people we think we understand or feel we communicate with are simply the ones who have tried to talk to us and we have therefore been aroused to try to talk back. Washington, as a historic figure, stands for that kind of aloofness that just doesn't give. For me it's the antithesis of what poetry is. It's also basically what I fought in myself all my life. I am extremely shy. It's really hard for me to talk to people. It took many years of writing poetry and then approaching people by talking to them about poetry to get away from this. I sat in Greece for three months this summer and literally did not have a conversation with anyone except one huge quarrel that I had with a man about poetry. And it's not because people bore me. It's because I'm really frightened of them and I am not able to give and they don't want to communicate, and they do seem boring to me. It's always been easier for me to go off and read a book. Poetry is the next thing to reading a book. By putting it down on paper and then by publishing it you're doing the same thing to people as if you had a conversation with them. But for me it's easier because I can do it by myself. I still really fear to communicate with people, unless I have that symbol.

Do you think your surrealism goes closer to the tremendous emotional impact of all that is in conflict?

Surrealism is a fascinating subject, and it's very easy to have a different idea about it every day. What I would say today about surrealism is that as a technique for writing it's a fascinating way of trying to combine your intellectual perceptions and your emotions about it. All those bizarre placements of things have to do with the fact that every day of our lives we have this bizarre mind living in a body that could be someone else's. Seeing too much and knowing so much more. I've never been an athlete or had any kind of physical prowess of any sort. And I often wonder if athletes, people like those Russian gymnasts, or acrobats you see in circuses, have a different kind of control over the world because I keep feeling how helpless we are. We know—I wonder, for instance, if they have more control over their emotions.

Because they seem to have so much practice.

To me emotions seem to come so much out of the body. A lot of my imagery is physiological imagery. I really do perceive my emotions as if they come out of different parts of my body. Different parts except my head. And I wonder if people who are wonderful athletes have in some way more of a sense of continuity with their emotions. My emotions are very strong and athletic, but my body just doesn't follow. I really think that part of what surrealism is about and why it's such a twentieth-century technique is that we have all developed our minds so much. They still live in these bodies which are so separate. It's a very good way of presenting that separate but together bizarreness.

What about recurring images in your work—oranges, blood, jewels, flowers, have they evolved?

Yes. I didn't start out knowing what I was doing, but after a few years of writing poetry I began to realize that there were certain things that were part of my fantasy life. Usually images are what to me seem very beautiful or very terrible things. And I realized that even before I became a poet I was going to be repeating myself. Those were the things I wanted to write about. I think at the point I became aware of that was the time I was taking Thom Gunn's class and even more important I was for the first time reading Wallace Stevens and beginning to understand that beautiful early poetry of his, and I was reading Lorca for the first time, and those are both poets who used very, very sensuous physical imagery, and it was particularly noticeable in the case of Lorca but equally true of Stevens. He used over and over again the same images. And I realized that they used them as symbols—that their landscape became part of their trademark or their voice, and it suddenly was one of those awarenesses that you have known for a long time without realizing it. That was so obvious. There was no reason why I had to keep trying not to write about those things. The thing to do was to be superconscious of writing about them and to make them into a network. So all of those things did stand for my own sense of what is beautiful and durable.

Also, the very short words, the very strong short words. Is that part of this network of symbols?

I think that has a lot to do with the fact that I always wanted to read my poems aloud and that I come from California and that we have a—I don't know what a good adjective is for the way we speak—but it's very matter of fact, and the poetry in general cannot have a matter-of-fact tone. One of my greatest battles is how to get my matter-of-factness, which I consider part of my vision of the world, into lines and still make it sound like poetry. It's very natural for me. It's my matter-of-fact way of trying to describe things. It's something that I have deliberately allowed myself to use and tried every possible way of using it to see if I could get away with it.

Another one of the things in addition to the short words is the assonance. Is this sought or does this just happen?

That's a very hard thing to talk about because it's talking about your perception of the use of language. I don't know if anyone, including a linguistic specialist, has really figured a successful way of assessing what that is in a person. I know that my own view of it is that I studied music for many years, that I started writing Shakespearean sonnets, that in the back of my mind I'm always going de-da, de-da, de-da, and that's the test for me, by the way. If my language gets too prose-y, too short, it means that at the back of my mind I've said, "Boy, you haven't been iambic for a while." I don't mean just iambic, but that's the easiest one to use. When I feel that there haven't been any regularly recurring rhythms, even though I don't feel required in any way to make even-length lines or subscribe to theories of meter (that strange thing which poetry is all about), I still keep pulling back to that kind of thing. Poetic language is everything that's beautiful. In some way it always comes out singing. And I'm sure that that has to do with my literal sense of what music is, and the way poetry is related to that.

What about the parallel line and the parallel structure that you use? That relates back to music, doesn't it?

That relates back to music, yes, and it also relates to the way I like to put things into neat little piles.

Do you find yourself practicing exercises to keep yourself in shape, writing sonnets and so forth?

I write short poems as exercises. It's hard for me to write short lines in short poems. Although in retrospect I've written an awful lot of them. Whenever I begin to get very long and discursive, which is when I'm writing a poem that I really wanted to write, I begin to feel myself just kind of dissolving out. I have a strong urge to just kind of pat things back in shape, and I write short poems. I haven't for a long, long, long time done any kind of experimentation with what is referred to as metrical forms. Because I started writing poetry that way. In high school poetry was a game for me. I don't mean I didn't take it seriously because I think when you're young, games are a serious part of your life—they were challenges—using language in certain rhythms, you'd get a rhyming dictionary, a thesaurus, it was really fun to do. The only thing was you couldn't say too much that way. And that's ideal for young people because you don't have much to say then except this is fun, who am I. You can boil it down to two or three statements, and you don't have to think about experiences to write about unless you want to write for *Seventeen* magazine. So I think game playing is a very good way of starting poetry. If you start writing poetry when you are older, I don't think that's a natural concern. Unless you have the particular sense of language which goes with that, which by the way is not a twentieth-century sense of language. But I periodically go into doing it again. I found a wonderful book of forms this summer. Its name has escaped me. It has I think every peculiar form ever invented. What is that crazy little book of forms and who is he?

But you do write in form. You have a sestina, for example, in **Inside the Blood Factory,** *which was five years ago, wasn't it?*

Sestinas are fun. If you break the rule for iamble pentameter, which I insist is an English rule and not a French rule, it's a fun-organizing form, because you keep coming back and back and back like a refrain. If you make yourself very conscious of making very long lines and very short lines then there are really interesting musical sounds to the language. I'm not sure that I could write an iambic pentameter sestina.

That was a free form sestina.

Yes. The idea of making thirty-six lines all the same length is like being in jail.

Do you keep a journal?

Oh, I'm a hopeless failure at keeping a journal. The most I can ever do is several weeks at a time.

What excuses do you make up for not keeping a journal? What excuses do you make when you don't write?

Well, I have a lot of excuses. I'm still enough of an old Puritan to have to have an excuse for myself when I'm not writing. I truly believe in my own self-discipline and that I write when I'm ready to write and if I'm not, nothing valuable will come out. I wrote very little this summer except a few critical articles, and my excuse is that I really am going through a big change in my personal life and in my poetry. This year is a very retrospective year. I'm looking back on what I've done. I don't feel very compulsive about writing anything. As far as I'm concerned I've written enough so that I don't have to worry about not writing any more. So I don't feel obliged to write. On the other hand, I write because I like to write. I am going to write again when I'm ready. I wrote three or four poems this summer, which will be included in my new book, some that I like very much. They're moving in other directions, much more—if you can make these distinctions Apollonian than Dionysian—and I'm much more interested in prose as a component of the poem, and for the first time in my life I'm really interested in writing some amount of criticism. I'm very interested in theories of poetry, and ideas of poetry and how poetry has changed in the last years and what it means, the kind of poetry that works, and why it works and so forth, and these never interested me. I mean they interested me in terms of how you made a poem, but not interested in how you made articles out of it. I sat down and wrote articles this summer because I really wanted to.

What writing method do you find most conducive to producing your work, writing in longhand or writing at the typewriter?

I'm very unhappy these days working in longhand, which is another reason these journals are not kept up. I don't write letters in longhand. I really like my typewriter. I started—I can remember being appalled once when someone told me he composed his poems on a typewriter. To me it was appalling, and he said, "Have you ever written a short story?" and I said, "Yes," and he said, "Did you write it in longhand?" and I said "Yes," and he said, "Well, what's the difference?" But I do notice that the more I compose on the typewriter, the prosier my poems are. I never compose those kind of exquisite little things—lyric poems—on the typewriter. I don't see any way of possibly composing a lyric poem on the typewriter, because that's the kind of thing where every word means something and the way you write it down and the shape of it. I have notebooks from when I was in college that have an almost shocking little strange elegant hand—my hand was very sloppy—that the poems were composed in. It was like a different state of organization.

The handwriting had to match it.

Yes, it had to match. There was a kind of elegant slowness, and just the act of writing down a line and then another line, I can just feel it. Every once in a while I get in that mood again. It's not the usual mood.

Do you have to be in a special mood to write a poem? Or if you feel one coming on, do you know . . .

I do. I think that's probably fairly typical. I can sit down at any time and write something. But the good things, the better things that I write—every once in a while I just sit down and write—my favorite poem last year—I was writing a letter to someone and I wanted to include a poem and I didn't have a thing I had written, so I just sat down and wrote it out and it's my favorite poem from that time. Actually I had done a lot of things that got me in the mood to write that poem, and I became aware of it in the process of sitting down and writing the letter.

How about revision? Do you revise a great deal?

I don't revise a great deal, but I revise after I read a poem aloud, and if there are what I call dead spots in it, I bring all my rhetorical skills to bear on it.

When you say read aloud, do you read to yourself or before an audience?

Preferably before an audience. But to myself if there is none. It's very hard for me to type something up, which is one of the reasons I appreciate hiring a typist. It's very hard for me to type things up and not want to change. My kind of revision is not what Dylan Thomas would call revision. Fifteen drafts or anything like that.

Then most of it comes through your original impulse.

The one part of every poem that I subject to rigorous rewrite is the last three or four lines. I love the last three or four lines of poems, and I think they are the easiest part to rewrite. You can rewrite a poem five days after you've written it and completely change that poem's meaning by changing the last four lines. Or you can turn what was a mediocre poem into an exciting poem. It's impossible for me to put a book manuscript together without meddling a little bit.

You were talking about craft before in relation to that workshop in California. Do you think craft is a conscious thing or something that just happens when enough bad stuff gets discarded in the process?

Well, obviously I think craftsmanship is something that can be acquired in a lot of different ways. Because I've always resisted authority even though I'm a very authoritarian person, it's hard for me to learn neat methodical ways and yet I always want to see other people learn that way. So the hit-or-miss method is my method of learning. In terms of the craft of writing, I think that you learn it by reading. I just don't see any other way for learning it. I think you learn more from reading than from hearing people talk. I don't see how anybody who writes poetry conscien-

tiously for ten years and reads can help but get better. I just don't see any way. In a way that's almost a dilemma with so many people writing today and so many, many creative writing programs because it means that any person with a certain amount of time and effort with a lot of reading and who has a certain kind of intelligence can write a respectable poem. That presents a whole other funny vehicle for poetry these days. No one really trusts reading one poem by a person. On the other hand, if you read one poem that you really like, you will remember it and you will go on and look for something else. Most people don't even see one poem that they really like in a magazine. On the other hand, they like the magazine. They say this is interesting, this is interesting and that could be and so forth. But it's a very controversial subject of what the value of publishing poems in magazines is. I know one value it has and that's purely professional, and that is you can't get a book published until you get published in a lot of magazines. They are your credentials for publishing a book. And they are the way a lot of people can get to know your name. But I don't know of a single positive value that I would say derives for people from reading poems in magazines. My feelings about this in the past few years have forced me to forget to submit poems to magazines. Lots of magazines ask you for poems and I'm always perfectly glad to submit them, but I never quite get around to typing them up, and by the time I sit and think about it, I know that those poems can be put in a book. The book will definitely have some readers. It's a very complicated subject, because if you ask me now if my conclusion is: should there be no poetry magazines, I wouldn't say that; I'd say it's even great to have poetry magazines for young writers to publish in. I can't reconcile that with the fact that I really don't think people read magazines. Obviously somewhere I'm working with a prejudice. Maybe my prejudice is that the magazines aren't good, or maybe my prejudice is even if they're good, you shouldn't submit to them.

What books do you recommend that your students read for craft principles? You said before that they have to read a lot. What do you recommend?

Well, there's just so many good books. I would like to suggest something very different from specific poets for people to read to learn craft. I think the way you learn craft is the same way you learn criticism. And that is by reading everything that you can find. I don't think you learn any kind of discrimination if you only read masterpieces. When you read a masterpiece, you may not like it. It may seem awful, and it's not until you read about a hundred more pieces that are nothing like masterpieces that you suddenly realize how good that was and when you start reading things that are badly written, and you suddenly recognize how badly written they are, you have already learned some craft. You can see students doing this, but you can't see them doing it if you say, "Now, read Sylvia Plath, and notice how she uses imagery here and so forth." There's nothing wrong with doing that in retrospect after they've read a lot, but if that's the way they learn, they will know that that's how Sylvia Plath knows how to use imagery and they know that Auden's lines are all scanned, and they know that and that, but they don't have any idea of why that is good poetry. They don't have any of the sensation that that's really exciting. When you go through a magazine and there's nothing that you can even stand to read and then suddenly there's this beautiful poem there. That's the experience they don't have because they only read masterpieces. They don't seem as masterful when they don't have a whole life of schlock around them, when we don't have a whole life of reading to compare them with. I think at any given time it helps to have models to write from. I learned to write from models. I think most people do. Anybody who learns on his own uses models. I started imitating Shakespeare's sonnets when I was in high school. It's still the best way to learn many many things. So I don't see anything wrong in putting whatever five or six books together at any given time, and I'm sure they change over the years, and reading them because it will give pleasure, and pointing out what you really like about poets, and they'll get some ideas. I've seen students that I would be willing to swear will not become poets, even if they have a certain amount of talent, write some nice pieces because they found a poem by someone that really excited them and they imitated it. And it was an exciting experience for them. But my real feeling is that if you read five books and that's all you're going to read, you're almost doing them a disservice. There should be some way that they could go out and have a lot available. This is done in the universities because the libraries are getting better and better and better. But you still have to go to the rare books room for most of the poetry books, and most students are shy about doing that. So they don't really get to sample anything. Another article that I wrote this summer—and it's a letter, a response to a man who teaches English at Kent State—and the whole subject of the letter is how it is possible to teach poetry today without being exclusive, because I think that's what the most exciting thing should be for the student—here's just this huge gamut of interesting stuff being written. Any time you make a reading list, it doesn't become a reading list, it becomes a list of what you leave out. And that's the biggest problem. And if you're in some place like Kent State, Ohio, maybe you stick around because you had a good teacher for a few years, but if you're in an ordinary college town, you don't have anything to browse in, to really see what's going on. So if they have one professor there who teaches Robert Lowell, they don't even know half the time that someone like Ginsberg exists. And Ginsberg is a different case because he's been in *Life* magazine. But they don't know the possibilities of poetry, they know that there's one, but they don't know that that one doesn't have to be in a quarrel with any other one. And they often don't find out that there are really ten or twelve things going on instead of two in a quarrel with each other. Because usually if somebody is teaching Robert Lowell and then he teaches anybody else, he'll teach someone and say, "Now this poet doesn't write anything like that." And they'll spend the time going over how much less good he is.

And you can't do that in writing. It destroys the whole idea of creativity.

The whole idea of making literature competitive the great story of your life if you are an artist and you love nature, is savoring the beautiful things that you've read and you've

heard, the masterpieces, but the masterpieces aren't beautiful because they're famous. They're beautiful because they're things that really hit you and you really like them, and there's no way that some young person is going to have your masterpiece experience. I may have loved Beethoven when I first heard him. But I didn't feel he was a master the way I now feel. And the real problem is that you have—I sometimes think that instead of lectures given by experts, the best teachers would be people who didn't know anything. I think the problem of teaching poetry today, I think it has to do with the way poetry is going to be taught in schools, and I can't—I'm usually very good at thinking of ideal systems, I can't think of any ideal system of teaching poetry. I just cannot think of it. Everything seems to be lacking. No matter what you do you seem to be putting something else down, or leaving something out. Maybe that's the way the poetry world is. They're always at each other's throats. You don't seem to be able to praise one poet without putting down another one.

How do you feel about the need for isolation in the life of a writer and how does it affect personal relationships?

Well, as I told you, I grew up extremely timid and shy and it was very very hard for me to even be interested in making friends with strangers. And consequently I always had a lot of enforced isolation in my life. And I grew up hating being alone, being terrified of being alone. And yet I spent a lot of time alone and it took me many years to learn to be alone and not freak out, to begin to appreciate that I really liked being alone and I didn't have enough privacy for being alone, and I got equally disturbed. And I approached it from the opposite side. I feel like you have to have a certain amount of privacy to sit down and work. But I don't feel that people interrupt that. I don't have that closed-door sanctuary attitude. I really am very seldom annoyed if someone disturbs me when working. And that's a result of compensation from when I was a kid and I would have been delighted if someone had disturbed me. My attitude is that it's natural for me to be alone, and if my life just flows its own way I'll find myself alone anyway, that I'm grateful when there are people there that I can talk to. I'm very much less flexible about it if somebody I don't like interrupts.

Have you ever done any experimenting with concrete poetry?

Not in the most literal sense. I've done a little series of what I call spells and chants. I did these a few years ago, many of which are just repetitions of words. I think of them as sound poetry. There is very little informational or emotional content. I think of that aspect of poetry as precisely that, an aspect of poetry. I'm not very satisfied with poems that only appeal to your eye on the page or can be listened to by your ear. It seems to me that an exciting poem can be seen on the page, and can sound good, and can also have all those other things.

Do you feel that you have a public image because of your readings?

I think that it's inevitable that anybody who gives as many readings as I do and I tend to give fairly consistent readings—I read many of the same poems—I present myself in one of two or three ways.

Is it a public image or images?

Well, that's a good question. I think the people think that I'm just as willing to talk to them in private as I am in my poems. Which may be true. I may be willing, but my old shyness and inhibitions arise and I don't find it very easy. And there's a real intimacy when I read my poems because many of them are very intimate gestures. And there's no way I could have a first conversation with a stranger that's anything like what I say in a poem. Now I think that's a hardship because I think they are disappointed. I keep telling people that if you love me, you should love me in my poems, and I could be a mass murderer or something. In fact, I have always felt that there is too much personality and silliness in the poetry world, so that if you like someone, you try to like their poems. I'm a victim of this too. You dislike someone, you find something wrong with their poems. I'm a very perverse person, and recently I've developed a dogma that you should be able to insult a person, somebody that you don't want to have anything to do with, you don't like him, you think he's stupid, and still like his poetry. And if you do, then he's written good poetry. Because you can transcend that. Now there are some people who just aren't honest enough to do that. I always admire people who can write wonderful poems and be rotten. It seems to me that they have achieved something. Poetry is a heroic form. People are idealizing themselves in a poem. I don't care what you say about confessional poetry and all of us presenting our weak sides, or our crazy sides, or whatever, we are presenting them to be loved, and we are presenting them in our most lovable form.

Do you write best early in the morning?

Yes, and I find it almost impossible to work at night. I don't find the dark conducive at all. I like real light, the sun, coming in.

Do you have a certain number of hours a day that you set aside for writing poetry?

Like my journals I'm always trying to do that, but I'm afraid it never did work out.

Do your dreams provide images for you?

They haven't for many years. I haven't written many poems in the last three years using dream imagery, but I don't really know why that is.

What do you do about fragments and unfinished lines?

I've always thought that's what journals ought to do. I have one in that journal.

Do you usually use them right away?

No, sometimes I use them five or six years later. I tend not to look through stuff like that. Because it's not exciting to me to keep a journal. I don't know and yet every once in a while I go through my papers. Sometimes when I'm going to edit a book and I want to put some poems together, I'll find fragments and write a poem from them. It always seems such a waste to have a fragment when you could sit for an hour longer and have a whole poem.

We talked about early workshop experiences, but was there any writer that you felt or you feel now did influence you when you began writing poetry?

Well, when I was younger I really didn't think anyone influenced me. It was all absolutely out of my head. But in retrospect, you see things slightly different. I really think Jerome Rothenberg had a profound influence on it. He was one of the people I met when I first came to New York and published my first little book of poems, which he liked because they used those surrealist kind of dream images and had a haunting sense of being terrified. It was a way of presenting the world that interested him. He translated a lot of German and Spanish poetry and he himself had this kind of Hassidic tradition. Even though I'm not Jewish, I've often felt like I've had a lot of the same emotional experiences in my life that the Jews associate with their history.

Do you have a sense of where you want your poetry to be, say, in five years?

No. I don't really know. I guess the best thing I could say is that I want to create the possibility of being as discursive as possible. And discursiveness is not really an attractive quality in poetry. It's like looking for ways to do something that I think basically unattractive.

Carole Ferrier (essay date 1975)

SOURCE: "Sexual Politics in Diane Wakoski's Poetry," in *Hecate*, Vol. 1, No. 1, July, 1975, pp. 89-94.

[*In the following essay that centers on* Virtuoso Literature for Two and Four Hands, *Ferrier takes up the issue of the feminist content of Wakoski's poetry. The critic notes that Wakoski's work details the difficulty and pain of women's lives, yet it often fails to present females that are "more free" than her typical, oppressed figures or that have completely given up conventional feminine roles and aspirations.*]

This is approximately the seventeenth volume of poetry that the American poet Diane Wakoski has published since her first, *Coins and Coffins,* in 1962. In it, many of the themes and concerns of the earlier volumes are taken up again and explored further. These themes include, centrally, problems of personal relationships, and the function and role of poetry, and art in general. Sexual politics are central to many of the poems; although an explicitly political context to the personal situation is not generally given; the politics of male/female relationships are scrutinised through the poet's focusing her attention on herself, as a typical woman.

Wakoski's intensely personal poetry demands personal interpretation, but, as in [Doris] Lessing's *The Golden Notebook* for example, it is hard to separate the persona of the central character from that of the author herself. In many of Wakoski's poems it is hard to find the detachment that partly informs Lessing's portrait of Anna Wulf, for example—in fact we are encouraged to read the poems as an account of Wakoski's own life "the poems in her published books give all the important information about her life" (*Smudging*). Are we to read all the poems as "The Confessions of Diane Wakoski," or does an ironic detachment inform some of the statements about dependence on men that we find in the poems? For feminists in reading this poetry, there is the problem of Wakoski as continual victim, and it's harder than it is in the works of Lessing or Plath to find a sense of irony that suggests ways out of subjection. In the earlier volumes we can perhaps trace a kind of split in Wakoski's attitude towards the men who stalk through their pages. *The Motorcycle Betrayal Poems* open with a defiant dedication "to all those men who betrayed me at one time or another, in hopes they will fall off their motorcycles and break their necks". But at the opposite pole is her **"The Pink Dress"** in which she herself is as limp and crumpled as the tossed-aside dress; and in which she recognizes

> the irony
> of my images.
> That you are the motorcycle rider
> Not I.
> I am perhaps,
> at best,
> the pink dress
> thrown against the back
> of the chair.

Wakoski here tells us about but doesn't, I feel, sufficiently analyse the contradictions of the position in which she finds herself. She has attempted to shake off, in subsequent volumes, some of her dependence on men. But even so, the macho males treated so tenderly at times in the pages of her books are a problem for women trying to shake off the mystique of these figures who reinforce a sense that "all men will leave me/if I love them" [**"The Father of My Country"**]. The Motorcycle Betrayer is the most recognizable enemy (recurring as a type in a whole range of American films from *Easy Rider* to *Five Easy Pieces*). Apparently more sensitive are the Man With the Silver Belt Buckle and the Golden Man these two incorporating some of the qualities of the mysterious King of Spain but they also leave a trail of destruction in their wake. In **"In Gratitude to Beethoven"**, Wakoski commented

> No one has loved me without trying to destroy me,
> there is no part of me that is not armoured,
> there is no moment when I am not expecting attack,

there is no one I trust,
there is no love in me that is not a wild flower,
growing at its own leisure with no cultivation
   period and no sense of order.

In an interview in 1971 [in *Chelsea* 32], Wakoski was asked whether her poems talked about the over-dependence on men and on interaction with them that is

> a lot of what Women's Liberation objects to the notion that in order to be truly happy we have to have this conventional, sexual kind of recognition from a man.

Wakoski did not have an adequate answer then to this question, replying that she saw a poet as "a humanist first, rather than a man or a woman, and what we care about is communication . . ." This problem for feminists in reading Wakoski is illustrated by this passage from an otherwise very 'strong' poem

> For a woman
> there is only one thing that makes sense:
> a man who loves her faithfully & keeps her warm at
>   night.
> If he goes, her life does not go,
> but it becomes a book with none of the pages in
>   the right order.
>
> [*Greed, Parts 8, 9, 11*]

In some areas, notably her attitude to suicide, Wakoski has a positive and unmasochistic position, outlining her view of life in her Foreword to **"The Water Element Song for Sylvia"** thus

> Living from day to day is a series of compromises that must be made by every human being. To feel that in some way you are above having to bow down to those compromises is a kind of greed which often makes you long for death, which can be a kind of purity or relief from those human situations where you cannot always do as you believe, cannot always lead the life you believe is honest or correct or right; that to stay alive is to give up your standards or compromise them in exchange for life. In this poem I try to address the destructive part of myself . . . and to use the legend of Sylvia Plath, a poet who felt compelled to kill herself, as a symbol of that alter ego, that Diane who could not or might not feel that when her husband leaves her, and the world does not honor her, and she cannot have or do the things she wants to do with her life, that she might in desperation be forced to take her own life.

> This poem is a protest against the deception of that sense of purity, that greed which does not allow us to accept life on its own terms, and which makes us feel as if we cannot summon up the strength to go on in the face of life's afflictions.

Although Wakoski here brings out contrasts between herself and Plath, "to make the male chauvinists of the world stop comparing me to Sylvia Plath as if all women of the world who write well must be similar", the two poets, nevertheless, do have similar preoccupations, especially that of destructive yet desired male influence the poem **"Dancing on the Grave of a Son of a Bitch",** for example, is very much Wakoski's "Daddy". Denise Levertov, writing soon after the suicide of Anne Sexton, points to those aspects of the "confessional" stance that Wakoski *is* concerned to resist:

> to raise our fears and insecurities into consciousness in order to confront them to deal with them is good; but if the pain is confused with art itself, then people at the receiving end of a poem describing pain and insecurity they share are not really brought to confront and deal with their problems, but are instead led into a false acceptance of them as signs or precursors of art, marks of kinship with the admired artist ["Light up the Cave," *Ramparts* 13, No. 5 (Dec. 1974–Jan. 1975)].

While Wakoski is aware of the dangers of a self-abnegating or conversely a totally self-centred position as far as this relates to the question of suicide—the attitude celebrated in Anne Sexton's "Sylvia's Death" she seems to show insufficient awareness of the fact that it is often these attitudes which pervade her account of relationships between men and women. When talking about suicide, her assertions are strong and self-reliant:

> I won't die for love, poetry, truth or a man who
>   betrays me;
> my grandparents were potato farmers
> and I have a bit of the simple potato
> in me.
> I have been a tree in winter
> and I did not scream when the birds
> flew out of my hair.
>
>   **[*Greed, Parts 8, 9, 11*]**

She is asserting here that she has broken out of the state of mind where one feels "inhabited by a cry / Nightly it flaps out / Looking, with its hooks, for something to love" [Sylvia Plath, "Elm"]. But nevertheless there has not been a real breaking away from the conditioned need of most women to create a world of happiness and love with a man at its centre. The awareness that this is a false direction and that one must have a wider perspective informs *The Golden Notebook* and much of Lessing's more recent writing, and it was beginning to be pervasive in Plath's last poems. Wakoski asserts [in the *Chelsea* interview] that she is prepared to stand by her emotional apprehension of her own experience

> the label 'confessional' is a misnomer, for the most part, because we're not trying to get rid of bad feelings or atone for sins by telling people what we've done. We really want people to know about some intimate feeling or reality that we've experienced that the world may not accept, but that we accept totally, and we want them to know why we accept it.

This means that we perhaps expect more of a direction from her on problems of a more common and everyday nature than suicide.

Wakoski's latest book, **Virtuoso Literature for Two and Four Hands,** is again an amalgam of defiance and acquiescence. In the title poem she talks of a depressing climate

> it was either cold or damp
> Weather than affects you like someone tracking mud
> onto your freshly scrubbed kitchen floor.

What is going on here? Is Wakoski trying to use imagery from the life of an ordinary woman? Are there still very many women who are distressed by people tracking mud onto "their" floor? In "The Emerald Essay" [published in **Virtuoso Literature for Two and Four Hands**] she comments (in relation to imagery) "Women have always been the interior decorators rather than the architects. I would like to propose that the image which used to be decoration in poetry is now becoming the building, the room itself." But will *these* kinds of images become rooms and houses different from the rooms of enclosure and madness that we find in Lessing's *The Four Gated City* or Murdoch's *The Unicorn*? The question relates to the current discussion about 'women's culture'—the rehabilitation of knitting and cooking as art forms—that is also raised in Janet Frame's novel *A State of Seige*:

> The women in those days made pictures from shells, from hair and leftover strands of cotton. They worked tapestry—tea roses, deer and highland cattle, their cooking was full of imagination. If cakes could be permanent they would be hung on the walls of homes and in Art Galleries as a National art . . . All those framed melting moments, Pavlova cakes, scottish pikelets, spanish cream, butterfly kisses—all interesting new collages . . .

Is Wakoski trying to write about the common experience of most women in which it is possible for a "common housewife" to "rise above her nature" and is this why her poetry presents problems for feminists who have gone some way towards trying to overcome their own conditioned subjection and acquiescence? She talks of being unable to be alone

> my mother always referred to herself as "a woman
>   alone".
> I learned it was a desperate and terrible condition.

The poem **"Alone"** in this volume makes some attempt to modify this assertion, but many of the longer poems in the book are preoccupied with the idea of "falling apart", especially **"The Story of Richard Maxfield",** an electronic composer who "wrote a piece called 'Cough Music', made up of the coughs of hundreds of people at concerts", but who, though "brilliant and well organised", suicided because he could not overcome his dependence on another person who could not fulfil his expectations. In **"Virtuoso Literature . . ."** Wakoski is preoccupied with the idea that one's life can "fall apart" to the point where one might wish to die

>   my life was falling apart,
> that is,

the man I loved was running away from me
as if I were a
leaking ceiling or a broken step, and he,
a homeowner, fatigued,
eschewing one more repair.

She comments

Whenever my life falls apart, I am reminded
that I still have not fallen apart.

The theme of music and of playing it is important in this volume, as it was in the earlier ones. References to various composers signify different moods and different approaches to life, and the actual playing of the piano is an important symbolic act, taking Wakoski back to her childhood and what having a piano meant to her then. The poem **"Thanking My Mother for Piano Lessons"**, prefigures another poem about her feelings towards her mother in this volume—**"Driving Gloves"**. It was Wakoski's mother, whom she now fears to resemble even in something as small as wearing gloves for driving, who paid, even when they were really poor, for Diane to have piano lessons, thus

all those years
keeping the memory of Beethoven
a deaf, tortured man,
in mind;
    of the beauty that can come
from even an ugly
past.
                    [**"Thanking My Mother for Piano Lessons"**]

In the poem **"Virtuoso Literature . . ."** it is suggested that at twenty one when she resolved

not to touch the piano again
to take the motion out of my hands
and transform it
into the energy of my life.

that she made some kind of choice about life or about art, that she wonders about when she yields to the temptation to go to the piano and play Chopin. Music for Wakoski has painful connotations:

When I type the word piano
my fingers often slip
They spell "Pain". Oh
How do we do it?
    Get from day to day
When nothing is simple or innocent,
not even poetry or music?

Wakoski in an interview comments on how she organises her poems:

In my poems, if you read a lot of them, you'll notice
I tend towards a certain bias, that is, I structure most
of them around metaphors and images.

Although dealing in many of her poems with the staple metaphors and images of confessional poems; "family" relationships and how to get (out of) them; before the images and metaphors can swell up to make rooms and houses for new freer people to live in, Wakoski may need to give more critical analysis of the innate assumptions about women's nature that are in many of her poems. But we must be very glad that there is no risk of her choosing to give up the struggle with life and with people: this is clear from her poem **"Second Chance"** about how she accidentally electrocuted herself:

A terrible experience, current vaulting out of the
    desk lamp
I held in my hand,
every nerve buzzing, whirring, charging through me,
as if I were a house in which someone were ringing
    the doorbell,
until I fell back on the floor
almost sure I was nearly dead . . .

Michael says it could not have killed me.
Not enough current in a small desk lamp,
and I defer to his knowledge of electrical
    appliances.
I know I thought I was dying
and it made me angry.

A friend commented to me, "Diane Wakoski has every reason and motivation for being a feminist poet on the basis of what she tells us in her books and yet somehow she isn't". Whether this is true, and some of the reasons why it is true if it *is,* I have only managed to touch on and outline here. Wakoski's problem is the common problem that we all share on the road to greater freedom and self-actualisation, and she is aware that literature can erect barriers rather than breaking them down. She commented in one of her most personal pieces

But critics, when you read this, I don't for once want
you to review it; I want you to review yourselves and
learn not about literature but about life how goodness,
or the desire for it, drives us mad.

                                        [*Greed Parts 5-7*]

Although Wakoski's poetry is important for it's capturing of the quality of the lives of most women now, it would be good to see the women in her poems becoming more free in the future.

Sandra M. Gilbert (essay date 1976)

SOURCE: "A Platoon of Poets," in *Chicago,* Vol. 128, No. 5, August, 1976, pp. 294-96.

[*In this mixed review of* Dancing on the Grave of a Son of a Bitch, *the critic praises Wakoski's imagery but criticizes her repetitiveness and a tendency toward self-parody.*]

Diane Wakoski, whose *Dancing on the Grave of a Son Of A Bitch* is her sixteenth book, is . . . at ease, established. . . . To be established in a place or a career, however, can mean being fixed, even stuck, as well as being comfortable and Wakoski, though she's a poet of unusual talent and vitality, seems to me to display a tendency toward staleness, flatness, repetitiveness in this book, a tendency, in other words, to self-parody. A fabulist, a weaver of gorgeous webs of imagery and a teller of archetypically glamorous tales, she's always attempted self-definition through self-mythologizing. "The poems were a way of inventing myself into a new life," she has said. Similarly, she's always tried to define the world by developing—to borrow Jerome Rothenberg's phrase—a technology of the sacred. But where in earlier books, *Inside the Blood Factory* for example, the rich secret world of George Washington and the King of Spain, Diane the moon goddess and her motorcycle betrayer, usually achieved a king of magical autonomy, in this collection the sacred figures seem at times profanely weary, despite the presence of marvelous fables like **"The Diamond Merchant."**

In choosing to write fairy tales about her secret self, Wakoski has always, of course, flirted with a little girl cuteness that threatens not to wear well, threatens to cloy as though the poet had decided to spend her life in an Alice in Wonderland costume wandering among not archetypes but stereotypes. Now, when the vitality of her imagination fails, the furry red lion of the sun, the cold sisterly moon maiden, the wise gentlemanly Buddha and the mustachioed motorcycle betrayer begin to seem like a collection of stuffed toys ranged on the shelves of some female Walter Mitty. And as her persistent imagery tires, Wakoski's language weakens, flattens. Lines like "Winter is a crystal. / Spring is a pool . . . Autumn is a crackle / a fire. . . ." or "A man's name / on my lips / thru all 4 / of the seasons" plainly try to draw on the naive strength that gave such poems as **"Blue Monday"** or **"The House of the Heart"** their extraordinary power, but the visionary energy falters. Perhaps, as someone once said of Wallace Stevens, Wakoski publishes too many "practice poems"? Certainly the title piece of this collection, an extended curse dedicated to "my motorcycle betrayer" and written "in the spirit of ritual recitation" seems oddly powerless compared to her earlier confessional incantations. Passages like

> You ride a broken motorcycle,
> You speak a dead language
> You are a bad plumber,
> And you write with an inkless pen.
> You were mean to me,
> and I've survived,
> God damn you,
> at last I am going to dance on your grave,
> old man. . . .

sound childish rather than childlike, and—more important—they appear to lack even the forward-driving, ritual force of rage.

And yet perhaps these problematically weary pieces are simply signs that Wakoski . . . has entered a transitional phase. **"The Astronomer Poems"** with which she begins this book seem, at any rate, to have a wonderful, newly speculative coolness and restraint. Apparently slight, brief flashes of light in a beautifully evoked darkness, the best of them combine the philosophical teasings of a poet like—yes—Stevens, with Wakoski's own characteristically mythic *Weltschmerz*. The endings of **"In the Secret Room,"** **"East of the Sun, West of the Moon"; "Those Trigger Fish Again";** and **"When Black Is a Color Because It Follows a Grey Day"** come particularly to mind. The first ends with a sure movement from myth to moral:

> Feeling the loneliness
> of my cold name,
> I live in a secret place,
> behind a carved door.
> My house is a diamond and my life
> is unspoken.
> There is music that rescues us all,
> and light into which
> we all fade.
> Life is its own metaphor. Silence speaks
> for itself.

The second achieves a moment of self-knowledge that is rendered with impressive calm:

> Knowing this vision of light
> at last I can love the darkness;
> at peace.
> Away from the terrible fires
> that once burned me up.
> As if I was the smallest planet in a tight orbit.
> As if I had no chance against
> that space,
> that night.

And the last goes beyond self-assertion to a wry objectivity that may finally help liberate Wakoski from the risks of self-parody her private mythology entails:

> That I do not love anyone
> in this night,
> so brilliant I am trying to understand it:
> that is a proposition
> like the lumps of sugar that fall into
> what they call
> "a black cup of coffee."

Diane Wakoski with Claire Healey (interview date 1974 and 1976)

SOURCE: An interview in *Contemporary Literature*, Vol. 18, No. 1, Winter, 1977, pp. 1-19.

[*In this interview, originally conducted in 1974 and updated in 1976, Wakoski discusses many aspects of poetry, including the role gender plays in writing, her concern with "beauty" and aesthetics, and the state of contemporary poetry.*]

[Healey]: *When did you first begin to write poetry?*

[Wakoski]: When I was about seven years old. I wrote many sonnets and began taking writing courses in the fifties at Berkeley. I was encouraged by Tom Parkinson and Josephine Miles, and admired Robinson Jeffers and T. S. Eliot. I think I was fortunate to be in college in the late fifties, at the time of the San Francisco poetry renaissance. Everyone around the college was as involved with contemporary poetry as people in the poetry scene in San Francisco, and that's unusual for universities. There were always the college professors who thought that poetry ended with Spenser or Milton, but there were many in the English Department like Tom Parkinson, who meant so much to me. He had the typical intellectual attitude that only history proves that something is great, which means that most people in the academic world aren't interested in things that are going on in the world now. I guess because Parkinson wrote poetry himself he was more involved, but he was very cynical. He was cruel to his students in that he loved to put them down, especially those who believed in God or had what he considered a romantic notion about the world. It meant a great deal to me to have my poetry praised by a man who was so willing to be unkind to other people.

Have you carried this over into your own criticism of other poets?

I try to do it without being a gratuitously mean person, because I still have a little of the Pollyanna in my personality, but I know how painful gratuitous criticism is. I read it all the time with my own work, but I would like the undergraduate or advanced students who study poetry with me to feel that if I praise a poem of theirs, it is really a good poem and really works. I've been told, especially by undergraduates, that it is very painful to be in a poetry workshop with me for the first few weeks, because I compare their poetry with everybody else's poetry. I never teach beginning classes because I'm afraid I would discourage people.

You have conducted many workshops. Do they contribute at all to your own writing?

I'm very fast to articulate experience but slow to absorb it. I'm not sure how typical this is of other poets; it takes me several years to absorb what I learn and use it in my poems. I seem to filter it through more parts of my body than just my mind. I've only been conducting poetry workshops for about three years, although I've always had informal sessions that were like workshops. When I first started as a writer-in-residence, I usually talked about my own poetry. Now I'm much more often in a position to talk about other people's poetry.

When you visited Montclair State College in 1973, you obviously enjoyed reading your own poetry. In this respect you are not unlike Amy Lowell who enjoyed reading her poetry in public.

I love reading my poetry, and, speaking of Amy Lowell, there have been a few poems, touchstones, that have helped me to create the kind of poetry I wanted to write. "Patterns" was one of those poems. So few people read anything by Lowell, and I'm happy that "Patterns" is one of the poems usually included in high school curricula, because I think it is one of the most terrific poems in terms of the narrative, the use of symbolic image, and the metaphor of using your own life for what life means. There's a poem by Mona Van Duyn called "Economics" which ends with a pun on "Christ! What are patterns for?" It's a poem about getting a grant from the National Endowment—a poem beautifully worked out. The poet is fascinated by the amount of money spent on a lavish dinner in Chinatown for a bunch of other poets, money spent on vacations, and justifying it because it was government money that wasn't going to the war. Whatever privileged thing it was spent on, it wasn't being spent to kill people, and she ends the poem: "Christ! What are poets for?"

It has been suggested that women writers are more subjective, internal, visceral, whereas male writers are objective, external, and perhaps less self-conscious. Do you subscribe to that overall generalization?

Not for the women poets that I know in the published history of poetry, but I think that since the women's movement, many people who would not normally write poetry do so. I don't know how accurate my observations are, but it seems to me it is easier for the women in poetry workshops to get at the material of poetry, and they're less apt to disguise it with the "accouterments of poetry." My observation has been that perhaps for beginning poets there is a certain advantage in being a woman—simply because women live more honestly with their feelings. They have to deal from an early age with the idea that if they couldn't earn a living or do something else for the world they were valueless people. So long as they are pretty, so long as they can cook, they are valuable. The girls who can't do those things don't really have a chance! But I very much dislike distinguishing between men and women poets, because there have been, relatively speaking, so few women who have "done things." We don't have a body of material to compare with. As far as I can see, poetry is a human art, and it really doesn't matter whether poets are black, white, Korean, or American—they are still appealing to the same internal forces, in some way trying to understand how you feel as against the way the world treats you.

When you read reviews of your own poetry, do the reviewers usually consider you as a woman writer, or as a poet?

They usually consider me as a woman writer, and it is something that bothers me very much. I still think it is a way of hedging, saying we can't really apply the same standards. You can look at it as an athletic or physical metaphor. Most people don't want men's and women's sports combined because the presumption is that men still are bigger and stronger than women. If we follow the physical metaphor, look at the tall girls we have had in the last twenty years. About five years ago I began to notice it—it seems as if there were just hundreds of six-feet-tall girls! It was like a science-fiction story, as if they had all been transplanted! We no longer feel that women have to be tiny, dainty things, which doesn't mean that we have gotten over all that cultural thing. You're a tall girl and may have grown up with a feeling of defeminization because of your tallness. To apply this to poetry, I think that the male and female roles have been divided for so long that even in the areas where theoretically there should be no division, there is. In the internal world of emotions (the world of poetry, for poetry may filter through the mind but goes back to the emotions), it is hard to say there is any difference. A man and a woman should feel love in the same way, should experience death in the same way, as filtered through their individual personalities.

You wrote: "My style is not light; it is heavy. / It is full of blueberry stains, and a light meal would make me thin. / I am not a thin writer / or a thin woman" ("From the Eleventh Finger"). Would you elaborate?

I am concerned with very painful subjects and very serious subjects. While I do have a sense of humor, it is much more a satirical sense of humor. It is very much connected with perceiving pain and finding there is only one alternative to that extent of pain, that is, to see how absurd it is for us who have minds to be caught up in situations which may be oppressive.

Have you at one time read a good deal of E. E. Cummings' poetry?

Not a great deal, but he was also one of the poets we read in high school. I felt liberated reading both E. E. Cummings and T. S. Eliot. That's interesting because I wrote metrical lines with end rhymes and found it extremely interesting to do so. My background in piano gave me an "ear" and my fairly large vocabulary made it very easy to find rhyme words. However, I found it difficult to make rhymes that were serious. They all seemed to turn to kind of jokes, and it's not my personality to be able to do so. I think one of the reasons I like comic novels is that I love to laugh, but I really don't know how to make other people laugh. When I wrote **"From the Eleventh Finger"** my wit was beginning to work whether I knew it or not, and I began to realize that there were people laughing at some of my poems. All of my life I wanted to be the life of the party, the person who could make other people laugh, and I loved it when it happened. Then I would go to the next poetry reading and be my same somber self. If what I had said had been witty or inadvertently funny, it was connected with the time and place, since there was nothing inherently comic in what I was saying. But I never learned to be a successful performing comedian. It seems to be an accident when I make the audience laugh. I realized I was straining to think of funny things to say, or to read poems which the audience would laugh at. The minute I started doing that it was disastrous. There's nothing worse than a somber person who is trying to be funny.

On more than one occasion in your poetry you are concerned with the beauty of women. You talk about beautiful women in "Movement to Establish My Identity" and in "Beauty," both detailed, sensitive statements about women.

I'm deeply concerned with beauty, and the longer I write, the more I realize that if one is to generalize about poetry, this is where Wallace Stevens is really my relative. What I am most concerned with is, in a way, aesthetics. At the point in my life when I wrote **Inside the Blood Factory** [1968], I was beginning to perceive beauty through myself. In all of my early poems I was trying to understand why there wasn't any beauty in my life. I couldn't accept the fact that there was no beauty because I was poor. Many of my **Greed** poems mention experiences such as the one about when I was a little girl going to a birthday party, seeing the silverware, and suddenly having a sense of awareness. I, like everyone else, have had a hard time coming to terms with myself, admitting things about myself. I grew up feeling pain and ugliness, didn't dwell as much on myself as on the social situations of being poor and living in an ugly world. I didn't make judgments on myself or know who I was until I was a fully formed person. I was an ugly little Polish leprechaun but didn't feel that that should be a condemnation, whereas I felt that in some way. I could condemn the world. I finally worked my way to self-examination in **Inside the Blood Factory,** in the [**The Motorcycle Betrayal Poems**] poems, and in some of the poems in **Magellanic Clouds.** That was the important next step. One of the reasons I am so enthusiastic about my next book is that I'm moving back to the aesthetic considerations, which I think is a healthy thing to do after you've examined yourself and seen how you fit into the mobile area in which you move.

In "Movement to Establish My Identity" you write that a woman wakes up and finds herself. Somehow it seems timely. Many women can relate to what you are suggesting.

I entitled these poems **"A Poet Recognizing the Echo of the Voice"** because I wrote a poem at the time when I began to realize that I had written a number of poems speaking about myself as a woman. I certainly meant it on the literal level, but I'm also trying to talk metaphysically about something that's always been more of a problem to me than being a woman; that is, being an intellectual and a poet in a world where that isn't accepted. I grew up in a poor world where if you had any intelligence you would use it to make your life better, i.e., have a better profession or a better career. It's ironic that I, choosing the world of books, wind up making more money than most of the people in my family. I don't think it has anything to do with me, whatever modest success I have had. It has a lot to do with the times. Recently, we have had an overflow of money for the scholars and artists. Many of us do the kinds of things we do because of worldly considerations. I often feel like a hypocrite talking to students and telling them not to become poets unless they are willing to starve or, less dramatically, work at jobs they hate all their lives, with nothing to do. Many of them now can get jobs as creative writing teachers—getting paid salaries and being respected, and dealing with students who like writing. When I wrote **"A Poet Recognizing the Echo of the**

Voice," I was very concerned with making the parallel (and I do this in many of my poems) between the world of the woman traditionally and the world of the artist. Both of them, the woman and the artist, have been excluded from the world of politics, finance, and banking, because they wish to cultivate their inner emotions. Those things are not useful to you when you have to make a decision in business that is basically screwing somebody's life.

Currently, the phrase "a room of one's own" has become a cliché. You make a point about "separation" in one of the poems in **Blood Factory.** *How important to the writer is separation, isolation?*

I think anyone who wants to write poetry can scribble poems anywhere. It is very inspiring to see young students scribbling their poems at a party or while they are listening to a poetry reading—at times this is insulting. It is reassuring to know that when you really need to write, you can find a place to do it. In some ways I think it is an advantage to grow up not having that privileged sense that here is my room, no one will bother me. If there is a study and a desk in the home, the man traditionally has it, even if the woman is a writer and the man is the owner of a linoleum store and all he does is write out his bills at the desk. I know an academic couple who are both getting their Ph.D.'s and the woman has already had many things published. She doesn't have a desk, but the man who has never published and will probably not write his dissertation has *the* desk; in fact, he has a whole room. She comes from a hierarchical, patriarchal Jewish family, where women have a definite and important role, but it is not at a desk. These are still the cultural differences between men and women. I think, however, that most writers, unless they are rich, have to earn a living, and have constant demands on their time. If you have to have a certain block of time every day in order to write, you're less likely to get it. I do think that the lives of men and women are changing so much it's difficult to make generalizations. There are a lot of customs connected with possessions, and things connected with possessions last the longest.

In your poems you have suggested that the poet, among other things, is in search of love: "The poet is the passionate man who lives quietly, knowing very well what he wants. It is love . . ." (**The Magellanic Clouds**).

Love is one of those words that I tell my students not to use in their poems because it has so many different meanings. I feel we're all working our way to some point where we are justified in using the word. In order to use it you have to define it. I was using it there as a sense of acceptance, and so many of my poems are about the sense of rejection. I often use physical and sexual love as a metaphor for some kind of acceptance, rather than as an absolute interest in sex. Basically almost all sexual discussion or images in my poems are metaphors for other things. Not to say that I am any less interested in sex than other people, but I am definitely not one who sees sex abstractly as interesting.

Operative metaphors are used deliberately?

I try to do that. I started writing poetry feeling that, first of all, there was nothing I could say about my life that would be earthshakingly interesting. Secondly, the few interesting things in my life were so painful, embarrassing, or shameful that I didn't want to talk about them. I think this is typical of most. What I learned was that poetry is the art of saying what you mean but disguising it. I discourage people from writing poetry which is too literal or too autobiographical when they are beginning, because I think you should save that great material to work up to. For me the discovery of surrealism and of an American poet like Wallace Stevens (who is surrealistic in his own American way) was a wonderful relief. It meant I could invent a life for myself; I could invent an "autobiography" dramatic enough for everyone to be interested in and poignant enough to satisfy me. There were parallels to what I really was trying to say but didn't reveal because it was too painful. Also, I didn't feel anybody had any business knowing it.

As a poet you are claiming a certain privacy. Robert Lowell, when asked if he were a "confessional poet," answered: "I confess only what I wish to confess."

That's right, and that's why the term "confessional poet" is such a misnomer, because none of us is going to "tell" anything we are the least bit ashamed of. Poetry is about controlling your life, control through words. We are reinventing the event on the page so that it can be controlled in a way we couldn't control it in our lives.

A minute ago you used the word "pain," and in **"Love Passes Beyond the Incredible Hawk of Innocence"** *you wrote about the lesson of innocence: "Innocence is suffering," but suffering protects people because it "keeps them involved in the situation at hand," and the "loss of that innocence is something to fear."*

I meant the paradox of the fact that some suffering is gratuitous—that is, it could be prevented if you were not too innocent to know enough to prevent it—and yet, when you are innocent enough you don't really understand how much you are suffering. It seems to me, innocence, in some strange way, promotes a great deal of unnecessary suffering. You don't "know," but at the same time, you don't know how much you are suffering. What I really wanted to get at was the paradox that innocence protects you from the bitterness, because there is nothing that makes you more bitter and angry than to think you are suffering unnecessarily. In some ways, innocence means not having a full awareness of how terrible it is.

What do you think the role of the poet is in our contemporary society? In **"Greed"** *you wrote: "[The poets] said what they had to say, / each one, / about the world." The TV audience saw one live poet at Kennedy's inauguration, a white-haired old man trying to read his poetry in the glare of the sun.*

I have always believed that the role of the artist, whether he is a poet or musician, is to focus on the conflict between the desire for beauty and the natural ugliness the world imposes on us, to create beautiful artifacts that in some way give other people a sense of beauty, other than just the physical beauty of the world. I see the role of the poet as writing poems that in some way touch, seem beautiful to people.

An artifact suggests form, composition, how a poem looks on the page something which concerned E. E. Cummings and other modern poets very much and which seems important to you.

E. E. Cummings was a great poet who influenced all of us far more than we really know. I think of the visual aspect of poetry as being especially important. We do want to read poetry aloud, and if we are to get any pleasure out of reading from the page, there has to be some clue as to the poet's voice and the deliberate kinds of things a poet does with the voice on the page. I spend a lot of time with students operating on poems, playing with what can be done with the voice on the page. Often now, the poem does not communicate anything to your eye, even for someone like you who has been reading poetry professionally for years. You hear the poet's reading and say, "Oh, that was wonderful!" and you go back to the page and sometimes it makes sense, but more often than not you feel it could have been different.

Amy Lowell apparently was able to captivate her audience when she read her own poetry.

It is interesting that we have a historical backlash against people who read their poems well; when they do, we don't take them seriously. I think that Edna St. Vincent Millay was a good poet, much better than she has been treated by history so far. I can only say that part of the reason is that she was such a popular poet, relatively speaking, in her lifetime, and she, too, read her poems well. Many assume that that couldn't be serious literature. I don't think people are going to feel that way in the future. Because Allen Ginsberg reads his poetry well, is he going to be considered no better than Rod Mc-Kuen?

Louis Simpson comments that your poems are full of experience, honestly expressed, and suggests that he is "constantly being surprised by new angles of vision."

One of the reasons that art is so important to me is that throughout my life I have seen life as filled with contradictions that don't make sense. I was very happy when I discovered Buddhism because there the paradox began to make some sense. I studied a bit about Buddhism; everyone did when I was in college. I'm not a Buddhist—I just found salvation in philosophies. I think we followed this up with existentialism.

Would you care to elaborate on the idea of paradox and contradiction?

I think one of the reasons books, music, and paintings always meant so much to me is that ambiguity in art reveals the world as a world of contradictions. So long as there is not a linear meaning involved, the paradoxes don't have to be contradicting. When someone says to you that you have to do something, then he doesn't also say you can't do it, because the two things aren't possible. In a poem, two things are possible, because in some way there is always inherent in the experience in the mind the possibility of doing it or not doing it. So long as you can conceptualize it, it can exist either way simultaneously—that's the paradox. In real life there is contradiction, and it's the kind of thing I've never been able to deal with. My life has been fraught with contradiction, and in some way I have been trying to abstract that and talk about it. Getting away from the physical to the metaphysical, though, I realize that we can't understand the metaphysical until we *see* the physical. For my vision of the world to be in balance, I have to keep this understanding. In life you have to make choices; there is something wrong, however, with making a choice unless there is a chance to conceptualize both possibilities. That, for me, is what poetry does, what the ambiguity of a poem is. There is nothing in the poem—as there is in life—to contradict either of the possibilities. In life the action will contradict it.

In one of your poems you write: "Choice is a watch never presented to me at graduation" ("Greed").

Again, I am concerned with poetry and its parallel with life. The difference between a good poet and a bad one is that a good poet has a marvelous sense of choice—the good poet makes the choices which are interesting and exciting. The artist is one who learns to choose well so that economy can exist. The fewer things you choose to make a whole, the better you are as an artist. I chose to be a poet and not continue to be a clinky piano player. I chose to be a poet and not remain in the academic world where surely I would have had a nervous breakdown. When I said choice is "a watch never presented to me at graduation." I meant that, in a realistic sense, I didn't have many choices about many things. One has to presume a degree of realism and live with it. After playing the piano for sixteen years and realizing that nobody wanted to listen to me, it was obvious that I couldn't spend my life that way. Many people wouldn't have seen that as an obvious choice. The prevailing idea is that ordinary people always get a watch for graduation, whereas, in reality, ordinary people get cars for graduation. What the ordinary person does not understand is that there are actually a few people who don't even get watches, and I was one of them. If I had really known as much about comfort and the bourgeois life as I know now, I might not have chosen to do many of the things I did. I might have chosen to live the calm, peaceful, comfortable life that I now know I would like to have.

One of the best things I have heard about you is that you were a landlady.

I sold my building at a tremendous loss! And one part of **"Greed"** is about being a "landlord of the emotions." Punishing because everyone hates you.

These are all parts of your identity, and in "At Welsh's Tomb" You are concerned with identity: "The journey one you must make to find your name." Do you think this search is important to a poet?

I think it's important to every human being, and one of the miseries of being young (whether you're rich or poor) is that you haven't created an identity for yourself, and you know that is something you have to do. Perhaps for a few young people (this is much less true in the present than in the past), the sense of coming from a large and important family is so overwhelming that they don't go through it. All the rest of us (99 percent of the human race) in some way realize that if we admire our parents we aren't them; if we hate them, we pray we're not like them. The most important thing is to get people to take us on our own terms.

Perhaps this is reflected in our contemporary scene. In the fifties you felt you knew what you wanted to do when you finished college. Now, that is not always the case. Do you think this identity problem is peculiar to our time?

I think every human experiences this, but we express it generationally in a different way. When I was young the real identity crises came when I was thirteen or fourteen. When I was a freshman I might not have known who I was, and I certainly didn't know what I was going to do. By the time I was a junior I was making choices which made it obvious what I was going to do. I was going to become a poet. Recently, young people really believed the whole doomsday thing and were surprised when they got to be eighteen and discovered they had to do something—go to college. They were surprised to graduate from college and to discover they were still alive and there was something for them to do. It was different when I was a young poet. Today, young poets have a whole set of stepping-stones to success: an M.F.A. degree, first-book prizes. None of that existed in the past. Oh yes, there was an M.F.A. program at Iowa, but that wasn't what you did to become a poet.

Because of these circumstances, do you think there will be a dilution, a weakening in the quality of the performance? I remember Richard Chase being concerned about the future of poetry when it was becoming so academically oriented—the phenomenon of the young poet being "apprenticed" to the older established poet.

I don't think we've ever not had that chain of succession, but I think we have it institutionalized in a way that's bad. There is an Iowa school of poetry. It's creating jobs for people to teach creative writing to other people! It's an industry. Imagine thinking of becoming a writer as part of an industry. Teaching people to do it for absolutely no purpose at all, which is kind of wonderful; I'm happy at least it doesn't have any purpose. But I don't feel like being a social prophet about the future. We do live in a healthy time for poetry.

What about the competition among authors concerning being published?

I have a new kind of anguish, and that is that at least one publisher will publish anything I write. I'm waiting for the day, maybe next year, when he suddenly realizes that not only will he not publish everything I write, but will consider me a has-been and not want to publish me at all. I think John Martin of Black Sparrow Press is a very loyal person, and it may take him ten or twenty years to do that. I have loyalty from the people at Doubleday who are interested in my work and want more. But I worry about this continuing. I experience competition on other levels. I'll probably never win a Pulitzer Prize or a National Book Award. I'm not friends with the right people, and at times this bugs me. Being a fairly conscientious person, I worry about another aspect of this. I'm not sure but it would be worse in relationship to Amy Lowell. What if you got to the point where the publisher is willing to publish you and everyone else considers it "garbage"? If I disregard the negative criticism, what do I have to go on? In some way I find totally gratuitous reviews which everyone looks at and says, "How can you take that seriously, Diane?" much more painful than positive reviews that contain a few reservations.

Perhaps this ultimately happened to the imagists who consistently reviewed and praised one another's poetry. Fletcher reviewed Lowell, Lowell reviewed Aldington etc. Not a healthy situation for poetry.

I see myself drawn into that for what I consider good reasons. I would really like to write an article about Eshleman's poetry because I don't think anyone realizes how good it is. But one of the reasons I would like to do it is that I'm a friend of Clayton's and I've been reading his poetry in a very careful way. Even if I write an article in terms of genuinely pointing out things that the reader can find in the poetry (which is what criticism should do), people will think it is just another of Diane Wakoski's articles about her best friend.

When you read your poetry at Montclair you talked about your letters. Are you going to use them deliberately in your poetry?

I've used prose in many long poems and decided it was time to do it in an even more ambitious way. I decided it would be interesting to work consciously on a long poem which was part prose and part poetry, the way *Paterson* is. At the time, I realized I was getting a great deal of satisfaction out of correspondence and, in my letters, was talking about a lot of the issues I was going to cover in my poetry. I started making carbon copies of my letters, thinking that if I could edit them in an interesting way, this would be the prose part. I love to receive letters and to write them, but I'm a very erratic correspondent.

Periodically, I realize how little excitement most people experience with poetry. I sometimes go through periods of this, too. I began to try to think of analogies I could apply to the reader's concern with poetry. Wouldn't it be interesting to try to invest some of the excitement you experience when reading a letter into the poetry of a poem? It's a fine analogy. That was the only period in my life when my typewriter seemed like a sexual object to me; I could hardly wait to get to it. I've never felt that way about writing. Oh, I've always had a good time once I made myself sit down at my typewriter. I wanted to try to create artificially a sense of excitement in myself and have it come over into my poetry. I wanted to edit my letters so that would be a primary thing.

Might you use them the way that Emerson used his journals?

Yes. I can't write journals, but I can write letters, especially if I get a correspondence going with someone for a month or more.

Dreams seem important to you. You refer to your "dream closet" and suggest, "I dream to offset my empty brain" ("The House of the Heart").

I love to sleep and I feel that my dreams are more interesting than my life. I've always been interested in the analogy that I would like to exist between the dream and the poem. I would like the reader to have the same sense after reading a poem, that you have when you wake up from a dream so vivid you can't get rid of it. I have noted that you can have that same sense from a dream that doesn't have one single interesting image in it or isn't one of those dreams that you can tell because it is funny, bizarre, or interesting. What interests me more is the dream that is not necessarily interesting but which nevertheless haunts you. What I'm looking for is the analogy between the experience and what you would like to create as an experience. And one of the things which I have discovered is that if you are going to use dream material at all, it has to be only those dreams that are metaphysical, symbolical, full of bizarre events and exciting images. Because if you try to tell someone that you dreamed someone's arm was around you, that it was the most wonderful feeling you ever had, that isn't very interesting, and you will not be able to convey the same sense that you had. It's a kinesthetic response and it's exciting. I think a good poem can touch many senses in a reader, or I would like to believe that it could, and the question really becomes how to create this process. The only thing you can recoup from dreams are the bizarre, the surrealist elements.

And this is what leads you to use surrealist techniques in your poetry?

At one time I thought this was just about the only thing you could do with dreams. I'm not sure I believe that now.

In surrealism there is no orderly sequence, is there?

One of the things I have noticed is that when you have a dream, part of what's fascinating about it is that things seem to be happening simultaneously, and one of the aspects of surrealism is try to get that sense of simultaneous experience by disordering and fragmenting images and events, so that you yourself have to say either it is hopeless and try to experience it, or you have to reorder it. I

have noticed that when you tell your dream to someone, you can't retell everything, but you try to re-create it in a linear sequence. To do this in a poem may be interesting. I think that, except for the ear, there is very little hope for just random images. I've totally rejected the surrealist manifesto as Breton wrote it, because I not only don't want to place the burden of arranging the images on the reader, but I actually resent that! I feel my only value as a poet is to present a series of images in terms of my perception of my experience arranged in my order. The poet is a person desperately trying to create order in his own world and communicate it to others so that, at least in two minds, the world is perceived in the same way. To that extent the poet wants to manipulate and control the reader.

In your George Washington poems you reveal the avarice and acquisitiveness of our society, and in "The Father of My Country" there seems to be a very personal tone.

On an abstract level what I was trying to do in those poems was to say that in some way, no matter how much we reject the culture that we live in, we are extensions of it. No matter how much we hate it, we should also look for an equal amount of love in order to balance the situation, because we are out to love ourselves. In those poems I am trying to search out the love-hate relationship we have with ourselves as expressed in the culture we can't totally accept. It both oppresses us and makes us what we are, and we can't deal with the positive or the negative parts until we see them both in perspective. Having always been a kind of misfit, I realize that in an odd way I've been a more patriotic, a more American person, than my less misfitted colleagues. In some strange way I really am more of the American spirit because I so rejected the negative aspects of it.

Do you think that being a misfit is an American phenomenon? We have so many poets who couldn't survive or comply with some of the demands of our culture: Hart Crane, Ezra Pound, Anne Sexton, John Berryman, Sylvia Plath, T. S. Eliot.

I think that is a serious question and I don't think I have enough of a historical perspective to answer that. We love the image of Robert Frost who is supposedly our pioneer father. But when you really look at his life, what a misfit he was. I'm not prepared to make generalizations. Perhaps intellectuals, artists, since they are classical people, are always misfits.

Do you think there is a "renaissance" in literature written by women, as some have suggested?

Renaissance presumes some kind of rebirth. It seems to me women writers haven't been active as a group. I don't think there is a renaissance, because I can't think of any period in history when women were predominant in anything. Right now we are living in a sort of golden age where anyone who has a chance to do something is doing it. It is one of the first times in history when women have as much, or almost as much, of a chance as men. Certainly in the literary world I think we do. However, I so rebel against looking at literature from a female-male perspective, that I haven't set up my mind to deal with it.

What about your latest book of poems?

Virtuoso Literature for Two and Four Hands is a shorter collection than others because many of the poems are new. In the past I've always dredged up things. There are a few earlier poems which fit in, and I'm republishing the very first adult poem I ever had published. The theme of the book is an aesthetic theme; that is, what does beauty mean in our lives and how do we re-create it. It's a very personal book for me because it looks at my life in a very retrospective way. Lots of flowers and garden imagery (California is so luxuriant with flowers!). There's even a poem about that. Another aspect about my childhood is playing the piano, which for me was pounding out the ugliness around me, making the sounds which were beautiful, to drown out everything else.

Have you changed your techniques, devices, or structure drastically in your latest poems?

The only thing I would say about them stylistically is that many of them are the prosiest I've ever written. One of the best is **"The Story of Richard Maxfield,"** and part of the aesthetic search is to understand the difference between the stories that poets tell and the stories fiction writers tell. Basically the poet is someone who loves a story but gets so sidetracked by the details and what it means, that he forgets to finish telling it. In this poem I don't really tell the story of Richard, which is summarized in the first line. Richard Maxfield committed suicide in southern California, and the poem is about not understanding why someone would take his life—which is another theme of my ***Greed*** poem about Sylvia Plath. When the search for beauty becomes an important factor in our lives, especially as artists, then we realize that the process of searching is part of the product of beauty. The process of writing a poem is part of what makes the poem interesting, which is very contemporary notion. This means you must have an educated reader, someone who can look for that process and is not just looking for what the poem says. The poet and his readers are special people, and my latest book embraces that proposition.

Do you think about an audience when you write?

I do, and to be truthful, I can't remember what my sense of the audience was ten or fifteen years ago. I know I had a sense of audience, but I don't know whether it has changed remarkably or not.

What last comment would you like to make about your life as a poet?

There's something really beautiful in being alive, and I don't know what, because I didn't grow up in happy circumstances; I didn't grow up in a beautiful world. I had to keep looking for it. The reason I get into all the problems I do is that I'm an optimist, even though all of my experiences should have made a pessimist of me. When I write about love and being a woman, in part, I am trying to make the point that I have never had an experience so bad (often I chronicle the badness so you know I'm not talking about nothing) that it makes me feel life is not worth living. In some ways it's when things are terrible that you perceive the beautiful things, you perceive them with a passion, and they mean so much. This is what produces art and makes life worth living.

Clayton Eshleman   (essay date 1982)

SOURCE: "Wakoski Poetry Aging with Concrete Realities," in *Los Angeles Times,* July 18, 1982, p. 11.

[*Eshleman is American poet and translator. In the following review, he praises the concrete imagery of* The Magician's Feastletters, *the specific objects that are the basis of the poems. Eshleman also comments on the book's theme of aging in contemporary American society.*]

I don't believe anyone has addressed the suddenness with which American poetry has gone abstract in the past decade. In fact the "new" has, overnight, become a kind of writing in which story has disappeared from narration, and narration itself has become so discontinuous that nonsense, in many instances, seems to have usurped imagination. While it is true that "A man died on the road" is not much of a line of poetry, neither is "Death on the deep knees of the fish."

At a mid-point between the literal and nonsensical, a line by Lorca, "Death on the deep roads of the guitar," might be said to stand for the imaginative. In my sense of poetry, it is always the imaginative that is at stake and always the imaginative that is fought, on one side by the dragons of the literal and, on the other, by the knights of nonsense.

Relative to this new abstract poetry (on one level no more than the return of the Surreal, or the revenge of Gertrude Stein's ghost), Diane Wakoski's poetry looks like Grant Wood's "American Gothic." It is about concrete realities and has a stubborn objectlike presence; a thing-possessed evolution of William Carlos Williams' "red wheel / barrow / glazed with rain / water / beside the white / chickens." At the same time, her sensibility, especially in these ravenously still new poems, is profoundly feminine and sensual, offering the language a kind of creamy substantiality of Ingres' women.

Here is the opening stanza of **"Making a Sacher Torte"**:

> Her hands, like albino frogs,
> on the keys of a Bosendorfer,
> nails short and thin like sliced almonds, fleshy
> fingers,
> with the lightning bolt gold and diamond wedding
> ring, zigzagging up to her fat knuckle,
> looking out of place
> on the heavy working hand.

While such lines might appear as merely descriptive, I find, rereading them, that they contain a lot of character, that they are packed with discontinuous sensations, and are a kind of amoebalike egg, turning on its own inward straining, out of which the snake of the poem will wind. All of the half-images in this stanza are picked up and worked in the course of the poem (the "albino frogs" of the "hands" become a "Frog Prince"), and are finally elaborated into a synthesis of memory and experience.

Wakoski's present collection is a fascinating continuation and elaboration of her last book, *Cap of Darkness*, where she began to take on the ramifications of aging in America, a real challenge given the American obsession, all across the board, with youth and novelty. In *Cap of Darkness* Wakoski began to reverse a whole system of frozen values geared to affirm youth / sexuality / summer / product and to denigrate aging / impotence / winter / soul. Especially in the light of current fashions in American poetry (where empty description is as touted as pretentious nonsense), Wakoski's poetry is extremely valuable. It is not enough to just say it is "about something," as opposed to "about nothing." She is increasingly able to register the contours of a world at once solid and bottomless in meditations across which the meaningfulness/meaninglessness of her own lived life is worked.

The Magician's Feastletters focuses on one aspect of aging tied up with converting sexual desire into sensual reception, where the need to perform must give way to a painstaking survey of the shapes of place into which the performance has bled. It is as if one awoke one morning (as one actually awakens throughout the span of a lifetime) in the grip of the details of, say, one's plants, or the food one enjoys cooking and eating—in short, to *one's 'own' things,* which had, in the turmoil of forging an identity, been left unattended.

Diane Wakoski's poetry is poised on an alchemical edge in which, I feel, the paths of her task will increasingly lead to a valuing of the temporal while its eternal hollows will demand to be mined. As an amulet, I offer her the final lines from a letter Antonin Artaud wrote Andre Breton in 1947: "My true state is inert, far beyond human life and captation, is that of my body when *he* is alone."

Kenneth Funsten (essay date 1984)

SOURCE: "More than Naive Confessions," in *The Los Angeles Times Book Review,* November 4, 1984, p. 4.

[*In this review of* The Collected Greed, Parts 1-13, *Funsten asserts that the collection represents Wakoski's maturity as a poet and that the work goes beyond the confessional style she is known for.*]

> This is
> an invitation
> for you to touch
> me, my body

> the tiger lily
> growing in the powdered coffee
> dirt

Since 1962, when Diane Wakoski's first book of poetry, *Coins and Coffins,* appeared, she has enchanted fans and offended critics. No one, it seems, straddles the line. One camp calls Wakoski entertaining, sincere, instructive; the other scoffs—and often with angry contempt—that she is prosy, crude, sentimental, moralizing. The only opinion that both seem to share is that Wakoski writes a form of "confessional poetry." But as her newest book, *The Collected Greed, Parts 1-13,* shows, Wakoski is writing something immensely more promising than naive confession.

Wakoski began *Greed* in 1967 at the behest of John Martin, who was looking for experimental poetry to publish at his new press, Black Sparrow. In the poem, she defines *greed* as *failing to choose,* "an unwillingness to give up one thing / for another." Polygamy is one form. The American norm of consumption—to have enough but want just a bit more—is another. In Part 2, Wakoski creates the metaphor of the kissing fish to describe the greed of poets: "The fish with the cupped and pale gold lips / swimming in the tank / gesture meaninglessly, / kissing constantly. Poets appear / endorsing the validity of each other's feelings. / They decide / who / really / feels / and / who's / a fake." But, she continues: "One kiss too many / and kisses lose their meaning."

Part 5, "The Shark—Parents & Children," begins confessionally: "I gave up my children when I was young / because I had no money, no husband. . . ." But after accepting her loss, the poem switches gears: "I want to talk about / the greed that makes a parent want a child / That makes a woman want to use her body / as a stretched, swollen, lumpy pocket in an old worn coat, / that makes a man want to see some squalling / smelly inarticulate baby animal take his name / and imitate his actions. / What is that greed? / That mirror / That desire for repeating ourselves. / Stamping ourselves on the world?" Wakoski's metaphor grows like a child, until it means more than just parenting, but stands for any type of creation.

Part 6, "Jealousy—A Confessional," begins, "Dear Diary, For the past few months these feelings have been exploding inside me," again drawing the reader into a confessional pretense. Pages later, Wakoski writes: "I never hear praise of anyone else without wanting to kill or destroy them. . . . I see every beautiful face as a reminder of my plain one. I see in fact anything which I have tried to associate myself with—*even ideas*—as my 33-year-old possessions and begin to feel drained, sucked dry, leeched out, the minute anyone else participates even for a minute in them. . . . This is sheer confession, by the way," the poet comments dryly and ironically.

Part 10 is a mystery. A portion of it appeared in a previous collection, *Cap of Darkness.* In *The Collected Greed,* there is only a small note between Parts 9 and 11, stating that 10 was conceived to be about the greed of "Love, Sex and Romance" but never completed. Wakoski doesn't believe she'll ever finish it; nevertheless, she writes, "I still retain the option. . . ." But isn't this greed on the poet's own part, claiming a territory but failing to choose between a set past and an open, uncertain future?

Part 12, **"The Greed to Be Fulfilled,"** is one of the two parts here previously unpublished, and it is a *tour de force*, a dream voyage in which the confessional "Diane" is transported by a Dalmatian to the desert, where inside a glass house is a beautiful garden in which sits George Washington, president of the Society for Western Flowers.

What follows is reminiscent of Chaucer's "Parliament of Fowls." Part 12 takes Wakoski's lyric "I" and moves it into the dramatic mode, where it becomes as much a representation of something as Washington is. George and Diane discuss what it is she has been searching for "all these years." "A feeling of completion, fulfillment," she responds. While Washington's guests don flower masks, the "main event" of the evening is a masque, "The Moon Loses Her Shoes," with actors playing the parts of Diane and George, as well as of the King of Spain, the Blue Moon Cowboy and others, all further distancing Wakoski from simple confession. Poet Charles Bukowski is even fictionalized as the event's emcee.

Finally, "Diane"—representing the poet at mid-life—confronts the unresolved problem of Part 10, choosing to stop fighting for her completion in **"Love, Sex and Romance"** in order to start fighting for her ideas. In effect, a character, the confessional voice of the self-centered ego, reaches a new plane of maturity when it decides that intellectual things, not emotional ones, are what matter.

As if to reinforce that choice, Part 13 is about an idea—poetry's analogy to music. Wakoski takes three Beethoven sonatas and uses verbal descriptions of their thematic structures as paradigms by which to create three poems. This uncovering of technique is the sign of a mature poet, unimpressed by obfuscation *or* autobiography for their own sakes, but intent upon illuminating substance. Listening to this poetry's thematic structure rather than its verbal one, *what* is said becomes more important than *how*. Reemphasizing content and idea, Wakoski strikes a most refreshing note amid a century and world overcome by form, technique and method.

Alicia Ostriker (essay date 1984)

SOURCE: "'What are Patterns For?': Anger and Polarization in Women's Poetry," in *Feminist Studies*, Vol. 10, No. 3, Fall, 1984, pp. 485-503.

[*Ostriker is an American poet and critic. In addition to poetry collections such as* The Imaginary Lover *(1986), Ostriker has published a number of analytical studies that apply feminist critical principles to the works of women writers. In the following excerpt, Ostriker addresses* The George Washington Poems, *exploring the way in which Wakoski uses the figure of Washington to critique the*

roles that men often assume in contemporary society. The critic also notes that while Washington is often portrayed as the antithesis of Wakoski's own persona in the poems, she also perceives him as "a necessary part of herself."]

Man as hero is . . . examined in Diane Wakoski's *The George Washington Poems,* twenty-three deadpan surrealist farces woven like Maypole ribbons around the stiff figure of the father of our country. As Wakoski explains in a preface, the poems "address some man in my life as well as his alter ego, George Washington"; both figures represent "'the man's world,' with its militaristic origins and its glorification of fact over feeling." Like Atwood, Wakoski enjoys surprise. Here is the opening of the first poem in the series, entitled **"George Washington and the Loss of His Teeth"**:

> The ultimate
> in the un-Romantic:
> False teeth
> > This room became a room where your heaviness
> > and my heaviness came together,
> > an overlay of flower petals once new and fresh
> > pasted together queerly, as if for some lady's
> hat,
> > and finally false and stiff, love fearing
> > to lose itself, locks and keys become inevitable.
> The truth is that George cut down his father's
> cherry tree,
> his ax making chips of wood so sweet with sap they
> could be
> sucked, and he stripped the bark like old bandages
> from the tree for kindling.
> In this tree he defied his dead father,
> the man who could not give him an education and
> left him to
> suffer the ranting of Adams and others,
> those fat sap-cheeked men who said George did not
> know
> enough to be president.

Several kinds of female outrageousness coalesce here. The most obvious is the deflation of male dignity in the opening three lines, but there is also the immediate digression from the historical subject to the poet's private life, the saucy "truth" compounded of history, biography, apocryphal anecdote, and the poet's lively imagination—which gives us an imaginary tree with real sweet chips cut from it—and the first-naming of "George," modeled perhaps on how we talk about female authors like "Emily" and "Jane," or popular politicians, or media celebrities.

The poem's narrative continues: after chopping the tree down, George naps and dreams that his dead father attacks him "with a large penis swung over his / shoulder." He retaliates by spitting a torrent of cherry pits at his father, but his teeth come out with the pits. Later he has false teeth made from the cherry wood, but since the tree was his father's, "His lips closed painfully over the stiff set."

A moment's dip below Wakoski's whimsical surface reveals considerable allegorical logic. The political rebellion sanctified by history has its private oedipal motives, and the end product is a son who defeats his father only to become a rigid and comfortless duplicate of him. The "false" teeth and the "false" love of the poem's opening are alike in that both represent a decline from nature to artifact, and both are associated with weapons. "We all come to such battles with our own flesh," Wakoski comments, and accuses her lover of spitting out "rocky white quartz sperm" that has ossified in her womb, and of getting his own false teeth from "This room . . . built with the lumber of my thigh" that is "heavy with hate."

This opening poem is the first and last time we see George Washington as a son, a person of passionate impulse. Subsequent poems depict him as an unemotional patriarch, propped up in the various masculine poses of governor, slaveowner and landowner, soldier, the face on coins and bills, the public figure waving at the crowd, a surrogate for the poet's absconding father, and the subject of a biography the poet quotes in the final piece, called, delightfully, GEORGE WASHINGTON, MAN AND MONUMENT. The Washington of popular lore also appears. The poet sleeps with her lover at an inn where Washington slept. She waits all night under the George Washington Bridge for George to keep a scholarly rendezvous with her, which of course he fails to do. He—or perhaps it is her lover—crosses the Delaware in a boat of razor blades. As Father of her Country, he is involved in a not-too-subtle anatomical pun. The poet's pose, meanwhile, is that of his earnest hero-worshiper, explainer, and amorous pursuer through a series of caricatured American landscapes.

Some of the fun Wakoski has with her ostensible idol is direct and personal. He is a "tight-lipped man" unable to love or to make anything grow on his plantation. In **"Patriotic Poem,"** the poet explains that she pines secretly for the more glamorous Alexander Hamilton, but is loyal to George because he is "first president / and I need those firsts," notwithstanding his "absolute inability / to feel anything personal, or communicate it." In **"George Washington and the Invention of Dynamite,"** she commiserates with him for not beating Nobel to the punch:

> We all
> know the story of the famous discovery
> the inventor's guilt
> and humanitarian needs.

George, she notices, is "different since this / crazy invention / and I wish I could restore you to your/ original polite calm." In one of several particularly anachronistic poems, poor George, naked with an erection, is tittered at by two ladies in bikinis at Martha's Vineyard. Another finds him glancing at his Bulova saying he has always been afraid of anachronisms, at the very moment Baudelaire drives up in a Ford.

The systematic derangement of chronology reinforces Wakoski's tacit undermining of objective history. The seriousness of history and the dignity of male leadership and power within it are deflated not by direct and solemn critique, but by the poet's spirit of play, and by her aggressive foregrounding of her own fascinations and obsessions. Interpolating Washington into dramas of disconnection and failure suggesting the flip side of the American Dream, she manipulates him much as political leaders manipulate populations. The hero of national fame is at the personal level false and stiff, a wooden puppet containing so little emotional sap that Wakoski, with her sweeping loves and hates, her moments of arrogant haughtiness and abject humility, her terror and pain on the one hand, and her penchant for wicked nonsense on the other, easily upstages him. Upstaging is the poet's form of victory, of course, not simply over this particular man, but over the mental and institutional structures mandated by masculinity. As political commentary, *The George Washington Poems* is both a fool's holiday and a declaration of independence, reminding us that authority resides where we the people bestow it, disappears where we withdraw it.

At the same time, to understand *The George Washington Poems* as predominantly satiric is to ignore their forceful emotionality. The long central poem **"The Father of My Country"** reconstructs the child Wakoski's desperate love and need of the absent, indifferent father who has both created her identity and betrayed her:

> Father living in my wide cheekbones and short feet,
> Father in my Polish tantrums and my American
> speech . . .
> Father who makes me dream in the dead of night of
> the
> falling cherry
> blossoms, Father who makes me know all men will
> leave me
> if I love them

When at the poem's conclusion the poet enlists George Washington as father figure, it is with the remembered incredulous ecstasy of the six year old playing outside when her father made an unannounced appearance. "Father," she cries three times, "have you really come home?"

Identified both with the indifferent lover and the indifferent father, Washington may also, the sequence hints, be a portion of herself. "We all come to such battles" marks one parallel. He and she write each other "inspiring letters," and he is her friend and confidant. She and he both have jewels (his are magic pearls he finds in his shoe) that fail to help in their romances. Her blood "perhaps was shipped from Mt. Vernon / which was once a blood factory," and "the white house of my corpuscles / asks for new blood." When Wakoski praises Washington's executive capacity—

> George, you could not love or make anything
> around you grow,
> but you built and pushed and forced
> and largely by will
> shaped and defended things—real, substantial—

she might be complimenting her own style as a poet. She is tempted to imitate him—"I should trim my hair straight . . . I should cut out all curves,—" though she rejects the

Wakoski.

temptation. In the sequence's last poem, ironically entitled **"George Washington: the Whole Man,"** the poet announces her disappointment with Washington as a great man, but also depicts him as shifting through time, caressing her body and brain, "squeezing the thalamus / fingering the spongy protrusions that make me dream," until he seems not only to touch but to dissolve into her identity. At least one interview confirms this subtext: "I guess I think of my world as so female or feminine, or so much in the spirit of the anima, that the things that populated it ought to be masculine and of animus . . . bursting through the mirror and reflecting back . . . these characters that are both completely outside the self and reflections of the self. The self you can never be in real life" [in Wakoski's *Toward A New Poetry,* 1980]. Whether as hero-father-lover or as animus, George Washington stands in an equivocal relation to Wakoski's "I." His world is public, hers private. He is emotionally arid, she is emotionally juicy. She despises and mocks him and the historical-political existence in which alone he lives and moves and has his being. Yet she also perceives him, and not only in jest, as her creator, a necessary part of herself, a thing she wants and needs—and can never possess, and there's the rub. As writers both Jungian and non-Jungian have found, what is experienced as the masculine principle within a female is more often a foe than a friend. Given Wakoski's sense of the relations between herself and men, she can win all her battles and still lose her war, for the feminine self needs

the masculine, but cannot believe it reciprocally needs her. Whether outside or within the self, the male remains Wakoski's antagonist.

Alan Williamson   (essay date 1984)

SOURCE: "The Future of Personal Poetry," in *Introspection and Contemporary Poetry,* Harvard University Press, 1984, pp. 159-65.

[*In this excerpt from his book-length study of contemporary poetry, Williamson analyzes several specific Wakoski poems to argue that, at her best, the poet presents complex works that are "extending the range of poetry." The critic notes that these poems show that Wakoski presents more than the "heart-on-the-sleeve confessionalism" for which she is often criticized.*]

Diane Wakoski has been one of the sadder casualties of the shift in taste in the last decade; she is so fixed in many readers' minds as an artless instance of heart-on-the-sleeve confessionalism that a serious, discriminating discussion of her work from the formal point of view is almost impossible to find. Wakoski has partly invited this reputation, by overproduction, self-repetition, and a peculiarly unfortunate habit of arguing with her critics in her own poems. Still, I don't think the reputation will survive even a cursory reading of her early poems, or a careful reading of the best of her later ones.

All of Wakoski's best poems do essentially the same thing: they use a governing image or group of images to look at the same situation from a number of perspectives, rather as a cubist painting (to use one of Wakoski's favorite points of comparison) might look at a chair from three sides at once. The images tend, especially in the early poems, to be splendid, scary, even over-romantic (gold scorpions, green horses, a girl joining hands with the wind). One feels that the legacy of Spanish surrealism came almost too ready to hand to a lonely young woman already inclined to prefer fantasy to reality. And yet the design of the poems works to correct this, from the very beginning. The cumulative effect of the repetition of images is claustrophobia, not escape. "There are so many ways / of telling the story," a very inventive poem concludes: but the feeling—in context—is clearly one of gloom and entrapment. The poems insistently speak of emotions as static things, "structures": "The structure of anger / is repetition"; "the structure of dream, / like a harness / lowered over my head." The macabre ending of the early poem **"Tour"**—

> I hope you will not be alarmed to learn
> that you may not leave this place again;
> because you have seen the black fox
> mate the white,
> and to satisfy your curiosity
> let me say,
> both animals are now
> dead

is paradigmatic both in its dry crispness, and in its sense of what it means to close a symbolic circuit, to purify and mate the mind's internal opposites. And one remembers that Wakoski's other early love, besides Lorca, was Stevens—the Stevens of *Harmonium,* whose rather chilly factorings of aesthetic impressions (think of "Domination of Black") convey the same sense of the mind's inability to escape from itself, in epistemological terms, that Wakoski's poems do in emotional terms.

Given these preoccupations, Wakoski would be a born writer of rather tight formal poems, and one can't help being ambivalent about the early identification with the idea of the avant-garde that steered her in other directions. A sestina, for instance, seems the perfect vehicle for her sense of proliferation and sameness, the mind trapped by its images; and when she in fact writes one, **"Sestina from the Home Gardener,"** it is at once one of her best poems and a strong contender for the best contemporary example of the form.

The choice of end-words tends to be the *pons asinorum* of sestina-writers. If the words are too emotionally laden, too wide in their applications, the poem gets easy and dull. If they are too narrow, it becomes gimmicky. Wakoski chooses with discrimination. Three of her words, "sections," "precise," and "pointed," are narrow enough to be a challenge, yet resonant: they can suggest the pleasant crispness of work with tools; they can also turn into images of self-division, dismemberment, aggression. ("Pointed" also carries a phallic suggestion, and a suggestion of direction or distance.) The other words run an ascending scale from the ambiguously mechanical to the unequivocally emotional: "removed," "unfamiliar," "losses."

The title suggests the poem's rather wistful, charming premise: a woman turns to fixing up house and garden (or a woman artist to art) to fill the empty time, and the emotional emptiness, after a marriage ends. But the tasks quickly become a language for her emotions and bodily sensations. There is a touch, here, of Plath's sense of being victimized to the point of being turned into a thing by one's relations to others; but with a difference:

> These dried-out paint brushes which fell from my
>   lips have
>   been removed
> with your departure; they are such minute losses
> compared with the light bulb gone from my brain,
>   the sections
> of chicken wire from my liver, the precise
> silver hammers in my ankles which delicately
>   banged and
>   pointed
> magnetically to you. Love has become unfamiliar

We feel at once how much more various in tone, and gently witty, Wakoski's images are than Plath's: from the gritty feel of the inner scratchiness, raggedness of lust (associated with the liver in Elizabethan physiology), to the wonderful image for a delicate, sexually self-

aware woman walking. Wakoski's poems from this early period are full of similarly arresting, original uses of mechanistic imagery to convey the helpless indwelling force of erotic feeling: "Blue of the heaps of beads poured into her breasts," or the "delicate / displacement of / love" that "has / pulled all my muscles / diagonal." These images surely enhance, at least as much as they diminish, the humanity and femininity of the speaker. Yet they have disturbing implications, which grow stronger as the sestina advances: that emotions, like tools, have an existence separate from the will and consciousness; that, like objects, they can be "removed"; that the poem's sense of the self is a fragmented one, allowing the possibility of integration through love, but not of self-integration.

The poem proves this, in a sense, by exploring all the avenues of autonomous integration. For a while, art seems stronger, more powerful, in the absence of the lover ("each day my paint brushes get softer and cleaner better tools, and losses / cease to mean loss"). Yet there is an uneasy awareness that parts of the self are becoming "unfamiliar," and so given over to nightmare or paranoiac projection: "the unfamiliar / corridors of my heart with strangers running in them, shouting"; the "sections / of my brain growing teeth" while "unfamiliar / hands tie strings through my eyes." The mind sinks, wittily and honestly, from art to money as a source both of power and of connection:

> and I explain autobiographically that George
>   Washington is
>   sympathetic to my losses;
> His face or name is everywhere. No one is
>   unfamiliar
> with the American dollar, and since you've been
>   removed
> from my life I can think of nothing else. A precise
>
> replacement for love can't be found. But art and
>   money are
>   precise
> ly for distraction. The stars popping out of my
>   blood are
>   pointed
> nowhere.

Not the least graceful aspect of the poem is the way in which this rather outrageously relaxed conversational voice—which points up the speaker's search for autonomy, and not incidentally breaks up the potentially drab unity of the form—plays off against the entrapping returns of surrealistic imagery. At last the speaker bursts out:

> But there are losses

> Of the spirit like vanished bicycle tires and losses
> of the body, like the whole bike, every precise
> bearing, spoke, gear, even the unfamiliar
> handbrakes vanished.

Only through the body does the self cease to be fragmented; and "the real body has been removed."

Removed by the ice tongs. If a puddle remains what
  losses
can those sections of glacier be? Perhaps a precise
count of drops will substitute the pointed mountain,
  far
    away, unfamiliar?

The concluding metaphor drives home the terrible central
insight: how the emotional equipment of the self in isolation is precisely the same as, yet utterly different from,
that of the self integrated in the body, through love; and
how nothing can be done about it. But the "precise count
of drops" is also, of course, the sestina form itself—its
exhaustive monotony, the sum of parts that will never be
a whole.

This poem is a perfect instance of the reflexive mode, in
its tightly drawn net of images, its unity-in-diversity, and
above all in the way in which the self is driven, fighting
all the way, to a recognition of the limits of its mastery
over itself. Other poems may use the method with a more
"cubist" clash of contradictory perspectives; they may also
lead it toward a happy ending, but with the same sense of
the mind's confusions and misdirections. Consider, for
instance, the lighter and happier **"Rescue Poem."** It is
another poem about tools: "the tools to chop down an
invisible telephone booth." The telephone booth is, fairly
clearly, the solipsistic sensibility, the "shadow foot between the real foot and the ground." The "tools" are the
body made vivid to itself, in the metaphorical extensions
of sexuality ("diamond breasts and a silver penis"), in an
almost frightening imagery of perception as incorporation
("an apple inside the ear"), and in a vision of passive
desires become active faculties ("teeth chipped out of the
navel," a "saw made of all the soft parts of / a cheek").
But if the images can proliferate endlessly, the event is
single, simple, and unexpected: "Need I say the obvious?
/ That you found the door?" And yet, the sealed consciousness is not, finally, left behind; rather, it becomes
one with the resurrected body—in what is at once a sexual
image and an image of the brain's electrical intricacy—as
the poet says

Join me
on the silver
wirey
inside.

It is a charming, rather Zen-like strategy: two incompatible endings which are in reality the same ending. And
again it enforces a sense of the mind's limitations, its
tendency to look in the wrong or the half-right place, its
need of the body, and of others, for its fulfillment.

Some readers, I suspect, will recognize the merit of these
early poems but still feel that the discursive turn Wakoski
has taken in the last ten years has been an unmitigated
disaster, given her lack of critical distance on feelings of
self-pity and defensive anger—so obviously unpromising
in a poet of wisdom. Four-fifths of the time, perhaps, these
readers would be right. Yet Wakoski continues to insist
that she is just as much interested in questions of form in

these later poems as in her early ones. And every once in
a while a poem comes along that is so ingenious in its
structural play with its bare and prosaic terms, that it triumphantly vindicates her.

One such poem is **"The Story of Richard Maxfield"** in
Virtuoso Literature for Two and Four Hands. The poem
deals with the suicide of a homosexual electronic composer, who once made a composition out of tapes of people
coughing at concerts, called "Cough Music." More centrally, the poem is a meditation on the mystery of psychic
strength: why it is available to some people and not to
others of equal intelligence and talent. From the beginning, Maxfield's death is at once an enigma and a banality:

He jumped out of a window.
Or did he shoot himself?
Was there a gun,
or was it pills?
Did anyone see blood?

Banality continues to be the poem's chosen method. It
drives home our ignorance concerning psychic strength by
its merciless, deliberate overuse of two conventional ques-
tion-begging expressions: a person who has such strength
is "well organized"; one who loses it "falls apart."

He was brilliant and well organized.
And then he fell apart.
He was homosexual and took drugs.
He was brilliant and well organized.
I loved "Cough Music" and could not see how such
  a fine
composer could fall apart as Richard fell apart.

But as the words are rubbed clean of what little explanatory value they ever had, the concepts are subtly, unex-
plicitly given new metaphorical bodies: music for organization—

                        a piano piece by
Debussy, delicate and sparse,
like a dress you can see through

—and the sensation of coughing for falling apart. And so
Maxfield's own subject becomes a way of refiguring and
elucidating his fate. The question, why do people cough
more during a piece like the Debussy, suggests rich if
unexhaustive answers to the question, why do people fall
apart? Is it a wish to draw attention to oneself; a wish, on
the contrary, "just to join the whole crowd"; or a kind of
panic in the face of the sexual and existential nakedness
of the clarified life? And the poet, restraining herself from
coughing during the Debussy though she feels the mysterious temptation to do so, arrives at a small illustration
and assurance of why "I would never fall apart." There is
a kind of structural genius in this poem, deliberately choosing the most unpromising materials in order to redeem
from within our commonplace, confused ways of "telling
our troubles." Most of Wakoski's more controlled later
poems aim at something like this, though only a few suc-

ceed so completely ("**Searching for the Canto Fermo**" is one that comes to mind). But at this level of accomplishment in extending the range of poetry, a few are enough; they deserve the envy of many writers who have gotten into the habit of dismissing Wakoski without reading her.

Estella Lauter   (essay date 1984)

SOURCE: "Diane Wakoski: Disentangling the Woman from the Moon," in *Women as Mythmakers: Poetry and Visual Art by Twentieth-Century Women,* Indiana University Press, 1984, pp. 98-113.

[*In the following essay, Lauter explores the developing relationship between women and nature in Wakoski's poetry, asserting that her association with nature, in particular the moon, evinces an appreciation of both nature and the feminine in life.*]

Perhaps Diane Wakoski's interest in the moon stems from its association with her given name. Whatever the reason, she transforms that coincidence into a remarkable exploration, over a ten-year span, of women's relationship to nature. In turn, by tracing the contours of her relationship with the moon through eight books of poems, I want to explore here some of the attitudes twentieth-century women might take toward nature. Specifically, I will argue that Wakoski effectively escapes two traps set by our cultural mythology: the radical separation of the human species from nature, which allows us to oppose culture to nature; and our curious exemption of women from the human category, which allows us to devalue women and all "things" feminine.

Diane Wakoski is known, and sometimes devalued, as a confessional poet whose primary concern is her relationships with men: her absent father, her (probably imaginary) suicidal brother, her several lovers, and her mythic images of masculine power—George Washington or fantasy figures such as "the King of Spain." But the term "confessional" is problematic. Wakoski's work reveals less about her life than it does about her imaginative confrontations with beauty and pain, love and rejection, greed and generosity, sacrifice and reward, or loyalty and betrayal. To name her "subjects" is to place her in a long line of Romantic poets who have mythologized their lives by relating themselves to aspects of the world with symbolic importance. Her poetry is valuable to us here precisely because she reveals her thought processes in an accessible, engaging style that allows her to connect the factual and the mythical, the mundane and the visionary, in the same poem. She holds our interest in the most ordinary aspects of our common experience by placing them in unexpected, often mythic, perspectives.

Wakoski not only relies heavily on nature for her imagery, but she makes its cosmic aspects (sun, moon, planets) a primary concern—even to the point of identifying herself with the moon at times. Thus her work raises questions for the feminist critic that extend well beyond the scope of poetry. She allows us to think about what happens when a woman raised in a scientific age identifies with nature, the object of science, and to ponder whether a woman can use the traditional equation of woman with nature for her own purposes. How does she, as subject, as creative agent, overcome centuries of efforts to domesticate nature and strip it of its mysteries? Such issues are difficult to resolve at present because we know so little about the worldviews that actually inform women's lives. While we wait for the accumulation of significant biographical and autobiographical materials and for the philosophical attention that will reveal the shape of women's contribution to Western thought, the questions press and multiply. My strategy here is to turn to a poet who, while eschewing the politics of feminism, nonetheless gives access to processes that may enable a collective re-envisioning of relationships between women and nature.

Wakoski's explorations began in her fourth book, *Inside the Blood Factory,* with a personification of the moon as a menstruating woman. The figure is at once stereotypic and bold, playing on masculine romantic-erotic visions of the inconstant female, but insisting on the presence of blood in the image. Wakoski pictures the moon bathing, breastfeeding her children, and sending messages to her lovers, but allowing herself to be taken away at the beginning of each day. The moon is a model of amicable separateness between lovers. Particularly in the poem's final lines, "she" becomes the "Virgin" figure that Mary Esther Harding describes [in *Woman's Mysteries: Ancient and Modern*] the female who, despite her attachments to men or children, defines her own purpose in life. Wakoski's speaker says:

> Oh how can I tell you, she loves you,
> but wants to be alone,
> wants to be in your wrist,
> a pulse,
> but not in your house. See,
> she is outside the window now.
> You look at her.
> It does not mean you should try
> to bring her inside.

"She" is also the speaker herself. The role of the moon in the poem is to justify the speaker's stance in a troubled relationship with a lover: "What we never speak of is that/ I love too many men/ and would not be unfaithful to myself." The moon is an utterly feminine model (both motherly and erotic) for the speaker, who asks "to be rebathed/ in thick plasma each night," yet desires to be independent by day.

The poem under consideration is called "**3 of Swords— for dark men under the white moon,**" and it appears in a series, based on the Tarot cards, that announces Wakoski's desire to "unlock" the sun and moon. The card, however, portends sorrow, separation, absence of a loved one; thus the poem is an attempt to avert such sorrow by explaining the kind of love the speaker bears. She begins by sharing fragments of her dreams with her lover, claiming that his sleep is only a "ghost sleep" because he is so constantly in her dreams. In her plea for him to dream of her, she claims willingness to be totally submissive, even masochistic in her love; but she is *not* willing to be permanently domesticated. In return for granting her the love that would restore him to his own sleep, he will remain free by day to pursue his own sword-like activity. The poem is an extended image of desired reciprocity, but one wonders how, starting from such an accommodating base, the woman can possibly win her bid for freedom. Only the inexorable logic of the final image drawn from nature saves the reader from incredulity. Just as the moon maintains both her independence and her "love," so will the speaker.

Inside the Blood Factory also announces Wakoski's interest in Isis, the Egyptian goddess who is mother, virgin, wise woman, and creator, all in one. The context is a modern ritual, the patriotic cocktail party where the melting eagle in the punch bowl becomes a symbol for the speaker of how men treat nature (in the form of the eagle), out of "fear of that great mystery/ the veiled woman, Isis/ mother, whom they fear to be greater than all else." **"The Ice Eagle,"** which Wakoski considers one of her best poems, clarifies one starting point in her thinking about the relationship between woman and nature: she understands that men prefer the beautiful surface of both and that they will allow the substance of both to disappear unnoticed into oblivion, like melting ice.

As if to accept a challenge, Wakoski moves into the slippery realm of Isis in her next book, *The Magellanic Clouds*. She briefly inhabits a mythic realm where human and non-human forces meet and merge, where the moon is "Queen of the Night," and the speaker *is* Isis in search of the sun god. Wearing the mask of a falcon, she watches over the course of history, burns through the veil that separates her from others, and navigates a porpoise under the ocean as if these were ordinary acts.

In the first of these energetic poems, **"Reaching Out with the Hands of the Sun,"** the speaker insists that she can attest to the effect of beautiful women on men because she has watched men through the masks and statues of Isis. In **"The Queen of the Night Walks Her Thin Dog,"** the speaker becomes the queen who walks the dog, "passing through every house," penetrating each "veil" by acts of drinking, seeing, touching, turning a key, and finally by burning through it, but primarily by "singing." Presumably each "house" is a body, and the speaker imagines that, as Isis, she is able to run through bodies with her "song" much as the moon traverses the sky. In the next poem, **"The Prince of Darkness Passing through this House,"** the house is under water, and it is a place where the Prince (Osiris) comes to be with the Queen (Isis). The navigator and her porpoise also come there to be initiated into love by "burning suns, moons, stars, meteors, comets, into our earlobes and eyelids / making our hands hold the live coals / of commitment. . . ." The poem ends with a non-human pact that gives the participants the "power of fish / living in strange waters."

In these poems, perhaps the moon is simply intended to symbolize a degree of passion that transcends the boundaries between male and female selves; Wakoski may be covertly describing moments of sexual orgasm and longing for them to be the rule rather than the exception in human relationships. But if so, her language and her imagination gain the upper hand, taking her into a realm where consciousness of differences within the order of things is transcended by images that eradicate those differences. The significance of this for our purposes is that the customary separateness of the human and the natural dissolves, as surely as the ice eagle did. Instead of using nature as a reference point, Wakoski becomes inseparable from it, as in the book's title poem, **"The Magellanic Clouds,"** in which the speaker imagines herself taking the place of the clouds. The dangers of this stance become apparent in her next book.

By *The Motorcycle Betrayal Poems* the speaker and the moon are interchangeable, so that she can say:

I am thinking about myself
now,
the moon,
. . . . .
Moon,
is what I am thinking about

Even though Wakoski returns to a conscious mode of imagining, the book shows traces of her "underwater" journey. For one thing, the poems reveal her discovery of the shadow or negative side of her personality, presented in these pages in images of herself as a shark, a tiger, a rock, and in her desire for vengeance against those who have wronged her. Out of these experiences emerges the *persona,* **"Lady Bank Dick,"** a tough cop who seduces the con men she chases, paying her own price in battered emotional health. This is the underside of her more ideal *persona,* Diane, who is part virgin goddess and part moon, but not fully reconciled to the exigencies of her human life; to her sorrow, she "must stand alone, for any effect at all."

In this book it is as if the scientific image of the moon has possessed Wakoski's consciousness; several poems show Diane grappling with its "negative" aspects—its deadness, lack of gravity and accepting them as descriptions of herself. In **"Caves"** for instance, she understands herself as a stony crust out of which empty cold caves have been carved. But in the poems where Wakoski allows herself to look directly at the equation of self and moon instead of letting it shape her language, she finds in her own images the equivalent of "a new element" for the scientist. The moon within her then becomes "only a dead crust / that I've learned to lift / in each foot." By contrast, the heavy new element (potassium in her blood), which creates an internal pressure and gives her poetry, bathes her in its own blue light. The outward form (dead crust) of the moon becomes relatively unimportant (a mere sliver) compared with its unknown interior.

Each of the three poems on the moon in this book repeats the same process, starting with an equation of the woman with nature, so that the new element the scientists look for is heavy enough to drag her heart down, arriving at an acceptance of the negative emotional valence of this act; and circuitously finding within the equation a way to revalue some aspect of the self. The revaluation is tentative and minimal compared with the weight of the traditional images, which dominate the book (as in "My rock doesn't crumble", or "I am the mountain / A frozen ocean / behind my eyes"). But it is a potential source of strength nonetheless. Thus, near the end of **"The Moon Being the Number 19,"** the heaviness within the woman becomes nothing less than the power to create, to become the "Superior Man" [*sic*] recommended by the *I Ching*.

In **"The Moon Has a Complicated Geography,"** the speaker explores the more mundane fact that the moon disappears from view in daylight, calling it a murder, and uses it to explain how one life is superceded by that of another or by thinking about life. Her own process of thinking not only reveals to her that she is dry and invisible (like the moon by day) to her lover, but also that she and the moon have a complicated geography, which continues to exist without the light of the sun. Although the poem ends with the desire for the moisture and coolness of the nighttime relationship among the planets, a liberating idea has emerged: the moon's geography may be interesting in its own right without reference to the sun.

"I Lay Next to You All Night, Trying Awake to Understand the Watering Places of the Moon" carries this line of thought a step further by imagining that the moon's geography includes "watering places," a position held by scientists long enough to cause the dark areas of the Moon to be called *mares* or seas. The speaker's daylight voice, which chides others to "burn like the sun," becomes at night a call for water; her arms try to gather the water, even though she knows

> there are no Li Pos left
> to drunkenly fall into a river
> attempting to hold its radiant face
> all night.

These are painful, brave poems, seeking to recognize the devalued internal potential of the moon and the woman at moments when the sun-man no longer serves to highlight their complicated geography.

The one poem in *Smudging* that is focused on the moon, **"The Moon Explodes in Autumn as a Milkweed Pod,"** continues the exploration of the self. It begins with a rhetorical question:

> Is there a moment when the moon explodes in
>   autumn
> as a milkweed pod
> wet wings of membrane unfolded
> clinging to the polished seed,
> sends light particles into the air
> flying to some secret reunion
> with the hidden parts of a man, woman
> keeping her secrets

The "moon" that does explode in this poem is a metaphor for multiple aspects of the self: on one level, a memory of the speaker's lover; on another, an image of herself under the lover's pillow; on yet another, the development of old wings behind her own eyes; and finally, of the self who cannot fly yet. The poem concerns an awakening of vision that gives the speaker the power to be alone with herself. She can no longer be found where the lover expects to find her. He must gain the secrets released in the explosion in order to bring her to the place of his expectations; he must follow her into the world of dreaming, where she is now comfortably alone with herself.

"The Moon Explodes . . ." marks a turning point in Wakoski's relationship with the moon. She had personified it as a woman in order to dignify her claim to loving independence as a *modus vivendi,* and she had entered its nighttime space to form a mysterious pact. She had sought her own inner "moistness" by penetrating beneath the astronomer's descriptions of the moon's surface and by insisting on the presence of a new element within her. The object of her quest, however, remained her lover's affection. The explosion (release of new life, shower of light, revelation of secrets deep inside herself) changes her attitude toward both her lover and herself. Neither the moon nor the self can any longer be encompassed by the lover's conventional descriptions. Both explode into secret parts.

Wakoski holds our interest in the most ordinary aspects of our comon experience by placing them in unexpected, often mythic, perspectives.

—Estella Lauter

The title poem from *Smudging,* which Wakoski also identifies as one of her best, suggests that her changing sense of the moon (and nature) is indeed part of a psychological shift in her attitude toward herself. Granted that we must be careful not to assign a speaker's attitudes too literally to the poet, the changing feeling-tone of the poet's imagery is too marked to ignore. In **"Smudging,"** Wakoski embeds an autobiographical story about her childhood fear of unruly laborers, who tended the smudging pots at night in the orange grove next to her flimsy house, into a poem that celebrates her ability to transcend that fear. The method of her transcendence is her identification with the orange prevented from freezing by the fire:

> That year
> I sought sunshine,
> looked for men who could work in a foundry,
> who were not afraid to touch hot metal.
> And I was the orange
> who began to love the dark groves at night,
> the dewy shake of the leaves,

and who believed these burnings in the night
were part of a ritual
that might someday be understood.

Her transcendence is not so much a matter of renouncing her fear (of men, of fire, of disorder) as it is a matter of allowing fear to co-exist with her orange-like need for warmth, and with the meteor-like fire within her head that allowed her (both figuratively and imaginatively) to get out of her house in the orange grove initially. In seeking ordinary sunshine and identifying with a mortal fruit, she grounds herself on earth. She trusts her imagination to prevent her from getting stuck there as she was stuck in her identification with the negative moon. As she says near the end of the poem, "Thank god for our visions. / That in our heads / we play many roles." The tone of this book is as full of pleasure in possibility as the previous one was full of anger in denigration.

Dancing on the Grave of a Son of a Bitch contains, in addition to the strident but also joyful poem that gives the book its title, a series called **"The Astronomer Poems"** which carry us further in our inquiry into possible relationships between women and nature. Wakoski's *persona* still identifies herself with the moon and claims to be in love with both the sun and the astronomer, "who defines her life," but the identification is more conscious and playful than in *The Magellanic Clouds*. The poet has an intonation that suggests a sense of power: the nonchalance apparent in the opening of **"Sun Gods Have Sun Spots"** ("I don't care if you are / the sun god") comes from her secret knowledge that

I am
also a ruler of the sun,
I am the woman
whose hair lights up in a dark room,
whose words are matches
who is a lion
on fire,
        burning in the woods,
at night.

The necessity for vengeance that arises from feeling oppressed is gone. The poet can turn her wit to clever reversals of stereotypes, as when she makes women the tenders of home-fires on the *sun* and then asserts that "The first man to land / on the sun / will scorch his feet." Her *persona* also has far more freedom, tentatively defined as being alone without having anyone notice, or as not being afraid of the dark. Now she can look for "a poet, an astronomer" to study *her* moon (or the contents of her overflowing trunk). She would *like* a man who would "locate" her when she is lost in her own ideas, which glow in the dark at night; she would like to be opened up. Some astronomer *should* love her. Yet she also understands that "All the light in the world/ will not penetrate my darkness."

It may be the case, as the parable called **"The Dream of Angling, the Dream of Cool Rain"** suggests, that Wakoski's boat called "Diane," or her more secure sense of

self, came to her through the love of a man at a time when water flooded her life and she could not swim. But I think it would be as true to say that her newfound sense of ease with herself and the world of this book comes from the increasing conviction that her imagination (or the kind of perception that arises when she fixes her attention on the sun or moon or smells the fragrance of flowers) is sufficient to the task of living. There is also just the slightest suggestion that her sense of belonging may relate to the discovery of another female figure who stands in a supportive relationship to her, an Isis who exists outside herself:

There is
an ancient priestess
whose tears make the spiderlilies grow.
She knows my name is darkness.
We are sisters.

But more of this figure later.

For the moment, it is enough to note that Wakoski's habit of thinking about herself in celestial terms produced the possibility of understanding that she too is the sun (with the capacity to scorch and singe others). There is also a new clarity about reality that comes from shifting her focus, so that the sun is simply an "old fire ball" with no intention of hurting the humans who would nonetheless melt on its surface. Significantly, her newfound sense of power and equanimity occurs in a volume of ritual chants stemming from her first sun poem in *Inside the Blood Factory,* where she was still looking for a key. Including poems in (mock?) celebration of the Buddha's birthday and outrageously imaginative psychological fables, *Dancing* restores the surreal image to the center of Wakoski's poetry.

In *Virtuoso Literature for Two and Four Hands,* Wakoski's requirements for the astronomer go up, and the moon becomes interchangeable with the poem rather than the poet. The astronomer, whom she still hopes to find, must be not only a reader of poetry but also a "magician who understands / what is invisible" and can turn the text of a poem into a "handful of silver, / something solid and real." This occurs in a poem called **"Story,"** in which the poet sees that the stories of her life (all lives) are like mushroom spores "dancing over the ground." In another extraordinary image of the woman moon, she remembers that

all stories are one story,
leaving a woman with a handful of silver
that turns to moonlight
slips away as air,
disappears with the sun,
she standing with her own hands open
and poetry which is music,
a song which haunts us all
is what she has left,
her reality mysteriously,
perhaps microscopically, gone
        to appear in some other patch
of damp ground.

Both realities (moonlight and woman) disappear only to appear again mysteriously, presumably in the poetry that the magician must *realize* in "a new kind of garden." Woman, moonlight, and poetry together become synonymous with the mysterious force that assures the continuation of life, but not with materiality itself.

Indeed, this is a book of survival stories—of Wakoski's resolution, after Richard Maxwell's death, never to fall apart; of her "second chance" after receiving an electric shock from a defective lamp; of her pleasure in playing Chopin (badly) after fifteen years of not having touched piano keys; of her reconciliation with the necessity of being alone; of love that endures in spite of the imperfections of the body; of mushrooms growing out of the earth—each survival as important as the other. They are poems of the conscious imagination, expressive of Wakoski's love of beautiful things; like Katherine Anne Porter's emeralds, they are "what comes out of life, not life itself."

In *Waiting for the King of Spain,* Wakoski has so loosened the ties binding her to the devalued moon in *The Motorcycle Betrayal Poems* that she can say "I once thought I was the moon. / Named Diane, I fought all day with the sun / which was trying so hard to obscure me." For the first time, she refers to the moon as male, remembering Harry Moon from her childhood anthology of verse, walking his dog much as the Queen of the Night walked hers in *The Magellanic Clouds.* And she writes fifteen poems for an unseen lunar eclipse, which turn up images for the moon that are separate from the self. Thus, the poet wishes the moon were more like the firm tomato, not like the old, mushy decaying one. Or she sees it floating on the ocean in her dreams and thinks "surely salt / kills moon creatures." Or it is an audience who sometimes applauds for a singer, but mostly sleeps. These images coexist with a poem that reaffirms the moon as one of the poet's many names, but not as her sole identity. Somehow, without heroic acts by an astronomer or anyone else, the silver coins the poet wished for from the moonlight in *Virtuoso Literature* pile up in mounds to her knees. *Waiting for the King of Spain* is full of poems that present the poet as throbbing with life:

> In my wrists
> the salmon return every spring
> and lay their shining eggs.
> We are faithful always
> to ourselves,
> those leapings and slidings which take us
> somewhere
> we feel
> we must go.

She no longer seeks fulfillment outside herself, although she waits patiently for the manifestations of the sun to appear in others as well as in herself.

At this point, Wakoski returns to the goddess imagery of her first books. She addresses **"Daughter Moon,"** one of her most beautiful poems, to a woman whom she sees as Penelope, "in the version of the story which gives her /

power over dark seduction." In Homer's *Odyssey,* Penelope uses her art as a ploy to keep her suitors at bay, weaving her tapestry by day and undoing her work at night. Wakoski steps into the myth, as Margaret Atwood did in her "Circe / Mud Poems," in order to imagine what Penelope does with her nights after the ritual unweaving is accomplished. In Wakoski's version of the story, Penelope moves, with the moon, to "a shrine of eucalyptus" where Hecate takes Penelope's head in her hands. Dressed in silver before an altar, like yet unlike the moon, the woman in the poem stands alone, worshipping simply by learning to "see in the dark." In so doing, she touches reality in a way that terrifies her suitors who hope to catch her off guard. From her perspective of reverence and contentment, marriage would seem like "a struggling fish," and all lovers would be interchangeable. The poet sees Penelope—and herself in the act of imagining her—as a witch, and she sees her poem as a means of re-establishing a "Broken line of contact." She identifies with Penelope's love of that "golden invisible man" (her Odysseus, Wakoski's King of Spain) whose mysterious light is "Only shown to women slipping down / soft silver stirways / of themselves." Again the image depends on the fact that the light of the sun is reflected by the moon at night and so is known then only through the moon. The attitude of worship celebrated in the poem is a withdrawal into the self, from which vantage point both darkness and light are known. The figure of the witch reestablishes the broken line of contact between the female self and her inner source of light at night, just as the poem establishes a line from Hecate to Penelope to the poet and her friend to the female reader. In its title, the poem also affirms the scientific theory that the moon was "daughter" of the earth.

In spite of Wakoski's negative pronouncements on the woman question, this is a feminist poem. That is, without denying the ultimate worth of the masculine principle (Odysseus or the King of Spain), but with no illusions about the general run of men, Wakoski creates a bond of sisterhood with the protégée of Hecate who sees in the dark and is confident of what she sees. The qualities she worships are no longer projected onto men but are visible in herself and in the world she observes when men are absent. The power of illumination the poet has attained in her quest is generalized to *women*—or at least to those women who are willing to slip down the "soft silver stairways / of themselves."

In a section of *The Man Who Shook Hands,* Wakoski narrates a literal journey in search of bald eagles in Wisconsin. The climax of the story is her arrival at the Mississippi River where the eagles are perched on the ice floe. On one level, the poet appears to be freer than ever before to turn her remarkable powers of observation outward to the external world. But her journey is mythical as well, taking place as it does astride another of her improbable beasts: a black camel "heavy-coated against / the winter snow," born perhaps in the convivial aftermath of a Lebanese dinner. She writes as one of the "new Americans," whose job it is "to invent new animals, / new elements." She is, by her own admission, "a good navigator / thru any world where I can ride / those magical beasts."

The reins she uses to steer them are her intimate knowledge of nature's rhythms. And the objective of this, as of all her journeys, is

> to find
> like some mythical goddess
> a satisfaction,
> a fulfillment,
> a partner, another rider
> of black camels
> for these trips.

Instead, she finds only the eagles. And within the narrative, she becomes a magician or goddess, showing the birds two tableaux of the moon. To her sorrow, the landscape of the moon is no more real to this endangered species than it is to the American for whom the birds serve as totem. Nor do all the capsules of the space program seem likely to *realize* the moon; that is the poet's office—to offer "an un-/ traditional / Ride" to an unknown realm. If we had wondered what she would do with the power she gained in her trans-human explorations, Wakoski lets us know her intent to use it on behalf of the non-human elements of the landscape.

To sum up Wakoski's progression on her journey to the moon and back, after the explosion of the moon-pod, the poet/*persona* became capable of surviving without the affection of a lover. As she began to understand the depth of her own mystery and realized that no one would be able to penetrate her darkness completely, she began to understand the darkness within her as the source of her power, her light, her poetry. As the pulse of life within her became stronger, the illumination more radiant, the sense of connection with other women more compelling, she became more free to observe the world and her fellow creatures with compassion.

We might say that she learned to value herself by identifying deeply with the moon. She learned to value both the moon and herself less romantically by adopting the perspective of the astronomer. She learned the limits of astronomy in the veritable explosion of the goddess-like imaginative source within her. She also felt the limits of her desire to shine alone in the empty sky. She resumed her mortal lineage, retaining the magician's and the poet's facility of making the invisible visible. She acknowledged her female ancestry as a source of strength. She became a naturalist—a defender of nature—for the sake of defending herself.

This was not an easy journey. Her first strategy, evident in **"3 of Swords,"** combined two characteristic ways of viewing nature in our culture: the "romantic" idea of moon as a lovingly feminine force, and the "materialist" view of it as a physical phenomenon with no special power over human life. The strategy was destined to fail because the male lover to whom she addressed the poem had nothing to gain from accepting this compound of loving independence.

Her second strategy, that of imagining herself to be a nature goddess, may have produced a momentary sense of pow-er, but it did not produce a permanent change in her sense of self-worth. She still had to deal with the problems of living a human life in a cultural setting. Not the least of her difficulties was having to live with the devalued aspects of nature after she had admitted her identification with them.

Wakoski got herself out of this predicament by mining science and by playing on the possibilities it offered for revaluing nature. In the case of the moon, she countered the image of the moon's unappealing surfaces with the image of water, drawn from the historical controversy over the origins of certain sea-like features of the moon. She used the disagreement about the moon's origins and its present composition for her own purposes, denying the theory that it is cold and dead, and affirming the possibility of its embodying a new element not known on earth.

At first, she embraced the information from the early space missions without giving up her identification with the moon. This position had its dangers. It is one thing to say, somewhat vaguely and poetically:

> I am a cloud
> dust on the desert,
> fog over the waters,
> gases in the sky

It is quite another to say,

> Oh the caves of cold iron ore
> I'm made of are so
> empty/

A less brave woman might have shrunk from the specificity science offered her, fearing its negative implications. A less clever poet might have taken fewer liberties with scientific hypotheses. But Wakoski used the idea of a "missing element" to sponsor a search for the missing element in herself.

Her next step was to explore the complicated geography or unused potential of herself, using the multiplicity and productivity of natural phenomena as touchstones. This exploration led to her insistence on her equality with the sun and with the men who had devalued both the moon and herself in their failure to notice what lay beneath the surface. With equality came responsibility. Thus she made herself responsible, through the medium of poetry, for the perpetuation of life in nature.

Wakoski did manage to use the traditional equation of woman and nature for her own purposes. At first it was little more than a crutch to develop a concept of herself. Later, however, the balance shifted completely, and she became a "naturalist," interested in preserving endangered phenomena outside herself through her imaginative powers of revealing reality to others. The transformation in her perspective took place because she dared to immerse herself in that endangered reality called "nature," challenging both the separateness of "man" from nature and the exclusion of "woman" from the human realm.

Holly Prado (essay date 1986)

SOURCE: "The Rings of Saturn by Diane Wakoski," in *Los Angeles Times Book Review*, October 16, 1986, p. 14.

[*In the following review, Prado affirms Wakoski's collection* The Rings of Saturn *and speaks of the poet's bitterness, curiosity, and her ability to transform elements of her life into accomplished poetry.*]

Diane Wakoski's latest book of poems is filled with landscapes; people, both friends and grotesques; and questions: She exists, in her writing, in a world fed by outer reality but not convinced by it. She's curious—and bitter; the bitterness is redeemed by the curiosity. Fearing decay, ignorance, and the inevitability of death, Wakoski writes with the intensity of someone fiercely alive, who still wants to unscramble failures, loneliness, the image of herself as the homely girl who was never acceptable. In describing a search for her own landscape, she says, "This icy planet / where I have banished myself. / This icy planet, / Saturn, / where I feel at home."

Wakoski has always been at home in the imagination. The titles of her many books abound with words like *dream, moon, magician.* And there are the well-known "Greed" poems, too: Her talent is often in her willingness to admit to the least exemplary human responses and to make magic of them in language. "The director told me at length now / he cares for his senile mother, / who is incontinent and who eats / everything she finds, like a baby. We saw / this at dinner, as she kept chewing / parts of her paper napkin." This is from a poem called, **"What Would Tennessee Williams Have Said,"** which explores the question, "Is there drama in everyday life?" The drama, although Wakoski insists that she sees only humiliation, is within the fine, taut description of the miserable dinner—a springboard for imagination, for imagining that a question of drama even exists and pondering, "What vision of myself, / the future, / this event was supposed to make me take / away?" It isn't enough for her to record experiences; she creates something from them that takes them far beyond the chewed napkin.

Perhaps, as she suspects, there are things too petty and cruel for art, but that suspicion doesn't keep her from writing about them and from believing in all that triggers imagination: ". . . what we cannot / forget / is how civilization and imagination / allow someone to take what is available / the salmon, / or the cherries, / the asparagus, / or millet, / or squid, / or milk, / a certain kind of grape, / rosemary growing wild, / and turn it into / a remarkable food." Wakoski, herself, is remarkable in her ability to question, to discover meaning behind the squid or the milk, to insist on her own vision when there are plenty of temptations to do otherwise.

In the book's final poem, **"Joyce Carol Oates Plays the Saturn Piano,"** she writes about literary disappointments, but admits that, "I hear a music / beyond what anyone can play." She hears her own intensity, which doesn't allow her the comforts of a settled or happy existence, but does allow a rich, disturbing poetry to be written, to be given to readers who can admire the mix of grit and dream, disgust and lushness, flat statement and beautifully wrought simile in her work.

As a book, ***The Rings of Saturn*** is a collection of poems related to each other through theme and image, but not a tightly woven group. The 11 poems that make up a real series at the end of the book are still more connected by image than by any one, overall idea. A reader would be unwise to try to nail down a precise, analytical logic in the arrangement of poems. The only ones, though, that don't carry much individual weight are the shortest ones. These are painterly, impressionistic, but without the bite of longer pieces. Wakoski needs length to travel in, the chance to open a poem farther and farther until it's fully exorcised.

It's dangerous to read any writing as a picture of the writer's personal life, yet Wakoski's revelations are, surely, a mirror, and not, probably, a particularly clouded one. She speaks of self-obsession in ways that remind readers to respect it; it can move one toward transformation. Using images of the weekly garbage truck and of herself as a chameleon in the orange fire of burning refuse, she asks, ". . . change me from / this garbage / into something pure. . . ." She reveals many privacies for the sake of acknowledging herself unstintingly with the faith—even if it's damaged faith—that there's hope for change. If her view is bitter, it's never suicidally exhausted or demeaning of life, and her curiosity about herself and the landscapes of her imagination is very valuable, indeed.

Paul Oppenheimer (essay date 1987)

SOURCE: "Ambushes of Amazement," in *The American Book Review,* Vol. 9, No. 4, September-October, 1987, p. 11.

[*Oppenheimer is a poet and critic. In the following review, he finds that the poems in* The Rings of Saturn *succeed when they skillfully employ surrealist techniques.*]

Modern surrealism, starting with Guillaume Apollinaire, who coined the word back in 1917, usually promises more than it delivers. If the promise, to quote André Breton's surrealist manifesto, is art and poetry full of "previously neglected forms of association," brimming with magic, leaps beyond reason, and hallucinations, the delivery, more often than not, is either trite or incomprehensible. "Automatic writing," another "method" favored by some surrealists, frequently combines perfectly trivial insights with failed grammar. These lapses are more apparent in surrealist poetry than in the painting, where the technical mastery of the artist—Max Ernst, say, or Duchamp or Dali or Klee—plus sheer intelligence and wit, may manage to steer what could be merely puzzling away from the totally private, the brutally introverted, the adolescent. In surrealism, the danger always matches the invitation. On the one hand, a dull talent may produce art or poetry that is pure show-biz dazzle, and about as powerful in the end as the timid Wizard of Oz, a charming knave full of bemused self-pity. On the other, there are Bosch and Rimbaud to be considered, geniuses anticipating surrealism, who invented realms of color, energy, and cleverness in which the subconscious plays with its torments and finds freedoms undreamed of in Horatio's philosophy, in which the miraculous "more" of things; their special mystery, appears in marvelous new ways.

Plainly too, as in any art that focuses exclusively on the "self," an imagined self really, the attitudes of the surrealist artist, his attitudes toward himself, determine the range and value of the art. This is not the case with other sorts of artists, who may use the startling, bizarre paradoxes of surrealism as possibilities, while remaining committed to reason. Shakespeare's attitudes toward himself play no role in his writings. Dante's despair, at the beginning of the *Inferno,* is cushioned by faith in God and faith in poetry. Whitman's celebration of himself is really a celebration of everyone else. Emily Dickinson allows her absolute trust in the discipline of the quatrain form, in which she nearly always writes, to transmute her private griefs into the gold of a public vision, and her hopefulness into an idea of the sublime, reaching far beyond herself. Dylan Thomas, at his surrealistic best, loses himself entirely in his devotion to the magic of words and the English language.

The poet Diane Wakoski has always ranked herself among the latest surrealists, taking the risks and sometimes succeeding. Her frequent goal is to create "extravagant surrealist imagery, like the girl riding naked on a zebra, wearing only diamonds." This was the promise, at any rate, in her preface to *Trilogy* (1974), a collection of her first three volumes of poems. The dream was perhaps that of a modern Lady Godiva, riding naked through suburbia and challenging Henry Miller's air-conditioned nightmare-America, perhaps on a bicycle or in a used car. But the intention was not to force her husband to lower the tax rates (that was Lady Godiva's purpose, in Coventry, in the feudal eleventh century). Instead it was to shock the sophistry put of the souls of so-called reasonable people.

Refreshingly enough, this was the effect produced by *The Motorcycle Betrayal Poems* (1971), with its striking dedication: "This book is dedicated to all those men who betrayed me at one time or another, in hopes that they will fall off their motorcycles and break their necks." The self-pity and likely self-delusion of this statement are arrestingly mocked by its irony, and by the steely clarity of the voice, a voice that often whispers its thunder. Through thirteen volumes of poems, with the first, *Coins and Coffins,* dating back to 1962, Wakoski has been honing her steel and polishing it. In *The Rings of Saturn,* her most recent volume, she offers a steel sometimes so polished as to become a mirror of surrealistic self-dramatization, as in **"Light"**:

> I live for books
> and light to read them in.
>   Waterlilies
> reaching up
> from the depths of the pond

algae dark,
the frog loves a jell of
blue-green water,
                    the bud
scales
a rope of stem,
then floats in sunshine. Like soap
in the morning bath.
This book I read
floats in my hand like a waterlily
coming out of the nutrient waters
of thought
and shines on us both,
the morning's breviary.

Books and light combine deliciously and surrealistically in these keen few lines, melting into algae, the "nutrient waters" of ponds and thought, buds, stems, shining, acts of creation, all swimming, traveling upward into the holiness of the "morning's breviary," the book itself. There is control here, a smart tension, and a release from self. The associations—of books with the making of life in light and primal clean waters—are public, poised, and original.

This ideal is not everywhere met, and *The Rings of Saturn,* through fifty-seven lyrics, offers the sort of unevenness to be expected of poems committed to a single tricky aesthetics, surrealism, rather than to several aesthetics at once, and to the balance they could provide together. Often a justifiable rage seems to organize these poems, substituting for insight, faith, and form, and weakening the lines. Often the plucky impertinence of Wakoski's voice, always a pleasure in itself, sinks into a peevishness of tone that might belong in a letter to a friend but lacks the resonance of poetry, as in **"The Lady Who Drove Me to the Airport"**: "How I hate the human voice / after being trapped on the Long Island Expressway / for nearly three hours with that woman's steady / chatter." Lines such as these do not simply fail. They abandon all effort at transforming experience into alive art. Surrealism droops into inconsequence.

This is to say that Wakoski's most recent collection is at its strongest when her gifts as a surrealist shine through. In **"The Handicapped at Risen Hotel,"** a boy who turns into a clock, a man whose hands "mistake themselves for pliers," and a girl whose ankles are "limbs of white birch / unbending" evoke "our interiors / with silence and some horror." **"Saturn's Rings,"** the sequence of eleven poems at the end, from which the volume takes its title, is an often captivating, often self-pitying cry from the depths, or from "a hotel balcony" on Saturn, "Where at last / whatever I create / may finally be / brilliantly, inexorably / my own." The cry is especially moving when uttered in the bright, chromic voice of Wakoski's most surrealistic lines. She is fine at depicting the possibility that "the world / is flying out of control," and that we may be living in "a disintegrating time." At these moments, her sense of humor, and even a demonic sort of satire, turn horror into solid shapes.

Surrealism surely tends to satire, perhaps because of its abruptness, its ambushes of amazement. It will tolerate compassion, nourish wit, adore high skill, and even accept a metallic scorn. All of these appear in abundance in the poetry of, say, Pablo Neruda, the century's finest surrealist poet so far, and in the surrealist films of Buñuel. What surrealism cannot abide, by definition, is mere bathos. It is an alchemist's aesthetics, forever seeking the alteration of the ordinary. When at their best Wakoski's poems show this understanding, they become pure nectar.

Gary Lenhart (essay date 1990)

SOURCE: A review of *Emerald Ice,* in *The American Book Review,* Vol. 12, No. 4, September-October, 1990, pp. 16-26.

[*In the following mixed review, the critic says the poetry is fueled by pain, anger and envy and that Wakoski defines herself in terms of men.*]

In December 1796, Samuel Taylor Coleridge wrote to his friend John Thelwall, "Do not let us introduce an Act of Uniformity against poets. I have room enough in my brain to admire, aye, and almost equally, the head and fancy of Akenside, and the heart and fancy of Bowles, the solemn lordliness of Milton, and the divine chit-chat of Cowper. And whatever a man's excellence is, that will be likewise his fault." Coleridge's words must apply to women poets too, or at least I was reminded of them, especially the last sentence, as I read *Emerald Ice: Selected Poems 1962-87* by Diane Wakoski.

Over the twenty-five years covered in this volume, Diane Wakoski's style has remained remarkably consistent. She writes a direct, unoccluded statement that is often close to transparent and never reaches for the elegant or sublime. Her poems are fueled by a deep font of pain, anger, and envy that erupts in passionate outbursts untempered by humor. She alludes frequently and with bitter class awareness to her Polish-American family, and often seems abashed by their crudity. Yet the vulgarity of her poems is a source of vitality and intimacy rare among her more patrician peers. Her honesty is unblinking and disarming. For instance, just as you are complaining of her near-sighted pettiness, she confesses that she is near-sighted and petty—like any fury. Her fury remains credible because her grudges are most often personal. She disdains the general wrath of the political and denounces those closest to her. Her self-righteousness seems painfully adolescent, conjuring the image of a smart, talented girl stewing because she's not voted the class's most beautiful. But then she has written,

> youth shouldn't be humble as
>   the tablecloth,
> but arrogant and fierce/
> we get toothless with age.

Arrogant and fierce Diane Wakoski has remained.

For as long as I've been conscious of contemporary American poetry, Diane Wakoski has been a prominent voice, gaining recognition early in her career on the strength of her "George Washington" poems. Reading that sequence in this volume, it's hard not to think of Sylvia Plath. The poems consist mainly of angry salvos fired by a daughter deserted by her father, "thirty years a chief petty officer, / always away from home." But when I first read these poems almost twenty years ago, I never thought to compare them with Plath but with Jack Spicer's "Billy the Kid." I thought Spicer's genius obvious and peculiar, and Billy the Kid one of his more magical inventions. Wakoski's immediate emotional relation with George Washington seemed similarly potent. That her rebellion was against the Father of Our Country instead of some undistinguished petty officer gave her disenchantment grandeur, plus a certain fashionable political edge. Now these poems read strictly as tales of familiar distress; then they suggested profound social alienation. I also remembered them as more surreal, more formally clever, playful, and surprising. There was still a glow around the New American Poetry, and Wakoski was prominent among the handful of women to benefit from its aura. Today the George Washington poems seem more mannered than avant-garde, their portrait of the American family so conventional as to obscure any experimental impetus. But the Spicer influence was salutary, and these poems still strike me as Wakoski's most startling work. The formal repetition tempered her predilection toward the preachy and took her to unpredictable destinations. The poems also established the patterns and strategies Wakoski would utilize most effectively throughout her subsequent work. She established her voice early, and it has changed little since.

Yet mention Diane Wakoski to most readers and their response is *The Motorcycle Betrayal Poems*. I find that unfortunate, because the poems in that sequence move increasingly closer to soap opera. If one reads them immediately after the George Washington poems, the very universe seems to constrict. One is confronted by no overflow of magic literary spirit, but by pathetic lack. As Wakoski put it,

> some of us have bad vision, are
>   crippled, have defects, and
> our reality is a different one, not the
> correct and ascertainable one,
> and sometimes it makes us dotty
>   and lonely
> but also it makes us poets.

During this stretch of her life, Wakoski was apparently suffering through romantic episodes with some real jerks. How about this litany?

> You hurt me.
> You locked me in a room and
>   took away my glasses when
>   you found me
> reading a book by a man you hated;
> you pounded my head against the
>   floor when I wouldn't change my
>   name;
> you tried to lock me in a mental

institution when I wanted to
go to a writer's conference for
two weeks,
you called up my friends and said
you'd castrate them if they
talked to me;
you hit me in the mouth every time
I disagreed with you;
you would not let me answer the
phone or open my own mail

The list goes on. Surely no one would say the poet lacked cause for complaint. But as poems and lovers pile up, all blend into one, a one nowhere near as compelling as George Washington. It's disturbing in a volume of such openly confessional verse to gain no sense of the other actors. Neither her parents nor her lovers ever step forward as individuals. All seem mere occasions for Wakoski's disappointments. Even when she writes an elegy for composer Richard Maxfield, it's primarily about Diane Wakoski's strength of will. Of course, she *is* strong-willed, and her disappointments are always credible. There is plenty of posturing in these poems, but no faking. It is her credibility that lifts Wakoski from the pack of versifiers penning interchangeable poems and demands that one deal with her as a particular witness to the space between the American dream and the reality of an actual American life.

I use the definite article before dream because Wakoski's version of it permits such simplification. She seems to feel entitled to be rich, famous, and all those other Hollywood qualities, like beautiful and glamorous. Much of her anger comes from her frustration at being cursed with a common lot. What amazes is that she convinces us that her lot is common, as she strips it of all elaboration and reduces it to a morality play that could be titled "I Will Survive" or something equally banal. Wakoski frequently returns to anecdotes she finds crucial, and one of her favorites indicates too well exactly what she pursues. Wakoski was once a serious piano student at Berkeley who adored Chopin and Beethoven.

How I hated the rich girls in my
class
who were being
expensively
psychoanalysed (how I needed
to tell
my histories),
and who played Bach
sitting decorously, neatly, on the
piano bench
like little hair brushes,
while I grimaced and swayed and
rocked on the bench

For her the piano represented "the beauty that can come / from even an ugly / past." But when she decided to make poetry her primary endeavor, she vowed that she would not play the piano again until after she won a Pulitzer Prize (which she anticipated receiving by age forty). Even

if we concede that thirty years ago the Pulitzer was a more esteemed accolade, her decision to abjure beauty for the sake of an annual literary prize sounds more like the stuff of mass market paperbacks than a sign of poetic vocation.

She illustrates further the quality of her imagination in **"Telling You True, about My Fantasy Life."** Throughout Wakoski's poetry, she continues to define herself in terms of the men in her life. In this poem, after recounting some fantasies about meeting men who walk right off the pages of Danielle Steel, she admits that she still wants to "feel assured that a man might take care of me / someday." Uncharacteristically abashed but characteristically frank, she then confesses that her fantasy life "reads like Esquire or Playboy / or worse / The Ladies' Home Journal."

Wakoski moved on from her Motorcycle Betrayer to the King of Spain, not a husband this time but a Prince Charming who enters her life at unlikely moments and transports her to fantastic realms. Though it isn't clear whether these realms are in fairyland or Beverly Hills (do the rich and famous still live there?), the King of Spain is more attractive than her other lovers and as a projection of her imagination a hopeful turn. But he is not insinuated into the poems in the way that George Washington and the Motorcycle Betrayer were. Perhaps he is simply too farfetched. For as one makes one's way through the last third of this volume, it's clear that Wakoski is not ripe for hope. When her ire is directed at targets as specific as her ex-mother-in-law, she is withering. When she generalizes from private circumstances to essay a larger statement, she often offends or embarrasses. For instance, although I don't live a sheltered life, I was jolted to come across in a book of contemporary poems her declaration that it's time "to let men be lovers / not faggots." Just as in the movies or the Iran-Contra hearings, there is in Wakoski's poems no middle ground. Her world is peopled by those who suffer and those who don't understand; or as she would have it, the poets and the others. In this case, there are men who love women and men who aren't lovers. Curiously, this is entirely gratuitous, as the poem is not a diatribe against homosexuals but against thin women, to whom she is just as aggressively and unjustly antagonistic. What might have become in other hands a witty plea for juicier flesh becomes in Wakoski's clutches a rage against "faggots and their thin bodies." It is only later in this collection that we discover that Wakoski's ex-husband is gay, a fact that we instantly realize to be more pertinent to her emotional disorder than the incidence of ectomorphism among homosexual men.

For most of us, this is an example of outrageously sloppy thinking. For others, it is merely a failure of taste. I think the problem is more fundamental. The sincerity of Wakoski's passions cannot hide the failure of imagination in her later poems. When a fifty-year-old woman treats the existence of male homosexuality as personal rejection, one can only suggest that the quality of her imagination may even be inferior to that found in *Playboy* or the *Ladies' Home Journal.*

Lest readers think this a one-issue failure, I direct them to the following bit of arrogance.

> Anne, Sylvia, John, Virginia,
> you were cowards . . .
> We all suffer.

I don't want to be cavalier about Wakoski's suffering, which is obviously much more profound than mine if she can go toe-to-toe with the successfully suicidal. But it offends my sense of the mystery and autonomy of human personality when someone pronounces with such authority on things she can't intimately know. Perhaps she was feeling somewhat repentant a little later when she wrote, "how easy it is to condemn, / how hard to be compassionate." If so, the repentant mood didn't last long, for she outdoes her own grand bad taste in **"How Do You Tell a Story?"** where she returns to the subject of suicide to single out Anne Sexton for extended attack. In this case, one feels that Wakoski's more brutal class instincts overwhelm her. She seems incapable of entertaining the notion that a beautiful woman of moderate wealth might have some grounds for discontent. Callously dismissing Sexton's misery as that of a weak sister, she offers her own survival, despite her less than beautiful face and college professor's salary, as heroic comparison. Then she goes on to attack the root of the problem—beauty.

> I want to tell you
> that beauty itself
> creates
> injustice,
> and that while everyone suffers,
> only beauty is allowed any mercy
> from the suffering.
> I have said it before,
> the ones who need love most
> are the unlovable.
> And how much more difficult to be
>   ugly and sensitive and still to
>   survive?

At this point, some may feel that Wakoski has yet to make a forceful case for her sensitivity. Frankly, I find her Savonarolan sense of justice scary. I confess to being of the party of Goethe, who wrote, "The beautiful is a manifestation of secret laws of Nature which, but for this appearance, had been forever concealed from us." Wakoski's is a radically democratic sensibility, which finds it more desirable that all be equal than that all be seen for what they are. The source of this sensibility is revealed in two poems near the end of the collection: **"Un Morceau en Forme de Poire"** and **"Making a Sacher Torte."** Both are genuinely poignant accounts of a young, lower-class girl of the 1950s being introduced to a range of bourgeois pleasures. Limning the teachers who befriended and educated the girl, Wakoski is almost congenial. We are nearly convinced that she didn't really intend to hatchet beauty, couldn't really help baiting the dead or raging against homosexuality. We remember her admission that there

> is no way I can imagine
> love, sex or romance
> without pain

and feel a sympathy toward her that she refuses to others.

Emerald Ice is a grating but undeniable testament to sheer will power. It is also a reminder that beauty, fame, and riches have an allure that won't be moderated by mutual aid societies or tamed by infusions of high culture. Class is still among the most undiscussed subjects in writing about poetry. What Wakoski says is often distasteful and, as I believe she would be first to admit, ugly. But she pronounces an unyielding, sad truth, that the powerfully ordinary claims of ego and envy can be more powerful than the beauty created by Chopin or Beethoven. All happy instances of beauty are vulnerable to the attacks of a jealous, unyielding justice. Because we recognize pain and deprivation as sources for such notions, they sometimes have the power to elicit our sympathy and even complicity. It's a bitter fruit this cactus bears, but for those of us from the lower classes, I'm afraid it's not at all exotic.

Thomas Gladysz   (essay date 1991)

SOURCE: A review of *Medea the Sorceress,* in *Small Press,* Vol. 9, No. 4, Fall, 1991, p. 74.

[*In the following review, Gladysz discusses the first volume of Wakoski's multi-volume set* The Archeology of Movies and Books. *The critic finds* Medea the Sorceress *to be an ambitious and original book that uses the work of other writers and filmmakers in the "unearthing of personal meaning."*]

For her last book, ***Emerald Ice: Selected Poems 1962-1987,*** Diane Wakoski was awarded the Poetry Society of America William Carlos Williams Award. That award is a fitting tribute, for Wakoski draws on Williams' book-length poem *Paterson* as a model for her recent volume, ***Medea the Sorceress***.

Medea the Sorceress—apparently volume one of a longer work entitled ***The Archeology of Movies and Books***—is a more ambitious project than Wakoski's initial attempt at a book-length work, the ongoing ***Greed*** poems. Wakoski draws upon Williams' example of incorporating short lyric poems, letters to various friends, prose fragments from other authors and meditations on various subjects (notably the new physics and Hollywood movies) into an overall layered verse structure. And like *Paterson,* Wakoski enables a specific geography to speak to larger concerns.

However, Wakoski's specific geography (outlined by a map in the beginning of the book) is not an actual location but a poetic locale that expands across two continents and the poet's own lifetime. As in the short imagistic and lyric poems for which she is well known, Wakoski utilizes the material of her own life in the creation of a personal mythology. The result, in ***Medea the Sorceress,*** is an original work that expands upon earlier attempts at the long form.

The proposed title for this multi-volume work—*The Archeology of Movies and Books,* which is also the title of a remarkable poem in the present volume—suggests the unearthing of personal meaning as found in film and literature. This title hints at what the art critic Donald Kuspit calls "archaeologism," or postmodernism as excavation. Kuspit—linking such a practice to Freud's use of the archeological metaphor to explain the psychoanalytic method and Michel Foucault's archeological analysis—sees archaeologism as a method of establishing meaning from the discursive and fragmented depths of the unconscious. *Medea the Sorceress* may be read in this light. Come prepared with trowels that dig at metaphor.

Diane Wakoski (essay date 1992)

SOURCE: "Color is a Poet's Tool," in *Poets' Perspectives: Reading, Writing, and Teaching Poetry,* edited by Charles R. Duke and Sally A. Jacobson, Boynton/Cook Publishers, 1992, pp. 24-30.

[*In the following essay, Wakoski discusses her use of color as a primary organizing image in her work and uses her poem "The Pink Dress" as an example of her process.*]

In a poem called "What you should know to be a poet," Gary Snyder [in *Regarding Wave*] says that, basically, poets have to know everything, but he starts with this catalogue:

all you can about animals as persons.
the names of trees and flowers and weeds.
names of stars, and the movements of the planets
     and the moon.

your own six senses, with a watchful and elegant
     mind.

at least one kind of traditional magic:
divination, astrology, the *book of changes*, the tarot;

As a young writer I agreed with Snyder that poets had to know everything, but I didn't quite understand how one conveyed that knowledge in poems. I loved the wisdom of Shakespeare on the subjects of love and aging and beauty in his sonnets, but when I tried to write that way, I simply sounded pompous or corny. And his images never made me see pictures. They were abstractions which gave me ideas, but when I tried with similar images of the moon or sun or stars or trees, sketched as they are in Shakespeare, I simply was trite, banal, more clichéd even than I was in ordinary talk.

What I needed, then, was some system for presenting this material in poems. And it was a combination of poets and poetry which assaulted me during my first two years of college, teaching me about images, surrealism, big metaphors, incantation. And it was reading poems and imitating them which finally led to my own prosody and craft.

A poem that inspired me deeply and continues to move me is Lorca's "Somnambule Ballad." Of course I read this in translation. In fact it was because a student friend of mine, Michael Rossman, was passionately and diligently translating Lorca's gypsy poems that I was introduced to this work. The poem offered me so much that was exciting. And more, so much that was new to me at the time. I don't think repetition or incantation were part of my tradition. And the poetry I had read and most enjoyed was not ecstatic poetry, so the use of the intensely lyrical repetition, "Green, how much I want you green. / Green wind. Green branches." thrilled me. And the use of repetition as an organizing device, as well as a means of conveying passionate feeling, excited my desire to try the same.

Because I am a visually oriented person, poems that used vivid imagistic description appealed enormously to me. But I had not, at that time, read a great deal of poetry that did this. Heavy in our curriculum were poems of narrative, or lyric poems which barely touched the visual world, or did so as Shakespeare's sonnets did, with the mind rather than the painterly eye. I am sure the use of color as an organizing device was one of the aspects of this poem which implanted in me so firmly and which gave me permission to continue to use color for the rest of my life, not as decoration, but as a device for organizing a poem.

In the "Somnambule Ballad," Lorca uses the folk tradition of the gypsy world along with twentieth-century surrealist images, and they come together surprisingly well. The simplification of images, and symbolic speech, which is in all folk poetry and painting ("Your white shirt bears/ three hundred dark roses," or "eyes of cold silver," or "I want to change/ my horse for your house,/ my saddle for your mirror,/ my knife for your blanket."), meshes well with the surreal images such as calling the girl "green flesh, hair of green," or referring to "the fish of darkness/ that opens the road of dawn," or referring to the stars as "a thousand crystal tambourines" which were "piercing the dawn."

Taking this poem into my heart entirely, and accepting the gift of its structures, I wrote a whole group of college poems in which I tried to make the world respond to my visions of color. The most successful of these was a poem using blue. In it, my love of the music of Debussy, of early Chinese poems which I had just begun to read, of this Lorca poem, all combined with my own desperately unhappy adolescent life. My longing for love I could not seem to find. My desire for lovers who did not desire me. And a wish for a world of the past, more structured, more orderly, and perhaps more royal or elegant. The poem was a dramatic monologue in which I spoke as the "blue jester" whose lady is royal and throws him out at dawn because he isn't good enough for the world to know that he's her lover. Speaking in the voice of the man rejected by the woman, I think I felt freer than if I had tried to speak in my own desperate adolescent girl's voice then. But I knew well the theme of lost love, as every 20-year-

old does, and the lost love of the "Somnambule Ballad"
glittering through its images, repeated by its refrain, embodied by the color green, inspired me to use those devices to talk about my own life through the story of the blue
jester.

About five years later I was again to use color to organize
another of my best poems. Probably each year of my life
since I discovered this Lorca poem, I have written at least
one poem in which color has been the primary organizing
structure. Often I have tried different techniques, but always the color domination has worked best when I am
attempting a theme of lost love, as was presented in my
early model. A poem that I must have discovered at about
the same time in my undergraduate life that I began to
read Lorca was / is Wallace Stevens' "Domination of
Black." This poem uses the image of blackness to present
a dramatic feeling about death or closure. Perhaps in my
mind this reinforced the power of color being associated
with pain or with loss or grief. For I think it is almost
always true that the most successful color poems I write
are explorations of those themes.

In the following poem, I was again attempting to talk about
lost love.

The Pink Dress

I could not wear that pink dress tonight.
The velvet one
lace tinting the cuffs with all
the coffee
of longing. My bare shoulder
slipping whiter
than foam
out of the night to remind me
of my own
vulnerability.

I could not wear that pink dress tonight
because it is a dress
that slips memories like
the hands
of obscene strangers
all over my body.
And in my fatigue I could not fight away the
    images
and their mean touching.
I couldn't wear that pink dress,
the velvet one you had made for me,
all year, you know.

I thought I would tonight because
once again
you have let me enter your house
and look at myself
some mornings
in your mirrors.
                    But
I could not wear that pink dress tonight
because it reminded me
of everything

that hurts.
It reminded me of a whole year
during which
I wandered,
a gypsy,
and could not come into your house.
It reminded me of the picture of a blond girl
you took with you to Vermont
and shared your woods with.
The pretty face you left over your bed to stare
at me
and remind me
each night
that you preferred her face to mine,
and which you left there to stare at me
even when you saw how it
broke me,
my calm,
like a stick smashing across my own
plain lonesome face,
and a face which you only
took down
from your wall
after I had mutilated it
and pushed pins into it to get those smug
smiling eyes off my cold
winter
body.

I couldn't wear that pink dress tonight
because it reminded me
of the girl who made it,
whom you slept with,
last year while I was sitting in hotel rooms
wondering why I had to live
with a face
so stony no man could love it.

I could not wear that pink dress
because it reminded me
of how I camp on your doorstep now,
still a gypsy,
still a colorful imaginative beggar
in my pink dress,
building a fire in the landowner's
woods, and my own fierceness
that deserts me
when a man
no, when you,
show a little care and concern
for my presence.

I could not wear that pink dress tonight.
It betrayed all that was strong in me.
The leather boots I wear to stomp through the
    world
and remind everyone
of the silver and gold and diamonds
from fairy tales
glittering in their lives.
And of the heavy responsibility
we all must bear

just being so joyfully alive
just letting the blood take its own course
in intact vessels
in veins.
That pink dress betrayed my one favorite image
—the motorcyclist riding along the highway
    independent
    alone
    exhilarated with movement
    a blackbird
    more beautiful than any white ones.

But I went off
not wearing the pink dress,
thinking how much I love you
and how if a woman loves a man who does not
    love her,
it is, as some good poet said,
a pain in the ass.
For both of them.

I went off thinking about all the girls
you preferred to me.
Leaving behind that dress,
remembering one of the colors
of pain
Remembering that my needs
affront you,
my face is not beautiful to you;
you would not share your woods with me.
And the irony
of my images.
That you are the motorcycle rider.
Not I.
I am perhaps,
at best,
the pink dress
thrown against the back
of the chair.
The dress I could not wear
tonight.

In this poem, the obvious narration of lost love is implemented through the image of the pink dress. To me, the idea that women are symbolized by pink has always been hateful. Perhaps because pink is a pastel color, an off shade, a dilution of the primary and powerful color red. Red, of course, is the color of blood and is often used to represent anger. In my poem, the pink dress becomes that dilution of person that a woman is to a man in our culture. Since red would be the color of blood, there is something of the stain of blood, death, and pain about this dream which is the diluted color of blood. And the diluted color of anger.

In **"The Pink Dress"** I wanted the idea of the color to represent again the emotions I was experiencing, this time not through a verbal pun, but through the symbols of the color itself. In fact, the whole poem works with symbol. The dress itself is a symbol for woman as she is seen by most men, a decorative object, and as she chooses to present herself through her clothes. She is no more than

the dress. So both the dress itself and its color, pink, are working as symbols throughout the poem.

Symbol and image are two of the major tools of figurative language. They are a vivid and real part of anyone's life and can be used most powerfully, I think, when they come naturally out of the matrix of one's life. I knew this, theoretically, when I was young and first starting to write, but I did not know how to apply what I knew until I began to discover how to talk personally about my own life in ways that were not obscure or embarrassingly intimate. It was the wonderful examples of poets who also had a painterly, visual vision of the world, like Garcia Lorca and Wallace Stevens, who led me away from cliché, banal language, and trite phrases, permitting me to talk somewhat originally about the clichéd, banal, and trite subject of lost love and the pain of rejection which was to become a major theme in my work. Perhaps **"The Pink Dress"** can be used by students as a model for writing poems that use organizational devices that they might not have thought of previously, in particular, color.

FURTHER READING

Bibliography

Newton, Robert. *Diane Wakoski: A Descriptive Bibliography.*
Jefferson, N.C.: McFarland & Company, Inc., 1987, 136 p.
    Bibliography of works by and about Wakoski that contains descriptions of many of the publications and quotes from critical works on the author.

Criticism

Blazek, Douglas. "Falling into Triteness." *Poetry* 124, No. 3 (June 1974): 167-78.
    Review of *Smudging* that declares that Wakoski "comes close to being terrible," but concludes that her work remains important because of her remarkable skills as a poet.

Malkoff, Karl. "Wakoski, Diane." In *Crowell's Handbook of Contemporary American Poetry*, pp. 317-19. New York: Thomas Y. Crowell Company, 1973.
    Analyzes Wakoski's earlier works and talks about her reputation as an imagist.

Martin, Taffy Wynne. "Diane Wakoski's Personal Mythology: Dionysian Music, Created Presence." *Boundary 2* X, No. 3 (Spring 1982): 155-72.
    A lengthy scholarly analysis of Wakoski's poetry that focuses on her use of Dionysian mythology.

Wagner, Linda W. "Wakoski and Rukeyser." In *American Modern Essays in Fiction and Poetry,* pp. 235-37. Port Washington, N.Y.: National University Publications/Kennikat Press, 1980.
    Wakoski's work is compared with that of Rukeyser.

Wakoski, Diane. "Eye and Ear: A Manifesto." *Ohio Review* 38 (1987): 14-19.

Wakoski presents her thoughts on how contemporary poetry tends to emphasize sound more than the visual appearance of the work.

Weller, Sheila. "The Mercy and Ironies of Memory: The Poetry of Diane Wakoski." *Ms.* 4, No. 9 (March 1976): 82-3.

Review of *Virtuoso Literature for Two and Four Hands* that also recounts biographical information on Wakoski.

Interview

Bartlett, Lee. "Diane Wakoski: Listening for Whatever There Was to Hear." In *Talking Poetry: Conversations in the Workshop with Contemporary Poets,* pp. 234-54. Albuquerque: University of New Mexico Press, 1987.

Wakoski discusses a number of issues, including the effect aging has had on her work, literary trends, and her publication history.

Bunge, Nancy L. "Diane Wakoski." In *Finding the Words: Conversations with Writers Who Teach,* pp. 128-44. Athens: Ohio University Press, 1985.

Wakoski presents her views on poetry as they relate to teaching.

Martin, Taffy. "An Interview by Taffy Martin with Diane Wakoski." *Dalhousie Review* 61, No. 3 (Autumn 1981): 476-96.

Wakoski considers the role of memory and mythology in her poetry and discusses her literary influences, among other topics.

Smith, Larry. "A Conversation with Diane Wakoski." *Chicago Review* 29, No. 1, (Summer 1977): 114-25.

Discussion of the types of verse Wakoski writes as well as her views on general trends in poetry.

Additional coverage of Wakoski's life and career is contained in the following sources published by Gale Research: *Contemporary Authors,* **Vols. 13-16 (rev. ed.);** *Contemporary Authors New Revision Series,* **Vol. 9;** *Contemporary Authors Autobiography Series,* **Vol. 1;** *Contemporary Literary Criticism,* **Vols. 2, 4, 7, 9, 11, 40; and** *Dictionary of Literary Biography,* **Vol. 5.**

Poetry Criticism
INDEXES

*Literary Criticism Series
Cumulative Author Index*

Cumulative Nationality Index

Cumulative Title Index

How to Use This Index

The main references

> **Calvino, Italo**
> 1923-1985.....CLC 5, 8, 11, 22, 33, 39,
> 73; SSC 3

list all author entries in the following Gale Literary Criticism series:

BLC = *Black Literature Criticism*
CLC = *Contemporary Literary Criticism*
CLR = *Children's Literature Review*
CMLC = *Classical and Medieval Literature Criticism*
DA = *DISCovering Authors*
DC = *Drama Criticism*
HLC = *Hispanic Literature Criticism*
LC = *Literature Criticism from 1400 to 1800*
NCLC = *Nineteenth-Century Literature Criticism*
PC = *Poetry Criticism*
SSC = *Short Story Criticism*
TCLC = *Twentieth-Century Literary Criticism*
WLC = *World Literature Criticism, 1500 to the Present*

The cross-references

> See also CANR 23; CA 85-88;
> obituary CA 116

list all author entries in the following Gale biographical and literary sources:

AAYA = *Authors & Artists for Young Adults*
AITN = *Authors in the News*
BEST = *Bestsellers*
BW = *Black Writers*
CA = *Contemporary Authors*
CAAS = *Contemporary Authors Autobiography Series*
CABS = *Contemporary Authors Bibliographical Series*
CANR = *Contemporary Authors New Revision Series*
CAP = *Contemporary Authors Permanent Series*
CDALB = *Concise Dictionary of American Literary Biography*
CDBLB = *Concise Dictionary of British Literary Biography*
DLB = *Dictionary of Literary Biography*
DLBD = *Dictionary of Literary Biography Documentary Series*
DLBY = *Dictionary of Literary Biography Yearbook*
HW = *Hispanic Writers*
JRDA = *Junior DISCovering Authors*
MAICYA = *Major Authors and Illustrators for Children and Young Adults*
MTCW = *Major 20th-Century Writers*
NNAL = *Native North American Literature*
SAAS = *Something about the Author Autobiography Series*
SATA = *Something about the Author*
YABC = *Yesterday's Authors of Books for Children*

Literary Criticism Series
Cumulative Author Index

Albert the Great　1200(?)-1280.... **CMLC 16**
See also DLB 115

Alcala-Galiano, Juan Valera y
See Valera y Alcala-Galiano, Juan

Alcott, Amos Bronson　1799-1888 .. **NCLC 1**
See also DLB 1

Alcott, Louisa May
1832-1888 .... **NCLC 6; DA; DAB;**
DAC; WLC
See also CDALB 1865-1917; CLR 1, 38;
DAM MST, NOV; DLB 1, 42, 79; JRDA;
MAICYA; YABC 1

Aldanov, M. A.
See Aldanov, Mark (Alexandrovich)

Aldanov, Mark (Alexandrovich)
1886(?)-1957 .... **TCLC 23**
See also CA 118

Aldington, Richard　1892-1962...... **CLC 49**
See also CA 85-88; CANR 45; DLB 20, 36,
100, 149

Aldiss, Brian W(ilson)
1925- .... **CLC 5, 14, 40**
See also CA 5-8R; CAAS 2; CANR 5, 28;
DAM NOV; DLB 14; MTCW; SATA 34

Alegria, Claribel　1924-........... **CLC 75**
See also CA 131; CAAS 15; DAM MULT;
DLB 145; HW

Alegria, Fernando　1918-.......... **CLC 57**
See also CA 9-12R; CANR 5, 32; HW

Aleichem, Sholom .... **TCLC 1, 35**
See also Rabinovitch, Sholem

Aleixandre, Vicente
1898-1984 .... **CLC 9, 36; PC 15**
See also CA 85-88; 114; CANR 26;
DAM POET; DLB 108; HW; MTCW

Alepoudelis, Odysseus
See Elytis, Odysseus

Aleshkovsky, Joseph　1929-
See Aleshkovsky, Yuz
See also CA 121; 128

Aleshkovsky, Yuz .... **CLC 44**
See also Aleshkovsky, Joseph

Alexander, Lloyd (Chudley)　1924- .. **CLC 35**
See also AAYA 1; CA 1-4R; CANR 1, 24,
38; CLR 1, 5; DLB 52; JRDA; MAICYA;
MTCW; SAAS 19; SATA 3, 49, 81

Alfau, Felipe　1902-............... **CLC 66**
See also CA 137

Alger, Horatio, Jr.　1832-1899 ..... **NCLC 8**
See also DLB 42; SATA 16

Algren, Nelson　1909-1981 .... **CLC 4, 10, 33**
See also CA 13-16R; 103; CANR 20;
CDALB 1941-1968; DLB 9; DLBY 81,
82; MTCW

Ali, Ahmed　1910-................. **CLC 69**
See also CA 25-28R; CANR 15, 34

Alighieri, Dante　1265-1321 .... **CMLC 3, 18**

Allan, John B.
See Westlake, Donald E(dwin)

Allen, Edward　1948-.............. **CLC 59**

Allen, Paula Gunn　1939-.......... **CLC 84**
See also CA 112; 143; DAM MULT;
NNAL

Allen, Roland
See Ayckbourn, Alan

Allen, Sarah A.
See Hopkins, Pauline Elizabeth

Allen, Woody　1935-........... **CLC 16, 52**
See also AAYA 10; CA 33-36R; CANR 27,
38; DAM POP; DLB 44; MTCW

Allende, Isabel　1942-.... **CLC 39, 57; HLC**
See also AAYA 18; CA 125; 130;
CANR 51; DAM MULT, NOV;
DLB 145; HW; INT 130; MTCW

Alleyn, Ellen
See Rossetti, Christina (Georgina)

Allingham, Margery (Louise)
1904-1966 .... **CLC 19**
See also CA 5-8R; 25-28R; CANR 4;
DLB 77; MTCW

Allingham, William　1824-1889 ... **NCLC 25**
See also DLB 35

Allison, Dorothy E.　1949- .... **CLC 78**
See also CA 140

Allston, Washington　1779-1843.... **NCLC 2**
See also DLB 1

Almedingen, E. M. .... **CLC 12**
See also Almedingen, Martha Edith von
See also SATA 3

Almedingen, Martha Edith von　1898-1971
See Almedingen, E. M.
See also CA 1-4R; CANR 1

Almqvist, Carl Jonas Love
1793-1866 .... **NCLC 42**

Alonso, Damaso　1898-1990 .... **CLC 14**
See also CA 110; 131; 130; DLB 108; HW

Alov
See Gogol, Nikolai (Vasilyevich)

Alta　1942-...................... **CLC 19**
See also CA 57-60

Alter, Robert B(ernard)　1935-...... **CLC 34**
See also CA 49-52; CANR 1, 47

Alther, Lisa　1944-............. **CLC 7, 41**
See also CA 65-68; CANR 12, 30, 51;
MTCW

Altman, Robert　1925-............. **CLC 16**
See also CA 73-76; CANR 43

Alvarez, A(lfred)　1929-.......... **CLC 5, 13**
See also CA 1-4R; CANR 3, 33; DLB 14,
40

Alvarez, Alejandro Rodriguez　1903-1965
See Casona, Alejandro
See also CA 131; 93-96; HW

Alvarez, Julia　1950-............. **CLC 93**
See also CA 147

Alvaro, Corrado　1896-1956 .... **TCLC 60**

Amado, Jorge　1912-..... **CLC 13, 40; HLC**
See also CA 77-80; CANR 35;
DAM MULT, NOV; DLB 113; MTCW

Ambler, Eric　1909-............. **CLC 4, 6, 9**
See also CA 9-12R; CANR 7, 38; DLB 77;
MTCW

Amichai, Yehuda　1924- ...... **CLC 9, 22, 57**
See also CA 85-88; CANR 46; MTCW

Amiel, Henri Frederic　1821-1881 .. **NCLC 4**

Amis, Kingsley (William)
1922-1995 ..... **CLC 1, 2, 3, 5, 8, 13, 40,**
44; DA; DAB; DAC
See also AITN 2; CA 9-12R; 150; CANR 8,
28; CDBLB 1945-1960; DAM MST,
NOV; DLB 15, 27, 100, 139;
INT CANR-8; MTCW

Amis, Martin (Louis)
1949-.................. **CLC 4, 9, 38, 62**
See also BEST 90:3; CA 65-68; CANR 8,
27; DLB 14; INT CANR-27

Ammons, A(rchie) R(andolph)
1926- ... **CLC 2, 3, 5, 8, 9, 25, 57; PC 16**
See also AITN 1; CA 9-12R; CANR 6, 36,
51; DAM POET; DLB 5, 165; MTCW

Amo, Tauraatua i
See Adams, Henry (Brooks)

Anand, Mulk Raj　1905-........ **CLC 23, 93**
See also CA 65-68; CANR 32; DAM NOV;
MTCW

Anatol
See Schnitzler, Arthur

Anaya, Rudolfo A(lfonso)
1937-.................. **CLC 23; HLC**
See also CA 45-48; CAAS 4; CANR 1, 32,
51; DAM MULT, NOV; DLB 82; HW 1;
MTCW

Andersen, Hans Christian
1805-1875 .... **NCLC 7; DA; DAB;**
DAC; SSC 6; WLC
See also CLR 6; DAM MST, POP;
MAICYA; YABC 1

Anderson, C. Farley
See Mencken, H(enry) L(ouis); Nathan,
George Jean

Anderson, Jessica (Margaret) Queale
.... **CLC 37**
See also CA 9-12R; CANR 4

Anderson, Jon (Victor)　1940- .... **CLC 9**
See also CA 25-28R; CANR 20;
DAM POET

Anderson, Lindsay (Gordon)
1923-1994 .... **CLC 20**
See also CA 125; 128; 146

Anderson, Maxwell　1888-1959 ..... **TCLC 2**
See also CA 105; DAM DRAM; DLB 7

Anderson, Poul (William)　1926- .... **CLC 15**
See also AAYA 5; CA 1-4R; CAAS 2;
CANR 2, 15, 34; DLB 8; INT CANR-15;
MTCW; SATA-Brief 39

Anderson, Robert (Woodruff)
1917-...................... **CLC 23**
See also AITN 1; CA 21-24R; CANR 32;
DAM DRAM; DLB 7

Anderson, Sherwood
1876-1941 .... **TCLC 1, 10, 24; DA;**
DAB; DAC; SSC 1; WLC
See also CA 104; 121; CDALB 1917-1929;
DAM MST, NOV; DLB 4, 9, 86;
DLBD 1; MTCW

Andier, Pierre
See Desnos, Robert

Andouard
See Giraudoux, (Hippolyte) Jean

Andrade, Carlos Drummond de ...... **CLC 18**
See also Drummond de Andrade, Carlos

Andrade, Mario de   1893-1945 . . . . . **TCLC 43**

Andreae, Johann V(alentin)
    1586-1654 . . . . **LC 32**
    See also DLB 164

Andreas-Salome, Lou   1861-1937 . . . **TCLC 56**
    See also DLB 66

Andrewes, Lancelot   1555-1626 . . . . **LC 5**
    See also DLB 151

Andrews, Cicily Fairfield
    See West, Rebecca

Andrews, Elton V.
    See Pohl, Frederik

Andreyev, Leonid (Nikolaevich)
    1871-1919 . . . . **TCLC 3**
    See also CA 104

Andric, Ivo   1892-1975 . . . . **CLC 8**
    See also CA 81-84; 57-60; CANR 43;
    DLB 147; MTCW

Angelique, Pierre
    See Bataille, Georges

Angell, Roger   1920- . . . . **CLC 26**
    See also CA 57-60; CANR 13, 44

Angelou, Maya
    1928- . . . . **CLC 12, 35, 64, 77; BLC; DA;
                        DAB; DAC**
    See also AAYA 7; BW 2; CA 65-68;
    CANR 19, 42; DAM MST, MULT,
    POET, POP; DLB 38; MTCW; SATA 49

Annensky, Innokenty Fyodorovich
    1856-1909 . . . . **TCLC 14**
    See also CA 110

Anon, Charles Robert
    See Pessoa, Fernando (Antonio Nogueira)

Anouilh, Jean (Marie Lucien Pierre)
    1910-1987 . . . . . . **CLC 1, 3, 8, 13, 40, 50**
    See also CA 17-20R; 123; CANR 32;
    DAM DRAM; MTCW

Anthony, Florence
    See Ai

Anthony, John
    See Ciardi, John (Anthony)

Anthony, Peter
    See Shaffer, Anthony (Joshua); Shaffer,
    Peter (Levin)

Anthony, Piers   1934- . . . . **CLC 35**
    See also AAYA 11; CA 21-24R; CANR 28;
    DAM POP; DLB 8; MTCW; SAAS 22;
    SATA 84

Antoine, Marc
    See Proust, (Valentin-Louis-George-Eugene-)
    Marcel

Antoninus, Brother
    See Everson, William (Oliver)

Antonioni, Michelangelo   1912- . . . . . **CLC 20**
    See also CA 73-76; CANR 45

Antschel, Paul   1920-1970
    See Celan, Paul
    See also CA 85-88; CANR 33; MTCW

Anwar, Chairil   1922-1949 . . . . **TCLC 22**
    See also CA 121

Apollinaire, Guillaume . . **TCLC 3, 8, 51; PC 7**
    See also Kostrowitzki, Wilhelm Apollinaris
    de
    See also DAM POET

Appelfeld, Aharon   1932- . . . . **CLC 23, 47**
    See also CA 112; 133

Apple, Max (Isaac)   1941- . . . . **CLC 9, 33**
    See also CA 81-84; CANR 19; DLB 130

Appleman, Philip (Dean)   1926- . . . . . **CLC 51**
    See also CA 13-16R; CAAS 18; CANR 6,
    29

Appleton, Lawrence
    See Lovecraft, H(oward) P(hillips)

Apteryx
    See Eliot, T(homas) S(tearns)

Apuleius, (Lucius Madaurensis)
    125(?)-175(?) . . . . **CMLC 1**

Aquin, Hubert   1929-1977 . . . . **CLC 15**
    See also CA 105; DLB 53

Aragon, Louis   1897-1982 . . . . **CLC 3, 22**
    See also CA 69-72; 108; CANR 28;
    DAM NOV, POET; DLB 72; MTCW

Arany, Janos   1817-1882 . . . . **NCLC 34**

Arbuthnot, John   1667-1735 . . . . **LC 1**
    See also DLB 101

Archer, Herbert Winslow
    See Mencken, H(enry) L(ouis)

Archer, Jeffrey (Howard)   1940- . . . . **CLC 28**
    See also AAYA 16; BEST 89:3; CA 77-80;
    CANR 22, 52; DAM POP;
    INT CANR-22

Archer, Jules   1915- . . . . **CLC 12**
    See also CA 9-12R; CANR 6; SAAS 5;
    SATA 4, 85

Archer, Lee
    See Ellison, Harlan (Jay)

Arden, John   1930- . . . . **CLC 6, 13, 15**
    See also CA 13-16R; CAAS 4; CANR 31;
    DAM DRAM; DLB 13; MTCW

Arenas, Reinaldo
    1943-1990 . . . . **CLC 41; HLC**
    See also CA 124; 128; 133; DAM MULT;
    DLB 145; HW

Arendt, Hannah   1906-1975 . . . . **CLC 66**
    See also CA 17-20R; 61-64; CANR 26;
    MTCW

Aretino, Pietro   1492-1556 . . . . **LC 12**

Arghezi, Tudor . . . . **CLC 80**
    See also Theodorescu, Ion N.

Arguedas, Jose Maria
    1911-1969 . . . . **CLC 10, 18**
    See also CA 89-92; DLB 113; HW

Argueta, Manlio   1936- . . . . **CLC 31**
    See also CA 131; DLB 145; HW

Ariosto, Ludovico   1474-1533 . . . . **LC 6**

Aristides
    See Epstein, Joseph

Aristophanes
    450B.C.-385B.C. . . . . **CMLC 4; DA;
                        DAB; DAC; DC 2**
    See also DAM DRAM, MST

Arlt, Roberto (Godofredo Christophersen)
    1900-1942 . . . . **TCLC 29; HLC**
    See also CA 123; 131; DAM MULT; HW

Armah, Ayi Kwei   1939- . . . . **CLC 5, 33; BLC**
    See also BW 1; CA 61-64; CANR 21;
    DAM MULT, POET; DLB 117; MTCW

Armatrading, Joan   1950- . . . . **CLC 17**
    See also CA 114

Arnette, Robert
    See Silverberg, Robert

Arnim, Achim von (Ludwig Joachim von
    Arnim)   1781-1831 . . . . **NCLC 5**
    See also DLB 90

Arnim, Bettina von   1785-1859 . . . . **NCLC 38**
    See also DLB 90

Arnold, Matthew
    1822-1888 . . . . . **NCLC 6, 29; DA; DAB;
                        DAC; PC 5; WLC**
    See also CDBLB 1832-1890; DAM MST,
    POET; DLB 32, 57

Arnold, Thomas   1795-1842 . . . . . . **NCLC 18**
    See also DLB 55

Arnow, Harriette (Louisa) Simpson
    1908-1986 . . . . **CLC 2, 7, 18**
    See also CA 9-12R; 118; CANR 14; DLB 6;
    MTCW; SATA 42; SATA-Obit 47

Arp, Hans
    See Arp, Jean

Arp, Jean   1887-1966 . . . . **CLC 5**
    See also CA 81-84; 25-28R; CANR 42

Arrabal
    See Arrabal, Fernando

Arrabal, Fernando   1932- . . . **CLC 2, 9, 18, 58**
    See also CA 9-12R; CANR 15

Arrick, Fran . . . . **CLC 30**
    See also Gaberman, Judie Angell

Artaud, Antonin (Marie Joseph)
    1896-1948 . . . . **TCLC 3, 36**
    See also CA 104; 149; DAM DRAM

Arthur, Ruth M(abel)   1905-1979 . . . . **CLC 12**
    See also CA 9-12R; 85-88; CANR 4;
    SATA 7, 26

Artsybashev, Mikhail (Petrovich)
    1878-1927 . . . . **TCLC 31**

Arundel, Honor (Morfydd)
    1919-1973 . . . . **CLC 17**
    See also CA 21-22; 41-44R; CAP 2;
    CLR 35; SATA 4; SATA-Obit 24

Asch, Sholem   1880-1957 . . . . **TCLC 3**
    See also CA 105 `

Ash, Shalom
    See Asch, Sholem

Ashbery, John (Lawrence)
    1927- . . . . . . **CLC 2, 3, 4, 6, 9, 13, 15, 25,
                        41, 77**
    See also CA 5-8R; CANR 9, 37;
    DAM POET; DLB 5, 165; DLBY 81;
    INT CANR-9; MTCW

Ashdown, Clifford
    See Freeman, R(ichard) Austin

Ashe, Gordon
    See Creasey, John

Ashton-Warner, Sylvia (Constance)
    1908-1984 . . . . **CLC 19**
    See also CA 69-72; 112; CANR 29; MTCW

Baldwin, James (Arthur)
1924-1987 . . . . . . **CLC 1, 2, 3, 4, 5, 8, 13, 15, 17, 42, 50, 67, 90; BLC; DA; DAB; DAC; DC 1; SSC 10; WLC**
See also AAYA 4; BW 1; CA 1-4R; 124; CABS 1; CANR 3, 24; CDALB 1941-1968; DAM MST, MULT, NOV, POP; DLB 2, 7, 33; DLBY 87; MTCW; SATA 9; SATA-Obit 54

Ballard, J(ames) G(raham)
1930- . . . . **CLC 3, 6, 14, 36; SSC 1**
See also AAYA 3; CA 5-8R; CANR 15, 39; DAM NOV, POP; DLB 14; MTCW

Balmont, Konstantin (Dmitriyevich)
1867-1943 . . . . **TCLC 11**
See also CA 109

Balzac, Honore de
1799-1850 . . . . **NCLC 5, 35, 53; DA; DAB; DAC; SSC 5; WLC**
See also DAM MST, NOV; DLB 119

Bambara, Toni Cade
1939-1995 . . . . . . **CLC 19, 88; BLC; DA; DAC**
See also AAYA 5; BW 2; CA 29-32R; 150; CANR 24, 49; DAM MST, MULT; DLB 38; MTCW

Bamdad, A.
See Shamlu, Ahmad

Banat, D. R.
See Bradbury, Ray (Douglas)

Bancroft, Laura
See Baum, L(yman) Frank

Banim, John 1798-1842 . . . . **NCLC 13**
See also DLB 116, 158, 159

Banim, Michael 1796-1874 . . . . . . **NCLC 13**
See also DLB 158, 159

Banks, Iain
See Banks, Iain M(enzies)

Banks, Iain M(enzies) 1954- . . . . **CLC 34**
See also CA 123; 128; INT 128

Banks, Lynne Reid . . . . **CLC 23**
See also Reid Banks, Lynne
See also AAYA 6

Banks, Russell 1940- . . . . **CLC 37, 72**
See also CA 65-68; CAAS 15; CANR 19, 52; DLB 130

Banville, John 1945- . . . . **CLC 46**
See also CA 117; 128; DLB 14; INT 128

Banville, Theodore (Faullain) de
1832-1891 . . . . **NCLC 9**

Baraka, Amiri
1934- . . . . **CLC 1, 2, 3, 5, 10, 14, 33; BLC; DA; DAC; DC 6; PC 4**
See also Jones, LeRoi
See also BW 2; CA 21-24R; CABS 3; CANR 27, 38; CDALB 1941-1968; DAM MST, MULT, POET, POP; DLB 5, 7, 16, 38; DLBD 8; MTCW

Barbauld, Anna Laetitia
1743-1825 . . . . **NCLC 50**
See also DLB 107, 109, 142, 158

Barbellion, W. N. P. . . . . **TCLC 24**
See also Cummings, Bruce F(rederick)

Barbera, Jack (Vincent) 1945- . . . . . . **CLC 44**
See also CA 110; CANR 45

Barbey d'Aurevilly, Jules Amedee
1808-1889 . . . . **NCLC 1; SSC 17**
See also DLB 119

Barbusse, Henri 1873-1935 . . . . **TCLC 5**
See also CA 105; DLB 65

Barclay, Bill
See Moorcock, Michael (John)

Barclay, William Ewert
See Moorcock, Michael (John)

Barea, Arturo 1897-1957 . . . . **TCLC 14**
See also CA 111

Barfoot, Joan 1946- . . . . **CLC 18**
See also CA 105

Baring, Maurice 1874-1945 . . . . **TCLC 8**
See also CA 105; DLB 34

Barker, Clive 1952- . . . . **CLC 52**
See also AAYA 10; BEST 90:3; CA 121; 129; DAM POP; INT 129; MTCW

Barker, George Granville
1913-1991 . . . . **CLC 8, 48**
See also CA 9-12R; 135; CANR 7, 38; DAM POET; DLB 20; MTCW

Barker, Harley Granville
See Granville-Barker, Harley
See also DLB 10

Barker, Howard 1946- . . . . **CLC 37**
See also CA 102; DLB 13

Barker, Pat(ricia) 1943- . . . . **CLC 32, 94**
See also CA 117; 122; CANR 50; INT 122

Barlow, Joel 1754-1812 . . . . **NCLC 23**
See also DLB 37

Barnard, Mary (Ethel) 1909- . . . . **CLC 48**
See also CA 21-22; CAP 2

Barnes, Djuna
1892-1982 . . . **CLC 3, 4, 8, 11, 29; SSC 3**
See also CA 9-12R; 107; CANR 16; DLB 4, 9, 45; MTCW

Barnes, Julian 1946- . . . . **CLC 42; DAB**
See also CA 102; CANR 19; DLBY 93

Barnes, Peter 1931- . . . . **CLC 5, 56**
See also CA 65-68; CAAS 12; CANR 33, 34; DLB 13; MTCW

Baroja (y Nessi), Pio
1872-1956 . . . . **TCLC 8; HLC**
See also CA 104

Baron, David
See Pinter, Harold

Baron Corvo
See Rolfe, Frederick (William Serafino Austin Lewis Mary)

Barondess, Sue K(aufman)
1926-1977 . . . . **CLC 8**
See also Kaufman, Sue
See also CA 1-4R; 69-72; CANR 1

Baron de Teive
See Pessoa, Fernando (Antonio Nogueira)

Barres, Maurice 1862-1923 . . . . **TCLC 47**
See also DLB 123

Barreto, Afonso Henrique de Lima
See Lima Barreto, Afonso Henrique de

Barrett, (Roger) Syd 1946- . . . . **CLC 35**

Barrett, William (Christopher)
1913-1992 . . . . **CLC 27**
See also CA 13-16R; 139; CANR 11; INT CANR-11

Barrie, J(ames) M(atthew)
1860-1937 . . . . **TCLC 2; DAB**
See also CA 104; 136; CDBLB 1890-1914; CLR 16; DAM DRAM; DLB 10, 141, 156; MAICYA; YABC 1

Barrington, Michael
See Moorcock, Michael (John)

Barrol, Grady
See Bograd, Larry

Barry, Mike
See Malzberg, Barry N(athaniel)

Barry, Philip 1896-1949 . . . . **TCLC 11**
See also CA 109; DLB 7

Bart, Andre Schwarz
See Schwarz-Bart, Andre

Barth, John (Simmons)
1930- . . . . . . **CLC 1, 2, 3, 5, 7, 9, 10, 14, 27, 51, 89; SSC 10**
See also AITN 1, 2; CA 1-4R; CABS 1; CANR 5, 23, 49; DAM NOV; DLB 2; MTCW

Barthelme, Donald
1931-1989 . . . . . . **CLC 1, 2, 3, 5, 6, 8, 13, 23, 46, 59; SSC 2**
See also CA 21-24R; 129; CANR 20; DAM NOV; DLB 2; DLBY 80, 89; MTCW; SATA 7; SATA-Obit 62

Barthelme, Frederick 1943- . . . . **CLC 36**
See also CA 114; 122; DLBY 85; INT 122

Barthes, Roland (Gerard)
1915-1980 . . . . **CLC 24, 83**
See also CA 130; 97-100; MTCW

Barzun, Jacques (Martin) 1907- . . . . **CLC 51**
See also CA 61-64; CANR 22

Bashevis, Isaac
See Singer, Isaac Bashevis

Bashkirtseff, Marie 1859-1884 . . . **NCLC 27**

Basho
See Matsuo Basho

Bass, Kingsley B., Jr.
See Bullins, Ed

Bass, Rick 1958- . . . . **CLC 79**
See also CA 126

Bassani, Giorgio 1916- . . . . **CLC 9**
See also CA 65-68; CANR 33; DLB 128; MTCW

Bastos, Augusto (Antonio) Roa
See Roa Bastos, Augusto (Antonio)

Bataille, Georges 1897-1962 . . . . **CLC 29**
See also CA 101; 89-92

Bates, H(erbert) E(rnest)
1905-1974 . . . . . . **CLC 46; DAB; SSC 10**
See also CA 93-96; 45-48; CANR 34; DAM POP; DLB 162; MTCW

Bauchart
See Camus, Albert

Baudelaire, Charles
1821-1867 . . . . **NCLC 6, 29, 55; DA; DAB; DAC; PC 1; SSC 18; WLC**
See also DAM MST, POET

Baudrillard, Jean 1929- . . . . **CLC 60**

Author Index

Booth, Philip 1925-............... **CLC 23**
See also CA 5-8R; CANR 5; DLBY 82

Booth, Wayne C(layson) 1921- ..... **CLC 24**
See also CA 1-4R; CAAS 5; CANR 3, 43;
DLB 67

Borchert, Wolfgang 1921-1947 ..... **TCLC 5**
See also CA 104; DLB 69, 124

Borel, Petrus 1809-1859......... **NCLC 41**

Borges, Jorge Luis
1899-1986 ... **CLC 1, 2, 3, 4, 6, 8, 9, 10,**
13, 19, 44, 48, 83; DA; DAB; DAC;
HLC; SSC 4; WLC
See also CA 21-24R; CANR 19, 33;
DAM MST, MULT; DLB 113; DLBY 86;
HW; MTCW

Borowski, Tadeusz 1922-1951...... **TCLC 9**
See also CA 106

Borrow, George (Henry)
1803-1881 .... **NCLC 9**
See also DLB 21, 55, 166

Bosman, Herman Charles
1905-1951 .... **TCLC 49**

Bosschere, Jean de 1878(?)-1953... **TCLC 19**
See also CA 115

Boswell, James
1740-1795 ...... **LC 4; DA; DAB; DAC;**
WLC
See also CDBLB 1660-1789; DAM MST;
DLB 104, 142

Bottoms, David 1949-............. **CLC 53**
See also CA 105; CANR 22; DLB 120;
DLBY 83

Boucicault, Dion 1820-1890...... **NCLC 41**

Boucolon, Maryse 1937-
See Conde, Maryse
See also CA 110; CANR 30

Bourget, Paul (Charles Joseph)
1852-1935 .... **TCLC 12**
See also CA 107; DLB 123

Bourjaily, Vance (Nye) 1922- .... **CLC 8, 62**
See also CA 1-4R; CAAS 1; CANR 2;
DLB 2, 143

Bourne, Randolph S(illiman)
1886-1918 .... **TCLC 16**
See also CA 117; DLB 63

Bova, Ben(jamin William) 1932-.... **CLC 45**
See also AAYA 16; CA 5-8R; CAAS 18;
CANR 11; CLR 3; DLBY 81;
INT CANR-11; MAICYA; MTCW;
SATA 6, 68

Bowen, Elizabeth (Dorothea Cole)
1899-1973 ...... **CLC 1, 3, 6, 11, 15, 22;**
SSC 3
See also CA 17-18; 41-44R; CANR 35;
CAP 2; CDBLB 1945-1960; DAM NOV;
DLB 15, 162; MTCW

Bowering, George 1935-........ **CLC 15, 47**
See also CA 21-24R; CAAS 16; CANR 10;
DLB 53

Bowering, Marilyn R(uthe) 1949-... **CLC 32**
See also CA 101; CANR 49

Bowers, Edgar 1924- .... **CLC 9**
See also CA 5-8R; CANR 24; DLB 5

Bowie, David..................... **CLC 17**
See also Jones, David Robert

Bowles, Jane (Sydney)
1917-1973 .... **CLC 3, 68**
See also CA 19-20; 41-44R; CAP 2

Bowles, Paul (Frederick)
1910-.......... **CLC 1, 2, 19, 53; SSC 3**
See also CA 1-4R; CAAS 1; CANR 1, 19,
50; DLB 5, 6; MTCW

Box, Edgar
See Vidal, Gore

Boyd, Nancy
See Millay, Edna St. Vincent

Boyd, William 1952-........ **CLC 28, 53, 70**
See also CA 114; 120; CANR 51

Boyle, Kay
1902-1992 ..... **CLC 1, 5, 19, 58; SSC 5**
See also CA 13-16R; 140; CAAS 1;
CANR 29; DLB 4, 9, 48, 86; DLBY 93;
MTCW

Boyle, Mark
See Kienzle, William X(avier)

Boyle, Patrick 1905-1982......... **CLC 19**
See also CA 127

Boyle, T. C. 1948-
See Boyle, T(homas) Coraghessan

Boyle, T(homas) Coraghessan
1948- .... **CLC 36, 55, 90; SSC 16**
See also BEST 90:4; CA 120; CANR 44;
DAM POP; DLBY 86

Boz
See Dickens, Charles (John Huffam)

Brackenridge, Hugh Henry
1748-1816 .... **NCLC 7**
See also DLB 11, 37

Bradbury, Edward P.
See Moorcock, Michael (John)

Bradbury, Malcolm (Stanley)
1932- .... **CLC 32, 61**
See also CA 1-4R; CANR 1, 33;
DAM NOV; DLB 14; MTCW

Bradbury, Ray (Douglas)
1920- .... **CLC 1, 3, 10, 15, 42; DA;**
DAB; DAC; WLC
See also AAYA 15; AITN 1, 2; CA 1-4R;
CANR 2, 30; CDALB 1968-1988;
DAM MST, NOV, POP; DLB 2, 8;
INT CANR-30; MTCW; SATA 11, 64

Bradford, Gamaliel 1863-1932..... **TCLC 36**
See also DLB 17

Bradley, David (Henry, Jr.)
1950- .... **CLC 23; BLC**
See also BW 1; CA 104; CANR 26;
DAM MULT; DLB 33

Bradley, John Ed(mund, Jr.)
1958-...................... **CLC 55**
See also CA 139

Bradley, Marion Zimmer 1930-..... **CLC 30**
See also AAYA 9; CA 57-60; CAAS 10;
CANR 7, 31, 51; DAM POP; DLB 8;
MTCW

Bradstreet, Anne
1612(?)-1672 ...... **LC 4, 30; DA; DAC;**
PC 10
See also CDALB 1640-1865; DAM MST,
POET; DLB 24

Brady, Joan 1939- .... **CLC 86**
See also CA 141

Bragg, Melvyn 1939- .... **CLC 10**
See also BEST 89:3; CA 57-60; CANR 10,
48; DLB 14

Braine, John (Gerard)
1922-1986 .... **CLC 1, 3, 41**
See also CA 1-4R; 120; CANR 1, 33;
CDBLB 1945-1960; DLB 15; DLBY 86;
MTCW

Brammer, William 1930(?)-1978 .... **CLC 31**
See also CA 77-80

Brancati, Vitaliano 1907-1954..... **TCLC 12**
See also CA 109

Brancato, Robin F(idler) 1936-..... **CLC 35**
See also AAYA 9; CA 69-72; CANR 11,
45; CLR 32; JRDA; SAAS 9; SATA 23

Brand, Max
See Faust, Frederick (Schiller)

Brand, Millen 1906-1980.......... **CLC 7**
See also CA 21-24R; 97-100

Branden, Barbara .... **CLC 44**
See also CA 148

Brandes, Georg (Morris Cohen)
1842-1927 .... **TCLC 10**
See also CA 105

Brandys, Kazimierz 1916-......... **CLC 62**

Branley, Franklyn M(ansfield)
1915- .... **CLC 21**
See also CA 33-36R; CANR 14, 39;
CLR 13; MAICYA; SAAS 16; SATA 4,
68

Brathwaite, Edward Kamau 1930-... **CLC 11**
See also BW 2; CA 25-28R; CANR 11, 26,
47; DAM POET; DLB 125

Brautigan, Richard (Gary)
1935-1984 ..... **CLC 1, 3, 5, 9, 12, 34, 42**
See also CA 53-56; 113; CANR 34;
DAM NOV; DLB 2, 5; DLBY 80, 84;
MTCW; SATA 56

Brave Bird, Mary 1953-
See Crow Dog, Mary
See also NNAL

Braverman, Kate 1950- .... **CLC 67**
See also CA 89-92

Brecht, Bertolt
1898-1956 ...... **TCLC 1, 6, 13, 35; DA;**
DAB; DAC; DC 3; WLC
See also CA 104; 133; DAM DRAM, MST;
DLB 56, 124; MTCW

Brecht, Eugen Berthold Friedrich
See Brecht, Bertolt

Bremer, Fredrika 1801-1865 ..... **NCLC 11**

Brennan, Christopher John
1870-1932 .... **TCLC 17**
See also CA 117

Brennan, Maeve 1917-............. **CLC 5**
See also CA 81-84

Brentano, Clemens (Maria)
1778-1842 .... **NCLC 1**
See also DLB 90

Brent of Bin Bin
See Franklin, (Stella Maraia Sarah) Miles

Brenton, Howard 1942-.......... **CLC 31**
See also CA 69-72; CANR 33; DLB 13;
MTCW

Brulls, Christian
See Simenon, Georges (Jacques Christian)

Brunner, John (Kilian Houston)
1934-1995 . . . . **CLC 8, 10**
See also CA 1-4R; 149; CAAS 8; CANR 2,
37; DAM POP; MTCW

Bruno, Giordano 1548-1600 . . . . **LC 27**

Brutus, Dennis 1924- . . . . **CLC 43; BLC**
See also BW 2; CA 49-52; CAAS 14;
CANR 2, 27, 42; DAM MULT, POET;
DLB 117

Bryan, C(ourtlandt) D(ixon) B(arnes)
1936- . . . . **CLC 29**
See also CA 73-76; CANR 13;
INT CANR-13

Bryan, Michael
See Moore, Brian

Bryant, William Cullen
1794-1878 . . . . . **NCLC 6, 46; DA; DAB;
DAC**
See also CDALB 1640-1865; DAM MST,
POET; DLB 3, 43, 59

Bryusov, Valery Yakovlevich
1873-1924 . . . . **TCLC 10**
See also CA 107

Buchan, John 1875-1940 . . . **TCLC 41; DAB**
See also CA 108; 145; DAM POP; DLB 34,
70, 156; YABC 2

Buchanan, George 1506-1582 . . . . **LC 4**

Buchheim, Lothar-Guenther 1918- . . . **CLC 6**
See also CA 85-88

Buchner, (Karl) Georg
1813-1837 . . . . **NCLC 26**

Buchwald, Art(hur) 1925- . . . . **CLC 33**
See also AITN 1; CA 5-8R; CANR 21;
MTCW; SATA 10

Buck, Pearl S(ydenstricker)
1892-1973 . . . . **CLC 7, 11, 18; DA; DAB;
DAC**
See also AITN 1; CA 1-4R; 41-44R;
CANR 1, 34; DAM MST, NOV; DLB 9,
102; MTCW; SATA 1, 25

Buckler, Ernest 1908-1984 . . . . **CLC 13; DAC**
See also CA 11-12; 114; CAP 1;
DAM MST; DLB 68; SATA 47

Buckley, Vincent (Thomas)
1925-1988 . . . . **CLC 57**
See also CA 101

Buckley, William F(rank), Jr.
1925- . . . . **CLC 7, 18, 37**
See also AITN 1; CA 1-4R; CANR 1, 24;
DAM POP; DLB 137; DLBY 80;
INT CANR-24; MTCW

Buechner, (Carl) Frederick
1926- . . . . **CLC 2, 4, 6, 9**
See also CA 13-16R; CANR 11, 39;
DAM NOV; DLBY 80; INT CANR-11;
MTCW

Buell, John (Edward) 1927- . . . . **CLC 10**
See also CA 1-4R; DLB 53

Buero Vallejo, Antonio 1916- . . . **CLC 15, 46**
See also CA 106; CANR 24, 49; HW;
MTCW

Bufalino, Gesualdo 1920(?)- . . . . **CLC 74**

Bugayev, Boris Nikolayevich 1880-1934
See Bely, Andrey
See also CA 104

Bukowski, Charles
1920-1994 . . . . **CLC 2, 5, 9, 41, 82**
See also CA 17-20R; 144; CANR 40;
DAM NOV, POET; DLB 5, 130; MTCW

Bulgakov, Mikhail (Afanas'evich)
1891-1940 . . . . **TCLC 2, 16; SSC 18**
See also CA 105; DAM DRAM, NOV

Bulgya, Alexander Alexandrovich
1901-1956 . . . . **TCLC 53**
See also Fadeyev, Alexander
See also CA 117

Bullins, Ed 1935- . . **CLC 1, 5, 7; BLC; DC 6**
See also BW 2; CA 49-52; CAAS 16;
CANR 24, 46; DAM DRAM, MULT;
DLB 7, 38; MTCW

Bulwer-Lytton, Edward (George Earle Lytton)
1803-1873 . . . . **NCLC 1, 45**
See also DLB 21

Bunin, Ivan Alexeyevich
1870-1953 . . . . **TCLC 6; SSC 5**
See also CA 104

Bunting, Basil 1900-1985 . . . . **CLC 10, 39, 47**
See also CA 53-56; 115; CANR 7;
DAM POET; DLB 20

Bunuel, Luis 1900-1983 . . **CLC 16, 80; HLC**
See also CA 101; 110; CANR 32;
DAM MULT; HW

Bunyan, John
1628-1688 . . . . . . **LC 4; DA; DAB; DAC;
WLC**
See also CDBLB 1660-1789; DAM MST;
DLB 39

Burckhardt, Jacob (Christoph)
1818-1897 . . . . **NCLC 49**

Burford, Eleanor
See Hibbert, Eleanor Alice Burford

Burgess, Anthony
. **CLC 1, 2, 4, 5, 8, 10, 13, 15, 22, 40, 62,
81, 94; DAB**
See also Wilson, John (Anthony) Burgess
See also AITN 1; CDBLB 1960 to Present;
DLB 14

Burke, Edmund
1729(?)-1797 . . . . **LC 7; DA; DAB; DAC;
WLC**
See also DAM MST; DLB 104

Burke, Kenneth (Duva)
1897-1993 . . . . **CLC 2, 24**
See also CA 5-8R; 143; CANR 39; DLB 45,
63; MTCW

Burke, Leda
See Garnett, David

Burke, Ralph
See Silverberg, Robert

Burke, Thomas 1886-1945 . . . . **TCLC 63**
See also CA 113

Burney, Fanny 1752-1840 . . . . **NCLC 12, 54**
See also DLB 39

Burns, Robert 1759-1796 . . . . **PC 6**
See also CDBLB 1789-1832; DA; DAB;
DAC; DAM MST, POET; DLB 109;
WLC

Burns, Tex
See L'Amour, Louis (Dearborn)

Burnshaw, Stanley 1906- . . . . . **CLC 3, 13, 44**
See also CA 9-12R; DLB 48

Burr, Anne 1937- . . . . **CLC 6**
See also CA 25-28R

Burroughs, Edgar Rice
1875-1950 . . . . **TCLC 2, 32**
See also AAYA 11; CA 104; 132;
DAM NOV; DLB 8; MTCW; SATA 41

Burroughs, William S(eward)
1914- . . . . . . **CLC 1, 2, 5, 15, 22, 42, 75;
DA; DAB; DAC; WLC**
See also AITN 2; CA 9-12R; CANR 20, 52;
DAM MST, NOV, POP; DLB 2, 8, 16,
152; DLBY 81; MTCW

Burton, Richard F. 1821-1890 . . . . **NCLC 42**
See also DLB 55

Busch, Frederick 1941- . . . **CLC 7, 10, 18, 47**
See also CA 33-36R; CAAS 1; CANR 45;
DLB 6

Bush, Ronald 1946- . . . . **CLC 34**
See also CA 136

Bustos, F(rancisco)
See Borges, Jorge Luis

Bustos Domecq, H(onorio)
See Bioy Casares, Adolfo; Borges, Jorge
Luis

Butler, Octavia E(stelle) 1947- . . . . . **CLC 38**
See also AAYA 18; BW 2; CA 73-76;
CANR 12, 24, 38; DAM MULT, POP;
DLB 33; MTCW; SATA 84

Butler, Robert Olen (Jr.) 1945- . . . . . **CLC 81**
See also CA 112; DAM POP; INT 112

Butler, Samuel 1612-1680 . . . . **LC 16**
See also DLB 101, 126

Butler, Samuel
1835-1902 . . . . . . **TCLC 1, 33; DA; DAB;
DAC; WLC**
See also CA 143; CDBLB 1890-1914;
DAM MST, NOV; DLB 18, 57

Butler, Walter C.
See Faust, Frederick (Schiller)

Butor, Michel (Marie Francois)
1926- . . . . **CLC 1, 3, 8, 11, 15**
See also CA 9-12R; CANR 33; DLB 83;
MTCW

Buzo, Alexander (John) 1944- . . . . **CLC 61**
See also CA 97-100; CANR 17, 39

Buzzati, Dino 1906-1972 . . . . **CLC 36**
See also CA 33-36R

Byars, Betsy (Cromer) 1928- . . . . **CLC 35**
See also CA 33-36R; CANR 18, 36; CLR 1,
16; DLB 52; INT CANR-18; JRDA;
MAICYA; MTCW; SAAS 1; SATA 4,
46, 80

Byatt, A(ntonia) S(usan Drabble)
1936- . . . . **CLC 19, 65**
See also CA 13-16R; CANR 13, 33, 50;
DAM NOV, POP; DLB 14; MTCW

Byrne, David 1952- . . . . **CLC 26**
See also CA 127

Byrne, John Keyes 1926-
See Leonard, Hugh
See also CA 102; INT 102

Byron, George Gordon (Noel)
1788-1824 . . . . . NCLC 2, 12; DA; DAB;
DAC; PC 16; WLC
See also CDBLB 1789-1832; DAM MST,
POET; DLB 96, 110

C. 3. 3.
See Wilde, Oscar (Fingal O'Flahertie Wills)

Caballero, Fernan 1796-1877. . . . . NCLC 10

Cabell, James Branch 1879-1958 . . . TCLC 6
See also CA 105; DLB 9, 78

Cable, George Washington
1844-1925 . . . . TCLC 4; SSC 4
See also CA 104; DLB 12, 74; DLBD 13

Cabral de Melo Neto, Joao 1920-. . . CLC 76
See also CA 151; DAM MULT

Cabrera Infante, G(uillermo)
1929- . . . . CLC 5, 25, 45; HLC
See also CA 85-88; CANR 29;
DAM MULT; DLB 113; HW; MTCW

Cade, Toni
See Bambara, Toni Cade

Cadmus and Harmonia
See Buchan, John

Caedmon fl. 658-680. . . . . CMLC 7
See also DLB 146

Caeiro, Alberto
See Pessoa, Fernando (Antonio Nogueira)

Cage, John (Milton, Jr.) 1912- . . . . . CLC 41
See also CA 13-16R; CANR 9;
INT CANR-9

Cain, G.
See Cabrera Infante, G(uillermo)

Cain, Guillermo
See Cabrera Infante, G(uillermo)

Cain, James M(allahan)
1892-1977 . . . . CLC 3, 11, 28
See also AITN 1; CA 17-20R; 73-76;
CANR 8, 34; MTCW

Caine, Mark
See Raphael, Frederic (Michael)

Calasso, Roberto 1941- . . . . CLC 81
See also CA 143

Calderon de la Barca, Pedro
1600-1681 . . . . LC 23; DC 3

Caldwell, Erskine (Preston)
1903-1987 . . . . CLC 1, 8, 14, 50, 60;
SSC 19
See also AITN 1; CA 1-4R; 121; CAAS 1;
CANR 2, 33; DAM NOV; DLB 9, 86;
MTCW

Caldwell, (Janet Miriam) Taylor (Holland)
1900-1985 . . . . CLC 2, 28, 39
See also CA 5-8R; 116; CANR 5;
DAM NOV, POP

Calhoun, John Caldwell
1782-1850 . . . . NCLC 15
See also DLB 3

Calisher, Hortense
1911- . . . . CLC 2, 4, 8, 38; SSC 15
See also CA 1-4R; CANR 1, 22;
DAM NOV; DLB 2; INT CANR-22;
MTCW

Callaghan, Morley Edward
1903-1990 . . . . . CLC 3, 14, 41, 65; DAC
See also CA 9-12R; 132; CANR 33;
DAM MST; DLB 68; MTCW

Callimachus
c. 305B.C.-c. 240B.C. . . . . CMLC 18

Calvino, Italo
1923-1985 . . . . . CLC 5, 8, 11, 22, 33, 39,
73; SSC 3
See also CA 85-88; 116; CANR 23;
DAM NOV; MTCW

Cameron, Carey 1952- . . . . CLC 59
See also CA 135

Cameron, Peter 1959-. . . . . CLC 44
See also CA 125; CANR 50

Campana, Dino 1885-1932. . . . . . . TCLC 20
See also CA 117; DLB 114

Campanella, Tommaso 1568-1639 . . . . LC 32

Campbell, John W(ood, Jr.)
1910-1971 . . . . CLC 32
See also CA 21-22; 29-32R; CANR 34;
CAP 2; DLB 8; MTCW

Campbell, Joseph 1904-1987 . . . . CLC 69
See also AAYA 3; BEST 89:2; CA 1-4R;
124; CANR 3, 28; MTCW

Campbell, Maria 1940-. . . . . . CLC 85; DAC
See also CA 102; NNAL

Campbell, (John) Ramsey
1946- . . . . CLC 42; SSC 19
See also CA 57-60; CANR 7; INT CANR-7

Campbell, (Ignatius) Roy (Dunnachie)
1901-1957 . . . . TCLC 5
See also CA 104; DLB 20

Campbell, Thomas 1777-1844 . . . . NCLC 19
See also DLB 93; 144

**Campbell, Wilfred. . . . . TCLC 9
See also Campbell, William

Campbell, William 1858(?)-1918
See Campbell, Wilfred
See also CA 106; DLB 92

**Campion, Jane. . . . . CLC 95
See also CA 138

Campos, Alvaro de
See Pessoa, Fernando (Antonio Nogueira)

Camus, Albert
1913-1960 . . . . CLC 1, 2, 4, 9, 11, 14, 32,
63, 69; DA; DAB; DAC; DC 2; SSC 9;
WLC
See also CA 89-92; DAM DRAM, MST,
NOV; DLB 72; MTCW

Canby, Vincent 1924-. . . . . CLC 13
See also CA 81-84

Cancale
See Desnos, Robert

Canetti, Elias
1905-1994 . . . . CLC 3, 14, 25, 75, 86
See also CA 21-24R; 146; CANR 23;
DLB 85, 124; MTCW

Canin, Ethan 1960-. . . . . CLC 55
See also CA 131; 135

Cannon, Curt
See Hunter, Evan

Cape, Judith
See Page, P(atricia) K(athleen)

Capek, Karel
1890-1938 . . . . . . TCLC 6, 37; DA; DAB;
DAC; DC 1; WLC
See also CA 104; 140; DAM DRAM, MST,
NOV

Capote, Truman
1924-1984 . . . . . . CLC 1, 3, 8, 13, 19, 34,
38, 58; DA; DAB; DAC; SSC 2; WLC
See also CA 5-8R; 113; CANR 18;
CDALB 1941-1968; DAM MST, NOV,
POP; DLB 2; DLBY 80, 84; MTCW

Capra, Frank 1897-1991. . . . . CLC 16
See also CA 61-64; 135

Caputo, Philip 1941-. . . . . CLC 32
See also CA 73-76; CANR 40

Card, Orson Scott 1951- . . . . CLC 44, 47, 50
See also AAYA 11; CA 102; CANR 27, 47;
DAM POP; INT CANR-27; MTCW;
SATA 83

Cardenal, Ernesto 1925-. . . . . CLC 31; HLC
See also CA 49-52; CANR 2, 32;
DAM MULT, POET; HW; MTCW

Cardozo, Benjamin N(athan)
1870-1938 . . . . TCLC 65
See also CA 117

Carducci, Giosue 1835-1907. . . . . . TCLC 32

Carew, Thomas 1595(?)-1640. . . . . . . LC 13
See also DLB 126

Carey, Ernestine Gilbreth 1908-. . . . CLC 17
See also CA 5-8R; SATA 2

Carey, Peter 1943-. . . . . CLC 40, 55
See also CA 123; 127; INT 127; MTCW

Carleton, William 1794-1869. . . . . . NCLC 3
See also DLB 159

Carlisle, Henry (Coffin) 1926-. . . . . . CLC 33
See also CA 13-16R; CANR 15

Carlsen, Chris
See Holdstock, Robert P.

Carlson, Ron(ald F.) 1947-. . . . . CLC 54
See also CA 105; CANR 27

Carlyle, Thomas
1795-1881 . . NCLC 22; DA; DAB; DAC
See also CDBLB 1789-1832; DAM MST;
DLB 55; 144

Carman, (William) Bliss
1861-1929 . . . . TCLC 7; DAC
See also CA 104; DLB 92

Carnegie, Dale 1888-1955 . . . . TCLC 53

Carossa, Hans 1878-1956. . . . . TCLC 48
See also DLB 66

Carpenter, Don(ald Richard)
1931-1995 . . . . CLC 41
See also CA 45-48; 149; CANR 1

Carpentier (y Valmont), Alejo
1904-1980 . . . . CLC 8, 11, 38; HLC
See also CA 65-68; 97-100; CANR 11;
DAM MULT; DLB 113; HW

Carr, Caleb 1955(?)-. . . . . CLC 86
See also CA 147

Carr, Emily 1871-1945. . . . . TCLC 32
See also DLB 68

Carr, John Dickson 1906-1977 . . . . . . CLC 3
See also CA 49-52; 69-72; CANR 3, 33;
MTCW

Carr, Philippa
See Hibbert, Eleanor Alice Burford

Carr, Virginia Spencer 1929- .... **CLC 34**
See also CA 61-64; DLB 111

Carrere, Emmanuel 1957- .... **CLC 89**

Carrier, Roch 1937- ..... **CLC 13, 78; DAC**
See also CA 130; DAM MST; DLB 53

Carroll, James P. 1943(?)- .... **CLC 38**
See also CA 81-84

Carroll, Jim 1951- .... **CLC 35**
See also AAYA 17; CA 45-48; CANR 42

Carroll, Lewis .... **NCLC 2, 53; WLC**
See also Dodgson, Charles Lutwidge
See also CDBLB 1832-1890; CLR 2, 18;
DLB 18, 163; JRDA

Carroll, Paul Vincent 1900-1968.... **CLC 10**
See also CA 9-12R; 25-28R; DLB 10

Carruth, Hayden
1921- ...... **CLC 4, 7, 10, 18, 84; PC 10**
See also CA 9-12R; CANR 4, 38; DLB 5,
165; INT CANR-4; MTCW; SATA 47

Carson, Rachel Louise 1907-1964... **CLC 71**
See also CA 77-80; CANR 35; DAM POP;
MTCW; SATA 23

Carter, Angela (Olive)
1940-1992 ...... **CLC 5, 41, 76; SSC 13**
See also CA 53-56; 136; CANR 12, 36;
DLB 14; MTCW; SATA 66;
SATA-Obit 70

Carter, Nick
See Smith, Martin Cruz

Carver, Raymond
1938-1988 ... **CLC 22, 36, 53, 55; SSC 8**
See also CA 33-36R; 126; CANR 17, 34;
DAM NOV; DLB 130; DLBY 84, 88;
MTCW

Cary, Elizabeth, Lady Falkland
1585-1639 .... **LC 30**

Cary, (Arthur) Joyce (Lunel)
1888-1957 .... **TCLC 1, 29**
See also CA 104; CDBLB 1914-1945;
DLB 15, 100

Casanova de Seingalt, Giovanni Jacopo
1725-1798 .... **LC 13**

Casares, Adolfo Bioy
See Bioy Casares, Adolfo

Casely-Hayford, J(oseph) E(phraim)
1866-1930 .... **TCLC 24; BLC**
See also BW 2; CA 123; DAM MULT

Casey, John (Dudley) 1939- .... **CLC 59**
See also BEST 90:2; CA 69-72; CANR 23

Casey, Michael 1947- .... **CLC 2**
See also CA 65-68; DLB 5

Casey, Patrick
See Thurman, Wallace (Henry)

Casey, Warren (Peter) 1935-1988... **CLC 12**
See also CA 101; 127; INT 101

Casona, Alejandro .... **CLC 49**
See also Alvarez, Alejandro Rodriguez

Cassavetes, John 1929-1989........ **CLC 20**
See also CA 85-88; 127

Cassill, R(onald) V(erlin) 1919- ... **CLC 4, 23**
See also CA 9-12R; CAAS 1; CANR 7, 45;
DLB 6

Cassirer, Ernst 1874-1945 .... **TCLC 61**

Cassity, (Allen) Turner 1929- ... **CLC 6, 42**
See also CA 17-20R; CAAS 8; CANR 11;
DLB 105

Castaneda, Carlos 1931(?)-........ **CLC 12**
See also CA 25-28R; CANR 32; HW;
MTCW

Castedo, Elena 1937- .... **CLC 65**
See also CA 132

Castedo-Ellerman, Elena
See Castedo, Elena

Castellanos, Rosario
1925-1974 .... **CLC 66; HLC**
See also CA 131; 53-56; DAM MULT;
DLB 113; HW

Castelvetro, Lodovico 1505-1571..... **LC 12**

Castiglione, Baldassare 1478-1529 ... **LC 12**

Castle, Robert
See Hamilton, Edmond

Castro, Guillen de 1569-1631........ **LC 19**

Castro, Rosalia de 1837-1885 ..... **NCLC 3**
See also DAM MULT

Cather, Willa
See Cather, Willa Sibert

Cather, Willa Sibert
1873-1947 .... **TCLC 1, 11, 31; DA;**
DAB; DAC; SSC 2; WLC
See also CA 104; 128; CDALB 1865-1917;
DAM MST, NOV; DLB 9, 54, 78;
DLBD 1; MTCW; SATA 30

Catton, (Charles) Bruce
1899-1978 .... **CLC 35**
See also AITN 1; CA 5-8R; 81-84;
CANR 7; DLB 17; SATA 2;
SATA-Obit 24

Catullus c. 84B.C.-c. 54B.C. ..... **CMLC 18**

Cauldwell, Frank
See King, Francis (Henry)

Caunitz, William J. 1933- .... **CLC 34**
See also BEST 89:3; CA 125; 130; INT 130

Causley, Charles (Stanley) 1917-..... **CLC 7**
See also CA 9-12R; CANR 5, 35; CLR 30;
DLB 27; MTCW; SATA 3, 66

Caute, David 1936-............... **CLC 29**
See also CA 1-4R; CAAS 4; CANR 1, 33;
DAM NOV; DLB 14

Cavafy, C(onstantine) P(eter)
1863-1933 .... **TCLC 2, 7**
See also Kavafis, Konstantinos Petrou
See also CA 148; DAM POET

Cavallo, Evelyn
See Spark, Muriel (Sarah)

Cavanna, Betty .... **CLC 12**
See also Harrison, Elizabeth Cavanna
See also JRDA; MAICYA; SAAS 4;
SATA 1, 30

Cavendish, Margaret Lucas
1623-1673 .... **LC 30**
See also DLB 131

Caxton, William 1421(?)-1491(?)..... **LC 17**

Cayrol, Jean 1911-............... **CLC 11**
See also CA 89-92; DLB 83

Cela, Camilo Jose
1916- .... **CLC 4, 13, 59; HLC**
See also BEST 90:2; CA 21-24R; CAAS 10;
CANR 21, 32; DAM MULT; DLBY 89;
HW; MTCW

Celan, Paul ...... **CLC 10, 19, 53, 82; PC 10**
See also Antschel, Paul
See also DLB 69

Celine, Louis-Ferdinand
.... **CLC 1, 3, 4, 7, 9, 15, 47**
See also Destouches, Louis-Ferdinand
See also DLB 72

Cellini, Benvenuto 1500-1571 .... **LC 7**

Cendrars, Blaise .... **CLC 18**
See also Sauser-Hall, Frederic

Cernuda (y Bidon), Luis
1902-1963 .... **CLC 54**
See also CA 131; 89-92; DAM POET;
DLB 134; HW

Cervantes (Saavedra), Miguel de
1547-1616 .... **LC 6, 23; DA; DAB;**
DAC; SSC 12; WLC
See also DAM MST, NOV

Cesaire, Aime (Fernand)
1913- .... **CLC 19, 32; BLC**
See also BW 2; CA 65-68; CANR 24, 43;
DAM MULT, POET; MTCW

Chabon, Michael 1965(?)- .... **CLC 55**
See also CA 139

Chabrol, Claude 1930- .... **CLC 16**
See also CA 110

Challans, Mary 1905-1983
See Renault, Mary
See also CA 81-84; 111; SATA 23;
SATA-Obit 36

Challis, George
See Faust, Frederick (Schiller)

Chambers, Aidan 1934- .... **CLC 35**
See also CA 25-28R; CANR 12, 31; JRDA;
MAICYA; SAAS 12; SATA 1, 69

Chambers, James 1948-
See Cliff, Jimmy
See also CA 124

Chambers, Jessie
See Lawrence, D(avid) H(erbert Richards)

Chambers, Robert W. 1865-1933... **TCLC 41**

Chandler, Raymond (Thornton)
1888-1959 .... **TCLC 1, 7; SSC 23**
See also CA 104; 129; CDALB 1929-1941;
DLBD 6; MTCW

Chang, Jung 1952- .... **CLC 71**
See also CA 142

Channing, William Ellery
1780-1842 .... **NCLC 17**
See also DLB 1, 59

Chaplin, Charles Spencer
1889-1977 .... **CLC 16**
See also Chaplin, Charlie
See also CA 81-84; 73-76

Chaplin, Charlie
See Chaplin, Charles Spencer
See also DLB 44

Chapman, George 1559(?)-1634...... **LC 22**
See also DAM DRAM; DLB 62, 121

Chapman, Graham 1941-1989 . . . . . **CLC 21**
See also Monty Python
See also CA 116; 129; CANR 35

Chapman, John Jay 1862-1933 . . . . . **TCLC 7**
See also CA 104

Chapman, Walker
See Silverberg, Robert

Chappell, Fred (Davis) 1936- . . . . **CLC 40, 78**
See also CA 5-8R; CAAS 4; CANR 8, 33;
DLB 6, 105

Char, Rene(-Emile)
1907-1988 . . . . **CLC 9, 11, 14, 55**
See also CA 13-16R; 124; CANR 32;
DAM POET; MTCW

Charby, Jay
See Ellison, Harlan (Jay)

Chardin, Pierre Teilhard de
See Teilhard de Chardin, (Marie Joseph)
Pierre

Charles I 1600-1649 . . . . **LC 13**

Charyn, Jerome 1937- . . . . **CLC 5, 8, 18**
See also CA 5-8R; CAAS 1; CANR 7;
DLBY 83; MTCW

Chase, Mary (Coyle) 1907-1981 . . . . . . **DC 1**
See also CA 77-80; 105; SATA 17;
SATA-Obit 29

Chase, Mary Ellen 1887-1973 . . . . **CLC 2**
See also CA 13-16; 41-44R; CAP 1;
SATA 10

Chase, Nicholas
See Hyde, Anthony

Chateaubriand, Francois Rene de
1768-1848 . . . . **NCLC 3**
See also DLB 119

Chatterje, Sarat Chandra 1876-1936(?)
See Chatterji, Saratchandra
See also CA 109

Chatterji, Bankim Chandra
1838-1894 . . . . **NCLC 19**

Chatterji, Saratchandra . . . . **TCLC 13**
See also Chatterje, Sarat Chandra

Chatterton, Thomas 1752-1770 . . . . **LC 3**
See also DAM POET; DLB 109

Chatwin, (Charles) Bruce
1940-1989 . . . . **CLC 28, 57, 59**
See also AAYA 4; BEST 90:1; CA 85-88;
127; DAM POP

Chaucer, Daniel
See Ford, Ford Madox

Chaucer, Geoffrey
1340(?)-1400 . . . **LC 17; DA; DAB; DAC**
See also CDBLB Before 1660; DAM MST,
POET; DLB 146

Chaviaras, Strates 1935-
See Haviaras, Stratis
See also CA 105

Chayefsky, Paddy . . . . **CLC 23**
See also Chayefsky, Sidney
See also DLB 7, 44; DLBY 81

Chayefsky, Sidney 1923-1981
See Chayefsky, Paddy
See also CA 9-12R; 104; CANR 18;
DAM DRAM

Chedid, Andree 1920- . . . . **CLC 47**
See also CA 145

Cheever, John
1912-1982 . . . . . . **CLC 3, 7, 8, 11, 15, 25,**
64; DA; DAB; DAC; SSC 1; WLC
See also CA 5-8R; 106; CABS 1; CANR 5,
27; CDALB 1941-1968; DAM MST,
NOV, POP; DLB 2, 102; DLBY 80, 82;
INT CANR-5; MTCW

Cheever, Susan 1943- . . . . **CLC 18, 48**
See also CA 103; CANR 27, 51; DLBY 82;
INT CANR-27

Chekhonte, Antosha
See Chekhov, Anton (Pavlovich)

Chekhov, Anton (Pavlovich)
1860-1904 . . . . . **TCLC 3, 10, 31, 55; DA;**
DAB; DAC; SSC 2; WLC
See also CA 104; 124; DAM DRAM, MST

Chernyshevsky, Nikolay Gavrilovich
1828-1889 . . . . **NCLC 1**

Cherry, Carolyn Janice 1942-
See Cherryh, C. J.
See also CA 65-68; CANR 10

Cherryh, C. J. . . . . **CLC 35**
See also Cherry, Carolyn Janice
See also DLBY 80

Chesnutt, Charles W(addell)
1858-1932 . . . . **TCLC 5, 39; BLC; SSC 7**
See also BW 1; CA 106; 125; DAM MULT;
DLB 12, 50, 78; MTCW

Chester, Alfred 1929(?)-1971 . . . . **CLC 49**
See also CA 33-36R; DLB 130

Chesterton, G(ilbert) K(eith)
1874-1936 . . . . **TCLC 1, 6, 64; SSC 1**
See also CA 104; 132; CDBLB 1914-1945;
DAM NOV, POET; DLB 10, 19, 34, 70,
98, 149; MTCW; SATA 27

Chiang Pin-chin 1904-1986
See Ding Ling
See also CA 118

Ch'ien Chung-shu 1910- . . . . **CLC 22**
See also CA 130; MTCW

Child, L. Maria
See Child, Lydia Maria

Child, Lydia Maria 1802-1880 . . . . **NCLC 6**
See also DLB 1, 74; SATA 67

Child, Mrs.
See Child, Lydia Maria

Child, Philip 1898-1978 . . . . **CLC 19, 68**
See also CA 13-14; CAP 1; SATA 47

Childers, (Robert) Erskine
1870-1922 . . . . **TCLC 65**
See also CA 113; DLB 70

Childress, Alice
1920-1994 . . **CLC 12, 15, 86; BLC; DC 4**
See also AAYA 8; BW 2; CA 45-48; 146;
CANR 3, 27, 50; CLR 14; DAM DRAM,
MULT, NOV; DLB 7, 38; JRDA;
MAICYA; MTCW; SATA 7, 48, 81

Chislett, (Margaret) Anne 1943- . . . . **CLC 34**
See also CA 151

Chitty, Thomas Willes 1926- . . . . **CLC 11**
See also Hinde, Thomas
See also CA 5-8R

Chivers, Thomas Holley
1809-1858 . . . . **NCLC 49**
See also DLB 3

Chomette, Rene Lucien 1898-1981
See Clair, Rene
See also CA 103

Chopin, Kate
. . . . **TCLC 5, 14; DA; DAB; SSC 8**
See also Chopin, Katherine
See also CDALB 1865-1917; DLB 12, 78

Chopin, Katherine 1851-1904
See Chopin, Kate
See also CA 104; 122; DAC; DAM MST,
NOV

Chretien de Troyes
c. 12th cent. - . . . . **CMLC 10**

Christie
See Ichikawa, Kon

Christie, Agatha (Mary Clarissa)
1890-1976 . . . . . . **CLC 1, 6, 8, 12, 39, 48;**
DAB; DAC
See also AAYA 9; AITN 1, 2; CA 17-20R;
61-64; CANR 10, 37; CDBLB 1914-1945;
DAM NOV; DLB 13, 77; MTCW;
SATA 36

Christie, (Ann) Philippa
See Pearce, Philippa
See also CA 5-8R; CANR 4

Christine de Pizan 1365(?)-1431(?) . . . . **LC 9**

Chubb, Elmer
See Masters, Edgar Lee

Chulkov, Mikhail Dmitrievich
1743-1792 . . . . **LC 2**
See also DLB 150

Churchill, Caryl 1938- . . . **CLC 31, 55; DC 5**
See also CA 102; CANR 22, 46; DLB 13;
MTCW

Churchill, Charles 1731-1764 . . . . **LC 3**
See also DLB 109

Chute, Carolyn 1947- . . . . **CLC 39**
See also CA 123

Ciardi, John (Anthony)
1916-1986 . . . . **CLC 10, 40, 44**
See also CA 5-8R; 118; CAAS 2; CANR 5,
33; CLR 19; DAM POET; DLB 5;
DLBY 86; INT CANR-5; MAICYA;
MTCW; SATA 1, 65; SATA-Obit 46

Cicero, Marcus Tullius
106B.C.-43B.C. . . . . **CMLC 3**

Cimino, Michael 1943- . . . . **CLC 16**
See also CA 105

Cioran, E(mil) M. 1911-1995 . . . . **CLC 64**
See also CA 25-28R; 149

Cisneros, Sandra 1954- . . . . . . **CLC 69; HLC**
See also AAYA 9; CA 131; DAM MULT;
DLB 122, 152; HW

Cixous, Helene 1937- . . . . **CLC 92**
See also CA 126; DLB 83; MTCW

Clair, Rene . . . . **CLC 20**
See also Chomette, Rene Lucien

Clampitt, Amy 1920-1994 . . . . **CLC 32**
See also CA 110; 146; CANR 29; DLB 105

Clancy, Thomas L., Jr. 1947-
See Clancy, Tom
See also CA 125; 131; INT 131; MTCW

Clancy, Tom. . . . . CLC 45
See also Clancy, Thomas L., Jr.
See also AAYA 9; BEST 89:1, 90:1;
DAM NOV, POP

Clare, John   1793-1864 . . . . . . NCLC 9; DAB
See also DAM POET; DLB 55, 96

Clarin
See Alas (y Urena), Leopoldo (Enrique
Garcia)

Clark, Al C.
See Goines, Donald

Clark, (Robert) Brian   1932- . . . . CLC 29
See also CA 41-44R

Clark, Curt
See Westlake, Donald E(dwin)

Clark, Eleanor   1913-1996 . . . . CLC 5, 19
See also CA 9-12R; .151; CANR 41; DLB 6

Clark, J. P.
See Clark, John Pepper
See also DLB 117

Clark, John Pepper
1935- . . . . CLC 38; BLC; DC 5
See also Clark, J. P.
See also BW 1; CA 65-68; CANR 16;
DAM DRAM, MULT

Clark, M. R.
See Clark, Mavis Thorpe

Clark, Mavis Thorpe   1909- . . . . CLC 12
See also CA 57-60; CANR 8, 37; CLR 30;
MAICYA; SAAS 5; SATA 8, 74

Clark, Walter Van Tilburg
1909-1971 . . . . CLC 28
See also CA 9-12R; 33-36R; DLB 9;
SATA 8

Clarke, Arthur C(harles)
1917- . . . . . . CLC 1, 4, 13, 18, 35; SSC 3
See also AAYA 4; CA 1-4R; CANR 2, 28;
DAM POP; JRDA; MAICYA; MTCW;
SATA 13, 70

Clarke, Austin   1896-1974 . . . . CLC 6, 9
See also CA 29-32; 49-52; CAP 2;
DAM POET; DLB 10, 20

Clarke, Austin C(hesterfield)
1934- . . . . CLC 8, 53; BLC; DAC
See also BW 1; CA 25-28R; CAAS 16;
CANR 14, 32; DAM MULT; DLB 53,
125

Clarke, Gillian   1937- . . . . CLC 61
See also CA 106; DLB 40

Clarke, Marcus (Andrew Hislop)
1846-1881 . . . . NCLC 19

Clarke, Shirley   1925- . . . . CLC 16

Clash, The
See Headon, (Nicky) Topper; Jones, Mick;
Simonon, Paul; Strummer, Joe

Claudel, Paul (Louis Charles Marie)
1868-1955 . . . . TCLC 2, 10
See also CA 104

Clavell, James (duMaresq)
1925-1994 . . . . CLC 6, 25, 87
See also CA 25-28R; 146; CANR 26, 48;
DAM NOV, POP; MTCW

Cleaver, (Leroy) Eldridge
1935- . . . . CLC 30; BLC
See also BW 1; CA 21-24R; CANR 16;
DAM MULT

Cleese, John (Marwood)   1939- . . . . . CLC 21
See also Monty Python
See also CA 112; 116; CANR 35; MTCW

Cleishbotham, Jebediah
See Scott, Walter

Cleland, John   1710-1789 . . . . LC 2
See also DLB 39

Clemens, Samuel Langhorne   1835-1910
See Twain, Mark
See also CA 104; 135; CDALB 1865-1917;
DA; DAB; DAC; DAM MST, NOV;
DLB 11, 12, 23, 64, 74; JRDA;
MAICYA; YABC 2

Cleophil
See Congreve, William

Clerihew, E.
See Bentley, E(dmund) C(lerihew)

Clerk, N. W.
See Lewis, C(live) S(taples)

Cliff, Jimmy. CLC 21
See also Chambers, James

Clifton, (Thelma) Lucille
1936- . . . . CLC 19, 66; BLC
See also BW 2; CA 49-52; CANR 2, 24, 42;
CLR 5; DAM MULT, POET; DLB 5, 41;
MAICYA; MTCW; SATA 20, 69

Clinton, Dirk
See Silverberg, Robert

Clough, Arthur Hugh   1819-1861 . . NCLC 27
See also DLB 32

Clutha, Janet Paterson Frame   1924-
See Frame, Janet
See also CA 1-4R; CANR 2, 36; MTCW

Clyne, Terence
See Blatty, William Peter

Cobalt, Martin
See Mayne, William (James Carter)

Cobbett, William   1763-1835 . . . . . NCLC 49
See also DLB 43, 107, 158

Coburn, D(onald) L(ee)   1938- . . . . . . CLC 10
See also CA 89-92

Cocteau, Jean (Maurice Eugene Clement)
1889-1963 . . . . CLC 1, 8, 15, 16, 43; DA;
DAB; DAC; WLC
See also CA 25-28; CANR 40; CAP 2;
DAM DRAM, MST, NOV; DLB 65;
MTCW

Codrescu, Andrei   1946- . . . . CLC 46
See also CA 33-36R; CAAS 19; CANR 13,
34; DAM POET

Coe, Max
See Bourne, Randolph S(illiman)

Coe, Tucker
See Westlake, Donald E(dwin)

Coetzee, J(ohn) M(ichael)
1940- . . . . CLC 23, 33, 66
See also CA 77-80; CANR 41; DAM NOV;
MTCW

Coffey, Brian
See Koontz, Dean R(ay)

Cohan, George M.   1878-1942 . . . . . TCLC 60

Cohen, Arthur A(llen)
1928-1986 . . . . CLC 7, 31
See also CA 1-4R; 120; CANR 1, 17, 42;
DLB 28

Cohen, Leonard (Norman)
1934- . . . . CLC 3, 38; DAC
See also CA 21-24R; CANR 14;
DAM MST; DLB 53; MTCW

Cohen, Matt   1942- . . . . CLC 19; DAC
See also CA 61-64; CAAS 18; CANR 40;
DLB 53

Cohen-Solal, Annie   19(?)- . . . . CLC 50

Colegate, Isabel   1931- . . . . CLC 36
See also CA 17-20R; CANR 8, 22; DLB 14;
INT CANR-22; MTCW

Coleman, Emmett
See Reed, Ishmael

Coleridge, Samuel Taylor
1772-1834 . . . . . NCLC 9, 54; DA; DAB;
DAC; PC 11; WLC
See also CDBLB 1789-1832; DAM MST,
POET; DLB 93, 107

Coleridge, Sara   1802-1852 . . . . NCLC 31

Coles, Don   1928- . . . . CLC 46
See also CA 115; CANR 38

Colette, (Sidonie-Gabrielle)
1873-1954 . . . . . . TCLC 1, 5, 16; SSC 10
See also CA 104; 131; DAM NOV; DLB 65;
MTCW

Collett, (Jacobine) Camilla (Wergeland)
1813-1895 . . . . NCLC 22

Collier, Christopher   1930- . . . . CLC 30
See also AAYA 13; CA 33-36R; CANR 13,
33; JRDA; MAICYA; SATA 16, 70

Collier, James L(incoln)   1928- . . . . . CLC 30
See also AAYA 13; CA 9-12R; CANR 4,
33; CLR 3; DAM POP; JRDA;
MAICYA; SAAS 21; SATA 8, 70

Collier, Jeremy   1650-1726 . . . . LC 6

Collier, John   1901-1980 . . . . SSC 19
See also CA 65-68; 97-100; CANR 10;
DLB 77

Collins, Hunt
See Hunter, Evan

Collins, Linda   1931- . . . . CLC 44
See also CA 125

Collins, (William) Wilkie
1824-1889 . . . . NCLC 1, 18
See also CDBLB 1832-1890; DLB 18, 70,
159

Collins, William   1721-1759 . . . . LC 4
See also DAM POET; DLB 109

Collodi, Carlo   1826-1890 . . . . NCLC 54
See also Lorenzini, Carlo
See also CLR 5

Colman, George
See Glassco, John

Colt, Winchester Remington
See Hubbard, L(afayette) Ron(ald)

Colter, Cyrus   1910- . . . . CLC 58
See also BW 1; CA 65-68; CANR 10;
DLB 33

Colton, James
See Hansen, Joseph

Colum, Padraic 1881-1972......... **CLC 28**
See also CA 73-76; 33-36R; CANR 35;
CLR 36; MAICYA; MTCW; SATA 15

Colvin, James
See Moorcock, Michael (John)

Colwin, Laurie (E.)
1944-1992 .... **CLC 5, 13, 23, 84**
See also CA 89-92; 139; CANR 20, 46;
DLBY 80; MTCW

Comfort, Alex(ander) 1920-......... **CLC 7**
See also CA 1-4R; CANR 1, 45; DAM POP

Comfort, Montgomery
See Campbell, (John) Ramsey

Compton-Burnett, I(vy)
1884(?)-1969 ...... **CLC 1, 3, 10, 15, 34**
See also CA 1-4R; 25-28R; CANR 4;
DAM NOV; DLB 36; MTCW

Comstock, Anthony 1844-1915 .... **TCLC 13**
See also CA 110

Comte, Auguste 1798-1857....... **NCLC 54**

Conan Doyle, Arthur
See Doyle, Arthur Conan

Conde, Maryse 1937-......... **CLC 52, 92**
See also Boucolon, Maryse
See also BW 2; DAM MULT

Condillac, Etienne Bonnot de
1714-1780 .... **LC 26**

Condon, Richard (Thomas)
1915-1996 .... **CLC 4, 6, 8, 10, 45**
See also BEST 90:3; CA 1-4R; 151;
CAAS 1; CANR 2, 23; DAM NOV;
INT CANR-23; MTCW

Congreve, William
1670-1729 .... **LC 5, 21; DA; DAB;**
DAC; DC 2; WLC
See also CDBLB 1660-1789; DAM DRAM,
MST, POET; DLB 39, 84

Connell, Evan S(helby), Jr.
1924- .... **CLC 4, 6, 45**
See also AAYA 7; CA 1-4R; CAAS 2;
CANR 2, 39; DAM NOV; DLB 2;
DLBY 81; MTCW

Connelly, Marc(us Cook)
1890-1980 .... **CLC 7**
See also CA 85-88; 102; CANR 30; DLB 7;
DLBY 80; SATA-Obit 25

Connor, Ralph .... **TCLC 31**
See also Gordon, Charles William
See also DLB 92

Conrad, Joseph
1857-1924 .... **TCLC 1, 6, 13, 25, 43, 57;**
DA; DAB; DAC; SSC 9; WLC
See also CA 104; 131; CDBLB 1890-1914;
DAM MST, NOV; DLB 10, 34, 98, 156;
MTCW; SATA 27

Conrad, Robert Arnold
See Hart, Moss

Conroy, Pat 1945-............. **CLC 30, 74**
See also AAYA 8; AITN 1; CA 85-88;
CANR 24; DAM NOV, POP; DLB 6;
MTCW

Constant (de Rebecque), (Henri) Benjamin
1767-1830 .... **NCLC 6**
See also DLB 119

Conybeare, Charles Augustus
See Eliot, T(homas) S(tearns)

Cook, Michael 1933- .... **CLC 58**
See also CA 93-96; DLB 53

Cook, Robin 1940- .... **CLC 14**
See also BEST 90:2; CA 108; 111;
CANR 41; DAM POP; INT 111

Cook, Roy
See Silverberg, Robert

Cooke, Elizabeth 1948- .... **CLC 55**
See also CA 129

Cooke, John Esten 1830-1886 ..... **NCLC 5**
See also DLB 3

Cooke, John Estes
See Baum, L(yman) Frank

Cooke, M. E.
See Creasey, John

Cooke, Margaret
See Creasey, John

Cook-Lynn, Elizabeth 1930- .... **CLC 93**
See also CA 133; DAM MULT; NNAL

Cooney, Ray .... **CLC 62**

Cooper, Douglas 1960-........... **CLC 86**

Cooper, Henry St. John
See Creasey, John

Cooper, J. California............... **CLC 56**
See also AAYA 12; BW 1; CA 125;
DAM MULT

Cooper, James Fenimore
1789-1851 .... **NCLC 1, 27, 54**
See also CDALB 1640-1865; DLB 3;
SATA 19

Coover, Robert (Lowell)
1932- .. **CLC 3, 7, 15, 32, 46, 87; SSC 15**
See also CA 45-48; CANR 3, 37;
DAM NOV; DLB 2; DLBY 81; MTCW

Copeland, Stewart (Armstrong)
1952- .... **CLC 26**

Coppard, A(lfred) E(dgar)
1878-1957 .... **TCLC 5; SSC 21**
See also CA 114; DLB 162; YABC 1

Coppee, Francois 1842-1908 ...... **TCLC 25**

Coppola, Francis Ford 1939-....... **CLC 16**
See also CA 77-80; CANR 40; DLB 44

Corbiere, Tristan 1845-1875 ..... **NCLC 43**

Corcoran, Barbara 1911-.......... **CLC 17**
See also AAYA 14; CA 21-24R; CAAS 2;
CANR 11, 28, 48; DLB 52; JRDA;
SAAS 20; SATA 3, 77

Cordelier, Maurice
See Giraudoux, (Hippolyte) Jean

Corelli, Marie 1855-1924......... **TCLC 51**
See also Mackay, Mary
See also DLB 34, 156

Corman, Cid...................... **CLC 9**
See also Corman, Sidney
See also CAAS 2; DLB 5

Corman, Sidney 1924-
See Corman, Cid
See also CA 85-88; CANR 44; DAM POET

Cormier, Robert (Edmund)
1925- ..... **CLC 12, 30; DA; DAB; DAC**
See also AAYA 3; CA 1-4R; CANR 5, 23;
CDALB 1968-1988; CLR 12; DAM MST,
NOV; DLB 52; INT CANR-23; JRDA;
MAICYA; MTCW; SATA 10, 45, 83

Corn, Alfred (DeWitt III) 1943-.... **CLC 33**
See also CA 104; CANR 44; DLB 120;
DLBY 80

Corneille, Pierre 1606-1684.... **LC 28; DAB**
See also DAM MST

Cornwell, David (John Moore)
1931- .... **CLC 9, 15**
See also le Carre, John
See also CA 5-8R; CANR 13, 33;
DAM POP; MTCW

Corso, (Nunzio) Gregory 1930-... **CLC 1, 11**
See also CA 5-8R; CANR 41; DLB 5, 16;
MTCW

Cortazar, Julio
1914-1984 ...... **CLC 2, 3, 5, 10, 13, 15,**
33, 34, 92; HLC; SSC 7
See also CA 21-24R; CANR 12, 32;
DAM MULT, NOV; DLB 113; HW;
MTCW

CORTES, HERNAN 1484-1547..... **LC 31**

Corwin, Cecil
See Kornbluth, C(yril) M.

Cosic, Dobrica 1921- .... **CLC 14**
See also CA 122; 138

Costain, Thomas B(ertram)
1885-1965 .... **CLC 30**
See also CA 5-8R; 25-28R; DLB 9

Costantini, Humberto
1924(?)-1987 .... **CLC 49**
See also CA 131; 122; HW

Costello, Elvis 1955-.............. **CLC 21**

Cotter, Joseph Seamon Sr.
1861-1949 .... **TCLC 28; BLC**
See also BW 1; CA 124; DAM MULT;
DLB 50

Couch, Arthur Thomas Quiller
See Quiller-Couch, Arthur Thomas

Coulton, James
See Hansen, Joseph

Couperus, Louis (Marie Anne)
1863-1923 .... **TCLC 15**
See also CA 115

Coupland, Douglas 1961-..... **CLC 85; DAC**
See also CA 142; DAM POP

Court, Wesli
See Turco, Lewis (Putnam)

Courtenay, Bryce 1933-........... **CLC 59**
See also CA 138

Courtney, Robert
See Ellison, Harlan (Jay)

Cousteau, Jacques-Yves 1910-...... **CLC 30**
See also CA 65-68; CANR 15; MTCW;
SATA 38

Coward, Noel (Peirce)
1899-1973 .... **CLC 1, 9, 29, 51**
See also AITN 1; CA 17-18; 41-44R;
CANR 35; CAP 2; CDBLB 1914-1945;
DAM DRAM; DLB 10; MTCW

Cowley, Malcolm 1898-1989 .... **CLC 39**
See also CA 5-8R; 128; CANR 3; DLB 4,
48; DLBY 81, 89; MTCW

Cowper, William 1731-1800....... **NCLC 8**
See also DAM POET; DLB 104, 109

Cox, William Trevor 1928- ... **CLC 9, 14, 71**
See also Trevor, William
See also CA 9-12R; CANR 4, 37;
DAM NOV; DLB 14; INT CANR-37;
MTCW

Coyne, P. J.
See Masters, Hilary

Cozzens, James Gould
1903-1978 .... **CLC 1, 4, 11, 92**
See also CA 9-12R; 81-84; CANR 19;
CDALB 1941-1968; DLB 9; DLBD 2;
DLBY 84; MTCW

Crabbe, George 1754-1832...... **NCLC 26**
See also DLB 93

Craddock, Charles Egbert
See Murfree, Mary Noailles

Craig, A. A.
See Anderson, Poul (William)

Craik, Dinah Maria (Mulock)
1826-1887 .... **NCLC 38**
See also DLB 35, 163; MAICYA; SATA 34

Cram, Ralph Adams 1863-1942.... **TCLC 45**

Crane, (Harold) Hart
1899-1932 ...... **TCLC 2, 5; DA; DAB;
DAC; PC 3; WLC**
See also CA 104; 127; CDALB 1917-1929;
DAM MST, POET; DLB 4, 48; MTCW

Crane, R(onald) S(almon)
1886-1967 .... **CLC 27**
See also CA 85-88; DLB 63

Crane, Stephen (Townley)
1871-1900 ...... **TCLC 11, 17, 32; DA;
DAB; DAC; SSC 7; WLC**
See also CA 109; 140; CDALB 1865-1917;
DAM MST, NOV, POET; DLB 12, 54,
78; YABC 2

Crase, Douglas 1944-............. **CLC 58**
See also CA 106

Crashaw, Richard 1612(?)-1649...... **LC 24**
See also DLB 126

Craven, Margaret
1901-1980 .... **CLC 17; DAC**
See also CA 103

Crawford, F(rancis) Marion
1854-1909 .... **TCLC 10**
See also CA 107; DLB 71

Crawford, Isabella Valancy
1850-1887 .... **NCLC 12**
See also DLB 92

Crayon, Geoffrey
See Irving, Washington

Creasey, John 1908-1973.......... **CLC 11**
See also CA 5-8R; 41-44R; CANR 8;
DLB 77; MTCW

Crebillon, Claude Prosper Jolyot de (fils)
1707-1777 .... **LC 28**

Credo
See Creasey, John

Creeley, Robert (White)
1926- ..... **CLC 1, 2, 4, 8, 11, 15, 36, 78**
See also CA 1-4R; CAAS 10; CANR 23, 43;
DAM POET; DLB 5, 16; MTCW

Crews, Harry (Eugene)
1935- .... **CLC 6, 23, 49**
See also AITN 1; CA 25-28R; CANR 20;
DLB 6, 143; MTCW

Crichton, (John) Michael
1942- .... **CLC 2, 6, 54, 90**
See also AAYA 10; AITN 2; CA 25-28R;
CANR 13, 40; DAM NOV, POP;
DLBY 81; INT CANR-13; JRDA;
MTCW; SATA 9

Crispin, Edmund .... **CLC 22**
See also Montgomery, (Robert) Bruce
See also DLB 87

Cristofer, Michael 1945(?)- .... **CLC 28**
See also CA 110; DAM DRAM; DLB 7

Croce, Benedetto 1866-1952 ...... **TCLC 37**
See also CA 120

Crockett, David 1786-1836 .... **NCLC 8**
See also DLB 3, 11

Crockett, Davy
See Crockett, David

Crofts, Freeman Wills
1879-1957 .... **TCLC 55**
See also CA 115; DLB 77

Croker, John Wilson 1780-1857 .. **NCLC 10**
See also DLB 110

Crommelynck, Fernand 1885-1970 .. **CLC 75**
See also CA 89-92

Cronin, A(rchibald) J(oseph)
1896-1981 .... **CLC 32**
See also CA 1-4R; 102; CANR 5; SATA 47;
SATA-Obit 25

Cross, Amanda
See Heilbrun, Carolyn G(old)

Crothers, Rachel 1878(?)-1958..... **TCLC 19**
See also CA 113; DLB 7

Croves, Hal
See Traven, B.

Crow Dog, Mary .... **CLC 93**
See also Brave Bird, Mary

Crowfield, Christopher
See Stowe, Harriet (Elizabeth) Beecher

Crowley, Aleister .... **TCLC 7**
See also Crowley, Edward Alexander

Crowley, Edward Alexander 1875-1947
See Crowley, Aleister
See also CA 104

Crowley, John 1942-.............. **CLC 57**
See also CA 61-64; CANR 43; DLBY 82;
SATA 65

Crud
See Crumb, R(obert)

Crumarums
See Crumb, R(obert)

Crumb, R(obert) 1943-............ **CLC 17**
See also CA 106

Crumbum
See Crumb, R(obert)

Crumski
See Crumb, R(obert)

Crum the Bum
See Crumb, R(obert)

Crunk
See Crumb, R(obert)

Crustt
See Crumb, R(obert)

Cryer, Gretchen (Kiger) 1935-...... **CLC 21**
See also CA 114; 123

Csath, Geza 1887-1919.......... **TCLC 13**
See also CA 111

Cudlip, David 1933- .... **CLC 34**

Cullen, Countee
1903-1946 ...... **TCLC 4, 37; BLC; DA;
DAC**
See also BW 1; CA 108; 124;
CDALB 1917-1929; DAM MST, MULT,
POET; DLB 4, 48, 51; MTCW; SATA 18

Cum, R.
See Crumb, R(obert)

Cummings, Bruce F(rederick) 1889-1919
See Barbellion, W. N. P.
See also CA 123

Cummings, E(dward) E(stlin)
1894-1962 ...... **CLC 1, 3, 8, 12, 15, 68;
DA; DAB; DAC; PC 5; WLC 2**
See also CA 73-76; CANR 31;
CDALB 1929-1941; DAM MST, POET;
DLB 4, 48; MTCW

Cunha, Euclides (Rodrigues Pimenta) da
1866-1909 .... **TCLC 24**
See also CA 123

Cunningham, E. V.
See Fast, Howard (Melvin)

Cunningham, J(ames) V(incent)
1911-1985 .... **CLC 3, 31**
See also CA 1-4R; 115; CANR 1, DLB 5

Cunningham, Julia (Woolfolk)
1916- .... **CLC 12**
See also CA 9-12R; CANR 4, 19, 36;
JRDA; MAICYA; SAAS 2; SATA 1, 26

Cunningham, Michael 1952- .... **CLC 34**
See also CA 136

Cunninghame Graham, R(obert) B(ontine)
1852-1936 .... **TCLC 19**
See also Graham, R(obert) B(ontine)
Cunninghame
See also CA 119; DLB 98

Currie, Ellen 19(?)-.............. **CLC 44**

Curtin, Philip
See Lowndes, Marie Adelaide (Belloc)

Curtis, Price
See Ellison, Harlan (Jay)

Cutrate, Joe
See Spiegelman, Art

Czaczkes, Shmuel Yosef
See Agnon, S(hmuel) Y(osef Halevi)

Dabrowska, Maria (Szumska)
1889-1965 .... **CLC 15**
See also CA 106

Dabydeen, David 1955- .... **CLC 34**
See also BW 1; CA 125

Dacey, Philip 1939- .... **CLC 51**
See also CA 37-40R; CAAS 17; CANR 14,
32; DLB 105

Dagerman, Stig (Halvard)
1923-1954 .... **TCLC 17**
See also CA 117

de la Mare, Walter (John)
1873-1956 .... **TCLC 4, 53; DAB; DAC;**
SSC 14; WLC
See also CDBLB 1914-1945; CLR 23;
DAM MST, POET; DLB 162; SATA 16

Delaney, Franey
See O'Hara, John (Henry)

Delaney, Shelagh 1939- .... **CLC 29**
See also CA 17-20R; CANR 30;
CDBLB 1960 to Present; DAM DRAM;
DLB 13; MTCW

Delany, Mary (Granville Pendarves)
1700-1788 .... **LC 12**

Delany, Samuel R(ay, Jr.)
1942- .... **CLC 8, 14, 38; BLC**
See also BW 2; CA 81-84; CANR 27, 43;
DAM MULT; DLB 8, 33; MTCW

De La Ramee, (Marie) Louise 1839-1908
See Ouida
See also SATA 20

de la Roche, Mazo 1879-1961 ...... **CLC 14**
See also CA 85-88; CANR 30; DLB 68;
SATA 64

Delbanco, Nicholas (Franklin)
1942- .... **CLC 6, 13**
See also CA 17-20R; CAAS 2; CANR 29;
DLB 6

del Castillo, Michel 1933- .... **CLC 38**
See also CA 109

Deledda, Grazia (Cosima)
1875(?)-1936 .... **TCLC 23**
See also CA 123

Delibes, Miguel .... **CLC 8, 18**
See also Delibes Setien, Miguel

Delibes Setien, Miguel 1920-
See Delibes, Miguel
See also CA 45-48; CANR 1, 32; HW;
MTCW

DeLillo, Don
1936- ..... **CLC 8, 10, 13, 27, 39, 54, 76**
See also BEST 89:1; CA 81-84; CANR 21;
DAM NOV, POP; DLB 6; MTCW

de Lisser, H. G.
See De Lisser, Herbert George
See also DLB 117

De Lisser, Herbert George
1878-1944 .... **TCLC 12**
See also de Lisser, H. G.
See also BW 2; CA 109

Deloria, Vine (Victor), Jr. 1933-.... **CLC 21**
See also CA 53-56; CANR 5, 20, 48;
DAM MULT; MTCW; NNAL; SATA 21

Del Vecchio, John M(ichael)
1947- .... **CLC 29**
See also CA 110; DLBD 9

de Man, Paul (Adolph Michel)
1919-1983 .... **CLC 55**
See also CA 128; 111; DLB 67; MTCW

De Marinis, Rick 1934- .... **CLC 54**
See also CA 57-60; CANR 9, 25, 50

Dembry, R. Emmet
See Murfree, Mary Noailles

Demby, William 1922-....... **CLC 53; BLC**
See also BW 1; CA 81-84; DAM MULT;
DLB 33

Demijohn, Thom
See Disch, Thomas M(ichael)

de Montherlant, Henry (Milon)
See Montherlant, Henry (Milon) de

Demosthenes 384B.C.-322B.C. .... **CMLC 13**

de Natale, Francine
See Malzberg, Barry N(athaniel)

Denby, Edwin (Orr) 1903-1983..... **CLC 48**
See also CA 138; 110

Denis, Julio
See Cortazar, Julio

Denmark, Harrison
See Zelazny, Roger (Joseph)

Dennis, John 1658-1734............ **LC 11**
See also DLB 101

Dennis, Nigel (Forbes) 1912-1989.... **CLC 8**
See also CA 25-28R; 129; DLB 13, 15;
MTCW

De Palma, Brian (Russell) 1940-.... **CLC 20**
See also CA 109

De Quincey, Thomas 1785-1859 ... **NCLC 4**
See also CDBLB 1789-1832; DLB 110; 144

Deren, Eleanora 1908(?)-1961
See Deren, Maya
See also CA 111

Deren, Maya .... **CLC 16**
See also Deren, Eleanora

Derleth, August (William)
1909-1971 .... **CLC 31**
See also CA 1-4R; 29-32R; CANR 4;
DLB 9; SATA 5

Der Nister 1884-1950............ **TCLC 56**

de Routisie, Albert
See Aragon, Louis

Derrida, Jacques 1930-......... **CLC 24, 87**
See also CA 124; 127

Derry Down Derry
See Lear, Edward

Dersonnes, Jacques
See Simenon, Georges (Jacques Christian)

Desai, Anita 1937- ...... **CLC 19, 37; DAB**
See also CA 81-84; CANR 33; DAM NOV;
MTCW; SATA 63

de Saint-Luc, Jean
See Glassco, John

de Saint Roman, Arnaud
See Aragon, Louis

Descartes, Rene 1596-1650 .... **LC 20**

De Sica, Vittorio 1901(?)-1974 ..... **CLC 20**
See also CA 117

Desnos, Robert 1900-1945........ **TCLC 22**
See also CA 121; 151

Destouches, Louis-Ferdinand
1894-1961 .... **CLC 9, 15**
See also Celine, Louis-Ferdinand
See also CA 85-88; CANR 28; MTCW

Deutsch, Babette 1895-1982 .... **CLC 18**
See also CA 1-4R; 108; CANR 4; DLB 45;
SATA 1; SATA-Obit 33

Devenant, William 1606-1649 ...... **LC 13**

Devkota, Laxmiprasad
1909-1959 .... **TCLC 23**
See also CA 123

De Voto, Bernard (Augustine)
1897-1955 .... **TCLC 29**
See also CA 113; DLB 9

De Vries, Peter
1910-1993 .... **CLC 1, 2, 3, 7, 10, 28, 46**
See also CA 17-20R; 142; CANR 41;
DAM NOV; DLB 6; DLBY 82; MTCW

Dexter, Martin
See Faust, Frederick (Schiller)

Dexter, Pete 1943-............. **CLC 34, 55**
See also BEST 89:2; CA 127; 131;
DAM POP; INT 131; MTCW

Diamano, Silmang
See Senghor, Leopold Sedar

Diamond, Neil 1941- .... **CLC 30**
See also CA 108

Diaz del Castillo, Bernal 1496-1584 .. **LC 31**

di Bassetto, Corno
See Shaw, George Bernard

Dick, Philip K(indred)
1928-1982 .... **CLC 10, 30, 72**
See also CA 49-52; 106; CANR 2, 16;
DAM NOV, POP; DLB 8; MTCW

Dickens, Charles (John Huffam)
1812-1870 ...... **NCLC 3, 8, 18, 26, 37,**
50; DA; DAB; DAC; SSC 17; WLC
See also CDBLB 1832-1890; DAM MST,
NOV; DLB 21, 55, 70, 159, 166; JRDA;
MAICYA; SATA 15

Dickey, James (Lafayette)
1923- .... **CLC 1, 2, 4, 7, 10, 15, 47**
See also AITN 1, 2; CA 9-12R; CABS 2;
CANR 10, 48; CDALB 1968-1988;
DAM NOV, POET, POP; DLB 5;
DLBD 7; DLBY 82, 93; INT CANR-10;
MTCW

Dickey, William 1928-1994 ...... **CLC 3, 28**
See also CA 9-12R; 145; CANR 24; DLB 5

Dickinson, Charles 1951-.......... **CLC 49**
See also CA 128

Dickinson, Emily (Elizabeth)
1830-1886 .... **NCLC 21; DA; DAB;**
DAC; PC 1; WLC
See also CDALB 1865-1917; DAM MST,
POET; DLB 1; SATA 29

Dickinson, Peter (Malcolm)
1927- .... **CLC 12, 35**
See also AAYA 9; CA 41-44R; CANR 31;
CLR 29; DLB 87, 161; JRDA; MAICYA;
SATA 5, 62

Dickson, Carr
See Carr, John Dickson

Dickson, Carter
See Carr, John Dickson

Diderot, Denis 1713-1784 .... **LC 26**

Didion, Joan 1934-..... **CLC 1, 3, 8, 14, 32**
See also AITN 1; CA 5-8R; CANR 14, 52;
CDALB 1968-1988; DAM NOV; DLB 2;
DLBY 81, 86; MTCW

Dietrich, Robert
See Hunt, E(verette) Howard, (Jr.)

Dillard, Annie 1945-............ **CLC 9, 60**
See also AAYA 6; CA 49-52; CANR 3, 43;
DAM NOV; DLBY 80; MTCW;
SATA 10

Dreiser, Theodore (Herman Albert)
1871-1945 . . . . **TCLC 10, 18, 35; DA;**
DAC; WLC
See also CA 106; 132; CDALB 1865-1917;
DAM MST, NOV; DLB 9, 12, 102, 137;
DLBD 1; MTCW

Drexler, Rosalyn 1926- . . . . **CLC 2, 6**
See also CA 81-84

Dreyer, Carl Theodor 1889-1968. . . . **CLC 16**
See also CA 116

Drieu la Rochelle, Pierre(-Eugene)
1893-1945 . . . . **TCLC 21**
See also CA 117; DLB 72

Drinkwater, John 1882-1937. . . . . . **TCLC 57**
See also CA 109; 149; DLB 10, 19, 149

Drop Shot
See Cable, George Washington

Droste-Hulshoff, Annette Freiin von
1797-1848 . . . . **NCLC 3**
See also DLB 133

Drummond, Walter
See Silverberg, Robert

Drummond, William Henry
1854-1907 . . . . **TCLC 25**
See also DLB 92

Drummond de Andrade, Carlos
1902-1987 . . . . **CLC 18**
See also Andrade, Carlos Drummond de
See also CA 132; 123

Drury, Allen (Stuart) 1918- . . . . **CLC 37**
See also CA 57-60; CANR 18, 52;
INT CANR-18

Dryden, John
1631-1700 . . . . **LC 3, 21; DA; DAB;**
DAC; DC 3; WLC
See also CDBLB 1660-1789; DAM DRAM,
MST, POET; DLB 80, 101, 131

Duberman, Martin 1930- . . . . **CLC 8**
See also CA 1-4R; CANR 2

Dubie, Norman (Evans) 1945- . . . . . . **CLC 36**
See also CA 69-72; CANR 12; DLB 120

Du Bois, W(illiam) E(dward) B(urghardt)
1868-1963 . . . . . . **CLC 1, 2, 13, 64; BLC;**
DA; DAC; WLC
See also BW 1; CA 85-88; CANR 34;
CDALB 1865-1917; DAM MST, MULT,
NOV; DLB 47, 50, 91; MTCW; SATA 42

Dubus, Andre 1936- . . . **CLC 13, 36; SSC 15**
See also CA 21-24R; CANR 17; DLB 130;
INT CANR-17

Duca Minimo
See D'Annunzio, Gabriele

Ducharme, Rejean 1941- . . . . **CLC 74**
See also DLB 60

Duclos, Charles Pinot 1704-1772 . . . . . **LC 1**

Dudek, Louis 1918- . . . . **CLC 11, 19**
See also CA 45-48; CAAS 14; CANR 1;
DLB 88

Duerrenmatt, Friedrich
1921-1990 . . . . . . **CLC 1, 4, 8, 11, 15, 43**
See also CA 17-20R; CANR 33;
DAM DRAM; DLB 69, 124; MTCW

Duffy, Bruce (?)- . . . . **CLC 50**

Duffy, Maureen 1933- . . . . **CLC 37**
See also CA 25-28R; CANR 33; DLB 14;
MTCW

Dugan, Alan 1923- . . . . **CLC 2, 6**
See also CA 81-84; DLB 5

du Gard, Roger Martin
See Martin du Gard, Roger

Duhamel, Georges 1884-1966 . . . . **CLC 8**
See also CA 81-84; 25-28R; CANR 35;
DLB 65; MTCW

Dujardin, Edouard (Emile Louis)
1861-1949 . . . . **TCLC 13**
See also CA 109; DLB 123

Dumas, Alexandre (Davy de la Pailleterie)
1802-1870 . . . . **NCLC 11; DA; DAB;**
DAC; WLC
See also DAM MST, NOV; DLB 119;
SATA 18

Dumas, Alexandre
1824-1895 . . . . **NCLC 9; DC 1**

Dumas, Claudine
See Malzberg, Barry N(athaniel)

Dumas, Henry L. 1934-1968 . . . . . **CLC 6, 62**
See also BW 1; CA 85-88; DLB 41

du Maurier, Daphne
1907-1989 . . . . **CLC 6, 11, 59; DAB;**
DAC; SSC 18
See also CA 5-8R; 128; CANR 6;
DAM MST, POP; MTCW; SATA 27;
SATA-Obit 60

Dunbar, Paul Laurence
1872-1906 . . . . . . **TCLC 2, 12; BLC; DA;**
DAC; PC 5; SSC 8; WLC
See also BW 1; CA 104; 124;
CDALB 1865-1917; DAM MST, MULT,
POET; DLB 50, 54, 78; SATA 34

Dunbar, William 1460(?)-1530(?) . . . . **LC 20**
See also DLB 132, 146

Duncan, Lois 1934- . . . . **CLC 26**
See also AAYA 4; CA 1-4R; CANR 2, 23,
36; CLR 29; JRDA; MAICYA; SAAS 2;
SATA 1, 36, 75

Duncan, Robert (Edward)
1919-1988 . . . . **CLC 1, 2, 4, 7, 15, 41, 55;**
PC 2
See also CA 9-12R; 124; CANR 28;
DAM POET; DLB 5, 16; MTCW

Duncan, Sara Jeannette
1861-1922 . . . . **TCLC 60**
See also DLB 92

Dunlap, William 1766-1839 . . . . **NCLC 2**
See also DLB 30, 37, 59

Dunn, Douglas (Eaglesham)
1942- . . . . **CLC 6, 40**
See also CA 45-48; CANR 2, 33; DLB 40;
MTCW

Dunn, Katherine (Karen) 1945- . . . . . **CLC 71**
See also CA 33-36R

Dunn, Stephen 1939- . . . . **CLC 36**
See also CA 33-36R; CANR 12, 48;
DLB 105

Dunne, Finley Peter 1867-1936. . . . **TCLC 28**
See also CA 108; DLB 11, 23

Dunne, John Gregory 1932- . . . . **CLC 28**
See also CA 25-28R; CANR 14, 50;
DLBY 80

Dunsany, Edward John Moreton Drax
Plunkett 1878-1957
See Dunsany, Lord
See also CA 104; 148; DLB 10

Dunsany, Lord . . . . **TCLC 2, 59**
See also Dunsany, Edward John Moreton
Drax Plunkett
See also DLB 77, 153, 156

du Perry, Jean
See Simenon, Georges (Jacques Christian)

Durang, Christopher (Ferdinand)
1949- . . . . **CLC 27, 38**
See also CA 105; CANR 50

Duras, Marguerite
1914-1996 . . **CLC 3, 6, 11, 20, 34, 40, 68**
See also CA 25-28R; 151; CANR 50;
DLB 83; MTCW

Durban, (Rosa) Pam 1947- . . . . **CLC 39**
See also CA 123

Durcan, Paul 1944- . . . . **CLC 43, 70**
See also CA 134; DAM POET

Durkheim, Emile 1858-1917 . . . . . . **TCLC 55**

Durrell, Lawrence (George)
1912-1990 . . . . **CLC 1, 4, 6, 8, 13, 27, 41**
See also CA 9-12R; 132; CANR 40;
CDBLB 1945-1960; DAM NOV; DLB 15,
27; DLBY 90; MTCW

Durrenmatt, Friedrich
See Duerrenmatt, Friedrich

Dutt, Toru 1856-1877. . . . . **NCLC 29**

Dwight, Timothy 1752-1817. . . . . . **NCLC 13**
See also DLB 37

Dworkin, Andrea 1946- . . . . **CLC 43**
See also CA 77-80; CAAS 21; CANR 16,
39; INT CANR-16; MTCW

Dwyer, Deanna
See Koontz, Dean R(ay)

Dwyer, K. R.
See Koontz, Dean R(ay)

Dylan, Bob 1941- . . . . . . **CLC 3, 4, 6, 12, 77**
See also CA 41-44R; DLB 16

Eagleton, Terence (Francis) 1943-
See Eagleton, Terry
See also CA 57-60; CANR 7, 23; MTCW

Eagleton, Terry . . . . **CLC 63**
See also Eagleton, Terence (Francis)

Early, Jack
See Scoppettone, Sandra

East, Michael
See West, Morris L(anglo)

Eastaway, Edward
See Thomas, (Philip) Edward

Eastlake, William (Derry) 1917- . . . . . **CLC 8**
See also CA 5-8R; CAAS 1; CANR 5;
DLB 6; INT CANR-5

Eastman, Charles A(lexander)
1858-1939 . . . . **TCLC 55**
See also DAM MULT; NNAL; YABC 1

Eberhart, Richard (Ghormley)
1904- . . . . **CLC 3, 11, 19, 56**
See also CA 1-4R; CANR 2;
CDALB 1941-1968; DAM POET;
DLB 48; MTCW

Eberstadt, Fernanda 1960-......... **CLC 39**
See also CA 136

Echegaray (y Eizaguirre), Jose (Maria Waldo)
1832-1916 .... **TCLC 4**
See also CA 104; CANR 32; HW; MTCW

Echeverria, (Jose) Esteban (Antonino)
1805-1851 .... **NCLC 18**

Echo
See Proust, (Valentin-Louis-George-Eugene-)
Marcel

Eckert, Allan W. 1931- .... **CLC 17**
See also AAYA 18; CA 13-16R; CANR 14,
45; INT CANR-14; SAAS 21; SATA 29;
SATA-Brief 27

Eckhart, Meister 1260(?)-1328(?) .. **CMLC 9**
See also DLB 115

Eckmar, F. R.
See de Hartog, Jan

Eco, Umberto 1932-........... **CLC 28, 60**
See also BEST 90:1; CA 77-80; CANR 12,
33; DAM NOV, POP; MTCW

Eddison, E(ric) R(ucker)
1882-1945 .... **TCLC 15**
See also CA 109

Edel, (Joseph) Leon 1907-...... **CLC 29, 34**
See also CA 1-4R; CANR 1, 22; DLB 103;
INT CANR-22

Eden, Emily 1797-1869 .... **NCLC 10**

Edgar, David 1948-.............. **CLC 42**
See also CA 57-60; CANR 12;
DAM DRAM; DLB 13; MTCW

Edgerton, Clyde (Carlyle) 1944-.... **CLC 39**
See also AAYA 17; CA 118; 134; INT 134

Edgeworth, Maria 1768-1849... **NCLC 1, 51**
See also DLB 116, 159, 163; SATA 21

Edmonds, Paul
See Kuttner, Henry

Edmonds, Walter D(umaux) 1903-.. **CLC 35**
See also CA 5-8R; CANR 2; DLB 9;
MAICYA; SAAS 4; SATA 1, 27

Edmondson, Wallace
See Ellison, Harlan (Jay)

Edson, Russell.................... **CLC 13**
See also CA 33-36R

Edwards, Bronwen Elizabeth
See Rose, Wendy

Edwards, G(erald) B(asil)
1899-1976 .... **CLC 25**
See also CA 110

Edwards, Gus 1939-.............. **CLC 43**
See also CA 108; INT 108

Edwards, Jonathan
1703-1758 .... **LC 7; DA; DAC**
See also DAM MST; DLB 24

Efron, Marina Ivanovna Tsvetaeva
See Tsvetaeva (Efron), Marina (Ivanovna)

Ehle, John (Marsden, Jr.) 1925-.... **CLC 27**
See also CA 9-12R

Ehrenbourg, Ilya (Grigoryevich)
See Ehrenburg, Ilya (Grigoryevich)

Ehrenburg, Ilya (Grigoryevich)
1891-1967 .... **CLC 18, 34, 62**
See also CA 102; 25-28R

Ehrenburg, Ilyo (Grigoryevich)
See Ehrenburg, Ilya (Grigoryevich)

Eich, Guenter 1907-1972 .... **CLC 15**
See also CA 111; 93-96; DLB 69, 124

Eichendorff, Joseph Freiherr von
1788-1857 .... **NCLC 8**
See also DLB 90

Eigner, Larry..................... **CLC 9**
See also Eigner, Laurence (Joel)
See also CAAS 23; DLB 5

Eigner, Laurence (Joel) 1927-1996
See Eigner, Larry
See also CA 9-12R; 151; CANR 6

Einstein, Albert 1879-1955 ...... **TCLC 65**
See also CA 121; 133; MTCW

Eiseley, Loren Corey 1907-1977..... **CLC 7**
See also AAYA 5; CA 1-4R; 73-76;
CANR 6

Eisenstadt, Jill 1963-............. **CLC 50**
See also CA 140

Eisenstein, Sergei (Mikhailovich)
1898-1948 .... **TCLC 57**
See also CA 114; 149

Eisner, Simon
See Kornbluth, C(yril) M.

Ekeloef, (Bengt) Gunnar
1907-1968 .... **CLC 27**
See also CA 123; 25-28R; DAM POET

Ekelof, (Bengt) Gunnar
See Ekeloef, (Bengt) Gunnar

Ekwensi, C. O. D.
See Ekwensi, Cyprian (Odiatu Duaka)

Ekwensi, Cyprian (Odiatu Duaka)
1921- .... **CLC 4; BLC**
See also BW 2; CA 29-32R; CANR 18, 42;
DAM MULT; DLB 117; MTCW;
SATA 66

Elaine........................ **TCLC 18**
See also Leverson, Ada

El Crummo
See Crumb, R(obert)

Elia
See Lamb, Charles

Eliade, Mircea 1907-1986 .... **CLC 19**
See also CA 65-68; 119; CANR 30; MTCW

Eliot, A. D.
See Jewett, (Theodora) Sarah Orne

Eliot, Alice
See Jewett, (Theodora) Sarah Orne

Eliot, Dan
See Silverberg, Robert

Eliot, George
1819-1880 ..... **NCLC 4, 13, 23, 41, 49;**
DA; DAB; DAC; WLC
See also CDBLB 1832-1890; DAM MST,
NOV; DLB 21, 35, 55

Eliot, John 1604-1690 .... **LC 5**
See also DLB 24

Eliot, T(homas) S(tearns)
1888-1965 ..... **CLC 1, 2, 3, 6, 9, 10, 13,**
15, 24, 34, 41, 55, 57; DA; DAB; DAC;
PC 5; WLC 2
See also CA 5-8R; 25-28R; CANR 41;
CDALB 1929-1941; DAM DRAM, MST,
POET; DLB 7, 10, 45, 63; DLBY 88;
MTCW

Elizabeth 1866-1941............. **TCLC 41**

Elkin, Stanley L(awrence)
1930-1995 ...... **CLC 4, 6, 9, 14, 27, 51,**
91; SSC 12
See also CA 9-12R; 148; CANR 8, 46;
DAM NOV, POP; DLB 2, 28; DLBY 80;
INT CANR-8; MTCW

Elledge, Scott.................... **CLC 34**

Elliott, Don
See Silverberg, Robert

Elliott, George P(aul) 1918-1980..... **CLC 2**
See also CA 1-4R; 97-100; CANR 2

Elliott, Janice 1931-.............. **CLC 47**
See also CA 13-16R; CANR 8, 29; DLB 14

Elliott, Sumner Locke 1917-1991 ... **CLC 38**
See also CA 5-8R; 134; CANR 2, 21

Elliott, William
See Bradbury, Ray (Douglas)

Ellis, A. E........................ **CLC 7**

Ellis, Alice Thomas................ **CLC 40**
See also Haycraft, Anna

Ellis, Bret Easton 1964-........ **CLC 39, 71**
See also AAYA 2; CA 118; 123; CANR 51;
DAM POP; INT 123

Ellis, (Henry) Havelock
1859-1939 .... **TCLC 14**
See also CA 109

Ellis, Landon
See Ellison, Harlan (Jay)

Ellis, Trey 1962-................. **CLC 55**
See also CA 146

Ellison, Harlan (Jay)
1934- .... **CLC 1, 13, 42; SSC 14**
See also CA 5-8R; CANR 5, 46;
DAM POP; DLB 8; INT CANR-5;
MTCW

Ellison, Ralph (Waldo)
1914-1994 .... **CLC 1, 3, 11, 54, 86;**
BLC; DA; DAB; DAC; WLC
See also BW 1; CA 9-12R; 145; CANR 24;
CDALB 1941-1968; DAM MST, MULT,
NOV; DLB 2, 76; DLBY 94; MTCW

Ellmann, Lucy (Elizabeth) 1956-.... **CLC 61**
See also CA 128

Ellmann, Richard (David)
1918-1987 .... **CLC 50**
See also BEST 89:2; CA 1-4R; 122;
CANR 2, 28; DLB 103; DLBY 87;
MTCW

Elman, Richard 1934-.............. **CLC 19**
See also CA 17-20R; CAAS 3; CANR 47

Elron
See Hubbard, L(afayette) Ron(ald)

Eluard, Paul.................... **TCLC 7, 41**
See also Grindel, Eugene

Elyot, Sir Thomas 1490(?)-1546 ..... **LC 11**

Elytis, Odysseus 1911-1996..... **CLC 15, 49**
See also CA 102; 151; DAM POET; MTCW

Emecheta, (Florence Onye) Buchi
1944-.............. **CLC 14, 48; BLC**
See also BW 2; CA 81-84; CANR 27;
DAM MULT; DLB 117; MTCW;
SATA 66

Emerson, Ralph Waldo
1803-1882 ..... **NCLC 1, 38; DA; DAB;**
DAC; WLC
See also CDALB 1640-1865; DAM MST,
POET; DLB 1, 59, 73

Eminescu, Mihail 1850-1889 ..... **NCLC 33**

Empson, William
1906-1984 .... **CLC 3, 8, 19, 33, 34**
See also CA 17-20R; 112; CANR 31;
DLB 20; MTCW

Enchi Fumiko (Ueda) 1905-1986.... **CLC 31**
See also CA 129; 121

Ende, Michael (Andreas Helmuth)
1929-1995 .... **CLC 31**
See also CA 118; 124; 149; CANR 36;
CLR 14; DLB 75; MAICYA; SATA 61;
SATA-Brief 42; SATA-Obit 86

Endo, Shusaku 1923- ..... **CLC 7, 14, 19, 54**
See also CA 29-32R; CANR 21;
DAM NOV; MTCW

Engel, Marian 1933-1985.......... **CLC 36**
See also CA 25-28R; CANR 12; DLB 53;
INT CANR-12

Engelhardt, Frederick
See Hubbard, L(afayette) Ron(ald)

Enright, D(ennis) J(oseph)
1920-.................... **CLC 4, 8, 31**
See also CA 1-4R; CANR 1, 42; DLB 27;
SATA 25

Enzensberger, Hans Magnus
1929-...................... **CLC 43**
See also CA 116; 119

Ephron, Nora 1941-.......... **CLC 17, 31**
See also AITN 2; CA 65-68; CANR 12, 39

Epsilon
See Betjeman, John

Epstein, Daniel Mark 1948- .... **CLC 7**
See also CA 49-52; CANR 2

Epstein, Jacob 1956- .... **CLC 19**
See also CA 114

Epstein, Joseph 1937-............. **CLC 39**
See also CA 112; 119; CANR 50

Epstein, Leslie 1938- .... **CLC 27**
See also CA 73-76; CAAS 12; CANR 23

Equiano, Olaudah
1745(?)-1797 .... **LC 16; BLC**
See also DAM MULT; DLB 37, 50

Erasmus, Desiderius 1469(?)-1536.... **LC 16**

Erdman, Paul E(mil) 1932- .... **CLC 25**
See also AITN 1; CA 61-64; CANR 13, 43

Erdrich, Louise 1954-.......... **CLC 39, 54**
See also AAYA 10; BEST 89:1; CA 114;
CANR 41; DAM MULT, NOV, POP;
DLB 152; MTCW; NNAL

Erenburg, Ilya (Grigoryevich)
See Ehrenburg, Ilya (Grigoryevich)

Erickson, Stephen Michael 1950-
See Erickson, Steve
See also CA 129

Erickson, Steve .... **CLC 64**
See also Erickson, Stephen Michael

Ericson, Walter
See Fast, Howard (Melvin)

Eriksson, Buntel
See Bergman, (Ernst) Ingmar

Ernaux, Annie 1940- .... **CLC 88**
See also CA 147

Eschenbach, Wolfram von
See Wolfram von Eschenbach

Eseki, Bruno
See Mphahlele, Ezekiel

Esenin, Sergei (Alexandrovich)
1895-1925 .... **TCLC 4**
See also CA 104

Eshleman, Clayton 1935-.......... **CLC 7**
See also CA 33-36R; CAAS 6; DLB 5

Espriella, Don Manuel Alvarez
See Southey, Robert

Espriu, Salvador 1913-1985........ **CLC 9**
See also CA 115; DLB 134

Espronceda, Jose de 1808-1842... **NCLC 39**

Esse, James
See Stephens, James

Esterbrook, Tom
See Hubbard, L(afayette) Ron(ald)

Estleman, Loren D. 1952- .... **CLC 48**
See also CA 85-88; CANR 27; DAM NOV,
POP; INT CANR-27; MTCW

Eugenides, Jeffrey 1960(?)- .... **CLC 81**
See also CA 144

Euripides c. 485B.C.-406B.C. .... **DC 4**
See also DA; DAB; DAC; DAM DRAM,
MST

Evan, Evin
See Faust, Frederick (Schiller)

Evans, Evan
See Faust, Frederick (Schiller)

Evans, Marian
See Eliot, George

Evans, Mary Ann
See Eliot, George

Evarts, Esther
See Benson, Sally

Everett, Percival L. 1956- .... **CLC 57**
See also BW 2; CA 129

Everson, R(onald) G(ilmour)
1903-...................... **CLC 27**
See also CA 17-20R; DLB 88

Everson, William (Oliver)
1912-1994 .... **CLC 1, 5, 14**
See also CA 9-12R; 145; CANR 20; DLB 5,
16; MTCW

Evtushenko, Evgenii Aleksandrovich
See Yevtushenko, Yevgeny (Alexandrovich)

Ewart, Gavin (Buchanan)
1916-1995 .... **CLC 13, 46**
See also CA 89-92; 150; CANR 17, 46;
DLB 40; MTCW

Ewers, Hanns Heinz 1871-1943 ... **TCLC 12**
See also CA 109; 149

Ewing, Frederick R.
See Sturgeon, Theodore (Hamilton)

Exley, Frederick (Earl)
1929-1992 .... **CLC 6, 11**
See also AITN 2; CA 81-84; 138; DLB 143;
DLBY 81

Eynhardt, Guillermo
See Quiroga, Horacio (Sylvestre)

Ezekiel, Nissim 1924-............. **CLC 61**
See also CA 61-64

Ezekiel, Tish O'Dowd 1943-....... **CLC 34**
See also CA 129

Fadeyev, A.
See Bulgya, Alexander Alexandrovich

Fadeyev, Alexander.............. **TCLC 53**
See also Bulgya, Alexander Alexandrovich

Fagen, Donald 1948-.............. **CLC 26**

Fainzilberg, Ilya Arnoldovich 1897-1937
See Ilf, Ilya
See also CA 120

Fair, Ronald L. 1932-............. **CLC 18**
See also BW 1; CA 69-72; CANR 25;
DLB 33

Fairbairns, Zoe (Ann) 1948- .... **CLC 32**
See also CA 103; CANR 21

Falco, Gian
See Papini, Giovanni

Falconer, James
See Kirkup, James

Falconer, Kenneth
See Kornbluth, C(yril) M.

Falkland, Samuel
See Heijermans, Herman

Fallaci, Oriana 1930-............. **CLC 11**
See also CA 77-80; CANR 15; MTCW

Faludy, George 1913-............. **CLC 42**
See also CA 21-24R

Faludy, Gyoergy
See Faludy, George

Fanon, Frantz 1925-1961..... **CLC 74; BLC**
See also BW 1; CA 116; 89-92;
DAM MULT

Fanshawe, Ann 1625-1680 .... **LC 11**

Fante, John (Thomas) 1911-1983 ... **CLC 60**
See also CA 69-72; 109; CANR 23;
DLB 130; DLBY 83

Farah, Nuruddin 1945-....... **CLC 53; BLC**
See also BW 2; CA 106; DAM MULT;
DLB 125

Fargue, Leon-Paul 1876(?)-1947 ... **TCLC 11**
See also CA 109

Farigoule, Louis
See Romains, Jules

Farina, Richard 1936(?)-1966 .... **CLC 9**
See also CA 81-84; 25-28R

Farley, Walter (Lorimer)
1915-1989 .... **CLC 17**
See also CA 17-20R; CANR 8, 29; DLB 22;
JRDA; MAICYA; SATA 2, 43

Farmer, Philip Jose 1918-....... **CLC 1, 19**
See also CA 1-4R; CANR 4, 35; DLB 8;
MTCW

Farquhar, George 1677-1707........ **LC 21**
See also DAM DRAM; DLB 84

Farrell, J(ames) G(ordon)
1935-1979 .... **CLC 6**
See also CA 73-76; 89-92; CANR 36;
DLB 14; MTCW

Farrell, James T(homas)
1904-1979 .... **CLC 1, 4, 8, 11, 66**
See also CA 5-8R; 89-92; CANR 9; DLB 4,
9, 86; DLBD 2; MTCW

Farren, Richard J.
See Betjeman, John

Farren, Richard M.
See Betjeman, John

Fassbinder, Rainer Werner
1946-1982 .... **CLC 20**
See also CA 93-96; 106; CANR 31

Fast, Howard (Melvin) 1914- ...... **CLC 23**
See also AAYA 16; CA 1-4R; CAAS 18;
CANR 1, 33; DAM NOV; DLB 9;
INT CANR-33; SATA 7

Faulcon, Robert
See Holdstock, Robert P.

Faulkner, William (Cuthbert)
1897-1962 ..... **CLC 1, 3, 6, 8, 9, 11, 14,
18, 28, 52, 68; DA; DAB; DAC; SSC 1;
WLC**
See also AAYA 7; CA 81-84; CANR 33;
CDALB 1929-1941; DAM MST, NOV;
DLB 9, 11, 44, 102; DLBD 2; DLBY 86;
MTCW

Fauset, Jessie Redmon
1884(?)-1961 .... **CLC 19, 54; BLC**
See also BW 1; CA 109; DAM MULT;
DLB 51

Faust, Frederick (Schiller)
1892-1944(?) .... **TCLC 49**
See also CA 108; DAM POP

Faust, Irvin 1924-................ **CLC 8**
See also CA 33-36R; CANR 28; DLB 2, 28;
DLBY 80

Fawkes, Guy
See Benchley, Robert (Charles)

Fearing, Kenneth (Flexner)
1902-1961 .... **CLC 51**
See also CA 93-96; DLB 9

Fecamps, Elise
See Creasey, John

Federman, Raymond 1928- ...... **CLC 6, 47**
See also CA 17-20R; CAAS 8; CANR 10,
43; DLBY 80

Federspiel, J(uerg) F. 1931-........ **CLC 42**
See also CA 146

Feiffer, Jules (Ralph) 1929-.... **CLC 2, 8, 64**
See also AAYA 3; CA 17-20R; CANR 30;
DAM DRAM; DLB 7, 44;
INT CANR-30; MTCW; SATA 8, 61

Feige, Hermann Albert Otto Maximilian
See Traven, B.

Feinberg, David B. 1956-1994...... **CLC 59**
See also CA 135; 147

Feinstein, Elaine 1930-............ **CLC 36**
See also CA 69-72; CAAS 1; CANR 31;
DLB 14, 40; MTCW

Feldman, Irving (Mordecai) 1928-.... **CLC 7**
See also CA 1-4R; CANR 1

Fellini, Federico 1920-1993 ..... **CLC 16, 85**
See also CA 65-68; 143; CANR 33

Felsen, Henry Gregor 1916- .... **CLC 17**
See also CA 1-4R; CANR 1; SAAS 2;
SATA 1

Fenton, James Martin 1949-....... **CLC 32**
See also CA 102; DLB 40

Ferber, Edna 1887-1968........ **CLC 18, 93**
See also AITN 1; CA 5-8R; 25-28R; DLB 9,
28, 86; MTCW; SATA 7

Ferguson, Helen
See Kavan, Anna

Ferguson, Samuel 1810-1886..... **NCLC 33**
See also DLB 32

Fergusson, Robert 1750-1774 .... **LC 29**
See also DLB 109

Ferling, Lawrence
See Ferlinghetti, Lawrence (Monsanto)

Ferlinghetti, Lawrence (Monsanto)
1919(?)-........ **CLC 2, 6, 10, 27; PC 1**
See also CA 5-8R; CANR 3, 41;
CDALB 1941-1968; DAM POET; DLB 5,
16; MTCW

Fernandez, Vicente Garcia Huidobro
See Huidobro Fernandez, Vicente Garcia

Ferrer, Gabriel (Francisco Victor) Miro
See Miro (Ferrer), Gabriel (Francisco
Victor)

Ferrier, Susan (Edmonstone)
1782-1854 .... **NCLC 8**
See also DLB 116

Ferrigno, Robert 1948(?)-.......... **CLC 65**
See also CA 140

Ferron, Jacques 1921-1985 ... **CLC 94; DAC**
See also CA 117; 129; DLB 60

Feuchtwanger, Lion 1884-1958 ..... **TCLC 3**
See also CA 104; DLB 66

Feuillet, Octave 1821-1890 ...... **NCLC 45**

Feydeau, Georges (Leon Jules Marie)
1862-1921 .... **TCLC 22**
See also CA 113; DAM DRAM

Ficino, Marsilio 1433-1499 .... **LC 12**

Fiedeler, Hans
See Doeblin, Alfred

Fiedler, Leslie A(aron)
1917-.................. **CLC 4, 13, 24**
See also CA 9-12R; CANR 7; DLB 28, 67;
MTCW

Field, Andrew 1938-.............. **CLC 44**
See also CA 97-100; CANR 25

Field, Eugene 1850-1895 .... **NCLC 3**
See also DLB 23, 42, 140; DLBD 13;
MAICYA; SATA 16

Field, Gans T.
See Wellman, Manly Wade

Field, Michael .... **TCLC 43**

Field, Peter
See Hobson, Laura Z(ametkin)

Fielding, Henry
1707-1754 ...... **LC 1; DA; DAB; DAC;
WLC**
See also CDBLB 1660-1789; DAM DRAM,
MST, NOV; DLB 39, 84, 101

Fielding, Sarah 1710-1768........... **LC 1**
See also DLB 39

Fierstein, Harvey (Forbes) 1954- ... **CLC 33**
See also CA 123; 129; DAM DRAM, POP

Figes, Eva 1932-.................. **CLC 31**
See also CA 53-56; CANR 4, 44; DLB 14

Finch, Robert (Duer Claydon)
1900-....................... **CLC 18**
See also CA 57-60; CANR 9, 24, 49;
DLB 88

Findley, Timothy 1930- ...... **CLC 27; DAC**
See also CA 25-28R; CANR 12, 42;
DAM MST; DLB 53

Fink, William
See Mencken, H(enry) L(ouis)

Firbank, Louis 1942-
See Reed, Lou
See also CA 117

Firbank, (Arthur Annesley) Ronald
1886-1926 .... **TCLC 1**
See also CA 104; DLB 36

Fisher, M(ary) F(rances) K(ennedy)
1908-1992 .... **CLC 76, 87**
See also CA 77-80; 138; CANR 44

Fisher, Roy 1930-................ **CLC 25**
See also CA 81-84; CAAS 10; CANR 16;
DLB 40

Fisher, Rudolph
1897-1934 .... **TCLC 11; BLC**
See also BW 1; CA 107; 124; DAM MULT;
DLB 51, 102

Fisher, Vardis (Alvero) 1895-1968.... **CLC 7**
See also CA 5-8R; 25-28R; DLB 9

Fiske, Tarleton
See Bloch, Robert (Albert)

Fitch, Clarke
See Sinclair, Upton (Beall)

Fitch, John IV
See Cormier, Robert (Edmund)

Fitzgerald, Captain Hugh
See Baum, L(yman) Frank

FitzGerald, Edward 1809-1883 .... **NCLC 9**
See also DLB 32

Fitzgerald, F(rancis) Scott (Key)
1896-1940 .... **TCLC 1, 6, 14, 28, 55;
DA; DAB; DAC; SSC 6; WLC**
See also AITN 1; CA 110; 123;
CDALB 1917-1929; DAM MST, NOV;
DLB 4, 9, 86; DLBD 1; DLBY 81;
MTCW

Fitzgerald, Penelope 1916-... **CLC 19, 51, 61**
See also CA 85-88; CAAS 10; DLB 14

Fitzgerald, Robert (Stuart)
1910-1985 .... **CLC 39**
See also CA 1-4R; 114; CANR 1; DLBY 80

FitzGerald, Robert D(avid)
1902-1987 .... **CLC 19**
See also CA 17-20R

Author Index

Fitzgerald, Zelda (Sayre)
1900-1948 .... **TCLC 52**
See also CA 117; 126; DLBY 84

Flanagan, Thomas (James Bonner)
1923- .... **CLC 25, 52**
See also CA 108; DLBY 80; INT 108;
MTCW

Flaubert, Gustave
1821-1880 .... **NCLC 2, 10, 19; DA;
DAB; DAC; SSC 11; WLC**
See also DAM MST, NOV; DLB 119

Flecker, Herman Elroy
See Flecker, (Herman) James Elroy

Flecker, (Herman) James Elroy
1884-1915 .... **TCLC 43**
See also CA 109; 150; DLB 10, 19

Fleming, Ian (Lancaster)
1908-1964 .... **CLC 3, 30**
See also CA 5-8R; CDBLB 1945-1960;
DAM POP; DLB 87; MTCW; SATA 9

Fleming, Thomas (James) 1927- .... **CLC 37**
See also CA 5-8R; CANR 10;
INT CANR-10; SATA 8

Fletcher, John 1579-1625 ..... **LC 33; DC 6**
See also CDBLB Before 1660; DLB 58

Fletcher, John Gould 1886-1950 ... **TCLC 35**
See also CA 107; DLB 4, 45

Fleur, Paul
See Pohl, Frederik

Flooglebuckle, Al
See Spiegelman, Art

Flying Officer X
See Bates, H(erbert) E(rnest)

Fo, Dario 1926- .... **CLC 32**
See also CA 116; 128; DAM DRAM;
MTCW

Fogarty, Jonathan Titulescu Esq.
See Farrell, James T(homas)

Folke, Will
See Bloch, Robert (Albert)

Follett, Ken(neth Martin) 1949- .... **CLC 18**
See also AAYA 6; BEST 89:4; CA 81-84;
CANR 13, 33; DAM NOV, POP;
DLB 87; DLBY 81; INT CANR-33;
MTCW

Fontane, Theodor 1819-1898 ..... **NCLC 26**
See also DLB 129

Foote, Horton 1916- .... **CLC 51, 91**
See also CA 73-76; CANR 34, 51;
DAM DRAM; DLB 26; INT CANR-34

Foote, Shelby 1916- .... **CLC 75**
See also CA 5-8R; CANR 3, 45;
DAM NOV, POP; DLB 2, 17

Forbes, Esther 1891-1967 .... **CLC 12**
See also AAYA 17; CA 13-14; 25-28R;
CAP 1; CLR 27; DLB 22; JRDA;
MAICYA; SATA 2

Forche, Carolyn (Louise)
1950- .... **CLC 25, 83, 86; PC 10**
See also CA 109; 117; CANR 50;
DAM POET; DLB 5; INT 117

Ford, Elbur
See Hibbert, Eleanor Alice Burford

Ford, Ford Madox
1873-1939 .... **TCLC 1, 15, 39, 57**
See also CA 104; 132; CDBLB 1914-1945;
DAM NOV; DLB 162; MTCW

Ford, John 1895-1973 .... **CLC 16**
See also CA 45-48

Ford, Richard 1944- .... **CLC 46**
See also CA 69-72; CANR 11, 47

Ford, Webster
See Masters, Edgar Lee

Foreman, Richard 1937- .... **CLC 50**
See also CA 65-68; CANR 32

Forester, C(ecil) S(cott)
1899-1966 .... **CLC 35**
See also CA 73-76; 25-28R; SATA 13

Forez
See Mauriac, Francois (Charles)

Forman, James Douglas 1932- ...... **CLC 21**
See also AAYA 17; CA 9-12R; CANR 4,
19, 42; JRDA; MAICYA; SATA 8, 70

Fornes, Maria Irene 1930- ...... **CLC 39, 61**
See also CA 25-28R; CANR 28; DLB 7;
HW; INT CANR-28; MTCW

Forrest, Leon 1937- .... **CLC 4**
See also BW 2; CA 89-92; CAAS 7;
CANR 25, 52; DLB 33

Forster, E(dward) M(organ)
1879-1970 ..... **CLC 1, 2, 3, 4, 9, 10, 13,
15, 22, 45, 77; DA; DAB; DAC; WLC**
See also AAYA 2; CA 13-14; 25-28R;
CANR 45; CAP 1; CDBLB 1914-1945;
DAM MST, NOV; DLB 34, 98, 162;
DLBD 10; MTCW; SATA 57

Forster, John 1812-1876 .... **NCLC 11**
See also DLB 144

Forsyth, Frederick 1938- ...... **CLC 2, 5, 36**
See also BEST 89:4; CA 85-88; CANR 38;
DAM NOV, POP; DLB 87; MTCW

Forten, Charlotte L. .... **TCLC 16; BLC**
See also Grimke, Charlotte L(ottie) Forten
See also DLB 50

Foscolo, Ugo 1778-1827 .... **NCLC 8**

Fosse, Bob .... **CLC 20**
See also Fosse, Robert Louis

Fosse, Robert Louis 1927-1987
See Fosse, Bob
See also CA 110; 123

Foster, Stephen Collins
1826-1864 .... **NCLC 26**

Foucault, Michel
1926-1984 .... **CLC 31, 34, 69**
See also CA 105; 113; CANR 34; MTCW

Fouque, Friedrich (Heinrich Karl) de la Motte
1777-1843 .... **NCLC 2**
See also DLB 90

Fourier, Charles 1772-1837 ...... **NCLC 51**

Fournier, Henri Alban 1886-1914
See Alain-Fournier
See also CA 104

Fournier, Pierre 1916- .... **CLC 11**
See also Gascar, Pierre
See also CA 89-92; CANR 16, 40

Fowles, John
1926- ...... **CLC 1, 2, 3, 4, 6, 9, 10, 15,
33, 87; DAB; DAC**
See also CA 5-8R; CANR 25; CDBLB 1960
to Present; DAM MST; DLB 14, 139;
MTCW; SATA 22

Fox, Paula 1923- .... **CLC 2, 8**
See also AAYA 3; CA 73-76; CANR 20,
36; CLR 1; DLB 52; JRDA; MAICYA;
MTCW; SATA 17, 60

Fox, William Price (Jr.) 1926- ..... **CLC 22**
See also CA 17-20R; CAAS 19; CANR 11;
DLB 2; DLBY 81

Foxe, John 1516(?)-1587 .... **LC 14**

Frame, Janet .... **CLC 2, 3, 6, 22, 66**
See also Clutha, Janet Paterson Frame

France, Anatole .... **TCLC 9**
See also Thibault, Jacques Anatole Francois
See also DLB 123

Francis, Claude 19(?)- .... **CLC 50**

Francis, Dick 1920- .... **CLC 2, 22, 42**
See also AAYA 5; BEST 89:3; CA 5-8R;
CANR 9, 42; CDBLB 1960 to Present;
DAM POP; DLB 87; INT CANR-9;
MTCW

Francis, Robert (Churchill)
1901-1987 .... **CLC 15**
See also CA 1-4R; 123; CANR 1

Frank, Anne(lies Marie)
1929-1945 .... **TCLC 17; DA; DAB;
DAC; WLC**
See also AAYA 12; CA 113; 133;
DAM MST; MTCW; SATA 87;
SATA-Brief 42

Frank, Elizabeth 1945- .... **CLC 39**
See also CA 121; 126; INT 126

Frankl, Viktor E(mil) 1905- .... **CLC 93**
See also CA 65-68

Franklin, Benjamin
See Hasek, Jaroslav (Matej Frantisek)

Franklin, Benjamin
1706-1790 ..... **LC 25; DA; DAB; DAC**
See also CDALB 1640-1865; DAM MST;
DLB 24, 43, 73

Franklin, (Stella Maraia Sarah) Miles
1879-1954 .... **TCLC 7**
See also CA 104

Fraser, (Lady) Antonia (Pakenham)
1932- .... **CLC 32**
See also CA 85-88; CANR 44; MTCW;
SATA-Brief 32

Fraser, George MacDonald 1925- .... **CLC 7**
See also CA 45-48; CANR 2, 48

Fraser, Sylvia 1935- .... **CLC 64**
See also CA 45-48; CANR 1, 16

Frayn, Michael 1933- ...... **CLC 3, 7, 31, 47**
See also CA 5-8R; CANR 30;
DAM DRAM, NOV; DLB 13, 14;
MTCW

Fraze, Candida (Merrill) 1945- ..... **CLC 50**
See also CA 126

Frazer, J(ames) G(eorge)
1854-1941 .... **TCLC 32**
See also CA 118

Frazer, Robert Caine
See Creasey, John

Frazer, Sir James George
See Frazer, J(ames) G(eorge)

Frazier, Ian 1951-................. **CLC 46**
See also CA 130

Frederic, Harold 1856-1898...... **NCLC 10**
See also DLB 12, 23; DLBD 13

Frederick, John
See Faust, Frederick (Schiller)

Frederick the Great 1712-1786...... **LC 14**

Fredro, Aleksander 1793-1876..... **NCLC 8**

Freeling, Nicolas 1927- .... **CLC 38**
See also CA 49-52; CAAS 12; CANR 1, 17, 50; DLB 87

Freeman, Douglas Southall
1886-1953................... **TCLC 11**
See also CA 109; DLB 17

Freeman, Judith 1946-............ **CLC 55**
See also CA 148

Freeman, Mary Eleanor Wilkins
1852-1930............ **TCLC 9; SSC 1**
See also CA 106; DLB 12, 78

Freeman, R(ichard) Austin
1862-1943................... **TCLC 21**
See also CA 113; DLB 70

French, Albert 1943- .... **CLC 86**

French, Marilyn 1929-...... **CLC 10, 18, 60**
See also CA 69-72; CANR 3, 31; DAM DRAM, NOV, POP; INT CANR-31; MTCW

French, Paul
See Asimov, Isaac

Freneau, Philip Morin 1752-1832.. **NCLC 1**
See also DLB 37, 43

Freud, Sigmund 1856-1939....... **TCLC 52**
See also CA 115; 133; MTCW

Friedan, Betty (Naomi) 1921-...... **CLC 74**
See also CA 65-68; CANR 18, 45; MTCW

Friedlander, Saul 1932-........... **CLC 90**
See also CA 117; 130

Friedman, B(ernard) H(arper)
1926-....................... **CLC 7**
See also CA 1-4R; CANR 3, 48

Friedman, Bruce Jay 1930-.... **CLC 3, 5, 56**
See also CA 9-12R; CANR 25, 52; DLB 2, 28; INT CANR-25

Friel, Brian 1929-........... **CLC 5, 42, 59**
See also CA 21-24R; CANR 33; DLB 13; MTCW

Friis-Baastad, Babbis Ellinor
1921-1970................... **CLC 12**
See also CA 17-20R; 134; SATA 7

Frisch, Max (Rudolf)
1911-1991..... **CLC 3, 9, 14, 18, 32, 44**
See also CA 85-88; 134; CANR 32; DAM DRAM, NOV; DLB 69, 124; MTCW

Fromentin, Eugene (Samuel Auguste)
1820-1876................... **NCLC 10**
See also DLB 123

Frost, Frederick
See Faust, Frederick (Schiller)

Frost, Robert (Lee)
1874-1963.... **CLC 1, 3, 4, 9, 10, 13, 15, 26, 34, 44; DA; DAB; DAC; PC 1; WLC**
See also CA 89-92; CANR 33; CDALB 1917-1929; DAM MST, POET; DLB 54; DLBD 7; MTCW; SATA 14

Froude, James Anthony
1818-1894................... **NCLC 43**
See also DLB 18, 57, 144

Froy, Herald
See Waterhouse, Keith (Spencer)

Fry, Christopher 1907-....... **CLC 2, 10, 14**
See also CA 17-20R; CAAS 23; CANR 9, 30; DAM DRAM; DLB 13; MTCW; SATA 66

Frye, (Herman) Northrop
1912-1991............... **CLC 24, 70**
See also CA 5-8R; 133; CANR 8, 37; DLB 67, 68; MTCW

Fuchs, Daniel 1909-1993........ **CLC 8, 22**
See also CA 81-84; 142; CAAS 5; CANR 40; DLB 9, 26, 28; DLBY 93

Fuchs, Daniel 1934-............... **CLC 34**
See also CA 37-40R; CANR 14, 48

Fuentes, Carlos
1928-...... **CLC 3, 8, 10, 13, 22, 41, 60; DA; DAB; DAC; HLC; WLC**
See also AAYA 4; AITN 2; CA 69-72; CANR 10, 32; DAM MST, MULT, NOV; DLB 113; HW; MTCW

Fuentes, Gregorio Lopez y
See Lopez y Fuentes, Gregorio

Fugard, (Harold) Athol
1932-.... **CLC 5, 9, 14, 25, 40, 80; DC 3**
See also AAYA 17; CA 85-88; CANR 32; DAM DRAM; MTCW

Fugard, Sheila 1932-............. **CLC 48**
See also CA 125

Fuller, Charles (H., Jr.)
1939-............. **CLC 25; BLC; DC 1**
See also BW 2; CA 108; 112; DAM DRAM, MULT; DLB 38; INT 112; MTCW

Fuller, John (Leopold) 1937-....... **CLC 62**
See also CA 21-24R; CANR 9, 44; DLB 40

Fuller, Margaret.............. NCLC 5, 50
See also Ossoli, Sarah Margaret (Fuller marchesa d')

Fuller, Roy (Broadbent)
1912-1991................. **CLC 4, 28**
See also CA 5-8R; 135; CAAS 10; DLB 15, 20; SATA 87

Fulton, Alice 1952-............... **CLC 52**
See also CA 116

Furphy, Joseph 1843-1912....... **TCLC 25**

Fussell, Paul 1924-............... **CLC 74**
See also BEST 90:1; CA 17-20R; CANR 8, 21, 35; INT CANR-21; MTCW

Futabatei, Shimei 1864-1909...... **TCLC 44**

Futrelle, Jacques 1875-1912...... **TCLC 19**
See also CA 113

Gaboriau, Emile 1835-1873...... **NCLC 14**

Gadda, Carlo Emilio 1893-1973.... **CLC 11**
See also CA 89-92

Gaddis, William
1922-..... **CLC 1, 3, 6, 8, 10, 19, 43, 86**
See also CA 17-20R; CANR 21, 48; DLB 2; MTCW

Gaines, Ernest J(ames)
1933-......... **CLC 3, 11, 18, 86; BLC**
See also AAYA 18; AITN 1; BW 2; CA 9-12R; CANR 6, 24, 42; CDALB 1968-1988; DAM MULT; DLB 2, 33, 152; DLBY 80; MTCW; SATA 86

Gaitskill, Mary 1954-............. **CLC 69**
See also CA 128

Galdos, Benito Perez
See Perez Galdos, Benito

Gale, Zona 1874-1938............ **TCLC 7**
See also CA 105; DAM DRAM; DLB 9, 78

Galeano, Eduardo (Hughes) 1940-... **CLC 72**
See also CA 29-32R; CANR 13, 32; HW

Galiano, Juan Valera y Alcala
See Valera y Alcala-Galiano, Juan

Gallagher, Tess 1943-.... **CLC 18, 63; PC 9**
See also CA 106; DAM POET; DLB 120

Gallant, Mavis
1922-...... **CLC 7, 18, 38; DAC; SSC 5**
See also CA 69-72; CANR 29; DAM MST; DLB 53; MTCW

Gallant, Roy A(rthur) 1924- .... **CLC 17**
See also CA 5-8R; CANR 4, 29; CLR 30; MAICYA; SATA 4, 68

Gallico, Paul (William) 1897-1976... **CLC 2**
See also AITN 1; CA 5-8R; 69-72; CANR 23; DLB 9; MAICYA; SATA 13

Gallo, Max Louis 1932-........... **CLC 95**
See also CA 85-88

Gallois, Lucien
See Desnos, Robert

Gallup, Ralph
See Whitemore, Hugh (John)

Galsworthy, John
1867-1933...... **TCLC 1, 45; DA; DAB; DAC; SSC 22; WLC 2**
See also CA 104; 141; CDBLB 1890-1914; DAM DRAM, MST, NOV; DLB 10, 34, 98, 162

Galt, John 1779-1839............ **NCLC 1**
See also DLB 99, 116, 159

Galvin, James 1951-............... **CLC 38**
See also CA 108; CANR 26

Gamboa, Federico 1864-1939...... **TCLC 36**

Gandhi, M. K.
See Gandhi, Mohandas Karamchand

Gandhi, Mahatma
See Gandhi, Mohandas Karamchand

Gandhi, Mohandas Karamchand
1869-1948................. **TCLC 59**
See also CA 121; 132; DAM MULT; MTCW

Gann, Ernest Kellogg 1910-1991.... **CLC 23**
See also AITN 1; CA 1-4R; 136; CANR 1

Garcia, Cristina 1958-............ **CLC 76**
See also CA 141

Garcia Lorca, Federico
1898-1936 . . . **TCLC 1, 7, 49; DA; DAB;
DAC; DC 2; HLC; PC 3; WLC**
See also CA 104; 131; DAM DRAM, MST,
MULT, POET; DLB 108; HW; MTCW

Garcia Marquez, Gabriel (Jose)
1928- . . . . **CLC 2, 3, 8, 10, 15, 27, 47, 55,
68; DA; DAB; DAC; HLC; SSC 8; WLC**
See also AAYA 3; BEST 89:1, 90:4;
CA 33-36R; CANR 10, 28, 50;
DAM MST, MULT, NOV, POP;
DLB 113; HW; MTCW

Gard, Janice
See Latham, Jean Lee

Gard, Roger Martin du
See Martin du Gard, Roger

Gardam, Jane   1928- . . . . **CLC 43**
See also CA 49-52; CANR 2, 18, 33;
CLR 12; DLB 14, 161; MAICYA;
MTCW; SAAS 9; SATA 39, 76;
SATA-Brief 28

Gardner, Herb(ert)   1934- . . . . **CLC 44**
See also CA 149

Gardner, John (Champlin), Jr.
1933-1982 . . . . . **CLC 2, 3, 5, 7, 8, 10, 18,
28, 34; SSC 7**
See also AITN 1; CA 65-68; 107;
CANR 33; DAM NOV, POP; DLB 2;
DLBY 82; MTCW; SATA 40;
SATA-Obit 31

Gardner, John (Edmund)   1926- . . . . . **CLC 30**
See also CA 103; CANR 15; DAM POP;
MTCW

Gardner, Noel
See Kuttner, Henry

Gardons, S. S.
See Snodgrass, W(illiam) D(e Witt)

Garfield, Leon   1921- . . . . **CLC 12**
See also AAYA 8; CA 17-20R; CANR 38,
41; CLR 21; DLB 161; JRDA; MAICYA;
SATA 1, 32, 76

Garland, (Hannibal) Hamlin
1860-1940 . . . . **TCLC 3; SSC 18**
See also CA 104; DLB 12, 71, 78

Garneau, (Hector de) Saint-Denys
1912-1943 . . . . **TCLC 13**
See also CA 111; DLB 88

Garner, Alan   1934- . . . . **CLC 17; DAB**
See also AAYA 18; CA 73-76; CANR 15;
CLR 20; DAM POP; DLB 161;
MAICYA; MTCW; SATA 18, 69

Garner, Hugh   1913-1979 . . . . **CLC 13**
See also CA 69-72; CANR 31; DLB 68

Garnett, David   1892-1981 . . . . **CLC 3**
See also CA 5-8R; 103; CANR 17; DLB 34

Garos, Stephanie
See Katz, Steve

Garrett, George (Palmer)
1929- . . . . **CLC 3, 11, 51**
See also CA 1-4R; CAAS 5; CANR 1, 42;
DLB 2, 5, 130, 152; DLBY 83

Garrick, David   1717-1779 . . . . **LC 15**
See also DAM DRAM; DLB 84

Garrigue, Jean   1914-1972 . . . . **CLC 2, 8**
See also CA 5-8R; 37-40R; CANR 20

Garrison, Frederick
See Sinclair, Upton (Beall)

Garth, Will
See Hamilton, Edmond; Kuttner, Henry

Garvey, Marcus (Moziah, Jr.)
1887-1940 . . . . **TCLC 41; BLC**
See also BW 1; CA 120; 124; DAM MULT

Gary, Romain . . . . **CLC 25**
See also Kacew, Romain
See also DLB 83

Gascar, Pierre . . . . **CLC 11**
See also Fournier, Pierre

Gascoyne, David (Emery)   1916- . . . . **CLC 45**
See also CA 65-68; CANR 10, 28; DLB 20;
MTCW

Gaskell, Elizabeth Cleghorn
1810-1865 . . . . **NCLC 5; DAB**
See also CDBLB 1832-1890; DAM MST;
DLB 21, 144, 159

Gass, William H(oward)
1924- . . . **CLC 1, 2, 8, 11, 15, 39; SSC 12**
See also CA 17-20R; CANR 30; DLB 2;
MTCW

Gasset, Jose Ortega y
See Ortega y Gasset, Jose

Gates, Henry Louis, Jr.   1950- . . . . . . **CLC 65**
See also BW 2; CA 109; CANR 25;
DAM MULT; DLB 67

Gautier, Theophile
1811-1872 . . . . **NCLC 1; SSC 20**
See also DAM POET; DLB 119

Gawsworth, John
See Bates, H(erbert) E(rnest)

Gay, Oliver
See Gogarty, Oliver St. John

Gaye, Marvin (Penze)   1939-1984 . . . **CLC 26**
See also CA 112

Gebler, Carlo (Ernest)   1954- . . . . **CLC 39**
See also CA 119; 133

Gee, Maggie (Mary)   1948- . . . . **CLC 57**
See also CA 130

Gee, Maurice (Gough)   1931- . . . . **CLC 29**
See also CA 97-100; SATA 46

Gelbart, Larry (Simon)   1923- . . . **CLC 21, 61**
See also CA 73-76; CANR 45

Gelber, Jack   1932- . . . . **CLC 1, 6, 14, 79**
See also CA 1-4R; CANR 2; DLB 7

Gellhorn, Martha (Ellis)   1908- . . **CLC 14, 60**
See also CA 77-80; CANR 44; DLBY 82

Genet, Jean
1910-1986 . . . **CLC 1, 2, 5, 10, 14, 44, 46**
See also CA 13-16R; CANR 18;
DAM DRAM; DLB 72; DLBY 86;
MTCW

Gent, Peter   1942- . . . . **CLC 29**
See also AITN 1; CA 89-92; DLBY 82

Gentlewoman in New England, A
See Bradstreet, Anne

Gentlewoman in Those Parts, A
See Bradstreet, Anne

George, Jean Craighead   1919- . . . . . . **CLC 35**
See also AAYA 8; CA 5-8R; CANR 25;
CLR 1; DLB 52; JRDA; MAICYA;
SATA 2, 68

George, Stefan (Anton)
1868-1933 . . . . **TCLC 2, 14**
See also CA 104

Georges, Georges Martin
See Simenon, Georges (Jacques Christian)

Gerhardi, William Alexander
See Gerhardie, William Alexander

Gerhardie, William Alexander
1895-1977 . . . . **CLC 5**
See also CA 25-28R; 73-76; CANR 18;
DLB 36

Gerstler, Amy   1956- . . . . **CLC 70**
See also CA 146

Gertler, T. . . . . **CLC 34**
See also CA 116; 121; INT 121

Ghalib . . . . **NCLC 39**
See also Ghalib, Hsadullah Khan

Ghalib, Hsadullah Khan   1797-1869
See Ghalib
See also DAM POET

Ghelderode, Michel de
1898-1962 . . . . **CLC 6, 11**
See also CA 85-88; CANR 40;
DAM DRAM

Ghiselin, Brewster   1903- . . . . **CLC 23**
See also CA 13-16R; CAAS 10; CANR 13

Ghose, Zulfikar   1935- . . . . **CLC 42**
See also CA 65-68

Ghosh, Amitav   1956- . . . . **CLC 44**
See also CA 147

Giacosa, Giuseppe   1847-1906 . . . . . . **TCLC 7**
See also CA 104

Gibb, Lee
See Waterhouse, Keith (Spencer)

Gibbon, Lewis Grassic . . . . **TCLC 4**
See also Mitchell, James Leslie

Gibbons, Kaye   1960- . . . . **CLC 50, 88**
See also CA 151; DAM POP

Gibran, Kahlil
1883-1931 . . . . **TCLC 1, 9; PC 9**
See also CA 104; 150; DAM POET, POP

Gibran, Khalil
See Gibran, Kahlil

Gibson, William
1914- . . . . **CLC 23; DA; DAB; DAC**
See also CA 9-12R; CANR 9, 42;
DAM DRAM, MST; DLB 7; SATA 66

Gibson, William (Ford)   1948- . . . **CLC 39, 63**
See also AAYA 12; CA 126; 133;
CANR 52; DAM POP

Gide, Andre (Paul Guillaume)
1869-1951 . . . . **TCLC 5, 12, 36; DA;
DAB; DAC; SSC 13; WLC**
See also CA 104; 124; DAM MST, NOV;
DLB 65; MTCW

Gifford, Barry (Colby)   1946- . . . . **CLC 34**
See also CA 65-68; CANR 9, 30, 40

Gilbert, W(illiam) S(chwenck)
1836-1911 . . . . **TCLC 3**
See also CA 104; DAM DRAM, POET;
SATA 36

Gilbreth, Frank B., Jr.   1911- . . . . **CLC 17**
See also CA 9-12R; SATA 2

Gilchrist, Ellen 1935-.. **CLC 34, 48; SSC 14**
See also CA 113; 116; CANR 41;
DAM POP; DLB 130; MTCW

Giles, Molly 1942- .... **CLC 39**
See also CA 126

Gill, Patrick
See Creasey, John

Gilliam, Terry (Vance) 1940-....... **CLC 21**
See also Monty Python
See also CA 108; 113; CANR 35; INT 113

Gillian, Jerry
See Gilliam, Terry (Vance)

Gilliatt, Penelope (Ann Douglass)
1932-1993 .... **CLC 2, 10, 13, 53**
See also AITN 2; CA 13-16R; 141;
CANR 49; DLB 14

Gilman, Charlotte (Anna) Perkins (Stetson)
1860-1935 .... **TCLC 9, 37; SSC 13**
See also CA 106; 150

Gilmour, David 1949-............. **CLC 35**
See also CA 138, 147

Gilpin, William 1724-1804....... **NCLC 30**

Gilray, J. D.
See Mencken, H(enry) L(ouis)

Gilroy, Frank D(aniel) 1925-........ **CLC 2**
See also CA 81-84; CANR 32; DLB 7

Ginsberg, Allen
1926- ...... **CLC 1, 2, 3, 4, 6, 13, 36, 69;**
DA; DAB; DAC; PC 4; WLC 3
See also AITN 1; CA 1-4R; CANR 2, 41;
CDALB 1941-1968; DAM MST, POET;
DLB 5, 16; MTCW

Ginzburg, Natalia
1916-1991 .... **CLC 5, 11, 54, 70**
See also CA 85-88; 135; CANR 33; MTCW

Giono, Jean 1895-1970......... **CLC 4, 11**
See also CA 45-48; 29-32R; CANR 2, 35;
DLB 72; MTCW

Giovanni, Nikki
1943- ...... **CLC 2, 4, 19, 64; BLC; DA;**
DAB; DAC
See also AITN 1; BW 2; CA 29-32R;
CAAS 6; CANR 18, 41; CLR 6;
DAM MST, MULT, POET; DLB 5, 41;
INT CANR-18; MAICYA; MTCW;
SATA 24

Giovene, Andrea 1904-............. **CLC 7**
See also CA 85-88

Gippius, Zinaida (Nikolayevna) 1869-1945
See Hippius, Zinaida
See also CA 106

Giraudoux, (Hippolyte) Jean
1882-1944 .... **TCLC 2, 7**
See also CA 104; DAM DRAM; DLB 65

Gironella, Jose Maria 1917-........ **CLC 11**
See also CA 101

Gissing, George (Robert)
1857-1903 .... **TCLC 3, 24, 47**
See also CA 105; DLB 18, 135

Giurlani, Aldo
See Palazzeschi, Aldo

Gladkov, Fyodor (Vasilyevich)
1883-1958 .... **TCLC 27**

Glanville, Brian (Lester) 1931-...... **CLC 6**
See also CA 5-8R; CAAS 9; CANR 3;
DLB 15, 139; SATA 42

Glasgow, Ellen (Anderson Gholson)
1873(?)-1945 .... **TCLC 2, 7**
See also CA 104; DLB 9, 12

Glaspell, Susan (Keating)
1882(?)-1948 .... **TCLC 55**
See also CA 110; DLB 7, 9, 78; YABC 2

Glassco, John 1909-1981 .... **CLC 9**
See also CA 13-16R; 102; CANR 15;
DLB 68

Glasscock, Amnesia
See Steinbeck, John (Ernst)

Glasser, Ronald J. 1940(?)-........ **CLC 37**

Glassman, Joyce
See Johnson, Joyce

Glendinning, Victoria 1937-........ **CLC 50**
See also CA 120; 127; DLB 155

Glissant, Edouard 1928-........ **CLC 10, 68**
See also DAM MULT

Gloag, Julian 1930- .... **CLC 40**
See also AITN 1; CA 65-68; CANR 10

Glowacki, Aleksander
See Prus, Boleslaw

Gluck, Louise (Elisabeth)
1943- .... **CLC 7, 22, 44, 81; PC 16**
See also CA 33-36R; CANR 40;
DAM POET; DLB 5

Gobineau, Joseph Arthur (Comte) de
1816-1882 .... **NCLC 17**
See also DLB 123

Godard, Jean-Luc 1930-........... **CLC 20**
See also CA 93-96

Godden, (Margaret) Rumer 1907-... **CLC 53**
See also AAYA 6; CA 5-8R; CANR 4, 27,
36; CLR 20; DLB 161; MAICYA;
SAAS 12; SATA 3, 36

Godoy Alcayaga, Lucila 1889-1957
See Mistral, Gabriela
See also BW 2; CA 104; 131; DAM MULT;
HW; MTCW

Godwin, Gail (Kathleen)
1937- .... **CLC 5, 8, 22, 31, 69**
See also CA 29-32R; CANR 15, 43;
DAM POP; DLB 6; INT CANR-15;
MTCW

Godwin, William 1756-1836...... **NCLC 14**
See also CDBLB 1789-1832; DLB 39, 104,
142, 158, 163

Goethe, Johann Wolfgang von
1749-1832 .... **NCLC 4, 22, 34; DA;**
DAB; DAC; PC 5; WLC 3
See also DAM DRAM, MST, POET;
DLB 94

Gogarty, Oliver St. John
1878-1957 .... **TCLC 15**
See also CA 109; 150; DLB 15, 19

Gogol, Nikolai (Vasilyevich)
1809-1852 .... **NCLC 5, 15, 31; DA;**
DAB; DAC; DC 1; SSC 4; WLC
See also DAM DRAM, MST

Goines, Donald
1937(?)-1974 .... **CLC 80; BLC**
See also AITN 1; BW 1; CA 124; 114;
DAM MULT, POP; DLB 33

Gold, Herbert 1924-....... **CLC 4, 7, 14, 42**
See also CA 9-12R; CANR 17, 45; DLB 2;
DLBY 81

Goldbarth, Albert 1948-......... **CLC 5, 38**
See also CA 53-56; CANR 6, 40; DLB 120

Goldberg, Anatol 1910-1982 .... **CLC 34**
See also CA 131; 117

Goldemberg, Isaac 1945-.......... **CLC 52**
See also CA 69-72; CAAS 12; CANR 11,
32; HW

Golding, William (Gerald)
1911-1993 .... **CLC 1, 2, 3, 8, 10, 17, 27,**
58, 81; DA; DAB; DAC; WLC
See also AAYA 5; CA 5-8R; 141;
CANR 13, 33; CDBLB 1945-1960;
DAM MST, NOV; DLB 15, 100; MTCW

Goldman, Emma 1869-1940...... **TCLC 13**
See also CA 110; 150

Goldman, Francisco 1955-......... **CLC 76**

Goldman, William (W.) 1931-.... **CLC 1, 48**
See also CA 9-12R; CANR 29; DLB 44

Goldmann, Lucien 1913-1970 ...... **CLC 24**
See also CA 25-28; CAP 2

Goldoni, Carlo 1707-1793 .... **LC 4**
See also DAM DRAM

Goldsberry, Steven 1949-.......... **CLC 34**
See also CA 131

Goldsmith, Oliver
1728-1774 ...... **LC 2; DA; DAB; DAC;**
WLC
See also CDBLB 1660-1789; DAM DRAM,
MST, NOV, POET; DLB 39, 89, 104,
109, 142; SATA 26

Goldsmith, Peter
See Priestley, J(ohn) B(oynton)

Gombrowicz, Witold
1904-1969 .... **CLC 4, 7, 11, 49**
See also CA 19-20; 25-28R; CAP 2;
DAM DRAM

Gomez de la Serna, Ramon
1888-1963 .... **CLC 9**
See also CA 116; HW

Goncharov, Ivan Alexandrovich
1812-1891 .... **NCLC 1**

Goncourt, Edmond (Louis Antoine Huot) de
1822-1896 .... **NCLC 7**
See also DLB 123

Goncourt, Jules (Alfred Huot) de
1830-1870 .... **NCLC 7**
See also DLB 123

Gontier, Fernande 19(?)- .... **CLC 50**

Goodman, Paul 1911-1972.... **CLC 1, 2, 4, 7**
See also CA 19-20; 37-40R; CANR 34;
CAP 2; DLB 130; MTCW

Gordimer, Nadine
1923- .... **CLC 3, 5, 7, 10, 18, 33, 51, 70;**
DA; DAB; DAC; SSC 17
See also CA 5-8R; CANR 3, 28;
DAM MST, NOV; INT CANR-28;
MTCW

Gordon, Adam Lindsay
1833-1870 . . . . NCLC 21

Gordon, Caroline
1895-1981 . . . CLC 6, 13, 29, 83; SSC 15
See also CA 11-12; 103; CANR 36; CAP 1;
DLB 4, 9, 102; DLBY 81; MTCW

Gordon, Charles William 1860-1937
See Connor, Ralph
See also CA 109

Gordon, Mary (Catherine)
1949- . . . . CLC 13, 22
See also CA 102; CANR 44; DLB 6;
DLBY 81; INT 102; MTCW

Gordon, Sol 1923- . . . . CLC 26
See also CA 53-56; CANR 4; SATA 11

Gordone, Charles 1925-1995 . . . . . . CLC 1, 4
See also BW 1; CA 93-96; 150;
DAM DRAM; DLB 7; INT 93-96;
MTCW

Gorenko, Anna Andreevna
See Akhmatova, Anna

Gorky, Maxim . . . . TCLC 8; DAB; WLC
See also Peshkov, Alexei Maximovich

Goryan, Sirak
See Saroyan, William

Gosse, Edmund (William)
1849-1928 . . . . TCLC 28
See also CA 117; DLB 57, 144

Gotlieb, Phyllis Fay (Bloom)
1926- . . . . CLC 18
See also CA 13-16R; CANR 7; DLB 88

Gottesman, S. D.
See Kornbluth, C(yril) M.; Pohl, Frederik

Gottfried von Strassburg
fl. c. 1210- . . . . CMLC 10
See also DLB 138

Gould, Lois . . . . CLC 4, 10
See also CA 77-80; CANR 29; MTCW

Gourmont, Remy (-Marie-Charles) de
1858-1915 . . . . TCLC 17
See also CA 109; 150

Govier, Katherine 1948- . . . . CLC 51
See also CA 101; CANR 18, 40

Goyen, (Charles) William
1915-1983 . . . . CLC 5, 8, 14, 40
See also AITN 2; CA 5-8R; 110; CANR 6;
DLB 2; DLBY 83; INT CANR-6

Goytisolo, Juan
1931- . . . . CLC 5, 10, 23; HLC
See also CA 85-88; CANR 32;
DAM MULT; HW; MTCW

Gozzano, Guido 1883-1916 . . . . PC 10
See also DLB 114

Gozzi, (Conte) Carlo 1720-1806 . . NCLC 23

Grabbe, Christian Dietrich
1801-1836 . . . . NCLC 2
See also DLB 133

Grace, Patricia 1937- . . . . CLC 56

Gracian y Morales, Baltasar
1601-1658 . . . . LC 15

Gracq, Julien . . . . CLC 11, 48
See also Poirier, Louis
See also DLB 83

Grade, Chaim 1910-1982 . . . . CLC 10
See also CA 93-96; 107

Graduate of Oxford, A
See Ruskin, John

Graham, John
See Phillips, David Graham

Graham, Jorie 1951- . . . . CLC 48
See also CA 111; DLB 120

Graham, R(obert) B(ontine) Cunninghame
See Cunninghame Graham, R(obert)
B(ontine)
See also DLB 98, 135

Graham, Robert
See Haldeman, Joe (William)

Graham, Tom
See Lewis, (Harry) Sinclair

Graham, W(illiam) S(ydney)
1918-1986 . . . . CLC 29
See also CA 73-76; 118; DLB 20

Graham, Winston (Mawdsley)
1910- . . . . CLC 23
See also CA 49-52; CANR 2, 22, 45;
DLB 77

Grahame, Kenneth
1859-1932 . . . . TCLC 64; DAB
See also CA 108; 136; CLR 5; DLB 34, 141;
MAICYA; YABC 1

Grant, Skeeter
See Spiegelman, Art

Granville-Barker, Harley
1877-1946 . . . . TCLC 2
See also Barker, Harley Granville
See also CA 104; DAM DRAM

Grass, Guenter (Wilhelm)
1927- . . . . . CLC 1, 2, 4, 6, 11, 15, 22, 32,
49, 88; DA; DAB; DAC; WLC
See also CA 13-16R; CANR 20;
DAM MST, NOV; DLB 75, 124; MTCW

Gratton, Thomas
See Hulme, T(homas) E(rnest)

Grau, Shirley Ann
1929- . . . . CLC 4, 9; SSC 15
See also CA 89-92; CANR 22; DLB 2;
INT CANR-22; MTCW

Gravel, Fern
See Hall, James Norman

Graver, Elizabeth 1964- . . . . CLC 70
See also CA 135

Graves, Richard Perceval 1945- . . . . CLC 44
See also CA 65-68; CANR 9, 26, 51

Graves, Robert (von Ranke)
1895-1985 . . . . . . CLC 1, 2, 6, 11, 39, 44,
45; DAB; DAC; PC 6
See also CA 5-8R; 117; CANR 5, 36;
CDBLB 1914-1945; DAM MST, POET;
DLB 20, 100; DLBY 85; MTCW;
SATA 45

Gray, Alasdair (James) 1934- . . . . . . CLC 41
See also CA 126; CANR 47; INT 126;
MTCW

Gray, Amlin 1946- . . . . CLC 29
See also CA 138

Gray, Francine du Plessix 1930- . . . . CLC 22
See also BEST 90:3; CA 61-64; CAAS 2;
CANR 11, 33; DAM NOV;
INT CANR-11; MTCW

Gray, John (Henry) 1866-1934 . . . . TCLC 19
See also CA 119

Gray, Simon (James Holliday)
1936- . . . . CLC 9, 14, 36
See also AITN 1; CA 21-24R; CAAS 3;
CANR 32; DLB 13; MTCW

Gray, Spalding 1941- . . . . CLC 49
See also CA 128; DAM POP

Gray, Thomas
1716-1771 . . . . . . LC 4; DA; DAB; DAC;
PC 2; WLC
See also CDBLB 1660-1789; DAM MST;
DLB 109

Grayson, David
See Baker, Ray Stannard

Grayson, Richard (A.) 1951- . . . . CLC 38
See also CA 85-88; CANR 14, 31

Greeley, Andrew M(oran) 1928- . . . . CLC 28
See also CA 5-8R; CAAS 7; CANR 7, 43;
DAM POP; MTCW

Green, Anna Katharine
1846-1935 . . . . TCLC 63
See also CA 112

Green, Brian
See Card, Orson Scott

Green, Hannah
See Greenberg, Joanne (Goldenberg)

Green, Hannah . . . . CLC 3
See also CA 73-76

Green, Henry . . . . CLC 2, 13
See also Yorke, Henry Vincent
See also DLB 15

Green, Julian (Hartridge) 1900-
See Green, Julien
See also CA 21-24R; CANR 33; DLB 4, 72;
MTCW

Green, Julien . . . . CLC 3, 11, 77
See also Green, Julian (Hartridge)

Green, Paul (Eliot) 1894-1981 . . . . . . CLC 25
See also AITN 1; CA 5-8R; 103; CANR 3;
DAM DRAM; DLB 7, 9; DLBY 81

Greenberg, Ivan 1908-1973
See Rahv, Philip
See also CA 85-88

Greenberg, Joanne (Goldenberg)
1932- . . . . CLC 7, 30
See also AAYA 12; CA 5-8R; CANR 14,
32; SATA 25

Greenberg, Richard 1959(?)- . . . . CLC 57
See also CA 138

Greene, Bette 1934- . . . . CLC 30
See also AAYA 7; CA 53-56; CANR 4;
CLR 2; JRDA; MAICYA; SAAS 16;
SATA 8

Greene, Gael . . . . CLC 8
See also CA 13-16R; CANR 10

Harris, Mark 1922- .... **CLC 19**
See also CA 5-8R; CAAS 3; CANR 2;
DLB 2; DLBY 80

Harris, (Theodore) Wilson 1921-.... **CLC 25**
See also BW 2; CA 65-68; CAAS 16;
CANR 11, 27; DLB 117; MTCW

Harrison, Elizabeth Cavanna 1909-
See Cavanna, Betty
See also CA 9-12R; CANR 6, 27

Harrison, Harry (Max) 1925- ...... **CLC 42**
See also CA 1-4R; CANR 5, 21; DLB 8;
SATA 4

Harrison, James (Thomas)
1937- ...... **CLC 6, 14, 33, 66; SSC 19**
See also CA 13-16R; CANR 8, 51;
DLBY 82; INT CANR-8

Harrison, Jim
See Harrison, James (Thomas)

Harrison, Kathryn 1961- .... **CLC 70**
See also CA 144

Harrison, Tony 1937-............. **CLC 43**
See also CA 65-68; CANR 44; DLB 40;
MTCW

Harriss, Will(ard Irvin) 1922-...... **CLC 34**
See also CA 111

Harson, Sley
See Ellison, Harlan (Jay)

Hart, Ellis
See Ellison, Harlan (Jay)

Hart, Josephine 1942(?)- .... **CLC 70**
See also CA 138; DAM POP

Hart, Moss 1904-1961 .... **CLC 66**
See also CA 109; 89-92; DAM DRAM;
DLB 7

Harte, (Francis) Bret(t)
1836(?)-1902 .... **TCLC 1, 25; DA; DAC;**
                                    SSC 8; WLC
See also CA 104; 140; CDALB 1865-1917;
DAM MST; DLB 12, 64, 74, 79;
SATA 26

Hartley, L(eslie) P(oles)
1895-1972 .... **CLC 2, 22**
See also CA 45-48; 37-40R; CANR 33;
DLB 15, 139; MTCW

Hartman, Geoffrey H. 1929-....... **CLC 27**
See also CA 117; 125; DLB 67

Hartmann von Aue
c. 1160-c. 1205 .... **CMLC 15**
See also DLB 138

Hartmann von Aue 1170-1210.... **CMLC 15**

Haruf, Kent 1943- .... **CLC 34**
See also CA 149

Harwood, Ronald 1934-........... **CLC 32**
See also CA 1-4R; CANR 4; DAM DRAM,
MST; DLB 13

Hasek, Jaroslav (Matej Frantisek)
1883-1923 .... **TCLC 4**
See also CA 104; 129; MTCW

Hass, Robert 1941-..... **CLC 18, 39; PC 16**
See also CA 111; CANR 30, 50; DLB 105

Hastings, Hudson
See Kuttner, Henry

Hastings, Selina................... **CLC 44**

Hatteras, Amelia
See Mencken, H(enry) L(ouis)

Hatteras, Owen................. **TCLC 18**
See also Mencken, H(enry) L(ouis); Nathan,
George Jean

Hauptmann, Gerhart (Johann Robert)
1862-1946 .... **TCLC 4**
See also CA 104; DAM DRAM; DLB 66,
118

Havel, Vaclav
1936- .... **CLC 25, 58, 65; DC 6**
See also CA 104; CANR 36; DAM DRAM;
MTCW

Haviaras, Stratis.................. **CLC 33**
See also Chaviaras, Strates

Hawes, Stephen 1475(?)-1523(?) ..... **LC 17**

Hawkes, John (Clendennin Burne, Jr.)
1925- ...... **CLC 1, 2, 3, 4, 7, 9, 14, 15,**
                                    27, 49
See also CA 1-4R; CANR 2, 47; DLB 2, 7;
DLBY 80; MTCW

Hawking, S. W.
See Hawking, Stephen W(illiam)

Hawking, Stephen W(illiam)
1942- .... **CLC 63**
See also AAYA 13; BEST 89:1; CA 126;
129; CANR 48

Hawthorne, Julian 1846-1934 ..... **TCLC 25**

Hawthorne, Nathaniel
1804-1864 .... **NCLC 39; DA; DAB;**
                                    DAC; SSC 3; WLC
See also AAYA 18; CDALB 1640-1865;
DAM MST, NOV; DLB 1, 74; YABC 2

Haxton, Josephine Ayres 1921-
See Douglas, Ellen
See also CA 115; CANR 41

Hayaseca y Eizaguirre, Jorge
See Echegaray (y Eizaguirre), Jose (Maria
Waldo)

Hayashi Fumiko 1904-1951....... **TCLC 27**

Haycraft, Anna
See Ellis, Alice Thomas
See also CA 122

Hayden, Robert E(arl)
1913-1980 ...... **CLC 5, 9, 14, 37; BLC;**
                                    DA; DAC; PC 6
See also BW 1; CA 69-72; 97-100; CABS 2;
CANR 24; CDALB 1941-1968;
DAM MST, MULT, POET; DLB 5, 76;
MTCW; SATA 19; SATA-Obit 26

Hayford, J(oseph) E(phraim) Casely
See Casely-Hayford, J(oseph) E(phraim)

Hayman, Ronald 1932-............ **CLC 44**
See also CA 25-28R; CANR 18, 50;
DLB 155

Haywood, Eliza (Fowler)
1693(?)-1756 .... **LC 1**

Hazlitt, William 1778-1830...... **NCLC 29**
See also DLB 110, 158

Hazzard, Shirley 1931- .... **CLC 18**
See also CA 9-12R; CANR 4; DLBY 82;
MTCW

Head, Bessie 1937-1986... **CLC 25, 67; BLC**
See also BW 2; CA 29-32R; 119; CANR 25;
DAM MULT; DLB 117; MTCW

Headon, (Nicky) Topper 1956(?)- ... **CLC 30**

Heaney, Seamus (Justin)
1939- ...... **CLC 5, 7, 14, 25, 37, 74, 91;**
                                    DAB
See also CA 85-88; CANR 25, 48;
CDBLB 1960 to Present; DAM POET;
DLB 40; DLBY 95; MTCW

Hearn, (Patricio) Lafcadio (Tessima Carlos)
1850-1904 .... **TCLC 9**
See also CA 105; DLB 12, 78

Hearne, Vicki 1946-.............. **CLC 56**
See also CA 139

Hearon, Shelby 1931-............. **CLC 63**
See also AITN 2; CA 25-28R; CANR 18,
48

Heat-Moon, William Least......... **CLC 29**
See also Trogdon, William (Lewis)
See also AAYA 9

Hebbel, Friedrich 1813-1863..... **NCLC 43**
See also DAM DRAM; DLB 129

Hebert, Anne 1916- ... **CLC 4, 13, 29; DAC**
See also CA 85-88; DAM MST, POET;
DLB 68; MTCW

Hecht, Anthony (Evan)
1923- .... **CLC 8, 13, 19**
See also CA 9-12R; CANR 6; DAM POET;
DLB 5

Hecht, Ben 1894-1964 .... **CLC 8**
See also CA 85-88; DLB 7, 9, 25, 26, 28, 86

Hedayat, Sadeq 1903-1951....... **TCLC 21**
See also CA 120

Hegel, Georg Wilhelm Friedrich
1770-1831 .... **NCLC 46**
See also DLB 90

Heidegger, Martin 1889-1976 ...... **CLC 24**
See also CA 81-84; 65-68; CANR 34;
MTCW

Heidenstam, (Carl Gustaf) Verner von
1859-1940 .... **TCLC 5**
See also CA 104

Heifner, Jack 1946-.............. **CLC 11**
See also CA 105; CANR 47

Heijermans, Herman 1864-1924 ... **TCLC 24**
See also CA 123

Heilbrun, Carolyn G(old) 1926-..... **CLC 25**
See also CA 45-48; CANR 1, 28

Heine, Heinrich 1797-1856 .... **NCLC 4, 54**
See also DLB 90

Heinemann, Larry (Curtiss) 1944- .. **CLC 50**
See also CA 110; CAAS 21; CANR 31;
DLBD 9; INT CANR-31

Heiney, Donald (William) 1921-1993
See Harris, MacDonald
See also CA 1-4R; 142; CANR 3

Heinlein, Robert A(nson)
1907-1988 ...... **CLC 1, 3, 8, 14, 26, 55**
See also AAYA 17; CA 1-4R; 125;
CANR 1, 20; DAM POP; DLB 8; JRDA;
MAICYA; MTCW; SATA 9, 69;
SATA-Obit 56

Helforth, John
See Doolittle, Hilda

Hellenhofferu, Vojtech Kapristian z
See Hasek, Jaroslav (Matej Frantisek)

Heller, Joseph
   1923- .... **CLC 1, 3, 5, 8, 11, 36, 63; DA;
                  DAB; DAC; WLC**
   See also AITN 1; CA 5-8R; CABS 1;
      CANR 8, 42; DAM MST, NOV, POP;
      DLB 2, 28; DLBY 80; INT CANR-8;
      MTCW

Hellman, Lillian (Florence)
   1906-1984 ...... **CLC 2, 4, 8, 14, 18, 34,
                        44, 52; DC 1**
   See also AITN 1, 2; CA 13-16R; 112;
      CANR 33; DAM DRAM; DLB 7;
      DLBY 84; MTCW

Helprin, Mark 1947- ..... **CLC 7, 10, 22, 32**
   See also CA 81-84; CANR 47; DAM NOV,
      POP; DLBY 85; MTCW

Helvetius, Claude-Adrien
   1715-1771 .... **LC 26**

Helyar, Jane Penelope Josephine 1933-
   See Poole, Josephine
   See also CA 21-24R; CANR 10, 26;
      SATA 82

Hemans, Felicia 1793-1835 ...... **NCLC 29**
   See also DLB 96

Hemingway, Ernest (Miller)
   1899-1961 .... **CLC 1, 3, 6, 8, 10, 13, 19,
                     30, 34, 39, 41, 44, 50, 61, 80; DA; DAB;
                     DAC; SSC 1; WLC**
   See also CA 77-80; CANR 34;
      CDALB 1917-1929; DAM MST, NOV;
      DLB 4, 9, 102; DLBD 1; DLBY 81, 87;
      MTCW

Hempel, Amy 1951- .... **CLC 39**
   See also CA 118; 137

Henderson, F. C.
   See Mencken, H(enry) L(ouis)

Henderson, Sylvia
   See Ashton-Warner, Sylvia (Constance)

Henley, Beth .... **CLC 23; DC 6**
   See also Henley, Elizabeth Becker
   See also CABS 3; DLBY 86

Henley, Elizabeth Becker 1952-
   See Henley, Beth
   See also CA 107; CANR 32; DAM DRAM,
      MST; MTCW

Henley, William Ernest
   1849-1903 .... **TCLC 8**
   See also CA 105; DLB 19

Hennissart, Martha
   See Lathen, Emma
   See also CA 85-88

Henry, O. .... **TCLC 1, 19; SSC 5; WLC**
   See also Porter, William Sydney

Henry, Patrick 1736-1799 .... **LC 25**

Henryson, Robert 1430(?)-1506(?).... **LC 20**
   See also DLB 146

Henry VIII 1491-1547 .... **LC 10**

Henschke, Alfred
   See Klabund

Hentoff, Nat(han Irving) 1925- ..... **CLC 26**
   See also AAYA 4; CA 1-4R; CAAS 6;
      CANR 5, 25; CLR 1; INT CANR-25;
      JRDA; MAICYA; SATA 42, 69;
      SATA-Brief 27

Heppenstall, (John) Rayner
   1911-1981 .... **CLC 10**
   See also CA 1-4R; 103; CANR 29

Herbert, Frank (Patrick)
   1920-1986 ...... **CLC 12, 23, 35, 44, 85**
   See also CA 53-56; 118; CANR 5, 43;
      DAM POP; DLB 8; INT CANR-5;
      MTCW; SATA 9, 37; SATA-Obit 47

Herbert, George
   1593-1633 .... **LC 24; DAB; PC 4**
   See also CDBLB Before 1660; DAM POET;
      DLB 126

Herbert, Zbigniew 1924- .... **CLC 9, 43**
   See also CA 89-92; CANR 36;
      DAM POET; MTCW

Herbst, Josephine (Frey)
   1897-1969 .... **CLC 34**
   See also CA 5-8R; 25-28R; DLB 9

Hergesheimer, Joseph
   1880-1954 .... **TCLC 11**
   See also CA 109; DLB 102, 9

Herlihy, James Leo 1927-1993 ...... **CLC 6**
   See also CA 1-4R; 143; CANR 2

Hermogenes fl. c. 175- .... **CMLC 6**

Hernandez, Jose 1834-1886 ...... **NCLC 17**

Herodotus c. 484B.C.-429B.C..... **CMLC 17**

Herrick, Robert
   1591-1674 ..... **LC 13; DA; DAB; DAC;
                      PC 9**
   See also DAM MST, POP; DLB 126

Herring, Guilles
   See Somerville, Edith

Herriot, James 1916-1995 .... **CLC 12**
   See also Wight, James Alfred
   See also AAYA 1; CA 148; CANR 40;
      DAM POP; SATA 86

Herrmann, Dorothy 1941- .... **CLC 44**
   See also CA 107

Herrmann, Taffy
   See Herrmann, Dorothy

Hersey, John (Richard)
   1914-1993 .... **CLC 1, 2, 7, 9, 40, 81**
   See also CA 17-20R; 140; CANR 33;
      DAM POP; DLB 6; MTCW; SATA 25;
      SATA-Obit 76

Herzen, Aleksandr Ivanovich
   1812-1870 .... **NCLC 10**

Herzl, Theodor 1860-1904 .... **TCLC 36**

Herzog, Werner 1942- .... **CLC 16**
   See also CA 89-92

Hesiod c. 8th cent. B.C.- .... **CMLC 5**

Hesse, Hermann
   1877-1962 .... **CLC 1, 2, 3, 6, 11, 17, 25,
                     69; DA; DAB; DAC; SSC 9; WLC**
   See also CA 17-18; CAP 2; DAM MST,
      NOV; DLB 66; MTCW; SATA 50

Hewes, Cady
   See De Voto, Bernard (Augustine)

Heyen, William 1940- .... **CLC 13, 18**
   See also CA 33-36R; CAAS 9; DLB 5

Heyerdahl, Thor 1914- .... **CLC 26**
   See also CA 5-8R; CANR 5, 22; MTCW;
      SATA 2, 52

Heym, Georg (Theodor Franz Arthur)
   1887-1912 .... **TCLC 9**
   See also CA 106

Heym, Stefan 1913- .... **CLC 41**
   See also CA 9-12R; CANR 4; DLB 69

Heyse, Paul (Johann Ludwig von)
   1830-1914 .... **TCLC 8**
   See also CA 104; DLB 129

Heyward, (Edwin) DuBose
   1885-1940 .... **TCLC 59**
   See also CA 108; DLB 7, 9, 45; SATA 21

Hibbert, Eleanor Alice Burford
   1906-1993 .... **CLC 7**
   See also BEST 90:4; CA 17-20R; 140;
      CANR 9, 28; DAM POP; SATA 2;
      SATA-Obit 74

Hichens, Robert S. 1864-1950..... **TCLC 64**
   See also DLB 153

Higgins, George V(incent)
   1939- ....**CLC 4, 7, 10, 18**
   See also CA 77-80; CAAS 5; CANR 17, 51;
      DLB 2; DLBY 81; INT CANR-17;
      MTCW

Higginson, Thomas Wentworth
   1823-1911 .... **TCLC 36**
   See also DLB 1, 64

Highet, Helen
   See MacInnes, Helen (Clark)

Highsmith, (Mary) Patricia
   1921-1995 .... **CLC 2, 4, 14, 42**
   See also CA 1-4R; 147; CANR 1, 20, 48;
      DAM NOV, POP; MTCW

Highwater, Jamake (Mamake)
   1942(?)- .... **CLC 12**
   See also AAYA 7; CA 65-68; CAAS 7;
      CANR 10, 34; CLR 17; DLB 52;
      DLBY 85; JRDA; MAICYA; SATA 32,
      69; SATA-Brief 30

Highway, Tomson 1951-...... **CLC 92; DAC**
   See also CA 151; DAM MULT; NNAL

Higuchi, Ichiyo 1872-1896....... **NCLC 49**

Hijuelos, Oscar 1951- ...... **CLC 65; HLC**
   See also BEST 90:1; CA 123; CANR 50;
      DAM MULT, POP; DLB 145; HW

Hikmet, Nazim 1902(?)-1963....... **CLC 40**
   See also CA 141; 93-96

Hildesheimer, Wolfgang
   1916-1991 .... **CLC 49**
   See also CA 101; 135; DLB 69, 124

Hill, Geoffrey (William)
   1932- ....**CLC 5, 8, 18, 45**
   See also CA 81-84; CANR 21;
      CDBLB 1960 to Present; DAM POET;
      DLB 40; MTCW

Hill, George Roy 1921- .... **CLC 26**
   See also CA 110; 122

Hill, John
   See Koontz, Dean R(ay)

Hill, Susan (Elizabeth)
   1942- .... **CLC 4; DAB**
   See also CA 33-36R; CANR 29;
      DAM MST, NOV; DLB 14, 139; MTCW

Hillerman, Tony 1925- .... **CLC 62**
   See also AAYA 6; BEST 89:1; CA 29-32R;
      CANR 21, 42; DAM POP; SATA 6

Hillesum, Etty 1914-1943 . . . . **TCLC 49**
See also CA 137

Hilliard, Noel (Harvey) 1929- . . . . . . **CLC 15**
See also CA 9-12R; CANR 7

Hillis, Rick 1956- . . . . **CLC 66**
See also CA 134

Hilton, James 1900-1954 . . . . **TCLC 21**
See also CA 108; DLB 34, 77; SATA 34

Himes, Chester (Bomar)
1909-1984 . . . . **CLC 2, 4, 7, 18, 58; BLC**
See also BW 2; CA 25-28R; 114; CANR 22;
DAM MULT; DLB 2, 76, 143; MTCW

Hinde, Thomas . . . . **CLC 6, 11**
See also Chitty, Thomas Willes

Hindin, Nathan
See Bloch, Robert (Albert)

Hine, (William) Daryl 1936- . . . . **CLC 15**
See also CA 1-4R; CAAS 15; CANR 1, 20;
DLB 60

Hinkson, Katharine Tynan
See Tynan, Katharine

Hinton, S(usan) E(loise)
1950- . . . . **CLC 30; DA; DAB; DAC**
See also AAYA 2; CA 81-84; CANR 32;
CLR 3, 23; DAM MST, NOV; JRDA;
MAICYA; MTCW; SATA 19, 58

Hippius, Zinaida . . . . **TCLC 9**
See also Gippius, Zinaida (Nikolayevna)

Hiraoka, Kimitake 1925-1970
See Mishima, Yukio
See also CA 97-100; 29-32R; DAM DRAM;
MTCW

Hirsch, E(ric) D(onald), Jr. 1928- . . . **CLC 79**
See also CA 25-28R; CANR 27, 51;
DLB 67; INT CANR-27; MTCW

Hirsch, Edward 1950- . . . . **CLC 31, 50**
See also CA 104; CANR 20, 42; DLB 120

Hitchcock, Alfred (Joseph)
1899-1980 . . . . **CLC 16**
See also CA 97-100; SATA 27;
SATA-Obit 24

Hitler, Adolf 1889-1945 . . . . **TCLC 53**
See also CA 117; 147

Hoagland, Edward 1932- . . . . **CLC 28**
See also CA 1-4R; CANR 2, 31; DLB 6;
SATA 51

Hoban, Russell (Conwell) 1925- . . **CLC 7, 25**
See also CA 5-8R; CANR 23, 37; CLR 3;
DAM NOV; DLB 52; MAICYA;
MTCW; SATA 1, 40, 78

Hobbs, Perry
See Blackmur, R(ichard) P(almer)

Hobson, Laura Z(ametkin)
1900-1986 . . . . **CLC 7, 25**
See also CA 17-20R; 118; DLB 28;
SATA 52

Hochhuth, Rolf 1931- . . . . **CLC 4, 11, 18**
See also CA 5-8R; CANR 33;
DAM DRAM; DLB 124; MTCW

Hochman, Sandra 1936- . . . . **CLC 3, 8**
See also CA 5-8R; DLB 5

Hochwaelder, Fritz 1911-1986 . . . . . . **CLC 36**
See also CA 29-32R; 120; CANR 42;
DAM DRAM; MTCW

Hochwalder, Fritz
See Hochwaelder, Fritz

Hocking, Mary (Eunice) 1921- . . . . . **CLC 13**
See also CA 101; CANR 18, 40

Hodgins, Jack 1938- . . . . **CLC 23**
See also CA 93-96; DLB 60

Hodgson, William Hope
1877(?)-1918 . . . . **TCLC 13**
See also CA 111; DLB 70, 153, 156

Hoeg, Peter 1957- . . . . **CLC 95**
See also CA 151

Hoffman, Alice 1952- . . . . **CLC 51**
See also CA 77-80; CANR 34; DAM NOV;
MTCW

Hoffman, Daniel (Gerard)
1923- . . . . **CLC 6, 13, 23**
See also CA 1-4R; CANR 4; DLB 5

Hoffman, Stanley 1944- . . . . **CLC 5**
See also CA 77-80

Hoffman, William M(oses) 1939- . . . **CLC 40**
See also CA 57-60; CANR 11

Hoffmann, E(rnst) T(heodor) A(madeus)
1776-1822 . . . . **NCLC 2; SSC 13**
See also DLB 90; SATA 27

Hofmann, Gert 1931- . . . . **CLC 54**
See also CA 128

Hofmannsthal, Hugo von
1874-1929 . . . . **TCLC 11; DC 4**
See also CA 106; DAM DRAM; DLB 81,
118

Hogan, Linda 1947- . . . . **CLC 73**
See also CA 120; CANR 45; DAM MULT;
NNAL

Hogarth, Charles
See Creasey, John

Hogarth, Emmett
See Polonsky, Abraham (Lincoln)

Hogg, James 1770-1835 . . . . **NCLC 4**
See also DLB 93, 116, 159

Holbach, Paul Henri Thiry Baron
1723-1789 . . . . **LC 14**

Holberg, Ludvig 1684-1754 . . . . **LC 6**

Holden, Ursula 1921- . . . . **CLC 18**
See also CA 101; CAAS 8; CANR 22

Holderlin, (Johann Christian) Friedrich
1770-1843 . . . . **NCLC 16; PC 4**

Holdstock, Robert
See Holdstock, Robert P.

Holdstock, Robert P. 1948- . . . . **CLC 39**
See also CA 131

Holland, Isabelle 1920- . . . . **CLC 21**
See also AAYA 11; CA 21-24R; CANR 10,
25, 47; JRDA; MAICYA; SATA 8, 70

Holland, Marcus
See Caldwell, (Janet Miriam) Taylor
(Holland)

Hollander, John 1929- . . . . . . **CLC 2, 5, 8, 14**
See also CA 1-4R; CANR 1, 52; DLB 5;
SATA 13

Hollander, Paul
See Silverberg, Robert

Holleran, Andrew 1943(?)- . . . . **CLC 38**
See also CA 144

Hollinghurst, Alan 1954- . . . . **CLC 55, 91**
See also CA 114

Hollis, Jim
See Summers, Hollis (Spurgeon, Jr.)

Holly, Buddy 1936-1959 . . . . **TCLC 65**

Holmes, John
See Souster, (Holmes) Raymond

Holmes, John Clellon 1926-1988 . . . . **CLC 56**
See also CA 9-12R; 125; CANR 4; DLB 16

Holmes, Oliver Wendell
1809-1894 . . . . **NCLC 14**
See also CDALB 1640-1865; DLB 1;
SATA 34

Holmes, Raymond
See Souster, (Holmes) Raymond

Holt, Victoria
See Hibbert, Eleanor Alice Burford

Holub, Miroslav 1923- . . . . **CLC 4**
See also CA 21-24R; CANR 10

Homer
c. 8th cent. B.C.- . . . . . **CMLC 1, 16; DA;
DAB; DAC**
See also DAM MST, POET

Honig, Edwin 1919- . . . . **CLC 33**
See also CA 5-8R; CAAS 8; CANR 4, 45;
DLB 5

Hood, Hugh (John Blagdon)
1928- . . . . **CLC 15, 28**
See also CA 49-52; CAAS 17; CANR 1, 33;
DLB 53

Hood, Thomas 1799-1845 . . . . **NCLC 16**
See also DLB 96

Hooker, (Peter) Jeremy 1941- . . . . . . **CLC 43**
See also CA 77-80; CANR 22; DLB 40

hooks, bell . . . . **CLC 94**
See also Watkins, Gloria

Hope, A(lec) D(erwent) 1907- . . . . **CLC 3, 51**
See also CA 21-24R; CANR 33; MTCW

Hope, Brian
See Creasey, John

Hope, Christopher (David Tully)
1944- . . . . **CLC 52**
See also CA 106; CANR 47; SATA 62

Hopkins, Gerard Manley
1844-1889 . . . . **NCLC 17; DA; DAB;
DAC; PC 15; WLC**
See also CDBLB 1890-1914; DAM MST,
POET; DLB 35, 57

Hopkins, John (Richard) 1931- . . . . . . **CLC 4**
See also CA 85-88

Hopkins, Pauline Elizabeth
1859-1930 . . . . **TCLC 28; BLC**
See also BW 2; CA 141; DAM MULT;
DLB 50

Hopkinson, Francis 1737-1791 . . . . . . **LC 25**
See also DLB 31

Hopley-Woolrich, Cornell George 1903-1968
See Woolrich, Cornell
See also CA 13-14; CAP 1

Horatio
See Proust, (Valentin-Louis-George-Eugene-)
Marcel

Horgan, Paul (George Vincent O'Shaughnessy) 1903-1995 .... **CLC 9, 53**
See also CA 13-16R; 147; CANR 9, 35; DAM NOV; DLB 102; DLBY 85; INT CANR-9; MTCW; SATA 13; SATA-Obit 84

Horn, Peter
See Kuttner, Henry

Hornem, Horace Esq.
See Byron, George Gordon (Noel)

Hornung, E(rnest) W(illiam) 1866-1921 .... **TCLC 59**
See also CA 108; DLB 70

Horovitz, Israel (Arthur) 1939- ..... **CLC 56**
See also CA 33-36R; CANR 46; DAM DRAM; DLB 7

Horvath, Odon von
See Horvath, Oedoen von
See also DLB 85, 124

Horvath, Oedoen von 1901-1938... **TCLC 45**
See also Horvath, Odon von
See also CA 118

Horwitz, Julius 1920-1986........ **CLC 14**
See also CA 9-12R; 119; CANR 12

Hospital, Janette Turner 1942- ..... **CLC 42**
See also CA 108; CANR 48

Hostos, E. M. de
See Hostos (y Bonilla), Eugenio Maria de

Hostos, Eugenio M. de
See Hostos (y Bonilla), Eugenio Maria de

Hostos, Eugenio Maria
See Hostos (y Bonilla), Eugenio Maria de

Hostos (y Bonilla), Eugenio Maria de 1839-1903 .... **TCLC 24**
See also CA 123; 131; HW

Houdini
See Lovecraft, H(oward) P(hillips)

Hougan, Carolyn 1943- .... **CLC 34**
See also CA 139

Household, Geoffrey (Edward West) 1900-1988 .... **CLC 11**
See also CA 77-80; 126; DLB 87; SATA 14; SATA-Obit 59

Housman, A(lfred) E(dward) 1859-1936 ...... **TCLC 1, 10; DA; DAB; DAC; PC 2**
See also CA 104; 125; DAM MST, POET; DLB 19; MTCW

Housman, Laurence 1865-1959 ..... **TCLC 7**
See also CA 106; DLB 10; SATA 25

Howard, Elizabeth Jane 1923- ... **CLC 7, 29**
See also CA 5-8R; CANR 8

Howard, Maureen 1930- ..... **CLC 5, 14, 46**
See also CA 53-56; CANR 31; DLBY 83; INT CANR-31; MTCW

Howard, Richard 1929- ...... **CLC 7, 10, 47**
See also AITN 1; CA 85-88; CANR 25; DLB 5; INT CANR-25

Howard, Robert Ervin 1906-1936... **TCLC 8**
See also CA 105

Howard, Warren F.
See Pohl, Frederik

Howe, Fanny 1940- .... **CLC 47**
See also CA 117; SATA-Brief 52

Howe, Irving 1920-1993........... **CLC 85**
See also CA 9-12R; 141; CANR 21, 50; DLB 67; MTCW

Howe, Julia Ward 1819-1910 ..... **TCLC 21**
See also CA 117; DLB 1

Howe, Susan 1937-.............. **CLC 72**
See also DLB 120

Howe, Tina 1937-................ **CLC 48**
See also CA 109

Howell, James 1594(?)-1666 .... **LC 13**
See also DLB 151

Howells, W. D.
See Howells, William Dean

Howells, William D.
See Howells, William Dean

Howells, William Dean 1837-1920 .... **TCLC 7, 17, 41**
See also CA 104; 134; CDALB 1865-1917; DLB 12, 64, 74, 79

Howes, Barbara 1914-1996 .... **CLC 15**
See also CA 9-12R; 151; CAAS 3; SATA 5

Hrabal, Bohumil 1914-......... **CLC 13, 67**
See also CA 106; CAAS 12

Hsun, Lu
See Lu Hsun

Hubbard, L(afayette) Ron(ald) 1911-1986 .... **CLC 43**
See also CA 77-80; 118; CANR 52; DAM POP

Huch, Ricarda (Octavia) 1864-1947 .... **TCLC 13**
See also CA 111; DLB 66

Huddle, David 1942- .... **CLC 49**
See also CA 57-60; CAAS 20; DLB 130

Hudson, Jeffrey
See Crichton, (John) Michael

Hudson, W(illiam) H(enry) 1841-1922 .... **TCLC 29**
See also CA 115; DLB 98, 153; SATA 35

Hueffer, Ford Madox
See Ford, Ford Madox

Hughart, Barry 1934-............. **CLC 39**
See also CA 137

Hughes, Colin
See Creasey, John

Hughes, David (John) 1930- .... **CLC 48**
See also CA 116; 129; DLB 14

Hughes, Edward James
See Hughes, Ted
See also DAM MST, POET

Hughes, (James) Langston 1902-1967 ..... **CLC 1, 5, 10, 15, 35, 44; BLC; DA; DAB; DAC; DC 3; PC 1; SSC 6; WLC**
See also AAYA 12; BW 1; CA 1-4R; 25-28R; CANR 1, 34; CDALB 1929-1941; CLR 17; DAM DRAM, MST, MULT, POET; DLB 4, 7, 48, 51, 86; JRDA; MAICYA; MTCW; SATA 4, 33

Hughes, Richard (Arthur Warren) 1900-1976 .... **CLC 1, 11**
See also CA 5-8R; 65-68; CANR 4; DAM NOV; DLB 15, 161; MTCW; SATA 8; SATA-Obit 25

Hughes, Ted 1930- .... **CLC 2, 4, 9, 14, 37; DAB; DAC; PC 7**
See also Hughes, Edward James
See also CA 1-4R; CANR 1, 33; CLR 3; DLB 40, 161; MAICYA; MTCW; SATA 49; SATA-Brief 27

Hugo, Richard F(ranklin) 1923-1982 .... **CLC 6, 18, 32**
See also CA 49-52; 108; CANR 3; DAM POET; DLB 5

Hugo, Victor (Marie) 1802-1885 .... **NCLC 3, 10, 21; DA; DAB; DAC; WLC**
See also DAM DRAM, MST, NOV, POET; DLB 119; SATA 47

Huidobro, Vicente
See Huidobro Fernandez, Vicente Garcia

Huidobro Fernandez, Vicente Garcia 1893-1948 .... **TCLC 31**
See also CA 131; HW

Hulme, Keri 1947- .... **CLC 39**
See also CA 125; INT 125

Hulme, T(homas) E(rnest) 1883-1917 .... **TCLC 21**
See also CA 117; DLB 19

Hume, David 1711-1776............. **LC 7**
See also DLB 104

Humphrey, William 1924-......... **CLC 45**
See also CA 77-80; DLB 6

Humphreys, Emyr Owen 1919-..... **CLC 47**
See also CA 5-8R; CANR 3, 24; DLB 15

Humphreys, Josephine 1945-.... **CLC 34, 57**
See also CA 121; 127; INT 127

Huneker, James Gibbons 1857-1921 .... **TCLC 65**
See also DLB 71

Hungerford, Pixie
See Brinsmead, H(esba) F(ay)

Hunt, E(verette) Howard, (Jr.) 1918- .... **CLC 3**
See also AITN 1; CA 45-48; CANR 2, 47

Hunt, Kyle
See Creasey, John

Hunt, (James Henry) Leigh 1784-1859 .... **NCLC 1**
See also DAM POET

Hunt, Marsha 1946-.............. **CLC 70**
See also BW 2; CA 143

Hunt, Violet 1866-1942 .... **TCLC 53**
See also DLB 162

Hunter, E. Waldo
See Sturgeon, Theodore (Hamilton)

Hunter, Evan 1926- .... **CLC 11, 31**
See also CA 5-8R; CANR 5, 38; DAM POP; DLBY 82; INT CANR-5; MTCW; SATA 25

Hunter, Kristin (Eggleston) 1931-... **CLC 35**
See also AITN 1; BW 1; CA 13-16R; CANR 13; CLR 3; DLB 33; INT CANR-13; MAICYA; SAAS 10; SATA 12

Hunter, Mollie 1922- . . . . **CLC 21**
See also McIlwraith, Maureen Mollie
Hunter
See also AAYA 13; CANR 37; CLR 25;
DLB 161; JRDA; MAICYA; SAAS 7;
SATA 54

Hunter, Robert (?)-1734. . . . . **LC 7**

Hurston, Zora Neale
1903-1960 . . . . **CLC 7, 30, 61; BLC; DA;**
DAC; SSC 4
See also AAYA 15; BW 1; CA 85-88;
DAM MST, MULT, NOV; DLB 51, 86;
MTCW

Huston, John (Marcellus)
1906-1987 . . . . **CLC 20**
See also CA 73-76; 123; CANR 34; DLB 26

Hustvedt, Siri 1955- . . . . **CLC 76**
See also CA 137

Hutten, Ulrich von 1488-1523 . . . . **LC 16**

Huxley, Aldous (Leonard)
1894-1963 . . . . . **CLC 1, 3, 4, 5, 8, 11, 18,**
35, 79; DA; DAB; DAC; WLC
See also AAYA 11; CA 85-88; CANR 44;
CDBLB 1914-1945; DAM MST, NOV;
DLB 36, 100, 162; MTCW; SATA 63

Huysmans, Charles Marie Georges
1848-1907
See Huysmans, Joris-Karl
See also CA 104

Huysmans, Joris-Karl . . . . **TCLC 7**
See also Huysmans, Charles Marie Georges
See also DLB 123

Hwang, David Henry
1957- . . . . **CLC 55; DC 4**
See also CA 127; 132; DAM DRAM;
INT 132

Hyde, Anthony 1946- . . . . **CLC 42**
See also CA 136

Hyde, Margaret O(ldroyd) 1917- . . . **CLC 21**
See also CA 1-4R; CANR 1, 36; CLR 23;
JRDA; MAICYA; SAAS 8; SATA 1, 42,
76

Hynes, James 1956(?)- . . . . **CLC 65**

Ian, Janis 1951- . . . . **CLC 21**
See also CA 105

Ibanez, Vicente Blasco
See Blasco Ibanez, Vicente

Ibarguengoitia, Jorge 1928-1983 . . . . **CLC 37**
See also CA 124; 113; HW

Ibsen, Henrik (Johan)
1828-1906 . . . . **TCLC 2, 8, 16, 37, 52;**
DA; DAB; DAC; DC 2; WLC
See also CA 104; 141; DAM DRAM, MST

Ibuse Masuji 1898-1993 . . . . **CLC 22**
See also CA 127; 141

Ichikawa, Kon 1915- . . . . **CLC 20**
See also CA 121

Idle, Eric 1943- . . . . **CLC 21**
See also Monty Python
See also CA 116; CANR 35

Ignatow, David 1914- . . . . . . **CLC 4, 7, 14, 40**
See also CA 9-12R; CAAS 3; CANR 31;
DLB 5

Ihimaera, Witi 1944- . . . . **CLC 46**
See also CA 77-80

Ilf, Ilya . . . . **TCLC 21**
See also Fainzilberg, Ilya Arnoldovich

Illyes, Gyula 1902-1983 . . . . **PC 16**
See also CA 114; 109

Immermann, Karl (Lebrecht)
1796-1840 . . . . **NCLC 4, 49**
See also DLB 133

Inclan, Ramon (Maria) del Valle
See Valle-Inclan, Ramon (Maria) del

Infante, G(uillermo) Cabrera
See Cabrera Infante, G(uillermo)

Ingalls, Rachel (Holmes) 1940- . . . . . **CLC 42**
See also CA 123; 127

Ingamells, Rex 1913-1955 . . . . **TCLC 35**

Inge, William Motter
1913-1973 . . . . **CLC 1, 8, 19**
See also CA 9-12R; CDALB 1941-1968;
DAM DRAM; DLB 7; MTCW

Ingelow, Jean 1820-1897 . . . . **NCLC 39**
See also DLB 35, 163; SATA 33

Ingram, Willis J.
See Harris, Mark

Innaurato, Albert (F.) 1948(?)- . . **CLC 21, 60**
See also CA 115; 122; INT 122

Innes, Michael
See Stewart, J(ohn) I(nnes) M(ackintosh)

Ionesco, Eugene
1909-1994 . . . . **CLC 1, 4, 6, 9, 11, 15, 41,**
86; DA; DAB; DAC; WLC
See also CA 9-12R; 144; DAM DRAM,
MST; MTCW; SATA 7; SATA-Obit 79

Iqbal, Muhammad 1873-1938 . . . . . **TCLC 28**

Ireland, Patrick
See O'Doherty, Brian

Iron, Ralph
See Schreiner, Olive (Emilie Albertina)

Irving, John (Winslow)
1942- . . . . **CLC 13, 23, 38**
See also AAYA 8; BEST 89:3; CA 25-28R;
CANR 28; DAM NOV, POP; DLB 6;
DLBY 82; MTCW

Irving, Washington
1783-1859 . . . . . **NCLC 2, 19; DA; DAB;**
SSC 2; WLC
See also CDALB 1640-1865; DAM MST;
DLB 3, 11, 30, 59, 73, 74; YABC 2

Irwin, P. K.
See Page, P(atricia) K(athleen)

Isaacs, Susan 1943- . . . . **CLC 32**
See also BEST 89:1; CA 89-92; CANR 20,
41; DAM POP; INT CANR-20; MTCW

Isherwood, Christopher (William Bradshaw)
1904-1986 . . . . **CLC 1, 9, 11, 14, 44**
See also CA 13-16R; 117; CANR 35;
DAM DRAM, NOV; DLB 15; DLBY 86;
MTCW

Ishiguro, Kazuo 1954- . . . . . . **CLC 27, 56, 59**
See also BEST 90:2; CA 120; CANR 49;
DAM NOV; MTCW

Ishikawa, Takuboku
1886(?)-1912 . . . . **TCLC 15; PC 10**
See also CA 113; DAM POET

Iskander, Fazil 1929- . . . . **CLC 47**
See also CA 102

Isler, Alan . . . . **CLC 91**

Ivan IV 1530-1584 . . . . **LC 17**

Ivanov, Vyacheslav Ivanovich
1866-1949 . . . . **TCLC 33**
See also CA 122

Ivask, Ivar Vidrik 1927-1992 . . . . . . **CLC 14**
See also CA 37-40R; 139; CANR 24

J. R. S.
See Gogarty, Oliver St. John

Jabran, Kahlil
See Gibran, Kahlil

Jabran, Khalil
See Gibran, Kahlil

Jackson, Daniel
See Wingrove, David (John)

Jackson, Jesse 1908-1983 . . . . **CLC 12**
See also BW 1; CA 25-28R; 109; CANR 27;
CLR 28; MAICYA; SATA 2, 29;
SATA-Obit 48

Jackson, Laura (Riding) 1901-1991
See Riding, Laura
See also CA 65-68; 135; CANR 28; DLB 48

Jackson, Sam
See Trumbo, Dalton

Jackson, Sara
See Wingrove, David (John)

Jackson, Shirley
1919-1965 . . . . **CLC 11, 60, 87; DA;**
DAC; SSC 9; WLC
See also AAYA 9; CA 1-4R; 25-28R;
CANR 4, 52; CDALB 1941-1968;
DAM MST; DLB 6; SATA 2

Jacob, (Cyprien-)Max 1876-1944 . . . **TCLC 6**
See also CA 104

Jacobs, Jim 1942- . . . . **CLC 12**
See also CA 97-100; INT 97-100

Jacobs, W(illiam) W(ymark)
1863-1943 . . . . **TCLC 22**
See also CA 121; DLB 135

Jacobsen, Jens Peter 1847-1885 . . **NCLC 34**

Jacobsen, Josephine 1908- . . . . **CLC 48**
See also CA 33-36R; CAAS 18; CANR 23,
48

Jacobson, Dan 1929- . . . . **CLC 4, 14**
See also CA 1-4R; CANR 2, 25; DLB 14;
MTCW

Jacqueline
See Carpentier (y Valmont), Alejo

Jagger, Mick 1944- . . . . **CLC 17**

Jakes, John (William) 1932- . . . . **CLC 29**
See also BEST 89:4; CA 57-60; CANR 10,
43; DAM NOV, POP; DLBY 83;
INT CANR-10; MTCW; SATA 62

James, Andrew
See Kirkup, James

James, C(yril) L(ionel) R(obert)
1901-1989 . . . . **CLC 33**
See also BW 2; CA 117; 125; 128; DLB 125;
MTCW

James, Daniel (Lewis) 1911-1988
See Santiago, Danny
See also CA 125

James, Dynely
See Mayne, William (James Carter)

James, Henry Sr. 1811-1882..... **NCLC 53**

James, Henry
1843-1916 ...... **TCLC 2, 11, 24, 40, 47, 64; DA; DAB; DAC; SSC 8; WLC**
See also CA 104; 132; CDALB 1865-1917; DAM MST, NOV; DLB 12, 71, 74; DLBD 13; MTCW

James, M. R.
See James, Montague (Rhodes)
See also DLB 156

James, Montague (Rhodes)
1862-1936 .... **TCLC 6; SSC 16**
See also CA 104

James, P. D. .... **CLC 18, 46**
See also White, Phyllis Dorothy James
See also BEST 90:2; CDBLB 1960 to Present; DLB 87

James, Philip
See Moorcock, Michael (John)

James, William 1842-1910..... **TCLC 15, 32**
See also CA 109

James I 1394-1437 .... **LC 20**

Jameson, Anna 1794-1860 .... **NCLC 43**
See also DLB 99, 166

Jami, Nur al-Din 'Abd al-Rahman
1414-1492 .... **LC 9**

Jandl, Ernst 1925- .... **CLC 34**

Janowitz, Tama 1957- .... **CLC 43**
See also CA 106; CANR 52; DAM POP

Japrisot, Sebastien 1931-.......... **CLC 90**

Jarrell, Randall
1914-1965 .... **CLC 1, 2, 6, 9, 13, 49**
See also CA 5-8R; 25-28R; CABS 2; CANR 6, 34; CDALB 1941-1968; CLR 6; DAM POET; DLB 48, 52; MAICYA; MTCW; SATA 7

Jarry, Alfred
1873-1907 .... **TCLC 2, 14; SSC 20**
See also CA 104; DAM DRAM

Jarvis, E. K.
See Bloch, Robert (Albert); Ellison, Harlan (Jay); Silverberg, Robert

Jeake, Samuel, Jr.
See Aiken, Conrad (Potter)

Jean Paul 1763-1825 .... **NCLC 7**

Jefferies, (John) Richard
1848-1887 .... **NCLC 47**
See also DLB 98, 141; SATA 16

Jeffers, (John) Robinson
1887-1962 .... **CLC 2, 3, 11, 15, 54; DA; DAC; WLC**
See also CA 85-88; CANR 35; CDALB 1917-1929; DAM MST, POET; DLB 45; MTCW

Jefferson, Janet
See Mencken, H(enry) L(ouis)

Jefferson, Thomas 1743-1826 .... **NCLC 11**
See also CDALB 1640-1865; DLB 31

Jeffrey, Francis 1773-1850....... **NCLC 33**
See also DLB 107

Jelakowitch, Ivan
See Heijermans, Herman

Jellicoe, (Patricia) Ann 1927- ...... **CLC 27**
See also CA 85-88; DLB 13

Jen, Gish .... **CLC 70**
See also Jen, Lillian

Jen, Lillian 1956(?)-
See Jen, Gish
See also CA 135

Jenkins, (John) Robin 1912- .... **CLC 52**
See also CA 1-4R; CANR 1; DLB 14

Jennings, Elizabeth (Joan)
1926- .... **CLC 5, 14**
See also CA 61-64; CAAS 5; CANR 8, 39; DLB 27; MTCW; SATA 66

Jennings, Waylon 1937-........... **CLC 21**

Jensen, Johannes V. 1873-1950.... **TCLC 41**

Jensen, Laura (Linnea) 1948- ...... **CLC 37**
See also CA 103

Jerome, Jerome K(lapka)
1859-1927 .... **TCLC 23**
See also CA 119; DLB 10, 34, 135

Jerrold, Douglas William
1803-1857 .... **NCLC 2**
See also DLB 158, 159

Jewett, (Theodora) Sarah Orne
1849-1909 .... **TCLC 1, 22; SSC 6**
See also CA 108; 127; DLB 12, 74; SATA 15

Jewsbury, Geraldine (Endsor)
1812-1880 .... **NCLC 22**
See also DLB 21

Jhabvala, Ruth Prawer
1927- .... **CLC 4, 8, 29, 94; DAB**
See also CA 1-4R; CANR 2, 29, 51; DAM NOV; DLB 139; INT CANR-29; MTCW

Jibran, Kahlil
See Gibran, Kahlil

Jibran, Khalil
See Gibran, Kahlil

Jiles, Paulette 1943-........... **CLC 13, 58**
See also CA 101

Jimenez (Mantecon), Juan Ramon
1881-1958 .... **TCLC 4; HLC; PC 7**
See also CA 104; 131; DAM MULT, POET; DLB 134; HW; MTCW

Jimenez, Ramon
See Jimenez (Mantecon), Juan Ramon

Jimenez Mantecon, Juan
See Jimenez (Mantecon), Juan Ramon

Joel, Billy .... **CLC 26**
See also Joel, William Martin

Joel, William Martin 1949-
See Joel, Billy
See also CA 108

John of the Cross, St. 1542-1591 .... **LC 18**

Johnson, B(ryan) S(tanley William)
1933-1973 .... **CLC 6, 9**
See also CA 9-12R; 53-56; CANR 9; DLB 14, 40

Johnson, Benj. F. of Boo
See Riley, James Whitcomb

Johnson, Benjamin F. of Boo
See Riley, James Whitcomb

Johnson, Charles (Richard)
1948- .... **CLC 7, 51, 65; BLC**
See also BW 2; CA 116; CAAS 18; CANR 42; DAM MULT; DLB 33

Johnson, Denis 1949-............. **CLC 52**
See also CA 117; 121; DLB 120

Johnson, Diane 1934-........ **CLC 5, 13, 48**
See also CA 41-44R; CANR 17, 40; DLBY 80; INT CANR-17; MTCW

Johnson, Eyvind (Olof Verner)
1900-1976 .... **CLC 14**
See also CA 73-76; 69-72; CANR 34

Johnson, J. R.
See James, C(yril) L(ionel) R(obert)

Johnson, James Weldon
1871-1938 .... **TCLC 3, 19; BLC**
See also BW 1; CA 104; 125; CDALB 1917-1929; CLR 32; DAM MULT, POET; DLB 51; MTCW; SATA 31

Johnson, Joyce 1935-............. **CLC 58**
See also CA 125; 129

Johnson, Lionel (Pigot)
1867-1902 .... **TCLC 19**
See also CA 117; DLB 19

Johnson, Mel
See Malzberg, Barry N(athaniel)

Johnson, Pamela Hansford
1912-1981 .... **CLC 1, 7, 27**
See also CA 1-4R; 104; CANR 2, 28; DLB 15; MTCW

Johnson, Samuel
1709-1784 ..... **LC 15; DA; DAB; DAC; WLC**
See also CDBLB 1660-1789; DAM MST; DLB 39, 95, 104, 142

Johnson, Uwe
1934-1984 .... **CLC 5, 10, 15, 40**
See also CA 1-4R; 112; CANR 1, 39; DLB 75; MTCW

Johnston, George (Benson) 1913- ... **CLC 51**
See also CA 1-4R; CANR 5, 20; DLB 88

Johnston, Jennifer 1930-........... **CLC 7**
See also CA 85-88; DLB 14

Jolley, (Monica) Elizabeth
1923- .... **CLC 46; SSC 19**
See also CA 127; CAAS 13

Jones, Arthur Llewellyn 1863-1947
See Machen, Arthur
See also CA 104

Jones, D(ouglas) G(ordon) 1929-.... **CLC 10**
See also CA 29-32R; CANR 13; DLB 53

Jones, David (Michael)
1895-1974 .... **CLC 2, 4, 7, 13, 42**
See also CA 9-12R; 53-56; CANR 28; CDBLB 1945-1960; DLB 20, 100; MTCW

Jones, David Robert 1947-
See Bowie, David
See also CA 103

Jones, Diana Wynne 1934- .... **CLC 26**
See also AAYA 12; CA 49-52; CANR 4, 26; CLR 23; DLB 161; JRDA; MAICYA; SAAS 7; SATA 9, 70

Jones, Edward P. 1950-........... **CLC 76**
See also BW 2; CA 142

Kazan, Elia 1909-.......... **CLC 6, 16, 63**
See also CA 21-24R; CANR 32

Kazantzakis, Nikos
1883(?)-1957 .... **TCLC 2, 5, 33**
See also CA 105; 132; MTCW

Kazin, Alfred 1915- .... **CLC 34, 38**
See also CA 1-4R; CAAS 7; CANR 1, 45;
DLB 67

Keane, Mary Nesta (Skrine) 1904-1996
See Keane, Molly
See also CA 108; 114; 151

Keane, Molly..................... **CLC 31**
See also Keane, Mary Nesta (Skrine)
See also INT 114

Keates, Jonathan 19(?)-........... **CLC 34**

Keaton, Buster 1895-1966 .... **CLC 20**

Keats, John
1795-1821 .... **NCLC 8; DA; DAB;
DAC; PC 1; WLC**
See also CDBLB 1789-1832; DAM MST,
POET; DLB 96, 110

Keene, Donald 1922- .... **CLC 34**
See also CA 1-4R; CANR 5

Keillor, Garrison.................. **CLC 40**
See also Keillor, Gary (Edward)
See also AAYA 2; BEST 89:3; DLBY 87;
SATA 58

Keillor, Gary (Edward) 1942-
See Keillor, Garrison
See also CA 111; 117; CANR 36;
DAM POP; MTCW

Keith, Michael
See Hubbard, L(afayette) Ron(ald)

Keller, Gottfried 1819-1890 .... **NCLC 2**
See also DLB 129

Kellerman, Jonathan 1949- .... **CLC 44**
See also BEST 90:1; CA 106; CANR 29, 51;
DAM POP; INT CANR-29

Kelley, William Melvin 1937-...... **CLC 22**
See also BW 1; CA 77-80; CANR 27;
DLB 33

Kellogg, Marjorie 1922-............ **CLC 2**
See also CA 81-84

Kellow, Kathleen
See Hibbert, Eleanor Alice Burford

Kelly, M(ilton) T(erry) 1947-...... **CLC 55**
See also CA 97-100; CAAS 22; CANR 19,
43

Kelman, James 1946-......... **CLC 58, 86**
See also CA 148

Kemal, Yashar 1923- .... **CLC 14, 29**
See also CA 89-92; CANR 44

Kemble, Fanny 1809-1893 .... **NCLC 18**
See also DLB 32

Kemelman, Harry 1908-........... **CLC 2**
See also AITN 1; CA 9-12R; CANR 6;
DLB 28

Kempe, Margery 1373(?)-1440(?) ..... **LC 6**
See also DLB 146

Kempis, Thomas a 1380-1471 .... **LC 11**

Kendall, Henry 1839-1882....... **NCLC 12**

Keneally, Thomas (Michael)
1935-...... **CLC 5, 8, 10, 14, 19, 27, 43**
See also CA 85-88; CANR 10, 50;
DAM NOV; MTCW

Kennedy, Adrienne (Lita)
1931-............. **CLC 66; BLC; DC 5**
See also BW 2; CA 103; CAAS 20; CABS 3;
CANR 26; DAM MULT; DLB 38

Kennedy, John Pendleton
1795-1870 .... **NCLC 2**
See also DLB 3

Kennedy, Joseph Charles 1929-
See Kennedy, X. J.
See also CA 1-4R; CANR 4, 30, 40;
SATA 14, 86

Kennedy, William 1928-... **CLC 6, 28, 34, 53**
See also AAYA 1; CA 85-88; CANR 14,
31; DAM NOV; DLB 143; DLBY 85;
INT CANR-31; MTCW; SATA 57

Kennedy, X. J..................... **CLC 8, 42**
See also Kennedy, Joseph Charles
See also CAAS 9; CLR 27; DLB 5;
SAAS 22

Kenny, Maurice (Francis) 1929-.... **CLC 87**
See also CA 144; CAAS 22; DAM MULT;
NNAL

Kent, Kelvin
See Kuttner, Henry

Kenton, Maxwell
See Southern, Terry

Kenyon, Robert O.
See Kuttner, Henry

Kerouac, Jack ..... **CLC 1, 2, 3, 5, 14, 29, 61**
See also Kerouac, Jean-Louis Lebris de
See also CDALB 1941-1968; DLB 2, 16;
DLBD 3; DLBY 95

Kerouac, Jean-Louis Lebris de 1922-1969
See Kerouac, Jack
See also AITN 1; CA 5-8R; 25-28R;
CANR 26; DA; DAB; DAC; DAM MST,
NOV, POET, POP; MTCW; WLC

Kerr, Jean 1923-................. **CLC 22**
See also CA 5-8R; CANR 7; INT CANR-7

Kerr, M. E..................... **CLC 12, 35**
See also Meaker, Marijane (Agnes)
See also AAYA 2; CLR 29; SAAS 1

Kerr, Robert .... **CLC 55**

Kerrigan, (Thomas) Anthony
1918-.................... **CLC 4, 6**
See also CA 49-52; CAAS 11; CANR 4

Kerry, Lois
See Duncan, Lois

Kesey, Ken (Elton)
1935-...... **CLC 1, 3, 6, 11, 46, 64; DA;
DAB; DAC; WLC**
See also CA 1-4R; CANR 22, 38;
CDALB 1968-1988; DAM MST, NOV,
POP; DLB 2, 16; MTCW; SATA 66

Kesselring, Joseph (Otto)
1902-1967 .... **CLC 45**
See also CA 150; DAM DRAM, MST

Kessler, Jascha (Frederick) 1929-.... **CLC 4**
See also CA 17-20R; CANR 8, 48

Kettelkamp, Larry (Dale) 1933- .... **CLC 12**
See also CA 29-32R; CANR 16; SAAS 3;
SATA 2

Key, Ellen 1849-1926 .... **TCLC 65**

Keyber, Conny
See Fielding, Henry

Keyes, Daniel 1927-.... **CLC 80; DA; DAC**
See also CA 17-20R; CANR 10, 26;
DAM MST, NOV; SATA 37

Keynes, John Maynard
1883-1946 .... **TCLC 64**
See also CA 114; DLBD 10

Khanshendel, Chiron
See Rose, Wendy

Khayyam, Omar
1048-1131 .... **CMLC 11; PC 8**
See also DAM POET

Kherdian, David 1931-........... **CLC 6, 9**
See also CA 21-24R; CAAS 2; CANR 39;
CLR 24; JRDA; MAICYA; SATA 16, 74

Khlebnikov, Velimir .... **TCLC 20**
See also Khlebnikov, Viktor Vladimirovich

Khlebnikov, Viktor Vladimirovich 1885-1922
See Khlebnikov, Velimir
See also CA 117

Khodasevich, Vladislav (Felitsianovich)
1886-1939 .... **TCLC 15**
See also CA 115

Kielland, Alexander Lange
1849-1906 .... **TCLC 5**
See also CA 104

Kiely, Benedict 1919-.......... **CLC 23, 43**
See also CA 1-4R; CANR 2; DLB 15

Kienzle, William X(avier) 1928- .... **CLC 25**
See also CA 93-96; CAAS 1; CANR 9, 31;
DAM POP; INT CANR-31; MTCW

Kierkegaard, Soren 1813-1855.... **NCLC 34**

Killens, John Oliver 1916-1987..... **CLC 10**
See also BW 2; CA 77-80; 123; CAAS 2;
CANR 26; DLB 33

Killigrew, Anne 1660-1685........... **LC 4**
See also DLB 131

Kim
See Simenon, Georges (Jacques Christian)

Kincaid, Jamaica 1949- ... **CLC 43, 68; BLC**
See also AAYA 13; BW 2; CA 125;
CANR 47; DAM MULT, NOV;
DLB 157

King, Francis (Henry) 1923- ..... **CLC 8, 53**
See also CA 1-4R; CANR 1, 33;
DAM NOV; DLB 15, 139; MTCW

King, Martin Luther, Jr.
1929-1968 .... **CLC 83; BLC; DA; DAB;
DAC**
See also BW 2; CA 25-28; CANR 27, 44;
CAP 2; DAM MST, MULT; MTCW;
SATA 14

King, Stephen (Edwin)
1947-...... **CLC 12, 26, 37, 61; SSC 17**
See also AAYA 1, 17; BEST 90:1;
CA 61-64; CANR 1, 30, 52; DAM NOV,
POP; DLB 143; DLBY 80; JRDA;
MTCW; SATA 9, 55

King, Steve
See King, Stephen (Edwin)

King, Thomas 1943-......... **CLC 89; DAC**
See also CA 144; DAM MULT; NNAL

Kingman, Lee. CLC 17
See also Natti, (Mary) Lee
See also SAAS 3; SATA 1, 67

Kingsley, Charles 1819-1875 . . . . . NCLC 35
See also DLB 21, 32, 163; YABC 2

Kingsley, Sidney 1906-1995 . . . . CLC 44
See also CA 85-88; 147; DLB 7

Kingsolver, Barbara 1955- . . . . . . CLC 55, 81
See also AAYA 15; CA 129; 134;
DAM POP; INT 134

Kingston, Maxine (Ting Ting) Hong
1940- . . . . CLC 12, 19, 58
See also AAYA 8; CA 69-72; CANR 13,
38; DAM MULT, NOV; DLBY 80;
INT CANR-13; MTCW; SATA 53

Kinnell, Galway
1927- . . . . CLC 1, 2, 3, 5, 13, 29
See also CA 9-12R; CANR 10, 34; DLB 5;
DLBY 87; INT CANR-34; MTCW

Kinsella, Thomas 1928- . . . . CLC 4, 19
See also CA 17-20R; CANR 15; DLB 27;
MTCW

Kinsella, W(illiam) P(atrick)
1935- . . . . CLC 27, 43; DAC
See also AAYA 7; CA 97-100; CAAS 7;
CANR 21, 35; DAM NOV, POP;
INT CANR-21; MTCW

Kipling, (Joseph) Rudyard
1865-1936 . . . . . TCLC 8, 17; DA; DAB;
DAC; PC 3; SSC 5; WLC
See also CA 105; 120; CANR 33;
CDBLB 1890-1914; CLR 39; DAM MST,
POET; DLB 19, 34, 141, 156; MAICYA;
MTCW; YABC 2

Kirkup, James 1918- . . . . CLC 1
See also CA 1-4R; CAAS 4; CANR 2;
DLB 27; SATA 12

Kirkwood, James 1930(?)-1989 . . . . . . CLC 9
See also AITN 2; CA 1-4R; 128; CANR 6,
40

Kirshner, Sidney
See Kingsley, Sidney

Kis, Danilo 1935-1989 . . . . CLC 57
See also CA 109; 118; 129; MTCW

Kivi, Aleksis 1834-1872 . . . . NCLC 30

Kizer, Carolyn (Ashley)
1925- . . . . CLC 15, 39, 80
See also CA 65-68; CAAS 5; CANR 24;
DAM POET; DLB 5

Klabund 1890-1928 . . . . TCLC 44
See also DLB 66

Klappert, Peter 1942- . . . . CLC 57
See also CA 33-36R; DLB 5

Klein, A(braham) M(oses)
1909-1972 . . . . CLC 19; DAB; DAC
See also CA 101; 37-40R; DAM MST;
DLB 68

Klein, Norma 1938-1989 . . . . CLC 30
See also AAYA 2; CA 41-44R; 128;
CANR 15, 37; CLR 2, 19;
INT CANR-15; JRDA; MAICYA;
SAAS 1; SATA 7, 57

Klein, T(heodore) E(ibon) D(onald)
1947- . . . . CLC 34
See also CA 119; CANR 44

Kleist, Heinrich von
1777-1811 . . . . NCLC 2, 37; SSC 22
See also DAM DRAM; DLB 90

Klima, Ivan 1931- . . . . CLC 56
See also CA 25-28R; CANR 17, 50;
DAM NOV

Klimentov, Andrei Platonovich 1899-1951
See Platonov, Andrei
See also CA 108

Klinger, Friedrich Maximilian von
1752-1831 . . . . NCLC 1
See also DLB 94

Klopstock, Friedrich Gottlieb
1724-1803 . . . . NCLC 11
See also DLB 97

Knebel, Fletcher 1911-1993 . . . . CLC 14
See also AITN 1; CA 1-4R; 140; CAAS 3;
CANR 1, 36; SATA 36; SATA-Obit 75

Knickerbocker, Diedrich
See Irving, Washington

Knight, Etheridge
1931-1991 . . . . CLC 40; BLC; PC 14
See also BW 1; CA 21-24R; 133; CANR 23;
DAM POET; DLB 41

Knight, Sarah Kemble 1666-1727 . . . . . LC 7
See also DLB 24

Knister, Raymond 1899-1932 . . . . . . TCLC 56
See also DLB 68

Knowles, John
1926- . . . . . . CLC 1, 4, 10, 26; DA; DAC
See also AAYA 10; CA 17-20R; CANR 40;
CDALB 1968-1988; DAM MST, NOV;
DLB 6; MTCW; SATA 8

Knox, Calvin M.
See Silverberg, Robert

Knye, Cassandra
See Disch, Thomas M(ichael)

Koch, C(hristopher) J(ohn) 1932- . . . CLC 42
See also CA 127

Koch, Christopher
See Koch, C(hristopher) J(ohn)

Koch, Kenneth 1925- . . . . CLC 5, 8, 44
See also CA 1-4R; CANR 6, 36;
DAM POET; DLB 5; INT CANR-36;
SATA 65

Kochanowski, Jan 1530-1584 . . . . LC 10

Kock, Charles Paul de
1794-1871 . . . . NCLC 16

Koda Shigeyuki 1867-1947
See Rohan, Koda
See also CA 121

Koestler, Arthur
1905-1983 . . . . . . CLC 1, 3, 6, 8, 15, 33
See also CA 1-4R; 109; CANR 1, 33;
CDBLB 1945-1960; DLBY 83; MTCW

Kogawa, Joy Nozomi 1935- . . . CLC 78; DAC
See also CA 101; CANR 19; DAM MST,
MULT

Kohout, Pavel 1928- . . . . CLC 13
See also CA 45-48; CANR 3

Koizumi, Yakumo
See Hearn, (Patricio) Lafcadio (Tessima
Carlos)

Kolmar, Gertrud 1894-1943 . . . . . . TCLC 40

Komunyakaa, Yusef 1947- . . . . . . CLC 86, 94
See also CA 147; DLB 120

Konrad, George
See Konrad, Gyoergy

Konrad, Gyoergy 1933- . . . . . . CLC 4, 10, 73
See also CA 85-88

Konwicki, Tadeusz 1926- . . . . . CLC 8, 28, 54
See also CA 101; CAAS 9; CANR 39;
MTCW

Koontz, Dean R(ay) 1945- . . . . CLC 78
See also AAYA 9; BEST 89:3, 90:2;
CA 108; CANR 19, 36, 52; DAM NOV,
POP; MTCW

Kopit, Arthur (Lee) 1937- . . . . CLC 1, 18, 33
See also AITN 1; CA 81-84; CABS 3;
DAM DRAM; DLB 7; MTCW

Kops, Bernard 1926- . . . . CLC 4
See also CA 5-8R; DLB 13

Kornbluth, C(yril) M. 1923-1958 . . . . TCLC 8
See also CA 105; DLB 8

Korolenko, V. G.
See Korolenko, Vladimir Galaktionovich

Korolenko, Vladimir
See Korolenko, Vladimir Galaktionovich

Korolenko, Vladimir G.
See Korolenko, Vladimir Galaktionovich

Korolenko, Vladimir Galaktionovich
1853-1921 . . . . TCLC 22
See also CA 121

Korzybski, Alfred (Habdank Skarbek)
1879-1950 . . . . TCLC 61
See also CA 123

Kosinski, Jerzy (Nikodem)
1933-1991 . . . . CLC 1, 2, 3, 6, 10, 15, 53,
70
See also CA 17-20R; 134; CANR 9, 46;
DAM NOV; DLB 2; DLBY 82; MTCW

Kostelanetz, Richard (Cory) 1940- . . CLC 28
See also CA 13-16R; CAAS 8; CANR 38

Kostrowitzki, Wilhelm Apollinaris de
1880-1918
See Apollinaire, Guillaume
See also CA 104

Kotlowitz, Robert 1924- . . . . CLC 4
See also CA 33-36R; CANR 36

Kotzebue, August (Friedrich Ferdinand) von
1761-1819 . . . . NCLC 25
See also DLB 94

Kotzwinkle, William 1938- . . . CLC 5, 14, 35
See also CA 45-48; CANR 3, 44; CLR 6;
MAICYA; SATA 24, 70

Kozol, Jonathan 1936- . . . . CLC 17
See also CA 61-64; CANR 16, 45

Kozoll, Michael 1940(?)- . . . . CLC 35

Kramer, Kathryn 19(?)- . . . . CLC 34

Kramer, Larry 1935- . . . . CLC 42
See also CA 124; 126; DAM POP

Krasicki, Ignacy 1735-1801 . . . . NCLC 8

Krasinski, Zygmunt 1812-1859 . . . . NCLC 4

Kraus, Karl 1874-1936 . . . . TCLC 5
See also CA 104; DLB 118

Kreve (Mickevicius), Vincas
1882-1954 . . . . TCLC 27

Kristeva, Julia 1941- . . . . CLC 77

Kristofferson, Kris 1936- . . . . CLC 26
See also CA 104

Krizanc, John 1956- . . . . CLC 57

Krleza, Miroslav 1893-1981. . . . . CLC 8
See also CA 97-100; 105; CANR 50;
DLB 147

Kroetsch, Robert
1927- . . . . CLC 5, 23, 57; DAC
See also CA 17-20R; CANR 8, 38;
DAM POET; DLB 53; MTCW

Kroetz, Franz
See Kroetz, Franz Xaver

Kroetz, Franz Xaver 1946- . . . . CLC 41
See also CA 130

Kroker, Arthur 1945- . . . . CLC 77

Kropotkin, Peter (Aleksieevich)
1842-1921 . . . . TCLC 36
See also CA 119

Krotkov, Yuri 1917- . . . . CLC 19
See also CA 102

Krumb
See Crumb, R(obert)

Krumgold, Joseph (Quincy)
1908-1980 . . . . CLC 12
See also CA 9-12R; 101; CANR 7;
MAICYA; SATA 1, 48; SATA-Obit 23

Krumwitz
See Crumb, R(obert)

Krutch, Joseph Wood 1893-1970. . . . CLC 24
See also CA 1-4R; 25-28R; CANR 4;
DLB 63

Krutzch, Gus
See Eliot, T(homas) S(tearns)

Krylov, Ivan Andreevich
1768(?)-1844 . . . . NCLC 1
See also DLB 150

Kubin, Alfred (Leopold Isidor)
1877-1959 . . . . TCLC 23
See also CA 112; 149; DLB 81

Kubrick, Stanley 1928- . . . . CLC 16
See also CA 81-84; CANR 33; DLB 26

Kumin, Maxine (Winokur)
1925- . . . . CLC 5, 13, 28; PC 15
See also AITN 2; CA 1-4R; CAAS 8;
CANR 1, 21; DAM POET; DLB 5;
MTCW; SATA 12

Kundera, Milan
1929- . . . . CLC 4, 9, 19, 32, 68
See also AAYA 2; CA 85-88; CANR 19,
52; DAM NOV; MTCW

Kunene, Mazisi (Raymond) 1930- . . . CLC 85
See also BW 1; CA 125; DLB 117

Kunitz, Stanley (Jasspon)
1905- . . . . CLC 6, 11, 14
See also CA 41-44R; CANR 26; DLB 48;
INT CANR-26; MTCW

Kunze, Reiner 1933- . . . . CLC 10
See also CA 93-96; DLB 75

Kuprin, Aleksandr Ivanovich
1870-1938 . . . . TCLC 5
See also CA 104

Kureishi, Hanif 1954(?)- . . . . CLC 64
See also CA 139

Kurosawa, Akira 1910- . . . . CLC 16
See also AAYA 11; CA 101; CANR 46;
DAM MULT

Kushner, Tony 1957(?)- . . . . CLC 81
See also CA 144; DAM DRAM

Kuttner, Henry 1915-1958. . . . . TCLC 10
See also CA 107; DLB 8

Kuzma, Greg 1944- . . . . CLC 7
See also CA 33-36R

Kuzmin, Mikhail 1872(?)-1936 . . . . TCLC 40

Kyd, Thomas 1558-1594. . . . . . . LC 22; DC 3
See also DAM DRAM; DLB 62

Kyprianos, Iossif
See Samarakis, Antonis

La Bruyere, Jean de 1645-1696. . . . . . LC 17

Lacan, Jacques (Marie Emile)
1901-1981 . . . . CLC 75
See also CA 121; 104

Laclos, Pierre Ambroise Francois Choderlos
de 1741-1803 . . . . NCLC 4

Lacolere, Francois
See Aragon, Louis

La Colere, Francois
See Aragon, Louis

La Deshabilleuse
See Simenon, Georges (Jacques Christian)

Lady Gregory
See Gregory, Isabella Augusta (Persse)

Lady of Quality, A
See Bagnold, Enid

La Fayette, Marie (Madelaine Pioche de la
Vergne Comtes 1634-1693. . . . . . LC 2

Lafayette, Rene
See Hubbard, L(afayette) Ron(ald)

Laforgue, Jules
1860-1887 . . . . NCLC 5, 53; PC 14;
SSC 20

Lagerkvist, Paer (Fabian)
1891-1974 . . . . CLC 7, 10, 13, 54
See also Lagerkvist, Par
See also CA 85-88; 49-52; DAM DRAM,
NOV; MTCW

Lagerkvist, Par . . . . SSC 12
See also Lagerkvist, Paer (Fabian)

Lagerloef, Selma (Ottiliana Lovisa)
1858-1940 . . . . TCLC 4, 36
See also Lagerlof, Selma (Ottiliana Lovisa)
See also CA 108; SATA 15

Lagerlof, Selma (Ottiliana Lovisa)
See Lagerloef, Selma (Ottiliana Lovisa)
See also CLR 7; SATA 15

La Guma, (Justin) Alex(ander)
1925-1985 . . . . CLC 19
See also BW 1; CA 49-52; 118; CANR 25;
DAM NOV; DLB 117; MTCW

Laidlaw, A. K.
See Grieve, C(hristopher) M(urray)

Lainez, Manuel Mujica
See Mujica Lainez, Manuel
See also HW

Laing, R(onald) D(avid)
1927-1989 . . . . CLC 95
See also CA 107; 129; CANR 34; MTCW

Lamartine, Alphonse (Marie Louis Prat) de
1790-1869 . . . . NCLC 11; PC 16
See also DAM POET

Lamb, Charles
1775-1834 . . . . NCLC 10; DA; DAB;
DAC; WLC
See also CDBLB 1789-1832; DAM MST;
DLB 93, 107, 163; SATA 17

Lamb, Lady Caroline 1785-1828. . NCLC 38
See also DLB 116

Lamming, George (William)
1927- . . . . CLC 2, 4, 66; BLC
See also BW 2; CA 85-88; CANR 26;
DAM MULT; DLB 125; MTCW

L'Amour, Louis (Dearborn)
1908-1988 . . . . CLC 25, 55
See also AAYA 16; AITN 2; BEST 89:2;
CA 1-4R; 125; CANR 3, 25, 40;
DAM NOV, POP; DLBY 80; MTCW

Lampedusa, Giuseppe (Tomasi) di . . . TCLC 13
See also Tomasi di Lampedusa, Giuseppe

Lampman, Archibald 1861-1899 . . NCLC 25
See also DLB 92

Lancaster, Bruce 1896-1963. . . . . CLC 36
See also CA 9-10; CAP 1; SATA 9

Landau, Mark Alexandrovich
See Aldanov, Mark (Alexandrovich)

Landau-Aldanov, Mark Alexandrovich
See Aldanov, Mark (Alexandrovich)

Landis, John 1950- . . . . CLC 26
See also CA 112; 122

Landolfi, Tommaso 1908-1979. . . CLC 11, 49
See also CA 127; 117

Landon, Letitia Elizabeth
1802-1838 . . . . NCLC 15
See also DLB 96

Landor, Walter Savage
1775-1864 . . . . NCLC 14
See also DLB 93, 107

Landwirth, Heinz 1927-
See Lind, Jakov
See also CA 9-12R; CANR 7

Lane, Patrick 1939- . . . . CLC 25
See also CA 97-100; DAM POET; DLB 53;
INT 97-100

Lang, Andrew 1844-1912. . . . . TCLC 16
See also CA 114; 137; DLB 98, 141;
MAICYA; SATA 16

Lang, Fritz 1890-1976 . . . . CLC 20
See also CA 77-80; 69-72; CANR 30

Lange, John
See Crichton, (John) Michael

Langer, Elinor 1939- . . . . CLC 34
See also CA 121

Langland, William
1330(?)-1400(?) . . . . . . LC 19; DA; DAB;
DAC
See also DAM MST, POET; DLB 146

Langstaff, Launcelot
See Irving, Washington

Lanier, Sidney 1842-1881 . . . . NCLC 6
See also DAM POET; DLB 64; DLBD 13;
MAICYA; SATA 18

Lanyer, Aemilia 1569-1645 . . . . . . LC 10, 30
See also DLB 121

Lee, Willy
See Burroughs, William S(eward)

Lee-Hamilton, Eugene (Jacob)
1845-1907 . . . . **TCLC 22**
See also CA 117

Leet, Judith 1935- . . . . **CLC 11**

Le Fanu, Joseph Sheridan
1814-1873 . . . . **NCLC 9; SSC 14**
See also DAM POP; DLB 21, 70, 159

Leffland, Ella 1931- . . . . **CLC 19**
See also CA 29-32R; CANR 35; DLBY 84;
INT CANR-35; SATA 65

Leger, Alexis
See Leger, (Marie-Rene Auguste) Alexis
Saint-Leger

Leger, (Marie-Rene Auguste) Alexis
Saint-Leger 1887-1975 . . . . **CLC 11**
See also Perse, St.-John
See also CA 13-16R; 61-64; CANR 43;
DAM POET; MTCW

Leger, Saintleger
See Leger, (Marie-Rene Auguste) Alexis
Saint-Leger

Le Guin, Ursula K(roeber)
1929- . . . . . . CLC 8, 13, 22, 45, 71; DAB;
DAC; SSC 12
See also AAYA 9; AITN 1; CA 21-24R;
CANR 9, 32, 52; CDALB 1968-1988;
CLR 3, 28; DAM MST, POP; DLB 8, 52;
INT CANR-32; JRDA; MAICYA;
MTCW; SATA 4, 52

Lehmann, Rosamond (Nina)
1901-1990 . . . . **CLC 5**
See also CA 77-80; 131; CANR 8; DLB 15

Leiber, Fritz (Reuter, Jr.)
1910-1992 . . . . **CLC 25**
See also CA 45-48; 139; CANR 2, 40;
DLB 8; MTCW; SATA 45;
SATA-Obit 73

Leimbach, Martha 1963-
See Leimbach, Marti
See also CA 130

Leimbach, Marti . . . . **CLC 65**
See also Leimbach, Martha

Leino, Eino . . . . **TCLC 24**
See also Loennbohm, Armas Eino Leopold

Leiris, Michel (Julien) 1901-1990 . . . **CLC 61**
See also CA 119; 128; 132

Leithauser, Brad 1953- . . . . **CLC 27**
See also CA 107; CANR 27; DLB 120

Lelchuk, Alan 1938- . . . . **CLC 5**
See also CA 45-48; CAAS 20; CANR 1

Lem, Stanislaw 1921- . . . . **CLC 8, 15, 40**
See also CA 105; CAAS 1; CANR 32;
MTCW

Lemann, Nancy 1956- . . . . **CLC 39**
See also CA 118; 136

Lemonnier, (Antoine Louis) Camille
1844-1913 . . . . **TCLC 22**
See also CA 121

Lenau, Nikolaus 1802-1850 . . . . . . **NCLC 16**

L'Engle, Madeleine (Camp Franklin)
1918- . . . . **CLC 12**
See also AAYA 1; AITN 2; CA 1-4R;
CANR 3, 21, 39; CLR 1, 14; DAM POP;
DLB 52; JRDA; MAICYA; MTCW;
SAAS 15; SATA 1, 27, 75

Lengyel, Jozsef 1896-1975 . . . . **CLC 7**
See also CA 85-88; 57-60

Lennon, John (Ono)
1940-1980 . . . . **CLC 12, 35**
See also CA 102

Lennox, Charlotte Ramsay
1729(?)-1804 . . . . **NCLC 23**
See also DLB 39

Lentricchia, Frank (Jr.) 1940- . . . . . . **CLC 34**
See also CA 25-28R; CANR 19

Lenz, Siegfried 1926- . . . . **CLC 27**
See also CA 89-92; DLB 75

Leonard, Elmore (John, Jr.)
1925- . . . . **CLC 28, 34, 71**
See also AITN 1; BEST 89:1, 90:4;
CA 81-84; CANR 12, 28; DAM POP;
INT CANR-28; MTCW

Leonard, Hugh . . . . **CLC 19**
See also Byrne, John Keyes
See also DLB 13

Leonov, Leonid (Maximovich)
1899-1994 . . . . **CLC 92**
See also CA 129; DAM NOV; MTCW

Leopardi, (Conte) Giacomo
1798-1837 . . . . **NCLC 22**

Le Reveler
See Artaud, Antonin (Marie Joseph)

Lerman, Eleanor 1952- . . . . **CLC 9**
See also CA 85-88

Lerman, Rhoda 1936- . . . . **CLC 56**
See also CA 49-52

Lermontov, Mikhail Yuryevich
1814-1841 . . . . **NCLC 47**

Leroux, Gaston 1868-1927 . . . . **TCLC 25**
See also CA 108; 136; SATA 65

Lesage, Alain-Rene 1668-1747 . . . . . . **LC 28**

Leskov, Nikolai (Semyonovich)
1831-1895 . . . . **NCLC 25**

Lessing, Doris (May)
1919- . . . . . CLC 1, 2, 3, 6, 10, 15, 22, 40,
94; DA; DAB; DAC; SSC 6
See also CA 9-12R; CAAS 14; CANR 33;
CDBLB 1960 to Present; DAM MST,
NOV; DLB 15, 139; DLBY 85; MTCW

Lessing, Gotthold Ephraim
1729-1781 . . . . **LC 8**
See also DLB 97

Lester, Richard 1932- . . . . **CLC 20**

Lever, Charles (James)
1806-1872 . . . . **NCLC 23**
See also DLB 21

Leverson, Ada 1865(?)-1936(?) . . . . **TCLC 18**
See also Elaine
See also CA 117; DLB 153

Levertov, Denise
1923- . . . . . . CLC 1, 2, 3, 5, 8, 15, 28, 66;
PC 11
See also CA 1-4R; CAAS 19; CANR 3, 29,
50; DAM POET; DLB 5, 165;
INT CANR-29; MTCW

Levi, Jonathan . . . . **CLC 76**

Levi, Peter (Chad Tigar) 1931- . . . . . **CLC 41**
See also CA 5-8R; CANR 34; DLB 40

Levi, Primo
1919-1987 . . . . **CLC 37, 50; SSC 12**
See also CA 13-16R; 122; CANR 12, 33;
MTCW

Levin, Ira 1929- . . . . **CLC 3, 6**
See also CA 21-24R; CANR 17, 44;
DAM POP; MTCW; SATA 66

Levin, Meyer 1905-1981 . . . . **CLC 7**
See also AITN 1; CA 9-12R; 104;
CANR 15; DAM POP; DLB 9, 28;
DLBY 81; SATA 21; SATA-Obit 27

Levine, Norman 1924- . . . . **CLC 54**
See also CA 73-76; CAAS 23; CANR 14;
DLB 88

Levine, Philip 1928- . . CLC 2, 4, 5, 9, 14, 33
See also CA 9-12R; CANR 9, 37, 52;
DAM POET; DLB 5

Levinson, Deirdre 1931- . . . . **CLC 49**
See also CA 73-76

Levi-Strauss, Claude 1908- . . . . **CLC 38**
See also CA 1-4R; CANR 6, 32; MTCW

Levitin, Sonia (Wolff) 1934- . . . . **CLC 17**
See also AAYA 13; CA 29-32R; CANR 14,
32; JRDA; MAICYA; SAAS 2; SATA 4,
68

Levon, O. U.
See Kesey, Ken (Elton)

Lewes, George Henry
1817-1878 . . . . **NCLC 25**
See also DLB 55, 144

Lewis, Alun 1915-1944 . . . . **TCLC 3**
See also CA 104; DLB 20, 162

Lewis, C. Day
See Day Lewis, C(ecil)

Lewis, C(live) S(taples)
1898-1963 . . . . . CLC 1, 3, 6, 14, 27; DA;
DAB; DAC; WLC
See also AAYA 3; CA 81-84; CANR 33;
CDBLB 1945-1960; CLR 3, 27;
DAM MST, NOV, POP; DLB 15, 100,
160; JRDA; MAICYA; MTCW;
SATA 13

Lewis, Janet 1899- . . . . **CLC 41**
See also Winters, Janet Lewis
See also CA 9-12R; CANR 29; CAP 1;
DLBY 87

Lewis, Matthew Gregory
1775-1818 . . . . **NCLC 11**
See also DLB 39, 158

Lewis, (Harry) Sinclair
1885-1951 . . . . . TCLC 4, 13, 23, 39; DA;
DAB; DAC; WLC
See also CA 104; 133; CDALB 1917-1929;
DAM MST, NOV; DLB 9, 102; DLBD 1;
MTCW

Lewis, (Percy) Wyndham
    1884(?)-1957 . . . . TCLC 2, 9
    See also CA 104; DLB 15

Lewisohn, Ludwig 1883-1955 . . . . . . TCLC 19
    See also CA 107; DLB 4, 9, 28, 102

Leyner, Mark 1956- . . . . CLC 92
    See also CA 110; CANR 28

Lezama Lima, Jose 1910-1976 . . . CLC 4, 10
    See also CA 77-80; DAM MULT;
    DLB 113; HW

L'Heureux, John (Clarke) 1934- . . . . CLC 52
    See also CA 13-16R; CANR 23, 45

Liddell, C. H.
    See Kuttner, Henry

Lie, Jonas (Lauritz Idemil)
    1833-1908(?) . . . . TCLC 5
    See also CA 115

Lieber, Joel 1937-1971 . . . . CLC 6
    See also CA 73-76; 29-32R

Lieber, Stanley Martin
    See Lee, Stan

Lieberman, Laurence (James)
    1935- . . . . CLC 4, 36
    See also CA 17-20R; CANR 8, 36

Lieksman, Anders
    See Haavikko, Paavo Juhani

Li Fei-kan 1904-
    See Pa Chin
    See also CA 105

Lifton, Robert Jay 1926- . . . . CLC 67
    See also CA 17-20R; CANR 27;
    INT CANR-27; SATA 66

Lightfoot, Gordon 1938- . . . . CLC 26
    See also CA 109

Lightman, Alan P. 1948- . . . . CLC 81
    See also CA 141

Ligotti, Thomas (Robert)
    1953- . . . . CLC 44; SSC 16
    See also CA 123; CANR 49

Li Ho 791-817 . . . . PC 13

Liliencron, (Friedrich Adolf Axel) Detlev von
    1844-1909 . . . . TCLC 18
    See also CA 117

Lilly, William 1602-1681 . . . . LC 27

Lima, Jose Lezama
    See Lezama Lima, Jose

Lima Barreto, Afonso Henrique de
    1881-1922 . . . . TCLC 23
    See also CA 117

Limonov, Edward 1944- . . . . CLC 67
    See also CA 137

Lin, Frank
    See Atherton, Gertrude (Franklin Horn)

Lincoln, Abraham 1809-1865 . . . . . NCLC 18

Lind, Jakov . . . . CLC 1, 2, 4, 27, 82
    See also Landwirth, Heinz
    See also CAAS 4

Lindbergh, Anne (Spencer) Morrow
    1906- . . . . CLC 82
    See also CA 17-20R; CANR 16;
    DAM NOV; MTCW; SATA 33

Lindsay, David 1878-1945 . . . . TCLC 15
    See also CA 113

Lindsay, (Nicholas) Vachel
    1879-1931 . . . TCLC 17; DA; DAC; WLC
    See also CA 114; 135; CDALB 1865-1917;
    DAM MST, POET; DLB 54; SATA 40

Linke-Poot
    See Doeblin, Alfred

Linney, Romulus 1930- . . . . CLC 51
    See also CA 1-4R; CANR 40, 44

Linton, Eliza Lynn 1822-1898 . . . . NCLC 41
    See also DLB 18

Li Po 701-763 . . . . CMLC 2

Lipsius, Justus 1547-1606 . . . . LC 16

Lipsyte, Robert (Michael)
    1938- . . . . CLC 21; DA; DAC
    See also AAYA 7; CA 17-20R; CANR 8;
    CLR 23; DAM MST, NOV; JRDA;
    MAICYA; SATA 5, 68

Lish, Gordon (Jay) 1934- . . CLC 45; SSC 18
    See also CA 113; 117; DLB 130; INT 117

Lispector, Clarice 1925-1977 . . . . . . CLC 43
    See also CA 139; 116; DLB 113

Littell, Robert 1935(?)- . . . . CLC 42
    See also CA 109; 112

Little, Malcolm 1925-1965
    See Malcolm X
    See also BW 1; CA 125; 111; DA; DAB;
    DAC; DAM MST, MULT; MTCW

Littlewit, Humphrey Gent.
    See Lovecraft, H(oward) P(hillips)

Litwos
    See Sienkiewicz, Henryk (Adam Alexander
    Pius)

Liu E 1857-1909 . . . . TCLC 15
    See also CA 115

Lively, Penelope (Margaret)
    1933- . . . . CLC 32, 50
    See also CA 41-44R; CANR 29; CLR 7;
    DAM NOV; DLB 14, 161; JRDA;
    MAICYA; MTCW; SATA 7, 60

Livesay, Dorothy (Kathleen)
    1909- . . . . CLC 4, 15, 79; DAC
    See also AITN 2; CA 25-28R; CAAS 8;
    CANR 36; DAM MST, POET; DLB 68;
    MTCW

Livy c. 59B.C.-c. 17 . . . . CMLC 11

Lizardi, Jose Joaquin Fernandez de
    1776-1827 . . . . NCLC 30

Llewellyn, Richard
    See Llewellyn Lloyd, Richard Dafydd
    Vivian
    See also DLB 15

Llewellyn Lloyd, Richard Dafydd Vivian
    1906-1983 . . . . CLC 7, 80
    See also Llewellyn, Richard
    See also CA 53-56; 111; CANR 7;
    SATA 11; SATA-Obit 37

Llosa, (Jorge) Mario (Pedro) Vargas
    See Vargas Llosa, (Jorge) Mario (Pedro)

Lloyd Webber, Andrew 1948-
    See Webber, Andrew Lloyd
    See also AAYA 1; CA 116; 149;
    DAM DRAM; SATA 56

Llull, Ramon c. 1235-c. 1316 . . . . . CMLC 12

Locke, Alain (Le Roy)
    1886-1954 . . . . TCLC 43
    See also BW 1; CA 106; 124; DLB 51

Locke, John 1632-1704 . . . . LC 7
    See also DLB 101

Locke-Elliott, Sumner
    See Elliott, Sumner Locke

Lockhart, John Gibson
    1794-1854 . . . . NCLC 6
    See also DLB 110, 116, 144

Lodge, David (John) 1935- . . . . CLC 36
    See also BEST 90:1; CA 17-20R; CANR 19;
    DAM POP; DLB 14; INT CANR-19;
    MTCW

Loennbohm, Armas Eino Leopold 1878-1926
    See Leino, Eino
    See also CA 123

Loewinsohn, Ron(ald William)
    1937- . . . . CLC 52
    See also CA 25-28R

Logan, Jake
    See Smith, Martin Cruz

Logan, John (Burton) 1923-1987 . . . . . CLC 5
    See also CA 77-80; 124; CANR 45; DLB 5

Lo Kuan-chung 1330(?)-1400(?) . . . . . . LC 12

Lombard, Nap
    See Johnson, Pamela Hansford

London, Jack . . TCLC 9, 15, 39; SSC 4; WLC
    See also London, John Griffith
    See also AAYA 13; AITN 2;
    CDALB 1865-1917; DLB 8, 12, 78;
    SATA 18

London, John Griffith 1876-1916
    See London, Jack
    See also CA 110; 119; DA; DAB; DAC;
    DAM MST, NOV; JRDA; MAICYA;
    MTCW

Long, Emmett
    See Leonard, Elmore (John, Jr.)

Longbaugh, Harry
    See Goldman, William (W.)

Longfellow, Henry Wadsworth
    1807-1882 . . . . . NCLC 2, 45; DA; DAB;
    DAC
    See also CDALB 1640-1865; DAM MST,
    POET; DLB 1, 59; SATA 19

Longley, Michael 1939- . . . . CLC 29
    See also CA 102; DLB 40

Longus fl. c. 2nd cent. - . . . . CMLC 7

Longway, A. Hugh
    See Lang, Andrew

Lonnrot, Elias 1802-1884 . . . . NCLC 53

Lopate, Phillip 1943- . . . . CLC 29
    See also CA 97-100; DLBY 80; INT 97-100

Lopez Portillo (y Pacheco), Jose
    1920- . . . . CLC 46
    See also CA 129; HW

Lopez y Fuentes, Gregorio
    1897(?)-1966 . . . . CLC 32
    See also CA 131; HW

Lorca, Federico Garcia
    See Garcia Lorca, Federico

Machiavelli, Niccolo
1469-1527 ...... **LC 8; DA; DAB; DAC**
See also DAM MST

MacInnes, Colin 1914-1976...... **CLC 4, 23**
See also CA 69-72; 65-68; CANR 21;
DLB 14; MTCW

MacInnes, Helen (Clark)
1907-1985 .... **CLC 27, 39**
See also CA 1-4R; 117; CANR 1, 28;
DAM POP; DLB 87; MTCW; SATA 22;
SATA-Obit 44

Mackay, Mary 1855-1924
See Corelli, Marie
See also CA 118

Mackenzie, Compton (Edward Montague)
1883-1972 .... **CLC 18**
See also CA 21-22; 37-40R; CAP 2;
DLB 34, 100

Mackenzie, Henry 1745-1831 .... **NCLC 41**
See also DLB 39

Mackintosh, Elizabeth 1896(?)-1952
See Tey, Josephine
See also CA 110

MacLaren, James
See Grieve, C(hristopher) M(urray)

Mac Laverty, Bernard 1942-....... **CLC 31**
See also CA 116; 118; CANR 43; INT 118

MacLean, Alistair (Stuart)
1922-1987 .... **CLC 3, 13, 50, 63**
See also CA 57-60; 121; CANR 28;
DAM POP; MTCW; SATA 23;
SATA-Obit 50

Maclean, Norman (Fitzroy)
1902-1990 .... **CLC 78; SSC 13**
See also CA 102; 132; CANR 49;
DAM POP

MacLeish, Archibald
1892-1982 .... **CLC 3, 8, 14, 68**
See also CA 9-12R; 106; CANR 33;
DAM POET; DLB 4, 7, 45; DLBY 82;
MTCW

MacLennan, (John) Hugh
1907-1990 .... **CLC 2, 14, 92; DAC**
See also CA 5-8R; 142; CANR 33;
DAM MST; DLB 68; MTCW

MacLeod, Alistair 1936- ..... **CLC 56; DAC**
See also CA 123; DAM MST; DLB 60

MacNeice, (Frederick) Louis
1907-1963 ...... **CLC 1, 4, 10, 53; DAB**
See also CA 85-88; DAM POET; DLB 10,
20; MTCW

MacNeill, Dand
See Fraser, George MacDonald

Macpherson, James 1736-1796 ...... **LC 29**
See also DLB 109

Macpherson, (Jean) Jay 1931-...... **CLC 14**
See also CA 5-8R; DLB 53

MacShane, Frank 1927-........... **CLC 39**
See also CA 9-12R; CANR 3, 33; DLB 111

Macumber, Mari
See Sandoz, Mari(e Susette)

Madach, Imre 1823-1864........ **NCLC 19**

Madden, (Jerry) David 1933- .... **CLC 5, 15**
See also CA 1-4R; CAAS 3; CANR 4, 45;
DLB 6; MTCW

Maddern, Al(an)
Scc Ellison, Harlan (Jay)

Madhubuti, Haki R.
1942- .... **CLC 6, 73; BLC; PC 5**
See also Lee, Don L.
See also BW 2; CA 73-76; CANR 24, 51;
DAM MULT, POET; DLB 5, 41;
DLBD 8

Maepenn, Hugh
See Kuttner, Henry

Maepenn, K. H.
See Kuttner, Henry

Maeterlinck, Maurice 1862-1949 ... **TCLC 3**
See also CA 104; 136; DAM DRAM;
SATA 66

Maginn, William 1794-1842....... **NCLC 8**
See also DLB 110, 159

Mahapatra, Jayanta 1928-......... **CLC 33**
See also CA 73-76; CAAS 9; CANR 15, 33;
DAM MULT

Mahfouz, Naguib (Abdel Aziz Al-Sabilgi)
1911(?)-
See Mahfuz, Najib
See also BEST 89:2; CA 128; DAM NOV;
MTCW

Mahfuz, Najib................. **CLC 52, 55**
See also Mahfouz, Naguib (Abdel Aziz
Al-Sabilgi)
See also DLBY 88

Mahon, Derek 1941-............. **CLC 27**
See also CA 113; 128; DLB 40

Mailer, Norman
1923- ...... **CLC 1, 2, 3, 4, 5, 8, 11, 14,
28, 39, 74; DA; DAB; DAC**
See also AITN 2; CA 9-12R; CABS 1;
CANR 28; CDALB 1968-1988;
DAM MST, NOV, POP; DLB 2, 16, 28;
DLBD 3; DLBY 80, 83; MTCW

Maillet, Antonine 1929-...... **CLC 54; DAC**
See also CA 115; 120; CANR 46; DLB 60;
INT 120

Mais, Roger 1905-1955 .... **TCLC 8**
See also BW 1; CA 105; 124; DLB 125;
MTCW

Maistre, Joseph de 1753-1821.... **NCLC 37**

Maitland, Frederic 1850-1906..... **TCLC 65**

Maitland, Sara (Louise) 1950-...... **CLC 49**
See also CA 69-72; CANR 13

Major, Clarence
1936- .... **CLC 3, 19, 48; BLC**
See also BW 2; CA 21-24R; CAAS 6;
CANR 13, 25; DAM MULT; DLB 33

Major, Kevin (Gerald)
1949-................. **CLC 26; DAC**
See also AAYA 16; CA 97-100; CANR 21,
38; CLR 11; DLB 60; INT CANR-21;
JRDA; MAICYA; SATA 32, 82

Maki, James
See Ozu, Yasujiro

Malabaila, Damiano
See Levi, Primo

Malamud, Bernard
1914-1986 ...... **CLC 1, 2, 3, 5, 8, 9, 11,
18, 27, 44, 78, 85; DA; DAB; DAC;
SSC 15; WLC**
See also AAYA 16; CA 5-8R; 118; CABS 1;
CANR 28; CDALB 1941-1968;
DAM MST, NOV, POP; DLB 2, 28, 152;
DLBY 80, 86; MTCW

Malaparte, Curzio 1898-1957 ..... **TCLC 52**

Malcolm, Dan
See Silverberg, Robert

Malcolm X................. **CLC 82; BLC**
See also Little, Malcolm

Malherbe, Francois de 1555-1628..... **LC 5**

Mallarme, Stephane
1842-1898 .... **NCLC 4, 41; PC 4**
See also DAM POET

Mallet-Joris, Francoise 1930-...... **CLC 11**
See also CA 65-68; CANR 17; DLB 83

Malley, Ern
See McAuley, James Phillip

Mallowan, Agatha Christie
See Christie, Agatha (Mary Clarissa)

Maloff, Saul 1922-................. **CLC 5**
See also CA 33-36R

Malone, Louis
See MacNeice, (Frederick) Louis

Malone, Michael (Christopher)
1942-...................... **CLC 43**
See also CA 77-80; CANR 14, 32

Malory, (Sir) Thomas
1410(?)-1471(?) ...... **LC 11; DA; DAB;
DAC**
See also CDBLB Before 1660; DAM MST;
DLB 146; SATA 59; SATA-Brief 33

Malouf, (George Joseph) David
1934-.................... **CLC 28, 86**
See also CA 124; CANR 50

Malraux, (Georges-)Andre
1901-1976 ...... **CLC 1, 4, 9, 13, 15, 57**
See also CA 21-22; 69-72; CANR 34;
CAP 2; DAM NOV; DLB 72; MTCW

Malzberg, Barry N(athaniel) 1939-... **CLC 7**
See also CA 61-64; CAAS 4; CANR 16;
DLB 8

Mamet, David (Alan)
1947- ...... **CLC 9, 15, 34, 46, 91; DC 4**
See also AAYA 3; CA 81-84; CABS 3;
CANR 15, 41; DAM DRAM; DLB 7;
MTCW

Mamoulian, Rouben (Zachary)
1897-1987 .... **CLC 16**
See also CA 25-28R; 124

Mandelstam, Osip (Emilievich)
1891(?)-1938(?) ...... **TCLC 2, 6; PC 14**
See also CA 104; 150

Mander, (Mary) Jane 1877-1949... **TCLC 31**

Mandiargues, Andre Pieyre de....... **CLC 41**
See also Pieyre de Mandiargues, Andre
See also DLB 83

Mandrake, Ethel Belle
See Thurman, Wallace (Henry)

Mangan, James Clarence
1803-1849 .... **NCLC 27**

Maniere, J.-E.
See Giraudoux, (Hippolyte) Jean

Manley, (Mary) Delariviere
1672(?)-1724 . . . . LC 1
See also DLB 39, 80

Mann, Abel
See Creasey, John

Mann, (Luiz) Heinrich 1871-1950. . . TCLC 9
See also CA 106; DLB 66

Mann, (Paul) Thomas
1875-1955 . . . . TCLC 2, 8, 14, 21, 35, 44,
60; DA; DAB; DAC; SSC 5; WLC
See also CA 104; 128; DAM MST, NOV;
DLB 66; MTCW

Mannheim, Karl 1893-1947 . . . . . . TCLC 65

Manning, David
See Faust, Frederick (Schiller)

Manning, Frederic 1887(?)-1935 . . . TCLC 25
See also CA 124

Manning, Olivia 1915-1980 . . . . . . CLC 5, 19
See also CA 5-8R; 101; CANR 29; MTCW

Mano, D. Keith 1942- . . . . CLC 2, 10
See also CA 25-28R; CAAS 6; CANR 26;
DLB 6

Mansfield, Katherine
. . TCLC 2, 8, 39; DAB; SSC 9, 23; WLC
See also Beauchamp, Kathleen Mansfield
See also DLB 162

Manso, Peter 1940- . . . . CLC 39
See also CA 29-32R; CANR 44

Mantecon, Juan Jimenez
See Jimenez (Mantecon), Juan Ramon

Manton, Peter
See Creasey, John

Man Without a Spleen, A
See Chekhov, Anton (Pavlovich)

Manzoni, Alessandro 1785-1873 . . NCLC 29

Mapu, Abraham (ben Jekutiel)
1808-1867 . . . . NCLC 18

Mara, Sally
See Queneau, Raymond

Marat, Jean Paul 1743-1793 . . . . LC 10

Marcel, Gabriel Honore
1889-1973 . . . . CLC 15
See also CA 102; 45-48; MTCW

Marchbanks, Samuel
See Davies, (William) Robertson

Marchi, Giacomo
See Bassani, Giorgio

Margulies, Donald . . . . CLC 76

Marie de France c. 12th cent. - . . . . CMLC 8

Marie de l'Incarnation 1599-1672 . . . . LC 10

Mariner, Scott
See Pohl, Frederik

Marinetti, Filippo Tommaso
1876-1944 . . . . TCLC 10
See also CA 107; DLB 114

Marivaux, Pierre Carlet de Chamblain de
1688-1763 . . . . LC 4

Markandaya, Kamala . . . . CLC 8, 38
See also Taylor, Kamala (Purnaiya)

Markfield, Wallace 1926- . . . . CLC 8
See also CA 69-72; CAAS 3; DLB 2, 28

Markham, Edwin 1852-1940 . . . . . . TCLC 47
See also DLB 54

Markham, Robert
See Amis, Kingsley (William)

Marks, J
See Highwater, Jamake (Mamake)

Marks-Highwater, J
See Highwater, Jamake (Mamake)

Markson, David M(errill) 1927- . . . . CLC 67
See also CA 49-52; CANR 1

Marley, Bob . . . . CLC 17
See also Marley, Robert Nesta

Marley, Robert Nesta 1945-1981
See Marley, Bob
See also CA 107; 103

Marlowe, Christopher
1564-1593 . . . . . LC 22; DA; DAB; DAC;
DC 1; WLC
See also CDBLB Before 1660;
DAM DRAM, MST; DLB 62

Marmontel, Jean-Francois
1723-1799 . . . . LC 2

Marquand, John P(hillips)
1893-1960 . . . . CLC 2, 10
See also CA 85-88; DLB 9, 102

Marquez, Gabriel (Jose) Garcia
See Garcia Marquez, Gabriel (Jose)

Marquis, Don(ald Robert Perry)
1878-1937 . . . . TCLC 7
See also CA 104; DLB 11, 25

Marric, J. J.
See Creasey, John

Marrow, Bernard
See Moore, Brian

Marryat, Frederick 1792-1848 . . . . NCLC 3
See also DLB 21, 163

Marsden, James
See Creasey, John

Marsh, (Edith) Ngaio
1899-1982 . . . . CLC 7, 53
See also CA 9-12R; CANR 6; DAM POP;
DLB 77; MTCW

Marshall, Garry 1934- . . . . CLC 17
See also AAYA 3; CA 111; SATA 60

Marshall, Paule
1929- . . . . CLC 27, 72; BLC; SSC 3
See also BW 2; CA 77-80; CANR 25;
DAM MULT; DLB 157; MTCW

Marsten, Richard
See Hunter, Evan

Marston, John 1576-1634 . . . . LC 33
See also DAM DRAM; DLB 58

Martha, Henry
See Harris, Mark

Martial c. 40-c. 104 . . . . PC 10

Martin, Ken
See Hubbard, L(afayette) Ron(ald)

Martin, Richard
See Creasey, John

Martin, Steve 1945- . . . . CLC 30
See also CA 97-100; CANR 30; MTCW

Martin, Valerie 1948- . . . . CLC 89
See also BEST 90:2; CA 85-88; CANR 49

Martin, Violet Florence
1862-1915 . . . . TCLC 51

Martin, Webber
See Silverberg, Robert

Martindale, Patrick Victor
See White, Patrick (Victor Martindale)

Martin du Gard, Roger
1881-1958 . . . . TCLC 24
See also CA 118; DLB 65

Martineau, Harriet 1802-1876 . . . . NCLC 26
See also DLB 21, 55, 159, 163, 166;
YABC 2

Martines, Julia
See O'Faolain, Julia

Martinez, Jacinto Benavente y
See Benavente (y Martinez), Jacinto

Martinez Ruiz, Jose 1873-1967
See Azorin; Ruiz, Jose Martinez
See also CA 93-96; HW

Martinez Sierra, Gregorio
1881-1947 . . . . TCLC 6
See also CA 115

Martinez Sierra, Maria (de la O'LeJarraga)
1874-1974 . . . . TCLC 6
See also CA 115

Martinsen, Martin
See Follett, Ken(neth Martin)

Martinson, Harry (Edmund)
1904-1978 . . . . CLC 14
See also CA 77-80; CANR 34

Marut, Ret
See Traven, B.

Marut, Robert
See Traven, B.

Marvell, Andrew
1621-1678 . . . . . . LC 4; DA; DAB; DAC;
PC 10; WLC
See also CDBLB 1660-1789; DAM MST,
POET; DLB 131

Marx, Karl (Heinrich)
1818-1883 . . . . NCLC 17
See also DLB 129

Masaoka Shiki . . . . TCLC 18
See also Masaoka Tsunenori

Masaoka Tsunenori 1867-1902
See Masaoka Shiki
See also CA 117

Masefield, John (Edward)
1878-1967 . . . . CLC 11, 47
See also CA 19-20; 25-28R; CANR 33;
CAP 2; CDBLB 1890-1914; DAM POET;
DLB 10, 19, 153, 160; MTCW; SATA 19

Maso, Carole 19(?)- . . . . CLC 44

Mason, Bobbie Ann
1940- . . . . CLC 28, 43, 82; SSC 4
See also AAYA 5; CA 53-56; CANR 11,
31; DLBY 87; INT CANR-31; MTCW

Mason, Ernst
See Pohl, Frederik

Mason, Lee W.
See Malzberg, Barry N(athaniel)

Mason, Nick 1945- . . . . CLC 35

Mason, Tally
See Derleth, August (William)

Mass, William
See Gibson, William

Masters, Edgar Lee
1868-1950 ...... TCLC 2, 25; DA; DAC;
PC 1
See also CA 104; 133; CDALB 1865-1917;
DAM MST, POET; DLB 54; MTCW

Masters, Hilary 1928- .... CLC 48
See also CA 25-28R; CANR 13, 47

Mastrosimone, William 19(?)- ...... CLC 36

Mathe, Albert
See Camus, Albert

Matheson, Richard Burton 1926- ... CLC 37
See also CA 97-100; DLB 8, 44; INT 97-100

Mathews, Harry 1930- .... CLC 6, 52
See also CA 21-24R; CAAS 6; CANR 18,
40

Mathews, John Joseph 1894-1979... CLC 84
See also CA 19-20; 142; CANR 45; CAP 2;
DAM MULT; NNAL

Mathias, Roland (Glyn) 1915- ...... CLC 45
See also CA 97-100; CANR 19, 41; DLB 27

Matsuo Basho 1644-1694 .... PC 3
See also DAM POET

Mattheson, Rodney
See Creasey, John

Matthews, Greg 1949- .... CLC 45
See also CA 135

Matthews, William 1942- .... CLC 40
See also CA 29-32R; CAAS 18; CANR 12;
DLB 5

Matthias, John (Edward) 1941- ...... CLC 9
See also CA 33-36R

Matthiessen, Peter
1927- .... CLC 5, 7, 11, 32, 64
See also AAYA 6; BEST 90:4; CA 9-12R;
CANR 21, 50; DAM NOV; DLB 6;
MTCW; SATA 27

Maturin, Charles Robert
1780(?)-1824 .... NCLC 6

Matute (Ausejo), Ana Maria
1925- .... CLC 11
See also CA 89-92; MTCW

Maugham, W. S.
See Maugham, W(illiam) Somerset

Maugham, W(illiam) Somerset
1874-1965 .... CLC 1, 11, 15, 67, 93;
DA; DAB; DAC; SSC 8; WLC
See also CA 5-8R; 25-28R; CANR 40;
CDBLB 1914-1945; DAM DRAM, MST,
NOV; DLB 10, 36, 77, 100, 162; MTCW;
SATA 54

Maugham, William Somerset
See Maugham, W(illiam) Somerset

Maupassant, (Henri Rene Albert) Guy de
1850-1893 ..... NCLC 1, 42; DA; DAB;
DAC; SSC 1; WLC
See also DAM MST; DLB 123

Maupin, Armistead 1944- .... CLC 95
See also CA 125; 130; DAM POP; INT 130

Maurhut, Richard
See Traven, B.

Mauriac, Claude 1914- .... CLC 9
See also CA 89-92; DLB 83

Mauriac, Francois (Charles)
1885-1970 .... CLC 4, 9, 56
See also CA 25-28; CAP 2; DLB 65;
MTCW

Mavor, Osborne Henry 1888-1951
See Bridie, James
See also CA 104

Maxwell, William (Keepers, Jr.)
1908- .... CLC 19
See also CA 93-96; DLBY 80; INT 93-96

May, Elaine 1932- .... CLC 16
See also CA 124; 142; DLB 44

Mayakovski, Vladimir (Vladimirovich)
1893-1930 .... TCLC 4, 18
See also CA 104

Mayhew, Henry 1812-1887 ...... NCLC 31
See also DLB 18, 55

Mayle, Peter 1939(?)- .... CLC 89
See also CA 139

Maynard, Joyce 1953- .... CLC 23
See also CA 111; 129

Mayne, William (James Carter)
1928- .... CLC 12
See also CA 9-12R; CANR 37; CLR 25;
JRDA; MAICYA; SAAS 11; SATA 6, 68

Mayo, Jim
See L'Amour, Louis (Dearborn)

Maysles, Albert 1926- .... CLC 16
See also CA 29-32R

Maysles, David 1932- .... CLC 16

Mazer, Norma Fox 1931- .... CLC 26
See also AAYA 5; CA 69-72; CANR 12,
32; CLR 23; JRDA; MAICYA; SAAS 1;
SATA 24, 67

Mazzini, Guiseppe 1805-1872 .... NCLC 34

McAuley, James Phillip
1917-1976 .... CLC 45
See also CA 97-100

McBain, Ed
See Hunter, Evan

McBrien, William Augustine
1930- .... CLC 44
See also CA 107

McCaffrey, Anne (Inez) 1926- ...... CLC 17
See also AAYA 6; AITN 2; BEST 89:2;
CA 25-28R; CANR 15, 35; DAM NOV,
POP; DLB 8; JRDA; MAICYA; MTCW;
SAAS 11; SATA 8, 70

McCall, Nathan 1955(?)- .... CLC 86
See also CA 146

McCann, Arthur
See Campbell, John W(ood, Jr.)

McCann, Edson
See Pohl, Frederik

McCarthy, Charles, Jr. 1933-
See McCarthy, Cormac
See also CANR 42; DAM POP

McCarthy, Cormac 1933- ..... CLC 4, 57, 59
See also McCarthy, Charles, Jr.
See also DLB 6, 143

McCarthy, Mary (Therese)
1912-1989 ... CLC 1, 3, 5, 14, 24, 39, 59
See also CA 5-8R; 129; CANR 16, 50;
DLB 2; DLBY 81; INT CANR-16;
MTCW

McCartney, (James) Paul
1942- .... CLC 12, 35
See also CA 146

McCauley, Stephen (D.) 1955- ..... CLC 50
See also CA 141

McClure, Michael (Thomas)
1932- .... CLC 6, 10
See also CA 21-24R; CANR 17, 46;
DLB 16

McCorkle, Jill (Collins) 1958- ...... CLC 51
See also CA 121; DLBY 87

McCourt, James 1941- .... CLC 5
See also CA 57-60

McCoy, Horace (Stanley)
1897-1955 .... TCLC 28
See also CA 108; DLB 9

McCrae, John 1872-1918 .... TCLC 12
See also CA 109; DLB 92

McCreigh, James
See Pohl, Frederik

McCullers, (Lula) Carson (Smith)
1917-1967 .... CLC 1, 4, 10, 12, 48; DA;
DAB; DAC; SSC 9; WLC
See also CA 5-8R; 25-28R; CABS 1, 3;
CANR 18; CDALB 1941-1968;
DAM MST, NOV; DLB 2, 7; MTCW;
SATA 27

McCulloch, John Tyler
See Burroughs, Edgar Rice

McCullough, Colleen 1938(?)- ...... CLC 27
See also CA 81-84; CANR 17, 46;
DAM NOV, POP; MTCW

McDermott, Alice 1953- .... CLC 90
See also CA 109; CANR 40

McElroy, Joseph 1930- .... CLC 5, 47
See also CA 17-20R

McEwan, Ian (Russell) 1948- ... CLC 13, 66
See also BEST 90:4; CA 61-64; CANR 14,
41; DAM NOV; DLB 14; MTCW

McFadden, David 1940- .... CLC 48
See also CA 104; DLB 60; INT 104

McFarland, Dennis 1950- .... CLC 65

McGahern, John
1934- .... CLC 5, 9, 48; SSC 17
See also CA 17-20R; CANR 29; DLB 14;
MTCW

McGinley, Patrick (Anthony)
1937- .... CLC 41
See also CA 120; 127; INT 127

McGinley, Phyllis 1905-1978 ...... CLC 14
See also CA 9-12R; 77-80; CANR 19;
DLB 11, 48; SATA 2, 44; SATA-Obit 24

McGinniss, Joe 1942- .... CLC 32
See also AITN 2; BEST 89:2; CA 25-28R;
CANR 26; INT CANR-26

McGivern, Maureen Daly
See Daly, Maureen

McGrath, Patrick 1950- .... CLC 55
See also CA 136

McGrath, Thomas (Matthew)
1916-1990 .... CLC 28, 59
See also CA 9-12R; 132; CANR 6, 33;
DAM POET; MTCW; SATA 41;
SATA-Obit 66

McGuane, Thomas (Francis III)
1939- . . . . CLC 3, 7, 18, 45
See also AITN 2; CA 49-52; CANR 5, 24,
49; DLB 2; DLBY 80; INT CANR-24;
MTCW

McGuckian, Medbh 1950- . . . . CLC 48
See also CA 143; DAM POET; DLB 40

McHale, Tom 1942(?)-1982 . . . . CLC 3, 5
See also AITN 1; CA 77-80; 106

McIlvanney, William 1936- . . . . CLC 42
See also CA 25-28R; DLB 14

McIlwraith, Maureen Mollie Hunter
See Hunter, Mollie
See also SATA 2

McInerney, Jay 1955- . . . . CLC 34
See also AAYA 18; CA 116; 123;
CANR 45; DAM POP; INT 123

McIntyre, Vonda N(eel) 1948- . . . . . CLC 18
See also CA 81-84; CANR 17, 34; MTCW

McKay, Claude
. . . . TCLC 7, 41; BLC; DAB; PC 2
See also McKay, Festus Claudius
See also DLB 4, 45, 51, 117

McKay, Festus Claudius 1889-1948
See McKay, Claude
See also BW 1; CA 104; 124; DA; DAC;
DAM MST, MULT, NOV, POET;
MTCW; WLC

McKuen, Rod 1933- . . . . CLC 1, 3
See also AITN 1; CA 41-44R; CANR 40

McLoughlin, R. B.
See Mencken, H(enry) L(ouis)

McLuhan, (Herbert) Marshall
1911-1980 . . . . CLC 37, 83
See also CA 9-12R; 102; CANR 12, 34;
DLB 88; INT CANR-12; MTCW

McMillan, Terry (L.) 1951- . . . . . CLC 50, 61
See also BW 2; CA 140; DAM MULT,
NOV, POP

McMurtry, Larry (Jeff)
1936- . . . . CLC 2, 3, 7, 11, 27, 44
See also AAYA 15; AITN 2; BEST 89:2;
CA 5-8R; CANR 19, 43;
CDALB 1968-1988; DAM NOV, POP;
DLB 2, 143; DLBY 80, 87; MTCW

McNally, T. M. 1961- . . . . CLC 82

McNally, Terrence 1939- . . . CLC 4, 7, 41, 91
See also CA 45-48; CANR 2;
DAM DRAM; DLB 7

McNamer, Deirdre 1950- . . . . CLC 70

McNeile, Herman Cyril 1888-1937
See Sapper
See also DLB 77

McNickle, (William) D'Arcy
1904-1977 . . . . CLC 89
See also CA 9-12R; 85-88; CANR 5, 45;
DAM MULT; NNAL; SATA-Obit 22

McPhee, John (Angus) 1931- . . . . . . CLC 36
See also BEST 90:1; CA 65-68; CANR 20,
46; MTCW

McPherson, James Alan
1943- . . . . CLC 19, 77
See also BW 1; CA 25-28R; CAAS 17;
CANR 24; DLB 38; MTCW

McPherson, William (Alexander)
1933- . . . . CLC 34
See also CA 69-72; CANR 28;
INT CANR-28

Mead, Margaret 1901-1978 . . . . CLC 37
See also AITN 1; CA 1-4R; 81-84;
CANR 4; MTCW; SATA-Obit 20

Meaker, Marijane (Agnes) 1927-
See Kerr, M. E.
See also CA 107; CANR 37; INT 107;
JRDA; MAICYA; MTCW; SATA 20, 61

Medoff, Mark (Howard) 1940- . . . CLC 6, 23
See also AITN 1; CA 53-56; CANR 5;
DAM DRAM; DLB 7; INT CANR-5

Medvedev, P. N.
See Bakhtin, Mikhail Mikhailovich

Meged, Aharon
See Megged, Aharon

Meged, Aron
See Megged, Aharon

Megged, Aharon 1920- . . . . CLC 9
See also CA 49-52; CAAS 13; CANR 1

Mehta, Ved (Parkash) 1934- . . . . CLC 37
See also CA 1-4R; CANR 2, 23; MTCW

Melanter
See Blackmore, R(ichard) D(oddridge)

Melikow, Loris
See Hofmannsthal, Hugo von

Melmoth, Sebastian
See Wilde, Oscar (Fingal O'Flahertie Wills)

Meltzer, Milton 1915- . . . . CLC 26
See also AAYA 8; CA 13-16R; CANR 38;
CLR 13; DLB 61; JRDA; MAICYA;
SAAS 1; SATA 1, 50, 80

Melville, Herman
1819-1891 . . . . . NCLC 3, 12, 29, 45, 49;
DA; DAB; DAC; SSC 1, 17; WLC
See also CDALB 1640-1865; DAM MST,
NOV; DLB 3, 74; SATA 59

Menander
c. 342B.C.-c. 292B.C. . . . . CMLC 9; DC 3
See also DAM DRAM

Mencken, H(enry) L(ouis)
1880-1956 . . . . TCLC 13
See also CA 105; 125; CDALB 1917-1929;
DLB 11, 29, 63, 137; MTCW

Mercer, David 1928-1980 . . . . CLC 5
See also CA 9-12R; 102; CANR 23;
DAM DRAM; DLB 13; MTCW

Merchant, Paul
See Ellison, Harlan (Jay)

Meredith, George 1828-1909 . . . TCLC 17, 43
See also CA 117; CDBLB 1832-1890;
DAM POET; DLB 18, 35, 57, 159

Meredith, William (Morris)
1919- . . . . CLC 4, 13, 22, 55
See also CA 9-12R; CAAS 14; CANR 6, 40;
DAM POET; DLB 5

Merezhkovsky, Dmitry Sergeyevich
1865-1941 . . . . TCLC 29

Merimee, Prosper
1803-1870 . . . . NCLC 6; SSC 7
See also DLB 119

Merkin, Daphne 1954- . . . . CLC 44
See also CA 123

Merlin, Arthur
See Blish, James (Benjamin)

Merrill, James (Ingram)
1926-1995 . . . . CLC 2, 3, 6, 8, 13, 18, 34,
91
See also CA 13-16R; 147; CANR 10, 49;
DAM POET; DLB 5, 165; DLBY 85;
INT CANR-10; MTCW

Merriman, Alex
See Silverberg, Robert

Merritt, E. B.
See Waddington, Miriam

Merton, Thomas
1915-1968 . . CLC 1, 3, 11, 34, 83; PC 10
See also CA 5-8R; 25-28R; CANR 22;
DLB 48; DLBY 81; MTCW

Merwin, W(illiam) S(tanley)
1927- . . . . CLC 1, 2, 3, 5, 8, 13, 18, 45, 88
See also CA 13-16R; CANR 15, 51;
DAM POET; DLB 5; INT CANR-15;
MTCW

Metcalf, John 1938- . . . . CLC 37
See also CA 113; DLB 60

Metcalf, Suzanne
See Baum, L(yman) Frank

Mew, Charlotte (Mary)
1870-1928 . . . . TCLC 8
See also CA 105; DLB 19, 135

Mewshaw, Michael 1943- . . . . CLC 9
See also CA 53-56; CANR 7, 47; DLBY 80

Meyer, June
See Jordan, June

Meyer, Lynn
See Slavitt, David R(ytman)

Meyer-Meyrink, Gustav 1868-1932
See Meyrink, Gustav
See also CA 117

Meyers, Jeffrey 1939- . . . . CLC 39
See also CA 73-76; DLB 111

Meynell, Alice (Christina Gertrude Thompson)
1847-1922 . . . . TCLC 6
See also CA 104; DLB 19, 98

Meyrink, Gustav . . . . TCLC 21
See also Meyer-Meyrink, Gustav
See also DLB 81

Michaels, Leonard
1933- . . . . CLC 6, 25; SSC 16
See also CA 61-64; CANR 21; DLB 130;
MTCW

Michaux, Henri 1899-1984 . . . . . . CLC 8, 19
See also CA 85-88; 114

Michelangelo 1475-1564 . . . . LC 12

Michelet, Jules 1798-1874 . . . . NCLC 31

Michener, James A(lbert)
1907(?)- . . . . CLC 1, 5, 11, 29, 60
See also AITN 1; BEST 90:1; CA 5-8R;
CANR 21, 45; DAM NOV, POP; DLB 6;
MTCW

Mickiewicz, Adam 1798-1855 . . . . . NCLC 3

Middleton, Christopher 1926- . . . . . . CLC 13
See also CA 13-16R; CANR 29; DLB 40

Middleton, Richard (Barham)
1882-1911 . . . . TCLC 56
See also DLB 156

Montgomery, Marion H., Jr. 1925- .. CLC 7
See also AITN 1; CA 1-4R; CANR 3, 48;
DLB 6

Montgomery, Max
See Davenport, Guy (Mattison, Jr.)

Montherlant, Henry (Milon) de
1896-1972 .... CLC 8, 19
See also CA 85-88; 37-40R; DAM DRAM;
DLB 72; MTCW

Monty Python
See Chapman, Graham; Cleese, John
(Marwood); Gilliam, Terry (Vance); Idle,
Eric; Jones, Terence Graham Parry; Palin,
Michael (Edward)
See also AAYA 7

Moodie, Susanna (Strickland)
1803-1885 .... NCLC 14
See also DLB 99

Mooney, Edward 1951-
See Mooney, Ted
See also CA 130

Mooney, Ted .... CLC 25
See also Mooney, Edward

Moorcock, Michael (John)
1939- .... CLC 5, 27, 58
See also CA 45-48; CAAS 5; CANR 2, 17,
38; DLB 14; MTCW

Moore, Brian
1921- ...... CLC 1, 3, 5, 7, 8, 19, 32, 90;
DAB; DAC
See also CA 1-4R; CANR 1, 25, 42;
DAM MST; MTCW

Moore, Edward
See Muir, Edwin

Moore, George Augustus
1852-1933 .... TCLC 7; SSC 19
See also CA 104; DLB 10, 18, 57, 135

Moore, Lorrie .... CLC 39, 45, 68
See also Moore, Marie Lorena

Moore, Marianne (Craig)
1887-1972 .... CLC 1, 2, 4, 8, 10, 13, 19,
47; DA; DAB; DAC; PC 4
See also CA 1-4R; 33-36R; CANR 3;
CDALB 1929-1941; DAM MST, POET;
DLB 45; DLBD 7; MTCW; SATA 20

Moore, Marie Lorena 1957-
See Moore, Lorrie
See also CA 116; CANR 39

Moore, Thomas 1779-1852 .... NCLC 6
See also DLB 96, 144

Morand, Paul 1888-1976 .. CLC 41; SSC 22
See also CA 69-72; DLB 65

Morante, Elsa 1918-1985 .... CLC 8, 47
See also CA 85-88; 117; CANR 35; MTCW

Moravia, Alberto ...... CLC 2, 7, 11, 27, 46
See also Pincherle, Alberto

More, Hannah 1745-1833 .... NCLC 27
See also DLB 107, 109, 116, 158

More, Henry 1614-1687 .... LC 9
See also DLB 126

More, Sir Thomas 1478-1535 .... LC 10, 32

Moreas, Jean .... TCLC 18
See also Papadiamantopoulos, Johannes

Morgan, Berry 1919- .... CLC 6
See also CA 49-52; DLB 6

Morgan, Claire
See Highsmith, (Mary) Patricia

Morgan, Edwin (George) 1920- ..... CLC 31
See also CA 5-8R; CANR 3, 43; DLB 27

Morgan, (George) Frederick
1922- .... CLC 23
See also CA 17-20R; CANR 21

Morgan, Harriet
See Mencken, H(enry) L(ouis)

Morgan, Jane
See Cooper, James Fenimore

Morgan, Janet 1945- .... CLC 39
See also CA 65-68

Morgan, Lady 1776(?)-1859 ...... NCLC 29
See also DLB 116, 158

Morgan, Robin 1941- .... CLC 2
See also CA 69-72; CANR 29; MTCW;
SATA 80

Morgan, Scott
See Kuttner, Henry

Morgan, Seth 1949(?)-1990 .... CLC 65
See also CA 132

Morgenstern, Christian
1871-1914 .... TCLC 8
See also CA 105

Morgenstern, S.
See Goldman, William (W.)

Moricz, Zsigmond 1879-1942 ..... TCLC 33

Morike, Eduard (Friedrich)
1804-1875 .... NCLC 10
See also DLB 133

Mori Ogai .... TCLC 14
See also Mori Rintaro

Mori Rintaro 1862-1922
See Mori Ogai
See also CA 110

Moritz, Karl Philipp 1756-1793 ...... LC 2
See also DLB 94

Morland, Peter Henry
See Faust, Frederick (Schiller)

Morren, Theophil
See Hofmannsthal, Hugo von

Morris, Bill 1952- .... CLC 76

Morris, Julian
See West, Morris L(anglo)

Morris, Steveland Judkins 1950(?)-
See Wonder, Stevie
See also CA 111

Morris, William 1834-1896 ...... NCLC 4
See also CDBLB 1832-1890; DLB 18, 35,
57, 156

Morris, Wright 1910- ... CLC 1, 3, 7, 18, 37
See also CA 9-12R; CANR 21; DLB 2;
DLBY 81; MTCW

Morrison, Chloe Anthony Wofford
See Morrison, Toni

Morrison, James Douglas 1943-1971
See Morrison, Jim
See also CA 73-76; CANR 40

Morrison, Jim .... CLC 17
See also Morrison, James Douglas

Morrison, Toni
1931- .... CLC 4, 10, 22, 55, 81, 87;
BLC; DA; DAB; DAC
See also AAYA 1; BW 2; CA 29-32R;
CANR 27, 42; CDALB 1968-1988;
DAM MST, MULT, NOV, POP; DLB 6,
33, 143; DLBY 81; MTCW; SATA 57

Morrison, Van 1945- .... CLC 21
See also CA 116

Mortimer, John (Clifford)
1923- .... CLC 28, 43
See also CA 13-16R; CANR 21;
CDBLB 1960 to Present; DAM DRAM,
POP; DLB 13; INT CANR-21; MTCW

Mortimer, Penelope (Ruth) 1918- .... CLC 5
See also CA 57-60; CANR 45

Morton, Anthony
See Creasey, John

Mosher, Howard Frank 1943- ...... CLC 62
See also CA 139

Mosley, Nicholas 1923- .... CLC 43, 70
See also CA 69-72; CANR 41; DLB 14

Moss, Howard
1922-1987 .... CLC 7, 14, 45, 50
See also CA 1-4R; 123; CANR 1, 44;
DAM POET; DLB 5

Mossgiel, Rab
See Burns, Robert

Motion, Andrew (Peter) 1952- ...... CLC 47
See also CA 146; DLB 40

Motley, Willard (Francis)
1909-1965 .... CLC 18
See also BW 1; CA 117; 106; DLB 76, 143

Motoori, Norinaga 1730-1801 .... NCLC 45

Mott, Michael (Charles Alston)
1930- .... CLC 15, 34
See also CA 5-8R; CAAS 7; CANR 7, 29

Mountain Wolf Woman
1884-1960 .... CLC 92
See also CA 144; NNAL

Moure, Erin 1955- .... CLC 88
See also CA 113; DLB 60

Mowat, Farley (McGill)
1921- .... CLC 26; DAC
See also AAYA 1; CA 1-4R; CANR 4, 24,
42; CLR 20; DAM MST; DLB 68;
INT CANAR-24; JRDA; MAICYA;
MTCW; SATA 3, 55

Moyers, Bill 1934- .... CLC 74
See also AITN 2; CA 61-64; CANR 31, 52

Mphahlele, Es'kia
See Mphahlele, Ezekiel
See also DLB 125

Mphahlele, Ezekiel 1919- ..... CLC 25; BLC
See also Mphahlele, Es'kia
See also BW 2; CA 81-84; CANR 26;
DAM MULT

Mqhayi, S(amuel) E(dward) K(rune Loliwe)
1875-1945 .... TCLC 25; BLC
See also DAM MULT

Mr. Martin
See Burroughs, William S(eward)

Mrozek, Slawomir 1930- .... CLC 3, 13
See also CA 13-16R; CAAS 10; CANR 29;
MTCW

Mrs. Belloc-Lowndes
See Lowndes, Marie Adelaide (Belloc)

Mtwa, Percy (?)-..................CLC 47

Mueller, Lisel 1924-...........CLC 13, 51
See also CA 93-96; DLB 105

Muir, Edwin 1887-1959...........TCLC 2
See also CA 104; DLB 20, 100

Muir, John 1838-1914...........TCLC 28

Mujica Lainez, Manuel
1910-1984....................CLC 31
See also Lainez, Manuel Mujica
See also CA 81-84; 112; CANR 32; HW

Mukherjee, Bharati 1940-.........CLC 53
See also BEST 89:2; CA 107; CANR 45;
DAM NOV; DLB 60; MTCW

Muldoon, Paul 1951-...........CLC 32, 72
See also CA 113; 129; CANR 52;
DAM POET; DLB 40; INT 129

Mulisch, Harry 1927-............CLC 42
See also CA 9-12R; CANR 6, 26

Mull, Martin 1943-..............CLC 17
See also CA 105

Mulock, Dinah Maria
See Craik, Dinah Maria (Mulock)

Munford, Robert 1737(?)-1783.......LC 5
See also DLB 31

Mungo, Raymond 1946-..........CLC 72
See also CA 49-52; CANR 2

Munro, Alice
1931-......CLC 6, 10, 19, 50, 95; DAC;
SSC 3
See also AITN 2; CA 33-36R; CANR 33;
DAM MST, NOV; DLB 53; MTCW;
SATA 29

Munro, H(ector) H(ugh) 1870-1916
See Saki
See also CA 104; 130; CDBLB 1890-1914;
DA; DAB; DAC; DAM MST, NOV;
DLB 34, 162; MTCW; WLC

Murasaki, Lady.................CMLC 1

Murdoch, (Jean) Iris
1919-......CLC 1, 2, 3, 4, 6, 8, 11, 15,
22, 31, 51; DAB; DAC
See also CA 13-16R; CANR 8, 43;
CDBLB 1960 to Present; DAM MST,
NOV; DLB 14; INT CANR-8; MTCW

Murfree, Mary Noailles
1850-1922....................SSC 22
See also CA 122; DLB 12, 74

Murnau, Friedrich Wilhelm
See Plumpe, Friedrich Wilhelm

Murphy, Richard 1927-...........CLC 41
See also CA 29-32R; DLB 40

Murphy, Sylvia 1937-.............CLC 34
See also CA 121

Murphy, Thomas (Bernard) 1935-...CLC 51
See also CA 101

Murray, Albert L. 1916-..........CLC 73
See also BW 2; CA 49-52; CANR 26, 52;
DLB 38

Murray, Les(lie) A(llan) 1938-.....CLC 40
See also CA 21-24R; CANR 11, 27;
DAM POET

Murry, J. Middleton
See Murry, John Middleton

Murry, John Middleton
1889-1957..................TCLC 16
See also CA 118; DLB 149

Musgrave, Susan 1951-........CLC 13, 54
See also CA 69-72; CANR 45

Musil, Robert (Edler von)
1880-1942.........TCLC 12; SSC 18
See also CA 109; DLB 81, 124

Muske, Carol 1945-..............CLC 90
See also Muske-Dukes, Carol (Anne)

Muske-Dukes, Carol (Anne) 1945-
See Muske, Carol
See also CA 65-68; CANR 32

Musset, (Louis Charles) Alfred de
1810-1857..................NCLC 7

My Brother's Brother
See Chekhov, Anton (Pavlovich)

Myers, L. H. 1881-1944.........TCLC 59
See also DLB 15

Myers, Walter Dean 1937-...CLC 35; BLC
See also AAYA 4; BW 2; CA 33-36R;
CANR 20, 42; CLR 4, 16, 35;
DAM MULT, NOV; DLB 33;
INT CANR-20; JRDA; MAICYA;
SAAS 2; SATA 41, 71; SATA-Brief 27

Myers, Walter M.
See Myers, Walter Dean

Myles, Symon
See Follett, Ken(neth Martin)

Nabokov, Vladimir (Vladimirovich)
1899-1977.....CLC 1, 2, 3, 6, 8, 11, 15,
23, 44, 46, 64; DA; DAB; DAC; SSC 11;
WLC
See also CA 5-8R; 69-72; CANR 20;
CDALB 1941-1968; DAM MST, NOV;
DLB 2; DLBD 3; DLBY 80, 91; MTCW

Nagai Kafu....................TCLC 51
See also Nagai Sokichi

Nagai Sokichi 1879-1959
See Nagai Kafu
See also CA 117

Nagy, Laszlo 1925-1978...........CLC 7
See also CA 129; 112

Naipaul, Shiva(dhar Srinivasa)
1945-1985.................CLC 32, 39
See also CA 110; 112; 116; CANR 33;
DAM NOV; DLB 157; DLBY 85;
MTCW

Naipaul, V(idiadhar) S(urajprasad)
1932-....CLC 4, 7, 9, 13, 18, 37; DAB;
DAC
See also CA 1-4R; CANR 1, 33, 51;
CDBLB 1960 to Present; DAM MST,
NOV; DLB 125; DLBY 85; MTCW

Nakos, Lilika 1899(?)-...........CLC 29

Narayan, R(asipuram) K(rishnaswami)
1906-...................CLC 7, 28, 47
See also CA 81-84; CANR 33; DAM NOV;
MTCW; SATA 62

Nash, (Fredric) Ogden 1902-1971..CLC 23
See also CA 13-14; 29-32R; CANR 34;
CAP 1; DAM POET; DLB 11;
MAICYA; MTCW; SATA 2, 46

Nathan, Daniel
See Dannay, Frederic

Nathan, George Jean 1882-1958...TCLC 18
See also Hatteras, Owen
See also CA 114; DLB 137

Natsume, Kinnosuke 1867-1916
See Natsume, Soseki
See also CA 104

Natsume, Soseki..............TCLC 2, 10
See also Natsume, Kinnosuke

Natti, (Mary) Lee 1919-
See Kingman, Lee
See also CA 5-8R; CANR 2

Naylor, Gloria
1950-.....CLC 28, 52; BLC; DA; DAC
See also AAYA 6; BW 2; CA 107;
CANR 27, 51; DAM MST, MULT,
NOV, POP; MTCW

Neihardt, John Gneisenau
1881-1973...................CLC 32
See also CA 13-14; CAP 1; DLB 9, 54

Nekrasov, Nikolai Alekseevich
1821-1878..................NCLC 11

Nelligan, Emile 1879-1941........TCLC 14
See also CA 114; DLB 92

Nelson, Willie 1933-..............CLC 17
See also CA 107

Nemerov, Howard (Stanley)
1920-1991..............CLC 2, 6, 9, 36
See also CA 1-4R; 134; CABS 2; CANR 1,
27; DAM POET; DLB 5, 6; DLBY 83;
INT CANR-27; MTCW

Neruda, Pablo
1904-1973.....CLC 1, 2, 5, 7, 9, 28, 62;
DA; DAB; DAC; HLC; PC 4; WLC
See also CA 19-20; 45-48; CAP 2;
DAM MST, MULT, POET; HW; MTCW

Nerval, Gerard de
1808-1855.....NCLC 1; PC 13; SSC 18

Nervo, (Jose) Amado (Ruiz de)
1870-1919..................TCLC 11
See also CA 109; 131; HW

Nessi, Pio Baroja y
See Baroja (y Nessi), Pio

Nestroy, Johann 1801-1862......NCLC 42
See also DLB 133

Neufeld, John (Arthur) 1938-......CLC 17
See also AAYA 11; CA 25-28R; CANR 11,
37; MAICYA; SAAS 3; SATA 6, 81

Neville, Emily Cheney 1919-.......CLC 12
See also CA 5-8R; CANR 3, 37; JRDA;
MAICYA; SAAS 2; SATA 1

Newbound, Bernard Slade 1930-
See Slade, Bernard
See also CA 81-84; CANR 49;
DAM DRAM

Newby, P(ercy) H(oward)
1918-.....................CLC 2, 13
See also CA 5-8R; CANR 32; DAM NOV;
DLB 15; MTCW

Newlove, Donald 1928-.............CLC 6
See also CA 29-32R; CANR 25

Newlove, John (Herbert) 1938-.....CLC 14
See also CA 21-24R; CANR 9, 25

Newman, Charles 1938- . . . . CLC 2, 8
See also CA 21-24R

Newman, Edwin (Harold) 1919- . . . . CLC 14
See also AITN 1; CA 69-72; CANR 5

Newman, John Henry
1801-1890 . . . . NCLC 38
See also DLB 18, 32, 55

Newton, Suzanne 1936- . . . . CLC 35
See also CA 41-44R; CANR 14; JRDA;
SATA 5, 77

Nexo, Martin Andersen
1869-1954 . . . . TCLC 43

Nezval, Vitezslav 1900-1958 . . . . . TCLC 44
See also CA 123

Ng, Fae Myenne 1957(?)- . . . . CLC 81
See also CA 146

Ngema, Mbongeni 1955- . . . . CLC 57
See also BW 2; CA 143

Ngugi, James T(hiong'o) . . . . CLC 3, 7, 13
See also Ngugi wa Thiong'o

Ngugi wa Thiong'o 1938- . . . . . CLC 36; BLC
See also Ngugi, James T(hiong'o)
See also BW 2; CA 81-84; CANR 27;
DAM MULT, NOV; DLB 125; MTCW

Nichol, B(arrie) P(hillip)
1944-1988 . . . . CLC 18
See also CA 53-56; DLB 53; SATA 66

Nichols, John (Treadwell) 1940- . . . . CLC 38
See also CA 9-12R; CAAS 2; CANR 6;
DLBY 82

Nichols, Leigh
See Koontz, Dean R(ay)

Nichols, Peter (Richard)
1927- . . . . CLC 5, 36, 65
See also CA 104; CANR 33; DLB 13;
MTCW

Nicolas, F. R. E.
See Freeling, Nicolas

Niedecker, Lorine 1903-1970 . . . . CLC 10, 42
See also CA 25-28; CAP 2; DAM POET;
DLB 48

Nietzsche, Friedrich (Wilhelm)
1844-1900 . . . . TCLC 10, 18, 55
See also CA 107; 121; DLB 129

Nievo, Ippolito 1831-1861 . . . . NCLC 22

Nightingale, Anne Redmon 1943-
See Redmon, Anne
See also CA 103

Nik. T. O.
See Annensky, Innokenty Fyodorovich

Nin, Anais
1903-1977 . . . . . . CLC 1, 4, 8, 11, 14, 60;
SSC 10
See also AITN 2; CA 13-16R; 69-72;
CANR 22; DAM NOV, POP; DLB 2, 4,
152; MTCW

Nishiwaki, Junzaburo 1894-1982 . . . . PC 15
See also CA 107

Nissenson, Hugh 1933- . . . . CLC 4, 9
See also CA 17-20R; CANR 27; DLB 28

Niven, Larry . . . . CLC 8
See also Niven, Laurence Van Cott
See also DLB 8

Niven, Laurence Van Cott 1938-
See Niven, Larry
See also CA 21-24R; CAAS 12; CANR 14,
44; DAM POP; MTCW

Nixon, Agnes Eckhardt 1927- . . . . . . CLC 21
See also CA 110

Nizan, Paul 1905-1940 . . . . TCLC 40
See also DLB 72

Nkosi, Lewis 1936- . . . . CLC 45; BLC
See also BW 1; CA 65-68; CANR 27;
DAM MULT; DLB 157

Nodier, (Jean) Charles (Emmanuel)
1780-1844 . . . . NCLC 19
See also DLB 119

Nolan, Christopher 1965- . . . . CLC 58
See also CA 111

Noon, Jeff 1957- . . . . CLC 91
See also CA 148

Norden, Charles
See Durrell, Lawrence (George)

Nordhoff, Charles (Bernard)
1887-1947 . . . . TCLC 23
See also CA 108; DLB 9; SATA 23

Norfolk, Lawrence 1963- . . . . CLC 76
See also CA 144

Norman, Marsha 1947- . . . . CLC 28
See also CA 105; CABS 3; CANR 41;
DAM DRAM; DLBY 84

Norris, Benjamin Franklin, Jr.
1870-1902 . . . . TCLC 24
See also Norris, Frank
See also CA 110

Norris, Frank
See Norris, Benjamin Franklin, Jr.
See also CDALB 1865-1917; DLB 12, 71

Norris, Leslie 1921- . . . . CLC 14
See also CA 11-12; CANR 14; CAP 1;
DLB 27

North, Andrew
See Norton, Andre

North, Anthony
See Koontz, Dean R(ay)

North, Captain George
See Stevenson, Robert Louis (Balfour)

North, Milou
See Erdrich, Louise

Northrup, B. A.
See Hubbard, L(afayette) Ron(ald)

North Staffs
See Hulme, T(homas) E(rnest)

Norton, Alice Mary
See Norton, Andre
See also MAICYA; SATA 1, 43

Norton, Andre 1912- . . . . CLC 12
See also Norton, Alice Mary
See also AAYA 14; CA 1-4R; CANR 2, 31;
DLB 8, 52; JRDA; MTCW

Norton, Caroline 1808-1877 . . . . . . NCLC 47
See also DLB 21, 159

Norway, Nevil Shute 1899-1960
See Shute, Nevil
See also CA 102; 93-96

Norwid, Cyprian Kamil
1821-1883 . . . . NCLC 17

Nosille, Nabrah
See Ellison, Harlan (Jay)

Nossack, Hans Erich 1901-1978 . . . . . CLC 6
See also CA 93-96; 85-88; DLB 69

Nostradamus 1503-1566 . . . . LC 27

Nosu, Chuji
See Ozu, Yasujiro

Notenburg, Eleanora (Genrikhovna) von
See Guro, Elena

Nova, Craig 1945- . . . . CLC 7, 31
See also CA 45-48; CANR 2

Novak, Joseph
See Kosinski, Jerzy (Nikodem)

Novalis 1772-1801 . . . . NCLC 13
See also DLB 90

Nowlan, Alden (Albert)
1933-1983 . . . . CLC 15; DAC
See also CA 9-12R; CANR 5; DAM MST;
DLB 53

Noyes, Alfred 1880-1958 . . . . TCLC 7
See also CA 104; DLB 20

Nunn, Kem 19(?)- . . . . CLC 34

Nye, Robert 1939- . . . . CLC 13, 42
See also CA 33-36R; CANR 29;
DAM NOV; DLB 14; MTCW; SATA 6

Nyro, Laura 1947- . . . . CLC 17

Oates, Joyce Carol
1938- . . . . . . CLC 1, 2, 3, 6, 9, 11, 15, 19,
33, 52; DA; DAB; DAC; SSC 6; WLC
See also AAYA 15; BEST 89:2;
CA 5-8R; CANR 25, 45;
CDALB 1968-1988; DAM MST, NOV,
POP; DLB 2, 5, 130; DLBY 81;
INT CANR-25; MTCW

O'Brien, Darcy 1939- . . . . CLC 11
See also CA 21-24R; CANR 8

O'Brien, E. G.
See Clarke, Arthur C(harles)

O'Brien, Edna
1936- . . . CLC 3, 5, 8, 13, 36, 65; SSC 10
See also CA 1-4R; CANR 6, 41;
CDBLB 1960 to Present; DAM NOV;
DLB 14; MTCW

O'Brien, Fitz-James 1828-1862 . . . NCLC 21
See also DLB 74

O'Brien, Flann . . . . CLC 1, 4, 5, 7, 10, 47
See also O Nuallain, Brian

O'Brien, Richard 1942- . . . . CLC 17
See also CA 124

O'Brien, Tim 1946- . . . . CLC 7, 19, 40
See also AAYA 16; CA 85-88; CANR 40;
DAM POP; DLB 152; DLBD 9;
DLBY 80

Obstfelder, Sigbjoern 1866-1900 . . . TCLC 23
See also CA 123

O'Casey, Sean
1880-1964 . . . . . . CLC 1, 5, 9, 11, 15, 88;
DAB; DAC
See also CA 89-92; CDBLB 1914-1945;
DAM DRAM, MST; DLB 10; MTCW

O'Cathasaigh, Sean
See O'Casey, Sean

Ochs, Phil 1940-1976 . . . . CLC 17
See also CA 65-68

O'Connor, Edwin (Greene)
1918-1968 . . . . CLC 14
See also CA 93-96; 25-28R

O'Connor, (Mary) Flannery
1925-1964 . . . . CLC 1, 2, 3, 6, 10, 13, 15,
21, 66; DA; DAB; DAC; SSC 1, 23; WLC
See also AAYA 7; CA 1-4R; CANR 3, 41;
CDALB 1941-1968; DAM MST, NOV;
DLB 2, 152; DLBD 12; DLBY 80;
MTCW

O'Connor, Frank . . . . CLC 23; SSC 5
See also O'Donovan, Michael John
See also DLB 162

O'Dell, Scott 1898-1989 . . . . CLC 30
See also AAYA 3; CA 61-64; 129;
CANR 12, 30; CLR 1, 16; DLB 52;
JRDA; MAICYA; SATA 12, 60

Odets, Clifford
1906-1963 . . . . CLC 2, 28; DC 6
See also CA 85-88; DAM DRAM; DLB 7,
26; MTCW

O'Doherty, Brian 1934- . . . . CLC 76
See also CA 105

O'Donnell, K. M.
See Malzberg, Barry N(athaniel)

O'Donnell, Lawrence
See Kuttner, Henry

O'Donovan, Michael John
1903-1966 . . . . CLC 14
See also O'Connor, Frank
See also CA 93-96

Oe, Kenzaburo
1935- . . . . CLC 10, 36, 86; SSC 20
See also CA 97-100; CANR 36, 50;
DAM NOV; DLBY 94; MTCW

O'Faolain, Julia 1932- . . . . CLC 6, 19, 47
See also CA 81-84; CAAS 2; CANR 12;
DLB 14; MTCW

O'Faolain, Sean
1900-1991 . . . . CLC 1, 7, 14, 32, 70;
SSC 13
See also CA 61-64; 134; CANR 12;
DLB 15, 162; MTCW

O'Flaherty, Liam
1896-1984 . . . . CLC 5, 34; SSC 6
See also CA 101; 113; CANR 35; DLB 36,
162; DLBY 84; MTCW

Ogilvy, Gavin
See Barrie, J(ames) M(atthew)

O'Grady, Standish James
1846-1928 . . . . TCLC 5
See also CA 104

O'Grady, Timothy 1951- . . . . CLC 59
See also CA 138

O'Hara, Frank
1926-1966 . . . . CLC 2, 5, 13, 78
See also CA 9-12R; 25-28R; CANR 33;
DAM POET; DLB 5, 16; MTCW

O'Hara, John (Henry)
1905-1970 . . . . CLC 1, 2, 3, 6, 11, 42;
SSC 15
See also CA 5-8R; 25-28R; CANR 31;
CDALB 1929-1941; DAM NOV; DLB 9,
86; DLBD 2; MTCW

O Hehir, Diana 1922- . . . . CLC 41
See also CA 93-96

Okigbo, Christopher (Ifenayichukwu)
1932-1967 . . . . . CLC 25, 84; BLC; PC 7
See also BW 1; CA 77-80; DAM MULT,
POET; DLB 125; MTCW

Okri, Ben 1959- . . . . CLC 87
See also BW 2; CA 130; 138; DLB 157;
INT 138

Olds, Sharon 1942- . . . . CLC 32, 39, 85
See also CA 101; CANR 18, 41;
DAM POET; DLB 120

Oldstyle, Jonathan
See Irving, Washington

Olesha, Yuri (Karlovich)
1899-1960 . . . . CLC 8
See also CA 85-88

Oliphant, Laurence
1829(?)-1888 . . . . NCLC 47
See also DLB 18, 166

Oliphant, Margaret (Oliphant Wilson)
1828-1897 . . . . NCLC 11
See also DLB 18, 159

Oliver, Mary 1935- . . . . CLC 19, 34
See also CA 21-24R; CANR 9, 43; DLB 5

Olivier, Laurence (Kerr)
1907-1989 . . . . CLC 20
See also CA 111; 150; 129

Olsen, Tillie
1913- . . . . . CLC 4, 13; DA; DAB; DAC;
SSC 11
See also CA 1-4R; CANR 1, 43;
DAM MST; DLB 28; DLBY 80; MTCW

Olson, Charles (John)
1910-1970 . . . . . CLC 1, 2, 5, 6, 9, 11, 29
See also CA 13-16; 25-28R; CABS 2;
CANR 35; CAP 1; DAM POET; DLB 5,
16; MTCW

Olson, Toby 1937- . . . . CLC 28
See also CA 65-68; CANR 9, 31

Olyesha, Yuri
See Olesha, Yuri (Karlovich)

Ondaatje, (Philip) Michael
1943- . . . CLC 14, 29, 51, 76; DAB; DAC
See also CA 77-80; CANR 42; DAM MST;
DLB 60

Oneal, Elizabeth 1934-
See Oneal, Zibby
See also CA 106; CANR 28; MAICYA;
SATA 30, 82

Oneal, Zibby . . . . CLC 30
See also Oneal, Elizabeth
See also AAYA 5; CLR 13; JRDA

O'Neill, Eugene (Gladstone)
1888-1953 . . . . . TCLC 1, 6, 27, 49; DA;
DAB; DAC; WLC
See also AITN 1; CA 110; 132;
CDALB 1929-1941; DAM DRAM, MST;
DLB 7; MTCW

Onetti, Juan Carlos
1909-1994 . . . . CLC 7, 10; SSC 23
See also CA 85-88; 145; CANR 32;
DAM MULT, NOV; DLB 113; HW;
MTCW

O Nuallain, Brian 1911-1966
See O'Brien, Flann
See also CA 21-22; 25-28R; CAP 2

Oppen, George 1908-1984 . . . . CLC 7, 13, 34
See also CA 13-16R; 113; CANR 8; DLB 5,
165

Oppenheim, E(dward) Phillips
1866-1946 . . . . TCLC 45
See also CA 111; DLB 70

Orlovitz, Gil 1918-1973 . . . . CLC 22
See also CA 77-80; 45-48; DLB 2, 5

Orris
See Ingelow, Jean

Ortega y Gasset, Jose
1883-1955 . . . . TCLC 9; HLC
See also CA 106; 130; DAM MULT; HW;
MTCW

Ortese, Anna Maria 1914- . . . . CLC 89

Ortiz, Simon J(oseph) 1941- . . . . CLC 45
See also CA 134; DAM MULT, POET;
DLB 120; NNAL

Orton, Joe . . . . CLC 4, 13, 43; DC 3
See also Orton, John Kingsley
See also CDBLB 1960 to Present; DLB 13

Orton, John Kingsley 1933-1967
See Orton, Joe
See also CA 85-88; CANR 35;
DAM DRAM; MTCW

Orwell, George
. . . . . TCLC 2, 6, 15, 31, 51; DAB; WLC
See also Blair, Eric (Arthur)
See also CDBLB 1945-1960; DLB 15, 98

Osborne, David
See Silverberg, Robert

Osborne, George
See Silverberg, Robert

Osborne, John (James)
1929-1994 . . . . . CLC 1, 2, 5, 11, 45; DA;
DAB; DAC; WLC
See also CA 13-16R; 147; CANR 21;
CDBLB 1945-1960; DAM DRAM, MST;
DLB 13; MTCW

Osborne, Lawrence 1958- . . . . CLC 50

Oshima, Nagisa 1932- . . . . CLC 20
See also CA 116; 121

Oskison, John Milton
1874-1947 . . . . TCLC 35
See also CA 144; DAM MULT; NNAL

Ossoli, Sarah Margaret (Fuller marchesa d')
1810-1850
See Fuller, Margaret
See also SATA 25

Ostrovsky, Alexander
1823-1886 . . . . NCLC 30, 57

Otero, Blas de 1916-1979 . . . . CLC 11
See also CA 89-92; DLB 134

Otto, Whitney 1955- . . . . CLC 70
See also CA 140

Ouida . . . . TCLC 43
See also De La Ramee, (Marie) Louise
See also DLB 18, 156

Ousmane, Sembene 1923- . . . . CLC 66; BLC
See also BW 1; CA 117; 125; MTCW

Ovid 43B.C.-18(?) . . . . CMLC 7; PC 2
See also DAM POET

Owen, Hugh
See Faust, Frederick (Schiller)

Owen, Wilfred (Edward Salter)
1893-1918 ...... **TCLC 5, 27; DA; DAB;**
DAC; WLC
See also CA 104; 141; CDBLB 1914-1945;
DAM MST, POET; DLB 20

Owens, Rochelle 1936- .... **CLC 8**
See also CA 17-20R; CAAS 2; CANR 39

Oz, Amos 1939- ... **CLC 5, 8, 11, 27, 33, 54**
See also CA 53-56; CANR 27, 47;
DAM NOV; MTCW

Ozick, Cynthia
1928- .... **CLC 3, 7, 28, 62; SSC 15**
See also BEST 90:1; CA 17-20R; CANR 23;
DAM NOV, POP; DLB 28, 152;
DLBY 82; INT CANR-23; MTCW

Ozu, Yasujiro 1903-1963 .... **CLC 16**
See also CA 112

Pacheco, C.
See Pessoa, Fernando (Antonio Nogueira)

Pa Chin .... **CLC 18**
See also Li Fei-kan

Pack, Robert 1929- .... **CLC 13**
See also CA 1-4R; CANR 3, 44; DLB 5

Padgett, Lewis
See Kuttner, Henry

Padilla (Lorenzo), Heberto 1932- ... **CLC 38**
See also AITN 1; CA 123; 131; HW

Page, Jimmy 1944- .... **CLC 12**

Page, Louise 1955- .... **CLC 40**
See also CA 140

Page, P(atricia) K(athleen)
1916- .... **CLC 7, 18; DAC; PC 12**
See also CA 53-56; CANR 4, 22;
DAM MST; DLB 68; MTCW

Page, Thomas Nelson 1853-1922 .... **SSC 23**
See also CA 118; DLB 12, 78; DLBD 13

Paget, Violet 1856-1935
See Lee, Vernon
See also CA 104

Paget-Lowe, Henry
See Lovecraft, H(oward) P(hillips)

Paglia, Camille (Anna) 1947- .... **CLC 68**
See also CA 140

Paige, Richard
See Koontz, Dean R(ay)

Pakenham, Antonia
See Fraser, (Lady) Antonia (Pakenham)

Palamas, Kostes 1859-1943 .... **TCLC 5**
See also CA 105

Palazzeschi, Aldo 1885-1974 .... **CLC 11**
See also CA 89-92; 53-56; DLB 114

Paley, Grace 1922- .... **CLC 4, 6, 37; SSC 8**
See also CA 25-28R; CANR 13, 46;
DAM POP; DLB 28; INT CANR-13;
MTCW

Palin, Michael (Edward) 1943- ..... **CLC 21**
See also Monty Python
See also CA 107; CANR 35; SATA 67

Palliser, Charles 1947- .... **CLC 65**
See also CA 136

Palma, Ricardo 1833-1919 .... **TCLC 29**

Pancake, Breece Dexter 1952-1979
See Pancake, Breece D'J
See also CA 123; 109

Pancake, Breece D'J .... **CLC 29**
See also Pancake, Breece Dexter
See also DLB 130

Panko, Rudy
See Gogol, Nikolai (Vasilyevich)

Papadiamantis, Alexandros
1851-1911 .... **TCLC 29**

Papadiamantopoulos, Johannes 1856-1910
See Moreas, Jean
See also CA 117

Papini, Giovanni 1881-1956 ...... **TCLC 22**
See also CA 121

Paracelsus 1493-1541 .... **LC 14**

Parasol, Peter
See Stevens, Wallace

Parfenie, Maria
See Codrescu, Andrei

Parini, Jay (Lee) 1948- .... **CLC 54**
See also CA 97-100; CAAS 16; CANR 32

Park, Jordan
See Kornbluth, C(yril) M.; Pohl, Frederik

Parker, Bert
See Ellison, Harlan (Jay)

Parker, Dorothy (Rothschild)
1893-1967 .... **CLC 15, 68; SSC 2**
See also CA 19-20; 25-28R; CAP 2;
DAM POET; DLB 11, 45, 86; MTCW

Parker, Robert B(rown) 1932- ...... **CLC 27**
See also BEST 89:4; CA 49-52; CANR 1,
26, 52; DAM NOV, POP;
INT CANR-26; MTCW

Parkin, Frank 1940- .... **CLC 43**
See also CA 147

Parkman, Francis, Jr.
1823-1893 .... **NCLC 12**
See also DLB 1, 30

Parks, Gordon (Alexander Buchanan)
1912- .... **CLC 1, 16; BLC**
See also AITN 2; BW 2; CA 41-44R;
CANR 26; DAM MULT; DLB 33;
SATA 8

Parnell, Thomas 1679-1718 .... **LC 3**
See also DLB 94

Parra, Nicanor 1914- .... **CLC 2; HLC**
See also CA 85-88; CANR 32;
DAM MULT; HW; MTCW

Parrish, Mary Frances
See Fisher, M(ary) F(rances) K(ennedy)

Parson
See Coleridge, Samuel Taylor

Parson Lot
See Kingsley, Charles

Partridge, Anthony
See Oppenheim, E(dward) Phillips

Pascoli, Giovanni 1855-1912 ...... **TCLC 45**

Pasolini, Pier Paolo
1922-1975 .... **CLC 20, 37**
See also CA 93-96; 61-64; DLB 128;
MTCW

Pasquini
See Silone, Ignazio

Pastan, Linda (Olenik) 1932- ...... **CLC 27**
See also CA 61-64; CANR 18, 40;
DAM POET; DLB 5

Pasternak, Boris (Leonidovich)
1890-1960 ...... **CLC 7, 10, 18, 63; DA;**
DAB; DAC; PC 6; WLC
See also CA 127; 116; DAM MST, NOV,
POET; MTCW

Patchen, Kenneth 1911-1972 ... **CLC 1, 2, 18**
See also CA 1-4R; 33-36R; CANR 3, 35;
DAM POET; DLB 16, 48; MTCW

Pater, Walter (Horatio)
1839-1894 .... **NCLC 7**
See also CDBLB 1832-1890; DLB 57, 156

Paterson, A(ndrew) B(arton)
1864-1941 .... **TCLC 32**

Paterson, Katherine (Womeldorf)
1932- .... **CLC 12, 30**
See also AAYA 1; CA 21-24R; CANR 28;
CLR 7; DLB 52; JRDA; MAICYA;
MTCW; SATA 13, 53

Patmore, Coventry Kersey Dighton
1823-1896 .... **NCLC 9**
See also DLB 35, 98

Paton, Alan (Stewart)
1903-1988 ...... **CLC 4, 10, 25, 55; DA;**
DAB; DAC; WLC
See also CA 13-16; 125; CANR 22; CAP 1;
DAM MST, NOV; MTCW; SATA 11;
SATA-Obit 56

Paton Walsh, Gillian 1937-
See Walsh, Jill Paton
See also CANR 38; JRDA; MAICYA;
SAAS 3; SATA 4, 72

Paulding, James Kirke 1778-1860 .. **NCLC 2**
See also DLB 3, 59, 74

Paulin, Thomas Neilson 1949-
See Paulin, Tom
See also CA 123; 128

Paulin, Tom .... **CLC 37**
See also Paulin, Thomas Neilson
See also DLB 40

Paustovsky, Konstantin (Georgievich)
1892-1968 .... **CLC 40**
See also CA 93-96; 25-28R

Pavese, Cesare
1908-1950 ..... **TCLC 3; PC 13; SSC 19**
See also CA 104; DLB 128

Pavic, Milorad 1929- .... **CLC 60**
See also CA 136

Payne, Alan
See Jakes, John (William)

Paz, Gil
See Lugones, Leopoldo

Paz, Octavio
1914- .... **CLC 3, 4, 6, 10, 19, 51, 65;**
DA; DAB; DAC; HLC; PC 1; WLC
See also CA 73-76; CANR 32; DAM MST,
MULT, POET; DLBY 90; HW; MTCW

Peacock, Molly 1947- .... **CLC 60**
See also CA 103; CAAS 21; CANR 52;
DLB 120

Peacock, Thomas Love
1785-1866 .... **NCLC 22**
See also DLB 96, 116

Peake, Mervyn 1911-1968 .... **CLC 7, 54**
See also CA 5-8R; 25-28R; CANR 3;
DLB 15, 160; MTCW; SATA 23

Pirandello, Luigi
1867-1936 . . . . . . **TCLC 4, 29; DA; DAB;**
DAC; DC 5; SSC 22; WLC
See also CA 104; DAM DRAM, MST

Pirsig, Robert M(aynard)
1928- . . . . **CLC 4, 6, 73**
See also CA 53-56; CANR 42; DAM POP;
MTCW; SATA 39

Pisarev, Dmitry Ivanovich
1840-1868 . . . . **NCLC 25**

Pix, Mary (Griffith) 1666-1709 . . . . . . **LC 8**
See also DLB 80

Pixerecourt, Guilbert de
1773-1844 . . . . **NCLC 39**

Plaidy, Jean
See Hibbert, Eleanor Alice Burford

Planche, James Robinson
1796-1880 . . . . **NCLC 42**

Plant, Robert 1948- . . . . **CLC 12**

Plante, David (Robert)
1940- . . . . **CLC 7, 23, 38**
See also CA 37-40R; CANR 12, 36;
DAM NOV; DLBY 83; INT CANR-12;
MTCW

Plath, Sylvia
1932-1963 . . . . . **CLC 1, 2, 3, 5, 9, 11, 14,**
17, 50, 51, 62; DA; DAB; DAC; PC 1;
WLC
See also AAYA 13; CA 19-20; CANR 34;
CAP 2; CDALB 1941-1968; DAM MST,
POET; DLB 5, 6, 152; MTCW

Plato
428(?)B.C.-348(?)B.C. . . . . **CMLC 8; DA;**
DAB; DAC
See also DAM MST

Platonov, Andrei . . . . **TCLC 14**
See also Klimentov, Andrei Platonovich

Platt, Kin 1911- . . . . **CLC 26**
See also AAYA 11; CA 17-20R; CANR 11;
JRDA; SAAS 17; SATA 21, 86

Plautus c. 251B.C.-184B.C. . . . . **DC 6**

Plick et Plock
See Simenon, Georges (Jacques Christian)

Plimpton, George (Ames) 1927- . . . . . **CLC 36**
See also AITN 1; CA 21-24R; CANR 32;
MTCW; SATA 10

Plomer, William Charles Franklin
1903-1973 . . . . **CLC 4, 8**
See also CA 21-22; CANR 34; CAP 2;
DLB 20, 162; MTCW; SATA 24

Plowman, Piers
See Kavanagh, Patrick (Joseph)

Plum, J.
See Wodehouse, P(elham) G(renville)

Plumly, Stanley (Ross) 1939- . . . . . **CLC 33**
See also CA 108; 110; DLB 5; INT 110

Plumpe, Friedrich Wilhelm
1888-1931 . . . . **TCLC 53**
See also CA 112

Poe, Edgar Allan
1809-1849 . . . . **NCLC 1, 16, 55; DA;**
DAB; DAC; PC 1; SSC 1, 22; WLC
See also AAYA 14; CDALB 1640-1865;
DAM MST, POET; DLB 3, 59, 73, 74;
SATA 23

Poet of Titchfield Street, The
See Pound, Ezra (Weston Loomis)

Pohl, Frederik 1919- . . . . **CLC 18**
See also CA 61-64; CAAS 1; CANR 11, 37;
DLB 8; INT CANR-11; MTCW;
SATA 24

Poirier, Louis 1910-
See Gracq, Julien
See also CA 122; 126

Poitier, Sidney 1927- . . . . **CLC 26**
See also BW 1; CA 117

Polanski, Roman 1933- . . . . **CLC 16**
See also CA 77-80

Poliakoff, Stephen 1952- . . . . **CLC 38**
See also CA 106; DLB 13

Police, The
See Copeland, Stewart (Armstrong);
Summers, Andrew James; Sumner,
Gordon Matthew

Polidori, John William
1795-1821 . . . . **NCLC 51**
See also DLB 116

Pollitt, Katha 1949- . . . . **CLC 28**
See also CA 120; 122; MTCW

Pollock, (Mary) Sharon
1936- . . . . **CLC 50; DAC**
See also CA 141; DAM DRAM, MST;
DLB 60

Polo, Marco 1254-1324 . . . . **CMLC 15**

Polonsky, Abraham (Lincoln)
1910- . . . . **CLC 92**
See also CA 104; DLB 26; INT 104

Polybius c. 200B.C.-c. 118B.C. . . . . **CMLC 17**

Pomerance, Bernard 1940- . . . . **CLC 13**
See also CA 101; CANR 49; DAM DRAM

Ponge, Francis (Jean Gaston Alfred)
1899-1988 . . . . **CLC 6, 18**
See also CA 85-88; 126; CANR 40;
DAM POET

Pontoppidan, Henrik 1857-1943 . . . **TCLC 29**

Poole, Josephine . . . . **CLC 17**
See also Helyar, Jane Penelope Josephine
See also SAAS 2; SATA 5

Popa, Vasko 1922-1991 . . . . **CLC 19**
See also CA 112; 148

Pope, Alexander
1688-1744 . . . . . . **LC 3; DA; DAB; DAC;**
WLC
See also CDBLB 1660-1789; DAM MST,
POET; DLB 95, 101

Porter, Connie (Rose) 1959(?)- . . . . . **CLC 70**
See also BW 2; CA 142; SATA 81

Porter, Gene(va Grace) Stratton
1863(?)-1924 . . . . **TCLC 21**
See also CA 112

Porter, Katherine Anne
1890-1980 . . . . . . **CLC 1, 3, 7, 10, 13, 15,**
27; DA; DAB; DAC; SSC 4
See also AITN 2; CA 1-4R; 101; CANR 1;
DAM MST, NOV; DLB 4, 9, 102;
DLBD 12; DLBY 80; MTCW; SATA 39;
SATA-Obit 23

Porter, Peter (Neville Frederick)
1929- . . . . **CLC 5, 13, 33**
See also CA 85-88; DLB 40

Porter, William Sydney 1862-1910
See Henry, O.
See also CA 104; 131; CDALB 1865-1917;
DA; DAB; DAC; DAM MST; DLB 12,
78, 79; MTCW; YABC 2

Portillo (y Pacheco), Jose Lopez
See Lopez Portillo (y Pacheco), Jose

Post, Melville Davisson
1869-1930 . . . . **TCLC 39**
See also CA 110

Potok, Chaim 1929- . . . . **CLC 2, 7, 14, 26**
See also AAYA 15; AITN 1, 2; CA 17-20R;
CANR 19, 35; DAM NOV; DLB 28, 152;
INT CANR-19; MTCW; SATA 33

Potter, Beatrice
See Webb, (Martha) Beatrice (Potter)
See also MAICYA

Potter, Dennis (Christopher George)
1935-1994 . . . . **CLC 58, 86**
See also CA 107; 145; CANR 33; MTCW

Pound, Ezra (Weston Loomis)
1885-1972 . . . . . . **CLC 1, 2, 3, 4, 5, 7, 10,**
13, 18, 34, 48, 50; DA; DAB; DAC; PC 4;
WLC
See also CA 5-8R; 37-40R; CANR 40;
CDALB 1917-1929; DAM MST, POET;
DLB 4, 45, 63; MTCW

Povod, Reinaldo 1959-1994 . . . . **CLC 44**
See also CA 136; 146

Powell, Adam Clayton, Jr.
1908-1972 . . . . **CLC 89; BLC**
See also BW 1; CA 102; 33-36R;
DAM MULT

Powell, Anthony (Dymoke)
1905- . . . . **CLC 1, 3, 7, 9, 10, 31**
See also CA 1-4R; CANR 1, 32;
CDBLB 1945-1960; DLB 15; MTCW

Powell, Dawn 1897-1965 . . . . **CLC 66**
See also CA 5-8R

Powell, Padgett 1952- . . . . **CLC 34**
See also CA 126

Power, Susan . . . . **CLC 91**

Powers, J(ames) F(arl)
1917- . . . . **CLC 1, 4, 8, 57; SSC 4**
See also CA 1-4R; CANR 2; DLB 130;
MTCW

Powers, John J(ames) 1945-
See Powers, John R.
See also CA 69-72

Powers, John R. . . . . **CLC 66**
See also Powers, John J(ames)

Powers, Richard (S.) 1957- . . . . **CLC 93**
See also CA 148

Pownall, David 1938- . . . . **CLC 10**
See also CA 89-92; CAAS 18; CANR 49;
DLB 14

Powys, John Cowper
1872-1963 . . . . **CLC 7, 9, 15, 46**
See also CA 85-88; DLB 15; MTCW

Powys, T(heodore) F(rancis)
1875-1953 . . . . **TCLC 9**
See also CA 106; DLB 36, 162

Prager, Emily 1952- . . . . **CLC 56**

Pratt, E(dwin) J(ohn)
  1883(?)-1964 . . . . **CLC 19; DAC**
  See also CA 141; 93-96; DAM POET;
  DLB 92

Premchand . . . . **TCLC 21**
  See also Srivastava, Dhanpat Rai

Preussler, Otfried 1923- . . . . **CLC 17**
  See also CA 77-80; SATA 24

Prevert, Jacques (Henri Marie)
  1900-1977 . . . . **CLC 15**
  See also CA 77-80; 69-72; CANR 29;
  MTCW; SATA-Obit 30

Prevost, Abbe (Antoine Francois)
  1697-1763 . . . . **LC 1**

Price, (Edward) Reynolds
  1933- . . **CLC 3, 6, 13, 43, 50, 63; SSC 22**
  See also CA 1-4R; CANR 1, 37;
  DAM NOV; DLB 2; INT CANR-37

Price, Richard 1949- . . . . **CLC 6, 12**
  See also CA 49-52; CANR 3; DLBY 81

Prichard, Katharine Susannah
  1883-1969 . . . . **CLC 46**
  See also CA 11-12; CANR 33; CAP 1;
  MTCW; SATA 66

Priestley, J(ohn) B(oynton)
  1894-1984 . . . . **CLC 2, 5, 9, 34**
  See also CA 9-12R; 113; CANR 33;
  CDBLB 1914-1945; DAM DRAM, NOV;
  DLB 10, 34, 77, 100, 139; DLBY 84;
  MTCW

Prince 1958(?)- . . . . **CLC 35**

Prince, F(rank) T(empleton) 1912- . . **CLC 22**
  See also CA 101; CANR 43; DLB 20

Prince Kropotkin
  See Kropotkin, Peter (Alekseievich)

Prior, Matthew 1664-1721 . . . . **LC 4**
  See also DLB 95

Pritchard, William H(arrison)
  1932- . . . . **CLC 34**
  See also CA 65-68; CANR 23; DLB 111

Pritchett, V(ictor) S(awdon)
  1900- . . . . **CLC 5, 13, 15, 41; SSC 14**
  See also CA 61-64; CANR 31; DAM NOV;
  DLB 15, 139; MTCW

Private 19022
  See Manning, Frederic

Probst, Mark 1925- . . . . **CLC 59**
  See also CA 130

Prokosch, Frederic 1908-1989 . . . . **CLC 4, 48**
  See also CA 73-76; 128; DLB 48

Prophet, The
  See Dreiser, Theodore (Herman Albert)

Prose, Francine 1947- . . . . **CLC 45**
  See also CA 109; 112; CANR 46

Proudhon
  See Cunha, Euclides (Rodrigues Pimenta) da

Proulx, E. Annie 1935- . . . . **CLC 81**

Proust, (Valentin-Louis-George-Eugene-)
  Marcel
  1871-1922 . . . . **TCLC 7, 13, 33; DA;**
                          DAB; DAC; WLC
  See also CA 104; 120; DAM MST, NOV;
  DLB 65; MTCW

Prowler, Harley
  See Masters, Edgar Lee

Prus, Boleslaw 1845-1912 . . . . **TCLC 48**

Pryor, Richard (Franklin Lenox Thomas)
  1940- . . . . **CLC 26**
  See also CA 122

Przybyszewski, Stanislaw
  1868-1927 . . . . **TCLC 36**
  See also DLB 66

Pteleon
  See Grieve, C(hristopher) M(urray)
  See also DAM POET

Puckett, Lute
  See Masters, Edgar Lee

Puig, Manuel
  1932-1990 . . . **CLC 3, 5, 10, 28, 65; HLC**
  See also CA 45-48; CANR 2, 32;
  DAM MULT; DLB 113; HW; MTCW

Purdy, Al(fred Wellington)
  1918- . . . . **CLC 3, 6, 14, 50; DAC**
  See also CA 81-84; CAAS 17; CANR 42;
  DAM MST, POET; DLB 88

Purdy, James (Amos)
  1923- . . . . **CLC 2, 4, 10, 28, 52**
  See also CA 33-36R; CAAS 1; CANR 19,
  51; DLB 2; INT CANR-19; MTCW

Pure, Simon
  See Swinnerton, Frank Arthur

Pushkin, Alexander (Sergeyevich)
  1799-1837 . . . . . **NCLC 3, 27; DA; DAB;**
                       DAC; PC 10; WLC
  See also DAM DRAM, MST, POET;
  SATA 61

P'u Sung-ling 1640-1715 . . . . **LC 3**

Putnam, Arthur Lee
  See Alger, Horatio, Jr.

Puzo, Mario 1920- . . . . **CLC 1, 2, 6, 36**
  See also CA 65-68; CANR 4, 42;
  DAM NOV, POP; DLB 6; MTCW

Pym, Barbara (Mary Crampton)
  1913-1980 . . . . **CLC 13, 19, 37**
  See also CA 13-14; 97-100; CANR 13, 34;
  CAP 1; DLB 14; DLBY 87; MTCW

Pynchon, Thomas (Ruggles, Jr.)
  1937- . . . . . **CLC 2, 3, 6, 9, 11, 18, 33, 62,**
              72; DA; DAB; DAC; SSC 14; WLC
  See also BEST 90:2; CA 17-20R; CANR 22,
  46; DAM MST, NOV, POP; DLB 2;
  MTCW

Qian Zhongshu
  See Ch'ien Chung-shu

Qroll
  See Dagerman, Stig (Halvard)

Quarrington, Paul (Lewis) 1953- . . . . **CLC 65**
  See also CA 129

Quasimodo, Salvatore 1901-1968 . . . **CLC 10**
  See also CA 13-16; 25-28R; CAP 1;
  DLB 114; MTCW

Quay, Stephen 1947- . . . . **CLC 95**

Quay, The Brothers
  See Quay, Stephen; Quay, Timothy

Quay, Timothy 1947- . . . . **CLC 95**

Queen, Ellery . . . . **CLC 3, 11**
  See also Dannay, Frederic; Davidson,
  Avram; Lee, Manfred B(ennington);
  Sturgeon, Theodore (Hamilton); Vance,
  John Holbrook

Queen, Ellery, Jr.
  See Dannay, Frederic; Lee, Manfred
  B(ennington)

Queneau, Raymond
  1903-1976 . . . . **CLC 2, 5, 10, 42**
  See also CA 77-80; 69-72; CANR 32;
  DLB 72; MTCW

Quevedo, Francisco de 1580-1645 . . . . **LC 23**

Quiller-Couch, Arthur Thomas
  1863-1944 . . . . **TCLC 53**
  See also CA 118; DLB 135, 153

Quin, Ann (Marie) 1936-1973 . . . . **CLC 6**
  See also CA 9-12R; 45-48; DLB 14

Quinn, Martin
  See Smith, Martin Cruz

Quinn, Peter 1947- . . . . **CLC 91**

Quinn, Simon
  See Smith, Martin Cruz

Quiroga, Horacio (Sylvestre)
  1878-1937 . . . . **TCLC 20; HLC**
  See also CA 117; 131; DAM MULT; HW;
  MTCW

Quoirez, Francoise 1935- . . . . **CLC 9**
  See also Sagan, Francoise
  See also CA 49-52; CANR 6, 39; MTCW

Raabe, Wilhelm 1831-1910 . . . . **TCLC 45**
  See also DLB 129

Rabe, David (William) 1940- . . . **CLC 4, 8, 33**
  See also CA 85-88; CABS 3; DAM DRAM;
  DLB 7

Rabelais, Francois
  1483-1553 . . . . . . **LC 5; DA; DAB; DAC;**
                         WLC
  See also DAM MST

Rabinovitch, Sholem 1859-1916
  See Aleichem, Sholom
  See also CA 104

Racine, Jean 1639-1699 . . . . **LC 28; DAB**
  See also DAM MST

Radcliffe, Ann (Ward)
  1764-1823 . . . . **NCLC 6, 55**
  See also DLB 39

Radiguet, Raymond 1903-1923 . . . . **TCLC 29**
  See also DLB 65

Radnoti, Miklos 1909-1944 . . . . **TCLC 16**
  See also CA 118

Rado, James 1939- . . . . **CLC 17**
  See also CA 105

Radvanyi, Netty 1900-1983
  See Seghers, Anna
  See also CA 85-88; 110

Rae, Ben
  See Griffiths, Trevor

Raeburn, John (Hay) 1941- . . . . **CLC 34**
  See also CA 57-60

Ragni, Gerome 1942-1991 . . . . **CLC 17**
  See also CA 105; 134

Rahv, Philip 1908-1973 . . . . **CLC 24**
  See also Greenberg, Ivan
  See also DLB 137

Raine, Craig 1944- . . . . **CLC 32**
  See also CA 108; CANR 29, 51; DLB 40

Raine, Kathleen (Jessie) 1908- ... CLC 7, 45
See also CA 85-88; CANR 46; DLB 20;
MTCW

Rainis, Janis 1865-1929 .... TCLC 29

Rakosi, Carl .... CLC 47
See also Rawley, Callman
See also CAAS 5

Raleigh, Richard
See Lovecraft, H(oward) P(hillips)

Raleigh, Sir Walter 1554(?)-1618 .... LC 31
See also CDBLB Before 1660

Rallentando, H. P.
See Sayers, Dorothy L(eigh)

Ramal, Walter
See de la Mare, Walter (John)

Ramon, Juan
See Jimenez (Mantecon), Juan Ramon

Ramos, Graciliano 1892-1953 ..... TCLC 32

Rampersad, Arnold 1941- .... CLC 44
See also BW 2; CA 127; 133; DLB 111;
INT 133

Rampling, Anne
See Rice, Anne

Ramsay, Allan 1684(?)-1758 .... LC 29
See also DLB 95

Ramuz, Charles-Ferdinand
1878-1947 .... TCLC 33

Rand, Ayn
1905-1982 ...... CLC 3, 30, 44, 79; DA;
DAC; WLC
See also AAYA 10; CA 13-16R; 105;
CANR 27; DAM MST, NOV, POP;
MTCW

Randall, Dudley (Felker)
1914- .... CLC 1; BLC
See also BW 1; CA 25-28R; CANR 23;
DAM MULT; DLB 41

Randall, Robert
See Silverberg, Robert

Ranger, Ken
See Creasey, John

Ransom, John Crowe
1888-1974 .... CLC 2, 4, 5, 11, 24
See also CA 5-8R; 49-52; CANR 6, 34;
DAM POET; DLB 45, 63; MTCW

Rao, Raja 1909- .... CLC 25, 56
See also CA 73-76; CANR 51; DAM NOV;
MTCW

Raphael, Frederic (Michael)
1931- .... CLC 2, 14
See also CA 1-4R; CANR 1; DLB 14

Ratcliffe, James P.
See Mencken, H(enry) L(ouis)

Rathbone, Julian 1935- .... CLC 41
See also CA 101; CANR 34

Rattigan, Terence (Mervyn)
1911-1977 .... CLC 7
See also CA 85-88; 73-76;
CDBLB 1945-1960; DAM DRAM;
DLB 13; MTCW

Ratushinskaya, Irina 1954- .... CLC 54
See also CA 129

Raven, Simon (Arthur Noel)
1927- .... CLC 14
See also CA 81-84

Rawley, Callman 1903-
See Rakosi, Carl
See also CA 21-24R; CANR 12, 32

Rawlings, Marjorie Kinnan
1896-1953 .... TCLC 4
See also CA 104; 137; DLB 9, 22, 102;
JRDA; MAICYA; YABC 1

Ray, Satyajit 1921-1992 .... CLC 16, 76
See also CA 114; 137; DAM MULT

Read, Herbert Edward 1893-1968 .... CLC 4
See also CA 85-88; 25-28R; DLB 20, 149

Read, Piers Paul 1941- ...... CLC 4, 10, 25
See also CA 21-24R; CANR 38; DLB 14;
SATA 21

Reade, Charles 1814-1884 .... NCLC 2
See also DLB 21

Reade, Hamish
See Gray, Simon (James Holliday)

Reading, Peter 1946- .... CLC 47
See also CA 103; CANR 46; DLB 40

Reaney, James 1926- .... CLC 13; DAC
See also CA 41-44R; CAAS 15; CANR 42;
DAM MST; DLB 68; SATA 43

Rebreanu, Liviu 1885-1944 .... TCLC 28

Rechy, John (Francisco)
1934- .... CLC 1, 7, 14, 18; HLC
See also CA 5-8R; CAAS 4; CANR 6, 32;
DAM MULT; DLB 122; DLBY 82; HW;
INT CANR-6

Redcam, Tom 1870-1933 .... TCLC 25

Reddin, Keith .... CLC 67

Redgrove, Peter (William)
1932- .... CLC 6, 41
See also CA 1-4R; CANR 3, 39; DLB 40

Redmon, Anne .... CLC 22
See also Nightingale, Anne Redmon
See also DLBY 86

Reed, Eliot
See Ambler, Eric

Reed, Ishmael
1938- ... CLC 2, 3, 5, 6, 13, 32, 60; BLC
See also BW 2; CA 21-24R; CANR 25, 48;
DAM MULT; DLB 2, 5, 33; DLBD 8;
MTCW

Reed, John (Silas) 1887-1920 ...... TCLC 9
See also CA 106

Reed, Lou .... CLC 21
See also Firbank, Louis

Reeve, Clara 1729-1807 .... NCLC 19
See also DLB 39

Reich, Wilhelm 1897-1957 .... TCLC 57

Reid, Christopher (John) 1949- ..... CLC 33
See also CA 140; DLB 40

Reid, Desmond
See Moorcock, Michael (John)

Reid Banks, Lynne 1929-
See Banks, Lynne Reid
See also CA 1-4R; CANR 6, 22, 38;
CLR 24; JRDA; MAICYA; SATA 22, 75

Reilly, William K.
See Creasey, John

Reiner, Max
See Caldwell, (Janet Miriam) Taylor
(Holland)

Reis, Ricardo
See Pessoa, Fernando (Antonio Nogueira)

Remarque, Erich Maria
1898-1970 .... CLC 21; DA; DAB; DAC
See also CA 77-80; 29-32R; DAM MST,
NOV; DLB 56; MTCW

Remizov, A.
See Remizov, Aleksei (Mikhailovich)

Remizov, A. M.
See Remizov, Aleksei (Mikhailovich)

Remizov, Aleksei (Mikhailovich)
1877-1957 .... TCLC 27
See also CA 125; 133

Renan, Joseph Ernest
1823-1892 .... NCLC 26

Renard, Jules 1864-1910 .... TCLC 17
See also CA 117

Renault, Mary .... CLC 3, 11, 17
See also Challans, Mary
See also DLBY 83

Rendell, Ruth (Barbara) 1930- .. CLC 28, 48
See also Vine, Barbara
See also CA 109; CANR 32, 52;
DAM POP; DLB 87; INT CANR-32;
MTCW

Renoir, Jean 1894-1979 .... CLC 20
See also CA 129; 85-88

Resnais, Alain 1922- .... CLC 16

Reverdy, Pierre 1889-1960 .... CLC 53
See also CA 97-100; 89-92

Rexroth, Kenneth
1905-1982 ...... CLC 1, 2, 6, 11, 22, 49
See also CA 5-8R; 107; CANR 14, 34;
CDALB 1941-1968; DAM POET;
DLB 16, 48, 165; DLBY 82;
INT CANR-14; MTCW

Reyes, Alfonso 1889-1959 .... TCLC 33
See also CA 131; HW

Reyes y Basoalto, Ricardo Eliecer Neftali
See Neruda, Pablo

Reymont, Wladyslaw (Stanislaw)
1868(?)-1925 .... TCLC 5
See also CA 104

Reynolds, Jonathan 1942- .... CLC 6, 38
See also CA 65-68; CANR 28

Reynolds, Joshua 1723-1792 .... LC 15
See also DLB 104

Reynolds, Michael Shane 1937- .... CLC 44
See also CA 65-68; CANR 9

Reznikoff, Charles 1894-1976 .... CLC 9
See also CA 33-36; 61-64; CAP 2; DLB 28,
45

Rezzori (d'Arezzo), Gregor von
1914- .... CLC 25
See also CA 122; 136

Rhine, Richard
See Silverstein, Alvin

Rhodes, Eugene Manlove
1869-1934 .... TCLC 53

R'hoone
See Balzac, Honore de

Roddenberry, Eugene Wesley 1921-1991
  See Roddenberry, Gene
  See also CA 110; 135; CANR 37; SATA 45;
    SATA-Obit 69

Roddenberry, Gene . . . . CLC 17
  See also Roddenberry, Eugene Wesley
  See also AAYA 5; SATA-Obit 69

Rodgers, Mary 1931- . . . . CLC 12
  See also CA 49-52; CANR 8; CLR 20;
    INT CANR-8; JRDA; MAICYA;
    SATA 8

Rodgers, W(illiam) R(obert)
  1909-1969 . . . . CLC 7
  See also CA 85-88; DLB 20

Rodman, Eric
  See Silverberg, Robert

Rodman, Howard 1920(?)-1985 . . . . . CLC 65
  See also CA 118

Rodman, Maia
  See Wojciechowska, Maia (Teresa)

Rodriguez, Claudio 1934- . . . . CLC 10
  See also DLB 134

Roelvaag, O(le) E(dvart)
  1876-1931 . . . . TCLC 17
  See also CA 117; DLB 9

Roethke, Theodore (Huebner)
  1908-1963 . . . . . . CLC 1, 3, 8, 11, 19, 46;
                                                 PC 15
  See also CA 81-84; CABS 2;
    CDALB 1941-1968; DAM POET; DLB 5;
    MTCW

Rogers, Thomas Hunton 1927- . . . . . CLC 57
  See also CA 89-92; INT 89-92

Rogers, Will(iam Penn Adair)
  1879-1935 . . . . TCLC 8
  See also CA 105; 144; DAM MULT;
    DLB 11; NNAL

Rogin, Gilbert 1929- . . . . CLC 18
  See also CA 65-68; CANR 15

Rohan, Koda . . . . TCLC 22
  See also Koda Shigeyuki

Rohmer, Eric . . . . CLC 16
  See also Scherer, Jean-Marie Maurice

Rohmer, Sax . . . . TCLC 28
  See also Ward, Arthur Henry Sarsfield
  See also DLB 70

Roiphe, Anne (Richardson)
  1935- . . . . CLC 3, 9
  See also CA 89-92; CANR 45; DLBY 80;
    INT 89-92

Rojas, Fernando de 1465-1541 . . . . . . LC 23

Rolfe, Frederick (William Serafino Austin
  Lewis Mary) 1860-1913 . . . . . TCLC 12
  See also CA 107; DLB 34, 156

Rolland, Romain 1866-1944 . . . . . . TCLC 23
  See also CA 118; DLB 65

Rolvaag, O(le) E(dvart)
  See Roelvaag, O(le) E(dvart)

Romain Arnaud, Saint
  See Aragon, Louis

Romains, Jules 1885-1972 . . . . CLC 7
  See also CA 85-88; CANR 34; DLB 65;
    MTCW

Romero, Jose Ruben 1890-1952 . . . TCLC 14
  See also CA 114; 131; HW

Ronsard, Pierre de
  1524-1585 . . . . LC 6; PC 11

Rooke, Leon 1934- . . . . CLC 25, 34
  See also CA 25-28R; CANR 23; DAM POP

Roper, William 1498-1578 . . . . LC 10

Roquelaure, A. N.
  See Rice, Anne

Rosa, Joao Guimaraes 1908-1967 . . . CLC 23
  See also CA 89-92; DLB 113

Rose, Wendy 1948- . . . . CLC 85; PC 13
  See also CA 53-56; CANR 5, 51;
    DAM MULT; NNAL; SATA 12

Rosen, Richard (Dean) 1949- . . . . . . CLC 39
  See also CA 77-80; INT CANR-30

Rosenberg, Isaac 1890-1918 . . . . . . TCLC 12
  See also CA 107; DLB 20

Rosenblatt, Joe . . . . CLC 15
  See also Rosenblatt, Joseph

Rosenblatt, Joseph 1933-
  See Rosenblatt, Joe
  See also CA 89-92; INT 89-92

Rosenfeld, Samuel 1896-1963
  See Tzara, Tristan
  See also CA 89-92

Rosenthal, M(acha) L(ouis) 1917- . . . CLC 28
  See also CA 1-4R; CAAS 6; CANR 4, 51;
    DLB 5; SATA 59

Ross, Barnaby
  See Dannay, Frederic

Ross, Bernard L.
  See Follett, Ken(neth Martin)

Ross, J. H.
  See Lawrence, T(homas) E(dward)

Ross, Martin
  See Martin, Violet Florence
  See also DLB 135

Ross, (James) Sinclair
  1908- . . . . CLC 13; DAC
  See also CA 73-76; DAM MST; DLB 88

Rossetti, Christina (Georgina)
  1830-1894 . . . . . NCLC 2, 50; DA; DAB;
                                   DAC; PC 7; WLC
  See also DAM MST, POET; DLB 35, 163;
    MAICYA; SATA 20

Rossetti, Dante Gabriel
  1828-1882 . . . . NCLC 4; DA; DAB;
                                         DAC; WLC
  See also CDBLB 1832-1890; DAM MST,
    POET; DLB 35

Rossner, Judith (Perelman)
  1935- . . . . CLC 6, 9, 29
  See also AITN 2; BEST 90:3; CA 17-20R;
    CANR 18, 51; DLB 6; INT CANR-18;
    MTCW

Rostand, Edmond (Eugene Alexis)
  1868-1918 . . . . . . TCLC 6, 37; DA; DAB;
                                                  DAC
  See also CA 104; 126; DAM DRAM, MST;
    MTCW

Roth, Henry 1906-1995 . . . . CLC 2, 6, 11
  See also CA 11-12; 149; CANR 38; CAP 1;
    DLB 28; MTCW

Roth, Joseph 1894-1939 . . . . TCLC 33
  See also DLB 85

Roth, Philip (Milton)
  1933- . . . . . . CLC 1, 2, 3, 4, 6, 9, 15, 22,
    31, 47, 66, 86; DA; DAB; DAC; WLC
  See also BEST 90:3; CA 1-4R; CANR 1, 22,
    36; CDALB 1968-1988; DAM MST,
    NOV, POP; DLB 2, 28; DLBY 82;
    MTCW

Rothenberg, Jerome 1931- . . . . CLC 6, 57
  See also CA 45-48; CANR 1; DLB 5

Roumain, Jacques (Jean Baptiste)
  1907-1944 . . . . TCLC 19; BLC
  See also BW 1; CA 117; 125; DAM MULT

Rourke, Constance (Mayfield)
  1885-1941 . . . . TCLC 12
  See also CA 107; YABC 1

Rousseau, Jean-Baptiste 1671-1741 . . . LC 9

Rousseau, Jean-Jacques
  1712-1778 . . . . . LC 14; DA; DAB; DAC;
                                                    WLC
  See also DAM MST

Roussel, Raymond 1877-1933 . . . . . TCLC 20
  See also CA 117

Rovit, Earl (Herbert) 1927- . . . . CLC 7
  See also CA 5-8R; CANR 12

Rowe, Nicholas 1674-1718 . . . . LC 8
  See also DLB 84

Rowley, Ames Dorrance
  See Lovecraft, H(oward) P(hillips)

Rowson, Susanna Haswell
  1762(?)-1824 . . . . NCLC 5
  See also DLB 37

Roy, Gabrielle
  1909-1983 . . . . . CLC 10, 14; DAB; DAC
  See also CA 53-56; 110; CANR 5;
    DAM MST; DLB 68; MTCW

Rozewicz, Tadeusz 1921- . . . . CLC 9, 23
  See also CA 108; CANR 36; DAM POET;
    MTCW

Ruark, Gibbons 1941- . . . . CLC 3
  See also CA 33-36R; CAAS 23; CANR 14,
    31; DLB 120

Rubens, Bernice (Ruth) 1923- . . . CLC 19, 31
  See also CA 25-28R; CANR 33; DLB 14;
    MTCW

Rudkin, (James) David 1936- . . . . . . CLC 14
  See also CA 89-92; DLB 13

Rudnik, Raphael 1933- . . . . CLC 7
  See also CA 29-32R

Ruffian, M.
  See Hasek, Jaroslav (Matej Frantisek)

Ruiz, Jose Martinez . . . . CLC 11
  See also Martinez Ruiz, Jose

Rukeyser, Muriel
  1913-1980 . . . . CLC 6, 10, 15, 27; PC 12
  See also CA 5-8R; 93-96; CANR 26;
    DAM POET; DLB 48; MTCW;
    SATA-Obit 22

Rule, Jane (Vance) 1931- . . . . CLC 27
  See also CA 25-28R; CAAS 18; CANR 12;
    DLB 60

Rulfo, Juan 1918-1986 . . . . CLC 8, 80; HLC
  See also CA 85-88; 118; CANR 26;
    DAM MULT; DLB 113; HW; MTCW

Runeberg, Johan 1804-1877 . . . . . . NCLC 41

Runyon, (Alfred) Damon
1884(?)-1946 . . . . **TCLC 10**
See also CA 107; DLB 11, 86

Rush, Norman 1933- . . . . **CLC 44**
See also CA 121; 126; INT 126

Rushdie, (Ahmed) Salman
1947- . . . . . . **CLC 23, 31, 55; DAB; DAC**
See also BEST 89:3; CA 108; 111;
CANR 33; DAM MST, NOV, POP;
INT 111; MTCW

Rushforth, Peter (Scott) 1945- . . . . . **CLC 19**
See also CA 101

Ruskin, John 1819-1900 . . . . **TCLC 63**
See also CA 114; 129; CDBLB 1832-1890;
DLB 55, 163; SATA 24

Russ, Joanna 1937- . . . . **CLC 15**
See also CA 25-28R; CANR 11, 31; DLB 8;
MTCW

Russell, George William 1867-1935
See A. E.
See also CA 104; CDBLB 1890-1914;
DAM POET

Russell, (Henry) Ken(neth Alfred)
1927- . . . . **CLC 16**
See also CA 105

Russell, Willy 1947- . . . . **CLC 60**

Rutherford, Mark . . . . **TCLC 25**
See also White, William Hale
See also DLB 18

Ruyslinck, Ward 1929- . . . . **CLC 14**
See also Belser, Reimond Karel Maria de

Ryan, Cornelius (John) 1920-1974 . . . **CLC 7**
See also CA 69-72; 53-56; CANR 38

Ryan, Michael 1946- . . . . **CLC 65**
See also CA 49-52; DLBY 82

Rybakov, Anatoli (Naumovich)
1911- . . . . **CLC 23, 53**
See also CA 126; 135; SATA 79

Ryder, Jonathan
See Ludlum, Robert

Ryga, George 1932-1987 . . . . . **CLC 14; DAC**
See also CA 101; 124; CANR 43;
DAM MST; DLB 60

S. S.
See Sassoon, Siegfried (Lorraine)

Saba, Umberto 1883-1957 . . . . **TCLC 33**
See also CA 144; DLB 114

Sabatini, Rafael 1875-1950 . . . . . . **TCLC 47**

Sabato, Ernesto (R.)
1911- . . . . **CLC 10, 23; HLC**
See also CA 97-100; CANR 32;
DAM MULT; DLB 145; HW; MTCW

Sacastru, Martin
See Bioy Casares, Adolfo

Sacher-Masoch, Leopold von
1836(?)-1895 . . . . **NCLC 31**

Sachs, Marilyn (Stickle) 1927- . . . . . **CLC 35**
See also AAYA 2; CA 17-20R; CANR 13,
47; CLR 2; JRDA; MAICYA; SAAS 2;
SATA 3, 68

Sachs, Nelly 1891-1970 . . . . **CLC 14**
See also CA 17-18; 25-28R; CAP 2

Sackler, Howard (Oliver)
1929-1982 . . . . **CLC 14**
See also CA 61-64; 108; CANR 30; DLB 7

Sacks, Oliver (Wolf) 1933- . . . . **CLC 67**
See also CA 53-56; CANR 28, 50;
INT CANR-28; MTCW

Sade, Donatien Alphonse Francois Comte
1740-1814 . . . . **NCLC 47**

Sadoff, Ira 1945- . . . . **CLC 9**
See also CA 53-56; CANR 5, 21; DLB 120

Saetone
See Camus, Albert

Safire, William 1929- . . . . **CLC 10**
See also CA 17-20R; CANR 31

Sagan, Carl (Edward) 1934- . . . . **CLC 30**
See also AAYA 2; CA 25-28R; CANR 11,
36; MTCW; SATA 58

Sagan, Francoise . . . . **CLC 3, 6, 9, 17, 36**
See also Quoirez, Francoise
See also DLB 83

Sahgal, Nayantara (Pandit) 1927- . . . **CLC 41**
See also CA 9-12R; CANR 11

Saint, H(arry) F. 1941- . . . . **CLC 50**
See also CA 127

St. Aubin de Teran, Lisa 1953-
See Teran, Lisa St. Aubin de
See also CA 118; 126; INT 126

Sainte-Beuve, Charles Augustin
1804-1869 . . . . **NCLC 5**

Saint-Exupery, Antoine (Jean Baptiste Marie Roger) de
1900-1944 . . . . **TCLC 2, 56; WLC**
See also CA 108; 132; CLR 10; DAM NOV;
DLB 72; MAICYA; MTCW; SATA 20

St. John, David
See Hunt, E(verette) Howard, (Jr.)

Saint-John Perse
See Leger, (Marie-Rene Auguste) Alexis
Saint-Leger

Saintsbury, George (Edward Bateman)
1845-1933 . . . . **TCLC 31**
See also DLB 57, 149

Sait Faik . . . . **TCLC 23**
See also Abasiyanik, Sait Faik

Saki . . . . **TCLC 3; SSC 12**
See also Munro, H(ector) H(ugh)

Sala, George Augustus . . . . **NCLC 46**

Salama, Hannu 1936- . . . . **CLC 18**

Salamanca, J(ack) R(ichard)
1922- . . . . **CLC 4, 15**
See also CA 25-28R

Sale, J. Kirkpatrick
See Sale, Kirkpatrick

Sale, Kirkpatrick 1937- . . . . **CLC 68**
See also CA 13-16R; CANR 10

Salinas, Luis Omar 1937- . . . **CLC 90; HLC**
See also CA 131; DAM MULT; DLB 82;
HW

Salinas (y Serrano), Pedro
1891(?)-1951 . . . . **TCLC 17**
See also CA 117; DLB 134

Salinger, J(erome) D(avid)
1919- . . . . . . **CLC 1, 3, 8, 12, 55, 56; DA;**
DAB; DAC; SSC 2; WLC
See also AAYA 2; CA 5-8R; CANR 39;
CDALB 1941-1968; CLR 18; DAM MST,
NOV, POP; DLB 2, 102; MAICYA;
MTCW; SATA 67

Salisbury, John
See Caute, David

Salter, James 1925- . . . . **CLC 7, 52, 59**
See also CA 73-76; DLB 130

Saltus, Edgar (Everton)
1855-1921 . . . . **TCLC 8**
See also CA 105

Saltykov, Mikhail Evgrafovich
1826-1889 . . . . **NCLC 16**

Samarakis, Antonis 1919- . . . . **CLC 5**
See also CA 25-28R; CAAS 16; CANR 36

Sanchez, Florencio 1875-1910 . . . . . **TCLC 37**
See also HW

Sanchez, Luis Rafael 1936- . . . . **CLC 23**
See also CA 128; DLB 145; HW

Sanchez, Sonia 1934- . . . **CLC 5; BLC; PC 9**
See also BW 2; CA 33-36R; CANR 24, 49;
CLR 18; DAM MULT; DLB 41;
DLBD 8; MAICYA; MTCW; SATA 22

Sand, George
1804-1876 . . . . **NCLC 2, 42, 57; DA;**
DAB; DAC; WLC
See also DAM MST, NOV; DLB 119

Sandburg, Carl (August)
1878-1967 . . . . **CLC 1, 4, 10, 15, 35; DA;**
DAB; DAC; PC 2; WLC
See also CA 5-8R; 25-28R; CANR 35;
CDALB 1865-1917; DAM MST, POET;
DLB 17, 54; MAICYA; MTCW; SATA 8

Sandburg, Charles
See Sandburg, Carl (August)

Sandburg, Charles A.
See Sandburg, Carl (August)

Sanders, (James) Ed(ward) 1939- . . . **CLC 53**
See also CA 13-16R; CAAS 21; CANR 13,
44; DLB 16

Sanders, Lawrence 1920- . . . . **CLC 41**
See also BEST 89:4; CA 81-84; CANR 33;
DAM POP; MTCW

Sanders, Noah
See Blount, Roy (Alton), Jr.

Sanders, Winston P.
See Anderson, Poul (William)

Sandoz, Mari(e Susette)
1896-1966 . . . . **CLC 28**
See also CA 1-4R; 25-28R; CANR 17;
DLB 9; MTCW; SATA 5

Saner, Reg(inald Anthony) 1931- . . . . **CLC 9**
See also CA 65-68

Sannazaro, Jacopo 1456(?)-1530 . . . . . . **LC 8**

Sansom, William
1912-1976 . . . . **CLC 2, 6; SSC 21**
See also CA 5-8R; 65-68; CANR 42;
DAM NOV; DLB 139; MTCW

Santayana, George 1863-1952 . . . . . **TCLC 40**
See also CA 115; DLB 54, 71; DLBD 13

Santiago, Danny . . . . **CLC 33**
See also James, Daniel (Lewis)
See also DLB 122

Santmyer, Helen Hoover
1895-1986 . . . . **CLC 33**
See also CA 1-4R; 118; CANR 15, 33;
DLBY 84; MTCW

Santos, Bienvenido N(uqui)
1911-1996 . . . . **CLC 22**
See also CA 101; 151; CANR 19, 46;
DAM MULT

Sapper . . . . **TCLC 44**
See also McNeile, Herman Cyril

Sappho fl. 6th cent. B.C.-. . . . **CMLC 3; PC 5**
See also DAM POET

Sarduy, Severo 1937-1993 . . . . **CLC 6**
See also CA 89-92; 142; DLB 113; HW

Sargeson, Frank 1903-1982 . . . . **CLC 31**
See also CA 25-28R; 106; CANR 38

Sarmiento, Felix Ruben Garcia
See Dario, Ruben

Saroyan, William
1908-1981 . . . . . **CLC 1, 8, 10, 29, 34, 56;**
DA; DAB; DAC; SSC 21; WLC
See also CA 5-8R; 103; CANR 30;
DAM DRAM, MST, NOV; DLB 7, 9, 86;
DLBY 81; MTCW; SATA 23;
SATA-Obit 24

Sarraute, Nathalie
1900- . . . . **CLC 1, 2, 4, 8, 10, 31, 80**
See also CA 9-12R; CANR 23; DLB 83;
MTCW

Sarton, (Eleanor) May
1912-1995 . . . . **CLC 4, 14, 49, 91**
See also CA 1-4R; 149; CANR 1, 34;
DAM POET; DLB 48; DLBY 81;
INT CANR-34; MTCW; SATA 36;
SATA-Obit 86

Sartre, Jean-Paul
1905-1980 . . . . **CLC 1, 4, 7, 9, 13, 18, 24,**
44, 50, 52; DA; DAB; DAC; DC 3; WLC
See also CA 9-12R; 97-100; CANR 21;
DAM DRAM, MST, NOV; DLB 72;
MTCW

Sassoon, Siegfried (Lorraine)
1886-1967 . . . . **CLC 36; DAB; PC 12**
See also CA 104; 25-28R; CANR 36;
DAM MST, NOV, POET; DLB 20;
MTCW

Satterfield, Charles
See Pohl, Frederik

Saul, John (W. III) 1942- . . . . **CLC 46**
See also AAYA 10; BEST 90:4; CA 81-84;
CANR 16, 40; DAM NOV, POP

Saunders, Caleb
See Heinlein, Robert A(nson)

Saura (Atares), Carlos 1932-. . . . . . . **CLC 20**
See also CA 114; 131; HW

Sauser-Hall, Frederic 1887-1961. . . . **CLC 18**
See also Cendrars, Blaise
See also CA 102; 93-96; CANR 36; MTCW

Saussure, Ferdinand de
1857-1913 . . . . **TCLC 49**

Savage, Catharine
See Brosman, Catharine Savage

Savage, Thomas 1915- . . . . **CLC 40**
See also CA 126; 132; CAAS 15; INT 132

Savan, Glenn 19(?)- . . . . **CLC 50**

Sayers, Dorothy L(eigh)
1893-1957 . . . . **TCLC 2, 15**
See also CA 104; 119; CDBLB 1914-1945;
DAM POP; DLB 10, 36, 77, 100; MTCW

Sayers, Valerie 1952-. . . . . **CLC 50**
See also CA 134

Sayles, John (Thomas)
1950- . . . . **CLC 7, 10, 14**
See also CA 57-60; CANR 41; DLB 44

Scammell, Michael . . . . **CLC 34**

Scannell, Vernon 1922- . . . . **CLC 49**
See also CA 5-8R; CANR 8, 24; DLB 27;
SATA 59

Scarlett, Susan
See Streatfeild, (Mary) Noel

Schaeffer, Susan Fromberg
1941- . . . . **CLC 6, 11, 22**
See also CA 49-52; CANR 18; DLB 28;
MTCW; SATA 22

Schary, Jill
See Robinson, Jill

Schell, Jonathan 1943-. . . . . **CLC 35**
See also CA 73-76; CANR 12

Schelling, Friedrich Wilhelm Joseph von
1775-1854 . . . . **NCLC 30**
See also DLB 90

Schendel, Arthur van 1874-1946. . . **TCLC 56**

Scherer, Jean-Marie Maurice 1920-
See Rohmer, Eric
See also CA 110

Schevill, James (Erwin) 1920-. . . . . . . **CLC 7**
See also CA 5-8R; CAAS 12

Schiller, Friedrich 1759-1805 . . . . **NCLC 39**
See also DAM DRAM; DLB 94

Schisgal, Murray (Joseph) 1926-. . . . . . **CLC 6**
See also CA 21-24R; CANR 48

Schlee, Ann 1934-. . . . . **CLC 35**
See also CA 101; CANR 29; SATA 44;
SATA-Brief 36

Schlegel, August Wilhelm von
1767-1845 . . . . **NCLC 15**
See also DLB 94

Schlegel, Friedrich 1772-1829 . . . . **NCLC 45**
See also DLB 90

Schlegel, Johann Elias (von)
1719(?)-1749 . . . . **LC 5**

Schlesinger, Arthur M(eier), Jr.
1917- . . . . **CLC 84**
See also AITN 1; CA 1-4R; CANR 1, 28;
DLB 17; INT CANR-28; MTCW;
SATA 61

Schmidt, Arno (Otto) 1914-1979. . . . **CLC 56**
See also CA 128; 109; DLB 69

Schmitz, Aron Hector 1861-1928
See Svevo, Italo
See also CA 104; 122; MTCW

Schnackenberg, Gjertrud 1953-. . . . . **CLC 40**
See also CA 116; DLB 120

Schneider, Leonard Alfred 1925-1966
See Bruce, Lenny
See also CA 89-92

Schnitzler, Arthur
1862-1931 . . . . **TCLC 4; SSC 15**
See also CA 104; DLB 81, 118

Schopenhauer, Arthur
1788-1860 . . . . **NCLC 51**
See also DLB 90

Schor, Sandra (M.) 1932(?)-1990 . . . **CLC 65**
See also CA 132

Schorer, Mark 1908-1977 . . . . **CLC 9**
See also CA 5-8R; 73-76; CANR 7;
DLB 103

Schrader, Paul (Joseph) 1946-. . . . . . **CLC 26**
See also CA 37-40R; CANR 41; DLB 44

Schreiner, Olive (Emilie Albertina)
1855-1920 . . . . **TCLC 9**
See also CA 105; DLB 18, 156

Schulberg, Budd (Wilson)
1914- . . . . **CLC 7, 48**
See also CA 25-28R; CANR 19; DLB 6, 26,
28; DLBY 81

Schulz, Bruno
1892-1942 . . . . **TCLC 5, 51; SSC 13**
See also CA 115; 123

Schulz, Charles M(onroe) 1922-. . . . **CLC 12**
See also CA 9-12R; CANR 6;
INT CANR-6; SATA 10

Schumacher, E(rnst) F(riedrich)
1911-1977 . . . . **CLC 80**
See also CA 81-84; 73-76; CANR 34

Schuyler, James Marcus
1923-1991 . . . . **CLC 5, 23**
See also CA 101; 134; DAM POET; DLB 5;
INT 101

Schwartz, Delmore (David)
1913-1966 . . . **CLC 2, 4, 10, 45, 87; PC 8**
See also CA 17-18; 25-28R; CANR 35;
CAP 2; DLB 28, 48; MTCW

Schwartz, Ernst
See Ozu, Yasujiro

Schwartz, John Burnham 1965- . . . . **CLC 59**
See also CA 132

Schwartz, Lynne Sharon 1939-. . . . . **CLC 31**
See also CA 103; CANR 44

Schwartz, Muriel A.
See Eliot, T(homas) S(tearns)

Schwarz-Bart, Andre 1928-. . . . . . . **CLC 2, 4**
See also CA 89-92

Schwarz-Bart, Simone 1938-. . . . . **CLC 7**
See also BW 2; CA 97-100

Schwob, (Mayer Andre) Marcel
1867-1905 . . . . **TCLC 20**
See also CA 117; DLB 123

Sciascia, Leonardo
1921-1989 . . . . **CLC 8, 9, 41**
See also CA 85-88; 130; CANR 35; MTCW

Scoppettone, Sandra 1936-. . . . . **CLC 26**
See also AAYA 11; CA 5-8R; CANR 41;
SATA 9

Scorsese, Martin 1942- . . . . **CLC 20, 89**
See also CA 110; 114; CANR 46

Scotland, Jay
See Jakes, John (William)

Scott, Duncan Campbell
1862-1947 . . . . **TCLC 6; DAC**
See also CA 104; DLB 92

Shaw, George Bernard
1856-1950 ... **TCLC 3, 9, 21; DA; DAB;**
DAC; WLC
See also Shaw, Bernard
See also CA 104; 128; CDBLB 1914-1945;
DAM DRAM, MST; DLB 10, 57;
MTCW

Shaw, Henry Wheeler
1818-1885 .... **NCLC 15**
See also DLB 11

Shaw, Irwin 1913-1984 ...... **CLC 7, 23, 34**
See also AITN 1; CA 13-16R; 112;
CANR 21; CDALB 1941-1968;
DAM DRAM, POP; DLB 6, 102;
DLBY 84; MTCW

Shaw, Robert 1927-1978 .... **CLC 5**
See also AITN 1; CA 1-4R; 81-84;
CANR 4; DLB 13, 14

Shaw, T. E.
See Lawrence, T(homas) E(dward)

Shawn, Wallace 1943- .... **CLC 41**
See also CA 112

Shea, Lisa 1953- .... **CLC 86**
See also CA 147

Sheed, Wilfrid (John Joseph)
1930- .... **CLC 2, 4, 10, 53**
See also CA 65-68; CANR 30; DLB 6;
MTCW

Sheldon, Alice Hastings Bradley
1915(?)-1987
See Tiptree, James, Jr.
See also CA 108; 122; CANR 34; INT 108;
MTCW

Sheldon, John
See Bloch, Robert (Albert)

Shelley, Mary Wollstonecraft (Godwin)
1797-1851 .... **NCLC 14; DA; DAB;**
DAC; WLC
See also CDBLB 1789-1832; DAM MST,
NOV; DLB 110, 116, 159; SATA 29

Shelley, Percy Bysshe
1792-1822 .... **NCLC 18; DA; DAB;**
DAC; PC 14; WLC
See also CDBLB 1789-1832; DAM MST,
POET; DLB 96, 110, 158

Shepard, Jim 1956- .... **CLC 36**
See also CA 137

Shepard, Lucius 1947- .... **CLC 34**
See also CA 128; 141

Shepard, Sam
1943- .... **CLC 4, 6, 17, 34, 41, 44; DC 5**
See also AAYA 1; CA 69-72; CABS 3;
CANR 22; DAM DRAM; DLB 7;
MTCW

Shepherd, Michael
See Ludlum, Robert

Sherburne, Zoa (Morin) 1912- ...... **CLC 30**
See also AAYA 13; CA 1-4R; CANR 3, 37;
MAICYA; SAAS 18; SATA 3

Sheridan, Frances 1724-1766 .... **LC 7**
See also DLB 39, 84

Sheridan, Richard Brinsley
1751-1816 .... **NCLC 5; DA; DAB;**
DAC; DC 1; WLC
See also CDBLB 1660-1789; DAM DRAM,
MST; DLB 89

Sherman, Jonathan Marc .... **CLC 55**

Sherman, Martin 1941(?)- .... **CLC 19**
See also CA 116; 123

Sherwin, Judith Johnson 1936-... **CLC 7, 15**
See also CA 25-28R; CANR 34

Sherwood, Frances 1940- .... **CLC 81**
See also CA 146

Sherwood, Robert E(mmet)
1896-1955 .... **TCLC 3**
See also CA 104; DAM DRAM; DLB 7, 26

Shestov, Lev 1866-1938 .... **TCLC 56**

Shevchenko, Taras 1814-1861 .... **NCLC 54**

Shiel, M(atthew) P(hipps)
1865-1947 .... **TCLC 8**
See also CA 106; DLB 153

Shields, Carol 1935- .... **CLC 91; DAC**
See also CA 81-84; CANR 51

Shiga, Naoya 1883-1971... **CLC 33; SSC 23**
See also CA 101; 33-36R

Shilts, Randy 1951-1994 .... **CLC 85**
See also CA 115; 127; 144; CANR 45;
INT 127

Shimazaki, Haruki 1872-1943
See Shimazaki Toson
See also CA 105; 134

Shimazaki Toson .... **TCLC 5**
See also Shimazaki, Haruki

Sholokhov, Mikhail (Aleksandrovich)
1905-1984 .... **CLC 7, 15**
See also CA 101; 112; MTCW;
SATA-Obit 36

Shone, Patric
See Hanley, James

Shreve, Susan Richards 1939- ...... **CLC 23**
See also CA 49-52; CAAS 5; CANR 5, 38;
MAICYA; SATA 46; SATA-Brief 41

Shue, Larry 1946-1985 .... **CLC 52**
See also CA 145; 117; DAM DRAM

Shu-Jen, Chou 1881-1936
See Lu Hsun
See also CA 104

Shulman, Alix Kates 1932- ...... **CLC 2, 10**
See also CA 29-32R; CANR 43; SATA 7

Shuster, Joe 1914- .... **CLC 21**

Shute, Nevil .... **CLC 30**
See also Norway, Nevil Shute

Shuttle, Penelope (Diane) 1947- ..... **CLC 7**
See also CA 93-96; CANR 39; DLB 14, 40

Sidney, Mary 1561-1621 .... **LC 19**

Sidney, Sir Philip
1554-1586 ..... **LC 19; DA; DAB; DAC**
See also CDBLB Before 1660; DAM MST,
POET; DLB 167

Siegel, Jerome 1914-1996 .... **CLC 21**
See also CA 116; 151

Siegel, Jerry
See Siegel, Jerome

Sienkiewicz, Henryk (Adam Alexander Pius)
1846-1916 .... **TCLC 3**
See also CA 104; 134

Sierra, Gregorio Martinez
See Martinez Sierra, Gregorio

Sierra, Maria (de la O'LeJarraga) Martinez
See Martinez Sierra, Maria (de la
O'LeJarraga)

Sigal, Clancy 1926- .... **CLC 7**
See also CA 1-4R

Sigourney, Lydia Howard (Huntley)
1791-1865 .... **NCLC 21**
See also DLB 1, 42, 73

Siguenza y Gongora, Carlos de
1645-1700 .... **LC 8**

Sigurjonsson, Johann 1880-1919... **TCLC 27**

Sikelianos, Angelos 1884-1951 .... **TCLC 39**

Silkin, Jon 1930- .... **CLC 2, 6, 43**
See also CA 5-8R; CAAS 5; DLB 27

Silko, Leslie (Marmon)
1948- .... **CLC 23, 74; DA; DAC**
See also AAYA 14; CA 115; 122;
CANR 45; DAM MST, MULT, POP;
DLB 143; NNAL

Sillanpaa, Frans Eemil 1888-1964... **CLC 19**
See also CA 129; 93-96; MTCW

Sillitoe, Alan
1928- ...... **CLC 1, 3, 6, 10, 19, 57**
See also AITN 1; CA 9-12R; CAAS 2;
CANR 8, 26; CDBLB 1960 to Present;
DLB 14, 139; MTCW; SATA 61

Silone, Ignazio 1900-1978 .... **CLC 4**
See also CA 25-28; 81-84; CANR 34;
CAP 2; MTCW

Silver, Joan Micklin 1935- .... **CLC 20**
See also CA 114; 121; INT 121

Silver, Nicholas
See Faust, Frederick (Schiller)

Silverberg, Robert 1935- .... **CLC 7**
See also CA 1-4R; CAAS 3; CANR 1, 20,
36; DAM POP; DLB 8; INT CANR-20;
MAICYA; MTCW; SATA 13

Silverstein, Alvin 1933- .... **CLC 17**
See also CA 49-52; CANR 2; CLR 25;
JRDA; MAICYA; SATA 8, 69

Silverstein, Virginia B(arbara Opshelor)
1937- .... **CLC 17**
See also CA 49-52; CANR 2; CLR 25;
JRDA; MAICYA; SATA 8, 69

Sim, Georges
See Simenon, Georges (Jacques Christian)

Simak, Clifford D(onald)
1904-1988 .... **CLC 1, 55**
See also CA 1-4R; 125; CANR 1, 35;
DLB 8; MTCW; SATA-Obit 56

Simenon, Georges (Jacques Christian)
1903-1989 .... **CLC 1, 2, 3, 8, 18, 47**
See also CA 85-88; 129; CANR 35;
DAM POP; DLB 72; DLBY 89; MTCW

Simic, Charles 1938-... **CLC 6, 9, 22, 49, 68**
See also CA 29-32R; CAAS 4; CANR 12,
33, 52; DAM POET; DLB 105

Simmel, Georg 1858-1918 .... **TCLC 64**

Simmons, Charles (Paul) 1924- ..... **CLC 57**
See also CA 89-92; INT 89-92

Simmons, Dan 1948- .... **CLC 44**
See also AAYA 16; CA 138; DAM POP

Simmons, James (Stewart Alexander)
1933- .... **CLC 43**
See also CA 105; CAAS 21; DLB 40

Snyder, Gary (Sherman)
1930- . . . . CLC 1, 2, 5, 9, 32
See also CA 17-20R; CANR 30;
DAM POET; DLB 5, 16, 165

Snyder, Zilpha Keatley 1927- . . . . . . CLC 17
See also AAYA 15; CA 9-12R; CANR 38;
CLR 31; JRDA; MAICYA; SAAS 2;
SATA 1, 28, 75

Soares, Bernardo
See Pessoa, Fernando (Antonio Nogueira)

Sobh, A.
See Shamlu, Ahmad

Sobol, Joshua. CLC 60

Soderberg, Hjalmar 1869-1941 . . . . TCLC 39

Sodergran, Edith (Irene)
See Soedergran, Edith (Irene)

Soedergran, Edith (Irene)
1892-1923 . . . . TCLC 31

Softly, Edgar
See Lovecraft, H(oward) P(hillips)

Softly, Edward
See Lovecraft, H(oward) P(hillips)

Sokolov, Raymond 1941- . . . . CLC 7
See also CA 85-88

Solo, Jay
See Ellison, Harlan (Jay)

Sologub, Fyodor . . . . TCLC 9
See also Teternikov, Fyodor Kuzmich

Solomons, Ikey Esquir
See Thackeray, William Makepeace

Solomos, Dionysios 1798-1857 . . . NCLC 15

Solwoska, Mara
See French, Marilyn

Solzhenitsyn, Aleksandr I(sayevich)
1918- . . . . . . CLC 1, 2, 4, 7, 9, 10, 18, 26,
34, 78; DA; DAB; DAC; WLC
See also AITN 1; CA 69-72; CANR 40;
DAM MST, NOV; MTCW

Somers, Jane
See Lessing, Doris (May)

Somerville, Edith 1858-1949 . . . . . . TCLC 51
See also DLB 135

Somerville & Ross
See Martin, Violet Florence; Somerville,
Edith

Sommer, Scott 1951- . . . . CLC 25
See also CA 106

Sondheim, Stephen (Joshua)
1930- . . . . CLC 30, 39
See also AAYA 11; CA 103; CANR 47;
DAM DRAM

Sontag, Susan 1933- . . . CLC 1, 2, 10, 13, 31
See also CA 17-20R; CANR 25, 51;
DAM POP; DLB 2, 67; MTCW

Sophocles
496(?)B.C.-406(?)B.C. . . . . CMLC 2; DA;
DAB; DAC; DC 1
See also DAM DRAM, MST

Sordello 1189-1269. . . . . CMLC 15

Sorel, Julia
See Drexler, Rosalyn

Sorrentino, Gilbert
1929- . . . . CLC 3, 7, 14, 22, 40
See also CA 77-80; CANR 14, 33; DLB 5;
DLBY 80; INT CANR-14

Soto, Gary 1952-. . . . . . . CLC 32, 80; HLC
See also AAYA 10; CA 119; 125;
CANR 50; CLR 38; DAM MULT;
DLB 82; HW; INT 125; JRDA; SATA 80

Soupault, Philippe 1897-1990 . . . . . . CLC 68
See also CA 116; 147; 131

Souster, (Holmes) Raymond
1921- . . . . CLC 5, 14; DAC
See also CA 13-16R; CAAS 14; CANR 13,
29; DAM POET; DLB 88; SATA 63

Southern, Terry 1924(?)-1995 . . . . . . CLC 7
See also CA 1-4R; 150; CANR 1; DLB 2

Southey, Robert 1774-1843 . . . . NCLC 8
See also DLB 93, 107, 142; SATA 54

Southworth, Emma Dorothy Eliza Nevitte
1819-1899 . . . . NCLC 26

Souza, Ernest
See Scott, Evelyn

Soyinka, Wole
1934- . . . . CLC 3, 5, 14, 36, 44; BLC;
DA; DAB; DAC; DC 2; WLC
See also BW 2; CA 13-16R; CANR 27, 39;
DAM DRAM, MST, MULT; DLB 125;
MTCW

Spackman, W(illiam) M(ode)
1905-1990 . . . . CLC 46
See also CA 81-84; 132

Spacks, Barry 1931- . . . . CLC 14
See also CA 29-32R; CANR 33; DLB 105

Spanidou, Irini 1946- . . . . CLC 44

Spark, Muriel (Sarah)
1918- . . . . . CLC 2, 3, 5, 8, 13, 18, 40, 94;
DAB; DAC; SSC 10
See also CA 5-8R; CANR 12, 36;
CDBLB 1945-1960; DAM MST, NOV;
DLB 15, 139; INT CANR-12; MTCW

Spaulding, Douglas
See Bradbury, Ray (Douglas)

Spaulding, Leonard
See Bradbury, Ray (Douglas)

Spence, J. A. D.
See Eliot, T(homas) S(tearns)

Spencer, Elizabeth 1921- . . . . CLC 22
See also CA 13-16R; CANR 32; DLB 6;
MTCW; SATA 14

Spencer, Leonard G.
See Silverberg, Robert

Spencer, Scott 1945-. . . . . CLC 30
See also CA 113; CANR 51; DLBY 86

Spender, Stephen (Harold)
1909-1995 . . . . . . CLC 1, 2, 5, 10, 41, 91
See also CA 9-12R; 149; CANR 31;
CDBLB 1945-1960; DAM POET;
DLB 20; MTCW

Spengler, Oswald (Arnold Gottfried)
1880-1936 . . . . TCLC 25
See also CA 118

Spenser, Edmund
1552(?)-1599 . . . . LC 5; DA; DAB; DAC;
PC 8; WLC
See also CDBLB Before 1660; DAM MST,
POET; DLB 167

Spicer, Jack 1925-1965 . . . . . . CLC 8, 18, 72
See also CA 85-88; DAM POET; DLB 5, 16

Spiegelman, Art 1948- . . . . CLC 76
See also AAYA 10; CA 125; CANR 41

Spielberg, Peter 1929- . . . . CLC 6
See also CA 5-8R; CANR 4, 48; DLBY 81

Spielberg, Steven 1947- . . . . CLC 20
See also AAYA 8; CA 77-80; CANR 32;
SATA 32

Spillane, Frank Morrison 1918-
See Spillane, Mickey
See also CA 25-28R; CANR 28; MTCW;
SATA 66

Spillane, Mickey . . . . CLC 3, 13
See also Spillane, Frank Morrison

Spinoza, Benedictus de 1632-1677 . . . . LC 9

Spinrad, Norman (Richard) 1940-. . . CLC 46
See also CA 37-40R; CAAS 19; CANR 20;
DLB 8; INT CANR-20

Spitteler, Carl (Friedrich Georg)
1845-1924 . . . . TCLC 12
See also CA 109; DLB 129

Spivack, Kathleen (Romola Drucker)
1938- . . . . CLC 6
See also CA 49-52

Spoto, Donald 1941-. . . . . CLC 39
See also CA 65-68; CANR 11

Springsteen, Bruce (F.) 1949- . . . . . . CLC 17
See also CA 111

Spurling, Hilary 1940- . . . . CLC 34
See also CA 104; CANR 25, 52

Spyker, John Howland
See Elman, Richard

Squires, (James) Radcliffe
1917-1993 . . . . CLC 51
See also CA 1-4R; 140; CANR 6, 21

Srivastava, Dhanpat Rai 1880(?)-1936
See Premchand
See also CA 118

Stacy, Donald
See Pohl, Frederik

Stael, Germaine de
See Stael-Holstein, Anne Louise Germaine
Necker Baronn
See also DLB 119

Stael-Holstein, Anne Louise Germaine Necker
Baronn 1766-1817 . . . . NCLC 3
See also Stael, Germaine de

Stafford, Jean 1915-1979. . . CLC 4, 7, 19, 68
See also CA 1-4R; 85-88; CANR 3; DLB 2;
MTCW; SATA-Obit 22

Stafford, William (Edgar)
1914-1993 . . . . CLC 4, 7, 29
See also CA 5-8R; 142; CAAS 3; CANR 5,
22; DAM POET; DLB 5; INT CANR-22

Staines, Trevor
See Brunner, John (Kilian Houston)

Stairs, Gordon
See Austin, Mary (Hunter)

Stannard, Martin 1947- . . . . **CLC 44**
See also CA 142; DLB 155

Stanton, Maura 1946- . . . . **CLC 9**
See also CA 89-92; CANR 15; DLB 120

Stanton, Schuyler
See Baum, L(yman) Frank

Stapledon, (William) Olaf
1886-1950 . . . . **TCLC 22**
See also CA 111; DLB 15

Starbuck, George (Edwin) 1931- . . . . **CLC 53**
See also CA 21-24R; CANR 23;
DAM POET

Stark, Richard
See Westlake, Donald E(dwin)

Staunton, Schuyler
See Baum, L(yman) Frank

Stead, Christina (Ellen)
1902-1983 . . . . **CLC 2, 5, 8, 32, 80**
See also CA 13-16R; 109; CANR 33, 40;
MTCW

Stead, William Thomas
1849-1912 . . . . **TCLC 48**

Steele, Richard 1672-1729 . . . . **LC 18**
See also CDBLB 1660-1789; DLB 84, 101

Steele, Timothy (Reid) 1948- . . . . **CLC 45**
See also CA 93-96; CANR 16, 50; DLB 120

Steffens, (Joseph) Lincoln
1866-1936 . . . . **TCLC 20**
See also CA 117

Stegner, Wallace (Earle)
1909-1993 . . . . **CLC 9, 49, 81**
See also AITN 1; BEST 90:3; CA 1-4R;
141; CAAS 9; CANR 1, 21, 46;
DAM NOV; DLB 9; DLBY 93; MTCW

Stein, Gertrude
1874-1946 . . . . . . **TCLC 1, 6, 28, 48; DA;**
DAB; DAC; WLC
See also CA 104; 132; CDALB 1917-1929;
DAM MST, NOV, POET; DLB 4, 54, 86;
MTCW

Steinbeck, John (Ernst)
1902-1968 . . . . . . **CLC 1, 5, 9, 13, 21, 34,**
45, 75; DA; DAB; DAC; SSC 11; WLC
See also AAYA 12; CA 1-4R; 25-28R;
CANR 1, 35; CDALB 1929-1941;
DAM DRAM, MST, NOV; DLB 7, 9;
DLBD 2; MTCW; SATA 9

Steinem, Gloria 1934- . . . . **CLC 63**
See also CA 53-56; CANR 28, 51; MTCW

Steiner, George 1929- . . . . **CLC 24**
See also CA 73-76; CANR 31; DAM NOV;
DLB 67; MTCW; SATA 62

Steiner, K. Leslie
See Delany, Samuel R(ay, Jr.)

Steiner, Rudolf 1861-1925 . . . . **TCLC 13**
See also CA 107

Stendhal
1783-1842 . . . . **NCLC 23, 46; DA; DAB;**
DAC; WLC
See also DAM MST, NOV; DLB 119

Stephen, Leslie 1832-1904 . . . . **TCLC 23**
See also CA 123; DLB 57, 144

Stephen, Sir Leslie
See Stephen, Leslie

Stephen, Virginia
See Woolf, (Adeline) Virginia

Stephens, James 1882(?)-1950 . . . . . **TCLC 4**
See also CA 104; DLB 19, 153, 162

Stephens, Reed
See Donaldson, Stephen R.

Steptoe, Lydia
See Barnes, Djuna

Sterchi, Beat 1949- . . . . **CLC 65**

Sterling, Brett
See Bradbury, Ray (Douglas); Hamilton,
Edmond

Sterling, Bruce 1954- . . . . **CLC 72**
See also CA 119; CANR 44

Sterling, George 1869-1926 . . . . **TCLC 20**
See also CA 117; DLB 54

Stern, Gerald 1925- . . . . **CLC 40**
See also CA 81-84; CANR 28; DLB 105

Stern, Richard (Gustave) 1928- . . . **CLC 4, 39**
See also CA 1-4R; CANR 1, 25, 52;
DLBY 87; INT CANR-25

Sternberg, Josef von 1894-1969 . . . . . **CLC 20**
See also CA 81-84

Sterne, Laurence
1713-1768 . . . . . . **LC 2; DA; DAB; DAC;**
WLC
See also CDBLB 1660-1789; DAM MST,
NOV; DLB 39

Sternheim, (William Adolf) Carl
1878-1942 . . . . **TCLC 8**
See also CA 105; DLB 56, 118

Stevens, Mark 1951- . . . . **CLC 34**
See also CA 122

Stevens, Wallace
1879-1955 . . . . **TCLC 3, 12, 45; DA;**
DAB; DAC; PC 6; WLC
See also CA 104; 124; CDALB 1929-1941;
DAM MST, POET; DLB 54; MTCW

Stevenson, Anne (Katharine)
1933- . . . . **CLC 7, 33**
See also CA 17-20R; CAAS 9; CANR 9, 33;
DLB 40; MTCW

Stevenson, Robert Louis (Balfour)
1850-1894 . . . . . **NCLC 5, 14; DA; DAB;**
DAC; SSC 11; WLC
See also CDBLB 1890-1914; CLR 10, 11;
DAM MST, NOV; DLB 18, 57, 141, 156;
DLBD 13; JRDA; MAICYA; YABC 2

Stewart, J(ohn) I(nnes) M(ackintosh)
1906-1994 . . . . **CLC 7, 14, 32**
See also CA 85-88; 147; CAAS 3;
CANR 47; MTCW

Stewart, Mary (Florence Elinor)
1916- . . . . **CLC 7, 35; DAB**
See also CA 1-4R; CANR 1; SATA 12

Stewart, Mary Rainbow
See Stewart, Mary (Florence Elinor)

Stifle, June
See Campbell, Maria

Stifter, Adalbert 1805-1868 . . . . . . **NCLC 41**
See also DLB 133

Still, James 1906- . . . . **CLC 49**
See also CA 65-68; CAAS 17; CANR 10,
26; DLB 9; SATA 29

Sting
See Sumner, Gordon Matthew

Stirling, Arthur
See Sinclair, Upton (Beall)

Stitt, Milan 1941- . . . . **CLC 29**
See also CA 69-72

Stockton, Francis Richard 1834-1902
See Stockton, Frank R.
See also CA 108; 137; MAICYA; SATA 44

Stockton, Frank R. . . . . **TCLC 47**
See also Stockton, Francis Richard
See also DLB 42, 74; DLBD 13;
SATA-Brief 32

Stoddard, Charles
See Kuttner, Henry

Stoker, Abraham 1847-1912
See Stoker, Bram
See also CA 105; DA; DAC; DAM MST,
NOV; SATA 29

Stoker, Bram
1847-1912 . . . . **TCLC 8; DAB; WLC**
See also Stoker, Abraham
See also CA 150; CDBLB 1890-1914;
DLB 36, 70

Stolz, Mary (Slattery) 1920- . . . . **CLC 12**
See also AAYA 8; AITN 1; CA 5-8R;
CANR 13, 41; JRDA; MAICYA;
SAAS 3; SATA 10, 71

Stone, Irving 1903-1989 . . . . **CLC 7**
See also AITN 1; CA 1-4R; 129; CAAS 3;
CANR 1, 23; DAM POP;
INT CANR-23; MTCW; SATA 3;
SATA-Obit 64

Stone, Oliver 1946- . . . . **CLC 73**
See also AAYA 15; CA 110

Stone, Robert (Anthony)
1937- . . . . **CLC 5, 23, 42**
See also CA 85-88; CANR 23; DLB 152;
INT CANR-23; MTCW

Stone, Zachary
See Follett, Ken(neth Martin)

Stoppard, Tom
1937- . . . . . . **CLC 1, 3, 4, 5, 8, 15, 29, 34,**
63, 91; DA; DAB; DAC; DC 6; WLC
See also CA 81-84; CANR 39;
CDBLB 1960 to Present; DAM DRAM,
MST; DLB 13; DLBY 85; MTCW

Storey, David (Malcolm)
1933- . . . . **CLC 2, 4, 5, 8**
See also CA 81-84; CANR 36;
DAM DRAM; DLB 13, 14; MTCW

Storm, Hyemeyohsts 1935- . . . . **CLC 3**
See also CA 81-84; CANR 45;
DAM MULT; NNAL

Storm, (Hans) Theodor (Woldsen)
1817-1888 . . . . **NCLC 1**

Storni, Alfonsina
1892-1938 . . . . **TCLC 5; HLC**
See also CA 104; 131; DAM MULT; HW

Stout, Rex (Todhunter) 1886-1975 . . . **CLC 3**
See also AITN 2; CA 61-64

Stow, (Julian) Randolph 1935- . . **CLC 23, 48**
See also CA 13-16R; CANR 33; MTCW

Stowe, Harriet (Elizabeth) Beecher
1811-1896 . . . . . NCLC 3, 50; DA; DAB;
DAC; WLC
See also CDALB 1865-1917; DAM MST,
NOV; DLB 1, 12, 42, 74; JRDA;
MAICYA; YABC 1

Strachey, (Giles) Lytton
1880-1932 . . . . TCLC 12
See also CA 110; DLB 149; DLBD 10

Strand, Mark   1934- . . . . . . CLC 6, 18, 41, 71
See also CA 21-24R; CANR 40;
DAM POET; DLB 5; SATA 41

Straub, Peter (Francis)   1943- . . . . . . CLC 28
See also BEST 89:1; CA 85-88; CANR 28;
DAM POP; DLBY 84; MTCW

Strauss, Botho   1944- . . . . CLC 22
See also DLB 124

Streatfeild, (Mary) Noel
1895(?)-1986 . . . . CLC 21
See also CA 81-84; 120; CANR 31;
CLR 17; DLB 160; MAICYA; SATA 20;
SATA-Obit 48

Stribling, T(homas) S(igismund)
1881-1965 . . . . CLC 23
See also CA 107; DLB 9

Strindberg, (Johan) August
1849-1912 . . . . . . TCLC 1, 8, 21, 47; DA;
DAB; DAC; WLC
See also CA 104; 135; DAM DRAM, MST

Stringer, Arthur   1874-1950 . . . . TCLC 37
See also DLB 92

Stringer, David
See Roberts, Keith (John Kingston)

Strugatskii, Arkadii (Natanovich)
1925-1991 . . . . CLC 27
See also CA 106; 135

Strugatskii, Boris (Natanovich)
1933- . . . . CLC 27
See also CA 106

Strummer, Joe   1953(?)- . . . . CLC 30

Stuart, Don A.
See Campbell, John W(ood, Jr.)

Stuart, Ian
See MacLean, Alistair (Stuart)

Stuart, Jesse (Hilton)
1906-1984 . . . . CLC 1, 8, 11, 14, 34
See also CA 5-8R; 112; CANR 31; DLB 9,
48, 102; DLBY 84; SATA 2;
SATA-Obit 36

Sturgeon, Theodore (Hamilton)
1918-1985 . . . . CLC 22, 39
See also Queen, Ellery
See also CA 81-84; 116; CANR 32; DLB 8;
DLBY 85; MTCW

Sturges, Preston   1898-1959 . . . . TCLC 48
See also CA 114; 149; DLB 26

Styron, William
1925- . . . . CLC 1, 3, 5, 11, 15, 60
See also BEST 90:4; CA 5-8R; CANR 6, 33;
CDALB 1968-1988; DAM NOV, POP;
DLB 2, 143; DLBY 80; INT CANR-6;
MTCW

Suarez Lynch, B.
See Bioy Casares, Adolfo; Borges, Jorge
Luis

Su Chien   1884-1918
See Su Man-shu
See also CA 123

Suckow, Ruth   1892-1960 . . . . SSC 18
See also CA 113; DLB 9, 102

Sudermann, Hermann   1857-1928 . . TCLC 15
See also CA 107; DLB 118

Sue, Eugene   1804-1857 . . . . NCLC 1
See also DLB 119

Sueskind, Patrick   1949- . . . . CLC 44
See also Suskind, Patrick

Sukenick, Ronald   1932- . . . . . CLC 3, 4, 6, 48
See also CA 25-28R; CAAS 8; CANR 32;
DLBY 81

Suknaski, Andrew   1942- . . . . CLC 19
See also CA 101; DLB 53

Sullivan, Vernon
See Vian, Boris

Sully Prudhomme   1839-1907 . . . . . . TCLC 31

Su Man-shu . . . . TCLC 24
See also Su Chien

Summerforest, Ivy B.
See Kirkup, James

Summers, Andrew James   1942- . . . . . CLC 26

Summers, Andy
See Summers, Andrew James

Summers, Hollis (Spurgeon, Jr.)
1916- . . . . CLC 10
See also CA 5-8R; CANR 3; DLB 6

Summers, (Alphonsus Joseph-Mary Augustus)
Montague   1880-1948 . . . . TCLC 16
See also CA 118

Sumner, Gordon Matthew   1951- . . . . CLC 26

Surtees, Robert Smith
1803-1864 . . . . NCLC 14
See also DLB 21

Susann, Jacqueline   1921-1974 . . . . . . CLC 3
See also AITN 1; CA 65-68; 53-56; MTCW

Su Shih   1036-1101 . . . . CMLC 15

Suskind, Patrick
See Sueskind, Patrick
See also CA 145

Sutcliff, Rosemary
1920-1992 . . . . CLC 26; DAB; DAC
See also AAYA 10; CA 5-8R; 139;
CANR 37; CLR 1, 37; DAM MST, POP;
JRDA; MAICYA; SATA 6, 44, 78;
SATA-Obit 73

Sutro, Alfred   1863-1933 . . . . TCLC 6
See also CA 105; DLB 10

Sutton, Henry
See Slavitt, David R(ytman)

Svevo, Italo . . . . TCLC 2, 35
See also Schmitz, Aron Hector

Swados, Elizabeth (A.)   1951- . . . . CLC 12
See also CA 97-100; CANR 49; INT 97-100

Swados, Harvey   1920-1972 . . . . CLC 5
See also CA 5-8R; 37-40R; CANR 6;
DLB 2

Swan, Gladys   1934- . . . . CLC 69
See also CA 101; CANR 17, 39

Swarthout, Glendon (Fred)
1918-1992 . . . . CLC 35
See also CA 1-4R; 139; CANR 1, 47;
SATA 26

Sweet, Sarah C.
See Jewett, (Theodora) Sarah Orne

Swenson, May
1919-1989 . . . . CLC 4, 14, 61; DA; DAB;
DAC; PC 14
See also CA 5-8R; 130; CANR 36;
DAM MST, POET; DLB 5; MTCW;
SATA 15

Swift, Augustus
See Lovecraft, H(oward) P(hillips)

Swift, Graham (Colin)   1949- . . . . CLC 41, 88
See also CA 117; 122; CANR 46

Swift, Jonathan
1667-1745 . . . . . . LC 1; DA; DAB; DAC;
PC 9; WLC
See also CDBLB 1660-1789; DAM MST,
NOV, POET; DLB 39, 95, 101; SATA 19

Swinburne, Algernon Charles
1837-1909 . . . . . . TCLC 8, 36; DA; DAB;
DAC; WLC
See also CA 105; 140; CDBLB 1832-1890;
DAM MST, POET; DLB 35, 57

Swinfen, Ann . . . . CLC 34

Swinnerton, Frank Arthur
1884-1982 . . . . CLC 31
See also CA 108; DLB 34

Swithen, John
See King, Stephen (Edwin)

Sylvia
See Ashton-Warner, Sylvia (Constance)

Symmes, Robert Edward
See Duncan, Robert (Edward)

Symonds, John Addington
1840-1893 . . . . NCLC 34
See also DLB 57, 144

Symons, Arthur   1865-1945 . . . . TCLC 11
See also CA 107; DLB 19, 57, 149

Symons, Julian (Gustave)
1912-1994 . . . . CLC 2, 14, 32
See also CA 49-52; 147; CAAS 3; CANR 3,
33; DLB 87, 155; DLBY 92; MTCW

Synge, (Edmund) J(ohn) M(illington)
1871-1909 . . . . TCLC 6, 37; DC 2
See also CA 104; 141; CDBLB 1890-1914;
DAM DRAM; DLB 10, 19

Syruc, J.
See Milosz, Czeslaw

Szirtes, George   1948- . . . . CLC 46
See also CA 109; CANR 27

Tabori, George   1914- . . . . CLC 19
See also CA 49-52; CANR 4

Tagore, Rabindranath
1861-1941 . . . . TCLC 3, 53; PC 8
See also CA 104; 120; DAM DRAM,
POET; MTCW

Taine, Hippolyte Adolphe
1828-1893 . . . . NCLC 15

Talese, Gay   1932- . . . . CLC 37
See also AITN 1; CA 1-4R; CANR 9;
INT CANR-9; MTCW

Tallent, Elizabeth (Ann) 1954- ..... **CLC 45**
See also CA 117; DLB 130

Tally, Ted 1952- .... **CLC 42**
See also CA 120; 124; INT 124

Tamayo y Baus, Manuel
1829-1898 .... **NCLC 1**

Tammsaare, A(nton) H(ansen)
1878-1940 .... **TCLC 27**

Tan, Amy 1952- .... **CLC 59**
See also AAYA 9; BEST 89:3; CA 136;
DAM MULT, NOV, POP; SATA 75

Tandem, Felix
See Spitteler, Carl (Friedrich Georg)

Tanizaki, Jun'ichiro
1886-1965 ...... **CLC 8, 14, 28; SSC 21**
See also CA 93-96; 25-28R

Tanner, William
See Amis, Kingsley (William)

Tao Lao
See Storni, Alfonsina

Tarassoff, Lev
See Troyat, Henri

Tarbell, Ida M(inerva)
1857-1944 .... **TCLC 40**
See also CA 122; DLB 47

Tarkington, (Newton) Booth
1869-1946 .... **TCLC 9**
See also CA 110; 143; DLB 9, 102;
SATA 17

Tarkovsky, Andrei (Arsenyevich)
1932-1986 .... **CLC 75**
See also CA 127

Tartt, Donna 1964(?)- .... **CLC 76**
See also CA 142

Tasso, Torquato 1544-1595 .... **LC 5**

Tate, (John Orley) Allen
1899-1979 .... **CLC 2, 4, 6, 9, 11, 14, 24**
See also CA 5-8R; 85-88; CANR 32;
DLB 4, 45, 63; MTCW

Tate, Ellalice
See Hibbert, Eleanor Alice Burford

Tate, James (Vincent) 1943- ... **CLC 2, 6, 25**
See also CA 21-24R; CANR 29; DLB 5

Tavel, Ronald 1940- .... **CLC 6**
See also CA 21-24R; CANR 33

Taylor, C(ecil) P(hilip) 1929-1981... **CLC 27**
See also CA 25-28R; 105; CANR 47

Taylor, Edward
1642(?)-1729 ... **LC 11; DA; DAB; DAC**
See also DAM MST, POET; DLB 24

Taylor, Eleanor Ross 1920- .... **CLC 5**
See also CA 81-84

Taylor, Elizabeth 1912-1975 ... **CLC 2, 4, 29**
See also CA 13-16R; CANR 9; DLB 139;
MTCW; SATA 13

Taylor, Henry (Splawn) 1942- ...... **CLC 44**
See also CA 33-36R; CAAS 7; CANR 31;
DLB 5

Taylor, Kamala (Purnaiya) 1924-
See Markandaya, Kamala
See also CA 77-80

Taylor, Mildred D. .... **CLC 21**
See also AAYA 10; BW 1; CA 85-88;
CANR 25; CLR 9; DLB 52; JRDA;
MAICYA; SAAS 5; SATA 15, 70

Taylor, Peter (Hillsman)
1917-1994 ..... **CLC 1, 4, 18, 37, 44, 50,
71; SSC 10**
See also CA 13-16R; 147; CANR 9, 50;
DLBY 81, 94; INT CANR-9; MTCW

Taylor, Robert Lewis 1912- .... **CLC 14**
See also CA 1-4R; CANR 3; SATA 10

Tchekhov, Anton
See Chekhov, Anton (Pavlovich)

Teasdale, Sara 1884-1933 .... **TCLC 4**
See also CA 104; DLB 45; SATA 32

Tegner, Esaias 1782-1846 .... **NCLC 2**

Teilhard de Chardin, (Marie Joseph) Pierre
1881-1955 .... **TCLC 9**
See also CA 105

Temple, Ann
See Mortimer, Penelope (Ruth)

Tennant, Emma (Christina)
1937- .... **CLC 13, 52**
See also CA 65-68; CAAS 9; CANR 10, 38;
DLB 14

Tenneshaw, S. M.
See Silverberg, Robert

Tennyson, Alfred
1809-1892 .... **NCLC 30; DA; DAB;
DAC; PC 6; WLC**
See also CDBLB 1832-1890; DAM MST,
POET; DLB 32

Teran, Lisa St. Aubin de .... **CLC 36**
See also St. Aubin de Teran, Lisa

Terence 195(?)B.C.-159B.C. ...... **CMLC 14**

Teresa de Jesus, St. 1515-1582 ...... **LC 18**

Terkel, Louis 1912-
See Terkel, Studs
See also CA 57-60; CANR 18, 45; MTCW

Terkel, Studs .... **CLC 38**
See also Terkel, Louis
See also AITN 1

Terry, C. V.
See Slaughter, Frank G(ill)

Terry, Megan 1932- .... **CLC 19**
See also CA 77-80; CABS 3; CANR 43;
DLB 7

Tertz, Abram
See Sinyavsky, Andrei (Donatevich)

Tesich, Steve 1943(?)- .... **CLC 40, 69**
See also CA 105; DLBY 83

Teternikov, Fyodor Kuzmich 1863-1927
See Sologub, Fyodor
See also CA 104

Tevis, Walter 1928-1984 .... **CLC 42**
See also CA 113

Tey, Josephine .... **TCLC 14**
See also Mackintosh, Elizabeth
See also DLB 77

Thackeray, William Makepeace
1811-1863 .... **NCLC 5, 14, 22, 43; DA;
DAB; DAC; WLC**
See also CDBLB 1832-1890; DAM MST,
NOV; DLB 21, 55, 159, 163; SATA 23

Thakura, Ravindranatha
See Tagore, Rabindranath

Tharoor, Shashi 1956- .... **CLC 70**
See also CA 141

Thelwell, Michael Miles 1939- ..... **CLC 22**
See also BW 2; CA 101

Theobald, Lewis, Jr.
See Lovecraft, H(oward) P(hillips)

Theodorescu, Ion N. 1880-1967
See Arghezi, Tudor
See also CA 116

Theriault, Yves 1915-1983 .... **CLC 79; DAC**
See also CA 102; DAM MST; DLB 88

Theroux, Alexander (Louis)
1939- .... **CLC 2, 25**
See also CA 85-88; CANR 20

Theroux, Paul (Edward)
1941- .... **CLC 5, 8, 11, 15, 28, 46**
See also BEST 89:4; CA 33-36R; CANR 20,
45; DAM POP; DLB 2; MTCW;
SATA 44

Thesen, Sharon 1946- .... **CLC 56**

Thevenin, Denis
See Duhamel, Georges

Thibault, Jacques Anatole Francois
1844-1924
See France, Anatole
See also CA 106; 127; DAM NOV; MTCW

Thiele, Colin (Milton) 1920- .... **CLC 17**
See also CA 29-32R; CANR 12, 28;
CLR 27; MAICYA; SAAS 2; SATA 14,
72

Thomas, Audrey (Callahan)
1935- .... **CLC 7, 13, 37; SSC 20**
See also AITN 2; CA 21-24R; CAAS 19;
CANR 36; DLB 60; MTCW

Thomas, D(onald) M(ichael)
1935- .... **CLC 13, 22, 31**
See also CA 61-64; CAAS 11; CANR 17,
45; CDBLB 1960 to Present; DLB 40;
INT CANR-17; MTCW

Thomas, Dylan (Marlais)
1914-1953 ... **TCLC 1, 8, 45; DA; DAB;
DAC; PC 2; SSC 3; WLC**
See also CA 104; 120; CDBLB 1945-1960;
DAM DRAM, MST, POET; DLB 13, 20,
139; MTCW; SATA 60

Thomas, (Philip) Edward
1878-1917 .... **TCLC 10**
See also CA 106; DAM POET; DLB 19

Thomas, Joyce Carol 1938- .... **CLC 35**
See also AAYA 12; BW 2; CA 113; 116;
CANR 48; CLR 19; DLB 33; INT 116;
JRDA; MAICYA; MTCW; SAAS 7;
SATA 40, 78

Thomas, Lewis 1913-1993 .... **CLC 35**
See also CA 85-88; 143; CANR 38; MTCW

Thomas, Paul
See Mann, (Paul) Thomas

Thomas, Piri 1928- .... **CLC 17**
See also CA 73-76; HW

Thomas, R(onald) S(tuart)
1913- .... **CLC 6, 13, 48; DAB**
See also CA 89-92; CAAS 4; CANR 30;
CDBLB 1960 to Present; DAM POET;
DLB 27; MTCW

Thomas, Ross (Elmore) 1926-1995 . . **CLC 39**
See also CA 33-36R; 150; CANR 22

Thompson, Francis Clegg
See Mencken, H(enry) L(ouis)

Thompson, Francis Joseph
1859-1907 . . . . **TCLC 4**
See also CA 104; CDBLB 1890-1914;
DLB 19

Thompson, Hunter S(tockton)
1939- . . . . **CLC 9, 17, 40**
See also BEST 89:1; CA 17-20R; CANR 23,
46; DAM POP; MTCW

Thompson, James Myers
See Thompson, Jim (Myers)

Thompson, Jim (Myers)
1906-1977(?) . . . . **CLC 69**
See also CA 140

Thompson, Judith . . . . **CLC 39**

Thomson, James 1700-1748 . . . . . . **LC 16, 29**
See also DAM POET; DLB 95

Thomson, James 1834-1882 . . . . . . **NCLC 18**
See also DAM POET; DLB 35

Thoreau, Henry David
1817-1862 . . . . . **NCLC 7, 21; DA; DAB;
DAC; WLC**
See also CDALB 1640-1865; DAM MST;
DLB 1

Thornton, Hall
See Silverberg, Robert

Thucydides c. 455B.C.-399B.C. . . . . **CMLC 17**

Thurber, James (Grover)
1894-1961 . . . . **CLC 5, 11, 25; DA; DAB;
DAC; SSC 1**
See also CA 73-76; CANR 17, 39;
CDALB 1929-1941; DAM DRAM, MST,
NOV; DLB 4, 11, 22, 102; MAICYA;
MTCW; SATA 13

Thurman, Wallace (Henry)
1902-1934 . . . . **TCLC 6; BLC**
See also BW 1; CA 104; 124; DAM MULT;
DLB 51

Ticheburn, Cheviot
See Ainsworth, William Harrison

Tieck, (Johann) Ludwig
1773-1853 . . . . **NCLC 5, 46**
See also DLB 90

Tiger, Derry
See Ellison, Harlan (Jay)

Tilghman, Christopher 1948(?)- . . . . **CLC 65**

Tillinghast, Richard (Williford)
1940- . . . . **CLC 29**
See also CA 29-32R; CAAS 23; CANR 26,
51

Timrod, Henry 1828-1867 . . . . **NCLC 25**
See also DLB 3

Tindall, Gillian 1938- . . . . **CLC 7**
See also CA 21-24R; CANR 11

Tiptree, James, Jr. . . . . **CLC 48, 50**
See also Sheldon, Alice Hastings Bradley
See also DLB 8

Titmarsh, Michael Angelo
See Thackeray, William Makepeace

**Tocqueville, Alexis (Charles Henri Maurice
Clerel Comte)** 1805-1859 . . . . . **NCLC 7**

Tolkien, J(ohn) R(onald) R(euel)
1892-1973 . . . . . . **CLC 1, 2, 3, 8, 12, 38;
DA; DAB; DAC; WLC**
See also AAYA 10; AITN 1; CA 17-18;
45-48; CANR 36; CAP 2;
CDBLB 1914-1945; DAM MST, NOV,
POP; DLB 15, 160; JRDA; MAICYA;
MTCW; SATA 2, 32; SATA-Obit 24

Toller, Ernst 1893-1939 . . . . **TCLC 10**
See also CA 107; DLB 124

Tolson, M. B.
See Tolson, Melvin B(eaunorus)

Tolson, Melvin B(eaunorus)
1898(?)-1966 . . . . **CLC 36; BLC**
See also BW 1; CA 124; 89-92;
DAM MULT, POET; DLB 48, 76

Tolstoi, Aleksei Nikolaevich
See Tolstoy, Alexey Nikolaevich

Tolstoy, Alexey Nikolaevich
1882-1945 . . . . **TCLC 18**
See also CA 107

Tolstoy, Count Leo
See Tolstoy, Leo (Nikolaevich)

Tolstoy, Leo (Nikolaevich)
1828-1910 . . . . . . **TCLC 4, 11, 17, 28, 44;
DA; DAB; DAC; SSC 9; WLC**
See also CA 104; 123; DAM MST, NOV;
SATA 26

Tomasi di Lampedusa, Giuseppe 1896-1957
See Lampedusa, Giuseppe (Tomasi) di
See also CA 111

Tomlin, Lily . . . . **CLC 17**
See also Tomlin, Mary Jean

Tomlin, Mary Jean 1939(?)-
See Tomlin, Lily
See also CA 117

Tomlinson, (Alfred) Charles
1927- . . . . **CLC 2, 4, 6, 13, 45**
See also CA 5-8R; CANR 33; DAM POET;
DLB 40

Tonson, Jacob
See Bennett, (Enoch) Arnold

Toole, John Kennedy
1937-1969 . . . . **CLC 19, 64**
See also CA 104; DLBY 81

Toomer, Jean
1894-1967 . . . . . . **CLC 1, 4, 13, 22; BLC;
PC 7; SSC 1**
See also BW 1; CA 85-88;
CDALB 1917-1929; DAM MULT;
DLB 45, 51; MTCW

Torley, Luke
See Blish, James (Benjamin)

Tornimparte, Alessandra
See Ginzburg, Natalia

Torre, Raoul della
See Mencken, H(enry) L(ouis)

Torrey, E(dwin) Fuller 1937- . . . . . . **CLC 34**
See also CA 119

Torsvan, Ben Traven
See Traven, B.

Torsvan, Benno Traven
See Traven, B.

Torsvan, Berick Traven
See Traven, B.

Torsvan, Berwick Traven
See Traven, B.

Torsvan, Bruno Traven
See Traven, B.

Torsvan, Traven
See Traven, B.

Tournier, Michel (Edouard)
1924- . . . . **CLC 6, 23, 36, 95**
See also CA 49-52; CANR 3, 36; DLB 83;
MTCW; SATA 23

Tournimparte, Alessandra
See Ginzburg, Natalia

Towers, Ivar
See Kornbluth, C(yril) M.

Towne, Robert (Burton) 1936(?)- . . . . **CLC 87**
See also CA 108; DLB 44

Townsend, Sue 1946- . . **CLC 61; DAB; DAC**
See also CA 119; 127; INT 127; MTCW;
SATA 55; SATA-Brief 48

Townshend, Peter (Dennis Blandford)
1945- . . . . **CLC 17, 42**
See also CA 107

Tozzi, Federigo 1883-1920 . . . . **TCLC 31**

Traill, Catharine Parr
1802-1899 . . . . **NCLC 31**
See also DLB 99

Trakl, Georg 1887-1914 . . . . **TCLC 5**
See also CA 104

Transtroemer, Tomas (Goesta)
1931- . . . . **CLC 52, 65**
See also CA 117; 129; CAAS 17;
DAM POET

Transtromer, Tomas Gosta
See Transtroemer, Tomas (Goesta)

Traven, B. (?)-1969 . . . . **CLC 8, 11**
See also CA 19-20; 25-28R; CAP 2; DLB 9,
56; MTCW

Treitel, Jonathan 1959- . . . . **CLC 70**

Tremain, Rose 1943- . . . . **CLC 42**
See also CA 97-100; CANR 44; DLB 14

Tremblay, Michel 1942- . . . . . . **CLC 29; DAC**
See also CA 116; 128; DAM MST; DLB 60;
MTCW

Trevanian . . . . **CLC 29**
See also Whitaker, Rod(ney)

Trevor, Glen
See Hilton, James

Trevor, William
1928- . . . . . **CLC 7, 9, 14, 25, 71; SSC 21**
See also Cox, William Trevor
See also DLB 14, 139

Trifonov, Yuri (Valentinovich)
1925-1981 . . . . **CLC 45**
See also CA 126; 103; MTCW

Trilling, Lionel 1905-1975 . . . . **CLC 9, 11, 24**
See also CA 9-12R; 61-64; CANR 10;
DLB 28, 63; INT CANR-10; MTCW

Trimball, W. H.
See Mencken, H(enry) L(ouis)

Tristan
See Gomez de la Serna, Ramon

Tristram
See Housman, A(lfred) E(dward)

Vance, John Holbrook 1916-
See Queen, Ellery; Vance, Jack
See also CA 29-32R; CANR 17; MTCW

Van Den Bogarde, Derek Jules Gaspard Ulric Niven 1921-
See Bogarde, Dirk
See also CA 77-80

Vandenburgh, Jane . . . . **CLC 59**

Vanderhaeghe, Guy 1951- . . . . **CLC 41**
See also CA 113

van der Post, Laurens (Jan) 1906- . . . **CLC 5**
See also CA 5-8R; CANR 35

van de Wetering, Janwillem 1931- . . **CLC 47**
See also CA 49-52; CANR 4

Van Dine, S. S. . . . . **TCLC 23**
See also Wright, Willard Huntington

Van Doren, Carl (Clinton)
1885-1950 . . . . **TCLC 18**
See also CA 111

Van Doren, Mark 1894-1972 . . . . **CLC 6, 10**
See also CA 1-4R; 37-40R; CANR 3;
DLB 45; MTCW

Van Druten, John (William)
1901-1957 . . . . **TCLC 2**
See also CA 104; DLB 10

Van Duyn, Mona (Jane)
1921- . . . . **CLC 3, 7, 63**
See also CA 9-12R; CANR 7, 38;
DAM POET; DLB 5

Van Dyne, Edith
See Baum, L(yman) Frank

van Itallie, Jean-Claude 1936- . . . . **CLC 3**
See also CA 45-48; CAAS 2; CANR 1, 48;
DLB 7

van Ostaijen, Paul 1896-1928 . . . . . **TCLC 33**

Van Peebles, Melvin 1932- . . . . . . **CLC 2, 20**
See also BW 2; CA 85-88; CANR 27;
DAM MULT

Vansittart, Peter 1920- . . . . **CLC 42**
See also CA 1-4R; CANR 3, 49

Van Vechten, Carl 1880-1964 . . . . . . **CLC 33**
See also CA 89-92; DLB 4, 9, 51

Van Vogt, A(lfred) E(lton) 1912- . . . . . **CLC 1**
See also CA 21-24R; CANR 28; DLB 8;
SATA 14

Varda, Agnes 1928- . . . . **CLC 16**
See also CA 116; 122

Vargas Llosa, (Jorge) Mario (Pedro)
1936- . . . . **CLC 3, 6, 9, 10, 15, 31, 42, 85;
DA; DAB; DAC; HLC**
See also CA 73-76; CANR 18, 32, 42;
DAM MST, MULT, NOV; DLB 145;
HW; MTCW

Vasiliu, Gheorghe 1881-1957
See Bacovia, George
See also CA 123

Vassa, Gustavus
See Equiano, Olaudah

Vassilikos, Vassilis 1933- . . . . **CLC 4, 8**
See also CA 81-84

Vaughan, Henry 1621-1695 . . . . **LC 27**
See also DLB 131

Vaughn, Stephanie . . . . **CLC 62**

Vazov, Ivan (Minchov)
1850-1921 . . . . **TCLC 25**
See also CA 121; DLB 147

Veblen, Thorstein (Bunde)
1857-1929 . . . . **TCLC 31**
See also CA 115

Vega, Lope de 1562-1635 . . . . **LC 23**

Venison, Alfred
See Pound, Ezra (Weston Loomis)

Verdi, Marie de
See Mencken, H(enry) L(ouis)

Verdu, Matilde
See Cela, Camilo Jose

Verga, Giovanni (Carmelo)
1840-1922 . . . . **TCLC 3; SSC 21**
See also CA 104; 123

Vergil
70B.C.-19B.C. . . . . . **CMLC 9; DA; DAB;
DAC; PC 12**
See also DAM MST, POET

Verhaeren, Emile (Adolphe Gustave)
1855-1916 . . . . **TCLC 12**
See also CA 109

Verlaine, Paul (Marie)
1844-1896 . . . . **NCLC 2, 51; PC 2**
See also DAM POET

Verne, Jules (Gabriel)
1828-1905 . . . . **TCLC 6, 52**
See also AAYA 16; CA 110; 131; DLB 123;
JRDA; MAICYA; SATA 21

Very, Jones 1813-1880 . . . . **NCLC 9**
See also DLB 1

Vesaas, Tarjei 1897-1970 . . . . **CLC 48**
See also CA 29-32R

Vialis, Gaston
See Simenon, Georges (Jacques Christian)

Vian, Boris 1920-1959 . . . . **TCLC 9**
See also CA 106; DLB 72

Viaud, (Louis Marie) Julien 1850-1923
See Loti, Pierre
See also CA 107

Vicar, Henry
See Felsen, Henry Gregor

Vicker, Angus
See Felsen, Henry Gregor

Vidal, Gore
1925- . . . . . **CLC 2, 4, 6, 8, 10, 22, 33, 72**
See also AITN 1; BEST 90:2; CA 5-8R;
CANR 13, 45; DAM NOV, POP; DLB 6,
152; INT CANR-13; MTCW

Viereck, Peter (Robert Edwin)
1916- . . . . **CLC 4**
See also CA 1-4R; CANR 1, 47; DLB 5

Vigny, Alfred (Victor) de
1797-1863 . . . . **NCLC 7**
See also DAM POET; DLB 119

Vilakazi, Benedict Wallet
1906-1947 . . . . **TCLC 37**

**Villiers de l'Isle Adam, Jean Marie Mathias
Philippe Auguste Comte**
1838-1889 . . . . **NCLC 3; SSC 14**
See also DLB 123

Villon, Francois 1431-1463(?) . . . . **PC 13**

Vinci, Leonardo da 1452-1519 . . . . **LC 12**

Vine, Barbara . . . . **CLC 50**
See also Rendell, Ruth (Barbara)
See also BEST 90:4

Vinge, Joan D(ennison) 1948- . . . . . . **CLC 30**
See also CA 93-96; SATA 36

Violis, G.
See Simenon, Georges (Jacques Christian)

Visconti, Luchino 1906-1976 . . . . **CLC 16**
See also CA 81-84; 65-68; CANR 39

Vittorini, Elio 1908-1966 . . . . . . **CLC 6, 9, 14**
See also CA 133; 25-28R

Vizinczey, Stephen 1933- . . . . **CLC 40**
See also CA 128; INT 128

Vliet, R(ussell) G(ordon)
1929-1984 . . . . **CLC 22**
See also CA 37-40R; 112; CANR 18

Vogau, Boris Andreyevich 1894-1937(?)
See Pilnyak, Boris
See also CA 123

Vogel, Paula A(nne) 1951- . . . . **CLC 76**
See also CA 108

Voight, Ellen Bryant 1943- . . . . **CLC 54**
See also CA 69-72; CANR 11, 29; DLB 120

Voigt, Cynthia 1942- . . . . **CLC 30**
See also AAYA 3; CA 106; CANR 18, 37,
40; CLR 13; INT CANR-18; JRDA;
MAICYA; SATA 48, 79; SATA-Brief 33

Voinovich, Vladimir (Nikolaevich)
1932- . . . . **CLC 10, 49**
See also CA 81-84; CAAS 12; CANR 33;
MTCW

Vollmann, William T. 1959- . . . . **CLC 89**
See also CA 134; DAM NOV, POP

Voloshinov, V. N.
See Bakhtin, Mikhail Mikhailovich

Voltaire
1694-1778 . . . . . **LC 14; DA; DAB; DAC;
SSC 12; WLC**
See also DAM DRAM, MST

von Daeniken, Erich 1935- . . . . **CLC 30**
See also AITN 1; CA 37-40R; CANR 17,
44

von Daniken, Erich
See von Daeniken, Erich

von Heidenstam, (Carl Gustaf) Verner
See Heidenstam, (Carl Gustaf) Verner von

von Heyse, Paul (Johann Ludwig)
See Heyse, Paul (Johann Ludwig von)

von Hofmannsthal, Hugo
See Hofmannsthal, Hugo von

von Horvath, Odon
See Horvath, Oedoen von

von Horvath, Oedoen
See Horvath, Oedoen von

von Liliencron, (Friedrich Adolf Axel) Detlev
See Liliencron, (Friedrich Adolf Axel)
Detlev von

Vonnegut, Kurt, Jr.
1922- . . . . . . **CLC 1, 2, 3, 4, 5, 8, 12, 22,
40, 60; DA; DAB; DAC; SSC 8; WLC**
See also AAYA 6; AITN 1; BEST 90:4;
CA 1-4R; CANR 1, 25, 49;
CDALB 1968-1988; DAM MST, NOV,
POP; DLB 2, 8, 152; DLBD 3; DLBY 80;
MTCW

Von Rachen, Kurt
See Hubbard, L(afayette) Ron(ald)

von Rezzori (d'Arezzo), Gregor
See Rezzori (d'Arezzo), Gregor von

von Sternberg, Josef
See Sternberg, Josef von

Vorster, Gordon 1924- . . . . CLC 34
See also CA 133

Vosce, Trudie
See Ozick, Cynthia

Voznesensky, Andrei (Andreievich)
1933- . . . . CLC 1, 15, 57
See also CA 89-92; CANR 37;
DAM POET; MTCW

Waddington, Miriam 1917- . . . . CLC 28
See also CA 21-24R; CANR 12, 30;
DLB 68

Wagman, Fredrica 1937- . . . . CLC 7
See also CA 97-100; INT 97-100

Wagner, Richard 1813-1883. . . . . . . NCLC 9
See also DLB 129

Wagner-Martin, Linda 1936- . . . . CLC 50

Wagoner, David (Russell)
1926- . . . . CLC 3, 5, 15
See also CA 1-4R; CAAS 3; CANR 2;
DLB 5; SATA 14

Wah, Fred(erick James) 1939- . . . . . . CLC 44
See also CA 107; 141; DLB 60

Wahloo, Per 1926-1975 . . . . CLC 7
See also CA 61-64

Wahloo, Peter
See Wahloo, Per

Wain, John (Barrington)
1925-1994 . . . . CLC 2, 11, 15, 46
See also CA 5-8R; 145; CAAS 4; CANR 23;
CDBLB 1960 to Present; DLB 15, 27,
139, 155; MTCW

Wajda, Andrzej 1926- . . . . CLC 16
See also CA 102

Wakefield, Dan 1932- . . . . CLC 7
See also CA 21-24R; CAAS 7

Wakoski, Diane
1937- . . . . . CLC 2, 4, 7, 9, 11, 40; PC 15
See also CA 13-16R; CAAS 1; CANR 9;
DAM POET; DLB 5; INT CANR-9

Wakoski-Sherbell, Diane
See Wakoski, Diane

Walcott, Derek (Alton)
1930- . . . . CLC 2, 4, 9, 14, 25, 42, 67, 76;
BLC; DAB; DAC
See also BW 2; CA 89-92; CANR 26, 47;
DAM MST, MULT, POET; DLB 117;
DLBY 81; MTCW

Waldman, Anne 1945- . . . . CLC 7
See also CA 37-40R; CAAS 17; CANR 34;
DLB 16

Waldo, E. Hunter
See Sturgeon, Theodore (Hamilton)

Waldo, Edward Hamilton
See Sturgeon, Theodore (Hamilton)

Walker, Alice (Malsenior)
1944- . . . . CLC 5, 6, 9, 19, 27, 46, 58;
BLC; DA; DAB; DAC; SSC 5
See also AAYA 3; BEST 89:4; BW 2;
CA 37-40R; CANR 9, 27, 49;
CDALB 1968-1988; DAM MST, MULT,
NOV, POET, POP; DLB 6, 33, 143;
INT CANR-27; MTCW; SATA 31

Walker, David Harry 1911-1992. . . . CLC 14
See also CA 1-4R; 137; CANR 1; SATA 8;
SATA-Obit 71

Walker, Edward Joseph 1934-
See Walker, Ted
See also CA 21-24R; CANR 12, 28

Walker, George F.
1947- . . . . CLC 44, 61; DAB; DAC
See also CA 103; CANR 21, 43;
DAM MST; DLB 60

Walker, Joseph A. 1935- . . . . CLC 19
See also BW 1; CA 89-92; CANR 26;
DAM DRAM, MST; DLB 38

Walker, Margaret (Abigail)
1915- . . . . CLC 1, 6; BLC
See also BW 2; CA 73-76; CANR 26;
DAM MULT; DLB 76, 152; MTCW

Walker, Ted . . . . CLC 13
See also Walker, Edward Joseph
See also DLB 40

Wallace, David Foster 1962- . . . . CLC 50
See also CA 132

Wallace, Dexter
See Masters, Edgar Lee

Wallace, (Richard Horatio) Edgar
1875-1932 . . . . TCLC 57
See also CA 115; DLB 70

Wallace, Irving 1916-1990 . . . . . . CLC 7, 13
See also AITN 1; CA 1-4R; 132; CAAS 1;
CANR 1, 27; DAM NOV, POP;
INT CANR-27; MTCW

Wallant, Edward Lewis
1926-1962 . . . . CLC 5, 10
See also CA 1-4R; CANR 22; DLB 2, 28,
143; MTCW

Walley, Byron
See Card, Orson Scott

Walpole, Horace 1717-1797. . . . . LC 2
See also DLB 39, 104

Walpole, Hugh (Seymour)
1884-1941 . . . . TCLC 5
See also CA 104; DLB 34

Walser, Martin 1927- . . . . CLC 27
See also CA 57-60; CANR 8, 46; DLB 75,
124

Walser, Robert
1878-1956 . . . . TCLC 18; SSC 20
See also CA 118; DLB 66

Walsh, Jill Paton. . . . . CLC 35
See also Paton Walsh, Gillian
See also AAYA 11; CLR 2; DLB 161;
SAAS 3

Walter, Villiam Christian
See Andersen, Hans Christian

Wambaugh, Joseph (Aloysius, Jr.)
1937- . . . . CLC 3, 18
See also AITN 1; BEST 89:3; CA 33-36R;
CANR 42; DAM NOV, POP; DLB 6;
DLBY 83; MTCW

Ward, Arthur Henry Sarsfield 1883-1959
See Rohmer, Sax
See also CA 108

Ward, Douglas Turner 1930- . . . . CLC 19
See also BW 1; CA 81-84; CANR 27;
DLB 7, 38

Ward, Mary Augusta
See Ward, Mrs. Humphry

Ward, Mrs. Humphry
1851-1920 . . . . TCLC 55
See also DLB 18

Ward, Peter
See Faust, Frederick (Schiller)

Warhol, Andy 1928(?)-1987. . . . . . . CLC 20
See also AAYA 12; BEST 89:4; CA 89-92;
121; CANR 34

Warner, Francis (Robert le Plastrier)
1937- . . . . CLC 14
See also CA 53-56; CANR 11

Warner, Marina 1946- . . . . CLC 59
See also CA 65-68; CANR 21

Warner, Rex (Ernest) 1905-1986. . . . CLC 45
See also CA 89-92; 119; DLB 15

Warner, Susan (Bogert)
1819-1885 . . . . NCLC 31
See also DLB 3, 42

Warner, Sylvia (Constance) Ashton
See Ashton-Warner, Sylvia (Constance)

Warner, Sylvia Townsend
1893-1978 . . . . CLC 7, 19; SSC 23
See also CA 61-64; 77-80; CANR 16;
DLB 34, 139; MTCW

Warren, Mercy Otis 1728-1814. . . NCLC 13
See also DLB 31

Warren, Robert Penn
1905-1989 . . . . CLC 1, 4, 6, 8, 10, 13, 18,
39, 53, 59; DA; DAB; DAC; SSC 4; WLC
See also AITN 1; CA 13-16R; 129;
CANR 10, 47; CDALB 1968-1988;
DAM MST, NOV, POET; DLB 2, 48,
152; DLBY 80, 89; INT CANR-10;
MTCW; SATA 46; SATA-Obit 63

Warshofsky, Isaac
See Singer, Isaac Bashevis

Warton, Thomas 1728-1790. . . . . LC 15
See also DAM POET; DLB 104, 109

Waruk, Kona
See Harris, (Theodore) Wilson

Warung, Price 1855-1911. . . . . TCLC 45

Warwick, Jarvis
See Garner, Hugh

Washington, Alex
See Harris, Mark

Washington, Booker T(aliaferro)
1856-1915 . . . . TCLC 10; BLC
See also BW 1; CA 114; 125; DAM MULT;
SATA 28

Washington, George 1732-1799. . . . . . LC 25
See also DLB 31

Wassermann, (Karl) Jakob
1873-1934 . . . . **TCLC 6**
See also CA 104; DLB 66

Wasserstein, Wendy
1950- . . . . **CLC 32, 59, 90; DC 4**
See also CA 121; 129; CABS 3;
DAM DRAM; INT 129

Waterhouse, Keith (Spencer)
1929- . . . . **CLC 47**
See also CA 5-8R; CANR 38; DLB 13, 15;
MTCW

Waters, Frank (Joseph)
1902-1995 . . . . **CLC 88**
See also CA 5-8R; 149; CAAS 13; CANR 3,
18; DLBY 86

Waters, Roger   1944- . . . . **CLC 35**

Watkins, Frances Ellen
See Harper, Frances Ellen Watkins

Watkins, Gerrold
See Malzberg, Barry N(athaniel)

Watkins, Gloria   1955(?)-
See hooks, bell
See also BW 2; CA 143

Watkins, Paul   1964- . . . . **CLC 55**
See also CA 132

Watkins, Vernon Phillips
1906-1967 . . . . **CLC 43**
See also CA 9-10; 25-28R; CAP 1; DLB 20

Watson, Irving S.
See Mencken, H(enry) L(ouis)

Watson, John H.
See Farmer, Philip Jose

Watson, Richard F.
See Silverberg, Robert

Waugh, Auberon (Alexander)   1939- . . **CLC 7**
See also CA 45-48; CANR 6, 22; DLB 14

Waugh, Evelyn (Arthur St. John)
1903-1966 . . . . . . **CLC 1, 3, 8, 13, 19, 27,
44; DA; DAB; DAC; WLC**
See also CA 85-88; 25-28R; CANR 22;
CDBLB 1914-1945; DAM MST, NOV,
POP; DLB 15, 162; MTCW

Waugh, Harriet   1944- . . . . **CLC 6**
See also CA 85-88; CANR 22

Ways, C. R.
See Blount, Roy (Alton), Jr.

Waystaff, Simon
See Swift, Jonathan

Webb, (Martha) Beatrice (Potter)
1858-1943 . . . . **TCLC 22**
See also Potter, Beatrice
See also CA 117

Webb, Charles (Richard)   1939- . . . . . . **CLC 7**
See also CA 25-28R

Webb, James H(enry), Jr.   1946- . . . . **CLC 22**
See also CA 81-84

Webb, Mary (Gladys Meredith)
1881-1927 . . . . **TCLC 24**
See also CA 123; DLB 34

Webb, Mrs. Sidney
See Webb, (Martha) Beatrice (Potter)

Webb, Phyllis   1927- . . . . **CLC 18**
See also CA 104; CANR 23; DLB 53

Webb, Sidney (James)
1859-1947 . . . . **TCLC 22**
See also CA 117

Webber, Andrew Lloyd. . . . . **CLC 21**
See also Lloyd Webber, Andrew

Weber, Lenora Mattingly
1895-1971 . . . . **CLC 12**
See also CA 19-20; 29-32R; CAP 1;
SATA 2; SATA-Obit 26

Webster, John
1579(?)-1634(?) . . . . . . **LC 33; DA; DAB;
DAC; DC 2; WLC**
See also CDBLB Before 1660;
DAM DRAM, MST; DLB 58

Webster, Noah   1758-1843 . . . . **NCLC 30**

Wedekind, (Benjamin) Frank(lin)
1864-1918 . . . . **TCLC 7**
See also CA 104; DAM DRAM; DLB 118

Weidman, Jerome   1913- . . . . **CLC 7**
See also AITN 2; CA 1-4R; CANR 1;
DLB 28

Weil, Simone (Adolphine)
1909-1943 . . . . **TCLC 23**
See also CA 117

Weinstein, Nathan
See West, Nathanael

Weinstein, Nathan von Wallenstein
See West, Nathanael

Weir, Peter (Lindsay)   1944- . . . . **CLC 20**
See also CA 113; 123

Weiss, Peter (Ulrich)
1916-1982 . . . . **CLC 3, 15, 51**
See also CA 45-48; 106; CANR 3;
DAM DRAM; DLB 69, 124

Weiss, Theodore (Russell)
1916- . . . . **CLC 3, 8, 14**
See also CA 9-12R; CAAS 2; CANR 46;
DLB 5

Welch, (Maurice) Denton
1915-1948 . . . . **TCLC 22**
See also CA 121; 148

Welch, James   1940- . . . . **CLC 6, 14, 52**
See also CA 85-88; CANR 42;
DAM MULT, POP; NNAL

Weldon, Fay
1933- . . . . **CLC 6, 9, 11, 19, 36, 59**
See also CA 21-24R; CANR 16, 46;
CDBLB 1960 to Present; DAM POP;
DLB 14; INT CANR-16; MTCW

Wellek, Rene   1903-1995. . . . . **CLC 28**
See also CA 5-8R; 150; CAAS 7; CANR 8;
DLB 63; INT CANR-8

Weller, Michael   1942- . . . . **CLC 10, 53**
See also CA 85-88

Weller, Paul   1958- . . . . **CLC 26**

Wellershoff, Dieter   1925- . . . . **CLC 46**
See also CA 89-92; CANR 16, 37

Welles, (George) Orson
1915-1985 . . . . **CLC 20, 80**
See also CA 93-96; 117

Wellman, Mac   1945- . . . . **CLC 65**

Wellman, Manly Wade   1903-1986 . . **CLC 49**
See also CA 1-4R; 118; CANR 6, 16, 44;
SATA 6; SATA-Obit 47

Wells, Carolyn   1869(?)-1942 . . . . . . **TCLC 35**
See also CA 113; DLB 11

Wells, H(erbert) G(eorge)
1866-1946 . . . . **TCLC 6, 12, 19; DA;
DAB; DAC; SSC 6; WLC**
See also AAYA 18; CA 110; 121;
CDBLB 1914-1945; DAM MST, NOV;
DLB 34, 70, 156; MTCW; SATA 20

Wells, Rosemary   1943- . . . . **CLC 12**
See also AAYA 13; CA 85-88; CANR 48;
CLR 16; MAICYA; SAAS 1; SATA 18,
69

Welty, Eudora
1909- . . . . . . **CLC 1, 2, 5, 14, 22, 33; DA;
DAB; DAC; SSC 1; WLC**
See also CA 9-12R; CABS 1; CANR 32;
CDALB 1941-1968; DAM MST, NOV;
DLB 2, 102, 143; DLBD 12; DLBY 87;
MTCW

Wen I-to   1899-1946 . . . . **TCLC 28**

Wentworth, Robert
See Hamilton, Edmond

Werfel, Franz (V.)   1890-1945 . . . . . . **TCLC 8**
See also CA 104; DLB 81, 124

Wergeland, Henrik Arnold
1808-1845 . . . . **NCLC 5**

Wersba, Barbara   1932- . . . . **CLC 30**
See also AAYA 2; CA 29-32R; CANR 16,
38; CLR 3; DLB 52; JRDA; MAICYA;
SAAS 2; SATA 1, 58

Wertmueller, Lina   1928- . . . . **CLC 16**
See also CA 97-100; CANR 39

Wescott, Glenway   1901-1987. . . . . . . **CLC 13**
See also CA 13-16R; 121; CANR 23;
DLB 4, 9, 102

Wesker, Arnold   1932- . . **CLC 3, 5, 42; DAB**
See also CA 1-4R; CAAS 7; CANR 1, 33;
CDBLB 1960 to Present; DAM DRAM;
DLB 13; MTCW

Wesley, Richard (Errol)   1945- . . . . **CLC 7**
See also BW 1; CA 57-60; CANR 27;
DLB 38

Wessel, Johan Herman   1742-1785 . . . . **LC 7**

West, Anthony (Panther)
1914-1987 . . . . **CLC 50**
See also CA 45-48; 124; CANR 3, 19;
DLB 15

West, C. P.
See Wodehouse, P(elham) G(renville)

West, (Mary) Jessamyn
1902-1984 . . . . **CLC 7, 17**
See also CA 9-12R; 112; CANR 27; DLB 6;
DLBY 84; MTCW; SATA-Obit 37

West, Morris L(anglo)   1916- . . . . . . **CLC 6, 33**
See also CA 5-8R; CANR 24, 49; MTCW

West, Nathanael
1903-1940 . . . . . **TCLC 1, 14, 44; SSC 16**
See also CA 104; 125; CDALB 1929-1941;
DLB 4, 9, 28; MTCW

West, Owen
See Koontz, Dean R(ay)

West, Paul   1930- . . . . **CLC 7, 14**
See also CA 13-16R; CAAS 7; CANR 22;
DLB 14; INT CANR-22

West, Rebecca 1892-1983 . . CLC 7, 9, 31, 50
See also CA 5-8R; 109; CANR 19; DLB 36;
DLBY 83; MTCW

Westall, Robert (Atkinson)
1929-1993 . . . . CLC 17
See also AAYA 12; CA 69-72; 141;
CANR 18; CLR 13; JRDA; MAICYA;
SAAS 2; SATA 23, 69; SATA-Obit 75

Westlake, Donald E(dwin)
1933- . . . . CLC 7, 33
See also CA 17-20R; CAAS 13; CANR 16,
44; DAM POP; INT CANR-16

Westmacott, Mary
See Christie, Agatha (Mary Clarissa)

Weston, Allen
See Norton, Andre

Wetcheek, J. L.
See Feuchtwanger, Lion

Wetering, Janwillem van de
See van de Wetering, Janwillem

Wetherell, Elizabeth
See Warner, Susan (Bogert)

Whale, James 1889-1957 . . . . TCLC 63

Whalen, Philip 1923- . . . . CLC 6, 29
See also CA 9-12R; CANR 5, 39; DLB 16

Wharton, Edith (Newbold Jones)
1862-1937 . . . . . . TCLC 3, 9, 27, 53; DA;
DAB; DAC; SSC 6; WLC
See also CA 104; 132; CDALB 1865-1917;
DAM MST, NOV; DLB 4, 9, 12, 78;
DLBD 13; MTCW

Wharton, James
See Mencken, H(enry) L(ouis)

Wharton, William (a pseudonym)
. . . . CLC 18, 37
See also CA 93-96; DLBY 80; INT 93-96

Wheatley (Peters), Phillis
1754(?)-1784 . . . . LC 3; BLC; DA; DAC;
PC 3; WLC
See also CDALB 1640-1865; DAM MST,
MULT, POET; DLB 31, 50

Wheelock, John Hall 1886-1978 . . . . CLC 14
See also CA 13-16R; 77-80; CANR 14;
DLB 45

White, E(lwyn) B(rooks)
1899-1985 . . . . CLC 10, 34, 39
See also AITN 2; CA 13-16R; 116;
CANR 16, 37; CLR 1, 21; DAM POP;
DLB 11, 22; MAICYA; MTCW;
SATA 2, 29; SATA-Obit 44

White, Edmund (Valentine III)
1940- . . . . CLC 27
See also AAYA 7; CA 45-48; CANR 3, 19,
36; DAM POP; MTCW

White, Patrick (Victor Martindale)
1912-1990 . . CLC 3, 4, 5, 7, 9, 18, 65, 69
See also CA 81-84; 132; CANR 43; MTCW

White, Phyllis Dorothy James 1920-
See James, P. D.
See also CA 21-24R; CANR 17, 43;
DAM POP; MTCW

White, T(erence) H(anbury)
1906-1964 . . . . CLC 30
See also CA 73-76; CANR 37; DLB 160;
JRDA; MAICYA; SATA 12

White, Terence de Vere
1912-1994 . . . . CLC 49
See also CA 49-52; 145; CANR 3

White, Walter F(rancis)
1893-1955 . . . . TCLC 15
See also White, Walter
See also BW 1; CA 115; 124; DLB 51

White, William Hale 1831-1913
See Rutherford, Mark
See also CA 121

Whitehead, E(dward) A(nthony)
1933- . . . . CLC 5
See also CA 65-68

Whitemore, Hugh (John) 1936- . . . . . CLC 37
See also CA 132; INT 132

Whitman, Sarah Helen (Power)
1803-1878 . . . . NCLC 19
See also DLB 1

Whitman, Walt(er)
1819-1892 . . . . . NCLC 4, 31; DA; DAB;
DAC; PC 3; WLC
See also CDALB 1640-1865; DAM MST,
POET; DLB 3, 64; SATA 20

Whitney, Phyllis A(yame) 1903- . . . . CLC 42
See also AITN 2; BEST 90:3; CA 1-4R;
CANR 3, 25, 38; DAM POP; JRDA;
MAICYA; SATA 1, 30

Whittemore, (Edward) Reed (Jr.)
1919- . . . . CLC 4
See also CA 9-12R; CAAS 8; CANR 4;
DLB 5

Whittier, John Greenleaf
1807-1892 . . . . NCLC 8, 57
See also CDALB 1640-1865; DAM POET;
DLB 1

Whittlebot, Hernia
See Coward, Noel (Peirce)

Wicker, Thomas Grey 1926-
See Wicker, Tom
See also CA 65-68; CANR 21, 46

Wicker, Tom . . . . CLC 7
See also Wicker, Thomas Grey

Wideman, John Edgar
1941- . . . . CLC 5, 34, 36, 67; BLC
See also BW 2; CA 85-88; CANR 14, 42;
DAM MULT; DLB 33, 143

Wiebe, Rudy (Henry)
1934- . . . . CLC 6, 11, 14; DAC
See also CA 37-40R; CANR 42;
DAM MST; DLB 60

Wieland, Christoph Martin
1733-1813 . . . . NCLC 17
See also DLB 97

Wiene, Robert 1881-1938 . . . . TCLC 56

Wieners, John 1934- . . . . CLC 7
See also CA 13-16R; DLB 16

Wiesel, Elie(zer)
1928- . . . . . . CLC 3, 5, 11, 37; DA; DAB;
DAC
See also AAYA 7; AITN 1; CA 5-8R;
CAAS 4; CANR 8, 40; DAM MST,
NOV; DLB 83; DLBY 87; INT CANR-8;
MTCW; SATA 56

Wiggins, Marianne 1947- . . . . CLC 57
See also BEST 89:3; CA 130

Wight, James Alfred 1916-
See Herriot, James
See also CA 77-80; SATA 55;
SATA-Brief 44

Wilbur, Richard (Purdy)
1921- . . . CLC 3, 6, 9, 14, 53; DA; DAB;
DAC
See also CA 1-4R; CABS 2; CANR 2, 29;
DAM MST, POET; DLB 5;
INT CANR-29; MTCW; SATA 9

Wild, Peter 1940- . . . . CLC 14
See also CA 37-40R; DLB 5

Wilde, Oscar (Fingal O'Flahertie Wills)
1854(?)-1900 . . . . TCLC 1, 8, 23, 41; DA;
DAB; DAC; SSC 11; WLC
See also CA 104; 119; CDBLB 1890-1914;
DAM DRAM, MST, NOV; DLB 10, 19,
34, 57, 141, 156; SATA 24

Wilder, Billy . . . . CLC 20
See also Wilder, Samuel
See also DLB 26

Wilder, Samuel 1906-
See Wilder, Billy
See also CA 89-92

Wilder, Thornton (Niven)
1897-1975 . . . . . . CLC 1, 5, 6, 10, 15, 35,
82; DA; DAB; DAC; DC 1; WLC
See also AITN 2; CA 13-16R; 61-64;
CANR 40; DAM DRAM, MST, NOV;
DLB 4, 7, 9; MTCW

Wilding, Michael 1942- . . . . CLC 73
See also CA 104; CANR 24, 49

Wiley, Richard 1944- . . . . CLC 44
See also CA 121; 129

Wilhelm, Kate . . . . CLC 7
See also Wilhelm, Katie Gertrude
See also CAAS 5; DLB 8; INT CANR-17

Wilhelm, Katie Gertrude 1928-
See Wilhelm, Kate
See also CA 37-40R; CANR 17, 36; MTCW

Wilkins, Mary
See Freeman, Mary Eleanor Wilkins

Willard, Nancy 1936- . . . . CLC 7, 37
See also CA 89-92; CANR 10, 39; CLR 5;
DLB 5, 52; MAICYA; MTCW;
SATA 37, 71; SATA-Brief 30

Williams, C(harles) K(enneth)
1936- . . . . CLC 33, 56
See also CA 37-40R; DAM POET; DLB 5

Williams, Charles
See Collier, James L(incoln)

Williams, Charles (Walter Stansby)
1886-1945 . . . . TCLC 1, 11
See also CA 104; DLB 100, 153

Williams, (George) Emlyn
1905-1987 . . . . CLC 15
See also CA 104; 123; CANR 36;
DAM DRAM; DLB 10, 77; MTCW

Williams, Hugo 1942- . . . . CLC 42
See also CA 17-20R; CANR 45; DLB 40

Williams, J. Walker
See Wodehouse, P(elham) G(renville)

Williams, John A(lfred)
1925- .... **CLC 5, 13; BLC**
See also BW 2; CA 53-56; CAAS 3;
CANR 6, 26, 51; DAM MULT; DLB 2,
33; INT CANR-6

Williams, Jonathan (Chamberlain)
1929- .... **CLC 13**
See also CA 9-12R; CAAS 12; CANR 8;
DLB 5

Williams, Joy 1944- .... **CLC 31**
See also CA 41-44R; CANR 22, 48

Williams, Norman 1952- .... **CLC 39**
See also CA 118

Williams, Sherley Anne
1944- .... **CLC 89; BLC**
See also BW 2; CA 73-76; CANR 25;
DAM MULT, POET; DLB 41;
INT CANR-25; SATA 78

Williams, Shirley
See Williams, Sherley Anne

Williams, Tennessee
1911-1983 ..... **CLC 1, 2, 5, 7, 8, 11, 15,
19, 30, 39, 45, 71; DA; DAB; DAC;
DC 4; WLC**
See also AITN 1, 2; CA 5-8R; 108;
CABS 3; CANR 31; CDALB 1941-1968;
DAM DRAM, MST; DLB 7; DLBD 4;
DLBY 83; MTCW

Williams, Thomas (Alonzo)
1926-1990 .... **CLC 14**
See also CA 1-4R; 132; CANR 2

Williams, William C.
See Williams, William Carlos

Williams, William Carlos
1883-1963 .... **CLC 1, 2, 5, 9, 13, 22, 42,
67; DA; DAB; DAC; PC 7**
See also CA 89-92; CANR 34;
CDALB 1917-1929; DAM MST, POET;
DLB 4, 16, 54, 86; MTCW

Williamson, David (Keith) 1942-.... **CLC 56**
See also CA 103; CANR 41

Williamson, Ellen Douglas 1905-1984
See Douglas, Ellen
See also CA 17-20R; 114; CANR 39

Williamson, Jack................... **CLC 29**
See also Williamson, John Stewart
See also CAAS 8; DLB 8

Williamson, John Stewart 1908-
See Williamson, Jack
See also CA 17-20R; CANR 23

Willie, Frederick
See Lovecraft, H(oward) P(hillips)

Willingham, Calder (Baynard, Jr.)
1922-1995 .... **CLC 5, 51**
See also CA 5-8R; 147; CANR 3; DLB 2,
44; MTCW

Willis, Charles
See Clarke, Arthur C(harles)

Willy
See Colette, (Sidonie-Gabrielle)

Willy, Colette
See Colette, (Sidonie-Gabrielle)

Wilson, A(ndrew) N(orman) 1950- .. **CLC 33**
See also CA 112; 122; DLB 14, 155

Wilson, Angus (Frank Johnstone)
1913-1991 .. **CLC 2, 3, 5, 25, 34; SSC 21**
See also CA 5-8R; 134; CANR 21; DLB 15,
139, 155; MTCW

Wilson, August
1945- .... **CLC 39, 50, 63; BLC; DA;
DAB; DAC; DC 2**
See also AAYA 16; BW 2; CA 115; 122;
CANR 42; DAM DRAM, MST, MULT;
MTCW

Wilson, Brian 1942-.............. **CLC 12**

Wilson, Colin 1931- .... **CLC 3, 14**
See also CA 1-4R; CAAS 5; CANR 1, 22,
33; DLB 14; MTCW

Wilson, Dirk
See Pohl, Frederik

Wilson, Edmund
1895-1972 .... **CLC 1, 2, 3, 8, 24**
See also CA 1-4R; 37-40R; CANR 1, 46;
DLB 63; MTCW

Wilson, Ethel Davis (Bryant)
1888(?)-1980 .... **CLC 13; DAC**
See also CA 102; DAM POET; DLB 68;
MTCW

Wilson, John 1785-1854......... **NCLC 5**

Wilson, John (Anthony) Burgess 1917-1993
See Burgess, Anthony
See also CA 1-4R; 143; CANR 2, 46; DAC;
DAM NOV; MTCW

Wilson, Lanford 1937-....... **CLC 7, 14, 36**
See also CA 17-20R; CABS 3; CANR 45;
DAM DRAM; DLB 7

Wilson, Robert M. 1944-......... **CLC 7, 9**
See also CA 49-52; CANR 2, 41; MTCW

Wilson, Robert McLiam 1964-..... **CLC 59**
See also CA 132

Wilson, Sloan 1920-.............. **CLC 32**
See also CA 1-4R; CANR 1, 44

Wilson, Snoo 1948-............... **CLC 33**
See also CA 69-72

Wilson, William S(mith) 1932- ..... **CLC 49**
See also CA 81-84

Winchilsea, Anne (Kingsmill) Finch Counte
1661-1720 .... **LC 3**

Windham, Basil
See Wodehouse, P(elham) G(renville)

Wingrove, David (John) 1954-...... **CLC 68**
See also CA 133

Winters, Janet Lewis .... **CLC 41**
See also Lewis, Janet
See also DLBY 87

Winters, (Arthur) Yvor
1900-1968 .... **CLC 4, 8, 32**
See also CA 11-12; 25-28R; CAP 1;
DLB 48; MTCW

Winterson, Jeanette 1959-......... **CLC 64**
See also CA 136; DAM POP

Winthrop, John 1588-1649......... **LC 31**
See also DLB 24, 30

Wiseman, Frederick 1930-........ **CLC 20**

Wister, Owen 1860-1938 .... **TCLC 21**
See also CA 108; DLB 9, 78; SATA 62

Witkacy
See Witkiewicz, Stanislaw Ignacy

Witkiewicz, Stanislaw Ignacy
1885-1939 .... **TCLC 8**
See also CA 105

Wittgenstein, Ludwig (Josef Johann)
1889-1951 .... **TCLC 59**
See also CA 113

Wittig, Monique 1935(?)-.......... **CLC 22**
See also CA 116; 135; DLB 83

Wittlin, Jozef 1896-1976 .... **CLC 25**
See also CA 49-52; 65-68; CANR 3

Wodehouse, P(elham) G(renville)
1881-1975 ... **CLC 1, 2, 5, 10, 22; DAB;
DAC; SSC 2**
See also AITN 2; CA 45-48; 57-60;
CANR 3, 33; CDBLB 1914-1945;
DAM NOV; DLB 34, 162; MTCW;
SATA 22

Woiwode, L.
See Woiwode, Larry (Alfred)

Woiwode, Larry (Alfred) 1941-... **CLC 6, 10**
See also CA 73-76; CANR 16; DLB 6;
INT CANR-16

Wojciechowska, Maia (Teresa)
1927- .... **CLC 26**
See also AAYA 8; CA 9-12R; CANR 4, 41;
CLR 1; JRDA; MAICYA; SAAS 1;
SATA 1, 28, 83

Wolf, Christa 1929- .... **CLC 14, 29, 58**
See also CA 85-88; CANR 45; DLB 75;
MTCW

Wolfe, Gene (Rodman) 1931-....... **CLC 25**
See also CA 57-60; CAAS 9; CANR 6, 32;
DAM POP; DLB 8

Wolfe, George C. 1954- .... **CLC 49**
See also CA 149

Wolfe, Thomas (Clayton)
1900-1938 ..... **TCLC 4, 13, 29, 61; DA;
DAB; DAC; WLC**
See also CA 104; 132; CDALB 1929-1941;
DAM MST, NOV; DLB 9, 102; DLBD 2;
DLBY 85; MTCW

Wolfe, Thomas Kennerly, Jr. 1931-
See Wolfe, Tom
See also CA 13-16R; CANR 9, 33;
DAM POP; INT CANR-9; MTCW

Wolfe, Tom .... **CLC 1, 2, 9, 15, 35, 51**
See also Wolfe, Thomas Kennerly, Jr.
See also AAYA 8; AITN 2; BEST 89:1;
DLB 152

Wolff, Geoffrey (Ansell) 1937- ..... **CLC 41**
See also CA 29-32R; CANR 29, 43

Wolff, Sonia
See Levitin, Sonia (Wolff)

Wolff, Tobias (Jonathan Ansell)
1945- .... **CLC 39, 64**
See also AAYA 16; BEST 90:2; CA 114;
117; CAAS 22; DLB 130; INT 117

Wolfram von Eschenbach
c. 1170-c. 1220 .... **CMLC 5**
See also DLB 138

Wolitzer, Hilma 1930-............ **CLC 17**
See also CA 65-68; CANR 18, 40;
INT CANR-18; SATA 31

Wollstonecraft, Mary 1759-1797...... **LC 5**
See also CDBLB 1789-1832; DLB 39, 104,
158

Zappa, Francis Vincent, Jr.   1940-1993
See Zappa, Frank
See also CA 108; 143

Zappa, Frank.................... **CLC 17**
See also Zappa, Francis Vincent, Jr.

Zaturenska, Marya   1902-1982.... **CLC 6, 11**
See also CA 13-16R; 105; CANR 22

Zelazny, Roger (Joseph)
   1937-1995 .... **CLC 21**
See also AAYA 7; CA 21-24R; 148;
   CANR 26; DLB 8; MTCW; SATA 57;
   SATA-Brief 39

Zhdanov, Andrei A(lexandrovich)
   1896-1948 .... **TCLC 18**
See also CA 117

Zhukovsky, Vasily   1783-1852 .... **NCLC 35**

Ziegenhagen, Eric .... **CLC 55**

Zimmer, Jill Schary
See Robinson, Jill

Zimmerman, Robert
See Dylan, Bob

Zindel, Paul
   1936- ..... **CLC 6, 26; DA; DAB; DAC;**
                                   DC 5
See also AAYA 2; CA 73-76; CANR 31;
   CLR 3; DAM DRAM, MST, NOV;
   DLB 7, 52; JRDA; MAICYA; MTCW;
   SATA 16, 58

Zinov'Ev, A. A.
See Zinoviev, Alexander (Aleksandrovich)

Zinoviev, Alexander (Aleksandrovich)
   1922- .... **CLC 19**
See also CA 116; 133; CAAS 10

Zoilus
See Lovecraft, H(oward) P(hillips)

Zola, Emile (Edouard Charles Antoine)
   1840-1902 ...... **TCLC 1, 6, 21, 41; DA;**
                            DAB; DAC; WLC
See also CA 104; 138; DAM MST, NOV;
   DLB 123

Zoline, Pamela   1941-............. **CLC 62**

Zorrilla y Moral, Jose   1817-1893.. **NCLC 6**

Zoshchenko, Mikhail (Mikhailovich)
   1895-1958 .... **TCLC 15; SSC 15**
See also CA 115

Zuckmayer, Carl   1896-1977........ **CLC 18**
See also CA 69-72; DLB 56, 124

Zuk, Georges
See Skelton, Robin

Zukofsky, Louis
   1904-1978 .... **CLC 1, 2, 4, 7, 11, 18;**
                                   PC 11
See also CA 9-12R; 77-80; CANR 39;
   DAM POET; DLB 5, 165; MTCW

Zweig, Paul   1935-1984........ **CLC 34, 42**
See also CA 85-88; 113

Zweig, Stefan   1881-1942 .... **TCLC 17**
See also CA 112; DLB 81, 118

PC Cumulative Nationality Index

PC Cumulative Title Index

Title Index

Title Index

Title Index

Title Index